KRLA ARCHIVES

KRLA
Chronological Archives
Volume 5

May 28, 1966, to November 5, 1966

KRLA ARCHIVES

The times, they were a-changing. In the very first issue included in this volume, the Beat reported that the British Invasion was losing its power. Nevertheless, The Beatles, The Rolling Stones, and Hollies still received giood coverage in the issue and the next issue featured a two page spread on what the British liked and didn't like about Americans.

KRLA continued to promote itself through an occassional column (and the Beat publication itself) and announced that it would be hosting its first all-request concert featuring the Beach Boys together with the Byrds, The Outsiders, The Sir Douglas Quintet, Percy Sledge and Captain Beefheart. Clearly, the station understood the value of marketing itself beyond the limitations of the airwaves on which it broadcast.

The Beatles, the Rolling Stones and other english bands continued to get their share of Beat attention. Articles also featured Leslie Gore, The Lovin' Spoonful, Neil Diamond, The Young Rascals, The Walker Brothers, The Turtles, Donovan, Bob Dylan, and Jan Berry who had just had his disasterous accident. The Sunrays even received a feature treatment.

Sonny and Cher, The Mamas and the Papas, and the Beach Boys continued to be American favorite for Beat coverage, and the Monkees started their huge coverage during these issues.

The Adventures of Robin Boyd, originally conceived as a short series of articles, continued to make a presence in most issues, as did a movie feature. There were articles on what to do if you met a star And The back cover featured ads including those for Hullabaloo. Everything you could want on a weekly basis.

In presenting these original issues, we've moved a few of the pages around to ensure that the spreads still lined up. Not a big deal to most people unless you are severly OCD and have access to the original issues.

Copyright © 2016 White Lightning Publishing

KRLA ARCHIVES

America's Largest Teen NEWSpaper 15¢

KRLA Edition BEAT
MAY 28, 1966

BEAT Art: Jan Walker

KRLA ARCHIVES

KRLA BEAT

Volume 2, Number 11 — May 28, 1966

British Invasion Losing Its Power

By Louise Criscione

The circle has been completed and the American artists are back to reigning on all of the music charts. Before the Beatles hit Stateside in February '64, American artists had dominated the world's record charts and were the supreme rulers of what was musically "in" and what was definitely "out."

Then, of course, the Beatles and company landed and the whole music world made a complete turn with the English taking over where the Americans had once been.

The take-over grew to such huge proportions that practically every artist who happened to be English made it onto our charts on that merit alone. Some had talent and some didn't but the only thing that really mattered was that they were British.

People such as the Honeycombs, Searchers, Zombies, Gerry and the Pacemakers, Billy J. Kramer, Sounds Incorporated, the Moody Blues, the Seekers, Freddie and the Dreamers and the Unit Four Plus Two came and went so fast that their departure was hardly even noticed.

Now it's Spring of '66, roughly 27 months since the British invasion began, and the Americans are again ruling the roost. Now the English singers on the charts are the exceptions instead of the other way around. No longer does being English assure you of a hit record in America. But then again, being American is not enough to place

(Turn to Page 11)

...COMING BACK BY POPULAR DEMAND.

BRUMMELS SUED FOR ONE MILLION DOLLARS

The Beau Brummels along with their former managers, Tom Donahue and Robert Mitchell, and their present manager Carl Scott are being sued by Declan Mulligan, former member of the group. Mulligan is seeking damages totaling $1,250,000 from his former partners.

Mulligan, if you remember, was one of the original Brummels who left the group about a year ago.

Several months after his split the other Brummels told *The BEAT* Mulligan had left for several reasons, one of which was his desire to go back to his native Ireland.

At that time, Sal Valentino stated that he felt the group had not suffered a tremendous loss when Mulligan made his exit but Ron Elliott disagreed saying that they had lost because they were minus one guitar — thus, changing their sound to a certain extent.

Mulligan now declares that *he* was the founder and leader of the group and charged in a San Francisco Superior Court that his four fellow Brummels had frozen him out of the business a year ago and have excluded him from their profits ever since.

The attorney for Mulligan said the Brummels have had two hit singles and two hit albums, grossing sales in excess of one million dollars since they began recording in 1964.

Their biggest hit, "Laugh, Laugh," sold more than 500,000 copies and was one of the biggest American-made records sold in England.

Mulligan is, therefore, seeking $250,000 in general damages and one million dollars in punitive damages plus the dissolution of his oral partnership with the other Brummels and a settlement of what they allegedly owe him.

At the time of this printing, the Brummels were filling concert dates on the East Coast and their manager was unavailable for comment.

Herman Set For U.S. Tour

Herman and his Hermits have announced the schedule for their summer tour of the United States and Canada. The tour, which will begin on July 1, will take the group to almost every major city in the U.S. It was originally set to last four weeks but the tour is now being extended in an attempt to meet the new offers which have been pouring in.

The tour schedule as it stands right now lists the starting date in Honolulu on July 1; San Francisco, July 2; Los Angeles, July 3; Seattle, July 5; Toronto, July 7; Des Moines, July 12; Tulsa, July 14; Dallas, July 16; Houston, July 17; Little Rock, July 18; Atlanta, July 20; Memphis, July 21; Montgomery, July 22; Birmingham, July 23; Chicago and Milwaukee, July 31; Atlantic City, August 1; Baltimore, August 4; Boston and Hartford, August 5; Toronto, August 6; Pittsburgh, August 7; Providence, August 8.

Herman and his Hermits have decided to do things up proper this time around and will travel by chartered plane with the press accompanying them at various times. Huge press conferences will be held in each city upon arrival. Thus far, the only two groups to use this technique to their distinct advantage have been the Beatles and Stones.

To match their string of unbroken hit records, Herman would very

(Turn to Page 4)

Inside the BEAT

On The Beat	2
The Ignored Stone	3
For Girls Only	4
Adventures Of Robin Boyd	6
Yardbird Ramblings	7
A Plastic Happening	13
A Living Legend	14
Beat Goes To The Movies	15

OLD TIME BEAU BRUMMELS, way back when Declan Mulligan (left) was a member of the group. Mulligan is now suing the Brummels and their managers for over one million dollars in general and punitive damages.

...WAYNE FONTANA AND THE MINDBENDERS NO LONGER EXIST.

A Horror Movie Inspired Wayne And Mindbenders

By Bruce S. McDougall

The Mindbenders originated in a horror movie. No, Eric, Ric and Bob are not the sons of Frankenstein. But they did get the idea for their name from a horror flick. Apparently some peculiar bloke in the film went around bending minds.

We first came to know the Mindbenders when they broke into the U.K. and U.S. disc scene with Wayne Fontana. Well, Wayne decided to go his own way and that was the last we heard of him. He has had minor hits but he is still looking for that big one (aren't we all.)

The Mindbenders, on the other hand, have been raving it up from John 'O Groats to Lands End with their latest song, "A Groovy Kind of Love." From where I sit at my typewriter it looks as if the boys will be doing the same thing Stateside.

Worried

When Wayne Fontana left the group, the Mindbenders were very worried about their future. After all, Wayne was the main attraction in the group, and the boys' fans were quite likely to get up and follow Wayne.

As it turned out, the Mindbenders proved themselves to be stars in their own right. Even before their present hit, the popularity of the Mindbenders was soaring. One of the best gauges of popularity in England is the concert tour. The group turned out to be a very big pull in the theaters. Perhaps pop fans aren't as fickle as some people think.

The Mindbenders new hit was written by seventeen-year-old American Toni Weil, and they are just as crazy about her composing ability as she is about their performing ability. The song first came to the attention of the Mindbenders by way of a demo disc (remember Eden in The BEAT told all America that one of the best ways for a budding composer to get his or her work recorded was to make a demo?)

According to the Mindbenders the version of the song by Toni would have been a hit in itself, but for some reason nobody picked it up. Not to worry however, now that Toni Weil has written one hit, the stars will be lined up outside her door.

When asked the standard questions in an interview, the Mindbenders usually come up with standard answers. For instance: they all love coke – providing it is given that Scotchy Beatle touch; they all like singers such as Jerry Lee Lewis, Little Richard, Fats Domino and John and Paul; they all like Lennon and McCartney compositions, and finally their biggest ambition in life is to go on making money.

Crashing

All pretty normal answers from pop singers, but Ric at least comes up with a different answer to the question, "What was your most thrilling experience." Believe it or not but Ric's most thrilling experience was crashing on the M.I. The M.I. is a six lane highway between London and Birmingham. It is also the big scene for he Rockers. This is their favorite highway for "doing the ton." I don't know whether Ric was "doing a ton down the M.I." but he sure wasn't in low gear.

For quite some time it appeared that the Mindbenders had disappeared into that never-never time zone, which is usually referred to as "Whatever happpened to-----?" I am glad to say that this is no longer so. People no longer say "Whatever happened to Wayne Fontana and the Mindbenders?" No indeed, they just say "Whatever happened to Wayne Fontana?"

On the BEAT

By Louise Criscione

Holly, Tony Hicks, didn't dig the Stones' British LP, "Aftermath," much at all. Said the backing sounded like a 12 string out of tune. Can't imagine why Tony didn't like the album – he only played it full blast and succeeded in driving practically everyone on our entire floor completely crazy, not to mention deaf!

We received a nice surprise this week when chief Papa, John Philips, wandered into The BEAT offices for a cup of coffee, a sandwich and a chat. Have to admit I had come to think of all the Mama's and Papa's as Bohemian type characters – rather groovy but in a weird, far-out sort of way.

Groovy Papa

However, I don't mind telling you that I still consider John rather groovy but not weird at all. Fact is, he's a very down-to-earth individual who also happens to be extremely brave – he actually drank a whole cup of my coffee without so much as making a face! And, believe me, *that* takes real courage. Horrible stuff, my coffee!

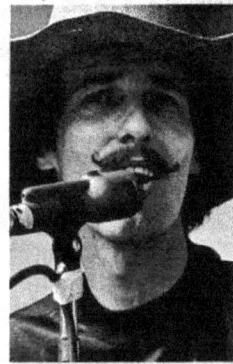

...JOHN PHILIPS

Would you believe that Mick Jagger discovered Nico, female singer in the Velvet Underground? Apparently, Mick came running into Andrew Oldham's office one day, dragging Nico behind him and shouting that he had discovered the next Joan Baez. He then proceeded to make Nico sing, thoroughly convinced that she was wonderful. However, Oldham came to the conclusion that she was "bloody awful" and everyone else agreed, which completely shot Mick down. After hearing her sing I must say my opinion stands somewhere between Mick's and Andrew's but considerably closer to Andrew's.

The Bobby Fuller Four are finally moving from the Hollywood scene to play the Ondine in New York, followed by a stand at the Phone Booth beginning June 13.

Sat next to Ryan O'Neal and Barbara Parkins at Andy Warhol's Plastic Inevitable Show the other night at The Trip and heard Ryan state as he sat among the long-hairs that he was sure glad his hair wasn't – long, that is. Barbara (who, incidently, boys, looks as good off camera as on) became downright shocked at times but seemed to really enjoy the show anyway.

Sloopy Hangin' On

The Beatles are number one in Argentina, Italy, New Zealand and Norway with "Michelle." Plus, they top the charts in Australia with "Norwegian Wood." But that's nothing – "Hang On Sloopy" is number one in the Philippines. Which is not at all fantastic until you see that it's the Newbeats' version of "Sloopy" hanging up there on the top, if you can believe that!!!

One time Searcher, Chris Curtis, has left the group to become a record producer for Pye Records in London. Chris was a Searcher for five years but apparently became fed up with the group scene and is now the possessor of a contract from Pye declaring that he can record who and what he likes (including himself) with any vocal or instrumental combination he wishes to use.

Keith Richard has purchased a fifteenth century house in Sussex, England. It's really old world with a thatched roof and a moat circling the house. Keith, who should be all moved in and settled by now, says: "I'll have to keep a large stock of bread as the moat has an added attraction – ducks."

The Stones have earned their third gold LP within six months for their latest album, "Big Hits (High Tide And Green Grass)." The LP features 10 pages of Stone photos, all done in color and all totally fantastic. The third gold LP was awarded the Stones last week as it surpassed the one million dollar mark in sales. Other gold winners were "December's Children" and "Out Of Our Heads," both of which are still high on the album charts.

Break Out

The Hideaways, one of the most popular groups in Liverpool and the last to play on the famous Cavern stage, are still trying to break out of Northern England and conquer the rest of the Island. I understand they're pretty good, so sooner or later we'll probably be hearing from them Stateside.

Personal to Brian Wilson – Wish

...BRIAN WILSON

you'd smile a little more when you come up to visit us. Doesn't hurt and besides we rather dig the Beach Boys up here – myself included.

KRLA ARCHIVES

The Ignored Stone

...CONCENTRATING

...CRACKING UP

...SAYING "HI"

By Louise Criscione

Why is it Keith Richard is the Stone who receives the least amount of publicity or fanfare? Of the three eligible Stones, Keith is the most romantically unattached member of the group. Mick has been steadily dating Chrissie Shrimpton for ages, Brian seems to change girl friends quite often but always manages to have at least *one* steady all the time. So, you really would think Keith would be the main object of Stone fans' daydreams, wouldn't you? But for some totally unaccountable reason, it just doesn't work that way.

On stage, Mick's movements and Brian's blond hair share the spotlight while Keith's jet black hair and usually dark clothes occupy the extreme stage left. Sometimes he stands motionless with only his fingers flying up and down his guitar strings. Other times he grins from ear to ear as his feet jump wildly to avoid objects hurled in his direction.

Ignored

But motionless or moving, Keith is never the center of attention. On television, Keith comes across on the extreme right of your screen—*if* he is seen at all. For some reason television cameramen, caught up in attempting to beam the many faces of Jagger across to the audience, seem to completely ignore Keith.

When they do move from Mick, they tend to concentrate on the gum-chewing face of Bill Wyman or the unchangeable face of Charlie Watts. But once off Jagger, they would really rather devote their attention to Brian Jones whose face lights up and whose lips spread into an enormous grin whenever he catches sight of himself on the television monitor.

Because Keith is so often in the background, people have come to believe that he is rather shy with a somewhat drab personality. But don't believe it. Keith's personality is *anything* but drab! He jokes and kids around as much, if not more, than the other Stones.

Big Ears

He's a reporter's delight because no matter what you ask him, Keith always manages to come out with a witty answer. Over and over the question of long hair will come up but instead of answering the monotonous question with a simple "because we want to" or "it's really none of your business," Keith thinks up a different reply each time. Probably his best was a straight-faced: "I wear mine long because I have big ears!"

I particularly remember one Stones' press conference when an older reporter insisted upon dwelling on the subject of long hair and unsatisfied with Keith's answers, demanded to know if Keith would ever cut his hair—to which Keith replied, again straight-faced: "Well, not unless it falls out!"

Still unsatisfied, the reporter grudgingly admitted that it was probably all right for the Stones to wear their hair long as they were entertainers—but what about the ordinary kids?

Keith knew the reporter was pressing for some sort of an opinion on "ordinary kids" wearing their hair long and was not about to give up until he had cornered Keith into giving one. So, Keith obliged.

He got his opinion but he got it with a Richard twist to it when Keith answered: "If they like it, they should wear it—and, anyway, *we're* ordinary kids."

As the room burst into laughter, the reporter considered himself properly put down. He had lost in the battle of wits, lost to a long-haired ordinary kid named Keith Richard, so he quietly retreated to a chair in the back of the room and was not heard from again during the conference.

Keith will answer any question put to him. But the answer will depend on two things—the question itself and how it's asked. If it is a serious question, Keith will answer seriously and honestly. But if it's a question asked in a sarcastic tone of voice, Keith will shoot back an equally sarcastic answer but he'll do it in such a way that he comes out on top with whoever asked the question looking very much like the dope of the year.

Keith's a firm believer in "a stupid question deserves a stupid answer." A perfect example occurred when a reporter asked out of the clear blue if the Stones had ever broken any bones—to which Keith deadpanned: "No, they don't break." Another time a reporter suggested that the Stones had never travelled to any Communist countries because they were afraid. Keith, looking very offended, replied: "*I'm* not afraid of the Commies, sir."

The other Stones tease Keith incessantly about his love for the guitar. They say that if it was possible for a person to marry his guitar, Keith would be the first in line! And it is true that Keith is particularly attached to the guitar. Even during a break in a recording session, you'll see Keith head for the pizza or coffee machine with his guitar still strapped around his neck.

Paid Off

His attachment to the guitar has paid off for him, though. Many declare Keith one of the best, if not *the* best, guitarist on the scene today. He rarely makes audible mistakes. In fact, I can remember only one time when he did goof. It was at a recording session and he breezed through hours minus one mistake and then on about the fifth take of a song, Keith played the wrong chord. All Stones halted and Keith said simply: "Sorry," as he began the count again.

Keith is the most obviously nervous Stone. He unconsciously chews his fingernails and is seldom found without a cigarette in his hand. Perhaps he's the worrier of the group and while concentrating on whatever happens to be worrying him at the time will pick up any wad of paper which is lying around and stick it into his mouth.

One time he did that on a plane and when the man sitting next to him went to light a cigarette, Keith (without thinking) stuck the end of the paper up for a light. Not knowing what Keith was up to, the man obligingly lit the end of the paper and at the smell of something burning somewhere, Keith finally came back from his contemplation just in time to discover that the burning was coming from somewhere very near the end of his nose!

A witty, friendly, good-looking and highly intelligent young man is Keith Richard. I wonder why more people don't appreciate him?

KRLA ARCHIVES

BEAT Photo: Chuck Boyd

AN OPEN LETTER
To Sonny And Cher

Dear Mr. and Mrs. Bono,

I don't suppose I have to tell you that you have two hit records in our UK charts at the moment. One is "Bang, Bang" which is only being held away from the top spot by Dusty Springfield's "You Don't Have To Say You Love Me." The other is "What Now My Love?" – which is a surprise best-seller since the same title made our Top Ten not too far back via a completely different recording.

Things are happening for you on the album front too. "The Wondrous World Of Sonny And Cher" has been tipped as a potential jackpot-winner and "The Sonny Side Of Cher" has been getting great reviews in our trade papers.

In addition to all this you're getting fairly wide TV exposure in a sort of remote-control fashion because shows like our "Tops Of The Pops" have got hold of several frequently-screened film clips which are keeping your faces in front of Britain's viewing public.

Maybe you're wondering why I am writing this open letter. I'll come to that in a moment. It's basically because I admire your talents – as a singing duo, as individual solo performers and as something above-average in the songwriting field.

In fact I saw your act long before most people over here in the UK. I watched what I think was your very first concert performance at Long Beach sometime around the end of October, 1964. The bill-toppers on that occasion were Gerry and the Pacemakers and Billy J. Kramer with the Dakotas, groups with whom I was traveling. Even then you had something excitingly different to offer in the way of a live performance and I'm sure you'll be the first to agree that you've come a very long way since then.

Last year you hit the pop headlines on both sides of the Atlantic with a mighty bang. So many of your records came across here in a space of two or three months that everyone said you'd burn yourselves out popularity-wise through overexposure. But that didn't happen and the 1966 UK charts prove the fact.

So I'll get the to point. It seems that your British representative has all kinds of exciting plans in mind for you over here. He wants to talk about them. He wants to talk UK television, UK concerts, UK promotion generally.

A few days ago Larry Page (he's your British representative, or so he understands) had some strong words to say. He told reporters here that he just couldn't locate either of you despite his great efforts. "All kinds of rumors are coming over about them but every time I get a new number and call them I find it's been changed again" he claimed. "It's impossible to reach Sonny and Cher. Perhaps they've become so big in their own country that they're not interested in Britain anymore."

Now I, for one, refuse to believe that you're not interested in Britain any more. From a business angle I'm sure you know the cash value of scoring Top Ten hits in Britain. From an artistic angle I'm sure you appreciate how many loyal fans there are in Britain and just how big a welcome you'd get from them as soon as you touched down here at London Airport.

So, maybe you didn't realize that Mr. Larry Page has been burning up the transatlantic telephone cables in his efforts to reach you. Or maybe your British Representative has been exaggerating. I don't know. In fact, I see no point in getting myself involved in someone else's argument.

But I do see plenty of point in persuading you to make another trip to Britain in the not too distant future. So maybe you'll decide that it's your turn to make a telephone call to London. A transatlantic chat with Larry Page would set the record straight. And just in case you have any difficulty reaching Mr. Page, here's a note of his London office number – it's Temple Bar 4864.

Hope we can look forward to seeing you both in Britain later this year.

With good wishes,
Yours sincerely,
TONY BARROW
HOTLINE LONDON

For Girls Only
By Shirley Poston

I'm numb, I tell you, numb.

I suppose you're thinking that you've just been treated to another in a long series of typographical errors. Well, you're all wrong (which figures because you sure wouldn't be reading this column if you were all right.) An N was not accidentally substituted for a D in that opening sentence.

Now, if I can summon me wits about me (which won't be easy because in order to summon one's wits, one must first have wits to summon) I'll tell you what I'm babbling about.

I'm numb (as in D) because I've finally done it! Finally gone and dreamed a realie that not only exceeds my fondest hopes but goes well beyond me wildest imagination (and man, that's going some.)

Needless to say, it was about GEORGE. And needless-er to say, if I could tell you about it, I'd have at least come back to earth by now. However, I would be happy to ugzj hkxipn rkvhqnigzjs zug ejgza svgeenv.

Apologies

Down, girl and/or Shirl. And apologize to all the nice people who didn't send in for your code and therefore haven't the foggiest notion what you're trying to say. (Then apologize to all the nice people who did send in for your code and still don't have the foggiest notion what you're trying to say.) (No one is perfect.)

Speaking of George (in low, hoarse whispers) ... er ... I mean speaking of codes, I have the feeling that both of my many readers are forming a war party and massing in the direction of The BEAT office. On account of because some of the codes arrived a little late (as in the early spring of 1967.)

You see, it's this way. The other night I was sleeping peacefully (actually, I was thrashing about making up another George whopper but I wouldn't want to shatter my cool, calm image) when I discovered that I was not alone.

Well, as you may have guessed (knowing the direction in which my luck seems to be running these days), the large lump under the mattress turned out to be a huge envelope containing almost two hundred un-answered code letters. Sorry about that.

Speaking of the village idiot himself, a lot of you who have been trying to coax me into at least giving my age away (I won't, but I might believe selling it if the price is right) have figured out that I have to be over sixteen because I refer to the aforementioned V.I. as my "little brother." Well, don't consider this a hint, but my term of reference doesn't necessarily apply to his age. However, it describes him perfectly above the eyebrows.

Oh, before I forget. I have to tell you something really embarrassing. While I was dreaming up an adventure for Robin Boyd and George of Genie fame, I suddenly found myself dreaming up an adventure for Shirley Poston and George of Genie fame.

If I suddenly feel my arm being yanked clean out of the socket, I'm going to wonder if a little bird isn't trying to tell me something. Something like keep your remaining hand off my George!

Gasp. That reminds me. I'm confused (this is news?), but delirously so. Remember the Robin Boyd Was Here stickers I told you about? Well, I saw one pasted in a telephone booth! It was handmade (the sticker, not the telephone booth) and looked so groovey I fairly flipped!

Luvly Idea

What I want to know is where did all this start, anyroad? I LUV the idea, but the girl who sent me the stickers didn't explain where the brainstorm came from. Will someone please clue me in? I'd like to at least thank the genius who thought up this zingwhammer!

Oh, I've just thought of the greatest line I should have said a couple of paragraphs back. I should have said that although Robin probably was in that phone booth, if I know R.I.B. (and, I sure do), she wasn't there alone! (A-hem.) Well, better late than never, I always say. (I always say that.)

This time I would like to call your attention to the fact that I have passed the half-way point (not to mention the one of no return) in this column without uttering so much as a sensible, rational word. Just thought you'd like to know.

I am also about to forget to mention my big boo-boo in the Beatles at the Cavern thingy. Did you catch the part where I said something about the yeah-yeah-yeah parts in "Kansas City." No, no, no, Shirl. They're coming for you again, and what's more, they're bringing stronger nets.

Hey-Hey-Hey

I, of course, meant to say the hey-hey-hey-hey parts, which never fail to reduce me to a quivering lump. Say, that's just given me an idea. Why don't we make up a list of Beatle Mindblowers? You know, things that really make one rattle the bars of the olde cage. If you'll send in your fave thingys, I'll make up said list and threaten someone into mimeographing about a million copies. (No, no, I won't use your names.) (Cowards.) Then I'll send said copies to whomever (my grammar is improving) (so's my speling) wants one.

I guess I shouldn't limit it to just the Beatles. Not if I want to live long. (Right, Stones-people?) So, after I complete this project (would you believe the early spring of 1968?) we'll do an all-star list, okay?

By the way, Paul-people, two of my all-time goosebumpers are the way your own true luv sings a certain line in "P.S. I Love You" and the way he looked when he sang "The Night Before" in "Help."

Hmmmmm. I think it's about time I said something I've been meaning to impart for several moons. If I ever give anyone the impression that I'm not a Ringo fan, it just ain't so. You're so right about Richard Starkey. He is beautiful.

Big John

I ask you. Am I in a Beatle mood? Answer – I'm in a Beatle mood. And since I've discussed all of them (a comment not without a certain amount of truth to it) (huh?) except John, I must tell you a song parody I wrote in his honor. (Also in pencil.) It's sung to the tune of "Big Bad John" and come to think of it, I must NOT tell you.

Gulp and blub. I've just read this insanity over and I really must apologize for being so out of my gourd (not to mention about as subtle as a steam-roller.)

I promise to be in more normal (ho) condition next week, providing I don't have another of those dreams. (If I do have another, I'll be in Surrey next week.)

And, since you were so kind and understanding and put up with me this column, my next collection of ravings will include an extra-special (as in super-bonus-fabgear) announcement.

Now what? I'll never tell. But, if by any remote possibility, a certain someone you sorta like is going to be passing through town within the next few months, and you'd kindof enjoy meetin him in person, stick around.

There ... that's better. Now I don't feel so lonely up here on Cloud Four.

Army Keeps Sadler Busy

S/Sgt. Barry Sadler is a very busy man.

Since he recorded his album and single, both called "The Ballad of the Green Beret," he spends much of his time on assignment away from Ft. Bragg doing public relations and recruitment work for the Army.

A glance at his schedule in the past month proves he's had little time to himself. For example, he appeared in Atlanta for the Red Cross one day, and presided the next day as Grand Marshall of the Apple Blossom Parade there.

Then he traveled to Danville, Va., to meet the Veterans of Foreign Wars. From Virginia he flew to Chicago to attend the Military Order of World Wars Association.

In addition to all his public relations work, S/Sgt. Sadler has recorded a new single, "The A Team."

Herman Comin'
(Continued from Page 1)

much like to leave behind him a string of broken attendance records and, accordingly, the group has been booked into large auditoriums and stadiums all across the country. During their previous tour the Hermits broke attendance records in 12 cities, but this time they're aiming for all 27 cities!

And judging by the way their records have a habit of becoming hits, Herman's Hermits just might succeed in selling-out everywhere they go!

KRLA ARCHIVES

...TONY HICKS ...GRAHAM NASH ...ALLAN CLARKE ...ERIC HAYDOCK ...BOBBY ELLIOT

The Hollies Take Over The BEAT

By Carol Deck

They came, they saw, they created chaos, they captured our hearts, our dog and one of our albums, and they left, we *think* — there may still be one under a desk somewhere.

The Hollies — Graham Nash, Allan Clarke, Tony Hicks, Eric Haydock and Bobby Elliot — took over *The BEAT* one day and completely destroyed one entire afternoon.

It all started the day after they arrived on the West Coast. We met them at a champagne reception given by Imperial Records in their honor.

They came up to the office the next day.

It went something like this. At the appointed hour the door flew open and in poured five Hollies, one road manager and we still haven't figured out who all else.

They immediately scattered to all the twelve hundred corners of our offices and introduced themselves to everyone who happened to be around and would listen.

We had cleverly put their album on the record player just before they came in. They promptly took that off and put on the Stones' "Aftermath," which we're not supposed to have because it hasn't been released here yet.

I decided to try and conduct an interview with the Hollies (fool that I am) and started attempting to round them all into one office.

I found Allan sitting in a corner holding the Boss's dog, Suzie, who never lets *anyone* but the Boss hold her.

The rest were still running around the office reading everything — back issues of *The BEAT*, notices on the bulletin board, hieroglyphic notes scribbled on scraps of paper and even the label on the coffee can.

After a bit of maneuvering I finally got them all into one office, whereupon they promptly sent their road manager out for cokes and coffee.

"OK," I said.

"OK," said Tony sprawling himself across the desk in front of me and looking up at me from a distance of approximately two inches from the end of my eye lashes.

"I don't like Batman," he stated, "But I like the Beverly Hillbillies."

And he was off. The first thing that became apparent about Tony is that he's no problem to interview — he talks constantly.

He told me that L. Ransford, the name of the writer of most of the songs on their album, is actually himself, Graham and Allan.

He told me how proud they are of the fact that they never put anything on record that they can't reproduce exactly on stage. "It's disgraceful not to," he said.

He told me about all their legal problems — they had trouble getting in the country, then were denied permits to do television appearances and were allowed only a very few live appearances.

FIVE HOLLIES AREN'T ENOUGH — WOULD YOU BELIEVE FIFTEEN?

At one point, in Detroit, they were so disgusted they booked flights for home and even sent their equipment home. After being talked into visiting the West Coast, they did manage to get clearance for a few live appearances and had to borrow equipment to perform.

But then it occurred to me that there were four other Hollies and despite Tony's overwhelming charm, I had better see what they were up to, so I politely tried to shut Tony up.

He finally jumped up, called Graham up to occupy the space he vacated across the desk in front of me and walked out of the room.

He rather startled *BEAT* reporter Louise Criscione when he strolled into her office and announced that I had kicked him out 'cause he talked too much. Thanks a lot Tony, you almost blew my job.

And so it went, each one making himself at home in the middle of the desk I was trying to take notes on, all except Eric, he doesn't talk.

Bobby told me a secret about Eric though, "He talks a lot when he's alone."

So after each one had told me his life story (more or less) and wandered out to investigate the office, I found myself alone with Eric, and Bobby was right, he does talk!

He said he is a big fan of Bob Dylan and Jimmy Smith and that the name Hollies started out as a joke name — that's about all he said, but at least now I'm sure he does talk.

Graham also clued me in to why Herman is more popular here than in England. He says it's because America "thinks he's Hitler and is going to take over the country."

Asked what *he* thought about Herman and his Hermits, Graham replied, "As a group, rubbish, but as a fellow, quite nice. I'll say one thing for him though, he never professes to be anything else."

Then Graham strolled out, took the Stones off the record player and put on the Everly Brothers, listened to one track, took the record off, stomped back in the office and said, "The Everly Brothers are fantastic, and that's my last comment."

"What do you think of the Everly Brothers, Graham?" I asked.

"No comment," he said and walked out with our Everly Brothers album, followed, we think, by the rest of the group.

THEY WERE PRETTY CALM HERE, but the next day they created total chaos in The BEAT office.

KRLA ARCHIVES

...BOB LIND

Mr. Bob Lind: 'I Want The Public To Love Me'

By Jeanne Castle

Bob Lind is a very quiet, conservative individual. So, it took three cups of coffee to get him wound up. To be completely honest, Bob is one of the most interesting performers I have interviewed, one who possesses a most unusual philosophy of life. He wants to sing and write songs for anyone who will listen and this plus singing to make people happy gives him complete satisfaction.

Bob started singing just about the time he started talking but it took him 11 years to begin playing the guitar. He managed to struggle through four guitar lessons before his teacher quit! However, Bob assured me that it wasn't *his* fault the teacher left but he grinned when he said it so I imagine Bob had a *little* bit to do with his instructor's early departure!

Singing has always been Bob's only love because singing makes him happy. Having a career never even entered his mind as he was much more interested in writing songs.

But now it appears that singing makes up a huge part of his life because he just couldn't wait to sing some of his songs for us. So, the interview was temporarily put aside while Bob gave a sneak preview of several of his compositions.

The willingness of Bob to perform so readily after he had spent the last two days and nights recording was beyond my imagination but it didn't seem to faze Bob at all. The feelings which go into the songs he writes are all feelings which he has actually experienced during his lifetime.

I asked if there were times when Bob was really down and had to worry about where his next meal was coming from and surprisingly enough he replied: "Definitely, yes." But then Bob hastened to add that when he least expected it someone always came to his rescue and found him a job singing in some small coffee house or cafe.

Bob has tremendous faith in people and believes that, "Wherever you are or whatever you do — you are never alone."

When asked what the turning point in his career was, Bob immediately answered: "Meeting Charlie Greene and Brian Stone." Greene and Stone were formerly the managers of Sonny and Cher and are now attempting to do for Bob what they achieved for Sonny and Cher.

I asked Bob how public life had affected his private life. "It affects me to a great extent. I want the public to love me and know me for what I am — just a happy individual who wants to spend his life singing and writing songs," said Bob Lind, one of the happiest individuals I have ever met.

Say you saw it in The BEAT

Adventures of Robin Boyd

By Shirley Poston

CHAPTER TWENTY-NINE

If there was one thing Robin Boyd learned the time she signed up for an easy-sounding class and found herself in an R.O.T.C. unit, it was to not give up easily. And it looked as though her commando training was about to come in handy.

Much as she disliked having to resort to violence, there seemed to be no other solution. She'd already tried the old lay-it-on-the-line explanation bit. And what had her understanding genie done when she'd broken the news about having to attend the prom tonight with John D. (as in Dolt) Winston (due to a rash promise of six months ago?)

George had understandingly broken both her ear lobes, that's what!

So, left with no other choice, Robin stood on tippy-toe, grasped George in a gentle but firm Half-Nelson and marched him off to the nearest phone booth.

Ummmmmmmmmm!

"*Robin Irene Boyd,*" he gasped, looking very shocked and displeased as she stood on tippier-toe and took careful aim. (Some afternoon when George has nothing to do, he should put his acting talents to better use and win a nice Oscar for his mantle.) "Ummmmmm," he added as she applied a hammerlock (not to mention fresh lipstick) and fired.

And, being the sort of person who is very dedicated to her work (as in nice if you can get it), Robin didn't even give up when the opposition began to show signs of unconditional surrender. Instead, she stuck to her guns until the enemy was totally destroyed.

Then she released her stranglehold on same and smiled innocently. (Speaking of Academy Awards . . .) "Now can I go to the prom?" she simpered.

Making an effort to pull himself together and failing, George fell out of the phone booth. But it didn't take him long to regain his Liverpudlian compsure (otherwise known as Pool Cool.) Nor did it take him long to yank her out after him. (It did, however, take him longer than it *would* have if he'd bothered to open the door first.)

"All right, you *nit*," he bellowed. "You can go, but don't think *I* won't be there. I *will* be, and I'll be watchin' every move you make!"

For a second, Robin looked a bit dismayed. (Not that she minded the thought of George keeping an eye on her. It was just that she suddenly realized there were several changes to be made in the *Way To A Man's Heart* sampler she was embroidering in Home Economics.) But, before George started re-yanking, she put on a happy face (fortunately, she had one with her)

"And I'll be thinking of you every moment," she syruped.

George gave her a menacing glint of the olde eye. "I hope so," he warned. "So do *you,*" he further warned. Then, before she could ask him what he meant by *that,* he vanished into thin air.

Hoping to high Heaven that she never had to find *out* what he meant by that, Robin looked at her watch and broke into a graceful (you bet) gallop.

Several hours later, she sat in the living room in all her glory (also in a chair), waiting for *It* to arrive. She looked reasonably calm and reasonably gorgeous (if she did say so herself) (and, you guessed it, she did), but she felt about as relaxed as an undernourished piranha fish.

Snit-Throwing

And, what's more (or, if you prefer, less) (and you're just the type), she was utterly exhausted. Having had her fair share of problems that morning, she had spent the afternoon coping with a series of liberal second helpings. Therefore, she had not only *exceeded* her two-tantrums-per-day limit. She was now the possessor of a new world's record for snit-throwing.

The main event had occurred at approximately 1 p.m. After briskly searching (as in hysterically plowing) through her closet, she had discovered that her one (excuse for) an evening gown simply would not do. (Not do for the prom, that is.) (It would do just *fine* for her next piano recital.) (Providing she wore matching anklets.)

To make a short story long, it had taken over ten minutes of post-graduate heel-kicking to convince her mother in twenty-five (thousand) words or less that she not *only* didn't have a thing to wear but intended to *prove* it.

Then, when she'd finally won temporary custody of the Boyd charge-plate, there had been a leisurely trip downtown for the purpose of carefully selecting a new formal. (As in race out to the garage, shriek "Liverpool," flap to the nearest store, snatch a dress off the nearest rack and hope for the best.)

Staggering

This was followed by a chain of events which stagger, among other things, the imagination. For instance, the hair-dryer chose this particular day to blow a fuse (too), Ringo sewed clean through two of Robin's favorite ribs while making a stab (amen) at helping with last minute alterations, and the dog devoured one of Robin's evening slippers without having so much as the courtesy to wait until she (Robin, not the dog) had removed her foot (from the slipper, from the slipper.)

But, despite this change of pace on the part of the someone up there who had previously seemed to at least *tolerate* if not actually *like* her, Robin had to smile when the doorbell heralded the arrival of the aforementioned *It.*

How could she possibly have *helped* but smile? Thanks to her "way" with electrical devices (as in Explosions, Inc.) the aforementioned doorbell now played the entire first chorus of "Girl," complete with a Lennonesque gasp (known in some circles as a real knee-knocker if there ever was one.)

Fortunately, *It* thought she was smiling at him. A pleasant change that helped him bear up under the physical and emotional strain of making Ringo's acquaintance. (The buxom brat had broken her Ludwig droomstick earlier in the day, but in an attempt to remain in character, was busily spearing him with a knitting needle.) (And don't think he didn't get the point.)

Runnin' Dad

After introducing *It* to her parents (no, make that parent, as Robin's dad was out of town again) (considering what was running *in* his family, it's no small wonder that he spent a great deal of time running *from* his family) Robin sailed majestically down the front steps.

Settling herself comfortably on the arm rest of *It's* father's car door, she was surprised to find herself in a slightly better mood (the desire to take large bits of innocent passers-by had been reduced to small bites.) Then she was equally surprised to feel a sudden tightness in her throat.

But, the feeling was purely transitory (and didn't last long, either) so she dismissed it as a budding case of hard-earned larangitis. And it's just as well that she did.

Having quite enough problems at the moment, thank you (you're welcome, you're welcome), it was better that Robin be temporarily spared the truth.

She would find out soon *enough* that the *real* cause of her momentary discomfort was an invisible collar which had been clamped about her lily white neck.

She would also find out that the other end of her *leash* was clutched in the clenched fist of another title-holder.

Namely, the World's Teed-Offest Genie.

14 New Songs From Bob Dylan

HOLLYWOOD — Bob Dylan has just completed a brand new album, entirely recorded in February in Nashville. The A&R work was done once again by Bob Johnston.

In an exclusive to *The BEAT*, we have learned that Bob's new LP will be a *double-set* — two records contained in the album which will be titled "Blonde on Blonde."

On the first side of the album, the new songs will be: "Rainy Day Women, #12 & 35;" "Pledging My Time;" "Visions of Johanna" (this one is the longest on the side, seven minutes and thirty seconds); "One of Us Must Know (Sooner or Later);"

Second side of the album contains "I Want You;" "Memphis Blues Again;" "Leopard-skin Pill-Box Hat;" and "Just Like A Woman."

The first side of the second record in the set will offer "Most Likely You Go Your Way and I'll Go Mine," "Temporary Like Achilles;" "Absolutely Sweet Marie;" "4th Time Around;" and "Obviously 5 Believers."

The fourth and final side will contain only one song — 11 minutes, 23 seconds — entitled "Sad Eyed Lady of the Lowlands."

It's a brand new album by a singer-composer who managed to revolutionize the pop music industry during 1965. It's a new year now, and a slightly different pop scene. But we might just be in for another revolution from the very revolutionary Mr. Dylan.

KRLA ARCHIVES

...THE YARDBIRDS (l. to r. Sam Smith, Keith Relf, Jeff Beck, Jim McCarty and Chris Dreja.

Shapes Of Ramblings From Yardbirds

(ED. NOTE: One of The BEAT's London based correspondents recently spent some time with the Yardbirds, so he immediately mailed us some Yardbird rantings and ravings which we thought you might be interested in reading.)

By Michael Mitchell

The Yardbirds are thoroughly fed up with the British pop music scene. A complete drag – nothing refreshing happening. America – the greatest – can't praise its music enough.

Keith, Paul and Jim think that the Lovin' Spoonful are the greatest group around. They think American recording facilities are far superior to Britain's – 100% more responsive.

Keith thinks "in" clubs are a monumental drag but only last week they set an all time record for attendance at the Marquee Club... Keith says: "We weren't at our best that night because we were so tired after three weeks of one-nighters."

Keith's wife, April, was there too so I had a chat with her. Apparently, she met Keith at a Beatle concert in London. When the show was over she went around to the back door of the theater and waited until the Yardbirds came out. Eighteen months later April and Keith were married – so keep your chin up girls, there might be some hope for you after all!

What with Keith, Chris and Jeff married and Paul going very steady it looks as if only Jim McCarty is left in the matrimonial stakes. Jeff is seeking a divorce from his wife at the moment, so there may be another contender soon. Jeff tells me he can't wait to return to California because there's a special film starlet he particularly digs who lives there.

I don't know why, but trouble with the Immigration Department in America seems to be one of the hazards of being a Yardbird. The first time they visited the U.S. they were threatened with deportation if they didn't leave immediately and on their last visit they again had trouble with the immigration officials. But, surprisingly enough, they are not bitter. Says Paul "Sam" Smith: "All we want to do is get along with everyone and that includes the Musician's Union."

There have been a lot of rumors floating around that the Yardbirds cannot reproduce their record sound on stage. Well, it's just not true! Every effect on record is faithfully reproduced "live," even the difficult guitar break in "Shapes Of Things." On stage they do a version of "Smoke Stack Lightning" which is so different from the original that even Howlin' Wolf's mother wouldn't recognize it! But it's a knockout.

They all dig Bob Dylan's music very much but seem to prefer Bob Lind's songwriting. Keith Relf is, in fact, set to record a Bob Lind number as a solo artist.

Their future plans include an exciting new idea in live performances incorporating 45 minute sets of constant music without any breaks between the songs! They also hope to make albums like this too. Jeff Beck asked me if I thought the idea would go down well in the States. I think it would – how about you?

In conclusion, I would like to say that I found the Yardbirds the most approachable group I have ever met – very alive, aware and just bursting with talent. I am convinced that we're due to hear a lot more from the Yardbirds in the future and I, for one, welcome it.

DISCussion

Probably the greatest record to come out of England by a female singer in a long, long while is Dusty Springfield's fantastic new disc, "You Don't Have to Say You Love Me."

Anyone with any kind of perceptive hearing just *has* to love both Dusty and her song as soon as they hear it, 'cause it is really a *gas!*

The lyrics are poignant and powerful and the melody builds up to an overwhelming conclusion. If this doesn't become a hit, then America may possibly be in dire need of an eye, ear, nose and throat doctor.

* * *

P.F. Sloan has released a great new disc – probably the most commercial record he has cut in a long while – entitled "City Woman." Great lyrics and a good beat should endear this disc to the dancing young-folk of the pop nation, and for the rest of you musical connoiseurs.

* * *

James Brown released "It's A Man's, Man's, Man's World," and everybody immediately flipped. The disc is soaring up musical charts across the nation – rhythm and blues as well as pop. Looks like still another smash for the Man of Soul.

* * *

If you recall a man named "Mr. Jones" who didn't seem to be hip to what was happening a few months ago, you will probably remember the Grass Roots who were trying to tell him.

Well, the Grass Roots are back, only this time they are doing some asking. For example, "Where Were You When I Needed You?"

Hope they find the answer with this brand new platter, 'cause it really deserves some good chart action. Give it a listen next time you're hanging 'round your favorite radio dial.

* * *

The Rascals will probably be releasing a new single any heart beat now, and if you know what's good for you – you *will* like it and make it a hit!

Why? Well, not only 'cause they are a very good group, but 'cause the Young Rascals are just that... little *rascals*, and great followers of the fine art of mischief! You never *know* who's pony tail they're gonna dunk in the ink well next if their records aren't all hits!

* * *

Stones' latest single in this country is "Paint It Black." Pretty good – considering the take-off on Beatle instrumentation, pardon-my satire-but, why so gloomy? Seems as how the Stones were in a morbid mood that day.

Well, it's going to be another hit for the boys, and probably much bigger than "Get Off Of My Cloud." But then, as the man says: *"Everybody must get STONED!"*

* * *

Happiness Incorporated: New Beatle disc will be ready for our anxious ear lobes on June 6. Titles: "Rain," and "Paperback Writer." Haven't heard the disc as yet, but I'm pretty certain it will be great. I mean, after all – isn't that the true definition of the word, "Beatle?"

* * *

Jimmie Rodger's latest, "It's Over" is probably one of the most beautiful songs he has ever recorded. He wrote it himself, and it looks as though it will be a large hit for him.

The beautiful, touching lyrics and the gentle melody will make this a contemporary favorite as well as a standard for some time to come. Look for many others to vocalize on this new tune as well.

* * *

Private to Bob Lind: Glad to see that you are sharing your music with the world, Bob. And rest assured, you *are* reaching out and touching a great many people.

KRLA ARCHIVES

Sean Connery LOSES HIS MARBLES OVER Joanne Woodward, Jean Seberg (AND A FEW OTHER LOVELY CHICKS) IN "A Fine Madness" A JEROME HELLMAN Production

We should all be so crazy

any time... any place... at any game... Samson Shillitoe can out-fox them all!

EXCLUSIVE ENGAGEMENT NOW PLAYING!

Co-starring PATRICK O'NEAL · COLLEEN DEWHURST
CLIVE REVILL · WERNER PETERS · JOHN FIEDLER · KAY MEDFORD
JACKIE COOGAN · ZOHRA LAMPERT · SORRELL BOOKE and SUE ANE LANGDON
Music Composed and Conducted by John Addison · Screenplay by ELLIOTT BAKER
Produced by JEROME HELLMAN · Directed by IRVIN KERSHNER
TECHNICOLOR® FROM WARNER BROS.

PACIFIC'S HOLLYWOOD
PANTAGES
HOLLYWOOD BLVD. at VINE
Crossroad of the Stars!
HO 9-2211

Inside KRLA
By Eden

Requests, requests, requests... everywhere you turn at KRLA there are requests flying all over the place. Not only for music, but for just about everything imaginable!

Dave Hull has put in several requests for a brand new, gold-plated, diamond-studded trumpet with which to accompany Herbie Alpert and his Brass. (Watch out, Herbie baby, the Hullabalooer is at it again!) And the Old Scuzz has already begun his annual turkey-shoot contest plugging...some six months early!

Then there's Bob Eubanks who keeps requesting a Magic Lasso with which he hopes to round up Nancy Sinatra.

And the Emp keeps requesting our Congress to declare a day on which the nation could celebrate his magnificence.

Your Radio

Quite a number of our KRLA listeners have had some requests of their own. So many in fact, that KRLA has made some requests of their own to the telephone company for some additional lines on which to take the many listener's calls.

This is *your* radio now, your music the way you want to hear it. Request radio in its finest hours. Funniest requests of all from some of the lazier-type KRLA DJ's who want to know when *you* are going to start running *your* radio. Like, when the weather is just perfect for them to go surfing, for example!

John-John (hallowed be his Bat Name!) has put in a request for a new door, since he can't seem to remove the Bat Manager sign from the one he has now.

Jim Steck has put in a request for a towel — he seems to have torn the last one he had up in several hundred tiny pieces!

"Star Operators"

KRLA has often hosted visiting celebrities in the past, but now we are sharing our house guests with you. In the last week or so, KRLA listeners have been able to speak to The Association, Roy Orbison, The Leaves, and Petula Clark as they answered our ever-ringing phones here at KRLA. There will be many, many more famous telephone "operators" coming up in the near future.

I had the pleasure of dropping in on Casey just the other eve as he was filming his telly-show, "Shebang." The night I was there, the Caser was celebrating Mother's Day, and for that special show he had as his guests many smiling mother-types and Mr. Roy Orbison.

Casey A Go Go?

The mothers were all very excited about being before the cameras, and several of them even danced. Which reminds me...they weren't the *only* ones dancing that night. Believe it or not — the old Caser got out on the dance floor — briefly, *very* briefly! — and turned a few steps around for the camera. Pardon my chortling, Casey-luv, but would you believe a Lebanese Fred Astaire?

KRLA ARCHIVES

French Frown On Fake Leopard Skin

Screaming Lord Sutch lost the election in Britain against Harold Wilson and this week found himself threatened with immediate expulsion from France—not because he lost the election but because he attempted to leave the plane dressed only in a fake leopard skin!

Screaming Lord Sutch, whose real name is David Sutch, is one of the wildest pop singers in England. During the recently held elections in Britain, Sutch ran against Prime Minister Wilson on the National Teenage Party ticket. No one knows for sure how many votes Sutch received but they do know for certain that he lost!

Axes And Swords

Screaming Lord, booked into a Paris teen club, decided to make his entry into France as noticeable as possible. So, he donned his fake leopard skin and came soaring down the plane's steps brandishing an oversized axe and shouting wildly while two members of his band staged a sword duel.

French fans gathered at the airport to greet Sutch upon his arrival thought the whole thing was magnificent but, unfortunately, the air police remained unimpressed and held Screaming Lord and his entire group for over an hour before Sutch finally agreed to dress in normal clothes.

Normal Attire

Those *normal* clothes which won French approval included a huge green 18th century coachman's hat, a highly colored shirt and bright green corduroy pants! Dressed accordingly, Sutch was officially admitted into France.

But the parting shot belonged enitely to Screaming Lord, for as he stepped down on French soil he declared: "As I failed to beat Wilson in the elections, I think I might stand against General De Gaulle over here."

As Sutch ambled off and was englufed by his adoring fans, the French police just shook their heads and muttered under their breath—"He *was* kidding, *wasn't he???*"

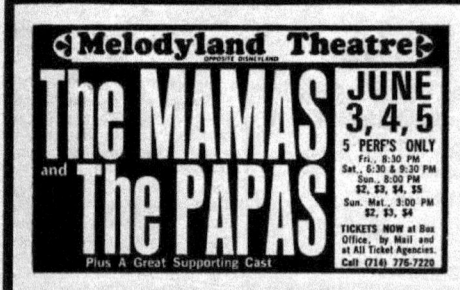

KRLA ARCHIVES

KRLA Night At The Cocoanut Grove!!!

BEAT Photos: Howard L. Bingham

... "COME ON DOWNTOWN," sings Pet.

... PETULA CLARK, STAR OF THE SHOW

... WINNERS DANCING

... AND TALKING

By Louise Criscione

It was KRLA night at the Cocoanut Grove with a most definitely talented Petula Clark as star of the show. For several weeks KRLA listeners from all over Southern California were diligently sending in post cards with their names and addresses in prominent view, hoping that when time for the drawing arrived *their* cards would be one of the ones pulled for an evening of dinner, dancing and appreciating Pet ark.

Thousands entered the contest but, unfortunately, only 25 could be winners. When the cards were drawn, those lucky winners were Steve Dundee, Tom Rizer, Phyllis Elliott, Cindy Adam and Dave Hall, Bob Graham, Marc Solomon, Linda Gilbert, John Beischel, Barbara Title, Pat Riley, Mr. & Mrs. Wayne Connally, Ginger Renshaw, Carole Beck, John D. Truxaw, George L. Dean, Cathi DuFrense, E. Mandell, Sharon Held, Mark D. Mann, Marilyn Spak and John Bright, Roberta Ronquillo, Cynthia Deleon, Bonnie Moe, and Tony Scott.

Notification of the winners caused general havoc as it meant the girls rushed for beauty parlor appointments and the boys begged off work early. Each winner received a ticket for himself and a guest and when April 29 finally rolled around all 25 couples gathered in the lobby of the Grove at 8 o'clock.

Once inside the winners mingled with such movie stars as Loretta Young and Yvette Mimieux, were treated to a marvelous dinner, plenty of dancing and one of the most professional shows ever put on stage.

If you ever have the opportunity to see Pet, do yourself a favor and don't miss it – she's great! She went down practically the whole musical spectrum singing everything from "Sign of The Times" to "Getting To Know You" to "Hello Dolly." She joked and ad libbed with the audience and was forced to come back on stage twice after her performance had officially ended because her audience simply refused to let her go.

Pet sang all of her hit singles and even succeeded in slipping in a Beatle song, "I Wanta Hold Your Hand," which she admitted was "heavily disguised" but which was great anyway!

The evening went off without one single hitch and all of the winners expressed their delight in being chosen by KRLA to spend an evening at one of the most famous showplaces in the world. Each and every one of them asked *The BEAT* to publically thank KRLA (which we just did!) and to tell everyone what a groovy station KRLA really is (which you already know.)

Anyway, all of the station personnel would like to thank not only the lucky winners, but everyone who entered the contest for making it such a resounding success. Congratulations to the winners, better luck next time to everyone else and keep your dial on 1110 for the next out of sight contest on KRLA!

ONE TABLE OF WINNERS enjoying the show are (l. to r.) Marc Solomon, Pat Riley, Mr. & Mrs. Riley, Mr. Elliott – and, no the last one is **not** a KRLA winner; she's **BEAT** reporter, our own Louise Criscione.

KRLA ARCHIVES

U.S. Dominates Disc Scene!

(Continued From Page 1)

you in the charts either. It has to be a good record first, regardless of nationality—and that's the way it should be.

This week's national top ten is lived in by such artists as the Mama's and Papa's, the Young Rascals, the Righteous Brothers, the Beach Boys, Bob Dylan, the Shadows of Knight, Johnny Rivers and the Outsiders, while the only British entertainer listed is Herman.

Ever since the Beatles arrived, people have been predicting the death of the English groups. They're still predicting it but don't fool yourself. It hasn't happened yet—at least, not the way they thought it would.

True, the Americans are once again dominating the record scene and perspectives have more or less returned to normal so that the measuring stick for a hit record is quality rather than nationality but the two most popular groups in the country are still the Beatles and Rolling Stones. Not because they're English but because they *are* the two best groups in their fields.

Critics

I don't know about you, but I'm really sick and tired of so-called critics crying to whomever will listen that looks and nationality make an artist, that talent has very little, if anything, to do with the success or failure of an artist.

To listen to them you'd think that the Beatles made it because they have long hair, Sonny only because he wears fur, Cher because she wears bell bottoms, the Stones because they wear whatever they feel like wearing, the Young Rascals because they wear knickers and the Beach Boys because they wear white pants and striped shirts.

In simple language what it all means is that you'd better have some talent in reserve when your gimmick wears itself thin—*if* you aim to stay around for awhile, that is. You'd better be flexible and able to bend. You'd better not become categorized because when your particular category dies, baby, you go down with it.

Timing

However, talent and individuality by themselves are most often not enough to assure an artist of a hit record. There's that all important aspect of timing. Record buyers probably don't give it much thought but people putting out records had *better* think about it because it can mean the difference between a hit and a bomb.

For instance, if the Beatles or Stones have just released a new single, it does no good for anyone else aiming at that number one spot to release a single. If it's at all possible, you will never find two top groups releasing a single at the same time.

The Stones have held up singles in order not to collide with a brand new Beatle record and although they've never admitted to holding up a single until the Stones are safely on their way down I'm sure the Beatles have, at least, given it considerable thought.

So, the see-saw continues moving with no one really sure which end will be up next month—or even tomorrow. It is more than useless and certainly foolish to declare that the British Invasion has been successfully thwarted because they just might come back stronger than ever.

Spoil It

Of course, if we knew exactly what was going to happen next, what sound was going to be "in," or what group would never again be able to come up with a smash it would spoil all the fun and excitement of witnessing the rise of a new group or the take-over of a fresh sound. Maybe it's best that the music business is just the way it is—so totally unpredictable that just when you think you've gotten the whole thing figured out something new comes along and destroys all of your predictions.

Actually, about the only safe thing you can say is that records will continue being made and hits and artists will continue flying up and down the charts. But just which record or what particular artist is *anybody's* guess!

Barry McGuire Chicken Rancher

"I'm going to be a rancher... a *chicken* rancher! I've got a 35-acre ranch and I'm going to raise chickens!" These were the latest words to The BEAT from... believe it or not!... Barry McGuire.

He told BEAT reporters that he has just purchased four chickens to inhabit his newly-acquired 35-acre ranch, at which point we quickly asked him why only four?

"Well, I believe in giving chickens a lot of room!" replied the effervescent Mr. McGuire. "I don't like to keep them *cooped* up! You may think that's an awfully large ranch for just four chickens—but you haven't seen my chickens! They each weigh *100 pounds*—I'm just going to put a saddle on each one and *ride them!*"

Aside from these new "fowl" activities, Barry has just released a new record—"Cloudy Summer Afternoon"—which may very well start a whole new trend of Rag 'n' Roll. And if it is anywhere near as successful as his first record, he won't have to wonder where his next bag of chicken feed is coming from for a long while!

Outside Album

The Outsiders hit the charts with their first single, "Time Won't Let Me," and now they've found the time to release their first album.

It carries the same name as the single and includes "Keep On Running," "Listen People," "My Girl," "She Cried," "Rockin' Robin" and five originals written by Tom King, leader of the group.

Matt Monro – A Well Respected Englishman

By Carol Deck

RESPECT—that's the only word that can really be used to describe the feeling surrounding Matt Monro, the British singer who has brought us such classics as "Softly, As I Leave You."

Matt's just finished cutting his first album in America and the sessions for that album really show the kind of entertainer he is.

He was working with an entire new set of musicians, a new arranger and a new producer. You'd think things would be a little strained just because they had never worked together before and didn't know each other.

But Matt really showed his stuff during the four day session. Unlike many artists Matt cuts a record together with the entire orchestra at the same time—most artists like to cut each set of instruments individually and then add the voices.

Not Matt, he walks into the recording booth, surrounded by a full orchestra and cuts each record all at once.

No Strain

And he cuts a first rate album in just four days—no artistic temperament, no late night sessions, no hair pulling, name calling strained emotions.

The greatest compliments a performer can receive are from his fellow entertainers and the people in the business. These people are not impressed by over night successes or gimmicks. They respect consistency and talent.

And that's the way it is with Matt. After a session you hear an engineer say, "I cut that same song with Nancy Wilson but I never *heard* the song until this afternoon."

You hear the arranger tell Matt, "you phrase a lyric beautifully."

You hear the musicians talk about how easy going he is and how he's the kind of guy you just naturally want to do great things for.

And that's really the secret of Matt Monro. He's a modest kind of guy who doesn't make demands, so you just naturally want to give him the world.

Someone at the session apologizes for being late and Matt says, "You weren't late actually, I was early."

Yet, it's respect he gets and not awe. He's not a God—he's a living, breathing, intelligent human being who happens to possess a powerfully beautiful voice.

Another Petula?

He's been called the male Petula Clark and says he has no objection whatsoever about the label. He'd be happy if he sold as many records as she does and he's sure getting a fast start on it.

He's had five albums out over here, all top sellers, and any number of big singles including "Softly, As I Leave You," "My Kind Of Girl," "Walk Away" and his latest, "Born Free," the title song from the movie of the same name.

His first album cut here is titled "This Is Life" and should be released soon. It includes some great numbers by Andre Previn.

Matt possesses one of the finest male voices around, but if you try and tell him that he passes your compliments on to the material. "That's a beautiful song," he says, or "It's great material."

He always seems to be passing compliments that were aimed at him on to some one else. He'll talk about song writers or his manager.

His manager, John Barry, is also a songwriter whose credits include "Walk Away," "Thunderball" and Born Free.

"He doesn't really need to manage me," Matt says.

Matt's manager may not need him, but we do. He's a great singer, a great entertainer and a great man—the world always needs people like that.

KRLA ARCHIVES

Pictured above on Tory Jeffery, are a few of the Mod-type styles featured at Lenny's. Musketeer boot — tured at Lenny's. Musketeer boot — Brown, Black, White — $35.00. Wide-wale cords, low-rise pant — Brown, Blue, Gold, Olive, Burgundy — $17.00. 2" belt, black — $5.00. Cowhide vest, Dk. or Lt. Brown, Burgundy, Olive, Gold — $21.00. The highest collar (4") 3-button cuff Mod shirt in wild floral or paisley prints. Name a color. Also available with contrasting collar & cuff — $10.00. For the head — corduroy cap — $10.00 or in velour $7.50 in S.M.L.

LENNY'S BOOT PARLOR
1448 GOWER ST.
HOLLYWOOD, CALIF.
466-7092

*Use order form below for items shown in picture. When ordering slacks, give waist and hip size since they are worn very low. State second color choice on all items. Your name will be added to our mailing list for our forthcoming illustrated brochure.

NAME _____
ADDRESS _____
CITY _____ STATE _____

NAME OF ITEM	1st COLOR	2nd COLOR	SIZE	PRICE

Please allow 30 days for delivery.
No COD's or stamps accepted. Money orders only.
*4% Calif. Res. Sales Tax
Postage
Total Enclosed

ENGLAND
We Knew Her When

"It's just a phase you're going through."

How many times have you heard those words? A few million, probably.

Used to bug you, didn't it? But it doesn't anymore. Like, why fight them when it's so much easier to just sit back and wait for them to join you? Which they will because the chances of a "teenage fad" turning into a national craze now falls into the sure-thing category.

Well, don't look now, but you've just been joined again. Two and a half years ago, someone switched on the Beatle beam high atop Liverpool City Hall and the younger generation went batty over the British.

Now this "phase" we were going through has *everyone* swtiched on. And whether you're fifteen or fifty, England is what's happening baby.

U.K. Mania

During this period of time when we could still call the "fad" our own, U-K-Mania was more personal than it was commercial. Not that you didn't spend your whole year's allowance on discs by British artists, spend next year's on tickets to see them perform in person, and/or donate most of your present wardrobe to the Goodwill and beg openly for loot to buy boots.

But you did a lot of other things. In those days, a large part of the British bag was seeing just how English you could act, sound and most important, feel.

If your folks didn't protest too violently, you let your hair grow. If they did, you grudgingly settled for a bumper crop of bangs.

Your friends became your mates and you learned to abbreviate fabulous. You got permanent writer's cramp from trying to correspond with anyone and everyone in Jolly Olde. And you got waspish glares from teachers who rather doubted that your new way of spelling colour and realise was purely "accidental."

Ball Snowballed

Those were the good old days. A real ball. Too much so not to be noticed by that other generation. So, the ball snowballed. And before it stopped rolling, U-K-Mania was no longer a feeling. It was an industry.

Teenagers built the bridge over the Atlantic, but adult acceptance of the red-coats was what paved it with a red carpet.

And the British had soon added another iron to every home fire America had burning for it.

The motion picture industry, for instance. In the past, most British films were only modestly successful in the U.S. Which is a crying shame because so many of them were so great.

Today, English flicks are so popular, it costs almost as much to see one as it does to produce one.

And remember when Hollywood's top stars came from Ohio or Texas or maybe even Cornbread, South Dakota?

Now they come from England. Last year's top Oscars went to Britons Rex Harrison and Julie Andrews. And "My Fair Lady" took another for best pic. This year, England's Julie Christie chalked up an additional point for their side.

Then there was the time when this country's major fashion influences came straight out of Paris. Now these come from England, too.

And let's not forget the vast wasteland. This season's telly schedule includes a number of BBC-ers.

ABC-TV's imported series, "The Avengers," does a masterful job of avenging some of our own networks' half-hearted attempts at tongue-in-cheek violence.

Diana Rigg, who plays the role of Mrs. Emma Peel, not only makes her unlikely monicker sound like it means business. She also makes a few of our hardier heroines look more like librarians.

And, although her co-star, Patrick Macnee, isn't what you'd call photo-on-the-wall material, he makes up for it in cool.

The Saint

"The Saint," which stars Roger Moore as "the famous Simon Templar" is, oddly enough, the most important British product on American television. The oddly-enough explained by the fact that it is a syndicated show which appears only in certain areas of the country. Also, it's programmed at odd hours. 11:15 on a Sunday night in some areas, for instance.

But, without much help from anyone, the series has come up through the ranks and will next season be a prime time show, in color yet!

Whether success will go to its head remains to be seen. Hopefully, it will remain a fast-moving, habit-forming, weekly glimpse at a saint who ain't, and will continue to guest star British talent like Jane Asher and others we rarely have the opportunity to see in action.

On the other side of the coin is "Secret Agent," a show that's had everything possible going for it. Half a season on CBS. Saturday night in a good time slot. Much success in the United Kingdom, where it appears under the title of "Danger Man." And a hard, handsome star (Patrick McGoohan) who was once neck-and-neck with Sean Connery for the James Bond role.

But, despite an increasing interest in the show, a growing fascination for its Irish headliner, and the fact that its theme song was recently the number one song in the nation, "Secret Agent" has already gone into re-runs and bites the dust come September. Another smooth move in a long line of same, brought to you by Sponsorville; land of the debb, home of the duff.

England matters elsewhere, too. Not just in the realms of entertainment and fashion. All British exports have had a shot in the sales arm. Everything from the Rootes Group's Hillman (forever immortalized by a small, non-speaking part in "Help") to Sundew's Double-Gloucchester cheese (manufactured just a hop, skip and a curd from the Harrison haven in Surrey) is selling bigger and better.

There's new interest in everything from the Rolls Royce to Carr's Assorted Biscuits (if you've never tasted their table water wafer, you haven't lived) (at least you haven't lived *right*.)

And America isn't the only place where England is happening. It's happening everywhere. There's always a city, one city that is really where it's at. And, in today's world, it's London.

Three years ago, this city was an international institution. Today it's a swinging Mecca for the tired traveler and another temporary plaything for the tiresome jet set.

And aye, there's the rub.

Times Change

The bridge between England and America was long overdue. Good things have come across it. The American way of life is less limited since it learned to speak with a British accent. But nothing ever lasts. Nothing this commercial, anyway, because as the times change, so do public tastes.

So, the grand-slam-large-scale fascination for anything English will fade. British phrases and fancies will disappear from the vocabularies and the lives of the people who made the big British boom possible. Restaurants will close their doors for a few days while they put away the ale tankards, sweep up the sawdust and hopefully drag out the checkered tablecloths which have been gathering dust since the demise of the big Italian boom.

And although they won't forget England completely, she won't be remembered much or with love because that other generation made its treasured memories years ago.

Maybe then it'll be our turn again. Not to take up where we left off, it'll be too late for that. But we *can* remember with love, because we won't be recalling a big fad or craze. We'll remember feeling a feeling all the money in the world couldn't buy, and recall the time you could whip off your John Lennon hat, face East, whisper thanks to someone or something that would never hear you and *mean* it.

And we're not about to forget England. After all, we knew her when.

Say you saw it in The BEAT

KRLA ARCHIVES

A Happening!

What is it? It's Andy Warhol, it's The Plastic Inevitable, it's The Velvet Underground, it's Nico, it's a pair of dancers, a candle, two whips, a candy bar, a violin, a pop bottle and movies.

It's from New York and it's on the West Coast for the first time at The Trip in Hollywood. It's going to other parts of the nation soon.

It's drawing crowds of curious celebrities and it's confusing crowds of curious.

It's happening.

See it for yourself, no questions allowed.

BEAT Photos: Howard L. Bingham

"Out of sight"... Sonny Bono, actor.

"It's like eating a banana nut Brillo Pad"... David Crosby, Byrd.

"It doesn't leave anything for the imagination"... Tony Hicks, Holly.

"It's where entertaining's going"... John Phillips, Papa.

"I'm glad I've got short hair"... Ryan O'Neal, Rodney

"The Velvet Underground should go back underground and practice"... Barry McGuire, chicken rancher.

KRLA ARCHIVES

A Living Legend In His Time

By Eden

BEAT Photos: Howard L. Bingham

"They're the greatest guys I ever worked with in my life... they're *down to earth!* People haven't really heard the Beatles yet. They are one of the most talented groups, I think, that has ever, ever been from any place or any time.

"You talk about rhythm and blues -- I love the Rolling Stones, I think that they're fantastic -- but you've got to hear the Beatles sing rhythm and blues! The people have got something coming! They are fantastic!!"

These are the words of the man who claims he started rock and roll in 1956, who feels that the Beatles are but imitations of his own unique stylings. These are the words of Richard Penniman -- Little Richard.

Has Respect

Little Richard does have a great deal of respect for the talents of both the Stones and the Beatles, and especially admires each group for its respective experimentations in the field of rhythm and blues. For Little Richard is by all rights an R&B artist -- one of the very first to carry his success over into the field of popular music, and he is truly an artist of great soul.

"To me, 'soul' is not *tricks;* to me, 'soul' is more than that. 'Soul' is when a man sings from his heart and it reaches *another* heart."

Little Richard went on to explain that he had been a life-long fan of country music, and that he considered it to be a "white man's blues."

Not a man to pretend false modesty, Little Richard is only too willing to tell you proudly of his many accomplishments in his chosen field.

"I thank God and all of the kids everywhere for the acceptance I have received. I have been in show business twenty years -- since I was eight years old! -- and I have sold 32 million records. And isn't it amazing... through all these years, the kids still know me and receive me. That can happen only to a person that the people accept."

A "Long-Hair"

In a musical age of long-haired singers, Little Richard stands as one of the originators of the much-disputed trend. His own locks have been worn quite long since the mid '50's, however it is only recently that he has discovered any difficulty as a consequence of his hair style.

In the last few weeks, he has been refused by various television shows to be allowed to make an appearance unless he would agree to trim his long hair.

Hurt and confused, Little Richard explains: "I was very hurt, because I *started* this and *everybody's* wearing long hair. This is *my* style and this is my *living*.

"Dick Clark has been very sweet to me -- he has let me come on his shows whenever I get ready, and others have been very sweet to me and let me come on their shows because I'm a legend -- and I'm still alive!"

He obtained his B.A. in theology, with minors in business administration and psychology, and then decided that he could no longer ignore the field of entertainment which he so loved, and so he decided to return.

Living Legend

Indeed he *is* a living legend in the field of rock and roll; and his praises have been sung by nearly every top artist and group of artists in the business -- including the Beatles who are among his most ardent fans.

But this is one legend who hasn't caught himself in the trap of monotony; several years ago he decided to relinquish the world of fame and fortune and went off to study theology so that he might become a minister in the church of Seventh Day Adventists.

He explains, "This is really my life; I thought I could just sit down and rest out of this -- but I can't make it. Not only financially, but it's the love of this field. A soul singer never loses that feeling.

"Once I hear a song, I wish I were singing it! The music just makes my toes and my hair move!"

Little Richard has made a great many toes move over the last pop decade... and if he has his way about it, he'll move a great many more toes before he's through!!

"Once I hear a song, I wish I were singing it! The music just makes my toes and my hair move!"

"To me, 'soul' is not tricks; to me, 'soul' is more than that. 'Soul' is when a man sings from his heart and it reaches another heart."

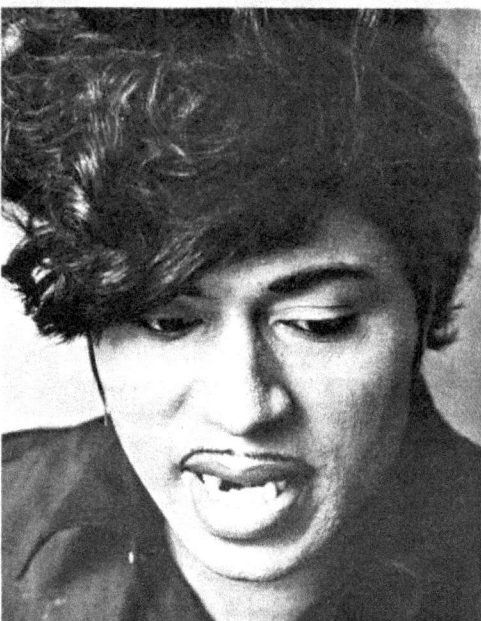

"You talk about rhythm and blues -- I love the Rolling Stones, I think that they're fantastic -- but you've got to hear the Beatles sing rhythm and blues! The people have got something coming! They are really fantastic!"

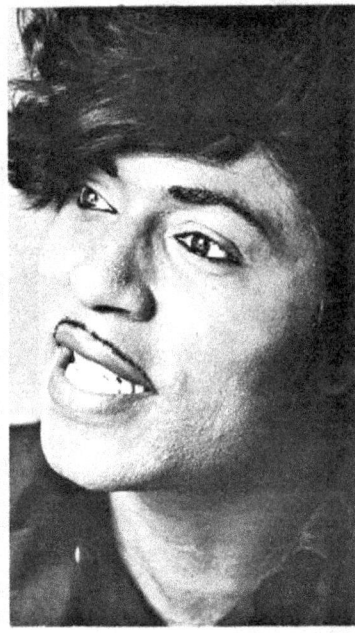

"People haven't really heard the Beatles yet. They are one of the most talented groups, I think, that has ever, ever been from any place or any time."

KRLA ARCHIVES

The BEAT Goes To The Movies
'THUNDERBALL'

By Jim Hamblin
(The BEAT Movie Editor)

It is still nice to be able to go back to the origin of all this spy jazz, and see some real professionals at work. The re-creation on the screen of the James Bond character by Ian Fleming has turned the whole world into one big spy story. Every new movie, every new TV show will be spies, superspies, and spoofs on spies for another several months. Happily it will all then fade away, as some new fad comes clattering down the walkway.

James Bond was the first of the spy pictures, and remains the best (with all due regard for Dean Martin's Matt Helm, the funniest) and very likely will stay that way for at least two more movies. Sean Connery, who has been portraying Bond, wants out, and will leave the cloak and dagger stuff after his contract expires... which means *two* James Bonds, as "Casino Royale" will be released in a few months, starring Peter Sellers!

There's a new vintage Bond beginning to appear with this movie. There are fewer gimmicks, less show of super force, and perhaps a little more sense of humor than the previous Bond flicks.

With this new found essence of maturity, the picture is maybe a little more entertaining, as well. It is attracting what may turn out to be the all-time box office gross in history.

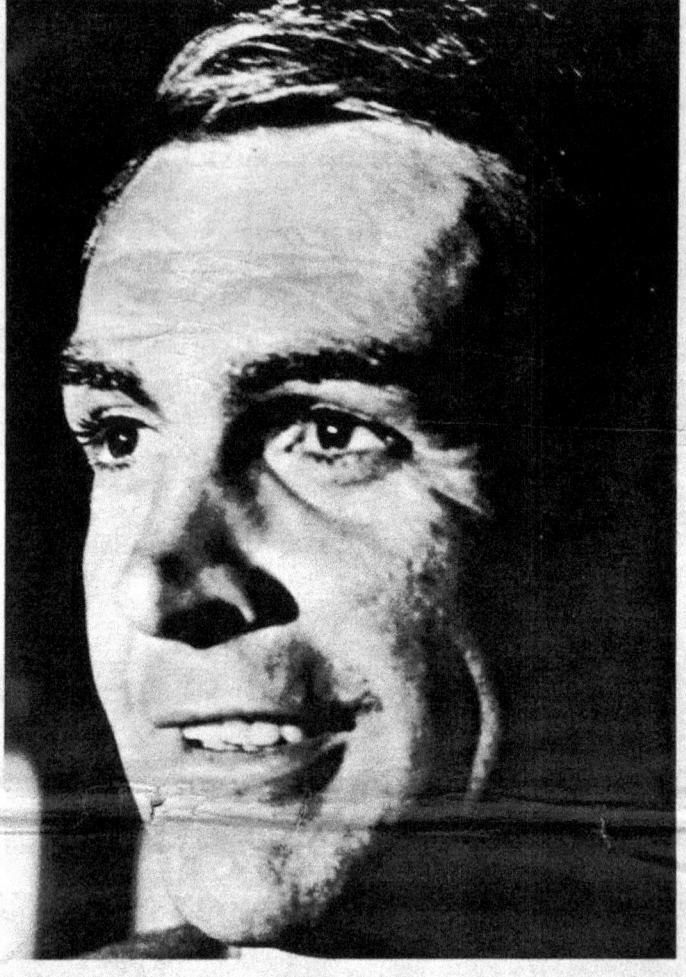

...BOND WANTS OUT

THE MORE DIFFICULT SIDE of movie making!! Three of the famous "Bond girls" who appear in this latest 007 flick-adventure.

A Man And His Music

Frank Sinatra, without a doubt, promises to be the most honored performer of the year... give or take a couple of minor accolades.

The Leader, hands-down, in individual awards during the recent National Academy of Recording Arts and Sciences tributes, Sinatra garnered a total of seven separate Grammy Awards for his "It Was A Very Good Year" single and "September of My Years" album in addition to being named "Outstanding Male Vocalist of the Year."

A few weeks later, the slim singer's video special, "Sinatra—A Man and His Music" was accorded a coveted Peabody Award and nominated a contender for this season's Emmy honors in several categories.

The much-hailed television special rated such outstanding viewer and critical response that NBC-TV will re-run the hour-long telecast on Sunday, May 15th at 10:00 p.m., immediately following "Bonanza."

To reiterate one of Sinatra's title tunes, it was indeed a "Very Good Year" for the slim singer.

Time has wrought many changes in the music world, but the Sinatra fame has held fast since the 30's when he first proved himself an undisputed champ. Today, as we are all aware, even a talented artist can become an overnight success and still wind up as a has-been before he collects the first royalty check on a million-seller record.

It is even rumored in some corners that things are moving so rapidly that rock and roll groups may soon run out of original names and, before long, resort to an identification system built around code numbers a la the digit dialing system conceived to facilitiate telephone communication.

Despite this acceleration in the demand for popular music, there always seems to be room at the top when Sinatra readies a new release.

A well-trained singer, with a special appreciation for the lyric, Sinatra on his recent one-man television show demonstrated a few of the reasons he is still a King in his field. Uncluttered by guest stars, dancers, an over-plus of dialogue or complicated sets, the telecast permitted Sinatra to go before the cameras and simply do the thing he does best... sing.

Credit should also be given to the direction of Dwight Hemion, who created the equally outstanding Barbra Streisand specials, as well as to Gordon Jenkins and Nelson Riddle, who conducted the orchestra for "Sinatra—A Man and His Music."

The re-run of this telecast on Sunday, May 15, is not only a program worthy of one's attention, but it is also a reminder that Frank Sinatra was once one of those recording stars whom many considered just another overnight hit and 'who lacked staying power required by the truly big personalities.'

Perhaps, in another thirty years, you will have the opportunity of pointing out a similar story to your own youngsters when one of today's "overnight successes" takes off into that super orbit with a certain something destined to make him a legend in his time.

KRLA ARCHIVES

KRLA Tunedex

This Week	Last Week	Title	Artist
1	1	WHEN A MAN LOVES A WOMAN	Percy Sledge
2	3	HEY JOE	The Leaves
3	5	A GROOVY KIND OF LOVE	The Mindbenders
4	7	ALONG COMES MARY	The Association
5	2	MONDAY, MONDAY	The Mama's & Papa's
6	4	RAINY DAY WOMEN #12 & 35	Bob Dylan
7	17	IN MY LITTLE RED BOOK	The Love
8	9	THE SUN AIN'T GONNA SHINE (ANYMORE)	Walker Bros.
9	13	LEANING ON THE LAMP POST/HOLD ON	Herman's Hermits
10	—	PAINT IT BLACK/STUPID GIRL	The Rolling Stones
11	6	TIME WON'T LET ME	The Outsiders
12	8	SOUL AND INSPIRATION	Righteous Bros.
13	25	FUNNY HOW LOVE CAN BE	Danny Hutton
14	33	DID YOU EVER HAVE TO MAKE UP YOUR MIND?	Lovin' Spoonful
15	20	LOVE IS LIKE AN ITCHING IN MY HEART	The Supremes
16	19	FALLING SUGAR	The Palace Guard
17	18	TEEN-AGE FAILURE	Chad & Jeremy
18	38	IT'S A MAN'S, MAN'S, MAN'S WORLD	James Brown
19	30	YOUNGER GIRL	The Hondells
20	—	DON'T BRING ME DOWN	The Animals
21	29	CAROLINE, NO	Brian Wilson
22	27	RIVER DEEP—MOUNTAIN HIGH	Ike and Tina Turner
23	37	I AM A ROCK	Simon & Garfunkel
24	31	DADDY YOU GOTTA LET HIM IN	The Satisfactions
25	—	HOLD ON! I'M A COMIN'	Sam & Dave
26	34	THE CRUEL WAR	Peter, Paul & Mary
27	32	GOT MY MOJO WORKING	Jimmy Smith
28	39	GREEN GRASS	Gary Lewis & The Playboys
29	—	DEDICATED FOLLOWER OF FASHION	The Kinks
30	—	DIDDY WAH DIDDY	Captain Beefheart & Magic Band
31	35	STRANGER WITH A BLACK DOVE/THERE'S NO LIVING WITHOUT YOUR LOVING	Peter & Gordon
32	36	COME AND GET ME	Jackie DeShannon
33	—	TRULY JULIE'S BLUES	Bob Lind
34	—	DIDDY WAH DIDDY	The Remains
35	—	BETTER USE YOUR HEAD	Little Anthony & The Imperials
36	—	YOU DIDN'T HAVE TO SAY YOU LOVE ME	Dusty Springfield
37	—	AIN'T TOO PROUD TO BEG	The Temptations
38	—	OPUS 17 (DON'T YOU WORRY 'BOUT ME)	4 Seasons
39	—	BAREFOOTIN'	Robert Parker
40	—	TWINKLE TOES	Roy Orbison

DAVE HULL

BOB EUBANKS

DICK BIONDI

JOHNNY HAYES

EMPEROR HUDSON

CASEY KASEM

CHARLIE O'DONNELL

BILL SLATER

KRLA BEAT Subscription

☐ 1 YEAR — 52 Issues — $5.00   ☐ 2 YEARS — $8.00   ☐ 6 MONTHS — $3.00
Enclosed is _____   ☐ CASH   ☐ CHECK   PLEASE PRINT — Include Your Zip Code

Send to: .... Age: ....
Address: .... City: ....
State: .... Zip: ....
Foreign Rate: $9.00 — 52 Issues

MAIL YOUR ORDER TO:
KRLA BEAT
6290 Sunset, Suite 504
Hollywood, Calif. 90028

KRLA ARCHIVES

America's Largest Teen NEWSpaper 15¢

KRLA *Edition* BEAT

JUNE 4, 1966

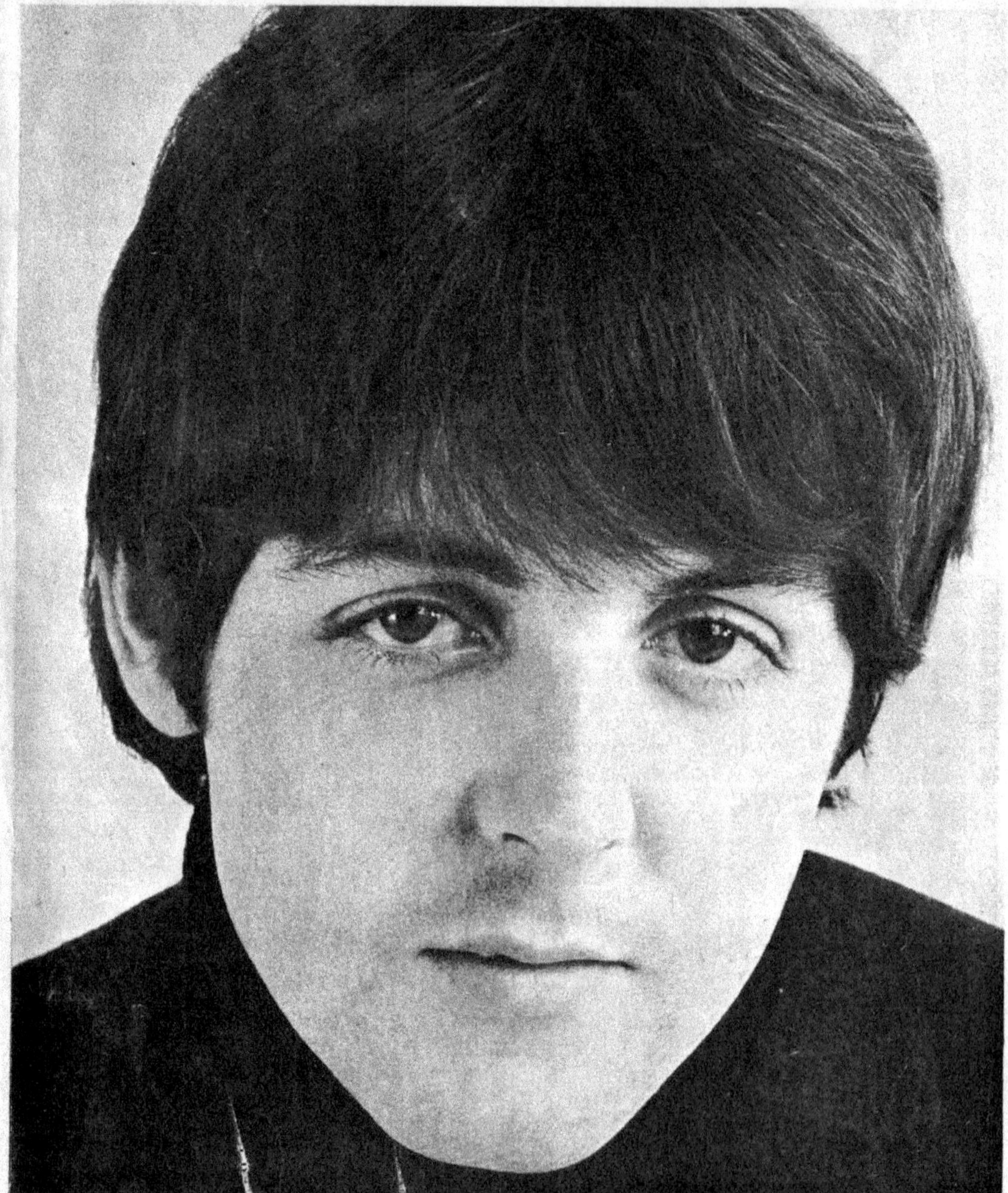

KRLA ARCHIVES

KRLA BEAT

Volume 2, Number 12   June 4, 1966

Beatle Single Is Minus The Sitar

By Tony Barrow

The first products of The Beatles' marathon series of April and May recording sessions will America on June 6 and in the UK on June 10. The titles are "Paperback Writer" and "Rain."

The first thing likely to surprise everyone who hears "Paperback Writer" is that the group's instrumental sounds are limited to their regular line-up of two guitars, bass guitar and drums. Most people had expected to hear all sorts of weird and wonderful innovations including, perhaps, George Harrison playing sitar. But for those special new sounds we must wait until August or September – the earliest planned release date for the album which the boys have been working on since Easter. Only seven album tracks have been completed to date. Some additional material has yet to be written.

Back to "Paperback Writer" – it's a fast-mover with a drumbeat which drives hard. The lyrics tell the story of a man who has written a novel and is trying to have it published. He's composing "Dear Sir or Madam" letters to book publishers pleading with them to read the 1,000 page work.

"Paperback Writer" opens up with a three-pronged vocal attack featuring John, Paul and George. Then Paul takes over the solo vocal side of things to be joined again by the other two for the chorus segments. Towards the end, there are some terrific guitar figures and a reverberating echo effect on the boys' voices.

Even if this deck doesn't boast an assortment of off-beat instrumental sounds it's certainly packed with technical specialties which took The Beatles and their recording manager, George Martin, plenty of thought to work out.

Mostly I find I need to hear any new Beatles' record five or six times before the tune sticks in my mind. Not so with "Paperback Writer." It has an instantly infectious tune, dominated by the much-repeated and multi-voiced title phrase.

The second side, "Rain," is a much less complex number which gives the vocal spotlight to John Lennon. Paul and George join him occasionally and contribute a se-
(Turn to Page 2)

'ONLY LOVERS LEFT ALIVE'

Stones Roll Ahead Of Beatles By Nine Hundred Thousand

The five Rolling Stones, who have taken to gathering money and leaving the moss behind, have officially stripped the Beatles of their monopoly of the young money-making set by receiving *one million dollars* for their motion picture debut! The Stones' figure is $950,000 higher than that received by the Beatles for their first film, "A Hard Day's Night."

The vehicle selected for the Stones' long-awaited debut on the motion picture screen is the current controversial (would the Stones have it any other way?) English novel, "Only Lovers Left Alive." The story was chosen by the Stones' business manager, Allen Klein, and revolves around an imaginary takeover of England by the country's violent and rebellious teenagers.

The first news of the Stones' film debut came directly from the Stones themselves. At a press conference at the Beverly Rodeo Hotel on December 8, Mick Jagger revealed that their first movie was "Back, Behind and In Front."

He admitted that the title was tentative, that it was scheduled to have begun filming in mid-April, would take seven or eight weeks to complete and would be shot entirely in Europe.

All five Stones emphatically stated that the movie would have a definite plot and would not be a hastily thrown together piece of garbage released for monetary reasons only.

"If we merely wanted to make money," said Keith, "We would have made one of those pop films two years ago."

"It won't be a vehicle for singing," declared Mick. "We have to sing but we want it to be something with a story."

Asked if the Stones were going to play themselves in the film, Charlie answered for himself by saying: "Certainly not. I shall be acting!"

The Stones were most explicit about what they wanted and didn't want in their first film, but other than that they gave no hint as to
(Continued on Page Four)

Paul McCartney With 48 Per Cent

By Shirley Poston

The Beatles Survey compiled by April Orcutt of Tustin, Calif. and printed in Shirley Poston's "For Girls Only" column shows Paul to be the most popular Beatle.

He received almost 50% of the votes, followed by George with less than 25%, then John and finally Ringo.

"Yesterday" proved to be the most popular Beatle song with "Mr. Moonlight" the least popular and "Help" showed up as more popular than "Hard Day's Night."

From comments received over 80% of the readers who responded feel the Beatles will last "forever."

Following are the questions and answers along with many of the comments received.

The opinions found in the parentheses are those of April's and not necessarily either Shirley's or *The BEAT'S*.

1. Who is your favorite Beatle and why?

PAUL — 48%. Reasons: cute - friendly - sweet - enjoys life - sense of humor - has that "something" - bouncy - his looks at John - sad and sexy voice - witty - big, droopy eyes.

GEORGE — 24%. Reasons: mysterious - good looking - polite - takes music seriously - accent - lonely eyes - tall, thin, sexy body - thick, tousled mop - big feet.

JOHN — 21%. Reasons: Handsome - warm - fascinating - wit - sexy - clever - mature - humorous - can feel it from head to toe when you look at him.

RINGO — 7%. Reasons: cute, especially his nose - funny - serious - sad blue eyes - neat smile - lifts our spirits.

2. What is your favorite Beatle song?

Winners were (1) "Yesterday," (2) "And I Love Her," (3) "Michelle," (4) "She Loves You," (5) "We Can Work It Out."
(Turn to Page Fourteen)

Them Coming To America Thanks To BEAT Readers

You did it, fans. You convinced the U.S. Immigration Authorities that you really want to see Them in this country.

A few issues ago *The BEAT* reported then that the Irish singing group had planned a tour of the U.S. and then had to cancel it because they couldn't get work permits from the authorities, so their American representatives had come to *The BEAT* asking for help.

We asked you to send in everything that had ever been printed about Them in any publication to prove to the authorities that they are a big group over here and that there is a demand for them.

Well, you came through. You flooded us with not only clippings but petitions and letters.

The authorities were impressed and this week we got a call from Washington saying that work permits had been issued for the group which will allow them to do television as well as live appearances.

All they lack now is visas – permits to enter the country – and there should be no problem there. The work permits were the major problem.

Thanks to you, *BEAT* readers, Them should be arriving in New York within the month for a nationwide tour that will bring them to the West Coast in just a few short weeks.

Inside the BEAT

Tokens And Middle Age	2
Second British Invasion	3
Beatle Likes And Dislikes	4-5
Elvis Is Told On	7
U.N.C.L.E. Noel Harrison	10
Two Many Diddy Wahs	11
For Girls Only	13
The BEAT Goes To The Movies	15

The BEAT is published weekly by BEAT Publications, Inc., editorial and advertising offices at 6290 Sunset Blvd., Suite 504, Hollywood, California 90028. U.S. bureaus in Hollywood, San Francisco, New York, Chicago and Nashville, overseas correspondents in London, Liverpool and Manchester, England. Sale price, 15 cents. Subscription price, U.S. and possessions, $5 per year; Canada and foreign rates, $9 per year. Second class postage prepaid at Los Angeles, California.

KRLA ARCHIVES

The Tokens Want To Appeal To Middle Aged Women!

By Carol Deck

The Tokens are a multi-talented group of guys from Booklyn who don't really need to put out records.

They first burst forth a few years back with a song they wrote, produced and recorded called "Tonight I Fell In Love," which established them as an up and coming rock group.

Then they surprised everyone by making the transition to folk and recording the smash hit, "The Lion Sleeps Tonight."

But that was some time ago. Ask them what they've been doing since and they'll tell you they've put out a number of fairly successful records and a larger number of very successful commercials for radio and television.

If you think you haven't heard much from them lately, you're wrong. You've probably heard them practically every day.

Busy Men

They've formed their own company, Bright Tunes Production Co., and through it they write, produce and perform commercials, their own records and many of the records by The Chiffons.

The radio commercials they've produced include "Ford Mustang," "Ford Galaxie," "Score Hair Cream," "Dentyne Chewing Gum," "Adams Sour Gum," "Ideal Toys," "Scott Paper," "Clairol," and "The Dodge Rebellion."

And on top of all this they are currently working on an adult night club act with the help of Kirby Stone of the Kirby Stone Four.

And, of course, they have just released a new single, "The Greatest Moments in A Girl's Life," as a followup to "I Hear Trumpets Blow."

These five guys — Jay Siegel, Hank Medress, Phil Margo, Stephen "Brute" Friedland and Mitch Margo — are very serious, very talented musicians who are not afraid to try many different fields of entertaining.

Ask them what their goals are and they'll frankly tell you they want to be the best group in the world.

"We want to be known as a great club act," says Mitch. "We want to win Academy Awards and Grammys."

"We just want to be admired as professional entertainers," says Hank, who is currently sporting a beard.

A Hairy Subject

Hair is the key topic with the Tokens. They have short hair and are proud of it, but they don't put down groups who let theirs grow.

"They have the right to long hair," explains Mitch. "But we just couldn't see it for ourselves."

"We're hoping," says Brute, "that when this long hair thing blows over people will remember that we had short hair all along."

"We want to appeal to middle age women and divorcees," adds Hank.

They were on the West Coast recently to film a number of television shows and, like every visitor to California, they wanted to see Disneyland.

"It seems to be what everywhere else isn't," said Mitch.

"It's in a close proximity to Europe," added Jay.

The Tokens have been and are a very busy group, trying to keep up with all the various facets of their career.

Jay sums it all up with, "we've been together six years and we're friends."

That alone is amazing, but on top of all they've done in those six years they are truly unbelievable, and a truly unbelievably nice group of guys too.

Beatle Single—A Weather Forecast

(Continued from Page 1)

ries of ear-catching falsetto effects. "Rain" has as its theme the idea that whatever the weather is like somebody is ready to moan – if the sun shines too strongly we rush into the shade and if it rains we want the sun back again.

At the end of May, The Beatles filmed on location around London a series of television clips for "Paperback Writer" and "Rain." These will be made in colour and in black and white and are designed for TV screening on a worldwide scale.

Otherwise John, Paul, George and Ringo are finding plenty of activities to fill their days. They've been spending some time seeing top journalists from German newspapers prior to their late-June dates in Hamburg, Munich and Essen. John's place down in Weybridge, Surrey, has become the group's favorite meeting place for the moment. There all four boys gather to write or rehearse new album numbers before each new recording session. Quite frequently they give themselves a break from more serious work and shoot off some zany home movies in John's vast garden.

On the BEAT

By Louise Criscione

Nosed around a little bit and discovered some of the dates for the next Stones' Stateside tour. Following their June 29 opener in Montreal, they head for Toronto on the same day, then to New York on July 2 for an appearance at the Forest Hills Tennis Stadium. Next date is Detroit on July 9, Chicago on the 10th, the Hollywood Bowl (a Stones' first) on July 25, San Francisco on the 26th and Honolulu on July 28.

Cities still negotiating for Stone concerts are Portland, Seattle, Washington, Vancouver and San Jose. When the tour winds up the Stones will spend several days in Hollywood at their RCA camping grounds to record the sound track for "Only Lovers Left Alive."

The Stones then head back to England and immediately begin filming the movie, hopefully finishing most of it before starting out on their British tour, which is scheduled to kick off on September 23.

The Lovin' Spoonful did so well on their first tour of England that they're set to pay a return visit in the fall. The group's manager, Daniel Moriarty revealed the reason for their almost back-to-back British tours as being simply because "the boys enjoyed themselves so much" the last time.

Wayne Fontana is apparently not very happy over the success of his former group members, the Mindbenders. Says: "Really, we hated each others guts but when we split we were told not to cause friction. Keep it 'nicey nicey' they told us. But we're still friends — we're the best of enemies."

You understand all of that? Afraid, I don't, but that's what the man said.

The Dave Clark Five had their share of problems when they played Hong Kong. Seems that the Five were being chased by fans, so they barricaded themselves in their hotel room and called the riot police — only to be informed that the riot police had to be booked two weeks in advance! As they all lived to tell about it, I suppose their fans finally gave up and left the guys alone — at least, most of them failed to get through the barricade.

Bob Dylan arrived in England last week to the dismay of the British press. They formally met Bob at a press conference and found him in such a funny mood that he refused to give one straight answer during the whole conference. Of course, some of the questions were so ridiculous that they didn't deserve *any* answer at all.

However, some of the questions made an attempt at seriousness but even they didn't get straight answers. One confused reporter asked Dylan why his last several singles (and especially "Rainy Day Women #12 & 35) bore titles which had nothing whatsoever to do with the lyrics.

To which Dylan replied: "It has significance. Have you ever been down in North Mexico? The reporter admitted that he hadn't so Dylan shot back: "Well, I can't explain it to you then!" He has to be the world's funniest comedian!!

Petula Clark is going to make an American movie. She's wanted to make one ever since "Downtown" but was searching for just the right movie, one which was "artistically worthwhile." Now she's found it — a light drama, "9th Floor Of The Plaza." Final plans will be made within the next month and until then the proposed film has no director and no cast — only Petula, which is probably all they need anyway.

The Animals extended their American tour several days in order to play three concerts in Ohio with James Brown. Would've loved to have been there to see Eric Burdon and James Brown on the same stage. Must have been out of sight!

Finally saw a picture of Keith Richard's new house in Sussex, England. The huge Tudor-styled home sits a few hundred yards from a main road but is completely hidden from it and separated by a moat running all around the house, which serves to keep Keith in and his fans out. Keith's driveway is lined with fruit trees and the whole place is really beautiful and quite a change from his tiny flat, huh?

...KEITH RICHARD

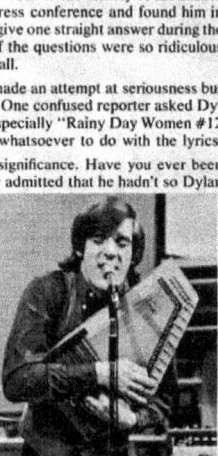

...JOHN SEBASTIAN

KRLA ARCHIVES

Here Come The British!

By Louise Criscione

Better get ready, the second tidal wave of British recording artists is set to hit Stateside throughout the summer months. One after the other (and sometimes together) the English groups will be landing on American soil to the delight of their fans and the terror of their parents.

Leading the parade will be the Yardbirds – *if* they can get into the country, that is! Last time around the Yardbirds almost succeeded in getting themselves deported and were then told not to count on coming Stateside again. However, they hope things will be straightened out enough to allow them into the country for a mammoth show at Yankee Stadium on June 10.

The Dave Clark Five kick off their *fifth* U.S. tour on June 12 with yet another appearance on "Ed Sullivan," followed by a cross-country string of personal appearances.

Stoned In June

The first of the big Three, the Rolling Stones, invade the U.S. on June 29 for a tour scheduled to last 20 days. Dates already set, include Los Angeles, New York, San Francisco, Chicago and Detroit. As usually happens when the Stones reach L.A., they will utilize the RCA Studios in Hollywood for recording sessions.

Herman's Hermits and the Animals will be making a joint tour of the U.S., arriving shortly after the Stones. The double-headlined bill starts its run in Hawaii on July 1 and as of now winds up on August 8 (for a complete itinerary of the tour see last week's *BEAT*.)

It should be interesting to see which tour will draw the biggest crowds and the most publicity – Herman/Animals or the Rolling Stones? Judging from past tours, one would have to give the edge to the Stones, who seem to have a natural talent for making headlines, evoking riots and smashing attendance records. *But* Herman certainly hasn't done badly for himself either – on his last tour, he broke attendance records in twelve cities.

The Animals, on the other hand, have enjoyed neither wide publicity nor a long string of broken gate records. I can't imagine why the press hasn't paid more attention to Eric Burdon. He is one of the most controversial and outspoken entertainers today and can certainly provide some of the most interesting interviews ever read.

Bent Minds In July

Arriving Stateside the same day as Herman and company will be the Mindbenders, those "Groovy Kind Of Love" guys. To begin their five week U.S. tour on July 1 with the majority of their dates set for colleges and state fairs. It's rather a novel concept in summertime tours but that's the way the Mindbenders obviously want it – so that's the way it's going to be. It stands to either set a new trend in tours or prove to be the biggest bomb of the summer. The month of July will provide the verdict.

While the Stones, DC5, Herman, the Animals and the Mindbenders are thinking of winding up their respective tours, the Hollies will be embarking upon their second major U.S. tour July 28.

When the Hollies landed in London last week from their just-completed U.S. tour (which was plagued with problems from the minute they set foot in the country until they boarded their London-bound jet at Los Angeles International Airport) they discovered that they have been set to return Stateside for over a month.

The Hollies will remain in the U.S. until September 4 with their time spent here in concerts, ballroom appearances, club dates and television shows. We at *The BEAT* heard the Holly news with decidedly mixed reactions. We've only just managed to get things back to normal around here – and now they're coming back!

Beatles In August

Two short weeks after the Hollies arrive, the Beatles' plane will touch down in Chicago spilling out John, Paul, George and Ringo for their third American summer tour beginning August 12.

Cities to be hit by the Beatles this time around include Detroit, Washington, Philadelphia, Boston, Memphis, New York, San Francisco and Los Angeles.

September is the month set aside for your recuperation – but it's also the month you should again replenish your supply of cash for a quick trip to Las Vegas in October.

And just who is going to be in Vegas in October? Tom Jones – the office hero!! Tom is set for a four week stint at Caesar's Palace beginning the end of October (how's that for clarity?) If you can't possibly swing a Vegas trip in October, don't worry. Tom will play two more month-long engagements at Caesar's during the next year.

You may now consider yourself duly warned of what is in store for you this summer – a fantastic time! Never have so many top British groups played the States in so short a time span – it ought to drive your parents out of their minds!

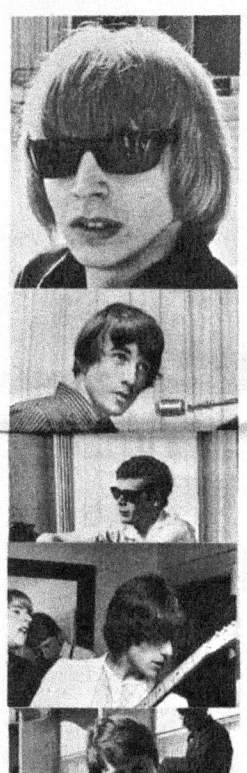

KRLA ARCHIVES

Like And Dislike About Americans

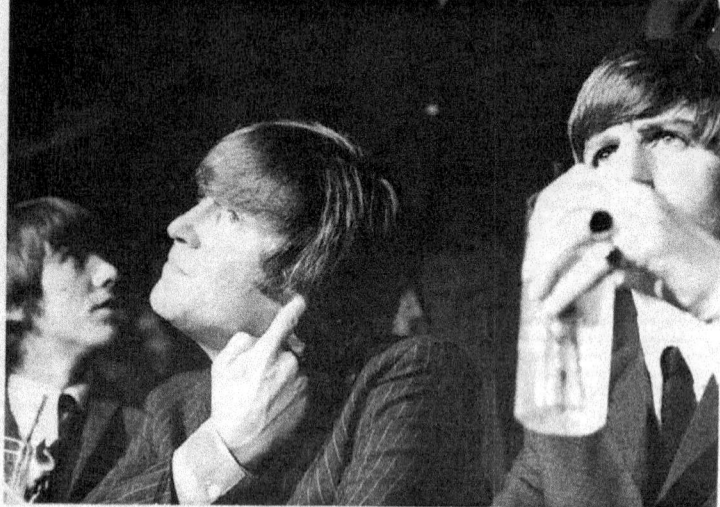

..."IS MY HEARING OFF, or are these reporters soft?"

..."AFTER ALL, they're paying the money."

..."WELL, it's cold in London."

By Gil McDougall

The Beatle press conference was going very well. It was already half over and both the press and the Beatles seemed pleased and in good humour. So far all of the reporters except one had stuck to asking sensible questions. The one exception seemed to have suicidal tendencies as all of his somewhat absurd questions were directed at John Lennon.

The reporter asked John one foolish question after another. Usually John made an attempt to answer, but it was obvious that his temper was becoming frayed at the edges and his answers were becoming very sarcastic indeed. Paul McCartney tried to help out by jumping in and answering some of the questions that the man directed at Lennon.

A reporter that the Beatles respected then stood up and asked John: "Are you writing a book at this time?" John grinned and answered: "No, not right at the moment, I'm talking to you."

"You"

Everybody laughed, and then the man with the suicidal tendencies stood up and said to Lennon: "What is it that you dislike most about America?" Quick as a wink John flashed back the answer: "YOU."

People like this, who apparently find it impossible to believe that Beatle fans could be interested in anything other than what kind of toothpaste the boys use, are very high on the four Liverpool lads list of dislikes.

During a press conference the press usually assumes that the Beatles are too busy answering queries to notice one individual reporter. The truth is that the four actually get a kick out of singling out the reporters that they consider to be intelligent enough to warrant a fair answer.

There are many things that the Beatles like about America and most of their problems during a tour are very minor. When you attend a Beatle concert you most probably go there and scream your lungs out. The Beatles consider this situation from two viewpoints.

Without Screams

In the first place they couldn't care less how much you scream or yell. They feel that if this indicates your enjoyment, then their visit to your town has been more than worthwhile. Paul was asked about the noise during a performance and he said: "The fans pay their money to come in and if they want to scream then that's their perogative. We don't mind if they scream. Why should we. The only thing that counts is that they are having a good time for their money." Paul continued: "Anyway five years ago we were playing without the screams, and friend, it wasn't half as nice. I mean the bread is important too y'know."

All of the other Beatles concurred with Paul, and John had something to say on the other view point of the fantastic noise that happens at all Beatle performances: "We can be heard if there is a decent mike system. Most of the people responsible for the concerts just don't want to spend the money necessary. In Atlanta they had a real good system. The fans screamed just as loudly, but they also heard us because of the superior equipment. We don't mind the screaming at all if it's what the fans want. After all they are paying the money, but it is possible for the kids to hear us and scream at us at the same time. Atlanta was great. Our best American concert yet."

The Beatles really get a kick out of seeing how loyal their fans are, but there are some things about the scene that they wouldn't be sorry to see go. Perhaps number one would be the objects fanatical fans chuck at the stage. The boys don't mind you crowding around the stage (providing that nobody gets hurt as so often happened during the 1965 tour) but they really would appreciate it if you would stop throwing things at them. Those items that you chuck so lovingly could cause one of the group a permanent injury.

Mostly though the Beatles love America as much as America loves the Beatles—and that is really going some! Before starting their 1965 trip they were a little concerned about rumours that they were dead in the U.S. However, the way in which these false stories were quickly dispelled pleased them very much. It is doubtful that there will be a reoccurance of the same situation. The Beatles have proved that they are here to stay and in 1966 the rumours will never get off the ground.

Meeting El

They all really enjoyed their stay in California. One big spot during their stay in Los Angeles was their meeting with Elvis Presley. All four got a kick out of that. Even though they were supposed to be resting up in L.A., Paul and George took time out to visit a recording session that the Byrds were doing. One funny part of the tour was that the Beatles met more fans than anyone had ever expected.

These are the kind of incidents that made the Beatles like America. Fans and stars alike, all were welcomed into the Beatles' house if it was at all possible. They enjoyed just meeting Americans because this was the best way possible to get to know America. And Americans enjoyed meeting the Beatles, even if they had to do it in a concert hall. It was as if four of the greatest friends of their life had just come to make their annual visit to town. And they were, and they did, and they will again this year.

ROBERT POORE (left) receives help from Johnny Rivers and Little Richard in his American teenage time capsule scavenger hunt, which will preserve our teenage generation for posterity.

Now A Teen Time Capsule!

Robert Poore—former recording artist and agent, who lead a double-edged career as a teen idol, and then as an agent who booked his own contemporaries, reminds us that we are thoroughly immersed in what is irrefutably—the TEEN AGE.

Hence—that Poore boy, who is richly endowed with experience and perception beyond his years, feels that the American Teen Age should be recorded for posterity—not just for the next hundred years, but for the next *thousand*.

He stands behind his conviction by beginning the construction of a time capsule which will be loaded with artifacts and memorabilia of the American Teen Age from 1955 through June of 1966.

Thus, in tribute to the fans who gave him national recognition, Robert (Bobby) Poore is inaugurating the American Teen Age Time Capsule *Scavenger Hunt*, which invites teenagers in all states and possessions of the U.S. to contribute objects, documents, stories, facts, etc. which will represent each year from ,and including, 1955 through June of this year.

Bob is preparing to launch a world-wide talent search for his forthcoming film project which will be directed primarily at the teenage market.

His Wide World of Talent Search will have no geographical or age boundaries. If you have ambition to become an actor, singer, dancer or novelty entertainer, send information regarding your background and/or dramatic training to Robert Poore, 1245 N. Vine St., Hollywood, California 90028.

Include a good, clear photograph of yourself ,alone. which does not have to be returned, plus a description of yourself, and a return address where you may be contacted by mail or telephone.

Batman
is not
Robert Poore

The Green Hornet
is not
Robert Poore

Matt Helm
is not
Robert Poore

Derek Flint
is not
Robert Poore

**Robert Poore
Is Real**

**Robert Poore
Remembers!**

**Robert Poore
Is!**

**Who Is
Robert Poore?**

Stones Rolling On
(Continued From Page 1)

what the movie would be about. It is now several months since the Stones made their private movie thoughts public—far past that mid-April starting date. Obviously, they ran into some kind of trouble but just where, they aren't saying.

Quite probably, "Only Lovers Left Alive" was not the story they were going to title "Back, Behind And In Front." Perhaps the Stones picked the title before they had even *found* a suitable script. Perhaps the whole thing was a Stone put-on, but that's doubtful. What probably happened was that the Stones decided to make a movie, but just which movie and for what price they didn't know. And now they do—"Only Lovers Left Alive" for a million dollars.

Allen Klein, who made some news for himself by purchasing 50,000 shares of MGM stock and, thus, causing people to believe that MGM will release the movie Stateside, concedes that the film fee is small compared to the three million dollar recording contract which he recently negotiated for the Stones with Decca Records, Ltd. It is Decca which is also guaranteeing the one million dollar movie salary, scheduled to begin filming in August.

Klein will co-produce the film with Andrew Oldham, Stones' 22-year-old manager and record producer. The pair are currently holding discussions with a screen writer, director and distributor and plan to film the movie in black and white, *and* in color, entirely on location in England.

The earning history of the Rolling Stones has certainly been an impressive array of figures in the millions. Their last American tour grossed $2,000,000 and their upcoming Stateside tour, beginning June 29, will assuredly pull in an excess of two million (for further tour details see Tony Barrow's Hotline London.)

Their motion picture contract is worth five million dollars and their latest album, "Big Hits (High Tide And Green Grass,") surpassed the million dollar mark in sales before the LP had even been out a month!

Now with the million dollar film fee, the Stones jump into the ranks of such show business giants as Barbra Streisand, Elizabeth Taylor, Richard Burton and Audrey Hepburn.

Would you believe the Stones could now easily *buy* the whole Hollywood Palace and turn it into a giant zoo—or maybe a distillery?

What Beatles

... "THE BREAD is important too, y'know."

... "THIS IS George Harrison, of the Beatles."

KRLA ARCHIVES

Writers' Revolution In Pop World

"The songs are insanely honest, not meaning t twist any heads an written only for the reason that i myself me alone wanted and needed to write them. i've conceded the fact there is no understanding of anything. at best, just winks of the eye an that is all i'm lookin for now i guess."

Bob Dylan's explanation of the songs he sings, the poetry he writes. His record company, Columbia, has defined him as a "millionaire" and one of the hottest properties on the label. The critics and journalists who have studied him have given him the definition of "poet," and "prophet."

But definitions have little value when you're speaking in the abstract; and Dylan is an abstract, for he'll never fit into the narrow restrictions of translation.

Somehow, this 24-year old poet-prophet from Hibbing, Minnesota has managed to take poetry—in its broadest definition—and walk it down the streets of the city.

He has taken it out of dusty libraries and brought it into the minds of men and women of all ages, and in the process—he has started a revolution.

Bob Dylan is the song writer who sings of life the way *he* sees it, and once you have heard his songs—your own eyesight must be forever altered. He does that to you.

He has also done a great deal for the lyric content of all the pop songs on the market today. Listening audiences are beginning to demand more and more lyrically ,their performers, and the entertainers themselves are searching for greater depth and substance in the material they select.

A large measure of responsibility for this "cultural" revolution in contemporary music must be placed on the slender shoulders of Bob Dylan who remains seemingly untouched himself through it all.

He has said: "The songs are what I do. What I do is write the songs and sing them. And perform them. That's what I do. The aftermath, whatever happens before and after is really not important to me. Just the time on the stage and the time we're singing the songs and performing them. Or really *not* performing them even, just letting them be there."

Bob Dylan has let a wealth of his material "just be there," while nearly everyone in the music industry has flocked there to try their vocal cords at a Dylan tune.

He has irrevocably touched this field of music and changed it, probably for the better. In years to come, when Dylan is studied as a contemporary classic poet in universities, someone somewhere may recall that once he was a pop singer.

ELUSIVE BUTTERFLY STARTED MAD RUSH

One of the top newspapers in London has sent a reporter to Hollywood to follow Bob Lind around for two weeks in order to obtain an in-depth interview with one of the most talented and most talked about young songwriters in the world.

This is a very sharp break from precedent, but Bob himself is a very unusual sort of boy. Not Hippy Hollywood, or Tin-Pan-Alley-King-For-A-Day. He is a very honest, truly talented young man who is shaking up the world of popular music.

Since the release and subsequent hit of his first record—"Elusive Butterfly"—there has been a mad rush to record almost anything written by this soft-spoken blue-eyed wonder, and the stampede shows no signs of abating now.

Bob is also a "spontaneous" writer, explaining that "I can't say, 'well, it's four o'clock in the afternoon . . . it's my writing time!' Songs, generally, are nothing more than pictures that I get when I feel a certain way.

"Generally the pictures that I see in my mind are pictures that I draw when I write, in my words. Actually, I have very little knowledge of what I'm doing when I sit down to write. I don't think structure; I think there's a song in my head that I want to get *out*, and any way it gets out is all right with me as long as it gets out!"

Bob argues that the lyrics in his songs are not complicated and don't require analysis in order to understand them. "All that are in my songs are words that should be just taken the way they are. In other words, *listen* to the words and if they make you feel a certain way—that's all that's important, because analyzing isn't going to make you like the song anymore! It won't make the feeling any more real to you."

Bob says, "I used to think that you could change people's minds writing music, but you can never really tell anyone something that they don't know, so my responsibility is not to people who say, 'all right, tell me about something I don't know; describe to me a feeling I've never felt.' I can't do that.

"The only thing I want to do is kind of like trying to reach out to somebody and saying, 'Do you know this? And if you do, isn't it good to talk about it, to feel it together, to know that someone else feels it?' There are so few times when people can be close to each other—people generally aren't."

There is, and Bob seems to have found it because a great many people are sharing his feelings about things with him. There seems to be a sort of universal language which Bob has found and it is a language quite readily understood by many. His songs are being spoken of and recorded the world over, and it seems quite certain that Bob will remain one of the most important and lasting influences on the music industry.

Bob is an important leader in the lyrical revolution in music: the movement toward better music, and more meaningful words. His songs are truly music of the emotions, music which tries to reach out and touch the hearts and souls of others.

Music which attempts to share at least a small portion of life with someone else. And generosity was never more apreciated.

EXHAUSTION HELPS PAPA'S WRITING

If anyone were to ask you just what was *happening* in the world of recording, you might be apt to reply: "The Mama's and Papa's, of course." You wouldn't be too far off, 'cause the M's and P's are definitely causing waves in our Pop Pond.

Papa John Phillips is the warm, witty, rebel-intellectual of the group who is responsible for the composing of most of their material. He has also become one of the most popular of contemporary songwriters almost over-night.

He says, "I have to write spontaneously. I can't just sit down and say, 'I'm going to write a song today.' I never consciously try to cause you get a much more artificial feeling that way."

Perhaps that is the secret of John's musical success: his songs are very *real*, not artificial. They are songs which say what they want to simply, effectively, and beautifully.

John says very earnestly that "I don't think there will ever be a big group again that doesn't write their own material. You're very close to the music you write, and I don't think that people can sing the songs the way the people who wrote them can."

John has written specifically for the Kingston Trio (with John Stuart) and has also written a tune (the title of which he has forgotten!) for Anthony Newley which was a large hit for the British star in his own country several years ago.

Genius works in many ways, and John explains: "I have to be really exhausted to write. I guess that's because my life is so crowded with other things that you have to sort of close yourself out to get back and write again. You can't just sit down and do it."

John is very concerned with the quality of the music he produces, and tells us: "I write a lot of poetry and one thing that bothers me about songwriting in the popular market, is that there are many ways to express an idea and perhaps the way you really want to express it — you know is too esoteric, and so you have to bring it to a conversation level.

"And that's the trick, the really hard thing about it: to make it person-to-person, so you don't have to search into it for meanings and things."

"I try to keep it simple; *simple* but meaningful."

An innovator himself, John likes to experiment with new and better sound combinations with the group and says that the new LP— which will consist primarily of original material—will tend more towards jazz. Not only that, but the album will have *13* tracks, and one song will last for only *one minute!*

After several moments of thought, John explained: "At this point in the music business, the major writers—like Lennon and McCartney—well, it's hard to go further than *they* have gone, until *they* go there! For me, anyway."

Then he adds, laughing, "But on the new album, we're doing some pretty strange things!!"

John sums up his views on the current musical situation: "To really be a good songwriter these days, you have to really exercise the vicarious part of you—to experience someone else's emotions and put them down.

KRLA ARCHIVES

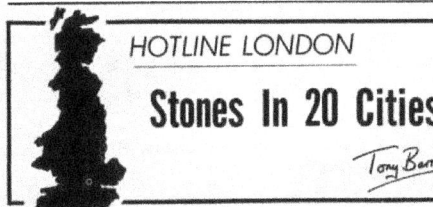

HOTLINE LONDON
Stones In 20 Cities
Tony Barrow

Two weeks ago in HOTLINE LONDON I revealed that THE ROLLING STONES' summertime plans included a short series of major concert appearances in America. Since then the US tour schedule has been built up and the final list of dates is likely to include concerts in as many as twenty cities in America and Canada. The tour kicks off up in Montreal on June 29 and that's followed by a date in Toronto. In July the cities to be visited include Los Angeles, San Francisco, New York, Detroit and Chicago.

In Los Angeles, The Stones hope to get into the recording studios and start work on their next album.

In the UK it looks as though The Stones are all set to claim the No. 1 chart spot with their newie "Paint It Black." They're likely to replace MANFRED MANN and "Pretty Flamingo." There's every chance that Jagger and Company will hold onto the top pop position until the middle of June when everyone is expecting to see The Beatles up there with "PaperbackWriter."

One way and another that seems to take care of the UK Number One spot from now until the middle of July. Otherwise I think a brand-new all-action group called THE TROGGS might have touched the top with "Wild Thing," penned for them by Chip Taylor who gave The Hollies their recent chart-smasher "I Can't Let Go."

Lead singer with The Troggs is Reg Presley who has written the group's next UK single "With A Girl Like You."

In America, Atlantic Records have taken the unusual step of releasing two singles by the Troggs – "Wild Thing" *and* "With A Girl Like You" – immediately.

At a series of sessions in Pye's London recording studios with a 30-piece orchestra, NANCY SINATRA made twelve new tracks in as many hours. Titles included "The More I See You," "On Broadway," and "Wishin' and Hopin'." From these sessions it is possible that two tracks will be selected for Nancy's next UK single due in June.

NEWS BRIEFS . . . JOHN JULIAN LENNON, who celebrated his third birthday in April, started to attend nursery school at the beginning of May . . . TOM JONES has been warned not to smoke, drink or strain his voice following the recent operation to remove his tonsils. If he fails to obey medical advice, he's been told his voice will be ruined for singing by Christmas! . . . THE ANIMALS are joining HERMAN'S HERMITS for July/August US tour . . . GEORGE HARRISON and London deejay ALAN FREEMAN open plushy 120,000 dollar London discotheque in June. It's named *Sibylla's* after former debutante Sibylla, the 21-year-old daughter of The Dowager Lady Edmonstone . . . In my opinion it now looks as though NANCY SINTARA will fail to make our Top Five with "Grab You" . . . Next single from Brian Epstein's folk unit THE SILKIE likely to be a re-styled version of the old hit "Born To Be With You" . . . THE WALKER BROTHERS turned down June 10 appearance at New York's mighty Yankee Stadium. Instead THE YARDBIRDS will join THE BEACH BOYS, RAY CHARLES and STEVIE WONDER on the show . . . GEORGE HARRISON loaned one of his 12-string guitars to MOODY BLUE DENNY LANE when Denny's instrument was stolen . . . THE ROLLING STONES start a three-week UK concert tour at London's large Royal Albert Hall on September 23 . . . THE HOLLIES have recorded "After The Fox," title song from the upcoming Peter Sellers movie . . . When FREDDIE AND THE DREAMERS finish their four-week US tour on August 1, they'll fly to the Far East and on to Australia. Latest Freddie single in the UK is "Playboy" . . . MGM movie executives in London discussing major Hollywood production for THE SMALL FACES who hope to make a promotional trip to America in July . . . 21-year-old BARRY BENSON, formerly P.J. PROBY'S personal hairdresser in London, has made his first record.

TAN, don't burn
USE **COPPERTONE**®

Get a faster, deeper tan
—with maximum protection
against sunburn—
than with any other leading product!

Use Coppertone
whenever you're
exposed to
the sun.

. . . DONNA AND ELVIS IN A SCENE FROM "FRANKIE AND JOHNNY."

BEAT EXCLUSIVE
Elvis 'Keeps To Himself' Says Leading Lady Donna Douglas

To most people, "Elvis Presley" is just a name on a record label or a face in a film. But to Donna Douglas, TV's Elly May from "The Beverly Hillbillies," this elusive star was a concrete co-star for two months while they filmed his latest, "Frankie and Johnny."

But Donna, one of the prettiest of El's always gorgeous leading ladies, claims that though they were on the set together daily, she hardly knew him! "He's so reserved," she explained. "He keeps to himself a lot – not that he's anti-social or anything like that, but somehow you just don't get to know him."

Despite Elvis' natural reserve, the cast and crew of "Frankie and Johnn," Donna's first film, was a lively one. "It was every bit as pleasant and family-like as our 'Hillbillies' set and we've been together for four years! Elvis may not chatter a lot, but a man who is always smiling throws a crew into high spirits, not into the dumps."

As her roles in TV and this film would suggest, Donna is a real live country girl, born and raised on a farm near Baton Rouge, Louisiana. She recalls, "I was a tomboy – always hunting, fishing, playing ball. Then suddenly I hit my teens and I was a girl!" And some girl she was. Immediately she began winning beauty contest after beauty contest. A year in New York as an illustration model led to a screen test and trip to Hollywood. When Donna heard that the producers of "The Beverly Hillbillies" needed someone to play an innocent young Southern girl – well, who else could play the part?

Following her four years in a top TV series, Donna's now branching out into films. "I hope I can make people as happy in movies as we do in the series. I like to think that people are smiling and laughing after watching a program I'm in. I guess that's my 'bag,' as teenagers would say!"

. . . "ELVIS THREW THE CREW INTO HIGH SPIRITS," SAYS DONNA.

KRLA ARCHIVES

JOSH WHITE, concert folk singer, appears at Doug Weston's Troubadour May 24 through June 5. White, whose career has been filled with tragedy, became a protege of the late Mrs. Eleanor Roosevelt through his terrifying ballads about the Black South.

Bus Service Expanding In Los Angeles

Good news for students in the Los Angeles area—discounts on bus service are now available to many more people.

The student discount bus fare program has been expanded to include millions of Southland students, it was announced by the Southern California Rapid Transit District.

The RTD Student Privilege Cards, which provide a 40% fare discount, will now be honored throughout the week at any hour except during the weekday evening rush hours.

The cards will also qualify students for reduced rate admission to many Southern California cultural, recreational and entertainment events, according to Dr. Norman Topping, director of RTD and president of the University of Southern California.

The cards may be purchased now for 50 cents by any student under 21 now enrolled in any school or college in the four RTD county service areas.

Trip Closed!

The Trip has been closed and bonded by court order! The popular teen club, one of the Strip's biggest attractions is having problems concerning ownership of the club itself as well as ownership of the liquor license.

The Trip has been officially closed since May 13 and if the case goes into litigation it will take at least five months before the club is re-opened.

Andy Warhol's Plastic Inevitable show was the last to play The Trip and Andy just barely got his possessions out of the club before the court bonded it. Now nothing can be either taken out of The Trip or brought into it.

KRLA ARCHIVES

Inside KRLA

Wow! Request Radio has really taken over Los Angeles, and I do mean with a capital KRLA!!! The phone circuits have been so jammed with calls that we've had to install even *more* additional lines! The calls were logged at one time at over 150,000 calls per hour!!!

In the last week, KRLA has had its Request Lines answered by the Leaves, the Palace Guard, Dean Torrance, Captain Beefheart and his Magic Band, the Spats, the Association, and the Midnighters.

Call KRLA and you never know *who* is going to answer the phone!

Now I have *really* big news for you. We all know how successful KRLA's new Request Radio has been, and here at KRLA we are well aware that it was *you*, our listeners, who made it a success.

So just to show our gratitude to you, KRLA is presenting live, and for the first time, *Request Concert*—to be held June 25 in the Hollywood Bowl.

Request Hits

The show will feature the songs which *you* have made into hits through requests over the last month or so, sung by the artists who made them popular.

Featured on the show will be the Beach Boys, the Lovin' Spoonful, the Byrds, Chad and Jeremy, Percy Sledge, the Outsiders, the Sir Douglas Quintet, the Leaves, Captain Beefheart and his Magic Band and the Love.

It's your show, by your request, with the songs you want to hear and the people you want to see. Keep your dial fixated on the 1110 position on your radio doohicky for further details about tickets 'n' things.

And remember—you heard it *first*—and *best* on KRLA!!!

Would you believe that we lost again? Yes, Ringo (our KRLA *Request Turtle!*) entered the Turtle Race at Cal State last week and lost with flying colors!

Not only that, but we had a chance to have the *slowest* turtle in the race—but Ringo finked out and moved his leg!

Congratulations

Congratulations to Less Robb, Jr. who won $1110 in the latest KRLA contest by guessing the most requested tune for the week of May 7.

Special notice to Bat fans: The Son of Sticky-type Bat Dealies are now available in Bat stores everywhere. (No . . . I *don't* believe it!!)

I think we've solved the Bat Manager mystery at long last. All my Bat clues and findings lead me to believe that it was actually the infamous, insidious Amazing Pancake Man who plastered the Bat Manager sign on John-John's door.

Hmmmm . . . I wonder who the Amazing Pancake Man *really* is!!!

Eve's APPAREL
See if you can BEAT our prices on our new Jr. and missy lines. Samples at wholesale or less.
1800 N. Vermont, Hollywood, Calif.
NO 3-4456

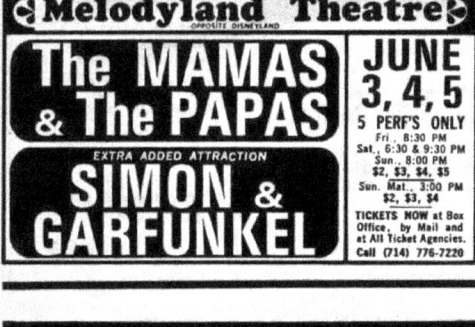

Melodyland Theatre
OPPOSITE DISNEYLAND

The MAMAS & The PAPAS

EXTRA ADDED ATTRACTION
SIMON & GARFUNKEL

JUNE 3, 4, 5
5 PERF'S ONLY
Fri. 8:30 PM
Sat. 6:30 & 9:30 PM
Sun. 8:00 PM
$2, $3, $4, $5
Sun. Mat. 3:00 PM
$2, $3, $4

TICKETS NOW at Box Office, by Mail and at All Ticket Agencies.
Call (714) 776-7220

MAY 24 — JUNE 5
The Legendary
JOSH WHITE
AT DOUG WESTON'S
Troubadour
9083 SANTA MONICA BLVD.
L.A. NEAR DOHENY

RESERVATIONS CR 6-6168

COMING SOON! **JOE & EDDIE**

Guitar & Drum SPECIALISTS

FOLK GUITARS
Go everywhere!!! Your Guitar & Drum specialist individually checks, adjusts, tunes & guarantees them. Famous brands tailored to your style, haircut & bankroll.
from **$13.95***

*Water Skis not included, but service always is at G&D specialists.

Nothing Fishy about the G&D values
Ukes from $3.99
Harmonicas from $1.00
Regular $10.00 chromatics $4.75
and Kazoos (what's that?) 15¢

Guitars—Gibson, Fender, Vox, and many others
Drums—Ludwig, Rogers-Gretsch-Slingerland and many others

GUITAR & AMP
Luster finished electric guitar plus big power amp for that wild Surf Sound—Usually priced at $39.50 each. Now $29.95 each. Combination Guitar and Amp.
$57.50* Complete

DRUM SET
Your choice of Blue, Red, or Gold Sparkle—This beautiful 4-piece drum set has chrome plated rims on six ply hardwood shells with durable mylar heads to give many years of keeping neighbors awake.
$189.50*

*Boat & Bikini extra, but Boss Bargains are bountiful at the G&D specialists.

YOUR LOCAL G&D SPECIALIST IS...

IN BUENA PARK	IN HUNTINGTON BEACH	IN VAN NUYS
Kay Kalie Music 8408 ON THE MALL	**Manolios Music** 18547 MAIN STREET (5 POINTS SHOPPING CENTER)	**Adler Music Co.** 14115 VICTORY BLVD. (AT HAZELTINE)
IN SANTA FE SPRINGS	IN TUSTIN	IN SIMI
Kay Kalie Music 11504 TELEGRAPH RD. (THE SHOPPING CENTER)	**Winn's Music** 540 E. 1st STREET (IN LARWIN SQUARE)	**Adler Music Co.** 1792 ERRINGER ROAD (NEXT TO SAFEWAY)

KRLA ARCHIVES

NOEL HARRISON JOINS 'GIRL FROM U.N.C.L.E.'

"A young girl" 'died' and the son of a famous British actor was cast into a spotlight all his own.

Noel Harrison was an entertainer in England for many years, but had to move to New York and record "A Young Girl" before Americans discovered him.

As the record climbed steadily up the charts across the nation he set out on a string of night club appearances to prove that he is more than "just Rex Harrison's son."

And that he has done — in The Living Room in New York, in the Hungry i in San Francisco and many others. He's proven himself a sincere and talented entertainer.

Now he's expanding even more by going into television. He's coming to the West Coast this month to start filming NBC-TV's new series, "The Girl From U.N.C.L.E.," which he co-stars in with Stefanie Powers.

Noel first came to the U.S. in 1960 for two appearances on the Ed Sullivan Show. The reaction to his performances was so great that he remained for a few club engagements.

Likes It Here

He then decided he liked America and brought his wife and four children over to New York to live in the top half of a town house where their downstairs neighbor was English friend, actress Georgia Brown.

Noel is noted for the relaxed and sincere manner in which he performs. He chooses his repertoire as though he were selecting poems. He believes it should be possible to print lyrics separately without losing either their value or their beauty.

"A good song is poetry," he declares. His material ranges from French classics by Jacques Brel and Charles Aznavour to American standards by Bob Dylan.

"I think Dylan is the greatest poet now writing," says Noel. "Though he, Dylan that is, won't play supper clubs, it's exciting for me to present his songs to an audience they might not otherwise reach."

A highly trained musician who often accompanies himself with guitar, Noel recently discovered the wide-ranging possibilities of the electric guitar and has now incorporated it into his act.

Noel feels that his career actually started in France where he learned French material well enough to perform locally in the language.

Another Language

He found that many songs were easier to perform in French, especially the French classics which often lose something in translation.

Since that time he's learned to speak, act and sing in four languages — German and Italian in addition to French and English.

He's quite a ski enthusiast and was a member of the British National Ski Team and competed in two Olympics, but one of his fondest dreams is to own a house in sunny Italy so he can spend a portion of each year there with his family.

Singer, skier, poet, actor, philosopher — yes, Noel Harrison is quite a bit more than "just Rex Harrison's son."

Bachelors Call To Say They're On Their Way

Three charming Irishmen called The Bachelors arrived in New York this week and promptly telephoned The BEAT to say they're on their way to the West Coast for a series of live and television appearances.

They're only going to be in America for a little over two weeks, but for them that's a long time. They've come over several times before, but for only a few days at a time.

During their brief stay in New York they're filming "The Ed Sullivan Show" and "The Tonight Show."

Then Here

Then they fly out here to do "Shivaree," "Shebang," "Lloyd Thaxton," "Where The Action Is" and "9th Street West."

They'll be performing their latest single, "Love Me With All Your Heart," on all of these shows.

They all seemed to be in fine spirits when they called but they did have a few complaints.

"We're working to death," said Dec Cluskey, the youngest of the three. "And the weather is dreadful in New York. It was lovely when we left London."

He was even more disappointed to learn that there had been slight rains in California.

"But it's supposed to be warm there," said John Stokes.

Some Problems

Con Cluskey, Dec's older brother, told us that they ran into strong head winds during the flight over and had to stop over in Canada before coming into New York.

"But it was fun," he added. "At least we got to see Canada."

After a two day stopover in Las Vegas, "just to look around," The Bachelors will be making their first trip to the West Coast to spread a little of that Irish charm our way.

Say you read it in The BEAT

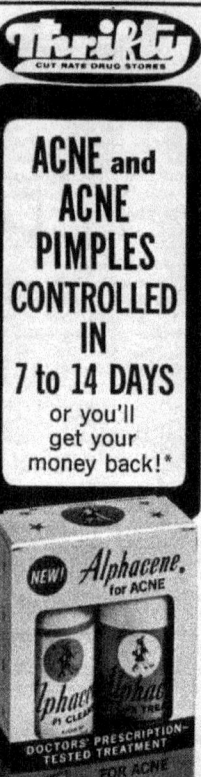

ACNE and ACNE PIMPLES CONTROLLED IN 7 to 14 DAYS or you'll get your money back!*

ALPHACENE. Really Works!

This two-step cleanser and treatment is a thoroughly tested and proven prescription, developed by a group of noted dermatological MDs. You'll get startlingly happy results with Alphacene. No prescription needed.

1. CLEANSER
and
2. TREATMENT
BOTH FOR **$3.98**

Buy Alphacene® at Your Nearby Thrifty Drug Store or use the Mail Order

--- MAIL ORDER ---
Thrifty Drug Store Co. Inc., Dept. M
Box 2363 Terminal Annex, L.A. 54, Calif.
Please send me _____ Alphacene® Cleanser and Treatment at $3.98. Enclose check or money order.

Name _____
Address _____
City _____ State _____ Zip _____
Add 4% Sales Tax

*If not completely satisfied, return unused portion to manufacturer for full refund.

KRLA ARCHIVES

Too Many 'Diddy Wahs'

"REMAINING" AMERICAN

PLAYING BRITISH

By Louise Criscione

One group is from Boston and claims to be protesting the British influence on American music. The other group is from California and proudly declares that they are often mistaken for an English R&B group.

They both have recorded the same song, "Diddy Wah Diddy," and neither group seems to be pulling very far ahead of the other. A decision is going to have to be made and only you can make it. So, The BEAT has decided to devote equal space to the Remains and Captain Beefheart and his Magic Band, introducing both groups to you and letting you decide which group will score a hit and which group will have to give it one more try.

Captain Beefheart and his Magic Band merged less than a year ago in the small desert town of Lancaster, California. Their first big break occurred when they played the Teen-Age Fair at the Hollywood Palladium. They were on stage only twice but they made such an impact on the audience that numerous fan clubs sprouted up before they even had a recording contract!

Boston Boys

The Remains decided to form their group in the fall of '64 while all four boys were still attending Boston University. Their first date was at The Ratskeller Club in Boston where they appeared on Monday nights. They, too, had a phenomenal impact on their audiences and before long the Ratskeller became the place to go in Boston.

The local action generated by both groups drew the attention of record companies, who are continually on the look-out for new talent. So, when word of the Remains spread as far as New York a representative from Epic Records flew up to listen to the group and became so excited over what he heard that he immediately herded them to New York for an audition. Passing the audition with room to spare, the Remains were signed to a contract and, thus, one "Diddy Wah Diddy" was born.

Meanwhile, Captain Beefheart and his group were playing gigs all over the state. The result was more fan clubs but still no recording contract. It was certainly not in vain, however, because with each pulbic appearance the group's stage technique improved until they reached the point where they could work their audience into a state of frenzy and then easily switch to a slow blues number and lure the crowd into quietly listening and watching.

Second "Diddy"

And, as happened with the Remains, wind of what Captain Beefheart was accomplishing spread down to the Los Angeles-based record companies. When all offers were weighed it was the Herb Alpert-Jerry Moss label, A&M Records, which finally signed the group to a contract. And "Diddy Wah Diddy" number two was released.

In terms of exposure, one would have to give the edge to the Remains. They've already appeared on the "Ed Sullivan Show" and the now-dumped "Hullabaloo," as well as being chosen the group to open one of New York's newest discotheques, the Ondine.

Taken individually, the members of Captain Beefheart et al. seem to share some of the same likes as the Reamins but as groups one gets the distinct impression that they're miles apart.

Captain Beefheart's Magic Band possesses five members—all of whom dig the real down-home blues. Musically their tastes run to such R&B giants as Howlin' Wolf, Sonny Boy Williamson, Lightning Hopkins, Jimmy Reed, James Brown and Johnny "Guitar" Watson.

Captain Beefheart is really Alex St. Clair and happens to like, among other things, Donna Loren, dogs, guns, hunting, fishing and Hemingway.

The Magic Band line up as Don Van Vliet, Doug Moon, Jerry Handley and Paul Blakeley. Don's tastes run the gamut from good brandy to falconry with sparrows, from fine cuisine to National Geographic.

Doug has decided that he is definitely in favor of sweet potatoes, egg nog, slim slacks, baggy sweaters, pretty girls with long hair, sports cars, pop art and poetry.

Jerry has given the whole subject plenty of thought and has finally emerged with the notion that he digs pork chops and intelligent girls. Oh, and I almost forgot—he considers Smokey the Bear totally out of sight!

The remaining (sorry 'bout that) Magic Band member is Paul, referred to by his friends as P.G. Paul is the only member of the group to actually hail from Lancaster and we must admit that his list of likes impress us most as he declares that he officially digs,

"Gene Krupa, Bill Cosby, Don Adams and The BEAT!"

The four Remains are Barry Tashian, Chip Damiani, William Briggs and Vern Miller. Barry is the lead guitarist and vocalist for the group. His musical tastes rather agree with his rivals as he prefers Muddy Waters, Otis Redding and is frequently called "the white James Brown."

Chip met the rest of the Remains when he enrolled at Boston University. He is the only group member who was not an experienced musician prior to joining the Remains.

William, or Briggs as he is usually called, is the perfectionist in the group. Because of his wide knowledge of electronics, he is only satisfied when the equipment and stage set-up are perfect.

Briggs spends his spare time writing songs and declares: "I write in a creatively simple vein because I want the kids to understand it. They lose interest if its too complex and then the communication is lost too."

Vern is the Remains' most serious student of music, perhaps because his father is a music teacher and composer. Vern is the group's second composer but in the future wants to go into writing music for movies and television.

So, there you have them—the Remains and Captain Beefheart and his Magic Band. Now that you've been formally introduced, which group will you buy and which one will you ignore? Or will you decide to like them both?

...WOULD YOU BELIEVE THESE ARE THE REMAINS? CAPTAIN BEEFHEART, MAYBE?

KRLA ARCHIVES

ANOTHER AWARD for KRLA news staff, presented by AP Executive Warren Jacobs, accepted by Tom Beck.

SHEBANG with CASEY KASEM — EVERY WEEKDAY AT 5:00 P.M. ON KTLA 5

 Bob Eubanks Says it!  Dave Hull Says it!  Emperor Hudson Says it!  Charlie O'Donnell Says it!

Everybody's Saying It!

You gotta get your new RTD STUDENT PRIVILEGE CARD Before School Closes!

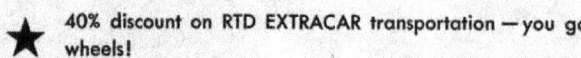

Don't be left out this summer—get your Student Privilege Card at school and go where the fun is—at a big discount! New RTD Student Privilege Card gives you

★ 40% discount on RTD EXTRACAR transportation—you got wheels!

★ Big discounts at all Pacific Walk-in and Drive-in theatres!

★ 50% discount at Hollywood Bowl!

★ Discounts at Greek Theatre, Pacific Ocean Park, Movieland Wax Museum—more deals being added!

Good now—all summer—and until Feb. 1967!

Only 50¢

Not sold at box offices—available only at your school student store or business/finance office.

Go where the action is by

(Squares call it a "bus")

Ready whenever you are!

KRLA ARCHIVES

Many Days In Roy's Life

By Kimmi Kobashigawa

For over a decade now, Roy Orbison has been one of America's foremost ambassadors of good will around the world through his music. A talented man of great versatility, Roy has consistently produced hit records in this country and in countries throughout the world.

Although he is accepted as a hit maker and a great talent in his own country, it is left to the British to make a pop idol of him. In Britain, Roy has been voted the Number One Favorite Male Vocalist on pop polls several years in a row, and he is considered to be one of the two top American singers in that island country.

Roy has just completed a highly successful tour of Great Britain with the Walker Brothers and Lulu, and during his brief stay here, *The BEAT* obtained this exclusive interview:

Roy told us that he is currently planning a movie, to begin filming about August of this year which will be called "The Fastest Gun In The West." The movie will be about the Civil War, and will be Roy's first film venture.

There will be nine songs, plus the theme, in the movie which Roy will compose himself, and he has high hopes that this will be the beginning of many successful motion pictures for him.

It won't be a pop film because Roy feels that "that would be just 'a day in the life of Roy Orbison' and I have enough of those!" But it will be a serious acting endeavor, and Roy is hopeful of being able to continue in this new field in the future.

Although he is an enthusiastic, active young man, Roy has every right to sit back and relax whenever he can find a few spare moments to do so, because those moments are few and far between for him.

For Roy is on the road at least ten months out of every year—and that includes his many tours abroad, as well. Roy explains that he doesn't really have very much time of his own in which he can indulge in many hobbies or outside activities, but he would like to continue his acting and possibly go into producing records for other artists.

We asked Roy if he was aware of any new trends which might be developing in pop music, and he laughed and replied: "No, but I wish I did—I'd jump right into it! I don't see anything new; just something a little dressed up from what was in the past."

Has Roy noticed many differences between the pop music situations in America and Britain? He says there isn't really too much of a difference, except: "I think they probably pay more attention to pop music, and it's accepted much more in England as a form of entertainment than it is in the States. We sell more records, but it seems to be a more important part of their lives.

Roy seems to be one of those very fortunate individuals who has been extremely successful in the field of entertainment, and yet has been surprisingly successful in being able to escape the horrors of a "label" of any kind being tagged on him.

He admits that he has been called the "King of the Beat-Ballads," but other than that he is usually spoken of in terms of his talent. "Soul" is a label attached to many (although Roy received it only after his largest hit, "Pretty Woman") and Roy describes soul music this way:

"Soul music, to me, would mean if you *really* knew what you were talking about and you sang it with feeling. Soul would be any kind of music that had feeling. If you really know what you are saying—that's soul to me."

In his spare time Roy enjoys listening to string music—Mantovani, and the Jackie Gleason orchestra. But he explains, "When most people say that they are going to listen to 'good music,' *I* go and try to *write* some good music."

Author of a lot of very "good" music, and singer of even more—Roy Orbison remains a star of great magnitude . . . and a human being of great warmth. Although he is one of our largest international stars in the field of pop music, his feet are still planted firmly on the ground—and his head is still well out of the clouds.

Definitely America's Ambassador of Good Will, Roy is a talented messenger bringing a lot of pleasure to people the world over.

BEAT Photo: Chuck Boyd

For Girls Only

Well, hello there!

Welcome to another fascinating segment of "For *Get* It" - I mean - "For Girls Only."

Hmmm, what's that odd rumbling sound I hear? Oh, you're trying to tell me something, right? You're trying to tell me you know exactly what I'm up to and that I'd better stop sounding so rational and sensible this MINUTE and explain the remark I made at the close of my last (don't you wish) (dreamer) column, right?

Oh, wrong. *What* last column? And what's more, you've never even *heard* of me? Well, if I were you, I'd make every possible effort to keep it that way and turn the page *quick!*

Ah, me (as in Eleanor) (that's an in joke for Beatlemaniacs only), now that we have ridded ourselves of the sane set, let's get down to cases (of S. and coke, for instance.)

Last week I brought things to a shuddering halt by muttering something about a certain reader of this column getting to meet a certain star. Well, here's what I have in mind (?). Remember how I told you (no, no, I hope you've forgotten *how* I told you) about me meeting George (or is it my meeting George?) (no, it's *me* meeting *MY* George) . . . crumbs, where was I?

Anyrut (hey, there's a new one), I managed to accomplish this by throwing a series of snits that would make Robin Boyd look like an amateur (or amatuer, take your pick.)

And, as a tantrum-tosser of some experience, I'll just bet that if I really put my mind to it (no remarks, pliz) I could fling a few thousand more and come up with a way for one of me . . . down, girl . . . one of you to meet *your* toe-nail-curler!

Anyway, I'm sure going to try. It can't happen right away, but there's no time like the present to get started thinking about it.

Tell you what. I'll be wondering about how to handle my end of the bargain (as in take another course in post graduate hysterics) and you be pondering how the "winner" could be chosen.

Actually, I think the second part will be harder than the first because it's going to be ghastly having to choose one person when both of my many readers would give their eye-teeth (whatever those are) (oh, who cares) to be the "looky kind." (Thank you, John.)

Like, just sorta think it over. It'll have to be a contest of some kind I suppose, but it's got to be the type that would really *mean* something, if you know what I mean (and, if you do, watch out because they're out looking for *you*, too.) Oh, stop gabbling. They know what you're trying (as in very) to say. The "winner" should be someone who not only *wants* to see someone in person, but, but *needs* to.

Boy, next I'll be getting out the violins! More on this subject soon, so think away.

Oh, (as in well, anyroad, boy, zap and GEORGE HARRISON) (well, I had to sneak him in there somewhere, didn't I?) here's a good beginning for a make-up type dream. I started it but haven't had the time to continue because I'm too busy staying up nights trying to dream another of those *real* ones) (as in GASP), but maybe you can take it from there . . . I mean, here . . . oh, *somewhere!*

Anyway, you go to a press conference (don't ask me how) (if I knew I'd be AT one) and ask a really twitchin' (cough) question that tears everyone up. Afterwards, the stars just *have* to meet you, and you just have to offer to drive them around town because they're not having any fun stuck off in that hideaway of theirs (oh, *sure* they're not.)

Naturally, the accept, especially when they find out that your car happens to be a Volkswagon bus-type-dealie with window curtains yet!

See, everything's perfect! There's no need for them to worry about being recognized. Well, what are you waiting for? Get going! And let me know how things work out. (Either that or meet me at the nearest VW lot.)

Before I proceed to the next boring subject, I wish to announce that I am not going to accept any more bribes. If, for instance, Shelly Heber of 6057½ Alcott St. in Los Angeles thinks I'm going to mention the fact that she has a club called "The American Society For the Prevention Of The Extinction of Yardbirds," just because she sent me some delicious *Beatle* pix, she is obviously out of her *mind*. However, if I *were* the sort of person who *would* fall for this sort of thing, I would also mention that dues are a pound minus $1.87.

There, now I feel *sooo* much better. Honesty truly is the best policy.

And *another* thing! If you think that I've run across several more unanswered codes and maybe even about eleven rawhides, lurking under a huge pile of something-or-other, you're wrong. (No, no, *I* wasn't lurking under the pile, the letters were.) (The letters I didn't find, remember?)

Well! I'm certainly glad *that* matter is cleared up! (What matter?) (How should I know?)

At this juncture I would like to thank someone from La Canada, California for sending me a very unusual letter. It told all about how this someone has been reading "Robin Boyd" and this (excuse for a) column to George each week.

It went on to say that George had replied. Written an answer with his very own hand (oh, pain, glorious pain!)

He said it's the funniest thing he's ever read, especially his new middle name (as in Pant.) He was also quite honored to have a genie named after him, and said to keep up the good work.

However, there was a small clump of paper taped at the close of the letter, which I was to open after reading the other for even *more* of a surprise. (Impossible.)

Me? Get mad just because the P.S. said *Belated April Fool? I???* Of course not! Why, those were some of the most exciting moments of my life (shiver, shake, not to mention rattle and roll.)

However, it's not quite the same story with me mum. In fact, I don't think she's *ever* going to stop being furious about that rug!

Any suggestions, someone from La Canada?

In closing, did you hear what George said in an interview when a reporter asked if he really *snai bszuuzar zaipn unqzingazga* (spelled wrong, probably) *zapzb ozvipqghbxzi?*

He said "*Zsgbai nfgyijh ogvn . . . zsgb yklnvnq szip rkkbncjnbp.*"

Join the crowd, boy. Join the crowd.

KRLA ARCHIVES

The Adventures of Robin Boyd...
By Shirley Poston

CHAPTER THIRTY

Robin Boyd ground another half-pound of teeth as John S. (as in *simp*) Winston stumbled toward her.

"I believe it's our dance again," he wheezed.

"Would you believe it's . . . ." Robin began, but her voice trailed off to nothing. (There was no point in wasting one of her clever quips on *this* utter mutt.) (Besides, she couldn't *think* of one of her clever quips at the moment, if nobody minded.) (Nobody did.)

It seemed there was just no escaping the aforementioned mutt. And, as she watched his glasses steam over again, she suddenly felt rather guilty for having tried so hard to elude him (tried to lose him, too.)

After all, due to circumstances beyond her control (not to mention her wildest nightmares), she *was* his date for the prom. And, since George had been kind (kind of livid with rage, that is) enough to let her attend, she might as well make the best of the situation.

So, curling her lip at the band for striking up a slow song, she fell eagerly into the waiting arms of her perspiring partner. (When Robin Irene Boyd decides to make the best of a situation, Robin Irene Boyd doesn't mess around.)

Needless to say, John R. (as in *retch*) Winston was somewhat taken aback, but he was one to make not only the best but the *most* of a situation. So, after an evening of trying to dance cheek-to-cheek and finding himself unable to combat Robin's preference for thumb-to-thumb, he held her closely (for those interested, the closely is located just down the road from the farley.) And he didn't trust himself to speak until a slight miscalculation in his version of the fox-trot severed her left foot just above the ankle.

"Sorry about that," he apologized originally. But Robin failed to answer.

"Did I hurt oo?" he nice-doggied tenderly, leaning back to stare into her upturned face.

It was then that he realized that Robin was not seeing him through new eyes *after* all (although she could sure use a couple) (of new eyes, of new eyes.) She wasn't seeing anything!

No Cooperation

Robin wasn't *cooperating*. Robin was *unconscious*.

But she wasn't for long because she suddenly pushed him away. "Stop *choking* me," she hissed, putting a hand (her own, in fact) to her throat.

John P. (as in *ptui*) Winston's mouth dropped open, revealing not only his surprise but several cavities. "I *didn't!*" he protested. And, what's more, he *hadn't*. He did have certain plans concerning her neck, but those were to be realized much later in the evening, after he'd cleverly run out of gas.

Robin swallowed hard. She could have sworn (and has been known to in moments of this nature) she had just been subjected to a stranglehold. And that wasn't the first time it had happened either! Something had been trying to tangle with her tonsils all *evening*!

Then Robin gasped. Why on earth was she standing there worrying about what was probably a budding (and hard-earned) case of larangitis when something incredible had just happened? When she had, during her recent bit of lip-curling, recognized four very familiar faces on the nearby bandstand?

Grasping John Y. (as in *yick*) Winston firmly, she took the lead and propelled him gracefully (as in herded him hysterically) to a spot very close to the foursome.

However, after a few preliminary squints, her face fell (and very nearly hurt itself). Ratzafratz! From a distance, they'd looked just like the Beatles. But, no such luck. It had just been her myopia making a spectacle of itself again.

Suddenly, her face lifted. (A trick which was going to come in handy in later years.) Maybe it wasn't the Beatles, but it was something almost as good. On account of because it was *Teddy and the Bears*!

Robin jumped excitedly on John V. (as in *three guesses*) Winston's penny loafers. Why, T. and the B. were just about the greatest group in California! Thanks to her, she added mentally, not to mention modestly.

Working Bird

(Robin, as you know, was at one time the hardest-working bird in all of groupie-dom. Directorship of the T&B fan club was only one of the several million activities she had dropped the day she had been forced to choose between turning in her feathers and turning into a grease spot. Then, as a reward for her tireless efforts, she had found the famous tea pot containing the famous Ringo . . . whoops . . . George of genie fame. What with George and her magic power to turn herself into a *real* robin, so much had happened since that day (welcome to the understatement of the century) (hey, you *can* put parentheses in parentheses), she'd forgotten all *about* Teddy!)

However, as the dashing leader caught her eye (a painful experience but well worth the agony) and flashed an engaging grin (as in give me a ring), she remembered in one large hurry.

Closeness

And, when he gave her the olde look, Robin blushed a rather peculiar shade of panther pink and give him a bat of the olde eyelash.

Robin and Teddy, as you may have guessed, were at one time rather close (make that *several* times.) In the olde days, the olde-look-and-lash bit had been a signal between them, meaning, of course, dig-you-now-not-to-mention-later.

Naturally, that was all in the past, now that she belonged to George (if she knew what was good for her) (and, she did) (you'd better believe it.) But that didn't stop her from re-blushing and re-batting.

After all, she figured, a little flirting never hurt anyone.

Anyone but me, she shrieked inwardly when, in the very next instant, her head was severed just slightly below ear level.

Clutching the remaining portions of her lily white, she turned as white as a lily (Repition Rules.) Just what was her major malfunction, anyroad? (Never answer that question.)

"Another frog in your throat?" John A. (as in *arghhh*) Winston inquired helpfully.

Robin shook the remaining portion of her head. "Seven *thousand* frogs," she squeaked when the rattling had ceased. "Doing the *frug*," she added.

Just then this romantic interchange was interrupted by a sudden fan-fare and John T.I.G.R. (as in *this is getting ridiculous*) Winston brightened.

"I have a surprise for you," he leered.

I'll just *bet* you do, Robin thought murderously, patting the pint of petrol concealed in her evening bag.

"I've been selected as the Grand Prince of the prom," he further leered. "You know, because of my excellent grades in Spruce-Pruning! And since you're my date, you're going to be crowned Queen Of The May!"

Doing her best to keep from becoming ill, Robin nonetheless giggled rather pleasantly.

"Me?" she simpered, for ridiculous as the title was, it really was quite an honor.

"You!" John X. – oh you know, that *person* – reaffirmed.

And, hoping that she wouldn't fall into another spasm right in the middle of the coronation, Robin took his offered arm (reminding herself at the time not to forget to return it later) and sailed majestically toward the stage.

Hoping she looked reasonably presentable, she began to trip gracefully (that is getting ridiculous, too) up the stairs.

Matching Set

She needn't have worried. Of course, the invisible *collar* that George had clamped around her neck earlier that evening *was no longer invisible*, and her beauteous blue formal was now being off-set by a matching *leash* which dragged train-like behind her, but aside from those minor details, she looked just fine!

Had she known of her condition, she would have done the only sensible thing.

She would have *killed* herself. Because when one had a jealous genie on one's hands, one is often in for a fate that makes death look like a lark in the park! Especially when said genie's ingenious method of curbing her wandering eye had *failed*, leaving him with no choice but to go on to bigger and better things.

But, she was totally oblivious. And, dismissing a smattering of twitters as sheer jealousy, she grinned greedily as the sparkling crown was placed atop her red hair.

Then, as a whoosh of appreciation spread through the gymnasium, Robin took a proud breath of oddly scented air (a rather disturbing mixture of carnations and evil-smelling sneakers) and turned to accept the congratulations of her fellow students.

Then she proceeded to turn green, blue and purple.

Was anyone even looking her way? No! They were too busy gaping at a certain couple across the crowded room.

Not only because said couple had chosen this particular moment to whirl into a waltz.

Also because they were Mr. and Mrs. George Harrison.

(To Be Continued Next Week)

Beatle Poll Shows Paul The Favorite

(Continued from Page 1)

3. What is your least favorite Beatle song?
Losers were (1) "Mr. Moonlight," (2) "Act Naturally," (3) "Matchbox."

4. Why do you like the Beatles?
Continually original - not phonies - fab composers - very talented - lovable - entertaining - care about fans - warm - witty - magnetic - cheer us up - enjoy themselves - deserving - great performers and people - little things they do - faith to stick with it when all was against them - "make you feel great just being alive" - something in their eyes that says "I care" - "They don't go around shouting 'I can't get no girlie action'" (I *love* that answer) - "I'd have been so much the poorer had I never known the ecstasy, warmth and magic of loving a Beatle" (how true!!!!).

5. What other groups do you like?
Winners in the order of their appearance were Herman's Hermits, the Rolling Stones, the Byrds the Animals and Sonny & Cher.

6. What is your opinion of the movie "A Hard Day's Night?"
The majority loved it; 9% liked it better than "Help," 6% didn't like it and 3% didn't see it. Comments: fantastic - sheer magic - new and fresh - one of a kind - full of charm and quick wit - no plot but certainly sufficient for us Beatlemaniacs - more emotional than "Help" - showed their true greatness - "rapid transport to utter bliss" - a photographic masterpiece - "stunk" (that's sure not *my* opinion.)

7. What is your opinion of the movie "Help?"
Again, the majority loved the film. 26% liked it better than "HDN" and only 5% of those who replied hadn't seen it.
Comments: exciting - imaginative - original - thrilling - marv - wild - great hidden lines - never knew what would come next - better acting and photography - "fantastic when you see it, but you can't quite believe it when it's over."

8. Which Beatle do you think is the best actor?
John – 40%, Ringo – 29%, Paul – 25%, George – 6%.

9. Which Beatle do you think has the best singing voice?
Paul – 49%, John – 31%, George – 16%, Ringo – 4%.

10. Do you think you'll still like the Beatles when and if Paul and George get married? (At the time the survey started, George was still a bachelor.)
Yes – 97%, maybe – 2%, no – 1%.

11. Why or why not?
"They've made us so happy we can't deny them happiness – impossible to stop loving them and to ignore their talent – we'll be happy if they're happy – marriage won't change their looks, personalities, songs, voices or humor . . . only the last names of their fave girls – John and Ringo are married and are still number one – it's their business, not ours – we can't all marry them – "why let some other girl spoil all MY fun?"

12. Do you think the Beatles will last?
FOREVER! – 85%, For A Few Years – 10%, No – 5%.

13. Why or why not?
Always original and a bit ahead of the rest – versatile – totally unique – talent always lasts – their records keep improving – their music has made a lasting impression – "they've lasted this long . . . why not longer?" – are loved by so many – entertainers in the true sense of the word – have an enduring quality – not always on top but will be around – "In MY heart they'll last" – "Who wants to worship a person 50 years old?" (*I* do!!!!) – "Everything has to end… too bad, that's life."

14. What do your parents think of the Beatles?
39% like them, 25% tolerate them, 12% dislike them. In 24% of the cases, the mother likes them but the father doesn't.
Comments: "They try not to like them" – "My parents don't appreciate good music" – "Dad knew they'd go far" – like them more than Elvis – don't like their screaming fans.
Parents' Comments: "They're okay if you can hear them" – "George has a needs-to-be-mothered look" – "I wish they'd go back to England and stay there" – "Give me a pair of scissors and five minutes."

15. Which Beatle is the you-know-whattiest?
JOHN – UNANIMOUSLY!!!!

KRLA ARCHIVES

The BEAT Goes To The Movies
'Night Of The Grizzly'

By Jim Hamblin
(The BEAT Movie Editor)

What? A movie with kids, a big grizzly bear, and even a dog... that Walt Disney didn't produce? Yes!

NIGHT stars the biggest man alive, Clint Walker, in a tussle with the biggest, meanest, orneriest, trickiest bear there ever was. The story comes from the cameras of Paramount Pictures, and tells of a man settling in the new frontier, with all the usual enemies, plus one. A big black bear by the name of Satan, who kills for fun, if he runs out of other reasons.

Practically the whole movie is taken over by blonde Victoria Paige Meyerink. The 4-year-old begins her adventures in the new town they've come to by undercovering a pole-cat. (That's a skunk!) "Here kitty kitty," says she.

"Out of the house," orders Dad Clint, when he smells her arriving back at the ranch.

Between bouts with that vicious b'ar, there are several exquisitely funny scenes involving some of the fine cast put together for the occasion. Included are Sammy Jackson, Jack Elam, Keenan Wynn, and co-star Martha Hyer.

Surprisingly, the beautiful scenery all comes from a part of California just an hour away from Hollywood, in the San Bernardino National Forest.

Recommended heartily as one of the finest family entertainment films of the year.

THE BIGGEST MAN, THE CUTEST GIRL...

...AND THE MEANEST BEAR ALIVE.

BETTER WATCH OUT, this little girl is plenty strong and mighty mean.

TOWN BUM Jack Elam is informed by cute Victoria Meyerink that he looks like her favorite caterpillar.

HANK AND GYPSY gave some thought to taking their act on the road, 'till this tangled mess got started.

SOMEBODY SPIKED 18 year old Candy Moore's punch — what a shock.

KRLA Tunedex

This Week	Last Week	Title	Artist
1	3	A GROOVY KIND OF LOVE	The Mindbenders
2	1	WHEN A MAN LOVES A WOMAN	Percy Sledge
3	10	PAINT IT, BLACK	The Rolling Stones
4	4	ALONG COMES MARY	The Association
5	2	HEY, JOE	The Leaves
6	7	MY LITTLE RED BOOK	Love
7	14	DID YOU EVER HAVE TO MAKE UP YOUR MIND	The Lovin' Spoonful
8	5	MONDAY, MONDAY	The Mama's & The Papa's
9	13	FUNNY HOW LOVE CAN BE	Danny Hutton
10	8	THE SUN AIN'T GONNA SHINE	The Walker Bros.
11	6	RAINY DAY WOMEN #12 & 35	Bob Dylan
12	19	YOUNGER GIRL	The Hondells
13	18	IT'S A MAN'S, MAN'S, MAN'S WORLD	James Brown
14	20	DON'T BRING ME DOWN	The Animals
15	9	LEANING ON THE LAMP POST/HOLD ON	Herman's Hermits
16	15	LOVE IS LIKE AN ITCHING IN MY HEART	The Supremes
17	23	I AM A ROCK	Simon & Garfunkel
18	25	HOLD ON! I'M A COMIN'	Sam & Dave
19	16	FALLING SUGAR	The Palace Guard
20	22	RIVER DEEP — MOUNTAIN HIGH	Ike & Tina Turner
21	17	TEEN-AGE FAILURE	Chad & Jeremy
22	28	GREEN GRASS	Gary Lewis & The Playboys
23	24	DADDY YOU GOTTA LET HIM IN	The Satisfactions
24	27	GOT MY MOJO WORKIN'	Jimmy Smith
25	21	CAROLINE, NO	Brian Wilson
26	29	DEDICATED FOLLOWER OF FASHION	The Kinks
27	30	DIDDY WAH DIDDY	Captain Beefheart & His Magic Band
28	31	STRANGER WITH A BLACK DOVE/THERE'S NO LIVING WITHOUT YOUR LOVING	Peter & Gordon
29	36	YOU DON'T HAVE TO SAY YOU LOVE ME	Dusty Springfield
30	35	BETTER USE YOUR HEAD	Little Anthony & The Imperials
31	32	COME AND GET ME	Jackie DeShannon
32	33	TRULY JULIE'S BLUES	Bob Lind
33	38	OPUS 17 (DON'T YOU WORRY 'BOUT ME)	4 Seasons
34	—	DIRTY WATER	The Standells
35	39	BAREFOOTIN'	Robert Parker
36	—	LOVE SPECIAL DELIVERY	The Midnighters
37	37	AIN'T TOO PROUD TO BEG	The Temptations
38	40	TWINKLE TOES	Roy Orbison
39	—	SOMEBODY HELP ME	Spencer Davis Group
40	—	BOYS ARE MADE TO LOVE	Karen Small

DAVE HULL

BOB EUBANKS

DICK BIONDI

JOHNNY HAYES

EMPEROR HUDSON

CASEY KASEM

CHARLIE O'DONNELL

BILL SLATER

KRLA BEAT Subscription

☐ 1 YEAR — 52 Issues — $5.00   ☐ 2 YEARS — $8.00   ☐ 6 MONTHS — $3.00

Enclosed is _____   ☐ CASH   ☐ CHECK   PLEASE PRINT — Include Your Zip Code

Send to: .... Age: ....
Address: .... City: ....
State: .... Zip: ....

Foreign Rate: $9.00 — 52 Issues

MAIL YOUR ORDER TO:
KRLA BEAT
6290 Sunset, Suite 504
Hollywood, Calif. 90028

KRLA ARCHIVES

America's Largest Teen NEWSpaper 15¢

KRLA BEAT
Edition

JUNE 11, 1966

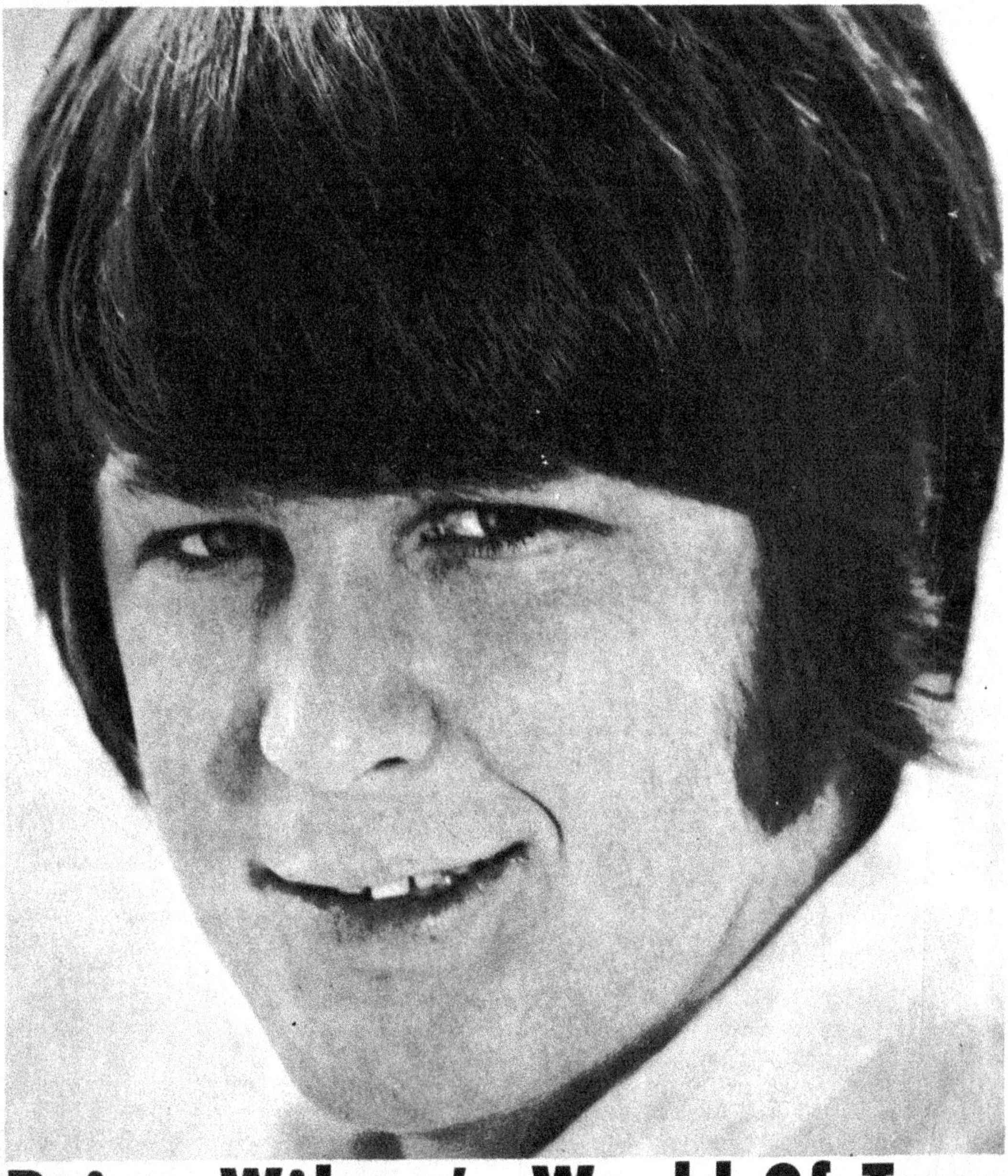

Brian Wilson's World Of Toys

KRLA BEAT

Volume 2, Number 13   June 11, 1966

HOTLINE LONDON SPECIAL

Stones In A Starkly Dramatic Film Debut

By Tony Barrow

Californian summer concert dates for the Rolling Stones were announced in London—together with the news that the group will spend the first part of August in Los Angeles recording soundtrack songs for their first motion picture!

The "Paint It Black" gang will play the Hollywood Bowl, July 25, and San Francisco, July 26. Prior to these performances they're likely to add in a mid-July San Jose date, a probably late-extra to their existing coast-to-coast tour schedule.

The final concert of the series will be on July 28 in Honolulu.

Shooting on The Stones' first movie will begin on location in England around the middle of August. The story will be based on "Only Lovers Left Alive" written early in 1964 by English novelist/schoolteacher Dave Willis. It describes what might happen if teenage hoodlums staged a violent revolution and took over the government of Britain. The script will give all five Stones major acting roles and they will not be featured as themselves. "Only Lovers Left Alive" is a starkly dramatic story which pulls no punches. This will be the first time a top pop attraction has taken part in this type of screen production.

The group's built-in songwriting team of Keith Richard and Mick Jagger is already hard at work on new material for the soundtrack. This will include seven songs plus a great deal of original music which will be used as the background instrumental score throughout the picture.

From Honolulu, The Rolling Stones and Andrew Oldham will fly back to Los Angeles where the first week of August will be spent in a Hollywood recording studio. The plan is to record all the movie material in advance on the West Coast.

Reports here indicate that "Only Lovers Left Alive" will guarantee The Stones a basic one million dollars plus a hefty percentage of the eventual gross when the picture is shown worldwide.

It looks as though The Stones' movie will be ready for screening on both sides of the Atlantic before The Beatles complete their third picture. The Beatles' producer, Walter Shenson, confirms his earlier report that there's still no definite conclusion to his year-long search for a suitable script for John, Paul, George and Ringo.

...STOP — WE HAVEN'T DONE ANYTHING WRONG.

Brummels Deny All Charges

In the May 28 issue of *The BEAT* we printed that the Beau Brummels were being sued for $1,250,000 by former group member, Declan Mulligan. At that time, The Brummels were filling dates on the East Coast and were unavailable for comment. However, we promised to let you know their side of the story as soon as they returned.

The four Brummels—Ron Elliott, John Peterson, Ron Meagher and Sal Valentino—deny each and every one of Mulligan's allegations. Mulligan charges that he was the founder and leader of the Brummels, that he was frozen out of the group a year ago and has been excluded from all profits ever since.

Trouble

The Brummels' attorney, Robert Cartwright, is filing their answer to Mulligan's suit in which they state that Mulligan caused dissention in the group, refused to co-operate and came unprepared to rehearsals, etc. They also emphatically deny that Mulligan was "frozen out." According to the Brummels, he left of his own free will and volition.

Mulligan's attorney has stated the Brummels have had two hit singles and two hit albums, grossing sales in excess of one million dollars since they began recording in 1964. Their biggest hit to date has been "Laugh, Laugh" which sold more than 500,000 copies and was one of the best-selling American records in England.

Therefore, Mulligan feels that the Brummels owe him $250,000 in general damages and has asked for an additional one million in punitive damages. In addition to damages, Mulligan asks the court to dissolve his oral partnership with the other Brummels and a settlement of what they allegedly owe him.

Ever since Mulligan left the group, the Brummels have refused to knock him. When asked why he made his exit, the Brummels have repeatedly stated that he departed for many reasons, one of which was his desire to return to his home in Ireland.

Shocked

At no time have the Brummels ever made any uncomplimentary remarks about their former group member. So, undoubtedly, they were surprised and shocked to learn that he was suing them for over a million dollars! The case is now pending in a San Francisco Superior Court. When a decision is made, or a settlement reached, *The BEAT* will, of course, let you know the outcome.

Yardbirds Not Changing

The Yardbirds are *not* changing their image as has been announced in all of the British music papers. *The BEAT* received a surprise phone call today from the Yardbirds' new manager, Simon Napier-Bell.

Reports have been filtering over the ocean to the effect that the Yardbirds were going to shear their hair and wear classy stage outfits, so we immediately put the question to their manager.

"No, they're not changing their image. They haven't *cut* their hair but they have *washed* it," laughed Napier-Bell. "They have new white stage outfits which look quite smart.

"Keith's solo record has been released in Britain and is doing quite well. It's a Bob Lind song, 'Mr. Zero.' And, you know, Jeff will be cutting a solo disc shortly on which he will sing."

Another rumor which has been floating in the air for several months is that Jeff Beck, Yardbird lead guitar extraordinaire, wants out of the group. But Simon says it isn't so. "No, they're very happy together," he declared.

Jeff was taken rather seriously ill in Paris some weeks back but Simon reveals that "he's much better now. Almost completely recovered. Of course, he still must have his tonsils out."

Simon also revealed to *The BEAT* that the Yardbirds will tour Stateside in August for five weeks. Their two previous tours have been plagued with endless immigration and work permit problems but Napier-Bell believes that the Yardbirds will get into the country this summer "with little trouble."

The Yardbirds have recorded their follow-up to "Shapes Of Things." The "A" side is a song with the unlikely title of "Over, Under, Sideways, Down." It's a group composition in which both Keith Relf (regular lead singer for the group) and drummer, Jim McCarty, sing. This marks the first time that Jim has lent his voice to the group, though he has had a mighty hand in the composition of many of their hits.

...COMING STATESIDE IN AUGUST.

Inside the BEAT

At Home With Eric Burdon 2
Brian Wilson's Toys 2
On The Beat 3
Stones—All In America 4-5
A Triumphant Johnny Rivers 7
Hits The Mann Way 10
A Wild Dusty Springfield 11
Walkers Overthrow Orbison 13
Herbie—Blowing Up Smashes 14
The BEAT Goes to The Movies ... 15

The BEAT is published weekly by BEAT Publications, Inc., editorial and advertising offices at 6290 Sunset Blvd., Suite 504, Hollywood, California 90028. U.S. bureaus in Hollywood, San Francisco, New York, Chicago and Nashville; overseas correspondents in London, Liverpool and Manchester, England. Sale price, 15 cents. Subscription price, U.S. and possessions, $5 per year, Canada and foreign rates, $9 per year. Second class postage prepaid at Los Angeles, California.

KRLA ARCHIVES

BEAT EXCLUSIVE
An At-Home Chat With Eric Burdon

By Michael Mitchell

Today could truly be called "Animal Meeting Day" in London. I'm quite sure if I had been out looking for the lads I couldn't have found them so easily.

Walking down Regent Street at lunch-time I bumped into Hilton Valentine on his way to do some last minute shopping for his trip to the Bahamas. Hilton wanted me to say hello to all his friends in America for him.

On the way home tonight as I was walking 'round Piccadilly Circus I met John Steele, the Animals' former drummer. John explained that he didn't leave the group because of any bad feeling between members of the Animals but simply because he wanted to stay at home with his wife.

He now lives back in Newcastle (Animal territory) where he has opened a small boutique and only comes down to London occasionally to visit the Animals at their office in Gerrard Street.

An Omen

After meeting two of the group in succession I figured it must be some kind of omen, so I hailed a taxi and proceeded 'round to Eric Burdon's flat in Duke Street.

Eric answered the door looking his usual dishelvelled self, complete with brown cowboy boots and blue jeans. He invited me into his new apartment which I will endeavor to describe to you. Basically, it's just a normal three room apartment but Eric's furnishings are *anything* but normal!

In one corner of the living room is the biggest German flag I've ever seen, the walls are covered with fire-arms of various description and the wall shelves are laden with steel helmets, including one which dates back to the Middle Ages.

Eric also has one of the biggest hi-fi's in existance, all done in Swedish wood. The bedroom and kitchen are likewise adorned with army momentoes. Very colorful.

"He's Fantastic"

I asked Eric how his new drummer, ex-Nashville Teen—Barry Jenkins, was fitting into the group. "Great! You see, he was fantastic to begin with but he just seems to excel himself when he plays with us."

What about the Animals' plans for the future? "We intend to make less commercial records in the future and concentrate more on deeper blues. And what with our new record company wanting 47 sides a year from us it looks like we'll be able to do it," said Eric.

The Animals were about to embark on a trip to the Bahamas, so I asked about it. "We do two weeks there, mostly recording and a couple of shows," answered Eric. "I hope to get a bit of a tan while we're there."

Eric is one of the many people who enjoy London's clubs, says "it's the only place I can get a drink in peace."

After wishing him goodbye, I was on my way downstairs and guess who I met? No, not another Animal — *two* of them, Chas Chandler and the new drummer himself, Barry Jenkins.

Well, if everyday is like today it looks as if living here in London will never be dull!

..."WE INTEND TO make less commercial records in the future and concentrate more on deeper blues."

Brian Wilson: 'Toys Are Gonna Happen!'

By Jamie McCluskey III

Well, Brian Wilson has discovered the wonderful world of toys. Yep—he has discovered a whole new world of things to get into and you probably wouldn't believe it, but come along anyway as Brian lets us take a peek at some of the latest additions to his toy chest.

Brian explains that he first met a young toy salesman in a Hollywood toy shop about six or seven months ago who promptly mistook him for a weird hippy-type who just flipped out over toys.

Went Along

With his usual amount of straight-faced humor, ultra-cool Brian went along with the joke and became friends with the young man—allowing him to demonstrate all of his latest and weirdest toys which had come into the shop.

Brian explained to us that the salesman "thought I was some sort of pseudo-hippy getting some sort of pseudo-kick from all of it. I went along with it, but actually I think there was some sort of deeper meaning to it.

"Actually, I think that buying these toys represents some fantasy of childhood that we are trying to relive."

Brian purchased, among other things, some silly putty—which can be pressed against a comic strip in the newspaper and will exactly reproduce the print.

Then there is the "cop car" which Brian was delighted with—until the battery fell out! When I asked the Chief Beach Boy just why he had purchased a police car, he explained that he felt that it was protecting him in some way. "I'll never have to worry about being protected by the police because I'll have my own police car!"

But Brian laughs as he describes the noises which his little "cop car" makes when it is turned on: "It gives very uncool, very square police calls! One of them says, 'you are completely surrounded by the police. Come out and you will not be harmed!' And a siren plays in the background."

Brian also has a monster robot which is capable of saying four wonderful things, one of which is: "I am a mighty man and I have one million volts of electricity stored up inside of me. I'm bullet proof too!!' (Then it begins to laugh . . . Ha, Ha, Ha!)"

Toy Boat

One of the toys which Brian recently acquired was a little boat, complete with two outboard motors on it which is run by batteries. The night after he purchased it, he was all set to journey over to brother Carl's house in order to sail it in his pool, however it never quite worked out. Oh well—there's always the bath tub!

In closing, Brian just gathered all of his brand new toys around him, and looking up very solemnly (well, as solemnly as anyone could look if one happened to be a Beach Boy!) prophetically proclaimed for all *BEAT* ears: "Toys Are Gonna Happen!"

... BRIAN ON STAGE

... BRIAN AND HIS DOG.

KRLA ARCHIVES

On the BEAT
By Louise Criscione

Most Beatle fans are plenty annoyed at the lengthy delay between Beatle movies and the long wait for their next LP. Well, if you're interested, Ringo thinks the whole thing is ridiculous too. "I wish somebody would decide on something, and quck," said Mr. Starr. "I think we've waited too long already for a follow-up picture, just as we've waited too long to do this LP."

Ringo also had some comments to make on the script chosen by the Stones for their first movie: "The Stones' film sounds quite interesting but I'm not sure about their decision not to do any numbers in it. I presume they're going to have their music in the background. That's all right if it's a serious dramatic thing but ours are semi-musicals and we must do numbers in front of the cameras."

Ringo To Sing

Ringo confirmed reports that he will have one vocal track on the Beatles up-coming album—*if* it's ever finished! "John and Paul have written a song which they think is for me but if I mess it up then we might have to find another country and western song off somebody else's LP," says the supreme C&W fan, Ringo.

Some words of wisdom from Spoonful, Zal Yanovsky: "Easy music is driving music. There's nothing in the world to compare with driving down the West Coast and listening to 'California Girls' by the Beach Boys or 'California Dreamin'' by the Mama's and Papa's. You've got the sunshine roof open and the feel of the surf spray in the air and wheels humming along the road. Driving music – great!"

...RINGO STARR

Saw Johnny Rivers the other night at the Whiskey and I'm now ready to eat any unkind remarks I may have *ever* made about Johnny's performances. I used to think he was rather dull on stage!!! Well, we all make mistakes once in a while. Anyway, the guy's great – and that's all I'm gonna say.

Mick's Dream

Mick Jagger was in a thinking-back mood recently and recalled the old days when "the group was everything to Brian and Keith and me. It was our dream, our whole world. Even when Andrew saw us first, the limit of our ambition was to make big money in clubs around London. And it wasn't until the Beatles came along that we thought maybe we could make a record and be like them. Six months before that it was a different story altogether. We felt like giving up."

Herbie Alpert and his TJ Brass have just returned from a record breaking tour of the U.S. and are planning a giant European tour in the fall. Meanwhile, they're living nicely off their hit albums. This week finds *six* TJB albums on the nation's charts, monopolizing the top three positions with "What Now My Love," "Going Places" and "Whipped Cream and Other Delights." The big thing in the business these days is attempting to out-sell Herbie!

QUICK ONES: The Jagger/Richard team has penned a song, "Sittin' On The Fence," for two Andrew Oldham discoveries – David Skinner and Andrew Rose . . . At last count, six Jagger/Richard compositions from their British LP, "Aftermath," have been covered by other artists . . . While they were in England, the Everly Brothers cut a Hollies' composition – which must have made the Hollies quite proud as they are such staunch supporters of Don and Phil.

...CHRIS DREJA

The Yardbirds are enthused to hear that Statesiders have taken to them so well. Says Chris Dreja: "They tell us that all the hippies and intellectuals are listening to our discs instead of Dylan's now." So are the rest of us, Chris!!

With everyone claiming to have introduced the sitar to pop music, the Yardbirds felt obliged to get into the act. "We were one of the first groups to introduce the sitar," remarked Sam. He also revealed that we're in store for some experimental electronic sounds from the Yardbirds. But he hastens to add that he still considers the Yardbirds musicians rather than electricians. Which is reassuring, don't you think?

SMOTHERS Invite Teen Press
By Tammy Hitchcock

The editors and reporters show their passes at the door and make their way to their seats in the conference room. Some carry large note pads, others have small tablets. A few tote camera cases and begin to set up their equipment to shoot photos for their publications. There is a bit of quiet conversation in the room but everything is businesslike and efficient.

A White House Press Conference? A State Department briefing? No, it's a new journalistic phenomena—a teenage press conference. One of the most effective utilizers of this new press format are the Smothers Brothers.

Recently, in various cities around the country the music and comedy team of Tommy and Dick Smothers have held such press conferences. The result has been a fast-paced but informative session with their fans who get direct answers to the questions they want to ask.

The teen press conference has been so successful in bringing teenage writers together with the Brothers that the spontaneous humor, wit and sometimes hilarity of the session may form the basis for a future Smothers Brothers' album.

How does the teen press conference work? Very much like such an event for the "adult" press. Whenever the Brothers are appearing in a particular locale, letters of invitation are sent to the high schools, junior colleges and colleges in the area asking if they would like to attend the press session and meet the Smothers in person.

..."TOMMY would say stupid things in school."

Each invitation bears an attached ticket authorizing a member of the staff of the school's paper to get into the press session while giving all pertinent data about the conference.

At each conference held so far, the Smothers answer questions thrown at them for about an hour and a half, enjoying it as much as the teen correspondents.

"We really enjoy these press conferences," said Tommy. "We like the questions and we like to see the young people. After all, at this point if we can stay in step with these young people, we feel we'll have a certain longevity in this business. So, it's important that we talk to teenagers—and we like it too," he added.

The following are some of the questions and answers asked at one of the Smothers' teen press conferences. As you will see, the questions are every bit as (and sometimes more) intelligent than those asked by certain members of the "adult" press.

QUESTION: How did you get the name Smothers?
TOMMY: It was a matter of heredity. We couldn't help ourselves.
QUESTION: What about your educational background?
TOMMY: I went to the eighth grade.
DICK: I was in my sophomore year at San Jose State when we started singing.
TOMMY: I went there too—only I wasn't doing too well with only an eighth grade education.
QUESTION: Were you both always comic personalities?
DICK: Tommy especially would say stupid things in school. He was always getting laughs.
QUESTION: How do you relax?
DICK: I have several hobbies.
TOMMY: I drink a lot and hang around with street gangs. No, we both enjoy sailing very much and we both like motorcycling.
QUESTION: How do you develop a comedy routine?
TOMMY: We don't rehearse. It's sort of ad-lib that we revise continually. We just go out and sing and start adding in the nonsense.
QUESTION: Did Dick ever do the comedy and Tommy the straight parts?
TOMMY: Dickie tries to be funny every now and then—but he's not very funny.

And so the questions and answers go—on and on for over an hour. Apparently, the Smothers' use of the teen press conferences has paid off handsomely for the two brothers because they continue breaking gross and attendance records everywhere they go. They even broke their *own* record when they played Melodyland in Anaheim, California.

Since the teen press conference is such a rewarding innovation, The BEAT wonders why more entertainers don't employ it—might do them lots of good!

..."IT WAS A MATTER of heredity, we couldn't help ourselves."

KRLA ARCHIVES

The Jagger: 'It's All Right Here

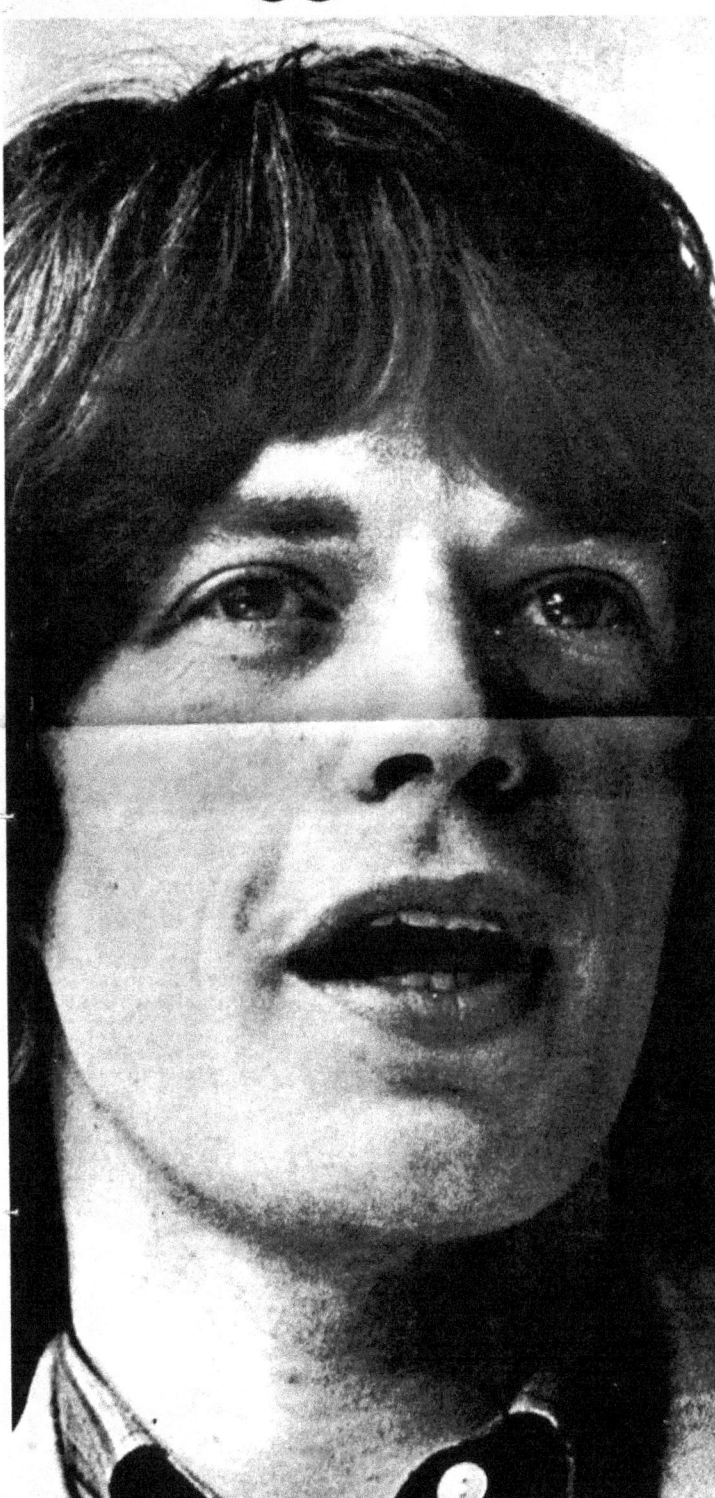

... HERMAN'S MUSIC IS "WET AND WATERY."

Many try to describe, categorize and analyze the five Rolling Stones. Most fail. Partly because they don't really know the Stones and are only going by what they hear, or what they want to believe. They can't conceive of a long-haired group of don't-give-a-damn-guys making so much money, causing such hysterical screaming or possessing so many devoted fans.

Perhaps if they just sat down and spoke with Mick, Brian, Keith, Charlie and Bill they'd find the answers.

But maybe they're afraid to do that—afraid that they might discover an ample amount of brains hidden behind that long hair. More brains perhaps than even *they* have. And they're afraid too that they will be shot down with clever remarks for which they have no answers. And if they ask ridiculous questions they *will* be put down, make no mistake about it.

Frank Stones

Because the Stones are frank—so frank that it makes some reporters shudder. Ask Mick Jagger about Herman and he'll fire back: "I wish people would stop asking us what we think of him. It's like this. He isn't a bad guy and he's very young. But the truth is that I don't think about him at all. To me his music is kind of wet and watery and doesn't have much significance."

Ask about the group scene in England and the Jagger will shrug his thin shoulder, brush a lock of hair from his forehead, stare the questioner directly in the eye and reply: "There's not a person or a group in England today that I would go to see to learn something. It's that simple; it's all right here in America and you've got to come here to see it."

Most reporters aren't used to that kind of frankness. They're accustomed to interviewing people with a publicity man sitting next to the artist making sure he doesn't put *anyone* or *anything* down. Frank and open answers, honest opinions and true feelings do not usually come forth if there is one chance in a million that it will cause the smallest amount of controversy.

But when you talk to the Stones you talk to them alone. They say what they want to say—not what some publicity man *wants* them to say. Occasionally you can even ask a question and come up with five different answers because the Stones do not always agree among themselves on matters not directly involving the group.

Eric Best

Once, in front of Mick, Brian Jones told a reporter that as far as he was concerned, "Eric Burdon is probably the best lead singer in England right now." Mick didn't bat an eyelash—maybe he feels that way, too.

Ask the Stones about the Beatles and Brian will say: "We're as close friends of the Beatles as anybody in the business. And they are good and I think they like us too, despite the feuds that some of the music papers in England have tried to generate between us."

The Stones have been on the receiving end of some rather hard knocks for putting a sitar on "Paint It Black," because the Beatles have used it before. The way some people have been carrying on you'd think the Beatles *invented* the sitar—which, in case you didn't know, they did not.

The Stones are not particularly worried about being referred to as copy-cats, because they're not. Ask Keith Richard about the sitar and he'll explain: "As we had the sitars, we thought we'd try them out in the studio. To get the right sound on this song, we found the sitar fit perfectly. We tried a guitar but you can't bend it enough."

"Don't Ask Me"

There is a rather odd looking comma hanging in the title of Paint It, Black" and if you're brave enough to inquire what it's doing there, Keith will reply: "Don't ask me what the comma is in the title. That's Decca. I suppose they could have put 'black' in brackets."

Did you ever wonder why the Stones record exclusively now in America and why they always choose Dave Hassinger as their engineer? If you'd bother to ask, Keith would be glad to inform you that "the sound is much better than it is in England. We find it pays to record here, we go to America so much. When we go to the studios, we make enough records to keep us going until next time."

And Dave Hassinger? "The important thing is that he gets on with Andrew. We don't have to see them but they work well together. He's a nice young chap. Quiet."

Because many reporters don't talk directly to Charlie, the misconception has been generated that Charlie simply *does not talk*. Wrong. And if you don't believe it, just read what Charlie had to say about the Stones on stage.

"I can't see much in front of me because of the bright lights. I'm in a world of my own really. I don't look at my drums, I play by feel and put my head on one side to keep an eye on Keith.

"As far as sound goes, I can't hear much at all because I usually have to belt the drums as hard as I can to make my presence felt. About the only thing that I'm aware of is Bill's bass—that usually shakes the stage. In the smaller places I can hear a few of Mick's words as they bounce back from the far end of the theater, *if* I'm lucky."

So, you think Charlie doesn't talk, huh?

Bill Wyman has also acquired about him the image of a Silent Stone. And yet he is not. True, when a question is asked to all five Stones, Mick, Keith and Brian are quick to get heir opinions in first and by the time it's Charlie's and Bill's turn they seem to find nothing left to add.

Perhaps this is what has prompted the Silent Stone label to fall equally on Charlie and Bill. It's when you can get either Bill or Charlie alone that they are fast to tell you what they think, what they feel and what they want.

Ask Bill his initial impression of Keith, Brian and Mick and he'll tell you a hilarious story of their

KRLA ARCHIVES

In America'

first meeting at the Whetherby Arms.

"There weren't too many people about this time of the night. But over at the bar were two geysers with long hair and scuffy clothes. I mean, I was reasonably well-dressed, I suppose, because at least I was earning some money — but these two were ridiculous!"

Scuff Called Mick

Those "ridiculous two" turned out to be Keith Richard and Brian Jones. They were soon joined by Mick, described by Bill as "another long-haired scuff called Mick."

The Stones have always been the object of mass attack by the "adult" press. Much more before, a little less now.

It was the frustration of not being taken seriously as musicians which caused Brian to once burst out: "These ruddy reporters do not seem to want to take us seriously. Well, that's okay. We'll make them eat their lousy words one day. We'll make them take our music seriously."

Brian's prediction, issued in the heat of anger, has now come true. No one dusts the Stone sound off as fly-by-night; their music is now taken seriously. It's a shame the five Stones who *make* that music aren't taken seriously, aren't understood as individuals and are thrown into that "dirty, unkempt, long-haired" bag. They really don't belong there — too bad a lot of people don't realize that.

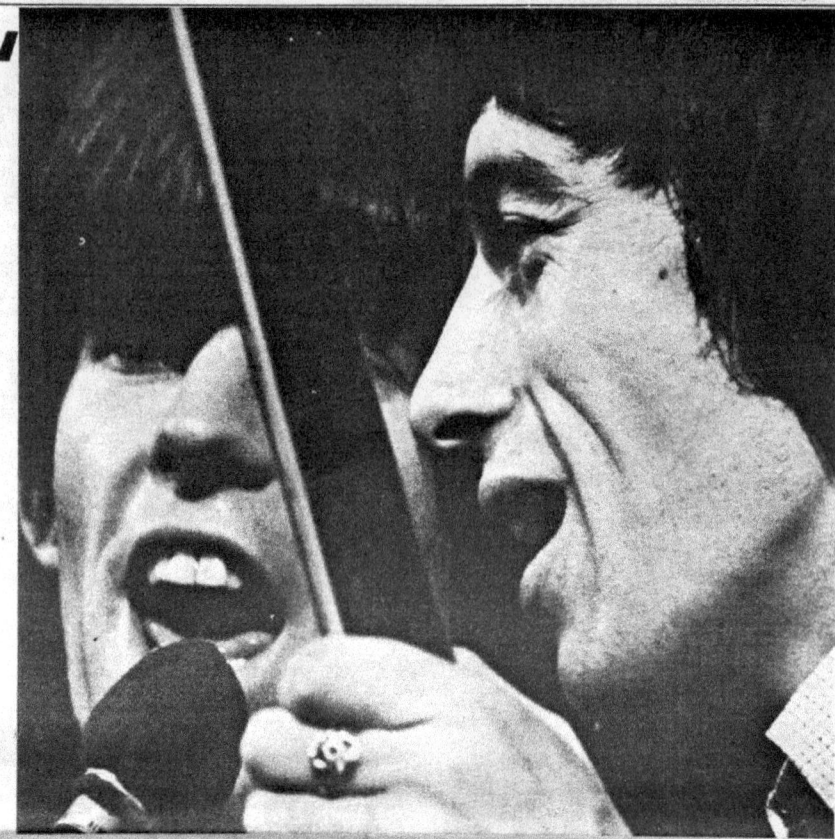

...BILL DESCRIBES KEITH AS A "GEYSER WITH LONG HAIR."

..."ERIC BURDON IS THE BEST LEAD SINGER IN ENGLAND."

..."I'M IN A WORLD OF MY OWN REALLY."

KRLA ARCHIVES

The Adventures of Robin Boyd

©1965 By Shirley Poston
CHAPTER THIRTY-ONE

There are some people in this world who would have a slight problem trying to leave a heavily chaperoned (in more ways than one) prom to "go home and get some toothache medicine." And Robin Boyd was one of them.

But, hoping that the paper she'd stuffed in her cheek wouldn't fall out, she continued begging until the two teachers at the door (death's, she hoped) finally agreed to let her depart.

As she did exactly that in a high run, the teachers exchanged a flip-you-for-who-gets-to-smell-her-breath-on-the-way-back-in look and raced off to borrow the necessary coins.

If the truth were known (and it seldom is because it's been known to smart a lot), they'd have smelled her breath on the way *out*.

Punch (Ahem)

But, being one step ahead of them, Robin had already removed her tell-tale collar and leash. And the faculty had been too busy at the punch (ahem) bowl to have noticed that, moments ago, the prom had been slightly disrupted (as in Chaos, Ltd.) by the sudden appearance and disappearance of Mr. and Mrs. George Harrison.

Naturally, Robin was also one step ahead of herself, and fell flat on her face as she raced down the darkened street.

Picking herself up (which is quite an accomplishment any way you look at it), she dusted off the remaining shreds of her blue formal.

Well, at least she wouldn't have to worry about the aforementioned paper falling out. It was now firmly lodged just north of her liver. (Actually, it had been rather tasty — the paper, not her liver — but she would have preferred it in a salad.)

'Pool

Then, having seen too many old TV shows on TV, she catapulted to the nearest phone booth, whispered "Liverpool" (as in *call the hawgs again Mable — I don't think they heard you in Seattle*), turned into a *real* robin and flapped wildly home.

Ducking around the corner of the house, she said the other magic word ("Ketchup") (formerly Worchestershire" and changed for reasons obvious) (well, can *you* pronounce it?) that turned her back (and her front, and her front) into her sixteen-year-old self.

Robin then tippy-toed noisily (no one is perfect) through the front door and stumbled to the olde English tea pot on the mantle.

Yanking a long red hair clean out of its socket, she chomped on it furiously.

That had *not* been the real Mr. and Mrs. George Harrison at the prom! In the first place, they were in England. In the second place, they would have been too polite to distract everyone at the very moment when a nice kid like Robin Irene Boyd was being crowned Queen Of The May (try not to get any on you.)

Digging George

In the third place, this was obviously the (dirty) work of *another* George (as in jealous Genie). And just as soon as she'd finished digging the fourth place, he'd be in it.

After one final chomp, Robin gasped a lot (paper, si ... spraynet, no) and strategically placed the aforementioned long red on the lid of the tea pot.

There! If George managed to sneak home before she returned, he wouldn't be able to escape her wrath. If that hair had been moved one *hair* (as you may have noticed, repition contines to rule), she'd know he was cowering in his pot and could proceed to cook his goose.

Mission accomplished, she re-stuffed her cheek with a corner torn from a nearby copy of *The BEAT* (known in some circles as chewing a plug) and winged back to the prom.

Re-entering the carnation-scented gymnasium (oh, *sure*) proved to be no problem at all. The two teachers were still making the rounds of the faculty members. Having given up on ever finding nickles, they had decided to believe pennies.

It took Robin exactly one hour to accomplish the second part of her mission. Which was, of course, getting rid of John C. (as in cripes, are we going to start *that* again?) Winston.

True to form, her date had declined all offers of post-prom parties in hopes of roping Robin (with real rope, if necessary) into a quiet drive in the country (of Mexico, if possible.)

Resisting the irresistable urge (repetition will *always* rule) to tell him he'd been out of gas for years, Robin complained violently of her aching tooth, and insisted upon tying her stole mumpily about her jaw.

When this failed to keep him from urging her to join him in a hamburger (providing, of course, there was room for both of them), she further assured him that she wasn't hungry.

"I had some paper and hair spray earlier," she explained. "But thanks anyway."

"You're welcome," he quaked in stark terror, rubberizing six blocks of pavement. (Actually, he drove rather carefully, but we wouldn't want to shatter his un-cool, un-calm image.)

When he refused to settle for a goodnight handshake, Robin resisted the urge to settle him several feet beneath the Boyd lawn and gave him a chaste peck (as in *yick*) on the cheek.

Racing into the house, she gargled briskly with Comet Cleanser (a person can't be too careful these days.) Then she murderously stalked up to the tea pot. Which, if George knew what was good for him, he'd better be in, or else. (Or else what? Don't confuse the girl — this is her first stalk-up.)

"*Ratzafratz*," she soon boomed, waking the entire neighborhood (not to mention the dead) (an unnecessary comment because in her part of town, they were one and the same.) George obviously had *other* opinions as to what was good for him because the long red hadn't been distubed.

Robin re-gasped. Realizing *why* George wasn't in his pot, she promptly went out of her persimmon.

He was with *her!* That vile, ghastly, horrible girl who, come to think of it, hadn't looked a *bit* like the georgeous (ahem) Pattie Harrison.

And, if Robin knew her George like she *knew* she knew her George (which she did) (don't you just know it), he had loved every moment of the masquerade and was now somewhere trying to make a career of it.

The question was *where?* And the only sensible answer was *find out in one large hurry!*

"Liverpool, Liverpool, Liverpool" Robin blithered as she rushed into her room and yanked the window clean out of its socket. Unfortunately, this turned her into *three* real robins, but she was soon able to pull herself together (a messy but necessary move.) At which time she began flapping frantically about the city.

She searched everywhere. Flying at sidewalk level past restaurants, terrorizing snoring pigeons in the park, and nearly smashing her Byrd glasses when she careened into the screen at the drive-in movie (where she remained for a few moments to catch her breath) (actually, she stayed to watch the cartoon, but we wouldn't want to shatter her — oh, you know.)

Finally, when she had continued getting nowhere faster than usual to the point where her feathers were starting to ache (an agonizing experience to be wished upon bitter enemies only), there was nothing to do but return home.

She did not arrive a second too early, for just as she perched exhaustedly atop the Boyd house (not to be confused with the boid house), a Jaguar rolled into the driveway.

Ordinarily, Robin would have placed a (collect) call to the nearest zoo, but this Jaguar happened to be of the automotive variety. And when two people emerged from the car, Robin ceased panting and curled her lip - er - beak in an unladylike manner.

It was George, all right. *And*, that *girl!*

Robin's eyes narrowed. The very *idea!* Her bringing *him* home! *Her* walking *him* to the door. *Her* kissing *him* goodnight.

Robin lurched and slid down seven shingles (which also smarts a lot.) *Her* doing *WHAT?*

Robin then slid back *up* seven shingles (smarts is not the *word*.) Why, you ask? Because George was *whatting* his unsavory companion right *back*, in his usual thorough fashion, that's what!

"I've got to stop them, stop them, stop them," Robin babbled. But how, how, how?

And it was then that Robin knew what she must do. (Just as soon as she could stop chortling and untangle herself from a nearby rose bush, that is.)

Actually, two purposes would be served. Her plan would not only successfully interrupt the touching scene at the doorstep. It would also give George a greater appreciation of literature.

For, the next time he heard that cute little poem about being glad that cows don't fly, it would have a deeper, more personal meaning.
(To Be Continued Next Week)

Percy Sledge—Fairy Tale Beginning With A Twist

"When A Man Loves A Woman" is one of those rare songs that kills two birds with one disc and hits both the pop and rhythm and blues lists. Even more spectacular, "When A Man Loves A Woman" did so in a matter of *days.*

The dynamic young singer who has performed this feat is Percy Sledge, a 25-year-old soul singer from Leighton, Alabama with a sound that is intense, genuine and sincere.

Sledge has been singing since he was 15, first as an amateur in his hometown. Then he graduated to professional singing and toured Alabama and Mississippi with a group known as The Esquires Combo. During this time he spent many weekends playing for fraternity parties at Ole Miss, the University of Mississippi.

Percy Sledge's road to success sounds like a Hollywood movie. After years of hard work, he dropped into a record shop in Sheffield, Ala., on the advice of a friend. He met the owner of the shop, who had been a disc jockey for many years and just happened to own a recording studio.

The owner of the shop handed Sledge a copy of "When A Man Loves A Woman." Sledge sang it once and the record shop owner decided he should record it immediately.

Backed by Quin Ivy (the owner of the record shop) and Marlin Greene, Sledge recorded the song which is now a sensational success.

Sledge is releasing his first album this month under the title, "When A Man Loves A Woman." It contains a powerful collection of soul songs performed in the warm, moving style which is uniquely his own.

KRLA ARCHIVES

The Expressions Of A Mighty River

BEAT Photos: Chuck Boyd

Capacity Crowds Welcome Johnny Rivers Back Home

By Eden

HOLLYWOOD: Johnny Rivers has made his triumphant return to the Whisky a Go Go in Hollywood, and it is a return never to be forgotten. Just back from a tour of Viet Nam where he performed for our fighting men, Johnny returned to the world famous discotheque where it all started... *after* Johnny gave it its beginning.

Originally the band leader at the Hollywood night spot, Johnny eventually became the headlining performer, drawing capacity crowds nightly and eventually making a huge name for himself all over the world.

On an evening not long ago, Johnny—complete with tux and a brand new hair cut—returned once again to the small, dimly-lit stage and proceeded to hypnotize the capacity crowd for about an hour.

Pleased with the reaction he received on opening night? Yes, very definitely, and pleased also with the attitude of the crowd to the whole idea of his music. "It seems to be stronger now than it was before, which is really unusual because everybody thought it was gone and dead.

"Great!"

"The audience was great... it was just like it used to be, except there were more people. All my old friends came out to see me and a lot of new, younger people."

We mentioned earlier that Johnny had just returned from a successful and very well-received tour of Viet Nam with Ann-Margaret, and he was very enthusiastic about the results of the trip.

He explained that he found the morale of our G.I.'s to be generally very high. "It was fantastic... no one complained. Actually, even though there was a war going on, you weren't really aware of it until you visited the hospitals."

They Were Fine

Johnny did a very nice thing during his frequent visits to those hospitals. "I had a tape recorder along and I made recordings with the guys in the hospitals and sent them to their families here when I got back. They wanted to say 'Hi' to their families and that they were fine.

"No matter how bad they were hurt—they all said they were fine! They were all okay."

Johnny went on to explain that the majority of the men he met were between the ages of 18 and 20 and many of them had heard and played his records back in the States, so during the performances they all joined in and sang along.

It was a spirit lifting thing for everyone and Johnny remembers the great appreciation that the men all had for the entertainment which he and his troupe brought to them. It was one of the few lighter moments in their very heavy days of fighting.

Something else Johnny is very excited about right now is the brand new record company which he is in the process of forming.

He explains that it is "something I always wanted to do; it's what I started out to do," and is very enthusiastic about the first artist he has signed to his Soul Town label.

The young man's name is J.B. Bingham and he is a talented and very *soulful* young singer, who also writes the majority of his own material.

Johnny has no plans at present to ever record on his own label as he is pleased with his current record company—Imperial—and believes in remaining on one label.

Johnny himself is leaning farther and farther into the field of rhythm and blues with his own vocalizing. His latest album—"Johnny Rivers ... Recorded Live" (and then some!) contains a predominance of rhythm and blues selections—all very great, I might add!

And speaking of "soul," the man tells us that: "Anybody can have soul. It's kind of hard to explain. If you really *feel* it when you're singing—that's soul.

"I think Tony Bennett has soul; Frank Sinatra does—on *some* of his things! It's a feeling when you get someone who really gets hung up on what he's singing and really feels it."

Whatever that soul is—Johnny Rivers is definitely in the possession of same! He has broken attendance records in night clubs around the country, and *made* records in people's hearts around the world.

And *The BEAT* would like to join all of Johnny's fans in congratulating him on a very triumphant return to the Whisky—the place where it all began!!

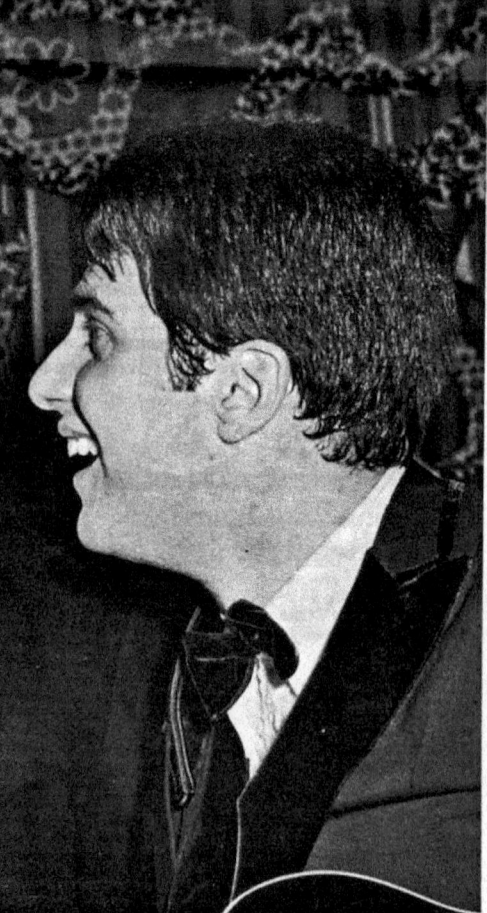

..."THE AUDIENCE WAS GREAT!"

KRLA ARCHIVES

...THE LOVIN' SPOONFUL

KRLA To Host Bowl Concert

KRLA, the first station to offer all-request radio along with dedications in Los Angeles, is now adding another first to their long list—the first all-request concert.

The concert will be held June 25 in the Hollywood Bowl, the site of many top pop concerts by the likes of the Beatles, Sonny and Cher and this summer, the Rolling Stones.

Featured will be the artists and songs that have shown up repeatedly in requests phoned into KRLA.

Headlining will be the Beach Boys doing their latest hits, "Sloop John B" and "Caroline, No." This concert will also mark one of Brian Wilson's rare appearances with the group. He has stopped traveling with the group so he can devote his time to writing and producing their records; however, there is a definite possibility that he will appear at this date.

Also appearing will be the Byrds with "Eight Miles High," the Lovin' Spoonful with "Did You Ever Have to Make Up Your Mind?" the Outsiders with "Time Won't Let Me," the Leaves and "Hey, Joe," the Sir Douglas Quintet and "Rain," Percy Sledge and "When A Man Loves A Woman," the Love with "In My Little Red Book," and Captain Beefheart and his Magic Band with their first hit, "Diddy Wah Diddy."

For ticket information contact the Hollywood Bowl.

See you there.

...THE BEACH BOYS

A PEACHY STORY — The Blood Brothers, a new singing group who visited the station recently, autograph their latest record, "I Can't Grow Peaches on a Cherry Tree," and present cans of peaches to Charlie O'Donnell and station manager John Barrett, also known as the illusive BatManager of station KRLA.

ROY ORBISON sure has a well stocked library. He keeps his copies of The BEAT right in there with Shakespeare and the encyclopedias.

KRLA ARCHIVES

Inside KRLA
By Eden

Everybody seems pretty excited about KRLA's first big Request Concert. It is the concert featuring the songs and artists that *you* have asked for over the last couple of months and it's gonna be about the most exciting thing in town... with the possible exception of the brand new issue of the Son-of-Sticky-Type-Bat-Dealies!!!

For tickets, please contact the Hollywood Bowl by phone or mail as soon as possible, as the tickets are going, *going* very fast. Prices are from $5.75 on down to $2.75.

Speaking of requests, KRLA played host to another group of visiting "phone operators," this time in the very personable persons of the three handsome and talented Bachelors from Ireland.

The boys were over here briefly on a promotion tour for their latest record—"Love Me With All Your Heart"—and they stopped by the station during Dick Biondi's program to say hello and chat awhile.

Dick Whatever

The boys chatted for awhile with our own Ugly-Skinny-Son-of-Sticky-type-and-what-have-you (or *whatever*!) DJ—Richard, the Biondi One—and then spent about the next 12 hours answering our phones which were ding-donging it off their little old hooks. But they told us they loved every minute of it, and we invited them back often (we can always use a good phone crew out here!)

The old Scuzzabalooer, Charlo, and Uncle DM stopped by the small party which London records threw for the Bachelors to introduce them to Los Angeles—and everyone is still wondering how The Scuzz managed to do away with every available shrimp appetizer in sight! Well, he *is* a growing Hullabalooer you know, and that does require a great deal of energy!!!!

Wouldja believe that rhythm and blues is taking over the world? Well, congratulations to Percy Sledge anyway for a groovy Number Oner. *Howsumever*... everybody better start making all kinds of Number One style room for our Boys the Beatles now that their record is being played all over KRLA Country.

I mean, there just ain't no kinda *nobody* no *how* who's gonna overtake the Beatles when it comes to taking up permanent residence at the top of our survey!

Cool It, Shirl!

Ahem... small aside to Shirley Poston: What's this I hear about Mark Lindsay's legs being very commercial? Ya better *cool it* babe or I'm gonna clip Robin's wings!!!!

Well, all right... you can steal a few small peeks, but only if you hold a picture of George in one hand and recite the Beatle National Anthem while doing so!!!

Keep your requests pouring in, people, and for those of you who have requested the request number, they are 681-3601 for the Los Angeles County, and 523-4330 in Orange County. And if anybody lives in the San Fernando Valley (but as the Scuzz often says, "Who lives out there????") the number for you to call is 989-2500.

All right group—get in there and request something!

From the Beach..

Where G&D Folk Guitars are the favorites!!!

Steel strings or nylon, they sound great. Famous brands—fully guaranteed and tailored to your style, haircut and bankroll.

from **$13.95***

Beach Bunnies not included, but service is always "standard equipment" at the G&D Specialists.

..to the Big Time!

For the pro and the aspiring musician, the right instrument makes the difference. Come in today to discuss your needs with your GUITAR and DRUM SPECIALIST featuring Fender, Gibson, Gretsch, and Vox Guitars and Amps, Ludwig, Rogers, Gretsch, and Slingerland Drums.

GUITAR & AMP
Luster finished electric guitar plus big power amp for that wild Surf Sound—Usually priced at $39.50 each. Now $29.95 each. Combination Guitar and Amp.

$57.50* Complete

DRUM SET
Your choice of Blue, Red, or Gold Sparkle—This beautiful 4-piece drum set has chrome plated rims on six ply hardwood shells with durable mylar heads to give many years of keeping neighbors awake.

$189.50*

*TV jobs not included, but your G&D specialist knows the Beatles... Would you believe Lawrence Welk? Mrs. Miller???

Stop by today and talk to your G&D Specialist...

IN BUENA PARK	IN HUNTINGTON BEACH	IN VAN NUYS
Kay Kalie Music	**Manolios Music**	**Adler Music Co.**
8408 ON THE MALL	18547 MAIN STREET (5 POINTS SHOPPING CENTER)	14115 VICTORY BLVD. (AT HAZELTINE)

IN SANTA FE SPRINGS	IN TUSTIN	IN SIMI
Kay Kalie Music	**Winn's Music**	**Adler Music Co.**
11504 TELEGRAPH RD. (THE SHOPPING CENTER)	540 E. 1st STREET (IN LARWIN SQUARE)	1792 ERRINGER ROAD (NEXT TO SAFEWAY)

IN EAST LOS ANGELES	IN WEST COVINA	IN BURBANK
Phillips Music Co.	**WC Music Center**	**Killeen Music**
2455 BROOKLYN AVE.	235 NO. AZUSA AVE. (JUST NO. OF FREEWAY)	316 N. SAN FERNANDO

UNLIKE ANYTHING YOU'VE EVER SEEN!

WARNER BROS. SUPER CINERAMA PRODUCTION
BATTLE OF THE BULGE

WARNER BROS. PICTURES PRESENTS A CINERAMA, INC. PRODUCTION "BATTLE OF THE BULGE" Starring HENRY FONDA • ROBERT SHAW • ROBERT RYAN • DANA ANDREWS • PIER ANGELI • BARBARA WERLE • GEORGE MONTGOMERY • TY HARDIN • CHARLES BRONSON • HANS CHRISTIAN BLECH • WERNER PETERS • JAMES MacARTHUR and TELLY SAVALAS • Written by Philip Yordan, Milton Sperling, JOHN MELSON • Produced by MILTON SPERLING, PHILIP YORDAN • Directed by KEN ANNAKIN • A SIDNEY HARMOR IN ASSOCIATION WITH UNITED STATES PICTURES, INC. PRODUCTION • TECHNICOLOR® • ULTRA-PANAVISION®

PACIFIC'S CINERAMA DOME Magnificent Theatre SUNSET AT VINE • HOLLYWOOD **NOW PLAYING!**

For Reserved Seats Information Please Call HO. 6-3401 • For Theatre Parties & Group Sales Call TR. 8-2915

Melodyland Theatre
OPPOSITE DISNEYLAND, ANAHEIM

● ● ON STAGE ● ● ● IN PERSON ● ●

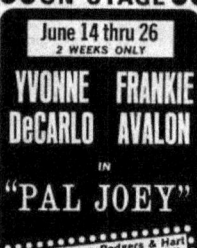

June 14 thru 26 — 2 WEEKS ONLY

YVONNE DeCARLO & **FRANKIE AVALON** IN "PAL JOEY"

Featuring these Rodgers & Hart songs: "Chicago," "I Could Write A Book," "Zip," "Bewitched, Bothered and Bewildered"

June 28 thru July 3 — 1 Week Only

The Roger Miller Show STARRING **ROGER MILLER** SPECIAL GUEST STAR **PETER NERO** AND HIS TRIO

SEATS NOW

Tickets NOW ON SALE at Box Office, by Mail, and at all Ticket Agencies
For Information Call (714) 776-7220

KRLA ARCHIVES

...BARRY AND CYNTHIA SHOW PAUL REVERE AND HIS RAIDERS HOW TO GET THEIR "KICKS."

Creating Number One Singles, Mann-Style

By Louise Criscione

Did you ever wonder how the Righteous Brothers came up with "Soul And Inspiration," how Paul Revere and the Raiders came up with "Kicks," or how the Animals found "We Gotta Get Out Of This Place?"

Well, they all found their hits through the help of a young songwriting team – that of Barry and Cynthia Mann. The Mann's have had unbelievable luck in writing number one songs time after time. They're looked to by many as *the* leaders and trend-setters in the world of pop – and actually they are.

They possess a rather loose-fitting formula for penning hits – they believe what they write. "It's important to believe what you're writing," 26 year old Barry will tell you. "We don't start out just to write a 'message song.' If by the time a demo record has been made, we still feel the contents are important we go ahead with it," with it."

A Giggle

The story of how Barry and Cynthia first met and began writing together is probably not unique but is certainly funny. They both happened to appear in the offices of theatrical manager, Ken Greengrass. Both had written a song (each with another partner) which was eventually recorded on opposite sides of a then popular Teddy Randazzo single. "I'm not sure it was love at first sight," Cynthia says now, "but I certainly wanted to see him again."

Her goal firmly set, Cynthia decided to take full advantage of the fact that Barry was under contract to Don Kirshner and Alden Music Publishing. Kirshner, who had played a major role in the development of both their careers, soon discovered that Cynthia was spending an extraordinary amount of time in his outer reception area!

"Sometimes I thought Barry would never show up," admits Cynthia. "I sat in that office for days!"

But Barry did arrive and soon the two were dating and then decided to get married. Not long after their marriage, they began to collaborate on song writing.

Hit After Hit

That was four years ago and since that time the talented Mann team has produced hit after hit. A cross-sampling of their achievements would be the Righteous Brothers' "You've Lost That Lovin' Feeling," the Drifters' "On Broadway," Gene Pitney's "I'm Gonna Be Strong" and "Looking Through The Eyes of Love," the Crystals' "Uptown," Glenn Yarborough's "It's Gonna Be Fine" and Jody Miller's "Home Of The Brave."

Cynthia Weil was born in Manhattan and after completing her studies at Sarah Lawrence she pursued her theatrical ambitions for awhile, winning the part of Sammy's girl friend on TV's "Goldberg" series.

Cynthia didn't receive what could be termed *lengthy* scripts in the series. In fact, she says: "In a good scene for me, the long speeches were to either say 'yes, Sammy' or 'no, Sammy.'"

Needless to say, this type of "acting" didn't appeal to Cynthia much so she found a job writing special material. From that, she went on to Alden Music as a full-time lyricist.

Born in Brooklyn, Barry acquired an appreciation of music rather early when he began composing small pieces after he found that he could play piano by ear.

Music, however, was only a hobby for Barry, one which he never imagined would blossom into a successful business later in his life.

When Barry graduated from high school, he decided on a career in architecture. In order to earn enough money for college, Barry worked in various resort hotels as a bus boy. It was during these bus boy days that Barry entered and won numerous talent contests.

When he acquired sufficient funds to enter college, Barry put music behind him and enrolled in the Pratt Institute of Art and Design. His acrchitect ambitions lasted for only a year before Barry quit school and began composing full-time, determined to learn about the music business firsthand.

Barry's first hit single came along in 1959 when the Diamonds chose to record "She Say." It was quickly followed by "Who Put The Bomp (in the Bomp, Bomp, Bomp)," "Footsteps" by Steve Lawrence, "Patches" by Dickie Lee, "Come Back Silly Girl" by the Lettermen and "I'll Never Dance Again" by Bobby Rydell.

Writing pop music has often been scorned upon. "It's easy," say the critics. "Nothing to that junk," cry the cynics. But Barry and Cynthia Mann vehemently disagree.

"Good rock and roll is not just an interesting melody," says Barry, "one must be constantly aware of the various sounds and instruments as well as their final synthesis.

Demos

"The production of demos," continues Barry, "is a more important part of our work than is generally known. Many times new songs are done over and over until the right sound emerges. Where we're successful, the demo showcases a song in the kind of performance that will lead to its production as a hit record.

"An artist or record producer may merely use our demo as a guideline for his final record," continues Barry, "but frequently our performances are copied almost to the note – one of the greatest compliments we can receive."

The Manns don't dream small – they're big time. Their goal for the future is the creation of a Broadway musical, an ambition which was prompted by Leonard Bernstein's magnificent "West Side Story."

Their more immediate plans include scoring the musical version of "Rebel Without A Cause." Barry's talking about a vocal deal with Capitol Records but Cynthia insists that she has no desire to be "another Cher."

Despite the pressures of their obviously successful careers, Barry and Cynthia try to regularly save time for just themselves. They share a newly-purchased Manhattan apartment with their German Shepherd and their Siamese cat.

Winter weekends are spent skiing in Massachusetts and, of course, they do devote considerable time (not to mention talent) to penning hit records. That's why *The BEAT* thought we'd showcase Barry and Cynthia this week – because without them you'd never have had "Soul And Inspiration," "Kicks," "Magic Town," etc., etc., etc.

Would have been rather dull, wouldn't it?

Loren, Laine Sing Of War

Capitol Records has gone to war – to records dealing with war, that is.

Two new records just released by Capitol this month deal with war.

One by Donna Loren is titled "Play Music Box, Play" and tells of a boy going off to war and leaving a music box for his girl to remember him by.

The other is "Johnny Willow" by Frankie Laine. It's the saga of a soldier fighting in Viet Nam.

Could this be the start of another protest period?

KRLA ARCHIVES

HOTLINE LONDON
A Long-Haired Zak
Tony Barrow

THE BEATLES, THE ROLLING STONES and BOB DYLAN got together several times during Dylan's first week in the U.K. In fact, Dylan met up with Paul McCartney, Keith Richard and Brian Jones less than twelve hours after he flew into London. By coincidence all four boys chose to spend that evening at Dolly's discotheque.

At around one in the morning they left Dolly's and went back to Bob's suite at the Mayfair Hotel. There Paul played some of the tracks from The Beatles' next album. Not to be outdone Dylan produced copies of tracks he'd just made for *his* next album before the beginning of the tour.

Later, before Dylan left for Dublin, the rest of The Beatles spent most of one night chatting with him and discussing trans-atlantic recording trends.

Roy C. Hits

One of the surprise '66 record hits in England right now is something called "Shotgun Wedding" by ROY C. It's a Top Ten best-seller throughout our nation mainly because the pop pirate ships — Radio Caroline, Radio London and Radio 390 — have been giving the deck heavy airplay over the past few weeks.

Roy Charles Hammond is a 23-year-old New Yorker whose "Shotgun Wedding" was issued on your side of the Atlantic last summer. Many U.S. deejays refused to air the record because they considered the lyrics immoral!

I'm pleased to know that THE HOLLIES have been booked for a further extensive U.S. tour which will run from July 28 to September 4. Apart from a string of concerts, they will play some important TV engagements and the possibility of recording sessions is not out of the question.

Mrs. Miller

NEWS BRIEFS . . . CILLA BLACK just back from sun-soaking Portugal vacation to promote her June record release, "Don't Answer Me" . . . THE MINDBENDERS are to play college and fair dates in America all thru July . . . NORMA TANEGA and GENE PITNEY due in London during June. LOVIN' SPOONFUL will be back with us for two weeks in August and we're hoping to see THE MAMA'S AND THE PAPA'S in the latter half of September . . . Danish newspaper tampered with a picture of RINGO'S baby, Zak, gave the infant a superimposed Beatle mop complete with long sideburns! . . . New U.K. single by BARBRA STREISAND is "Sam You Made The Pants Too Long" . . . They say THE TROGGS will be the biggest new British group of 1966 — and I'm inclined to believe it! . . . Every pop trade paper in London carried hard-hitting attacks on THE MINDBENDERS by the group's former singing star WAYNE FONTANA who is currently enjoying solo success via the single "Come On Home" . . . Half our record critics are disgusted with Capitol for releasing "Downtown" by MRS. MILLER whilst the other half fall about with laughter at the mention of the lady's name! . . . BRIAN EPSTEIN spent the second half of May at his hideaway villa in Spain. A regular visitor to that country, Brian has become an avid bullfight fan. He broke his vacation and flew back to London for two days so that he could watch THE BEATLES filming "Paperback Writer" and "Rain" sequences for television . . . CLIFF BENNETT AND THE REBEL ROUSERS will be with THE BEATLES for their six end-of-June concerts in Germany . . .

Dusty: 'Hip' And 'Wild?'

By Louise Criscione

Dusty Springfield pulls no punches. She's honest and frank, surprisingly so. She's been described as "hip" and "rather wild." She probably is hip and she does throw wild parties which end up with practically everything movable being hurled thru the air. And if that's what is meant by "wild," then Dusty Springfield is an out of sight kind of wild.

If she digs something, she tells everyone how great it is. Dusty digs R&B and Motown but she believes that she "is certainly not an R&B singer." Months before Motown was ever even heard of in England, Dusty was busily singing its praises to anyone who would listen.

When a huge Motown package visited England several months ago, people went in small droves to see this Motown which Dusty Springfield seemed to endorse so completely. The tour bombed. Dusty still digs it but she thinks she understands why her fellow Britons obviously did not.

Too Advanced

"Motown is (though it used not to be) a mass-produced article and it's very well done," said Dusty. "I also think it's too advanced. I know they only use the same chords but I happen to like them. They orchestrate it fully and it's a smooth sound and I think that people are knocking it because it's too glossy for them."

Dusty had been having her own share of problems in America. She couldn't come up with a hit. "I don't know why," she told me not long ago and then added with a shrug of her shoulder, "it's just one of those things."

She later admitted that she probably wasn't Stateside enough and still later blamed her record company for her lack of hit singles. But perhaps she picked an inopportune time to publically blame the company because the words were no sooner out of her mouth when "You Don't Have To Say You Love Me" began it's lightning-paced climb up the nation's charts.

It's about time Dusty had a smash. She's one of the most talented female performers in the pop field today. It's always a shock to watch Dusty stride up to the microphone looking very much like she invented "cool" and then proceed to belt out song after song.

Shocking

But it's even more of a shock to meet her. She retains at all times an element of the unexpected about her. She never looks the same twice. She will appear quite foreign looking with all the chic of a girl at Portofinio or Santo Stephano.

Then she'll change into white capris and a striped shirt, every inch of her 5'3" frame looking like a native-born Southern Californian. A girl who never fully realized what a hat or a pair of gloves were used for. A girl who thinks the only way to go is on a surfboard. But then she opens her mouth and the words tumble out at a fantastic rate, clipped and very British.

She's a kick and a teaser. A reporter once demanded to know what luxury she would most like to own and Dusty replied, completely deadpan: "All of the Twentieth Century Fox musicals. I could sit in bed, push a button and get any movie I wanted."

Another reporter, unaware of the extent of the Springfield wit, asked what her greatest handicap in starting out had been. Before he was even finished speaking, Dusty was answering: "My face and middle-class background. The upper and lower classes are uninhibited; the middle-class is too restricted."

She's a practical joker of unique ability. She once had cans and cans of gasoline sent to a friend's house and another time filled the Shangri-las' boots with anchovies!

Dusty receives as much as she dishes out. For instance, there was the time she opened her purse to find it filled with soap powder just wet enough to make a gigantic mess and total ruin of everything unfortunately residing in her purse at the time!

Whenever her slim 112 pound figure adds a few ounces her faithful friends send her dresses which could only have been made at the tent and awning company. Still, she laughs — and why shouldn't she? That's what life is for. At least, that's what Dusty Springfield's life is for.

Yet, she is serious about her career. "I enjoy it. I love singing. I like doing tours but I also like clubs because they give you the chance to progress," says Dusty.

It's hard to picture her as a nervous person, or as one who even worries. But she *is* nervous and does occasionally even worry. "If I'm doing a week somewhere I'm nervous the first night," admits Dusty. "But when it's some big occasion, then I'm nervous the whole time."

Nervous on the inside but cool on the outside. No one ever knows or even suspects that behind the calm figure and belting voice there is a twinge of anxiety. Because Dusty *is* anxious — anxious to be accepted and liked as a performer. Behind the shrug of the shoulder and the "it's just one of those things" there is a strong desire to be a hit-making artist.

She's got her hit now. Will she have another? If all's fair (which it isn't) she should have hit after hit, but if she doesn't, one gets the impression that Mary O'Brien will go back to the laundry assistant, the record salesgirl or the department store clerk which she once was.

But you can bet your last Dusty Springfield smash that she'll make whatever job she has a load of laughs. She's like that, you know — making the best of everything and giving everything her best. That's the Springfield way.

. . . "SO, YOU THINK SO, HUH?"
BEAT Photo: Robert Custer

KRLA ARCHIVES

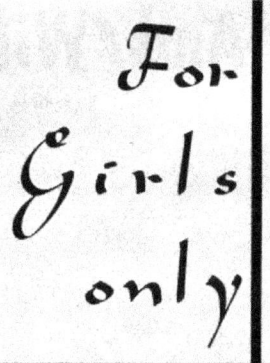

For Girls only
by shirley poston

By Shirley Poston

If any of you have decided to come for me with a long rope, please join the large, noisy line which has been forming to the right for some months.

In other words, I have done it again! True to form, I have sent several of you blank sheets of paper instead of codes! And after I finish murdering my little (as in pea-brain) brother, feel perfectly welcome to hurl poisonous darts in my direction.

That *nit* swore up and down that he'd checked through all the mimeographed copies to make sure none of them were blank, but from what I've been hearing (simply by lifting a window) *he's* done it again, too.

Promises, Promises

Sorry about that. I've already re-raced to the post office to correct said glaring errors, and promise (as in *promises, promises*) never to let it happen again.

Now, about those star pix chain letters. Thanks so much for including me in several chains (which is the best idea you've had for days), and please don't stop speaking to me because I always open them too late to get involved, or lose them before I get around to it.

I think it would be better if you'd sorta include me out until I get organized (would you believe the year 2000?) But, if someone will write and tell me how to start a chain, I'll print the info so everyone can get in on the fun.

Anygeorge, (which, as everyone knows, is the *only way* to go) before I forget, my girlfriend has made up a cool new saying.

For the past couple of weeks, every time we'd see a really spectacular boy, she'd mutter "that's *money*" or "he's got *money*."

Naturally, I immediately assumed she'd become a gold-digger and lectured her promptly. (For those interested, the promptly is located —oh, never mind.)

After she'd finished laughing at me, she explained that this was only her way of saying "I'll buy that." Or something. Well, *I* thought it was interesting.

John?

Speaking of John—what am I *saying?* Guess I must have been thinking about him on account of because "Alfy" from Redlands, Calif. sent me a copy of the Lennon poem that appeared in the December issue of McCalls.

Godfrey, is it *too much!* It's titled "Toy Boy" and is something no Be-at-le fan should miss.

Guess what . . . I'm about to make another of those rash offers that keep me up nights. If you'll send me a stabbed, undressed envelope, I'll mimeograph copies and send them to you. I'll also send "When England Went To War" if you like (remember, it's pretty gory, but great.)

Be sure to write the letters T.B. in the lower left hand corner of the envelope . . . no, no, no, Shirl. That just doesn't sound right. Better write "John" instead.

Warning

A warning . . . please give me at least three weeks before you start stalking toward *The BEAT* office with axes in hand. It'll take me at least that long to "fill the orders."

My, the postman is certainly going to be happy to hear I have another goodie going. He has now come to the point where he flings the mail at the door and runs for his life.

Now I have approximately seven million things to say thanks for.
(1) Thanks to the person who sent me those marbles. Unfortunately, they weren't mine, but there's a good chance they belong to another member of the family. Sorry I can't thank you by name. My dog ate the box you mailed them in.

(2) Thanks for all the fantarvelous (choke) envelopes you've been sending! We're going to photograph some of the winners just as soon as I can crawl out from under a pile of "Ravers." (Which makes no sense unless you're a regular reader of these blitherings.) (Which, come to think of it, makes no sense, *period!*)

Petition

(3) Thanks to Jan Krekemeyer of El Segundo, who sent a petition requesting that this column run a whole page in *The BEAT!* With 103 signatures, yet! Jeez, I about *flipped!* I am now working on getting up the nerve to submit it to der boss.

(4) Thanks *eight* million times for your letters about the Beatles-at-the-Cavern thingy. I was so scared I was getting too . . . well, you know . . . mushy or something. It's so hard for me to write about things that are terribly important to me, because I always get too carried away. Your letters posed a couple of very interesting questions which I'm now trying to answer in an article for a future *BEAT*.

I probably shouldn't say this, but I should be the one writing thank-you letters to *you* instead of the other way around (fortunately, this column seems to be turning into one.) Before I found out that I wasn't the only one in the world who's completely crackers, I couldn't even *say* what I really feel, much less let it appear in *print!*

(5) Thanks to whoever (whomever?) (how should I know?) wrote and told me that George's middle name is Hilton! I've been *dying* to find out! George Hilton Harrison. Veddy important sounding, don't yah think? (I don't) (think, that is) (ever, I mean.)

Hey, I wonder why they don't open a hotel called the Harrison Hilton? (Meet you in the lobby when they do.)

Speaking of George (and, for once, I was) (for *once???*), I keep getting letters saying my column should be re-titled that! Well, I don't agree. *"That"* would be a *ridiculous* name for a column!

Down, girl. What I really meant to say was you've been suggesting this mess be called "Speaking of George." Hmmmmm. I wonder what ever gave you that idea? Which has to be the best one I've ever heard, incidentally!

(6) Thanks to Bobby Tanner of Los Angeles for sending me a bumper sticker that reads: "GEORGE IS MINE!" Gasp, pant and moose mumps. Oh, Bobby's letter had a gastric P.S. that read: "I'm a boy and it's okay if you put my name in *The BEAT*. You know, in 'For Gawd's Sake'."

A special message to Sandy Scott of San Jose . . . As I told you, I *never* take bribes, so surely you don't think I'm going to write about Paul Revere & The Raiders just because you sent me all those HEAVENLY pix of G.H.H. Why, I'm not even going to say that I think Mark Lindsay has the most commercial pair of legs since Betty Grable. I ask you, would I say a thing like *that?*

Beatle Babies

And another thing. If B.B. from 671 Castro St. in San Francisco thinks I'm going to announce that she's sponsoring a survey to see which Beatle Baby (as in John Jr. and Zak) is the most "popular" with Beatle fans, she has obviously been at the cooking sherry.

She tried to coax me into this by writing *Shirley & George Always* all over the envelope. Aren't you glad I am completely immune and her scheme just didn't work? Besides, I don't even *know* anyone named George Always.

Well, now that I haven't uttered one sensible, rational word, it's time to close with our secret message of the week. So get out your Captain Midnight decoders and live! (It down, that is.)

Yipes . . . I nearly forgot. If you've found the code to be confusing, join the crowd. What I mean is, when I want to say the letter in the left hand column, I use the letter beside it in the right hand column instead. (I hope that's perfectly clear now.) (If it is, someone will be dropping a net over you soon.)

Remember last week's gabblings about George reading this column and Robin Boyd? The April Fool thingy, I mean. *Well* . . . I've heard from a very reliable source (I HOPE!) that *okip rpbvrn gaq egizn vngquh vglzarb!* The person said that George's *ukipnv bglnb ngyp ypgeinv kcvkoza* and that they especially dig it because it seems to be written *gokmi ipnu!!!*

Naturally, I'm so embarrassed I could croak, but delirious too! I'm trying to find out now if this is really true. Will let you know.

Will also try to see you next week if the men in white don't see me first. (If they think *that's* bad, they sould see me *fifth!*)

THE TWO "DOWNTOWN" GIRLS, Petula Clark and Mrs. Miller, gave each other a hug backstage at the Cocoanut Grove where Pet was packing them in for three weeks. Pet made "Downtown" a million seller and now Mrs. Miller has the song out and is surprisingly doing quite well with it. The world of pop music is certainly crazy, isn't it?

Big Pen on Campus!

UTILITY by Lindy

#460-M MEDIUM POINT
non-refillable Ball Pen

The perfect school pen for every writing and drawing need... perfectly balanced to lessen writing fatigue.

GIANT INK SUPPLY

The pen you never refill...oversize ink cartridge assures many months of skip-free, clog-free writing.

12 BRILLIANT INK COLORS

Manufactured by LINDY PEN CO. INC., North Hollywood, Calif. 91605, U.S.A.

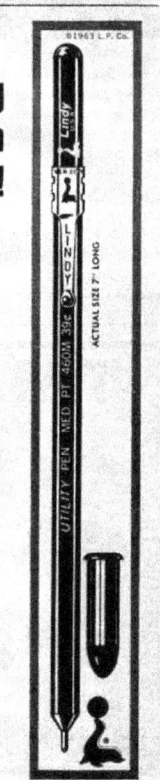

KRLA ARCHIVES

LESLEY GORE
A Normal School Girl?

By Tammy Hitchcock

Successful female pop singers are unique in themselves but Lesley Gore manages to be even more than unique, she's about as unusual as they come! She's not far-out, she's not a hippie. It's her beliefs and the way she stands up for what she believes which is unusual for an entertainer.

The best example is her attendance at Sarah Lawrence College in Bronxville, New York. "When I decided to go to college full-time, most people in show business were skeptical about the whole thing," admitted Lesley. "So many talented teenagers drop out of school at the start of a career 'temporarily' but they never go back. All the success in the world can't replace an education."

And so Lesley limits her career activities to weekends and school vacations. She's turned down a television series and a choice Broadway musical role in order to continue her education.

School Girl

That's unique. You'd be hard put to find another popular entertainer who has remained in school when the stardom and money of a prospering career beckoned. But that is exactly what Lesley has done. At the very beginning of her career she stated that she wanted to remain "a normal school girl interested in education, music and boys." Needless to say, no one believed her. At least, they didn't believe she'd stick to her "normal school girl" image. But she has.

Of course, Lesley's whole career has been rather unusual. After singing at a friend's birthday party in early 1963, someone suggested to Lesley that she get a dub of the song and send it to a record company.

Several days later the dub was made and promptly shipped off to Mercury Records in Chicago. It took the record company only one listening of "It's My Party" before they signed Lesley to a contract.

Four Million

"It's My Party" was followed by "It's Judy's Turn To Cry" which automatically became Lesley's second nation-wide smash. In one year Lesley had become the nation's number one female vocalist with an impressive total of over four million sales in singles and 200,000 in albums.

At that time Lesley was still in high school, attending Dwight School for Girls in Englewood, New Jersey. It was there that she began making unusual news by passing up offers for television appearances in order to sing with her school choir!

Lesley's decision to place her education above her career was met with the approval of her parents. Although quite excited about their daugher's success, they were worried that she would decide to drop-out of school to concentrate on her career.

Yet her family is certainly not against her career. In fact, they participate in it. Her father handles the business arrangements, her mother handles her fan mail while her grandmother supervises the fan club correspondence.

Most recently, her 14 year old brother got into the act by penning two songs for Lesley, "I Won't Love You Anymore (Sorry)" and "We Know We're In Love"—both of which Lesley has already recorded.

While her college work keeps Lesley at Sarah Lawrence during the week, it doesn't stop her from doing concerts on the weekends. And then, of course, there's the summer months. Last summer Lesley appeared in night clubs for the first time in an act she worked up herself. But in September it was back to the books and studies at college where Lesley is a sophomore and majoring in World Literature.

"I know it is easy for people in show business to become completely preoccupied with themselves and their careers to the exclusion of all else.

"I want to grow as a person and that's why I feel that college, or any education for that matter, is important," said Lesley.

That Lesley Gore has managed to combine her college education and her career is a credit to both the 20 year old singer and her family. And it just goes to prove what I said in the first paragraph— Lesley Gore is more than unique, she's downright unusual!

Walkers Overthrow Orbison

The Walker Brothers kicked off their act in Southern California in 1964 but failed to draw much of a response and so headed for England in '65. It was a smart move, as everyone knows, because the Walkers became *the* big new act of the year.

They bombarded the British record charts with hit after hit and slowly their name as well as their records filtered back across the ocean—back to the same place which had only a year before, categorized them as "just another group."

Even though their discs have done well Stateside (especially their latest, "The Sun Ain't Gonna Shine Anymore"), the Walkers are reluctant to come home. Reluctant because they don't really consider America home anymore and because they're not sure how their performances would be received.

It's gotten to the point in Britain where every single one of the Walkers' concerts is torn with screams and hysterical mobbings. So many injuries have befallen the three Walker Brothers that they recently took to wearing crash helmets while making their way to and from the stage. They've become notoriously well-known for wild performances and have succeeded in making local police shudder when they even *suspect* that the Walkers are coming to their town.

But despite all that they've achieved in the past year, they really outdid themselves on their last British tour. They had second billing to Roy Orbison, an artist who has managed to hold onto a large and loyal following in England even when he has had trouble getting hits in the U.S.

The tour was announced in all of the British papers as being the "Roy Orbison Tour" when, in fact, it should have been tabbed the "Walker Brothers Tour" because that's exactly what it was. *They* were the stars of the show— they were the headliners.

Concert after concert belonged to the Walkers. The fans crowding into every theater along the tour route reminded the veteran press of those throngs which habitually follow the Beatles and Rolling Stones—except that now they were following the Walker Bros.

Hysteria

The tour kicked off at London's Finsbury Park with an ambulance parked outside the theater and patrol cars prowling the entire neighborhood. When the Walkers were announced the place went wild, the screams were deafening and the crowd was almost uncontrollable.

But when Orbison appeared on stage he was greeted by a handful of screams and several polite whistles. He stood almost deathly still at the microphone with the spotlights shining off his dark glasses. A few people even got up and left while Roy was still on stage. It just wasn't his audience, nor was it his tour.

It belonged exclusively to the Walker Brothers. Billing Orbison on top of the Walkers in England was as suicidal as billing the Byrds on top of the Stones here in America (or in England for that matter.)

Reluctant

Because of all the headlines the Walkers have made within the past year, because of all the mobbings and because of their successful coup on the Orbison tour the Walkers' are reluctant to tour Stateside.

You see, it is highly doubtful that they would be able to duplicate their British popularity in America. They could not sell-out everywhere nor could they evoke the same hysterical riots at each concert. And because they couldn't, in the eyes of their English fans they would look as if they've failed a second time in the U.S.

The Walkers wouldn't like that, so they probably won't come back. At least, not until they're positive they will receive the same amount of attention they receive in Britain.

KRLA ARCHIVES

Herbie: Blowin' Up Hits

...NO WONDER HERBIE'S SMILING!

Just recently Herbie Alpert made one of his infrequent appearances on television screens across the nation as he performed three of his award-winning songs on the Grammy Awards spectacular.

And while Herbie blew up a storm, feminine hearts all over the country sighed right along with him. Herbie has succeeded in capturing a good many hearts over the last few months with the happy strains of Mexican music which he and his TJ Brass produce.

Well, actually it isn't really Mexican music, but neither is Herbie. Mexican, that is. Or, to rephrase it in his kind of terminology, he's a lot closer to being a motzoh than a taco!

Still in his twenties, Herbie is typically tall, dark, and out of sight. He is also the author of a very unique sound in popular music, sometimes referred to as "Quasi-Mexican" which is sort of a combination of American and Mariachi music... a la Alpert.

Brass Beginning

Success came to Herbie on the winds of a bull fight—in "The Lonely Bull," which was the first record he recorded with the Spanish flavor. Herbie recollects now the very beginnings of that smash hit, which also served as the beginning for the TJ Brass.

"One night a friend of mine, Sol Lake, was playing a tune on the piano—something called 'Twinkle Star,' one of those persistent melodies that pops into your head when you wake up, and refuses to go away. It seemed to me to lend itself perfectly to a Spanish tempo.

"We worked with it for a while, adding trumpet, piano, bass drums and mandolin, using my voice and that of the mandolin player, plus a girl singer.

"Then we incorporated the sounds of the Tijuana arena—the trumpet call as the bull comes out, the roar of the crowd, all the noise and excitement of the bull ring."

New Trend

Thus, a whole new trend in music was begun and Herbie became a hit record maker as well as a popular record breaker. For example, his latest album, "What Now My Love," took only three weeks to reach the top of the LP charts!! A fantastic achievement for *any* artist and especially for an instrumental group.

"You have to know where you're going," says Herbie and he certainly knows where he's going—before the public in theaters and auditoriums all across the country. Before this year is over, Herbie and his Brass will have played before at least a million people!

He's made a habit out of selling-out everywhere he goes and is booked months and months in advance. The TJB fly around the States in their own plane, playing cards, laughing and pulling jokes on each other while their plane soars above the heads of people who would give anything in the world to be Herbie Alpert right now.

Herb would like to make a movie but is being hung up by the writes to the movie score. Herb, along with Jerry Moss, owns A&M Records and if they made a movie A&M would have to retain the music rights. Although several movie companies have offered Herbie films, he has turned them all down because of the squabble over the music rights.

Naturally, all of Herbie's fans wish he would make a film. At least, that way they could see him as often as they wish. What with his busy schedule, he is seldom in one town longer than a week. And most times it is only one or two days for each city.

Before long, the TJB should be heading back to England for their second visit. About two months ago they flew over for a quick three day trip and received such a tremendous reception that they're dying to go back. Brian Epstein promoted a huge concert for the group in London and as always with Herbie it was completely sold-out in a matter of days.

Only Two

This year, Herbie will make only two television appearances (apart from his all too brief appearance on the Grammies) which will include a "Hollywood Palace" and a special all his own.

With several gold records already to their credit, this promises to be a very bright year for Herbie and his crew—bright as Brass, in fact! Absolutely no one plays like Herbie Alpert and his Tijuana Brass from Hollywood, California!

DISCussion
By Eden

Rhythm and blues seems to have taken over the world lately and the pop charts across the nation are finding themselves dominated by this soulful music.

Otis Redding has released a brand new record—"My Lover's Prayer"—which shows every indication of bounding up the rhythm and blues charts at a fast clip. Good strong blues sound here, but nothing very distinctive so don't look for too much action on the pop charts.

* * *

The Shadows of Knight released "Gloria," originally a hit only in Los Angeles for Them and enjoyed a large amount of nationwide success with the disc.

The boys are back with a tune entitled "Oh Yeah." Prognosis! Oh *no!* Good catchy tune, and a driving beat make this a possible Top 20 item, but not overly probable. Very dull lyrically.

* * *

Sonny and Cher have invaded the pop scene once again with "Have I Stayed Too Long?" a Sonny Bono "What Now My Love" sound-alike composition. Cher sounds pretty great but Sonny should either learn to sing (at least on key if nothing else) or consider fading a little bit.

* * *

Mitch Ryder and the Detroit Wheels have released "Break Out" as their latest single, but it's really a shame, 'cause the flip side of the disc—"I Need Help"—is really a groove while the plug side just doesn't make it! Dear Mr. D.J.—please play the other side.

* * *

"Double Shot (Of My Baby's Love)" by the Swinging Medallions takes this week's award as the most disgusting disc of the week. A very poor attempt at suggestive, pre-adolescent lyrics really drag this platter down about a floor below gutter-level.

* * *

Maybe it's a new trend or something... don't really know, but even Ray Charles is doing it. His new soul sound is "Let's Go Get Stoned." It's great. But aside from that, do you suppose that The Genius of Soul has been listening to a few too many Dylan discs?

Jan Better

HOLLYWOOD: Jan Berry, one half of the popular singing duo Jan and Dean, is now out of the coma in which he remained for over two weeks after his recent automobile accident in Beverly Hills.

Jan, now completely conscious, has been taken out of the intensive care unit of the hospital and is in a private room. Although he is as yet unable to speak, Jan has begun to feed himself and is able to sit up for some periods of time now.

Doctors caring for the handsome blond singer feel confident that Jan will make a full and complete recovery from the serious accident which threatened to put a permanent end to his short but shining career.

As we go to press, Jan is due to begin physical therapy and it is felt that there will be no permanent speech impediment so we can all look forward to more great hits from Jan and his singing partner, Dean Torrence, as soon as Jan is fully recovered.

The *BEAT* would like to join Jan's many fans in wishing him a speedy recovery.

WHILE IN New York for dates at the Ondine and Phone Booth, Bobby Fuller Four pose with Carolyn Hester.

KRLA ARCHIVES

June 11, 1966 — THE BEAT — Page 15

The BEAT Goes To The Movies

A Fine Madness

By Jim Hamblin
(The BEAT Movie Editor)

We knew it had to be an important preview. There on the sidewalk in front of Hollywood's PANTAGES THEATRE was millionaire and *bon vivant* Jolly Jack Warner.

With his usual smile, his always present flower, and exquisite grooming, Mr. Big Time was watching the folks go in to see his newest movie. Most of the crowd, there to see the regular picture playing, hardly noticed him. But the *in-group* certainly did.

With his first hundred years now behind him, Jack L. Warner is a man with massive self-confidence. He has guided his studio through some hectic years, and is one of the tiny handfuls of executives who are still at the job. A few years back (39 of them) Jack Warner had made the first sound movie, and he's seen a lot of Hollywood since then.

This night he was there to see what public reaction was going to be for the world's second Sean Connery film in which the super-star does not portray James Bond.

We are happy to report a success.

Stunned by the appearance of such a film magnate, I remarked to the girl inside that we had "royalty" among us. The obviously jaded popcorn girl said, "Oh, you mean Warner? He comes here all the time."

With that put-down, the movie started.

The title also happens to be a fair description of what goes on. Much may be unconsciously compared to Agent 007, but the film hardly suffers for that.

It begins with the seduction of a secretary (our spy has switched careers to carpet cleaner) and then on to other problems. Like for instance *where does a poet work?*

Samson Shillitoe is his name, and except for a few brief moments when Connery's thick Scotch brogue forces its way through, he becomes a real and identifiable personality.

Some of the funniest scenes occur while he's talking to a psychiatrist, and later to a patient who hears recordings of all his wife's confessions, dutifully played for him by our poet.

Academy Award winner Joanne Woodward protrays Samson's determined wife, but it's the psychiatrist's lady who joins him in the sauna room... but then that's telling part of the story.

It seems the world's most type-cast actor may be breaking his Bonds after all.

...BREAKING THE JAMES BOND IMAGE.

CAN A MAN EVER ESCAPE the Bond that made him a fast million dollars virtually overnight?

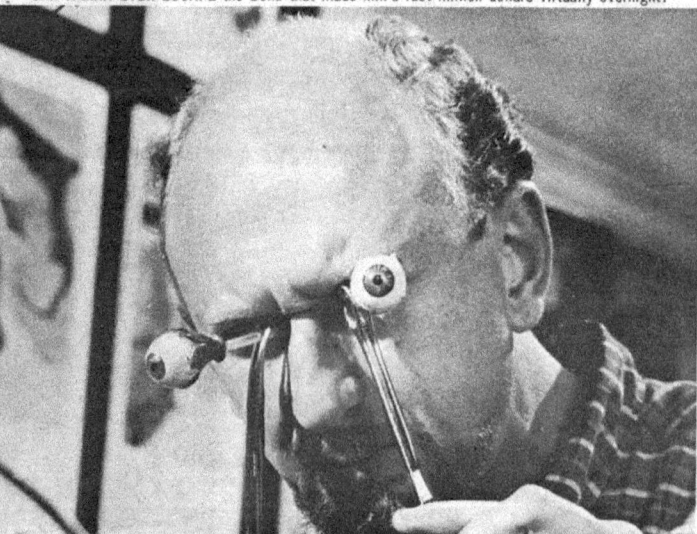

"IS DOIN' WHAT comes naturally always mean you're a nut?" "DON'T HAVE TO BE, BUT IT HELPS," says film director Irvin Kershner, offering a demonstration.

KRLA ARCHIVES

KRLA Tunedex

This Week	Last Week	Title	Artist
1	1	A GROOVY KIND OF LOVE	The Mindbenders
2	2	WHEN A MAN LOVES A WOMAN	Percy Sledge
3	4	ALONG COMES MARY	The Association
4	3	PAINT IT, BLACK	Rolling Stones
5	7	DID YOU EVER HAVE TO MAKE UP YOUR MIND?	Lovin' Spoonful
6	5	HEY JOE	The Leaves
7	12	YOUNGER GIRL	The Hondells
8	6	MY LITTLE RED BOOK	Love
9	14	DON'T BRING ME DOWN	The Animals
10	17	I AM A ROCK	Simon & Garfunkel
11	13	IT'S A MAN'S, MAN'S, MAN'S WORLD	James Brown
12	10	THE SUN AIN'T GONNA SHINE ANYMORE	Walker Bros.
13	18	HOLD ON! I'M COMIN'	Sam & Dave
14	9	FUNNY HOW LOVE CAN BE	Danny Hutton
15	8	MONDAY, MONDAY	The Mama's & Papa's
16	11	RAINY DAY WOMEN #12 & 35	Bob Dylan
17	29	YOU DON'T HAVE TO SAY YOU LOVE ME	Dusty Springfield
18	22	GREEN GRASS	Gary Lewis
19	16	LOVE IS LIKE AN ITCHING IN MY HEART	The Supremes
20	20	RIVER DEEP — MOUNTAIN HIGH	Ike & Tina Turner
21	33	OPUS 17 (DON'T WORRY 'BOUT ME)	The 4 Seasons
22	24	GOT MY MOJO WORKIN'	Jimmy Smith
23	27	DIDDY WAH DIDDY	Captain Beefheart & His Magic Band
24	30	BETTER USE YOUR HEAD	Anthony & The Imperials
25	15	LEANING ON THE LAMP POST/HOLD ON	Herman's Hermits
26	26	DEDICATED FOLLOWER OF FASHION	The Kinks
27	34	DIRTY WATER	The Standells
28	28	STRANGER WITH A BLACK DOVE/THERE'S NO LIVING WITHOUT YOUR LOVING	Peter & Gordon
29	35	BAREFOOTIN'	Robert Parker
30	31	COME AND GET ME	Jackie DeShannon
31	36	LOVE SPECIAL DELIVERY	Thee Midniters
32	37	AIN'T TOO PROUD TO BEG	The Temptations
33	40	BOYS ARE MADE TO LOVE	Karen Small
34	—	LITTLE GIRL	Syndicate of Sound
35	—	DOUBLE SHOT (OF MY BABY'S LOVE)	The Medallions
36	—	OH, HOW HAPPY	Shades of Blue
37	—	GRIM REAPER OF LOVE	The Turtles
38	—	LOVING YOU IS SWEETER THAN EVER	The 4 Tops
39	—	SEARCHIN' FOR MY LOVE	Bobby Moore
40	—	SOLITARY MAN	Neil Diamond

DAVE HULL

BOB EUBANKS

DICK BIONDI

JOHNNY HAYES

EMPEROR HUDSON

CASEY KASEM

CHARLIE O'DONNELL

BILL SLATER

KRLA BEAT Subscription

- ☐ 1 YEAR — 52 Issues — $5.00
- ☐ 2 YEARS — $8.00
- ☐ 6 MONTHS — $3.00

Enclosed is _____ ☐ CASH ☐ CHECK PLEASE PRINT — Include Your Zip Code

Send to: .... Age: ....
Address: .... City: ....
State: .... Zip: ....
Foreign Rate: $9.00 — 52 Issues

MAIL YOUR ORDER TO:
KRLA BEAT
6290 Sunset, Suite 504
Hollywood, Calif. 90028

KRLA ARCHIVES

America's Largest Teen NEWSpaper

15¢

KRLA BEAT
Edition
JUNE 18, 1966

JAN BERRY

Same Car—Same Street—Before It Struck

KRLA BEAT

Volume 2, Number 14 — June 18, 1966

HOTLINE LONDON SPECIAL

Behind The Scene With The Beatles

By Tony Barrow

The 'remote control' June 5 appearance of THE BEATLES on CBS Television's "Ed Sullivan Show" was pre-taped in color by Brian Epstein's Subafilms production unit in London on May 19. John, Paul, George and Ringo broke into their current prolonged series of album recording sessions to go in front of the color TV cameras. Location was the EMI recording studios in St. John's Wood, North London, where the boys worked in the massive No. 1 studio for the best part of five hours on the special Sullivan insert.

They arrived for shooting at 9:45 a.m., a ridiculously early start to a Beatleday. By ten they were ready for the first take of "Rain." Two hours later they were ready for a belated breakfast and roadmanager Mal Evans brought in four boiled eggs plus a plateful of bread and butter.

At one o'clock they moved onto the second title—"Paperback Writer." For this all four Beatles wore shades—John and Paul used shades with orange tinted glass, George's were green and Ringo's were blue. For this sequence, John and George perched themselves on a grand piano while Paul sat on a stool raised up on a sort of lectern-type rostrum immediately in front of the camera.

Before breaking for lunch the boys taped a special introductory segment of talk to be slotted into the Sullivan Show. In this they said that they'd have loved to make a live-on-the-spot appearance on this particular edition of the Sullivan Show but it just wasn't feasible because of their tight album-making schedule.

The color taping was just one part of a two-day project. Throughout the afternoon of the first day The Beatles stayed in the EMI recording studio to make a series of black and white inserts for screening via various British television shows—the first of these being the BBC "Top Of The Pops" program seen throughout the UK on June 9, the day before the "Paperback Writer"/"Rain" single is issued on our side of the Atlantic.

On the second day the boys traveled out to the West London district of Chiswick where they used the grounds of the impressive Chiswick House as the picturesque open-air setting for further

(Turn to Page 3)

Are Long-Haired Boys Actually Revolting?

A well-known psychiatrist offers an interesting explanation for the current long-hair trend.

Dr. Wladimir Eliasberg of New York, former president of the American Society of Psychoanalytic Physicians, says it's all a passing fad for boys to look like girls and girls to look like boys. He comments:

"It's not psychiatric. It's not biological. It's not neurotic. It can be traced directly to social factors. It is rebellion—rebellion by the youngsters against their parents and against society."

Dr. Eliasberg says there's nothing for adults to be alarmed about—that it's all just a wave. He goes on to say:

"It's strictly a revolt against the world—starting with the parents first, then older people generally, and finally the secretary of defense. They glare at older people on the street—as if they're enemies—and some burn draft cards."

The psychiatrist adds:

"But after a while, girls will want their men to be strong again and the boys will start drifting toward the effeminate girls. Then we will sit back and wait for another wave."

Actually, Dr. Eliasberg's explanation that boys who wear long hair are revolutionaries is nothing new. A long-haired 18th century farmer, George Washington, was one of our better-known revolutionaries.

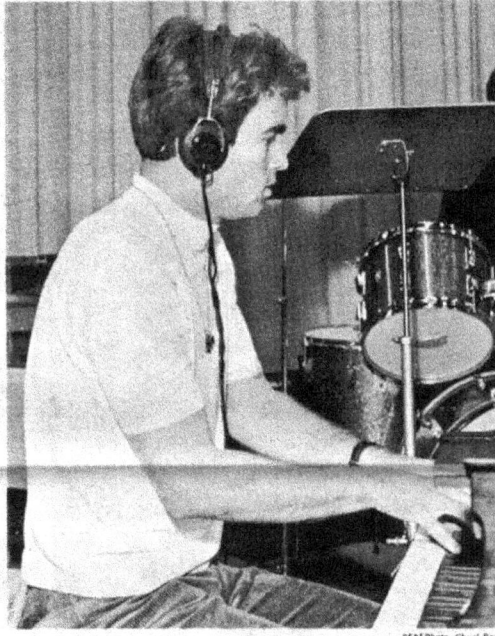

...JAN CUTTING "POPSICLES"

...DAYS BEFORE ACCIDENT

Jan Is Improving

Good news comes to The BEAT this week from Lou Adler, President of Dunhill Records, who informs us that successful young singer, Jan Berry is showing great improvement.

Jan was critically injured in an automobile accident on April 12 and has only recently come out of his coma. Reports now show that Jan is "progressing and is awake but is paralyzed on one side and it is too early to tell if the paralysis is permanent."

When Jan came out of his coma his power of speech was completely gone and Jan is presently learning to speak all over again. However, he is able to say a few words and is also undergoing physical therapy in order to regain complete control of his speech.

Lou happily revealed that Jan's spirits have picked up considerably in the last few days and he seems to be making a rapid emergence from the deep depression into which he had fallen after regaining consciousness.

Ironically, Jan has been studying to become a doctor but during the past few months has spent more time in the hospital as a patient than as a med student.

September was the month Jan and his singing partner, Dean Torrance began their movie. The movie was interrupted when Jan became the victim of a one-in-a-million accident on the set. Result—a very badly broken left leg.

The film was, at that time, scheduled to begin shooting again in the Spring but April had barely arrived when Jan was struck again. Now no one knows when, or if, the movie will ever be finished.

In between accidents, Jan had conducted a symphonic orchestra and recorded an album titled, "The Jan and Dean Symphony Number One—In Twelve Movements." Jan wanted very much to perform the selections at the Los Angeles Music Center, using the proceeds to build a children's hospital and research foundation.

"After all," Jan told The BEAT months ago, "the kids paid for it. They're the ones who went to see our concerts and who bought our records. Why not build it?"

Jan has remained very serious about becoming a doctor, despite the fact that he is tremendously successful as a singer. "I want to practice when I receive my M.D. degree; it isn't just something to fall back on."

Jan and Dean began singing together in 1958 and conducted their first recording sessions in Jan's

(Turn to Page 10)

Inside the BEAT

Beatles—Yesterday and Today	2
So, What's A Lovin' Spoonful	3
Sonny On Piano	4
Neil Diamond—A Solitary Man	5
The Young Rascals	7
Don't Worry 'Bout 4 Seasons	11
An Everly Gig	12
Outsiders Digging In	13
Bachelors—Talking Their Way	14
Beat Goes To The Movies	15

The BEAT is published weekly by BEAT Publications, Inc., editorial and advertising offices at 6290 Sunset Blvd., Suite 504, Hollywood, California 90028 U.S. bureaus in Hollywood, San Francisco, New York, Chicago and Nashville; overseas correspondents in London, Liverpool and Manchester, England. Sale price, 15 cents. Subscription price: U.S. and possessions, $5 per year; Canada and foreign rates, $9 per year. Second class postage prepaid at Los Angeles, California.

...BUSY FILMING TV INSERTS

KRLA ARCHIVES

..."HOW COME I ONLY GOT ONE?"

..."'CAUSE THAT'S ALL YOU DESERVED."

BEAT Photo: Howard L. Bingham

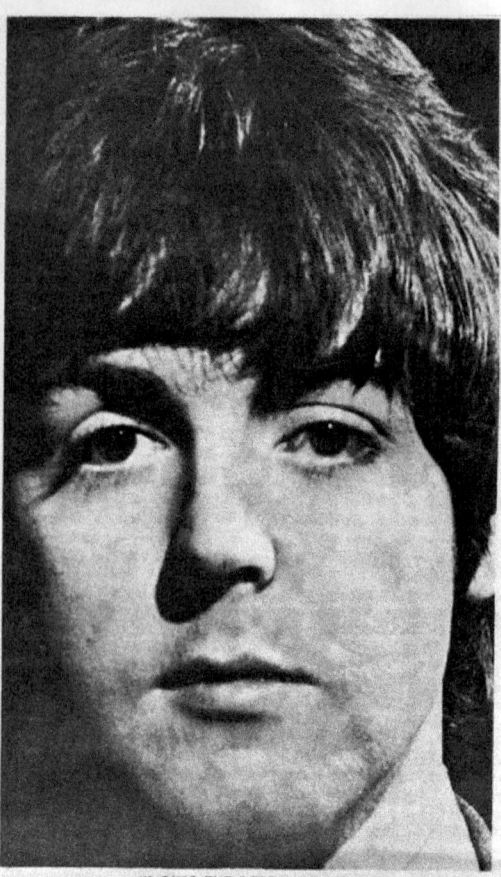

..."I SING THE BEST ANYWAY."

..."YOU MUST BE KIDDING!"

New Beatle Album: 'Yesterday – Today'

Get ready everyone, 'cause here they come again. Talking about the Beatles who are once again about to upset the entire recording industry.

In the last month since the announcement of the release date of the new Beatle single was made, nearly every top group about to release a record of their own went into rush production in order to get their product out before the Beatles' new disc came along and whipped up the charts.

Release Date

It looks as though it's about to begin once again, as the Beatles have tentatively scheduled June 15 as the release date for their brand new album.

Entitled "Yesterday . . . and Today" there will be eleven new tunes on the LP and the new single — "Paperback Writer" b/w "Rain" — will *not* be included.

Many people have protested the choice of Beatle tunes which are included among the American versions of the Beatle albums as well as the number of tunes which are included.

A representative of Capitol records explained to The BEAT that the reason for this is primarily a financial one. In this country, a record company must pay the composer of a song two cents for each song in royalties.

Therefore, on a normal 12-cut record, the composer (if he composed all 12 tunes) would be receiving 24 cents for each album sold. For this reason, if the full 14 to 16 tracks which are on the British LP were included on the American version, it would increase the royalties paid to approximately 32 cents per album.

Extra Tunes

If this were done, the record company, in turn, would be forced to increase the price of the whole album to the general public by at least one dollar. Capitol admits, however, that they are perfectly willing to include the extra tunes if the Beatlemaniacs who are purchasing the albums are equally willing to shell out the extra portions of their allowances.

In the meantime, we can probably expect some rush-releasing of albums from people such as the Association, the Lovin' Spoonful, the Animals, and maybe even Bob Dylan.

There is also a good possibility that this new album by the Fabulous Foursome will be another "Rubber Soul" sort of thing, as reports coming in to The BEAT from across the foam indicate a very extensive use of unusual instruments and instrument combinations as well as some very unusual technical effects.

So, we extend fair warning to all pop performers with an eager eye glued greedily to the nation's charts: Watch out, 'cause the Beatles are coming back!

KRLA ARCHIVES

On the BEAT
By Louise Criscione

This was a week for pop people to speak out and, of course, leading the pack was Mick Jagger. There just does not exist a more frank or out-spoken person than Mr. J. His latest? "I hate America. I like certain things in America. I like Los Angeles because it's always warm and it makes a change from England. It's a great country if there weren't any people there." End Of Words Of Wisdom From Mick.

His remarks will probably make a lot of people angry. But they shouldn't really. If that's the way he feels — that's the way he feels and, at least, he's honest about it which is more than I can say for some people.

Mitch Ryder had a few things to say this week too. You know, he's so hung-up on rhythm 'n' blues that he revealed: "I'd rather have a song on the rhythm and blues charts than a number one pop hit. That would be a personal accomplishment for us and would give us great satisfaction."

U.S. Blues

Mitch went on to take a little dig at the British R&B performers. "This blues sound belongs to America. It's our heritage and we ought not to let the British take the lead and show us how it's done."

The Kinks have withdrawn from a scheduled appearance at a huge pop show in England because both the Kinks and the Small Faces wanted to top the bill!

... MICK JAGGER
BEAT Photo: Chuck Boyd

They're having their share of problems getting into the U.S. too. "I don't know what it's all about," admitted Ray Davies. "We went twice last year and our records do well there. I think it must be 'Our Man Flint' after us. Or perhaps the Americans are fed up with James Bond and the Beatles taking all their money."

The Hollies have recorded the title song from the next Peter Sellers movie, "After The Fox." Immediately following the session, the Hollies left for a three week tour of the Continent along with Bernie Calver who is taking Eric Haydock's place on bass guitar while Eric is recovering from nervous exhaustion.

By the way, if you're an Association fan and want to write them a letter or something, you can be sure they'll get it if you address it in c/o The BEAT. At least one of them drops by our office every single day and the worst offender – Russ. They're a funny bunch, though, and we're all glad to see that they are finally making some chart noise.

Herman Sellin'

Herman's up-coming tour of the U.S. is assured of two sell-outs already. In Birmingham, Alabama, 12,000 out of 15,000 tickets were sold during the first week. Ditto for Chicago where 14,000 tickets were sold without any promotion whatsoever! Now, if Herman can only keep that up for the other 25 cities...

The Animals have just completed a tour of Stateside colleges and have definitely noted a difference between a "young" and a college audience. But they're not saying which they like the best. However, Eric Burdon was so impressed with the audience at Cornell University that he personally thanked the audience for making the Animals closing date so fantastic.

Incidentally, the Animals broke gate records at many of the colleges they played and were obviously very much impressed with the fact that their audiences seemed to be really listening to each one of their songs. Quite a change for the Animals – to be actually *heard!*

Anthony and the Imperials, however, are not impressed (fact is, they're disgusted) with playing colleges. Said Anthony: "Quite a few colleges, about seven out of ten, are providing poor working conditions." By that Anthony means that the PA systems don't work properly, they are often without a stage and are practically never provided with capable back-up musicians.

"If colleges want a top act," continued an angry Anthony, "they should be able to provide a top band for the act to work with. Now, riders on our contracts will call for seven to nine qualified musicians who can read music, decent dressing rooms and that all shows will be in concert halls with seats."

... ERIC BURDON

So, What Is A Lovin' Spoonful?

Don't be too upset if you don't know what a Lovin' Spoonful is. And for heaven's sake — don't ask John Sebastian, Zal Yanovsky, Steve Boone or Joe Butler to explain it to you. You'll be very sorry if you do. We know, because we did and we are!

The Lovin' Spoonful decided to do us a favor and actually write an article about themselves for us. We thought it was a fabulous idea – but we won't make that mistake again. Because, word for word and punctuation mark for punctuation mark, this is exactly what we got:

"Zal and I just wandered around the West Village telling each other that when we needed a bass player and a drummer, one would appear."

John Sebastian, 21, plays guitar,

Beatle Scope
(Continued From Page 1)

television tapes of the same two songs.

By having these special TV performances pre-taped by the Subafilms unit, The Beatles gave themselves considerable scope so far as background locations are concerned. Much greater scope than they could have been offered in the TV studios where shows like "Top Of The Pops," "Scene At 6:30" and "Thank Your Lucky Stars" are produced. In color or in black and white, the "Paperback Writer" and "Rain" tapes will be made available for TV screenings in more than a dozen different countries all over the world.

harmonica and autoharp. Born and raised in Greenwich Village, started playing harmonica as a child and guitar at 12. Lived in Italy for five years. After a year as a guitar-makers' apprentice, worked on my own as a studio harmonica player, working with jug bands and some of the young city-country blues musicians.

Driven to despair by the byzantine power play of commercial folk music, retired to Marblehead, Mass. where I intended to make sails. But the man who said he wanted a sailmaker really wanted someone to paint bottoms of boats with rust paint. Allergic to rust paint so I went back to New York and combined forces with Zal.

"... and I don't know how it happened, but all of a sudden no more things for free and like that, and there I was, playing with John."

Zal Yanovsky, 20, lead guitarist from Toronto, Canada, started playing folk music at 15. Quit high school at 16 and became a folk singer. Went to Israel for 10 months, returned, lived on streets —"... then I lived in a laudromat for 7 months ..." Got a job as accompanist for the Halifax Three for 10 months. Crashed in flames in California, returned via two-passenger M.G. with two other people and luggage, and there was a snow storm in Albuquerque.

Met John Sebastian in New York, and vectored back to Toronto, but it wasn't the same etc. So I went to Washington, D.C. where I met an electric guitar and people said they would give me things if I played it. So I did and someone gave me thousands of dollars, a fat pad with four telephones, and a twelve string guitar and bins full of assorted electrical musical equipment. Later I met John again.

"I was going to quit rock and roll, go to Europe, go to school, and be straight but I was knocked out and awed by the musicians there."

Steve Boone, born in Camp Le Jeune Naval Hospital in North Carolina, 21, 6 feet 3 inches tall, and related to Daniel Boone's brother. I also maintain my family once owned the Times-Tower building in Manhattan and one-fifth of Delaware. Started playing rhythm guitar at 17 after an accident which had me in traction for two months. Got many thousands of dollars for the accident. For several years, played in a swing band, played rock and roll and spent money. Went to Europe, came back, met John and Zal. I play electric bass.

"They really didn't have much choice at the time I was the only person I know who lived in the Village who didn't play guitar."

Joe Butler, 21, born in Glen Cove, Long Island. Started playing drums early, accompanying an accordion player when he was 13. After high school went to college, and played and sang in a twist band in several of the gay clubs in Long Island. Met Steve Boone while playing on the Island. Moved to New York where I was working with a band in the village when Steve and I met John and Zal.

And that – or rather those – are what a Lovin' Spoonful is. "It had to happen," says John.

KRLA ARCHIVES

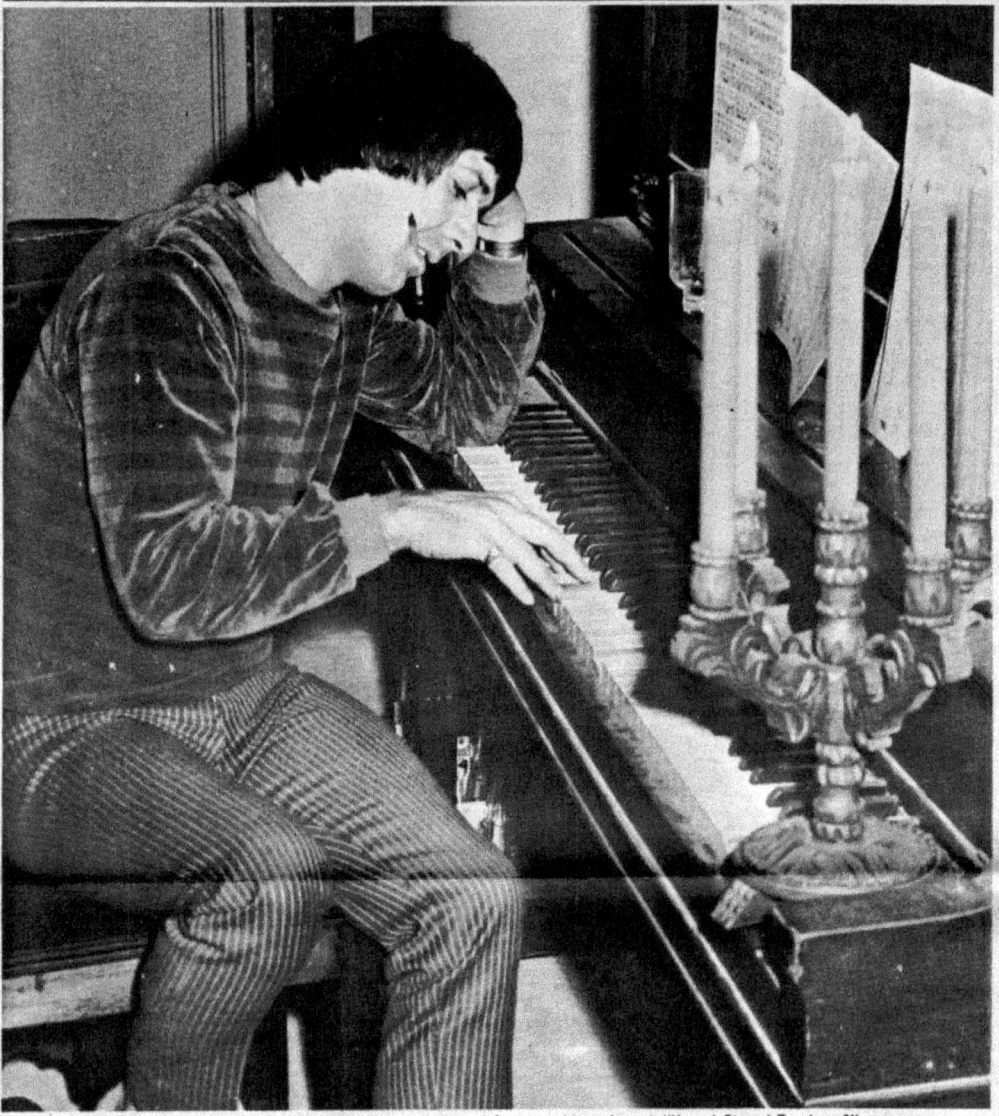

...**THE BEAT** catches a picture of Sonny as he works out "Have I Stayed Too Long?"

And Now—Sonny On Piano

By Jeanne Castle

How does Sonny Bono manage to come up with hit after hit? Simple—he just needs a few basic ingredients. Like one garage—loaded with left over furniture, rolled rugs, extra paintings, empty coke bottles, newspapers, and beat-up, half-written lead sheets.

Sonny also requires one wrought iron candelabra—borrowed from the formal dining room (when Cher isn't looking.) And, of course, matches to light the candelabra.

Old Piano

Then there's Sonny's old, rickety, battered piano which possesses numerous keys which don't work and broken pedals. The piano itself is covered with rolls and rolls of wall paper and Sonny swears he wouldn't part with his piano for a million dollars.

Sonny demands a pencil on which to chew while he's thinking, and if you don't believe me just look closely at the above picture of Sonny. That photo was taken while I watched Sonny pound out "Have I Stayed Too Long?"

I didn't intentionally visit Sonny & Cher to watch Sonny compose. Actually, I was viewing their magnificent new home when Sonny insisted upon showing me what *he* considers to be the most important room in the entire house. You guessed it—the garage!

Sonny opened the door to his inner sanctum and instantly seemed to forget that our photographer and myself were even alive! He stared at the piano, turned around and went into the formal dining room to secure a beautiful wrought iron candelabra and a book of matches.

Candelabra placed on top of the piano, Sonny proceeded to finger thru the partially written lead sheets (some of which were upside down) and then sat down and lit the candles.

His bare foot began moving as he muttered some of the song's lyrics. His fingers moved up and down the keyboard until he found a section of the piano which possessed some keys which worked and slowly "Have I Stayed Too Long?" was born—right there in front of me! What a thrill that was.

How?

Very curious to find out how Sonny had managed to write the entire song in less than a half an hour, I asked him what had brought that particular song to his mind as he stepped foot into the garage.

"Jeanne, I took one look at my old piano," said Sonny, "and the keys seemed to start playing a tune —the keys which work, that is!"

How about Cher? She wasn't anywhere around while Sonny was writing—doesn't she usually listen to what Sonny is composing? "I get Cher out here and have her listen to it when it's finished," answered Sonny. "She comments on it — sings it thru with me and that's it!"

It occurred to me that Sonny must spend hours in that garage but he assured me that "it just depends on when I get an idea. Ideas don't come at any special time. Sometimes late at night I can't sleep when I get an idea so I'm out there in the wee hours of the morning."

Although Sonny's piano is rather wretched looking, it is obviously very precious to him because when I suggested that perhaps he should buy a new one, he screamed: "Are you kidding? I wouldn't get rid of this piano for a million bucks!"

Guess I don't blame Sonny—after all, that old, rickety piano has certainly produced it's fair share of hit songs. And I'd like to thank both Sonny and Cher for inviting us over to their home and letting us in on how one of their smash singles is actually written.

A Look

By Louise Criscione

Neil Diamond is real. And in the record business, that's unusual. In a world of phonies and "yes" men, a real person stands out like a wrong note on a Beatle record. Neil doesn't have long hair (though his side-burns remind one of a very early Elvis) and he doesn't wear wild clothes. Yet, he's cool. Not a hippie cool but a know-what's-happening sort of cool.

You'd probably dig him if you knew him. But you probably won't get the chance because he's a "Solitary Man." "It's my nature to be alone," Neil tells you frankly. "I'm a loner from the word 'go.' I don't think I could ever play with a group again. I must have played with 40 groups in my life, sometimes just for a couple of nights. I was young then, 17. I'm 22 now and it was very good experience playing with so many people. Something that a 17 year old kid doesn't usually get."

You Know It

Neil is from New York and it shows. The way he talks, the words he uses, the clothes he wears all spell New York. He walked into *The BEAT* offices alone, and it fit him perfectly. You'd be shocked if a publicity man had come with him. Carol Deck, one of our illustrious reporters, glanced up from her typewriter, caught a glimpse of Neil and immediately tagged him "Stormy—a guy my mother would call 'a diamond in the rough.'" But when the coffee arrives he fixes yours for you, laughs at the fact that you don't possess a spoon and so stirs the coffee with a fork and you know that the diamond has already been polished.

He tells you right off that he "really got started two years ago. Before it was just to make a buck. I used to write poems and things and then I started putting them to music and I liked what I was able to do.

"I wrote for other people—Sonny & Cher, Bobby Vinton, Andy Williams, the Vogues, the Bachelors—but I really wanted to do it myself. Of course, you don't make much money that way. If it's a choice between you and Bobby Vinton, you give it to Vinton.

"'Solitary Man' I wrote just for myself. It was a personal thing to me and I didn't want to record it. After about three months of arguing I decided to do it. It was cut in a small but very soulful studio in New York, where the Rascals record. But even after the session I didn't want to release it.

Gone

"Now, it's lost that personal feeling. If you sing an emotional thing enough times it doesn't really mean the same thing anymore. It's a song I love and a song I love to sing, but it doesn't stick me everytime I sing it. I'm very happy that they did put it out."

You decide that Neil did not enjoy writing exclusively for other artists and discover that you're right when he says: "Before, I felt like I was a speech-writer for a

KRLA ARCHIVES

Inside A Rather 'Solitary Man'

politician. People were singing things that I believed and felt. They were things that I wanted to record. Whenever I heard one of my songs it would always get me — that I should have done it."

He *has* done it now and his first smash is keeping him busy flying around the country. You know where he is right now but where's he going? "Back to New York, then to the Midwest. They released 'Solitary Man' a week ago in England and they say it's doing great, so I'm going to England, right?"

Your initial impression of Neil as an angry young man continues to fade as he continues to talk and you wonder where you *ever* got such an idea when he begins telling you about his biggest fault — no sense of direction.

Always Lost

"I always get lost in every city," he grins. "So, if I know I have to be somewhere and it's going to take a half an hour to get there I leave an *hour* and a half early! That way I know I'm gonna get lost but I enjoy it and see the sights. In England, it's going to be ridiculous — they drive on the wrong side of the road! I'm going to add one day to each day of my schedule so I get to see it. I've been to an awful lot of towns but I never get to see them."

It's a funny thing about most entertainers, no matter how personally different they are they all seem to have the same sort of goals. To get a nation-wide chart topper, to play the Hollywood Bowl, to pack Shea Stadium. Except Neil, he has an ambition that was completely new to me — he wants to go to Russia!!!

"What I'd really like to do is a rock 'n' roll show in Moscow because they're so restricted there that I have a feeling if they went to a rock 'n' roll show they'd really go out of their heads. It's that type of thing for me. It's sort of like when you let a guy out of prison and he sees the sun again.

"Of course, they wouldn't understand a word. But I'm really going to do that. I'm going to talk to some people and see if they'll let me go. They probably won't but I'm going to ask anyway."

You don't exactly inquire about Neil's hobby — first because you don't know what it is and secondly because you're not in the habit of asking about hobbies. But he tells you anyway. Only he starts out by saying, "Most people think it's kooky," so you're ready for Neil to inform you that he raises elephants in his backyard. And you're naturally relieved to learn that it's pianos — not elephants.

"I buy upright pianos and guitars. I never pay more than $50 for an upright. I must have bought 15 pianos in the last year. An instrument has personality of its own. I buy them because every once in a while I find one which has a sound I love.

"I used to have that hang-up with guitars. Once in New York I found this beautiful, great looking guitar in a hock shop and now that's the only guitar I ever use. I don't go anywhere without that guitar. The funny thing is that I bought the guitar without even playing it because it looked so great!

"People say it's ridiculous but it doesn't sound ridiculous to me and it's important to get an instrument that says something back to me."

Asked if his home wasn't getting a bit crowded with 15 upright pianos living there, Neil was quick to set the whole thing straight. "No, I just buy one piano at a time. There's this guy in New York who makes his living by moving my pianos!"

Wanta Know?

Since you're not a songwriter, you've always wondered how a song is actually written. You've asked that question before but you've never received a very satisfactory answer. You don't think you'll get one this time either — but you're wrong. You not only get an answer — you get an example.

"I was in San Francisco last week and after a show in this big auditorium I saw a girl in a corner all by herself and there were tears in her eyes. It affected me. I went over and asked if I could buy her a coke or something. She'd had a fight with her boy friend, I guess. Anyway, when I got back to the hotel that night I wrote a song about what I thought might have happened. That's the way a song comes. Maybe no one will ever hear it but it was just something I had to say.

"I've written maybe a 100 songs. Some people can write a song in 20 minutes but it usually takes me a long time because it's like I have to *pull* it out of myself. I have to keep at it until I finish. I mean, I can stop to sleep but then I go right back to it. When it's finished, I say: 'Thank, God.' That's the nice part — when you've finished it. Then when you sing it, it brings back certain memories.

"I'm very happy being a songwriter. It's kind of a fulfillment to me. I'd be happy if I never made a dime. It adds a lot when someone comes up and says they feel that way too. When I write a song I think about me, so it's a nice feeling when you find that someone else feels that way too.

"That happened in San Francisco. After a show this boy came back to tell me that he had come to the show because 'Solitary Man' was the way *he* felt."

Reluctantly

Neil tells you that he has to leave. Sometimes you can hardly wait to get an artist or a group out of the office but today, right now, you're reluctant to see Neil go. Unfortunately for you, but fortunately for Neil and his fans, he's on his way to film a "Never Too Young" segment.

"They've given me a few lines of dialogue. I've never done dialogue before. The dialogue on that show is very simplified so I'm looking forward to it. I've never acted before and the only thing I can do is die. I've been practicing that for years! You know, if somebody says 'Bang, you're dead,' then I know how to die," says Neil, clutching his side in the agony of imaginary pain.

Right at the precise moment that Neil has chosen to "die" the sound of the Rascals' new record, "You Better Run," comes blaring out of the radio and the whole office staff makes a mass beeline for the nearest radio. And leading the mad dash? Neil Diamond.

"I saw them in a club in Jersey when they were first the Rascals," Neil reveals. "They were out of sight then. They're great guys." He listens to a few more lyrics and then announces for anyone who happens to be interested: "That's Felix singing. Great little guy."

The record ends and apparently Neil takes it's title to heart — he runs. You watch him swing his car into the noontime traffic and you wonder if he'll get lost before he ever gets anywhere *near* the "Never Too Young" set. But you sort of shrug your shoulders and smile as you think: "Well, at least he'll see some sights!"

KRLA ARCHIVES

The Adventures of Robin Boyd . . .

©1965 By Shirley Poston

CHAPTER THIRTY-TWO

By the time George came lurching through the front door, Robin had already flown through her bedroom window, returned to her sixteen-year-old self, and was sitting calmly on the couch.

"Robin Irene Boyd," George hissed in livid Liverpudlian, mopping his brow (among other things.) "How DARE you?"

Robin looked up and smiled innocently. "How dare I what?"

George literally gurgled with fury. "You bloomin' well know what, you twit!"

Robin shrugged. "Don't rave on so, you'll wake me mum," she lied. (Anticipating a bit of a row, she had placed galvanized ear muffs on her snoozing mother and snoring sister.) (And, just for good measure, she had blindfolded the gossipy Boyd dog with an old sock.)

George lunged at her with outstretched talons. Fortunately, he collided with the coffee table and directly on his head.

Casually flicking through a magazine, Robin allowed George to lie there in peace (no, make that pieces.) Then, as he groaned to his feet and stumbled to a chair, she decided to take advantage of of his slightly dazed (as in Addled, Inc.) condition.

Why?

"George, dear," she sugared. "Why did you send me to the prom on a leash? Don't you trust me, George?"

"Never!" George moaned, remopping. "Anyroad, never again?"

Robin grinned nastily. "And why did you show up at the prom and ruin my big moment by pretending to be Mr. and Mrs. George Harrison? With that thing . . . that . . . that person!"

George stopped blithering to himself and snarled. "Because you were . . . well, you know what you were doing to that singer . . . that Tad and the Poles!"

"Teddy and the Bears," she corrected coldly. "And, if it's any of your business, I was merely greeting an old friend! Which, I might add, and come to think of it will, is more than I can say for that finale you just presented on the doorstep!"

George re-snarled. "I wasn't aware of the fact that I had an audience. Not until you . . . you . . ." At this point, George's voice drifted off as he turned a speechless shade of Sanka.

Robin re-shrugged. "I did no such thing. Mayhaps it was a pigeon."

As he hurled himself at her again, Robin cleverly rolled a hassock into his oncoming path (not to mention his shins) and felled him neatly on a throw rug. (Which, being the sort to take things rather literally, he immediately threw at her.)

"George Dear"

"George, dear," Robin simpered, addressing his prostrate form. "Who was that girl, George?"

"What girl?"

"The one you were trying your best to devour!" (A statement which began in the key of B flat and ended on high C.) (Someday when Robin has nothing better to do, she should consider a series of personal appearances at the Met.)

"She's an old friend of mine," George thundered. "Her name is Ann."

Robin cracked her knuckles disinterestedly. "Ann Thrax, I presume."

George looked confused. "I don't get it."

"Well, I'll keep hoping," she recracked. "It couldn't happen to a nicer person."

What Robin really wanted to do was crack her knuckles on that utter wretch's chin, but rather than shatter her cool, calm image, she contented herself with biting off her index finger.

Realizing for the first time that Robin wasn't just giving him the business, but was truly beside herself (and, at the moment, they made a most unpleasant couple), it was then that George knew what he must do.

Pullin' A Robin

He must pull a Robin Irene Boyd.

Since there was no phone booth in sight, the couch had to suffice. And for the first few moments it seemed as though the abovementioned tactics were working (they've been known to, you know) (don't you just know it.) That is to say, if Robin's bellows of protest didn't exactly cease, they were at least well muffled. Shortly thereafter (about three hours, to be exact) (a joke, a joke), Robin pushed him away with all her might (not to mention her fist.)

"How dare YOU?" she ranted. George grinned that one grin. "How dare I what?" he drawled.

Robin drew herself up haughtily. "Lips that touch Ann Thrax will never touch mine," she decreed. "Again, that is," she added, because it was then that she knew what she must do.

Not Mutch

She must teach George The Genie (not to be confused with George The Harrison (not mutch) a lesson. If she let him get away with the events of this evening, Heaven only knew (and very probably wished it did not) what he'd dream up the next time she so much as batted the olde lash at another. (At another boy, not another lash.) (Silly.)

"George," she insisted as he rolled off the couch in hysterical laughter (having gotten Ann Thrax at last) (again, it couldn't happen to a nicer person.) "I don't happen to be kidding. In fact, I'd like to know where I can apply for a substitute genie!!"

George leaped to his feet (not to mention hers.) "What did you say?"

"You heard me," Robin said firmly. "Is such a thing possible?"

"It certainly is not!" George re-thundered. "Is not very often done," he added hurriedly as a bolt of lightning grazed his left eyebrow.

Robin gave a gesture of indifference. "Well, how do I get one?"

George narrowed his eyes. "Just for the askin', luv," he said in no longer livid but deadly Liverpudlian. "Just for the askin'."

"Well-then-there-now," Robin mused, having seen not nearly enough old James Dean movies on the telly. "I'm askin'!"

If you've a mind (a debatable point considering what you're reading at the moment) to think that some of Robin's never-give-up-easily-itis hasn't worn off on George, you're out of same.

When he re-realized that she was serious, he left no stone (gasp) unturned.

Having gotten nowhere fast by raining kisses on her upturned face (again, try not to get any on you), he resorted to stronger measures.

First he yanked both her arms and her legs clean out of the sockets. Then he shook her until his teeth rattled. And, for an encore, he re-pierced her ears.

But he re-got nowhere even faster, for Robin (what remained of her) stood her ground.

"Go!" she commanded, pointing a trembling finger toward the door. "Never to darken my tea pot again!"

George's georgeous (ahem) face became suddenly serious. Ahhh—thought Robin. Here it comes. Now he would absolutely refuse to leave hearth and home, and she would let him stew in that pot for at least a month before she so much as even spoke to him.

However, the serious look faded just as suddenly into a fiendish thingy . . . er . . . smile.

"Groovy, Girl"

"I can't say it hasn't been groovey, girl," he said in the you-know-whattiest voice in this entire world. Then, laying a finger aside of his nose and giving a nod, up the chimney he rose.

"Santa—I mean GEORGE!" she wailed, grabbing for a disappearing winklepicker and catching only a snootful of soot. "Come back! I was only kidding!"

But it was too late. He was gone. (Join the crowd, George, join the crowd.)

It is difficult to predict what Robin might have done if she hadn't taken several blither-blinded steps backward and tripped over Ringo (as in Boyd.)

It is even more difficult to predict what she is going to do next because the very moment she and her sturdy sister struggled to their feet, they tripped over Ringo (as in Starr.)

(To Be Continued Next Week)

. . . HOLD ON! — SAM & DAVE ARE COMIN'!

KRLA ARCHIVES

the young rascals

The Young Rascals are hard edge, there are no softening effects in their music. Frenetic, fast and driving, they have the kind of sound that is stripped naked. They are pop... blown up, bold, brilliant and tough. They are bang-bang and drop dead. They are super-everything. They don't mess around; they play for keeps.

In their own scene, they are just right and from the guts, which means that there is a whole lot of private personality in their playing. They have a restlessness about music. "We haven't reached it yet" sort of attitude about things. There is never one whole, completed, set arrangement to a song. Every night is discovery night. They go at a song the way a sailor on leave goes after a town... running, jumping, standing... the Age Of Anxiety in four parts.

They are an eminently visual group without doing anything hokey. One is not embarrassed watching them. No adolescent humor. They don't like to do TV shows where they have to lip-sync the words... it's not honest. Only when they have to lip-sync do they resort to some kind of natural kidding just to keep the show in their own hands.

The most typical thing about them, and perhaps the only predictable thing, is that they finish off each evening with one song which has become their trademark: "Cute," an improvised musical goofball that relaxes all their tensions and throws out every stray hang-up and left-over emotion that they have accumulated during the night. It is, in effect, the link between rock and roll and jazz... a link which is getting stronger. The song may well run over fifteen minutes and is guaranteed to settle all scores.

Rightly enough, on record, they have the same effect as they do in a club. They do not like being identifiable, but there is something which is identifiable... the way a Gershwin song is. There is always a telltale signature somewhere in the work. They are, as one has said, particularly New York. What Gershwin tried to do in the twenties, they try in the sixties. They are all the things that are the city. The crowds, the swinging, the smoke, the noise, the sweat, the beautiful people out for kicks, the waiting, screaming teen-agers, the pushy doormen, the romantic, glamorous sink of the city on the make.

They are not tired businessmen thinking young, impossible thoughts, nor dolled up matrons in too-tight girdles. They are today, tonight and the morning after; the drive, the chutzpah, the lights, the action, and all the questions when it's four A.M. and there's no place else to go, and you wonder what it all means anyway.

One By One

FELIX CAVALIERE – Organ

When Felix Cavaliere was in high school in Pelham, he let his hair grow long. This had great annoyance value. What can squares do against that? He is the son of a dentist and was slated to be a doctor. Two years stay at Syracuse University proved that he didn't really want to be a doctor. It is just as well. Now he has something he is dedicated to – a career as a fine musician.

Although there is no leader, he is the spokesman for the group which means that he occasionally gets a word in edgeways, if Gene and Eddie have nothing to say. He is the official worrier of the group.

Felix usually smokes a pipe which gives him a thoughtful air... which is no fake because he is an intelligent boy who is a gentleman too. He is very articulate about the aims of the group. It is refreshing to talk with someone of his age who can talk about Aldous Huxley. The name of that author comes into the conversation when Felix tells what he wants to achieve... it's the "total sound" of the organ in *Brave New World* which completely saturates the listener in sound. Felix feels that music is sensual so why fight it.

...DINO DANELLI

...FELIX CAVALIERE   ...GENE CORNISH

...EDDIE BRIGATI

DINO DANELLI – Drums

Dino Danelli may well be the best drummer in the whole world. He is certainly one of the greatest. He has been playing professionally since he was fifteen and has sat in with practically every big band in existence. He is a fascinating person to watch on stage. He has assumed a manner which will probably be imitated to death. He is about the coolest looking chap around. He plays completely straight face with only his head turning in a kind of mechanical doll movement which exactly matches his rhythm. His high-arched eyebrows give the effect of "couldn't care less." He plays at a fast, lickety split rate with the sticks twirling around on the upbeat at a clip that seems faster than light. He has a superb sense not only of timing but of showmanship.

In conversation, Dino likes to remain mysterious and usually lets the others who are all eager to talk do so. However, when he does talk, it's usually about music.

GENE CORNISH – Guitar

Gene Cornish, who originally came from Canada, is the only non-Italian in the group but he tells everybody that his favorite food is Italian. "It has to be," he says realistically. Actually, his favorite food is Chinese but he knows where is pasta fazoole is coming from. Anyway, Gene is an affable young man. His conversation, which often takes on the aspects of a monologue, veers crazily from the serious to the outrageous and back again with what is usually described as "bewildering speed." He usually warns people by saying, "I was only kidding," but by then one has more or less gotten the point... Gene is a nut!

He now calls Rochester, N.Y. his hometown because his family lives there, but he lives in Manhattan. He originally came to the city with his own group which duly starved and scraped and scrounged to try to make it. The others finally couldn't take it anymore and went back, but Gene stayed. He lived in the city and subsisted on berries and roots until he met the other Young Rascals. Gene plays the guitar with the group and also raises his voice in song – sometimes he just raises his voice.

EDDIE BRIGATI – Vocal

Eddie looks like a Dead End kid... sometimes he acts like one. He is quite a level-headed young man who has the drive and ambition of the British fleet against the Spanish Armada. A teacher would hate to have him in a classroom... but he is what they call "a diamond in the rough" and would get away with murder. During an interview, he can be impossible but then he lights a lady's cigarette and you know he really has been kidding around. However, he still needs an occasional rap in the mouth.

Eddie is Italian... and that explains everything... the pride, the sensitivity, the orneriness, the big mouth and the music... the appreciation of the fine point, the exact detail, the calculated indiscretion.

He likes Claude Raines as an actor... so what can be bad about someone like that? He is devoted to his family and very close. Girls think he's cute and I suspect they baby him. I don't doubt that he takes advantage of this but doesn't really like the idea.

KRLA ARCHIVES

KRLA Tunedex

This Week	Last Week	Title	Artist
1	1	A GROOVY KIND OF LOVE	The Mindbenders
2	39	SEARCHIN' FOR MY LOVE	Bobby Moore
3	3	ALONG COMES MARY	The Association
4	5	DID YOU EVER HAVE TO MAKE UP YOUR MIND?	The Lovin' Spoonful
5	2	WHEN A MAN LOVES A WOMAN	Percy Sledge
6	4	PAINT IT, BLACK	Rolling Stones
7	7	YOUNGER GIRL	The Hondells
8	6	HEY, JOE	The Leaves
9	17	YOU DON'T HAVE TO SAY YOU LOVE ME	Dusty Springfield
10	9	DON'T BRING ME DOWN	The Animals
11	10	I AM A ROCK	Simon & Garfunkel
12	13	HOLD ON! I'M COMIN'	Sam & Dave
13	8	MY LITTLE RED BOOK	Love
14	11	IT'S A MAN'S, MAN'S, MAN'S WORLD	James Brown
15	27	DIRTY WATER	The Standells
16	21	OPUS 17 (DON'T WORRY 'BOUT ME)	The 4 Seasons
17	29	BAREFOOTIN'	Robert Parker
18	35	DOUBLE SHOT (OF MY BABY'S LOVE)	The Medallions
19	18	GREEN GRASS	Gary Lewis
20	34	LITTLE GIRL	Syndicate of Sound
21	24	BETTER USE YOUR HEAD	Anthony & The Imperials
22	23	DIDDY WAH DIDDY	Capt. Beefheart & His Magic Band
23	40	SOLITARY MAN	Neil Diamond
24	26	DEDICATED FOLLOWER OF FASHION	The Kinks
25	36	OH, HOW HAPPY	Shades of Blue
26	33	BOYS ARE MADE TO LOVE	Karen Small
27	—	WHERE WERE YOU WHEN I NEEDED YOU	Grassroots
28	—	PAPERBACK WRITER/RAIN	The Beatles
29	—	STRANGERS IN THE NIGHT	Frank Sinatra
30	32	AIN'T TOO PROUD TO BEG	The Temptations

DAVE HULL

BOB EUBANKS

DICK BIONDI

JOHNNY HAYES

EMPEROR HUDSON

CASEY KASEM

CHARLIE O'DONNELL

BILL SLATER

KRLA's Giving Prizes To Teens In Love

Summer is on its way now, and with it a brand new exciting contest for all of KRLA's listeners. The contest is the "For Young Love Sweepstakes" and it will be running for 30 days.

During that time, KRLA will be giving away a set of his and her prizes each day—and wait until you hear about the prizes!

Included in the list of fantastic gifts which you can win are twin Suzukis, Packard Bell radios, All-transistorized portable phonographs complete with portable transistor radios inside, Vox guitars, custom-made surf boards by Hal Jacobs for the boy and girl, and many, many more which we'll be telling you about in the next few weeks.

In order to enter the Sweepstakes, just pick up an entry blank in record stores with the KRLA-Lettermen "A New Song For Young Love" display, or stop into a Suzuki dealer with streamers advertising this fantastic new contest for young people in love in the window.

Two lucky winners will receive a phone installed free in their homes—and the installation fees and the phone bills for the first three months up to ten dollars will be paid! Now what two young people in love wouldn't like that?

BOB EUBANKS points out some of the prizes in KRLA'S latest contest.

Bob Eubanks Says it!

Dave Hull Says it!

Emperor Hudson Says it!

Charlie O'Donnell Says it!

Everybody's Saying It!

You gotta get your new RTD STUDENT PRIVILEGE CARD Before School Closes!

Don't be left out this summer—get your Student Privilege Card at school and go where the fun is—at a big discount! New RTD Student Privilege Card gives you

★ 40% discount on RTD EXTRACAR transportation—you got wheels!

★ Big discounts at all Pacific Walk-in and Drive-in theatres!

★ 50% discount at Hollywood Bowl!

★ Discounts at Greek Theatre, Pacific Ocean Park, Movieland Wax Museum—more deals being added!

Good now—all summer—and until Feb. 1967!

Only 50¢

Not sold at box offices—available only at your school student store or business/finance office.

Go where the action is by

(Squares call it a "bus")

Ready whenever you are!

KRLA ARCHIVES

Inside KRLA
By Eden

The Byrds flew into the KRLA studios for a brief visit this past week and answered a few million phones while they were at it. And while they were busy talking to several million KRLA listeners on our request lines, the old Scuzzabalooer was keeping himself mighty busy answering requests for Byrd tunes.

Request lines have been handled for us by the Love and Neil Diamond this week along with the Byrds and there will be many, many more guest phone operators in weeks to come, so keep your earlobes at 1110 — your Request Radio in KRLA-Land.

Speaking of Bill Slater (I don't know; you'd better ask Shirley Poston about that one!), it seems that our fave-rave all night DJ-type has gone into the cupid business in his spare time.

Don't really know what it's all about yet, but William has been spreading all kinds of rumors about Mark Lindsay of Paul Revere and the Raiders and a certain member of the KRLA BEAT staff.

Charlio has finally completed a fantastic painting which he was working on for quite some time and I'm very excited about seeing it. Cheery Charlio promised to show it to me before he sent it back to a friend, but if all else fails he will take a picture of it, so maybe you'll get a peek too.

GIANT DOUBLE BILL
Co-Starring

THE DEEP SIX
and
THE PAIR EXTRAORDINAIRE
May 31 — June 5

THE PAIR EXTRAORDINAIRE
June 7 — 14
and
STAN WILSON
June 7 — 26

at

The ICE HOUSE — GLENDALE
folk music in concert
234 S. Brand, Glendale
Reservations: 245-5043

and in Pasadena

BUD DASHIEL
(formerly of Bud & Travis)
May 31 — June 5

PAUL SYKES
June 7 — 26

at

The ICE HOUSE — PASADENA
folk music in concert
24 N. Mentor, Pasadena
Reservations: MU 19942

UNLIKE ANYTHING YOU'VE EVER SEEN!
SUPER CINERAMA
BATTLE OF THE BULGE

WARNER BROS. PICTURES PRESENTS A CINERAMA, INC. PRODUCTION "BATTLE OF THE BULGE" Starring HENRY FONDA · ROBERT SHAW · ROBERT RYAN · DANA ANDREWS · PIER ANGELI · BARBARA WERLE · GEORGE MONTGOMERY · TY HARDIN · CHARLES BRONSON · HANS CHRISTIAN BLECH · WERNER PETERS · JAMES MacARTHUR and TELLY SAVALAS · Written by Philip Yordan, Milton Sperling, John Melson · Produced by MILTON SPERLING, PHILIP YORDAN · Directed by KEN ANNAKIN · A SIDNEY HARMON IN ASSOCIATION WITH UNITED STATES PICTURES, INC. PRODUCTION · TECHNICOLOR® · ULTRA-PANAVISION®

PACIFIC'S CINERAMA DOME Theatre
SUNSET AT VINE · HOLLYWOOD
NOW PLAYING!

KRLA BEAT Subscription
SAVE 33% Of Regular Price

☐ 1 YEAR — 52 Issues — $5.00   ☐ 2 YEARS — $8.00
☐ 6 MONTHS — $3.00

Enclosed is _____   ☐ CASH   ☐ CHECK
PLEASE PRINT — Include Your Zip Code

Send to: .... Age: ....
Address: .... City: ....
State: .... Zip: ....

MAIL YOUR ORDER TO: KRLA BEAT
6290 Sunset, Suite 504
Hollywood, Calif. 90028

Foreign Rate: $9.00 — 52 Issues

GUITAR & DRUM
SPECIALISTS
From the Beach..

Where G&D Folk Guitars are the favorites!!!

Steel strings or nylon, they sound great. Famous brands — fully guaranteed and tailored to your style, haircut and bankroll.

from **$13.95***

Beach Bunnies not included, but service is always "standard equipment" at the G&D Specialists.

..to the Big Time!

For the pro and the aspiring musician, the right instrument makes the difference. Come in today to discuss your needs with your GUITAR and DRUM SPECIALIST featuring Fender, Gibson, Gretsch, and Vox Guitars and Amps. Ludwig, Rogers, Gretsch, and Slingerland Drums.

GUITAR & AMP
Luster finished electric guitar plus big power amp for that wild Surf Sound — Usually priced at $39.50 each. Now $29.95 each. Combination Guitar and Amp.

$57.50* Complete

DRUM SET
Your choice of Blue, Red, or Gold Sparkle — This beautiful 4-piece drum set has chrome plated rims on six ply hardwood shells with durable mylar heads to give many years of keeping neighbors awake.

$189.50*

*TV jobs not included, but your G&D specialist knows the Beatles . . . Would you believe Lawrence Welk? Mrs. Miller???

Stop by today and talk to your G&D Specialist . . .

IN BUENA PARK	IN HUNTINGTON BEACH	IN VAN NUYS
Kay Kalie Music	**Manolios Music**	**Adler Music Co.**
8408 ON THE MALL	18547 MAIN STREET (5 POINTS SHOPPING CENTER)	14115 VICTORY BLVD. (AT HAZELTINE)
IN SANTA FE SPRINGS	IN TUSTIN	IN SIMI
Kay Kalie Music	**Winn's Music**	**Adler Music Co.**
11504 TELEGRAPH RD. (THE SHOPPING CENTER)	540 E. 1st STREET (IN LARWIN SQUARE)	1792 ERRINGER ROAD (NEXT TO SAFEWAY)
IN EAST LOS ANGELES	IN WEST COVINA	IN BURBANK
Phillips Music Co.	**WC Music Center**	**Killeen Music**
2455 BROOKLYN AVE.	235 NO. AZUSA AVE. (JUST NO. OF FREEWAY)	316 N. SAN FERNANDO

KRLA ARCHIVES

For Girls only

by shirley poston

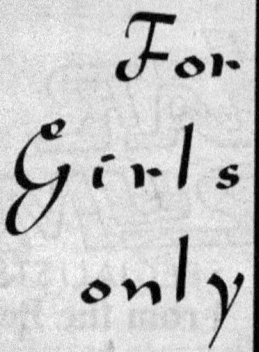

Now, don't take me wrong. (In fact, *please* don't because it matches me right and I hate to break up the set.) I am not referring to the mental condition of both of my many readers.

I'm simply (amen) trying to say that Olde Shirle Postum has done it again. This morning when I left home (by popular demand) I meant to bring this whole big bunch of goddies . . . I beg your pardon . . . goodies to write about in my pillar (sorry, I get tired of saying column all the time.)

Really fantastic thingys I've been getting in the mail, I mean. But, true to form, I'll have to tell you about them next week because I left them lying on the couch.

Course, by the time I get home, my dog will have them torn into seven million shreds (she works part-time for the Easter Bunny), but I'll do my best to pick up the pieces (of my shattered life, that is.)

No Bombs

Have you ever stopped to think how much of your valuable time I waste telling you about things I'm not going to tell you about until next week (as in late autumn of 1975?) Well, please don't. None of the interesting packages I've been receiving have contained bombs, and I'd just as soon keep it that way.

Now, before I lose my head (which would be promptly returned because who else would *want* it?) and start ranting about you-know-who, two things I don't want to forget.

Thingy One: An urgent plea from one crazy gypsy lady to another . . . please get in touch with me immediately if not sooner. Your "Beatle Movie" was FAB and I need to know if I can print it! Write fast!

Thingy Two: A gentle hint to the girls who participated in a five-mile chase down a certain street several Saturdays ago, trying to get a look at the person who was driving the car with the "George Is Mine" bumper sticker. It wasn't me, but you're getting warmer.

SPEAKING OF GEORGE... (Hey, I can finally say that for realsville!) (I mean, I really *was* speaking of it. (When, pray tell, am I *not????*)

Say, before I continue speaking of George S.S.F.M. Harrison (the S.S.F.M. stands for . . . no, on second thought, I'd get fired) (with real matches), I've just had an impromtu zingwhammer (came to me all of a sudden, too.)

We're always honoring some inventor or another, but has anyone even bothered to even so much as mention one of the true greats of all time? No! (I tell you!)

Well! I think it is high (and I *know* I am) time that all of us joined together to pay tribute to the utter genius who invented the parenthesis!

Therefore, I hereby decree the last week of June as International Parentheses Week! (Or else.)

I shall be expecting to receive all sorts of parenthesized letters during that week. And if you'd *really* like to celebrate, you could even make buttons and posters and all them there sticky-type kook dealies! To say nothing of making everyone scurry for the nearest Yellow Pages.

Oh, what the heck. Even if they do bag an extra-large net-full of us that week, at least we'll be together in that padded cell.

George Again

Now, back to George (who *left?*) Two of my fiendish friends have played the most ultra-dirty-rotten trick in history on yours (and George's) truly.

I hope I can explain it somewhat rationally (rotsa ruck), because in spite of the fact that I'd luv to bean both of them, it was really hypercool.

Lemme see . . . what they did was this. One girl got on the phone (comfort isn't everything) and called me. Then the other girl picked up the extension, and when I answered, they started talking to each other. You know, like I wasn't even there (no cutting remarks, please.)

One pretended to be Pattie Harrison, and she was telling the other girl all sorts of *marvelous* things about George. For a few minutes, I actually thought there was some kind of crossed connection or something and that I was actually hearing an actual conversation by accident.

I've heard of this sort of trick (as in ultra-dirty-rotten) before, but I still about flipped! Next time you're in a fiendish mood, try it on one of your soon-to-be-ex-friends. If nothing else, it's a lot more fun than calling all the Tracy's in the phone book and asking for Dick.

Oh, I have another thingy I mustn't (it would have been so much simpler to have said must not, but you know how it is) forget.

Mark's Legs

Thingy Three: To Sherry who suggested that I leave Mark Lindsay's legs out of this column if I know what's good for me (which, as you may have guessed, I do) . . . sorry about that. Didn't mean to infringe on your territory. From now on, you stick to Mark and I'll stick to George. Tell ya what . . . I'll even bring the glue.

On the other hand, if I do get carried away again (in a cage, I fear), I'll — no, come to think of it, I have a wart on the other hand, so forget the whole thing.

You know something? I'll bet you're all very proud of me because I don't do nasty-bad things like using my column to solicit bribes. Well, aren't you even prouder that I don't use it to convey personal messages?

I somehow knew you would be.

Now, before der boss starts coming for me with a large scoop, I'd better close (my yap, for instance.)

Two more boring items before I do, however.

First, you'll notice there's no coded message this week. Well, there *isn't* going to be one until I stop finding code letters (of the unanswered variety) peeking out from under piles of total chaos (not to mention total strangers.) Soon, I promise (not to mention hope.) No, really. I'm going to go through that whole room tonight and get that mess straightened out. Providing, of course, that I can find an Alpine guide between now and then.

Daddy Too!

Second, when I started writing for *The BEAT*, my dad just sorta patted me on the head (as in nice-doggie) and smiled patiently. Now he reads my ravings every week, especially Robin (A.I.B.) (As In Blither.)

However, I fail to understand the only actual comment he has ever made about my "work" (aside from a few hysterical howls.)

What precisely did that wonderful man (he's bigger than I am) mean when he said I sounded like *"a cuckoo in its cups?"*

I ask you!!

Jan Berry

(Continued from Page 1)

garage. While people were busy laughing at the very idea of making a record in a garage, "Baby Talk" was smashing up the nation's charts.

And they haven't stopped making hits yet – even though they *have* moved out of Jan's garage! They've grabbed a hold of crazes, watched them die and watched themselves live on in the charts.

They really hit it big with the surf sound, though Jan was vehement in denying that there ever was such a thing as "a surf sound." "There is no real surf music," Jan once told us. "There is just the 'sound' of the individual artists. We don't have a 'surf sound.'"

Maybe not – but they certainly have a sound which is selling just as fast today as it did eight years ago. While Jan is recovering in the hospital, their latest release, "Popsicles" – recorded before Jan's accident – has been released and is a heavily requested item on radio stations all across the country.

If you would like to help Jan along the road to what we all hope will be a very speedy recovery, why don't you send Jan a get-well card (or whatever) to Jan Berry c/o Dunhill Records, 321 South Beverly Drive, Beverly Hills, California. We know Jan would appreciate knowing that you are thinking about him. *Now* is the time he needs you the most – please don't let him down.

Brenda Lee Celebrates 15 Years Of Success

Brenda Lee rhymes with tenderly, and that's not a rhyme without reason.

A balladeer who, in the face of somersaulting trends, sticks with what she does best, it's not just coincidence that every record she has cut since 1959 has made the charts – all but two of them with both sides. You might call it long-playing talent.

Her manager, Dub Allbritten, analyzes the Lee appeal in this way: "Brenda has always had three separate audiences. The kids liked her from the beginning, because she was one of them. Adults like her because she has the appeal of a little girl, with the aplomb of a woman; and ever since her records began hitting the charts, the teenagers have gone for her. Since she appeals to all of those markets, she and her audiences can't outgrow each other."

Brenda started out on the kiddie contest circuit, but went professional age of six. She signed her first recording contract when she was eleven, back in 1957.

The record that set her career sinning was "Sweet Nothin's," a slow-starting, long-lasting hit that took a good six months to make the charts.

An Enigma?

It may seem pretentious to apply the word enigma to anyone as uncomplicated and forthright as Brenda, but it seems to fit.

Certainly it is hard to explain the riddle of her consistent success, year after year, when admittedly she has had very few number one records.

At twenty-one, the little girl with the big voice is a veteran of fifteen years in show business, she has appeared on every major television show, and her nightclub and concert tours have taken her to every state in the Union, and to thirty-two foreign countries.

In the States she tries to keep to a schedule of two weeks on tour, two weeks at home, in order to have some time with husband Ronnie Shacklett and their year-old daughter.

She has played a command performance for the Queen of England, Brazil's president has called her "America's finest good will ambassador," and in another South American city she generated so much excitement that six national police were assigned to 24 admirers.

On tour she is backed by The Casuals, six young bachelors who, with two exceptions, have been with her for nine years.

Likes Japan

She considers England, Japan and South America "the most exciting" places she has visited, but Japan ranks as her favorite. "It's the one country in the world," says 58-inch Brenda, "where I can look people in the eye!"

The diminutive singer is a giant in the foreign market. Last year she cut eight sides in Hamburg for release in Germany and the United States, and has recently recorded in Japanese and English, for Japanese release.

"I don't think much about recording or singing when I'm at home in Nashville," says Brenda, "but Dub gave me all my old recordings in leather-bound volumes for Christmas, and I've had fun and some laughs, listening to those early records. My voice sounded very high, to me. It's changed a lot since 'Sweet Nothin's,' but a good deal of my phrasing is the same."

Perhaps that's the secret of her success – the basic changelessness, the consistent integrity, which keeps her on the charts year after year.

The BEAT extends a hardy "congratulations" to 'lil bit' on the 15th anniversary of her start in show business.

Say you saw it in The BEAT

KRLA ARCHIVES

DISCussion
By Eden

Young Rascals have returned to cause some mischief around the old turntables and they're in for some mighty powerful mischief with their brand new 45er, "You Better Run." These boys have an awful lot of soul and it's pretty difficult to imagine this new disc going any place but up.

* * *

Neil Diamond's "Solitary Man" is a good, strong sound, very reminiscent of some of Sal Valentino's distinctive vocal stylings. Pretty song.

* * *

Knickerbockers have begun their third smash in a row with their new release, "High On Love." Have you gotten into those lyrics yet? Wheww! It's a winner.

* * *

The Cindermen have a smash hit in their Moonglow release, "Don't Do It Some More ('Cause It Hurts So Good.")" It has become one of the most requested tunes on radio surveys and will probably start moving up the nationwide charts shortly.

* * *

The We Five had a hit with their very first release, "You Were On My Mind," but haven't succeeded in establishing a permanent residence on our charts as yet.

Their newest is "There Stands The Door" and may be able to place them back in the pop spotlight. It's a pretty song, pleasant to listen to, but not really outstanding.

* * *

Bob Lind's managers, Charlie Greene and Brian Stone, have taken on a brand new group called The Troggs. They hail from England and their first release in this country is "With A Girl Like You."

The disc is coming on as a double-sided smash for the boys in England, but so far hasn't made too many dents in our surveys.

* * *

Blue-eyed wonder Robert Goulet has decided to launch an attack on the pop charts and his initial weapon is one entitled "Daydreamer," from the motion picture of the same name. As usual, it's a pretty tune... but, *pop*????

* * *

Johnny Rivers is sticking to the rhythm and blues thing he is all hung up on now and his new release is "Muddy Water." Hitsville for the A Go Go boy.

P.S. Not to infringe on Tracy Albert's territory but pick up a copy of Johnny's new LP – "And I Know You Wanna Dance" – and listen to it a lot. Great!

* * *

Hot new rumor in town is that Cher is currently penning her first tune which she'll record if it turns out well. How 'bout a brand new LP, "Sonny Sings Cher."

* * *

"Hungry" is the brand new single by Paul Revere and the Raiders. "Hungry" is a hard-driving, fast-moving, big-beat number. "Hungry" is about to attack the pop charts and take over in a big way. "Hungry" is a smash hit... and so are the Raiders.

...THE FOUR SEASONS (l. to r.) Joe Long, Tommy deVito, Frankie Valli and Bob Gaudio

The Same Four Seasons Don't Worry 'Bout Them

By Kimmi Kobashigawa

When you think of the Four Seasons, perhaps the first thing which will come to mind is their distinctive sound, characterized by very high voices.

Any long time fans of the Seasons will remember the first records the boys made – all-time favorites such as "Sherry," "Big Girls Don't Cry," and "Dawn." These tunes, among many other hits by the successful foursome, established the Four Seasons in the hearts of many, and also succeeded in establishing a very unique sort of sound.

And it is that sound, primarily a high-range vocal, which lead singer Frankie Valli is responsible for. It isn't too unlikely, therefore, to associate Frankie with the sound of the Four Seasons.

Just like any other successful group, the Four Seasons are constantly plagued with the vicious rumors that one or another member of the group is planning on quitting. And Frankie, credited with being responsible for the distinctive sound of the group as a whole, is the member most frequently assaulted with this rumor.

In answer to these rumors, Frankie patiently explains: "One of the things I get asked all the time is whether I'm leaving the group. Since I made ('You're Gonna) Hurt Yourself' as a single, folks seem to assume this is the first step in me breaking away and becoming a solo artist. And I'm sure glad to tell you that there's no chance of that.

"You see, the Four Seasons are a corporation, a corporate body. We split everything into equal shares. So I make a hit single and it makes a lot of loot and... well, we all share in it.

"I figure that anything that can help the Seasons is just fine and dandy with me. Let's be fair, primarily we're all interested in making money.

"There's the glamour and the fame and the trimmings, but what we're all doing – guess you're the same – is keeping our bank managers happy.

"So the Four Seasons remain as we are. That's a promise. But it's sure flattering to have so many people worrying about us and our future."

Being in the public eye as much as they are, the Four Seasons are, of course, constantly subjected to many questions. But recently they let themselves in for even more by recording a song under another name. But we'll let Frankie tell that story.

"People ask me about that record me made under the name of 'The Wonder Who?' Maybe you remember it, 'Don't Think Twice, It's Alright!' Let me tell you about that. We were in the studios and cutting an album which was to feature six Burt Bacharach numbers and six from Bobby Dylan. Came to the end when I started doing this particular song, and it was all a bit of a joke.

"I didn't even know they had the tapes going. I was fooling about. Afterwards, we listened and figured: 'It's so way out maybe we could get away with it, using a different name.'

"We also guessed people wouldn't recognize us." Well, people did, but they went right ahead to make it a huge hit for the Four Seasons anyway.

Currently the Seasons are riding high on the pop charts with their latest release, "Opus 17," and although the group no longer sticks strictly to the ultra-high tones of their first smash, "Sherry," they *are* still sticking strictly together.

..."NO CHANCE of that"

Get the **Lindy** Pen that really adds up!

Auditor's
FINE POINT / BALL PEN

Check the features that put the Lindy in a class by itself: Perfect balance, fine point for sharp, detailed writing, giant ink supply, permanent, non-smudging, non-transferable, and in economical 7" and compact new 5" sizes. Any way you figure it, the Auditor's Pen is a great value.

only **49¢** ea.

© LP Co., Inc. 1963

12 BRILLIANT INK COLORS
color of pen is color of ink

Manufactured by LINDY PEN CO INC. North Hollywood, Calif. 91605, U S A

KRLA ARCHIVES

Wanta Come Along On An Everly Gig?

...FIRST STOP—Ireland

...CHECKING at the Genealogical Office to see if they're Irish.

...RECOGNIZE three important heads? Who are they digging so much?

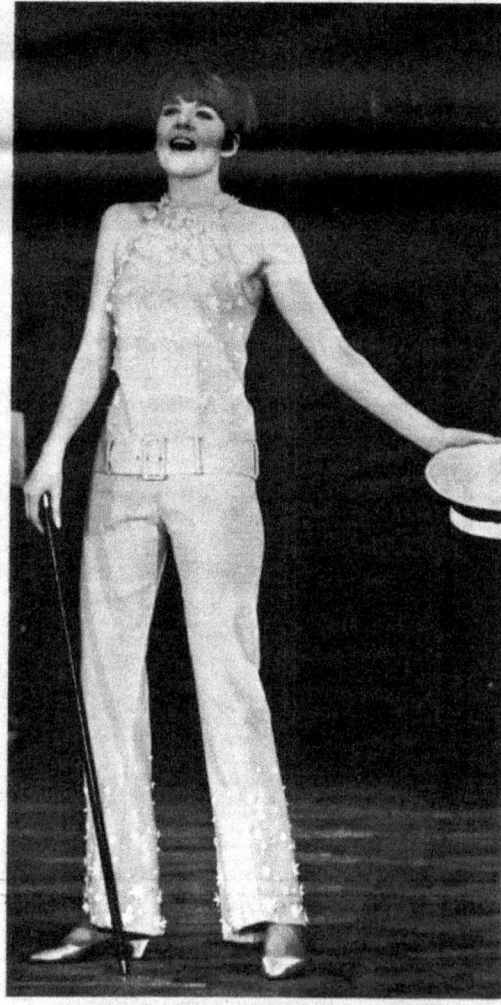
...CILLA BLACK at London's Savoy, of course!

It's always great to hear that countries other than our own really appreciate the fantastic Everly Brothers. Don and Phil have just returned from a European tour which took them to Ireland, Germany and France. Outcome? Capacity crowds everywhere!

When the Everly plane touched down in Ireland, Don and Phil stepped rather reluctantly from the plane, uncertain of the reception they would receive. Although they are huge in England, they had never been to Ireland and, unfortunately (they thought) had chosen to arrive when the country was being plagued by horrible weather.

However, their two-week stay in Ireland proved to be so successful that they were mobbed on practically every date they played!

During their Irish visit, the Everlys made two rather important side trips. One was to the Genealogical Office to try to discover if "Everly" was really an Irish name. They never did find out—so if any of you know, Don and Phil would certainly like to be in on the secret!

Their second side trip was a quick flight to London where they re-visited an old friend and ex-tour mate, Cilla Black. Cilla was about to appear at London's famed Savoy to film a color television special for American audiences and, naturally, Cilla extended an invitation to Don and Phil to watch her show.

Of course, they accepted and to see what they thought of Cilla's performance, take a very close look at the picture directly above. You guessed it—they pronounced Cilla, "out of sight!"

The Everlys spent several days in England, utilizing their time to cut six new songs—all of which were composed by the Hollies. The Everlys and Hollies seem to have a real mutual admiration society going between them. The Everlys record Hollies — and Hollies swipe Everly albums from The BEAT office!

Germany and France were next on the Everlys' agenda. They played military clubs throughout both countries and broke every existing attendance record in the process. Reports filtering back to America reveal that there wasn't even *standing room* left.

The Everlys are now playing clubs on the East Coast, secure in the knowledge that their tour was a smashing success—even if they never did learn if they have Irish blood running through them or not!

KRLA ARCHIVES

HOTLINE LONDON
Film Rush

By Tony Barrow

Last week's news about initial plans for the making of the first motion picture to star THE ROLLING STONES seems to have sparked off a pop-scene rush to get in on the movie act!

Indeed several of this week's most important pop stories involve the making of movies by big-name British chart favorites. THE SPENCER DAVIS GROUP will have acting and playing roles in a 60-minute color comedy to be made on location at Windsor and elsewhere in or around the London area in July. A leading comedian will be cast in the part of the group's manager and several other pop attractions are expected to guest in the production which is, as yet, untitled.

DC 5 Movie

Tentative plans are going ahead for the DAVE CLARK FIVE to film a crime story called "You'll Never Get Away With It." Shooting is scheduled to start at the end of August in London. Dave himself contributed the basic ideas for the script—which concerns a London robbery—but the DC5 will not be seen performing any new numbers in the picture. They will write and play the soundtrack music but are not expected to sing since their dramatic roles do not cast them as members of a group.

That curiously if intriguingly named quintet DAVE DEE, DOZY, BEAKY, MICK and TICH will make a brief guest appearance in the MGM movie "The Blow Up" which is being made in London right now. They will film their contribution almost immediately and it will show them performing their major UK disc hit "Hold Tight."

The week's pop movie headlines also include a surprise confession from DC5 leader DAVE CLARK. According to him, the story "Only Lovers Left Alive" was offered to The Dave Clark Five as a motion picture subject at the end of last year. Dave claims he turned down the script on the grounds that it was too violent and too horrific for his group to involve themselves with. Now, five months after that rejection, "Only Lovers Left Alive" has been announced as the story selected for THE ROLLING STONES to film later this year!

Where're The Girls?

So far, Britain's girl singers don't seem to be making much headway in the screen race. Chart-toppers like DUSTY SPRINGFIELD, SANDIE SHAW, PETULA CLARK and CILLA BLACK have yet to make movies—although there are rumors that more than one important producer has made approaches about Cilla's availability for a picture.

In the meantime only diminutive Scottish red-head LULU has concrete movie plans. She's to have a straight dramatic role as a schoolgirl in "To Sir With Love" which Columbia is making at the Pinewood studios this month. Songstress Lulu will play opposite SIDNEY POITIER who will be her school-teacher. The picture will be set in London's East End.

NEWS BRIEFS... Next single from GERRY AND THE PACEMAKERS likely to be the American number "Girl On A Swing" sent to him by Laurie Records' New York executives... RINGO STARR thoroughly proud of the fact that baby Zak took his first two unaided steps last week!... Union problems have brought about the formal cancellation of 5-week June/July US tour planned for THE KINKS... Lengthy late-summer return visit to the UK set for THE LOVIN' SPOONFUL... If "Sorrow" is a US chart-smasher for THE MERSEYS they'll be making the trip to your side of the Atlantic for additional promotion work this summer... TV studio row led the mass walkout by THE SMALL FACES when they couldn't agree to billing position put forward by "Top Of The Pops" producer... "Strangers In The Night" composer BERT KAEMPFERT cannot hope to match the popularity of the FRANK SINATRA recording with his own instrumental version. Good to see Frank back in our Top Ten with the most commercial piece of material he's recorded in years!... Bass guitarist ERIC HAYDOCK latest pop personality to be struck down with nervous exhaustion. His place with THE HOLLIES has been taken by unknown instrumentalist BERNIE CALVERT during the group's current June concert tour of Europe... THE WHO are to undertake a lengthy concert tour of Britain in September and October. Co-starring with them will be THE MERSEYS... Several top London R&B musicians supplying brass sounds for at least one of the tracks featured on the upcoming BEATLES album... Long overdue return visit to America and Canada now looks possible in September and October for GERRY AND THE PACEMAKERS... BEATLES studying special designs and materials for new stage suits which should be ready in time for the August US tour... Rumors — plus an emphatic denial from the Tom Parker offices — reached London this week regarding ELVIS PRESLEY. The rumors linked his name romantically with that of the ultra-attractive PAT BEAULIEU... Two months ago who would have imagined that THE STONES would have been involved in a US Top Ten chart race with THE MINDBENDERS!

THE OUTSIDERS are running with two hit singles and a smash LP. They are (from left) Ricky Baker, Tom King, Sonny Geraci, Bill Bruno and Mert Madsen. Remember their faces—they aim to stay around awhile!

Outsiders Digging 'In'

Cleveland has a baseball team that is leading the American League and a recording group that is batting one thousand in the tough recording league. The latter is The Outsiders, the hottest new group to hit the country since The Beatles.

The first single cut by The Outsiders for Capitol, "Time Won't Let Me," has been on the best seller list since it was released in late January. Their first LP album, with the same title as their smash single, sold more copies in the first thirty days than was originally projected for ninety days, requiring additional pressings. "Girl In Love," their second single, hit the best seller list in the first week of release and is currently zooming upwards.

"In" Not "Out"

To put it bluntly, The Outsiders are "in" and, according to their leader, Tom King, the group plans to keep their fans interested in them for a long, long time.

"There are many acts," Tom said thoughtfully, "that have made overnight hits and when it comes time to follow that first record with another, they can't. They can't think of what to do, so they simply record another song, one that sounds exactly like the first one. Then they try a third time. It sells, but much less than either of the first two. Before you know it, they're recording flops."

Tom, who has been writing most of the songs The Outsiders record (he wrote both "Time Won't Let Me" and "Girl In Love") has done a great deal of thinking about the typical group, its rise and fall.

"It would be easy for us," Tom explained, "to ride the standard pattern—this is, follow our first big hit with a song that sounds exactly like it. In fact, a number of people urged us to. But we don't want to be like that, we want to be around for a long time. Take a look at some of the big, successful groups. The Beatles and The Beach Boys, for instance. Their songs don't follow the same pattern nor do they all sound the same. That's one of the reasons they continue to be popular. They offer some variety.

Follow-Up

"We'd like to do the same. That's why we came out with a ballad ('Girl In Love') for a second record. Naturally we took a chance, went against advice that said play it safe... give everyone another song that sounds exactly like 'Time Won't Let Me.' We said no. We feel that it is important for groups to add to their repertoire in order to keep their fans interested in them."

The group recently completed a highly successful Eastern tour with Gene Pitney and are now back in Cleveland recording their second LP album for Capitol titled "Girl In Love." The album will contain six original tunes by Tom King with lyrics by Chet Kelley. The album will be released the end of June.

Spectaculars

When the album is completed the group will embark on a tour that will bring them to Hollywood for the first time. They will appear as one of the featured groups in the Beach Boys' two mammoth "Summer Spectaculars" which will be staged June 24, at the San Francisco Cow Palace and June 25, at the Hollywood Bowl.

The Outsiders are: Tom King, leader and rhythm guitarist, who also writes most of the songs for the group; Sonny Geraci, who is lead singer; Bill Bruno, lead guitar; Merdin Prince Gunnar Madsen (call him Mert), bass-guitar and harmonica player; Ricky Baker, drummer.

HEY FELLAS, you're missing one.

KRLA ARCHIVES

'We Can Talk Our Way Out Of Anything'– The Bachelors

By Carol Deck

The Bachelors are an illusive trio of Irishmen who don't seem to fit nicely into any of the categories we make up for pop people.

And they're rather proud of that fact. They planned it that way.

"We've done a very clever thing," says Dec Cluskey, youngest of the three. "In England we haven't said exactly what we are and our records don't fit anywhere into any category."

The reason their records don't fit anywhere is that every time anyone gets close to finding a category for them they change just to keep everyone wondering.

From their first hit, "Charmaine," they went into a string of several somewhat similar things.

"Then we decided to change it before people categorized us and we did 'I Believe' in a Ray Coniff style," continues Dec.

"Then people said 'We know what you are, you sing oldies,' so, quick as a wink, we recorded a newie.

"Now they just call us singers," he adds proudly, for that's just about the only category they feel they do fall in all the time.

Not A Group

However, Dec's older brother Con, being an older brother, hastens to add that Americans are still trying to categorize them, but Americans have found the only real slot they fall into is that of "group" and "We're not a group, we're an act," he notes.

The funny thing about them in America is that the so-called good-music stations say they are one of the rare pop groups who appeal to good-music audiences and the pop stations say they're one of the few good-music groups who appeal to pop audiences.

While everyone searches for a nice nitch to put them in, the Bachelors sit back and think up new ways of staying out of categories.

"We recorded 'Hello Dolly' for no apparent reason, just to confuse people," they admit.

But they never sit back for long, because they are one of the most popular acts in England and they're working 49 weeks out of the year.

The other three weeks are supposed to be for vacation but they keep giving up their vacation time in order to come to America. Last year they spent a week over here, thereby limiting their vacation to two weeks and now they've just returned to England after two weeks over here, so they've only got one week's rest coming this year.

They Know

One of the most remarkable things about the Bachelors is that, even though they try very hard not to let other people figure them out, *they* have a very clear knowledge of exactly what they are.

And what they are is one of England's most talented and popular groups, but America is just now beginning to discover them. But they know that, they're very aware of their place. They didn't come trooping over here demanding to be treated like the stars they are back home.

At home they limit the number of television shows they do every year to avoid overexposure, yet they came over here and filmed practically every pop TV show in the country because they realize that's what they have to do here.

Actually we should feel very lucky, they filmed more TV over here in two weeks than they have in many months in Britain.

They were a little surprised too, by the way American TV shows are filmed. For one thing they're used to rehearsing much more for each show than they did for *all* the shows they did while they were here.

And another thing, they ran into lip-syncing again. Miming, as they call it in England, has been all but banned over there, but the Bachelors don't really seem to mind lip-syncing.

"The thing about singing live is you're depending entirely on the sound technician," says John Stokes.

"We've been very lucky when we've sung live though," adds Dec. "I think it's because most of the sound technicians are middle-aged and they say 'thank goodness, someone who can sing,' just because we have short hair."

Aside from looking and sounding about as great as possible, they also come up with a very quick brand of Irish humor.

A Manager?

They seem to have a lot of fun introducing people to their manager. You see their manager is one very young and attractive lass by the name of Dorothy Solomon and most people just don't believe that anyone that young and pretty could really be their manager. People are always asking 'is she really your *manager?*'

They also use their Irish heritage to their best advantage. While they are touring their fans will often find out which hotel they are in and the phone rings constantly.

They always give most of the calls to Dec, the only real bachelor in the Bachelors, but Dec doesn't seem to worry about the calls.

"We don't worry about that. We can talk our way out of anything with this Irish blarney," he says with a very Irish twinkle in his green eyes.

All in all, the Bachelors are three very talented, handsome, interesting guys, who possess a remarkably huge amounts of that good old Irish charm that enables them to appeal to everyone from grandmothers to grandchildren.

They've gone back home now, but they left us their latest album, "Hits of the '60's," and single, "Love Me With All Your Heart."

Gene Pitney – A Very Unusual Star

In the last two years since The Beatles first conquered these Continental shores, the world of pop music has been just that—a truly international sphere of entertainment.

We have shared many artists with other countries over the years, and especially recently we have traded a good many artists with Great Britain. Groups and single artists alike have crossed the Big Pond from Merrie Olde and established permanent friendships here on our side.

For the most part, these entertainers have enjoyed more or less equal support from both countries, but there are still a few performers who are more highly favored in one country.

The two most unusual examples are two of our own American exports: Gene Pitney and Roy Orbison. Both are extremely talented singer-composer-musicians both are Americans, and both are British stars of great magnitude. And both are all but ignored in their native land. Unusual, yes?

Super-Star

Gene Pitney has enjoyed a number of successful disc hits here in America but he doesn't consistently top charts in this country and he isn't generally considered by us to be one of our top pop idols.

Quite the contrary in England, where Gene is unable to walk down the street without being mobbed. He is a super-star and a romantic idol in his own right.

Having traveled 'round the world many times, Gene is now something of a connoisseur in the fine art of dating and has a wonderful characterization of the different girls around the globe.

"Today there are so many pretty girls around the world, that's why traveling never bores me. American girls? They're too independent and hard. They make it easy for a guy to like other girls.

"English girls prefer to be women and be liked for it. I don't think there's much of a difference between French and Italian girls.

A little more serious and a little more candid, Gene reflected about this thing called love: "Love is a thing I talk about a lot and I sing about all the time. I think singing about it so much must make some impression on you.

"On a date, for instance, I'm quite romantic. I take a girl flowers

and things like that. I know how much little things mean to a girl when she's in love—or *thinks* she is...

"Myself, I think I know the difference between love and infatuation. Love takes time, it has to. Infatuation? Well, it's just a wonderful feeling that's too good to last forever."

Chart Topper

It is taken for granted that whenever Gene releases a record in England, it will immediately race to the top-most position on the pop charts. And now, Mr. Pitney has become about the hottest performer in all of Italy.

A talented singer and one of the nicest young men in the pop world today, Gene Pitney is definitely one American pop star well worth reclaiming.

THE BACHELORS MEET QUEEN ELIZABETH AFTER PERFORMANCE.

KRLA ARCHIVES

"NO STRAPS?" asks Quinn. "I thought I told you this was a FAMILY MOVIE!"

SPECIAL RE-ISSUE brings back one of the most ambitious films made, as Allies fight German war machine.

The BEAT Goes To The Movies

THE GUNS OF NAVARONE

By Jim Hamblin
(The BEAT Movie Editor)

The time and the place is World War Two. On a Mediterranean chunk of land once owned by the free Greeks, the Germans have now established strong fortifications. So strong that an all-out invasion is due from the Allies. But there are over 2,000 prisoners being held by the Nazis, all of whom will be killed if they cannot be liberated before the attack.

But giant guns sit on a rocky ledge called Navarone. The biggest guns ever made at the time, they can pop a ship out of the sea like a cork out of a champagne bottle. The answer is to sneak behind the lines and blow up the guns. And for the job, head spy man James Roberston Justice (who is also heard as the narrator) appoints Gregory Peck, Anthony Quinn, Anthony Quayle, James Darren, Stanley Baker, and David Niven. Notable for the fact that it is one war movie that does NOT star Henry Fonda, this feature is one of the most exciting and certainly one of the best-made pictures of its kind. So good, it deserves a second look. Which is what it will get the first week in June. Made originally in 1961, Columbia Pictures is re-releasing it nationwide.

Perhaps the most remarkable scene involves a grey eyed beauty, one of the local girls, who is discovered collaborating with the Nazis to save her own skin. Fearing that she will rat-fink on the plan to blow the guns, it is decided that she must be executed. In the usual Hollywood-type drama, all would agree it *should* be done, but then there is no one willing to pull the trigger. In this Carl Foreman-produced epic, the harsh reality of what the men are up against is brought home forcefully by the grim conclusion to the scene.

The music score is exceptionally well done, and at the time of its first release, became a best-selling record. And by coincidence a top name in music is also in the cast. James (*Goodbye Cruel World, Her Royal Majesty, etc.*) Darren portrays a young good looking Greek fighting for his country.

Firmly established as classic fare, *The Guns Of Navarone* is another entry into the rush of battle movies. They *all* prove just how hard it is to get a good bag of french fries and a Coke when there's a war on!

... SINGER JAMES DARREN

... AND A COUNTERFEIT NAZI.

NOW you see his real nature. "Rough" Tony and his Sealyham pup.

KRLA ARCHIVES

"HERE COMES THE NIGHT"
"BABY, PLEASE DON'T GO"
"GLORIA"
"MYSTIC EYES"

Whisky A Go Go
8901 Sunset Strip
Telephone: 652-4202

1st American Club Appearance
JUNE 2-18

THEM

also 5 weekend afternoon matinees for all ages! Saturdays: June 4, 11 & 18! Sundays: June 5 & 12! Time: 4 P.M.

COMING:

GENE CLARK AND THE GROUP

JUNE 22-JULY 10

Food & Fun Till 2 A.M. - Age 18 & Up Welcome

KRLA ARCHIVES

America's Largest Teen NEWSpaper 15¢

KRLA Edition BEAT

JUNE 25, 1966

BEAT Photo: Robert Young

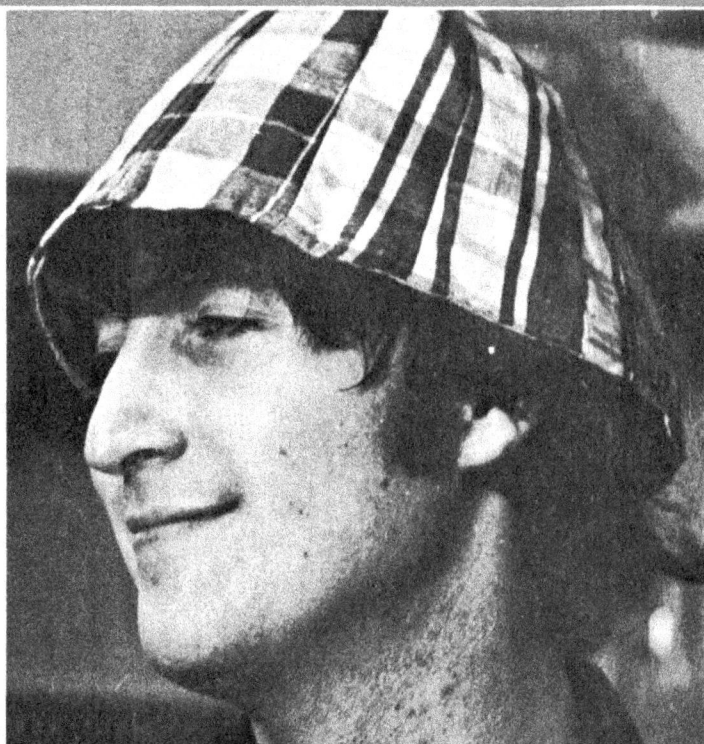

BEAT Photo: Robert Custer

How Individually Important Are They?

KRLA BEAT

Volume 2, Number 15   June 25, 1966

HOTLINE LONDON SPECIAL

Two New Beatle Albums Due Here This Summer

By Tony Barrow

Almost certainly American Beatle People will have the chance of hearing TWO new albums by John, Paul, George and Ringo this summer! Capitol Records plan to issue the first of these within the next few weeks and the second should follow around the time of the '66 U.S. concert tour.

The first album has the program title "Yesterday and Today" and it will include three tracks made during The Beatles' lengthy series of current sessions in London. The three are "And Your Bird Can Sing" (subtitled "You Don't Get Me"), "Dr. Robert" and "I'm Only Sleeping."

"Dr. Robert" was made just two days after the boys completed "Paperback Writer" and "Rain." It was recorded at sessions which took place over the Easter holiday weekend and most of the finishing touches were put to the composition on the studio floor.

"I'm Only Sleeping" took time to perfect. John had in mind a particular sound to create a lazy instrumental backing. At two different sessions all the boys agreed that the sound they were getting was far too wide-awake for the feel of the song. At a third-time-lucky work-out they managed to get the effect they'd been waiting for. That was on Friday, May 6.

Other titles included in the "Yesterday And Today" Selection range from Ringo's "What Goes On" and "Act Naturally" to George's "If I Needed Someone." Also in the album are "We Can Work It Out," "Day Tripper," "Nowhere Man," "Drive My Car" and Paul's solo ballad "Yesterday."

The scheduled Capitol release date for this album means that Beatle people on your side of the Atlantic will hear three brand-new titles at least four to six weeks ahead of their U.K. counterparts. Over here in Britain, Parlophone records do not plan to issue a new album by the Beatles before the beginning of August.

Long Hair Groups: 'A Collection Of Tramps,' Declares Len Barry

NEW YORK—Len Barry, who professes to own a clean-cut, good-looking, well-dressed image, today informed his booking agency, William Morris, that he no longer wants to work any extended tours or nitery engagements with what he terms "long-haired, dirty-looking, sloppily-dressed groups.

"I've had it with them," said Barry in one of the most outspoken comments on long-hair groups ever issued. "It isn't only that they look like a collection of tramps, they act that way and it's the way they really are. They're completely indifferent to the kids who have made them and their personal habits are disgusting.

"I have too much respect for my audience," continued Len, "Whether it's adult or teen, for show business and for myself to ever work with them again.

"They're appealing to the lowest possible common denominator in their appearance, performance and in some cases in their material as well. I know dozens of artists who feel the way I do and I hope that my speaking up will encourage them to do the same. It'll make this a better business for all of us."

Len, who has had three hit singles—"1-2-3," "Like A Baby" and "Somewhere"—pointed to the Beatles as an example. "I enjoy their records but I think that they're probably one of the worst in-person acts I've ever seen.

"They make a joke out of the kids who love them. They ridicule the very people who took them out of the gutter and made them stars. The Rolling Stones don't perform, they just stand there and fake. Dylan is another completely aloof, nothing personality.

"I don't mind long hair in talented kids like Freddie and the Dreamers, Herman's Hermits and the McCoys but when it's used as a replacement for talent, as it is with the Animals, the Lovin' Spoonful, the Changin' Times and most of the others, it's something I want to dissociate myself from completely," concluded Len.

The BEAT would like to make it quite clear that we do not agree with most of Len's statements. We DO agree that there are certain artists who are "completely indifferent to the kids who have made them" but these artists are NOT exclusive to long-haired
(Turn to Page 11)

... "I'VE HAD IT WITH THEM," says Barry

Supremes Score At Fairmont

Chalk up another triumph for the Supremes! There probably doesn't exist a top night club in the world which the Supremes have not graced with their combined talent and personalities.

The staid Fairmont Hotel was the latest to fall in the path of the Supremes. They opened at the Fairmont amid thunderous applause and wall-to-wall people.

Everybody who was anybody (and even some who weren't) turned out to see Diana, Mary and Florence go through their paces.

And they weren't disappointed as the Supremes proved once again why they are without a doubt the number one female singing group in the entire world.

During their busy schedule, the Supremes took time out to visit some of the soldiers wounded in Vietnam and recuperating in San Francisco. Although the girls said nothing about the reason for their visit, a reliable source revealed that the Supremes were so upset by the refusal of the Chicago Hilton to allow recovering soldiers to attend one of the hotel's shows that the Supremes decided to go and perform for the soldiers.

... THE SUPREMES SWINGING AT THE FAIRMONT
BEAT Photo: Howard L. Bingham

George's Club

In the early stages of Beatlemania, when the press was desperately searching for individual tags to apply to each of the foursome, they dubbed George Harrison the "businessman" of the group.

Whether this was an actual fact, or whether George was just giving biographers the business, is a good question. Whatever the case, he is definitely living up to the title.

His most publicized investment to date is Sibylla's, the discotheque he's opened just off London's famed Picadilly Circus.

Early reports stated that the $120,000 nitery was being financially backed by George and British disc jockey Alan Freeman. It has since been learned that several others are involved in the venture.

Among them are Terry Howard (George's 26-year-old photographer friend who accompanied the Harrisons during part of their honeymoon in the Barbados), Bruce Higham (a 24-year-old property man), Keven McDonald (a young ad man who is the cousin of Viscount Rothemere, the press lord) and Sir William Pigott-Brown.

The latter, who provided half of the finances, is a millionaire baronet. At the age of 19, Sir William was the Amateur Steeplechase Champion of England. Now at 25, he's taken to running first in the entertainment race.
(Turn to Page 6)

Inside the BEAT

Walkers Killing Myths	2
Do You Demand Stand-Outs?	3
Cher's Surprise Party	4
Beatle Talk	4
Turtles Meet Dylan	5
A Sunrays' Concert	6-7
The Mysterious Them	12
Day For Decision	13
Beat Goes To The Movies	15

The BEAT is published weekly by BEAT Publications, Inc., editorial and advertising offices at 6290 Sunset Blvd., Suite 504, Hollywood, California 90028. U.S. bureaus in Hollywood, San Francisco, New York, Chicago and Nashville; overseas correspondents in London, Liverpool and Manchester, England. Sale price: 15 cents. Subscription price: U.S. and possessions, $5 per year; Canada and foreign rates, $9 per year. Second class postage prepaid at Los Angeles, California.

KRLA ARCHIVES

...JOHN MAUS, SCOTT ENGEL AND GARY LEEDS — THE WALKER BROTHERS.

Walkers Killing Myths

Myths die hard. One of the myths that seems to be taking an impossibly long time to die is the one that says that all pop stars come from England to America. To disprove this, there is a goodly contingent of Americans in England who head the charts and create riots. Pre-eminent among those who do create this kind of excitement is a trio of unrelated young men who call themselves "The Walker Brothers." With a sound that has been described as "just like the Righteous Brothers only completely different" the boys and their rioting fans have created more official headaches than anything since the Boston Tea Party.

They came, the 3 of them, from Hollywood where the drugstores are full of starlets and out-of-work actors hanging around waiting for someone to discover them. The Walker Brothers did their hitch-hanging around but then began to make it (that is, John and Scott did ... they met Gary later on in a car wreck), then went to London with hope of really making it there.

The fact is that they went like Yankee Doodle Dandy to London and took the place by storm. They didn't arrive in any whirlwind of advance publicity and one is certain there were no grave omens taken by soothsayers, but from a simple, unheralded arrival which was almost certainly not first class, they have become the darling of the British pop fans.

The effect of the boys on the British fans is a little hard to describe and hard to believe. They have the kind of good looks which foreigners think is typically American and Americans would like to think was too ... the cowboy build ... long legs, blue eyes, tousled hair, and animal magnetism. The girls respond by screaming and ripping clothes (off the boys, that is).

The boys don't really hate the idea but it's expensive and often frightening. In fact, they are insured for $270,000.

A projected return to the States is underway and there is the problem: will Americans give them the same kind of attention? Prophets are notoriously unhonored in their own country. But the Walker Brothers are not prophets ... they're musicians ... good ones too, and they have a magnetism which isn't confined to England. Their records are selling here too and interest in them is high.

There is nothing people like so well as a winner, particularly if the person won from a foreign country. Swimming the English Channel is more glamorous than swimming Lake Michigan. The Walker Brothers went to England, conquered hands down and will return to their own country with all that glamour ... and don't forget the talent too.

On the BEAT

By Louise Criscione

The Beatles, rather unwillingly, became the object of considerable controversy in the Mid-west. It seems some disc jockey in Pittsburgh played an alledged telephone interview with the Beatles in which they slammed Barry Sadler and his "Green Berets," tabbing the record "rubbish."

Well, it made Mid-west teens so furious they threatened to boycott all stores unless *all* Beatle records were removed from the racks! And several distributors supposedly phoned Capitol Records to request that the Beatles "cool it with this kind of talk."

On the London end of the controversy, however, it was vehemently denied that the Beatles had even *given* an interview to any American disc jockey. And, as of now, the mystery remains just that — a mystery.

Poor, Paul

Speaking of the Beatles, didn't realize how badly Paul had chipped his tooth and cut his lip until I saw him on "Ed Sullivan." No wonder he didn't smile much!

Are you ready for the latest "in" craze? I'm not sure I am, but Howard Kalan of the Turtles was up here last week hyping us on the Cisco Kid Fan Club. I swear. He even sang us their theme song (or whatever they call it!) and with a straight-face revealed that he was on the level. We sort of think it's a put-on. But then, with Howard you just never know!

...PAUL McCARTNEY

It's like I told you before — Mick Jagger forever has his mouth open. This week he's been busy knocking the Beach Boys. Says the Jagger: "I hate the Beach Boys but I like Brian Wilson. If you saw the Beach Boys play 'live' you wouldn't believe it. The drummer can't seem to keep time to save his life."

Mick then went on to say that he thinks the Beach Boys' latest album, "Pet Sounds," is "good" but he doesn't particularly dig the songs although he does think they're "great records" and "Brian Wilson is a great record producer."

A Beateles?

Incidentally, Mick says in ten years he hopes he'll be an actor. Hope that doesn't mean we'll have to wait a decade for "Only Lovers Left Alive." What're the Stones trying to pull — a Beatles?

The Mindbenders are going to be in a movie, "To Sir With Love." The film stars Sidney Poitier and went into production last week in England. The Mindbenders will sing the title song over the movie credits and will also be seen in a club sequence. The score for the film is being penned by Barry and Cynthia Mann — naturally, don't they write everything?

Well, Herman has a new baby sister and he's done the honors of choosing her name himself. I must say Herman has excellent taste, he named his sister, Louise.

The Standells are cracking up over the use of their record, "Dirty Water," as the theme of a mid-western city's fight against water pollution! 'Course, it was a great promotion for the record, which looks as if it might be a nation-wide smash for the guys.

Sinatra On Top!

Are you ready for Frank Sinatra making it all the way to number one on the British charts with his "Strangers In The Night?" It's the first time in a long time for the Chairman of the Board. Actually, the record's okay — it's just that "dooby, dooby, do" part at the end which is making people giggle a lot.

Yardbirds' Stateside tour kicks off on August 1 and lasts for five weeks. It's set to include concerts, club dates and television appearances.

Motown has decided to expand — and, baby, are they ever. They're heading for movies, television and Broadway! They're currently searching for good scripts and are willing to invest up to $600,000 on a Broadway play. As far as television is concerned, the Motown people are thinking seriously of specials for some of their artists, especially the Supremes.

...DIANA ROSS

KRLA ARCHIVES

Do You Honestly Demand A Stand-Out?

By Eden

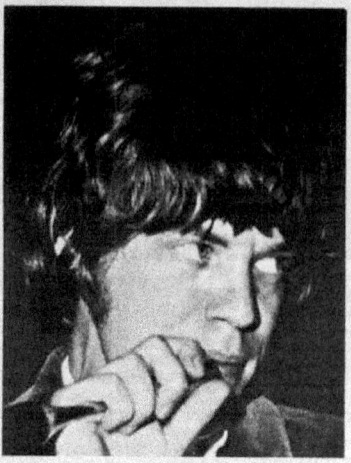

... MICK STONE
BEAT Photo: Chuck Boyd

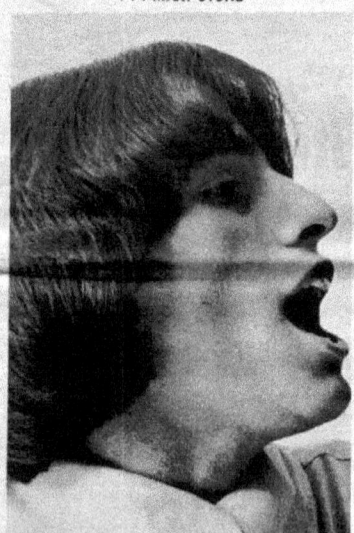

... EDDIE RASCAL

... BRIAN BEACH BOY

... JOHN SPOONFUL

... MARK RAIDER

... ERIC ANIMAL
BEAT Photo: Chuck Boyd

How many times have you heard your favorite disc jockey announce the next record by "Eric Burdon and the Animals," "Mick Jagger and the Rolling Stones," or "John Sebastian and the Lovin' Spoonful?"

If you are like many loyal fans of these groups, you have found yourself somewhat upset, complaining that these are *groups*—not just individuals accompanied by some additional long-haired musicians.

However, your complaints are usually to no avail, as the DJ's go right on announcing in the same old way. As long as we can't seem to put an end to this slightly irritating habit, perhaps we can at least find out why it is done.

The Beatles have always been unique (you should pardon the understatement!), and the fact that they have always been treated as four individuals within a group is no exception to their rule of individuality.

The Stones have not been quite so fortunate, however. And time after time you will hear their latest disc being introduced with "Mick Jagger and the Stones" attached to it.

Why? Perhaps in the Stones' case it is because Mick really is the personality of the group onstage. He is the one who does nearly all of the singing, with the exception of some occasional harmony from Keith. It is the dynamic Jagger personality which is the symbol of the group, the human representation which stands for everything which the Stones are to their fans.

Soulful Eric

One of the most outstanding examples of a lead singer being singled out of the group is Eric Burdon of the Animals. But here there is quite a good reason for the separation.

In England, Eric is generally regarded as being *the* most fantastic soul singer who has ever existed in time and space. He has earned this reputation and he deserves it, and is held in high esteem by nearly all of his colleagues in the field of pop music.

In many instances, it is a talent above-and-beyond the mere performance level which singles out a singer for public attention. For example, many of the lead singers in the big groups today are responsible for writing and arranging and even producing the music which the group is performing.

John Sebastian is one of these creative people who has been singled out not so much because he is the lead singer for the Lovin' Spoonful, but because he is also thought to be an outstanding writer and producer.

Brian Wilson is the name which generally preceeds the introduction of the Beach Boys, but perhaps he of all people has distinctly earned this accolade.

Brian has now entirely discontinued his live performances with the group. Brian Johnston has taken his place with the boys when they are on the concert stage or in front of the television cameras.

But it is behind the piece of wax which we place upon our stereos in order to hear the unique Beach Boys music where Brian takes command and is the star. For Brian is not only a very talented songwriter, but probably one of the most talented and creative record producers in popular music today.

Often, it is the group's appearance onstage which will single out the lead singer for public identification. For example, Mark Lindsay who is the lead singer for Paul Revere and the Raiders, is frequently thought by those not yet acquainted with the group to be Paul Revere.

Most probably, this is because Mark is the dynamo of talent and energy who is *all over* the stage during the Raiders' performances. The entire group is a wild and fun-loving bunch of guys, but Mark is probably the wildest onstage.

One of the most popular new groups in America is The Young Rascals, and though he isn't always their lead singer, the tiny fireball of nervous energy they affectionately refer to as Eddie is already being singled out for distinction in the public's affection.

Eddie is usually caught playing the tambourine (well, he *is* about the best tambourine man this side of Fifth Avenue!), but he does a lot of singing for the group, and a whole *lot* of the *moving* onstage!

Talent Is First

There are other groups who have been individually "torn asunder" by the press and the public—the Hermits, the Brummels, the Yardbirds, the Byrds, and the Mama's and Papa's have all been victims at one time or another.

Why? Once again we ask that question, and once again the answer is difficult to find. Possibly on the basis of talent; talent beyond just the vocal attributes displayed onstage. Possibly it is on the basis of a distinctive physical appearance; a certain "look" about someone.

Or perhaps it is even larger than that. Today we live in a pop world of *groups*. There are very few individuals to be found, and have you ever tried asking someone for their favorite male singer? They usually don't have one, but that could just be because there *aren't* any.

Most of the pop idols are members of groups, and while the fans in America and England are still as group happy as ever—there is still that basic need to identify with something, or someone. Especially with a single someone.

It is not always simple to dream about an entire group, but few girls would find any difficulty in focusing their sighs individually on Paul McCartney, Mick Jagger, Eddie Brigatti, Mark Lindsay, or Keith Relf. It is this need to individually recognize—and be recognized *by*—one person which seems to be behind this whole thing.

It is far easier to think in terms of one at a time, and let that one represent many. And so we have Mick and The Stones, Eric and The Animals, Brian and The Beach Boys, and so on. But even that is all right. The important thing is—we *have* them!

KRLA ARCHIVES

A Surprise Birthday Party For Cher

BEAT Photos: Cora Filipeli

By Jeanne Castle

HOLLYWOOD: A combination surprise birthday party for Cher and a sneak preview of the new Sonny and Cher clothing line occurred the other night at one of

The club was packed with the curious, the well-wishers and the friends. Many sat with their eyes glued to the large screen set up to the left of the bandstand which was showing continuous color pictures from Sonny and Cher's first feature film, "Good Times."

While all of this was going on I got word that Sonny and Cher were about to make their appearance, so I made my way through the cluster of photographers and out to the front of the club. I had no sooner planted myself at the curb than one of Sonny and Cher's custom-made, gold-painted Mustangs pulled up and deposited the famous pair right at my feet.

Looking at them I found it hard to believe that they had spent the entire day on the set of "Good Times." Cher looked absolutely ravishing in a beautiful black and white sequin outfit, topped with a black and white fur coat.

The duo was escorted (with some difficulty) through the ever-present mob of photographers and into It's Boss where a fashion show of Sonny and Cher's new fall line of specially designed Gordon and Marx clothes was in progress.

I might add that the clothes were fabulous (Sonny and Cher wear them in their movie) and I'm sure it won't be long before thousands of teens across the nation will be sporting the "S&C Originals."

Following the fashion show, a huge (two feet by two feet), white birthday cake, trimmed in mounds of beautiful pink swirls, was wheeled in and the audience broke into "Happy Birthday, Cher."

But Cher herself was so surprised that she was actually *speechless* for several minutes! After kissing Cher Happy Birthday, Sonny helped cut the cake which was then served to all of the guests. Strangely enough, instead of eating the cake many of the guests were as souveniers.

Cake all eaten (or stowed away) Sonny and Cher signed autographs and posed for pictures as long as the crowds lasted. And you *know* they lasted for hours!

Typical of the audience's reaction to the whole affair was reflected in the remark made by one of the young reporters, Cara Marie Filipeli: "This is the most important day in my life and I will never forget it as long as I live. Sonny and Cher are two of the most wonderful artists in the world."

And I guess they are.

What The Beatles Say About Their Movies

By Jamie McCluskey III

Nearly everyone in the wide and wonderful world of pop music is anxiously awaiting the next Beatle movie, now long over-due. At this writing, the boys have still to find an acceptable script, however, they are still searching. Hopefully, they will be able to begin filming — if a script is found — sometime this fall.

In the meantime, we are all going to have to content ourselves with watching re-runs of "A Hard Day's Night," and "Help" about 357 times or so.

And speaking of those two fab films now of the past, did you ever wonder what the Beatles themselves had to say about their work in "Help"? Well, we did, and if you're interested we'll share their answers to some of our prying questions with you.

Ringo: "'Help'? I thought I'd probably need it when we were shooting on location in the Bahamas. I had to jump into the sea from a boat in one scene and I was a bit scared about it.

"I mean, I don't mind splashing about in a pool, swimming from side to side in about five feet — but leaping into the ocean, that's a different matter!

"I'd like to end up in films, though I always hate myself on the screen and I don't particularly like my voice. But I'd like to be able to get enough confidence to be a good actor — and to be asked to do films because I'm an actor and not just because of being a Beatle."

Paul: "What I liked most about the film is the way the songs were photographed. There's much more variety than there was in the songs from out first film.

"I don't really know what our performances were like — I don't think we improved very much as actors — but I can tell you that the color photography was fabulous.

George: "I enjoyed making this much more than "A Hard Day's Night." We had great actors with us and we were always having a laugh. In fact, from the day we got on the plane to go to the Bahamas we were always laughing.

"And in Austria it was even more hilarious. I don't know why but people always seemed to be rushing up to us and babbling away in strange languages. We just felt about.

"One of the funniest things that happened was the crazy relay race we had round the huge lawn when we were filming at Cliveden. We decided to challenge the film crew and about six teams lined up. And I might tell you that the Beatles team won!!

John: "This time it was mostly visual humor — there wasn't so much of us making smart remarks. I think there is a lot of scope for us in films which hasn't been exploited.

"I mean, it took us three or four records before we really got our sound. I suppose it will be the same with films. When we've made three or four we'll probably hit the right formula. But I wouldn't like to concentrate on films. I still prefer playing to a live audience to anything else."

Now, then — if we can only find the right script for the third Beatle flick.

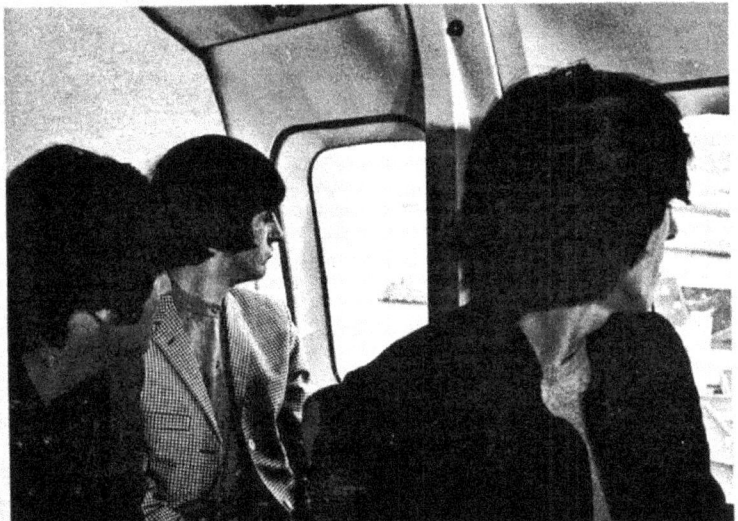

...JOHN, RINGO AND GEORGE searching for a suitable script?

Tokyo Prepares Itself For A Beatle Invasion

The Beatles' forthcoming visit to Tokyo is drawing such enthusiastic support from Japanese students that local authorities are beginning to worry. More than 200,000 applicants have registered for tickets and only 30,000 will be admitted to each one of the three performances beginning June 30.

A lottery was set up to decide which of the lucky applicants would be permitted to buy tickets. Seats are ranging from 1,500 to 2,100 yen ($4.17 to $5.84), but newspaper entertainment reporters expect the tickets to bring exhorbitant prices from speculators.

The concerts will be held at the 10,000 seat Budokan Hall, a templelike building where the Olympic judo competition and other important sport events have been held.

But while police have, at least for the present, solved the touchy problem of attendance, they are still concerned with the security of the Beatles.

The huge turnout of well-wishers expected to greet the Britons is still a problem. One suggestion is that the Japan Air Lines plane, which arrives June 30, be diverted to one of the United States Air Force bases near Tokyo, where the public is not admitted.

Another suggestion is that the Beatles be taken from the airport to the city to avoid the huge traffic pileup that is expected.

Housing for the world-famous group remains one of the most pressing problems for Tokyo authorities. It seems that no hotel is willing to accomodate the Beatles for fear of property damages that might result when screaming Beatle fans over-run the hotel.

Already, Tokyo is thinking Beatle. Much of the city's male population has grown shoulder-length hair and local wigmakers are enjoying a big boom in business.

KRLA ARCHIVES

...**THE TURTLES** (l. to r. Al, Mark, Don, Howard, Jim and Chuck) sing their latest smash, "Grim Reaper Of Love."

Turtles Meet Dylan

By Jamie McCluskey III

Lunching with a Turtle can be one of life's most unusual – and most *enjoyable* – experiences. And it *was* just the other day when Turtle Howard Kaylan joined me for a pleasant chat over a bowl of chili.

Being on the road as much as he is with the group, Howard has a great opportunity to meet many people and from these associations came the story he told on himself about the night he met Bob Dylan.

"We were playing the Phone Booth in New York, and it's a beautiful club – and everyone was just great. *Everybody* – all our good friends came down to see us: Jay and the Americans, Bobby Goldsboro and Brian Highland, the Brummels stopped in – it was just great, *every*body stopped in.

"But, I developed a tonsilitis problem while I was there, because every night I had been singing, for like three months solid without a night off. So I developed this trouble.

"Well, the night before my 'trouble,' Andrew Loog Oldham came in with the Rolling Stones, and we'd never met them before. And it's a very frightening feeling when a group like the Stones comes in and sits down in the front row and *gapes* at you and wants you to please them. It's a very scary thing!

"So we did the show, and we went into some electronic music and evidently the guys had never heard an American group do it before and they flipped out. Brian Jones was really thrilled and he came up and told us 'Wow, you guys were great, and I'm gonna come back!' And we thought, *sure* you are. But it was great having him flatter us like that.

"Well, Brian and the boys came back like *every* night for a week, and it was a tremendously gratifying feeling.

"But, I reached a point where, all of a sudden I decided it was gonna be impossible for me to sing – it was hurting me something terrible. I couldn't squeak out a note to save my soul!

"So, I sat myself down in the audience and watched the other fellow Turtles take over. And it made it really rough on Mark, who's like second in command. He had to sing stuff I wrote that he didn't know, so I was like faking the words to him from the audience!

"And then, in walks Brian, and Andrew, and George Harrison, and Chrissie Shrimpton, and Monti Rock III, and all of these society people and I felt *terrible*. I was in a corner feeling very low and depressed, and watching the other five Turtles onstage, and all of a sudden, who walks in but *Bob Dylan!!*

"I'd never met Bob Dylan before. He'd written 'It Ain't Me, Babe' and it was very successful for both of us, but we'd never met him ... and there's Dylan!

"I *sunk* under the table!!! I was never so depressed in my life! But, no one else saw him except Jim. Jim was onstage and looked down into the audience and went ... 'Unhhhhhhhhhh!!' So they went right on playing and the manager of the club found out and he grabbed a piece of paper and a crayon and scribbled on it and brought it up to Mark.

"In between songs, Mark looks at the paper – didn't know what was happening – and thought it was paging someone. So he said, 'Paging Mr. Bob Dy ... D ... D ... D' – crumbled up the note with a very shocked expression on his face, and goes 'Oh no! What are we gonna do, what're we gonna do?!!'

"So, there's Dylan in the audience, the five Turtles onstage, and *me* under the table! Mark went up to the microphone and said, 'Ladies and gentlemen, we have in our audience, the fantastic Mr. Bob Dylan and everybody stood up and applauded, and Mark went on:

'Our lead singer, Howard, has tonsilitis and hasn't been singing with us all night. But, I think you'll give him a rousing hand of applause and have him come up here and just for Bob Dylan, sing the song that made us famous.'

"I felt like a complete *moron* as I crawled out from under my table (no, he didn't say *shell!*), and all the people are standing up applauding me.

"I walked up there and set my voice back approximately *four* days. I *ruined* it – but I *had* to sing 'It Ain't Me, Babe.' I *had* to – there was *Bob Dylan!*

Other than that, the Turtles have been moving at a very fast pace the past few months, cramming recording dates, television appearances, and a tour into their hectic schedule.

Just returned from a lengthy cross-country tour, part of which was done in conjunction with the Dick Clark "Action" tour, Howard had many words of praise for Dick Clark, and all the Turtles' audiences across the nation, and for several of the other groups with whom they toured, especially the Young Rascals.

Although they are a comparatively new group, the Rascals have been tearing up all of New York the last few months and are currently extending their invasion to the rest of the States. Howard agrees with the great reception given to this new group, and adds that they are "beautiful, groovy people."

From here, the Turtles will wrap up a marathon series of recording sessions in which they are experimenting with many new kinds of music – Howard says this next group of songs will probably be one of the best ever from the Turtles – and a number of top television shows which will beam the six smiling Turtle faces your way in the near future.

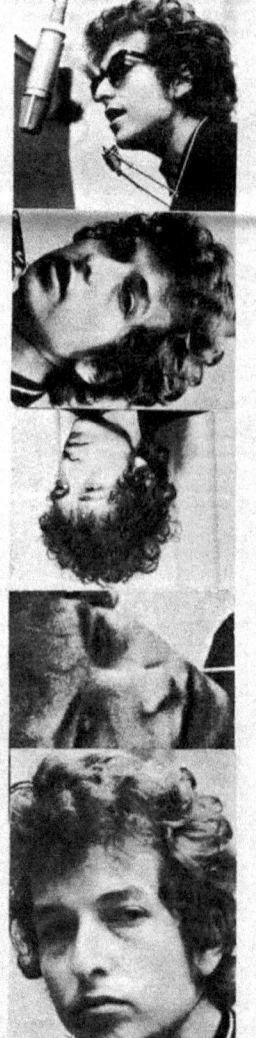

..."AND THEN in walks Dylan."

KRLA ARCHIVES

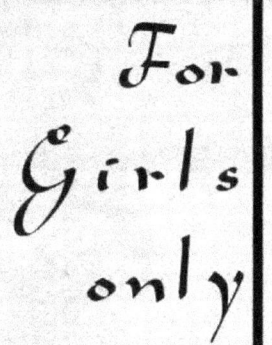

For Girls only

by shirley poston

George has had it.

As of this moment, we have split the olde orange blanket (which I certainly have on the brain this week) (well, I have to have *something* on it.)

What do I have against George? No, let me re-phrase that question — I don't trust myself to answer it in its present form. Why am I *furious* at George? Well, it's this way.

I realize I should have told you about George and me some time ago (would you believe George and I?) (or are you having enough trouble believing George and *me*?). But I just couldn't bring myself to confess.

Homsomever (rather than go to all the trouble of re-typing that, just turn the first m upside down, okay?) I am now ready to tell all.

George and I have been seeing each other for some time (especially since we got glasses) (never you mind glasses of *what*.) But never again. Not after last Monday night!

George *knows* (I tell you) that I have to write Robin Boyd on Monday night. I mean, I don't have to, but I *have* to. You know, because I always *have*. (Anyone who wishes to know what I am gibbering about is invited to join the throng.)

Hot Typewriter

Anyrut, what did George do but tempt me into going out on Monday instead of cackling over a hot cauldron - er - typewriter.

And what did I do but chomp into the olde apple and allow myself to be convinced. (If the truth were known, the last date I turned down was a stuffed Dromedary.)

Well, do you realize that I *waited* and *waited* and *waited* for that twink to arrive? Do you also realize that by the time it finally dawned on me that he wasn't *going* to, I was so livid I couldn't have written my *name* (had I known it, that is!)

He's called three times since, but if he thinks I'll ever speak to him again, he's out of his tulip! In fact, every time he telephones, I encourage my discouraging brother (as in Jimmy The Jerk) to play his coronet very close to the receiver.

I once wrote a long open letter to George. I am about to write another more abbreviated version.

Dear George Black: Dropinze *dead!*

Black Routine

What's this *Black* routine? What do you *mean* what? (*Whatt???*) Oh, I'll bet you thought I was speaking of George *Harrison!* I certainly can't imagine whatever gave you *that* idea! I intended to make it perfectly clear that I was speaking of another George. Perhaps it slipped my mind. (And why not? Everything else has.)

And to think that I only went out with him in the first place because his name is the same as Harrison's first one (not to be confused with Lennon's first two) (remember that?) (I'm still trying (very) to forget it) (so is Lennon) (down, girl.) (Happy International Parentheses Week!) (Or lese . . . crumbs . . . else!)

Serially, I think that is the ratriest, dirty-low-down-sneakiest-type-trick anyone can do to anyone. Stand them up, I mean. Crikeys, it makes you get all panic-stricken and you start hurling yourself into corners even if you really don't even care that much for the alleged person who's causing your problem (at the moment.)

I hope that when all of you start speaking to me again (not to mention *of* me in angry mutters), no one will write and ask me if I'd go out with the *real* George (GASP) if I had the chance. You know, all things considered and all. That would be some question to have to decide on an answer for. (At this point, only my hairdresser knows for sure, but would you believe rxi *YKJQ?*)

There I go with that #59$*!©! code again, when I've promised myself (as in I-done-tole-me-and-tole-me) fo cease and desist until I'm absolutely *certain* that I've answered all those last-minute lurkers I've been finding.

Speaking of godes . . . help . . . I mean, codes . . . no, come to think of it, that isn't what I mean at all. What I was going to say was thanks! To everyone who wrote and told me that I did *not* have the Herman album contest, that is.

I would also like to thank everyone who wrote and told me that I *did* have the Herman album contest.

It is always nice to be among friends. (Even if we are chained together.)

I would also like to thank Lynn Burgermeister who wrote me a gastric letter about the day she drove several million miles an hour to get to the *BEAT* office and back during a free period. Just to see *me*, yet! (Brag it up, kid — they'll be here soon.)

When she found out that I wasn't there (which certainly is not any military secret), she commented to a girl in the office about the Cavern chapter of Robin Boyd.

And here, in Lynn's own words, is the answer she received.

The girl smiled. "I can't write like that either," she said. "Probably because I'm *sane*."

It is also nice to be *surrounded* by friends.

Personally, I'd rather be surrounded by George. (The mere thought of which fairly gives me willywackers on the wezand.)

Oh, more thanks. This time to Jane Sanborn from Walnut Creek, Calif. who sent me a whole list of possible titles (as in re) for this (and I use the word (looslier) (hah?) column.

Sub Titles

Among them were "More Tall Heavy," "No Blokes Allowed," "A Moldy Moldy Girl," "Beatle Blithering," "Gone Bonkers" and my favorite, which was "It Won't Be Long" (Sub Title: Until The Little Men In White Come.)

Something tells me that Jane and I have been plagarizing from - er - reading the same books (Let's hear it for J.W.L.M.B.E.) (Better yet, let's hear *from* him!)

Narcissa Nash, don't just stand there! I need your help. A girl named Kathy has sent a dream for you to analyze, and I quote:

"My best friend Carol and I were somehow in London (what a shame.) We were walking by this alley and Paul and Jane were standing there by a trash can, with a minister!

"Carol started to scream, but I just stood there and cried. This attracted Paul's attention and he came over to me (pant, pant.) He put his arm around me and said 'don't cry, luv, it's only a joke.'

"Then he kissed me sweetly and Jane jumped into the trash can and Carol jumped in after her.

"That's it. Can you explain it, or have N.N. do it?"

Since I am having trouble explaining my room to the Board Of Health, I think I'd best leave this one to the legendary N.N.

Speaking of leaving, I'd best do that, too, as the swish of nets is swiftly becoming a roar. Well, if they do catch up with me, I'll go quietly. But that doesn't mean I'll *stay* quiet.

George's Place

(Continued from Page 1)

There seems to be little doubt that the club will be a rousing success. Named after a friend of the backers, Miss Sibylla Edmonstone (a grand-daughter of Marshall Field), it's already received several take-over bids from large, established corporations.

Bids so far have been refused, and will most likely continue to be. Everyone involved in the venture seems not only optimistic about but fascintated by the project.

As George himself puts it, "it'll be a laugh."

Sibylla's sounds like a swinging spot for today's ravers, and it also looks the part. George and company commissioned one of their country's most "in" decorators to design the club.

This was Beatle-mopped, 26-year-old David Mlinaric's first attempt at nitery decor, but he thought positively from the beginning.

Being of the opinion that most nightclubs are filled with old junk, Mlinaric attempted to and succeeded in giving *Sibylla's* a "feeling of under-decoration, with the simplicity that goes with today's clothes." The main color theme throughout is a twilight blue.

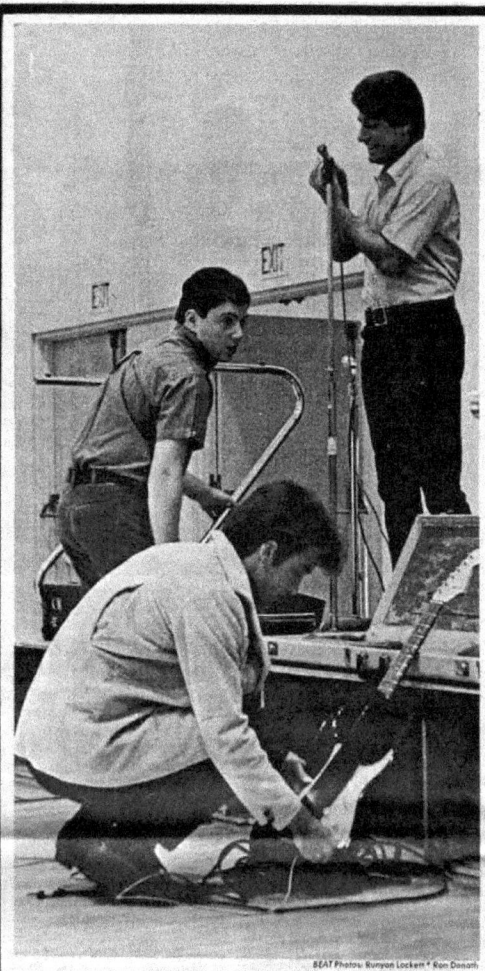

...SUNRAYS setting up their equipment

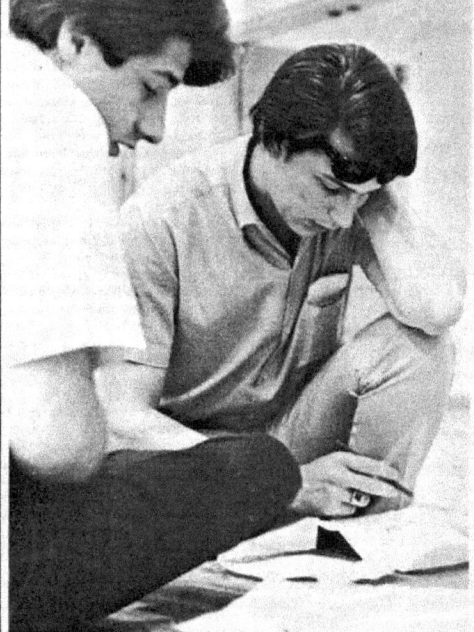

...EDDIE and Vince go over the program and choose their songs

KRLA ARCHIVES

... **FINALLY** on stage the five Sunrays (l. to r. Marty, Byron, Eddie, Rick and Vince) introduce their latest disc, "Don't Take Yourself Too Seriously."

Behind The Curtains At A Sunrays' Concert

You file in and take your seat in the auditorium. You glance around, size up the rest of the audience and settle back for waht you hope will be a short wait until the show gets underway. And usually without warning, it happens. The curtains part, the MC steps to the mike and the show which you have shelled out three of four dollars to see finally begins.

If you're lucky, everything runs smoothly. There are no huge hang-ups, the performers head out one after the other, mass confusion and obvious goofs are missing. You watch, you laugh, you scream, you cry. Or maybe you just sit there and applaude.

And then as suddenly as it had begun — it's over. For minutes, perhaps only for seconds, you sit perfectly still hoping that your favorite will re-appear. When he doesn't, you slowly wander out of the auditorium and pile into your car, linger at ths bus stop, or wait for your family car to pull into sight.

Through the entire ordeal you have found your mind being constantly plagued with the re-occuring question: "What's going on backstage." What IS happening behind those curtains which separate you from him?

To find out, we enlisted the aid of the five Sunrays and being extremely helpful guys they invited *The BEAT* and hired their OWN photographers to snap shots of exactly what went on backstage at one of their college dates.

Actually, the Sunrays were naturals for this kind of a feature as they spend a good deal of their time playing "live" dates and while they admit frankly that nothing can beat the excitement of a concert, they are quick to reveal that it's not ALL fun and games.

There is a tremendous amount of work involved, long hours of rehearsal, the loading and the unloading of instruments and a million small (but vitally important) details which must be worked out.

To the Sunrays, each concert is a new challenge but a challenge which they are eager to accept. Their hard work has paid off well for them because they are now known as "crowd pleasers." And quite honestly, they are. They enjoy performing and this becomes immediately obvious to their audiences, making for a harmonious feeling throughout the whole auditorium.

So, thanks to the Sunrays the next time you attend a concert you won't wonder what your favorites are doing—you'll know.

... **EDDIE** chats with **The BEAT** before leaving.

... **BYRON**, Marty and Rick take down the equipment which they had set up less than two hours before.

KRLA ARCHIVES

KRLA Tunedex

DAVE HULL

BOB EUBANKS

DICK BIONDI

JOHNNY HAYES

EMPEROR HUDSON

CASEY KASEM

CHARLIE O'DONNELL

BILL SLATER

This Week	Last Week	Title	Artist
1	2	SEARCHIN' FOR MY LOVE	Bobby Moore
2	1	A GROOVY KIND OF LOVE	The Mindbenders
3	6	PAINT IT, BLACK	Rolling Stones
4	3	ALONG COMES MARY	The Association
5	5	WHEN A MAN LOVES A WOMAN	Percy Sledge
6	18	DOUBLE SHOT (OF MY BABY'S LOVE)	Swingin' Medallions
7	15	DIRTY WATER	The Standells
8	8	HEY, JOE	The Leaves
9	12	HOLD ON! I'M COMIN'	Sam & Dave
10	9	YOU DON'T HAVE TO SAY YOU LOVE ME	Dusty Springfield
11	10	DON'T BRING ME DOWN	The Animals
12	4	DID YOU EVER HAVE TO MAKE UP YOUR MIND?	Lovin' Spoonful
13	20	LITTLE GIRL	Syndicate of Sound
14	29	STRANGERS IN THE NIGHT	Frank Sinatra
15	7	YOUNGER GIRL	The Hondells
16	11	I AM A ROCK	Simon & Garfunkel
17	17	BAREFOOTIN'	Robert Parker
18	28	PAPERBACK WRITER/RAIN	The Beatles
19	23	SOLITARY MAN	Neil Diamond
20	16	OPUS 17 (DON'T WORRY 'BOUT ME)	The Four Seasons
21	27	WHERE WERE YOU WHEN I NEEDED YOU?	Grass Roots
22	22	DIDDY WAH DIDDY	Captain Beefheart & His Magic Band
23	25	OH, HOW HAPPY	Shades of Blue
24	19	GREEN GRASS	Gary Lewis
25	21	BETTER USE YOUR HEAD	Anthony & The Imperials
26	—	DAY FOR DECISION	Johnny Sea
27	—	HANKY PANKY	Tommy James & The Shondells
28	26	BOYS WERE MADE TO LOVE	Karen Small
29	31	LOVE SPECIAL DELIVERY	Thee Midniters
30	33	HAVE I STAYED TOO LONG?	Sonny & Cher
31	30	AIN'T TOO PROUD TO BEG	The Temptations
32	—	HE WILL BREAK YOUR HEART/HE	Righteous Brothers
33	32	SHE DONE MOVED	The Spats
34	37	SWEET TALKIN' GUY	The Chiffons
35	40	(I'M A) ROAD RUNNER	Jr. Walker
36	34	LOVING YOU IS SWEETER THAN EVER	The 4 Tops
37	—	IT'S OVER	Jimmie Rodgers
38	38	COOL JERK	The Capitols
39	—	YOU BETTER RUN	The Young Rascals
40	39	DON'T DO IT SOME MORE	The Cindermen

Them Break The Barrier — Appear In American Club

Irish singing group Them have broken the barrier for groups from the British Isles performing in America.

Until now visiting British groups have appeared in America only in concert. The few groups that have actually appeared in clubs here have done so "in concert," that is, where dancing and serving of food or drinks is not allowed.

But the rule stopping British groups from appearing in clubs has fallen once and may fall more often now.

Them have appeared for an 18 day engagement at Hollywood's Whisky A Go Go.

The historic booking was accomplished by going through the America Guild of Variety Artists instead of the Musician's Union, which doesn't allow such bookings.

About the Musician's Union, Elmer Valentine, owner of the Whisky said, "The ones who are complaining are the older musicians who can't find work because they didn't adjust to the new music."

Valentine feels that now that they've done it once they should be able to book many more British groups into the Whisky and he is planning a trip to England to negotiate for the Animals, Kinks and Yardbirds.

Them may also turn out to be the first British group to cut a live album in an American club. Plans are currently being discussed for Them to cut a live LP during their stay at the Whisky.

The only other artists who've cut live albums there are Johnny Rivers and Otis Redding.

If this turns out to be the beginning of something and not just the exception to the rule, you may soon be able to see top British acts in the close quarters of American clubs where you can dance to their performance.

HELP!

HELP!
Needed: a manager for a girl's group. Also, members for the group. Write to *Sherry Eagles, 2070 Wickshire Ave., Hacienda Heights, Calif.*

HELP!
Wanted: One hard-cover 3-ring notebook that says "Beatles" on the cover. Also, one Beatle doll, with bobbing head, used in cars. Anyone having either of these for sale or knowing where they can be obtained please write to *Ferne Habush, 16023 Cantloy St., Van Nuys, Calif. 91406.*

HELP!
I would like to buy a 45 r.p.m. record entitled "One by One," by Diane and Anita. Anyone knowing a store where it is sold write *Ferne Habush, 16023 Cantloy, Van Nuys, Calif.*

HELP!
None of my pictures of the Beatles, taken at Balboa Stadium on Aug. 28, 1965, came out. Will pay for copies of shots taken there. Or at the Hollywood Bowl. *Suzy Harrison, 811 North Towner St., Santa Ana, Calif. 92703.*

HELP!
I play guitar and am very interested in starting a singing group just for fun. I want a girl who can play a nylon string guitar (no electric, yet) and a girl who can play the drums both between the ages of 12 and 14. Must live near Inglewood-Hawthorne area and be willing to practice. Contact *Janey Segal PL 5-1914.*

HELP!
We would like to start a Fan Club for the great new group, The Sons of Adam. Anyone knowing how we can obtain more information on them, please contact us. *Marlene and Kathy Bartraw, 15503 Domart, Norwalk, Calif. 90651.*

HELP!
One pen pal needed for another pen pal (of my pen pal). Her name and address is Crystal White, 342 Trincomalee Street, Kandy, Ceylon.

HELP!
I'm looking for anyone who knows the Preachers fan club address. If you have any information please write me. *Jenny Turpin, 547 Gray Street, Colton, California.*

FROM THE BAY AREA comes the Syndicate of Sound with their first hit, "Little Girl." From left to right, standing, Bob Gonzales, Don Baskin and John Duckworth; seated, John Sharkey and Jim Sawyers.

Inside KRLA
By Eden

It's been an unbelievable week out here at KRLA and I don't really think that we have recovered yet! We have had a large number of guests out at the station, including Paul Revere's Raiders, the Beach Boys, Simon and Garfunkel, the Standells, Them, the Mama's and Papa's, and about five thousand KRLA listeners!

Along about the end of the week, Mark Lindsay and Phil Volk (Fang) of the Raiders, came out to the station to answer a few calls on our Request Lines, and it was along about then that complete pandemonium struck.

About eight hundred very excited Raider fans (mostly girls) journeyed on out to Pasadena in order to greet the boys in person, and it really was something else. Mark and Fang were installed in a small room in the back of the studio where the Request Lines are located and they began to answer the calls from their many fans, most of them requesting songs from one of the Raiders' albums.

Lost Key

While they talked on the phone and signed autographs, one of their loyal fans managed to get a hold of Mark's car keys which he had accidentally left in his car. When it came time for the boys to leave, the keys were nowhere to be found.

Poor Mark went into an immediate state of panic while Fang began to search under Sticky-type Bat Dealies, complaining that he had also misplaced his keys.

Several hasty but intensive searches and a few short minutes later, Dick Moreland appeared holding a very furry yellow thingie to which was attached some keys.

"Did you lose something, Mark?" he inquired intelligently. With a great sigh of relief, Mark agreed that he had, but protested that when he lost them—they hadn't been attached to anything even slightly yellow *or* furry! "But thank you anyway" he said into the air to the unknown girl responsible for the furry achievement.

Smiles 'N' Tails!

Aided by about eight of KRLA's male-types, including the powerful Uncle DM himself, the two Raiders then began to attempt their getaway. Fang armed himself with his widest, toothiest grin, while Mark tucked his pony tail inside his collar and tried to smile a lot—and they both disappeared into the mob of female-types in the lobby.

The last thing I could see was a female hand reaching for Mark's head, but I was unable to see anything else. (I think I had just fainted!)

Have you been keeping a thought in mind for the great new For Young Love Sweepstakes on KRLA? You should, 'cause the prizes being given away are really something else!

The His and Hers prizes—one pair to be awarded each day for a total of 30 days—will include Vox guitars, pairs of slot car racing sets, stuffed mice, His and Her fashions of Ninth Street East, electric manicure kits, electric shaver kits, and watches.

Summer Salary

Also, KRLA will be awarding a salary (the amount has not yet been determined) for the entire summer to one boy and girl. Pretty great, huh? Right, so why don't you get out there and start entering?

Just fall by your nearest record counter and pick up an entry blank in the For Young Love Sweepstakes.

Special note to my little friend in the San Fernando Valley. Of course there are people in the Valley, but it's always fun to joke about it—especially when it was actually the old Scuzzabalooers' joke anyway! Besides, I live out there myself—right in the heart of Sonny and Cher territory!

And for all of you who have complained that you couldn't get through on KRLA's request lines, believe us when we say that it isn't for lack of phone lines.

KRLA has had to install several additional lines in order to accommodate our flooded switchboards. The only problem is that there are more of you—*many* more of you!—than there are phone lines in the *universe*, maybe! Well, would you believe in the *studio*?!

If you can't get through on the first few rings, just keep on trying and you will eventually get through. And, yes Virginia—KRLA *does* play all of the songs which are requested.

Till next week, then—remember the Amazing Pancake Man and keep the Cisco Kid in mind, will you?

HEY JOE — Look who dropped by KRLA to answer phone requests. Johnny Hayes shows the Leaves some of the station equipment. You just never know who's going to answer the phone when you call KRLA.

KRLA BEAT Subscription
SAVE 33% Of Regular Price

☐ 1 YEAR — 52 Issues — $5.00   ☐ 2 YEARS — $8.00
☐ 6 MONTHS — $3.00

Enclosed is _____ ☐ CASH ☐ CHECK
PLEASE PRINT — Include Your Zip Code

Send to: .... Age: ....
Address: .... City: ....
State: .... Zip: ....

MAIL YOUR ORDER TO: KRLA BEAT
6290 Sunset, Suite 504
Hollywood, Calif. 90028

Foreign Rate: $9.00 — 52 Issues

KRLA ARCHIVES

The Adventures of Robin Boyd

©1965 By Shirley Poston
CHAPTER THIRTY-FOUR

Robin Boyd had been in many different kinds of pickles in her life (dill, bread & butter, and hamburger-slice, just to mention a few), but never one like this.

Ringo (as in Starr) had disappeared the moment she and Ringo (as in Boyd) fell all over him. Whether he had vanished by choice or been trampled into the rug, Robin couldn't say for sure. But, whatever the case, his exit had been just a little too late, for Ringo (A.I.B.) had gotten herself a good look at (not to mention a large bite of) her idol (Ringo) (A.I.S.) (get the nets.)

"*Ringo!*" wailed Ringo. (If you think *this* is confusing, you should have been around during the adventures of Batman and *Robin*.)

"*Shurrup!!*" Robin demanded, stuffing a sofa pillow into her sturdy relative's blithering yap. "Do you want to wake mum?"

"Of course she does," Mrs. Boyd soothed sardonically from the doorway. "Now, what precisely is going on here?"

"N-n-nothing," Robin stammered, wishing she'd silenced her sister with a lamp instead of a pillow.

English Phase

Mrs. Boyd gave *her* a look. "Then precisely why are you batting each other about in the wee small?" (Don't look now, but Robin's *mother* may be starting to go through an English phase.) (Stranger things have happened.) (And will continue to, so stick around.)

"Because Ringo was here," gurgled Ringo, leaping to everyone's feet. "My very own Richie Starkey, in this very *house*."

Robin shuddered, sinking deeper into the proverbial brine of this particular pickle (if you think Peter-Piper-picked-a-peck-of is rough, try *that* one.)

She'd already lost George. Now, should she be forced to explain the unexplained presence of the aforementioned very own Richie (in this very house), she would also lose her magic powers. Not to mention the remainder of her marbles.

Suddenly she stopped shuddering, for it was then that she knew what she must do. (In other words, get set for another whopper because here we go again.)

"I can explain everything," Robin said calmly. (In fact, give her a moment and she can explain *anything*.) "I happen to know that Ringo had a pizza sundae before bed, and she's simply had another of her nightmares."

No Dream

Ringo stared at her aghast and then speared same with an unusually pointed droomstick. "I did not have no dream," she screeched negatively (make that a double.)

"You did not have *a* dream," Mrs. Boyd corrected wearily.

"I knew you'd see it my way," Ringo agreed smugly. "My very own Richie *was* here! In this very house, I tell you!"

Noticing that Robin was creeping out of the room on all fours (at any rate, on all of the fours she had with her), Mrs. Boyd murderously motioned her to a chair.

Realizing that her mum was in one of *those* moods again (known in some circles as a super-snit), Robin met her demands half way. Where she didn't exactly sit in the offered chair, she did hide behind it.

Mrs. Boyd returned her attention to her rotund twelve-year-old. "You're on," she said wearily-er (not to mention warily-er.) "Begin at the beginning." (Which is always nice.)

Being the sort of person who dislikes being the center of attraction (not to mention being the president of the Flannel Mouth Society), Ringo began at the beginning. (Repetition 4 *Ever!*)

"I was sound asleep when all of a sudden I heard this big commotion in the living room," she began in particularly annoying once-upon-a-time tones. "Naturally, I came running out here to see what was happening and I found Robin trying to crawl up the chimney yelling *George!*"

Mrs. Boyd moaned. "Was *Robin* yelling George or was the *chimney* yelling George?" (She might well ask.)

Ringo thought for a moment (told you stranger things would continue to happen.) "Robin was," she decided, at which time her older sister stopped hiding behind the chair and hid *under* it.

"Then she walked backwards across the room and tripped over me."

"Backwards across the room . . ." Mrs. Boyd echoed.

Ringo Realie

Ringo nodded. "Then both of us turned around and tripped over *Ringo!* Ringo *realie!*"

Mrs. Boyd made a cats cradle with the belt of her bathrobe. "Then what?" she re-moaned.

"I don't know! He just vanished into thin air, I tell you. But he was here . . ."

"In this very house," Mrs. Boyd interrupted, now fashioning a noose. Then she pondered momentarily, eyeing her creation as a possible solution to not only this but *all* of her problems.

"*Robin Irene Boyd*," she thundered at last.

Robin peered at her meekly (oh, don't be silly—*everyone* knows where *that's* located) from beneath the chair. "Yesss?" she hisped with three S's.

"I don't know what you're doing, but I want you to stop doing it this instant," her mother ordered. "Is that clearly understood?"

"Huh?—I mean, definitely," Robin hurried, spearing her ear on a loose spring.

Campused

"And what's more, you are campused for two weeks!" Mrs. Boyd continued. "And so are *you*, Ringo Irene Boyd," she completed, having forgotten her younger daughter's name ages ago (not to mention her own.)

"Now go to your rooms," she re-thundered. "Both of you - you -." Then, words failing her, she walked slowly in the direction of the cooking sherry. (At moments like these, later with the yellow pages.)

After stalking into her room, Robin flang off her formal, yanked on pajamas, and flang herself bitterly into her trundle. But it was utterly pointless to even try to sleep. Her eyes just wouldn't stay shut, not even when she weighted the lids down with elderly gum wads.

So, she soon flang herself back out of bed and paced frantically about. (About what?) (Name it, kiddo.)

"*George*," she whispered in agony (a nice place to visit, but you wouldn't really want to live there.) "Come *back*, George. Come back, *Ringo!* Come back *Shane* and *Little Sheba!* Hello, *ANYBODY!*"

Then it happened. The room was suddenly filled with a strange light accompanied by an odd flapping sound. And, as everything went very bright, Ringo (as in Starkey) slowly descended through the ceiling.

Robin (as in Starkers) (that's an out joke) gasped and leaped gracefully into a robe.

"Hullo," he said, a blanket statement if there ever was one. (Orange, that is.) (As in popsickle.)

Robin tried to untangle her left leg from the right sleeve. "What are you doing here?"

"You called me, didn't you?"

Where's George?

Robin re-tangled. "No . . . I mean yes . . . I mean where is George and why were you here before and *were* you here before *and* will someone please tell me what is going *ON?*"

Ringo silenced her by lifting a hand. (One of his own, oddly enough.) "One—I don't know where George is. Two—I was here before because he summoned me, although I seem to have arrived at the wrong moment—sorry about that. Three—I'm here now because I'm your substitute genie. Sort of," he added.

"Sort of?" Robin echoed.

Ringo turned beet red. "Well, my powers are—you might say—limited to granting only—you might say—*unselfish* wishes. And, ummm, I won't be able to extend some of the - er - services George so generously provided . . . understand?"

"Nary a word, you might say."

Ringo cleared his throat. "What I mean is . . . your telephone booth tactics won't work on me."

Robin turned *BEAT* red (never let it be said that this girl doesn't know where it's buttered.) "I *beg your pardon?*" she sniffed haughtily.

Ringo smiled. "You've had a day," he said with unruffled patience. "Go to sleep now and we'll straighten things out tomorrow. And don't you go worrying about anything."

Robin clutched at him for support (not as in alimony.) "Will I get him back?"

Finer Things

Ringo looked deeply into her eyes (not to mention her bangs.) "You may not want him back. There are far finer things in life, you know."

Then he turned to leave, and it was then that Robin knew EX-ACTLY what was going on. At first, she stared openly. Then she seethed openly.

George had not only deserted her. He had cooked *her* goose! The georgeous, jealous, marvelous, evil-tempered, luvley Liverpudlian genie who had been known to shake her until her teeth rattled (in more ways than one) (you better believe it) had seen to it that he was replaced by another absolute angel.

Only *this* one had *wings*.

(To Be Continued Next Week)

. . . THE CHIFFONS ARE WARNING YOU ABOUT THAT "SWEET TALKIN' GUY."

©LP CO., 1965
Starts Writing Instantly
#915
UTILITY MARKER
by **Lindy**®
America's Largest Selling Markers

the one that writes better
Big assortment of Brilliant Colors
Writes on most anything
With the Magic Secret Point

39¢ each

Lindy since 1945

QUALITY IS OUR MOST IMPORTANT PRODUCT

LINDY PEN CO.
north hollywood, calif. 91605 u.s.a.

©LP CO., 1965
Starts Writing Instantly
#916
POCKET SIGN™ PEN
by **Lindy**®
America's Largest Selling Markers

Writes on most anything
Brilliant Ink Colors
Color of Cap and Point Guard is Color of ink
With the Magic Secret Point

49¢ each

Lindy since 1945

QUALITY IS OUR MOST IMPORTANT PRODUCT

LINDY PEN CO.
north hollywood, calif. 91605 u.s.a.

KRLA ARCHIVES

... THE ROBBS (l. to r. Bruce, Dee, Joe and Craig) win their "Race With The Wind."

The Robbs Play For Keeps

By Louise Criscione

Every so often, amid a show packed with top names, a new group wins the opportunity to display their talents—to test whether they've got what it takes to find their own special niche in the overcrowded world of pop. Sometimes they make it — more often they don't.

They're really not expected to. How *can* they hope to surpass, or even equal the stage presence and know-how of an experienced, hit-producing group? The truth is, they usually can't.

But the few who *can*, the select handful who manage to hold an audience which has quite obviously come to see someone else, who don't look entirely amateurish along-side an experienced group, are the ones you can bet will be around for awhile.

In April

You can also bet that it doesn't happen very often but it did happen in April. The group was the Robbs and the place was the Chicago Amphitheatre during Dick Clark's Teen Fair. The thousands of assembled teens had come to see Paul Revere and the Raiders, the Young Rascals, Lou Christie and Freddie Cannon. And into this line-up of "names," were thrown the Robbs.

They had been playing together for almost two years, hitting the usual school dances and civic affairs. People had told them they possessed an unusual amount of talent and naturally they had reeled in the priase — but they had never before been faced with the very *real* problem of matching their talent against that of popular and well-known groups, of holding an audience which did not belong to them.

You probably aren't far off if you think they were nervous and slightly scared. No doubt they were. It was their making or breaking point and no one knew it better then they.

Yet, the four Robbs strode onto the stage with all the calm and cool of a group with ten smash singles behind them, and immediately burst into their first record, "Race With The Wind."

Playin' For Keeps

They took a tremendous chance doing that but they were playing for keeps—or not at all. Here they were, an unknown group singing an unknown song. Either the audience would dig it — or they'd boo the Robbs off the stage with screams of "We want the Raiders" or shouts of "We want the Rascals." But the Robbs felt strongly about the song which Dee Robb had penned and they decided to stick with it.

Specifically, the song details the lament of an individual who is free of social pretensions and sham and who sees things going on about him which his friends don't recognize. Ultimately, "Race With The Wind" is a song about honesty — a person being honest with himself.

It's a rather universal song, as Dee says it stems from an experience which "almost everyone has had happen to them." And so, because they believed in the song, because they felt the audience could identify with it, they went ahead and sang it — sang it for people who had never even *heard* of them before.

And their gamble paid off. They weren't even through the first verse when they began to feel the audience warming up to them and by the time they had finished the song the entire Chicago Amphitheatre was thundering its approval and screaming its acceptance of the Robbs.

They made it — they were "in." Teens began flooding record stores in the Chicago area asking for "Race With The Wind" but the record hadn't even been released yet! When they couldn't find it in the stores, they began phoning the executive offices of Mercury Records in an effort to get their hands on the record.

The Robbs (reminiscent of the Beach Boys) consist of three brothers and a cousin. The brothers are Dee, Joe and Bruce, their cousin is Craig and all four boys sport the last name, Robb.

Dee is the group's perfectionist, admitting: "I'm never quite satisfied with anything I do. Nothing is good enough."

Joe is the extravagant Robb: "When I see something I want, I feel I have to buy it whether I can afford it or not."

Bruce is the witty, funny Robb; his main worries in life are that "smog will obliterate the sun, Batman will be revealed and work will be stopped on the Toledo freeway."

Craig is the poet. He's already had some of his poems published in magazines and spends part of his spare time tracking down books of poetry to add to his collection.

But once on-stage the perfectionist, the extravagant, the witty and the poet become one group of wild and dynamic performers. They've broken in now and they aim to stay. The question is — are you going to let them?

'Folk' Started By The Kingston Trio

By Shannon Leigh

Folk music has become a very important influence on the popular music of today, extending as far as the Beatles, the Stones, and nearly every other successful singing group.

Nearly all of the top groups today have experimented with this form of music in one form or another, whether it was classical folk music or the sort of folk music which Bob Dylan has been credited with writing.

But folk music in the pop field has come a long, long way, and if you think back a few years—you may remember that it found its true beginnings in a hit record which topped the pop charts for many weeks. It was sung by the Kingston Trio and it was a little tune entitled "Tom Dooley."

Folk Artists

After the smash success of that record, the Kingston Trio became established as folk artists and folk music became established as an acceptable form of popular music.

Nearly a decade later, folk music is still going strong in the pop field—and so is the Kingston Trio, however, John Stuart explains:

"We never claimed to be folk *singers* — we're folk *entertainers*. I think if you have to put labels on something — a folk singer is someone who presents folk songs because they're folk songs and the entertainment is within the songs, and not within the presentation.

"We sing many types of songs and we sing them with folk instruments and with folky harmonies, rather than modern harmonies and folky instrumentation.

"When folk music was really popular—then 'Shindig' and the Beatles came along and the pop music fans didn't want to drop their folk root, so the performers adopted both the electricity of 'Shindig' and the Beatles and the folk idiom, and then combined them.

"It seems that all popular music is combined into one now — country and western has a big influence on groups like the Lovin' Spoonful, who are in no way country and western."

Nick Reynolds picked up the conversation here to explain that he did feel that the Trio has been responsible for the pop trend in groups — trios, quartets, and folk choirs—but continued: "I'm not going to say that there would have been no Bobby Dylan without the Kingston Trio!

"But, maybe his interest got started back then with some folk group or singer, but I don't know."

Over the last nine years, the Kingston Trio has produced 26 albums—each and every one of them long-time best-sellers. But never let it be said that these trend-setters allow themselves to get caught *behind* a trend.

Something Else

On their latest album, they have taken the very modern pop sound of electrified instruments — something not traditionally used in the folk medium—and produced an album titled "Something Else" composed of selections rendered entirely in a pop vein.

The new LP is "Something Else"—and so are the Kingston Trio. They may not be folk *singers* —but the *entertainment* which these "folks" have produced for the last decade will appeal to just about everyone.

... THE KINGSTON TRIO (Bob, Nick and John)

KRLA ARCHIVES

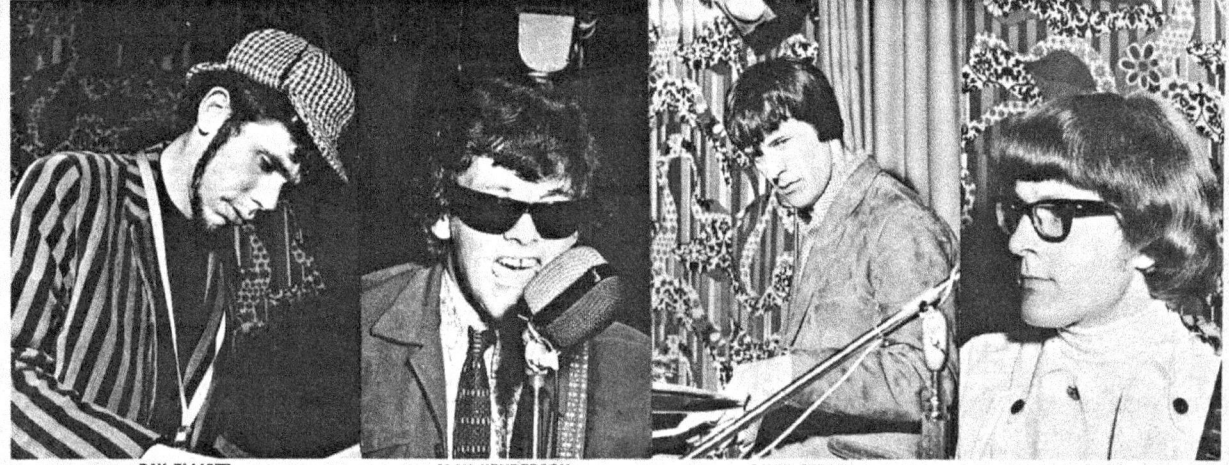

RAY ELLIOTT   ALAN HENDERSON   DAVID TURFEY   JIM ARMSTRONG

The Intense and Mysterious Them

BEAT Photos: Chuck Boyd

By Carol Deck

Them are more than just an awkward name to fit grammatically into a sentence.

Them are an electrified soul sound, kind of like shock with soul. They've taken the intensity of electrification and given it the depth of rhythm and blues with just a touch of jazz.

Them are five distinct, individual human beings from Ireland.

Van Morrison is a tiny bundle of intensity who's almost frightening to watch on stage. But somehow you know that this mystifying bundle isn't really going to explode; he's just going to smoulder.

He's been called a genius, withdrawn and moody. He doesn't talk a lot and particularly doesn't like to be questioned about why or how he wrote any of his songs.

Opening night of their first American club date at Hollywood's Whisky-A-Go-Go — the first time any British group had appeared in an American club out of concert — while the other members of the group met and talked with various other performers, members of the press and fans, Van slipped quietly into an empty booth in the back, slouched down and sat there, all by himself, watching people, until some fans noticed him and asked for autographs.

All Alone

Somehow you got the impression he could have just sat there, all by himself, until he had to go on stage.

Alan Henderson, who with Van is one of the two remaining members of the original group, is a wild dresser but a rather quiet guy who recedes behind his ever-present dark glasses and, like Van, watches people.

On stage he seems to *feel* the real heart of the music more than the others, except for Van, who at times *is* the real heart of their music.

Alan's the one who drives the girls insane.

The brightest dresser of the group has got to be Ray Elliott, who's also a little more talkative than the others.

He's a fan of "funky, modern jazz and blues" and can really belt it out on his sax.

At first meeting he seems to put down a lot of people, but once you gain his respect he's quite an outgoing fellow. He's the cool one of the group.

Jim Armstrong looks like everybody. He looks like a Peter Asher that grew up and stopped grinning. Or maybe he's a Chad Stuart that threw away that motley old brown coat and got a sexy white shinny one.

He's a frank, honest person who seems to be the stabilizing factor in the group. He says their goal is just "to let things happen."

Rare Drummer

David Tufrey, the newest member, is a friendly, outgoing character who smiles a lot (rather rare among drummers) and has quite a memory for names.

He's a fan of "old time jazz, like Thelonious Monk."

Together they are an easy going group, not "uptight" as the expression goes. They seem to have no major hangups.

They do, however, seem very much alone, in a field by themselves. There don't appear to be many hangers-on with this group.

It's not because no one cares, but because Them don't *need* to be constantly surrounded by adoring people.

You can't always understand the lyrics when Van really gets going, but it seems unimportant. He's creating a mood — a mood that's often similar to an electric shock, but with a lot of real down to earth soul.

And singing is just about the only self-expression Van has. He just doesn't communicate with people, so if you want to know Van, listen to him sing.

He says more when he's singing than he'll ever say in conversation.

He says everything he has to say in the songs he writes and sings.

So listen to him.

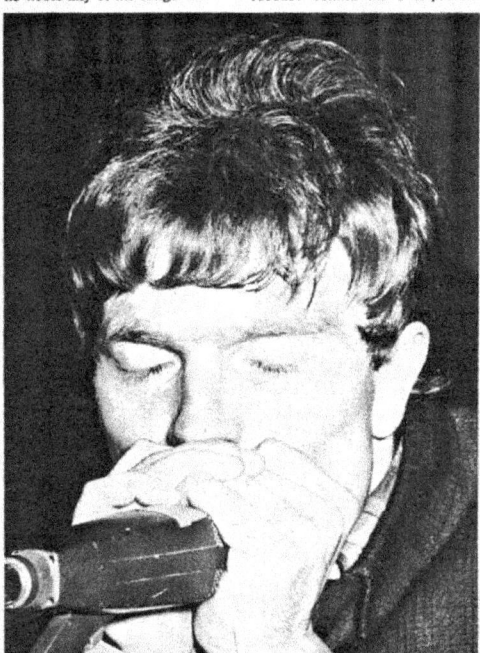

VAN MORRISON — TINY BUNDLE OF SMOULDERING INTENSITY   ... A RARE PICTURE OF THEM FOOLING AROUND. NOTE — EVEN VAN SMILING.

KRLA ARCHIVES

'Day For Decision'

While many people are still debating the merits of Johnny Sea's "Day For Decision," others are making it one of the fastest rising and most popular records in the nation.

The single, a patriotic narrative against a musical background, moved so fast that Warner Brothers was forced to charter an airplane to move 12,000 copies into Chicago last week. Sales in the first three days of release exceeded 80,000.

The record has overcome an obstacle that threatened its early success. Radio stations were at first hesitant about playing it because of its unusual length. But listener reaction in most instances was so positive that stations were soon forced to play it. In many cases a single play by a station brought a deluge of telephone calls requesting more plays.

Decca Records has released a 3-1/2 minute version (Sea's is a lengthy five minute version) sung by Buddy Starcher. But the Decca record is somewhat altered and it looks like it would have an almost impossible time overtaking Sea's recording for Warner Brothers.

Several radio stations were so impressed with Sea's record and its overnight popularity that they announced that the disc was a "must" for every show even if it was necessary to triple advertising spots to get it in. And in St. Louis a radio station pre-empted a five minute newscast to play the record.

In Chicago, three high schools sent special messengers to the local distributing company for copies of the record to play at their assemblies. Many religious groups have also approved of the record, and a number of churches in the Chicago area played the record during their Sunday services.

And in areas where "all talk" shows have become popular, "Day For Decision" has been played continually to stimulate phone-in discussions.

Orlando, Florida had an even more striking reaction to the controversial disc. The single became the number one phone requested record after only one play by a local station. This was typical of the widespread audience reaction to the song.

Other Views

But on the other side of the fence, "Day For Decision" is drawing violent negative reactions. Several radio stations have banned the song from the air and held firm in their original policy. And the song has become a symbol for political groups on many of the nation's college campuses. It has been accepted by many conservatives and condemned by most liberals.

Most of the charges against the song are that it is extremely reactionary and encourages war, and that it commercializes upon something that should be intrinsic.

Most of the entertainers interviewed by The BEAT said they disagreed with the total concept of the song, but some said it was poorly written lyrics that made the song distasteful to them.

But the real test of any record lies in its ability to sell, and under this standard "Day For Decision" is a highly successful recording. It is tabbed as a million seller, and it is already more than halfway there.

"Day For Decision" wasn't the first recording by Johnny Sea, but it certainly will be his biggest and it is easily his most controversial. It also was his first disc to be accepted on the pop music scene, with all his other's appealing to a country and western audience.

Ironically, Sea's agent, Stan Hoffman, says the record wasn't necessarily aimed at the younger audience. "It was just aimed at Americans in general," he said last week. "Johnny, myself and everybody associated with the record felt it was simply something that needed to be said . . . to everyone."

Johnny Sea obviously feels more needs to be said because he is now recording an album—entitled "Day For Decision"—that will be released shortly. It is his first album.

It was only for the album to follow after the widespread acceptance of "Day For Decision." Hoffman says the album will contain songs like the original hit as well as some slow country and western music.

Country Singer

Johnny Sea is generally considered strictly a country and western singer. He received a fair amount of prominence in this field after his recordings of "Frankie's Man Johnny," "Nobody's Darlin' But Mine," "My Baby Walks All Over Me" and "My Old Faded Rose." But "Day For Decision" threatens to sell more records than all of his other singles combined.

Johnny got his start in professional singing after he won a state talent competition in Georgia at the age of 17. A talent scout heard him and immediately signed him to a contract.

After recording on two different labels, he moved to Nashville where he appeared almost regularly on the Grand Ole Opry, the number one country and western variety show in America.

Alan Peltelrer, who is affiliated with Sea, first heard "Day of Decision" in Nashville several months ago and contacted Johnny and told him about it.

Sea and his manager both liked the song and they signed with Warner Brothers to produce it.

Sea was placed in immediate demand for appearances after the release of his single. He agreed to the Berlin goodwill tour, has been booked on the Ed Sullivan show and Time magazine is rushing a feature article on him.

Whether Sea will quit country and western singing and devote full time to this type of song even after the release of his album is speculation. He is in Berlin now on an entertaining tour of American service bases. He is scheduled to return later this month.

. . . JOHNNY SEA

Entertainers Divided On 'Day For Decision'

Some have called them cruel and facist, others have praised them and lauded their patriotism . . . few have ignored them.

The war in Viet Nam has had a greater impact upon the popular music scene than perhaps any other single event in history. More than 300 records dealing with the war have been released, and current indications point to more of the same.

If anything, you can look for an increase in both the number of Viet Nam records released and their firm pro-or-con position concerning the war.

Basically, the war songs are divided into two distinct groups. They are the super-patriotic songs that condemn American apathy, and the ones that aim against war in general. The first category greatly leads the second in both total releases and total sales.

S/Sgt. Barry Sadler, who was in a U. S. hospital recovering from a wound he received in Viet Nam, found the greatest success with war songs. His "Green Berets" single topped nationwide charts for many weeks and he followed that up with the number one album in the country.

As can be expected, both groups of songs have been met by heavy criticism on some fronts, praise on others. The war song controversy was extended and intensified late last month with the release of John Sea's "Day of Decision." There are those who label it "korny" and "a deliberate attempt to undermine our position in Viet Nam." Others firmly believe it is a sincere effort to aid American patriotism. Entertainers, for the most part, disagree with the concept of war songs.

"I think they're very commercial things," said Russ Giguere of the Association. "I'm not saying that the people who make them do so just to make money, but right now almost anything along that line will sell. It seems like they're just capitalizing on a tragedy.

"Then again, I don't like the songs protesting war. I think they have very little to offer. Yet they leave a lasting impression. Bob Dylan, for instance, hasn't written protest songs for several years, but he's still considered a protest singer."

Howard Kalan of the Turtles had even stronger feelings about war songs.

"Negative isn't the word for my feelings about war songs," he said. "They all seem to be trying to give the impression that 'the fatherland is invincible.' They tell you that America is so mighty and so innately right that we should go to war with anybody who disagrees with us."

On Barry Sadler — "I hate to see a military man spring up and become a star overnight. He glorifies the concept of war. One line from 'Green Berets' really made me sick. It was the one where the guy is dying and he says 'O.K., just make sure my son fights and dies like I did.' This is a heckova thing for a young widow to look forward to."

"Now don't get me wrong, I dig patriotism. There are some lines from "Day of Decision" that I think are groovy. But the total concept of this and other war songs encourages hate, war and destruction."

The popularity of this type song, however, can't be questioned. "Day of Decision" is one of the fastest rising records on the charts and one of the most requested.

"Eve of Destruction" by Barry McGuire was involved in the same kind of controversy prior to "Day of Decision." It was immensely popular on most of the nation's college campuses, but many radio stations refused to play it on the air because of such staunch, varied reaction to it.

But whether it is pro or con, war songs are drawing a reaction and are being talked about. It looks like they'll be around for a while.

And Sonny Says . . .

"I haven't been impressed with any of the so-called war or protest songs. But I don't automatically condemn a song just because it deals with that kind of topic."

"I think a thing — any thing — can be said very beautifully or it can be said very distastefully. When I look at a song this is what I look at and this is how I form my reaction to it."

"I didn't particularly like 'Eve of Destruction' or 'Day For Decision' because I didn't like the way they said what they had to say. Both dealt with important, worthwhile subjects but yet they seemed to have little to offer me."

KRLA ARCHIVES

GLENN YARBROUGH
The Portrait Of A Man

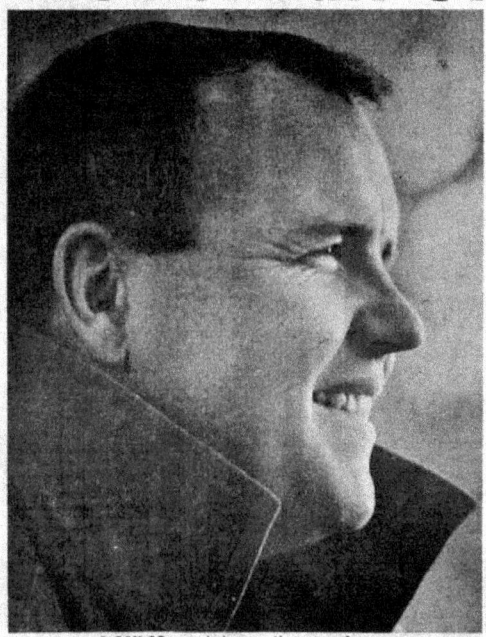

... A SAILOR, a scholar — then a performer

By Shannon Leigh

"THANK YOU"

"As a sailor I am grateful for simple things: a good breeze, a sturdy craft, and a safe harbor. But as a singer, my appreciation goes beyond those things, and I must say thanks to the people who compose and arrange the songs I sing, to the musicians who bring those songs to life, and most of all, to you, the audience, whose appreciation makes it all worthwhile."

The words of Glenn Yarbrough: words of a sailor, a scholar, a singer. The words of a man.

Glenn has been singing since early childhood and has been the recipient of vocal scholarships in high school as well as in universities.

When given the freedom of choice, Glenn prefers the study of philosophy – classical Greek and pre-Socratic – and the restless wind which blows his boat, The Pilgrim, over boundless seas to the confines of entertainment. But when he faces his profession as a singer, it is a headlong collision and he is talent and professionalism all the way.

"I just try to do good songs. I don't care whether their pedigree is Broadway, folk or rock and roll. It is vital that the melody be so good that it becomes a vehicle for the words; it must be good enough to stay in the background. The words must have the most importance."

As a man of the sea, Glenn explains: "Another thing the sea does for me is it removes me from the pressing details of my other life and allows me to spend long periods of contemplation."

And Glenn's contemplations extend into many different fields of thought. For example, to youth: "Kids are a lot smarter than they used to be, and they're not hung up with sociological problems that turn to cruelty and violence. I think there's a lot more brotherly love."

And life? It sort of revolves around the question 'why?' "That's life, actually. I think that the minute you stop asking *why*, you might as well be *dead* because that's the whole point of it. I don't think we're ever going to find the answers but the whole purpose of life is the *search*."

Searching

Glenn Yarbrough is a man of constant search. He is constantly seeking new songs with great lyrics, and in his search for better material he has found another man who shares with him a love of life and living. The man is Rod McKuen, also a singer, and a highly sensitive and talented songwriter.

Glenn has formed a strong union with Rod – both in their business ventures with a joint publishing company, and even more importantly in their unique composer-performer relationship.

Just recently, Glenn recorded an album entitled "Glenn Yarbrough – The Lonely Things." It is a beautiful collection of the love songs of Rod McKuen – sung as only Glenn can sing, or should I say *live* them – forming a story told in twelve poignant verses.

A scholar himself, Glenn is currently involved in the formation of long-range plans which he is making for a school which he hopes to establish within the next four to five years.

It will be a very special school, tutoring children from broken homes, orphans, displaced children, from all over the country. The school will be a complete entity within itself, where the children will live and learn guided by highly trained instructors, at the head of whom will be Glenn himself.

Wide-Scope Plans

It is a plan tremendous in scope, but one which Glenn has been developing for a number of years, and has now brought to the very brink of its realization. The only further necessity is a financial one, and this is one of Glenn's main purposes for being an entertainer.

He has frequently admitted that he doesn't really enjoy his life as a singer, the pressures and grinds of a performer. He has always freely admitted that his original purpose in becoming a performer was only to gain enough money to enable him to continue his studies. But it continued beyond that, and it was a continuation which eventually led Glenn to one of his many solitary sojourns across the mighty ocean.

He left the world of people and music and pressures for the calm of the sea where he could think things out. He found something among those salty waves: the realization that he was pushing forward in a business he didn't really enjoy so that he could one day establish his school, and further develop the process of cultivating and enriching the human mind.

Greater Peace

And when he returned, he returned with a little greater sense of peace within himself. The world will lose something of great value when Glenn retires to his school. The high, clear, sweet notes of his voice will no longer conduct a love affair with the walls of coffee houses and concert halls. But as we lose, so shall we gain. A teacher, a father, a philosopher, a pioneer – all these will be *our* benefits.

Glenn Yarbrough is less a folk singer, less a performer, than he is a man. But he is a great man.

Len Barry

(Continued from Page 1)

groups. They are found in short-haired, "well-dressed" groups and artists as well.

Long hair should never be used as a replacement for talent, but who can possibly say that the Spoonful and the Animals are not talented? Granted, they are not in the same bag Barry's in but in their own fields they are talented.

Another interesting question, and one which William Morris is probably acquiring tremendous headaches over, is: "If Len doesn't want to be booked with long-haired groups, who in the world CAN he be booked with?"

Would you believe Len is trying desperately to break into the adult night club bag and doesn't want to be booked with any pop performers? It is the only place in the entertainment field where rock groups and solo artists are not widely accepted. There are, however, certain groups who ARE accepted by both the teen and adult markets. You don't suppose Len is attempting to become one of these select few, do you? Or could it be that Len has decided he doesn't want to have anything at all to do with the teen market?

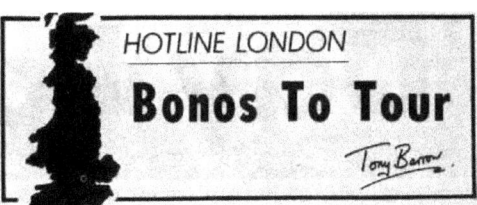

HOTLINE LONDON
Bonos To Tour

Tony Barrow

A few weeks ago in *BEAT* you may have read my HOTLINE LONDON open letter to SONNY AND CHER, drawing the attention of Mr. and Mrs. Bono to the fact that the twosome's London representative, Larry Page, was having problems getting hold of them via transatlantic telephone.

My piece in *BEAT* had positive and immediate results – within hours of the publication of that particular issue Sonny used the London telephone number I printed in my Open Letter to call up Larry Page. Sonny explained that the Bono number had to be changed almost daily because of the fantastic volume of fan calls which came through.

Larry Page tells me he enjoyed a long and friendly conversation with Sonny and made concrete plans for the return of Sonny and Cher to the UK this summer. The popular duo will undertake one major television spectacular in London and are expected to make just a single concert appearance here.

Larry is hoping to line up London's impressive Royal Albert Hall as the concert venue and Britain's "Wild Thing" chart-toppers THE TROGGS will appear with Sonny and Cher on the show.

Thank you, Mr. and Mrs. B. for taking care of the problem so promptly, proving in the process your obvious interest in what's happening on the UK side of the Atlantic. Look forward to seeing you here in London next month!

RAVI SHANKAR, the Indian classical musician whose work has inspired the Byrds, Yardbirds, Stones and Beatles to turn their ears towards the mystic music of the East, is in London all thru June. In fact his very first U.K. single record was issued here on June 10, the day The Beatles released "Paperback Writer" on our side of the Atlantic.

Of all the pop guitarists who have taken to experimenting with sitar sounds, I guess Beatle GEORGE HARRISON is the most dedicated student of Eastern musical culture. It's highly likely that George will spend time with Shankar in London before the end of June and the most obvious meeting place for the pair is the headquarters of the Asian Music Circle.

We're always hearing about internal on-stage and off-duty arguments within top British beat groups. Much of the information has very little truth in it and starts as a rumor which gains in exaggerated falsehoods as it passes from mouth to mouth.

On the other hand there's a certain amount of evidence to support the idea that friction exists within THE KINKS and THE WHO. Latest trouble led to Who drummer KEITH MOON threatening that he'd quit the group. The threat followed an incident during a provincial concert performance when Who leader PETE TOWNSEND swung his guitar around with violent force and Keith sustained not only a black eye but a leg injury which took three stitches to close the cut.

Whether the injuries were the result of a willful attack or a serious error of judgment on Pete's part we may never know, but Keith Moon left the stage with wounds which cannot be collected during any average pop performance!

NEWS BRIEFS ... BEATLES cannot claim that their just-completed album-making sessions set up any kind of long-run record – next YARDBIRDS album has been in slow but concentrated production since last November! ... TAMLA MOTOWN power in Britain shrinking swiftly – U.K. visits for MARTHA AND THE VANDELLAS plus STEVIE WONDER called off ... In all other U.K. charts THE ROLLING STONES made top spot after two weeks with "Paint It, Black" but *Disc and Music Echo* placed them second and put newcomers THE TROGGS and "Wild Thing" at Number One ... RAY DAVIES has penned "Sunny Afternoon" for new KINKS single. Composition is a sequel to "Well Respected Man" and "Dedicated Follower Of Fashion" ... "From Nowhere Came THE TROGGS" is the thoroughly appropriate album title chosen by our "Wild Thing" hitmaking unit ... KINKS in Spain and other European countries during the period they were scheduled for their summer U.S. visit ... PERCY SLEDGE, fast-rising Top Twenty climber in the U.K., due here mid-July for TV and concerts ... JAY AND THE AMERICANS hope to record single plus album by THE WALKER BROTHERS at least a month before it is released in the U.K.... 77 year old MISS RUBY MILLER is pathetic U.K. answer to MRS. ELVA MILLER ... EVERLY BROTHERS will record several original numbers passed to them by THE HOLLIES ... Beach Boy BRUCE JOHNSTON is expected to supervise a series of London recording sessions this summer when he'll produce various British groups. U.K. surf-styled combo TONY RIVERS AND THE CASTAWAYS could be amongst them ... Unlikely to click in England – the shoal of third-rate BATMAN records which are flooding the U.K. market this month.

KRLA ARCHIVES

The BEAT Goes To The Movies
"Maya"

By Jim Hamblin

Our first question was how do you pronounce the title of the picture? It it MY-yuh, not MAY-yuh. And Maya is a big friendly elephant, who has a little baby elephant. And Maya dies fighting for that little elephant ... who is a very special one, a sacred white elephant.

This picture should have been entitled, *"Dennis The Menace Goes To India"*, and 13-year old Jay North isn't any better fighting Pythons and cheetahs than he was as the mean little kid. As a matter of fact the humans in the film are downright *insipid*.

Produced by the King Brothers, who also gave us *"The Brave One"*, this adventure story is, however, a first-rate film for any kiddie matinee. And if you happen to be a kiddie, or know someone who is, we recommend it.

But mostly because of Maya. Clint Walker shuffles through this one in the most vague performance of his career.

But shooting on location in India, the camera could hardly miss the grandeur of the natural scenery, and the cleverness of the animals used.

MOST EXCITING SCENE: A one-eyed bad guy has tried to hurt Maya's baby, and got her mad, and now he steals the little one altogether. Maya goes on a rampage, tearing apart whole houses to find the villain. Finally after toppling a bus he's hiding in, and watching it slide into a lake, Maya is happy and calm once again.

There is an old legend that the lion is the "king of beasts" in the jungle, but that was probably a rumor started by Metro-Goldwyn-Mayer (whose Leo adorns their trademark) but Maya shows you who is *really* the boss!

... An Angry Mama rips down a few obstacles in the path of revenge.

... Huck Finn and his raft, done the hard way ...

The BEAT Goes To Another Movie
"The Lost Command"

By Jim Hamblin
(The BEAT Movie Editor)

The men are parachuted in to re-inforce a vicious attack. They are machine-gunned to death as they float down. Most of them are dead by the time they reach the ground. Others are massacred shortly after they touch down and still struggle with their canopy. The slaughter is being watched helplessly by Anthony Quinn, who suddenly lurches out and rescues at least two of the men. The place is French Indo-China. But since 1954 it's been called *Viet Nam*, and that is what makes this film so timely. Maybe you have a brother or son fighting there. This will not be a pleasant picture to watch, but it may give you an insight into the fighting.

The picture is not all that easy to follow. The action is seemingly un-motivated at times. Buy all in all there's enough excitement to keep any audience interested.

It deals only with the very early years of the fighting, and only concerns the French. Quinn portrays a soldier of fortune who wants a General's star as much as he wants anything. He is a rough trainer. And he has one rule for fighting a war. And maybe you'll agree it's a good one: "Don't die!"

... The prelude to the Viet Nam war frames a background for a Columbia feature.

KRLA ARCHIVES

KRLA ARCHIVES

America's Largest Teen NEWSpaper 15¢

KRLA Edition BEAT
JULY 2, 1966

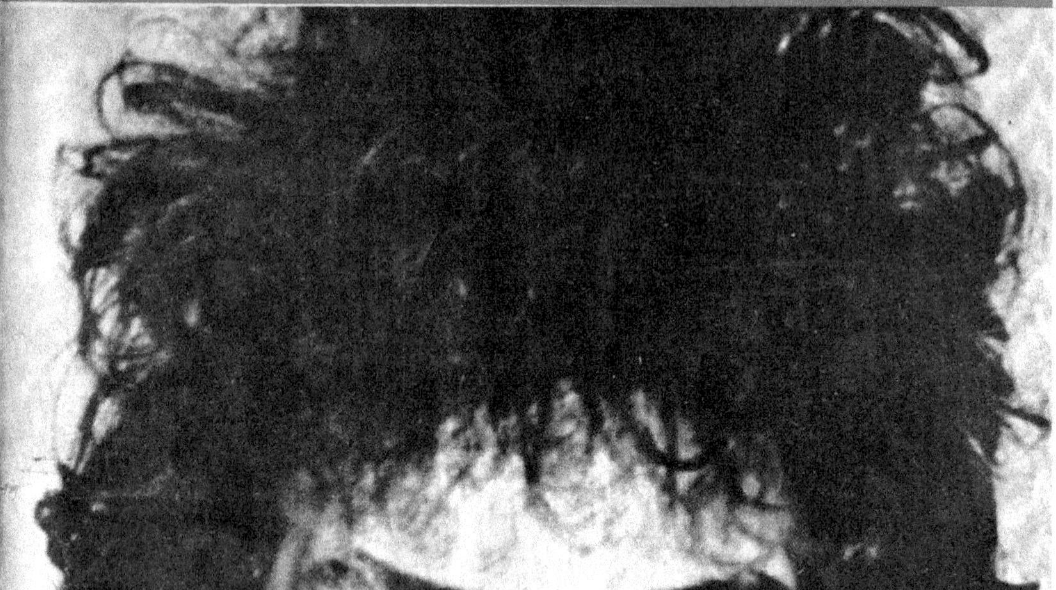

Bob Dylan — Europe's Fall Of An Idol?

KRLA BEAT

Volume 2, Number 16   July 2, 1966

Dylan A Complete Bomb In Europe

By Tony Barrow

Bob Dylan's British concert tour ended with a mighty bang at London's Royal Albert Hall. Dylan seemed determined to break off between items and deliver a series of pungent speeches to his audience on subjects ranging from rock 'n roll to "drug songs."

At one point, Dylan declared that he would never play any more concerts in England. Matters came to a head at the start of his second segment when the star brought on his group and the crowd objected to the over-loud instrumental backings from the two guitars, thundering organ and pounding drums.

In *Disc* and *Music Echo*, critic Ray Coleman comments: "Dylan is great but with that sort of row going on behind him he insults his own talent."

During the second half of the show, a section of the audience yelled and booed. Many stormed out of the hall while Dylan fought back with angry words from the platform.

We've never seen anything like it before. Nor had the Beatles, who were amongst the concert audience that night.

AND IN PARIS...

Dylan ran into the same sort of resistance from his audiences. It was Bob's first visit to France and his concert at the Paris Olympia was a complete sell-out. However, Dylan's Paris audience was as shocked as his British audience when Bob took roughly a ten minute break between each song, utilizing the time to tune his guitar.

At one point in the Olympia concert, the audience began whistling loudly during the long break between songs and Dylan looked down on them and said: "I'm just as anxious to go home as you are. Don't you have any paper to read?"

As expected, Dylan was crucified by the French press. One paper carried the banner headline: "Bob Dylan, Go Home..." while another and more conservative paper described Dylan's concert as, "the fall of an idol."

Amid Controversy Troggs Break-Out

By Louise Criscione

Probably never before has a *totally* unknown group caused the amount of comment and controversy (not to mention record sales) as the Troggs from England and their "Wild Thing." In the midst of a heated argument between Atco and Fontana Records, "Wild Thing" began its national break-out and the Troggs launched their quest for public recognition.

The conflict between Atco and Fontana is simple—they *both* claim the Troggs' disc belongs to them and, thus, have each issued the record on their respective labels.

But the Troggs don't seem the least bit upset about the label mix-up; they're too happy with their newly-discovered success. One gets the definite impression that deep down they never *really* thought they'd make it. They've been together only since the early part of '66 but in the span of those few months they've received more publicity than many established groups. In fact, Tony Barrow has been mentioning them in *The BEAT* for weeks and weeks now.

(Turn to Page 8)

Inside the BEAT

Letters To The Editor 2
Beatles Banned Cover 3
Young Rascals At Phone Booth 4-5
For Girls Only 6
Mama's And Papa's 7
Beatles On TV—A Bomb? 10
D.J. Awards 11
Vic Slams Len 12
Adventures Of Robin Boyd 14
Beat Goes To The Movies 15

The BEAT is published weekly by BEAT Publications, Inc., editorial and advertising offices at 6290 Sunset Blvd., Suite 504, Hollywood, California 90028, U.S. bureaus in Hollywood, San Francisco, New York, Chicago and Nashville, overseas correspondents in London, Liverpool and Manchester, England. Sale price, 15 cents. Subscription price, U.S. and possessions, $5 per year, Canada and foreign rates, $9 per year. Second class postage prepaid at Los Angeles, California.

'Green Berets' Banned by Reds

"Ballad of the Green Berets" is rapidly becoming the number one song in East Germany even though it has been banned and is not available in sheet music or records.

The song, written and originally sung by S/Sgt. Barry Sadler, is being picked up by East German youth behind the Iron Curtain via tape recording from the U.S. military's Armed Forces Network stations in West Berlin and West Germany.

The Communist Youth newspaper Junge Welt (Young World) said that the song, praising U.S. special forces in Viet Nam, is being sung all over East Germany by youth and is being played at many dances.

While the song is generally popular with the East Germans, however, some youths greatly disapprove of it. After hearing the song played at a dance, one youth wrote to Junge Welt: "I was outraged at this brazen display of disloyalty to our Socialist ideals. We do not need such songs from 'the other side'. We have enough good songs of our own."

But the general concensus among youth is that the song is greatly acceptable. One girl "amazed" Junge Welt editors when she said she often heard the song and liked it.

The song is at the top of music charts in West Germany under the title "Hundert Mann und ein Befehl."

KRLA ARCHIVES

Letters TO THE EDITOR

Not All Phil Spector

Dear BEAT:

After reading the May 7th issue of The BEAT, I simply had to sit down and write to you. The front page article entitled "Spector's Side Of The Brothers Story" made my blood boil.

First of all, let me start by saying that I, personally, consider Phil somewhat of a musical genius and do not wish to put him down in any way; however, some of the statements quoted from Danny Davis are so erroneous that I just couldn't let them pass by. For instance, I do not think all the credit for the Righteous Brothers' success should be given to Phil. Granted, the record "You've Lost That Lovin' Feeling" was a sensational recording and brought them national recognition, but they weren't quite "unknown" before that.

Phil most certainly did not find them in Orange County, earning $15 a night. When he became interested in them, they were one of Southern and Northern California's biggest names; had already had a chart record behind them, "Little Latin Lupe Lu;" and had appeared with the Beatles on their first American tour. As their agent at that time, I can assure you that they were making no small amount of money and were already in the $1500 to $2000 a night category on the West Coast.

As a matter of fact, in addition to all that, they were appearing as regulars on a network television show. All this was prior to their association with Mr. Spector.

With regard to the current legal feud going on between Phil and the boys, I know nothing and will say nothing. But having been their agent for the first two years of their career, I am well familiar with their past. I am aware of the progress they have made and of the significance of their relationship with Phil Spector and Philles Records and do not intend to belittle this in any way. However, neither do I feel that it is fair to minimize the talent of Bob and Bill and insinuate that without any one person they would have amounted to nothing.

With their talent, sooner or later, one way or another, they would have become an important part of the music world. I'm just happy that it happened quickly, for they deserve it; and I am proud to know that I had a small part of helping them along the way; and even prouder to have them as friends.

Thanks for listening.

Julie Steddom

'Animals Are Indeed Dead'

Dear BEAT:

I am a BEAT subscriber and I wish to voice a brief opinion, if there is such a thing! This letter refers to the article, "The Animals Are Dead."

The author of this article must surely be an aware person and a highly competent one. The fine obituary by B.A. Tremayne was very realistic and not the least bit fatalistic. I hope that many people besides myself noticed that.

The Animals are indeed dead. Ever since "It's My Life" their records have decreased in quality. They've been making very few live performances and those they've made they've pretty well botched up. They've lost their "soul" and their "certain something."

When they lost Alan Price they lost their foothold. Alan Price was more than just an organist, just as James Brown is more than just a singer. Alan was a unique person, perhaps the "backbone" of the Animals. Alan is something that could never be replaced by a Dave Rowberry, or for that matter anybody else.

When John Steel departed the grave stone was put in position.

Gone is the innefably talented group that gave us personality, charm and our money's worth for an album.

K.E. Thomas

Animals Alive

Dear BEAT:

You printed one side of the Animal story. Now, I hope you print the other. True, Alan and Johnny are gone but that's no reason to condemn the whole group. They have two great guys taking their place.

I don't think there will ever be as great a drummer as Johnny, but it doesn't mean the group's sound or blues feeling and beat is gone with the wind. Look at their new disc, "Don't Bring Me Down." You can't say that has a dead sound!

B.A. Tremayne has bats in his brain. He has no right to say the Animals cannot sing anymore just because two of the originals have left the group. Maybe two of the Animals are dead but the Animals' sound is very much alive.

Prissy Martin

Beatles Stink!

Dear BEAT:

The Beatles' latest single just proves what I've always thought—they can put out anything and it'll sell! When are people gonna wise up? They're "Paperback Writer" stinks! And for that matter, so have their last several releases.

Howard Evans

GI's Say Thanks

Dear BEAT:

I would like to convey my congratulations and on behalf of the many GI's here at the 93rd Signal Battalion in Darmstadt, Germany for your great newspaper, The BEAT.

I have had my sister in California send the issues of BEAT each week. Believe me, I feel that I can speak for the many who admire your newspaper. It makes us feel as if we were back home reading up-to-date, inside information on the pop music world.

Pvt. Jesse Mendoza

P.S. To show how great The BEAT is, this month's issue of Tiger BEAT show's Mick Jagger reading the article, "Stoned," which recently appeared in The BEAT!!!

Thanks for your fab letter—makes us proud to know we're dug in Germany! Our best to the 93rd and we hope you'll all be coming Stateside soon.

The BEAT

Beatle Survey

Dear BEAT:

I would like to tell you how deeply grateful I am to you and Shirley Poston for printing the questions and results to my Beatle Survey. Thank you so very, very, much. And what a great honor—the results printed on page one!!

I'll be buying about eight extra copies of The BEAT for my pen pals. Again, my deepest thanks and keep up the fantastic work on the world's greatest pop paper.

April Orcutt

P.S. The picture of Paul on the cover was definitely one of the best I've ever seen of him. Wow!!!

Even Wet Suits

Dear BEAT:

As a boy, I don't give a darn if a group has long hair, short hair, wears suits, knickers or shorts! If they have talent and a good sound, they're okay by me.

As far as the Young Rascals go, I think they've got a great sound (saw them in person several times) so I'd go to see them again even if they wore wet suits!

Gary Miles

Rascals

Dear BEAT:

Since The BEAT is the paper with the best coverage of the Young Rascals and even better than what I have found in magazines, I wish, and am asking for a reply on where I can write to them, the Young Rascals as a group and individually.

Thank you and keep up the good work.

Carolyn Keuther

You may write to the Rascals at 1841 Broadway, New York 23, New York.

The BEAT

A Groovy Love

Dear BEAT:

Thank you very much for giving us the story behind the Mindbenders' beautiful song, "A Groovy Kind Of Love." It's a nice success story and I wish there were some way to let the Mindbenders know how much I appreciate their song.

It's really a pleasure to listen to—pretty in the best sense of the word. The tempo is smooth and relaxing, the melody is flowing, the lyrics are tender and the lead singer's tone is so sincere that we know he means it. He must be in love himself to be able to sing of love so convincingly. Certainly he gives hope to those of us who haven't found true love yet.

Carol Anne Riis

Local Groups?

Dear BEAT:

It would sure be nice to have a few articles about what's going on locally in San Francisco. Maybe not in every issue but occasionally. For instance, the Lovin' Spoonful came to Sausalito during their engagement at the hungry i. The We Five once lived here and return as often as they can. The Beau Brummels are often around.

The Supremes are at the Fairmont and Herman, the Beatles, the Stones and many other groups are returning to San Francisco this summer.

Donna Rodriguez

Beach Boys

Dear BEAT:

I really think Tony Barrow's recent article, "What Do You Really Want From Your Favorite Group?" was a little weird.

The American sounds are a little alike. I mean, our U.S. groups usually put out recordings which sound like the records before. What would you do if the Beach Boys, for instance, changed their sound completely?

You wouldn't buy their records anymore, right? They have experimented with a little change here and there but, fortunately, they haven't made any drastic changes in their music. We like them for what they are, not what they could be.

Nancy Fox

Brian Wilson, will, no doubt, be overjoyed to hear that you don't think the Beach Boys' sound has changed much!

The BEAT

English Finks!

Dear BEAT:

So Mick Jagger hates America does he? And what else is new? I thought all Englishmen in general, and members of English pop groups in particular, hated America. I mean, Herman doesn't like it. The Beatles don't like it... fact is, I don't recall reading anything complimentary... no, wait a minute. That's not true. When the English pop stars are in America, they say complimentary things... it's when they get back to England we discover how two-faced they are.

I've pretty much concluded the English are endowed with rotten dispositions (they don't give opinions—they issue critiques... snide, snotty, or simpering), and who should expect them to like anything—or anyone (there is a poem that goes—roughly—thusly: ('the French hate the Germans, the Germans hate the Dutch, and the English don't like anybody very much.') I believe it.

I don't suppose this 'hatred' will be mutual. Americans are masochists. I expect we'll accept the insults and overlook the bad mouths. But not this American broad. As far as I'm concerned, the English are a herd of finks, snobs, and parasites who have mastered the art of looking down their noses. I hope they grow warts. In all the wrong places.

Jackie Genovese

BEAT Lacking?

Dear BEAT:

I have been reading your newspaper ever since it first came out and I must say that it is really great. Everytime I get a BEAT I can't wait to read the ravings of Shirley Poston or the Adventures of the dear Robin Boyd. I always look forward to Hotline London and On The Beat by Louise Criscione.

But I think that The BEAT is lacking in one area. This area is the personal side of any newspaper, big or small. Even the huge newspaper chains have a Dear Abby or a Dear Ann Landers column. And I think, being a loyal BEAT reader, that is all you lack.

Terri Hamann

How about the rest of you? Think we need a personal column?

The BEAT

Resents Mold

Dear BEAT:

I just read the article called "What Do You Really Want From Your Favorite Group?" and I'm mad! I do respect Tony Barrow's views but really, what right does he have to lump all teen American record buyers into one dull mold?

He's practically saying that British pop fans are more intelligent! It all depends on how you look at it. I mean, there are intelligent pop fans in the U.S. too. A lot of people I know can't stand half of the ordinary-type songs on the charts today. They are very careful of what records they buy. This goes for me too.

And that bit about the Beatles spending extra long hours recording a number to get it just right. Well, I do respect them for it and I know many others who do too. Haven't record sales proven anything?

Well, I've said my piece. I know this probably won't be printed but I just had to let you know that I truly resent being thrust into one mold.

Kathy Torres

KRLA ARCHIVES

On the BEAT
By Louise Criscione

What a week this was! Jay (of Jay and the Americans) informed the world of his tastes in music, Jeff Beck admitted that he can't really play the sitar, the Rascals formed their own publishing firm, Chas Chandler said some nasty things about America, Eric Burdon is going to make a movie, one of the Fortunes split, Pete Quaife of the Kinks was injured in a car accident and Mick Jagger didn't have anything to say! And quite sadly, Roy Orbison's wife, Claudette, was killed in a motorcycle accident.

The BEAT would like to express our sympathy to Roy Orbison. He and his wife were returning on separate motorcycles from a racing function in Tenn. A car pulled into an intersection without stopping and Mrs. Orbison's motorcycle ploughed into the side of the car. She was taken to the Summer County Memorial Hospital where she died two hours later. The driver of the car is being held by local police on charges of involuntary manslaughter.

Doesn't Dig Barry

On a little happier note, I guess, is Jay Black's musical tastes. "People buy records to escape from the troubles of the world; they don't want to hear about the war or Vietnam. I don't like Barry Sadler's records because they bring fighting and death into records. There's another one who did that—Barry McGuire. 'Eve Of Destruction' was the same thing."

Jeff Beck, genius of the guitar, says he can't play the sitar. "I've messed around with one," confessed Jeff, "but I can't play well enough to play it commercially. I haven't got one of my own."

... JAY BLACK

The Young Rascals have formed their own publishing firm which is affiliated with BMI. The first songs in the new publishing firm are "You Better Run," "Love Is A Beautiful Thing" and "Do You Feel It." I'd give you three guesses as to the name of their publishing firm but you wouldn't even need that many. It's SLACSAR. Rascals spelled backwards. Naturally.

I keep telling you—if there's a more outspoken group than the Stones it has to be Eric Burdon and his Animals (or what's left of them.) This week it was Chas Chandler's turn to knock America (newest "in" craze in England.) Anyway, Chas says about America: "It's all a big drag. No matter how good a time you have on stage in the States, it's the attitude over there that begins to get you down."

I wonder, then, why the Animals keep coming back? They're all set to co-star with Herman on a giant Stateside tour kicking off in July. Maybe it's the American money they like?

Eric's Movie

However, I guess they don't dig the money all that much either because they're cutting short their Stateside tour in order for Eric Burdon to make a movie. Apparently, the rest of the group isn't too jazzed about Eric's movie plans because it was strongly hinted in England that the group all but broke up over the situation.

But Eric's movie really does sound great. It is being made by Universal and will star Eric in a dramatic role, playing a pop singer who builds a religion around himself. The purpose of the film is to show the hold pop stars have on their fans.

Glen Dale has left the Fortunes. "I felt I was being pushed to the background. I am just not happy being a background vocalist. I am planning a new career as a solo singer." Best of luck to Glen and to the Fortunes who will replace Glen with singer-rhythm guitarist, Shel Macrae.

... PETE QUAIFE

Pete Quaife, bass guitarist for the plague-stricken Kinks, was injured in a car accident last week. He's currently in the Warrington Infirmary recovering from multiple fractures of his left foot and cuts on his head which required stitches. Reports out of England say Pete should be in the hospital for at least a week and then must rest at home for another week. Hope you get well soon, Pete.

Mick Jagger didn't say a quotable word all week!!!

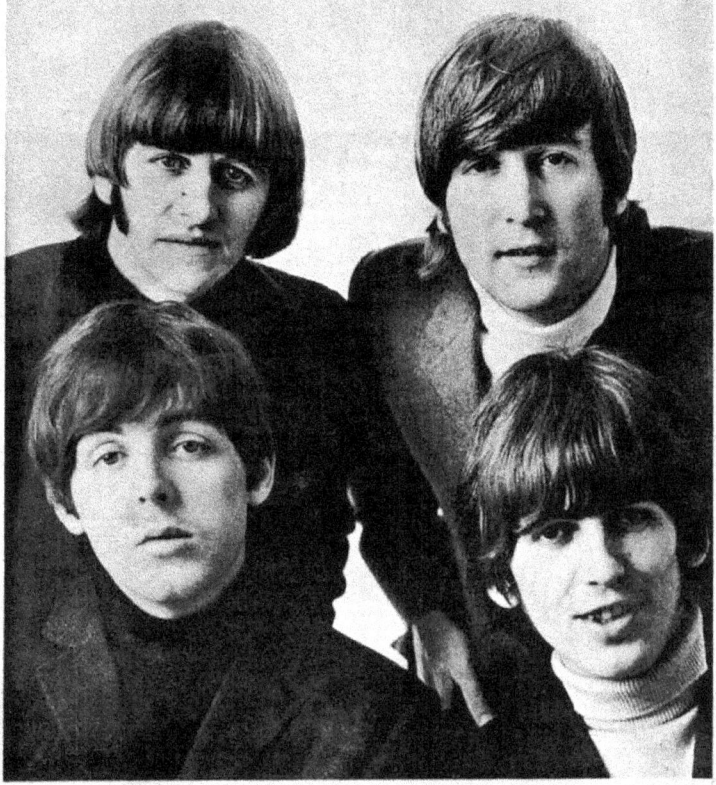

Beatle L.P. Cover Banned

The Beatles have turned out the most nauseating album cover ever seen in the U.S. The jacket is in color and shows the four Beatles in butcher outfits with chopped up raw meat (the meat of what we don't know) lying all over them. If this isn't bad enough, on top of the meat and the Beatles are decapitated baby dolls.

At the very last minute (after 800,000 of these covers had been distributed across the country) someone had brains enough to ban the album cover and demand that no one attempt to sell the album while it is still reposing in that cover.

But the damage is already done. Enough people have already seen the cover and they're all asking the same question—why? Why would a group who will obviously sell a million copies of the album no matter what they put on it stoop to posing and giving their blessing to such a ridiculous attempt at humor, or shock, or whatever it was meant to evoke?

Because it was the Beatles who did it and because no one is supposed to knock them, the comments and opinions which we received from those who had seen the cover will be anonymous. However, we *will* tell you that they were all given by people in someway connected with the entertainment business.

Not even one person who saw the banned album cover liked it. No one found it even *slightly* amusing. In short, they all felt it was the most sickening spectacle they'd ever seen. Many agreed that it must have been done for pure shock value. And this poses a question—why do the Beatles feel they must resort to shock to sell an album? Are they afraid that despite all their previous million selling LP's, if they don't put something shocking on the cover of this one, it won't sell?

Others felt that the whole thing came out of John Lennon's head. "If you've read his books," said one of our anonymous souls, "you *know* Lennon came up with the idea for the cover. Only he could think of something as morbid as that."

Gary Lewis was one performer who did agree to let *The BEAT* use his name along with his opinion of the cover. "I don't get it. Why? What does it mean? I hate that. They did it just so people would say, 'I hate that.' Harrison looks like he's chopping up another one back there."

Telling Us?

Some were of the opinion that the Beatles were trying to tell us something. "I think they're trying to tell us that this is the beginning of the end," said one. And another added, "You know, we've been getting this strange mail concerning the Beatles. The letters have been pouring in and all have been asking the same questions — 'what is happening to the Beatles?' 'Why are they becoming so weird?' Personally, I think the Beatles are now so far from their public that they don't even know what their public wants any more.

Actually, ever since the Beatles first were introduced to America, people have been predicting their downfall. But those wise in the ways of the entertainment business have stuck to the same thought throughout the Beatle reign—"No one can kill the Beatles, except the Beatles themselves." And perhaps they're doing it now.

For months and months the Beatles have been doing nothing—at least, nothing that can be seen. They've been looking for a third movie script. And after almost a year of looking, they say they still can't find one. We're all for the Beatles turning out a fantastic movie but *there's no way* they would have been diligently looking for an entire year and still not be able to find one. There has to be a hang-up somewhere.

Follow-Up

Then, too, the Beatles have been busy recording a follow-up album to "Rubber Soul." Well, "Rubber Soul" has been on the LP charts for 26 weeks. For someone as popular as the Beatles that's a long time to wait between albums. Because, you see, this new album of theirs (the one with the banned cover) contains only *three* songs which you haven't heard before—"I'm Only Sleeping," "Dr. Robert" and "And Your Bird Can Sing." It also contains "Drive My Car" which you've heard but which has never been released on an album here in the U.S.

We'd be very interested in hearing your comments on the banned cover. Do you think it was done for shock value, that they were trying to tell us something, or that it means nothing?

KRLA ARCHIVES

THE YOUNG RASCALS

...EDDIE AND GENE SNEAK an admiring glance at Felix's new Hammond organ, which isn't even available to the public!

...CELEBS AT THE PHONE BOOTH to see the Rascals included "old timers" such as Harry Belafonte, Buddy Hackett and Gordon MacRae.

By Louise Criscione

Outside it's cold. Very. This time of the year in New York always is. Inside the Phone Booth it's hot—Los Angeles during August. But the people don't seem to mind because mixed in with the heat and sweat is a feeling of excitement which is thick enough to slice with a switchblade.

To a person from another planet (if such a person exists) the scene inside the crowded Phone Booth would have made him wonder if he hadn't stepped into some sort of a psycho ward.

In various shapes and sizes, the Phone Booth clientele had one - no, two - things in common. They had come to see the Young Rascals and they were all wearing Rascal buttons, thoughtfully provided for them by the group's clever publicity man, Billy Smith.

It looked rather odd, you know— The Rolling Stones, Bob Dylan, Herman, the Lovin' Spoonful, the bell bottoms, the hip-huggers, the formals. All wearing Rascal buttons. All dancing. All shrugging off the anxieties and frustrations of life in the Mix-Mastered world of '66.

Old And Young

What looked even funnier, though, was the social blending of the old and the young. The Phone Booth is not usually noted as a hang-out for those unfortunate enough to be out of their twenties. And yet tonight, among the Jaggers and the Hermans are seen the Buddy Hacketts, the Harry Belafontes and the Gordon McRaes.

All those people who usually stick close to Arthur's (mecca for the "elderly") are holding up the walls of the Phone Booth tonight. Because tonight the Young Rascals open. Tonight the Phone Booth is where it's all happening. So, tonight the segment of the "in" world, the world of the happening people, is grooving at the Phone Booth. You probably wouldn't want it any other way.

The Rascals certainly wouldn't. Quite simply, they know where it's at. And right now *they're* where it's at. And that's funny too. Not hah, hah. Just a great sort of funny. The Rascals have all been around for awhile. People think they're new. They're not. They've all played in other groups.

But in January of '65, Felix Cavaliere simply got tired, or fed up, or both, with playing organ for Sandu Scott and Her Scotties. He wanted out, he wanted a group of his own.

Horse's Tail

Felix is, above all, persuasive. They say he could talk the tail off a horse. Perhaps he could, but I doubt if he's ever tried. He *did* talk Sandu Scott's drummer, Dino Danelli, into quitting and joining forces with him. It proved to be a smart move, but then Felix is smart.

Smart enough to realize that a drummer and an organist are not enough to set the pop world on fire, no matter how great they are. Felix had been around long enough to see a hundred groups

KRLA ARCHIVES

..."RINGO WHO?????"

...RASCALS TAKING IT EASY (l. to r. Felix, Gene, Dino and, naturally, that's Eddie on the floor! Who else?).

...SAYIN' IT with Soul

Inside A Phone Booth

struggle out of the womb and into the spotlights of a small club. And then graduate into smaller clubs. And then die.

He wanted to live and to do so he knew he had to find at least two other talented members for his infant group. He knew too that they had to be more than merely talented — they had to have that something extra which separates a talented *person* from a talented *performer*.

It's a quality you can't touch but one which you can feel. And Felix felt it when he tore Eddie Brigati and Gene Cornish from the Joey Dee Band. Eddie and Gene probably didn't shed many tears over their departure from the Joey Dee outfit. After all, the twist was dead.

So, the Rascals as a musical unit were complete. But as a business enterprise they were far from whole. Frankly, they needed capital. But they needed publicity and bookings even more. Again, Felix put his oratorical ability to work and persuaded Bill Smith to leave Sandu Scott and work as the Rascals publicity man.

That left only the bookings and the money. They took care of the booking part by begging, stealing or borrowing (none will say) a job at the Choo Choo Club in Garfield, New Jersey. Not a very impressive start you say?

The Barge was just about set to open and the owners of the club were searching for a new group to set the Barge swinging, to make it the "in" place on the Sound.

They heard about the Rascals. But they'd *heard* about a hundred new groups. Would this one be any different? They took a chance, traveled to the Choo Choo, liked what they saw and the Rascals christened the Barge in the summer of '65.

Southampton, where the Barge is located, is a summer resort area. To escape the engulfing heat of the city, New Yorkers headed in droves to the Sound. Once there, they spent their days lying in the sun and their nights swinging at the Barge. And when they returned to the city, they talked. About a lot of things but especially about this fantastic new group, the Rascals.

It was this word of mouth "reporting" which lead Sid Bernstein, businessman extraordinare, to the Barge to see for himself what was so great about a group of long-hairs who called themselves the Rascals. Well, he saw, he dug, he became their manager. The capital was in the bag.

And tonight they open at the Phone Booth. Tonight, with the Stones, Herman, the Spoonful, Dylan — *everybody* watching, they have to prove that they have it. Scared? Probably. But they needn't have been. They had it. They were happening. And that's all that counts.

The Phone Booth opening night is behind the Rascals now — thousands of miles, a hundred ordinary looking hotel rooms, three hit records and two cowboy hats behind. A long, long way.

...SO, WHAT'S ZAL find so funny?

...PERHAPS IT'S Barry McGuire?

KRLA ARCHIVES

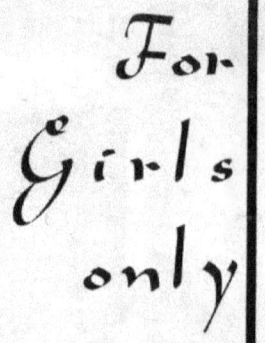

For Girls only

by shirley poston

Narcissa Nash has re-struck. And I quote...

"After reading the beginning of your Beatle dream in *The BEAT'S* June 4th witty, I dropped off (to sleep) and finished it. So, with further ado, here 'tis:

With the Beatles settled comfortably in the back of me VW bus, which I have affectionately re-named Nigel, I gun the motor (as in bang, bang) and tear off (all the rubber on the front tire).

As we jog along, I hear the Beatles exchanging questionable witticisms, when suddenly all of a suddy Paul jumps up (knocking a 9-1/2 inch hole through the roof of me bus) (I always wanted a convertible) and shrieks matter-of-factly, "Cor, it's hot in here."

John (never at a loss for words) (never at a loss, period) replies: "Maybe it's because your pants are on fire."

George adds, "Why didn't you think of that, you twit?"

At this point, I pull Nigel to a screeching halt and up to a fire hydrant. But before I can turn the water on Paul, he has shed his trousers and is now headed toward the nearest fountain with purple-polka-dot shorts on. (No comment.) As he leaps into a posh fountain in front of a posh bank, a loud sizzling is heard and a great mass of steam rises.

Indecent Exposure

At which time Paul is arrested for indecent exposure and for contributing to air pollution (the steamin' nit).

Paul protests: "But I'm Ringo!"

The cop answers, "They all say that these days."

Then, while Paul's solicitor is coming to his rescue, John, George, Ringo and I play darts. Ringo half-heartedly stabs a woman in the street and says, "I thought she was a sandwich."

Then everyone (but John and I) runs off to get help for Ringo whose sacrificial ring won't come off his sacrificial.

Meanwhile, John and I are kidnapped by Victor Spaghetti, who locks us up in the trunk of a Hillman for six years.

What a drag it is getting out."

Hmmmmm. Something tells me that Ringo (as in Boyd) isn't the only one who eats pizza sundaes before going to bed.

Now, before I start gibbering incessantly about nothing. I would like to gibber incessantly about something. Therefore, I must resort to my list tactics to keep my thoughts organized (ordinarily, I keep them in a net).

1. Sorry that last shipment of codes was such a mess, but I had to type them myself, which should explain everything.

2. My undying thanks to the person who informed me that GASP stands for George Adores Shirley Poston. (Would you believe George *avoids* Shirley Poston?) (If he values his life.)

3. No, no, no, I can't *really* send you all the details of my *real* George dream, The men in white are already looking for me. I'd hate for them to be joined by the Postmaster.

4. A special message to J.S. of W.G. — If it's the slightest bit of help, I know just how you feel. Sometimes I wish they were just boys instead of men; loving them would be so much less complicated.

5. Hysterical thank-yous to Susan Maynard and Claudia Davis, who sent me a whole batch of *Robin Boyd Was Here* tapes, (you know, the kind you make with those tape guns) (I have got to be kidding) (why can't I ever explain anything?) S&C also told me about visiting *The BEAT* office on a field day trip, and related a comment made by one of the staff members. About me, yet.

"Shirley's material is very hard to proofread," said she. "It's hard to tell if it's a mistake or just her."

I have the feeling I'm among friends again.

6. I have been informed by Robin Morris (any relation to Phillip?) that I am misinformed about George's middle name. It not only isn't Hilton. It isn't, period. (Of *course* it isn't, who would name a child George *Period* Harrison??) (I ask you!) What I mean is, she says he doesn't have one (doesn't have a middle name either).

No Middle

She quoted a line from a letter she'd received from George's mother, which was: "No dear, we didn't give George a middle name."

Well, I did. And George *Pant* Harrison rules (I dare say it?) the world! However, I still think someone should open a Harrison Hilton (re-pant).

7. Two more groovey suggestions for re-titling this gritty-witty "Shirley You Jest" and "For Grorge Only." Keep them coming!

8. Yes, yes, I too am absolutely miserable when Robin and George (of Genie frame . . . whoops . . . fame) are apart. Don't worry, they won't be for long. You know how Robin will go to any length to get her way, and I'm becoming a little tired of having to duck under an awning every time I see a bird.

Oh, enough of this listitis. But before I go (an unnecessary move as I've been gone for years), must tell you about a somewhat *unusual* (as in whattt???) package I received from Cheryl Barrett and Manar Johansen.

It contained (1) A Christmas present which I immediately opened despite do-not-open-until warnings. Whoopee! Inside were ten full-page pix of George! (2) An orange popsickle stick. No, I mean a stick from an orange popsickle. They were going to send the entire popsickle, but you know how it is. (3) A magnet, in case I ever run into George wearing metal (hah?). Well, all I can say is this . . . if I ever do, the metal he's wearing had better be a suit of armor.) (Send can openers, quick.)

(4) Some more of that very nice paper than many of my readers think is stationery. Fortunately, it came in handy because my nose was running at the time. (Down the street in search of George's nose, that is.)

(5) A 45-rpm record spindle with this note: "This was broken in Florida (legend has it) when George stepped on it. (Actually, Cheryl bit and broke it, but don't let it get around.)"

(6) Last but not least, a Rolling Stones record ("Heart Of Stone") which they almost didn't put in because it "weighs a lot". (Puns upon a time . . .) And, best of all, there was an 11X14 COLOR pic of you-know-who on the back of the package. (Pant, stoke and chip-a-tooth.)

Speaking of George, you know something else that sends me into quivering lumpsville? When he leaves the top oxqqka kcpzb bpzvi open.

Well, I've gotta run. And I'm not kidding. They're gaining on me again.

KRLA ARCHIVES

Cass Goes to England 'To Get' Beatles' John

By Mike Tuck

Would you believe . . . Cass of the Mamas and Papas is going to England to "get John Lennon." And judging by the reverence and dedication with which the forceful Mama spoke of the Beatle at the Melodyland Folk Festival she might do just that.

Cass was still wide-eyed about John calling a friend of hers and saying he wanted to meet Cass when he comes to Los Angeles late this summer.

"I was thrilled," Cass said. "Can you imagine that . . . John calling about me . . . saying, 'I want to meet the big bird!'" But Cass can't wait until September – she's going to England and John . . . NOW.

We thought at the time she was kidding. But, sure enough, right after the show Lou Adler, manager of the Mamas and Papas, announced the group was going to England "to do nothing really" except to give Cass a shot at her idol.

The trip will probably serve as a vacation for the busy group. They recently released their latest single, "I Saw Her Last Night," which could be a double-sided hit with "Even If I Could." John wrote "Even If I Could," and John and Denny both wrote the flip side.

Cass was discussing Paul's swollen lip and chipped tooth with the other Mama, Michelle Gilliam, and both concluded that "all Paul really needs is a kiss from a Mama." We failed to see how this remedy could restore the tooth but it could conceivably effect the swollen lip.

The group had just given another excellent performance in the Anaheim theatre. Their presence offered an interesting balance of acts . . . with the soft, melancholy lyrics of Simon and Garfunkel contrasting their own hard rock folk sound. But while the contrast was appealing from an overall view of the acts, we did get the impression that perhaps both groups overdid their specialty a bit.

The accompanyment of the Mamas and Papas, while it showed excellent cohesion with the singing, was noticeably too loud. It occasionally drowned out the singing completely and almost made "Monday Monday" and "California Dreamin'" sound like any other loud, unmemorable arrangement. And neither is.

But the group was still tremendously popular with the audience. To our disappointment, however, they failed to sing either of their new songs.

In the show, the genius of Paul Simon's lyrics and composition was observable in the fact that the group was effective even though their stage props were limited to one guitar, two chairs and a microphone.

The lyrics were more easily discernable this way, but even so we felt one or two more orchestral instruments could have been used to give their songs the same effect they produce on record. "I Am A Rock" and "Sounds of Silence" could have both been made a little more familiar sounding with either another guitar or a drum or both accompanying.

Simon added to the effect of his act with his wide variety of funny stories that covered everything from immodest sparrows in New York City to Garfunkel's embarrasing, child-like sleeping habits. The billing of Simon and Garfunkel opposite the Mamas and Papas was a natural, as both groups have publicly admired each other's compositions. Simon and Garfunkel have said they were considering recording some of John Phillips' compositions while the Mamas and Papas have commented that they would like to do something by Simon.

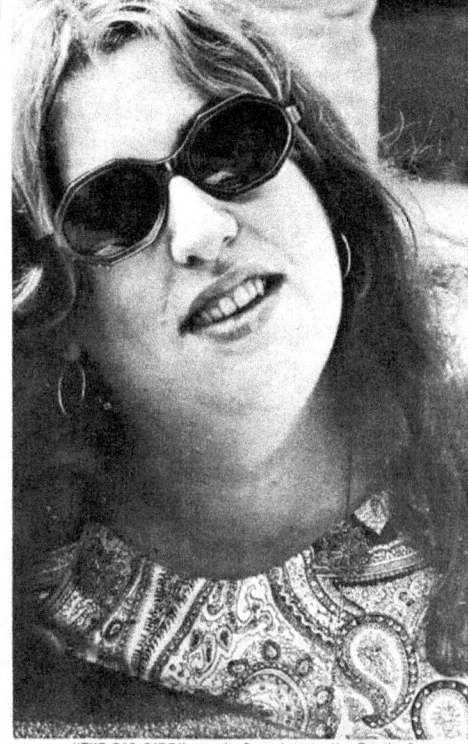
"THE BIG BIRD" . . . Is Cass lost to the Beatles?

"WE HATE TO WORK" . . . Denny, Mamas and Papas take English vacation. Also known as a John Lennon Hunt.

MICHELLE, JOHN, DENNY AND CASS . . . to be broken up by the Beatles? Only Cass and John know.

HEAD PAPA . . . John keeps on composing. Latest are "I Saw Her Last Night" and "Even If I Could." Double-sided smash — naturally!

KRLA ARCHIVES

KRLA Tunedex

DAVE HULL

BOB EUBANKS

DICK BIONDI

JOHNNY HAYES

EMPEROR HUDSON

CASEY KASEM

CHARLIE O'DONNELL

BILL SLATER

This Week	Last Week	Title	Artist
1	7	DIRTY WATER	The Standells
2	1	SEARCHIN' FOR MY LOVE	Bobby Moore
3	6	DOUBLE SHOT (OF MY BABY'S LOVE)	The Swingin' Medallions
4	2	A GROOVY KIND OF LOVE	The Mindbenders
5	10	YOU DON'T HAVE TO SAY YOU LOVE ME	Dusty Springfield
6	3	PAINT IT, BLACK	The Rolling Stones
7	4	ALONG COMES MARY	The Assoication
8	18	PAPERBACK WRITER/RAIN	The Beatles
9	14	STRANGERS IN THE NIGHT	Frank Sinatra
10	13	LITTLE GIRL	Syndicate of Sound
11	9	HOLD ON! I'M COMIN'	Sam & Dave
12	19	SOLITARY MAN	Neil Diamond
13	11	DON'T BRING ME DOWN	The Animals
14	23	OH HOW HAPPY	Shades Of Blue
15	5	WHEN A MAN LOVES A WOMAN	Percy Sledge
16	15	YOUNGER GIRL	The Hondells
17	21	WHERE WERE YOU WHEN I NEEDED YOU	The Grass Roots
18	16	I AM A ROCK	Simon & Garfunkel
19	12	DID YOU EVER HAVE TO MAKE UP YOUR MIND	The Lovin' Spoonful
20	20	OPUS 17 (DON'T WORRY 'BOUT ME)	The 4 Seasons
21	26	DAY FOR DECISION	Johnny Sea
22	17	BAREFOOTIN'	Robert Parker
23	27	HANKY PANKY	Tommy James & The Shondells
24	34	SWEET TALKING GUY	The Chiffons
25	25	BETTER USE YOUR HEAD	Little Anthony & The Imperials
26	22	DIDDY WAH DIDDY	Captain Beefheart & His Magic Band
27	35	(I'M A) ROAD RUNNER	Jr. Walker & The All Stars
28	49	WILD THING	The Troggs
29	29	LOVE SPECIAL DELIVERY	Thee Midniters
30	32	HE WILL BREAK YOUR HEART/HE	Righteous Bros.

Troggs In Caves?

(Continued from Page 1)

The Troggs consist of Reg Presley, lead singer; Chris Britton, lead guitarist; Peter Staples, bass guitarist; and Ronnie Bone, drummer. They admit to deriving the name from "troglodyte," an ethnological term which means "someone who creeps into holes or caverns" or "dwells in caves."

The Troggs are currently getting their biggest kick from meeting pop stars. You see, the Troggs didn't quite believe that popular entertainers were human beings. However, now that *they* are falling into that popular bag they're meeting their fellow performers and are discovering to their delight that they all seem to possess two arms, two legs, one head—the whole bit.

Their increase in revenue hasn't seemed to travel as far as their heads. Fact is, Reg Presley (who is no relation to Elvis) says: "Money? We're worse off than before we were in the hit parade. We just draw a salary every week. The rest of the money we don't see. In fact, I've probably got less in my pocket today than when we were back in Andover."

The feelings of the Troggs about their instantaneous success is explained by Chris Britton: "We can't really describe how we feel. It's starting to sink in now but the sort of exhilaration we imagined hasn't happened. It's a different sort of feeling."

Chris went on to hastily add: "I don't think we'll ever go wild and extravagant the way some people do. We're not that sort. I can't imagine any of us rushing out and buying a big car or something like that. It's just not like us."

Probably what sets the Troggs apart from other groups is their unique sound. Whether they *are* actually unique or whether they merely achieved a "different" sort of sound on one record is, of course, impossible to determine this early.

However, basing an opinion on "Wild Thing" alone, one would be forced to conclude that there is something a little special hidden in the Troggs. But the four Troggs aren't exacly sure if they agree with that "different" tag. Says Chris: "People say we have a different sound but we can't vouch for that. The sound we produce is just us, the way we've always played since we joined up together."

Surprisingly enough, the sudden fame and glory of the whole thing has not yet reached the Troggs. They're still polite. And they have been actually heard to utter the unexcusable "sir" and "ma'm" when speaking to people older then they... A totally foreign idea to many "big" performers.

Another thing the Troggs don't go for is the business of entertainers attacking other entertainers in the press. "If someone attacks us in print, naturally we feel resentful and might have a go back privately, but not publically," said Reg.

THE SUNRAYS
JOIN THE GALAXY OF STARS APPEARING IN

THE BEACH BOYS SUMMER SPECTACULAR

COW PALACE	HOLLYWOOD BOWL
SAN FRANCISCO	LOS ANGELES
FRIDAY, JUNE 24th	SATURDAY, JUNE 25th
8 P.M.	8 P.M.

THE SUNRAYS
("Don't Take Yourself Too Seriously")

KRLA ARCHIVES

Leaves Fall By KRLA

SPECIAL BONUS – SUBSCRIBE NOW and receive a free copy of The Bobby Fuller Four's best selling album, "I Fought The Law."

KRLA BEAT Subscription
SAVE 33% Of Regular Price

☐ 1 YEAR – 52 Issues – $5.00   ☐ 2 YEARS – $8.00
☐ 6 MONTHS – $3.00

Enclosed is _____   ☐ CASH   ☐ CHECK
PLEASE PRINT – Include Your Zip Code

Send to: .... Age: ......
Address: .... City: ....
State: .... Zip: ....

MAIL YOUR ORDER TO: KRLA BEAT
6290 Sunset, Suite 504
Hollywood, Calif. 90028

Foreign Rate: $9.00 – 52 Issues

Sean Connery LOSES HIS MARBLES OVER **Joanne Woodward, Jean Seberg** (AND A FEW OTHER LOVELY CHICKS) IN "A Fine Madness"
A JEROME HELLMAN Production
PATRICK O'NEAL · COLLEEN DEWHURST
CLIVE REVILL · WERNER PETERS · JOHN FIEDLER · KAY MEDFORD
JACKIE COOGAN · ZOHRA LAMPERT · SORRELL BOOKE · SUE ANE LANGDON
Screenplay by ELLIOTT BAKER · Produced by JEROME HELLMAN · Directed by IRVIN KERSHNER
TECHNICOLOR® · FROM WARNER BROS.

PACIFIC'S HOLLYWOOD **PANTAGES**
HOLLYWOOD BLVD. at VINE
Crossroad of the Stars!
HO 9-2211

AHHH... SUCCESS AT LAST! It's not that we don't love this bunch of fun-loving guys or anything, it's just that after having five mischievous Leaves trapped within the KRLA studios for a week, it's sorta nice to have them free-falling about the rest of society once again. Watch out, 'cause they might fall your way.

Whisky à Go Go
8901 SUNSET STRIP
TELEPHONE: 652-4202

for the first time EVER
GENE CLARK & THE GROUP
hear their new-new music!

Also Mexico's #1 Group
The LOCOS

MOVIES   MOVIES   MOVIES
2 to 4 a.m. eat & be merry
FOOD till 2 A.M.   AGE 18 AND UP WELCOME

KRLA ARCHIVES

TEEN PANEL DISCUSSION

Beatles On TV: A Bomb?

This is another in The BEAT'S series of teen panel discussions. As always, the session was taped in complete privacy and later transcribed. Since we want to hear what teenagers really have to say, panelists participate on a "pen-name" basis.

The tape remains un-edited, with one exception. Conversation which doesn't apply to the subject at hand does not appear in print because it would consume too much space.

Stay tuned to The BEAT for more discussions, and for information as to how you can become a member of a future teen panel.

* * *

The topic of today's discussion is the same subject everyone has been talking about since Sunday, June 5. Namely, the Beatles' appearance on "The Ed Sullivan Show."

For some time, there hasn't been much difference of opinion where the Beatles are concerned. Not among teenagers, anyway, as most of us dig them in our own individual ways.

The Sullivan stint has prompted a return of pro vs. con. Many viewers praised the performance, but just as many have panned it.

The following is an analysis of their appearance, made by five of the millions of teenagers who made the Beatles the stars they are today.

Participating are Tim (14), Penny (18), Gary (17), Georgia (15) and Jillian (16), who begins the discussion.

Jillian—"I can sum up entire opinion in one sentence. I love the Beatles, but I sure didn't like them on 'Ed Sullivan'."

Tim—"What do you think they did wrong?"

Jillian—"I don't know. They really didn't do anything wrong. But they looked so different; that was the worst part. Especially the bit with Paul's tooth. That really put me off."

Georgia—"It did me, too. I've heard so much about how conscious Paul is of his appearance. I just couldn't believe he'd appear on television in that condition. Especially on a show that's seen by millions of people, and right before a tour."

Penny—"I doubt if he had any choice. The arrangements were probably made months ago, and how was anyone to know he'd fall off a motorcycle in the meantime? They probably tried to cancel out after Paul had the accident."

"Do It!"

Gary—"Get serious... Remember who we're talking about here. If the Beatles have to cancel something, they don't just try—they do it... Even if the whole show was planned months in advance, they could have found a substitute. My uncle works for a TV network and sometimes they have to make substitutions the day a show is filmed..."

Penny—"Maybe so, but I'll bet there's some good reason why they went on anyway. It could be they figured we would want to see them in *any* condition. I, for one, would. I'd rather see Paul without a tooth in his head than not see him at all."

Tim—"There's another possibility. Maybe they didn't see the tape before it went on the air, and didn't know about the bad close-ups of Paul."

Penny—"Even if they *did* see it, that doesn't make them responsible for how it turned out. It's not up to the performer to decide on camera angles. If anyone's at fault, it's the director who was in charge of the taping. He should have had more brains than to allow such unflattering shots. It almost seemed like someone was *trying* to make them look ridiculous."

Georgia—"Well, they didn't help matters much with those sunglasses. My best friend says that's the first phony thing she's ever seen the Beatles do."

"Crazy"

Jillian—"Then she's crazy. There's nothing phony about sunglasses. Everyone wears them now because they're in the vogue."

Georgia—"I was just about to add that I don't agree about the phoniness part. But I do think they had on the wrong style of shades. Some people just don't look good in weird-shaped glasses. Ringo's looked cute on him, but the rest detracted from their looks instead of the other way around."

Jillian—"Frankly, Ringo was about the only one who looked like himself. George's hair was all weird on top, and I almost didn't recognize John. His new hairstyle is rather cool, though."

Tim—"I don't see why you're all steamed up about the way they looked. What does that have to do with anything? Aren't looks supposed to be the most unimportant part of a person, especially someone you care about? I can understand girls being more aware of the Beatles' looks than we are, but aren't you going overboard on the subject?"

Care

Penny—"Personally, I was so glad to see them, I didn't pay much attention to the way they looked. But you've got to realize that no two people 'care' alike or to the same degree. You might not understand that because you aren't a girl and like the Beatles in a different way."

Jillian—"I'll say... I'll bet *you've* never stayed up all night crying about Paul..."

Tim—"Let's *hope* not, but back to what Penny was saying. I don't think I'm reading you."

Penny—"I wasn't finished. I was going to say that even though I don't share the feeling, I can understand someone being shook up by a sudden physical change. When you love a certain face and you're used to seeing it a certain way, it's natural to be sort of revolted by a chipped tooth or a cut lip. If you 'care' on that particular level, I mean."

Georgia—"What's wrong with caring on that level? You make it sound childish."

Penny—"I don't mean to because it isn't. I think most everyone goes through this stage if they're really attracted to someone, but after awhile, if you keep caring, you stop seeing someone with your eyes and, if I may get slightly sickening, start seeing them with your heart. That's why marriages don't break up when wives get fat and husbands stop shaving on weekends. These things matter terribly at the beginning, but they keep mattering less and less as your feeling for someone gets stronger. Wow—I'd better shut up..."

Georgia—"You've just reminded me of something. I wasn't all that shocked by the way the Beatles looked. I was glad to see them, too. But my folks raised such hell—excuse me, but they did—about it. They kept saying 'how can you scream over *that*? I don't expect the Beatles to cater to adults, but you'd think they'd make it as easy on us as they could. They've always looked sharp before, and they could help a lot by just cooling it a little and not giving our folks any legitimate gripes against them. They would help themselves, too. After all, parents have a lot of control over the way teenagers spend money."

Jillian—"This is going to sound moronic, I suppose, but the only other thing I didn't like about the show was the lack of screams. Not that people should have been shrieking all through their numbers, but even on shows like Ed Sullivan's there have always been enough Beatle fans to blither a little and set the mood. This time, when the Beatles were announced, no one in the audience even breathed heavily. There probably wasn't anyone young enough to have the strength to. That was a mistake on someone's part. It made the appearance seem so cold and impersonal."

"Old Drummer"

Penny—"That's a good point. I'm not a screamer . . . I wouldn't dare be or people would stop laughing at me for still loving the Beatles and start *pointing*. But I love to hear the old roar, and I missed it, too."

Gary—"I'm beginning to wonder if anyone is ever going to get down to the less *emotional* aspects of this subject. The Beatles are mainly musicians, and we haven't said one word about anything remotely connected with music."

Tim—"So keep going before they start up again..."

Gary—"Okay. I'd like to ask all of you one question, and please answer it honestly... What do you really think of the new Beatle record—the one they did that night on the show?"

Jillian—"I LOVE it... Especially 'Paperback Writer'..."

Gary—"Why? Because Paul sings the lead?"

Jillian—"That's one of the reasons. I also dig the song, and the other side also. John sounds so groovy I can't believe it."

Georgia—"I like the record, but it's hard to hear the words on both numbers. That's the only thing I don't like about it."

Tim—"I don't think either side is up to par. They can do so much better and have, but that's just my personal opinion. I expect the Beatles to maintain a certain standard, which really isn't fair because it's my standard and not theirs. This record might be great in their eyes because we have different tastes in music."

Penny—"I don't care that much for either side, but I agree with Tim. That doesn't mean they aren't good songs. I honestly wouldn't have bought this record if it hadn't been by the Beatles, but I'd have bought most of their records if they'd been by the Bull Frogs... You can't please everyone all the time, but I commend the Beatles for being able to please *enough* people all of the time. That's really all a performer has to do to sustain his popularity."

Medicore

Gary—"I won't argue with any of those answers—most of them made a lot of sense. But think about this. All five of us dig the Beatles in one way or another, and the majroity of us agree that we aren't really all that gone on their latest record. So why are we sitting around looking for reasons why we weren't that wild about their performance? Looks and screams and emotions aside, the Beatles performed two songs that don't exactly fall into the mindblower category. What better reason is there for their appearance to have been on the mediocre side? A performer is as good as his material, and this time they were doing songs that aren't as well-received as a lot of their past stuff. I'll go one step further than any of you and say that I think both sides are *technically* bad.

Penny—"There's another element we've forgotten. Neither of the songs they performed are what you might call *participation* numbers. You know what I mean. There wasn't much for Paul to bounce about, so he didn't. In person, they're a lot better when they do songs they can really get *into*. Any performer is. So it wasn't one of their greatest moments. So what? There are a million reasons why this could have happened. After all the Beatles are *people*—and to quote a well-known 'bird,' no one is perfect. I think it's about time we stopped expecting them to be something none of us ever *will* be..."

Gary—"I agree. People always make too big a deal out of a performance that isn't the greatest, when they themselves couldn't do one-tenth as well."

Tim—"I agree, too. And now I feel sort of stupid for sitting here trying to analyze something that really doesn't matter that much."

Georgia—"Penny is right about the perfection bit—that's too much to expect from anyone because it just isn't possible. But I don't think we should feel stupid for talking about all this. Some of the things we brought up were valid points, and I'll bet the Beatles will really be interested in what we've said when they read this in *The BEAT*."

Jillian—"Maybe no one is perfect, but man, that's coming close... Incidentally Paul, how much do you want for that chip?"

Thrifty
CUT RATE DRUG STORES

ACNE and ACNE PIMPLES CONTROLLED IN 7 to 14 DAYS or you'll get your money back!*

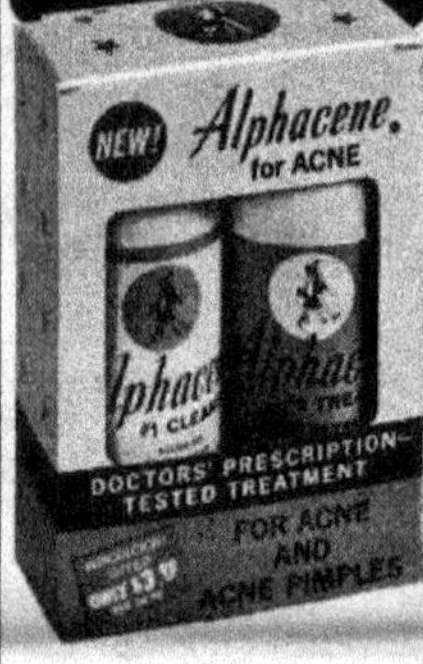

NEW!
Alphacene,
for ACNE
DOCTORS' PRESCRIPTION-TESTED TREATMENT
FOR ACNE AND ACNE PIMPLES

ALPHACENE. Really Works!

This two-step cleanser and treatment is a thoroughly tested and proven prescription, developed by a group of noted dermatological MDs. You'll get startlingly happy results with Alphacene. No prescription needed.

1. CLEANSER
and
2. TREATMENT

BOTH FOR $3.98

Buy Alphacene® at Your Nearby Thrifty Drug Store
or use the Mail Order

MAIL ORDER
Thrifty Drug Store Co. Inc., Dept. M
Box 2363 Terminal Annex, L.A. 54, Calif.
Please send me ______ Alphacene® Cleanser and Treatment at $3.98. Enclose check or money order.
Name ______
Address ______
City ______ State ______ Zip ______
Add 4% Sales Tax

*If not completely satisfied, return unused portion to manufacturer for full refund.

Thrifty
CUT RATE DRUG STORES

KRLA ARCHIVES

HOTLINE LONDON
George And Ravi

Tony Barrow

By Tony Barrow

An important concert marked the arrival in the U.K. of Indian instrumental virtuoso and classical sitar expert RAVI SHANKAR. GEORGE HARRISON attended Shankar's opening performance in London's famous Royal Festival Hall, home of the capital's finest symphony concerts. To be there the Beatle left his three colleagues in the middle of a recording session at E.M.I.'s North London studios! With him to watch the Shankar recital went George's wife Patti.

Immediately afterwards George returned to E.M.I. and the recording session continued until nearly three o'clock the following morning. By that time one of the final tracks for the group's forthcoming album had been completed. Now the boys have still got to rehearse and record four further titles and the 14 numbers for their August U.K. album will be ready.

Beatle Comfort

Six years ago during their first visits to Germany, THE BEATLES slept alongside members of two or three other beat groups in one large room of an unfurnished attic apartment in Hamburg. This month when John, Paul, George and Ringo round off their three-day six-show German tour in Hamburg, their accommodation will be somewhat less cramped. They will stay for two nights in a huge, ancient and very historical German castle built high on a hill 20 miles to the north of Hamburg.

On the second day of the tour the group will use its own special train to move between Munich, Essen and Hamburg. The party will spend twelve hours in the luxuriously equipped Pullman rail carriages which will have a television lounge, restaurant section and sleeping quarters.

It goes without saying that The Beatles will not be playing Hamburg's Star Club this trip. That's where they gained some of their first major success. Now they'll play a considerably larger venue holding more than 12,000 people.

Spencer Tops

Meanwhile the Star Club continues to flourish. Latest favorite there is our SPENCER DAVIS GROUP who drew a record-splintering crowd of two and a half thousand fans just a couple of weeks ago. The club announced that the Davis' attendance was the biggest since the Beatle days of '61 and '62 when the Star Club had just opened.

This summer Spencer Davis tours Norway and Sweden before making a return visit to Germany. The group hopes to finalize details of a full-scale U.S. tour for the month of October but this may depend upon the success of "Somebody Help Me" on your side of the Atlantic.

National D.J. Winners

Cash Box has compiled it's annual poll of disc jockeys to determine the most programmed artists of the year. The results of the cross-country poll will, undoubtedly, surprise many of you and will come as no shock to others. Listed are the categories (with the top five winners) which we thought you would be most interested in.

Frank Sinatra, whose "Strangers In The Night" is currently topping the nation's charts, swept the honors in the Male Vocalist category with Elvis Presley second; Bob Dylan, third; Andy Williams, fourth; and Dean Martin, fifth.

Darling Petula Clark came in first in the Female Vocalist category with Barbra Streisand, Cher, Nancy Sinatra and Nancy Wilson trailing respectively behind Pet.

It should come as a surprise to absolutely no one that the Vocal Group category was topped by the Beatles. Who else? The Supremes came in second and are the only female vocal group in this category's top winners. Rounding out the Vocal Group winners are Herman's Hermits, third; the Rolling Stones, fourth; and the Beach Boys, fifth.

Herbie Alpert, who has made a habit out of winning awards, naturally won his fair share in the D.J. poll. Herbie and his TJB easily stole the first place in the Instrumentalist and Orchestra categories. Following Herb in the Instrumentalist category were Al Hirt, second; Ramsey Lewis, third; Peter Nero, fourth; and the T-Bones fifth.

Lining up behind Herbie in the Orchestra category were Henry Mancini, second; Bert Kaempfert, third; Si Zentner, fourth; and Billy Vaughn, fifth.

First place in the Up And Coming Male Vocalist category was a tie with both Bob Lind and Frankie Randall fighting for the top honors. Barry Sadler found himself in second place, John Gary in third, Lou Christie in fourth and Mel Carter in fifth.

Nancy Sinatra, who placed fourth in the Female Vocalist category, made it all the way to the top spot in the Up And Coming Female Vocalist category. Second place was held down by Marilyn Maye but the third place winner was Pet Clark! What??? Pet was voted the top Female Vocalist and then the D.J.'s turned around and named her an Up And Coming Female Vocalist. Just how far up can she go? Bobbie Norris was fourth in this category and Cher came in fifth.

The Up And Coming Vocal Group was, of course, won by the Mama's and Papa's with the Lovin' Spoonful coming in second, the We Five were third, Simon and Garfunkel were fourth and Paul Revere and the Raiders held the number five position.

The Stones' "Satisfaction" tied for first place with "Ballad Of The Green Berets" for the Single Of The Year.

And so went the results of the Cash Box National D.J. Poll. Do you agree with the winners?

KRLA ARCHIVES

Vic Dana Says Len Barry Chose The Wrong Groups

By Susan Ann Van Meter

Vic Dana leaned back in one of our office chairs to study a copy of The BEAT. His eyes were glued to the front page story we ran last week – Len Barry's refusal to appear on the same bill as "long-haired, dirty-looking, sloppily-dress groups."

Dana finished reading the article and looked up, remarking "A great deal of what he has to say is true, but I don't agree with the groups he names." Barry had pointed out the Beatles, Stones, Animals and Bob Dylan as prime examples of what he called "a collection of tramps."

"Long hair doesn't matter," Dana said, "it's the way a singer or a group appears and acts in public. For instance, the Beatles dress well and neatly."

But Dana abhors groups who don't care how they appear, how often they bathe or how rude they are to their audience. "Groups like this show contempt, not respect, for their audiences." And the worst part of it, Dana feels, is that the singers influence their listeners in their dress, their attitude and their actions.

While Dana is a short-haired American singer in an era of long-haired Englishmen, he doesn't feel this has hurt him a bit.

Most surprisingly, Dana credits the Beatles with helping his career – not personally but professionally. "They introduced a very hard sound and radio stations played it day and night. Finally, it had to be broken up."

And this is where the handsome, intense young singer with the smoothly perfect voice feels he belongs – in a field of soft, melodic songs. In fact, he cut some hard rock records at one time, but each failed miserably.

"The record buying public is getting younger, but they are also brighter. They demand that you stay in the element best for you," he said.

But Vic Dana wants, more than anything else, to be good in all fields of entertainment. He has sung in shows, nightclubs, college tours and toys with the idea of eventually trying Broadway. And he is also a creditable actor, having performed for both television and movies.

He has just completed an unusual television program, "Shadow Over Elveron," with Jim Franciscus, part of a new color series for the fall. Two hours long, the program, entitled "Project 120," will be shown on U.S. television but released in Europe as a movie.

Dana also released an album last week "Town and Country." It was cut after his single, "I Love You, Drops," became a hit. Though the album is definitely country music, Dana is quick to point out that it is far from the horse and saddle sound.

Europe is one of Dana's biggest markets, with The Netherlands adn Italy boosting his sales the most. An Italian-American, Dana fell in love with Italy on his last European tour and is making plans to maintain a residence in a small Swiss town, Lugano, on the Swiss-Italian border. He will use this residence as headquarters on his European tours.

Since he recorded "More", "Shangri-La," "Red Roses For a Blue Lady," and others, Dana has been a hit with both teens and adults. Last February, he made the finals in the San Remo Festival, the famous Italian music contest where one of the stipulations is that all songs must be sung in Italian.

European audiences, Dana feels are unlike American audiences in that they are more concerned with whether or not a performer has something legitimate to offer. They tend to look past a hit record or a singer's dress, he says, to see whether he truly has talent.

Dana is returning to Europe in the fall, which he considers "an untapped market." Meanwhile, he will spend the summer attending Air Force Summer Camp and after that will journey to Montreal and Puerto Rico.

...*"LONG HAIR DOESN'T MATTER"*

Brenda Lee—Ten Golden Years And Discovery Of The Beatles

By Mike Tuck

Few performers can boast a ten year history of success as can Brenda Lee, but even fewer can make claims of discovering the Beatles.

Now celebrating her tenth golden year of professional entertaining, Brenda recalls the Beatles when they were playing for pennies in the slums of Liverpool.

"I first saw them when Peter Best was with them some years ago," she remembers. "I knew right away they had something so I came back to the United States and tried to get Decca Records to sign them. But, naturally, they refused."

Decca Records has probably never gotten over not heeding Miss Lee's advice.

Brenda Lee has changed greatly in her ten years of entertaining... changed from a shy little girl with an off key voice to a mature young woman with a throaty, captivating audience appeal.

She is not what is currently known as a "hippie" but she would have to be classified as "cool" by any standards. She is outspoken and honest and you get the impression she is much more mature than her 21 years indicates.

She has soft features and stands just a shade under five feet and when you see her on stage you understand why she has been labeled the "little girl with the big voice."

After ten years of singing and entertaining it would seem logical that Brenda, if anybody, could offer predictions of where pop music is headed.

But not even Brenda Lee can do that. "I wish I could," she laughed . . . "I'd make a million dollars."

Brenda likes much of the current pop music, but she doesn't limit herself to just that. "I just don't see how anybody that has been exposed to Tony Bennett or Andy Williams can help but like that type of music, too," she said.

It has been a while since Brenda has turned out one of her many hit records, but she says she definitely hasn't quit pop music. "If something worthwhile comes along," she said, "most certainly I'd record it."

She has been playing before mostly adult audiences recently, but she says her audience – the one that has made her the number one female singer in America for many years – hasn't changed.

Brenda has probably sold more records overseas than any other American singer. Her songs have done especially well in Japan, a country Brenda has visited many times and one that has become her favorite.

Asked what she likes most about Japan, Brenda answered without a second of thought. "The people," she said. "I think the Japanese are the most friendly people in the world, and they have always been very warm and hospitable to me.

"They always give gifts as a token of their friendship," she said. "Once I had an appointment to see a young man in Tokyo and when he greeted me he handed me a small package. When I opened it I found a beautiful gold medal – a gold medal he had won in the Olympic games."

When Brenda finished with this story someone sitting next to her suggested that the real reason for her fondness of the Japanese was that they were her own size. She couldn't disagree.

Brenda was married last year and now has a young son. Her singing tours have naturally become limited but she still travels quite a lot.

Asked if her profession interferred with her marriage she said: "No . . . I don't let it."

And somehow, you get the impression she means everything she says.

KRLA ARCHIVES

LSP-3531 STEREO

CHET ATKINS picks on the Beatles
"Mr. Guitar" plays

- Yesterday
- Hard Day's Night
- I Feel Fine
- She Loves You
- Michelle
- I'll Follow the Sun
- Can't Buy Me Love
- I'll Cry Instead
- And I Love Her
- She's a Woman
- If I Fell
- Things We Said Today

RCA VICTOR DYNAGROOVE RECORDING

RCA Presents—
CHET ATKINS PICKS ON THE BEATLES

Beatle George Harrison says: ".... I have appreciated Chet Atkins as a musician since long before the tracks on this album were written; in fact, since I was the ripe young age of seventeen. Since then I have lost count of the number of Chet's albums I have acquired, but I have not been disappointed with any of them.

"For me, the great thing about Mr. Atkins is not the fact that he is capable of playing almost every type of music but the conviction in the way he does it. Whilst listening to CHET ATKINS PICKS ON THE BEATLES I got the feeling that these songs had been written specifically with Chet in mind."

...Beatle Chet

Thrifty CUT RATE DRUG STORES

Cut Rate Prices And Blue Chip Stamps, Too!

KRLA ARCHIVES

The Adventures of Robin Boyd...

©1965 By Shirley Poston

Robin smiled sneakily into her Triple-Fudgie-Wudgie-Teener-Treat. (Where some malt shop menu-writers have only been at the vanilla vat, this one had obviously been canned off his head).

"Ringo," she ahemed, addressing the familiar face across the table. "You're really an angel, huh?"

Ringo flexed his wings beneath the corduroy cape he'd thrown over same. (Genies, she had discovered, were not the only incurable hams in this world). (Make that *any* world).

"I am that, I am," he replied.

Robin scooped up another shovel-full of whipped cream. It figured, it did. She'd often wondered why he hadn't been in on the Cavern caper with George, Paul and John. And why the three of them had spoken, in hallowed tones, of calling on him *only* if all else failed.

"Why do you arsk?" arsked Ringo.

Robin inhaled half a banana. "I suppose angels always tell the truth, huh?"

"Heavens, yes..." Ringo announced stoutly.

Robin chortled inwardly. "Then tell me the real reason why the four of you look so much like the four of them..." (A question which will be fully understood by Beatle-maniacs only). (On second thought leave off the Beatle).

Ringo twisted uncomfortably (not to mention old-hattedly) (no one is perfect) (whoops, there goes that lightning bolt again).

Menacingly dangling a cherry, Robin hummed a chorus of "The George Washington Blues."

"Okay, okay," Ringo writhed. "I'll tell you. We look so much like them because everyone in our country looks like someone who has brought happiness to the world."

Robin choked on a half-ton of strawberry ripple. "Your country?"

Country!

Ringo reddened. "Our *country*." (Someone is going to have to do something about the echo in this place, but don't hold your breath.) (Please don't... you look like heck in purple). (Not to mention Helen Green).

Having grown mellow (as in marsh) in her old age, Robin decided to let that one pass (away would be nice.) "Who looks like who first?" she asked hopefully. (Hoping, that is, that the man with the net hadn't overheard *that* one).

Ringo re-wrothe. "Five years after a person is born, it's determined what he will contribute to society. If he qualifies, a genie is born in his image."

"Determined by whom?" Robin insisted. "Re-whoops," she added, dodging another you-know-what. Then she suddenly started counting on her fingers, toes and the other half of the banana.

"Cheers..." she soon screeched. "That means George, *my* George, is only 18, by George..." Which was good news despite the fact that she wouldn't be able to add D.O.M. to the list of blood-boilers she intended to call him upon his return. Oh well, it wouldn't be all that much trouble to change the O. to Y. and add E.S.

"So, why are you an angel instead of a genie?" she raved on.

"One in every four," he explained. "It's planned that way. Saves us the trouble of hiring bobbies."

Robin looked confused (amen to that). "Bobbie's what?"

"As in policeman, as in policeman," Ringo grouched.

"But why *you*?" she persisted.

"Well," he began, "Paul wasn't a very likely candidate."

Robin nodded in agreement, recalling velvety eyes with non-angelic tendencies.

"And John didn't exacly qualify," he continued..

"I'll say," she snorted into her sundae (not to mention the other seven) (as in eight daze a week).

"And George," he finished. "Well, you know *George*."

Robin, who sure did, slid cackling beneath the table. "I see what you mean," she whooped, clutching her sides.

No Comment

But she suddenly sobered (up would be nice), for Ringo was looking at her askance. (No comment).

"What's the prob?" she asked, crawling back into her chair.

Ringo took another look at her askance. (Still no comment). "Now that I've revealed all me deep-darks, I'd say it's my turn to ask a few questions."

Robin re-attacked the aforementioned Triple-Fudgie-Wudgie-Teener-Treat. "Shoot," she slurped. And he did, with both barrels. Because his first question was—"Whatever happened to a sweet, sixteen-year-old rare bird by the name of Robin Irene Boyd?"

Robin gulped. *"Hah?* I mean, she's right here... No, I mean *I'm* right here."

"Wrong," said Ringo sadly— "I mean the Robin Irene Boyd who never screamed or fainted, only gasped at concerts, and never *ever* told whoppers."

"Oh," Robin shrugged. "She died."

"It's not foony," Ringo remorsed. "Not when I'm sitting across the table from her corpse."

"Thanks a bunch of sour *grapes*," Robin bristled. "I suppose you think *you're* perfect? Well, you're not... And everyone *nose* why..."

"Physical chops are the lowest form of humor," Ringo grimaced. "Not to mention par for the coarse."

Robin moaned and pushed away the dish (as in washtub) containing one last bite of Triple—oh, *you* know. "There you've done it," she sagged. "Ruined me very appetite, you have."

But Ringo wasn't listening. "It was George's fault, I suppose," he said, almost to himself. "Unhealthy influence, that boy. Tried me best with him, but could never quite reach the lad."

"Too *tall* for you?" Robin rebristled. "There is *nothing* wrong with George. He may be an utter wretch, but he's a simply *super human being!*"

"That's just the point," Ringo snapped. "He isn't *supposed* to be a human being. He's supposed to be a *genie*, and *help* people."

Robin seethed. "I'll have you know he's helped me *thousands of times*!"

"Helped you find the nearest telephone booth, that is," Ringo said sarcastically.

"I mean no such *thingy!*" Robin raged. "I *luv* George and I want him *back* and I'm going to *get* him back if it's the last thing(y) I every *do...*"

Ringo smiled smugly. "I'm afraid the matter is quite out of your hands. It is now in mine."

Robin started to tell him to keep his hands *off* her matter, thank you (you're welcome) but she suddenly thought better of it. Ringo wasn't kidding...

"You mean it's up to *you* to decide whether George can be my genie again?"

"It is up to him to decide whether he *wants* to be," Ringo corrected. "Then it's up to me to decide whether he'll be *allowed* to return."

Robin put a hand to her throat. (His, in fact). (His hand, not his throat). (At a moment like this, *anyone* can get mixed up). (No, make that *everyone*).

"I'll do it..." she blithered. "I'll do it... Tell me what to do and I'll do it... I'll do anything you tell me, I tell you..." (Don't look now, but Robin may just have written a hit song).

"Good..." Ringo replied. "All I ask is that you mend your ways."

"Quick, pass the thread..." Robin blathered.

"Stop needling me," Ringo reprimanded. "I'm serious... I'm going to give you a list of resolutions to keep, and although I'm not through writing them up, first and foremost on the list is this... you will not so much as even *speak* to George until you've reformed. Is that *clear?*"

"As mud," she muttered, and the word had a deeper, more personal meaning now that it was her new last name.

"Good..." Ringo repeated (repetition remains unsurped) (it still rules, too). "Now, I have a treat for you... We're going to see a movie..."

"Which one, pray tell," Robin smirked. "'*Help*' or '*Hard Day's Night*'?"

Double Ham

"Both," Ringo confessed, and was immediately re-classified as a *double*-ham. "They're playing at the drive-in cinema just down the street."

"*Drive-in?*" Robin bellowed righteously. "What kind of girl do you think I *am*?"

"I don't *think*," he said sternly. "I *know*."

Robin curled her lip in the most unladylike manner in lip-curling history (my, wasn't *that* a mouthful). "Don't worry, dahling," she snarled. "I promise to control myself."

"And that's *one* promise I won't have *any* trouble keeping," she added mentally. A statement which will someday be remembered as the *grondfather* of ALL famous last words.

(To Be Continued Next Week)

Ian Likes U.S.; Leaves Britian

By Carol Deck

Ian Whitcomb wandered by The BEAT offices this week and we casually asked what he'd been doing lately, thinking we hadn't seen much of him.

Well, although *we* haven't seen much of him lately, a lot of other people have. He's been a very busy entertainer.

Since he was in California last December he's been to England, Ireland and France.

He witnessed a riot at a Stone concert in Paris and he appeared at the "Internationale Rallye Du Rock" in Monte Carlo, where he was billed as "Yan Witcob," an American representative."

Ian's very honest about the fact that, although he's actually English, he works more outside of Britian.

"I've never worked in England," he says. "And when I work in France, I work as an American artist."

Aside from singing as Ian Whitcomb, he also does a lot of sessions as a musician and has been putting out instrumental records under the names Sir Arthur and Bluesville.

Marvelous Mae

And he's just finished working on an album that may turn out to be the biggest thing since Mrs. Miller. It's by Mae West and includes many of the top rock hits of the last year.

It includes "Nervous" and "You Turn Me On," both done by Ian, and "When a Woman Loves a Man," the answer song to Percy Sledge's current hit.

Ian seems to be branching out in many different directions. He also wants to put out a spoken single, but is a little worried about it.

He wants to record a poem from the novel, "In Cold Blood." The poem was written by one of the murderers in the nonfiction book and just happened to fit a melody that Ian had written.

"I'm frightened about putting it out because it might be in bad taste," he says.

The label of the record would read, written by Ian Whitcomb and the name of the murdered and the date he was executed by the state for the murder.

"It's a most strange thing," he notes.

And he also has a new single coming out soon called "Poor Little Bird," which he wrote.

A Pub Sound

He calls it the English pub sound and says it was recorded under the influence of a couple hundred pounds of beer.

"We weren't really stoned, just feeling quite merry," he explains.

It's got a Salvation Army type band on it, complete with tubas, trumpets and trombones, but no guitars.

And he's got his fourth EP coming out in England. It's called "Where Did Robinson Crusoe Go?" and is a instrumental bluesy, jazz sort of thing.

And on top of recording everything from instrumentals to spoken records, he's also continuing his education.

He recently received his degree in history and is now considering doing graduate work at the University of California at Berkeley.

He's living in California now too, so we should be seeing much more of him. And with the way he's been working lately we should definitely be hearing more from him, although it may be in many different forms and under several different names.

KRLA ARCHIVES

The BEAT Goes To The Movies

"LT. ROBIN CRUSOE, U.S.N."

By Jim Hamblin
(The BEAT Movie Editor)

Some folks try to cure hiccups by putting their head between their knees, or using a paper bag. Or with a finger in an ear they hop around on one foot . . . the remedies are endless. But sailor man Robin Crusoe, lost on the Pacific Ocean in a teeny little raft, figures if he scares himself they'll go away.

In one of the most hilarious sequences ever filmed, Dick Van Dyke does battle with a survival kit, the smallest life raft in the world, a menacing shark, and his sleepwalking habit. In thrashing around with a knife to scare off the shark, he stabs the raft instead.

But somehow he finds an island, where he soon meets up with Floyd, the AstroChimp, who landed on the island after a space shot. And there's even a girl on the island, and soon *a whole island full of girls!*

Van Dyke, after scrapes with Jap submarines and bottles of *sake*, tries to teach a local mynah bird how to crow like a rooster. The idea is great, just like an automatic alarm clock. But something's wrong somewhere . . . on his first rehearsal the bird comes up with *"cock-a-diddle-doodle!"* (Look close and you'll see that it is audio-animatronic, just like the Tiki-birds at Disneyland).

The expected trouble with the girl's head-hunting father is not far away, but with the help of super-chimp Floyd it looks as though the United States Navy will win through to victory.

Portions of Robin Crusoe were shown on Disney's television show, but they logically left out some of the best parts — leaving them for your enjoyment inside a theatre.

Filmed largely on the island of Kauai, the picture is based on a story by Retlaw Yensid. Sound like an Asistic author you've heard of before? Try reading it backward when it comes on the screen.

This is easily the funniest film that Disney ever produced, and we delightfully recommend it for everybody of all ages. You'll find yourself chuckling over its memories for months to come.

. . . **Dad's** a little unhappy

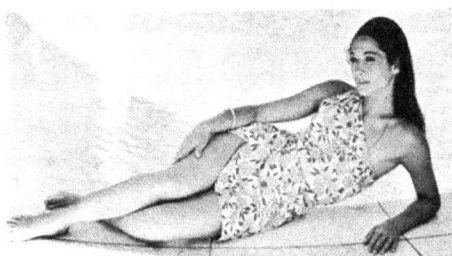

. . . "**It** shows we're somewhere between Cleveland and Cincinnati!"   . . . **Scene** stealing Astro-chimp   . . . **Crusoe's** girl Wednesday (ah, this island life!)

KRLA ARCHIVES

America's Largest Teen NEWSpaper

KRLA *Edition* BEAT

JULY 9, 1966

Sadler Sounds Off

KRLA BEAT

Volume 2, Number 17 — July 9, 1966

A BREAK-UP FOR THE MAMA'S AND PAPA'S?

A rumored "personality clash" between John Phillips and Michelle Gilliam of the Mama's and Papa's has Michelle reportedly being replaced by another female entertainer.

Michelle, pretty singer who recently attained a divorce from John, is said to have been at odds with the head Papa for some time. Reports say the group finally decided one of the singers would have to be replaced . . . and since John does most of the song writing, Michelle became the most dispensable.

The group is now supposedly searching for its fourth member. Rumors have at least ten different songstresses under consideration by the original Mama's and Papa's, and Michelle's replacement is expected to be named soon.

Finding a replacement for Michelle, however, will be no easy task; she was an integral and vital part of the group. She gave the group necessary balance, with her melancholy, mysterious presence contrasting the outgoing joviality of Cass.

Once a highly successful professional model, Michelle was one of the main attractions of the group's on-stage appearances. She carries herself well on stage and her withdrawn appearance made her tremendously popular.

She also has considerable talent as a song writer. She teamed with John to compose "California Dreamin'," the group's first nationwide number one hit.

John, Cass and Denny are now in England and are unavailable for comment. It is believed, however, that on their first appearance after returning to America, the newest Mama will make her debut.

The four original Mama's and Papa's had been together since they were the back-up group for Barry McGuire. They backed Barry on his second album and on a nationwide television special and they cut a single by themselves called "Go Where You Want To," which John had written.

Then they got their biggest boost when they released "California Dreamin'," which was written while John and Michelle were in the Bahamas.

The popularity of the Mama's and Papa's skyrocketed after this release and they quickly developed into one of the top groups in the world.

Whether the departure of Michelle will effect this status is still anyone's guess. The group's sound will undoubtedly change, as will their stage performances. And the biggest question in the minds of the Mama's and Papa's is will the change be for the better . . . or for the worse . . . ?

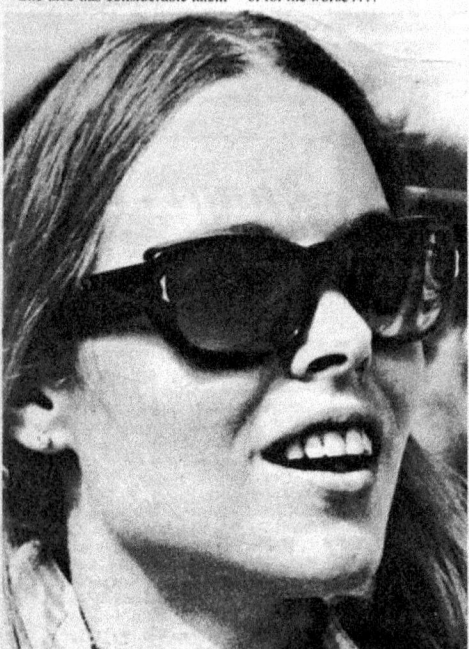

Barry Sadler: 'You Don't Have To Shake Dandruff'

By John Michaels

"I don't think you have to have shoulder-length hair and shake dandruff over the first three rows just to be able to sing."

No, the speaker wasn't Len Barry. It was a brash and outspoken American soldier who vaulted to fame after the release of his songs depicting the life of the Green Berets in Viet Nam. It was S/Sgt. Barry Sadler.

Sadler was talking to reporters between filmings at a local television studio where he was hosting a series of evening movies. He spoke quietly and with obvious restraint . . . the only time his voice picking up a knife edge sharpness was when the topic shifted to draft card burners, dissenters, or long haired groups — all of which he seemed to speak of with similar distaste.

"I Don't"

So why does he compete with such long-haired groups on the pop music charts? "I don't," he insisted. "My music is entirely different from that kind . . . when I write or record a song I don't even consider the rock 'n roll songs that are on the charts."

Nor does he like the current trend in music, which he says is "too loud." He is a country and western music fan, and his "Ballads of the Green Berets" reflects this preference.

Sadler's songs have become world-wide hits ("Green Berets" is number one even in East Germany, where the song has been banned), but they have also been the target for pointed commentary . . . especially in the United States and Britain.

Free Country

Concerning those who have called his records "trash", Sadler says: "It's a free country. People have the right not to like my songs . . . just as I have the right not to like them."

On a TV discussion show Sadler was recently quoted as saying that he got a certain satisfaction out of sighting down on a man running across an open field. But he says he was misinterpreted on this point. "I don't necessarily get pleasure out of killing a man," he reflected. "Maybe I do from making a good shot . . . just as a deer hunter likes to make a good shot . . . but I don't particularly like to kill a man."

Sadler's days as a fighting soldier are over. A poisoned spear made of sharpened bamboo sliced into his leg while he was in a thick Viet Nam jungle and gave him a permanent physical disability.

He now makes promotion tours throughout the United States for the Army. When he makes a public appearance while in uniform — which he generally does — he isn't permitted to accept the fee so he donates it to charity. A knowledgeable source, however, estimated that Sadler has already received more than $500,000 in personal income from recording and personal appearances in civilian clothes.

Sadler, after spending seven years in the service, had planned on making a career of it but now has different plans.

"If I stayed in the service I would be limited to a desk job," he said. "I just wouldn't feel right doing that. Somehow, I would never feel like one of the 'big boys'."

So after he is out of the service he hopes to continue singing "as long as there is a market for the type of songs that I do." He said he is recording songs, for one reason, "because I like making a buck just as much as the next fellow." He did say, however, that the draft card burning and dissent by American youth prompted "Ballads of the Green Berets."

Sadler, who writes all of his own songs, is now working on a new release for RCA Victor.

Symphony Conductor Applauds The Beatles

The Beatles have been praised the world over for their originality, but they recently got a pat on the back from a source that usually reserves judgment for the great Masters of classical music.

Elyakum Shapira, associate conductor of the Baltimore Symphony Orchestra, singled out the Beatles as a pop group that has "preserved originality in everything they do."

The way Shapira puts it . . . "The Beatles really do some clever things . . . musically, I mean. They are always experimenting . . . always trying something new. This is very unusual in the popular music field."

Shapira said the Beatles have obtained a wide variety of sounds and effects in their songs. To prove his point Shapira goes on . . . "There is a great difference between such upbeat numbers by the Beatles as "A Hard Day's Night' or 'All My Loving' and an intricate ballad like 'Yesterday.'"

Shapira said the main thing that has discouraged originality among pop groups is the strict emphasis on the dollar value of their profession.

Shapira adds . . . "The commercial pressures are so strong that once you do come up with something that goes over well, the typical tendency is to stick with it until you beat it to death."

The Beatles, he said, have reversed this trend and one of the basic reasons for their popularity is their lack of fear of something new . . . their thirst for originality.

Inside the BEAT

Letters To The Editor	2
Gene Clark's New Group	3
Stones Painting It	4-5
The East Side Kids	6
Is Love Lost	7
Miracles Not Going Beatles	10
The Burdon Of Eric	11
Simon Speaks	13
The Beat Goes To The Movies	15

The BEAT is published weekly by BEAT Publications, Inc., editorial and advertising offices at 6290 Sunset Blvd., Suite 504, Hollywood, California 90028 U.S. bureaus in Hollywood, San Francisco, New York, Chicago and Nashville, overseas correspondents in London, Liverpool and Manchester, England. Sale price: 15 cents. Subscription price: U.S. and possessions, $5 per year; Canada and foreign rates, $9 per year. Second class postage prepaid at Los Angeles, California.

KRLA ARCHIVES

Letters TO THE EDITOR

Barry Has None!

Dear *BEAT*:

I never read an article that made me as mad as the one on page one of the June 25 *BEAT*. Where does Len Barry get the idea he's an authority on talent. *He has none!* All his records have exactly the same sound with very little, if any, change except in the words.

The Beatles, Rolling Stones, Animals and Lovin' Spoonful have had an entirely new sound on each of their records. They are, I think, some of the finest musicians I've ever heard. I've seen the Stones and Beatles in concert and I've enjoyed both very, very much.

As for Freddie and the Dreamers—that's one group who got on the charts with a gimmick, not talent. Herman and the Hermits are cute but I don't think they are in the same league with the Beatles, Stones, Animals and Lovin' Spoonful.

Len Barry might be surprised to know that John Sebastian before he joined the Lovin' Spoonful was considered to be one of the best studio blues and folk mouth-harp players around. He was good enough to be chosen to be the mouth-harpist on the "Blues Project," an album on the finest in blues artists of today.

Len Barry's comments made me see red—thanks for letting me blow off steam.

Susan Sweet

Message To Len

Dear *BEAT*:

Could you please print this message to Len Barry?

Mr. Barry:

My father always used to tell me, "If you can't say anything nice about someone, keep your big fat mouth shut!" Get the message?

Maureen

Only The Beatles

Dear *BEAT*:

I got a sneak look at the Beatle cover that has been banned and I don't mind telling you I have never been more shocked. Only the Beatles would have the nerve to think they could get away with something like that. Somehow I just can't see the Stones, the Animals or Herman's Hermits ever doing anything so repulsive. The Beatles, obviously, still think people will go for anything they do ... no matter how degrading or unpleasant.

It is only fortunate—for the Beatles—that the album cover was banned before too many people saw it. I think it would even make Beatle fans a little sick.

Sue Herbert

Beatle Concept Not New

Dear *BEAT*:

I can't help but laugh when I see how upset people get when they talk about the Beatles' new album cover. They just can't believe their darling Beatles would stoop to something so "nauseating" and "unprofessional."

Actually, the concept of this type of thing is nothing new. Babies are starving all over the world; but you don't hear Beatle fans suddenly making any ghastly protests about this. The United States is doing much worse than the image on the album cover with napalm bombs in Viet Nam. But, again, this doesn't strike home like a simple publicity stunt by a singing group.

I wasn't disappointed when the Beatles put out the album cover; I was disappointed when they lost their nerve and withdrew it at the last minute.

Mike Gorham

Neil Diamond

Dear *BEAT*:

I just want to tell you how very much I enjoyed your interview with Neil Diamond in the June 18 issue of *The BEAT*. It was one of the most interesting articles I have ever read on a performer, especially a newcomer. Of course, Neil's comments were very interesting but Louise's comments and background added a great deal to it.

Also, I really enjoyed the article on the Young Rascals in the same issue. I only wish it had a by-line as I like to know who writes what.

And I appreciate the pic and bit on the Spoonful as they are number one in my book.

Donna Peters

Len Wrong

Dear *BEAT*:

After having read the article in the June 25 issue of *The BEAT* in which Len Barry said about the Beatles: "I enjoy their records but I think that they're probably one of the worst in-person acts I've ever seen."

Well, I'd just like to know where and when Mr. Barry happened to see the Beatles perform. I saw them last August and they're the greatest performers that I've ever watched.

Like I've told lots of other people, "If you can't say something nice about someone don't say anything at all." I'd appreciate it if you printed this or told Mr. Barry about it.

Thank you.

Jacque Garner

Cover Groovy

Dear *BEAT*:

The banned Beatle album cover is groovy! I mean, it really says something. It's about time something new was tried with album covers, because up to now they've all been so dull and alike. It looks like the Beatles are the only group with enough guts to take the first step forward.

So, it's a little gory ... so what? I still dig it and I think a lot of other people would have too if it wouldn't have been banned just because a few old ladies were complaining. But, anyway, maybe the album will clear the way for others and we can start having covers that are original and wild. Cheers for the Beatles, jeers for dumb old ladies.

Rod Sanger

Thanks For Stones

Dear *BEAT*:

I wish to compliment you on your articles about the Rolling Stones. The best article that I have ever read about the Stones was in the June 11th issue of *The BEAT*. Nowhere else has any paper or magazine given such true merit to the five boys.

Although there have been articles written for the purpose of praising the Stones in both magazines and papers they are mushy and skip over the basic facts and issues. If they do mention them they touch upon them lightly.

But this last article in *The BEAT* was to the point, so much in fact that I had to write to you and tell you how great it was. Keep up the good work. Maybe if others would follow in your footsteps people will stop thinking the Stones are rebellious and that they are dirty. But instead have talent, are intelligent and are clean and most important they have a purpose to teenagers.

Thank you again for your wonderful articles.

Patricia Ann Corney

Them Say Thanks

Dear *BEAT*:

Our sincere thanks and appreciation to the staff of *The BEAT* for all your help and co-operation, without which the group, Them, would have been unable to enter the United States. Also, for the help given us during our stay in America where everyone has made us feel very much at home.

Once again, we would like to take this opportunity to thank you.

Yours sincerely,
Jim Armstrong,
Van Morrison,
Alan Henderson,
Roy Elliott,
Dave Tuffrey,
(Them)

Capitol Explains

Dear *BEAT*:

The original Beatle cover, created in England, was intended as 'pop art satire.' However, a sampling of public opinion in the United States indicates that the cover design is subject to misinterpretation. For this reason, and to avoid any possible controversy or undeserved harm to the Beatles' image or reputation, Capitol has chosen to withdraw the LP and substitute a more generally acceptable design.

Alan Livingston,
President of Capitol Records

'in' people are talking about...

The Beatles becoming butchers and the Butchers' Union is wondering about dues ... What would happen if they sang "America" at their next party ... Why Dylan's new album is being delayed and if perhaps he's considering donning a butcher's jacket too ... What Mama Cass wants with John Lennon in the first place ... Why the Rascals are urging everybody to run ... Len Barry and whether he's sick or crazy or what ... Sonny and Cher's bomb and asking if they haven't stayed too long ... Groupies and their imaginative tales because if they knew all the people they claim to know there would have to be 64 hours in a day ... How Herbie Alpert can manage to look so totally out of sight and demanding to know who thinks up those groovy album covers.

PEOPLE ARE TALKING ABOUT Johnny Rivers and how he thinks he can get his hands clean in Muddy Water ... Why Beatle promoters for '66 are running scared and searching for things to blame their up-coming bombs on ... The Walker Brothers and their on-again, off-again Stateside tour ... Why Eric Burdon appears to despise razors so much ... Mick Jagger and his amazing mouth ... Why the phone company digs Bill Smith so much ... Paul McCartney's stop-over in L.A. and how in the world he pulled it off ... What it would take to satisfy Mark Lindsay's Hunger and how much he'd sell his pony tail for.

PEOPLE ARE TALKING ABOUT Howard Kaylan's Cisco Kid Fan Club ... Barry McGuire's tremendous ability to consume cokes ... *The BEAT* staff's futile attempts at brewing coffee and their obvious distaste for shoes ... The Beatles' decision to record backwards ... Why Eddie fell off the chair and wondering why he'd joke about something so serious ... Who Felix is waving at ... The jinx we have on the Beau Brummels ... The easiest way to differentiate between Bobby and Bill—or the long and short of the Brothers and which is which ... The pause that refreshes in the middle of "Wild Thing" ... Whether Papa John sang the wrong words or did it on purpose.

PEOPLE ARE TALKING ABOUT Frank Sinatra's Shiner In The Night ... The Stones painting it orange ... How rude a Spoonful can be ... The falling Leaves ... How much it cost Jerry ... Sam's attempt to sound like Mick and wondering why the kids are digging it ... What happened to the Shangri-las that will "never happen again" ... What it would take to make Dino Danelli grin ... Why the Yardbirds went Over so they could go Under but then turned Sideways and ended up Down ... The mess when Tony Hicks and Jeff Beck arrive in Hollywood on the same day ... How big Bobby Fuller is in New York when he couldn't move much in Hollywood ... Gene Cornish being the only one who isn't ... The way some things get flipped about, especially when there is an egotistical press agent behind the whole mess.

PEOPLE ARE TALKING ABOUT which two Lovers will be Left Alive ... How many years will go by before the Beatles find a movie script ... Why some adults say unquotable things about guys who wear long hair when their fathers or grandfathers wore even longer hair ... Why Them didn't release their first version of "Gloria" ... Why cynics say long hair on guys is feminine and wondering if they think long beards are feminine too ... How many versions of "If You Gotta Go, Go Now" will be banned and if Lyme and Cybel can get away with it when Manfred Mann and the Liverpool Five couldn't ... Why Cyrkle spells circle funny.

KRLA ARCHIVES

On the BEAT

By Louise Criscione

I found out only an hour before press time that the movie Eric Burdon was set to make has been cancelled! No explanation was given—the movie is simply off. It means that the Animals' original plans to stay in America until early September are on again. Following their Stateside tour with Herman, the Animals will kick off a British tour in October and then head Stateside again in November for a six week tour along the college trail.

Mick Jagger has been sick. A spokesman for the Stones reported from London that: "Mick's doctor has told him to rest. The group is on holiday, of course. But if they had had to work, the situation is that Mick would not have been allowed to." The Stones are due to land in the U.S. within the next few days—and that includes the mighty Jagger, we hope.

"Swinging World"

Dusty Springfield, the Yardbirds, Marianne Faithfull and Paul and Barry Ryan have filmed segments for a television special, "The Swinging World Of Youth," set to air Stateside on August 5.

The Kinks and Manfred Mann are having their share of headaches this week. As you know, Pete Quaife, bass guitarist for the Kinks, was injured in a car accident last week. The rest of the Kinks went onto Spain to fulfill a date in Madrid but were refused permission to work because Pete and not his replacement, John Dalton, was listed on their work permit! So, the Kinks turned tail and returned to London—mad. Pete will be out a month.

...ERIC BURDON

The Manfred Mann aren't too happy either. The big rumor has hit that Paul Jones, their lead singer, is leaving the group. Of course, rumors don't mean a thing *but* Paul won't deny the rumor! And what is worse, Paul has signed a management and agency deal for his work outside the Mann. To top the whole mess off, radio stations across the country are playing Lyme and Cybel's version of "If You Gotta Go, Go Now" when the Manfred Mann version was banned all over the country. Sometimes there's must no justice.

Dylan Shocked

Bob Dylan was reportedly shocked and surprised at the bad reception he received in England and France. Dylan said he couldn't understand why his English fans booed him—but then his English fans couldn't understand those pauses which just didn't refresh.

QUICK ONES: Herbie and his Brass are set to tour England in the fall... Pet Clark opened to an overflowing crowd at London's Savoy, her first major British personal appearance in four years... They're even gonna get Prime Minister Harold Wilson to attend the re-opening of the Cavern in July... The Sangri-las have been added to the Young Rascals show at Madison Square Garden in September... Beach Boys a smash at Yankee Stadium.

Clamike Records has brought suit against James Brown, King Records and Dynaton Music for damages in an alleged copyright infringement of Brown's hit single, "It's A Man's, Man's, Man's World."

Stone Dates

All of the Stones' dates have been announced. They are Cleveland, June 25; Pittsburgh, June 25 (evening show); Washington, D.C. June 26; Baltimore, June 26 (evening show); Hartford, June 27; Buffalo, June 28; Toronto, June 29; Montreal, June 30; Atlantic City, July 1; New York, July 2; Asbury Park, July 3; Virginia Beach, July 4; Syracuse, July 6; Detroit, July 8; Indianapolis, July 9; Chicago, July 10; Houston, July 11; St. Louis, July 12; Fargo, July 13; Winnipeg, July 14; Omaha, July 15; Portland, July 21; Sacramento, July 22; Phoenix, July 23; Los Angeles, July 25; San Francisco, July 26. Whew!!!!

...MICK JAGGER

The Mindbenders have just signed a new three year contract with Fontana Records, same label which released "A Groovy Kind Of Love." Mindbenders now set for a U.S. tour beginning July 1 and ending August 4.

Gene Clark: 'You Have To Hear It And See Yourself'

By Thermon Fisk

What happens to a group when it breaks up, or loses some of its members? Sometimes, the entire group disappears completely from the pop scene, never to be heard from again. Sometimes, some of the individual members join up with other groups, or even go out on their own as solo artists.

As a rule, few of these people ever attain the success they once had with the original group the second time around. Occasionally, they become far greater than that original group.

Unusual

Something very unusual has happened in the pop world recently, and it may have a widespread affect on many of its musical residents.

Several groups have been affected by break-ups—either of the entire group, or at least by the loss of one or two members. Among these, the Byrds—who lost Gene Clark; the MFQ—who are now completely defunct as a group; the Grass Roots—now minus their drummer, Joe Larson; and the Leaves, who lost their originator, Bill Rhinehart.

All of these young men were members of important groups, or groups about-to-become very important. Now, for the first time, all of these gentlemen—Gene Clark, Chip Taylor, Joe Larson, and Bill Rhinehart,—have left their respective groups and banded together to form their own group, collectively known as The Gene Clark Group.

The boys claim to have a very new and different sound, something which is uniquely their own, but something which they find extremely difficult to describe to anyone else. Gene explains simply: "I cannot describe our sound to you. You will just have to hear it and see it for yourself."

All four did agree that there won't be an electronic sound, or an Indian sound dominating their music, but they hope to return—at least, in part—to some of their more fundamental sounds of good, hard rock music. It will, of course, be more elaborate and strictly original, but still easier for the public to understand than some of the exaggerated sounds now being produced by other groups.

Vaudeville Routine?

Gene did hint that there might be a little vaudeville material creeping into their onstage appearances, and although I first thought him to be joking—after watching these four young men thoroughly destroying themselves—and our entire office—with their humor, it may very well be so.

All of the material which the group will be performing and recording in the future will be original, written and arranged by Gene in combination with the other members of the group. There is no album or single as yet recorded, but Gene hopes to have the group's first single in release within the next two or three months.

Each member of the group expressed an appreciation of the talents and efforts of their former associates, and complimented them on their new releases. Gene expressed the opinion that one of his favorite records right now is the new Byrd single, "5D."

They hope to incorporate a good deal of "soul music" into their material—both rhythm and blues and otherwise. They all agree that soul music is something which you feel, something which has to be said "that way," and at present—they are making some mighty big plans to say a number of things "that way"... *their* way.

They claim to be new and different; they say they will be great. Time—and *your* reaction—will prove their predictions true or false. But this could be the beginning of a whole new era in pop music. Who knows—someday we might even have an intermingling of the Beatles and the Stones.

Well, would you believe a combination of Dylan and the Mama's and Papa's?!

KRLA ARCHIVES

The Everlovin' Rolling Stones Are

...BRIAN FINDS SOMETHING INTERESTING TO LOOK AT BUT MICK IS TOO ABSORBED IN LOOKING AT THE CAMERA TO SEE MUCH ELSE!

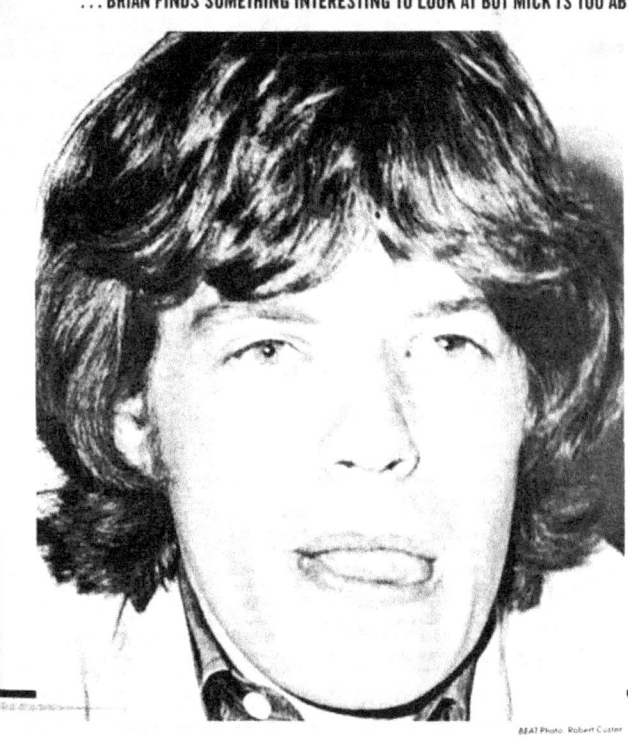

By Tammy Hitchcock

Inside the RCA Studios the atmosphere, while not tense, is certainly business-like. Guards keep vigil at all possible entrances to the huge building. They check for bubble gum stuck to locks (a neat trick fans have learned to let themselves in after a door has been locked) and they pull down the chain over the garage entrance after first looking over, under and around all the cars parked inside.

Clustered around the doors are long-haired girls in hip-huggers and short-haired girls with dangling earrings. Cameras, autograph books and stuffed toys with attached notes are seen in the hands of some while only rat-tail combs are clutched in the hands of others.

Why the tight security? Why the girls? Just why? "In" people driving or walking past RCA tonight (or any Stone night) *know* why. It's because the five Rolling Stones are locked securely inside Studio B along with Andrew Oldham, Dave Hassinger and a select and mighty few others. The Stones are cutting "Paint It, Black."

The scene never changes, the people seldom change—only the songs the Stones are recording change. It's become a common sight to residents of the downtown Hollywood area—the girls, the guards, the Stones. It happens everytime the Stones decide it's time to cut a new single or a new album and they seem to decide it's time to record *something* everytime they visit Stateside.

The Stones usually pick the evenings to record—evenings which can run all the way into the next morning's sun. And usually do. Outside the fans find the night dragging by but inside the studio it moves with increasing speed. Stone sounds blare out of the studio and into the lobby where the guards joke and laugh and tap their feet (despite themselves) in time to the infectious Stone music.

They occasionally mutter that they wish the Stones would hurry up and leave. Life's too complicated when they're utilizing the RCA Studios. But they probably don't mean it. Because *their* nights pass fast too when the Stones are there—they are rid of their usual problem of trying to keep awake when it's three a.m. and there's nothing to listen to but the creaking building.

The nearly empty building *still* creaks when the Stones are there but it doesn't stand a chance in a million of being heard as the Stone takes whiz past and the finished product winds up in the can.

KRLA ARCHIVES

Painting It Any Wild Color At All

...BUT BILL SEES IT.

...CHARLIE WONDERS ABOUT IT.

...AND KEITH? HE'S BUSY WITH HIS GUITAR, NATURALLY!

The coffee machine sometimes reposes in the lobby and every so often a Stone or two will wander out, pour himself a cup and then saunter back inside. The number of cups and the agility of the Stones in pouring and consuming them are sure ways of telling how the session's going and how tired the Stones are.

When the first break of the first session is called the Stones walk spritely to the coffee machine and between jokes and grins, manage to pour a cup without spilling. But at two a.m. on the last night of the session they sort of crawl out, their faces tired and drawn. They still pour the coffee and mix in the sugar and cream but they don't laugh. If you make a really hilarious remark they might smile. But forget the laughing and joking of the first night. It's gone.

Andrew Oldham watches the Stones carefully and when they begin making mistakes, he knows it's time for a dinner break. A break which can come anywhere from ten to midnight. And when it does finally arrive the five Stones file out of Studio B, through the lobby, past their fans and into their rented car.

Except once, when they decided to walk the short block to Martoni's. That will never happen again. The five Stones began walking, but ten steps later they started *running* as girls appeared out of nowhere and chased them down the darkened Hollywood streets. The Stones ran faster with the girls in hot pursuit and it wasn't until they retraced their steps and piled into their car that relieved grins spread across their faces. And Martoni's never *did* see the Stones that night – the Villa Capri did.

Dinner always seems to help the Stones as they inevitably file back into Studio B with lighter steps and with Mick toting a box of candy which he will, or will not, pass around – depending on his mood.

Roughly five minutes after they re-hit Studio B, the familiar sounds again blare forth and you have sort of mixed reactions. You look around and discover that there is only one other girl in the whole studio and she's with you! So, here you are watching the Stones put together "Paint It, Black" – an instant smash you're sure. And you wish all the Stones' fans could be here too, to witness the birth of a national number one record.

But, then again, you're glad they're not because then you wouldn't feel so extra special.

When the clock in the studio reaches the magic three a.m., you know you've gotta split. The dim lights inside Studio B and the driving sound of the Stones has not prepared you for the bright lights of the lobby nor the still deadness and deserted streets of downtown Hollywood at three a.m. on a Wednesday. The chilly morning air beats against your bare arms and you wish you were back inside the warm studio. You wave goodnight (or good morning, or whatever you're supposed to wave at three a.m.) to the guard as he lifts the garage chain to let you out.

And as you pull onto Sunset, you smile as you think what you've witnessed during the last eight hours – the birth of "Paint It, Black" and you wonder why people say those things about the Stones.

KRLA ARCHIVES

...THE EAST SIDE KIDS

'Living Room Music' With The 'Jewish Funky' Sound

By Ollie Tooms

There's a brand new group in the neighborhood this week, and they call themselves The East Side Kids. There are six members of the band, ranging in age from 18 to 21.

Now mind you, they *are* what might be called a "pop" group, but the music they play is ... are you ready? ... old Jewish folk songs with a beat backing!

They explain that it was sort of an abstract idea suggested to them by a friend. "We started thinking about looking for 'soul' in music, the soul of oppressed people, somebody who has had some problems. The music of people who have had problems usually has a lot of feeling in it.

Funky Rock

"So, we started listening to a lot of Jewish music and then combined it with a funky sort of rock and roll, for rhythm and blues soul. And we came up with the kind of stuff that is closely related to the East Indian music that's happening now."

That was Mike, the sometimes spokesman for the "Kids."

John Madrid, another of the "Kids" attempted to define soul music for us. "Soul music is something that is yourself."

Then Mike interjected that he thought Indian music was the epitome of soul music, because it is "improvision to the utmost, it all depends on the individual as to how the sound comes out, and that's the real, true soul."

At this point, all six of the "Kids" launched into a group reading—in harmony!—of *The BEAT*. After a few choruses in the keys of H and L minor (respectively), they decided to sound off on the comments of a gentleman named Len Barry, which they had found in a recent edition.

Bad Judge?

Dave Doud explained: "He judges people by their appearance and says he doesn't like long-haired groups because they don't like the people who put them there. Then he says that the long-haired groups are playing to the 'lowest common denominator.'

"Well, what does Len Barry dig? He doesn't seem to like *his* fans either! He's putting himself even lower by knocking them. If a person cuts his long hair off, what is he? He's still a person, except he doesn't have his long hair anymore. So Len Barry doesn't like long hair; then, all they have to do is cut their hair off and he'll like them. It doesn't make any sense."

Their first single, "Chocolate Motzos," is entirely instrumental. It is completely "Jewish Funky" music. However, the boys do intend to record tunes with lyrics in the future, just as they have been singing them in their live appearances.

The boys describe their music as being "living room music," because they create and develop it while sitting in their living room and "jamming" for hours on end. In this way they can work together to come up with newer and more unique sounds.

Also, Dave explained that the boys are definitely playing for the people, and although they incorporate all of the different ideas of the individuals in the group in their music, it is most important to them to play the sort of music which their audiences appreciate and enjoy.

Group Tastes

As a group, the boys appreciate the talents of the Beatles, the Beach Boys—"I don't like their songs, I like their *talent*"—and Paul Revere and the Raiders—"The best entertainers I've ever seen."

The future holds personal appearance tours and possible television appearances for the East Side Kids, and possibly—a hit record. Of course, it may just sound a little like the songs which your grandmother used to sing to you, but then—Grandma never had this much soul!

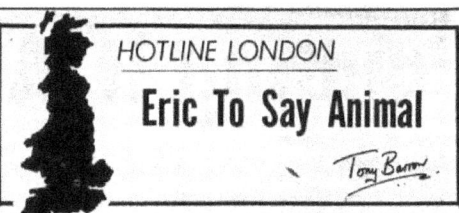

HOTLINE LONDON
Eric To Say Animal

Tony Barrow

By Tony Barrow

According to latest London reports, U.K. "Strangers In The Night" chart-topper FRANK SINATRA will almost certainly undertake at least one concert appearance in our capital at the Royal Festival Hall. If the show details are finalized, Sinatra will wait until he completes shooting of the movie "The Naked Runner" before making his first London concert appearance since 1962.

Various different stories are circulating about how JOHN LENNON achieved the curious vocal effects heard at the end of THE BEATLES' recording of "Rain." In fact that last segment of the record features the voice of Lennon IN REVERSE. He didn't try to sing backwards on the session—the actual strip of recording tape was reversed to give the desired effect.

Eric Stays

For the moment at least, ERIC BURDON has put a firm stop to extensive rumors suggesting he's to quit THE ANIMALS. It's true that the group will be unable to work any concerts, TV or recording dates all through August and September while Burdon makes his first motion picture. But Eric tells me there is no question of "Don't Bring Me Down" being the last record to be made by The Animals. Once his movie-making is over Burdon will return to the group and a new set of dates for The Animals will be fixed for October onwards.

In his screen debut picture Burdon will be featured in a demanding dramatic role. As yet untitled, the picture will deal with the tremendous influence which a typical big-name pop star can have over his fans. Shooting starts in England on August 1 which means that The Animals must cut short their July U.S. tour with Herman's Hermits so that Eric can be in London for final script rehearsals. He will be in front of the movie cameras for at least seven weeks. Meanwhile most of The Animals have been taking a pre-tour vacation before jetting in your direction. Burdon chose the island of Majorca for his sun-soaking fortnight.

After being involved in a motorway accident, it is not likely that PETE QUAIFE will rejoin THE KINKS before their July 17 concert date in Barcelona. The Kink sustained foot and head injuries when his car was involved in a 70 m.p.h. collision with a large truck. Without Pete, The Kinks continued their schedule of TV and radio appearances to coincide with the U.K. release of "Sunny Afternoon." Then they left to tour Spain and Denmark with John Dalton acting as temporary Kink in Quaife's place.

Glen Goes

Because the group's second solo singer ROD ALLEN is featured on both sides of the FORTUNES' new record—"Silent Street" and "You Gave Me Somebody To Love"—vocalist GLEN DALE is quitting to go out on his own. Scottish rhythm guitarist SHEL MACRAE left with THE FORTUNES for their brief tour of Germany last week and he's expected to stay with the unit as Glen Dale's permanent replacement. ... "Sunshine Superman" is the title of a new album by DONOVAN. In addition it's the single he's about to release on both sides of the Atlantic. Under this and two other cancelled titles, the same number was originally to have been issued as a Donovan single almost one year ago.

NEWS BRIEFS ... Sandie tells me Don told her the other Don is going to marry Dolores this side of September (Heck! Only an everly few folk will understand what that's all about!) ... ALFRED ("FREDDIE") LENNON, father of Beatle John, announced his intention to marry a 41-year-old mother of six children, the former Mrs. Trudie Harris, a part-time barmaid at a Surrey pub ... Star-stacked audience at London's Savoy Hotel saw PETULA CLARK'S cabaret opening. EDDY ARNOLD amongst the first-night guests. Pet started her own series of six weekly TV shows here last week ... New wave of rumors indicate substantial likelihood of MANFRED MANN lead vocal star PAUL JONES leaving the "Pretty Flamingo" group ... DA-DOO-RONETTES now join THE CYKLE as supporting attractions for BEATLES' August U.S. tour ... Revival of movie number "Hi Lili Hi Lo" is next record by ex-Animal Alan Price with THE ALAN PRICE SET ... Next WALKER BROTHERS single features another Bob Crewe composition, "You Don't Have To Tell Me Goodbye" ... Sitar jackets in fawn and black (selling for around 30 dollars) are latest line in Carnaby-street boutiques ... Much U.K. TV for HERMAN'S HERMITS to promote their newie "This Door Swings Both Ways" prior to July U.S. tour ... Hollywood showbiz publicist JERRY PAM in London last week. Also top New York deejay GARY STEVENS ... It was Gibby—of Brian Epstein's singing/playing trio PADDY, KLAUS AND GIBSON—who suggested to HOLLIE Graham Nash that he should show set of original new songs to DON AND PHIL EVERLY at their May Fair Hotel in London. Everlys selected seven Hollie numbers to record ... July 28 London hearing of drug charge case against DONOVAN and his manager Ashely Kozac unlikely to assist success of artist's next record "Sunshine Superman" ... CILLA BLACK singing her first Country & Western song, "I Can't Stop Loving You," in Blackpool "Holiday Startime 1966" summer season stage show ... Miami's RON O'QUINN making pop pirate station RADIO ENGLAND the most American-sounding of all the off-shore Top 40 ships around our coast ... MOODY BLUES, SOUNDS INCORPORATED and CLIFF BENNETT AND THE REBEL ROUSERS starring in TV spectacular to be made at London's underground beat city.

KRLA ARCHIVES

Is Love Lost?

...WHAT IS LOVE TRYING TO PULL?

BEAT Photo-Chuck Boyd

By Rochelle Reed

In the spirit of good reporters everywhere, BEAT staffers have braved screaming fans, flying bricks, press parties and other assorted hazards to bring you all the news of the music world.

At one time, BEAT reporters had to kick off their high heels and run for it, with Rolling Stones' fans hot in pursuit.

But even this didn't prepare us for LOVE.

LOVE is the group of five young men that placed "In My Little Red Book" on the top 10 and sold enough albums to give the group a strong foothold in the music world. Though they are wonderful entertainers, they are miserable at communicating.

The BEAT has been trying to interview LOVE for quite some time and when other interview sources failed to materialize, we invited them to our office.

Bryan

LOVE didn't show. Instead they called to say that Bryan was "sick in bed, unable to leave" and could we come out to their "castle?"

So we dropped everything and journeyed out to their hillside home, a huge, old, weird structure that might have been a set for a Dracula move.

We pulled up to the "castle" to find Bryan, who had been "sick in bed" dressed and talking intimately to a girl on the doorstep. Saying good-bye to her took Bryan a while, and the news that he was worse the next day came as no surprise.

Walk-Out

It was the first interview I almost walked out on. After numerous waits, we rounded up Arthur, Kenny and Bryan, but neither Kenny or Snoopy ever showed up.

Monosyllables and giggles were their only comments and my ire was really blown off when Bryan began complaining that I hadn't brought a tape recorder along to capture the profound conversation taking place at this tremendous meet. Arthur and Jon, meanwhile, sat on the floor, uncommunicable to everyone including themselves.

I experimented with all kinds of questions – hip and straight. Since the LOVE have no written biographical material, I had to get that information at the same time.

The big blow came when I asked LOVE how they got together. "We were walking down the railroad tracks..." said Arthur and John.

"No, it was in a gang fight – I was just about to hit Arthur over the head and..." Bryan disagreed.

That did it. "Let's go," I said.

LOVE reacted to this verbal slap in the face the way I had hoped. Arthur and John sat up and told Bryan to shut up. Then the interview began anew.

LOVE, I found out, is a new group timewise, as they've been playing together only six months.

Arthur Lee, lead singer and songwriter for the group, likes to explain their music as being "free-sounding." "It's self-expressive, I guess," he added, then shrugged into silence.

Within a minute, he continued his description. "It's spontaneous," he said, "with a little combustion thrown in," added Bryan brilliantly.

A Happening

It obviously wasn't my day. Apparently the group met in the same free-wheeling way that they describe their music. It just sort of happened.

Arthur and Johnny Echols, both 21, were playing together when they met 19 year old Bryan Maclean. Then they added Kenny Forssi, 23, and Snoopy Phfister, 19, the youngest of the group, for an engagement at "Brave New World," a coffeehouse.

Both Arthur and Johnny were born in Memphis and came to Los Angeles when they were very young. Bryan was born in Los Angeles while Snoopy hails from Switzerland.

Kenny is the only one in the group that doesn't sing, and he sticks to playing bass guitar. Arthur, John and Bryan play mainly guitar, although all play various other instruments. Snoopy alternates between drums and piano.

Original Songs

The group performs almost all original material and Arthur writes most of it. Their album features 11 songs by Arthur and one by Bryan.

Their next album, to be cut this month, will be "very different," they promise. "It will be prettier sounding," Arthur said before he was immediately lambasted by the other two.

"Anyway, it will be easier to listen to," he conceded, "with catchy parts." LOVE, unlike many other groups, does not choose to emphasis either the music or the lyrics, but tries for a balance of the two. They want their music to engulf the listener, much like they feel love engulfs the world.

What's Love?

Love means a lot to LOVE, they say, but they haven't decided exactly what. "It's all around us," says Arthur, but apparently naming the group LOVE was not a profound christening by Arthur but merely a name for lack of any other – several of which Arthur claims were more or less stolen by other big name groups.

The LOVE are a weird group – there's no doubt about it. Often rude. And they occupy their hillside "castle" in a world of their own. They don't live there for any romantic reason though – only because they were looking for a five bedroom place where they could practice.

No Put-On

"We're not a put-on. This is the way we really are," Arthur swears, but I got the distinct impression they weren't completely honest with themselves. Nothing means much to these young men, not even love.

The only thing LOVE wants out of life is to achieve success. "We're going to make it to the top," Arthur declares militantly, adding that he has no intention of staying in the small time.

Indeed, if LOVE could succeed on musical worth alone, they might make it to the top. But their offstage manners leave them in the venerable position of being just another group to fall by the wayside.

Only when a group really reaches the top can their careers withstand what they may suffer from being continually rude and uncaring to fans and reporters alike.

In my opinion, LOVE will soon be on many blacklists in the music industry, rather than "In My Little Red Book," where they want so badly to belong.

KRLA ARCHIVES

THE WORD HAS GOTTEN OUT — The place to find your favorite performer is at KRLA. Just about everyone drops by to answer phones. Beach Boy Dennis Wilson even stopped in the parking lot to sign autographs.

ANOTHER FAN caught Carl Wilson just outside the station door and collected another cherished autograph.

Inside KRLA
By Eden

Summer has definitely arrived at good old KRLA, and just to prove it — the last couple of weeks have hung right in there being just as hot and hectic as possible!

Over the last two weeks, we have had all kinds of great guests answering our request lines — and all kinds of mob scenes, with the many fans (mostly female-types!) who came down to see their favorite recording artists. Whewwww!

In the last 14-day period, we have played host to — and effectively planned getaways for — Paul Revere and the Raiders, the Beach Boys, the Standells, the Mama's and Papa's, Simon and Garfunkel, the Byrds, Them, the Vogues, the Hondells, the Lovin' Spoonful, Ian Whitcomb, and Joey Paige.

Beatle Cover

See what I mean? *Hectic!!!* Then, to add to all of the confusion, we had a Beatle album released, and a Beatle album *cover* which was *almost* released. By now, you have undoubtedly read about the controversial cover in the pages of *The BEAT*, and heard it discussed on KRLA, so you are well aware of the commotion stirred up by that one picture.

Dave Hull — the scuzzy old Hullabalooer — told me that, in his opinion, it was "horrible! I'd say it was extremely distasteful. I quizzed several kids here at the station about it. I showed the album cover to them and they didn't like it either."

Summer Re-Runs

Uncle DM confided to *The BEAT* that the Bat Cave is now well into its summer re-runs! Unfortunately, Super Sissy — originally set to act as host for the series of summer Bat Kave-RLA re-runs — has had to leave us temporarily in order to pay a warm and affectionate visit to one of his uncles. I believe the gentleman's name is *Sam*. Anchors Aweigh, Super-Sissy-Babe!

There's a brand new giveaway coming to KRLA (Son of a Bat Dealie!!!) and it's just for *you*. Now, for the first time in the history of modern radio, you can obtain your very own, personalized, KRLA Belly Button just made for *your* belly button.

Obviously, the purpose of the thing is to cover up your belly button (hallowed be its name!) so as to protect it from sunburn and other such unpleasant summer situations.

All you have to do to get your KRLA Belly Button — absolutely free of charge, as a community service — is to send a self-addressed, stamped envelope to Belly Buttons, KRLA, Pasadena. All right everyone — hold on to your belly buttons, and let's all get out there and COVER UP!!!!!!

Question Of The Week

Questions this week: Could Bill Slater ever succeed as Boy Wonder, and would his success have a damaging effect on his friendship with Robin?

Is it true that Casey Kasem has always wanted to be in movies, and hopes to someday do a revival of The Shiek of Araby in widescreen technicolor?

Is it true that Charlie is related to Van Gogh . . . on his right side?

Is there any truth to the report that Glenn Campbell is secretly plotting to sabotage Emperor Hudson's Nine Iron?

Is it *possible* that Dick Biondi was once a 285-pound gym teacher at UCLA?

Is there any truth to the rumor that Johnny Hayes is the best tambourine player in Los Angeles and has snagged the leading role in the Byrd's first film?

Why does the Amazing Pancake Man want revenge? And what have *I* got to do with it?

Dear Susan
By Susan Frish

How long will the Yardbirds be in the States on their summer tour?
Mae Washington
About six weeks.

On the Ed Sullivan show I noticed Paul McCartney had a chipped tooth. Why?
Jill Jameson
That was from his motorcycle accident.

What is Donovan's first record and what label does he record under?
Barbara Daurty
"Catch The Wind," and he records under Pye, or in the States Hickory.

How old is Mark Lindsay and Mike Smith of Paul Revere and The Raiders? *Malene Mahoney*
Mark is 24, and Mike 21.

Where can I write to Barry McGuire?
A Fan
Write Barry in care of, Dunhill Productions, 321 S. Beverly Dr., Beverly Hills, California.

Are the Searchers going to be coming to the States in the summer? *Joyce Smith*
Plans were made for July, but now they have cancelled them, so I doubt that they'll be coming now, at least not in the summer.

When will the Yardbirds be arriving in the States? *Sue McElliot*
They arrive in New York on August 1, and they'll be in L.A. on August 28.

Are the Troggs English or American? *Brenda Cashdin*
They are English.

What was Marianne Faithfull's first record, and what are her hobbies and her favorite color?
Mike Barrow
"As Tears Go By." Her hobbies are reading, particularly poetry, and as for her favorite color, or colors, she likes pink and brown.

How old are the Grassroots?
Diane Peepers
They are all 18.

Is Ray Davis of the Kinks married?
Debbie Moon
Yes, and he has a little girl named Louise.

What is Herman's address?
Mary Gould
9 Chestnut Lane, Roby, Liverpool, England.

KRLA BEAT Subscription
SAVE 33% Of Regular Price

☐ 1 YEAR — 52 Issues — $5.00   ☐ 2 YEARS — $8.00
☐ 6 MONTHS — $3.00

Enclosed is _____   ☐ CASH   ☐ CHECK
PLEASE PRINT — Include Your Zip Code

Send to: .... Age: ....
Address: .... City: ....
State: .... Zip: ....

MAIL YOUR ORDER TO: **KRLA BEAT**
6290 Sunset, Suite 504
Foreign Rate: $9.00 — 52 Issues   Hollywood, Calif. 90028

KRLA ARCHIVES

Time Capsule 'Hot Rod' To Preserve Teen Age

Parents often complain that teenagers rule the world and their complaint may be truer (happily) than they think.

Teenagers now occupy strategic positions in clothes design, art purchases, finance and business, and many teens write books, columns and plays.

And of course, teenage buying power is enough to turn any merchant's head — they influence the spending of $25 billion a year...

Finally, after recognition of the Ice Age, Air Age, Space Age and Nuclear Age, today's Teen Age is being celebrated by the planting of a teen age time capsule, scheduled to be preserved for 1000 years.

The capsule will actually be a hot rod vehicle loaded with memorablia representing the American Teen Age from 1955 to the present. The year 1955 is, of course, the year of Bill Haley and his Comets, and their "Rock Around the Clock," which actually rocked around the world to introduce rock 'n roll.

"Rock Around the Clock," which has sold more than any other rock 'n roll record (it's *still* selling), may give Bing Crosby's "White Christmas" a run for its money. Haley's hit started the wonderful madness that has produced Elvis Presley, the Beatles and all the others in between.

Now Robert Poore, a former teen singer himself, is looking for teen contributions from all over the country for placement in the capsule. Objects and documents of fashions, music, science and literature relating to the teen-age era from 1955 are being submitted in care of Poore at 1245 N. Vine St., Hollywood 90028.

The names of all donors whose objects or documents are selected for the capsule will appear on display as they are selected, until "drop" time. Afterwards, duplicates or replicas of the objects, with the donor's name, will be kept on display during all future public exhibitions of the capsule and its contents.

Poore has also launched a nationwide search for a hot rod car (any vintage from 1955) which will be used as the capsule and filled with teen memorabilia. The vehicle will be sealed, and lowered into the earth for preservation.

The selected hot rod will be on display along with the donor's name until "drop" time and then a replica will appear for future exhibitions.

Any car constructed by a teen or constructed when the person was a teen will be considered by Glenn Gregory at 1570 Gower St., Hollywood, Calif. 90028.

After considering many sites, Poore has decided to plant the capsule on the land of the proposed Silver Nugget Hotel in Las Vegas. It will be dropped later this month at the site.

Poore has invited well-known personalities to contribute articles for the capsule and one group to do so is The Outsiders, who have led the contributions by donating first copies of their two albums on the Capitol label.

Robert Poore, originator of the Teen Age time capsule, was a singer under his own name at one time. Then he took the name Beau Gentry and placed "Heartbreak of Love" in the top twelve.

After that, he went back to Bobby Poore and became an actor for stints in segments of Dobie Gillis, M Squad and Wagon Train, among others.

Then Poore decided to enter another phase of show business and became a theatrical booking agent. Now he has branched out into film production and is currently working on three pictures which will play to teenage audiences.

English Like Frank

Frank Sinatra has hit the top spot on British charts for the first time in 12 years with his "Strangers in the Night."

The last time Sinatra was Number one in Britian was with "Three Coins in a Fountain" in 1954. His daughter, Nancy, occupied the same position in English pop charts earlier in the year with "These Boots Are Made For Walkin," also on the Reprise label.

... THE OUTSIDERS

Local Girl Joins Otis Redding Show at the Apollo Theater

An attractive 23-year-old blond dancer from Hollywood is currently appearing at the Apollo Theater in New York with the fantastic Otis Redding Show.

Judy Guyer, who has been working as a Go-Goette at Hollywood's Whisky A Go Go for the last two years, is now dancing at the Apollo at the request of Otis Redding.

She's one of the first White artists to appear at the Apollo, and also one of the first to work with Redding.

Redding first noticed Judy when he appeared at the Whisky, where he cut a live album. Judy will also appear on the cover of that album, along with Daryle Ann Lynnely, the Whisky's other regular dancer and Slim Picken's daughter.

He asked the two girls then if they'd like to tour with him but later changes his mind.

"He's been touring the South and thought we'd get stoned," explained Judy.

He also had some second thoughts about Judy working at the Apollo.

"Otis is very cautious of my being White," added Judy, "so he asked me to take a Negro girl with me."

So Cynthia Webb, another local girl, is accompanying her.

"It's going to be quite an experience," Judy continued. "We'll probably be completely exhausted. We do five shows a day, from 2 p.m. to midnight.

"We might come back a little skinnier, which I have no objection to."

In addition to dancing at the Whisky, Judy does all of the choreography for the Go-Goettes and designs the outfits they wear.

THRU JULY 10
BACK HOME AGAIN!
JOE AND EDDIE
— plus —
BRITISH COMIC JONATHAN MOORE

AT DOUG WESTON'S
Troubadour
9083 SANTA MONICA BLVD.
L.A. NEAR DOHENY

RESERVATIONS CR 6-6168

COMING JULY 12 — MUDDY WATERS

KRLA ARCHIVES

The Miracles Are Not Going Beatles

"Us? . . . Why no, we hadn't really thought about it but . . ." Smokey Robinson was caught off guard by the question. He looked around the room and pondered the rumor about which he had just been questioned. It had the Miracles planning to record some of Paul McCartney's compositions.

Not that the Miracles really needed to, but word had gotten out that they were going to re-do some of the English group's songs.

The rumor didn't sound quite right to us either. Because if it's one thing the Miracles are it's original, and if anything it would seem likely that someone else would do their songs.

"We admire the Beatles very much," Smokey explained, "but we write all of our own songs, as well as writing some for the other Motown groups. We've never had any real desire to do anyone else's songs."

Smokey and his Miracles are one of the smoothest acts around today, and it seems hard to imagine them benefiting by a change. The group has been together since 1954 and in that time their versatility and talent has become a standard as they have not only turned out their own million sellers ("Shop Around"), but have written goldies for other groups ("My Girl" by the Temptations).

Their versatility has also been demonstrated by their touring schedule, which has been revamped and is now composed almost entirely of night clubs. It would seem natural that playing before older, more sophisticated audiences they would have to modify their style, but their audiences like them just the way they are.

"No matter who we're playing for," Smokey said, "we do pretty much the same things. We've never had any reason to change our act."

All four of the Miracles, Smokey, Pete, Bobby and Ronnie, are from Detroit and all four are married. Their tours have lessened in the last several years but when they're not touring they're kept busy at the Motown headquarters in Detroit.

The singing of the Miracles ranges from "soulful" rhythm & blues to classical rock 'n roll. But however you look at it, their style is still as up to date as today's headlines.

And Smokey knows what it takes to keep a group on top. "A group has to remain exciting to its audience," he said. "I think it's admirable for a group to be so popular that they get 'mobbed' occasionally. When they lose this, they've lost everything."

Smokey and his Miracles have been mobbed quite a few times.

... "A GROUP HAS TO REMAIN EXCITING" say the exciting Miracles.

 For Girls Only

By Shirley Poston

I have just informed my dad that I may never speak to him again.

As you may have already guessed, he had two comments to make regarding this threat. One was, "promises" and the other was "promises."

As you may also have guessed (do a lot of that, dont you?) (in this column, you *have* to) (I already know that I left the apostrep . . . that thingy that looks like this (') out of the don't up there, so dont start nagging me about it.)

Where?

Oh, where was I (a question I find myself asking all too often these days)? Ah, yes, I was about to say that you've probably guessed that I found out what he meant when he said my ravings sound like "a cuckoo in its cups."

According to Barb Harrison (gasp) of San Francisco, it means about the same thing as a *drunken do-do bird*. Thanks a lot there, pop. You, too, Barb.

Speaking of Harrisons (and I hardly ever do) (nt), I've had a few outrageously groovy Beatle dreams in me day (not to mention me nights), but last night I had the all-time oddie.

I dreamed I went to a press conference (in my *ugzqnackvuovg*) There was one big table with chairs for the Beatles on one side, and chairs for the press (your pants while you wait) on the other. What I mean is, the rows of press chairs started right on the other side of the table.

Right against it, I MEAN. (Horseradish! I can babble more than six hundred brooks.)

Anyspeedway, I sat down in the first row. Pretty soon Ringo came in and sat down right across from him. He was wearing the same thing as he had on the night of "Ed Sullivan," and carrying droomsticks.

I still can't believe this dream, but here's what I did. I gave him this soulful look and said "Why can't they all be here?" (I had Robin Boyd at the Cavern on the brain, maybe?) (It would be a nice change if I had *something* on it besides water.)

Well, he gave me this strange grin and said "I wouldn't run out for days."

Perfectly Logical

I haven't the foggiest what he meant by that, but in my dream it seemed a perfectly logical answer.

Then the rest of the Beatles walked in. And what did I do next, you arsk? I smiled, handed John a bottle of aspirin, and walked out.

Boy, don't think *that* one didn't wake me up in a large hurry. But I didn't have long to try figuring out what *that* meant because I went right back to sleep and dreamed that the Beatles were giving their second concert (whatever happened to their first?) in the backyard where I used to live.

There I go again. No, no, I didn't live in the backyard (although my folks did drop a few hints to that effect) (now they suggest such things openly.) Oh, you know what I mean.

Anyway, I was racing around trying to get a ticket, which was odd because I lived there at the time.

Woke Up

Then I woke up again. Well, all I can say is this. Narcissa Nash, unless you've started charging for your invaluable services, *helppp!*

Speaking of help, have I ever told you about the bit I have going with the Beatle record of the same name?

For the past year or so, every time I've really needed help (would you believe 24 hours a day?) (well, then, would you believe 25?), I've heard "Help" on the radio.

It's happened about ten or so times. You know, just enough to give me some more willywackers on the olde wezand. A friend (?) of mine suggested that I hear the song in such moments whether it's playing or not.

Scoffed

I immediately scoffed that one off (and placed a hysterical call to the station the next time it happened, just in case.)

Another reason I thought of it, is because it happened again just a few days ago. I had this violently important appointment (more about that later—it concerns someone you all know) and I was so scared my legs felt like tapioca pudding.

Just as I was turning off the car radio, there came "Help" again. Can't you just imagine what an ultra-groovy feeling that gives me? Even though they don't know me, they're right there when I need them, to sort of help pluck up the olde courage.

I guess they're right there for a lot of us . . . in a lot of ways. Sorry to get morbid and maudlin, but caring too much about someone sure teaches you about yourself. Boy, I could *kill* people who say that someone you don't even know can't have an effect on your life. George Pant Harrison has changed almost everything about me.

Wish he'd hurry up and get to work on my luck.

Gibbering

Well, I have once again wasted almost an entire column gibbering. Don't you ever get tired of reading all this frothing-at-the-typewriter? If you ever do, please tell me. I used to write a sensible, rational column. I probably could again if you ever find yourselves up to here with my inanity (feel free to add an *s* after that first syllable.) However, I wouldn't advise your making any large bets.

Fortunately, I've rambled on too long to tell you something I probably shouldn't tell you anyway (about the one really *funny* time "Help" played.) If I haven't come to my senses by next week, maybe I'll pick up where I left off. Providing, of course, that I can figure out *where* I left it.

One thingy for sure next column (and I use the word . . . sorry, words fail me.) I've made up my mind (go ahead *say* it) about how to handle my reader-meets-star "contest." So I'll be blithering on indefinitely (amen) about that next week.

A Word To The John Sebastian Fan Who Loves To Call John Sebastian John Sebastian: Hurry! On account of because they're trying to drop a net over you. No, seriously, I know just what you mean. The name just fits him, and it's such a nice name to say (or, if you prefer, moan) (and *you* would.)

Several Words To *All* John Sebastian Fans: Could I interest anyone in starting a *"Pnje Bingu Xe Ipkbn Jziijn Vkxaq Rjgbbnb* Club?"

I realize that George may never forgive me for that, but if he thinks *that's* unforgiveable, I wonder how he's going to feel about *August?*

August P. Schwartz, that is. You know, the nice man who's always trying to drop a net over *me*.

Say you read it in The BEAT

KRLA ARCHIVES

The Big Burdon Of Soul When It Belongs To Eric

...BURDON AT HOME

By Louise Criscione

He's wild, he's way-out, he's too frank for his own good. Plain and simple—he's Eric Burdon. Chief Animal, super-soul, the works. Brian Jones thinks he's the best lead singer in England today. And although he hasn't actually said so, I suspect Eric thinks so too—and he just may be right. If he's not the tops, at least he is one of the very best of the blue-eyes.

If you don't think so, watch his short and rather sturdy frame move on stage. Watch his face twist into unbelievable grimaces while he's wailing something soulful, something definitely Southern U.S. Then you'll know what soul is all about.

Controversy

But beyond soul, Eric possesses what reporters like most about a person. The man's controversial. Boiled or fried, it just means that Eric has a flare for making headlines. A flare which he has on many occasions turned into a raging fire. It comes naturally to Eric —he just opens his mouth and out come honest but often searing remarks. About a lot of things, but especially about discrimination.

Eric's preoccupation with discrimination began when he was a child. "I was a Protestant brought up in a mainly Catholic area in Newcastle," says Eric. "Kids can be pretty cruel when you are the only different one among them."

It must have been a painful childhood because Eric has never gotten over it. To this day he hates discrimination with the same amount of passion as he loves rhythm 'n' blues. He's presently writing a book, a book which may never be published and one which is sure to be banned in parts of the world. Eric says the book is about his friends and his experiences. The friends Eric lists are people like John Lee Hooker, James Brown and perhaps he'll even include the time he met Cassius Clay.

Out-Spoken

But beyond the stories, Eric will attempt to project his own ideals and beliefs. And this is where he might run into some problems for many think he is entirely too outspoken. An opinion which makes Eric laugh and frown almost at the same time.

Actually, Eric is a curious mixture. He tires on the tough-guy suit but sheds it for the nice-guy outfit when ladies are around. I remember once when the Animals were appearing on the now-deceased "Shindig." Eric was standing off in a corner, unshaven and scouling. Completely oblivious to scenery being moved, dancers practicing and cameramen lining up shots. His hair looked as if it could stand a good washing and his clothes could use a trip to the nearest laundry. He looked for the world like he had just stepped out of the slums somewhere.

And yet when he walked over to me his manners were those of a Beverly Hills executive. I don't mind telling you that it was a shock to discover that the Eric Burdon on the outside and the Eric Burdon on the inside are two different people.

Yet, those two people have one thing in common—they're sensitive. Eric will never win the Muscle Man Of The Year Award.

He looks in the mirror—he knows. So he laughs and calls himself, "overfed." And it's the same with discrimination. He grins as he reminisces about his childhood and yet he digs "Mississippi Goddamn" by Nina Simone.

Not Funny

People have been predicting the death of the Animals ever since Alan Price split and then when John Steele left they all went around sending flowers. But Eric made "Don't Bring Me Down" a smash. Now that Eric has decided to make a movie the death rumors are flying again. Only this time no one's laughing. They can't because the rest of the Animals were noticeably upset by Eric's movie move—one which he will make without them. It means that they're out of work until Eric finishes his movie —and they don't find that amusing at all.

When an English reporter asked Eric point-blank if there was unrest in the group, he nodded his head but refused to answer. Of course, the story was played up huge in all the papers, using the face that Eric refused to answer as sure proof that the Animals had made their last record as a group.

Only the Animals know for sure and they're not talking. But you can bet on one thing. Whatever Eric decides to do, he'll do—hang everything else. He's like that. You might call it bull-headed or you might just term it strong-willed. Personally, I'd just say it's Eric Burdon...frank, opinionated, untidy, talented, out of sight!

...BURDON ON STAGE

KRLA ARCHIVES

DLP 3717

It's 'Over' for Jimmie Rodgers

But Only On His New Album!

HEAR JIMMIE, EXCLUSIVE ON

... Jimmie Rodgers

KRLA ARCHIVES

Paul Simon Says Dylan's Too Arrogant

Simon and Garfunkel have become one of the most popular — and one of the most unusual — singing duos in all of the pop world today.

Their first three records have all been hits, including their latest, "I Am A Rock." All of the songs which Art and Paul perform and record are written by Paul Simon, who has earned himself the reputation of being one of the finest song writers — and poets — around today.

But Paul is a very modest and unassuming young man. He is a great talent — but not one given to constantly reminding those around him of his creative abilities. Of his songs he explains: "I wouldn't presume to preach in my songs.

"I can't tell people what they should do, I can only express my feelings, my opinions in a song. If their opinions happen to coincide with mine, fine, but what I sing is personal.

"I hope it will make whoever's listening sit up and recognize something they've been thinking themselves but didn't know how to say it."

Fallen Idol

Paul seems to feel very strongly about the attitudes and obligations of a writer and a singer, and he has some very definite opinions on the subject, especially when they concern someone who was once an idol of his.

Bob Dylan was once placed upon a pedastal of sorts in Paul's mind, but his feelings have been considerably altered in the last year or so. Paul gives us an insight into his own personality as well as his views on Dylan with his explanation:

"I had to get out of the Village. (Ed. note: Paul was born and raised in New York, and spent a good deal of time in Greenwich Village.) It was stifling. The people there have lost all the ability to communicate. Dylan was one of them:

"He's too arrogant. He preaches — doesn't explain. He generalizes, he tells everyone what he thinks is wrong with the world. Who cares what he thinks? He's lost the talent for talking to human beings.

"His arrogance has lost him many friends around the Village. People who fed him and gave him a roof over his head when he was down a few years ago, they've lost faith in him."

Sensitive Poet

Paul is a kind and considerate human being. He is a talented and creative writer who is able to artfully weave his great sensitivity and compassion for life and humanity into his songs and his poetry. And most of all, Paul Simon is a poet.

He isn't just someone who writes songs and occasionally hacks out a few rhymed verses which aren't meant to be sung. He is a perceptive interpreter of human emotions and feelings, and even his songs sound like works of great poetry rather than just so many words sung by a pop singer.

Paul says simply: Words — they're *everything*. How can anyone possibly do justice to them, communicate, express, describe, when they've got to stick to a tune, hold it in their head, and play a guitar? Words alone are enough."

In one of Paul's songs, "Sounds Of Silence," he says: "Hello darkness my old friend; I've come to speak to you again." Through the words of Paul Simon's songs and poems, he is speaking a language which is bringing light to thousands of people the world over.

... IT'S GARFUNKEL AND SIMON — NOT THE OTHER WAY AROUND.

So, What's With The Leaves?

... THE LEAVES AS THEY FALL TODAY.

Individualism is something a lot of people talk about but something few practice. It is courage to try something new even though there is no proof of its success. Individualism is what distinguishes a stereotyped group from five assorted young men with both collective and separate personalities. It is what sets the Leaves apart and the reason for their immediate success.

The Leaves . . . five men who make no effort to align their individual personalities just for the sake of a single, simplified image. There is Bob . . . the business-like scholar of the group; and Jim, whose nick name is "Gentleman Jim." And the sullen, withdrawn Bobby who is contrasted by the outgoing friendliness of Tom and John.

The Leaves are now going big time after a year of being labeled "a local group." The release of their latest album "Hey Joe," which contains one of the widest assortment of sounds of any LP released in a long time, is probably the reason why.

fornia, "War of Distortion." Bobby, who wrote the song, explained that it is a "freak out" song.

"We were playing at the Trip," he recalls, "when I got the idea for the song. The people dancing to our music was the 'war of distortion.'"

The Trip is one of many top entertainment spots where the Leaves have played. They have been booked at Ciro's on Sunset Strip, have done engagements in San Francisco and Santa Barbara, and the Summer Spectacular in the Hollywood Bowl. They will appear at "It's Boss" in two weeks.

The Leaves are a raw, vibrant lot, and this has been one of their main appeals in both live performances and on record. It would take an unusual name to depict them, and the name "Leaves," although other groups have assumed titles of both insects and animal life, is the first entrance into the botany field.

"We were all sitting out in the back yard one day trying to think up a title for our group," remembers Bob. "It was a windy afternoon and the leaves were falling to the ground. That's when we decided 'Leaves' would be our name."

KRLA ARCHIVES

The Adventures of Robin Boyd

©1965 By Shirley Poston

Half-way through "Hard Day's Night," Robin stared across the car and snorted inwardly. Which, of course, caused her to choke outwardly.

"What's the *matter?*" Ringo (A.I.A.R.) (As In Angel, Remember?) jumped, removing his eyes from the screen (a painful but necessary move.)

"*Nothing's* the matter," Robin fumed. "I was just thinking about how much *trouble* I'm having keeping my promise to *control* myself."

Ringo gave *her* a look. "Well, see that you *continue* keeping it," he admonished, returning his eyes to the screen (ahhh, that's better.)

"Don't *worry*, I will," Robin snarled under her breath. "*NOT!*" she added at the top of her lungs.

Fungus Among Us

Ringo re-jumped, smashing his face against the roof of the Facel Vega (repetition, you may have noticed, is still the fungus amongus.) "*Now* what?" he asked tiredly, not to mention toothlessly.

But Robin didn't answer. She was too busy staring aghast at the car which had just crashed to a stop beside them.

"*George!*" she gurgled as a tall, lean Liverpudlian leaped out of the all-too-familiar Jaguar (a messy sight as the digestive process had already begun) and retrieved what remained of the ex-speaker.

"*Robin Irene Boyd*," Ringo commanded, yanking her out of the glove compartment (not to mention the socket.)

But she *still* wasn't listening. "Just as I *thought!*" she screeched. "George is with *her!*"

"*Who?*" Ringo snapped, beginning to lose patience (not to mention his halo.)

"That . . . that *Ann Thrax* person. Who, come to *re-think* of it, is too dreadful and horrible to even faintly *resemble* Pattie Harrison!" babbled Robin.

"Shurrup and watch the movie," Ringo further ordered. "You know what I told you about George. You're not to have a thingy to do with him until you've completely reformed."

Let it not be said that Robin didn't make a sincere effort to comply with the wishes of her guard (and not as in *ian*) angel.

She, in fact, monkeyed around and followed his instructions for thirteen seconds. However, on the fourteenth, she went Harry Apers (that's British for bonkers.)

"I can't *STAND* it," she shrieked as the girl in the next car had several thingys to do with George and did them rather well.

"Then sit *down* and act like a *lady!*"

Robin moaned, again not hearing a thing Ringo said (which was just as well because this was a heck of a time for him to test her ability as an actress) (at moments like these, Oscar could go smell exhaust pipes.)

Suddenly she stopped moaning. She still didn't know exactly what sure that murder would do for openers.

Her quaking hand reached for the handle (see paragraph #6) (then learn to live with the situation.)

"Oh *no* you don't," Ringo said, lunging to stop her.

"Oh yes I *do!*" Robin writhed, yanking the door open. And, with this, she vaulted head first into another ex-speaker.

Picking herself up (a nice change), she started to race hysterically toward the steamy-windowed Jaguar.

Then she came to a screeching halt.

Ringo not only wasn't following her. He was nowhere to be seen.

"What have I done?" she asked, suddenly recalling the sound of a somewhat sickening *crunch*.

Ballet, Yet

"I have *really* done it, *that's* what," she soon answered as she returned to the other side of the car and witnessed what appeared to be the last act of "Swan Lake" during a tornado.

"*Ringo!*" she screamed, fighting her way through the cloud of feathers and slamming the car door back open.

"*George!*" she added hysterically as Ringo toppled unconscious out of the Facel Vega.

Robin will probably never known how what happened next happened (parddon?), but the next thing she knew, the Jaguar had disappeared and she was sandwiched between George and the remains of Ringo.

"What *happened?*" George bellowed, maneuvering the F.V. under the screen and out of the theater through a loose board in the fence. "And where's the nearest hospital?"

"I think I shut his wing in the car door and turn right at Left Street," she sobbed.

Winged

"Shut his wing in the *car door?*" George gaped. "How not to mention why not to mention where now?"

"I was coming over to kill you and he tried to stop me and turn left on Right Street," she re-sobbed.

"Left?" he echoed.

"Right," she replied.

(As any Californian can attest, there is no middle of the road where our street-naming is concerned. Streets must either accept being known by something as simple as A or B orpay the social consequences of being titled Apple-Plum Marmalade Manor.) (Blues.)

Fortunately for everyone concerned, this conversation soon ended as they permanently rubberized the emergency entrance of a hospital called, not unappropriately, Angel's Rest.

Drop-Out

Moments later, after Ringo had disappeared down the hall on a stretcher propelled by a slightly unnerved intern (who was to, in later years, refer to this incident as the moment that turned the tide of his life) (he left med school and became a plumber), Robin and George found themselves across the counter from an equally distraught nurse.

"I have a few questions," she trembled, brandishing an 84-page questionnaire.

"Now, *look*," George said sharply. "This place is called Angel's Rest, correct?"

"I think so," she quaked.

"Well, we've just brought in an angel. The rest of him is scattered all over a drive-in theater."

"I *see*," she re-quaked, seeing but hardly believing. "What about the bill?"

"*Blank* the bill," George replied, using a bit of Liverpudlian Robin had never heard before. (Others of us, having been around, *have* heard it and know better than to print it if we expect to *stay* around.)

"Scuse me scouse," he reddened. "I'll pay the bill, of course."

This being all the nurse really wanted to know (with the possible exception of which end was up), she raced down the hall (where she immediately turned in her bed pan and left the profession) (she later became a plumber's helper.)

For the next half-hour, Robin and George paced wordlessly about the waiting room. Then, shortly after George had started on his second carton of Senior Service and had been told for the thirty-second time that it was boy, a man in white staggered up to them.

After making sure that he wasn't carrying a net, Robin and George pounced. "How's Ringo?" they blithered in unison.

The doctor searched for words (not to mention his marbles.) "Your - er - friend will be just fine," he finally gulped. "We're making the necessary arrangements to repair his - er - we've sent out for ducks - um - the necessary arrangements are made."

"When can we see him?" Robin and George re-blithered.

"You can visit him tomorrow," the doctor replied nervously. "And don't worry about us talking. If Psychiatric gets wind of this, they'll never give us a chance to prove it."

"Thanks for that," George said warmly, shaking the doctor's hand. (An unnecessary move as the doctor's hand was already shaking plenty, thank you.) (You're welcome.) (Best learn to live with that, too.)

Breathing a series of relieved sighs, Robin and George returned to the car whese they sat for some time without speaking.

Finally George looked at Robin. And Robin looked back.

"*George*," she breathed.

"*Marcia*," he chortled. Then he reached an arm around her and kissed her so hard *everyone's* teeth rattled.

"I take it you missed me," he said modestly (not to mention later) (as in mutch.)

Robin suddenly stiffened. "Yeah," she said sourly. "I also missed getting the measles once."

George retreated to the other side of the car (a short not to mention a bum trip in a F.V.). "*Hah?*" he inquired.

"I forgot something," she sagged, and she told him the whole sad story. "And I'm to have nothing to do with you until I've completely *reformed!*" she finished tearfully.

After a few preliminary moans and several "change-one-hair-and I'll-yank-out-the-rests," George put his head in his hands. "Would it help if I talked to Ringo?"

Robin shook her head (which rattled a lot, as usual.) "No, he wouldn't listen."

George re-put his hands in his re-head. (There's something wrong with that sentence, but I hesitate to rewrite it as it seems to be part of a matched set.) (Willow pattern, I believe.) (And *I* would.) "Who *would* he listen to?"

"I dunno . . . someone who understands me . . . a grown up, maybe."

George grimaced. "A grown up who understands *you?* Impossible!"

"Impossible," Robin agreed.

And it was then that it hit her. It was also then that it hit her. It was also then that she knew what she must do.

"George, dear," she said smiling sneakily. "Let's go."

"Where?" he arksed (and Lord knows he might well.)

"Just turn into Out street and then go up Down."

George started the car. "But where are we going?"

Robin smiled sneakily-er. "Never mind," she said, humming a chorus of Alex Andersrag Time Band.

(*To Be Continued Next Week*)

KRLA ARCHIVES

The BEAT Goes To The Movies

"BOY, DID I GET A WRONG NUMBER!"

By Jim Hamblin
(The BEAT Movie Editor)

Bob Hope is these days something of a legend in his own lifetime. Now a multi-millionaire, he devotes a large amount of time to doing nice things for other people. Recently he appeared at the annual Celebrity Golf Tournament at March Air Force Base near Riverside.

After he came off the 18th hole he told us, "We're playing *my* kind of golf out here today . . . *cross-country!*"

And as a matter of historic interest, *Ski-nose* performed for the first time in front of troops at March Field on May 6th, 1941. At the recent golf tournament, Hope was introduced to an airman now stationed at March *who was born* on the day of that first show.

Appearing with Hope in this delightful comedy is Phyllis Diller, the stand-up comedian with a husband named Fang. They are an obvious hit in this movie, which involves the story of a runaway movie queen who winds up in Rocky Point, Oregon, where real estate man Bob Hope is just in the process of trying to unload "no-takers acres."

It is difficult to say just which is the best part of this film, but no red-blooded male can for long ignore the immense talents of German-born Elke Sommer. Seen in all her glory, she spends much of the time in one bubble bath or another.

She told us it was a very rough film to do. "Most of the stunts I had to do myself, and I really got scarred up," she lamented. Various scenes called for her to fall through a trap door while riding a skate board, and to slide down a rocky hill on a board, among other acrobatics.

In addition to being one of the great beauties on the screen, Elke is also a charming and intelligent woman who is outspoken about her life, her loves, and herself. "I think the *face* is the most important part of a woman," she observed, while autographing a life-size portrait of herself wearing only a small mink stole. "Men," she continued, "get tired of looking at just *bodies* all the time – what's all that laughing for? – while a face is a new and always changing part of a woman."

Well, Elke baby, you are certainly entitled to your opinion.

But she promised that she would not be wearing a bundle of clothes in her next picture. "No, that would ruin my image. Men," she says, "still like to see undressed women in movies, and thank Heaven they do!"

Audiences will see about as much of her as they ever have. This photoplay from Edward Small and United Artists is excellent fare for the entire family, and the whole story comes to the screen in very good taste and high humor.

Besides, there *must* be something hilarious about Elke Sommer and Phyllis Diller in the same movie!

...A WRONG NUMBER in anybody's book

...SHARING HIS OLIVES with the whole wide world

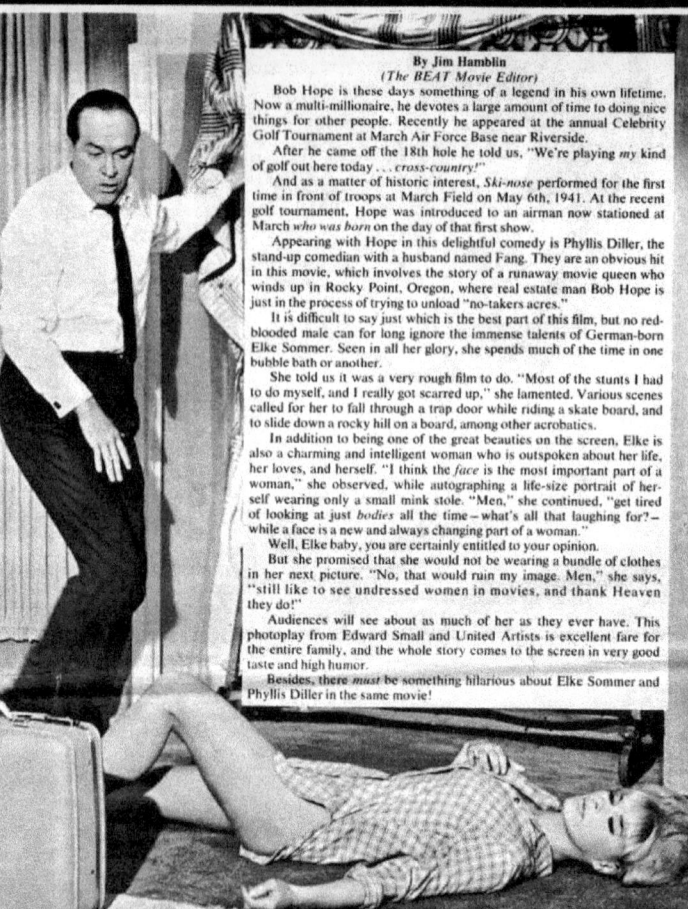

SOME OF THE BEST one-liners are traded between this great new comedy team in latest UA release.

SHE SAYS the face is the most important part of a woman's body.

KRLA ARCHIVES

KRLA Tunedex

This Week	Last Week	Title	Artist
1	2	SEARCHIN' FOR MY LOVE	Bobby Moore
2	3	DOUBLE SHOT (OF MY BABY'S LOVE)	Swingin' Medallions
3	9	STRANGERS IN THE NIGHT	Frank Sinatra
4	1	DIRTY WATER	The Standells
5	8	PAPERBACK WRITER/RAIN	The Beatles
6	10	LITTLE GIRL	Syndicate of Sound
7	5	YOU DON'T HAVE TO SAY YOU LOVE ME	Dusty Springfield
8	28	WILD THING	The Troggs
9	12	SOLITARY MAN	Neil Diamond
10	23	HANKY PANKY	Tommy James & The Shondells
11	6	PAINT IT, BLACK	Rolling Stones
12	4	A GROOVY KIND OF LOVE	The Mindbenders
13	7	ALONG COMES MARY	The Association
14	24	SWEET TALKING GUY	The Chiffons
15	17	WHERE WERE YOU WHEN I NEEDED YOU?	Grass Roots
16	14	OH, HOW HAPPY	Shades of Blue
17	11	HOLD ON! I'M COMIN'	Sam & Dave
18	18	I AM A ROCK	Simon & Garfunkel
19	16	YOUNGER GIRL	The Hondells
20	22	BAREFOOTIN'	Robert Parker
21	19	DID YOU EVER HAVE TO MAKE UP YOUR MIND?	Lovin' Spoonful
22	13	DON'T BRING ME DOWN	The Animals
23	15	WHEN A MAN LOVES A WOMAN	Percy Sledge
24	21	DAY FOR DECISION	Johnny Sea
25	20	OPUS 17 (DON'T WORRY 'BOUT ME)	The 4 Seasons
26	29	LOVE SPECIAL DELIVERY	Thee Midniters
27	34	AIN'T TOO PROUD TO BEG	The Temptations
28	25	BETTER USE YOUR HEAD	Anthony & Imperials
29	39	HUNGRY	Paul Revere & The Raiders
30	35	BAND OF GOLD	Mel Carter
31	30	HE WILL BREAK YOUR HEART/HE	Righteous Bros.
32	36	YOU BETTER RUN	The Young Rascals
33	26	DIDDY WAH DIDDY	Captain Beefheart & The Magic Band
34	27	(I'M A) ROAD RUNNER	Jr. Walker
35	—	LET'S GO GET STONED	Ray Charles
36	38	COOL JERK	The Capitols
37	33	THE MORE I SEE YOU	Chris Montez
38	32	GREEN GRASS	Gary Lewis
39	31	HAVE I STAYED TOO LONG	Sonny & Cher
40	—	MUDDY WATER	Johnny Rivers

DAVE HULL

BOB EUBANKS

DICK BIONDI

JOHNNY HAYES

EMPEROR HUDSON

CASEY KASEM

CHARLIE O'DONNELL

BILL SLATER

KRLA BEAT Subscription

☐ 1 YEAR — 52 Issues — $5.00   ☐ 2 YEARS — $8.00   ☐ 6 MONTHS — $3.00

Enclosed is _____   ☐ CASH   ☐ CHECK   PLEASE PRINT — Include Your Zip Code

Send to: ....   Age: ....
Address: ....   City: ....
State: ....   Zip: ....
Foreign Rate: $9.00 — 52 Issues

MAIL YOUR ORDER TO:
KRLA BEAT
6290 Sunset, Suite 504
Hollywood, Calif. 90028

KRLA ARCHIVES

America's Largest Teen NEWSpaper

KRLA Edition BEAT
MFP

15¢

JULY 16, 1966

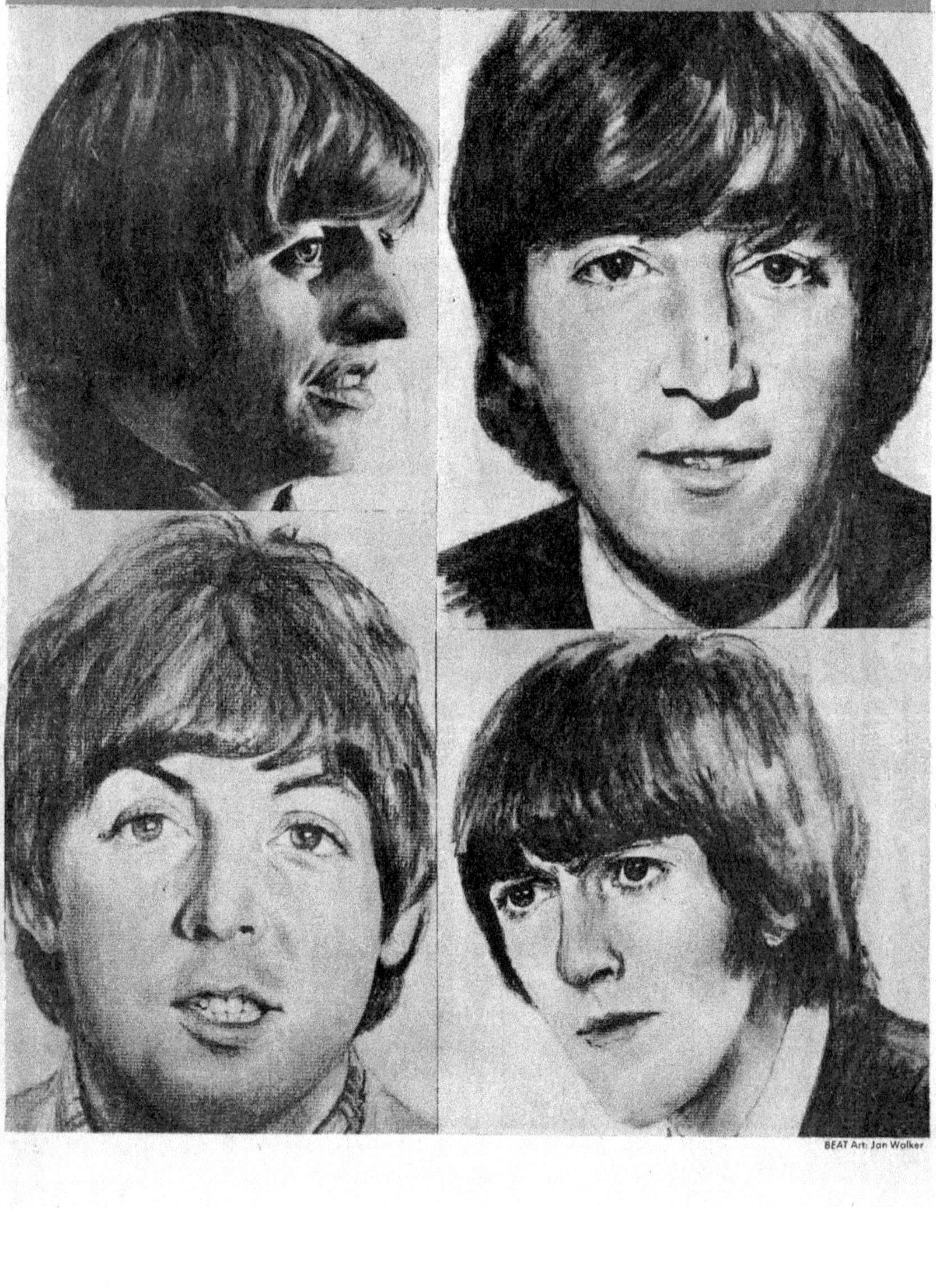

BEAT Art: Jon Walker

KRLA BEAT

Volume 2, Number 18   July 16, 1966

BEATLE CHANGE ERASES PROFIT

The Beatles have released a conventional album cover entitled "Yesterday and Today" after banning the first cover to the album because it was "misinterpreted." The untimely transfer cost Capitol Records and the Beatles at least $250,000.

More than 750,000 copies of the original album had been distributed across the United States and were poised for release when a backlash of protest from those who received advance copies forced the withdrawal.

Capitol officials made the decision to ban the cover. They quickly sent word to those who had received the advance copies and informed them the cover was being withdrawn.

The 750,000 albums were reclaimed, and then began the mountainous process: by hand, the records had to be taken out of the covers, and by hand again, stuffed into the new covers. Then they were re-shipped to the distributors.

But reclaiming and restuffing the covers was only part of the problems. Streamers that went to dealers, and other printed promotional material all had to be junked and new ones put out.

"It will cost us about $250,000," a record company spokesman said. "That wipes out the profit."

The Beatles had intended the first album cover as pop art. But it was vehemently rejected and some even charged it was cannibalistic. It showed John, George, Paul and Ringo in butchers smocks festooned with chunks of raw meat and the severed parts of a toy doll's body.

The new cover, however, is much more sedate. It shows the Beatles simply standing around a stage trunk.

But even though the album had hard luck in its early going, it is still expected to be a smash in sales. A Capitol spokesman said close to one million copies of the album with the new cover were shipped to distributors on release date. The initial allocation is one of the largest in Capitol's history.

Of the 11 tunes in the LP, none have ever before been released on an album. Five ("Drive My Car," "I'm Only Sleeping," "Dr. Robert," "And Your Bird Can Sing," "If I Needed Someone" have never been released in the U.S. The six other songs were all previously released as singles. They are: "Nowhere Man," "Yesterday," "Act Naturally," "We Can Work It Out," "What Goes On?" and "Day Tripper." All of the songs with the exception of "Act Naturally" (written by John Ressel/Voni Morrison) and "If I Needed Someone" (written by George Harrison) are Lennon-McCartney compositions.

Stones To Sue Hotels

Hotel proprietors have never been noted for their fondness of long-haired singing groups, but this time it looks like they might have gone a step too far.

The Rolling Stones, who stopped off in New York City while on a nationwide tour of the United States, last week charged 14 elite New York hotels with refusing them loding. At the same time the British group slapped the hotels with a $5 million civil suit.

The group is contending their civil rights have been violated. They said the hotel proprietors made no attempt to conceal the reason for their refusal of service,

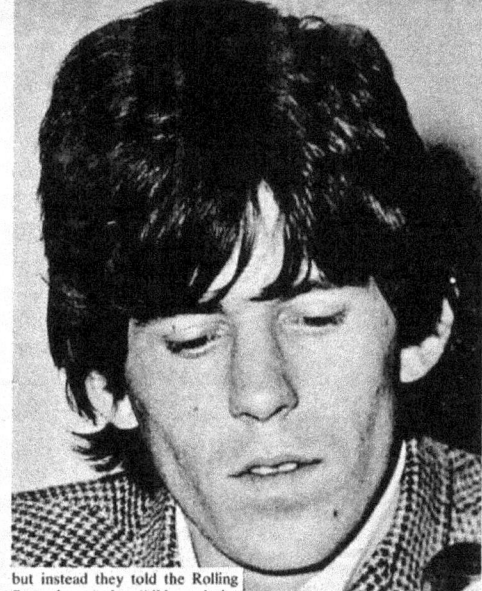

but instead they told the Rolling Stones' agent they "did not desire to lodge the plaintiffs and that they must go elsewhere."

The Stones thought the refusal of lodging had something to do with the fact that they were foreigners. They said the hotels discriminated against them "on account of their national origin."

Groups have often been refused service by hotels and other enterprises in the United States, but none have ever sued. The suit could possibly start a precedent making it unlawful to refuse vital services to anyone because of personal disapproval.

In the past, when a hotel refused service to a group it was generally on the premise that the group's presence in the hotel might cause chaos and damage to the hotel by eager teens who sought to get closer looks at the group.

But the 14 hotels in New York City didn't even use this excuse and now it might cost them $5 million.

Meanwhile, the Rolling Stone '66 Stateside tour began a triumphant run in Lynn, Mass. where the Stones were mobbed, barracades were smashed and several arrests were made.

Bob Dylan Gets Into The Album Controversy Too

By Carol Deck

Bob Dylan, way out wizard of the weird, has added a few more Dylan originals to the music of our times.

His new album, "Blonde On Blonde," will probably be talked about as much as the Beatle album cover that's just been withdrawn.

To start with, he's ignored the usual horizontal album cover and turned the cover on it's side to utilize the entire back surface for one long vertical picture.

The picture, Dylan leaning against a wall, is fuzzed out of focus just enough to annoy you.

And inside are 10 more photos, with no captions or explanations. In the center is a large picture of a girl but no one at Columbia Records seems to know who she is.

There's also a picture of some man who Columbia doesn't know who he is either. They do know, however, that he's not Al Grossman, Dylan's manager, or Bob Johnston, the producer of the album.

The only person on the album, besides Dylan, that they do know is Hargus Robbins, Dylan's organist. The back of his head appears in one of the pictures.

(Turn to Page 4)

Inside the BEAT

Letters To The Editor 2
Double Shot Of Medallions 3
A Beatle Recording Session 4-5
Adventures Of Robin Boyd 6
Manfred's Paul Jones 7
Conceited Crispian St. Peter? ... 10
What's A Yardbird? 11
Mark Lindsay's Two Worlds 12
Hotline London 13
Gary Slams Len 14
The BEAT Goes To The Movies 15

The BEAT is published weekly by BEAT Publications, Inc., editorial and advertising offices at 6290 Sunset Blvd., Suite 504, Hollywood, California 90028, U.S. bureaus in Hollywood, San Francisco, New York, Chicago and Nashville; overseas correspondents in London, Liverpool and Manchester, England. Sale price, 15 cents. Subscription price: U.S. and possessions, $5 per year; Canada and foreign rates, $9 per year. Second class postage prepaid at Los Angeles, California.

Sam Leaves Yardbirds; Will Continue Writing

Paul Samwell-Smith, bass guitarist and founder of the Yardbirds, rocked the popular music world last week when he announced he is leaving the quintet. "Sam," often called "the brains behind the group," is being replaced by one of the Yardbirds' session guitarists, Jimmy Page.

Sam will remain close to the Yardbirds, however, even though he will no longer make stage appearances or sit in on recording sessions with them.

Sam explained that he left the group to devote more time to writing and record production. He said he will continue to write almost exclusively for the Yardbirds and will co-produce their discs with manager Simon Napier-Bell.

Will the change affect the Yardbirds' sound? Remaining members of the group say they don't think so, even though Sam is an excellent guitarist and greatly accented the group's sound.

But the Yardbirds point out that Jimmy Page is also a good guitarist, and under the present arrangement Paul can supply them with more fresh material.

Sam, who played bass with two other groups before the Yardbirds existed, founded the original Yardbirds along with Keith Relf some time ago. But the rest of the personnel was different then and even though the group had a couple of resident stints at London jazz clubs, it was still virtually undiscovered.

Jeff Beck, Jim McCarty and Chris Dreja were then added to the group and their popularity increased somewhat, but for a while it looked as though their unorthodox style wasn't geared to the public taste.

Sam noted that while the group was not prepared to change its style just to get a hit, it was delighted to do "For Your Love."

The song made the top five in the United States and even higher in England. It helped the Yardbirds to their present status and paved the way for their other hits since then.

Sam has written most of the material for the Yardbirds, but as a member of the group he has recently been unable to devote much time to composing.

So now the Yardbirds might be losing a bass guitarist, but they're gaining a full-time composer.

KRLA ARCHIVES

Letters TO THE EDITOR

Uproar Is Ridiculous

Dear BEAT:
You will not want to print this letter and most likely won't because it is very contrary to your majority's views on a "controversial" subject. However, I am writing this, hopeful that someone will take notice in spite of some uncomplimentary references to persons who created the inspiration for it.

I will have to state first that the whole uproar over the Beatles' banned album cover is nothing short of ridiculous. When I heard it being described by DJs as "controversial" and/or "nauseating," I became curious and with a friend went to the station to find out what it was all about.

A DJ (I won't say which one) walked out with the partially hidden album cover under one arm and when he stopped to give an autograph, we asked him if we could please see it. He said, "Certainly," and he showed us.

The look of anticipation as if he expected us to groan or vomit or something was enough to make us want to laugh hysterically. So THAT was it! I shudder if someone even cuts his finger but this album cover looked no more nauseating than four little boys who had frolicked through the refrigerator steaks and then the toy box.

It's really surprising how one can shock half the nation into cardiac conditions with a bit of a messy album cover. SADISTIC? That really makes me laugh; and though I will agree that it is not in the best taste and certainly is not a very artistic idea, seeing these half-witted people's reactions to it was amusing enough in itself and maybe that is what the Beatles intended.

As they go further into their experimentation with sight, sound and mind they leave behind more and more angry, confused members of the general public who just can't understand.

And may I pose a question? How can people who will condemn a comparatively harmless photograph allow moral filth such as the song, "Double Shot (Of My Baby's Love)" and others which not only have disgusting lyrics but no musical quality at all to be available to teenagers—and with no comments from our quick-to-put-down-the-album-cover disc jockeys. If it weren't such a sad situation, it would really be a laugh.

— Sue

Beatle Art

Dear BEAT:
I am writing in response to the article in your latest issue about the cover of the new Beatle L.P. I thought the article was completely ridiculous and obviously the author had his doubts too because he didn't sign his name. I don't think I would admit to being that totally assinine either.

I have seen the album cover and although I'm sure the Beatles could have found a better one, I'm not going to crucify them for using the one they did. I can see where someone might say that it was in poor taste but to go so far as to scream that it is revolting and nauseating is ridiculous!

There are far worse paintings in thousands of art museums and galleries all over the country. I've seen many of them myself. Maybe if the Beatles had placed their album cover in museums throughout the country it might have gained artistic recognition instead of being attacked as an outrage and a disgrace.

I'm not saying that it is a work of art but that it seems ridiculous that when there are such grotesque paintings and exhibits accepted by the people as art they can still jump on the Beatles and say that they have put out a nauseating album cover.

Right now our nation is involved in a war, we are having riots inside our own country. I think we have much bigger things to criticize and worry about than a record cover. It's just being blown way out of proportion!
Thank you.

— Randi Vreeland

BEAT Vegetarian?

Dear BEAT:
Since you solicited them I am offering my comments on the recent Beatle record jacket and related subjects. All I have seen of the cover is what was reproduced in the newspapers, so I may not be qualified to judge its merits. My feeling, however, as well as that of everyone I have talked to (which, unfortunately, excludes show-biz folks) is that it is a charming and imaginative piece of work.

Perhaps whoever wrote the unsigned article in the July 2 BEAT is a vegetarian, in which case I can sympathize with the feelings of revulsion evoked by the jacket design. What I do find hard to understand is the statement that BEAT staffers and their fellow arbiters of teenage taste "felt it was the most sickening spectacle they'd ever seen."

Why is the sight of a few decapitated Barbie Dolls and freshly butchered sides of beef more sickening than the lurid daily photographs of the effectiveness of our bombing and napalming in Viet Nam? Is it because the baby dolls and steers are Anglo-Saxon while our human victims across the Pacific are merely Communist or Buddhist gooks?

— Thomas Ganiats

Cover Is Clever

Dear BEAT:
I certainly don't understand why so many people protested the cover of the Beatles' "Yesterday And Today" album. I saw a photo of it in a San Francisco paper and I felt it was not only clever but also very original. And as for the Beatles trying to shock us, well, all I have to say is "large charge."

I loved the whole idea for the picture as it was so unusual and unlike anything else. It seems a pity that some people can't accept something new and different. And it also seems that lately the Beatles can't do one darn thing without being criticized.

— Joni Sawnier

English Bad?

Dear BEAT:
It isn't very often that I feel so strongly about something that I will take the time and effort to write a letter. In your July 2 issue of The BEAT you featured what I think is the best description of what the English are like. I would like to congratulate Jackie Genovese for having the courage to write it and to congratulate The BEAT for printing it.

I lived near England nearly all my life and I know what the English are like. Two-faced is a mild name you might call them. The English like exactly what is good for the English, no matter who suffers. Their opinion of themselves is, "No one is, was, or will be as great as we are."

There is a poem the Irish have about them which I think is a good summary of them. "God made the Irish, the devil made the Dutch, whoever made the English sure didn't make much!"

Thank you very much for listening to my opinion.

— Jackie McGinty

To Be Funny

Dear BEAT:
Concerning the article on the Beatles' new LP cover and your question on what I thought it was done for I would like to say this. I think they did it because they thought it was funny. I thought it was funny when I heard the description of the cover.

Of course, hearing the description isn't as effective as seeing it. I would like to see it very much. It couldn't be so horrible in black and white.

— Elise Kurutz

Beatles Are Changing

Dear BEAT:
I have just finished reading the July 2 issue of The BEAT and now I just must comment on a few things.

On the Beatles new L.P. cover being banned, well, the Beatles have always been impossible to figure out and probably will always be! Maybe they are tired of the whole bit—the concerts, being famous, being on the move, etc. and want to stay home in England with their loved ones.

On their new single and album, the music world is changing and they can't have the same style of the days of their first few albums. (But oh how I wish!) If they did, we wouldn't have the greatest album ever made by anyone, "Rubber Soul!" As Paul said about their song, "It is not our best single but we're satisfied with it. We are experimenting all the time with our sound. We cannot stay in the same rut." And I agree.

The Beatles are my favorite group and always will be. Sure, a lot of their singles haven't been their greatest but someday they will find the new style that is awaiting them.

Lastly, that Jackie Genovese who said that about the Beatles not liking America must be losing a couple of her marbles! I have an English pen pal and she sends me papers (such as the great BEATS I send her) and everytime I see something the Beatles said about America it has been good! (And why not???!!!)

Thanks for reading this letter, now I'm happy I've said what I wanted to.

— Nancy Thune

Why The Big Fuss?

Dear BEAT:
Whatever happened to all that professed admiration for honesty? I refer to the "nauseating" Beatle album cover. I've had several graphic descriptions of it given me and can't for the life of me understand all this hue and cry.

Perhaps because I happen to dig the humor of the pose. Not many people will. Now, this doesn't put me above those who don't care for grisly jokes but I don't really think it should put them above me either! Has it ever occurred to any of you that the Beatles just liked the idea of posing that way and decided to do it?

You think the cover is nauseating. I happen to see the amusing side. Each of us is entitled to his opinion but my main point is contained in the beginning sentence. Is the Beatles' openness and their willingness to risk offense for what they care about and all the other "honest" things for which they are praised—are all these things laudable only when they don't offend anyone?

It takes neither honesty nor courage to produce a full album cover or to state, for instance, that a great deal of pop music is trash. Anyone familiar with the business will substantiate the last statement. It's true. But it does take at least a modicum of courage to expose oneself to the sort of witch-hunting which is being pursued by so many people against the Beatles because of this album cover. Maybe they thought it would be a crazy, fun thing to do—pose for that picture, I mean.

I'm being redundant. I've said too much and yet too little but hope I've got my point across. There seems to be a bit of hypocrisy lurking in the woodwork somewhere; let's see if we can smoke it out and kill it.

— Kathy Sedwick

Fans' Fault

Dear BEAT:
I've wanted to write to The BEAT for a long time but until now I haven't had the time. However, the letter about the "snobby" remarks that some English groups have made about the U.S. really stirred me up. I honestly think that the American fans of these groups are at fault. Sorry to say, I cannot exclude myself from the fans who have given these English guys a pretty rotten impression of America. I wish you'd print my letter so that maybe a few U.S. teens will see the light.

First of all, England means home to these groups. England is where their families and friends are. England is where they've spent most of their lives. Yet a lot of us don't think about that.

I've heard so many people say that the English groups don't spend enough time in the U.S. But why should they when just about all they see of our great country are stuffy hotel rooms. The only people they come into contact with are nosey reporters and screaming fans who are a constant threat to their very lives.

I mean, how would you like to have to sneak around and hide all the time from a bunch of nutty girls who are bent upon tearing you limb from limb! It's pretty frightening, you know.

Maybe someday—when the screams die out and another generation takes over the world of pop music—a one time Beatle or Stone or Hermit will come back to the U.S. and get a look at our really good side.

— Linda Reali

KRLA ARCHIVES

On the BEAT
By Louise Criscione

Are you ready for this? David Garrick has sent his recording of the Jagger/Richard composition, "Lady Jane," to the Queen of England because he says it relates to her ancestors. David goes on to say: "I think this song is a collectors' item – history brought it up to date." Could be, I guess, and knowing Mick Jagger it probably is!

Personally, I thought a lot of fuss was made over nothing when people made such a big thing over Paul's broken tooth. Well, he's had it capped now but I guess he felt he had to explain about it 'cause he told the whole story. "It was quite a serious accident at the time," says Paul. "It probably sounds daft, having a serious accident on a motorized bicycle but I came off hard and I got kicked about a bit. My head and lip were cut and I broke the tooth."

Paul's Fault

Paul admitted that it was entirely his own fault. Says he hit a stone in the road because, "It was a nice night and I was looking at the moon!" He probably won't be looking at the moon anymore because although he had his tooth fixed he still has a scar on his lip. And the moon just isn't worth it.

Forget the Hollies. They aren't coming Stateside for their tour scheduled to kick off on July 28. The reason? Work permits, naturally. They applied for work permits weeks ago and they haven't come through so the Hollies have decided to cancel their U.S. tour and take some other offers they have.

They do hope to visit us at the end of October for a four to five week tour and in the meantime they have a British tour lined up as well as a three week vacation.

... PAUL McCARTNEY

Mama Meets John

Well, Mama Cass finally met John Lennon and as an extra added bonus Paul McCartney showed up too! Guess Cass wasn't disappointed because she said after her meeting with John: "He was charming, courteous and intelligent. Witty, amusing and entertaining."

Cass said the two Beatles sat around and talked for hours and that Paul even played the piano. "They were everything I hoped they would be," finished up Cass.

While we're on the subject of Mama's and Papa's, the latest word on Michelle leaving the group is that today they are the same group – but there's always tomorrow and people closely connected with the group seem awfully upset at what tomorrow could bring. But until then – everything's groovy with the Mama's and Papa's.

Boy, Len Barry sure knows how to open his mouth and have people all over the world mad at him. Remember what he said about long-haired groups? Well, the mail has been pouring in and now even Gene Pitney's gotten into the act.

Gene said he didn't read what Len said but, of course, he heard about it. "When I was told I could only say that somewhere, somehow along the line, something went wrong. I can't believe Len said that. Maybe he did criticize long hair – to which my answer is that length, or shortness, of hair is quite irrelevant to a performer's talent or lack of it – but I don't think he meant to attack the Animals like that. They're obviously a talented, musical group."

Ego Factor

Gene had a few comments of his own to make on why groups wear long hair in the first place – he thinks it's an ego factor. "If you wear long hair," said the short-haired Gene, "you're instantly recognized as being on the pop scene – or at least a beatnik! I think it's a lot harder to go on stage looking absolutely straight but that's the way I prefer it. I rely on the show, on my singing style, rather than on something as irrelevant as hair length."

Gene's a great performer and an all around talented person. Too bad people in the States refuse to recognize the fact.

Have you heard the new Dylan album, "Blonde On Blonde," yet? Out of sight!

... GENE PITNEY

THE SWINGIN' MEDALLIONS (l. to r.) Joe Morris, Jimbo Doares, John McElrath, Steve Caldwell, Carroll Bledsoe, Jimmy Perkins, Charlie Webber and Brent Fortson. Yes, Virginia, **all** eight are Swingin' Medallions.

SWINGIN' MEDALLIONS SAY:
'Double Shot' Is A Fraternity Song

By Rochelle Reed

A little bit of Dixie came in to brighten up the office this week.

Four members of the Swingin' Medallions, wearing bright blue-green paisley trousers and blue shirts, dropped by for a quick interview before rushing off to do a local television show, where the other four Medallions were setting up.

The sameness of their outfits was overwhelming since hardly any group wears the same thing *together* anymore. "These are Southern collegiate clothes," John explained, "this type of outfit is not uncommon in the South." The other three, Jimbo, Jimmy and Brent, nodded their heads in agreement.

They should know, as all eight – that's right, eight – of the group are from the South, and all possess the famous charm of Dixie.

Since "Double Shot (Of My Baby's Love)" has brought them to national attention, however, the South has seen less and less of the Medallions as they travel from Los Angeles to Old Orchard Beach, Maine, to perform.

The group started playing together about five years ago, when John and Joe combined to fill a steadily growing series of engagements at Southern schools and other spots from Louisiana to North Carolina.

Then, not long ago, two Birmingham, Alabama radio stations began playing "Double Shot." It was an overnight sensation.

The song, however, has received wide criticism for it's lyrics, which compare a boy's involvement with a girl to the overwhelming effects of a drink. It has a party flavor, with shouting and talking in the background.

"The song is a fraternity song," John said, "it's how you take it."

He believes that today's listening audience is adult enough to accept the song, like they have accepted "Satisfaction," "Gloria," and others.

"Satisfaction," incidentally, is on the group's album, just released this week. "One side is all hits that have made it big in America – 'Wooly Bully,' 'Satisfaction' – while the other side has original songs either written for us or ones we wrote," John said. A single will also be pulled from the album but which song it will be the group hasn't decided yet.

Spokesman John is actually John McElrath, handsome 20 year old leader of the group who plays piano, organ, and is a junior at Lander College in So. Carolina. The other members are:

Joe Morris – 20, history major at Lander, drums.

Carrol Bledsoe – 22, teaches algebra at a junior high school, trumpet.

Brent Fortson – 19, pre-med at Erskine but plans to attend the University of So. Carolina next year, flute, piano, saxophone.

Jimmy Perkins – 19, a high school senior in Greenwood, S.C., tenor sax, electric bass.

Jimbo Doares – 20, a business senior at Lander, lead guitar.

Steve Caldwell – 20, a sophomore at Lander, sax, piano, drums.

Charlie Webber – 20, a former football player at Clemson University, trumpet.

It is difficult to categorize the sound of the Medallions by instrumentation since their versatility is remarkable. Unlike most of today's groups, they do not rely on guitars alone, but utilize a variety of instruments, including three saxophones, an electric piano, organ and flute – with one lonely guitar.

The group strongly disagrees with Them, who packed their saxophones away when advised that American audiences niether like nor appreciate the sax. The Swingin' Medallions feel that audiences do like and appreciate the sax, fortunate for them since they rely heavily on the instrument.

The group specializes in soul music, although "Double Shot" isn't soul. In the past five years, when they were performing fraternity parties and clubs, they played almost every type of music, from country to pop to soul, depending on their audience. "Versatile," said Brent, is about the only way to describe their music.

Though the group wears Mod styles, which they continually insist are "Southern collegiate," long hair is out, in the back anyway. Jimmy has some trouble seeing through his bangs, but no one in the group has hair around his collar.

At one time the group had very long hair but "everyone else started doing it so we cut our hair," John said. Now short hair, or *relatively* short hair, will stay with the Swingin' Medallions.

The name Medallions has been with the group even longer than their long-short hair. "We had the name Medallions," Jimbo says, "but then we found out a group in Chicago had the same name, so we added the 'Swingin'."

The group loves California, especially Disneyland. "We almost cried when it closed for the day," Jimbo confided.

The Swingin' Medallions, all eight of them, are undoubtedly one of the most charming groups to hit the pop music scene in a long time. Friendly, polite and talkative, the Medallions might be just as big a group even if they didn't sing a note. They could just stand on stage and smile!

KRLA ARCHIVES

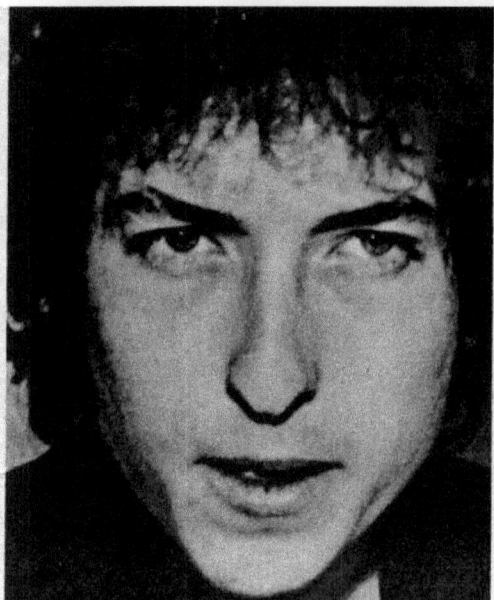

A Tender Dylan?

(CONTINUED from PAGE 1)

The album has been delayed for some time now and word had reached *The BEAT* that it was Dylan himself who delayed it.

It had been cut and mastered when he called it back to re-mix some of the numbers on it.

He also changed the title from the original "Blonde on Blond" to "Blonde on Blonde."

There *are* a few things missing on the album, like for instance photo credits and times on the tracks. We can report though, that one side of one record, in the two record set, is one song, titled "Sad Eyed Lady of the Lowland" and it's 11 minutes 23 seconds long.

As for the most important part of the album—the songs—you're in for a surprise if you're expecting more of his far out, highly symbolic babblings that he's becoming known for.

It does contain his latest two singles, "Rainy Day Women #12 and 35," "I Want You," but it also contains some numbers that are probably as close to tender and gentle as Dylan's come in a long time.

One track in particular, "Just Like A Woman," could almost be called a love song—something that we haven't heard from Dylan in quite a while.

Dylan seems to have come back one step closer to the earth in this album. Some of it is down right close to being *real*.

That Hat

One number however, will probably have people talking for quite a while. It's called "Leopard-Skin Pill-Box Hat," and it's pretty obviously not about a hat. We're rather curious to hear what people are going to get out of this number.

If you listen carefully to the entire album, you'll find some great blues things and, every now and then, a very *human* lyric or two.

For my personal opinion, as a *BEAT* reporter and sometimes Dylan fan, Dylan became a living, breathing, human being for the first time in my mind after I'd listened to this album about 10 times. He was never real to me before, but now I see in my mind a human being rather than just a mind.

We have to assume that all the material on this album is new—written recently—because Dylan doesn't usually regress and pick up material written some time ago.

So we have to assume that this album is Dylan now, as opposed to the Dylan that wrote "Blowing In The Wind," or even the Dylan that wrote, "Like A Rolling Stone."

We haven't seen Dylan for some time and probably won't see him again for a while. The only personal appearances he's made recently were his recent British tour.

Appearances

The only appearance he's even rumored to have scheduled is the Newport Folk Festival in Mass. However, he hasn't appeared at the festival for several years and it seems unlikely he'd go back to it. Dylan rarely goes back to anything once he's left it.

So all we have of Dylan now is this album, but there's enough of it to keep us busy a while.

Beatle fans may note one of the pictures inside shows Dylan holding a framed picture and a pair of pliers that looks very similar to the cover of John Lennon's last book.

True Dylan fans shouldn't be able to keep their eyes or ears off this album for some time.

The BEAT can't offer any explanation for anything Dylan does. We just have to assume that everything he does is deliberate. We *can* recommend that you take this album and give it a lot of concentrated attention.

It's Dylan and it's Dylan now. Maybe he's ahead of his time, or maybe he's outside of time all together. But this latest album is all we have of him as he is today. He won't be the same next time we hear from him.

Behind The Scenes At

Millions of words have already been written about the latest Beatle single, "Paperback Writer," b/w "Rain." Since its release just one month ago, this last single from the Fabulous Foursome has caused more talk and controversy than almost any other Beatle tune to date.

This is, of course, the first more or less electronic effort by the boys and it came as somewhat of a shock to the many Beatlemaniacs around the world. It took some longer than others to catch on to the new styles which the boys set down in this new record, but now everyone seems pretty generally agreed that—like all previous Beatle records—this one is also fantastic.

Instead of criticizing the songs further, then, *The BEAT* is going to take you *behind* the scenes at the actual recording session when the two controversial tunes were created on wax. Come along with us now as we journey to the Number 3 studio at the famous E.M.I. studios in London, and watch a private Beatle recording session.

Scattered all around the studio, you will notice a fantastic assortment of equipment, in the middle of which are the brand new, massive amplifiers the boys are using on this session. Arranged in great disorder around the rest of the room are all manners of pianos, grand pianos, guitars, percussion instruments, amplifiers, and various assorted unnamed pieces scattered about.

Four Beatles

Also situated about the studio are four Beatles. Paul is wearing his customary casual recording outfit, consisting of black trousers, black moccasin-type shoes, a white shirt with fawn-colored stripes, a black sleeveless pullover sweater, and a pair of bright-orange tinted glasses, probably the same specs he was wearing on the now-famous Ed Sullivan show of June 6.

John is clad in green velvet pants, a blue wool vest which he has buttoned up, and black suede boots.

Ringo looks very much like he always looks, in dark trousers and a black turtle neck sweater, but George has distinguished himself on this auspicious occasion with a Mongolian lamb fur coat, black courduroy "Lennon cap" and oblong metal glasses.

Now—the stage is set for an important recording session. Everyone seems tensed and ready to begin—with the possible exception of Ringo, who is calmly seated in one corner of the room behind a large screen where he is engrossed in a game of chess with road manager, Neil Aspinall.

A gentleman present leans over to Paul and asks what he is hoping to do with this record. Paul inquires if he has already heard the lyrics, and the man replies that he has and thinks them to be quite unusual. Paul leans back and explains, "The trouble is that we've done everything we can with four people, so it's always a problem to ring the changes and make it sound different. That's why we have got all these guitars and equipment here."

Elusive Bass Line

Paul then climbed down from the stool he had been perched on, gently placed the red-and-white Rickenbacker guitar he had been playing down, and strode over to the piano. John, George, and George Martin gathered around him in a close huddle and after a few preliminary attempts to find a new bass line, John got up and

..."WHERE'D ALL THE HORSES GO?"

KRLA ARCHIVES

The Beatles' London Recording Session

... BEATLES ARRIVE STATESIDE AUGUST 12.

tried to find the elusive notes on an orange-colored Gretsch guitar, while Paul got up once again and switched this time to a Vox organ.

The original concept for this particular number had been Paul's, and he makes a request for the engineer to play the track (already recorded the night before) back at half speed, so that John and George can add some vocal bits to it.

Once this has been done, they are ready to begin the hardest part of the vocal recording. As the recording light goes on, each Beatle clamps a microphone down upon his head to listen to the track being played back, and then John and George begin to sing, going after some of the very high notes.

Tea Time

But George stops and informs his fellow Beatles that "I don't think I can make it unless I have a cup of tea."

Mal Evans is recruited instantly and dispatched to secure some tea and biscuits. As an extra treat, Mal brings back some toast and strawberry jam which proves to be very popular.

Just as the "tea break" is just about over, Paul receives a sudden spark of inspiration which sends him flying to the nearest piano to tweak out a few notes of "Frere Jacques." He seems to think that it might be very interesting to have this melody line in their new record, and gathers John and George and George Martin around him to try it out.

A few experimental notes are heard from three Beatles, then Paul's head pops up and he asks, "Did you come in at the right place?" But John just grunts, "We can't hear it properly, and anyway I thought that was the end of it." George just glanced at John and explained that it was the *beginning!*

After a few more of these experimental bits are gotten down on tape, they are compared and the "Frere Jacques" idea seems to come up favorites. At this point, Ringo looks up briefly from his chess game to comment that it sounds as though John and Paul are singing through water.

Dum Dum Dee Dum

Those words are definitely *not* music to Paul's ears, so he's off to the organ once more to find a new sound.

Within seconds, Paul has begun creating a sound strongly resembling those made by the Scottish bag pipes. Almost immediately, John leaps across the studio crying, "*You've got it. You've got it!*" and Paul continues playing, adding a few "dum-dum-dee-dumm-dumms" to it. George Martin sticks his head over the piano to inform Paul, "I see what you mean," at which point Paul promptly informs George that he thinks someone else should play it. In other words—*George!*

John and Beatle George go back to the mikes to add some more vocals to the track, and then Paul asks them if they think they are singing right. George Harrison turns around very slowly to Paul, lowering his tinted shades, and looking very much like a rather superior school teacher, replies: To the best of our ability, Paul!"

At last, the tracks are all completed, and all four Beatles seem satisfied with their efforts. It has taken over ten hours of studio time until this tune is finally pronounced "in the can!" but now it is finished and it sounds like a hit to everyone present. Oh yes—they have decided to call it "Paperback Writer." Sounds like a good title for a Beatle record, don't you think?

... "HERE THEY ARE."

KRLA ARCHIVES

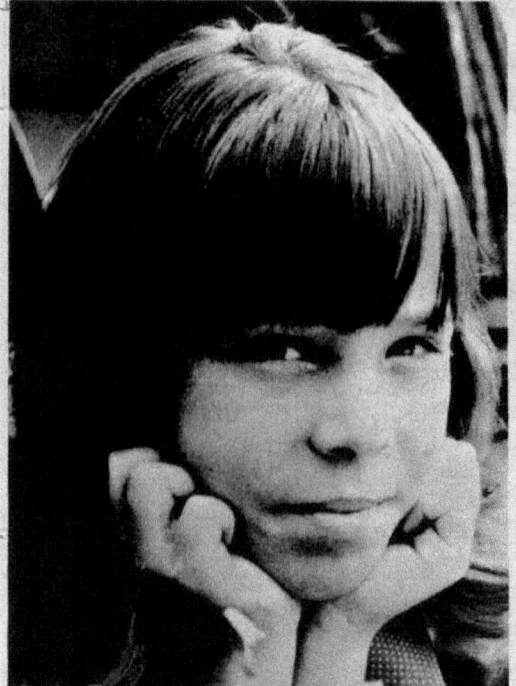

Little Lisa—The Motown Swinger

No matter what the age group, people seem to be the same all over.

Little Lisa, 9 year old Motown singer, says success brought her three things: her teacher gave her better grades, her vice principal asked for her record and everyone in school wanted to be her friend.

"Everyone seems to like me at school," says the pint-sized bright-eyed singer, "it wasn't like that before."

Charming Miss

Not that Little Lisa, whose full name is Lisa Miller, is unfriendly —far from it. She's a charming miss, with a disarming smile that shows a row of brand new adult teeth and a remarkable resemblance to Cher of Sonny and Cher. She's the sister everyone would like to have—and she can sing, too.

Lisa's recording career came about more or less by coincidence. "I used to sing around the house and no one used to listen," she confides, but one day her mother and aunt decided to have Lisa record one of the songs they had written, more or less as a lark.

She is currently on the VIP label, a division of Motown. Her mother and sister also write and record for Motown under the name of the Lewis Sisters.

After her demonstration record was approved by Motown, Lisa left her dolls and bike to become a very busy girl. She flew to Detroit where she recorded her first disc, "Puppet On A String/Hang On Bill." This led to appearances on "Swinging Summertime" in Detroit and other television shows, plus hops in Philadelphia and Cleveland.

Back in Los Angeles again, she performed on Hullabaloo and other shows, often with another young group, The Bantams, who Lisa feels look much smaller than their 10, 11 and 12 years.

Lisa has a remarkable sound for her age. She belts out songs in a voice much older than her years, and often gives the impression of being a much older person trying to sound younger.

She has accepted success with an off-handed shrug. "One day I was one kid and the next day I was something else," she says.

Being "something else" has brought Lisa into contact with many people, the majority of whom she likes. However, one of her pet peeves is the person who attempts to talk down to her age level. Lisa would much rather not understand someone than to listen to inane baby talk aimed her way.

Lisa has no special fondness for adults, and prefers teenagers for an audience any day. "I think they know how I feel on stage and they know how it feels to be made fun of, so they don't do it," she says. "After all, they were children a couple of years ago."

Normal Life

Lisa has all the problems of any performer, but she still attempts to lead a normal life among her friends and attends regular school. Often she slips off to contemplate her current state of affairs with her two pets—a dog named Shalley, (it's a mixture of Shepherd and Collie) and a cat named very simply, Babe.

Lisa has no intentions of being another Shirley Temple, though she "loves to watch her old movies." She just wants to be a singer and a good one. Little Lisa has big hopes, and with her drive, she just might make it.

The Adventures Of Robin Boyd

©1965 By Shirley Poston

Robin was half-way out of her bedroom window when her mother's voice stopped her short (the exact location of her short is a long story.)

"Where do you think *you're* going?" Mrs. Boyd bellered.

Robin gulped. "I have an appointment to meet Dr. Andersrag," she lied truthfully.

Mrs. Boyd moaned. "Is it customary for you to leave through the window when your father paid all that money to have a door installed?"

"Of course," Robin soothed.

"Then you'd best *hurry* and see Dr. Andersrag," Mrs. Boyd remoaned.

Hurry isn't the *word* for it, Robin thought as she raced gracefully (as in chip-a-toof) to the corner where George was waiting for her behind the wheel of Ringo's car.

"Forward!" Robin cried, leaping into the front seat.

Groping the unfamiliar gears, George set the car in motion and they zoomed down the street in reverse.

"Ahem," Robin admonished, trying to catch her false eyelashes (no one is perfect) as they flapped away to join a nearby flutter of butterflies.

Giving her the all-time yank, George applied the same drastic measures to the shift and got nowhere fast. "Would you believe *backward?*" he growled.

Anything

"At this point in my life, I'd believe anything," Robin groaned. And moments later, after having sent countless motorists off in search of the yellow pages, they backed supersonically into the parking lot of Angel's Rest Hospital.

"Are you sure this is going to work?" George asked, barely missing a male nurse (who brandished his purse menacingly) as he careened to a halt.

"It's *got* to," Robin breathed, crossing her fingers, toes, and for good measure, her eyes. "You said Ringo might listen to an adult who understands me, and if there's one adult in this world who understands me, it's Dr. Alex Andersrag."

"You rang?" boomed the good (using the term loosely) doctor (that one, too), slamming the car door open and giving Robin a bear hug. "How's my favorite nut?"

Between giggles, Robin managed to introduce George to her friendly (I'll say) psychiatrist, and the three of them were off (I'll-say that also) to Ringo's room.

"Take it from the top one more time," said Dr. Andersrag, pausing in the hospital corridor.

Translating his request, Robin took a deep breath of alcohol-scented (rubbing-unfortunately) air. "The . . . um . . . person we're going to see insists that I change my ways," she explained. "If I don't, I'll have to . . . er . . . stop seeing George. However, if I *do*, George is going to stop seeing me. Understand?

"Of course not," the doctor soothed. "And you want me to convince this person that you're perfect(ly ridiculous) the way you are, right?"

"Right!" chorused Robin and George, but suddenly sobered (as in up.)

"There's just one more thingy," she quaked. "You may find this . . . ah . . . person somewhat unusual."

The doctor shrugged complacently. "Kiddo, see one and you've seen 'em all."

However, when they walked through the door, the doctor began to wonder if he'd seen *anything* yet (which he hadn't.)

"*Groovy!*" chortled Andersrag. "Aren't you one of the Beatles? And aren't you one, too?" he added, taking another look at George.

"No," quipped Ringo as he sat up and started to exercise his bandage-swathed wing.

As the doctor stared open-mouthedly, Robin realized it was up to her to get things moving. So she moved over to the gaping psychiatrist and administered a swift kick right to his left shin.

She then led him to Ringo's bedside. "Ringo, I'd like you to meet Dr. Andersrag, who would like to say a few words in my behalf."

Ringo looked stern. "Nothing is going to change my mind," he announced firmly. "Since Robin Irene Boyd fell under the influence of George the Genie, she has changed into, among *other* things, a gasping, fainting, trouble-making whopper-teller! She must reform, or else, I tell you!"

Speaking of gasping, Robin did exactly that at this (apt) description of herself.

But the good doctor (oh, *sure*) remained unruffled. "Man, you gotta be puttin' me on," he said in his best bedside manner (and man, if you think that's bad, you should see his *worst*.) "I mean, you can't tame a *wild thing*, baby!"

It was Ringo's turn to gasp. Not only at the language Andersrag had chosen to convey his "few words." Also because the opener-mouthed nurse, who had been seated across the room polishing a bright object, let same clatter to the floor.

Looms Large

"Careful with that halo," Robin warned. "It looms large in his legend."

"*Shurrup!*" Ringo thundered angelically, returning his attention to the doctor. "Don't you think some of these traits *warrant* changing?"

Robin jumped up and down on the remains of the doctor's remaining foot. "Did you hear *that?*" she screeched. "He said *some!* Maybe I won't have to *completely* reform. Couldn't I just stop telling whoppers?" she begged, batting her eyelashes (hmmm) at Ringo.

"*You* could stop gabbling and wait in the *hall*, you could," Ringo ordered, pointing to the door.

Narrowing her eyes to mere murderous slits, Robin yanked the knob clean out of the socket and stomped out of the room.

After what seemed like seven hours of post-graduate-pacing, and after being told several times that it was a girl, Robin saw Dr. Andersrag emerge into the hallway.

"Did it work?" she blithered, re-jumping to his side (not to mention the rest of him) (and let's not.)

He gave an addled, expressionless nod. "Yes . . . you're to stop telling whoppers and promise to stay out of trouble. George is ironing out all the details, and you're to meet him in the car."

"YIPPEE! I mean, I *promise*, I *promise!*" Robin caterwauled, causing a surgeon on the next floor to hemstitch himself to a rather attractive nurse's aid (who was heard to remark "sew what else is new?")

Dr. Andersrag, still looking odd, muttered something unintelligible. (Robin couldn't hear what he said, either.)

"What's the matter with *you?*" she inquired.

"Beatles," he re-muttered. "Genies . . . angels with their wings in slings . . . maybe life really *does* begin at forty."

Wild Thing

Then he looked deeply into Robin's bangs. "Wild thing, I think I love you . . . I mean how old did you say you were?"

"*Hah?* . . . er . . . sixteen."

The doctor smiled. "I'll wait," he said reverently. Then, after a quick look at his watch, Robin's psychiatrist bombed off down the hall to keep an appointment with *his* psychiatrist.

Fortunately, Robin was able to control herself until he had disappeared from view. When he did, she leaned against the wall and laughed hysterically.

Only when a man in white came along and offered to help her into a most unstylish jacket did she race for the parking lot and collapse in the car.

About fifteen minutes later, she stopped laughing and started snarling. *Ratzafratz!* What was keeping George, anycowpath?

She continued to re-ask herself this question for *another* fifteen minutes, during which she squirmed, only to learn that getting comfortable was another of the many things one cannot do in a sports car (such as play tennis and/or perform an appendectomy.)

Finally, out of desperation (not to mention her gourd), she checked to see that no one was looking and whispered "Liverpool." When the magic word had turned her into a *real* robin, she pecked open the glove compartment and nestled cozily in . . . you guessed it . . . a glove.

That was the last thing Robin knew for several hours.

The next thing she knew, she was jolted awake by the *closing* of the glove compartment.

And the *next* thing she knew, as she straightened her Byrd glasses and peered through the keyhole, was that she was already in a whole lot of the trouble she'd just promised to stay out of.

(To Be Continued Next Week)

KRLA ARCHIVES

Manfred Stand-Out: A Bloke Named Paul

By Louise Criscione

Manfred Mann is a group but like most top groups they possess one member who stands out, who is immediately recognizable, who is "it." The funny thing is, he's not Manfred Mann. He's rather fair-haired, he'll say anything and usually does. He's Manfred Mann's lead singer and they call him Paul Jones. Sometimes they just call him one of the Jones Boys.

Paul likes being the center of attraction and says so. He enjoys the screams, the excitement, everything. "For me, it's a way of winning attention. I was a very spoiled kid. My parents expected great things of me," says Paul and then adds with a sort of half-attempted grin, "They're bitterly disappointed."

Paul's brother is a minister and the fact that his parents are very proud of him probably hurts Paul deeply but he won't admit it — at least, not out loud. "I was doing all right until I was twelve," recalled Paul. "I was quite an athlete. I liked that, showing off in front of an audience. Then when I was twelve I went to seed. Got in with the wrong crowd. I missed the audience. I suppose that's why I left Oxford and started singing and leaping about. Singers are always like that in a group. They always want to be the center of attraction."

Complex is the only word I can think of to aptly describe Paul. He's very much a joker and yet he can be serious. He's not afraid to make decisions and doesn't dodge responsibility. He married young, has two small children and doesn't hide the fact the way some performers do.

He does keep his family out of the spotlight, however, and is quick to tell you about it. "I don't like to push my wife into the limelight, so I don't have photos of her taken often, or go into great discussions about my sons, Matthew and Jacob. Nevertheless, I have an enormously high regard for my wife and all she is and stands for in my personal life."

Phony people rate first in Paul's list of dislikes. Being in the entertainment field has, of course, given Paul the opportunity to meet and learn to dislike all kinds of phonies. He doesn't fight with them, exactly. He just puts them on. "I dislike false people. Why shouldn't I take it out of them?" And he does, too. The minute he spots someone trying to be hip, he immediately moans: "Hello daddyo, what fab gear, man."

It's been a long time between American hits for the Manfreds but it looks as if they've come up with another smash in the form of "Pretty Flamingo." But the Manfreds seem to have a positive knack for recording songs whose lyrics are criticized and which are even occasionally banned.

Whether you know it or not, the Manfreds recorded "If You Gotta Go," almost a year ago but it was denyed air play because of alledged "filthy" lyrics. The whole controversy made the group furious and they lost no time in lashing out at those responsible for the banning. Then they recorded "With God On Our Side" — you never heard that one either.

So, now they've recorded "Pretty Flamingo" and, wonder of wonders, the record is actually being played and thus far there have been no words of lyric criticism on our side of the Atlantic, but, of course, in England the disc has been knocked around quite a bit.

"The man who wrote the song claims he doesn't know what Flamingo means. I don't particularly care whether he knew what it meant or not — I really can't see he could be that naive — but still, it's not that important," says Paul.

"I don't go ga-ga over the song. It's commercial and it gives me a chance to be my usual cheeky self, which I've come to quite like." Paul goes on to add that he doesn't really believe the record buying public listens to words of a song but rather, "Mostly, people catch a tune and a phrase or so and that's all."

Paul appreciates his fans — he loathes being mobbed. Girls that tug, pull and scratch turn Paul completely off. And besides that, "They rather embarrass me," says Paul. He is realistic to a terrific degree and knows that his fans are the only ones responsible for his success. Without them, he just wouldn't be. Yet, he stares you down and states frankly: "It's great that they scream, bless them, but I don't like them all personally."

So goes Paul Jones — king Mann, super singer, speaker of wise words, sometimes just speaker. One of the Jones Boys, really.

... PAUL JONES

... THE MANFRED MANN

AN ARTY sort of shot Paul particularly digs.

KRLA ARCHIVES

THE FABULOUS KNICKERBOCKERS re-opened The Trip on Sunset Blvd. after it had been closed due to legal difficulties. After a 10 day stay there the group is off on a nationwide tour for "Where The Action Is."

IT'S ASSOCIATION WEEK — The Glendale Ice House and the City of Glendale are hosting "Association Week" this week, July 12-17, marked by the group's homecoming to the Ice House, July 12 for a week's engagement which will feature songs from their forthcoming album, that is set for release this week.

Inside KRLA

Well, it's happened. KRLA Belly Buttons are *taking over!* They are spreading all over the Southland, covering everything from *real* belly buttons to door knobs and doughnut holes! I guess it had to happen, but who could ever have predicted it?

People here at KRLA still haven't gotten over the Beach Boys' Summer Spectacular at the Bowl — probably won't for many weeks to come! — 'cause it really was a swingin' affair.

Hope you all went along for all the fun and excitement.

Jarvis the Janitor has been very active lately; in fact, just last week he decided to sub-lease the Downstairs Subterranean Bat Cave for the summer. Believe it or not, his first tenant turned out to be the Amazing Pancake Man — who is still out for *revenge!*

One of the funniest lines of the year has to be the one Dave Hull dropped on the air about our favorite Emperor the other day.

The Scuzzabalooer explained that many people had been asking just how it was that Hudson came to be an Emperor in the first place.

"Well," continued Dave, "he was spreading some margarine on a piece of bread one day, and all of a sudden this crown just popped onto his head . . ."

Beatle people will be glad to know that once again KRLA will be proudly presenting the Fantabulous Foursome to you in concert again this August, and we should have full information on how you can obtain your tickets by next week.

It will certainly be great to have the Beatles back in the Southland once again. It's too bad that they won't be able to stay longer. Although they have spent several days just resting on vacation here during their last two visits, present plans include only a one or two-day stopover in our area during this tour.

Speaking of the Beatles, last week we mentioned that there had been some confusion concerning the erroneous release of a rather unusual Beatle album cover.

This week, however, the situation seems to have been straightened out and the correct cover — appropriately attached to the album jacket containing a very normal record — has been issued and is now impatiently waiting to be received by your eager little hands in record stores all over the area.

Now that we have spoken about the outside of the package, what do you think about the contents *inside* the album? Do you like the new songs by the Fab Four?

They are a bit unusual, to be sure, but they do provide us with just a taste of some of the things which we will find on the second Beatle album to be released sometime this summer — probably to coincide with their U.S. tour.

The boys have tried many new things on this album, ranging from the electronic sounds on "Paperback Writer" and "Rain," to some brass trumpets and jazz influences which you will be hearing on the new LP. It's amazing how they always manage to come up with something new and different. But then, that's the Beatles!

And don't forget — KRLA will be bringing the Beatles to *you* in concert at Dodger Stadium this August, so KRLA Beatlemaniacs of Southern California — *stand by!*

Them Honored By Their Hometown

A city in Ireland has instituted an award to honor the singing groups who put the city on the pop map.

The Citybeat Golden Guitar Award, the first of its kind in Ireland, has been presented for the first time by Ulster to Them, the first and only group from that area to put a record on the national and international charts.

They hit the international charts first with "Baby Please Don't Go," then followed that with "Here Comes the Night."

THE SWINGING MEDALLIONS — all eight of them — dropped by Casey Kasem's "Shebang" with their hit, "Double Shot (Of My Baby's Love.)"

FUNTEEN BONUS COUPON OFFERINGS

Coupon	Merchant	Offering
"C"	San Fernando Valley Teen Center, 17400 Victory Blvd.	2 for 1 admission
"D"	Drum City-Guitar Town, 15255 Sherman Way, Van Nuys; 5611 Jumilla, Woodland Hills; 6226 Santa Monica Blvd., L.A.	2 free "Crazy Fill" book covers plus $5 gift certificate with $15 one-time or accumulated purchase. Member's friends may purchase on his accumulation.
"G"	Gazzarri's, 319 N. La Cienega	2 for 1 admission to Teen Night every Sunday (7 pm-12 midnight)
"H"	Hullabaloo, 6230 Sunset Blvd.	2 for 1 admission
"J"	Michael's Jewelers, 7510 Woodman, Van Nuys	Free Beatle jewelry piece
"K"	World on Wheels Show, Rose Bowl, Sunday, Aug. 7	2 for 1 admission 8 am-4:30 pm
"M"	Northridge Valley Skateland, 18140 Parthenia, Northridge	2 for 1 admission, with or without skates.
"N"	Extra's Oasis, 316 N. La Cienega	"Most anything on the menu" at 2 for 1
"O"	Orange Julius, 6001 W. Pico, L.A.	2 Orange Juliuses for price of 1
"P"	Pasadena Civic Auditorium, 300 E. Green	Free admission for member and 1 guest to dance ever Saturday (8:30-11:30). Dresses for girls, dress shirts, tie and slacks for boys. Same offer good at DeWald's Ballroom, 831 W. Las Tunis Drive, San Gabriel
"Q"	Orange Julius, 1715 Pico Blvd., Santa Monica	Free Orange Julius with any purchase
"S"	Shirt Shack, 1900J Lincoln, Santa Monica	$5 gift certificate with $15 one-time or accumulated purchase. Member's friends may purchase on his accumulation
"T"	Ice House, 24 N. Mentor, Pas.	2 for 1 admission
"U"	Ice House, 234 S. Brand, Glendale	2 for 1 admission

Membership Card: Swinging Young Adults Club of Los Angeles. Dancing every Sunday, 2-10 p.m. Only 75c for members with card. Old Dixie Ballroom, 4269 S. Western.

KRLA BEAT Subscription
SAVE 33% OF REGULAR PRICE

☐ 1 YEAR — 52 Issues — $5.00   ☐ 2 YEARS — $8.00   ☐ 6 MONTHS — $3.00

Enclosed is _____   ☐ CASH   ☐ CHECK

PLEASE PRINT — Include Your Zip Code

Send to: .... Age ....

Address: .... City ....

State: .... Zip: ....

Foreign Rate: $9.00 — 52 Issues

MAIL YOUR ORDER TO: KRLA BEAT, 6290 Sunset, Suite 504, Hollywood, Calif. 90028

KRLA ARCHIVES

Youth Oriented Beauty Salon Opens In May Co. Topanga

"The Rockin' Roller," the first youth-oriented Beauty Salon in Southern California is open in May Company Topanga's Beauty Salon.

Open every Wednesday, 4:30 to 7:30 P.M., the shop will provide complete beauty salon services and will serve as an information and demonstration center where teenagers may keep up-to-the minute on hairstyling techniques, make-up and good grooming. May Co. Teen Board Members will serves as hostesses.

Girls will be allowed to use the facilities including rollers, pins, hair dryers and other professional equipment to set their hair or that of their friends at no charge.

A youth stylist, an expert on the new looks and styles, will be there to offer suggestions on how an individual girl should wear her hair. She will also be available to shapoo, cut and style for a minimal charge.

Clinics will cover all facets of complexion care and use of cosmetics and perfumes.

```
Present This Coupon
For Free Gift
May Co. Topanga
Beauty Salon
July 13 – ONLY
```

WELCOME to the "Rockin' Roller"

Beatlemania Hits Los Angeles Again

The voice at the other end of the trans-Atlantic telephone was brisk but friendly, still retaining a trace of Liverpudlian accent.

"I suppose that takes care of everything. We're looking forward to seeing Los Angeles again. Dodger Stadium should be quite an experience, you know."

"At the rate the ticket orders are pouring in, even Dodger Stadium may not be big enough. There seems to be even more enthusiasm this year."

"Marvelous! Well, give the rest of the fellows at KRLA our regards."

"Thanks. Tell the boys we've never seen Los Angeles so excited. It's going to be a fantastic

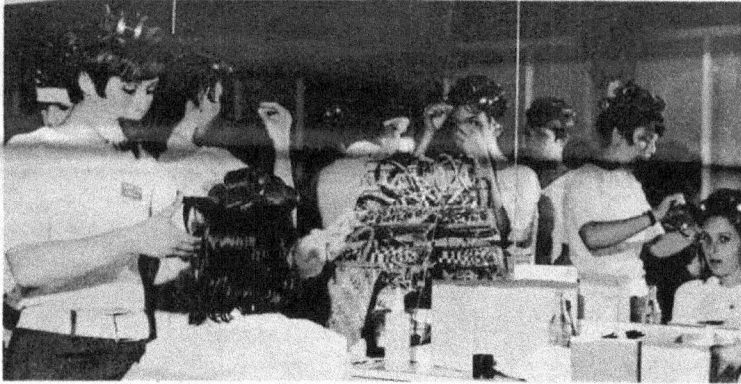

YOU'RE ALLOWED to use all facilities including rollers and pins.

Ignited by the recent announcement over KRLA, Los Angeles is again throbbing with an annual summer madness known as Beatlemania.

Ticket orders are pouring in—the deluge began the instant it was announced—for the KRLA Beatle Concert at Dodger Stadium Aug. 28.

To make the concert even more enjoyable, the Beatles are bringing their own special sound system with them to accommodate the large outdoor crowd.

The KRLA disc jockeys will also take part in the program, serving as emcees. It will begin at 8 p.m.

Tickets are priced at $6.00, $5.50, $4.50 and $3.00 and there is a limit of four per order.

Send a certified check or money order, payable to Beatles KRLA along with the coupon below to BEATLES KRLA, Pasadena, Calif.

Be sure to include a stamped, self-addressed envelope and specify the number of tickets desired.

See you there.

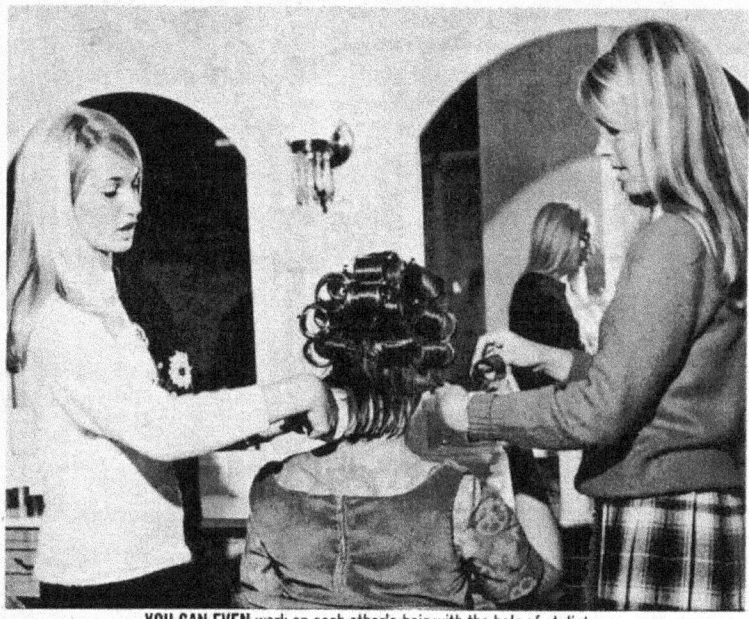

YOU CAN EVEN work on each other's hair with the help of stylists.

```
KRLA BEATLE CONCERT 1966
Dodger Stadium, August 28, 8 P.M.
NAME_____
ADDRESS_____
CITY_____
ZIP CODE_____
PHONE_____
```

TICKET PRICE	NUMBER OF TICKETS
$6	1 2 3 4
$5.50	1 2 3 4
$4.50	1 2 3 4
$3.00	1 2 3 4

KRLA ARCHIVES

For Girls Only
By Shirley Poston

Well, I'm loose again.

Surely they didn't think those little old heavy-duty-jungle-weave nets were going to hold *me*. No, I don't suppose they did, but I'll bet they sure hoped a lot.

Fortunately, I happened to have my wire-cutters with me (I carry them around a lot, in case I have to cut any wires) (well, maybe it *is* repititious, but you've got to admit it's *logical*), and managed to snip my way out of my imprisoning bonds (which I immediately cashed.)

All right, Shirl. That will *do*. Say something sensible, okay? Okay.

Speaking of Paul! Har, I bet that *really* fooled you, didditnot? And now that I *am* speaking of him, I dearly hope I'll be able to explain something without getting totally confusing (not to mention arrested.)

Y'see, I got this letter from someone (another coward who prefers to remain anonymous) who thinks she has Beatlemania down to a science. Like, she thinks she can tell what sort of person a person is (beautiful, Shirl) by what Beatle the person (that word and I are becoming very close friends) likes.

See if you agree with her analysis. (If you don't throw things at *her*, not me.)

If you like Paul best (which the majority of Beatle fans seem to), you are probably under the age of eighteen. You are, at times, honestly concerned about the difference between your age and Paul's. You are less inclined to lie awake nights, dreaming up desert-island situations, and more inclined to dream about marrying Paul. And you are heartsick at the thought of him marrying someone else because (among other reasons) you will feel guilty about loving him when he belongs to someone else.

You are of average intelligence, you have a warm sense of humor, and you have a tendency to take things rather seriously. Particularly your feelings for Paul, which is probably your first real love.

If you like Ringo best, you are a gentle person, and a lot deeper than you let on. You're rather shy (even if you manage to hide it), but once you do get acquainted, you're an extremely loyal friend.

You have a tendency to be more understanding and tolerant than most people, and you rarely become impatient. After the initial shock had passed, you found it possible to accept Ringo's wife and son and make them a part of your feeling for him. And you found it much easier to accept his family than do the fans of the other Beatles.

If you like George best (and there's a rumor going around that I do), you like making your own rules, you have many different moods, and you're unusually easy-going, on the outside anyway.

You're acutely aware of yourself, and of George, and to you he's more of a man than a boy. You don't feel guilty that he still tears you up even though he's no longer a bachelor.

You have a tendency to worry, to analyze yourself, and to stick up for anyone who isn't getting a fair shake.

If you like John best (would you believe *second*-best?), you are mature for your age in almost every respect, and somewhat frustrated by your feeling for him. (You don't want to just meet him; you actually *need* to *know* him.)

When you do something you don't enjoy, you do it badly. You have a clever way with words, you try not to take anything too seriously, and your jokes are often cover-ups to hide your true feelings.

There is no one who knows everything about you, you are of above-average intelligence (although most of your grades don't show it) and you never scream at Beatle concerts.

Well, there you have it. I can't say I agree with everything she said. How about you? I think she was really trying to say that a person likes the Beatle she is most like (whatever *that* means.)

If this is the case, I only have one comment about my similarity to George. Which is, Viva Le Difference!

Oops. Before I forget. Mucho thanks to Barbara Burhop for helping April Orcutt compile the Bealte survey that was printed several *BEATS* ago. And also for being the person who originated the H.S.T.O.M.O.O.P.M.H. thingy. Which, as any reader of this column can tell you (on visiting day, that is) means Help Stamp Thoughts Of Marriage Out Of Paul McCartney's Head.

Sepaking of people who can't spell speaking ... (I was going to say George just for the heck of it, but I blew the whole thing.) (Come to think of it, I'll say it anyway ... George just for the heck of it.)

Two more thingys to tell you before they come around waving those nets again.

One – I've found an utterly *georgeous* (stoke) way to really drive people out of their trees (especially those whose feet fit so well on a branch) (whooo, me?)

Last week, a couple of friends and I were having this big intellectual (you *bet*) argument about whether English groups *started* the British trend or whether they were just part of it. (Hah?)

Anytoad (sorry about that) (I must have a frog in my throat today), I was going to say something very profound, like "which came first, the chicken or the egg?"

Well, it didn't come out quite that way. For some reason, I said "which came first, the chicken or the *horse?*"

After we finished rolling all over the floor (in a *restaurant*, yet) we started making up all sorts of thingys just like that. You know, murdering old cliches until they don't make a *whit* of sense. And we've been saying them ever since, very seriously of course, and you should *see* people go screaming off into the sunset.

That started us off on another kick, which is making up your own cliches from scratch (providing, of course, that it itches at the time.) And man, some of them are really ridiculous.

I hate to admit it, but my jerky brother came up with a good one this morning. My mother was bawling him out for one of his smoother moves, and after she got through yelling (I mean *discussing* – sorry, mum) he shrugged and said, in deep philosophical tones ... "Ah well, just another cobweb in the bucket of life."

Two – About that meet-your-star bit I've been mentioning lately. I've real all of your letters of suggestion, and most everyone agrees that the only way to handle it is have each person write, as briefly as possible, *why* it's so *important* that she get to meet her fave.

Also, if you'd like to "nominate" a friend who might be embarrassed to write on her own, please do.

Better start writing those letters now, for obvious reasons. When your masterpiece is finished, send it to me right away at The BEAT address. And please don't forget to draw a star in the lower left hand corner of the envelope so these letters won't get mixed up with the nine million other things I still haven't done (like send out "Toy Boy") (soon, I tell you, soon!)

I'm going to pick twenty-five of the best letters, and then I'll ask for volunteers to help me pick the "winner." Remember, it can be any star at all, because most everyone will either be in the States this summer or is already here.

I don't like to put a time limit on this, but I'd better. So let's say the "contest" will end two weeks from the date on the cover of this issue.

Now, if I expect to still be working here two weeks from now, I had better close. My yap, for instance.

'I Keep Having This Same Dream' Says Mr. St. Peter

By Jamie McCluskey III

The lyrics of the song say, "Follow me, I'm the Pied Piper, and I'll show you where life's at." Perhaps it would seem that one would have to be quite conceited to make a statement of that sort. But then, we would have to remind ourselves that these are only the words of a song, and not necessarily the opinion of the artist who is singing them.

In the case of Crispian St. Peters, however, these lyrics really *do* seem to express the feelings of the singer. Crispian has earned himself quite a reputation in the duration of his short career in his native country, Britain. He seems to have a habit of constantly having his mouth open – and unfortunately, it islant *always* employed in the act of singing at the time!

Crispian seems to be forever knocking one or another of his competitors in pop music, and he has done some mighty large-style sounding-off in the past. For example: "I still maintain that I write better songs than John and Paul. The Beatles haven't got any act. They just jump up and down, sing and play guitars."

That's just an *example*. Crispian has also claimed that he would  someday be bigger than Elvis Presley. He went on to explain, "At the moment Elvis is just making films. His recent discs were recorded years ago. But if he came over here (Britain) now and played to a 'live' audience he would get a bigger reception than I would – but he'd have to work very hard to get it!!"

In his time, Crispian has also been known to claim that he could do anything that Sammy Davis Jr. could do – and probably even better! Well, confidence *is* supposed to be good for an entertainer!

Asked if he would like to travel to America soon, he replied: "I'd like to go to America for a lot of reasons – to see how I go down as a singer and a performer, and I'd like to see some of the Grand Ol' Opry stars."

Currently, Crispian's latest release, "Pied Piper" – already a moderate hit in this country – seems to be doing fairly well for itself on this side of the Big Pond. But it is going to be interesting to see whether or not Crispian in person – accompanied by his mouth! – will be successful as a performer in our country.

Just recently Crispian confided to a British newspaper: "I keep having this same dream that someone shoots me when I'm singing onstage. I can see the packed audience out front. Then there's a flash and a shot and I'm lying there on the stage in a pool of blood and the crowd's in an uproar."

Very strange words for a pop singer to be speaking. But then, Crispian St. Peters is a very strange young man – pop singer or *no!* It remains to be seen now only whether or not Crispian will be able to succeed in this country, and whether or not he will have continued success in England.

KRLA ARCHIVES

Who Is This Group Called Yardbirds?

By Louise Criscione

A Yardbird of the musical variety is a difficult thing to define. And four Yardbirds are totally out of the question. 'Cause they're super everything. They're noise, excitement, ear-splitting electronics. What they really are is alive and happening. And what else is there?

The blond thread-thin one — the one in the middle with the ever-present harmonica in his hand — is the center of attraction. No one can argue that point. When he lifts the harmonica to his mouth, his hands hide his face and what his hands don't cover his long blond strands manage to conceal. But no one minds because the sounds coming from the four Yardbirds make everything else seem small and inconsequential. Which is the way they want it.

Every so often, Keith relinquishes his position in the middle and the lead guitar player on the extreme end of the stage takes over the spotlight. Many have tried but no one can imitate Jeff Beck. He's the master.

Jeff can do more things with a guitar than a rich man can do with money. And that's a lot. He can literally play it "Over, Under, Sideways and Down." Fact is, he can set it down on the stage, move five feet away and still make it play... But what's even better — Jeff makes the most unbelievable faces you've ever seen. People say, and I rather agree with them, that Jeff could make a fortune as a face comedian.

Except those agonizing faces he makes when he's playing something like "Jeff's Boogie." I don't think he even realizes he's making those faces. He's concentrating too hard to realize anything except his fingers on the guitar. It's like a student taking a final who comes to a question he can see the answer to but can't think of what it is.

A drummer is usually the most inconspicuous member of a group. Mostly because he sits behind the rest and is partially hidden from his audience. Jim McCarty is sometimes like that. He moves with the beat but if you're not watching him closely you don't see. But you feel. Because his beat is always there.

Jim is really a bit of a clown and he especially shines during the break between songs. I suspect he likes being behind the rest of the group because it gives him the opportunity to make faces at them which only the audience can see. An opportunity Jim takes full advantage of.

Chris has changed more than the rest. I don't know why but I'm glad he has. Chris used to just stand there and play rythmn. That's all. The only time he moved was to adjust his amplifier. He looked lost up there and his expression never changed.

But all that's behind him now. Now, he's alive too. He moves and he smiles and he sings and he joked with the audience. He's one of the Yardbirds — finally.

...THE YARDBIRDS

The 4 Seasons Just Keep Comin' Back

Several years ago, Dick Clark made a prediction as he was looking over the future of pop music: "A lot of new names will come and go but The 4 Seasons will probably last forever."

Clark's prediction was not merely a wild speculation, but then few of Clark's predictions are. In the topsy-turvy world of popular music, few singing groups can boast of the continuing success and audience acceptance accorded the four New Jersey singers known everywhere as The 4 Seasons. Like their calendar namesake, the winds of change blow but the Seasons keep returning, year after year.

Recently, one of the few changes in the Seasons' ten year history occured when Joe Long replaced retiring Nick Massi with the group. Otherwise, the Seasons' line-up has remained the same with Tommy diVito, Bob Gaudio and, of course, the "sound" of Frankie Valli that has clearly established a unique quality of every 4 Seasons' release.

The near-institutional aspect of The 4 Seasons as a singing group can best be seen in their continuing success in the record market. Their current smash is, of course, "Opus 17" but it's only one more in a long string of hits for the veteran Seasons.

Last year the group became some sort of phenomena in the pop music field when their "Let's Hang on" hit the top three at the same time another Seasons' pressing under the pseudonym of The Wonder Who bounced into the charts with the song "Don't Think Twice."

Looking back on previous seasons, the group can point to a steady succession of hits that gives credence to the Dick Clark prediction of years ago. They now have three best-selling albums, "The 4 Seasons Gold Vault of Hits," "Working My Way Back To You" and "The 4 Seasons Sing Big Hits by Burt Bacarach, Hal David and Bob Dylan."

The 4 Seasons' success may well be attributed to their professional attitude toward their recording. Bob Gaudio, who has written the majority of the Seasons' material, says the group's schedule only allows them to record every three months. He also explained how they develop their new material: "We never cut a song without a full scale conference first." In these discussions, ideas for harmony, arrangements and songs are argued out.

In one such session, the idea that developed into the Wonder Who was hatched. Frankie Valli suggested recording under another name just to see if the group could get a hit without the identifying impetus of the established name. The idea was to see if 4 Season's songs were hitting merely because they were done by the Seasons or because the public really liked the song. The success of "Don't Think Twice" provided the answer. They have released another single under their pseudonym but they emphatically deny that it will ever, under any circumstances, replace the name 4 Seasons.

Dick Clark offers this as the formula for The 4 Seasons staying power with a variety of audiences: "They're not a teenage group fresh up from the ranks. They have a good solid well-rehearsed act and sound which will be able to take them through night clubs and concert dates in both the teen and adult field."

Even the Seasons' newest member, Joe, is a pro with established credentials in the music business. First, he hails from a musical family. He became an instrumentalist at age 8, a professional musician at 20 and played nation-wide dates with his own groups. Like the other members of the Seasons, Joe is a resident of New Jersey.

Tommy diVito is the firm baritone of the Seasons while Frankie Valli, smallest in size, has the biggest voice — the penetrating high soaring sound that has become virtually The 4 Seasons' personal trademark.

Today, The 4 Seasons continue to play a heavy itinerary of personal dates at clubs, concerts and colleges. Usually, their booking keeps them performing three nights out of every week in the year.

Glancing back over their long and successful career, it looks as if they chose their name well: Year after year The 4 Seasons return. A rather re-assuring occurence, don't you think?

...THE PERENNIAL 4 SEASONS

KRLA ARCHIVES

Mark Lindsay's Two Worlds

By Eden

Onstage, beneath the multi-colored lights, he is the tall, dark, and handsome ponytailed Raider who commandeers the microphone and leads Paul's merry band of men—along with the audience—through musical storms of fun and excitement.

He is dynamic, captivating, forceful, and powerfully entertaining. He sings happy songs—and you laugh; he sings sad songs and you feel the pain and share his tears. He lets his powerful voice go and he is the personification of *soul*.

In his physical appearance, he seems to represent everything the Raiders are supposed to be. He is dashing, gallant-looking, sometimes reminiscent of Captain Kid.

He is an explosive bundle of energy, seeming to fill the entire stage with his presence, continually exploding into millions of musical fragments of happiness which he rains down upon his audience. And that is just a *part* of Mark Lindsay—onstage.

A Long Road

But, when the glaring klieg lights have been dimmed for the evening, and the final curtain rung down, Mark Lindsay—*Raider* walks off the stage, and becomes Mark Allen Lindsay—human being. He walks into a very different world then, a world which is all his own. And for Mark Lindsay—it's a long road in between.

The world of Mark Lindsay came into existence in Eugene, Oregon, on March 9, 1944. Rapid growth and expansion filled that world over the next few years, rushing Mark headlong into manhood.

As a child, Mark had never formally studied music or any musical instruments, but he has been singing since he was four years old. At first, it was mostly to himself. Unlike the man Mark has become, the young boy was shy and somewhat introverted.

But music—and, especially singing—was, and is, his whole world. "The kind of music I like to sing—my favorite kind—would have to be something that you could pretty much get into, that you could *feel*."

A very important part of Mark Lindsay's world today consists of *creating* the music which he performs. He is very deeply involved in songwriting, and takes his creative efforts in this area very seriously.

Make 'Em Happy

"If I could make people happy with my music, I would like that very much. That's what I would like to be able to do.

"Or write songs that make people happy, or give people a good feeling, or tell them something, or songs which they can relate to."

If it were possible to sum Mark's entire world up in one small word, the only word which I could supply would be "love." If we were to split that word into two, it would probably be fairly evenly divided between "music" and "people."

When the truth is told, it must be admitted that Mark Lindsay is an irrepressible *people-lover*. He loves to talk with them, to observe them, to just be among them.

"Communication between people is probably the most important factor in well-being with your fellow man. Singing is a very important form of communication with me, because when we're doing a concert, you can tell whether you're getting through to people or not by their reactions.

"Speaking to people—you know, just getting them off alone and talking to them is also very important. Any form of communication—singing or just talking ... or shouting, or whispering!—is *all* good."

Unlike many people, Mark places no restrictions upon the kind of people with whom he communicates; he is genuinely interested in nearly *everyone*. "Each individual person has certain things about them you are attracted to, or repelled by, or that you relate to, or that you try to bring to. I try to treat each person as an individual, and not have any set pattern. I try to adapt myself to each person."

In the area of entertainment, there are no boundary lines in Mark's world. He wants to walk through as many fields as possible. "I would like to be fairly proficient on all the instruments I now play (sax, trumpet, flute, guitar, and piano.)

"I would like to get into acting—that kind of performing. Instead of interpreting music, it is interpreting words. *Thoughts*, is basically what it is; *emotions*.

"I would like to get into all kinds of fields of music, and be able to convey a distinct impression of what I got into in each case. No matter what field I was going for—I would like to be able to achieve it all the way, so people wouldn't say 'What's he trying to do?' They would *know, absolutely*, what I was trying to do because I would be *doing it*."

"Friendship and Love"

An important key to understanding the world in which Mark lives, is the understanding of the way in which he defines "friendship" and "love" in his life.

"*Friendship*—feels warm; friendship is people around you that you care for. These people care what you're trying to do, and what happens to you. Basically, friendship is someone you can rely on. I hate to be dependent upon anyone, but it's nice to think that someone *would* be there if you're ever really down and out.

"Friendship, I suppose, is trying to understand you and trying to help you. I suppose a true friend would be very interested in what you were trying to do with yourself and with others, and would try to help you find the right way.

"*Love*—to me, right now—means appreciation, wonder, just

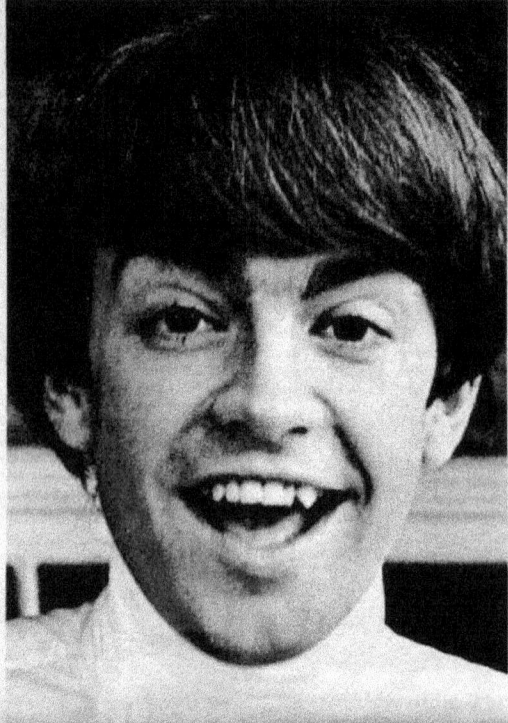

BEAT Photo: Gino Rossi

marveling at so many things. *Love* is a word that describes a feeling, or an emotion, that you get when you are doing things that you really enjoy doing, or when you love a person.

"*Love* is the epitome of *feeling*. Love is one of the values we place on things all around us. Love is something that expands and fills everything—or, *should*.

"Someone once asked me, 'If you could say one thing to the whole world—what would you say?' I thought for a very brief moment, and said it would have to be like something that was written long ago that people should follow but a lot don't: *love one another*."

His is a world of music, a world of other people and their lives. The world of Mark Lindsay is a spinning globe of activity, overflowing the insufficient number of hours which have been closed within the narrow confines of each single day.

It is a very beautiful world which, ultimately, only *he* can live in—but a world which he is willing to *share* with *everyone*.

Bobby Hebb—'Sunny' Outlook

By Walt Syers

For some entertainers, show business is simply an occupation—a means, like almost any other, of making a dollar. For Bobby Hebb, show business is a way of life ... certainly not always an easy life but the only one he has ever wanted.

Bobby admits he has been "down" many times and he wasn't always sure what he'd be doing the next day, but he never quit. He once teamed with a songstress named Sylvia, but they split up. His first record bombed out.

He's made it now but by all practicability he should have quit the business a long time ago. He just had too much determination. And because of that determination he is now a highly respected entertainer with his latest release, "Sunny," stealthily climbing the charts.

His thirst for entertaining began early. He had a stormy childhood but he still dreamed of show business. Both of his parents were blind ... but both were fine, trained guitarists and Bobby right away learned to love music.

All through grade school he concentrated on music. Then, at 12, he got his first real professional break.

Roy Acuff, the great fiddler-singer who is enshrined in the Country and Western Hall of Fame, saw Bobby perform. He was impressed and Bobby consequently became the only Negro to perform in the large "Grand Ole Opry" cast. Bobby played the "spoons" and sang with the Smoky Mountain Boys.

But when Bobby left the show he was almost right back where he started. He found that there wasn't much demand for "spoon" players, and although he sat in on a few Bo Diddley recording sessions he was still on the same old treadmill.

His approach was all wrong. Several years later Bobby was in the Navy, and one night he and a friend went to a performance at the famed Lighthouse, the jazz citadel in Hermosa Beach, California. Barney Kessel was headlining the show.

At that show Bobby remembers, he, for the first time saw what real jazz was ... what it can do to both the audience and the musicians. He admits he was dazzled by what Kessel put down.

Determined to master the techniques of the music that so moved him, Bobby returned to his home after he was discharged from the Navy and began work on the guitar. It was awkward and offkey at first, but with the help of Chet Atkins and Hank Garland, old friends from his Roy Acuff days, he learned valuable lessons in "soul" music. In 1964, Bobby went into Brandy's on E. 84th St. in Manhattan. He has been there over two years as a solo. During that time he continued his active interest in songwriting, and recently penned his current hit, "Sunny."

KRLA ARCHIVES

HOTLINE LONDON
Beatle Fourteen

By Tony Barrow

Immediately prior to their Germany/Tokyo/Manila tour THE BEATLES made their first live U.K. television appearance of 1966. On "Top Of The Pops" they did both "Paperback Writer" and "Rain." The last-minute decision for them to appear on the show was made by Brian Epstein after thousands of fan requests had poured into his office, into the U.K. fan club headquarters and into the production suites of just about every major TV company in London!

In Germany the foursome's concert at the Munich Circus Krone was video-taped for subsequent screening as a 45-minute TV spectacular and in Japan Tokyo's NTV channel made a 60-minute Beatle Special out of the boys' Budo Kan Hall concert performance plus newsreel film material.

Kiddie Song

On the day of the "Top Of The Pops" appearance, The Beatles also undertook a late-night recording session at which they completed one of the final tracks for their upcoming U.K. album. Now they have a total of 14 all-new recordings, including the three already available on your side of the Atlantic via Capitol's "Yesterday and Today." GEORGE has penned three new numbers for the set and every one of the others is a LENNON/McCARTNEY composition. Although Ringo has not been involved as a writer, he is certainly featured vocally on one stand-out track which the boys themselves describe as a "special kiddie song."

As previously reported in this column, the eleven new numbers as yet unreleased in America or England are likely to make another U.S. Capitol album later this summer.

Exaggerated reports about MICK JAGGER'S state of health circulated around London immediately prior to the departure of THE STONES for their current U.S. tour. It was said that Jagger was on the brink of a nervous breakdown and that he had collapsed. In fact, the truth was that Mick had been overworking, one way and another, and was just exhausted. At no time was there any question of him having to miss the American trip although he did spend his final week in London under doctor's orders to take it easy and get plenty of rest. There was not, and is not any longterm worry over Mick's condition.

Because his plans to begin a solo motion picture career would have clashed with so many '66 dates with THE ANIMALS, ERIC BURDON has postponed indefinitely his dramatic screen debut. His first picture was to have gone into production on August 1 which would have forced the Animals to cut short their lengthy summer tour of America. Burdon has confirmed his continued desire to act in a full-length screen drama but he will wait until the group's engagement diary is less full.

Busy Pet

Between October and January a fantastic new series of U.S. dates has been lined up for international songstress PETULA CLARK. Currently completing a highly successful cabaret starring stint at our plushy Savoy Hotel in the Strand, Pet is also seen every week in her own network TV show throughout the U.K.

When she returns to America she'll start off with guest appearances on the Ed Sullivan, Andy Williams and Roger Miller shows. Then she's at New York's Copa nighterie for a 4-week season prior to doing the Danny Kaye program. In December she's in Reno for the entire month and in the new year she has a Dean Martin TV date before heading for Europe and a much-deserved 6-week vacation. Meanwhile it looks as though the prolific Pet will have another Top Ten U.K. hit via her latest record, "I Couldn't Live Without Your Love," a number penned jointy by recording manager and musical director Tony Hatch and British songstress Jackie Trent.

NEWS BRIEFS ... New York's WMCA Good Guy GARY STEVENS is likely to have his own show on latest of our pop pirate stations Radio England ... PAUL McCARTNEY has had that chipped-off front tooth capped. Now the damage doesn't show even on TV close-ups ... "Shotgun Wedding" hitmaker ROY C. plans lengthy stay in the U.K. and may make his permanent home in London ... Talk of RADIO CAROLINE and England's GRANADA TELEVISION companies setting up independent record production units with their own labels ... October and November college dates in U.S. being set for THE FORTUNES ... KINK RAY DAVIES shaved his moustache after strong fan protests! ... Massive press coverage of June London vacational trip by PAPA JOHN PHILLIPS and MAMA CASS ELLIOT ... In Stockholm THE WHO shattered Scandinavian concert attendance records set up by THE ROLLING STONES ... Composer LIONEL BART named his pair of Alsation pups SIMON AND GARFUNKEL ... Nose operation still part of summer plans for TOM JONES ... PAUL McCARTNEY purchased a 200 acre farm way up in the Highlands of North East Scotland as hideaway retreat for off-duty relaxation ... In some U.K. charts FRANK SINATRA stopped THE BEATLES going straight to Number One with "Paperback Writer" ... MANFRED MANN lead singer PAUL JONES has signed personal management and agency contract to take care of his own ventures outside the group on an individual basis. Paul produced debut disc with newcomers THE RAM HOLDER BROTHERS ... PADDY, KLAUS AND GIBSON, singing/playing threesome signed by Brian Epstein a few months ago, disbanded although their "Quick Before They Catch Us" TV title recording is still heard every Saturday via BBC Television's teen-drama series of the same name

Patty Michaels: A 'Little Girl?'

By John Walters

Patty Michaels says she's "tired of being a little girl," but at first glance a guy is inclined to believe she's grown up.

The young songstress dropped by the office the other day, thoroughly disrupted the male inhabitants here and then made this seemingly facetious statment. But when you consider Patty played the part of a little girl for four years in the Broadway epic "Sound of Music," the statement doesn't seem quite as ridiculous.

Concentrating

Patty, whose record, "Something Happens (Deep Inside Me)," has just been released on the West Coast, is now out of the theater completely and is concentrating on recording.

Patty Michaels is not an easy person to interview. She's much too pretty . . . and if you're fortunate enough to get a coherent question out, the chances are it will be answered with either one word or a shrug. Not that she's stuck for an answer . . . she's just quiet and somewhat reserved and when she does say something you get the impression she means it.

So it is only natural that her choice of the opposite sex would be someone who "is quiet, sincere, and 'nice'." But people like this are pretty scarce so "I don't date very much."

Patty makes no obvious effort to project an image. She is down to earth and doesn't try to imitate anyone, although she admires Sandra Dee and Brigette Bardot and with her long blond hair falling over her shoulder she looks very much like the latter.

One of the things that has turned Patty against Broadway is the long demanding schedule she has had to face. It limited her social life somewhat, but she still managed to go horseback riding and swimming during her few free hours.

She cut her first solo record last year, "Mrs. Johnnie," which in her own words "bombed out." Her latest record is on the Epic label and has a good arrangement that looks promising, but she still will venture no prediction of its success.

Will she record again? "If this record does well," she evaluated in one of her longer statements of the day, "then I will keep on recording. I like pop singing very much."

She likes what she is doing now better than the theatre, for one reason, because "I like being with people like myself."

Long Time

It has taken Patty a long time to be with people like herself. Her entire family was in show business and Patty began her career when she was five weeks old. She was selected as a Harry Conover model at that time and made her first public appearance. When she was seven she was chosen "Miss Sunbeam" by the quality Bakers of America. For that honor Patty was chosen out of about 1,000 girls who auditioned for the title.

In addition to singing she can also dance, and has appeared with numerous groups and solo performers, including The Lovin' Spoonful, The McCoys, The Wild Ones, The Beau Brummels, Paul Revere and the Raiders, The Shangri-Las, Little Stevie Wonder, Joe Tex and Mary Wells.

KRLA ARCHIVES

Len Is Killing Himself—Gary Lewis

By Carol Deck

Gary Lewis is usually a pretty easy going guy, but he became near violent while reading in *The BEAT* Len Barry's decision not to appear with long haired groups anymore.

Gary himself is not exactly what you'd call a long haired singer, but he came quickly to the defense of those Barry described as "a collection of tramps."

"He's killing himself by saying that. You have to have long haired groups on a show," he said adamantly.

Sitting in the living room of his spacious Beverly Hills home, Gary violently ripped the paper in pieces, saying that Barry's examples of groups who "use it (long hair) as a replacement for talent" are ridiculous.

"The Animals are a gas," he said. "And the Spoonful are only about two points below the Beatles. John Sebastian's going to be up there in the Lennon-McCartney category."

Len Barry also used the Stones as one of his examples, saying "they just stand there and fake." Gary completely disagrees.

Digs It

"I dig their show because each one has his own little thing going on stage."

But then Gary calmed down a bit—enough to show what a true performer he really is. You see, he sat there and placed personal calls to five girls back East who had won a chance to meet him after one of his performances there but had been unable to, due to some technical difficulty.

So Gary called each of the winners and chatted briefly on the phone with each girl. He's one performer who really tries to do nice things for his fans.

Gary also had a little time to tell us what he's been doing lately and where he's going next.

He recently completed the Dick Clark Tour and then returned home to receive an "Oscarette" from the Junior Philharmonic Orchestra. He's the first pop artist to receive the award since Johnny Mathis got it three years ago.

At the climax of the presentation of the award Gary got to lead a 110 piece orchestra—and that's a little different from standing in front of a rock and roll group.

He's got a busy month ahead of him now. He makes his legitimate stage debut in the next few weeks as Birdie in "Bye Bye Birdie" at the outdoor Starlight Bowl in Kansas City.

His Own Show

Then shortly after that he goes back on the road with five or six other acts, in what's being billed as The Gary Lewis Show.

Sometime later he hopes to grab a vacation in Hawaii. Good Luck Gary.

But right now he's working on the release of his latest single, "My Heart's Symphony," and racing about town in his new car, a GT Mustang.

Life's not all beautiful for Gary though; he does have one ever present worry—the draft.

He very frankly admits, "I'm 1-A and can be called at any time."

That can kind of hang up a career a lot, but Gary's not just sitting back waiting for it to happen. He's keeping very busy with traveling, performing and conducting a 110 piece orchestra.

Just before he left on his next jaunt, he did leave one final command with *The BEAT* on a subject which he has repeatedly stated his opinion.

"There must be long hair on girls," sayeth Gary Lewis.

Gary Lewis and an old friend ... Ed Sullivan

Thomas Group Likes 'Sexy' Indian Sound

By Jamie McCluskey III

They call themselves The Thomas Group. It's possible that the name has something to do with their drummer. His name is *Tony Thomas*. He also has the distinction of being the founder of the group. Oh yes—he also happens to be related—by blood!—to a rather famous Lebanese, who curiously enough, *also* happens to bear the name Thomas. As in, *Danny Thomas!*

Tony was born in Los Angeles, California on December 7, 1948, and is so fond of his drums that they are the only instrument he plays.

The lead singer for the group is a tall, handsome lady-killer type, who smilingly bears the name Greg Gilford. Greg arranged to make his worldly debut on September 30, 1948, also in the City of the Angels, in sunny Southern California. However, contrary to popular opinion, he bears no relation to a tall, dark Lebanese comedian.

88-Man

Unlike Tony, Greg finds it difficult to be faithful to just one instrument, and boasts nine years of lessons on the piano, and an ability to create many musical sounds on the 88's along with the organ (which he plays in the group) and the tambourine.

The group's lead guitarist, Myron Howard, is the only member of the youthful band who has done any songwriting for the group, though the others admit to a "little bit of fooling around" in this area.

When I asked Greg what sort of music the group as a whole preferred to play, he responded simply: "Folk rock." At which juncture, Tony Thomas (of the drum fame) promptly fell into a fit on a nearby floor, simultaneously commanding poor Greg to "get yourself out of *that* one!"

So, after helping Tony back to his seat, Greg patiently re-explained the group's musical preferences: "We like to play rock and roll, a *little* folk rock (he said quietly, casting a sly look at friend Tony who was slyly turning green!) but mostly the stuff that's 'in' like the swingin' rock stuff."

Folk Rock???

The Thomas Group has recently released its first record—introduced on the nation's Number One pop show, the Ed Sullivan Show!—and Greg describes the disc, entitled "Autumn," as "A happy summer sound-like thing. It's not too folk rock (Tony winced again!) and it's not too way-out-swinging-stuff."

And what about the musical trends in the pop field today? Just what is happening and what is important? For the answers to these all-important questions, we turned to the ever-present, ever-smiling Leader of the Group (Thomas, that is)—Tony, who immediately elucidated upon the topic:

"I feel that the Indian music and the Arabic beat have infiltrated through the rock and roll today. It's a steady percussion sound and it swings. It's very *sexy!*"

Mr. Thomas was temporarily unavailable for comment regarding an explanation of that last adjective, so any curious *BEAT* readers who have some questions to ask—will please *fake* it, in the approximate key of L Minor!

... THE THOMAS GROUP AND YOU CAN JUST GUESS WHICH ONE IS DANNY'S SON!

KRLA ARCHIVES

The BEAT Goes To The Movies

"ASSAULT ON A QUEEN"

By Jim Hamblin
(The BEAT Movie Editor)

The scene: Waterfront.
The man: Frank Sinatra, who operates a fishing boat charter with his friend Linc, have just had a visit. The landlord demanded the back rent, and has been thrown into the ocean by the pair.
LINC: "Can he swim?"
SINATRA: "We'll check the morning papers."

This may give you a hint of some of the dialogue throughout most of *Queen*. The reason is obvious when you notice who did it: Rod Serling. That master of prose and wit who has given us many a notable night on the Tube with *Twilight Zone* — and even more recently constructed the final words spoken over the body of a man who will be very much missed in Tinsel Town, Mr. Ed Wynn.

Titles that grab an audience are always a special delight, and this one certainly does that. In conversation it invariably is understood as "Salt On A Queen," but it's a good movie just the same.

It is difficult to separate the Man from the Character when Frank Sinatra is on the screen. First of all because he is probably paying for the film, and secondly because he is the most sought-after entertainer in the biz, he can leisurely pick and choose his roles without regard to what it might do to his career.

It is a matter of historic record that he consistently chooses roles that involve military people, and this one comes pretty close. Paramount Pictures has rather generously compared the excitement in this film to *Von Ryan's Express*, a film made by Sinatra for a rival studio. Perhaps they hope to duplicate the financial success.

The story revolves around an ex-Nazi submarine commander who talks them into trying to hi-jack the luxury liner Queen Mary, using an old crusty U-boat they just happen to have in dry dock.

There are a few unexplained oddities in the film. Sinatra, as the diver, first goes down in an old type diver's suit, with the canvas material and metal head bubble and all that, but then when they dive again for the submarine he suddenly appears in a modern SCUBA diving rig.

In a burst of questionable logic, the producers hired on Duke Ellington to create a very forgettable music score. With no music at all in places where it needs some, the rest of the picture is sandbagged by some razz-matazz combo group tootling away. Dimitri Tiomkin would have a stroke.

Tony Franciosa had a terribly difficult role to play, and we last week asked him what the reaction has been so far. He agreed that it was a very unsympathetic role, and that tends to get people confused about making a judgment of the performance, rather than the character being portrayed.

But with Chairman of the Board Frank Sinatra at the helm, who needs to worry? The picture is well-done and exciting, with a particularly fine job by veteran actor Richard Conte, who at one point gets fed up with Franciosa, grabs a wrench and asks, "What are we gonna do with this guy? Somebody make a suggestion."

Our suggestion is take in a movie tonight. This one.

DURING ONE WEEK of filming, a severe smog attack hit Hollywood. Here's one man's answer to problem.

RICHARD CONTE pulls the switch on what had been a perfect plan.

. . . **VIRNA LISI** adds interest

TONY FRANCIOSA in an unsympathetic role

THAT MAN goes anywhere to get away from smog.

KRLA ARCHIVES

LIMITED SUMMER BONUS FOR BEAT READERS —

$200 in Values *Only* **$2** in Price!

FUNTEEN CLUB

GO-GUIDE COUPON BOOK

More than 100 coupons for Free Admissions, Discounts up to 50% or 2 for 1 offerings. Activities and Products listed below, plus many others.

Movies	Revell
Clubs	Statewide Theatres
Dancing	So. Cal. Bowl. Assn
Sports	Troubador
Food	Ash Grove
Clothing	Orange Julius
Records	Hullabaloo
Jewelry	Gazzari's
Cosmetics	P.O.P.
Shows	Pasadena Civic
Fairs	Sports Show
Horseback Riding	L. A. Blades
Bowling	Ice House
Folk Music	World On Wheels
Plays	Independ. Theatres
Slot Car Racing	Vivian Woodward
Billiards	Fashion Tops
Skating	Mademoiselle

Dial F-U-N-T-E-E-N For More Information

ORDER NOW WHILE THEY LAST!

FUNTEEN GO-GUIDE
c/o KRLA BEAT
6290 Sunset, Suite 504
Hollywood, Calif. 90028

Please send me _____ copies of the 1966 FUNTEEN GO-GUIDE (Valid thru Dec. 31, 1966) at the special summer rate of only $2.00 each. I enclose $_____

NAME:_____
ADDRESS:_____
CITY:_____ STATE:_____ ZIP:_____

KRLA ARCHIVES

America's Largest Teen NEWSpaper

KRLA Edition BEAT
JULY 23, 1966 — 15¢

Animals Arrive! Exclusive Photos

Hermits to Split?

Brand New Mama

KRLA ARCHIVES

KRLA BEAT

Volume 2, Number 19   July 23, 1966

Police Use Tear Gas To Save The Stones

Police were forced to use tear gas to save the five Rolling Stones from being mobbed by 5,000 wild fans at a concert in Lynn, Mass. An audience of over ten thousand had paid to see the Stones and just as they came on the stage of the Manning Bowl, the sky opened up and drenched the audience with a steady downpour.

The 75 man police wall crumbed when the weight of 5,000 fans rammed into it, injuring dozens of fans as well as several policemen. The Stones made it safely to their car as tear gas exploded all around them but the screaming fans smashed their car windows with wooden planks torn loose from police barricades.

Groups from the audience completely surrounded the car, grabbed the bumpers and bounced the Stones around as they continued to scream and yell their devotion to the five Stones trapped inside a car which was unable to move without hitting crowds of teenagers pressed tightly around the suffocated car.

Police finally cleared the mob away from the crowd by popping more tear gas grenades near the cars as the "fans" continued battering it with broken timbers. However, as the Stone car pulled out of the field two fans were seen still clutching the back bumpers. And about this time 20 bearded motorcyclists decided to get into the act but the Stones reached Boston Airport miraculously uninjured and boarded their plane for the next stop on their American tour.

...THE MAMA'S AND PAPA'S — TODAY.
BEAT Photo: Guy Webster

Michelle's Out!

As reported in the July 9 issue of *The BEAT*, Michelle Gilliam is officially out of the Mama's and Papa's. While Papa Denny took care of the heart-throb department for the female fans, the small, lithsome, lovely, Michelle soothed the eyes of the male fans.

No reason was given for Michelle's departure at the peak of the group's newly-found popularity. But a reason really isn't needed. She's gone — and that's all there is.

There is a new Mama now but the group vehemently denies that she is a replacement for Michelle. They prefer to think of her as "just a new Mama." Her name is Jill Gibson and she is 22 years old. She is Jan Berry's girlfriend and has been friends with the Mama's and Papa's for the last seven years, so it was almost natural that she should eventually join the group.

Lou Adler, an executive of Dunhill Productions and producer of all the group's hit records, explained to *The BEAT* that: "This isn't a group that's strictly worried about an image, just a 'show business thing.'

"If they weren't recording they would still be singing. These are four fantastic, individual people who love to sing and really enjoy their singing. We would never have looked for a replacement for Michelle. Jill is joining only because she happened to fit in and if she hadn't been there the group probably would have gone on as three. They wouldn't have gone out and tried to replace Michelle."

Lou describes the new Mama as a "very artistic and aesthetic person. She paints and she loves flowers. She knows every flower there is to know. Beauty is the most important thing of all to her."

Besides singing, Jill is also a talented songwriter, having written several hit songs for Jan and Dean. Should be interesting to see if she will collaborate with Papa John on some new songs for the group.

The group is currently preparing to begin a series of recording sessions for their second album, an album which will contain Jill's voice instead of Michelle's. However, the nation will not get a glimpse of the new Mama until August when the group undertakes an extensive cross-country tour. Following the tour, the group will begin filming a television special for Fall viewing.

Jill has already become an integral member of the group, and just as she has been accepted by her fellow Mama's and Papa's, we hope she will be accepted by their many fans.

Two Thousand Guard Beatles

Beatlemania struck the shores of Japan last week and caught the population off-guard. The Phenomenal Foursome made their debut performance in Japan before a capacity crowd of 10,000 teenagers — predominantly female, and predominantly hysterical.

The concert was held at the Martial Arts Hall, which is right outside of the Emperor's Palace in Tokyo. The Tokyo police assigned a record number of 1,700 policemen to protect both the quartet and the fans inside and around the hall.

The fire department in Tokyo ordered an additional 500 men, plus a number of ambulances and first-aid stations for the hectic occasion.

Japanese authorities said it was the first time that such heavy security precautions had been necessitated for an entertainment event of this sort. Fortunately, there were no serious injuries or incidents to mar the hysterical — but happy — event.

In the meantime, Beatle Paul McCartney and long-time girlfriend Jane Asher traveled to a remote area of Scotland to inspect a 183-acre dairy farm which he hopes to purchase.

The couple roamed about the property for some time, and then were invited to join farmer John Brown and wife Janet at a meal of bacon and eggs.

According to a spokesman for the Beatles, Paul has hopes of purchasing the farm and would like to move in before the end of the year.

A reliable source informs us that, "To farm has been a lifelong ambition of his and he'd like to go where he can get away from it all."

Inside the BEAT

Letters To The Beat 2
Animals Join Herman 4-5
Jaggered By Mick 7
Davis A Traitor? 10
Keith Relf Speaks 11
A Well-Tanned DC 5 13

The BEAT is published weekly by BEAT Publications, Inc., editorial and advertising offices at 6290 Sunset Blvd., Suite 504, Hollywood, California 90028. U. S. bureaus in Hollywood, San Francisco, New York, Chicago and Nashville; overseas correspondents in London, Liverpool and Manchester, England. Sale price, 15 cents. Subscription price: U.S. and possessions, $5 per year; Canada and foreign rates, $9 per year. Second class postage prepaid at Los Angeles, California.

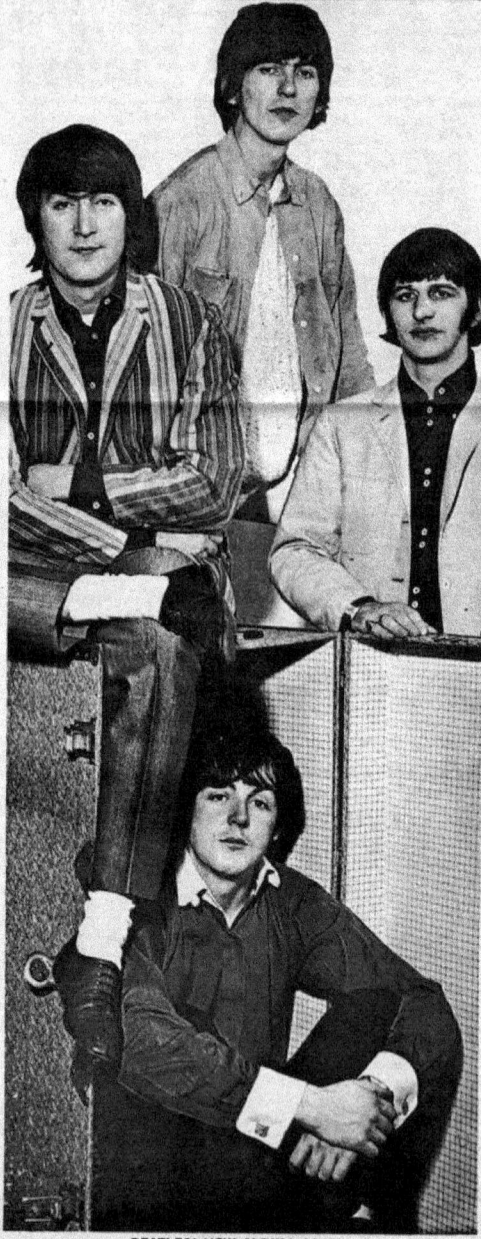

...BEATLES' NEW ALBUM COVER

KRLA ARCHIVES

Letters TO THE EDITOR

Beatles Insulting?

Dear *BEAT*:

I am an ardent Beatle fan. One who stayed awake nights crying when the Paul-Jane marriage rumors began, not because I was jealous but I thought that Jane was putting him on and taking advantage of him.

I stayed awake over a cut and swollen lip and a chipped tooth as though it were acute appendicitis. In other words, I love the Beatles, especially Paul. I think everyone who is a Beatle fan *now* has gone through the test. By test, I mean, Beatle marriages without being jealous and fickle, seeing through the nasty rumors, the whole bit.

They're the real ones, the ones that'll last forever. We (I am happy to put myself in this category) stuck with them because they were magnetic, they knew what we wanted and they made us feel good to just be living. Now, they're losing it and they can't blame anyone but themselves. Instead of doing personal appearances, they make a tape and sell it.

The new single isn't as good as it could be but it's good. The Beatles know it's not up to par. In a recent article, Paul said: "It's not as good as it should be, but we're satisfied." Well, so are their fans—but *just* satisfied. Before the Beatles weren't satisfied with just being "satisfied." Maybe that sounds weird but, isn't it true? That when Paul and John used to write a song they'd put their very lives into writing and performing it? It's not like that anymore and it scares me because I don't understand.

I've defended the Beatles from silly things that other people say more times than you could shake a stick at. I'm not saying they owe me anything because any star's fan defends him from petty, meaningless things. But when the nauseating album cover came out, I had no want to offer defense. I pitied them and glared at them at the same time. I pitied them because I wondered if they knew what they were doing. And I glared at them because I didn't understand "why" they did it if they did know what they were doing.

The cover is the most grotesque thing I've ever seen. I think they're trying to tell us something, but not what you said. Maybe they're trying to show us how "cute" they can be, if they want to. If the gallows humor did come from the mouth of Lennon, he's not the only one to blame. Why did the others allow it?

Why do they want to connect themselves with infanticide? Are they insulting teenagers by saying that this is what we *want?* I mean, what do they think we are?

Are they trying to give us an abrupt picture of what they're really like? They know they have captured the thoughts of numerous teenagers. Although parents can control whether or not their teenagers buy Beatle merchandise, they can't control our thoughts! Maybe the Beatles want to convince us of the new "in" way to live. If this is the way their album cover is, it's no small wonder they can't find a movie script to suit them!!!

Don't get me wrong, I don't dislike the Beatles now, even though it sounds that way. I'm just upset and puzzled with them. There must be some explanation, one certainly is in order. And I hope *The BEAT* doesn't hesitate to ask for one this August at a press conference. I bet a lot of Beatle fans, including me, hope a lot of questions are answered.

I don't care what you do with this letter—print it, burn it, acknowledge it, ignore it. I really don't care. I'm only glad there is finally *someone* who wants the fans' opinion of the people they can make or break.

A Puzzled Beatle fan

Gripping Pop Stars

Dear *BEAT*:

A lot of time has been given to the many pop stars to air their grievances such as lack of privacy, constant traveling and overwork resulting in nervous breakdowns.

These problems seem to irk them very much. And I don't blame them. But if they hate such popularity, why did they seek it in the first place? Maybe just for money, but in that case they won't last very long.

I've read about many pop stars leaving their groups because the pace was too fast. They just could not take it. Well, why must a group be constantly on the go, knocking themselves out to do one-nighters or record a song into the early hours of the morning?

They get tired, feel miserable and blame it on their fame. I know they're trying to please their fans and I love them for it but, man, it's a real pain when some pop star you really like leaves the "pop world."

Can't they just take it all a bit easier? I don't think I'm about to go off and die just 'cause my favorites don't bring out a new record every week. And can't they have their concert dates spread out more, so it won't be a show every night in a different town? Maybe it all has to do with managers, promoters, etc. . . . ; I don't know enough about that.

I hope I've gotten my point across. I wish very much that you'd get some groups' opinions about this because it's really bothering me.

Jenny Clarke

Flipped Cool

Dear *BEAT*:

As I understand it (and as the *BEAT* reporters reported it) the Beatles planned this album cover to be a satire on pop-art. Since I don't know much about pop-art, I do not want to judge them or the cover on this. But, if the article in *The BEAT* is true, that they did it for shock value, I think some Beatle has flipped his cool. Since when have the Beatles needed shocks to sell an album?

Well, judging from their last five songs, I think it's now! The only reason I like their last songs is because I love Paul's voice. If they cannot produce any better songs or anything better than a shock album cover, then they're sick. But if those songs were a bad experiment, or I have bad taste in songs and the cover was meant to be a pop-art satire, then my faith in their good intentions is justified. And I hope so because I love the Beatles and I want them to be the top group for a long time.

Lisa Mason

Why Fuss?

Dear *BEAT*:

I have just finished reading the article regarding the cover on the latest Beatle album. I have seen the cover and, in my opinion, it isn't as bad as people put on. True, it isn't the most desirable cover to look at and I can't really say that I like it, but I honestly can't understand why everyone is making such a fuss over it.

In your article you asked the question, "why would the Beatles put out something like that?" I suppose everyone was too busy knocking the cover to give any thought as to what the meaning *behind* it might be. Did any one of you ever stop to think that they may have been referring to war and how ugly and distasteful that is?

The Beatles don't have to resort to "shock" in order to sell a record or an album, and it seems rather idiotic that some people would think so. If you want a frank and honest answer as to why they put it out and what the true meaning was behind it, why don't you ask the Beatles themselves before you condemn and criticize.

Linda Wheeler

Hatching Of John

Dear *BEAT*:

I read your article on the banned L.P. cover of the Beatles. Let me say this, I agree with those "anonymous commentators." It had to be a hatching of John Lennon's thoughts. I don't care what anyone says, they can argue with me 'til the moon is blue—John Lennon is sick, mentally, but only in certain things.

For instance, most of the songs he writes are beautiful basically, but I think he's still a child in other respects. He hasn't gotten over his father leaving. He takes people on when they offend him just like a boy of maybe five.

The album cover was probably done for shock value. I don't know. No one can say. All I can say is; it made me sick! I felt three things when I read your article. First; the illness. Second; I was mad. Mad because I get the impression that the Beatles are getting lazy. That's a terrible illness. Third; I cried. The reason I did this was because I felt sorry for the four men in my life—the only men in my life.

It used to be that they were so full of life or something. Now they seem dying or dead. I still love them but what's happening? Why are they changing so much? I need an answer to this badly.

Confused

P.S. I can't sign my name because I'd have a very rough time with my friends.

Hanging On

Dear *BEAT*:

This is concerning the Beatles' L.P. cover. I agree with the person who brought up the point, "no one can kill the Beatles except the Beatles themselves."

I feel that the Beatles are trying to hang onto their popularity by causing some controversy as they did when they first started out with their long hair because they *are* losing a lot of their popularity and now some respect too.

I don't think I know one person around my age level whose favorite group is the Beatles. Somehow, though, I can't imagine the music scene without the Beatles. Although it is time for them to move over and let another group rule. But as far as I'm concerned, the Stones already rule.

Toni DeVito

Jeff Married?

Dear *BEAT*:

First of all, I am a true fan of the Yardbirds and when I read that Jeff was ill I was shocked. Do you know what kind of meningitis he had? I hope and pray that it is not the incurable kind.

Secondly, it was stated in *The BEAT* that Chris and Jeff of the Yardbirds were married. True, Chris is married but it is Keith Relf, and not Jeff, who is married.

Toni Hammerlock

You'll be glad to know that Jeff is almost fully recovered, Toni. However, you probably won't be too happy to hear that Jeff is married. But he is supposedly seeking a divorce at the moment.

The BEAT

Goody-Goodies

Dear *BEAT*:

I'm writing about the Beatle L.P. cover. Just before all this controversy broke out, I was wondering if the Beatles were about to be pushed aside as goody-goodies. They dressed nicely, were fairly polite and generally good boys.

Anyroad, I was thinking if they don't shock us they might be stuck in a closet. So, now they have. I did not think the cover was so shocking or gruesome. I've seen a lot worse things and I have not been around long. And in answer to someone's suggestion, I am definitely *not* going to cut off my sister's head just because my beloved Beatles were holding so mangled dolls.

I didn't think it was a good picture for an album cover because it lacked color and the right punch to make me want to buy that picture. It was the kind of picture you see in a magazine and laugh about and maybe notice how groovy Paul looks.

Speaking of Paul, he can't help it if his tooth is chipped. The poor boy goes on with the show and everyone complains. Now really, is that fair?

About their songs—they may be weird but they have some great things. "I'm Only Sleeping" creates the effect of sleeping without actually being tiresome and "Paperback Writer" has a great comment if you like to look for deeper meanings in songs.

Oh, you asked what doing the cover means, well, who knows what an author or a poet means when he writes a piece of work?

However, I do think they ought to get out among their fans if they wish to remain The Fab Four.

A Fan Who is Tired of Reminiscing

Human Carnage

Dear *BEAT*:

The banning of the new Beatle album cover reminds me of the way some people carried on over the song "Eve Of Destruction." Anything that jerks our heads up out of the sand, we criticize. Perhaps the cover does represent human carnage, but there's enough of it going on in this world.

I saw the album cover and I thought it was great. I agree with that boy who said he respected the Beatles for coming out with it. I also agree with the boy who said he was disappointed with the Beatles for withdrawing the cover.

Instead of chopping the Beatles down, their fans ought to be proud of their guts!

Sherry Matthews

KRLA ARCHIVES

On the BEAT
By Louise Criscione

Stones settled their accommodation problem in New York by hiring a yacht, the SS Sea Panther. After 14 elite New York hotels refused them lodging, the Stones slapped each and every one of them with a $5 million civil suit and then set about finding a place to stay. They found the Sea Panther and that solved the problem of housing but as far as I know they're going to go ahead with the law suit charging "discrimination on account of nationality."

It's safe to say the Fortunes will never play the Isle Of Man again. Not after the mauling they received from their audience the night they played the Palace Ballroom in Douglas. Barry was dragged off stage and knocked unconscious. His gold ring and gold cuff links were stolen by fans as "souvenirs." Barry had to be taken to the hospital and the Fortunes swore they're *never* going back to the Isle of Man. Gettin' risking being a pop star.

Manfred's Mad

The Manfred Mann are furious with EMI's HMV label for releasing "You Gave Me Somebody To Love." Manfred has now switched labels but what made him really mad is the fact that "You Gave Me Somebody To Love" was recorded before "Pretty Flamingo" and rejected by the group as not being up to their usual standard. EMI answered Manfred with: "'You Gave Me Somebody To Love' is one of a number of unissued Manfred Mann tracks that we have and we think it's an excellent follow-up to 'Pretty Flamingo.'" Manfred doesn't think so, but then he didn't think "Pretty Flamingo" would be a hit either."

... BARRY PRITCHARD

Herman was recently contemplating all the money he's made and has tentatively decided what he's going to do with it. "I shall probably buy a house for my parents in Switzerland. I don't really know. I'm sure Dad would like it—he speaks German as well—but I haven't asked me Mum yet, and then there's all the kids and that. Maybe I'll get a business there, you never know."

Dave Isn't

Although the Kinks sing about a "Dedicated Follower Of Fashion," Dave Davies says he isn't. "I wear them. I like colorful clothes, even in the winter. I'm not a follower of fashion, I just buy what I like. Fashions in general are now fantastic, there is such a variety. Anybody can look nice these days. I think boys' clothes are getting more effeminate every year and will go on doing so until it gets absolutely ridiculous." End of Davies clothes talk.

Found out a little bit about the new Yardbird, Jimmy Page. He's been one of Britain's top session men for the past two years. Jimmy is not exactly sure what his role in the Yardbirds will be. "At the moment I'm playing bass guitar but maybe I'll do a few things with a second guitar. Jeff Beck and I have had a lot of very interesting talks about using two lead guitars," says Jimmy. The new Yardbird is looking forward to coming to the U.S., especially to California because "The Californians are interested in the electronics and all that — whereas, the rest of the U.S. aren't quite so keen."

Cliff Likes To Talk

Cliff Richard, England's answer to Elvis, has religion. "About four years ago, I started looking into it," he says. "You have to study the theory of it, then it becomes far more interesting and easy to understand." Cliff says he used to dislike talking about religion, but now "I like to talk about it. Some people say it's soft and sissy to be religious today, but I feel that much stronger by being able to say I'm a Christian."

Talk has it that Cliff is going to study for the ministry. Wonder if he will pull a Little Richard? He has a lot of fans in England who don't want to lose him but Cliff says: "Two years ago, I didn't think of anything buy show business, now I think if it ended tomorrow I wouldn't care." Hmmm.

... CLIFF RICHARD

... TOMMY ROE

From The South—Tommy Roe
By Jamie McCluskey III

What do you see when you listen to your favorite record playing on the radio? Not a whole heck of a lot, right? Mostly, it's just the radio dial which hangs into view—and that *just don't get it* when one wishes to *see* the physical manifestation of the voice coming through the radio tubes!

Therefore, as a public service to all faithful *BEAT* readers, we are now going to present to you a picture of a young man who currently has a record which is coming through a lot of radio tubes across tha nation.

His record is called "Sweet Pea," and his name is Tommy Roe. Now, then—picture in your mind's eye one twenty-one year old young man. Medium-long golden-brown hair, bright blue eyes, and the most mischievous smile on earth.

Labels, Anyone?

Got that? Okay, from there let's go on to his label. Oh yes!—*everyone* must have a label, you know. Tommy . . . would you believe, *folk singer*?

"Oh yeah! I like folk music very much and I don't mind being classified as a folk singer, but of course—I've had most of my success in the teenage Top 40 market."

(Ed note: at this point, please insert one medium-heavy Southern accent, slightly set off by one heavy cold.)

The BEAT was curious as to just where this particular label came from, and we asked Tommy just what folk music really is. He leaned forward and placed his elbows on the boss's desk (sorry boss!) and explained:

"I think folk music is the real raw-type mountain music that is written in the modern day about modern times, but still has the old mountain flavor to it; or, what we call from the South—the *hillbilly* sound.

"I think folk music, basically, tells a story. It's always got a real interesting story—sometimes sad, sometimes happy."

Hits Help!

Tommy writes all of the music which he records, as well as a few pieces for some other artists. He is responsible for the penning of both of his first two hits—"Everybody," and "Sheila," as well as the current chart-buster, "Sweet Pea."

When I asked Tommy what type of music he prefers to write, he flashed one of his most mischievous grins and replied: "Anything that's a hit—that always helps!!"

By his own admission, Tommy will never be a member of the "Blue-eyed Soul Singers Club," however—that doesn't prevent him from holding a few "soulful" opinions of his own on the subject:

"I think 'soul music' is something that you have to really *feel*; it comes from your heart. If you're singing about something you've experienced or if you can really relate yourself to a certain experience—then you can really sing with soul.

"It's very hard to do. A lot of people *imitate* soul and I can always tell it, myself. I'm not a soul singer, and I don't claim to be and I wouldn't even try it."

Some White Soul

"Usually, you associate 'soul' with the colored race, but today you have a lot of white artists that are singing pretty soulfully!

"But I think that real soul comes from the South, where I'm from—like Otis Redding, Percy Sledge—people like this are real soul singers."

Tommy is very conscientious about the music which he—and his fellow entertainers—are creating. And while he reserves the right to critically comment on it—he still manages to keep a sense of humor about the whole situation.

When I asked if he tried to keep one certain 'sound' in all of his records, he replied: "I don't think an artist can afford to. Let me say that I've not been one of the hottest artists in the world—but I've been pretty consistent. I mean, I'll come up with a hit every once in a while if you don't watch me!

"But, you take artists who try to stay in the same groove constantly, and I really think they lose ground. It's good to change.

Cross Your Fingers

Tommy has a number of plans for the future, among which is a career in acting. "This is what I'm very much interested in. I've lived in New York for the last year and a half going to dramatic school."

Right now Tommy is up for a leading role in an upcoming motion picture, and he smilingly confided to us that: "All I can do there is keep my fingers crossed and hope I get lucky like I did in the record business!"

Tommy has been very lucky in the record business. He is one of the biggest artists in the South and he is currently working on his third national hit single.

Along with his dramatic studies and his own recording activities, Tommy manages to produce records for other artists as well as writing a few songs now and then, and within the next two weeks he will take wing (as in *jet*) and fly off to England for his *fifth* visit to the foggy isle.

All in all, Tommy paints a very nice picture on *any* radio dial. Don't you wish *yours* had one?!!

KRLA ARCHIVES

Chaos At The Airport—

By Carol Deck

It looked for sure like we'd lost Herman this time, but somehow he really did make it on the plane and then who should join him and his Hermits but the Animals. It was quite an hour.

It all started about noon one Wednesday when the Hermits made a brief stopover in Los Angeles on their way from New York to Hawaii, before returning for a couple of performances over the weekend.

Everything started out fine as the plane taxied in and several hundred excited fans gathered to greet the group.

Five ruffled and tired English lads tumbled out of the plane and somehow made their way through the fans into a side room for a press conference.

As they sat down at a long table a blast of flashbulbs hit them and Herman, pretending his hands were guns, shot them all down.

Dutch Boy

Then he took off his sun glasses and sat there looking for all the world like a little Dutch boy in his white coat, blue and white checked shirt and blue cap with his blue eyes shining.

Herman did most of the talking as they were asked about the seven figure deal they've just completed with MGM involving motion pictures and recordings.

He didn't really seem to know a lot about the group's next movie except that "it's going to be a comedy" and it's tentatively titled "Mrs. Brown You've Got A Lovely Daughter."

Someone asked what they do with all the money they make.

"We all invest money in a few things," Herman replied.

"Like what?"

There was a long pause, a slow smile, and finally he just said "property."

The conference continued, Herman making faces, and Karl yawning periodically—he seemed to be more tired than the rest of the group.

Back Again

Herman, still doing most of the talking, answered questions about writing—"We always write our B sides, but rarely the A sides;" Los Angeles—"It's always great here;" the Stones' "Aftermath" album—"I like that album myself;" and when they are coming back—"probably September or October."

Keith got his two cents in when someone noticed he hadn't combed his hair. "They mess it up out there," he said pointing to the mob of fans just outside the door.

Lek too, got in a few words when I got him off to one side and asked if he'd seen the Beatle album that was banned here.

"Why does everyone ask that?" he queried. I explained that it had caused quite a stir here and he said "everyone got all upset in England too."

As for his opinion of the cover, he said, "It's just a picture."

A few more questions and a few more pictures and the easy part was over.

Now came the fun and games known as getting five Hermits through about five hundred fans and into a waiting plane.

As I stood across the hall beside the door they had to go through to get to the plane I saw four Hermits disappear and then re-appear in front of my eyes. A couple of guards literally yanked them through the fans and onto the plane.

But then came Herman and I thought it was all over. He paused for a moment at the door to hand his sunglasses and hat to someone and the next thing I knew he too disappeared into the mob of fans.

But when he finally did appear again he was headed in the wrong direction—down the hall instead of across it.

Waving his hands and running madly down the corridor with several hundred fans after him, he really looked like maybe he might never make it to that plane.

But *BEAT* photographer Chuck Boyd outran the fans, stopped him and showed him another way down to the plane.

When I walked onto the plane he was sitting down with a seat belt laying loosely across him, smiling and joking like nothing had happened—and he had his sunglasses and hat back on.

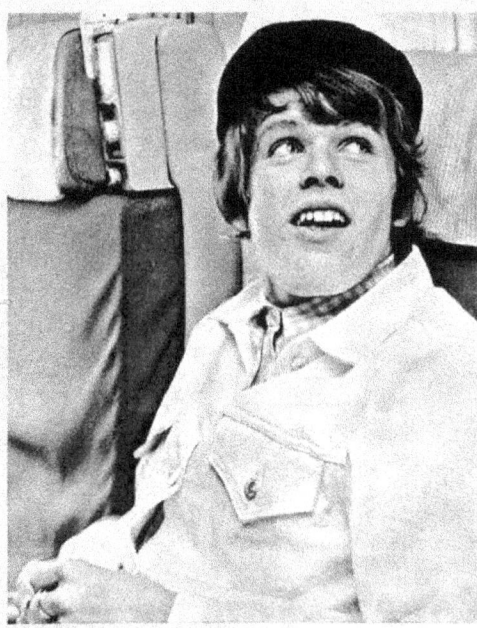

HERMAN, with his hat back, looks calm after nearly missing his plane.

BARRY WHITWAM and Karl Green didn't get a chance to say much.

BARRY IN THE COCKPIT

LEK AND A "FRIEND"

KARL — TIREDEST OF THE GROUP

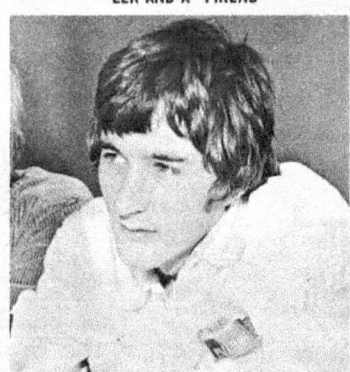

KEITH — A LITTLE MESSED UP

KRLA ARCHIVES

Animals Join Herman

As the other Hermits made their way to their seats, all noticing the attractive stewardesses dressed in Hawaiian sarongs, Lek casually sat a large stuffed something-er-other that had been given to them in the seat next to him, fastened a seat belt around it, held it's hand (paw maybe?) and told it there was nothing to fear.

Then there was quite a discussion about who wanted to go back and watch the movie. They were afraid it would be the same movie they'd seen on their way out, but it turned out to be another, Debbie Reynolds' "Singing Nun." None of them seemed over anxious to see it. I guess none of the Hermits are great Debbie Reynolds fans.

Then came the next big surprise of the day.

Animals Arrive

As I stood by the open door of the plane trying to convince myself that I really *did* have to get off the plane and that I really *didn't* want to hide somewhere on board and fly off to Hawaii with them, four rather scruffy looking guys came on board.

At first I didn't recognize them, but in the middle of them was one very short Eric Burdon looking better than I've ever seen him. He didn't need a shave, his hair was combed (somewhat) and he was even smiling!

So in strolled four of the Animals who were originally scheduled to meet with the Hermits in Hawaii but at the last minute had come into L.A. at the same time. They made a quick change of planes without being seen by anyone except this *BEAT* reporter, and our photographer took the exclusive pictures you see here, including some of the first shots of the newest Animal, Barry Jenkins.

No Hilton

Hilton Valentine wasn't with the others. He's staying with friends in New York and will meet the rest of the group in Hawaii.

There were a few short words of greeting and then the Hermits settled down in the front of the plane and the Animals made for the back — maybe the Animals are Debbie Reynolds' fans.

After somehow convincing myself to get off the plane, I walked back out into the still waiting gathering of Herman fans. I wondered what they would have thought if they'd known that the Animals were on board that plane also.

Rarely do you get to see two major British groups together like that, and Herman and the Animals are kind of a weird combination.

There seemed to be no great friendship or lack of it between the two groups. They just said hello and went their separate ways.

And *The BEAT* was there to report it all to you.

HERMAN AND HIS HERMITS during their brief stopover on their way from New York to Hawaii.

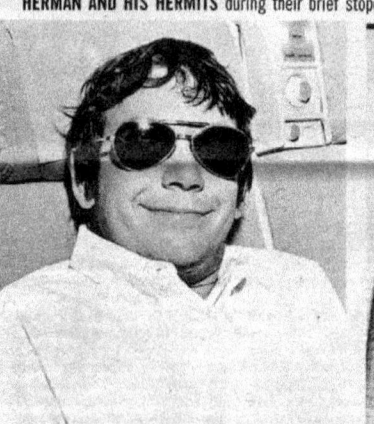
ERIC BURDON — A surprise meeting with Herman.

BARRY JENKINS — First picture of new Animal.

ON THE PLANE — Herman chats with Nola Leoni, publicist from the office of Connie De Nave, which handles all of the group's publicity.

CHAS AND DAVE — A little tired after the flight in from New York.

CHAS CHANDLER — On the way to Hawaii.

DAVE ROWBERRY — Headed for back of the plane.

KRLA ARCHIVES

BEAT EXCLUSIVE
Will This Be Beatle Movie Number Three?

A NOTE FROM SHIRLEY POSTON: Did you, by any chance, page hysterically through The BEAT, searching for your beloved "For Gawd's Sake"—whoops—"For Girls Only," only to discover that it was gone?

Seriously (oh sure), there's a good reason why my weekly ravings don't appear in this issue. And you're about to read that reason. Which happens to be an entire Beatle movie, sent to me by one of both of my many readers.

After reading it 42,000 times, I decided it was just too good to keep to myself, so I wheedled the boss into printing it in The BEAT. She agreed on one condition. Since the "movie" was so long, someone was going to have to donate some of their space so it could appear.

However, it's worth giving up my chance to blither about George (ache) for one week. I think you'll think so too (hah?) when you read the masterpiece dreamed up by Linda Souza of Oakland, Calif.

I suppose Linda will kill me for blabbing that after she completes a "film" (each one takes several months and she's done several), she also dreams up a premiere and an Academy Awards ceremony where her stars win Oscars.

But Linda sure deserves one of those Oscars! Like pass the popcorn and see for yourselves as The BEAT presents...

THE RIGHT GUARD(IAN)
OR
ONE BOBBY GIVES YOU 24 HOURS PROTE TION

The movie begins n English park where Paul is strumming his guitar and singing as his partner in crime, a young girl named Jill, is dancing with members of the crowd. The camera occasionally zooms in for a close up and stop action of Jill cleverly lifting a ring off her dancing partner's finger, or taking a wallet from his pocket. During these stop action periods, the credits are superimposed over the scene.

One of the fellows Jill dances with is Napoleon Solo. Jill easily relieves him of his tie clip, but fails to recognize his identity.

Missing Badge

As the song comes to a close, Jill accepts one more partner—a charming policeman named Ringo. When the song ends, Paul and Jill make a quick bow then casually stroll away. Ringo, too, begins to depart, but after taking two steps, he notices that his badge is missing.

Before the bobby can utter a sound, Paul begins shouting orders to him. Acting like an officer of the law, Paul waves the stolen badge about, and gruffly commands Ringo to stand against the wall.

The stunned Ringo complies, and Paul frisks him, pocketing anything of value. After Paul briefly but soundly reprimands the befuddled bobby for various offenses, he and Jill depart. Ringo stands thinking for a moment, then faces the camera and delivers his conclusion: "I've been bamboozled."

The hoodwinked bobby again gives chase, this time blowing his whistle as he runs. The fleeing couple turns a corner only to find three more bobbies waiting there.

The duo is captured and taken to the local police station where Jill is ordered to hand over the stolen items. She does, with one exception, concealing the spared loot in her long hair. Paul and Jill are then locked in a cell already occupied by one other person. A cunning rogue named John.

The camera has followed Ringo back to the station where a visiting commissioner is telling the officers that one of them is to be given a special and dangerous 24-hour assignment. Facing the lineup of bobbies, the commissioner asks for all volunteers to take one step forward.

All the men except Ringo take two steps backward, leaving Ringo standing alone. The commissioner profusely thanks Ringo for volunteering, but it's a puzzled Ringo who shakes the commissioner's hand.

Meanwhile, back in the cell, Jill and Paul are arguing over who is to blame for their incarceration. As the argument grows more heated, Jill tells Paul she is much more clever than he as she has managed to save part of the loot.

As she hands the tie clip to Paul, Constable Ringo enters, followed by George, who has come to bail out John. However, he decided to bail out Jill instead! Jill, not one to let opportunity knock in vain, accepts George's offer.

"Jill-Ted"

Both John and Paul are outraged. As the trio leaves, John sinks back to his bunk and mumbles: "I believe we've been Jill-ted, mate."

Paul, in anger, slams the tie clip against the cement wall. A small explosion occurs, and the wall crumbles. Paul and John are startled, but they hurriedly make their escape, followed by Ringo.

Not too far away, Ringo encounters the escapees in a dark alley. But as he approaches them, the bumbling bobby knocks over a stack of crates which tumble on John. John lies on the ground, motionless. Ringo is horrified. Paul goes to John, takes his arm and puts the wrist to his (Paul) ear. He gives it a thump and again places the wrist to his ear as if he were listening to a watch.

"He's dead," Paul gasps as the shocked Ringo's eyes grow wider. "Of course you know what this means," Paul continues. "Murder of this sort can send a bumbling bobby like you to prison for a long time. And, as a witness to this foul crime, I am going to see that you get everything that's coming to you!"

Paul goes on terrifying Ringo and finally persuades him to flee the scene, leaving Paul to dispose of the body. Ringo reluctantly leaves, vowing someday he will put Paul behind bars for this treacherous act of blackmail. When the defeated policeman departs, John dusts himself off and he and Paul start out in search of George and Jill.

The camera finds George and Jill leisurely having dinner in a dimly lit, romantic Italian restaurant. Four musicians stroll over to their table and serenade them with a soft ballad. The musicians bear a remarkable resemblance to the Beatles, but look very Italian in their mustaches.

As George continues to woo the sticky-fingered miss, she interrupts to explain that she must go back and rescue Paul. George is not very understanding or keen on the idea, but pursues Jill as she leaves for the police station.

While snooping about the station, George and Jill eavesdrop on a conversation between Ringo and the commissioner, who are discussing the special assignment.

A great treasure is coming to the United Kingdom. In every country where it has been displayed, it has been stolen at least twice. Scotland Yard, however, is determined not to lose the treasure to plunderers, and has devised a plan to thwart the villians.

One man is to take charge of the priceless article. Where he hides it will be known only to him, and his identity is to be kept a secret.

Then, from a brown paper bag, the commissioner removes an exquisite, jewel-laden tiara. Twenty-four hours from now it is to be presented to the Queen and then taken to the Tower Of London to be displayed with the other royal jewels. Until that time, the tiara will be left in Ringo's charge.

George and Jill can hardly believe their ears. How easy it will be to follow Ringo and snatch the tiara! But as they prepare to do just that, Ringo recognizes them and has them questioned for over an hour. When they're finally released, Ringo has left the station and George and Jill must search the streets for him.

Bickering

However, John and Paul find George and Jill before the latter two find Ringo. On the street corner where they meet, the four immediately plunge into an argument. As the bickering continues, a newsstand keeper calls in two bobbies to restore order.

They recognize Paul and John and another chase is on.

John ducks into a house, seats himself at an empty place at the table, and begins to make "small talk" with the others seated there. Paul enters a pub by the front door, while Jill and George stuff themselves into the dark sidedoorway of the same building. The policemen carry on down the street, passing them by.

John finishes his cuppa, then bids a jibberish adieu to his astonished "hosts." Paul opens the door George and Jill are leaning against. George, appearing not to be the least bit surprised, fingers Paul's navy blue tie with white dots.

"The seagulls must be flying lower this year," he says. Paul is not amused. John joins the group complaining that "it's getting so no one is safe on the streets after dark."

The four venture into a pub, but when their drinks are finished, they've no money for the bill. Paul suggests a song and picks up his guitar (which he's been carrying all this time.) Jill then dances with the surly bartender, picks his pocket, and pays the tab. When they leave the pub, George and Paul escort Jill home. John goes off in another direction.

John whistles as he walks down the road. Noticing what appears to be a convention of cats, John invites himself to be guest speaker. At the conclusion of his "speech," there is applause from two hands. John turns around to take a bow and thoroughly surprises his audience of one. Namely, Ringo.

"Thought you were dead," says Ringo.

"I am," says John.

"Then watcha doin' here?"

"I'm yer guardian angel," replies John, quite seriously.

"Oh yeah? Where's yar halo and wings, then?" challenges Ringo.

"I'm a nonconformist."

"'Specially when it comes to obeyin' the law. Yer under arrest!"

Just then, George approaches. "Evening, guv'nor. Luvly night."

"Not for yer mate 'ere," Ringo growls.

In a loud "whisper," John tells Ringo, "he can't see or hear me because I've been deaded."

George, picking up the hint, asks "Who are you referrin' to, sir?"

"To that ruddy bloke standin' behind me." Ringo turns to face John, but he's hidden behind a mail box. "He's gimme the slip," sighs Ringo.

"Yeah, I believe you've slipped one, too," mutters George. "night, sir."

Invisible

Ringo watches George leave. John comes out and taps Ringo on the back.

"And where were you off to?" questions Ringo.

"I had to make meself invisible, so George couldn't see me."

"Rubbish, you were probably 'iding somewhere."

"Hold on, mate. If you don't believe me, I'll have to do something drastic to prove I am what I am. (On those last five words, John executes a bit of the sailor's hornpipe, a la Popeye.) "I shall expose your secret."

"What secret?"

The information George had passed on to John, John now passes on to Ringo. "How did you find out?" gasps Ringo.

"E.S.P. (Extra Salty Peanuts)," cracks John.

"Are ya trying to tell me you can read me mind?"

"Well, I hate to brag, but we angels can do a few odd things."

"I'm beginnin' to believe that angel stuff, but I'm still not quite sure you're what you seem."

"Okay, I'll prove it," swaggers John. "I'll tell you where the tiara is hidden."

"If you can do that, I'll believe you." (Ringo is confident John can't.)

John takes out some paper and a pencil. "Write down the hidin' place here and I'll tell you what you've written down."

Ringo writes. "Why do I have to write it down? Why don't you just read me mind?"

"It's kind of a check—I read your mind, then we check the paper to see if I'm right. Now put the paper here."

Ringo places the piece of folded paper on top of the mailbox.

"Now think of what you've just written." Ringo thinks. "Think harder, the message isn't clear." Ringo thinks harder. "*Harder!*" Ringo closes his eyes, making an agonizing face, and thinks harder.

John, meanwhile, reads the note and quickly puts it back before Ringo opens his eyes. "Now, I'll tell you the hiding place and you check the note. The tiara is in the palace, under the throne, right?"

Ringo is amazed, not to mention duped. "Then you - you must be . . ."

"Said I was, didn't I? Say now, what time ya got?"

"'Alf past eleven," Ringo notes.

"Blimey! I'm due at a union meeting at twelve!"

"*Union* meeting?"

"Yeah, could you loan me a pound for dues?"

Ringo gives John a disgusted look and a pound for dues, and with that, John is off down the street.

"You Know"

Ringo calls after him. "Hey, what about me problem of protectin' the . . . the (he looks around, then softly adds) *you* know. Aren't you gonna help me?"

"I'll bring it up at the meeting."

"But it's a secret!"

"Okay, so I won't bring it up at the meeting."

As John turns the corner, Ringo mutters "typical."

The next day, George, John, Paul and Jill meet in the park to discuss plans for stealing the tiara. They decide that the best way to enter the palace is as guards and Paul suggests a costume shop where they would find such costumes.

They journey to the shop, find exactly what they need, but are several shillings short of the rental fee. However, John spots an organ-grinder's costume and asks to borrow the organ for half a mo'. Outside the shop, he grinds out a tune with George acting as monkey. An amused crowd gathers, tossing coins into George's tin cup. By the conclusion of the song, enough money is collected to pay for the uniforms.

Near the Palace, the four knaves don their costumes, then march to meet the real guards. Upon meeting them, John tricks them into believing they are being relieved early. In a matter of minutes, the imposters enter the Palace, snatch the tiara, and return to their assumed post. The real relief guards arrive, and ceremoniously change places with the charlatans, who make a hasty departure.

A few hours before a certain ceremony is to begin, Ringo and the commissioner enter the throne room and find the tiara gone. The commissioner is furious. Poor Ringo is to be drummed out of the corps and placed under arrest. Fortunately, Ringo gets away and wanders about the streets, a wanted man in search of his guardian angel.

In his search, he pokes his head into a church as four choir boys, closely resembling the Beatles, begin to sing. He enjoys the music for a brief moment, then continues

(Turn to Page 14)

KRLA ARCHIVES

...BOBBY MOORE

Bobby Moore Tells About His 'Search'

Recently, we noticed a fellow named Bobby Moore was occupying one of the top spots on the nation's music charts with "Searching For My Love." We couldn't place the name offhand, so we instinctively went to our biographical files to find out about the sudden upstart.

Only he wasn't listed there, either. And what was worse, no one in town seemed to know anything aobut Bobby Moore except that he had the number one record here.

This struck us a little funny, because we generally hear about every entertainer who has any hopes of ever making the top 200. And here was a guy with the hottest record going and nobody even heard of him. Didn't he believe in publicity firms?

Bewildered, we decided to write Checker Records (the label on which Bobby records) and see what they knew about our mystery man.

Sure Enough

Sure enough... Bobby must not believe in publicity firms. He handles that sort of thing himself. In a letter to The BEAT, Bobby told us the following about himself and his group, The Rhythm Aces:

"The Rhythm Aces were born in 1952 at an army base in Fort Benning, Georgia. A group of fellows from the regular army band, and I formed a swinging band. We played everything from jazz to rock and roll. I attended band school in Germany. However, nothing really happened big until I got out of the army.

"In 1961 I came to Montgomery, Alabama with my saxophone and a few dollars. A few weeks later the Rhythm Aces were reborn with the strong assistance of my manager, Mr. A.R. Seymour. His wonderful wife believed in our possibilities and invested her money in the uniforms and equipment for our band.

Bobby's Son

"The members of the band are Chico Jenkins, on guitar; John Baldwin Jr., on drums; Larry Moore, my son, on alto sax; Joe (Sleepy) Frank on bass guitar, Clifford Law on organ, and myself on tenor sax. "Searching For My Love" and "Hey Mr. D.J." is our first and only recording. We are very grateful and proud to be associated with Chess Records. We have just signed with Shaw Artists for exclusive booking.

"I was inspired by Ray Charles to further my musical career. I have promoted numerous shows during the time I have been in Montgomery. Most of the shows were backed up by my band, The Rhythm Aces. We have backed up such stars as Etta James, Kim Weston, Gene Chandler, Ruth Brown, Mittie Collier, Sam and Dave, Wilson Pickett, Joe Simon, the late Sam Cooke and Dinah Washington, Sugar Pie Desanto, The Kelly Brothers, The Drifters, Lee Dowsy, Solomon Burk, Otis Redding and Johnny Cash.

"It took a great deal of time, money and patience to get our band on the go, but with faith and hard work we feel we can go a long way." With that, the letter ended ... and Bobby Moore lost a little of his mystery. But not too much of it.

Want To Get Jaggered By The Mighty Mick?

By Eden

Have you ever been *Jaggered*? If you haven't, please believe us when we tell you that it is a feeling like no other. Especially when it is effected by the Mighty Mouth of Mick.

And wouldn't you just know it? The BEAT staff has gone and gotten itself *Jaggered* again this week. It all came about when we started listening to a few off-the-tongue comments from Michael Philip, himself.

It all began when Mick up and proclaimed: "I've got more private life than anybody thinks. Well, right away—I was all ears. As usual, the Mick was all *mouth* as he went on to explain: "People think I do nothing but work. But there's plenty of time to do things."

"Do-Nothing Jagger"

My first question had to be, *what* things, to which Mick politely replied: "Well, really I don't do anything. That's the whole thing. Now and then I feel I ought to get interested in things. But then I feel there's not really long enough. So most of the time I just sort of sit around.

"The trouble is that I'm always too busy to wonder what I can do besides what I'm doing already. I can't know, so I just put it aside and say 'Oh well, I'll think about that some other time.' I live in the present."

Being thoroughly *Jaggered* has a lot to do with *revelation*. The kind of revelations which Mick makes about his life and just how it came to be what it is. For example, Mick's reflections on the changes which have occurred to himself and his other Stony friends.

It Was Different Before

"It was different in the beginning. When I came into pop it didn't seem to me it was going to be such a permanent thing. And I don't think that anybody then could foresee how international it would all be.

"In those days, that just never happened to British artists. Cliff Richard was the nearest thing we had to an international artist. He did a bit in South Africa and he had a few records in Australia.

"But look at the kind of traveling the Beatles do today. Or us. When I started off buying old 78 records, who'd have known it'd be like this? This is Friday. Tomorrow we're flying to Brussels, then Amsterdam, Copenhagen, and Stockholm.

"Then we're back in England. Then we're off again. That's why I relax when I can instead of looking for new things to do!"

Have you ever wondered just how the fantastic sounds which eminate from your much-played Stone album came to be? Another very important part of being *Jaggered* centers around at least a partial understanding of how their music is created, so come along with The BEAT as M.P.J. takes us through the beginnings of another Stone hit.

"We've got our own way of

working. Keith works the tape recorder and takes things down as they come into our minds.

"If anyone else tried to play back the tape they wouldn't believe it, because we usually get about two hours of stuff. And it's all different songs and different ideas. Half a minute of this, then half a minute of that.

"Suddenly you find that one song has got into another one and two songs are joined together. Meanwhile I write out a list of fifty titles. Then the titles get into the songs. You might get three of them in the words of one song.

"Then we might take the verse out of one song and add it to the chorus of another. Then we might change the tempo. And when we've got all that done, I say 'Right, I'll write a lyric to it.'

"When we get to the studio, it's still a very skeleton thing, like a minute and a half of a song. So we have to put more bits to it, write an introduction, figure where the beat's on. Then the real work starts—making the record!"

Mime Along With Mick!

Has your head begun to swim yet? Or perhaps you see a wide variety of brightly flashing lights before your eyes? Possibly you hear strains of "Get Off My Cloud" passing through your disbelieving ears?

Well, if you are experiencing any one of these symptoms, or any combination of them—rest assured you are well on your way to being *Jaggered*!

Just to complete the job and further blow your minds, listen while Mick spouts off a few of his views on the current pop scene—including the controversial topic of miming.

"What's different about pop music today is that there's more improvisation, but it's disciplined. We rely on ourselves. The earlier pop singers had to rely on songwriters and rely on so many other people that they came out as if they were just another instrument. They weren't anything really creative.

"I like mime, too. People put it down, but half the time they don't know waht they're talking about. It's a lot more difficult to make an impact with a mimed show than in a live show, and if they do away with it I'll be very disappointed. (Ed. note: British pop fans are currently facing a possible ban of all miming on network TV pop shows).

"The great thing about it is that once you're with the song you can do anything you like, even put your head between your knees if you want to, and you can build up a far more exciting show.

"Jump around, go potty. What they forget is that you can't sing if you're three feet in the air. Mime helped to make the Rolling Stones!"

Well, there you have it. If you feel a little weak in the knees, or slightly uncertain as to what has just occurred—fear not; it's only the immediate *aftermath* of being *Jaggered*!

And if you decide that you like the feeling—hang around The BEAT, 'cause it usually hits us about once a week!

KRLA ARCHIVES

"IT'S ALWAYS A MADHOUSE BACKSTAGE at any DC5 show, and the performance at the Carousel Theater was no exception, but Dave still found time to read what's going on in a recent issue of The BEAT.

PICTURED ABOVE and to the right are three of the recent visitors to the KRLA studios in recent weeks. Above, Mark Lindsay is caught by our BEAT camea as he signs his John Hancock for one of the many fans waiting outside the door. In the upper right, Fang makes a valiant attempt to answer our request lines and sign autographs at the same time. Below right, Simon and Garfunkel drop in to take a few calls from their many fans in KRLA country.

..."FANG"

IT'S UNCLE DM to the rescue! KRLA DJ Dick Moreland fakes a smile as he bravely attempts to escort an unidentified guest to the KRLA studios out through the milling mob of female fans in the crowded lobby.

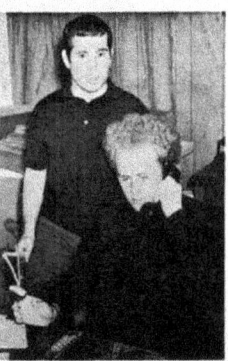

... SIMON AND GARFUNKEL

Inside KRLA

By Eden

The Beatles are headed back to the Southland and KRLA's got 'em... NATURALLY... There is nothing but excitement running rampant all over the studios out here, and if you ever wanted to see a nervous wreck in action — you should get a glimpse of the old Scuzzabalooer...

David can't quite control himself everytime he remembers that the Fab Four will be here in about a month, and it's all he can do to keep from blowing his horn in STEREO...

Bill Slater tells me that he just celebrated his second rear-end collision in six weeks.

I asked Bill how his car (happens to be a NEW one, too) looked now, and he replied: "Just like it did the LAST time I got it out of the shop..." P.S. It was Mrs. Slater's fault last time...

KRLA has gone all-request now, so here's your big chance. If you have a record you want to hear — just pick up your trusty telephone and call in on one of our many request lines. There is a number to serve every area in the Southland, and it's YOUR radio, YOUR request, so START DIALING...

You make the hits on KRLA...

Hope that you all were able to attend the KRLA Beach Boys' Summer Spectacular at the Hollywood Bowl on June 25. It was a wild and wonderful evening, and I know that everyone there had a blast.

All of the KRLA DJ's were there, even the Emperor, himself. Beautiful Bob came without his Royal Robes that evening. In fact, he didn't even wear a SUIT... He just donned his golf outfit, and clad in his sports trousers and pale blue golf sweater he put in his Royal Appearance. Oh well — that's an Emperor for you...

Oh, by the way — if you want Beatle tickets for the concert at Dodger Stadium this August, better not waste anymore time. Send a certified check or money order immediately to "Beatles," in care of KRLA in Pasadena. And be sure to specify the exact number and price of tickets which you wish to purchase.

Win a Surf Wagon

Winning a customized surf wagon with a Yamaha on the back, surf board on top and stereo tape player inside wouldn't be too bad, now would it?

Not really. And by simply sending in the coupon at the bottom of the next page you will be in the thick of a contest sponsored by KRLA and Capitol Records that will ultimately give one of the dream wagons away.

A new winner will be named each day until the end of the contest when a giant drawing will be held to determine the final winner of the wagon. Capitol, now celebrating the fourth anniversary of the Beach Boys' first hit, "Surfin' Safari," has authorized the production of the customized craft.

The cars are actually English-made Austin Mini-Mokes and are customized by George Barris of Kustom City. The jeep-type surfers come with a Yamaha Campus 60 strapped to the back in a special rack and surf board by Kon of California perched on top, complete with a half-block of cord and giant portable speakers, so that they can be hauled down to the beach and almost into the water.

So fill in the entry blank on the next page and get in on the fun.

THE ASSOCIATION
July 12 — 17
with their hit
"Along Comes Mary"
and album
"Along Comes The Association"
with
THE NEW FOLK TRIO
of
pepsi-cola fame

The ICE HOUSE   GLENDALE
folk music in concert   234 S. Brand, Glendale
Reservations: 245-5043

KRLA BEAT Subscription

SAVE 33% Of Regular Price

☐ 1 YEAR — 52 Issues — $5.00   ☐ 2 YEARS — $8.00
☐ 6 MONTHS — $3.00

Enclosed is _____   ☐ CASH   ☐ CHECK
PLEASE PRINT — Include Your Zip Code

Send to: ....Age: ....
Address: ....City: ....
State: ....Zip: ....

MAIL YOUR ORDER TO: KRLA BEAT
6290 Sunset, Suite 504
Foreign Rate: $9.00 — 52 Issues   Hollywood, Calif. 90028

KRLA ARCHIVES

WIN THIS MINI-SURFER!

Customized by George Barris, of Hollywood, this candy-striped Austin MINI-SURFER comes with a Yamaha Campus 60 strapped to the back, a custom surfboard by Kon of California cresting the top, a Borg-Warner 8-track stereo tape player, and two giant portable speakers with a half-block of cord!

it's KRLA's BEACH BOYS BIRTHDAY BLAST!

To join in the fun, just look for the Mini-Surfer display and the Beach Boys' newest album:

BEST OF THE BEACH BOYS

Surfin' U.S.A.
Little Honda
Fun, Fun, Fun
Wendy
...and more!

(D)T 2545

It's the easiest contest ever! Pick up an entry blank today!

HERE'S ALL YOU HAVE TO DO:
Write in your name, age, address and favorite all-time Beach Boys' song... Cut out coupon and drop in mail box.

TO: KRLA BEAT
BEACH BOYS BIRTHDAY BLAST!
1401 South Oak Knoll
Pasadena, California 91109

Name_____ Age_____
Address_____
City_____
State_____ Zip_____
Favorite Beach Boys' Song_____

Beach Boys and KRLA — A Smash At The Bowl

BEAT Photos: Chuck Boyd

DENNIS WILSON shows up sporting a new hair cut. **BUT BABY BEACH BOY** Carl Wilson still the same.

... **BYRDS JIM McGUINN AND CHRIS HILLMAN** grab a few quick minutes of rehearsal

PERCY SLEDGE autographs a lucky girls' purse.   ... **BRIAN WILSON** — Strictly a producer.

KRLA ARCHIVES

Davis Group Traitors?

By Anna Maria Alonzo

Just a few short months ago, a record called "Keep On Running," by a brand new British group, topped American pop charts across the nation.

The group was the Spencer Davis group, long recognized by other top British pop groups as one of the best R&B groups in England.

In their native country, they followed their first pop chart hit up with a second, "Somebody Help Me." Unfortunately, they were unable to duplicate their original success over here.

Like so many other groups who began in one field and then enjoyed success on the pop charts, the Spencer Davis group has been accused of being "traitors" to R&B; labeled "turncoats" who have crossed over and joined the ranks of the pop combos.

Frequently, their names are linked with those of the Yardbirds, another group who began in clubs with their own very distinctive brand of R&B and jazz who have since strayed off into the field of pop.

What Is "Pop?"

The question is, just what is "pop" music? Often, the term is just a synonym for a sound which is considered to be commercial; one which will sell on the popular markets.

The handsome leader of this talented group — Spencer Davis — explains: "I think it is a question of how much the fans will swing towards our kind of music. If it becomes popular then we will be pop."

Spencer also explained that there are many important factors involved in the creation of any musical sound — whether or not it is classified as *pop*.

"Material is very hard to come by. We write quite a bit of it ourselves. When choosing material, I have to consider the instruments, and Stevie's voice (the lead singer), which is all-important to the group, and also consider how much the sound and feeling on the record will be appreciated.

"But we always have considered these things. We didn't make records for our own enjoyment. We've always wanted to sell."

Affects On Group

All of the members of the group are aware of their commercial success and of its affects upon them. They are currently one of the three top groups in the main cities in Great Britain, and play to packed clubs and concert halls. This in itself might convince them to leave their older bluesy haunts for the more financially secure surroundings of pop, wouldn't it?

"It does to a point," is Spencer's reply. "We are impressed with all that has happened to us since 'Keep on Running.' But we were a group's group and we were highly thought of for our type of music. We don't want to go pop mad and turn out stuff that is too simple."

Their eighteen-year-old lead singer — Stevie Winwood — is considered to be one of the two top R&B "soul" singers in England today, Eric Burdon of the Animals running off with the top honors in that field. But Stevie adds his comments to Spencer's: "I don't wnat to do pure pop. It's not just the voice I'm thinking of, but the backing. It's very boring singing to a twelve bar backing. I like complicated music.

No Soul?

"I don't think I am a great soul singer though," he adds modestly. "No white singer can capture the feeling the Negroes get."

While they are aware of — and constantly reminded of — their pop success, Spencer determinedly maintains: "It's all too easy to let it affect you. You tell yourself you won't, but you can't help feeling pleased."

And their audience? Why the screaming, the worship, the adulation from their pop audiences? After briefly considering this, Spencer explains: "It is a question of splitting the audience into three. Some don't scream because they feel they shouldn't, for although they like us as stars — they understand our music.

"The others scream simply because we are four boys and we are famous, and the footlights add glamour.

"And the others don't scream, they just listen. The Hit Parade success means little to them. Yes, we like it, all of it, and we have had to work on keeping level-headed."

The Spencer Davis Group seems to have been able to *maintain their cool* — "levelheadedness" and all... — but their level of commercial success from here on out might just depend on whether or not they make the switch to pop complete.

In America, they will be accepted as just another British group — no srings, R&B or otherwise, attached. But in their native country across the Big Pond — they might have to play a game of Pop Goes the Group for a while.

Mathis Albums Big

"Johnny's Greatest Hits," the Johnny Mathis album which was issued in 1958 by Columbia Records, last week celebrated its 400th consecutive week on the Top LP chart. This week the Mathis album was No. 89 on the chart, up eight positions from the previous week.

Mathis is also on the chart with "Shadow of Your Smile" on Mercury. The Mercury Album, which climbed from No. 33 last week to No. 27 this week, has been on the chart for nine weeks and is expected to continue climbing.

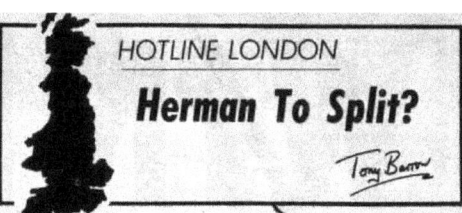

HOTLINE LONDON
Herman To Split?

By Tony Barrow

Will HERMAN'S HERMITS split up? The group looks set for new British success with a single called "This Door Swings Both Ways," but there are strong rumours here right now that the group is not swinging as much as it has done in the past. Bright, likeable Herman wants to try new ideas, whereas the Hermits seem quite happy with their current kind of music. Let's hope they work it out.

In spite of comments I made recently, the British pop scene now is literally being rocked by trouble among the groups — and it looks like it's getting worse. Apart from the almost weekly threats to leave by members of the Who (which most of us now ignore!), new rifts have taken place in the Animals, Yardbirds, Fortunes, Pinkerton's Assorted Colours and Manfred Mann.

The NEW MUSICAL EXPRESS carried a story that the ANIMALS' future seemed "uncertain" after lead singer ERIC BURDON had been offered a solo role in a film. Behind-the-scenes reports were that the rest of the group were unhappy because they would not be able to work for seven weeks while Burdon concentrated on the movie. There were dramatic discussions over the space of a weekend, however, and eventually the acting commitment was dropped. Eric and the Animals will now continue as before.

Sam's Gone

PAUL SAMWELL-SMITH has left the YARDBIRDS. Many fans considered the bass guitarist to have been an inspiration behind the group. He produced the Yardbirds' last three hits in this country (including "Over, Under, Sideways, Down"), but now he says he will concentrate on songwriting.

Paul claims that his departure was not due to arguments. He explained: "I am leaving because there is too much traveling involved." His replacement is a former session guitarist JIMMY PAGE.

The MANFRED MANN group has signed with a new label (Philips) and has already recorded without PAUL JONES. Both Paul and Manfred have been hotly denying a split, but it is now accepted that MICHAEL D'ABO, a former member of the now defunct BAND OF ANGELS, will take Paul's place with the Manfreds.

Paul is expected to stay with EMI as a solo artist. EMI have released "You Gave Me Somebody To Love" from their stockpile of Manfred recordings. The number is also on release by the FORTUNES.

Paul Turns Author

Incidentally, Paul has turned playwright. He and his wife SHEILA penned the play "They Put You Where You Are," which has just been screened by BBC-2 TV. It concerned a pop idol's reaction to his fans when they call on him in his dressing room.

The ASSORTED COLOUR who has departed the group is BARRIE BENARD, and he has been replaced by Yorkshire-born IAN COLMAN. Barrie has formed a new group called THE JIG SAW with three of THE MIGHTY AVENGERS and GLEN DALE, who has left the FORTUNES. His replacement is SHEL MACRAE.

CLIFF RICHARD's massive fan club is closing down. The big-name British singer is deeply religious and it is expected that early next year he will give up showbusiness to embark on a three-year course as a student of Divinity.

SYBILLA'S, the discotheque, opened by GEORGE HARRISON and d-j ALAN FREEMAN, has now opened in London. As expected, business is fantastic and the nightly clientele reads like a Who's Who of British showbusiness.

Before the BEATLES departure to Germany, PAUL McCARTney told Alan Smith in the NEW MUSICAL EXPRESS how he had injured himself when he fell from a motor scooter recently.

Said Paul: "It was quite a serious accident at the time. It probably sounds daft, as I was only doing about 30, but I came off hard and I got knocked about quite a bit. My head and lip were cut and I broke a tooth.

"I've now had it capped, but I had to make a few television appearances with the gap showing. Some people also said I looked tired and ill on TV, but it was only the effects of the accident.

"I was also a bit worn out after working long hours on our LP."

Paul added that the accident happened "because it was dark, and I was looking at the moon instead of the road. I hit a stone and went flying through the air!"

NEWS BRIEFS . . . DUSTY SPRINGFIELD, the WALKER BROTHERS, SPENCER DAVIS and many other artists are contributing to a special LP in aid of the United Nations Save The Children Fund . . . One of PAUL McCARTNEY's favorite records of the moment is IKE AND TINA TURNER's "River Deep — Mountain High" . . . HOLLIES scoring here again with a new one penned by GRAHAM GOULDMAN, who penned HERMAN'S "Listen People" — "Bus Stop" . . . TOM JONES needed 14 stitches in his head after an accident in his Jaguar sports car near London's Marble Arch . . . JERRY LEE LEWIS returning to Britain this fall . . . HOLLIES fourth British LP, just issued, includes Chinese-style song and "Fifi The Flea," one of their own compositions; this has been waxed by the EVERLY BROTHERS . . . Big success here for new Liverpool singer DAVID GARRICK covering MICK JAGGER song, "Lady Jane" . . . ROLLING STONES manager ANDREW OLDHAM once recorded as one half of a duo called BO and PEEP! . . . British Government more determined than ever to stamp our pirate radio stations here .

KRLA ARCHIVES

Keith Relf: A Man In Search

By Eden

JBL SOUND IS WHERE IT'S HAPPENING!

Trini Lopez, Chet Atkins, Johnny Rivers, The Beach Boys, The Rolling Stones make it with JBL sound.

JBL is the sound of the scene at the top!

Fender, Jordan, Ampeg, Gretsch, Standel, Guild, Gibson, C. F. Martin, Sunn amplifier systems groove with JBL loudspeakers.

High notes that won't quit, thundering bass at peak volume from JBL F-Series loudspeakers. Write us for free information about use and installation.

James B. Lansing Sound, Inc.
3249 Casitas Avenue
Los Angeles, California 90039

In this very weird world of pop music, there are some few individuals who leave a more lasting impression upon the people with whom they come in contact than just a few guitar chords, or some off-hand sarcastic remark.

There are some pop musicians who come across as human beings, and succeed in actually *touching* another human being, and in some way — affecting him.

Such a person is Keith Relf of the Yardbirds. Keith is small, and quiet; a person given to moods in their extremes. He is a sensitive young man, and seems not only to *hear* everything which is said to him, but to actually take it in, think about it, and *really feel* it somewhere within himself.

He is a sensitive person, and yet strong enough to stand up to the pressures placed upon him by the world in which he lives. He is strong enough to understand the burdens which he has taken as his own, and to accept them as a necessary part of his life; a life which he has chosen.

"Pop is all-demanding. It's my whole life at the moment. I've had lots of moments of doubt. Sometimes, late at night, you're traveling back after a bad gig and you think, 'Why should I go on?' Then you go to sleep, wake up the next morning and think what a twit you've been.

"This business has me by the ears. Or should I say by the hair?"

Sense of Proportion

Yes, he has still managed to retain a sense of humor. But he has also succeeded in hanging onto a sense of proportion, a vital necessity for anyone who hopes to survive in the field of entertainment.

Very thoughtfully, Keith explains: "I suppose I'm trapped in a group. I can't please myself whether I work or not. If you have a gig you can't get out of it. You *must* go there.

"I worked for people before the group. A lot of people. If I didn't want to go in, I stayed in bed all day or lay flat on my back in Richmond Park watching the clouds move across the sky.

"I can't do that now. If I missed out tonight, I would let down a thousand people who had planned to put Friday aside to see us, and had queued up for tickets, and had made us a part of their week.

"On four or five occasions we've missed a date . . . through illness or once through bad weather. I felt most awful."

Sincere Effort

It is important to Keith to fulfill what he considers to be his obligations to other people, and he usually will make a sincere effort to do so.

For the most part, he doesn't seem to really enjoy interviews. The whole aspect of being questioned and pryed at; of being dissected with a pen and typewriter — seems to claw at his mind, and sometimes nearly tears him apart.

And yet, he will nearly always try to get hold of himself long enough to go through with that interview, and to answer those questions to the best of his ability, and with as much patience, courtesy, and cooperation as possible.

He might not smile — but then, he doesn't smile too often anyway. And when he does, it is the infectious grin of a little boy, with all the trust and sincerity which he can pour into one small smile.

"A Good Keith"

And happiness for Keith is a very important thing. It might come in the form of a "good gig." "The sort of gig that really makes you happy is when there's great applause as soon as the audience sees you. You feel wonderful. The applause grows and grows, and you play better and better.

"You rise to a peak. You're built up because the audience is built up. Yet, sometimes you go on stage in a ballroom and you're faced with an apathetic, washed-out crowd.

"They've already seen two or three groups that week, and they don't care anymore. You can't do anything for them . . . they've been brainwashed somehow.

"You do two numbers and you think, 'Oh, my goodness — still forty minutes to go!' I hate that . . . arriving at a place full of enthusiasm then finding it a drag."

Keith isn't one to allow himself to be spread too thin if he can possibly help it. While others can constantly run to the escapism-atmosphere of the dimly-lighted, sense-destroying pop clubs, Keith prefers another sort of existence.

"I can go to a club and enjoy myself, but it doesn't make me want to go there again the next night. I can't stand the sort of society where you go to a club night after night, meeting the same people. People who do that must be rootless wanderers. I have a home to go to."

Yes, Keith does have a home — a new home now, with a new wife inside. Recently married to a girl from Kenya — April Liversidge — Keith now has a home, a shelter to which he can return from the hectic whirl of activity in which his pop activities involve him.

And yet, he seems still somewhat "rootless" himself. He seems to be searching for something which he has yet to find. You see it in his eyes as he searches your face while you are speaking to him.

Perhaps he hopes to find a friend there. You hear it in his voice as he confides one of his dreams to you. "It's a dream — perhaps an immature one — of mine to make an expedition into the wilds of darkest Alaska. It would be a two-month survival course. I'd have to rely on myself to fight the elements."

He seems to be searching for something, and yet — even he seems unsure of just what that something is. I have a hunch that he is only searching for himself — for a young man named Keith — and when he finally finds that man, it will most likely prove well worth his search.

BEAT Photos, Chuck Boyd

DISCussion

Spoonful's record, "Summer in the City," is a super-sized summer smash. There is some great production on this disc, and it really deserves to reach the top pop spot.

* * *

Herman has a new single out, "This Door Swings Both Ways." There are some pretty good ideas behind the lyric-lines, and some fairly good beginnings in the way of arrangement and production. But all put together and mixed-down, the resulting 45 RPMer *just doesn't make it!* Definitely not one of Peter's better efforts.

* * *

Brian Wilson of the Beach Boys tells us that the group's next single will be "God Only Knows," one of the best cuts off of their latest smash LP, "Pet Sounds."

The album is in the Number 10 position nationally, and is only in its second week on the charts. This new single is a good representation of the extensive thought and hard work poured into the album, and is really one of the prettiest Beach Boy discs you will hear.

"City Women," by P. F. Sloan, is one of the most commercial efforts by the talented young composer-singer. Although he and partner Steve Barri have been responsible for penning a number of hits for many of today's top groups, including Herman's Hermits, the Turtles, the Grass Roots, and many others — his own records have yet to be accepted by the public.

This new one is one of the best, however. It's blues-oriented, with a good, strong beat and it deserves to go straight to the top.

In America, the Stones' latest release is now "Mother's Little Helper" b/w "Lady Jane." "Mother's Little Helper" was accidentally played as the new Stone single several months ago, and now it has been released as the real thing.

Too bad, too, 'cause the Stones can do much better. The flip side — "Lady Jane" — is one of the best ever from the Five Rolling Ones, and it should set a trend for a number of other groups. Watch for many cover versions of this tune.

"Pretty Flamingo" is the first release which we have received from the Manfred Mann group in some time, and it really is a good disc.

In England, all of the top musical trade papers are giving volumes of praise to this new single, and claiming that it was well worth waiting for. However, I feel that the song still could have been done better. Still a pretty disc, though.

* * *

And then there is the case of "Somewhere My Love" by the Ray Conniff Singers which would be slow even for the "good music stations." The disc is currently getting air play on pop stations all around. Why?

* * *

The Righteous Brothers are slowly but surely climbing to the chart-tops once again with their latest single, "He."

This is another pretty ballad-Spector-style — for the soulful duo, but even so it seems kind of disappointing that with all of their talent they seem to feel that they must stick in one "bag" forever.

How about another helping of that "blue-eyed soul" which made them famous in the first place?

* * *

Good to see Paul Revere and the Raiders' "Hungry" heading toward the Number One area. They seem to be having a neck-and-neck race with their latest album — "Midnight Ride" — which is soaring up the LP charts. They're off and running...

Keep sending in your letters to let me know about your fave American groups, 'cause I still want to know who you're listening to.

KRLA ARCHIVES

...SAM AND BUDDY PHAROAHS

Twentieth Century Pharoah: A Texan Named Sam The Sham

By Louise Criscione

"Wooly Bully" and a beard. Turbans and sheet-like outfits. The whole thing seems like years ago but actually isn't. Since "Wooly Bully" Sam The Sham and the Pharoahs have seen movies, mobs, hit records, practically the whole world and a million cubby holes affectionately (though erroneously) tabbed dressing-rooms.

The beard has come and gone and come again. The turbans and sheets have been discarded and reclaimed. One never knows what tomorrow will bring—least of all Sam. "Wooly Bully" was one of the biggest rock records of the year. It seemed impossible that the group who made it would have to wait almost an entire year to find a follow-up as big as "Wooly Bully." And yet they did.

Finally

Fair-sized hits and fair-sized bombs came their way readily but that really big one—that partner to "Wooly Bully" failed to materialize until someone had the sense to dream up a song with the crazy title, "Lil' Red Riding Hood." And finally they had it—their second smash.

It is really something of a wonder that Sam and his Pharoahs are still intact. The anxiety and frustrations of not releasing hit records usually results in some sort of a major group split. And Sam *was* reported to be leaving the group. Fact is, several months ago, The BEAT got it straight from their publicity office that Sam had already flown.

We thought it was a definite character-switch for Sam. He's so determined—we couldn't see him giving up. And through the whole thing——the hit, the concerts, the screams, the excitement, the flash bulbs—Sam hadn't changed. He never became swell-headed, never assumed the role of "star."

Down-Home

He's big and you can't imagine him ever losing. His black hair and eyes, his strong jaw and broken nose resemble a Roman Emperor. Yet, he is everyone's idea of a cowboy. Probably because he has the soft and gentle manner associated with the South or West. His drawl is thick and his adjectives are strictly downhome. "Shaving my beard was like scraping a hog's hide," said Sam. City people just have to guess what he's talking about. Country people know.

Sam takes life in stride. He looks and he laughs. I doubt if he's ever cried. He's Texas. But his ideas of what constitutes a man and a woman are definitely Latin. To Sam, a man is not a big mouth, not someone who laughs so loud or speaks with such a tremendous volume that he can be heard all over the room.

Sam's a gentleman. Not phony, just natural. Only Sam's idea of a gentleman isn't someone who merely opens doors and lights ciragrettes for ladies. He's a man, too. And a fighter. Sam will jump into any fight to help a friend. He'll fight for himself too—make no mistake about it.

Yet, I suspect that he doesn't *enjoy* hurting. He's not above it; he just doesn't particularly dig it. Sam boxed at Arlington State College and lost only one match and that was by a decision. He stands six feet one inch and weighs in at 165 pounds. Which means that if he really lost his temper and hit someone—that someone would hurt, bad.

Singin' Opera

So, he looks like a Roman Emperor or a cowboy...depending. He's a gentleman and a fighter. He specializes in hard rock and yet he wants to be an opera singer. His biggest ambition is to sing at the Metropolitan Opera House and his dark eyes light up as he tells you: "No one can beat Jussi Bjorling...he was the greatest."

Funny, but Sam's most memorable moment was not when he found "Wooly Bully" perched at the top of the nation's record charts. It was when they played with James Brown and did so well that Brown had to work to get his audience back. "They underestimated us," said Sam frankly. And that's a mistake in anybody's book. You never under-estimate a man like Sam. If anything, you over-estimate him.

The formation of Sam and the Pharoahs isn't anything unusual. They just happened to be in the same place at the same time and decided to form a group. And the name? "All the others were taken," they chorus.

Life should be so easy.

Five Weld

By Carol Deck

HOLLYWOOD: Somewhere there's a guy who probably makes a living off providing the Dave Clark five with guitar straps. They seem to loose a set at practically every performance.

During the group's latest visit to America they lost, after just the first few performances, three drums, two sets of guitar straps and a tambourine and were expecting to loose more before the tour was over.

This annoys them but they've learned to accept it; as well as the fact that they're also going to loose a fair amount of buttoms from their stage outfits.

In fact they've given up even sewing buttons on their current outfits — balck pants, while puffy sleeved shirts with two rows of black buttons down the front and red, white and blue striped belts — they now just pin them on. They loose a lot of pins too, but it saves a lot of thread and time by not sewing them on.

On this, their eighth tour of America, they arrived on the West Coast straight from Hawaii with the most fantastic tans ever seen on a British group.

Along with their tans they also got the usual amount of burning and peeling and, by the time they reached California, looked like natives of the Golden State.

Usual Chaos

Their performance at the Carousel Theater in West Covina was the usual chaos they've learned to accept.

They arrived back stage just a few minutes before they were scheduled to go on, but there were a few hang-ups and they didn't make it on stage until about 15 minutes later.

They arrived wearing their stage outfits, already a little wrinkled from the trip over.

Dave had a few words about the over stiff collars on the shirts. "Your American laundries — they always make the collars too stiff. Buy don't get me wrong, I love America. It's just the way your laundries starch collars."

A young handicapped girl was brought into the dressing room and the guys all stopped, signed autographs and posed for a picture with her. Dave even took time out to chat with her for a few minutes. You could tell she'll be loyal to the DC5 for the rest of her life.

Then while Mike stood off in one corner softly singing "Hold On, I'm Coming," Dave cornered all the photographers in the room and asked them to help him built a montague.

He's got a wall at home he wants to cover with one huge montague of pictures of the group and their fans and the chaos at concerts. It's 10 feet square and he wants to make half of it British and half of it American.

A man from the theater came in and told Dave he'd have to cut the show short because they were running late.

Not Fair

Dave flatly said, "No, it's not fair to the fans to cut it short."

So they went on stage and did a full set. There was some confusion back stage over what their last number was.

The guards and light technicians had to know when they went into the last number so they could put into action the security precautions for getting the group safely off stage and into their waiting limousine.

There were two different lists of what they were going to sing and two different songs listed as the last number, so everyone just

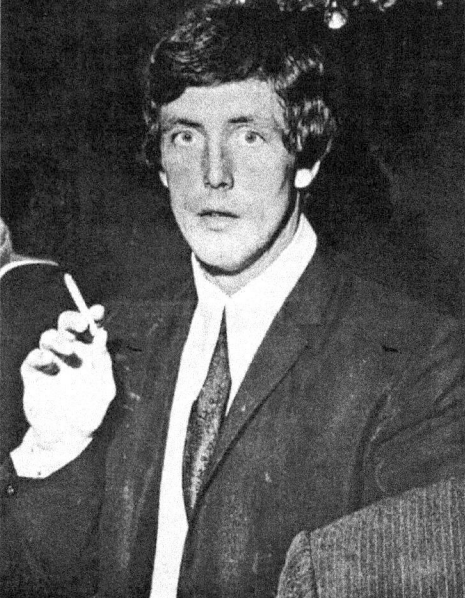

MIKE SMITH kept trying to hide in corners all during the press party until he found a piano, then he didn't move for the rest of the evening.

KRLA ARCHIVES

Tanned Englishmen On Tour

got ready to get them off stage at *any* time.

Somehow all five got safely out to the car and dissappeared into the night.

We saw them again the following night at a press party in their honor.

They arrived together, slightly late, and immediately separated to meet everyone in the room.

Except Mike Smith who headed straight for a corner but someone brought him out and started introducing everyone to him. Sometime later he *did* manage to slip off in a corner where he found a piano.

Nobody could seem to get him away from the piano so finally the rest of the group joined him to pose for a few group pictures.

Lenny chatted for a while about what's happening music-wise in England.

"There's something happening with groups like The Who, Pinkerton's Assorted Colours and Them", he said.

He also revealed that he's going to grab a vacation after this tour's over. He's been invited to spend some time at a villa in Portugal that belongs to Cliff Richard.

Great?

Someone said something about how great it must be to travel around the world and meet so many people.

"Yeah," Lenny said, "But you don't really get to know many of them."

"But then some of them aren't really worth getting to know," he added solemnly.

Dave, in a striking gold coat, was curiously amused that everyone in the room seemed to know his shoulders were peeling from too much sun.

There was talk of their next movie, which they're scheduled to start shooting in December, but no one would reveal the title or anything about the script.

We discovered later though that Dave himself thought up the basic idea for the script and turned it over to a professional script writer. Now he's looking for a title, preferably one word.

Five Days

Between parties and performances they spent a total of five days in Southern California this year and most of that time was spent lying around in the sun. They've got to be five of the best tanned Englishmen around.

Mike Smith also spent a good deal of time denying rumors, started in New York, that he's married to an English model. Mike once said, "When I get married the world will know," and he's intent on keeping that promise. So relax fans, until he tells you so himself, it ain't true.

Now the Dave Clark Five are off again, in their private jet, for more concerts, more chaos, more press parties, more lost equipment and buttons, and undoubtedly, more time in the sun.

HEY DAVE, WHERE'S YOUR DRUM STICK? Dave seems a little bewildered to find there's nothing in his hand — not even a drum stick!

DENNIS LETS GO with his sax during their latest performance in Calif.

"SOME PEOPLE really aren't worth getting to know," says Lenny.

DAVE CLARK AND BEAT REPORTER CAROL DECK BACK STAGE.

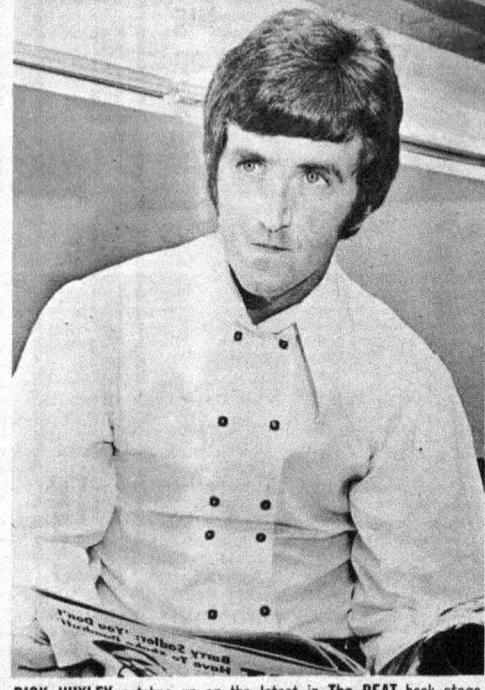
RICK HUXLEY catches up on the latest in The BEAT back stage.

KRLA ARCHIVES

The Adventures Of Robin Boyd

©1965 By Shirley Poston

There are some people in this world who would take a dim view of finding themselves locked in the glove compartment of a speeding auto.

It is, in fact, rather difficult to take a view *other* than dim because it's darker than Pauley's left eyebrow in the glove compartment of a speeding auto.

At any rate, Robin Irene Boyd was definitely one of those people. (See paragraph #1 if you've forgotten one of *what* people). (On second thought, consider yourself fortunate and leave well enough alone).

Repetition, Inc.

Re-adjusting her Byrd glasses, Robin re-peered through the keyhole and re-quaked.

Being locked in the glove compartment of a speeding auto was truly a problem to be reckoned with (and it will be just as soon as you've recovered from another message brought to you by Repitition, Incorporated).

Since the view from Robin's (disad)vantage point provided only a close look at a knee-cap, it was impossible for her to tell who was driving the S.A. (of G.C. fame). But it was simple (I'll say) to determine who was *NOT*.

If there was one thing George the Genie refused to do (a conservative estimate), it was wear purple-flowered bell bottoms, (*Pink*-flowered mayhaps, but never purple).

Robin put her head in her hands (which is not only difficult for a *real* robin, but also rather painful if one is badly in need of a manicure), (clawicure?) (forget it).

"Ratzafratz..." she muttered. "And turn off that *stereo!*" she added as the sounds of "Baby Don't Go" filtered through the key-hole.

Savagely severing the thumb of a glove she'd been nestling in, Robin settled down for a session of problem-reckoning-with, only to have her thoughts interrupted by the end of the world.

Well, it sure *felt* like it... Because Robin was suddenly blown several feet into the air (a slight exaggeration, but what the hey). Then, after landing tailfeather over teakettle and smashing her glasses into a million (bits and) pieces (threw that in there for you DC5-ers), she proceeded to freeze solid.

Realizing that the person who invented air conditioning for (speeding) autos had probably never been in a glove compartment when the feindish thing(y) was turned on (the A.C., not the G.C.), and therefore did not know that he should have at *least* installed subway straps, Robin still planned to peck him to death at the earliest possible opportunity.

(You have just visited another of the world's longest sentences). (Please enjoy the remainder of your trip). Meet you over Tokyo).

Suddenly, the great blizzard was switched off, as was the stereo and the car motor. And, just as suddenly, Robin blew the remainder of her cool (not to mention her alleged brains out).

In the past, Robin has been known to slightly joggle the olde seismograph with one of her smaller sneezes. But this particularly gargantuan (it was big, too) achoo measured 7.9 on the Richter scale.

It also blew the door of the glove compartment clean out of the socket.

The next thing Robin knew, she was cuddled in the palm of a tender hand, and blind as she was (as in six bats) without her ex-glasses, she was also beginning to see the light.

That hadn't been stereo at all... It had been the real thingy... On account of because the voice, the tender hand and the purple-flowered knee-cap belonged to none other than Mrs. Salvatore Bono...

As Robin twittered a feeble cheep of combination despair-delight, Cher raced up the driveway.

Sonny Honey

"Sonny..." she cried, bursting (not as a balloon) through the door. "Honey..." she added. "*Sonny honey!*" she finished.

Sonny, who was seated at the piano, thoughtfully swallowed the pencil he had just been thoughtfully gnawing.

"Hi," he said (when he was able), getting up (from the floor) to give his beautiful wife Jill (a joke, a joke) a kiss. "What's all the excitement?"

Cher glowed happily. "Look what I found in the glove compartment of our speeding auto..."

With this she tenderly transferred Robin from her tender hand to Sonny's tender hand.

"Hey," breathed Sonny. "It's a Robin..."

Fighting back the urge to faint from sheer joy, Robin lurched to her feet, gave a great shake (well, it wasn't really all *that* great) and smiled prettily.

Sonny looked at Robin. Cher looked at Robin. Robin looked at Sonny and Cher. Then Sonny looked at Cher. And Cher looked at Sonny. (No comment). (Words fail me). (And it's about time).

"It's trying to tell us it's hungry..." chorused Sonny and Cher. And they were right the first time. (Huh?).

Dig Worms

Tenderly re-transferring Robin from Sonny's tender hand to her own (tender hand), Cher started in the direction of the kitchen. "I'll warm some milk," she said over her shoulder. "And you dig worms."

Sonny gave her a hurt glance. Then he brightened. "Oh, sure... I'd forgotten that robins eat

May you forget it again SOON, Robin prayed, trying not to retch as he burst (again, not as in—oh, you know) out the door.

Unfortunately, his memory didn't fail him this time. Just as Cher was spooning the milk into an eye-dropper (an ill-named instrument if there ever was one, as it has probably never dropped an eye in its entire life), Sonny returned. And he was gingerly dangling a wriggling earthworm by its tail. (Actually, it could have been its head. This, you see, is a debatable point, of interest only to other earthworms, who often can't tell the difference either, but sure have their fair share of fun trying to find out).

Placing Robin gently on the table, Sonny re-dangled the worm right before her very (horrified, that is) eyes.

Wife Worm

"Mercy," whispered the worm, "I have a wife and six wormlets." (Worms, you can, *can* talk, but since they very rarely do, there's really no point in trying to start up a conversation the next time you happen to run across one). (Particularly if you happen to run across it with a motorbike).

"Don't worry your head . . . er. . . your . . . well, *whatever* it is, don't worry it..." Robin hissed, and with this she turned up her nose (an unnecessary move as it was plenty loud enough already).

Sonny shrugged. "I guess it isn't hungry after all."

Robin gasped, longing but not daring to bellow "the *ratzafratz* it isn't..." And, with visions of Dagwood sandwiches (with real Dagwoods) she hopped over to Cher and leaned coaxingly against her purple-flowered arm (she was wearing a suit, a suit).

Then she re-smiled and was soon greedily gulping from the eye-dropper.

Nap Time

gills with a half-quart of milk (well, it's better than nothing), Robin lay sprawled gracefully (you bet) on a satin pillow, plotting her exit.

Not that she really wanted to leave, but she had no choice. A few hours ago, she'd promised to stay out of trouble, which she was definitely now in (up to a point) (the one on her head).

In trouble with George, who would in turn be in it with Ringo, who would (in turn) turn a most un-angelic shade of purple (flowered bell-bottoms, probably) and re-revoke her genie privileges (a nice way of putting it, don't you agree?).

All things considered, she was going to have to wait until Sonny and Cher became engrossed (the three of them were on the couch, watching a spot of telly) and then fly off into the sunset through a nearby window.

And she *would* have if she hadn't suddenly been scooped up and tenderly placed in the *birdcage* that was hanging in front of that nearby window.

(To Be Continued Next Week)

Beatle Movie Number Three

(Continued From Page 6)

his pursuit—the music continues also.

This time it's members of a Salvation Army Band (also resembling the Beatles (who are playing. Ringo watches and listens for a few seconds, then to the accompaniment of the music, strolls to the zoo where he observes four monkeys (guess who?)

After leaving the park, Ringo turns a sharp corner and bumps (literally) into John, George, Paul and Jill. Paul drops the sack he was carrying and the tiara rolls out. A short silence follows, after which Ringo thanks John for his aid in capturing the crooks. Then George picks up the loot and runs down the street. Jill and Paul take off after him, and John and Ringo trail behind.

From an aerial view, the audience sees the first three enter a shop through the front door and exit at the rear on a bicycle built for three. Then John and Ringo enter and exit on a bicycle built for two.

The first part of the chase is viewed from the air. Above the background music, Ringo's police whistle is heard. Bobbies on bicycles (two by two, of course) give chase and through the countryside. The parade of bicycles grows and grows, as more officers join in.

There are close-ups of various puzzled spectators as they view George (wearing the tiara) at the front, Jill in the middle and Paul at the rear of their bike, being shadowed by John and Ringo on their bike, followed by fifty bobbies on twenty-five bikes.

But the race ends when George's vehicle skids and falls after narrowly missing a collision with an Astin Martin. Then Ringo's bike falls over, also spilling its passengers. The rest of the bikes pile up, too.

The driver of the car graciously aids Jill to her feet as the bobbies nab her companions. Jill fails to recognize the driver (James Bond, alias Sean Connery), and the driver fails to recognize his cuff-links have been swiped.

The movie comes to a close in the police station. The commissioner congratulates Ringo on his capturing the elusive marauders, and safely delivering the tiara to the Queen. (Ringo has failed to inform the authorities of his escapades with John.)

Back in the jail, Jill has a cell of her own and John, Paul and George occupy one opposite her. The fearless foursome are in the midst of saying goodbye when Jill tells Paul she has a little going away gift for him.

She produces the cuff links and holds one in each hand. Paul is quite pleased (can't say the same for George.) She tosses one cuff link to Paul, but he misses and the link strikes the wall, exploding with a pink poof.

Jill then tosses the other link against her cell wall with the same results.

The boys give her a round of applause—to which she makes a modest bow. Then the group blow a kiss to the remaining walls and ed man in search of this guardian.

Finis? It's About Time!

Big Pen on Campus!

UTILITY by Lindy

#460-M MEDIUM POINT
non-refillable Ball Pen

The perfect school pen for every writing and drawing need... perfectly balanced to lessen writing fatigue.

GIANT INK SUPPLY

The pen you never refill... oversize ink cartridge assures many months of skip-free, clog-free writing.

39¢

12 BRILLIANT INK COLORS

Manufactured by LINDY PEN CO. INC.,
North Hollywood, Calif. 91605, U.S.A.

The BEAT Goes To The Movies

"WHO'S AFRAID OF VIRGINIA WOOLF?"

By Jim Hamblin
(The BEAT Movie Editor)

Normally we try to spotlight films that are of general family interest, and especially those that young people would find entertaining. With so many good ones produced, though, we very often just do not have time or space to present anything about certain pictures that fit the category.

On rare occasions, a film of such compelling artistry comes along that it literally demands our attention. Such is this new Warner Brothers' picture, which has already blasted existing records at every theatre it has played. Perhaps because of the public clamor to see what is so special about the story, and why it is restricted to persons who are 18 years of age or older.

A New Chapter

Jack L. Warner (the last of the brothers) knew that the play by Edward Albee, from which this film is adapted, would require handling in good taste. But what he did to guarantee that only adult audiences would see the film established a new page in Hollywood history. Warner is the first to ever *classify* his own film. Every theatre that shows this movie must sign an agreement to admit only those persons under 18 who are accompanied by at least one parent. Naturally, anyone who is not permitted to see the film will wonder why.

What's In A Word?

Let us first say that Virginia Woolf is an uproarious comedy. It is a continuing flow of intellectual humor, side by side with gutter language. For it is what the characters *say* and the *words* they use that makes this film objectionable to youngsters.

There is nothing in it that any teen-ager has not perhaps heard from adults during a heated argument. And strictly speaking there are no *obscene* words in the dialogue either, just words never before heard on the screen. At least legally, anyway.

A Long Time Making

The director of the picture is Mike Nichols, the same fellow who was half of the Elaine May-Mike Nichols comedy team. He is so much in demand as a director on Broadway that he is completely booked until 1968. His direction of the four people in this cast is absolutely flawless. The cast and crew labored over the film for nearly six months, which is a monumentally long time for cameras to be rolling on any kind of picture.

Most of those who have seen the picture seem surprised that Elizabeth Taylor can act so well. And as for Richard Burton . . . has there ever been such an accomplished and magnificent actor on the screen?

The Future Topic

There will be several top contenders for Academy Awards next year but no future discussion of those gold statues with the funny name Oscar can ever leave out this film.

We remind you again that it is for sophisticated audiences only. Those who do see it are in for an evening of tragedy and pathos, grisly realism and high humor, and a look at a masterpiece of the film maker's art.

KRLA ARCHIVES

LIMITED SUMMER BONUS FOR BEAT READERS—

$200 in Values *Only* **$2** in Price!

FUNTEEN CLUB

GO-GUIDE COUPON BOOK

More than 100 coupons for Free Admissions, Discounts up to 50% or 2 for 1 offerings. Activities and Products listed below, plus many others.

Movies	Revell
Clubs	Statewide Theatres
Dancing	So. Cal. Bowl. Assn
Sports	Troubador
Food	Ash Grove
Clothing	Orange Julius
Records	Hullabaloo
Jewelry	Gazzari's
Cosmetics	P.O.P.
Shows	Pasadena Civic
Fairs	Sports Show
Horseback Riding	L. A. Blades
Bowling	Ice House
Folk Music	World On Wheels
Plays	Independ. Theatres
Slot Car Racing	Vivian Woodward
Billiards	Fashion Tops
Skating	Mademoiselle

Dial F-U-N-T-E-E-N For More Information

ORDER NOW WHILE THEY LAST!

FUNTEEN GO-GUIDE
c/o KRLA BEAT
6290 Sunset, Suite 504
Hollywood, Calif. 90028

Please send me _____ copies of the 1966 FUNTEEN GO-GUIDE (Valid thru Dec. 31, 1966) at the special summer rate of only $2.00 each. I enclose $_____

NAME:
ADDRESS:
CITY: _____ STATE: _____ ZIP: _____

KRLA ARCHIVES

America's Largest Teen NEWSpaper

KRLA Edition BEAT

JULY 30, 1966

15¢

Beatles Mauled
PAGE 1

Stone Hold On Beatles
PAGE 4-5

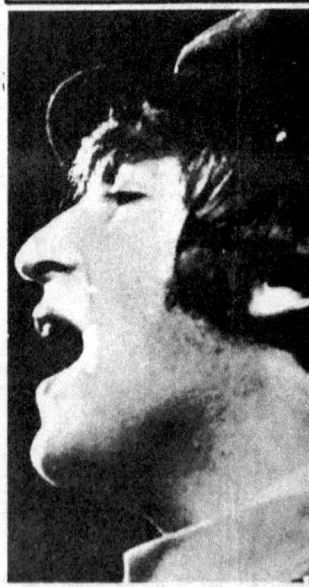

KRLA BEAT

Volume 2, Number 20   July 30, 1966

Regarding the black eye given him in New Delhi: "I got it from a policeman's baton in New Delhi and he was on our side!"

"We're going to have a couple of weeks to recuperate before we go and get beaten up by the Americans."

"We didn't even know about the invitation, must less receive it, until it was too late."

And John Lennon had this to say, "I didn't even know they had a President."

Beatles Cursed, Shoved By Mobs...America Next?

A barrage of apologies and clarifications has followed the shocking incident in Manila recently where the Beatles received the first maltreatment of their careers, but it looks as though the group may not be able to forget its alleged "snub" of Manila's First Lady for a long, long time.

Reports of the incident were heard around the world and the Beatles were victims of similar mob action in India, where Paul suffered a black eye.

Paul said he received the black eye when he was struck by the baton of a policeman who was attempting to protect the boys during the Indian riot.

The group's sudden unpopularity came about after the boys failed to keep a scheduled luncheon date with Mrs. Ferdinand Marcos, wife of the Filipino president. The Beatles denied they knew anything about the appointment.

Paul, speaking on behalf of his companions, apologized for standing Mrs. Marcos up, but said he and his companions simply knew nothing of the schedule.

At the time of the luncheon, Paul said he was sightseeing around Manila and the other three Beatles were sleeping in their hotel suite.

An angered John Lennon wasn't nearly so calm and apologetic as spokesman Paul. "I didn't even know the country had a president," he quipped.

The Manila incident, a harassing, violent send-off of the group at the Manila International Air-
(Turn to page 6)

Inside the BEAT

Letters To The Editor 2
Herman's New Movie Contract 3
Obscenity In Pop Music 4
Beatle Fans Turning To Stones 4-5
The Soul Of Jackie Wilson 6
Herman's Pop Satire 7
Adventures Of Robin Boyd 10
Righteous Brothers On Stage 11
Noel Harrison—Secret Agent 12
Spoon Of The Lovin' 13
Cyrkle Around The World 14

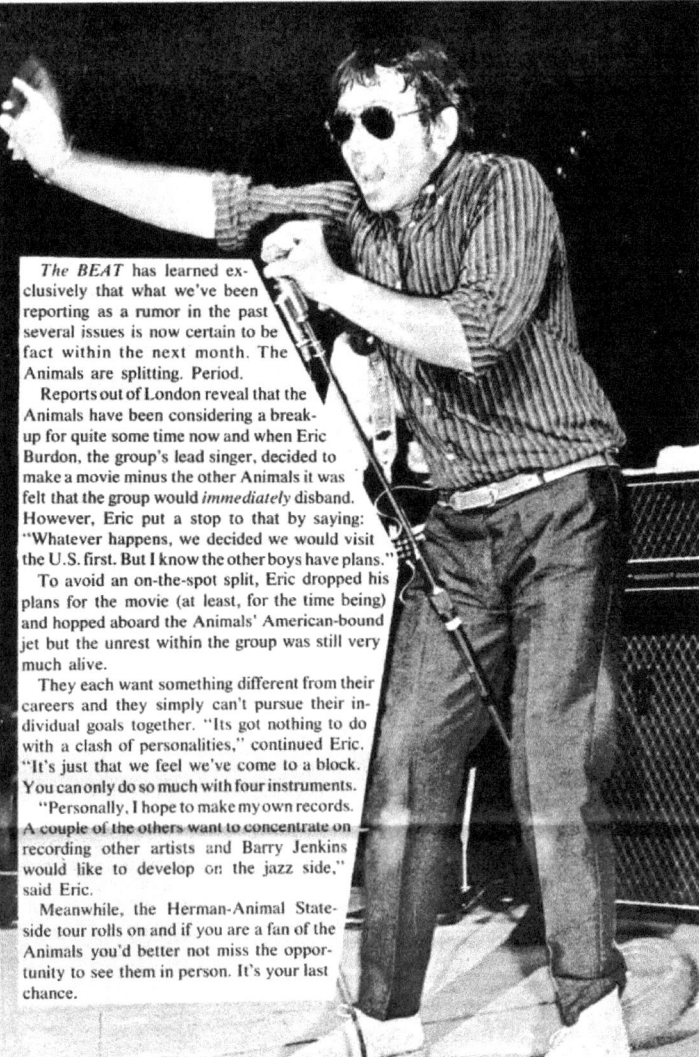

ERIC TO SOLO?

The BEAT has learned exclusively that what we've been reporting as a rumor in the past several issues is now certain to be fact within the next month. The Animals are splitting. Period.

Reports out of London reveal that the Animals have been considering a break-up for quite some time now and when Eric Burdon, the group's lead singer, decided to make a movie minus the other Animals it was felt that the group would *immediately* disband. However, Eric put a stop to that by saying: "Whatever happens, we decided we would visit the U.S. first. But I know the other boys have plans."

To avoid an on-the-spot split, Eric dropped his plans for the movie (at least, for the time being) and hopped aboard the Animals' American-bound jet but the unrest within the group was still very much alive.

They each want something different from their careers and they simply can't pursue their individual goals together. "Its got nothing to do with a clash of personalities," continued Eric. "It's just that we feel we've come to a block. You can only do so much with four instruments.

"Personally, I hope to make my own records. A couple of the others want to concentrate on recording other artists and Barry Jenkins would like to develop on the jazz side," said Eric.

Meanwhile, the Herman-Animal Stateside tour rolls on and if you are a fan of the Animals you'd better not miss the opportunity to see them in person. It's your last chance.

BEAT Photos, Chuck Boyd

Dave Clark Takes A Punch At A Phoenix Disc Joackey

The Dave Clark Five received an hour-long broadcast apology from a Phoenix, Arizona radio station after Dave and a station disc jockey had what might be described as a small scuffle.

"The crowd was getting pretty excited, but the Chief of Police was quite happy that things were under control," relates Dave, when 6'4" disc jockey, Dick Gray, rushed onto the stage in the middle of a number and told me to stop the show. I told him we would finish the number and then decide whether it was necessary. He went off and came back almost immediately, grabbed me by the shoulders from behind and kicked me, saying "If you don't get off the stage I will break your back.' I finished the number, followed Gray back-stage and gave him a right hander. That appeared to settle the situation and we continued the concert without further trouble."

MORE BEAT EXPANSION

The BEAT — America's most widely-read pop music newspaper — is preparing to begin another major expansion program.

It will result in an even larger newspaper, expanded coverage and a number of other improvements.

As a result we'll be experiencing growing pains for the next few weeks as the improvements are added and will temporarily publish on an every-other-week basis rather than weekly. Subscriptions will be extended accordingly.

You'll notice some of the changes in the next issue — two weeks from now. We hope you'll like them.

Letters TO THE EDITOR

Down On Stones

Dear BEAT:

I protest! How come everyone points out and criticizes the Beatles when they do something a little out of the ordinary, but never bring up the subject of the many rather nauseating things the Stones have done?

How come everyone expects the Beatles to be "nice little boys" all the time but when the Stones put out a song that is obviously about drugs ("Mother's Little Helper") everybody clams up and acts as if it's the most natural thing in the world?

The Beatles are human and prone to being a little out of line once in a while so how come everyone starts having fits when they put out an album cover that's not half as offensive as some things Brian Jones has done?

I think it's about time people started expecting new and weird things from the Beatles in the future like we all have been doing for the Stones. I hope somebody at least reads this and thinks about it for awhile because it means a lot to me and I just pray you have the space (or gall) to print this and hope that a few other people give the Beatles another chance.

Linda Casson

More Elvis?

Dear BEAT:

Why don't you have Elvis Presley in your paper? Is Elvis too good for you? If I'm not right, then why don't you have Elvis in it?

Believe me, your paper would sell a lot more if you did have Elvis in it. Will you write back and tell me why you don't have Elvis in your newspaper? I would like to know the reason why you can't have Elvis the King in The BEAT.

Bonnie Shaver

Elvis has been in The BEAT—many times! We dig Elvis as much as anyone else and we try to put him into the paper as often as possible.

The BEAT

Thanks For Eric

Dear BEAT:

I want to tell you how much I enjoy reading The BEAT and I'm glad you're putting in all my favorite stars! Especially the articles on Eric Burdon of the Animals.

Deana L. Hilton

The New Dylan

Dear BEAT:

In a recent issue about Dylan falling in Europe, I think he didn't go over well because Europe wasn't ready for Dylan—the new Dylan. They wanted the old Dylan but there is a new Dylan. His writings still have his own special meaning but to get them across now he adds more music so that more people will listen.

There is Dylan, the times change, Dylan changes slightly. But he is still the same young man, still writing what he feels so other people can hear it. Dylan wants people (especially young people) to hear his message, so he adds some rock 'n' roll.

England, France and Europe are not mature enough to grasp him. We (America) are far more mature in the music field than England and Europe will ever be with Dylan. So, Europe—wise up or you'll lose something great, wonderful and a beautiful human being—Bob Dylan.

Laura Figone

An Older Fan Speaks Up

Dear BEAT:

This letter is in reference to the article in the July 2 issue in which the assorted teenagers expressed their opinions about the Beatles. Noting their ages, I would like to express opinions from another age group.

I wonder if the Beatles are aware of their fans in the 25 to 35 year and up group? Most everyone I know, with a few exceptions (those who have never really listened to them) are very staunch fans! Let's face it, they are super talented and they have class.

They don't see us at their concerts because we would like to be able to see them at a place where we could see them and hear every note and word. We might have the urge to faint a bit too, but we would be polite about it. (In my case, if I ever got to see John Lennon, I would quietly slip to the floor with all the dignity I could muster.)

We don't write to them because we know they never see most of their mail.

We look forward to the few times they are on TV. However, this last time they let us down. People who I had asked to watch them "just once," will never again. And they really have their doubts about me too! And what can I say? I know they are fantastic no matter what, but they aren't going to win anyone new, or make it any easier on those of us who love them.

Let's just hope when they appear again, they'll make us proud again.

Mrs. Sheila Armistead

Jay Like Joe?

Dear BEAT:

I wonder how many other readers noticed a similarity in the appearance between the picture you printed of Jay Black (July 2 issue) and the Lovin' Spoonful's Joe Butler. I thought the resemblance was amazing. I had never seen Jay before, and when I saw the picture in The BEAT I thought maybe it was Joe.

I'd like to know if anyone else noticed the resemblance?

Also, on the subject of the Spoonful, I read in two of the English papers that John Sebastian is married. If you could give me any information about the marriage at all, I'd surely appreciate it.

Mary Miller

Seeds Are Great

Dear BEAT:

I just heard The Seeds album at a girlfriend's house and I think they're really great! How about a story on who they are and where they come from? How come I've never heard any of their records on the radio?

Thanks to the ad in the July 2 BEAT, at least I know all their names. But let's have more information.

Ann Divers

Write To Drake

Dear BEAT:

My friends from California often send me copies of your groovy BEAT, especially when you have things on the greatest group in the world—Paul Revere and the Raiders.

Recently in On The Beat, there was a bit on the group's lead guitarist, Drake Levin (now he's Pvt. Levin, though.) Several days ago, I received a letter from Drake and I'd like to do something nice for one of the nicest guys I know.

He mentioned that he'd love to hear from all his fans, since it gets pretty lonely down at Ft. Ord. You can write to him at: Pvt. Drake Levin NG 28815316, A-41 4th Platoon (BCT), Ft. Ord, California.

I know it'd make him so happy to know he hasn't been forgotten by his fans. Thank you for your time and consideration.

Evi Schuster

Three Cheers For Fakes

Dear BEAT:

In your June 25 issue of The BEAT you had an article about Len Barry and his opinion of long haired groups. First, he cut down the Beatles and the Stones, which is expected from anyone putting down long hair, but when he said Dylan was a nothing personality I blew up! I would like to say a few things to Mr. Barry.

So, you don't like the Beatles, Rolling Stones, Animals, Lovin' Spoonful or Bob Dylan. Let's see, that gives you about three fans left—yourself, Mister Morris, and your mother unless she happens to like one of the groups you "commented" on. Just who DO you like? Freddie and the Dreamers . . . who??? The McCoys. Herman's Hermits. Yeah, well.

Bob Dylan has done more for the improvement of songs than anybody in the business. And if you can gain talent like the Animals and Lovin' Spoonful by having long hair, you better start growing hair, Mr. Barry—fast!

As for your music, I hardly think that three hit (?) records gives you, or anyone, the right to such scathing criticism.

After I recovered from the initial shock, I began to feel sorry for you. If you can't appreciate or even see talent like Eric Burdon, John Lennon, Mick Jagger, Keith Richard, John Sebastian and Steve Boone, I pity you. You're missing the core of today's music. And if you see nothing in Dylan, nothing at all, then man, you're hardly even aware of the world that surrounds you.

All you have to do is open your ears and mind to the music of today and you'll realize that there's more to it than you think. Now that I've calmed down, I wonder—are you jealous? The name of Len Barry will mean nothing in five years but I dare say blues lovers will still acclaim Eric Burdon as the greatest blues singer ever, the Spoonful will be around with their jug band music, "Satisfaction" is already a rock classic and the Stones will be inciting riots for years, Lennon-McCartney will be sung by everyone from Lennon-McCartney to Frank Sinatra. And Bob Dylan will always be Bob Dylan.

Obviously, millions of fans don't agree with your opinion of "bad in-person acts." And the Rolling Stones "fake?" Fake what? Since when can you fake soul, writing, talent and love? If the Stones are fakes, three cheers for fakes!! Dylan has a nothing personality. That baffles me. Dylan has done so much for so many people. He has given poetry lovers dignity, he has awakened the music world to the realization of our crummy lyrics; he has put wisdom to music.

You must feel very empty if you feel nothing but contempt for these men. Can you judge a man's talent by the clothes he wears, or the length of his hair? Can you see his poetic or musical ability through his table manners or the way he walks. Don't deny them because of their appearance.

There's no success like failure—and failure is no success at all. It's a free country and you are entitled to your opinion. But then so are we. So when you get booed off the next stage—don't say you were warned.

Lyn Finfrock

'In's' Out?

Dear BEAT:

The "in" people that are talking about Sonny & Cher's so-called "bomb" and asking if they haven't stayed too long are the people that are on their way out.

"Have I Stayed Too Long" is another classic written by the great Sonny Bono. Sonny's voice combined with the beautiful Cher's voice harmonize to create another wonderful record by the great duo. Just because it was not recognized and raised to the top of the record survey is no reason to knock it.

I enjoy reading The BEAT and recently subscribed to it. I respect your opinions and hope you will respect mine by printing this letter.

Jim Canchola, Jr.

Is Herman Picked On?

Dear BEAT:

Everytime I pick up a magazine or a newspaper somebody's putting down Herman. This must be national "down with Herman" year and I am sickened and saddened by this continual criticism.

If these "know-it-alls" would only take the time to really listen to the Hermits' albums, they would change their tune. After hearing Herman sing "Jezebel" or "I Understand" or "Listen People" (to name a few) anyone would have to be out of his mind or just plain stubborn to say Herman has no talent.

Also, all you who think Herman's a silly kid should attend one of his concerts. Herman and the Hermits generate so much happiness and warmth it's hard to hate for days afterwards.

Herman doesn't have the same style, nor does he sing the same type of songs as the Animals or even the Beatles but this fact certainly doesn't make him any less of a performer or any less worthy of praise.

Herman's great...he possesses more talent and showmanship in his little toe than many highly praised groups could obtain in 100 years! It's time some people give credit where credit is due.

Thanks, BEAT, for letting me express my opinions. I only hope I opened someone's closed mind.

Peggy Briggs

KRLA ARCHIVES

On the BEAT

By Louise Criscione

Sonny and Cher have won the battle of the "Alfie" versions—at least, as far as the movie track is concerned. Cher will sing the title song over the credits from Paramount's up-coming motion picture, "Alfie." Sonny will produce this session and it marks the first time a title song has been added to a film which has already been released in Europe.

The Beatles have certainly been having a rough time, haven't they? Mauled in Manila and a black eye for Paul in New Delhi. George seems to think they'll get beaten up in the U.S. as well. I rather doubt that because, after all, it is highly unlikely President Johnson will invite them to lunch with Lady Bird...

The Kinks might make it behind the Iron Curtain at the end of October. Negotiations for Kink concerts in Russia and Hungary are now underway and if definite dates are set it will bring to 11 the number of European countries expecting the Kinks within the next three months.

Tommy Roe just walked in looking great, as usual. And then he dropped the bomb—he'd spent the weekend in the hospital recovering from exhaustion! Tommy's busy cutting an album and reveling in the success of his smash, "Sweat Pea." What a doll he is—sure hope he gets the movie part he's after. He'd be a sensation in the part (but we can't say just what part it is yet).

Are you ready for Dick Clark joining "Batman?" Don't know if I am but I guess Dick *is* 'cause he's set to play a bad guy in an episode entitled, "Shoot A Crooked Arrow."

...CHER

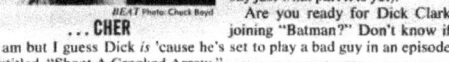

Bill Medley of the Righteous Brothers is temporarily out of commission following throat surgery. It's nothing serious, though, and the tall half of the Brothers will be ready to go in ten days. Meanwhile, the Brothers' next MGM single, "Go Ahead and Cry," has already drawn an advance order of over 650,000 copies. Which ain't bad!

Herman says one thing he particularly admires about himself is his "fantastic will-power." He has set certain goals for himself—goals which he swears he'll reach by the time he's 21. But from the looks of things, I'll bet he reaches them all before he's 20.

Speaking of Herman, I wonder if there really is tension within the Hermits. There usually is when one member is the *real* stand-out, the one everyone's always writing and talking about while the rest of the group remains in the "back-up" bag. Anyway, Herman's not talking and neither are the Hermits.

The on-again, off-again departure of Paul Jones from the Manfred Mann is now on-again. The rumor of Paul's split has been making the rounds for months now and Manfred has been steadily denying them. Paul's denials, however, have been half-hearted giving staunch support to the rift rumor.

But now they've decided it's no use keeping the break-up a secret so in a press conference this week Paul's departure has been confirmed. He will be replaced by Michael D'Abo who will join the Manfreds in Copenhagen in early August. Paul is going solo and has already signed a contract.

While his Stones are busy hot-tailing it across the U.S., Andrew Oldham has secured the Who's recording contract. Fact is, the Who made a surprise visit to New York last week to sign the contract. Stones' business manager, Allen Klein, has signed a deal by which the Who's American and Canadian releases will be through MGM.

The Mama's and Papa's are now set for a short tour of England sometime in October. They'll make only about eight or ten appearances and will appear in the second half of the show. The Lovin' Spoonful and Otis Redding are also set for British tours in the fall.

Donovan's "Sunshine Superman" out of sight. Best record Don's released.

...ANDREW OLDHAM

Jan Berry Leaves Hospital; Recovering Fast From Crash

By Anna Maria Alonzo

Good news comes to us this week on the condition of singing star Jan Berry.

Seriously injured some weeks ago in a near-fatal auto crash in Beverly Hills, Jan has been making miraculous progress on his road to recovery.

After the startling accident, there were many who held their breath in serious doubt that Jan would be able to overcome the seemingly insurmountable odds which were stacked against him.

He lay seriously ill in a coma for nearly three weeks, and friends and fans of the good-looking blond singer sadly admitted that the chances seemed quite slim for Jan to recover.

Then, almost through a miracle of fortune, Jan regained consciousness and came out of his coma for the first time. Suddenly there was hope once again for his recovery.

For some time after he regained consciousness, Jan was unable to speak at all, and had great difficulty in accomplishing any sort of physical activity. For this reason, nurses were required to be in attendance around the clock, and though his condition was still quite

(Turn to page 14)

'Wild Thing' Still Divided

"Wild Thing," by the Troggs, is one of the Top Ten songs in the nation this week, but the controversy over who really has the legal right to market the disk is still raging.

At present, there are two record companies claiming ownership of the hit—Atco and Fontana—and the injunction hearing has been stayed until September 1.

Because of this temporary delay, no decision can be reached immediately, and sales of the record will continue to be divided between the two companies throughout the summer.

This is the first time in nearly twenty years that two record companies have claimed ownership of the same record and simultaneously offered the same pop hit for sale. The last case of this sort revolved around a disc by Eileen Barton, entitled "If I Knew You Were Coming I'd Have Baked A Cake."

Rolling Stones In Columbia Club

The Columbia Records Club has acquired distribution rights to albums of the Rolling Stones. Members of the club will have an option on the albums six months after their initial release.

This means that "Aftermath," the Stones album released in the U.S. early this month, will be available through the club about December. The album, which was released to coincide with the Stones' fifth U.S. tour, contains their latest hit, "Paint It Black."

Hermits Contract Over $1 Million

Reactions to the first motion picture by Herman and his Hermits—"Hold On"—have been so favorable that MGM Records has announced the recent signing of the group to a brand new long-term contract.

The recording contract covers not only the recordings to be made by the group in the future, but also calls for Herman and Company to appear in motion pictures.

The new contract guarantees an excess of $1 million—a "seven figure mutliple deal" and makes provision for at least two movies and "as many albums as we want."

The contract was signed with Allen Klein, who is the President of Reverse Producers Corporation and who holds the exclusive United States and Canada rights on the group.

The group's record producer—Mickie Most—is signed to Reverse.

Brand New Beatle Album Out Soon?

Beatle fans in America and Great Britain are anxiously awaiting the new Beatle album, scheduled for release sometime this summer.

Although no title has been definitely decided upon as yet, Paul McCartney says some suggestions currently under consideration include "Magic Circles," "Beatles On Safari," and "Revolver"—which is John's favorite at the moment.

Some of the titles included on the new track will include a new sitar number written and performed by George, "Love You To," while Paul will be singing a rather sad new tune entitled "For No One," on which he will be accompanied by French horns.

Paul will also take vocal honors on the new tune, "Good Day Sunshine" which will feature the Beatles recording manager, George Martin, on honky-tonk piano in the background.

The Beatles have also made several references in the last few weeks to the idea of using some jazz musicians on these new tracks—an idea which has met with mixed reactions from members of several other top British groups.

All in all, it promises to be another fantastic album from The Beatles destined to chalk up still another smash summer success for the quartet.

Release of the long-awaited LP in this country may be scheduled to coincide with The Beatles' upcoming U.S. tour, which begins in Chicago on August 12.

KRLA ARCHIVES

OBSCENITY
..............in Pop Music?

A recent article in *Time* Magazine has aroused heated controversy in almost all segments of the pop music field.

Performers, composers, producers and record company executives have taken issue with *Time's* charges that today's song lyrics are smutty and suggestive, obsessed with "LSD and lechery."

Angry denials are also being voiced by a majority of the teenagers and young adults who either read the article or heard about it.

Among several hundred *BEAT* readers contacted, 87 per cent said they believed *Time's* allegations contained "no truth whatsoever," 11 percent regarded it as "true in isolated instances but highly exaggerated" and the remaining two percent described it as "largely accurate."

Listeners Unaware

Many stated they had not been aware of possible double meaning in the song lyrics before reading the *Time* article and that the magazine's interpretations had destroyed the personal meaning attached to many of their favorite records.

Most said they felt it was a matter of interpretation — that dirty meanings could be read into any song if the listeners were specifically trying to find smut. The same could hold true for Mother Goose rhymes.

They also pointed out that many of the hit songs recorded a decade or more ago — such classics as "Night and Day," "Body and Soul" and "All the Way" — could be censured on the same grounds as the modern hits criticized in the *Time* article.

A leading sociologist at the California Youth Study Center gave the *BEAT* an interesting evaluation of todays music morality.

Moral Fervor

"They tend to be the people with a great deal of moral fervor, the younger generation. And I think that songs *do* reflect some of the feeling of the younger generation — but, interestingly enough, *Time didn't* mention the fact that many of the current songs are concerned with civil rights; they're concerned with war, they're concerned with the problems of peace, and people getting along together.

"I think one would be hard put to demonstrate that the current interests of young people are more with lecherous or immoral things than with the real problems of our time. Many of the things young people are being criticized for *is* their *moral* fervor.

The sociologist went on to conclude that neither the books which are read nor the songs which are listened to by the younger generations are leading them down a trail of delinquency.

Nothing New

Laments such as those in the recent *Time* article are not new, of course. A few years ago critics were accusing Elvis Presley of vulgarisms and of causing a rise in juvenile delinquency. They insinuated that teenagers would start robbing banks after hearing Elvis sing "Jailhouse Rock."

To date there are no such cases on record.

A few years prior Frank Sinatra was the object of similar accusations, hurled at him over the noise created by his screaming, swooning female fans.

(Sinatra was also the target of an innuendo in the recent *Time* article, which stated that some "see Frank Sinatra's "Strangers in the Night," for example, as a song about a homosexual pickup.")

The Beatles also caught it from *Time*, which called them "the latest group to get into the act." In addition to a shocked reference to their controversial album cover, the article tells of obscene interpretations which can be given to "Norwegian Wood" and "Day Tripper."

Also Mentioned

Other recent hit records mentioned in the *Time* article were "Rainy Day Women" (*Time* said: "A 'Rainy-Day Woman,' as any junkie knows, is a marijuana cigarette."), "Let's Go Get Stoned," "Straight Shooter" (Junkie argot for someone who takes heroin intravenously, said *Time*), "You've Got Me High," "A Most Peculiar Man," "Little Girl," "Rhapsody in the Rain" and "Satisfaction."

Time is not alone in pursuing the search for hidden meanings and phrases in today's music. A majority of the recent hits have been branded as obscene by some self-appointed censors.

They think "Eight Miles High" refers to narcotics rather than the Byrds' recent plane trip to England; that "Along Comes Mary" is a reference to marijuana; that one popular version of "Louie, Louie" contains an obscene word which can sometimes be heard when the record is played at a slow speed.

Two of Petula Clark's records — "Downtown" and "I Know a Place" — have been called smutty by some of those who search for hidden meanings.

Warning Labels?

As one unsigned letter — evidently written by an adult with a long memory — stated: "I think all of today's songs are filthy. They ought to have to put a warning on them, just like on cigarette packages, saying WARNING: THESE SONGS MAY BE INJURIOUS TO YOUR MORALS." The letter concluded, "Sometimes I wonder whatever happened to Nelson Eddy."

Perhaps he's still chasing "Naughty Marietta."

(Inasmuch as the question of morality has been raised by TIME and others criticize today's music, The BEAT feels that frank and open discussion is the healthy way to resolve the question. Please send us a brief summary of your feelings, whether pro or con. We'll print as many letters as possible in future issues. — The Editor.

Mindbenders To Do Movie

The Beatles are doing it. The Stones are doing it. Herman's doing it. Now the Mindbenders are going to do it, too.

Make a movie, that is.

The Mindbenders, whose record "A Groovy Kind Of Love" made it to top of American charts, have been signed for their first motion picture. The Columbia film, "To Sir With Love," stars Sidney Poitier and Lulu.

Suit Filed On Donovan

British singer Donovan made it plain he doesn't like outdoor concerts, but as a result he is being sued for $10,000.

Donovan contracted to appear in Sweden at the Grona Lund-Tivoli, an outdoor scene, but refused to appear when he found out it was not an indoor concert hall. Donovan charged that there was too much going on all around him during his concert.

He made the show opening night, but then said he was leaving Stockholm if they couldn't offer him an indoor spot for his show for the contracted time. Grona Lund-Tivoli quickly answered that they would sue Donovan, asking for $10,000 in damages if he did not fulfill his contract.

Simon & Garfunkel to Russia

Simon and Garfunkel have jointed the growing list of global American pop stars, and may cop honors for the Most Traveled Duo of the Year.

Within the last month, the talented pair of composers-singers have appeared on television and in concerts in Paris, Holland, Aalberg, and Denmark — where they participated in the Danish Fourth of July celebration.

Upon returning to the U.S., Simon and Garfunkel embarked upon a strenuous cross-country tour of America, chalking up appearances in New York, New Hampshire, and Massachusetts.

Tentative plans for the duo at present include further traveling for the reaminder of the year, in addition to a possible jaunt to the Soviet Union.

Their latest hit disc was the Paul Simon composition, "I Am A Rock," which is still resting in the Top 20 nationally, while a number of other successful artists both here and in Great Britain have been recording other compositions by Paul.

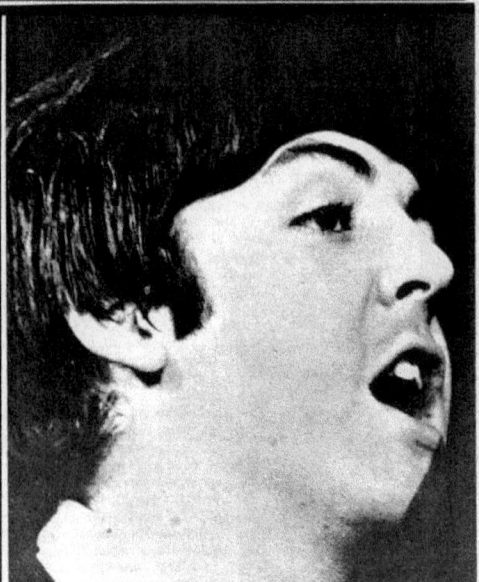

...PAUL McCARTNEY—MOST POPULAR.

Beatle Fans

By Eden

We build them up — we idolize them — we lay the physical manifestations of adulation, worship, and success at their feet.

And then we tear them down and destroy them. Pretend they never existed at all, and walk away to seek a new idol. These are the "teen idols" — the "pop stars" — the people who rise to fantastic heights because we tell them that we care.

But they are also people destined to plunge to the very bottom of failure if just once they fall out of favor with the public, their "fans" — the people who "put them where they are."

We sometimes speak a little harshly of our pop idols, criticizing them for not paying more attention to us. We say that they have gotten too big for their own good, and accuse them of forgetting their fans and all the other people who have supported them.

...BEATLES — BEATEN IN AMERICA?

KRLA ARCHIVES

...THE STONES ABOARD THE S.S. SEA PANTHER.

...SEE, CHARLIE CAN SMILE!

Defecting To Stone-Side Of Fence?

...THE MIGHTY JAGGER RELAXES

But we forget, too. Forget how very fickle we have been over the years. How many times we have built a performer up to fantastic heights—made a super-star of him, only to turn our backs on him entirely the first time he does something which displeases us in any way, or perhaps the first time we find someone new to lavish our affections upon?

We have done it countless times—and time and time again. And it seems as though we are almost ready to do it once more to the biggest of stars—to the most spectacular super-stars of this or any generation. Would you believe that there are people who now say they are ready to turn their backs on the Beatles?

It seems incredible, but the same "loyal," fanatically faithful, hysterical Beatlemaniacs who just one or two years ago were standing outside in the rain for four hours, or sleeping outside in the cold in order to get tickets to a Beatle performance are now packing their gear and heading off in other directions, some even defecting to the Stone-side of the fence.

Too many refuse to admit that one can enjoy both Beatles *and* Stones, and now are claiming that the Beatles have forgotten them and so they will transfer their affections and their "undying loyalty" to the Stones.

New Attacks

The Beatles have come under attack for a number of things during the brief span of their spectacular career to date; criticism is nothing new to these boys who have revolutionized the entire pop industry.

But none of the attacks—even those first heard when the Beatles initially appeared on our shores for the first time with their unusual new haircuts and distinctive styles of dressing—have been so vicious as the ones launched against them recently, protesting the release and hasty withdrawal of their controversal album cover.

Almost no one—admittedly—really understood the controversial album cover, either in meaning or in purpose. Yet everyone had an absolute judgment upon their lips, and seemed ready to pass instantaneous sentence upon the fabulous quartet.

Was it a pop art album cover? Was it in protest of the war in Viet Nam? Was it another example of Lennon's "sick humor?" Was it a badly misunderstood and misinterpreted joke? Was it really released erroneously, while it had originally been intended as a pop art joke for only the Beatles' eyes to see?

No Answers

No one has the answers to these questions at the moment. An executive of Capitol Records had said that the release of the album cover was a mistake, that the Beatles had never intended it to be the cover on this strictly American album.

And the Beatles themselves have been amazingly quiet about the whole thing. The less said the better, perhaps.

And yet, what could they really say? If they denied that they had been responsible for the release of the album cover, they would be severely criticized and accused of lying. If they assumed full responsibility for it, they would be lambasted as sadists and accused of falling from their once-supreme position in the pop world.

Only they can tell us what was really behind that cover, only they can tell us why it was released. And as Beatlemaniacs, it seems only fair to give them a chance to do so. The Beatles will be in our country this summer, and while they are here—The BEAT hopes to put these questions—and many others—to the boys, and give them an opportunity to speak out for themselves once and for all.

The *BEAT*, too, has come under attack of late, accused of switching sides and supporting only Stones; accused of deserting the Beatles we once avidly defended. But this is not so.

We write about many groups, and are able to appreciate and enjoy a number of groups—we don't feel as though we have to confine our support to just one group of artists. So it is that we do not find it incongrous to be able to enjoy the talents of both the Beatles *and* the Stones, simultaneously.

Each group is in a class all its own—there is no true comparison between the two, so why should we have to create a false one?

We haven't forsaken the Beatles—and if we have an opinion of a piece of their work—whether it is an album cover, a movie, or a performance . . . we can still remain loyal to the Beatles without having to lie about their work.

Being a true fan includes the ability to criticize as well as commend. *No one*—not the Beatles or The Stones or *anyone*—is truly perfect; we are all human and we all make mistakes.

Right now, we are being called upon *not* to make the mistake of ignorance by turning our backs on four of the most talented and most influential artists in the pop world today.

We put them up there upon a pedestal, and supported them and all of their work and their ideas. We said they represented *us*, and were indicative of the way *we* felt and thought.

If we turn away from them now—if we attempt to tear down this idol once again—it might just be *us* who winds up with the clay feet this time around.

KRLA ARCHIVES

Jackie's Knocking Em' Out With Soul, Rhythm & Blues

By Mike Tuck

HOLLYWOOD — The man came on in an olive green suit and black silken shirt that seemed to grab the reflection from every colored stage light and throw it back at you. Slowly, he made his way to the microphone, clutched it in his hand as one would a young, delicate bird . . . then screeched into it in a high, fervent wail as if it had just given him some sudden, unexpected burst of pleasure.

Jackie Wilson's voice at first had an almost mocking light pitch to it. His movements were easy; carefree little steps — like those of a man who was celebrating the lifting of a huge weight from his shoulders. He pranced around the circular stage at the Trip and completely ignored its restraining limitations.

But his original easy pace too confined Jackie Wilson. He had too much inside. It looked as though the man was so desperate in his drive to convey some innate substance that his body lost all earthly restrictions as it gyrated into inhumanly positions. His voice hit operatic summits as he rolled on the floor and struck out wildly with his arms.

The man continued his crescendo towards frenzy while a would-be sedate audience shouted "yeah man, yeah" and stood so they could see his every grimmace. It was more than a show . . . it was an unforseen phenomina.

Jackie Wilson has something a step beyond ESP. He doesn't even seem to try. He just feels something and everyone around him is aware of it and feels it themselves.

But even with all of his seeming intrinsic inspirations, "Mr. Excitement" was beginning to tire. His eyes projected an almost hollow effect. Little rivers of perspiration flowed steadily towards his chin where drops cascaded down to his already soaking shirt, which clung to his body and shone all the more intensely.

Then the band fell into deep, painful blues and a trembling Jackie Wilson dropped to his knees in a simulated praying position. He moaned low, melancholy notes that seemed almost like a plea.

His final song ended and Jackie Wilson rose to his feet and amidst a tumultous ovation he walked wearily towards the dressing rooms. He seemed to be sapped of all energy . . . like he had just given away a parcel of soul and was now empty.

... "SOULMAN" JACKIE WILSON

Beatles Mauled

(Continued from page 1)

port, was touched off when the Manila press reported the group deliberately snubbed Mrs. Marcos by not appearing at the designated time.

Manilan government officials, who issued an official apology over the incident, are now saying the group knew nothing of the appointment until it was too late.

The promoters of the Beatles' appearance in Manila lost their shirts over the concert. The Beatles played two shows in an auditorium which holds 100,000 but each night they drew only 40,000 to their concerts. Consequently, their promoters are now out of business.

President Marcos, who issued the statement, said, "There was no intention on the part of the Beatles to slight the First Lady or the government of the Republic of the Philippines." Marcos called the airport demonstration a "breach of Filipino hospitality."

The Beatles' unexpected encounter with the Manila mob at the airport was a nightmare for the group. "I just don't understand," said a stunned Paul McCartney as he pushed his way through the mob.

Almost all police protection and special considerations for the Beatles were cancelled and the Philippine tax bureau threatened for a time to hold up their departure until they made a declaration of their earnings as required by law.

The Beatles were forced to go through all the ordinary procedures required of departing passengers instead of being hustled through customs and immigration formalities.

As they stood inside the terminal waiting their turn, they were surrounded and harassed by an angry crowd who pushed, shoved and cursed the Beatles and their companions.

An unidentified member of the Beatle party was kicked to the ground. Shouts of "Scram," "Get out of our Country," and unprintable curses were hurled at the quartet as the boys tried to push their way through the jeering mob.

The raucous departure debacle was in sharp contrast to the rip-roaring welcome extended the Beatles on their arrival the previous Sunday by thousands of fans and a massive security cordon.

Only about 100 die-hard Beatle fans turned out Tuesday to cheer their idols but they were outnumbered and out-shouted by the newly organized Beatle-haters.

George, sitting alone and dejected afterwards, probably best summed up the new fears of the Beatles when he said, "Now I guess we can go to America and really get beaten up."

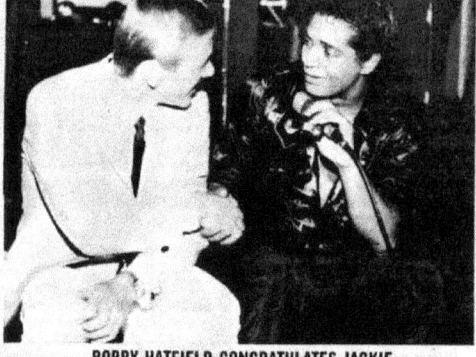

... BOBBY HATFIELD CONGRATULATES JACKIE

HOTLINE LONDON
Merseys Cancel
Tony Barrow

By Tony Barrow

ANIMAL troubles in the group are starkly revealed in a new film just premiered in London, "The World Of The Animals." It's a documentary which pulls no punches: in one revealing close-up Eric turns to the audience and says: "The last three years have been like one long one-night stand. Now it's time to slow down. I'm mentally and physically very, very tired."

The MERSEYS – very big in Britain with "Sorrow" – have postponed plans to visit the U.S. They now hope to be on your side September. Original plans for them were some recording and promotional dates in Los Angeles, and they were due to leave London a fortnight ago.

The duo have heavy bookings here, however, and were forced to break the date.

Beach Boys Arrive

The BEACH BOYS will now arrive in Britain on October 23 for a period of seven days before flying on to other parts of Europe.

FRANK SINATRA is due in London this month to record at the Pye studios, where PETULA CLARK makes all her English and French-language hits. Sinatra is on the crest of a big wave of chart popularity in Britain. Some of the more hip groups seem unhappy at his success, but "Strangers In The Night" is a phenomenal hit – so much that it recently knocked the STONES "Paint It Black" from No. 1.

Britain's IVY LEAGUE are due in the U.S. for a short promotional tour, July 26, and may visit California if time permits. They will also plug a new single, "The Willow Tree." DUSTY SPRINGFIELD is also trying for a Los Angeles visit this month.

Your own LOVIN' SPOONFUL will return the compliment in October. They fly to seven major European cities before coming into London for one week of TV appearances. Just rush-released here is the Spoonful's "Summer In The City."

Touch of Mitchum

New YARDBIRDS guitarist JIMMY PAGE is a tall, dark and handsome 20-year-old who is proving a wow with the girls. Jimmy has a slight touch of the ROBERT MITCHUMS – he has sleepy eyes beneath curly dark hair and smooth sideburns.

Hoping for a hit with his own group the MOCKINGBIRDS is Manchester-born Graham Gouldman, 19, the young songwriter who penned such chart smashes as HERMAN'S "Listen People," the YARDBIRDS "For Your Love," "Heart Full Of Soul" and "Evil Hearted You," and "Look Through Any Window" for the HOLLIES.

Graham also wrote the Hollies' new big one in Britain, "Bus Stop." With so much talent to his credit you'd think the Mockingbirds would have recorded one of his own songs. But they haven't – it's an American number, "One By One!"

Getting a lot of action on the pirate radio stations is a number called "Black Is Black" by a Spanish group with a German singer who sings in English: LOS BRAVOS. This is the first time anything like this has happened and with Los Bravos' good looks, I wouldn't be surprised to see them become smash favorites.

American Pirate

Britain's newest pirate, ship-based, radio station is Radio England, which features American d-j's and a hot-paced Top Forty format. Station is now going into concert promotion and its first venture is set for August with PERCY SLEDGE co-billing with CRISPIAN ST. PETERS, who hit the British No. 1 with "You Were On My Mind."

IN BRIEF...Ex-SEARCHER CHRIS CURTIS now busy producing discs by other artists; first effort is PAUL AND BARRY RYAN'S revival "I Love How You Love Me."...MARIANNE FAITHFULL issuing a BOB LIND song "Counting"...at time of writing, BEATLES still undecided on special British title for their next LP...that PAUL and BARRY RYAN single features a bagpipe sound; could this be the next 'in' trend? If so, watch out RAVI SHANKAR...Why did big U.S. popularity of FREDDIE and the DREAMERS fade?...BRIAN EPSTEIN believed to be in take-over bid for Kennedy Street Enterprises, agency of HERMAN...Big BOB DYLAN admirer is BRIAN JONES...SCOTT WALKER grew a beard but shaved it off a few days later...Big British name SPENCER DAVIS to appear in a ghost film...the HOLLIES cancelled plans for a U.S. tour this summer, but they want to visit in October...Cover versions of MICK JAGGER composition "Lady Jane" started off well, but now seem to be fading... CHRIS CURTIS has his first solo single out, "Aggravation"...Liverpool's famous CAVERN re-opening this month...at school, JOHN LENNON used to publish his own "newspaper" without teachers' knowledge; he called it "The Daily Howl"...ANIMAL CHAS CHANDLER plans to record a friend of his from Newcastle called ARTHUR FOGGIN – and there are no plans to change the name... BEATLES once toured here with CHRIS MONTEZ...Chris has his first British hit for some years with "The More I See You"...HERMAN planning to buy a mansion house in London.

KRLA ARCHIVES

Herman – The Master Of Pop Satire

By Jamie McCluskey III

HERMAN... the little boy next door, plotting a practical joke to be played on the household kitten.

HERMAN... the truant teenager playing hooky from his classes.

HERMAN... the well-dressed English lad who was voted one of the ten best dressed men in England by the British Clothing Manufacturers.

HERMAN... the tease who smiles impishly while hundreds of girls are tearing after him as he races for a plane.

HERMAN... the 5'10" blue-eyed blond who smiles like a little boy, sings up a storm, and has created musical chaos wherever he had traveled in the world of pop.

Just 18-years-old now, Herman looks like the perennial little boy. And yet, when he steps onstage – he is an experienced showman, a master performer – able to grip the audience in his hands and maneuver them in any direction which he sees fit.

He has recently completed a successful American tour, which he and the Hermits headlined, along with The Animals. All across the country, crowds gathered to watch the boys perform, and before he left our shores and returned home to his foggy isle – Herman had secured at least another million hearts as souvenirs of this latest American conquest.

Oddly enough – in an era of protest songs, war songs, and epics by Mrs. Miller – Herman sings *good* music. He sings songs which have a melody, songs which contain a lyric with some sort of meaning, rather than just two minutes of sheer nonsense.

Capable of singing pretty ballads, such as "Listen People," and "End of the World," Herman has also been responsible for introducing the wonderful element of satire into pop music, with his hit recordings of "Henry VIII," and "Mrs. Brown."

Just recently, the Hermits led by their now de-fanged leader, Herman, appeared in their first feature film – "Hold On" – which has been well-received all across the country.

So well received, in fact, was the flick, that the boys have been signed to a new, exclusive long-term contract with MGM. All of which means that we will be seeing a great deal more of Herman in the months and years to come.

There have been rumors flying of late that Herman might just want to venture off on his own, causing the breakup of the Hermits. It has been reported by *The BEAT's* Tony Barrow that Herman has some new ideas, musically, which he would like to experiment with, while the other Hermits are content to continue just as they are.

Problem here is that rumors of this sort are much too easily started, and even more easily continued – even when there is little reason for them.

Musically, Herman and the Hermits have succeeded in producing a wide variety of music, and have escaped falling into one "bag" and getting trapped there for any serious length of time.

And onstage, it is really only Herman who is the star of the show, cavorting all over the stage and stirring up general pandemonium among the Hermits and amplifiers who also join him under the spotlights.

So, it seems highly unlikely that the group would deny Herman the opportunity to make constructive suggestions about their work and the music which they will be producing in the future.

In the meantime, the boys will be concentrating on their next movie, tentatively titled "Mrs. Brown You've Got A Lovely Daughter," hoping to duplicate the success of their first feature film.

At the same time, their latest release – "This Door Swings Both Ways" is headed toward the top of all the national pop charts, and the door to success certainly seems to be swinging wide open for Herman. And if we know Herman – he's not about to let it swing shut too soon.

...HERMAN THE TEASE.

...HERMAN THE BOY NEXT DOOR.

'in' people are talking about...

Eric Burdon and what a talent he really is... Herman's joke about the tobacco and "Paperback Writer" and wondering what he found so funny... The way the Spoonful spend their summer in the city... Percy Sledge and how many versions of "When A Man Loves A Woman" we're going to be treated to before the song finally dies... the Vogues and asking for directions to that land they sing about... Ray Charles and his groovy idea... This girl in Hollywood who looks like Mama Cass but didn't fly off to London fast enough to convince John Lennon ...The Kinks and wondering when (or if) they'll ever stop being plagued with sickness and accidents...How much the truth hurts certain groups – especially when it's printed... How Neil Diamond could possible be a solitary man when he's so totally out of sight.

PEOPLE ARE TALKING ABOUT how long it will take Barry McGuire to get another big hit... What will happen to the Yardbirds now and hoping they'll be around for years... The Hollies not coming Stateside after all and supposing it means Jeff wins... Dave looking before leaping... How you *can* roller skate in a buffalo herd if you really put your mind to it... That word the Knickerbockers used to save their record from being banned... Susie thinking Felix is waving at her and asking if she hasn't *completely* flipped her cool... Henrietta and Isabella and how Carol didn't catch on... The Beatles in Manila and wondering what actually did happen... Brian Jones punching that guy who jumped on stage in New York... The way Barry sings "Sloppy"... Phil Spector supposedly dumping the music business in favor of movies and the Canter crowd is wondering if Phil will drop them for the Daisy people.

PEOPLE ARE TALKING ABOUT those stick-on belly buttons... Andrew Oldham's shaved beard and Keith Richard's polka-dot shirt and how it knocks your eyes out... That funky picture of Keith Relf... The new Mama and what's going to happen... The Stones releasing "Mother's Little Helper" instead of the more popular "Under My Thumb"... How important shaking dandruff is... Dave Harvey's words of wisdom: "Everyone must freak out at five o'clock at least once in his life"... Chubby Checker giving it one more try... The million versions of "Alfie" and wondering if he deserves all of it... How groups have taken to playing musical chairs lately... Nola Hola... The original two minutes and thirty eight seconds which turned into eleven minutes and thrity five seconds of "Goin' Home"... Jim McCarty's fake peach and how Jeff Beck almost ate it but Louise ended up with it... Sonny's new crewcut... Len's green-eyed soul ... Paul trying to knock over Farmer John... Granny Goose look-alikes who aren't provacative enough for anybody... Why no one saw Ian.

PEOPLE ARE TALKING ABOUT steaming album covers to discover things which were banned ... Why both the Animals and the Hermits skipped the Debbie Reynolds movie on their way to Hawaii... The way *The BEAT* staff fought over the British "Aftermath"... The slug Dave Clark gave that disc jockey on stage... The girl who wall-papered her bedroom with *BEATS*.

KRLA ARCHIVES

WIN THIS MINI-SURFER!

it's KRLA's **BEACH BOYS BIRTHDAY BLAST!**

Customized by George Barris, of Hollywood, this candy-striped Austin MINI-SURFER comes with a Yamaha Campus 60 strapped to the back, a custom surfboard by Kon of California cresting the top, a Borg-Warner 8-track stereo tape player, and two giant portable speakers with a half-block of cord!

HERE'S ALL YOU HAVE TO DO:
Write in your name, age, address and favorite all-time Beach Boys' song ... Cut out coupon and drop in mail box.

TO: KRLA BEAT
BEACH BOYS
BIRTHDAY BLAST!
1401 South Oak Knoll
Pasadena, California 91109

Name_____ Age____
Address_____
City_____
State_____ Zip_____
Favorite Beach Boys' Song_____

Inside KRLA
By Eden

In answer to all of your questions, there will *not* be a Top 40 Tunedex any more. The switch to All-Request Radio has been completed now, and KRLA is the first to make the big change all the way.

From now on, there will be a list compiled each week of the Top 40 Requested Tunes of the week.

So keep your calls coming in, because KRLA is Request Radio—*Your* radio.

More changes at the station include a switch-about of some of our great KRLA DJ's and the addition of a brand new disc jockey. Bill Slater—who has become just about everybody's favorite person from midnight to six in the morning—has been promoted to the position of Head of Production at the station. This will entail a great deal of writing and production work for Bill, and though we will still be able to hear him on many of the spots and commercials which will be used on the air—we will all miss the nightly get-togethers with Mr. Slater.

Groups!

Rehearse Where The Hits Are Recorded. Low Rates. Call Now and reserve your rehearsal time.

HO 7-5532

LIMITED SUMMER BONUS FOR BEAT READERS—

$200 in Values — Only $2 in Price!

GO-GUIDE COUPON BOOK

More than 100 coupons for Free Admissions, Discounts up to 50% or 2 for 1 offerings. Activities and Products listed below, plus many others.

Movies	Revell
Clubs	Statewide Theatres
Dancing	So. Cal. Bowl. Assn
Sports	Troubador
Food	Ash Grove
Clothing	Orange Julius
Records	Hullabaloo
Jewelry	Gazzari's
Cosmetics	P.O.P.
Shows	Pasadena Civic
Fairs	Sports Show
Horseback Riding	L. A. Blades
Bowling	Ice House
Folk Music	World On Wheels
Plays	Independ. Theatres
Slot Car Racing	Vivian Woodward
Billiards	Fashion Tops
Skating	Mademoiselle

Dial F-U-N-T-E-E-N For More Information

ORDER NOW WHILE THEY LAST!

FUNTEEN GO-GUIDE
c/o KRLA *BEAT*
6290 Sunset, Suite 504
Hollywood, Calif. 90028

Please send me ____ copies of the 1966 FUNTEEN GO-GUIDE (Valid thru Dec. 31, 1966) at the special summer rate of only $2.00 each. I enclose $____
NAME:
ADDRESS:
CITY:_____ STATE:____ ZIP:____

FUNTEEN BONUS COUPON OFFERINGS

Coupon	Merchant	Offering
"C"	San Fernando Valley Teen Center, 17400 Victory Blvd.	2 for 1 admission
"D"	Drum City – Guitar Town, 15255 Sherman Way, Van Nuys; 5611 Jumilla, Woodland Hills; 6226 Santa Monica Blvd., L.A.	2 free "Crazy Fill" book covers. $5 gift certificate with $15 one-time or accumulated purchase. Member's friends may purchase on his accumulation.
"E"	Hobby-Land Hobby Shop, 1828 S. Robertson Blvd., L.A.	Free Gift plus 20% discount on all purchases—with card.
"G"	Gazzarri's, 319 N. La Cienega	2 for 1 admission to Teen Night every Sunday (7 p.m.-12 midnight)
"H"	Hullabaloo, 6230 Sunset Blvd., Hollywood	2 for 1 admission
"J"	Michael's Jewelers, 7510 Woodman, Van Nuys	Free Beatle jewelry piece
"K"	Kookie Kapers, 7860 Santa Monica Blvd., L.A.	$5 certificate after $15 purchase
"M"	Northridge Valley Skateland, 18140 Parthenia, Northridge	2 for 1 admission, with or without skates
"N"	Ezra's Oasis, 316 N. La Cienega	"Most anything on the menu" at 2 for 1
"O"	Orange Julius, 6001 W. Pico, L.A.	2 Orange Juliuses for price of 1
"P"	Pasadena Civic Auditorium, 300 Green, Pasadena	Free admission for member and 1 guest to dance any Saturday (8:30-11:30 p.m.). Dresses for girls, dress shirts, tie and slacks for boys. Same offer good at De Wald's Ballroom, 831 W. Las Tunas Dr., San Gabriel
"Q"	Orange Julius, 1715 Pico Blvd., Santa Monica	Free Orange Julius with any purchase
"R"	Valley Ice Skating Center, 18361 Ventura Blvd., Tarzana	2 for the price of 1
"S"	Shirt Shack, 1900J Lincoln, Santa Monica	$5 gift certificate with $15 one-time or accumulated purchase. Member's friends may purchase on his accumulation.
"T"	Ice House, 24 N. Mentor, Pasadena	2 for 1 admission
"U"	Ice House, 234 S. Brand, Glendale	2 for 1 admission

Membership Card Admission: World on Wheels Show, Rose Bowl, Sunday, August 7. 8 a.m. til 5 p.m.

Membership Card Admission: Swinging Young Adults Club of Los Angeles. Dancing every Sunday, 2-10 p.m. Only 75¢ for members with card. Old Dixie Ballroom, 4269 S. Western.

SPECIAL ANNOUNCEMENT! All of the Statewide Theatre coupons in your Go-Guide are now good at any Statewide Theatre.

KRLA ARCHIVES

Sunrays at KRLA

THE SUNRAYS dropped by KRLA to answer the request lines and found DJ Johnny Hayes all willing to help.

EVEN CASEY KASEM stopped in for a few minutes to thank the guys for helping out with the many calls.

SUNRAY MARTI DI GIOVANNI signs a few autographs on his way out.

VINCE HOZIER AND BYRON CASE chat with fans in the lobby.

Drum City - Guitar Town
15255 Sherman Way, Van Nuys
5611 Jumilla, Woodland Hills
6226 Santa Monica Blvd. L.A.
2 free "Crazy Fill" book covers. $5 gift certificate with $15 one-time or accumulated purchase. Member's friends may purchase on his accumulation.
USE YOUR FUNTEEN BONUS COUPON "D"

July 12-24

The One And Only

BO DIDDLEY

And His Chicago Blues Band
Originators of the Big Beat

AT DOUG WESTON'S

Troubadour

9083 SANTA MONICA BLVD.
L.A. NEAR DOHENY

RESERVATIONS
CR 6-6168

Join the "In" Crowd!

Brave New World

(The Club where LOVE first started)

The wildest dance club in Hollywood! Hollywood's only private club for top and upcoming recording groups, dancers, talent scouts and those with a musical interest. And their firends.

We are considering applications for a limited time only.

The BRAVE NEW WORLD features dancing to live entertainment 10 p.m. to 2 a.m., starring the best of Hollywood's rock and roll groups.

Membership applications must include name, address, age (18 over only), musical interest or group and agency name, personal reference and a $3 membership fee.

Mail to the BRAVE NEW WORLD

1642 No. Cherrokee Ave.
Hollywood, California

Private Parties Are Also Arranged — Call 462-9826

Now A New Funteen Sponsor! Hobby-Land
HOBBY SHOP
1838 S. Robertson Blvd.
Let's Get Acquainted
Come In and See Our Complete Selection Of Handicraft Supplies: Plastic resins, crystals, paper mache, etc. Model Kits: Autos, planes, boats, animals, etc.
Phone 838-5802
Open weekdays 'til 7, Sat. 'til 3 p.m.

Use your Funteen Coupon "K"
Hosiery - Sportswear - Lingerie

Kookie Kapers
$5 certificate with $15 purchase
OL 4-9561 7860 Santa Monica Bl.
Store Hours 10-6:30 — Mon.-Fri. 9 p.m.

A WORLD ON WHEELS
Antiques, Classics, Sportscars, Custom and Experimental. Hotrods, Motorcycles and Competition Machines.
6 Great Shows in One
Sun. - Aug. 7 - Rose Bowl
8 A.M. 'til 5 P.M.

KRLA ARCHIVES

The Adventures of Robin Boyd

©1965 By Shirley Poston

Clinging to her perch with one hand—er—leg, Robin Irene Boyd gnawed another toenail off the other hand—er—leg and spat it into the bottom of the cage with an unladylike *ptui*.

"Ratzafratz on the fortisee," she moaned, not having the foggiest notion what a fortisee was but hoping for the worst.

She had been in several jams in her time (grape, peach, and apple-gooseberry, just to mention a few), but this one really put the lid on the olde jelly jar.

Squinting into the rising sun, Robin decided that it was morning. (One of her more brilliant deductions, you might say.) (And you *would*.)

"Morning"

"*Morning*," she mused hysterically but quietly. (Having heard the old adage about the early bird getting the worm and having come all too close to getting one of the same last night, she wasn't about to waken her benefactors any sooner than necessary.)

Re-squinting, Robin peered at the remaining glimmer of the north star and judged the time to be approximately six a.m. (Actually, the north star has practically nothing to do with what time it is, and besides, what she was really looking at was an unidentified flying object, but don't you think this poor kid has enough problems already?)

"Six *o'clock* in the *morning*," she re-moaned. Which meant that this particular jam was no longer confined to the area of genie-angel traumas. Her having not come home all night had by now broadened the circumference of the vicious circle to encompass a petrified, panting parent and a sobbing, sturdy sister.

This was, in other words (English, preferably) (yeah, yeah, yeah), one mell of a hess.

Staggering over to the mirror in her cage, Robin took a long look at the remains of her self.

"Ark," she cried hoarsely at the sight, and it was an understatement. Her beak was badly chapped from a night of trying to pry open the cage door, and her feathers were sadly in need of a curry (lobster would be nice).

Unfortunately, this same understatement was also the mating call of the Yellow-Bellied Sap Sucker and seven thousand of the same were soon flapping frantically at the window.

After making several signs of disinterest, Robin finally hit on the right one, not only dispersing the flock but leaving several of the more sensitive members emotionally scarred for life.

But she soon went on to bigger and better problems, because the noise had awakened Sonny and Cher, who came bounding into the living room wearing matching bathrobes. (The living room was wearing matching bathrobes, not Sonny and Cher.) (Which figures, as a living room would look rather ridiculous wearing Sonny and Cher.)

"Sonny, look," Cher said tenderly. "It's awake!"

"It's been *asleep*?" Robin thought nastily as she tried to smile prettily, forgetting that to un-birds, a *real* robin's smile appeared only to be a cavernous glimpse of the olde tonsils.

Hungry

"And it's hungry again," Sonny replied tenderly-er.

Cher brightened. "Go get the worm from last night and I'll warm some more milk."

Sonny unbrightened. "I flang it out," he admitted.

"Sonny, you *didn't!*"

"Yes, but I did it tenderly."

"Oh," shrugged Cher. "Well, go dig another one."

It was then that Robin knew what she must do. She knew she must kill herself the very second she said, in loud and clear tones. "Please don't bother, I hate worms."

Sonny smiled at Cher. Cher smiled at Sonny. Then they disappeared in the direction of the kitchen.

Suddenly, they reappeared in the direction of the bird cage.

"Cher," quaked Sonny. "Tell me that bird didn't just say *I hate worms.*"

"That bird did not *just* say *I hate worms*," Cher supplied obediently. "It also said *please don't bother*."

"Oh," said Sonny. "My Gawd," he added. But then his face broke (a painful experience, I tell you) into a smile. "So what?" he chortled. "You've obviously found a talking bird!"

"Polly want a cracker?" Robin squawked helpfully, playing along.

Sonny re-chortled and Cher joined in. "See if you can get it to say something else," Sonny urged.

Cher poked a tender finger (her own, oddly enough) through the bars of the cage and chucked Robin under the chin, humming a chorus of "Bang Bang" under her breath.

Believe It

Then Sonny poked a tender finger (his own, strangely believe it) through the bars of the cage, joining in both the chin-chucking and the "Bang Bang"-ing.

And it was then that Robin lost her head. That is to say, she suddenly threw it back, took a deep breath, puffed up with sheer pleasure (not to mention gas) at the thought of singing along with Sonny and Cher (later with Mitch) (mutch) and bellowed rapturously.

Everything went fine until just after the middle part where Robin belted out the necessary "HEYS!" and simulated a rather neat tambourine sound by clanging her remaining toenail against the side of the cage.

Suddenly Cher stopped singing. Then Sonny stopped singing. Finally, even Robin stopped singing.

Cher stared at Sonny. Sonny stared at Cher. Sonny and Cher turned to Robin. Sonny and Cher and Robin turned purple.

"I think your bird can sing, too," Sonny gulped.

Left Cold

"Oh," said Cher. "My Gawd," she added. And, with this, the two of them went bounding back *out* of the living room wearing matching bathrobes. (I'd go through that bit again, but I think it left you cold the first time.) (If you think *that's* cold, you should try bounding around at six a.m. *without* matching bathrobes.) And the famous twosome was last seen racing down the driveway, fearing for their ex-sanity.

"*OH NO!*" blithered Robin, leaping about the cage like a spastic gazelle. "Not to mention *LEMMEOUTTAHERE!*" she re-blithered, banging her head against a bar (no comments, please).

But she got nowhere even faster than usual, and it was then that she really *did* know what she must do.

She'd been toying with the idea all night, and had finally discarded it and looked for something safer to toy with. The pin of a live hand grenade, for instance.

But now she had no choice. She had to get out of that cage and make *some* explanation to Sonny and Cher before they had themselves committed to the nearest irrational ranch. And there was only one way she could do it. Maybe.

So, looking soulfully toward the Heavens, Robin quivered and whispered "ketchup" (which used to be "Worchestershire" but—oh, let's not go through all *that* again).

At the very mention of this magic word, Robin changed back into her sixteen-year-old self.

There was, however, one slight problem. She was, as she had feared she might be, *still in the bird cage!*

"*HELP!*" she shrieked into her navel, which was crammed just to the left of where her right (or was it her wrong?) (at such a moment, who knows?) ankle was jammed. "Not to mention *LIVERPOOL!*"

At the very mention of this other magic word, Robin returned to *real* bird form and fell senseless to the bottom of the cage.

She lay there for a moment, addled, and babbled. Then something stopped her short (the location if which is now an even *longer* story).

"Hark," she gibbered at the sound of a strange sound which, strangely enough, sounded like larfter.

(That paragraph may make you want to leap from the nearest window, but I wouldn't advise it. Those 7,000 Yellow-Bellied Sap Suckers are back out there again.) (They're not only somewhat persistent, they don't hear so good either.)

As the strange sound, which was now *unmistakably* larfter, grew louder, Robin gangled over to the side of the cage to investigate.

To her amazement, the room was filled with stars!

(To Be Continued Next Week)

DISCussion

By Eden

A few months ago, a handsome, talented young singer named Tommy Roe had a hit record resting at the top of all the pop charts in the Southern section of our country.

Now, six months later, that same disc – "Sweet Pea" – is bounding up charts all over the nation. Within the next couple of weeks it should find itself comfortably nestled within the Top Ten. It's a happy, sing-along record – and a big hit for a very nice guy.

* * *

Do you believe that Pete Seeger has released a new single entitled "The Draft Dodger Rag?" Okay, we'll go you one better than that. If you don't believe the 45 title tag – take a quick peek at the shot of Mr. S. on the cover of the LP by the same name. Wheewwww........

* * *

The "I'm Only Sleeping" cut off the new Beatles LP is really brilliant. The production and instrumentation really points out the hard work put into this track to the best advantage.

In case you've been wondering, the yawning affect you hear about three-quarters of the way through the song is accomplished with a guitar...

* * *

Little Stevie Wonder – who is no longer so very little – has a very big – and very commercial – R&B smash with his updated version of Dylan's "Blowin' In The Wind."

This is probably the first time you have heard the tune sung with soul, and the results are excellent.

* * *

The Everly Brothers are two of the most talented and professional performers to have emerged from the American pop music scene in the last decade.

Although they haven't received their due recognition in this country in the last few years, they are two of the biggest stars in England and in a number of other countries around the globe.

Their latest release is "Somebody Help Me" recently recorded by the British Spencer Davis Group. Their disc didn't cause too much action on our charts, but hopefully this new rendition by the Everlys will.

It features some of their fine, distinctive harmonies with a steady, "soulful" sort of beat.

* * *

Percy Sledge has a new soul-sound on the market tagged "Warm and Tender Love." Could be successful, but probably won't top the charts as did his first disc, "When A Man Loves A Woman."

* * *

Noel Harrison had a hit with his first record, "A Young Girl," and now he has returned with "Marieke." This is a French tune, originally penned by Jacques Brel, but Noel has recorded it with a brand new set of English lyrics which he has written.

It's a beautiful song which builds to a powerful and emotional climax, and with a little luck it might follow "Girl" right back into the Top Ten.

Big Pen on Campus!

UTILITY by Lindy

#460-M MEDIUM POINT
non-refillable Ball Pen

The perfect school pen for every writing and drawing need... perfectly balanced to lessen writing fatigue.

GIANT INK SUPPLY

The pen you never refill... oversize ink cartridge assures many months of skip-free, clog-free writing.

 39¢

12 BRILLIANT INK COLORS

Manufactured by LINDY PEN CO. INC.,
North Hollywood, Calif. 91605, U.S.A.

KRLA ARCHIVES

Two Righteous Brothers — On Stage!

By Jeanne Castle

It was opening night at the Coconut-Grove the audience was occupying every seat and spilling over into the aisles. But this was no ordinary audience. Not only was it different in that the constant buzz was reaching an almost monotonous pitch, but it was comprised of about an equal intermingling of teens and adults.

The teens looked somehow out of place but something gave you the impression they weren't. The Grove usually caters to almost all-adult audiences, but on this special night the featured act gave the audience a bond of unity . . . a single, driving interest that brought two generations together. Even if you didn't know the Righteous Brothers were about to come on you could tell something big was going to happen. You could feel something in the air and see it on the faces of those who stared at the empty, dark stage.

Then, after a standing ovation interrupted an unneeded introduction, a huge spotlight pierced the darkness and found Bobby and Bill in black tuxedos and standing side by side.

On stage there is something static about the Righteous Brothers. They don't sing . . . they just sort of feel to music. It's a contageous kind of feeling that is deep-rooted. It is Righteous.

Their music is "soul" music — they are about the only white singers to ever be called such — but other than that you can't really put a classification on them. It isn't limited to any age and can't be confined to the year 1966 or even 1970.

But one of the things you notice most about the Righteous Brothers is that they are singers. They have the natural range and tone to be opera singers. And they project . . . not only melodeous words and phrases but the forceful "Righteous" feeling that can't be defined.

At the Grove, Bill and Bobby reached back into their bag of hits and came up with the standards that have made them what they are and established them as unique in an otherwise almost stereo-typed world of popular music.

Theirs has been an almost overnight climb to stardom, but it surprisingly still has them a little baffled and amazed. The Grove appearance was one of the high points of their career, and after the show ended Bobby was reflecting on the pair's gusty entrance into bigtime show business.

"I didn't think anything this exciting could happen to us," he said, "and if anyone would have forecast this a few years ago, I'd have called them insane."

But it's no fluke that the Righteous Brothers are where they are today. They scored big with "You've Lost That Lovin' Feeling," their first real try at the popular market with good material. And they have taken timeless songs like "Unchained Melody" and turned them into "soulful" arrangements that appeared to have been originally written with the Righteous Brothers in mind.

Bill Medley and Bobby Hatfield were palying in a night club a few years ago. Those were the days before the rebirth of the Righteous Brothers and the duo had no real name. So after an especially bluesy number one of the patrons lept to the table and shouted "That's Righteous, brother."

The fellow didn't know it at the time but his impromptu desceiption of their music stayed with them . . . and probably always will.

James Brown—Soul For The Cool

BEAT Photos: Howard L. Bingham

By Mike Tuck

HOLLYWOOD — James Brown stood in the corner of the Villa Capri banquet room and began to relax. His first day in Los Angeles had been a rough one. He had almost been mobbed by well-wishers when he climbed out of his Lear jet earlier in the day, and then was rushed off to Ninth Street West where he did the entire show.

Now, the only thing that threatened him was an occasional question from reporters as they mingled about the press party and talked with fellow reporters and members of the James Brown troupe. Even now James kept all his poise, remaining polite and warm even though he at times was asked the same question three consecutive times by different people.

Spoke Freely

But the atmosphere in the plush surroundings was cordial and James Brown talked freely about his plane trip, his stay in Los Angeles and his relentless devotion to those who have been devoted to him.

You would think a man in his position would be at least a little bit cocky . . . but he isn't. "I just want everybody to know how deeply grateful I am to them for putting me where I am today," he said.

You see a lot of words describing James Brown as the king of soul men, but too often the human element of James Brown is overlooked. He shakes hands and talks to thousands of peoply every day, yet you seldom see him without his patented smile and he is never brash.

Self-Made

James Brown is a self-made man, but he still won't accept full credit for his success. He was born into desperate poverty in Georgia where he was reared in the traditional squalor of southern cotton fields.

"I used to sing a lot while I would work in the cotton fields," he remembers. "I always loved to sing and I did it every chance I got." His early days are still vivid in his memory, and he recalls his family was so poverty-stricken he had to wear clothes and undergarments made from flour sacks.

But the James Brown of today is a man who now has in excess of 500 suits and who seldom wears the same pair of shoes twice. He now gets his choice of everything, and he stays well-manicured and perfectly-groomed at all times.

He is appropriately called the King, and in every department — class, showmanship and personality — he may never be matched.

JAMES chats with BEAT Reporter, Mike Tuck.

. . . The Soul of the Man

KRLA ARCHIVES

Noel—New Secret Agent

Beginning September 13, he will be known to the public as a secret agent in "The Girl From U.N.C.L.E." but for right now—he is Noel Harrison... singer, actor, musician, and ex-member of the British Olympic skiing teams.

That's a rather complicated title for one man, but then Noel is a rather complex individual. At thirty-two years of age, he is beyond the usual age range of the typical pop star, yet he has just had a Number One single on the national charts, and boasts a far better knowledge of the technical aspects of today's pop music than most pop musicians!

Recently, "Time" magazine featured an article deploring the "evils" and "obscenity" of today's pop music. But Noel scoffs at this, insisting, "Obscenity is in the ears of the listener and the eyes of the beholder."

Pop Obscenity

While a number of adults and others in agreement with "Time" are occupying their time with worries about the mental state of the younger generation—as they are *subjected* to this "obscenity"—Noel has quite a different point of view.

"The problem lies with the *kids*, not with the lyrics. The exciting thing about pop music to me now, is that it's being written *honestly*.

"All art should be there so that people can provide their own interpretation. Now, if their interpretation of it is sick—that's *their* sickness, not the sickness of the writer."

One of the biggest and most important influences on pop music in Noel's opinion has been the widely-felt influence of Bob Dylan.

"I think his influence has been enormous. He's waved the flag, and everyone realizes that anything is allowed, and they can write anything that they feel."

Noel finds himself very "excited" by today's pop music; by the musical experimentation currently taking place, by the new wave of lyrical freedom being exercised by the new, young writers, and by the whole atmosphere of change. "I think everything about it is exciting!"

Noel agrees that "Why?"—that one-word question—is one of the most important discoveries which the younger generation has made, and explains: "The thing that's good at the moment is that all the kids—and the younger kids too—are questioning everything, and saying 'This isn't right and it's got to change.'

"Now, *hopefully*—they're not going to bring up *their* children rigidly and say, 'We've got the answer;' hopefully, they're going to say 'Go on—question it, question it! Move it, change it all the time.' Because, as long as it changes—it's good."

Freaking-Out

Although he doesn't do a great deal of experimentation on his own, Noel enjoys listening to almost anything which is new and different, which can display some thought and originality.

One of his favorite music forms right now is the Indian music of the sitar, specifically that of Ravi Shankar.

"I have *five* albums of Ravi Shankar! I sit with my eyes shut and *freak out* with it, I love it—you can go anywhere with that!!"

His vocabulary is sprinkled with "hip" expressions, but Noel is far from being a "Sunset Strip-Hippie." He has been called a "folksinger" by some, but he denies this.

He explains, "I *was* a folk singer at one time, although—even then, I said I *wasn't*! Folk music was a kind of semi-intellectual pastime for a rather grubby people, I thought!

"Everyone was trying to be *ethnic* and make the right noise. *Now*, on the other hand, I've heard some beautiful new songs. Dylan, again, has had so much influence there, that everyone is writing songs and a lot of the songs are good."

No Word Play

Noel does hold a great distaste for the entire game of "semantics" which he feels people play too often, and claims, "Words are very dangerous, because I may understand one thing by it and you may understand something quite different."

Communication is quite important to Noel, but he doesn't feel limited to the area of words alone in order to communicate with others. For Noel, communication is a "feeling"—the feeling which can be communicated between two people—rather than a mere verbal interchange.

Just recently, Noel has begun to doubt the ultimate importance of the spoken and written word, as well as the significance frequently given to the future as opposed to the present.

If you ask him what plans he has made for his career in the near future, he will smile and explain: "I haven't the faintest idea! I'm doing this now ('The Girl From U.N.C.L.E.'), and whatever happens, *happens*!"

Certainly, his future holds success—most likely because his present holds an abundance of talent. Within a few months, Noel will become the Man from "The Girl From U.N.C.L.E." but he will always remain a complex and fascinating individual.

... NOEL AND HIS BEST FRIEND.

... NOEL AND STEPHANIE POWERS.

Dobe Gray Into The Acting Bag

By Rochelle Reed

The "Leader of the 'In' Crowd" came into *The BEAT* office this week and almost didn't get out.

Dobie Gray, a slim, good-looking young man with big brown eyes, an infectious smile and natural vocal talent, charmed *The BEAT* staff so much we spent way over our interview time talking with him.

Dobie, famous for his "'In' Crowd" and "Look At Me," has released a new single, "Out On The Floor," and contemplates cutting another album in the near future.

But when Dobie first began breaking into the record world, he auditioned for Sonny Bono, an A & R man for a record company before he grew out his hair to become Sonny of Sonny and Cher.

"He sure looked a lot different then," Dobie recalls. "He had a crewcut and suit and tie." Sonny told Dobie he was singing the "wrong type" of songs—popular tunes—and referred him to another record man, for whom Dobie cut "a little airy ballad," which didn't sell.

But after that he recorded the song that started him on the road to success, "Look At Me." He followed it with the "In Crowd" and voila... Dobie had arrived.

But if Dobie hadn't arrived yet, he has thoughts on how he would do it all over again.

"If I were a new singer," he says, "I'd work harder, get better material and whether I was played on the air or not, I'd stick to my own guns."

Dobie doesn't think there is any formula for a sure hit. He says it doesn't take a good singer, a good song or a good arranger to produce a hit record.

Instead, it takes lots of luck, lots of air play and especially "a catchy tune you don't forget."

Two examples of catchy tunes which Dobie says sometimes haunt him are "Groovy Kind of Love" and "Funny How Love Can Be."

"White artists can sing soul, there's no doubt about it," Dobie says. "Soul is something you feel. It doesn't belong to any particular people," he added.

"An artist, an actor, a dancer can have soul," he says. Soul is mostly a "basicness" to Dobie, and being soulful is being "truthful." Even a bricklayer, he says, can have soul for what he is doing.

"My own favorite soul singer is Ray Charles," says Dobie, and his favorite among white soul singers are Dusty Springfield and the Righteous Bros.

"The Beatles and Stones are saying something, too," he adds, "and I do a lot of their material." He performs "Michelle," "Yesterday," "Satisfaction," "19th Nervous Breakdown," and "Paperback Writer."

Dobie is also branching into another entertainment field—acting. "That's my bag," says Dobie, and to prove it he is currently playing an office clerk in a little theater production. He has just completed the movie "Out of Sight," in which he plays himself.

But Dobie would like to stay in more serious dramatic acting, and is currently keeping his fingers crossed for a good role in the MGM movie, "Bloomer Girl."

Acting isn't new to Dobie—he's been doing it since his school days when he was active in drama and musical productions. After graduation, he began taking drama lessons and joined various little theater groups.

Dobie is soft-spoken and sensitive. He's worked hard for his success. He was once a cook in a Lebanese delicatessen, where he picked up not only the Lebanese tongue but Arabic, Hebrew and Spanish. He also washed dishes, put paper on hangers at a dry cleaning plant and operated an Ozalid (music reproduction) machine while waiting for his big break.

Today Dobie is a promising actor, an already accomplished singer and a wonderful personality. Relying on himself as his only "formula," Dobie will be around for a long time.

Beatles Score With Germans

First reports in on the recent German tour made by The Beatles indicate nothing but a smash success. German sales representatives are reporting the tour to be a classic in the history of record sales promotion, explaining that there has never been such an effective tie-in with a tour and a sales promotion as was achieved on the "Bravo Beatles Blitz-Tournee" — the German tag for the tour.

The tour was sponsored by "Bravo," a German magazine for young people in that country, which reports that the tour was a sales success even before the Beatles arrived in Essen for their debut German performance.

The record sales on Beatle discs increased by approximately *500 per cent* in Essen, Hamburg, and Munich—all three cities where the Beatles were booked for performances, and the increase soared to an astronomical and unprecedented *1,000* per cent before the end of the tour.

Final tabulations on the overall results of the tour are still in the process of completion, however trade officials in that country are already saying that there is little doubt that the tour will send Beatle record sales sky-rocketing to an all-time high in Germany.

The German tour was also one of sentimental—as well as financial—value to the Phenomenal Foursome.

KRLA ARCHIVES

...LOVIN' SPOONFUL

The Brilliance Of A Spoonful

By Rochelle Reed

"Summer In the City" is another lovin' spoonful from the group by the same name. It's wild, it's groovy and it's a hit.

Written by Spoonfuls John Sebastian, Steve Boone and John's younger brother Mark (a non-Spoonful), the song has spread from city to city like summertime itself. It's here, it's now and it's happening.

The Spoonful had been promising something *very different* in their newest single. Everyone did a lot of guessing, but no one was prepared for "Summer." In short, it's great.

A brilliant composition of notes, with a splash of sirens and auto horns, "Summer In the City" is one of the more unique things to come out of today's record industry. It captures the mood of burning streets and auto jams, long working days and nights that don't cool.

Gritty clothes and the city grime don't escape "Summer." It has captured the megalopolis in search of a supercity . . . the impatience of a pedestrain waiting for a red light to turn green . . . it touches on the endless search and ever-present mystique that belongs to the city alone.

Charmed

The latest hit for the Spoonful follows closely their return from Europe, where they charmed the people and press alike. They'll return again around the end of September for a tour which will take them to major European cities before they tour Britain for a week in October.

In addition to charming two continents, "Do You Believe In Magic?" and "You Didn't Have to Be So Nice," catapulted John, Steve, Zal and Jo to stardom, and just won them two awards for "Best New Male Group of 1966" as chosen by American disc jockeys.

The Spoonful are a creative group and worthy of their new honors, as they are more than a little different from their peers. Artists are never "one of the group" precisely because their artistic talents set them apart from the masses. It can be no other way. This life apart is an intense life, very intense, but a free-wheeling one too.

Vacation

For instance, Steve Boone says that if he had all the money in the world and a week's vacation, he would go to Sitges, Spain. "I was driving around the Mediterranean last year on a motor bike and I stopped there. I was going to stay the day and ended up staying three whole weeks. The people were great and the place was beautiful."

Most people, if they had all the money they could spend and a free week, would pick hundreds of places before choosing Sitges, Spain. But a Spoonful is one apart.

A Spoonful lists the qualities he would want in a girl as "to be on the quiet side, to think for herself and to be herself—and not to imitate other girls."

But this isn't only a Spoonful's idea of a girl. It's the group's general outlook on the people and places of the world. It pervades their entire way of living, for indeed, it *is* their way of living.

The Lovin' Spoonful are themselves. Their music is their own. Their last two hits have been uniquely different from each other, and "Summer In the City" is one more world away.

In one Spoonful's words, the group is volatile. They aren't flighty but they are fast movers. They *have* to be in order to keep up and adjust to a rapidly changing world.

Spoonful Zal is the nocturnal person that is common among musicians. His favorite type of people are "night people." "I like to stay up all night and wake up at 10 a.m.—but it ain't so practical," he laughs, "when I'm working."

The English press credited the Spoonful and especially lead singer John Sebastian with being the forerunners of folk-rock, which they assured their readers would sweep both continents and then some before the year is out.

Jug-Rock

But a Canadian paper credits the Spoonful, and again especially John, with graduating beyond folk-rock into what they call jug-rock—more or less Hillbilly blues.

"I dig jug bands," John says, and this influences his writing, but more subjectively than overtly . . . listen closely and mixed with the jug band sound you will find that John's songs are creations spawned from life in Greenwich Village and a roving existence, of disappointments and versatility, of many other things than just black dots on paper.

One more factor may begin to influence John's writing: newly married, John doesn't stray far from his bride except when he is performing.

The Lovin' Spoonful, who take their name from the spoonful of sugar or honey which follows one of bitter medicine, formed when John and Steve met Joe and Zal in New York while all were living in the Village.

Basement Life

Their first job was at the Night Owl Cafe, from which they were immediately dismissed. But with the conviction that sets a successful group apart from all the rest, they hid away in a basement for two months while they did a musical hibernation.

They played and practiced and played in a setting that might rival the best horror movie set. They lowered their instruments into the basement via freight elevator and laundry cart. Everyday they skirted around an enormous black pool which was full of water bugs, centipedes and sightless fish.

Plaster on the walls, shaken loose by the musical vibrations, rained down on them until they had to wear funny hats to keep their hair clean.

But after two months they developed professionalism, even though they were pale and blinking. The Night Owl rehired them for an indefinite time and at the owner's expense, printed up 1000 balloons reading "I Love You—The Lovin' Spoonful."

From then on, you know the story. "It had to happen," John says, and he's right.

For Girls Only

By Shirley Poston

Ahhh, that's more like it. Now things are back to normal. (Back?) (I didn't know they'd ever been there in the first place.)

As you can see, my week's respite (another great word for pronouncing just like it's spelled)from the rigors of column-writing (not to mention Mortis) (I'm not quite sure *I* get *that*) (and let's keep it that way)... where was I? Oh, yes. I was telling you all that rest didn't change a thing, but I guess I needn't have bothered.

As usual, this column speaks for itself. (It also speaks *to* itself.)

Boy, I sure can't write today (*today?*). The fact that I'm so tired I'm absolutely cross-eyed may have something to do with it, and the fact that I stayed up until four a.m. in the morning may have something to do with that. However, I doubt it. My sanity, that is.

Did I just say four a.m. in the morning? Oh, well, at least I didn't say four a.m. in the evening.

Speaking Of 'G'

Speaking of George, George, GEORGE, (sorry, got a little carried away there) (in a net) I haven't typed that name for one entire week. No, no, I'm not recovering from Harrison-itis. My typewriter has been in the hospital. You see, when I was composing my usual witty writty (Oh, *sure*) for the last *BEAT*, this lock of hair kept hanging in my eyes and driving me crazy (change the y to i and add er), so I finally grabbed a scissors and whacked it off.

Do I have to tell you that it fell in the typewriter and got all tangled up in some of those weird thingies and that a certain repairman is certain that someone is coming for me soon?

I hope not. I just don't think (I'll say) I could bear up under the strain of having to talk about it.

I'd much rather talk about something I've been forgetting to say for 42,000 months. Which is "Happy Birthday George, Pauley and Ringo", because I forgot to say it when I should have. I guess I've always been too exhausted from the antics we go through on Beatle B-days to have the strength to mention my good wishes here.

Two of my feinds (I meant to sat friends but I think I was right the first time) (or was it right *for* the first time?) (down, girl) and I have this regular ritual we go through on said special daze — whoops — days. I won't go into the whole gory story . . . say, on second thought, maybe I will. Not now, of course, because it would take up all my room and I have several more subjects to blither about.

Anyfootbath (I'm too tired to type that over, so please just turn the b upside down, okay?), I will go into ghastly detail if you'd like to hear how three reasonably respectacle kids make utter fools of themselves.

To give you an example, we start off the night before by each baking a one layer cake. Then, the next day, we put the layers together and frost and decorate them and all that. Only problem is, we never agree on what shape or size cakes to bake, so one layer is round and maybe the others are square or some gawdawful(ly funny) thing like that. (Well, *we* think it's funny.)

Beatle Pageant

I think that's my fave part of the whole celebration. Or is it our Beatle Pageant (which will have to undergo some, shall we say, *revisions*, before I can print it)? No, I guess it's roaming around searching for people with the same name as whatever Beatle the particular birthday happens to belong to (we have to find a specific number of same, that's part of the dealie).

Wait, on fourth thought, I think it's singing "Happy Birthday" on the busiest street corner in town.

Re-down, girl. I knew I'd never be able to get off the subject once I got on it. In any carton, let me know if you'd like to hear the entire bit. If so, I'll print it before John's birthday and maybe you can join us. Course, they'll come for you too if you do, but what the cell (as in padded)?

Cute Commercial

Two short items before they slip my alleged mind. 1 — I did *not*, as several of you have been hinting, serve as a model for the songwriter who came up with "They're Coming To Take Me Away". 2 — I would like to congratulate the Dairy Queen company on their groovy commercial where the girls chase the long-haired singer. It's really cute, and so different from most commercials that feature teenagers.

Usually, the kids look about forty and say and do stuff no teenager would be caught dead saying or doing (repition, you may have noticed, still numbers among my many virtues), but this one is kind of neat. (So is that guy!)

Thank-You

I now have approximately six thousand thank-yous to bellow at the top of me lungs, on account of because I have been getting the smashingest things in the mail. Rave, pant and chip-another-toof, I don't know what I ever did to deserve all of you (and I don't mean that the way it sounds), but WOW, don't stop now.

Oh, crumbs. I seem to have lost the letter that came with the all-time smasher, which happens to be a hand-made Robin Boyd doll, which now happens to be sitting on the lap of the George doll Linda Jackson made for me some time ago. All I can remember is the girl's name, so until I find the writty, Lisa Jenkins, I love you!

I also love Pam Jensen, who sent me a star-spangled net; and Bea Berkery, who made me a "Robin Boyd Was Here" rubber stamp (out of a big eraser, which must have taken ten years to "whittle"); and Debbie Rutherford, who's writing "The Adventures Of Shirley Poston" and sending me all the chapters (which send me, period); and a lot of others I'll be thanking here and by letter just as soon as I possibly can.

It there were only some way I could get all this done right away, and get all my rash promises fulfilled this instant! (A confession: I'm not quite finished with "Ravers" yet, and "Toy Boy" comes next, but forgive me most of all for *still* finding a stray "Code" or "RH" every once in awhile.)

Just please bear with me a little longer because I'm getting there slowly but shirley (ahem). And *PULLEASE* don't think I don't read every word you write me and flip out of my gourd over same. My folks are so sick of me crashing around the house, reading letters and giggling hysterically, one of you had better start cleaning up the olde guest room just in case.

Anytruck (don't ask me where I got *that* one) (or why), I just wasn't prepared for all this because I never realized how many fellow-retardos I have in this world, but I'm finally getting everything under control (not to mention the bed).

Also, things are looking up. Ever since I found out what "a cuckoo in its cups" means, has my dad been *nice* to me! He even hinted around that he might buy a whole big box of postcards so I could answer some more goodies without having to take my water pistol and hold up the nice man the the stamp window. And I've been whining around for him to hurry up ever since.

Lord, I'm out of room and this week I really did have something marvtastic (burp) to tell you in code. Next week, so help me. Help me find my marbles, that is.

Jan On The Road To Recovery

Continued from Page 3

serious — at least he seemed far more alive.

Jan remained in the Intensive Care section of the hospital for nearly a month, and hiscondition remained listed as "serious"on the hospital's records.

Slowly but surely, though, his condition continued to improve until finally he was allowed to be moved into a room of his own, although still with nurses in constant attendance.

At first, Jan's spirits were understandably very low. But as he continued to gain in strength and to make progress, he began to have a far more cheerful outlook than before.

At first, he was able to regain the power of speech which he had temporarily lost due to the brain injury sustained in the accident. It began with just a few words, and the weighty task of re-learning much of his vocal powers and attempting to reconnect, through other channels, a system of communications which had been temporarily disrupted by the crash.

After this major step forward, Jan had regained enough of his strength to begin a stiff — but important — program of physical therapy.

While he had at first been unable to do almost anything for himself after regaining consciousness, Jan could now use all of the muscles on his left side.

At this printing, Jan still remains paralyzed on the right side, however — this is, again, something which is a matter of time and requires painstaking hard work to get these muscles back into condition and functioning normally once again. But there is great hope now, as Jan is making great and rapid progress.

Just a short while ago, Jan was finally released from the hospital, and needless to say — it was a deliriously happy occasion for everyone concerned. It was a very long-awaited day for Jan and for his many friends. It was also a day which many had once feared might never come.

Back at home, Jan continued his physical therapy and has been making excellent progress with the program. So much so, on the second day of the Mama's and Papa's recording session for their brand new album, Jan felt well enough to go down to the studio for a visit with his friends.

Jan spent a good part of the day at the studio, chatting happily with the group and with many of their mutual friends who had stopped by. And throughout the day, Jan's spirits were very high, his attitude excellent, and his face constantly lighted with a cheerful smile.

It seems almost an unbelievable miracle that Jan has come as far as he has since his untimely accident. It has been a very long road, and one which at first seemed nearly impossible to travel, so littered was it with stones and boulders.

But Jan — with the help of many fine doctors and nurses, and the support of many loyal friends, fans, and members of his family — cleared that road and is now prepared to walk — standing tall! — down that road to a complete and successful recovery.

An Epstein Endorsement: The Cyrkle Is Happening

. . . DON DAWES OF THE CYRKLE

It wouldn't be too much of a venture to say that Brian Epstein knows a little about music and musicians. In fact, the statement is about as safe as saying Albert Einstein knows something about physics or John Steinbeck is a qualified writer.

So when Brian Epstein puts the stamp of approval on a group you know right away the group has something going for it. This Epstein endorsement is one thing The Cyrkle has in its favor. The second is the group's every-changing image.

The group used to be the Rhondells. That changed, as did its sound. Not only that, but the Cyrkle picked up a new manager and about the only thing that remained was three guys and some old Rhondell fan mail.

But the group had an alive sound and although it had just undergone a big upheaval, no one seemed to worry. Nathan Weiss, a New York attorney, became their manager, and although he had never been directly connected with a singing group he had been a personal friend of Epstein for some time.

Brian was in New York during Christmas of 1965 and he and Weiss went to the Downtown to watch the then Rhondells perform.

Brian takes up the story: "We were very enthusiastic about the group. Nat asked my advice and I told him I would be happy to give any help I could. Afterwards I met the three boys and went to their recording session — it was my first visit to a U.S. recording studio. Acetates were sent to me and from the three titles I chose 'Red Rubber Ball' as the best. It seems that everyone else thought the same way."

Brian was more than a little bit influential with the group. It was he who suggested they change their name to The Cyrkle, and he gave them other pointers that benefitted their style.

The Cyrkle is composed of Marty Fried, Don Dannemann and Tom Dawes. The trio met while they were attending Lafayette College in Pennsylvania and immediately formed a group that rose to high campus stature as they catered to dances and fraternity parties.

Until Don's July release from the U.S. Coast Guard Reserve, personal appearances for The Cyrkle must be limited to weekends when he can get a leave pass.

U.K. representation of The Cyrkle will be handled by Brian Epstein's Nems Enterprises organization in London and a European tour is planned for the group later this year.

KRLA ARCHIVES

| Sophia Loren | + | Gregory Peck | + | Henry Mancini | = |

Music from the film score -- on RCA

KRLA ARCHIVES

WHISKY A GO GO
8901 SUNSET STRIP • 652-4202

• JULY 13th to JULY 23rd

The Turtles
THE DOORS

• JULY 27th to AUGUST 7th

Johnny Rivers
King of the Go Go

THE CHAMBERS BROTHERS

• AUGUST 10th to AUGUST 27th

THE DOORS

FOOD & FUN TILL 2 A.M. — AGE 18 & OVER WITH I.D.

KRLA ARCHIVES

America's Largest Teen NEWSpaper

KRLA *Edition* BEAT

AUGUST 13, 1966

BOBBY FULLER'S STRANGE DEATH
PAGE 1

BEAT Photo: Chuck Boyd

CLOSE ONE FOR ERIC
PAGE 1

Words To Donovan's 'Sunshine Superman'
PAGE 16

BEAT Photo: Chuck Boyd

KRLA BEAT

Volume 2, Number 21 — August 13, 1966

DYLAN MARRIAGE RUMOR CONFIRMED

Bob Dylan's long rumored marriage to Sarah Lownds has been confirmed in an article by the Saturday Evening Post. The article also disclosed Dylan has fathered a son — Jesse Byron Dylan — in the past year.

Dylan, who has tried desperately to keep his marriage a secret, recently purchased a townhouse in Manhattan's fashionable East 30's, the article said.

When rumors of Dylan's marriage spread throughout Europe prior to his most recent tour there the Wizard of Words remained typically elusive on the subject. The Post story carried the first public admission of the marriage by a national magazine.

The article said Dylan has been married to the beautiful, black-haired Sarah Lownds for about a year. *The BEAT* was one of the first publications to mention Dylan's marriage, giving reports on the rumor of it for the past four months.

After the release of the Post article Dylan was unavailable for comment — and even if he were he would probably deny the marriage.

Pop Star's Death Probed

BOBBY FULLER — "Enjoyed people, had many friends — no excesses."

Body Discovered In Parked Auto

The small recording studio on Selma Boulevard was cloaked in a dirge-like atmosphere. Inside, people spoke very little — and when they did at all it was mostly to offer condolences.

In one corner of the downstairs reception room glittered Mustang Records' showcase . . . a large, glassed-in enclosure featuring momentos and milestones of the company's youngest and brightest star.

Five records, arranged in a chain from top to bottom, were flanked on every corner by pictures of a gentle looking fellow with dark, questioning eyes. And sprinkled throughout the showcase were buttons and stickers that read "Bobby Fuller 4 Ever . . ."

But Bobby Fuller didn't last forever. He was only 23 — a promising young singer from Texas whose friends said he "just liked to be around people" — when he was found dead in his car parked in front of his home.

And no one knew why.

A slight, restrained blend of conversation became noticeable as more reporters squeezed into the tiny office and joined some of Bobby's friends and close business associates. Somewhere in the background a big, somber-faced executive was telling a reporter why he thought the popular singer hadn't committed suicide, as first reports indicated.

"There was just no reason for him to take his own life," said Bob Keene, president of Mustang Records. "I've been closely associated with him for the past two years, during which time he has not given any indication of being unstable emotionally. He enjoyed people, had many friends and had no excesses."

But, he was reminded, when Bobby's body was discovered on the night of July 18 there were indications of suicide. The windows had all been rolled up and in the front seat with Bobby was a half-full gasoline can and a rubber hose. Gasoline saturated the upholstery but there was no obvious sign of a struggle.

Even the preliminary autopsy revealed that Bobby had consumed a large amount of gasoline — enough to kill a man.

"I know," Keene said, "but the preliminary autopsy did not say that was what necessarily killed him. We won't know that until the final autopsy is released later in the week.

"It just didn't make sense," the executive insisted. "Bobby was not in a depressed state of mind prior to his death. His mother supposedly told reporters last night that her son had become despondent in the last few days, but I talked to her this morning and she said she never made the statement."

Keene said that even during
(Turn to Page 15)

Eric Suffers Convulsions After Emergency Landing

Eric Burdon was almost hospitalized and the Animals/Herman's Hermits U.S. tour almost ended in tragedy recently, but with a bundle of determination and a stroke of luck both the troupe and Eric continued the barnstorming tour.

But it just wasn't in the cards for the entertainers to keep a scheduled engagement in Denver, Colorado.

First, the private plane carrying the 24-man troupe was forced to make an emergency landing in Farmington, N.M. while in route to Denver. Lack of sufficient oxygen in the cabin of the plane forced the landing.

Eric, who has a long history of asthma, suffered a mild convulsion. After a thorough doctor's examination, however, the Animal's lead singer was adjudged well enough to continue the tour.

Several other members of the troupe weren't so lucky, however. Two of the passengers — members of a group called the 3 and ½ that open shows for the Herman/Animal tour — were taken to the Farmington Hospital for recuperation after suffering convulsions.

There was still a chance for the two groups to keep their date at Denver that evening so Bob Levine, road manager for the troupe, arranged for extra oxygen to be rushed to the Farmington Airport. It was, and with the new supply of oxygen the boys were allowed to fly to Denver in time for their appearance in Bear Stadium. But alas, a hailstorm cancelled the performance.

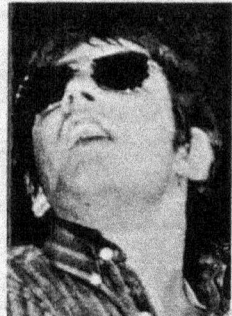

'Revolver' Is Title For New Beatle LP

By Tony Barrow

During their Germany/Far East tour THE BEATLES worked out a final running order for their upcoming U.K. album, due for Parlophone release August 5.

Having settled on a final sequence for the 14 all-new numbers, they held a series of concentrated discussions about a suitable title for the album. More than 50 different ideas were discussed but the unanimous choice favoured Paul's simple yet effective one-word suggestion—"REVOLVER."

GEORGE HARRISON has written three of the 14 numbers and on each of these he is the featured lead vocalist. They are "TAX MAN," "LOVE YOU TO" and "I WANT TO TELL YOU." On the second of these tracks George has created a terrific sitar introduction and on the third Paul plays piano in the background.

RINGO STARR'S vocal solo is "YELLOW SUBMARINE" and I'd say this kiddie-angled ditty is destined to become his most successful track to date. Paul, John and George join him vocally for the catchy chorus lines and there's a series of carefully-placed sound effects at appropriate points throughout the arrangement.

Of the remaining 10 Lennon-McCartney compositions, five have vocal leads handled by John and five feature Paul. The Lennon quintet runs like this: "I'M ONLY SLEEPING," "SHE SAID, SHE SAID," "AND YOUR BIRD CAN SING," "DOCTOR ROBERT," "TOMORROW NEVER KNOWS." That last number was given its title by Ringo and the track includes a host of weirdie sound effects created specially for the occasion by Paul.

Paul's set includes "ELEANOR RIGBY," "HERE, THERE AND EVERYWHERE," "GOOD DAY SUNSHINE," "FOR NO ONE" and "GOT TO GET YOU INTO MY LIFE."

"Eleanor Rigby is Paul's ballad specialty in the "REVOLVER" program. The precision-built lyrics tell a meaningful story and Paul is backed by strings just as he was for his two biggest previous ballad hits. For me this is one of the album's stand-out performances and the commercial chart potential of "Eleanor Rigby" is limitless.

(Turn to Page 5)

Inside the BEAT

Letters To The Editor	2
Lennon-McCartney Win Awards	3
Pictures In The News	6
Paul & Jane	7
Adventures Of Robin Boyd	8
Genderally Mindbenders	10
BEAT Meets New Groups	14
"Overnight" For The Shondells	15
Donovan — The Musical Magician	16-17
The Turtles Return	18-19
Pop Music Puzzlers	20
The Raiders By Candlelight	21
The BEAT Goes To The Movies	23

The BEAT is published bi-weekly by BEAT Publications, Inc., editorial and advertising offices at 6290 Sunset Blvd., Suite 504, Hollywood, California 90028. U.S. bureaus in Hollywood, San Francisco, New York, Chicago and Nashville; overseas correspondents in London, Liverpool and Manchester, England. Sale price, 15 cents. Subscription price: U.S. and possessions, $3 per year; Canada and foreign rates, $9 per year. Second class postage prepaid at Los Angeles, California.

Napoleon Is Record Star

With the sounds of sirens serving as backup music for a psychotic bemoaning the departure of his pet canine, "They're Coming To Take Me Away, Ha-Haaa..." is apparently the fastest breaking single pop recording of the year.

A mystery man who goes under the guise of Napoleon XIV is responsible for the smash recording, and he evidently has such a good thing going with the record he refuses to devulge his name.

As a result of the enormous response to the recording, Napoleon XIV is being beseiged with offers from booking agents, television shows and night clubs. Thus far he has not responded, as he prefers to remain incognito.

KRLA ARCHIVES

Letters TO THE EDITOR

Beatle, Stone Fans Unite!

Dear BEAT:
I saw a popular teen show recently where some "pro-Beatle" and "pro-Stone" fans had an impromtu debate which was the top singing group in the world.

First, I'll tell you where I stand. My favorites are still The Beatles and they probably will be for a long time to come. But I've purchased nearly all of the Rolling Stone albums and consider them a fantastic group also. I've seen both groups perform.

Now, I'd like to know why most kids insist upon "taking sides" — either for The Beatles or for the Stones. Each side tries to put its group on top of the other, which is ridiculous. Both groups are great because they're improving their styles constantly and becoming more versatile.

If a person insists upon putting these two groups "in order," the only possible way would be to use popularity as a basis. One can always say that this group is more popular than that one because it's statistical. But to say which group is better is a matter of opinion. In closing, I'd like to say: "Beatle and Stone fans of the world unite."
(That'll be the day...)
Alice Villanueva

QUESTIONS FOR BEATLES

Dear BEAT:
The Beatles do, indeed, seem to be killing themselves. Not over the album cover — to me, it's ridiculous to be getting all steamed up over such a silly thing. It's what's inside the cover that should matter, not what's on it.

Not over Manila, because what happened there wasn't their fault. How could they go to that reception if they didn't even know about it?

The Beatles are killing themselves — because they just don't seem to CARE anymore. Maybe it's because they've made their millions, and don't want to bother anymore. I don't know. They've stopped giving... they've stopped trying.

I'm not writing this because I hate the Beatles, because I don't. I love them more than anything, and always will. But what they've been doing (or haven't been doing) hurts. It hurts terribly, and I just wish that someone would ask them, WHY?
Hurt and Confused

Dear BEAT:
Well, the Beatles have done it now. For good. They can be excused for the pathetically poor album they just released and they might even be forgiven for the ridiculously distasteful cover accompanying the record. And there's probably some reason for losing their once-close contact with their fans.

But not even the Beatles can publicly insult an entire country and get away with it. National pride runs stronger than attachment to any singing group. They deserved everything they got at the Manila International Airport ..., and maybe they deserved more. At least they got more, when they went to India and received the same kind of reaction there.

Paul apologized and this might be interpreted as a partial compensation for their snub of the Philippine's First Lady, but John didn't even display that little bit of courtesy. "I didn't even know the country HAD a president," he said, and in effect further insulted the Philipinos.

But John may soon realize the folly of his sarcastic comments. Perhaps George best summed up the Beatle situation when he said, "Now we can go to America and really get beaten up." He may be right.
Eric Weiss

Dear BEAT:
The controversy over the new Beatle single seems to me to be a case of artists outdistancing their audience. In the past their music, though usually superior, was still only a reworking of standard forms employed by many others in the past. Now that they are accomplishing true innovations, many of the fans are afraid to accompany them. The fact that many of the girls were disappointed with their TV sequence stemmed from the absence of screams and is very telling.

I thought the sequence on the Sullivan show was very moving, and those who see only "weirdness" in the new songs reveal their own shallowness. If rock and roll is to become generally regarded as a serious musical force in our time and not just a field where amateurs with press agents grind out popular cliches to unsophisticated ears, then it must begin right here.
Lester Bangs

Dear BEAT:
It looks as though the sincere are separating from the phonies. The ones that liked the Beatles because everyone else did are starting to be recognizable.

On the television show I was just watching, the emcee read an excerpt from a newspaper article about the Beatles "snubbing" the wife of the president of the Philippines. I'm sure they had a good reason — Paul said that they didn't know about the invitation, but that isn't the point.

The kids were asked if the Beatles were "getting too big for their breeches." One girl said that they should go because the kids are "getting tired of them."

I think that any true-blue fan is going to love the Beatles come-what-may. I know I am.

Some people are putting the Beatles down. They're saying that their new song is bad. "Paperback Writer," in my opinion, is original. It's turn it over and play "Rain." Who else but the Beatles would think of singing backwards?

Any true fan could never dislike the Beatles, especially when they think about all the Beatles have done for them. If the Beatles' popularity is dying, it's because the phony fans are leaving; but the ones who still love them will hold them in their hearts forever.
Dorothy Dane

LOVE RUDE

Dear BEAT:
I've just read the article in the July 9th issue about "Love." I would luv Love to see and read this letter. It might do them some good. Here goes.

If any group has any appointment they should keep it. And not give a phony excuse like lazy Love did. And all the members should have been there. Love was missing two people, Kenny and Snoopy; that was rude. I got the feeling that Love will be better off if Bryan is told to shut up more often.

Musically they are a very good group. Individually they are all crummy people and that's no jive.

If they were all about 15 years younger and acted rude like that, I'd suggest what they need now is a whack or 10 across the bottom. It would probably help them or at least knock some sense into them.
Bonnie Phillips

Tell Me Chick

Dear BEAT:
In Rochelle Reed's article on Love she said, "it just wasn't my day." Tell me chick, has it ever been your day?
I think not.
(Unsigned)

Beatle Majority

Dear BEAT:
I really don't have much to say, but I hope Tony DeVito gets the message: Anyone who has to knock the Beatles to build up the Rolling Stones hasn't really convinced the Beatle fans, who are still, like it or not, the majority.
One of the majority.

Philipino Animals

Dear BEAT:
I have just read an article in the paper about the Philipino treatment of the Beatles at Manila International Airport, and "furious" is a mild word to describe how I feel about it.

Imagine people acting like animals because of the alleged snub of an invitation for lunch for the Philippino's First Lady. The Beatles were pushed, shoved, swung at and cursed at, while police stood by and watched! And then the Philippino President and First Lady managed to say only that they "regretted" the incident. If the Beatles had been injured, I'm afraid "regretting" wouldn't be of much help.

To top it off, the Beatles hadn't even received notice of an invitation, though even if they had and did ignore it, there would still be no excuse for the Philippino people's behavior.

Paul apologized over the radio for himself and John, George and Ringo. But the Beatles aren't the ones who should apologize, are they?
Sue Marston

Catchy Names Not Enough

Dear BEAT:
Recently I read an article in the BEAT concerning the group Love. Before I even read it, just seeing the title (Is Love Lost?) I knew exactly what it would be all about. It isn't hard at all to piece this example of their conduct together with their lousy performances and come up with a real bomb.

When the record "Little Red Book" came out, I really dug it and was actually looking forward to seeing them in person... that is until I DID see them! The description of them in The BEAT reminded me of what they were like; really bad. Their sound was O.K., but that singing you hear on the records is one fraud... That vocalist is terrible and they gave the overall impression of not being able to put forth or project anything. They were so bad, it was almost ridiculous to have them billed so highly, and was just as surprising as Rochelle Reed's interview (?). If they think they're going to make it, it's all in their minds, and the flame under that idea is fed by their all-consuming egos. Love is too good a name for them and they seem to be the greatest example of transparent (not to mention flat) personality now metabolizing. My friends and I, after witnessing that, are convinced that it takes more than recording studio tricks and catchy names to make a good group, and an attitude like theirs doesn't belong anywhere.
Pattie Golf

Love Letter

Dear BEAT:
I have been reading your magazine for some time now in hopes of finding an article about "Love." Finally in the July 9 issue, there it was — lucky page seven — a 1/2 page picture (unfortunately, not really up to BEAT standards), followed by a blizzard of words about all the trouble a reporter had while interviewing them.

I know it isn't always possible to interview a group and get the answers that will fit into a story. But, a reporter should be ingenious enough to know what questions to ask and how to ask them without being hostile.

I hope that the BEAT will have other articles about Love from unbiased reporters who will go and listen to Love and also see them perform. Maybe then they can write an article that contains "Love."
Billie

Thanks For Mark

Dear BEAT:
I just received my July 16 issue of the BEAT. The first thing I read was the article "Mark Lindsay's Two Worlds." I would like to thank you — Eden in particular — for this inspiring article.

I think Mark Lindsay is a wonderful person. He is talented, witty, sincere, sensitive and (as if this weren't enough) handsome. I have come to thoroughly respect him.

Seeing Mark, along with the other Raiders and "Uncle Paul," perform is an experience nobody should pass up.

Thanks again for the fantastic article.
Linn Davis
Inglewood, Calif.

Gary Right

Dear BEAT:
Is Gary Lewis the only one who has any sense around here? He was right. The Beatles used that cover just to see what people would say. And they hated it. They said it was horrible and morbid and sickening. That was what The Beatles wanted them to say. That was the idea.

In the article it said that not one person who saw the banned cover liked it. That was a lie. I liked it. So did my best friend. So did hundreds of other Beatle fans who went out and bought the album and steamed off the cover so they could have the other cover. I did too, and I'm keeping it even though the cover is ripped and half of John's and George's faces were ripped off.

Ralph Gleason described the cover as a "subtle protest against war". He's on the right track. It's just the people who have to be so critical who didn't like the cover. But Beatle fans will accept the Beatles in any way, and after
(Turn to Page 4)

KRLA ARCHIVES

On the BEAT
By Louise Criscione

I'd like to add my own personal condolences to the Fuller family. I didn't know Bobby too well but I thought he was a polite, talented and extremely nice person.

What's with the Mama's and Papa's? They've initiated a new policy whereby they're turning down all television guest spots and instead are going to do only their *own* specials! Right now they're busy recording with the new Mama and their photographer, Guy Webster, is in the process of shooting tons of pictures of the group. Naturally, all the ones with Michelle are being canned so an entirely new set is being shot.

Speaking of the M's & P's, Mama Cass and Papa Denny dropped by the Whiskey to see the Turtles. Same night, same place, we spotted the Stones, Them, Beach Boy Mike Love (complete with beard), Nino Tempo, Lyme, P. F. Sloan and three-fourths of the Gene Clark Group.

Just to show you how smart (?) I am, I thought all this time that the Yardbirds had penned "Respectable." Discovered it's an Isley Brothers' composition. Anyway, it's a fantastic song. No offense to the Outsiders, but I think the Yardbirds have the best version on their "Rave-Up" LP. 'Course, they never released it as a single. So...

I wonder if Phil Spector is really going to switch records for movies. Seems he is. His first production is set to be "The Last Movie" but it probably should have been titled "The Last Record." Whatever, it will no doubt be on the interesting side. It's a contemporary Western with guilt as the main theme. Phil says it will win the Cannes Film Festival. And knowing Spector, it probably will.

...MAMA CASS

How about this for a change? While the Beatles were putting the finishing touches on "Revolver," their van was parked outside. Fans, waiting for a glimpse of the Beatles, noticed the dirty state of the van and spent an entire hour cleaning it. However, their work was in vain—they had no sooner completed the washing when a new crop of fans appeared and proceeded to scribble names and messages all over the clean van. Oh, well.

Bobby Rydell has just finished his annual two week visit with Uncle Sam. He's in the Army Reserves and this year he spent his "vacation" at Indiantown Gap, Pa. I swear!

Now that the split has been officially announced, both Manfred Mann and Paul Jones are having their says. Manfred claims that the only thing worrying him is "inactivity." That's why he didn't want the news of Paul's departure made public until the last possible minute.

Paul admitted that they had been forced to be dishonest with the press. A move he termed "unfortunate." He then went on to say that there had been no fight with Manfred but "to be absolutely corny about it, I guess I'm a loner."

Pete Quaife is out of hospital following his car accident. Fact is, Pete put quite a scare in the Kinks when he slipped off for a week's vacation without telling anyone. You can imagine the confusion around the Kink office while the search for missing Pete was on. But when he had soaked up enough sun, Pete hobbled back to London and will join the Kinks when they take-off for their European tour.

Caught Bo Diddley's stage act the other night. If it wasn't for the fact that I was watching a rock phenomena in action I probably wouldn't have enjoyed the show much. It got downright boring in parts but if you listen closely to the man you can hear bits and pieces of the Animals and Yardbirds. Some say that Elvis saw Bo years ago and thus developed his famous stage antics. Anyway, if you ever get the chance go and see Bo Diddley—one of the artists who started it all.

...BO DIDDLEY

I didn't think it would ever happen but the Association have finally released their album! They've been recording it for the last six months (well, maybe not *six* months... would you believe three?) Russ brought us down a copy the other day and it really *is* good. It's titled "And Then ...Along Comes The Association" and the cover is a wild double exposure. Out of sight!

Lennon And McCartney Win Three Composer's Awards

Winners of the Ivor Novello Awards, presented annually for the outstanding British compositions of the year, have just been announced. As expected, the Beatles walked off with three of the awards. Lennon and McCartney took both the first place and runner-up trophies in the category of Highest Certified Record Sales for a British composition in 1965. In first place was "We Can Work It Out" and coming in second was the Beatles' "Help!"

Lennon and McCartney's third award was won by "Yesterday" as the Oustanding Song of 1965. Runner-up in that category was the Jackie Trent English hit, "Where Are You Now," written by Jackie and Tony Hatch.

Donovan's "Catch The Wind" was voted the Outstanding Folk Song of the Year and the Tom Jones smash, "It's Not Unusual" written by Gordon Mills and Les Reed, was named the Outstanding Beat Song of 1965.

The Seekers' first number one hit, "I'll Never Find Another You," was named the Most Performed Work of The Year. In the Oustanding Novelty Composition category "A Windmill In Old Amsterdam," written by Ted Dicks and Myles Rudge, took the top honors with "Mrs. Brown You've Got A Lovely Daughter" coming in a close second.

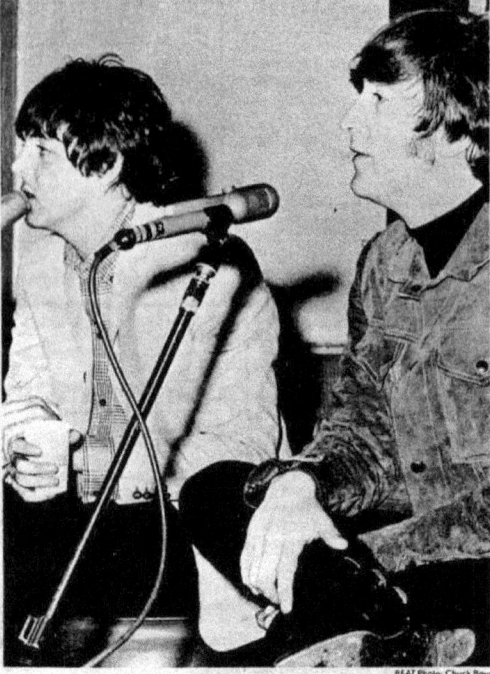
...McCARTNEY AND LENNON—TRIPLE WINNERS!

More Dates For Herman

Still more dates have been added to the long-term Herman's Hermits Stateside tour. The popular Hermits will add the Ohio State Fair to their tour where they will co-star with Perry Como on August 29, 30 and 31.

They then head for New York where they will play the Roosevelt Stadium on September 3 before flying back to England for a couple of weeks rest.

They return to the U.S. for a guest shot on "Ed Sullivan" on September 28 and the group won't get much of a chance to rest following the Sullivan stint because their agent, Danny Betesh, is negotiating a ten day Continental tour for the Hermits in October. Included will be three days in Germany, two days in Denmark, two days in Sweden and one day each in Norway, Austria and Switzerland.

Beach Boys Tour

The Beach Boys are set to arrive in England on October 25 but their dates still haven't been finalized! They have yet to decide if they'll do their Continental dates first or their British dates first. Either way, they're due to spend about a week in England.

Their "Pet Sounds" LP has just been released in Britain and made its debut at number nine on the album charts.

Eric Burdon Solo Singer; Paul Jones In Burdon Role

Eric Burdon is set to record his first solo effort upon his return from the U.S. The search for suitable material is already on but apparently nothing has been found yet.

No one has yet confirmed reports that the Animals will split immediately following their current Stateside tour and apparently Animal management is still hopeful that the group will resolve their differences before they reach England.

However, with Eric set to solo it doesn't look too hopeful that the Animals will continue as a group.

Paul Jones, ex-lead singer for the Manfred Mann, is taking Eric's place in "The Privilege." The movie began shooting on August 1 on location in London and Birmingham. The plot centers around a pop singer who turns into an "idol" and the power and effect he has on his fans.

Playing opposite Paul is England's top model, Jean Shrimpton. Neither Paul nor Jean have had any acting experience but Paul probably won't have to do much acting anyway since he *is* a pop singer who is something of an idol in England.

Immediately following the movie, Paul will head out on his first solo tour when he co-stars with the Hollies in October. The British tour will include 21 days but so far only ten dates have been confirmed.

On the record scene, Paul has just waxed his first solo for HMV and the record is expected to be released in mid-August.

...ERIC BURDON—solo singer.

KRLA ARCHIVES

Letters TO THE EDITOR

(Continued from Page 2)
all, it's the fans that account for most of the albums, so why cheat us? We resent what Capitol did, and we'll do anything to get the other cover. Why didn't they put out both covers so you could pick which ever one you wanted? Then maybe everybody would be happy.
Jane Powell

Hurt By Beatles

Dear *BEAT*:
I was one of those "few" who saw the Beatles' banned album cover for myself and I must say that I was not only shocked but deeply hurt. The Beatles used to mean so much to me and now they're like people I never knew. They've changed and I'm sorry. They no longer care about their fans — they're out only for themselves and their latest attempt at sick humor proves it.

Now they are out *only* to make money and I pity them for their loss of feeling. They've become hard and tough and what's worse, swell-headed. I know because I met them.

I think all their album cover was meant for was to have a good laugh at American fans, those people who have made them what they are today. You see, that cover was meant only for American release. The Beatles know the English market would avoid such an album cover like the plague. But they feel Americans are too stupid to avoid anything which has to do with the Beatles.

For what it's worth, that's my opinion. And I'm sorry it is because the four Beatles of two years ago were the greatest four people on the face of the earth. Too bad time changes most things.
Stella Nelson

Sponge It

BEAT:
For you Beatle fans that want "Yesterday . . . and Today," with the original cover, it's under the picture that's on now. Just take a sponge and hot water and very carefully peel off the top picture. You have to do it really slowly and carefully, or you'll wreck the bottom picture, too.
Vicke Lloyd

Open Season?

Dear *BEAT*:
I have just finished reading about the incident in the Philippines involving the Beatles. What is this . . . open season on the Beatles?

On top of all the things they're already supposed to be they now have been elected to the post of political ambassadors. Granted, they should put out a good image for their country but they shouldn't be obligated to do special shows for a nation's first family. I feel the discourtesy was on the part of the Filipinos. I could understand if the First Family was verbally insulted, but the people threw things and cursed at the Beatles without bothering to find out if there was a legitimate reason why the Beatles didn't show up. The Beatles claim they weren't told of the invitation and that is why they didn't show.

Whether this is true or not, this was still no excuse for the display that was put on. I think there should be a little apologizing on both sides.
Ann Marie

Sadler Wrong

Dear *BEAT*:
I'm writing in reference to the article you had in the July issue of *The BEAT*. It was about Sgt. Barry Sadler and the way he cut down long hair, this bit about shaking dandruff over the first three rows is ridiculous. I've had front row seats a lot of times for long-haired groups, and it's funny I've never gotten any dandruff shaken on me. If he thinks guys with long hair just shake their hair, then how come the long-haired groups are on the top charts all the time, for instance, the Stones. Has that Sadler ever really listened to some of Mick's songs? For that Sadler's own sake, why doesn't he just sit down and really listen to one of Mick's songs. They make sense; they all have meanings.

I do realize a lot of people are against long hair, but why can't they keep their feelings to themselves. You never see the Stones or any other long-haired group go through all the bother to write an article to cut down short hair. Why doesn't everyone just mind their own business and stop this cutting down and critizing. It's not really worth it all.
Mary Jean Tragna

A Reader Suggests

Dear *BEAT*:
I have to comment on several different topics in this one letter, so I hope you will print it all.

First: The idea of letters to the editor page is great. I would like to see a page devoted to this every week.

Second: Terri Hamann has a groovy idea in an advice column each week, as long as it is interesting and covers a wide range of problems.

Third: How about a classified section? At reasonable rates, it would be great for selling records, cars, pen pals and even a "Personals" section in which one could put in crazy messages.

Fourth: On Beatle L.P. cover. No one had a right to ban that. No one has a right to censor anything. That cover should have been put on the stands for those who wanted it. A lack of sales would have hurt the Beatles more than petty censorship.

Fifth: I am in love with Shirley Poston. I have to take seasick pills before and after reading her blitherings — she sends me on a trip into another world! Please print her picture so I can see the girl I love.

Thank you for all the space.
Mike Pearce

The BEAT welcomes your suggestions and comments, Mike. Let us know what you'd like to see included in your newspaper.
The BEAT

COMMENTS INVITED!
Send Correspondence To:
Letters, c/o The BEAT

Beatles Out?

Dear *BEAT*:
I can remember just a few months ago when it really was the "in" thing to say how great and talented The Beatles are and how fantastic "Rubber Soul" was. Now the "in" thing is to criticize them and to say how terrible and disgusting they are. Well, if that is how to be "in", I think I will be one of the "out" ones. To think that all of these people would completely change their minds about them just over one album is insanity. Anything can be taken wrong if you have a dirty mind.
A TRUE Beatle fan

'in' people are talking about...

The BEAT printing the words to "Enter The Young" months before the Association even decided to record it . . . Jerry Lewis' pussycat drowning . . . All of Bobby's friends refusing to believe it was the way they said it was . . . Jan recuperating from one and suing over another . . . Whether Dylan is or isn't . . . "Born To Raise Hell" and how gruesome and morbid some "songwriters" really are . . . Donovan's legal problems . . . The Stones popping up in Hollywood a week early . . . Them wanting to stay but possibly being forced to leave . . . Which "Louise" the Raiders are immortalizing on wax . . . The crazy buttons Russ wears.

PEOPLE ARE TALKING ABOUT the way Bo's Cookie can shake it . . . How the Kinks spend their sunny afternoons and wondering when they're going to cross

NAPOLEON XIV
Who he really is
Why he's being taken away
What his dog's name was
What he thinks is so funny
Why does he have the top disc

over . . . Whether Love is a four-letter word or a new sound . . . Don and Dolores having to read about it in *The BEAT* and what it all means to Cilla . . . Why thirteenth floor elevators are so hard to find . . . Money losing out to the Army . . . Dave's peeling shoulders . . . Sam's on-again, off-again beard and wishing it would stay off . . . How Paul originally wrote the words to "Paperback Writer" . . . Whether or not they'll find their names in Jim and Chris' book and most of them hoping they'll be forgotten . . . The time John Lennon got knocked down on the bus and if he remembers who did it and why . . . How the Stones thought they might walk on the waters while Ramsey is content with just wading in it . . . Nancy cooling off fast and wondering if it's temporary or permanent.

PEOPLE ARE TALKING ABOUT an unknown group having the number one record in the nation, proving how far a little hanky panky will go . . . The fuss over pop lyrics and just how much it all means anyway . . . The Righteous Brothers and their new choral group . . . How funny it would be if Paul Jones turned into a movie idol . . . Where Michelle has gone . . . Sinatra actually going through with it and wondering what he'd do if he heard the description of Mia currently making the rounds . . . Mike Love's beard and how you can only see his eyes now . . . Ringo's dreams and how much he digs the Would You Believe man . . . Ivor not being turned on to the Stones sound . . . That wild picture of Herman with a pint in one hand and a dart in the other . . . American pirates and what Uncle Sam will do.

PEOPLE ARE TALKING ABOUT the collapse James Brown had in California and wondering whose fault it was . . . The two up here who don't and the four who are among the 32 million who do . . . The Mothers freaking out . . . Mary having a baby girl . . . Donovan, the Rascals and Peter, Paul and Mary showing up for the Otis Redding show at the Apollo in New York . . . What happened to the Who . . . How many colors Pinkerton's Assorted wear . . . Whether George borrowed that straw hat from Pattie . . . Keith Richard being the only one available and keeping their fingers crossed.

KRLA ARCHIVES

HOTLINE LONDON
Dylan For Mann
Tony Barrow

After months of rumours, predictions and denials, I can tell you for sure that PAUL JONES is about to quit the MANFRED MANN five-some. Paul's replacement is singer MIKE D'ABO and he is featured on the first single cut by Manfred Mann for Philips Records in London. Title is "Just Like A Woman," penned by Bob Dylan.

Paul's final concert appearance with the Manfred team was on July 31 in Blackpool.

With "Sunny Afternoon" THE KINKS have scored their fourth Number One hit in the U.K. Now they're coming out with a new 14-title album made up of numbers which are all Kink-penned originals. After summer visits to a host of different European countries including Holland, Italy, Norway, Denmark, Finland and Austria, The Kinks hope to undertake their first tour behind the Iron Curtain where dates in Russia and Hungary are being lined up.

No less than 19 numbers will be woven into the action of the upcoming color movie "The Ghost Goes Gear" now in production here. The picture stars THE SPENCER DAVIS GROUP and DAVE BERRY plus several guest groups including the ST. LOUIS UNION. First scenes to be shot show Spencer and his boys in comedy sequences set in a stately home.

NEWS BRIEFS ... BEATLES bought sets of kimonos in Tokyo and sets of Indian sarees in New Delhi, luxury gifts for wives and friends ... Mystery still surrounds London recording plans of FRANK SINATRA now here for motion picture "The Naked Runner." Some reports say he will certainly go into the Pye studios to make an album and a single. Others say he has no intention of doing any sessions during his lengthy stay ... MANFRED MANN disc "Just Like A Woman" produced by American A&R man SHEL TALMY who was associated with all but most recent hits by THE WHO ... Next U.K. single by THE SPENCER DAVIS GROUP will be old Brenda Holloway fave "Till The End Of Time" ... While BEATLES in Far East MRS. CYNTHIA LENNON vacationed in Italy with infant JOHN JULIAN, MRS. PATTI HARRISON lazed in sunny South of France ... Married men with children—lead singer REG PRESLEY plus two of his TROGGS ... In the U.K. HERMAN'S Hollywood-made movie "Hold On" will go out next month as second feature with David McCallum/Robert Vaughn picture "One Of Our Spies Is Missing" ... DUSTY SPRINGFIELD to co-star with THE LOVIN' SPOONFUL for September/October U.K. concert tour ... South Londoner ROD CLARKE replaces retiring bass guitarist CLINT WARWICK in THE MOODY BLUES. KLAUS VOORMAN of now defunct PADDY, KLAUS and GIBSON group was offered the job but he turned it down to join MANFRED MANN instead ... Originally GEORGE HARRISON planned secret solo stopover in New Delhi to look at Indian musical instruments but other three Beatles plus Brian Epstein decided to join him.

Unfortunately this has to be my final "Hotline London" contribution to BEAT for the moment. As you can imagine things are getting a bit hectic for me in London now that the Beatles' August tour of the U.S. and Canada approaches. I've thoroughly enjoyed writing for you each week and I'm looking forward to meeting dozens of old and new friends when I'm in the area towards the end of August. Thanks for all your letters—see you soon.

— TONY BARROW

Beatle 'Revolver'

(Continued from Page 1)

"Got To Get You Into My Life" is the track we've heard so much about over the past few weeks although it has not been publicly named until now. Here a full-blooded brass sound backs Paul and I'd say those blasting trumpets constitute the nearest approach to the Memphis studio sound ever created on our side of the Atlantic. Forget the nonsense about this brass work being jazz-angled. It is R&B, but certainly not jazz.

I have no information (at the time of writing) about Capitol's plans to issue the "REVOLVER" material in America. Although three of the titles are already in your "Yesterday and Today" collection, eleven others remain un-issued in the U.S. and will obviously form Capitols' next album later this summer.

MY OVER-ALL REACTION TO THE "REVOLVER" MATERIAL ... Without doubt some younger Beatle People will find at least three or four of these recordings too complicated, too intelligent (musically) and/or too weird. On the other hand there is more than a fair sprinkling of perfectly straightforward performances ranging from Ringo's simple but extraordinarily infectious "Yellow Submarine" to the rocking "Doctor Robert," from the thoughtful "Eleanor Rigby" to the boisterous "Got To Get You Into My Life." On listening to the whole album, it becomes plain that The Beatles didn't waste any of those days and weeks between Easter and their June tour of Germany. Every track has been produced with perfectionist polish—one took over 55 hours of recording time to complete! Nobody is likely to be disappointed by the finished product—and that, after all, is the aim of any recording artist.

GARY LEWIS AND THE PLAYBOYS with their sailor host at the U.S. Naval Training Center in San Diego, California. As guests of the U.S. Navy, Gary and the group performed two concert shows for more than 20,000 service men and then were given a "grand tour" of the base and ships.

Gary Lewis Is Drafted

The draft board must have heard about the role Gary Lewis is playing in "Bye Bye Birdie" and liked it. Because the day after he arrived in Kansas City for rehearsals for the musical they drafted him.

Gary, who just received a coveted award as the most outstanding pop singer of the year, was ironically portraying a famous young rock and roll singer in the story who just got drafted. The musical can now be accused of type casting.

Gary said his Los Angeles draft board ordered him to report Dec. 5. That date was agreed on so he could go through with the scheduled performance dates for himself and the Playboys, his back-up group.

Gary, whose father is the famous entertainer Jerry Lewis, is currently riding the charts with "Green Grass." He will probably be allowed to record on a limited basis during his stay in the service.

Adults Dig Freckles

Freckle-faced teen-age girls who once took great pains to camouflage the marks need fret no longer. In fact, a current fad has made freckles so popular many girls with flawless complexions are painting freckles on their faces.

Once considered a handicap, freckles are now considered beauty marks to be coveted and admired. One beauty expert says the next step will be to match freckles to the color of a dress — for example, purple freckles with a purple dress. Polka-dot dresses might also provide some interesting combinations.

The fad isn't limited to teens alone. Indeed, it is the adults who are the greatest torchbearers of the trend.

Veteran makeup man Eddy Senz advises that painted freckles are not for every woman. He says the trend stems from adults' admiration of youth, but he warns:

"Freckles are part of the glow of youth and should not be hidden by the young. But it is wishful thinking for a mature woman to believe that freckles can do anything to improve her. The freckle fad is a part of this whole youth-worshipping kick."

Dionne Smash At Festival

Dionne Warwick and Oscar Brown got the Central Park Music Festival in New York off to a rousing start recently with capacity crowds the first and fourth nights when they appeared. Brown's show was entitled "Joy '66."

The house seating capacity is 4,400 and has 250 more spots for standing. Admission was one dollar per person.

The Beau Brummels and the Vargants drew a crowd of 2,800 the second night and the Sabicas drew 3,600 the third night.

KRLA ARCHIVES

PICTURES in the NEWS

AN ANNIVERSARY CAKE is enjoyed by The Kingston Trio (from left), Nick Reynolds, John Stewart and Bob Shane, at The Sahara Tahoe where the famed singing group is celebrating its 10th anniversary in show business. The cake was a surprise present from Mrs. Elva Miller, who is appearing at the hotel with the trio. The trio will record a 10th anniversary album for Decca release while at the Sahara Tahoe.

BRENDA LEE has been forced to cancel engagements for the first time in her 11-year career. An ear infection has become serious enough to confine her to her home in Nashville for at least a month.

DUSTY SPRINGFIELD'S Stateside tour has now been confirmed. After returning to Britain she is set to open with the Lovin' Spoonful at Finsbury Park on Sept. 7.

THE YOUNG RASCALS have just been awarded a Gold Record for their nationwide number one, "Good Lovin'." It marks the first Goldie for the group who received public recognition last summer. Their debut disc, "I Ain't Gonna Eat Out My Heart Anymore" was a fair-sized hit and they immediately followed it up with the million selling "Good Lovin'." They are scheduled for a series of one-nighters August 10-20 throughout California and then are to appear for one week in Hawaii. Tentative plans now have them scheduled for their European debut in October.

Dave Carr Is Married

Dave Carr, organist and pianist with the Fortunes, was recently married to a 19-year-old secretary. Dave, 21, was married to Beverly Spierden on July 21st at Wanstead, England, which is the bride's home town.

Dave was the second member of the group to take marriage vows. The other member of the Fortunes who is married is Barry Pritchard. The rest of the group were present at the ceremony and played later at the reception.

The Fortunes are currently negotiating for a series of dates in Belgium from September 8th.

...DAVE CARR

...ROD ALLEN

Rod Allen Is Injured

Rod Allen, the Fortunes' lead singer, was hurt at a Fortunes' personal appearance at the Lincoln Starlite Room when fans dragged him from the stage.

Allen injured his back as fans pulled him off the stage and he fell on top of his guitar. He was rushed to the hospital where his back was treated and will resume bookings with the group.

Allen's injury follows on the heels of a riot involving the Fortunes when they played the Isle Of Man. Rod escaped injury then but two of his fellow Fortunes were not so lucky.

THE SMOTHERS BROTHERS lost their television series but have come up with featured roles in an NBC special, "Alice Through The Looking Glass." The special is set to air Nov. 6.

KRLA ARCHIVES

HOTLINE LONDON SPECIAL

Cliff Bennett First To Cover 'Revolver'

By Tony Barrow

Whenever a new album by THE BEATLES goes on the market, we know to expect a flood of cover-version singles from different parts of the world.

The Beatles don't particularly mind the idea that anything from two to ten unknown groups and/or singers may well make the grade via Lennon-McCartney album numbers within the next couple of months. Like any other composing team they get brought down when they hear a cover version which is sub-standard. But then The Beatles have standards which are high, and they are always severely critical of badly produced recordings whether one of their own songs is involved or not.

Beatle Blessings

Over the years, The Beatles have been only too willing to co-operate with artists who want to record their material. There's a very long list of people who have hit the chart jackpot with Lennon-McCartney songs and done so with the fullest blessing of the boys themselves.

So far as British artists are concerned, early Beatle-penned material brought chart success to people ranging from CILLA BLACK and THE FOURMOST to BILLY J. KRAMER and even THE ROLLING STONES who once enjoyed fringe-of-the-charts sales with "I Wanna Be Your Man." I don't need to remind you of the value of Lennon-McCartney numbers in the rise to fame of PETER AND GORDON and THE SILKIE.

Now it looks as though another of Brian Epstein's acts — CLIFF BENNETT AND THE REBEL ROUSERS — will click on both sides of the Atlantic via the number "GOT TO GET YOU INTO MY LIFE" which comes from the "Revolver" program.

'Revolver' Named

Cliff was with The Beatles when they toured Germany at the end of June. In their backstage dressing room at the Grugahalle in Essen, John, Paul, George and Ringo were able to listen for the first time to a finished acetate of their new album. It was flown in specially from London so that the boys could agree on a final running order for the fourteen titles. At that stage the album didn't even have a name. It was not until the following week (in Tokyo) that The Beatles and Brian finally agreed to Paul's suggestion, "Revolver."

The dressing room at Essen was particularly crowded that night because the boys invited Cliff's Rebel Rousers to join them at that first exciting listening session. When they came to "GOT TO GET YOU INTO MY LIFE" it was Paul who turned to Cliff and remarked that this would be an ideal vehicle for the Bennett combo to record. Cliff listened to Paul's wildly rhythmic interpretation of the lyrics, to the blasts of brass and to the solid brick-built beat.

"This is the track everyone's been writing about without knowing the title" explained George. "We brought in three trumpets and a couple of tenors. We used jazz men so everyone got the idea they must be playing jazz for us. They're not as you can hear."

Cliff and his Rebel Rousers were very enthusiastic about the song. In the last 48 hours of the German tour the two groups went into a series of intense huddles exchanging ideas about a Cliff Bennett version of "GOT TO GET YOU INTO MY LIFE."

Then The Beatles flew on from Hamburg to Tokyo and the Rebel Rousers headed home to London.

Paul Assists

By the time The Beatles returned from Japan, Manila and New Delhi, Cliff was ready to take the new number into the recording studio. In fact, Paul attended the two sessions at which "GOT TO GET YOU INTO MY LIFE" was recorded. Cliff no longer works with an A & R man — he produces all his own records. On this occasion an unofficial assistant in the production of the session was Paul McCartney! Rush release for the Cliff Bennett single was organized and it came out in the U.K. on Friday, August 5 —

...CLIFF BENNETT

the same day that the same label (Parlophone) put out The Beatles' "Revolver" album. So CLIFF BENNETT AND THE REBEL ROUSERS became the first group to have produced a single from the "Revolver" bundle — and, to date, the only outfit to be invited by The Beatles to cover one of the 14 new numbers. There's a strong possibility that another of Brian's groups — THE FOURMOST — will record something from "Revolver" — there'll be between 20 and 30 re-

volver." Beyond that, I'm sure cordings from the album before the middle of September. Most of these won't even be heard by The Beatles until they're released. So we're left to wonder just who will and who won't crash into the Top Ten via "Revolver" titles. Apart from Cliff Bennett, I'll bet we have at least five other entirely new headline names amongst the best-sellers once the flood of "Revolver" cover versions reaches a peak!

Three Shangri-Las: Grooving In Utopia

An idyllic utopia, a hidden paradise. This is how Webster pictured a Shangri-la; as an exotic little dream world with deep, beautiful truths.

And in the steaming sixties the word has continued to pack its same asthetic qualities. It is the fitting title for three young girls who are so different and refreshing that they are in a sort of utopian category all their own.

The Shangri-las' sound is offbeat. It is a weird, distinct sensation with taunting lyrics that contain sometimes-overlooked, deep-rooted messages. It is something you would expect to hear in Greenwich Village or in a smoke-filled room housing a comglomeration of beat poets.

The Shangri-las' initial hit, "Remember (Walking In The Sand)," was number one on the charts from coast to coast. The song captured all the sounds of the sea — the cries of the gulls, the steady roar of the ocean and the soft crunch of sand underfoot.

It is a girl's unfading remembrance of soft nights with her lover by the ocean.

Most of the songs by the Shangri-las have that same element of beauty but all seem to contain the same degree of a serene sadness. Their latest release, "Past, Present and Future", which also is a top seller, is probably their most hauntingly sad song yet.

The success of the three girls from Queens, New York is said to have started a trend. In a time when almost everything musically successful is coming out of England, the Shangri-las are consistently listed in the top selling charts of every city in the country. Their popularity has spread from the shores of the U.S. to the Orient, Australia and to Europe where they finished a highly successful tour.

The girls are only recently out of high school, yet they have traveled most parts of the world and have swept across the United States many times.

RUMORS CONTINUE

Paul and Jane

By Sue Barry

There remains today one bachelor Beatle — his name is, of course, Paul McCartney. Two years ago no one would have bet a halfpenny that Paul would be the last single Beatle, for it is around him and Jane Asher that the most often and violent rumors of marriage have persisted. Yet today, after the marriage of George Harrison, Paul finds himself the only unmarried Beatle. But, although Paul does date other girls, it is common knowledge that he prefers the company of Jane Asher to that of any other girl.

Paul first met Jane in 1963. Jane was a young seventeen year old actress who had been asked to do an interview with the Beatles for a radio show.

The story goes that after the official business was completed the boys asked her to a party at a friend's flat.

For many months Paul and Jane kept their meetings secret, but eventually their privacy was shattered when in December of 1963 they were spotted together at the Prince of Wales Theater. From this date on they were completely harrassed by marriage rumors.

Some people claimed to have been at the wedding, seen copies of insurance policies for the two or to have seen the marriage certificate. An example of these fantasies was the case of Noel Harrison. He had been quoted saying that he had been at the wedding. His reply was: "Don't know how these stories got around. All I can say is that it is all a complete load of nonsense." This was even before we Americans had ever heard of the Beatles!

By the time the Beatles invaded "the colonies" in February, 1964, Paul and Jane were seeing quite a bit of each other.

On his return to England, Paul continued dating Jane, this time very much in the eye of the public, saying, "We are not going to dodge the cameras any longer. We are still not married. But if I ever marry Jane, there will be no engagement, just a swift, simple ceremony."

It was not long after this that Walter Winchell reported on March 14 that "Paul McCartney, 21, was secretly married 72 hours ago in London to Jane Asher, 22." This story was followed up a few weeks later by a quote from a letter that read: "For goodness sake, don't breathe this to a soul. Jane and Paul were married in London. I was at the wedding." Paul answered with a quick retort that he was not married.

But even the word of Paul himself would not stop the onslaught of marriage rumors and when Ringo and Maureen and Paul and Jane journeyed to the Virgin Islands in May of 1964, the press still insisted that a marriage between the two had taken place.

It was not until the day of Ringo's marriage that people became satisfied that if a Beatle got married he would let it be known to the world. Only then did the ugly rumors about Paul and Jane calm down a bit.

But what about Paul's girlfriend? What kind of a person is she? What does she hope for?

Jane Asher, a red haired, blue-eyed actress was born in London on April 5, 1946. She is 5-ft. 5-in. tall and weighs 112 pounds, lives with her parents in the Harley Street area of London where Paul often visits with her. Jane's shy manner has a hint of dignity inherited from her wealthy London background.

She and Paul are often seen together at the famous Ad Lib in London's West End when she is not working. For Miss Asher is an accomplished actress and was so long before she met Paul.

About her career Jane says, "My career as an actress is very important and I've got a long way to go before I could think of marriage. Acting is my life. At the moment this comes first." But looking ahead Jane says that her main ambition is: "The same as every other single girl. To eventually get married and have children. Nothing unusual."

To date Jane and Paul are still not married. No one knows when or where Paul will get married, but he says this, "When will I get married? That's simple, when I find someone I want to marry. And when I find her I'll marry her, career's end or not. I like my success, it's been great, but I don't think any Beatle would put it ahead of his personal happiness, do you?"

KRLA ARCHIVES

The Adventures Of Robin Boyd

©1965 Shirley Poston

When Robin Boyd discovered that Sonny and Cher's living room was filled with stars, she instantly regretted that they were of the five-cornered rather than the Hollywood variety.

She even instantly-er regretted that she was seeing the aforementioned stars because George the Genie had just yanked her out of the birdcage by her very beak, and Ringo the Famous (whoops.. angel) was banging her over the head with his halo.

Shrieking a number of things better left *un-*shrieked (and even *better* left un-*printed*) Robin severed George's thumb at his very wrist, chomped a nasty hole in Ringo's halo and fluttered toothlessly out of reach.

"Come *down* here," George commanded as she flapped wildly about. (About what?) (Get serious, kiddo).

Flying High

"Go smell exhaust pipes..." she bellowed, lighting on the chandelier (no pun intended).

Suddenly, the sound of larfter (not to be confused with the sound of musick) re-filled the air.

Robin glared at George, but he wasn't larfing. Then she glared at Ringo, but he wasn't larfing either. Robin shrugged. "And that goes for your cat, too..." she further bellowed.

Suddenly George *was* larfing. So was Ringo. So was Pauley, who appeared out of thin air and appeared to be rolling right on the very floor. And so was John, who appeared out of pleasingly-plump air and appeared to be rolling on the very floor right to the left of Pauley. (Hah?).

Meanwhile

Robin snarled. Glad as she was to see these utter wretches, it was hardly appropriate for them to be fiddling about while Rome (not to mention her mother) was burning and Sonny and Cher had gone out of their chords.

However, glowering a lot only increased rather than decreased their cackling and pointing. And finally, so mad she couldn't see straight (or wouldn't have been able to had she not already been blind as six bats), Robin took a deep breath and screeched "Liverpool!"

(An act she later referred to as her first mistake — in that particular set, of course — because if she thought she'd had problems during her *first* performance on a chandelier, she soon found that being smashed to smithereens on the lid of a tea pot had certain advantages over her encore).

In other words, (English would be appropriate) (not to mention appreciated), the moment she said the magic word, she turned back into her sixteen-year-old self, at which time both she *and* the chandelier shattered to the floor in a series of quivering lumps.

Now, a person would think (and scurry swiftly to the next page if they did) that at least *one* of the four other persons witnessing this tragedy would come to (that would be nice, also) the aid of the remains of the party of the first part. But, no... They were still having their own party...

In fact, the *lot* of them were now rolling hysterically about the floor.

"*Oafs*," she hisped, struggling to her ex-feet. "*Dolts*," she added, crunching George's remaining thumb, hauling out a handful of Pauley's midnight mop and stomping savagely on Ringo's sore wing.

For The Birds

"You twits are for the *birds!*" she bellowed at full volume, resisting the urge to bite John in the leg instead of kicking him.

Needless to say, this sent the aforementioned twits off into regales of larfter. Needless-er to say, Robin, who despite her anger was having trouble keeping a straight face (and frankly didn't much care to, as she was rather attached to her crooked one), began to snort noisily and was soon augmenting their rolling with a whole lot of hysterical rocking.

Then it happened. First George ceased his chortling and rushed rest of her) (and he's been known to).

"Are you okay?" he asked, patting her tenderly.

Robin wrenched away. (When she wanted her tenderly patted by *that* nit, she would ring a loud bell).

Then Ringo rasped his racous roaring to a sudden halt and winged (wang?) over to join them.

"You poor, dear child," he soothed.

Robin, feeling the former but hardly the latter, gave him her special Fangs-A-Lot-Fella snarl.

Then Pauley gasped a final giggle and John wheezed a last whoop (if *you* thing this is getting tiresome, how do you think I feel?) (I know, with me fingers, with me fingers), and dashed over to help in the simpering.

A Tender Pat

(If the truth were know, John also *re*-patted her tenderly, but let's leave well enough alone or George just might give them both a large pat in the olde pan). (Although Robin has turned into a *very* partial (as in plate) bird, John the Genie has been known to run George the Same a close second). (Not, however, to hear *him* tell it).

"But... but... not to mention but..." Robin sputtered cleverly at this unexpected burst of attention.

"But what?" they chorused kindly.

"But I got in the wrong car..." she began.

"So?" they chimed.

"But I didn't come home all *night!*" she continued.

Trouble Galore

"S'okay!" they re-chimed.

"But Sonny and Cher put me in a cage and I got carried away and talked and sang and now they're cowering somewhere and besides I totaled their chandelier and my Byrd glasses and am in all *kinds* of the trouble you told me to stay out of," she completed breathlessly.

"S'allright!" they re-*re*-chimed. Robin's chin dropped. "I don't get it," she said, picking it up.

"I've decided you don't need to reform after all, except for the whoppers," Ringo revealed.

"And your mother won't remember a thing about your latest moronic move — I mean, this particular incident," George grinned.

"And Sonny and Cher won't either," Pauley put in.

"And I'll meet you later," John joshed (you *bet*).

Then, as if by magic (if you don't believe in it yet, stick around) (in fact, stick around *long* enough and you'll believe *anything*), the chandelier re-grouped for its ex-crystals and tinkled intact to the ceiling.

"Gasp," Robin gasped. (Repition 4 *EVER!*) For it was then that she knew what she must do.

She must get the holy moley cause there was only one *possible* reason why these four afourmentioned oafs were being so nice to her in spite of all the chaos she'd caused.

They *wanted* something.

And if you think she turned purple at the thought of what that something might *be*, you should have seen her turn *plaid* when she found out...

(To Be Continued Next Week)

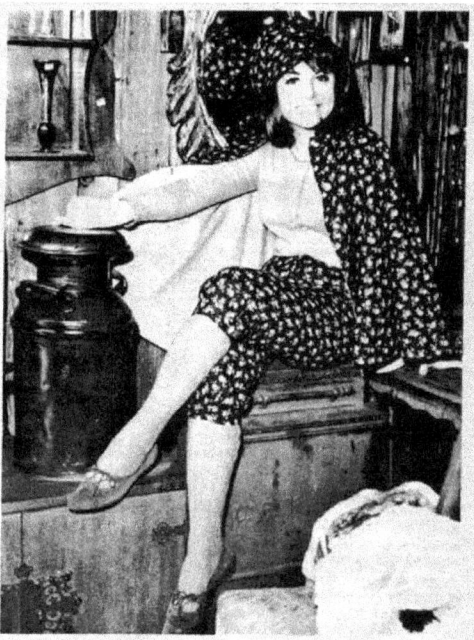

JONNA GAULT... the world's only female sincomperneer.

Ordinary Life? Not For Jonna

By Mike Tuck

Jonna Gault can do almost anything — and has. At 19, she is so independent it is sheer folly to try and predict anything she will do. And her talents are so intense and widely distributed she is often compared to Barbara Streisand.

Her mere presence causes a stir wherever she appears — whether at the Hungry i in San Francisco or on nationwide TV. She is now engrossed in her first production of "a hard-rock record," entitled "Come On Home," and is fulfilling a lifelong ambition.

"I always wanted to do this type of thing," she says, "but everytime I would attempt it I would get all this advice from people who wanted me to sound like someone else. The result was that I didn't really sound like anybody."

Some of the fiercest battles of modern history have taken place between Jonna Gault and record companies. "They just never let me do what I want," she says.

"I once had what I thought was a very funny record entitled 'Oh, Sob, You're the Cause of it All,'" and a record company brought me to New York to record it. Well... they seemed to think that Sob was a boy's name, and they insisted I change it to Bob."

That did it for that record company. Jonna switched.

But her affiliation with the next company was equally distasteful for Jonna. "I was recording a song and the producer kept screaming 'sing dumber, sing dumber,' and what in the world does 'sing dumber' mean?

It means Jonna Gault changed companies again.

Only with her present company, Reprise Records, she is in charge of every aspect of her records. It seemed the only solution. "Now I can arrange everything just the way I originally had in mind," she says. "I've really had a lot of fun doing my present record."

Jonna is now billed as the world's only female sincomprerneer (a combination of singer, composer, performer and engineer) and there aren't too many males who can make the same claim.

"The way I look at it," she reflected, "records allow you to utilize every facility of talent you have. Records are kind of immortal, in that you can play them back as many times as you like and they never really die."

Ever since Jonna Gault was old enough to talk she has been singing. Her parents were Russian Adagio dancers and she admittedly was "just a showbiz kid." It was during one of her parents' performances — while they were balanced in a delicate, precarious position — that she rushed onto the stage and made her unscheduled debut with "God Bless America."

"I was backstage and can still see the whole thing quite vividly," she remembers. "I don't know what made me do it... I just ran out and began singing. Ironically, the crowd loved it and after that we put it in the act."

Jonna Gault is like that — an individualist who does whatever she feels. About a year ago she was reading a novel by Ayn Rand and was so taken by the leading character she decided to use his name. The fact that his name was masculine was of little importance... with a little feminine ingenuity that could be changed. So "Jonna Gault" was born.

KRLA ARCHIVES

Freddie And Cilla Cancel Their Manila Appearances

Cilla Black and Freddie and the Dreamers have cancelled plans to appear in Manila following the treatment received by the Beatles when they allegedly snubbed the country's First Lady. Contradictory reports have since been filtering in. The Beatles claim they're innocent of any intentional snub while the promoters of their Manila concert declare that the Beatles knew of the invitation well in advance and that it was Brian Epstein who refused to allow the Beatles to attend the luncheon.

Anyway, the Beatles were roughed up at the Manila airport — regardless of whose fault it was. And now Freddie and Cilla have cancelled their scheduled stop-offs in Manila. However, Freddie's agent revealed that his cancellation was only partially due to the Beatle trouble. "The main factor is the financial position of the promoters, who should have sent us an advance deposit and the air tickets but have failed to do so," said the group's agent.

No reason was given for Cilla's decision not to play Manila but since Brian Epstein manages both the Beatles and Miss Black no reason was really needed.

Freddie and his Dreamers have just completed their American tour and have recorded their "Short Shorts" stage routine for release as their next Stateside single. They've been having considerable difficulty lately in producing a hit single here in America. But they're going to give it another try with the old "Short Shorts" — Freddie style.

...CILLA BLACK PREPARES TO TAKE-OFF WITH THE BACHELORS INSTEAD OF FREDDIE.

A Kink To N.Y.

Ray Davies, chief Kink, made a surprise visit to New York last week along with the Kinks' managers, Robert Wace and Grenville Collins. The visit was to meet with Allen Klein, business manager for the Rolling Stones.

Klein has recently been responsible for negotiating recording deals for the Stones, Herman's Hermits and the Who. The Kinks' records have been independently produced by Shel Talmy but released in America on the Warner Brothers label.

Supposedly, the Kinks are securely tied to both Talmy and Warner Brothers for some years to come. However, Klein has just made a deal with Talmy whereby Andrew Oldham has taken over the Who's recording contract from Talmy. Perhaps this is what he's after for the Kinks?

Anyway, the group isn't taking any chances on air strikes. They've chartered their own jet for an up-coming European tour. The tour kicks off on September 3 in Holland and goes to Rome on the 5th and 6th, Germany September 9-13 and Scandinavia 17-25.

Austria and Sweden will see the Kinks during the first two weeks of October. They are then scheduled to return to Britain but there is a possibility that late October will find the Kinks in Hungary and Russia. However, negotiations are still going on with no definite word as to whether or not the Kinks will be allowed behind the Iron Curtain.

The group's latest smash English single, "Sunny Afternoon," is still riding at the top of the charts and their new album, "Face To Face," is set for British release August 12.

Crispian's Coming

Crispian St. Peters, controversial British pop star, is set for a two week promotional tour of the U.S. in October. Crispian's version of "Pied Piper" is currently riding high on the U.S. charts but this will be the first glimpse of him on our side of the Atlantic.

The Stateside tour will come immediately after his three week tour of Australia and the Far East. As of now, no dates have been finalized but Lloyd Greenfield, U.S. agent for St. Peters, is busy negotiating dates for the Pied Piper.

Yardbirds Authors

The Yardbirds Stateside tour opened on August 2 but the group didn't sit still waiting for it to begin. On the contrary, they finished their latest album and every single track was written by the group!

Jim McCarty, Yardbirds' drummer, wrote the jacket notes and Chris Dreja, rhythm guitarist, designed the album cover.

Jim and Chris are working feverishly to finish up a book they're writing about life with the Yardbirds. They hope to have the whole thing completed before their American tour opens. Needless to say, Yardbird fans are already lining up in front of book stores demanding the book!

...JIM McCARTY — drummer turned author.

...CHRIS DREJA — writing book.

British Groups On See-Saw

The barrage of English pop groups currently touring the U.S. are having their ups and downs. The Rolling Stones played the Forest Hills Tennis Stadium in New York to an estimated audience of 9,000, leaving approximately 5,000 seats empty.

Herman and the Animals failed to sell-out when they played the Sports Arena in Los Angeles and the Dave Clark Five also faced some disappointments along their tour route.

Promoters are reasoning that meager attendance in certain cities is due simply to the fact that too many groups are touring at the same time and fans can't scrape up enough money to see them all.

LENNY'S BOOT PARLOR
1448 GOWER STREET
HOLLYWOOD, CALIFORNIA 90028

Send For It! Get It! **LENNY'S FREE CATALOG** with the latest in clothes and boots IS READY. Just your name and address on a 4c post card and it's yours.

KRLA ARCHIVES

...THE MINDBENDERS (l. to r.) Eric Stewart, Bob Lang and Ric Rothwell

Generally Mindbenders

By Rochelle Reed

When the first days of the air strike halted travel for many performers, one group that found their schedule bent out of shape were none other than the mindbending Mindbenders, three charming Englishmen who landed in Hollywood for exactly one day.

So naturally they dropped into The BEAT office.

"What are you doing in Hollywood?" I asked.

"Nothing," all three replied.

Then they leaped into a discussion of their visa problems, travel problems, their philosophies on each and how applications must be made by each individual promoter in each state where they appear.

Sadly

This, they said sadly, shaking their heads, was why they couldn't do television shows, club appearances or even go out and look around a radio station.

But on the brighter side, the Mindbenders reported that their newest single, "Ashes to Ashes," was about to be released any moment and they were anxiously waiting to hear it themselves.

"Ashes to Ashes," they explained, was written by the same teenage girls from New York who wrote "Groovy Kind of Love."

"They met us at the airport," Bob said, "They're complete idiots, but great fun," Ric added.

"Generalizing," blond Bob said, "'Ashes' is generally the same as 'Groovy.'"

It will be released with an LP, titled appropriately "Mindbenders," according to Bob, or "Groovy Kind of Love," according to Ric, or as Eric decided, "'Mindbenders,' subtitled 'Groovy Kind of Love.'"

Anyway, we got the idea.

The Mindbenders, who officially split with Wayne Fontana last October, are "on talking terms with Wayne," Bob said. There wasn't any argument, he explained, just that Wayne wanted to go on alone as a solo singer.

When he isn't singing, 19-year-old Bob is admittedly "a discotheque fiend." "I go to a place in Manchester called The Phonograph."

But both Ric and Eric were shaking their heads.

"He doesn't go there?" I asked.

"No, he goes there," Ric said, "I don't."

"Oh. Where do you go?"

"I go to Mr. Smith's."

Eric was still shaking his head. "They don't go there?" I asked.

"They go there. I don't."

"Oh again," I said. "Where do you go?"

"I don't."

"You don't go anywhere?" I asked.

He kept shaking his head. "I see enough of the sweet life on tour," Eric replied.

That ended that.

The weather intrigued all of us and the Mindbenders explained that their native Manchester right now is a little like San Francisco, but with an average temperature of about 50 to 60 degrees.

The Mindbenders, collectively, didn't like the controversial Beatle album cover, to put it mildly.

"Yeech..." said Ric.

"It's the sickest thing we've ever seen," they said jointly.

"Of course," Bob added, "the Beatles can afford to make a mistake – they're big enough."

The Mindbenders seriously disagree, however, with anyone who says that the Beatles are losing their hold on the music world.

"They aren't going down at all," Eric said. "They're still 10 years ahead of everybody."

Eric, a bit of an intellectual when it comes to observations on the music scene, is convinced that groups will last and not be overshadowed by solo singers, sometimes predicted as the next big craze.

"Groups have got to last," the 21-year-old singer said, "you couldn't put a solo singer in a ballroom. No, groups are your most transportable package."

In a fast moving conversation – much to fast for notes – the Mindbenders, their manager and I discussed the difference between American and British groups. The main thoughts of the Mindbenders were these:

They feel the majority of American groups just grow long hair, wear what they want and think they have captured what makes a British group.

But the Mindbenders say that British groups have a *sound* and *talent* that American groups either can't or won't imitate.

A Steal?

However, they confess that the British have taken American music – namely rhythm and blues – and watered it down to sell as their own.

"We stole it," Eric admits. But this doesn't mitigate the Mindbenders' feeling towards American groups.

An American group of a different variety – namely Indians – is a great favorite of one Mindbender.

Ric, 22, a small, tan, sunglassed package of a singer, announced that when he left Hollywood, they were going to Arizona to see Indians.

"Lots of Indians," he said. "I like Indians. Scalping. I like that, the way they scalp people."

I informed Ric that Phoenix wasn't full of scalp-hungry Indians, a fact that disappointed him immensely. So he decided to walk up and down Hollywood instead, looking for Elvis Presley.

California: Gangs, Vietniks and Surfers

By Gil McDougall

Reading press reports from California it is very easy for an Englishman to get a completely false impression of the Golden State. To the unitiated, California may seem to be a land of Vietniks, motorcycle gangs, and surfers. Naturally, anyone who is able to take time out and really get to know California finds this to be a false image. Right?

I have lived in California myself, but some of my friends who haven't had the opportunity, revealed their thoughts on Californians in the following descriptions.

Vietniks: Vietniks are usually college students, and come in various sizes – with or without guitars. Vietniks' idea of happiness is for the campus to be within walking distance of a fair-sized military base. Some of those posters are pretty heavy. Vietniks dislike draft cards, the local police force, Barry Sadler, Lyndon B. Jonson, and Hells Angels. Vietniks like beards, long hair, casual clothes (spelled s-l-o-p-p-y) Barry McGuire, Bob Dylan, folk music and the Beatles.

Visitors to California will easily recognize Vietniks as they are often carrying such signs as, "Yankee go home," and "Mao is gear." Vietniks often organize protest parties – anyone welcome but be sure to bring a supply of well worded protests – and the party will sometimes culminate with select members of the group burning their draft cards. After this ceremony the draft card burners will demonstrate their vocal capabilities as they are dragged away by the FBI.

Color them red.

Motorcycle gangs (who shall be nameless) also fancy beards and long hair. However, a close scrutiny will show the difference between Vietniks and the leather boys. A member of a motorcycle gang will often be found sporting a beard, a hangover, several swastikas, an unemployment check, a pocket edition of Mein Kampf, and a citation from the police department.

Motorcycle gangs like motorcycles, a good time, demonstrating against demonstrators, the fifth amendment, and the Beatles. They dislike Vietniks, the law, draft dodgers, and the draft.

Color them funny.

Teenagers, up to the age of thirty, can be surfers, mods or anything else but they appear in their youth to be the most unaffected of California's inhabitants. Teens like British beat groups, British styles, American money, and the Beatles. Refreshingly they don't dislike anything in particular. They do, however, have some misconceptions about the ways of the world. For instance, many of them believe that John Lennon's house in the country is called Chequers, and that Harold Wilson is Brian Epstein's assistant road manager.

Color them red, white and happy.

The teens' young brothers and sisters, preteens, are also happy with life, and their tastes are really very similar. Preteens like Batman, comic books, Buggs Bunny, Donald Duck, and Herman's Hermits.

And then there are the adults – the instigators of the whole scene. Adults like evening television, afternoon television, morning television, imitating their kids, bowling, their bank balance and the Beatles.

Color them bored.

Adults are dancing, acting, and living so much after the fashion of their children that it is often hard to tell them apart. Out on the highways, however, it is fairly easy, as adults apparently believe it to be illegal to drive in any lane other than the one on the extreme left.

Well, that's it. Would you believe that the preceding image is the image conveyed by California to the rest of the world?... Would you believe upper Michigan?

HERB ALPERT IN MOVIES

HERBIE IN "ICE CREAM SUIT."

Herbie Alpert is going to be a movie star yet! And why not? He's done everything else. The idea has been in Herbie's head for quite sometime but up until now he has been unable to find a suitable script.

Apparently, he has now found one because Alpert is making a deal for "The Wonderful Ice Cream Suit," the Ray Bradbury play which enjoyed about a year's run in 1965. Both Herb and Bradbury admit that the deal is about to be signed and Bradbury is set to begin writing the movie script.

The completed script is expected to be in Alpert's hands by December and will soon after go into production as a giant musical. Neither parties would reveal the price.

On the personal appearance side of the Herb Alpert story, it appears that Herbie and his TJB are now the proud record holders for attendance at the famous Greek Theatre.

KRLA ARCHIVES

ELVIS!

By Louise Criscione

It all seems like a million years ago. The long side-burns, the machine-operated hips, the outraged cries of "immorality" and "filth" which turned into a legend. A legend which is still living, still here, still the King.

The decade between 1956 and 1966 brought with it changes which were sometimes small but mostly drastic. Time has left absolutely nothing untouched. Perhaps no where has it left more of a mark than on the field of popular music.

To be sure, in 1956 the best-selling records were being called "pop music" but the name is the only thing which remains. Most of The Top are dead as far as the world of pop is concerned. Bill Haley, Fats Domino, Pat Boone, Frankie Avalon, Fabian, Rick Nelson. All gone. Some to other fields of entertainment. Some to oblivion.

Only The Legend

Only the Legend remains. The man they said couldn't last. The "horrible" spectacle who mothers attempted (unsuccessfully) to keep their daughters from liking. The man who has made more money, set more records and been heard by more people in the *world* than any other artist in the history of the record business.

Elvis is still here—he's today. And despite everything—time, rumors, criticism, out-of-date singles, a hitch in the Army, secrecy, the British invasion—Elvis Presley is every inch alive and happening.

No one, including the Beatles, has ever been able to match him. Quite naturally. How can anyone in the span of two years hope to accomplish what Elvis has achieved in ten?

The amazing aspect of Elvis' long career is not that he remains unequalled but rather that he remains at all. For the most part, the fans who discovered Elvis, who defied their elders and made him the biggest star in existence are now "elders" themselves. They're married and have children of their own. Yet, somehow Elvis has managed to keep the majority and add thousands more so that today he can sit back in secrecy and still chalk up box office smashes and best-selling albums.

Greta Garbo?

You'll never see an interview with Elvis. He doesn't give any. You seldom run across a picture of him. His entourage sees to that. Reporters stand a thread-thin chance of gaining admittance to his movie sets. Col. Parker makes sure of that. He makes no personal appearances and no television dates. He doesn't need to.

He is occasionally seen around the Hollywood clubs. Photographers and reporters are everywhere. But you'll never see pictorial evidence of Elvis' visit; nor will you read a quote obtained from Elvis. Because that's the way the Elvis of today operates.

I suppose you *could* conceivably catch a quick glimpse of Elvis if you found the narrow street up in Bel Air where the Presley manor is located and then waited patiently for hours (or days). If you were extremely lucky, Elvis' gold Cadillac would appear. You know, the one with the gold interior lights, the double row of gold plated engraved records, the center lounge, the gold refreshment bar that freezes its own ice cubes and the gold plated swivel television. And hidden in there somewhere, perhaps you'd see Elvis himself. But don't count on it. You're facing million to one odds.

That's what makes Elvis' continual success so fantastic. His physical absence. You can't see him except in his movies and perhaps this is what makes his movies so popular. And they *are* popular—make no mistake of that. To date they've grossed over $130 million! Quite a bit of which is profit since Presley movies are usually filmed in three or four weeks, whereas many films take months and months to complete.

GI Joe

The biggest threat to Elvis' career occurred in 1958 when the Army called his number. The world sat back waiting for Elvis to become an entertaining GI. But they were fooled. Elvis went into the Army as a regular GI Joe. He asked for, and received, no special privileges.

Critics heralded the fall of Presley. One even went so far as to say that before he even learned to salute properly his fans would have transferred their affections to someone else. They too were fooled. When Elvis returned from Germany he was every bit as popular as the day he left. He had not utilized the "star" bit and his Army buddies had found him no different than anyone else.

Civilian Again

He was released in early 1960, and during one of the worst snow storms in New Jersey, Elvis held his first press conference at Fort Dix. Newsmen from television, radio, magazines and newspapers trugged through the mountains of snow to get a close look at Sergeant Presley.

Many of the reporters were downright shocked to discover that Elvis had not changed. Nor had his show business star fallen one inch. He immediately launched into his first movie following his Army release, "GI Blues." A movie which broke all box office records. He renewed his unbroken chain of hit singles with "Stuck On You," "It's Now Or Never" and "Are You Lonesome Tonight." All were released during 1960 and all were million sellers.

The opposition was forced to surrender. Apparently, nothing could stop Elvis. Nothing could force him to abdicate his musical throne.

Pop idols came and went—none of them even came *near* to challenging Elvis. Then in 1964 the biggest contenders for Elvis' title appeared in the form of four charming, long-haired singers from Liverpool. The Beatles were big all right. Bigger than anyone since Elvis. Again the critics piped up: "The Beatles will overthrow Elvis."

Elvis himself didn't say anything about the Beatles. But then why should he? He has eight years over them. And that's a long time, a lot of money and an avalanche of prestige.

Anyway, how can you overthrow a legend?

1956

1957

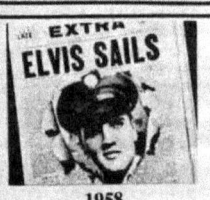
1958

1960

Elvis' Gold Cadillac

Elvis—1956

Elvis—1966

KRLA ARCHIVES

Top 40 Requests

THIS WEEK	TITLE	ARTIST	THIS WEEK	TITLE	ARTIST
1	THEY'RE COMING TO TAKE ME AWAY	Napoleon XIV	21	SEARCHIN' FOR MY LOVE	Bobby Moore
2	SUNSHINE SUPERMAN	Donovan	22	STRANGERS IN THE NIGHT	Frank Sinatra
3	SUNNY	Bobby Hebb	23	OVER UNDER SIDEWAYS DOWN	The Yardbirds
4	SWEET PEA	Tommy Roe	24	I WANT YOU	Bob Dylan
5	LIL' RED RIDING HOOD	Sam The Sham & The Pharoahs	25	DOUBLE SHOT (OF MY BABY'S LOVE)	The Medallions
6	SEVEN AND SEVEN IS	Love	26	LADY JANE/MOTHER'S LITTLE HELPER	The Rolling Stones
7	PAPERBACK WRITER	The Beatles	27	YOU DON'T HAVE TO SAY YOU LOVE ME	Dusty Springfield
8	SOMETIMES GOOD GUYS DON'T WEAR WHITE	The Standells	28	SWEET DREAMS	Tommy McLain
9	SUMMER IN THE CITY	The Lovin' Spoonful	29	SOMEWHERE MY LOVE	Ray Conniff
10	DISTANT SHORES	Chad & Jeremy	30	OH, HOW HAPPY	Shades Of Blue
11	ENTER THE YOUNG	The Association	31	THE WORK SONG	Herb Alpert
12	RED RUBBER BALL	The Cyrkle	32	SOLITARY MAN	Neil Diamond
13	DIRTY WATER	The Standells	33	LOVE LETTERS	Elvis Presley
14	ALFIE	Cher	34	LITTLE GIRL	Syndicate of Sound
15	THIS DOOR SWINGS BOTH WAYS	Herman's Hermits	35	5 D	The Byrds
16	HUNGRY	Paul Revere & The Raiders	36	A GROOVY KIND OF LOVE	The Mindbenders
17	HANKY PANKY	Tommy James & The Shondells	37	GUANTANAMERA	The Sandpipers
18	WILD THING	The Troggs	38	GO ON AND CRY	Righteous Brothers
19	MAGIC TOUCH	Bobby Fuller Four	39	MY HEART'S SYMPHONY	Gary Lewis & The Playboys
20	I SAW HER AGAIN	The Mama's & Papa's	40	BLOWIN' IN THE WIND	Stevie Wonder

OFFICIAL NATIONAL ROCK & ROLL BAND CHAMPIONSHIP
WESTERN REGION
Aug. 1 thru Sept. 3
AT PACIFIC OCEAN PARK
SANTA MONICA, CALIFORNIA

Sponsored by Tea Council of U.S.A. and VOX Guitars & Amplifiers

Calling all TEEN ROCK GROUPS!

WIN...
- $5000 in VOX Equipment.
- All Expense Trip to East – National Championships.
- Hundreds of other Prizes – Teen Tea Packets, LP Albums from Capitol Records, Trophies Given to All Winners, Season Passes to P.O.P.

All groups participating will be provided with VOX Guitars and Amplifiers for their use during competitions — the same equipment used by the Beatles, The Rolling Stones, Paul Revere and the Raiders, The Animals, The Dave Clark Five, and hundreds of others!

Drop by your Participating VOX dealer and register today!
Deadline Aug. 15, so HURRY! Free gifts to the first 50 registrations!

Adler Music Co., Inc.
(Larry Adler)
14115 Victory Blvd.
Van Nuys, California
781-3012

Adler Music Co., Inc.
(Larry Adler)
1792 Erringer Road
Simi, California

Schireson Brothers
(Stan Schireson)
344 South Broadway
Los Angeles, Calif.
628-9161

Beechler's Music
(Elmer Beechler)
18024 Ventura Blvd.
Encino, California
345-0773

Winn's Music
(Martin Winn)
540 East First St.
Tustin, California
(714) 544-3360

Kay Kalie Music
(Kay Kalie)
8408 On the Mall
Buena Park, Calif.
860-2600

Kay Kalie Music
(Kay Kalie)
11504 E. Telegraph Rd.
Santa Fe Springs, Calif.

Harris Music Co.
(Bill Harris)
1327 E. 4th Street
Ontario, California
(714) 986-7547

Harris Music Co.
(Bill Harris)
551 E. Holt Avenue
Pomona, California

Fred's Music Co.
(Pete Conn)
2753 E. Garvey
West Covina, Calif.
331-0931

Manolios Music
(John Manolios)
18547 Main St.
Huntington Beach, Calif.
(714) 847-4376

Moore & Livingston
(Phil Moore)
6726 Pacific
Huntington Park, Calif.
698-0251

Gilmore Music
(Glen Gilmore)
1935 East 7th Street
Long Beach, Calif.
HE 7-7469

Killeen's Music
(Larry Killeen)
316 N. San Fernando Rd.
Burbank, Calif.
846-4873

Lancaster Music
(Ronny Gay)
815 W. Lancaster Blvd.
Lancaster, California
(805) WH 2-4529

Pedrini, Inc.
Tom Pedrini
231 W. Main Street
Alhambra, Calif.
289-2041

Phinney-Hale Music
(Ed Phinney)
269 Wagon Wheel Rd.
Oxnard, Calif.
(805) 485-1918

Splevins Music Center
(Henry Splevin)
8834 Pico Blvd.
Los Angeles, Calif.
CR 4-2255

Inside KRLA
— By Eden

There are some days when you just can't keep up with *anything*, anymore. Like, for example, who's where on KRLA this week, and like that.

THIS WEEK – please look for blue-eyed and beautiful Boy Millionaire, Bob Eubanks, in the nine-to-noon spot, while smilin' Charlie is hanging out at the crack of dawn position of six-to-nine.

Of course, you could find Dick Moreland, Bill Slater, or almost *anybody* in the three-to-six position during the last couple of weeks while the old Scuzz was on vacation. But the President of the Southern California Beatles Fan Club has returned to us once again to thoroughly mess up our air waves, so things in the afternoon here at KRLA are right back to *abnormal* again!

And, speaking of the Phenomenal Foursome – have *you* sent in for your Beatle tickets yet? If you haven't, you'd better make tracks before you miss out on this year's concert – and it promises to be a gas, so get moving!

Guests this week have included the Sir Douglas Quintet, who stopped by our studios to answer phones and cause general mayhem in and around KRLA. And then of course there is the situation of Napoleon XIV and "They're Coming To Take Me Away." Well, somebody had better – and, fast... Hmmmm – do you suppose that Napoleon is really the Amazing Pancake Man in disguise, and this whole thing is really just a put-on? Do you *really suppose???*

On a more serious note, everyone here at KRLA and at *The BEAT* would like to extend our most sincere sympathy to the family and friends of Bobby Fuller. He was a friend to many people here at KRLA, and he will be sadly missed.

In case you've been wondering about the Tunedex – wonder no more, 'cause the Tunedex *is no more!* Instead of the Top Forty Tunedex which we all came to know and love, there is now a Top Forty Request List, compiled from the most-requested songs here at KRLA each week.

By the way, as a result of the recent week-long series of editorials concerning the recent allegations of obscenity in pop music, made by a national magazine, which you heard on the KRLA news broadcasts, KRLA is now co-operating with UHF educational TV station, KCET on a discussion program aimed at clarifying and solving the problems which have arisen in this area.

Station general manager for KRLA, John Barrett, is working closely with the TV station to develop a strong debate exploring the pros and cons of the so-called "hidden meanings" of today's music as compared with the content of pop music compositions of the past.

Once again KRLA is out in front to serve you in the best way possible.

KRLA ARCHIVES

Paul Drops 'Little Brother' TV Image

By Anna Maria Alonzo

He used to be just somebody's kid brother; Patty Duke's TV kid brother, to be exact. But Paul O'Keefe has come out of the shadow of an "older sister image" now, and headed straight into a huge beginning with The End.

What's that? Paul O'Keefe is the fifteen-year-old, blue-eyed blond who portrayed Ross Lane on the Patty Duke Show. With the demise of the series, Paul turned his attentions to another area in show business, and formed his own musical group—which he calls, "The End."

Paul plays rhythm guitar for the group, and is joined by Bob Bisno on lead guitar, Edie Adjamian — a girl singer — and Phil Erenberg on drums. The four have been together for only about two months—and they are still looking for a bass player...—but they have high hopes of being able to secure a recording contract as soon as possible.

Paul has been acting and performing professionally since he was seven-years-old, and has appeared in three Broadway musicals—Music Man, Sail Away, and Oliver—along with numerous television appearances, including his role in the Patty Duke series.

Now he has added the big Silver Screen to his list of achievements, as he portrays young Hans Christian Anderson in the Joe Levine production, "Daydreamer," soon to be released. Paul is hopeful of continuing in motion pictures, but is just as eager to play straight dramatic roles as the more humorous comedy parts.

Dirty Pop?

As a member of a new musical group now, Paul is beginning to observe the pop situation even more closely. One topic of conversation currently at the top of everyone's mind is the recent controversy over the alleged "obscenity" in the lyrics of contemporary music.

Paul doesn't find quite so much to be upset about though, and after considering the now-famous article printed in a national magazine, he staunchly claims: "I belong to the 11 percent group... Everybody and his brother has been raging about this, but I don't see how 87 percent of the kids can say that there are no lyrics of that kind in the songs—because there are, definitely.

"But, it's mostly isolated—it's not every song. I mean, if you wanted to—you could take 'London Bridges Falling Down' and find something dirty in it! And, when they can find something in 'Strangers In The Night—I give up!"

Bad For Kids

Paul does agree that there are a number of songs with rather questionable lyrics currently on the pop market, but feels that the only really harmful affects are on the very young audiences.

"That's the bad part about it. Younger kids might be influenced by that sort of lyric. I don't think songs like "Louie, Louie" should be allowed on the market, but it's a very individual thing—what might be dirty for one person, isn't for another. I think songs that are really bad, should be taken off the market."

In relation to his own group, Paul insists that "You don't have to put bad lyrics into a song to get somewhere with it"—and intends to select the best possible material for his group.

But, his main ambition is still to become the best actor he possibly can, and with his determination and talent—there's no "End" in sight for Paul O'Keefe.

SWINGIN' WHITE LEVI'S GUYS... Bill Champlin and his Sons of Champlin.

KRLA ARCHIVES

BEAT Spotlights New Groups

THE NU-LUVS

Last November, The Nu-Luvs won first place in a New York State Talent Contest and with the honor, a recording session. After the master was cut, the Nu-Luvs were notified that Mercury Records picked up their song and they signed a contract.

Their first release, "So Soft, So Warm," has received reviews like this: "Powerfilled and outstanding with huge vocal and instrumental sections, broken by heartbreaking recitations." The Nu-Luvs are "IN" with their unique sound and style of tomorrow.

The Daily Flash

The Daily Flash is the newest discovery of Charlie Green and Brian Stone, who have colored the pop scene with Sonny and Cher, The Troggs and Bob Lind, to name a few. The Daily Flash made their debut recently with the release of "Queen Jane Approximately." The group (left to right) Doug Hastings, Steve Lalor, Don MacAllister and John Kelihor, is slated to arrive in Hollywood within the next few weeks.

The Indigos

The Indigos, since they formed a year ago, have played clubs throughout Southern California. The leader of the group is 22 year old Russ Rizzotto, affectionately known as "boy leader" His favorite type of music is R & B.

John Bergman, better known as John E. Hoy, is more or less the clown prince of the Indigos. His onstage antics range from wild watusi dancing to doing back flips from Russ' shoulders. John has reddish blond hair and loves to sing slow meaningful ballads.

B. Jay Moreau designs the miniature guitars used by the Indigos since they are lighter and can be easily adapted to the group's choreography. B. Jay and John write most of the original material performed by the group.

Shakey, the group's drummer, is probably the backbone of the Indigos. The group's essence is his pulsating, driving drumbeat. Shakey does the talking for the group from the stage, and has a great flair for comedy.

... DDBM&T – TONGUE-TWISTING AGONY.

Dave Dee, Dozy, Beaky, Mick and Tich

Their name is a jawbreaker and the cause of the tongue-twisted agony to many an announcer... but it's part and parcel of their success as one of Britain's wildest and wittiest rock groups.

The group is currently hitting American shores with their second release, "Hideaway." And they've signed to appear in a new motion picture. The film is MGM's feature "The Blow-Up" which is presently being shot on location in Britain and in which the Dave Dee group will perform "Hold Tight," their first release.

Their antics on stage have also built a huge following for Dave Dee and friends. Their "act" combines every element of show business – vocals, slapstick, gags, one-liners, instrumental music (or virtually anything else that may strike the group at a given moment!)

The group was "discovered" about a year ago when they appeared on the same bill with the Honeycombs. That group's managers were so impressed by the boys that they signed Dave Dee. Since then, the Dave ensemble have brought their wild act to an increasing number of ballrooms, piers, shows and theaters all over England, Scotland and Wales.

The lead singer of this uniquely named congregation, Dave Dee, once considered becoming a plumber because he thought it was "dead interesting" (a phrase all the Dave Dee group like to use.) He soon found plumbing as a career "dear boring".

Dave Dee personally is very direct. "I hate all this soul and Ravi Shankar bit," he says. "I go to clubs to listen. Someone tells me its soul music. I can go out and come back five hours later, and it sounds like they are playing the same disc to me."

Dave Dee, Dozy, Beaky, Mick and Tich won't remain unknown in the U.S.A. very long.

KRLA ARCHIVES

Shondells: Three Years 'Overnight'

By Tammy Hitchcock

So, you think you know about ironic twists? Well, if you haven't heard the Tommy James and the Shondells story—you don't even know what ironic *means*! Three years ago an unknown group made a record entitled, "Hanky Panky." The record was a complete bomb and the group *remained* nationally unknown.

Then in 1966 a disc jockey somewhere in the country decided to take a look through his file of old records. He discovered "Hanky Panky," dug the sound and put it on the air. That was it. Nothing more, nothing less. Requests poured in, record stores sold out. "Hanky Panky" was on the charts and Tommy James and the Shondells were a three year "overnight" success!

Slow Starter

You'd think they'd be ecstatic with their newly found success. Actually, they are. Except for one small problem... "Hanky Panky" is *not* the sound of Tommy James and the Shondells. Three years is a long time. The Shondells are not a static group. They move, they change. Today, they're rhythm 'n' blues. Three years ago they were "handclapping music." Hanky Panky" has given way to "Please, Please, Please." How were they to know their "handclapping music" would be the number one record in the nation three years after it was released? I mean, they'd heard of slow-starting records but three years has to be the slowest yet!

The Shondells all come from around the Pittsburgh area. Really, they're from a little town called Greensboro but no one except its inhabitants know where it is. They've known each other for years but then, everyone in a small town knows each other.

Tommy James is set apart. He calls himself the "Outsider." Not because he doesn't fit in but because he was born in Ohio instead of Greensboro. And to top the whole thing off, Tommy didn't even meet the Shondells in Greensboro. He saw them play one night in Pittsburgh and decided they were the group he wanted to be in. So, he joined up. As simple as that.

An 'Oldie'

Tommy is nineteen years old but he's something of a show business "oldie." He made his first professional appearance at the mighty age of 11 when he was on a local television show. He started his first group in Niles, Michigan when he reached the age of 13. He picked out the name too—Tommy & The Tornadoes. But he blushes if you remind him of his former moniker and puts it down to "youthful indiscretion."

Tommy wears his brown hair on the short side, doesn't like dirty looking performers and prefers American artists over the British variety. Tommy's the one responsible for the name "Shondells." He admits that it means nothing in particular—"it just sounds right."

The Group

The Shondells line up as Joe Kessler, George Magura, Vinnie Pietropaoli, Ronnie Rosman and Mike Vale. Joe is the joker and the introvert of the group—even though that seems to be impossible. The thing is, Joe never has much to say about any given subject and yet what he *does* say is

...THE SHONDELLS (l. to r.) Ronnie, Joe, Vinnie, Tommy, George and Mike.

hilarious. The rest of the guys tease Joe continually because he's always late and is introverted. But he seems to enjoy it. He says he likes to take showers and that's why he's always late but he doesn't feel that he's wasting time because he sings loudly in the shower!

George might become a legend in his own time but he won't say why. He looks like he lives in Greenwich Village but was actually born in Svaby, Czechoslovakia and raised in Greensboro. He sports a goatee and wears those kind of glasses your father wore when he married your mother. He's the kind of musician who can play anything from a comb to a violin but the Shondells only allow him to play sax, bass and organ. Which is a large shame because the music world *needs* a goateed comb player!

Vinnie is the youngest Shondell (following Tommy by two and a half months) so he's described as "everybody's kid brother." Vinnie owns a perpetual grin, which is probably a defense mechanism because that way no one can get mad at him. He's not the least bit sophisticated and is incapable of faking anything. If you ask him what he plays, he'll tell you with a straight-face: "Drums, table taps, glasses and an occasional bald head." Then he puts his smile back on and informs the world that he likes Italian food.

Which Star?

Ronnie has one of those serious, pre-occupied looks about him. People say he resembles a movie star but won't say which one. His real name is Claren but since he claims to have a temper no one ever calls him Claren. Although Ronnie likes to talk, one gets the impression he's a lover of the slow and quiet life. He'd rather live in the country than the city, likes quiet and natural girls and prefers to spend an evening "just kidding around" with old friends. So, you can't really picture him grooving on the Sunset Strip or North Beach or New York City.

Mike says he wears his hair like Napoleon but with his goatee he actually looks more like George's Greenwich Village neighbor. Mike used to have shoulder-length hair but his neighbors stared at him so much that he finally cut it off. He's hung on blues... period. Because he used to wear his hair long, is extremely informal and split Greensboro for summers in New York City, you'd probably pick Mike out as the group's hippie. But you'd be wrong. He claims that he doesn't dig the wild scene but prefers "the companionship of a few close friends."

So, now you've been formally introduced to Tommy James and The Shondells. It's rather difficult to go up from the number one record in the nation but that's exactly where The Shondells want to go. They aim to be one of the best American representatives of the blues sound. And with three solid years of practice behind them—they just might make it.

...TOMMY JAMES

Bobby Fuller Dead

(Continued From Page 1)

times of stress—when the group had to spend long hours on the road or when things weren't going well—Bobby was never subject to moods of depression.

But just prior to his death, Keene said, Bobby was at the zenith of his career with everything going for him and should have had no worries. His recording of "I Fought The Law" had placed him in the national pop spotlight and "he never gave me any indication he was having personal difficulties," Keene said.

"He was making plans to move to a new apartment and was very happy about his career, which was blossoming beautifully," Keene recalled. "He left no notes or in any way gave any indication of being remorse prior to his death.

"In fact, just before he left his house the morning of his death he had called his girl friend in New York City and asked her to come to the West Coast and join him. (Ed. note—Bobby had only known the girl for about a week and a half but she was reported to be happy with Bobby's invitation.) He also told his brother and his road manager, who both lived with him, that he was pleased with the song he had just finished that very day.

"I saw him on Sunday, the day before his death, while he was with some friends of his from Texas and he was in his normal good spirits. Also at that time he mentioned that he wanted to purchase an automobile from another member of his group who has been drafted." (Ed. note—Bobby had a life-long history of asthma so he could have had no fear of being drafted.)

Did Keene think Bobby was murdered? "I just know he didn't take his own life... and that's all I have to say.

"But since I do feel that he did not die of his own intention," Keene picked up his last statement, "I have decided to support my belief. I have retained, through my attorney, the services of the necessary people to investigate his death to determine what actually happened."

And so the mysterious circumstances behind the death of one of America's brightest young singers—a fellow who obviously had everything to live for—still remained unknown.

KRLA ARCHIVES

All Girl Groups

By Mike Tuck

So you think men hold an exclusive corner on the rock 'n' roll music block, huh... then you're in for a surprise because if you'll look closely you'll notice a creeping trend of all-girl groups invading hte pop music scene.

Not that they're making any immediate threat to overshadow groups like The Rolling Stones or the Beatles, but female groups, at least on the East Coast and in Ivy League Colleges, are coming back to the limelight for the first time since the heyday of Phil Spitalny.

Males Dig 'Em

Record companies are now keeping a close watch on a number of female groups who do most of their entertaining for East Coast colleges. The groups have reportedly met with staggering success playing before live audiences, especially at colleges where the male enrollment outnumbers its counterpart.

And just because a group is comprised of all girls, that's no indication they "tone down" or alter their hard-rock songs. The girls use the same instrumentation, amplified guitars and drums as the male groups, and many even write their own songs.

Still, record companies, while keenly interested in the new groups, have accepted a position of watchful skepticism. They want conclusive proof that all-female groups would be nationally accepted before they endorse them.

Mixed groups, however, have unquestionably made their mark on the pop music market and in the process have opened the door a little wider for all-girl groups. The Mama's and Papa's, which features two girls, has become one of the top groups in the world.

Probably the biggest names in all-girl groups today are the Moppets, from Mt. Holyoke College in Massachusetts, and the New Pandoras from Boston.

Don't get the impression that just because they're girls they're meek and debate with no individuality. The Moppets have solved their transportation problem with a 1957 hearse, which they ride in to their engagements at Ivy League Colleges like Harvard, Yale and Cornell.

They have become so popular at eastern all-male colleges that they haven't been able to handle all requests for their performances. They have built up a solid reputation from Boston to Philadelphia.

New Pandoras

And the New Pandoras, probably the only rock group ever to play at the Harvard Club in Boston, is as popular and well-known in the Boston area as many of the groups that are currently riding high on the record charts.

Made up of a college senior and three Boston area high school girls, the New Pandoras were just recently the featured act at Seventeen Magazine's annual fashion show in New York.

The new groups are a natural for publicity... they are fresh and present a new angle to the Pop music world. The New York Times ran a feature on the Moppets; Women's Wear Daily had a story on the New Pandoras; and the Boston Globe also covered the Pandoras with a feature story.

Part of the appeal of the two groups is that they're very feminine in appearance. At least while on stage, they shun slacks and appear in sophisticated dresses. This, undoubtably, is a factor in their popularity at all-men's universities.

What is the future of all-girl groups as recording stars? For the Moppets and the Pandoras it is bright but neither group is trying to rush its recording career. The Moppets have declined record offers so far because they feel they aren't quite ready for them, and the Pandoras have reportedly been undergoing unhurried negotiations with seven record companies.

Japanese Song Hits America

First the British... now the Japanese.

Maybe not with the same resounding impact that the British artists have made, but Japanese artists are about to make what is expected to be a big entrance into American music.

Capitol Records has announced that "Kimi-To-Itsumadero," the largest selling record in the history of the Japanese record industry, will be released here soon. The single, which has topped the three million sales mark in Japan alone, was written and recorded by Japanese motion picture and singing star, Yuzo Kayama.

The last artist to record a song for Capitol in Japanese was Kyu Sakamoto. His single, "Sukiyaki," became a million-seller in 1963, expected to draw the same kind of reaction. The song will be sung entirely in Japanese on the American version.

"Kimi-To-Itsumadero," which means "Love Forever," is expected to draw the same kind of reaction. The song will be sung entirely in Japanese on the American version.

Released in December, 1965, it has stayed atop the Japanese charts for more then five months. Since the debut of the single, Kayama and his group, The Launchers, have been deluged with personal appearance offers and are now considered the most successful pop group Japan has ever had.

Stone Movie

An American all-star pop movie has just opened in England. The film, "Gather No Moss" stars the Rolling Stones as well as James Brown and his Famous Flames, the Beach Boys, Billy J. Kramer, Chuck Berry, the Supremes, Jan & Dean, Gerry and the Pacemakers, Marvin Gaye and the Miracles.

Sound familiar? It should. It has already played throughout America as the T.A.M.I. Show.

Instant Mischief On Bob Lind Tour

By Barri

Most people wouldn't consider the talented songwriter-singer, Bob Lind, to be a dangerous young man. They might have some doubts about his two nutty — but rich — managers, Charlie Greene and Brian Stone, however.

But put these three together and send them off to Merrie Olde England for a P.A. tour — and you have it: instant mischief...

While in the foggy isle on their recent tour, Bob, Brian, and Charlie were taken to a very typically old English restaurant where the diners mixed their food with song, as they all joined in on tunes brightly played by a little old English gentleman — complete with top hat and an old English upright piano.

The customers merrily sang along, while banging their forks and knives on the tables before them in time to the uptempo beat of "I'm Henry The VIII." After listening to a couple of choruses of the old English tune — made famous by a certain young — and toothy — English lad, just recently — Bob turned round to his host and cracked: "It sounds like a prison riot for better food..."

Brian and Charlie immediately picked up the cue and joined in the festivities with a little improvisation of their own, beginning with a giant Sugar Lump Battle of the Century, conducted with the occupants of a nearby table.

Then Charlie popped up brightly with the always-pertinent question: "Hey, isn't it luck to throw salt over your shoulder?" A very unsuspecting host replied that it was, whereupon Charlie immediately tossed a three-pound container of salt over his shoulder — which proceeded to bounce off the table, through a nearby window, and off into the Thames River below...

Charlie and Brian are in for either a very large dose of luck in the near future — or an even larger dose of English bills...

The Sunshine Superman
Words & Music by DONOVAN LEITCH

Sunshine came softly
Thru My window today
Could have tripped out easy
But I've changed my way
It'll take time I know it
But in a while
You're gonna be mine I know
it
We'll do it in style
'Cause I made my mind up
You're going to be mine
I'll tell you right now
Any trick in the book now
baby
That I can find
Everybody is hustling just
to have a little scene
When I say we'll be cool
I think that you know what
I mean
We stood on the beach at
sunset
Do you remember when?
I know a beach where baby
It never ends
When you've made your mind
up
Forever to be mine
Pick up your hands and
slowly
Blow your little mind
Cause I made my mind up
You're going to be mine
I'll tell you right now
Any trick in the book now
baby
All that I can find
Superman or Green
Lantern ain't got nothin'
on me
I can make like a turtle in
dark fog
A-float in the sea
You can just sit there thinkin'
On your Velvet throne
About all the rainbows you
can
Have for your own
When you've made your mind
up
Forever to be mine
Pick up your hands and
slowly
Blow your little mind
When you've made your mind
up
Forever to be mine

Lyrics Printed with Permission of Epic Records

DONOVAN — FACTS AND FACETS

REAL NAME — Donovan Phillips Leitch
BIRTHDATE — May 10, 1946
BIRTHPLACE — Maryhill, Glasgow, Scotland
PRESENT HOME — London
HEIGHT — 5' 6"
WEIGHT — 138 lbs.
COLOR EYES — Green
COLOR HAIR — Black
BROTHERS AND SISTERS — One brother, Gerry
MUSICAL INSTRUMENTS — Guitar, harmonica, kazoo
MUSICAL EDUCATION — Self-taught
ENTERED SHOW BUSINESS — At age 18
FIRST PUBLIC APPEARANCE — The Cock, St. Albans
BIGGEST BREAK — "Ready, Steady, Go!" and meeting my manager, Ashley Kozak
TV DEBUT — "Ready, Steady, Go!"
BIGGEST INFLUENCE ON CAREER — Woody Guthrie, Jack Elliott
HOBBIES — Living, listening to jazz
FAVORITE COLORS — Turquoise, tangerine, the rainbow
FAVORITE SINGERS — Hedy West, Righteous Brothers, Bob Dylan, Mick Jagger, Sonny and Cher
FAVORITE COMPOSERS — John Sebastian, Lennon and McCartney, Phil Ochs, Bob Lind
FAVORITE FOODS — Octopus, fresh bread, real — not plastic — potatoes
FAVORITE DRINK — Milk
FAVORITE CLOTHES — Edwardian shoes, lace cuffs, black cloaks
FAVORITE CAR — Old gangster-type sportscars
LIKES AND DISLIKES — I have less to hate and less to want
PERSONAL AMBITION — To buy an old English house with bay windows; to explore the ocean bottom
FAVORITE DAYDREAM — Complete interrelation of the arts; i.e., I'd have a concert with Allen Ginsberg recording a Beatles' song, John Lennon reading poetry, George Harrison playing the sitar, McCartney making electric tapes and Dylan taking tickets at the door or showing films.

KRLA ARCHIVES

DONOVAN: Magician of Music

By Debbie Weller
Hillary Bedell

He's only twenty years old, and already a man with a new, wierd type of sound. This man is Donovan Phillips Leitch, better known to the teen world as Donovan.

He calls his type of sound, in his own words, "Music just for now, 'now music,' 'cause it's changing so much."

As we sat talking with Donovan, caped in a black velvety floor length cape with dark sequins, it was obvious he had quite a wonderous, wonderful personality. Of himself, he says he has a "goody-goody" type personality. In addition to being a "goody" type, Donovan is a very deep thinking person and shows this by the lyrics of many of his songs.

At Home

When this magical, mystical musician isn't on tour, or doing a show, he likes to relax at his home in London, where he lives with Gypsy Dave. Gypsy must be a very still, and quiet person, because this is the type of people Donovan likes.

Before becoming a famous singer, Donovan traveled all around with the Gypsy. He said all of his adventures were fun and he had so many that one day he may write a book about them.

Donovan's younger brother, Jerry, who is fourteen, is also a musician. But contrary to Donovan's "now" sound, Jerry plays the classics. He is at present living in England.

Quiet Life

Many people must always be with crowds and the hubbub of the city, but Donovan prefers the quieter life. He prefers the country to the city because it is simple and quiet. His choice of a place to live is a Greek Island in the Mediterranean.

Many of Donovan's songs seem to show a deep feeling and he says he believes himself to be a very deep person. Donovan sometimes writes on inspiration and other times he writes on past experiences and the future. He says he must be alone when writing. Donovan says he doesn't have to get into a certain mood to write, because he is automatically in it when he is writing.

Other Jobs

Before Donovan gained fame as a singer, he had many adventures. He traveled up and down the lands of Great Britain with his friend, Gypsy Dave. Because singing couldn't always furnish his stomach with the food he needed, he worked at various jobs. When Donovan traveled the high and low, he did mostly labor jobs. When asked the types of work he had experienced he said, "I can't remember now, but there was diggin' the road . . . I didn't do a lot of work, used to work for a couple of weeks then moved away from it . . . don't like much doin' work."

Donovan helped soothe many of the hardships of traveling on the road by singing on his way. Ever since he can remember he's enjoyed singing.

Happy Now

Despite the carefree life of roaming the lands, he likes best what he's doing now. He says, "You can't bring back yesterday and live what you did before."

Donovan has many talents other than singing. He writes poems which he turns into songs, and he writes fairy tales. Bob Dylan is his favorite writer and Donovan seems to show this in some of his songs.

If you went up to an average Englishman visiting California and posed the question of the difference of England's fog compared with L.A.'s smog, he would probably give some everyday, usual answer. When we asked Donovan that, he answered: "I haven't seen any smog yet, but I saw a big, noisy car laying tar on the road, 'twas billowing and blowing, but the pure air sucked the dirt out," an example of his poetic charm.

Donovan gives some very unusual answers, but one of the most surprising seems to be the answer to the question "What was your most embarrasing moment?" After thinking of one, then crossing it out, and saying he didn't think he ever had one, an often moment came to his mind and he said, "Yeah, interviews are embarrassing. Sometimes embarrassing for the interviewed, and sometimes embarrassing for the interviewer, but they're embarrassing."

Exciting Moments

Another fascinating answer was to what his most exciting moment was. "Waking up every morning," he said. That seemed to show us what he would say when we asked him what he loved most in life. We were right — "life."

Many people listen to Donovan's works and think, "What is he trying to tell me?" While others can tell when they first listen to a song. Donovan says his songs say to, "Have fun . . . live . . . just listen to your own head, and laugh all the time, laugh with others, and dance all the time."

Most people are accustomed to seeing Donovan playing his usual six-string guitar. But when we visited a night club recently (where he was playing) we saw the different sounds he has.

He transferred from his quiet sound to the powerful sound of the electric guitar which showed his versatility with music. In singing one song (a fairy tale) "Guenivere," Donovan's quiet sounding guitar was accompanied by a rather unusually beautiful sounding Indian instrument called the 'sitar!'

Favorite Colors

In one of Donovan's past hit songs, "Colors," he sang about many different hues, but he doesn't even mention his two favorite ones. Maybe it's because they have too many syllables! They're torquoise and tangerine.

Donovan says he has so many favorite performers he could make a list, and they vary from the Beatles to Julian Bryme, of the classical guitar. Even though he has so many favorites, the biggest influence on his career was himself.

When Donovan went traveling through Europe, he had many pets which he calls "animal friends". At his stops they were waiting for him. Among them were mice, a guinea pig, afhhan hounds, birds, and a cat. He says he has pets all over the world.

We found Donovan to be a fabulously magical person. Who enhances just by the answers he gives.

THE EVER CHANGING DONOVAN — When he first came on the scene he appeared in denims and an old railroad cap and he sang about the wind and colors and things. After "Universal Soldier" was a huge hit for him, he disappeared for a while, then came back wearing velvet capes and ruffled shirts. Now he's back again with "Sunshine Superman" and he's become a man of the world in padded shoulder suits and immaculately styled hair.

TWO LUCKY GIRLS — Hillary Bedell, left, and Debbie Weller with Donovan, whom they found a "magical, mystical musician."

... IN DENIM

... VELVET CAPE

KRLA ARCHIVES

A Beatle Hunt Revisited

By Martie Henderson

With the August appearance of the fabulous Beatles just around the corner now, the waves of Beatlemania are once again reaching a crest and the familiar excitement of that happy affliction is once again at high tide.

But, it has been over two-and-a-half years since we were first introduced to the British quartet who have revolutionized the entire pop world — and by now, some of us have almost gotten used to the whole aura of Beatlemania.

But, I can remember the first time that I contracted the disease, and I bet that you have many of the same symptoms which I experienced.

Beatle Hunt

It was August of 1964 then, and after months and months of waiting — the Beatles had finally arrived. Hidden away in a private home which they rented during their stay, they were surrounded by police — who in turn, were surrounded by Beatle-hunters.

It was very unusual to see teenagers climbing fences, hiding under bushes, scaling walls, and digging tunnels in order to get at least a glimpse of these four young men they had heard so much about. But it wasn't *half* as unusual as seeing their *parents* — doing the very same thing!

Never one to be left behind, I decided to join in the fun and go on a Beatle hunt of my own. So, accompanied by a close friend — who is also a nut! — and armed with only our Beatlemania and a package of chocolate chip cookies, we began our first onslaught.

In order to get to the house, we had to first cross a wide ravine. However — this was no *ordinary* ravine. This one included a marvelous selection of overgrown shrubs, poison ivy, hideous spiders, oversized trees, and just for added effect — a couple of barbed wire fences. But what's a barbed wire fence where a Beatle is concerned, right?

Needless to say, by the time we had crossed through the jungle of mud and drippy shrubbery, we were drenched. And the fact that it was only six o'clock in the morning and the sun was still asleep didn't add to our comfort too much, either. But, onward in the names of John, Paul, George, and Ringo anyway.

When finally we arrived at our very last hurdle, we found ourselves just across the road from the Beatle house, separated only by the road — a few trees and plants — and a *barbed wire fence!*

We quickly exchanged hysterical glances, then forged ahead quickly to attempt to crawl underneath the dangerous obstacle. However, there wasn't really enough room between the fence and the ground — about an inch and a half to be exact — so we began looking about for an alternate route.

As we were doing so, we were joined by a group of about eight other boys and girls — all very noisy, and like us — all very wet.

Together, we decided that we would climb the tree in a nearby corner and avoid the wire fence.

Now, mind you — I have nothing personally against the Tom Sawyer life, or anything — but about the most climbing I had ever done in my life was up and down the two steps in front of my home. So you can probably imagine the joy which was inhabiting my heart as I began to *fake* my way up the side of the tree.

Well — I now have a two inch scar to prove that I once climbed over a barbed wire fence . . . but, on to better things. Once over the fence, we all cotton-tailed it across the narrow road to the side of the house, and hid ourselves beneath the shrubbery — which was still soaking wet, due to the fact that the people inside had been running the sprinklers the night before to ward off "guests" just like us.

Atmosphere???

It was very nice sitting on top of those wet and muddy leaves while the trees above us dripped upon us continuously for about two hours. It gave us sort of a feeling of *atmosphere*. You know, it was sort of foggy that morning, so we could pretend that we were doing all of this valiant suffering across the great foam in Jolly Olde. Oh, the loveliness of our little wet selves as we tried to munch on some equally drenched and soggy chocolate chip cookies.

For about two and one half miserable hours, we watched cars driving up and down that hallowed road. We saw such fave raves as Pat Boone, Pat Boone's children, and a number of young actors, actresses and singers driving by. Along with a rather large number of police patrol cars, also driving by, and as they did so — they spoke through a loud speaker the following immemorable lines: "Everyone out! If you do not come out of those bushes within five minutes, you will all go to jail!"

It was a toss up. Which was worse? The soggy, foggy, drippy underground retreat in which we were currently ensconced — or a nice, dry, warm, well-lighted jail complete with something warm to eat and drink? Well, the jail didn't include a glimpse of the Fab Foursome, so we continued to drippingly cower in great fear everytime a policeman drove by.

At long last, our waiting was rewarded though — we heard a great roar of engines, and a long procession of cars began to stream past us. One by one they drove by, complete with the police escort, until finally a long black limousine pulled into view.

Beatles

Yes — it really was J, P, G, and Ringo — all four waving and smiling at their many fans gathered by the road side. (The same fans who weren't supposed to be there...). So, being good-natured about the whole thing, we decided to wave back — and grinning as widely as possible — we dangled our hands — still clutching the soggy chocolate chip cookies — furiously about in the air above us.

Paul rewarded us with a smile and a wink — and then, they were gone.

And now it is two and a half years later. The Beatles will be returning very soon, and perhaps there will be other Beatle-hunts, in other places, with other Beatlemaniacs. Because Beatlemania, is indeed, an incurable disease — but probably one of the greatest and most enjoyable afflictions known to the human race.

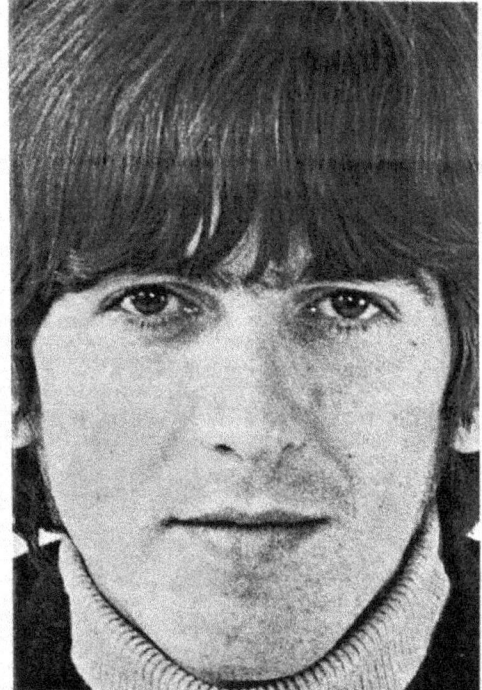

...OBJECT OF BEATLE HUNT

...HOWARD KAYLAN — THE "KING"

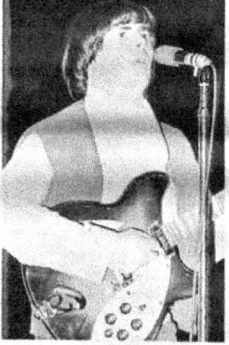

...AL "EASY SMILE"   ...MARK "KNOCK IT OVER"

...CHUCK "FRANKLIN"

KRLA ARCHIVES

The Turtles Return!

...THE TURTLES ON STAGE AT THE WHISKEY EXPLAINING YOU DON'T STAND AN "OUTSIDE CHANCE."

...TURTLES GOING FORMAL

HOLLYWOOD: The hot, cigarette-stale air belched out of the Whiskey and onto the Strip. The sardine-like inside of the club drew its breath from the thimbleful of fresh air which somehow managed to filter through the open door and spread itself thinly over the rows of crowded tables. The Turtles opened tonight and scattered throughout the Whiskey were those who remembered how long a year can be and how far 365 days can take you.

It was the same sort of hot, sticky day a year ago when you drove down the Strip to interview a virtually unknown group with the unlikely name, Turtles. They'd just released a record but it hadn't started to really happen yet. The record was "It Ain't Me, Babe" and it was the Turtles' very first interview.

Impressed

You remember being impressed with the group. Not so much because of their musical ability—a lot of groups have talent. But because they were real. They possessed that fresh sort of quality which is mixed with enthusiasm and a deep liking for what they're doing.

There was the official leader, or as they termed it — "our biggest goof," Howard Kaylan. You just couldn't help but like the guy. He was so down-to-earth, so sincere. Not phony sincere—the genuine stuff. His eyes took on this glow and his hands gestered continually as he told you the aims of the group. You know it sounds rather hackneyed to describe him like that. But that's how you remember him—so what can you do?

You recall that warm sort of feeling you had towards Chuck as he sat there with those funny little glasses perched half-way down his nose and asked, in what you probably mistook for deep concern, if you didn't think he looked a lot like Benjamin Franklin. And the harder you looked at him the more you actually *did* see a resemblance.

But then he began telling you all about Buffy St. Marie and her kind of folk music. He laughed quite a bit and afterwards you decided he probably didn't resemble Ben Franklin at all. Somehow you just couldn't see him standing out in the rain flying a kite.

Jim you liked immediately because of the crazy way he chewed his gum. You swear he never stopped and you found yourself wondering if he had a problem keeping the gum in his mouth and singing at the same time. But you decided that he probably had the technique down to a fine art by now and, thereupon, decided that in your book he was "okay."

The other guys said Mark was a "bumbling idiot." You just laughed but they told you to stick around a while and see for yourself. You assumed they were making a joke but in the hour you were there you witnessed the overthrow of a microphone, the fall of a loaded ashtray and the mess of a spilled coke. All neatly maneuvered by Mark. So, you made a mental note to keep clear of him if you didn't want to get hit in the head by a mike or cooled off by a coke in your lap.

Easy Smile

Al sat directly in front of you and put his easy smile into action. He said exactly what he thought but he didn't waste words. The Turtles chose a Dylan composition to record right at the peak of Dylan's entrance into the pop field. Dylan was "in" and you remember asking if that was why "It Ain't Me, Babe" was chosen. And you remember Al's short, but concise, answer: "We're not going to ride on it." And when he strode into the kitchen to get you a coke, you filed his name on your list of "dug people."

Don seemed to be the group's deep thinker. He was the one who searched for all the "whys." He complimented Al's short answers with long ones. He possessed a great sense of humor—one which shone through constantly—except when he bore his serious side. Then he didn't laugh at all.

Just as you started to leave, Howard asked if you couldn't print a group message. As you nodded your head, the group "message" was delivered by Howard: "Thanks to everyone who supported the record. We hope that we can continue putting out records which people will like."

Wishing

You remember wishing particularly hard that they *would* stay on the scene for years and years. But you couldn't predict that they would—only time could do that.

After all, hundreds of artists had one hit and then were never able to come up with another. Despite talent and good material, they just never made it again. You hoped the Turtles wouldn't fall into that bag but all you could do was wait and see.

An entire year has gone by since "It Ain't Me, Babe" and the Turtles are still here. Still recording hits and now opening at the Whiskey to a packed and enthusiastic audience. They've changed a bit—but then they said they would.

Don's gone now. He's been replaced by Johnny Barbata and as Johnny moves into the booth and plops down next to you, you silently commend the Turtles on their choice. But when he starts into his drum solo you remain silent no longer. The guy's a fantastic drummer. One who would fit into any group but who especially fits into the Turtles.

Proud

You feel proud as you watch the Turtles on stage. You haven't seen them perform in nearly a year so their improved stage presence hits you immediately. Actually, there is no reason *you* should feel proud—you had nothing to do with it. Except that you picked them out as winners a long time ago and they didn't let you down. Which is reason enough...

— Louise Criscione

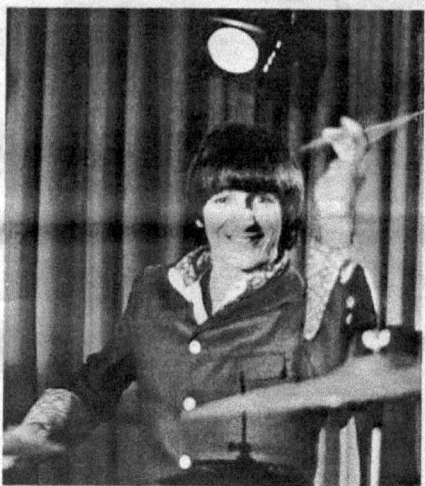

...JOHNNY BARBATA—DRUMMER EXTRAORDINAIRE.

...JIM "GUM CHEWER"

KRLA ARCHIVES

POP MUSIC PUZZLERS

Do you ever get the feeling that you, as a reader of The BEAT, know just about everything there is to know about the international pop scene? Of course you do! And rightly so! And here's your chance to prove it!

The quizzes on this page are designed to test your knowledge in several different areas of the music world, so don't just stand there. Grab a pencil and go-go!

The answers will appear in the very next issue of The BEAT, so stay tuned!

True Or False?

Some of the following twenty-five statements are true and some aren't. Can you tell the difference? Mark answers below.
1. David McCallum is recording an album of Beatle songs!
2. Bob Dylan is draft exempt!
3. Two of the Walker Brothers are really brothers!
4. Barry Ryan is three minutes older than his twin brother Paul!
5. The M.F.Q. stands for Modern Folk Quartette!
6. "Somewhere" was previously recorded by P.J. Proby!
7. Mick Jagger is a James Bond fan!
8. Lou Christie's real name is Geno Sacco!
9. Barry Sadler is a First Sergeant in the U.S. Special Forces!
10. The original Mama's and Papa's were named Cass, Michelle, John and Danny!
11. The Beatles have received nine gold records for single discs!
12. Len Barry was once a member of the Dovells!
13. There are five members in the Turtles!
14. Bobby Vinton is the new manager of the Village Stompers!
15. Zal Yanovsky sang the lead on the Spoonful's "Daydream"!
16. Herb Alpert is of Latin American ancestry!
17. "6-84;789" was a recent hit recording!
18. Sonny Bono had nothing to do with the recording of "Bang Bang"!
19. Mitch Ryder & The Detroit Wheels were once known as the Rivieras!
20. The Righteous Brothers have been giving college concerts!
21. Hilton Valentine is the lead singer of the Animals!
22. The DC5's first movie will be their last!
23. The Beatles will make a recording while they're in America this summer!
24. There was a mistake in the record "History Repeats Itself."
25. "Norwegian Wood" was taken from a John Lennon poem by same name.

1. T☐ F☐
2. T☐ F☐
3. T☐ F☒
4. T☐ F☐
5. T☐ F☒
6. T☒ F☐
7. T☒ F☐
8. T☐ F☐
9. T☐ F☐
10. T☐ F☐
11. T☐ F☐
12. T☒ F☐
13. T☐ F☒
14. T☐ F☐
15. T☐ F☒
16. T☐ F☐
17. T☒ F☐
18. T☐ F☐
19. T☐ F☐
20. T☐ F☒
21. T☐ F☐
22. T☐ F☐
23. T☐ F☐
24. T☐ F☐
25. T☐ F☐

Second Time Around
These present hits have been recorded previously. Match the discs in the left hand column with the original artists listed at the right.

1. "Gloria" — C
2. "Little Latin Lupe Lu" — E
3. "What Now My Love?" — D
4. "Got My Mojo Working" — A
5. "Young Love" — B

a. Manfred Mann
b. Tab Hunter
c. Them
d. Sonny & Cher
e. Righteous Bros.

BRAIN TEASER
These five songs were taken from "another medium" such as stage, TV, etc. Name where each originated, and then list the pop artists who made them hits!

1. "Somewhere" — Stage
2. "Phoenix Love Theme" — Motion Picture
3. "Secret Agent Man" — TV
4. "No Matter What Shape" — TV
5. "Leaning On The Lamp Post" — Motion Picture

THE 'FIRST NAME' GAME
Each of these five song titles contains a first name. Fill in the blanks and then name the artists who recently recorded them.

1. "Sloop John B" — Beach Boys
2. "I'm Coming Home Cindy" — Trini Lopez
3. "Caroline No" — Brian Wilson
4. "Message To Michael" — Dionne Warwick
5. "Frankie And Johnnie" — Elvis Presley

BEATLEMANIA

1. Who produced both the Beatle movies? Walter Shenson
2. A recent Beatle album included their version of "Words Of Love." What late great wrote this song? Buddy Holly
3. What is Mrs. Ringo Starr's first name? Maureen
4. Who played the part of the channel swimmer in "Help?" Mal Evans
5. What is Paul McCartney's middle name? Paul
6. Have any of the Beatle wives ever been to America? yes
7. Name the western type film the Beatles almost made. A Talent For Loving
8. The first Beatle song to hit the number one spot in America was "I Wanna Hold Your Hand." What was the second? I Saw Her Standing There
9. What drummer substituted for Ringo some time ago, when he was too ill to tour with the group? Jimmy Nichol
10. Name the George Harrison composition that appeared on the British but not the American "Rubber Soul" album. If I Needed Someone
11. A while back, the Beatles produced a record for another group. The song was "You've Got To Hide Your Love Away." What was the group? The Silkie
12. Paul McCartney wrote "Woman" under what pen name? Sebastian Webb
13. Name the disc recorded by John Lennon's father. It's My Life
14. In what city will the 1966 Beatle tour begin? Chicago
15. Who was the Beatles' drummer before Ringo Starr? Pete Best

MEMORY MAKERS
See if you can remember the first big hit single (in this country) by each of the following stars.

1. Herman's Hermits — I'm Into Something Good
2. Lovin' Spoonful — Do You Believe In Magic
3. Petula Clark — Downtown
4. Mitch Ryder & Detroit Wheels — Jenny Take A Ride
5. Gary Lewis & Playboys — This Diamond Ring
6. Bob Dylan — Like A Rolling Stone
7. Walker Brothers — Make It Easy On Yourself
8. Zombies — She's Not There
9. Joe Tex — Hold On To What You Got
10. Elvis Presley — Hound Dog

On The Flip Sides
How good is your music memory? Find out by matching the A sides in the left column with the B's at the right.

1. "Help" — J
2. "Sign Of The Times"
3. "We Can Work It Out" — D
4. "Lost That Lovin' Feelin'"
5. "Walkin' My Cat Named Dog"
6. "Yesterday" — H
7. "Caroline No"
8. "Monday Monday" — B
9. "Nowhere Man" — C
10. "The Cruel War"

a. "There's A Woman"
b. "Got A Feelin'"
c. "What Goes On"
d. "Day Tripper"
e. "Summer Means New Love"
f. "Time For Love"
g. "Mon Trai Destin"
h. "Act Naturally"
i. "I'm The Sky"
j. "I'm Down"

Spell Bound
There is a spelling error in each of the following ten names. Find it and correct it!

1. Norma Tanaga — Tanega
2. The Temtations — Temptations
3. Sam The Sham & The Pharoahs — Pharaohs
4. The Shadows Of Night — Knight
5. Diane Warwick — Dionne
6. Otis Reding — Redding
7. Simon And Garfunkle —
8. Leslie Gore — Lesley
9. Wilson Picket — Pickett
10. Johnnie Rivers

BEHIND THE SCENES
Match these five hits with the record producers who sent them spinning to the top of the charts.

1. "A Must To Avoid" — C
2. "Nowhere Man"
3. "Boots Were Made for Walkin'" — A
4. "19th Nervous Breakdown"
5. "Shapes Of Things" — D

a. Lee Hazlewood
b. Andrew Oldham
c. Mickie Most
d. Giorgio Gomelsky
e. George Martin

MERRY OLDE ENGLAND
Here are ten questions with a British flavor, so see how up to date you are on the U.K.!

1. What English group recently weathered a split with their leader and went on to have a hit record on their own? Mindbenders
2. What do the letters N.E.M.S (of Brian Epstein fame) stand for? _____
3. How are Noel Harrison and Rex Harrison related? Son & Father respectively
4. What group did Tom Jones put down in an interview? _____
5. Name the American singer-composer who recently completed a smash tour of Britain. Bob Dylan
6. Which member of the Yardbirds was married this last March? Keith Relf
7. Spencer Davis has a B.A. degree in what subject? _____
8. Paul McCartney and Jane Asher attended the premiere of Jane's latest movie. Name that film. _____
9. What English group this year lost a drummer named John Steel? Animals
10. There's a famous shop in London, patronized by pop people, called Hung On You. What kind of merchandise does it sell? _____

Answers To Pop Music Puzzlers Will Be In The Next Issue Of The BEAT

KRLA ARCHIVES

The Raiders By Candlelight

Somehow, you have the feeling that this will be a very special evening—an evening which you will never forget. And you are right; tonight *is* a very important, very special evening for tonight you will attend your very first recording session with Paul Revere and the Raiders.

There are very few people who are allowed to sit in on the Raiders' sessions, so you feel very privileged as you walk quietly into the studio and take your seat in front of the large glass window which separates you from the recording booth.

Behind you, is a massive piece of machinery responsible for all of the recording which will take place, and operating it is an engineer named Ray. Standing beside Ray is the Raiders' talented producer, Terry Melcher.

Probably the first thing which caught your eye as you entered the dimly-lit recording studio was the recording booth which is completely dark—with the exception of several flickering *candles!*

At first, it seemed almost religious, but then you discover that it was Mark Lindsay's doing. He nearly always records his lead vocals in absolute darkness, but for this track—which all of the Raiders are cutting—he decided that a little atmosphere was called for. And it really is quite impressive.

The engineer is ready and waiting, and a voice in the recording booth comes over the microphone, "Let's try and take one, Terry." Terry gives the okay, and after a few last minute instructions, the music begins.

This particular track doesn't have a name yet, but it is very unusual. As a matter of fact, it doesn't even sound like the Raiders you have known before. This tune is very strange, very romantic-sounding, very weird yet strangely beautiful.

Terry isn't satisfied with this take and calls for another. A short discussion takes place over the intercom and the Raiders try it again. There are several stops-and-starts, but it is important to get this track just right ... and very soon, it is.

"All right—c'mon in for a playback," Terry says, and the Raiders troop into the control booth where we are sitting, one by one.

They are very much absorbed in the music they are creating, so they might not notice you at first. But, be patient. Five Raiders scatter all over the small room—some on chairs, some sitting on the floor, and another perched atop a table. And they all listen, intently, to this track which they have just finished.

Terry wants to hear something very closely, so he climbs on top of a chair in order to stand right next to one of the four huge speakers which are hung above the large glass window.

The track is done and Terry discusses it with the boys. They decide that it could still be improved, and decide to try another take.

Before they file back to the recording booth, Mark comes over to welcome us and say hello, and he is quickly joined by Fang and Harpo who both smile broadly at everyone. Then, it's back to the booth and a couple more takes are attempted.

Another playback—more discussion—still another take with some new ideas to be added—another playback ... and, that's it. Everyone is satisfied that the track is complete, and the Raiders take a break.

Uncle Paul is dressed very casually in a pair of beige pants and a brown-and-white striped shirt. He slouches across a chair in a corner, and begins to joke with Harpo, who respectfully plays "straight man" to all of "Uncle Paul's" jokes.

Fang finds a new guitar in a corner, brought in by another musician, and ecstatic over the new "toy" he has found, sits down in a corner to try a few new chords.

Smitty decides that it is definitely time for coffee and a doughnut, and heads quickly for the nearby commissary, stopping briefly to say hello to us and say he's glad that we could make it.

Mark is lost for the moment in a discussion with Terry on some of the material which they will be recording this evening, and for a moment—the two boys sing back and forth at one another, working out a temporary arrangement in their minds which they will figure out completely a little later.

When he's finished, Mark strolls over in our direction—clad, as usual, in his own distinctive style of dress. Tonight he is wearing black pants, his black knee-length boots (natch!), and a black-and-white print puffy-sleeved shirt. Oh yes—and a black ribbon in his "queue!"

He's excited about a song which he has just written—a very satirical song—and he comes over to sing a few bars of it to us. It sounds like a hit, Mark. He says he hopes so and then disappears to round up some tea to soothe his throat before he continues singing.

In a few minutes, Terry calls the troops back to order and together, they all go into the recording booth. Gathered around a honky-tonk piano, the six of them work out some of their ideas for the arrangement of this next tune together, deciding just which harmonies will be used, and who will sing which parts.

Terry suddenly bursts through the door—excited and enthusiastic about the ideas he has for this track—and once again, recording begins. It is an intricate track, and the boys put a great deal of work into it. And before anyone realizes it, a couple more hours have gone by.

It does seem sort of dream-like—seeing all of the Raiders, with only the candles to light up their smiles for us.

THE EVERPRESENT FULLNESS:

Or The World From Big Sur

The Everpresent Fullness make people happy, and it's not because of their name.

Of course, their name always inspires a bit of humor, but it is a very earnest name—one that they feel describes the world from a vantage point at Big Sur. But that's another story.

The Everpresent Fullness are a quietly joyful group. A former employee said, "I've never seen a group make so many people so happy." The Fullness aren't equipped with bottles of laughing gas, just effervescent personalities, bubbling wit and attitudes that are free as the wind.

Solidified

Several of the group once lived in Big Sur but it was in Redondo Beach that the group solidified. They began playing at a coffeehouse where they commanded the salary of one dollar apiece per show and "all the coffee you could drink." This convinced Jack that they "weren't in it for the money."

Actually, everpresent fullness is a religion that just happens to serve as a collective title for a group of people who hum and strum and smile broadly when thinking of their single, "Wild About My Lovin'."

Jack sings lead on "Wild Lovin'," a task he does in a twangy, laconic, bantering fashion to the accompaniment of snarling mouth harps and jangling guitars and thundering drums played by the other four Fullness.

The Fullness are an honest group, so honest that two of their members actually admit they are married. Paul Johnson recently married a freckle-faced strawberry blonde, and Tom Carvey is married with a little son named Chad.

Twenty-year-old Tom has a wild wild thatch of hair that would defy any comb in captivity. Shoeless and hatless, he is most often seen in "beer-barrel-polka shorts." Tom's special hobby is photography. He also does a lot of thinking and prefers seas and trees to world events.

Individually, the Everpresent Fullness are bright, free-wheeling individuals. Sparkling-eyed Paul Johnson, who peers at the world from behind rimless glasses and a sun-bronzed face, spends his time playing games, "especially stadium checkers" (an elaborated version of Chinese checkers). On the road, he specializes in alphabetic games — finding words on signposts and billboards that start with all the letters of the alphabet. "Quaker State and Zenith signs," he says, "come in very handy."

Fruit Trees

Jack Ryan is 25, and while can't be described exactly as *starving*, one could say that he is lean and gaunt. Tall, gangling Jack lives by himself in Redondo Beach where he has a small garden containing "a bunch of fruit trees and stuff." Jack definitely isn't a poet.

Ingenious Jack has found a way of always winning at Paul's stadium checkers. "I just tip the board and all the marbles roll in the hole," he says.

Steve Pugh, bass guitarist for the Fullness, is currently "putting a lot of effort into growing a beard." A tall, friendly, dark-haired twenty-year-old, Steve lives with his father in Manhattan Beach. Steve's claim to fame is once being "almost thrown out of Disneyland"—or well—"asked to stay off the dance floor anyway." Steve likes "a smiling face and good personality" in a girl, qualities that he possesses himself.

Terry is the youngest of the Fullness—a mere nineteen. He spends most of his time "losing at Paul's games," but when he isn't losing, he likes to "walk or ride around with a friend." A sensitive, perceptive performer, he plays thundering drums for the group.

Though the group describes their sound as "indescribable," they arrive at the general conclusion that the Everpresent Fullness play "an integration of general folk, general rock 'n roll and country jug rock."

"Groups on the same type of trip," says Tom, have been their greatest inspiration—and by trip he means type of sound. "The Yardbirds and Ray Stevens" according to Paul, are specific groups that have affected their playing.

They like real music, which Jack describes as "genuine," Tom says is "solid," and Steve concludes is "true to themselves."

The Everpresent Fullness, are most of all, true to themselves. They are earnest, honest, happy and human. It would be hard to imagine the Everpresent Fullness ever being spoiled by success.

... THE EVERPRESENT FULLNESS (l. to r.) Paul, Terry, Steve, Tom and Jack.

KRLA ARCHIVES

For Girls Only

By Shirley Poston

Speaking of George, why is he just *standing* there? (*Where, where?*) Why isn't he *hurrying*? And why isn't he at the end of August (you know him) doing the same?

Now that I have things off to a blithering start, I shall endeavor to do something besides rant incessantly in this column. I won't succeed, of course, but at least I'm trying (as in very).

First of all, I'd like to explain a couple of expressions I've used in Robin Boyd recently (Lord knows some of them could sure *use* a little explaining) (to the police, for instance).

Of course, I'll only succeed in confusing you with my garbled way of putting thingys into words, but here goes.

Harry Apers

Not long ago, I said that Robin went "Harry Apers." Well, that's a slang dealie they use in England, which I happen to think is extraordinarily neat.

Instead of saying they're flat (as in broke), they say they're *flatters*, and sometimes put a Harry in front of the word (as in Harry Flatters). And the same word-type-game can apply to just about any word, all of which escape me at the moment.

If you have the slightest idea what I just finish babbling about, please join a very small crowd.

Speaking of Robin (foolydah again), I would like to scramble atop the nearest roof and screech seven million thank-yous to Judy Mancz of Dayton, Ohio. Judy (one of both of my many readers) sent me the all-time surprise, which just happened to be a complete chapter of Robin, completely illustrated... Like a comic strip, I mean...

Godfrey, how groovy. She used the chapter where George (groan) takes Robin to Jeweller's Cafe in Liverpool, and she meets Paul and John The Genies for the first time.

I've loaned the masterpiece to the boss, and am now wheedling and stomping a lot, in hopes that it can be printed in *The BEAT*. Course, it would take up a lot of room, and they still haven't quite recovered from that nine hundred page "Beatle Movie" I nagged them into printing, but I'll keep hoping. I know you'd flip over it, too.

Speaking of the "Beatle Movie" (my, this certainly must be your day for getting fooled) (parddon?), something sort of happened to the last line as you may have noticed. And I suppose you've been blaming me and thinking I typed it wrong, right? (Re-parddon?). Well, that's usually the case when there's a mistake in something that's passed through my (in)capable hands, so just as soon as I can find the original manuscript (would you believe the early spring of 1974?), I'll tell you what the last line really was.

Until then, *suffer*...

By the way, I have succeeded in wringing that borrowed ten dollars out of my brother (as in Jerk), and can announce the winners of the envelope contest next week... No, no, I won't forget to send out a George (as in Washington) to each of the winners. I hope...

I'm always bellowing around, on various soap boxes, about how great it is that everyone is so interested in music, and learning to play instruments and all that. Well, after defending several thousand friends who don't exactly have all the talent in the world but sure do have fun, I have been put to the test.

Droom Trouble

The boy next door has bought a set of *drooms!* There are a number of feet (in my mouth, generally) between our house and his, but at this point, I would somehow prefer *blocks*. (Would you believe *Miles?*).

However, I am going to stick to my guns (and aim one of them directly at my temple the next time he starts flailing those cymbals at six-thirty a.m.) and not complain. Besides, I may soon not be able to hear all the racket. I seem to be developing a slight problem. I don't know whether it's those drooms or the fact that since he bought them, I've been sleeping (or making a desperate attempt to) with my ears crammed full of used Juicy-Fruit.

Flays Dinstruments

Just remembered something. I have a friend who is also a writer (get in that *also*) (am I a dreamer or am I a dreamer?), and she wrote the funniest line about John Lennon. She said: "He can flay the guitar and other dinstruments."

Well... *I* thought it was funny.

Oh, quick, before canned soft drinks put pop bottles in the nearest museum, try another in the long series of dirty, rotten-type tricks I've been printing in this mes--er--column--er--mess.

I know I shouldn't write about stuff like this, because it only proves what a twink I truly am and encourages you to be equally as daft, but I've never been known to let *that* stop me.

One time, a bunch of us wanted to go I-forget-where and we had about thirteen cents between us. Soooo, we decided to gather up all the pop bottles we could find.

Well, that got us nowhere fast, so we then decided to go from door to door and ask. Rather than have it appear as though we were begging (don't think that hasn't occurred to us, too) (in fact, we've laid in a large supply of tin cups just in case all else fails), we invented a "Scavenger Hunt" and used that plan of attack on several unsuspecting housewives.

Naturally, by the time we'd collected enough bottles to finance whatever it was we wanted the loot for, we were so completely carried away, we kept at it the rest of the day. It's a good thing one of us had a car (and I say *had* because you don't know what a trunkfull of pop bottles can do to a set of already-sagging springs), because by the time we finally collapsed of sheer exhaustion, we had a total of *five hundred and eleven pop bottles!*

I have never had as much fun in my life as I did that day, and the next was just about as good. We all got together and took our haul to the nearest fence... whoops... market, and you should have seen the owner pop *his* bottle (not to mention his cork).

Say, just thought of an idea. This would be a great way to raise money for a charity (besides yourself) or a fan club. I think it may also be a great way to get arrested, but that is just one of the many chances one has to take in this life.

Money For Bonnie

Hlep... Not to mention Help... I keep forgetting to tell you that I know someone who is willing to pay a princely sum for a copy of the orignial "My Bonnie." The Beatle 45 that was recorded in Germany, I mean. If you know where one is available, let me know quick...

Just thought of another way to make money. Swipe - er - rescue lots of old thingys from your attic (although you probably don't have one) (be glad, if you did, someone would probably keep you chained up in it) and get your feinds - er - freidns (oh well, you get the idea!), to do the same. Then have a thingy sale (as in rummage!)

People seem to be going ultra-Harry Apers over the kookiest stuff these days, and you just might make many mons selling something your mother was going to throw away.

Code of the Week

Down, girl. It's time for your secret coded message of the week (no, make it of the year) (it's been awhile since I printed one because I keep finding code letters lurking about) (please, God, let me find no more.)

There are several reasons why I should have more sense than to mention this, but I've been trying for weeks and have finally given up. It's just too good to be true, and I can keep my flapping trap closed no longer.

While the Beatles are in California, no one really knows where they'll be going when, except to their concerts. But there's this one particular place I *know* they have to go (I can't say where or I'd either get fired or killed, and that's a difficult choice to make.) AND, *za kvqnv ik RNI ipnvn,* they will have to *QVZLN VZRPI OH PKXBN!!!!!*

Is that not the coolest ever created???? I don't know exactly when it will happen, so guess where I am going to spend several days! So, if you see anyone permanently perched on a curb, join me! (It's too late to confuse me.)

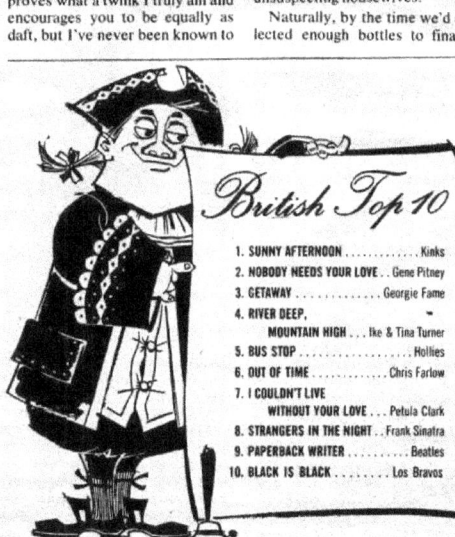

British Top 10

1. SUNNY AFTERNOON .... Kinks
2. NOBODY NEEDS YOUR LOVE ... Gene Pitney
3. GETAWAY .... Georgie Fame
4. RIVER DEEP, MOUNTAIN HIGH ... Ike & Tina Turner
5. BUS STOP .... Hollies
6. OUT OF TIME .... Chris Farlow
7. I COULDN'T LIVE WITHOUT YOUR LOVE ... Petula Clark
8. STRANGERS IN THE NIGHT ... Frank Sinatra
9. PAPERBACK WRITER .... Beatles
10. BLACK IS BLACK .... Los Bravos

KRLA ARCHIVES

The BEAT Goes To The Movies
"NEVADA SMITH"

By Jim Hamblin
(The BEAT Movie Editor)

Mr. Smith is a character born in a book called THE CARPETBAGGERS, which was made into a feature film starring George Peppard. The role of Nevada Smith was played by Alan Ladd, but before Paramount could get around to making the planned feature film of the story, Mr. Ladd suffered an unusual accident and died in Palm Springs. So the role was assigned to Steve McQueen.

The main guy's real name is Max Sand. Three men torture and kill his parents looking for gold that isn't there, and the rest of the picture tells the story of Max tracking down and killing all of them . . . except the last man. Just why and the reason for the phony name, is the basic idea of the story. There's a lot of action, and an impressive list of stars.

. . . THEY WENT THAT-A-WAY!

Out Of Sight

. . . EVEN BATMAN COULDN'T CATCH THE ZZR.

Until now, spy movies have been limited to the older set — Sean Connery, James Coburn, Dean Martin. Name a star and if he's over thirty, he's played Mr. Super Secret Agent.

Universal Pictures, however, decided teenagers shouldn't be left out in the cold. Hence the sparkling spoof and zany comedy, "Out Of Sight."

The picture is filled with all the usual fun and gyrations, but this time to the music of pop stars Gary Lewis and the Playboys, Freddie and the Dreamers, Dobie Gray, The Turtles, The Astronauts and The Knickerbockers. Their hip-swinging beat sets the tempo for the movie.

Heading the cast is Jonathan Daly who portrays the butler of a famed secret agent. He harbors a deep rooted desire to become a super spy himself and gets his big chance when he's mistaken for his employer.

Handsome Robert Pine plays a designer of wild hot rods and Karen's boyfriend. He's considered somewhat of a square by his friends since he'd rather work on an auto motor than dance among a bevy of bikini-clad beauties on the beach.

To round out the picture, well-rounded Rena Horton and midget Billy Curtis, agents of FLUSH, attempt to blow up a George Barris creation, the ZZR car.

. . . WELL-ROUNDED ACTRESS.

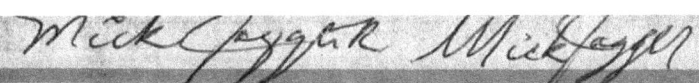

KRLA ARCHIVES

KRLA ARCHIVES

America's Largest Teen NEWSpaper 25¢

KRLA Edition BEAT
AUGUST 27, 1966

ARE BEATLES MORE POPULAR THAN JESUS?

'Burn The Beatles' — Ku Klux Klan
'Misinterpreted' — Author of Article
'Stay Out of Pennsylvania' — Sen. Fleming
'Perhaps They Are' — The Rev. Pritchard

KRLA ARCHIVES

KRLA BEAT

Volume 2, Number 22   August 27, 1966

'More Popular Than Jesus'
JOHN 8:4

What seemed to be a harmless interview at the time has touched off one of the most heated controversies of the modern generation. The following is an exert from the explosive text of Maureen Cleave's article on John Lennon that has caused the heated blasts against the Beatles.

Miss Cleave quoted Lennon as saying:

"Christianity will go. It will vanish and shrink. I needn't argue about that. I am right and will be proved right.

"We're more popular than Jesus right now. I don't know which will go first—rock 'n roll or Christianity. Jesus was all right, but his disciples were thick and ordinary. It's them twisting it that ruins it for me."

In the article, Miss Cleave said of Lennon, "Not that his mind is closed, but it's closed round whatever he's thinking at the time." She said Lennon had been conducting a thorough religious investigation for some time.

Beatles 'Ban-Wagon' Rolls!

John Goes Solo For New Film

With the Beatles stymied at the stormiest, most closely watched point in their careers, John Lennon quietly announced he is going on his own—at least temporarily.

The BEAT has learned that John, the brash focal point of the Beatles, plans to act in a movie—without the other Beatles—for the first time since the origin of the group.

A spokesman insists, however, that Lennon's single act will not involve a permanent split among the group. Lennon will be back with the other Beatles for the next group movie in January.

And, of course, it does not affect recording sessions or the Beatles' U.S. tour in August.

The Beatles are believed to have been disenchanted with the rigors of their singing routine for some time. Those close to the Beatles say the boys want to start doing more things individually.

Two Animals Leave Group

The BEAT has learned that at least two and maybe three members of the original Animals will be leaving the group. Both Hilton Valentine and Chas Chandler have said they will now concentrate on record production.

Drummer Barry Jenkins is expected to continue working with Eric Burdon, but the future of jazz organist Dave Rowberry is still unknown.

Inside the BEAT
Letters To The Editor 2
On The Beat 3
People Are Talking About 4
Herman's Low Guarantee 5
Rock On The Road 6
Pictures In The News 7
Johnny Rivers 9
Kinks—Musical Rebels 10
Open Letter To Mick Jagger 11
Is Dylan Weird? 15
Yardbirds "Over, Under, Sideways, Down" 19
Temptin' Temptations 21
The Beat Goes To The Movies ... 23

The BEAT is published bi-weekly by BEAT Publications, Inc., editorial and advertising offices at 6290 Sunset Blvd., Suite 504, Hollywood, California 90028. U.S. bureaus in Hollywood, San Francisco, New York, Chicago and Nashville, overseas correspondents in London, Liverpool and Manchester, England. Sole price, 15 cents. Subscription price: U.S. and possessions, $5 per year; Canada and foreign rates, $9 per year. Second class postage prepaid at Los Angeles, California.

JOHN — Storm Center

Epstein Fears Security Dangers During U.S. Tour

Embroiled in a controversy which produced more mass reaction than the Viet Nam war or big-city race riots, the Beatles launched their third American tour prepared for an uncertain reception.

Manager Brian Epstein, trying desperately to soothe ruffled feelings, openly expressed fears of security dangers while denying rumors that some of the 14 scheduled concerts might be cancelled.

Still unresolved was the intent of John Lennon's statement that the Beatles are "more popular than Jesus." The writer whose interview created the furore claimed the statement was taken out of context, and John quickly followed suit.

But many Americans were still dissatisfied and dozens of radio stations across the U.S. continued to ban Beatle records and organized mass burnings of Beatle records and photographs.

Subsequent statements by two other Beatles merely aggravated the situation.

Columnist Maureen Cleave appeared to ease hostile feelings when she stated that her article

READERS REACT TO BEATLE BAN PAGE 2

had been "completely misinterpreted and that Americans have the story entirely wrong."

Lennon Christian

Miss Cleave said that Lennon, whom she termed a "Christian with a young son who has also been Christened," deplored the lack of interest in the Christian Church.

Lennon, according to Miss Cleave, observed that the "power of Christianity was on the decline in the modern world and that things had reached such a ridiculous state that human beings (such as the Beatles) could be worshipped more religiously than religious figures."

She said that Lennon, far from approving this type of worship, was appalled by it.

But if Miss Cleave's explanation of the article eased feelings, ensuing statements by the other Beatles rekindled anti-Beatle sentiment.

Beatles Paul McCartney and George Harrison got in on the act while Manager Epstein was in New York City attempting to clarify Lennon's statements. McCartney said he found the American people's pursuit of money "sort of frightening," and Harrison said he wasn't really looking forward to the Beatles' current U.S. tour.

Doesn't Like U.S.

McCartney said he liked England better than the United States chiefly because of "the attitude of the people in America." He said, "They seem to think that money is everything.

"And this applies especially to the kind of people we meet — agents and corporation people. You get the feeling everybody's after it — money — and it's sort of frightening," Paul declared in a BBC radio interview.

Harrison, who earlier said the Beatles were "coming to America to get beaten up," eased his blast against the United States only when he spoke of California — where the Beatles finish their tour in late August.

"At least there," he said, "we
(Turn to Page 16)

BEAT MEDIATES
Eureka—a Solution!

The BEAT is proud to announce "The Great Compromise."

Acting as a voluntary mediator in the dispute which has strained relations with our closest ally and turned brother against brother and daughter against mother in America, The BEAT has successfully negotiated a reciprocal agreement with the Beatles.

After exhaustive negotiations they have agreed—in return for similar concessions on our part—that they will not attempt to interfere with our rights to freedom of speech or freedom of religion.

Nor will the Beatles try to force any Americans to praise England, provided we don't ask them to praise America. Most important of all, perhaps, the Beatles have unanimously agreed not to ban any American radio stations.

Thus, now that this really vital crisis has been settled, the world can return to less pressing problems such as Viet Nam, disarmament and starvation.

GEORGE — Dreads Tour   PAUL — dislikes U.S.

KRLA ARCHIVES

Letters TO THE EDITOR

Stones 'On Your Own'

Dear *BEAT*:

I would like to congratulate Linda Casson on her fine example of the most immature letter ever published. (Letters To The Editor, July 30, 1966, "Down On Stones.")

She definitely shows clear-cut symptoms of a defense reaction. She must defend the Beatles against a few charges by picking on the Stones.

I also believe that she has put her size 10½ foot into her size 12½ mouth by saying that the Beatles' album cover was not half as offensive as some things Brian Jones has done.

Some of the things Brian has done (not to mention some of the things John Lennon has done!) are not half as offensive to me, and probably many Stone and Beatle fans, as this ridiculous statement made by Miss Casson, who does not seem to know what offends and what does not.

Well, Linda. I have just one thing to say to you if you feel you must pick on someone—in the words of Ringo—"Go pick on your own nose!"

A Linda Casson fan forever,

Sue Willoughby

Stone-Side OK

Dear *BEAT*:

This letter is in reference to the article, "Beatle Fans Defecting to Stone-Side of Fence?", which appeared in the July 30 edition of *The BEAT*.

The reporter who wrote the article seemed quite dismayed that people were "turning their backs on the Beatles." She went on to say that some were even "defecting to the Stone-side of the fence."

Well, what's wrong with that? People have the right to change their minds if they want to do so. Maybe some people are tired of the Beatle sound; maybe they are looking for something new. No star can expect to stay super-popular forever. The Beatles themselves realize this.

Sure, the Beatles are great entertainers. I'm not disputing that. But maybe there are other groups who deserve to become just as popular as they have been. The Beatles' fans have been very good to them for a long time. Maybe it's someone else's turn now.

April Vargas

Time A 'Clean' Or 'Dirty?'

Dear *BEAT*:

I just read your article about "Obscenity in Popular Music" in your July 30 issue. I also read the article in Time Magazine which I thought was ridiculous.

Before I read the article, I found nothing wrong with "Day Tripper," "Rhapsody In The Rain," "Satisfaction," "Downtown," or any other songs that were mentioned.

Now, all of a sudden, these songs are bad, obscene, smutty or any other adjective these people want to tag on. This hidden meaning business is childish.

A lot of adults are always trying to find things wrong with our taste. First, they put down the groups, now they're finding things "wrong" with the songs.

I'd like to see one of these so called "critics" analyze songs like "Yesterday," "As Tears Go By," "Girl In Love," etc.

Perhaps we should ban Mother Goose because of the "sex adventures" of Georgie Porgie. Or how about this sweet little rhyme I found in my sister's Mother Goose book?

"Cry, baby, cry,
Put your finger in your eye,
And tell your mother it wasn't I."

Compared to that, what is wrong with a "Day Tripper?"

Wendy Nelson

Dear *BEAT*:

Teenagers, take a stand! Are you a "Clean" or a "Dirty?" I didn't even know the "Cleans and Dirties" existed until I read *Time* Magazine's ridiculous expose of the "really-look-and-you'll-find-it" obscenity in pop music.

Before the article in *Time* appeared, nobody gave a second thought to a possible "suggestive" lyric. Now that *Time* has made an issue out of it, there'll be some people who will carefully scrutinize the music they listen to, looking for the "dirt" that just isn't there. Yes, it seems that *Time* Magazine has invented a new "game"—the only question is, how many people are going to play?

Pam Ellison

Dear *BEAT*:

Does the "older generation" think we're sex maniacs? That's just about what it sizes up to be. That survey projects a good point. It's not the younger generation that's dirty minded—it's the adults.

When I hear our songs I don't think of Lesbians, LSD, or lechery. And I'm not an innocent teenager. You can make anything dirty if you have a mind for it.

Cheryl Crawford

Dear *BEAT*:

Recently there was an article in *Time* regarding obscenity in pop music. In my point of view, obscenity in anything depends on the person concerned. Tom Lehrer once said:

"When indirectly viewed,
Everything is lewd.
I could tell you things
About Peter Pan,
And the Wizard of Oz
Is a dirty old man."

When you think about it, anyone condemning a record for its obscene lyrics would already have to know all the tricks.

Paula Walker

Dear *BEAT*:

Thank you for the rebuttal of *Time* Magazine's ridiculous article on pop music but there is one point I would like to add. I think we can agree that suggestive songs are nothing new (you forgot to mention "Love For Sale," which speaks of out-and-out prostitution!) but, can you name a song written in the "good old days" (?) that can be compared to "Kicks," which is so obviously against the use of drugs, etc.?

And while I'm at it, I'd like to say a great big thank you to Bob Dylan, the Beatles, Stones, and all those wonderful geniuses for jolting me out of the horribly unrealistic world I used to live in. They made me open my eyes and start looking for a few answers (and they do exist if you look hard enough!).

Thanks for the fab reading matter.

A BEAT Subscriber

Dear *BEAT*:

When the article in *Time* was published, I read it. And for the most part, I laughed at it.

. . . Now—let's pretend that we're one of the "dirties" mentioned in *Time* magazine, one of the persons whose express purpose in life is to read obscenity into everything we see and hear.

For instance: Mother Goose's story of "Jack and Jill" is most certainly about a boy and a girl who go on an LSD trip and consequently lose their minds. "Puff The Magic Dragon" is about a boy's illusions under the influence of drugs, and "Universal Soldier" is about a homicidal maniac who runs around killing everybody he can get his hands on.

Of course, that's stretching it a bit—but isn't *Time* doing the same thing?

Poppie Chase

Dear *BEAT*:

I read the article in *Time*, "Rock 'n' Roll Going To Pot" and I don't blame the author for keeping his name out of it. If I had written it I wouldn't want anyone to know my name either. It seemed to me he or she knew a lot about rainy day women and getting stoned and straight shooters, and as Mr. X said "as any junkie knows . . ."

I also have to wonder about anyone who can listen to "Strangers In The Night" and end up thinking about a homosexual pick up.

The author goes on to talk about unwed mothers, a man who finds out that his girl is a prostitute, and Mick Jagger trying to make some girl. These things happen everyday, and are we supposed to just close our eyes and pretend it doesn't happen and just sing and write songs about sunshine and rainbows? I'm surprised this guy didn't pick "Mary Had A Little Lamb" apart.

J.T.W.

Beatle Controversy No. II

Dear *BEAT*:

Myself, my husband and my two teenage daughters are all Beatle fans. We've gone to the last two concerts they had here and have tickets for this year's concert. We surely hope this thing won't be blown up out of proportion and prevent them from coming here this year.

It's all a mistake I'm sure . . . and I think the most important thing your paper can do is to continue repeating that reporter Maureen Cleve in London said her quote from John was taken out of context. She said that John was only making a comment on the sad state of the world today. I know that even our own newspapers in America say that church attendance is down, and this is really no different than what John Lennon said.

Mrs. Gable

Dear *BEAT*:

The way John Lennon puts things it's sort of weird . . . it's like sarcasm. Sometimes you can't take him really seriously. He may have been throwing a little bit of sarcasm at society because not many people really go to church. Although they really believe in their religion they don't practice it that much. They support the Beatles wholeheartedly but they don't really support their church.

Dan Minnimede

Dear *BEAT*:

I feel John Lennon is just being sarcastic and I wouldn't hold it against him. And even if he weren't, I feel that everybody has the right to believe the way they want to about religion.

Eileen McMain

Dear *BEAT*:

John Lennon's statement on the state of Chrisitianity was taken the wrong way. I believe the man was saying, in a sense, that he doesn't like people to worship the Beatles so much. To follow them, yes, but not to worship them to the point that they just go way out of bounds.

The Beatles have done nothing in their private or public lives that is anything but clean.

I'm an adult and I've lived half of my life and even now I enjoy—and hope to continue enjoying—the Beatles in my home. I hope that every American mother will take what John Lennon said, describe it to her children, and break it down to what he meant and not what people are trying to read into it.

Mary Hudseth

Adults True Beatle Fans

Dear *BEAT*:

I object to the quote under George Harrison's picture on page one of the July 30 issue of your magazine. Even if he did say it, this certainly isn't the time, after all that's happened, to turn even more people away from the concert in August by printing it.

For some unknown reason, there seems to be a "hate the Beatles" movement afoot and I, for one, am greatly concerned over it. The overall news media has always resented them and takes fiendish delight in running them down, for what reason, I couldn't say.

I am an adult who happens to appreciate good music, whether it be rock or Bach. There are many more like me around. In the long run, it will be us adults and a few un-fickle, mature truly loyal teenagers who will be the solid core of the Beatle following.

How could anyone, young or old, have loved the Beatles two years ago and turn away from them today, when their music keeps getting better and better?

I hope their America tour will be successful and a happy venture for them, or we may never see them again.

Mrs. Roger Hayes

KRLA ARCHIVES

On the BEAT
By Louise Criscione

Well, everything's back to normal again with the Beatles in the midst of controversy and the Stone fans camped outside of the RCA Studios in Hollywood waiting for a glimpse of the fab five. Phoenix fans are up-in-arms over the Dave Clark Five appearance in their city and "I Saw Her Again," "Along Comes Mary," "Sweet Pea" and several other American hits are being recorded in Swedish and Norwegian. Other than that, nothing much is happening – except maybe Fire And Ice.

Something strange is definitely going on in the Beatle camp and no one in the business is quite sure what. Reports filtering out of England seem to indicate that Epstein is losing his control over John Lennon. Up until the last few months, all Beatle comments to the press were guarded. And now within the span of a month, John has told the world that he didn't even know the Philippines had a president and that "we're (the Beatles) more popular than Jesus now."

And, on top of his statements to the press, John is going to make "How I Won The War" minus Paul, George and Ringo. The whole mess adds up to "something wrong somewhere." People who know John (or who know those who do) are not in the least bit surprised about John's views on Christianity but they *are* surprised that Epstein would let John go ahead and make them public. John, naturally, has the right to his opinions but Epstein is a shrewd businessman, one who is well aware what adverse effects John's views would have in the U.S.

... JOHN LENNON

That is the fact which makes people wonder if Epstein isn't perhaps losing his control over John and I, for one, would give anything to find out what is *really* going on with the Beatles.

The Stones had their share of trouble this week too, thanks to the air strike. They had booked studio time at RCA but missed three entire days because they couldn't get a flight into Los Angeles. No small matter, you say? Well, it is when you're paying $40 an hour for a studio to sit empty!

Three Million Haul

However, the Stones managed to gross a neat three million on this tour so the dent in their pocketbooks is expected to recover nicely. Keith, on the other hand, may *never* recover from the shock of actually passing his driving test and possessing his own driver's license! It's been a long time coming (what with Keith continuing to fail the tough British exam) but this time around he made it and can now do his own driving rather than relying on his chauffeur.

Despite the fantastic amount of money made by the Stones on this tour, there were moments when they, no doubt, wished they'd have stayed in England. First off, you know about the New York hotel problem and the pending suit the Stones have filed against them. But did you know that only hours after they played their New York Forrest Hills date their equipment was stolen?

What made the Stones especially furious was the fact that their Dulcimer, Brian's favorite and the only electronic Dulcimer in the world, was among the stolen equipment. All equipment was custom made and the Stones had only two days in which to replace it. Needless to say, the Vox people worked night and day and succeeded in getting new equipment for the Stones.

... BRIAN JONES

Two Stories

Phoenix teens are plenty mad over the Dave Clark Punches Dick Gray story which appeared in *The BEAT*. It seems that Dave's version of the story differs with what the Phoenix audience witnessed. Since I wasn't there, I don't know who is right but I *do* know that this marks the first time the DC5 has gone really controversial.

It should be interesting to see if the world is ready for Fire And Ice. They're a new group who feature, among other things, a Negro female singer who is completely bald and a "very pretty" girl who is absolutely flat-chested and wears negligees when she sings. However, we're assured "they're the kind you can't see through." A fact which the boys will appreciate, I'm sure!

The Hollies Dump Haydock: Oppose Time Off For Birth

What is this, the year of musical chairs for pop groups? Apparently it is, and the Hollies didn't want to be left behind so they canned their bass guitarist, Eric Haydock.

Usually, the bow-out among groups is graceful with all sides admitting a "mutual decision." However, the Hollies have gone a step beyond this with Eric and the remaining Hollies each giving contradictory views on the split.

Eric claims "it was a raw deal and I am consulting my lawyers. It all hinges on the fact that I wanted a few days off in November when my wife is expecting a baby."

Graham Nash, speaking for the Hollies, emphasized that musically the Hollies had no gripe against Eric but that he was extremely unreliable. Nash stated that a replacement for Eric had to be called in for their Swedish tour and also for the recording session at which the Hollies' latest hit, "Bus Stop," was cut.

In answer to Graham's charges, Eric declared: "It's true that I've missed a few dates through illness but on each occasion I have produced a doctor's certificate."

Whichever side you choose to believe, the fact remains that Eric is out of the Hollies and has been permanently replaced by 23 year old Bern Calvert, former member of the Dolphins, and the bass guitarist who took Eric's place in Sweden.

... HAYDOCK—dumped because he asked time out for birth of baby.

Stones Sell Out Palace

The Rolling Stones, currently finishing their fifth record-breaking tour of the United States, sold out all 12,000 seats in San Francisco's Cow Palace in less than a week.

The ticket gross for the instant sell-out exceeded $81,000. For the Stones' 29-city U.S. tour the group is expected to earn at least $3,000,000.

Rascals First At Hawaii Fair

The Young Rascals, finishing up a ten day visit to California, are preparing to head for Hawaii where they will be the first American group to headline the Honolulu Teen Fair on August 24.

They hope to spend the next four days in Hawaii just loafing on the beach but it's doubtful whether their Hawaiin fans will go for that! It's also doubtful that the Rascals are capable of merely "resting."

The Rascals return to the Mainland on August 29 and will begin recording in New York City on September 6. Colleges throughout the U.S. will be hit by the Rascals from September 16-30 and October is the month set aside for Gene, Eddie, Dino and Felix's first visit to Europe.

Other than that the Rascals don't have a thing to do – except laze on the beach and gaze at the hula girls!

Cher Wins The Battle

Cher is emerging the winner in the battle of the "Alfie" versions. She's already been named to sing the title over the credits of the British movie, "Alfie," when it opens Stateside in the Fall.

Now, it appears that Cher's single is setting sales records, which is especially difficult since "Alfie" is the most recorded song since "Shadow Of Your Smile." Everyone from Jack Jones to Cher has recorded it but from all the sales reports it is Cher who is destined to have the biggest hit with the Burt Bacharach penned "Alfie."

Sonny's Out Of Solo Bag

To the great lament of music lovers, Sonny Bono has announced that he is leaving the solo business to concentrate on movies and record production.

However, Sonny assures us that he will still occasionally sing with Cher. But Sonny's bag is really turning to the movie screen now that he's had a taste of the big screen business with "Good Times."

"If you want longevity in this business," states Sonny, "you've got to make a move. No one's just stayed a singer and made it."

Sonny estimates that making "Good Times," the duo's first feature film, has cost the couple "over $250,000 in bookings." The movie took longer than expected to make and ran $550,000 over the original budget.

Along with the movie and Cher's success as a single artist (her version of "Alfie" has already sold over 200,000 copies), the Bonos also have quite a thing going in the clothing business. Cher designs, Sonny manages and their fans spend small fortunes buying Sonny & Cher originals.

Not bad for a guy who used to exist on cheese and crackers and wore short hair and suits, is it?

KRLA ARCHIVES

Letters TO THE EDITOR

DAVE CLARK CONTROVERSY

Bald Dylan

Dear BEAT:

After reading the Well-Wisher's letter, I hurriedly hurried home, unfolded my album cover, took out my warped record, whipped a sopping paper towel out of my drawer, and set to work. Much to my dismay, I discovered I had the wrong folded album cover. I had unwittingly (but rather charmingly, don't you think?) balderized Bob Dylan. He'll never be quite the same.

After I had simiarly ruined several album covers, it finally struck me as enlightening that I had no Yesterday or Today or Tomorrow for that matter. (I have been doomed.) I cautiously wended my way to the nearest store, trampling several persons. While the nasty storekeeper (also known as my father) had his back turned, I snitched a copy of "Yesterday and Today." Then, with sirens wailing in my ears, I calmly thumbed a ride home with the local patrolman.

Home once again, I cautiously skirted the Parent Trap and gleefully dashed into my bedlam - oops - bedroom. I re-went thru the whole dis-comfortable process. This time, however, and much to my surprise (just think, it's not even my birthday) I did uncover something . . . a soggy blank piece of cardboard. I wept, I cried, I cut my hair! Ah me, what could I do? I snitched another album, that's what!

The moral of this woe-filled, well-fed (it eats scraps) tale of woe is: Do not, under penalty of life, buy album covers unless you can plainly discern a figurement beneath the picture presently occupying the front of the Beatles' new album cover.
(Amen) *Jillian McIntyre*

P.A.T.A. Fan

Dear BEAT:

I just wanted to write and tell you how much I like your "People Are Talking About" column. People aren't always talking about the things mentioned there: they are too busy trying to figure out what the items in the column mean!

The placement of the column in the July 30th issue was very appropriate for one item. "Why no one saw Ian" could not go in any better place than under Chuck Boyd's pictures of the concert!

Now, if I may, I would like to add my own suggestions for the column. PEOPLE ARE TALKING ABOUT Frank on the Lomax show . . . The way Donovan always seems to be in court lately . . . The reason a certain column (hint: the initials are P.A.T.A.) has no byline . . . Barry Fisher (?) on the drums.

I do hereby promise to rush down to the news stands in two weeks and buy my next copy of The BEAT, because I want to see the next "People AreTalking About" column. I really do hope this is one of the new columns in the new BEAT.

I hope your success continues with the new policies. Take Care.
Linda Welker

Dylan's Hat

Dear BEAT:

After scanning your July 16 issue I must inquire how it is so obvious that Bob Dylan's "Leopard Skin Pill Box Hat" is not about a hat. How clearly must one speak before people will grope what's really happening?
Space Lady

Dear BEAT:

I am afraid you were misinformed by Dave Clark as to what happened during and after the DC-5 concert in Phoenix. He also did not explain what led to the event. While the local groups, such as the fabulous P-Nut Butter, were on, you were allowed to leave your seat to take pictures—but you had to go immediately back to your seat.

During the intermission before the DC-5 came on a small crowd began to gather in front of the front row seats. The police allowed them to stay there and as time went on the crowd grew. Finally, during the middle of the show the ropes broke and the crowd went up to the stage—but it wasn't any worse than any of our other concerts.

Then in the middle of "Try Too Hard" DJ Dick Gray came storming out and told Dave Clark to get off the stage, and Dave replied, "I ain't finished yet," and continued to play. I couldn't see if he was kicked or not. He went off at the end of the number, hit Dick Gray—but did not return to the stage (this caused the dropping of the last two numbers.)

Also, Mr. Gray did not apologize to Dave and the group. He made a short statement as to what happened but said that he felt, "If anyone should apologize it should be Dave Clark." Don't get me wrong, I am on the DC-5's side. I think Mr. Gray was wrong. But so was Dave Clark in his story to The BEAT. And two wrongs don't make a right. They just make Phoenix look bad and maybe stop others from appearing here.
Becky Carron
Phoenix

Dear BEAT:

I am a regular reader of your magazine but after your July 30 issue I may stop, as will many of my friends. We are up in arms about your statement saying that Dick Gray, one of our disc jockeys, apologized for his scuffle (as you call it) with Dave Clark.

The broadcast that you speak of said that they would not apologize. It stated, in fact, that Dave owed Dick Gray an apology. And until we get an apology from you and Dave for this article, Phoenix will be up in arms against you both.
Bill

In our July 30 issue we printed only Dave Clark's version of the incident in Phoenix. But every story has at least two sides, and we appreciate yours.
Editor

Fogey 'Love'

Dear BEAT:

This letter is concerning the song the Ray Conniff Singers made, "Somewhere My Love." Why do all the Pop stations play it? I mean, it's so slow and old fogey-like. I think it should be played on old people's stations—not the pop stations.
Cynthia Patton

Dear BEAT:

Boy, do I have some news for you. Does Dave Clark's memory need a little refreshing! I refer to your article "Dave Clark Takes Punch At Phoenix Disc Jockey." I don't know which concert he attended in Phoenix, but the one I went to was nothing like he described.

In the first, second, and third place there was absolutely no hour long apology from Dick Gray. If anything, it was an explanation of what happened at the concert.

Saying the crowd "was getting pretty excited" was the biggest understatement in history. It was out of control even before the DC-5 came on stage.

What happened in Phoenix has been blown up out of proportion so that the real truth will probably never be known.

The radio station was at fault because it failed to control the crowd before the DC-5 ever got on stage. The DC-5 was at fault because when the radio station asked to control the crowd, the group kept on playing.

All this now is publicity for the DC-5 and if this junk is what they want for publicity let them have it.
Cindy Stecker
Phoenix

Dear BEAT:

I have just read the article "Dave Clark Takes Punch At Phoenix Disc Jockey" and my mouth is still hanging open in disbelief. Obviously, the entire article was from Mr. Clark's point of view, but does he think the audience was blind? Or maybe he thought Phoenix would never see the article in The BEAT. In either case, he was wrong.

First off, I never did hear any hour-long broadcast apology, but I did hear the radio station make a statement that they did not feel they owed the Dave Clark Five an apology. The broadcast said the Dave Clark Five owed the audience and apology for not giving the radio station an opportunity to calm the crowd down. The crowd was getting pretty excited and there were some injuries along with the usual faintings.

Fearing further injuries, disc jockey Dick Gray asked the DC-5 and their manager to stop for five minutes in order to give the radio station a chance to calm the crowd. This they would not do. Consequently, the disc jockey went back on stage, placed his hand on Dave Clark's shoulder (he did not kick Clark) and told him to stop the show.

Angered by being stopped in mid-number Dave Clark and Mike Smith rushed backstage after the disc jockey and the swinging began.

Indeed it was unfortunate that the incident did happen, and perhaps the DC-5 is not too fond of Phoenix now, but then, maybe Phoenix is not too fond of it anymore, either.
Cecily Matter
Phoenix

'in' people are talking about...

The unbelievable ignorance and the total uncouth of the people at the Los Angeles International Airport coffee shop (opposite Continental Airlines) for refusing to serve the Turtles anything except water and menus and considering avoiding the place like they would an adult's suggestion to get a hair cut . . . The Eskimo-like outfit Johnny Rivers was wearing one night at the Whiskey . . . Whether Time is a four-letter word and why adults are always searching for dirt and when they're going to announce the *obscenity in church* hymns . . . What "drive my car" means in England . . . James Brown and what gives him the idea that money won't change you . . . Whether Alfie is a heel or a great guy and deciding he's probably a heel . . . The Hollies finally finding it at a bus stop after they thought they'd lost it looking through that window . . . How groovy it would be under Mick's thumb . . . How funny it would be to perch Tommy Roe on top of our water fountain . . . What you can do with tar and cement.

PEOPLE ARE TALKING ABOUT the money situation in Seattle . . . The location of that land of a 1,000 dances and coming to the conclusion that it's any club in New York, San Francisco or Hollywood where you can see Zal at the Phone Booth dancing with a girl who has shorter hair than he does, Barry McGuire dancing on everyone else's feet at the Avalon or the girl at the Whiskey who dances alone . . . The de-Animalization of Eric . . . The Warner Brothers' search for an 18 year old girl who looks 16 and can pass for a boy . . . What is blowin' in the wind . . . The impossible dream of being able to order a coke at a rock club and getting less than three-fourths water included with the thimble of coke . . . Whether one of the teenage authors of "A Groovy Kind Of Love" is related to Cynthia Wyle . . . How you have to watch out when the door swings the other way . . . A well-known trade paper calling the Young Rascals a "British" rock group.

PEOPLE ARE TALKING ABOUT who is going to get shot with the Beatles' revolver . . . Which joker went wild . . . The Mindbender who avoids Mr. Smith's . . . Good guys occasionally wearing white . . . What the young are entering . . . Brian's Anita excusing herself from Papa John at the Mama's & Papa's session to go out and buy some toys . . . Whether or not Sinatra is a frustrated prize fighter or at least a frustrated bouncer . . . How the King could possibly get love letters on the charts . . . How fab it is to be sunny . . . The door who looks like the spoonful if you have bad eyesight . . . Manfred's flamingo and whether or not Paul was right about its meaning . . . What kind of function is going on at the junction . . . The spell of Price . . . How long Shorty is . . . How you're bound to miss the 13th floor elevators since they don't exist . . . How many wipe outs the Surfaris can have before their boards disown them.

PEOPLE ARE TALKING ABOUT how no one recognized Willie when he shaved his beard. Even his own group didn't know him because they hadn't seen his face in a year and a half . . . What seven and seven really is . . . The pages which turned yellow . . . The Grass Roots getting thirsty and changing their name . . . Low guarantees against a large percentage of the gate and what happens when a group bombs . . . How the departure of Sonny from the solo ranks is making music lovers particularly sad . . . Locking up the doors . . . Which Donovan was the grooviest . . . Whether or not the Beatles will get beaten up in America and what it will mean if they do . . . Taking Bill and Bobby's suggestion . . . Lady Jane helping mother . . . Pied piping and how come Crispian thinks he can . . . Whether the Rascal ash trays were sent by a slow mule or galloping turtle and deciding they probably weren't sent at all.

KRLA ARCHIVES

Ray Charles Holds Inmates 'Captive'

LORTON, Va.—It is not often that a performer has a captive audience of 2,000 even before the curtain goes up. But that's what was waiting for Ray Charles and his band when he played to an "invitation only" audience at the Eleventh Annual Lorton Jazz Festival at the Lorton Reformatory in Lorton, Virginia.

Ray's appearance, arranged by the Catholic Chaplains of the Washington, D.C. Department of Corrections, followed an auspicious list of entertainers who have performed in the past for the inmates. Last year Frank Sinatra, Ella Fitzgerald and Count Basie appeared on the same bill.

Appearing with Ray at the benefit performance were the Raylettes, the Shirley Horn Trio, Charlie Rouse, The "ESP" and The Soulfuls.

The jazz festival was held on the institution's athletic field. A simple platform fitted with a canopy served as a stage. Bleachers were added to the regular stands to accommodate the audience and the dugouts were used as home base for the entertainers.

The first festival was held 11 years ago. What started out as a spontaneous performance by Sarah Vaughn has grown into this annual event. An inmate clerk, who was a jazz buff, wrote to Sarah and asked for her autograph. Instead of mailing it, she showed up in person at the reformatory and brought a combo with her. So impressive was the reaction of the prisoners, many serving long-term and life sentences, that the Catholic Chaplains took it upon themselves to produce and direct the benefit show on an annual basis.

Charles interrupted his schedule of one-nighters to fly to Washington for the special performance. Since kicking off his personal appearance tour, Charles has grossed over $500,000 in what have been almost uniformly standing-room-only audiences in major arenas in 52 cities from coast to coast.

Father Sheehy, Director of Catholic Chaplains who coordinated the event, called Charles' hour and forty-five minute performance one of the most stirring and enthusiastically received in Lorton's History.

Herman: Low Guarantee But Piles Of The Green

Never let it be said that Herman and his management are not smart people. The figures for the last six dates on their American tour are in and they clearly show Herman pulling in the green stuff.

In Tulsa, the Hermits brought in a $29,000 gross; Little Rock showed a gross of $29,000; Dallas was a sell-out with a $41,000 gross and a $20,000 guarantee for the group; Corpus Christi turned up a gross of $25,000 and in Jackson, Mississippi 3,000 fans were turned away at the gate with a $41,000 gross and $23,000 for the Hermits.

The unique part of the Herman's Hermits tour is that they are working on a considerably lower guarantee than most of the other big British groups but are consistently going into percentages based on ticket sales. The result is that they earn as much money but play to packed houses.

This '66 summer season has been rather hard on some promoters who have signed big name artists with huge guarantees only to have the group playing to empty houses. This, of course, means that the promoter has paid out top prices for the group but has failed to reciprocate at the gate. In other words, he's lost a pile.

Herman, on the other hand, does not demand a large guarantee. He relies on his drawing power by taking a certain percentage of the gate. Therefore, if he fails to draw he loses and not the promoter.

But Herman's drawing power is such that he doesn't often lose! Last year he broke twelve house records and earned over two million dollars in the U.S. This year, with a multi-million dollar MGM movie contract in his pocket, an unbroken string of hit records and a highly successful Stateside tour Herman and his Hermits have already passed the two million mark.

Nancy Sinatra: Coup Of Year

Nancy Sinatra has just been signed for three Ed Sullivan Show dates next season at $10,000 per appearance. Sullivan has shelled out that price before but the twist is that Nancy will receive a twelve minute segment introducing her new album. And *that* is unusual!

Sullivan is notoriously well-known for giving his guests extremely limited segments. A performer is lucky if he manages to be in front of the camera a full five minutes.

So, handing Nancy 12 minutes is indeed an honor for the daughter of the Chairman of the Board.

McCallum Demands New Deal

David McCallum, one of the men from U.N.C.L.E., has asked MGM for a new deal. McCallum originally signed with MGM three years ago for theatrical films.

But until he joined Robert Vaughn in the U.N.C.L.E. television series, he wasn't worth a whole lot to the studio. Now, however, he's quite valuable and that's why he wants a new contract.

Representatives for McCallum are asking for a brand new contract with "clarification" of terms of the original deal. Reportedly, McCallum is also seeking more money for his services in movies as well as more money for the series and a bigger say in the selection of features.

Neither MGM nor McCallum's co-star, Robert Vaughn, have released any statements on McCallum's move. But if McCallum is asking for more than the studio or Vaughn think he's worth, you can bet your "Revolver" MGM and Vaughn will be saying plenty!

Single For Beach Boys

Early sales figures indicate that the Beach Boys' new single, "God Only Knows," might be one of the biggest sellers ever taken from any Beach Boy album.

The single, taken from the group's "Pet Sounds" album, and released just last week by Capitol Records, picked up more than 250,000 orders for advance copies.

"God Only Knows" is the fourth single in a row to be taken from a Beach Boy album following the LP's release. Prior to this one, the group met success with "Barbara Ann," "California Girls," and "Help Me Rhonda," all from previous albums.

All of the three previous singles were in the Top 10 nationally and "Help Me Rhonda" hit the number one spot on every major survey. The four songs were all written by Beach Boy leader, Brian Wilson.

FRANK SINATRA SPECIAL NO. 11

Frank Sinatra has been signed for a second giant Sinatra special. "Frank Sinatra: A Man and His Music – Part II" will be a new hour musical inspired by one of the most highly-acclaimed specials in recent years, "Frank Sinatra: A Man and His Music."

The new Sinatra special will be aired on the CBS network at 9 p.m. on December 7. Sinatra's daughter, Nancy will be her father's guest on the show but otherwise the hour special will feature all new songs by Sinatra Sr.

Wild Ones Launch Massive Campaign

NEW YORK—One of the most extensive and elaborate tie-in campaigns ever made between a group and a major retailer was launched this week as the Wild Ones headed for the first of 44 promotions in Sears & Roebuck stores in cities all over the United States.

The group will be in Montgomery, Amarillo, Dallas, Fort Worth, Steubenville, Kansas City, Fort Meyers, Shreveport, Austin, Tulsa, San Antonio, Lubbock, Wichita, Omaha, Oklahoma City, Wilmington, Savannah, Washington D.C., Greenwood, Evansville, Chicago, Green Bay, Fort Wayne, Minneapolis, Milwaukee, Sandusky, Las Vegas, Harrisburg, Bakersfield, Salt Lake City, Ogden, El Monte, Baton Rouge, San Bernardino, Riverside, Tucson, Pittsburgh, Fresno, Reno and Stockton.

In order to make the dates, Sears has provided the Wild Ones with a private, eight-passenger Lear Jet, limousine service from the moment they touch down at the local airport until they leave the city and deluxe accomodations when they have to stay overnight.

In each city, local Sears promotion staffers have arranged television, radio and newspaper interviews, in-store personal appearances and performances, parking lot hops, fashion shows, motorcades and tie-ins with any local events that coincide with the Wild Ones' visit.

A single, "Come On Back" b/w "Here At Sears," is given away free to everyone who attends and is autographed by the group at in-store "signing sessions." The single was cut specifically for the Sears label and is available only when the Wild Ones make an appearance at a Sears store.

Greene And Stone To Wrestle Uncle Sam?

Charlie Greene and Brian Stone, discoverers of Sonny & Cher, are already pop music millionaires. They're considering establishing a pirate radio station (similar to the British pirates) off the coast of New York and now they're down in Mexico buying a music publishing business. Reason? To corner the "Mexican Ranchero" business.

Controversy is sure to rage if, and when, Greene and Stone start their pirate radio station. The U.S. Government is almost positive to heartily dislike the idea of a pirate ship anchored off the coast, especially because of all of the problems encountered by the British Government with their pirate ships.

Besides up-setting the Government, the pirate radio idea is extremely dangerous. Since it is outside the country's limit, no police protection is available to the ship and is probably the reason for the murder of Terry King aboard one of the British pirate ships only last month.

KRLA ARCHIVES

TROGGS MAD OVER 'SLAP'

LONDON—Just leave it to Jonathan King. He can make anyone mad by merely opening his mouth. But he really accomplished quite a feat when he made the mild-mannered Troggs see red.

King, who enjoyed a huge American chart success with his "Everyone's Gone To The Moon," apparently stated that if you dig the Troggs' follow-up to "Wild Thing," "A Girl Like You," (which is at the top of the British charts) you are "the very lowest common denominator in the pop audience."

Naturally, the Troggs were incensed with King's remark, not only because he put them down as musicians, but because he classified their fans as nothing short of morons. And that the Troggs refused to take silently.

Said Trogg Chris Britton: "Jonathan would appear to walk about with one foot in his mouth and the other in his typewriter." He went on to add that King could make as many remarks about the Troggs as he liked but "he can leave the fans alone."

King's attack on the Troggs and their fans was only another in a series of problems for the British group that came from nowhere and managed to secure the top spot in the U.S. charts with their "Wild Thing."

In the States there has been a continuing legal hassle over the rights to the Troggs' material with both Atco and Fontana issuing "Wild Thing" and "A Girl Like You." The case has been brought to court but postponed until September, meaning that the sales money from both discs will continue being divided between the two record labels until a court decision is reached.

Yardbirds Pass U.S. Inspection

The Yardbirds, despite previous hang-ups with the Immigration Department, have obtained an okay to tour the United States throughout August and the early part of September.

Their two other visits to America have been plagued with nothing but trouble over work permits and the group was once almost deported. However, the Yardbirds now have a new manager, Simon Napier-Bell, and apparently he has been able to iron out any difficulties formerly existing between the Yardbirds and the Government.

As of press time, the Yardbirds' schedule is Oklahoma City on August 19 and 20; Tucson on the 21; Los Angeles on the 22; Monterey on the 24; San Francisco on August 25; San Leandro on the 26; Santa Barbara on August 27; Pismo Beach on the 28; San Diego on August 29; and San Jose on August 30.

On September 1 the Yardbirds head to Santa Rosa, have a free traveling day and then appear in Salem, Oregon on September 3. Hawaii seems to be the new "in" place to play, so on September 4 the Yardbirds jet to the 50th state for an appearance in Honolulu.

MAMA'S AND PAPA'S TURN DOWN SULLIVAN

The Mama's and Papa's, the most non-conforming of the non-comforming groups, have pulled their wildest stunt yet. They've just turned down Ed Sullivan's three-package deal for the upcoming season!

With the death of "Lloyd Thaxton," "Shindig," "Hullabaloo" and "Ninth Street West" about the only top weekly show utilizing the talent of pop acts is the once conservative "Ed Sullivan Show." And Mr. Sullivan still remains ultra-conservative about booking a rock act for more than one appearance at a time.

However, after giving the matter careful consideration, the M's and P's decided that they didn't want to work *that* hard so they nixed Sullivan's offer and he still hasn't gotten over it!

Although the Mama's and Papa's have a mental block about too much work, they did jet to New York last week to appear at the Forest Hills Tennis Stadium. And they did manage to put the finishing touches on their second LP—a feat which made everyone quite happy.

In an age of contracts and money and act of God clauses, the Mama's and Papa's remain unique. No one is ever sure if tomorrow the group will decide to give it all up and go back to being beachcombers. And then, of course, there is always the chance Mama Cass might suddenly make up her mind to pay John Lennon another visit. In which case...

Gold Record Percy's First

Percy Sledge has received a Gold Record for his smash single, "When A Man Loves A Woman" which was certified as a million seller last week by the RIAA.

The record was Percy's first big hit and established him firmly in both the rock 'n' roll and in R&B fields. He is currently high on the charts with "Warm And Tender Love."

Stations Ban Napoleon XIV

"They're Coming To Take Me Away, Ha Haaa!" is being taken away.

The record, the fastest selling novelty disc in many years, has been banned from air play by many top 40 radio stations because it allegedly makes fun of the mentally unbalanced and is therefore offensive.

Several stations said listener response was so negative it forced the withdrawal. In other instances, station personnel disagreed with the subject matter of the disc.

The record — containing the rhythmic mumblings of a psychopath as he is being taken away by "nice young men in clean white coats"—is still selling 30 to 50,000 copies a week, however.

And it is still listed in the top five best-selling records, even by radio stations that refuse to play it.

The BEAT also learned last week that Napoleon XIV, who recorded the best-selling disc, has a real name after all. He's Jerry Samuels, a long-time record producer.

But at this stage, neither banning of the record by radio stations or revealment of Napoleon XIV's real name looks like it will hurt sales of the record.

Rock On The Road

SUNRAYS
AUGUST
15-18 — Tour Canada with Beach Boys
19 — Spokane, Washington
20 — Tour with Raiders
TURTLES
AUGUST
19-24 — Miami Beach, Fla.
25 — Baltimore, Maryland
27 — Society party in San Francisco
29-31 — Tape Hollywood Palace
GARY LEWIS
AUGUST
18-20 — Elmira, New York
21-27 — Steel Pier, Atlantic City
30-31 — Detroit, Michigan State Fair
PETULA CLARK
AUGUST 1-JANUARY 15
In the U.S. for TV shows and 30 concerts.
KNICKERBOCKERS
AUGUST
17-27 — Seattle, Washington
PAUL REVERE & THE RAIDERS
AUGUST
20 — Asbury Park, New Jersey
21 — Wallingford, Conn.
22 — Manchester, New Hampshire
23 — Holyoke, Mass.
24 — Cleveland, Ohio
25 — Baltimore, Maryland
26 — Jacksonville, Fla.
27 — Tampa, Fla.
28 — Orlando, Fla.
29 — Miami Beach, Fla.
30 — Lafayette, La.
31 — Omaha, Neb.
EVERLY BROTHERS
AUGUST
15-21 — Deerborn, Michigan
23 — Plainview, Texas
24 — Clovis, New Mexico
25 — Lubbock, Texas
26 — Odessa, Texas
27 — Amarillo, Texas
LOVE
AUGUST
18 — Fresno, California
27 — Longshoremans, San Francisco
P.J. PROBY
SEPTEMBER
14-28 — Tour in Australia
JOHNNY RIVERS
AUGUST
13-27 — Army Reserves
LOVIN' SPOONFUL
AUGUST
24 — Connecticut
27 — Ohio
28 — Ohio
31 — Michigan
SEPTEMBER
5-18 — Vacation
CYRKLE
AUGUST
12-29 — Beatle tour
31 — Phoenix
SEPTEMBER
3 — Ohio
4 — Illinois
ROY HEAD
AUGUST
21-28 — Regal Theater, Chicago
LEAVES
SEPTEMBER
2- 8 — Miami, Fla.
THEM
AUGUST
16-21 — Losers North, San Jose, California
23-28 — Same
SEPTEMBER
2- 3 — Longshoreman's, San Francisco
9 — Fresno, California
VOGUES
AUGUST
20 — Chicago, Ill.
26 — Illinois
30 to Sept. 4 — Texas tour
JERRY NAYLOR
AUGUST
21 — State Fair in Wisconsin
MITCH RYDER AND THE DETROIT WHEELS
AUGUST
19-28 — "Where the Action Is" — Dick Clark Tour
19 — Commack, Long Island
20 — Hershey, Pa.
21 — Cleveland, Ohio
22 — Johnstown, Pa.
23 — Ithaca, New York
24 — Providence, Rhode Island
25 — Worchester, Mass.
26 — Long Beach, L.I., N.Y.
27 — Newburg, Pa.
28 — Evansburg, Pa.
ANIMALS
AUGUST
17-23 — New York City, N.Y.
24 — Phoenix, Arizona
25 — Manatu Beach, Michigan
26 — Harbor Springs, Michigan
27 — Midland, Michigan
28 — Benton Harbor, Michigan
29 — Mendon, Mass.
30-Sept. 5 — Steel Pier, New Jersey (Atlantic City)
SEPTEMBER
5 — Return to England
YARDBIRDS
AUGUST
18 — Tulsa, Oklahoma
19-20 — Oklahoma City, Okla.
21 — Tucson, Arizona
22 — Los Angeles, California
23 — Avalon, Catalina Island
24 — Monterey, California
25 — San Francisco, California
26 — San Leandro, California
27 — Santa Barbara, California
28 — Pismo Beach, California
29 — San Diego, California
30 — San Jose, California
SEPTEMBER
1 — Santa Rosa, California
3 — Salem, Oregon
4 — Honolulu, Hawaii
BEAU BRUMMELS
AUGUST
14-31 — VACATION
SEPTEMBER
2 — Hastings, Nebraska
3 — Green Bay, Wisconsin
4 — Medina, Ohio
6 — Lima, Ohio
7 — Visalia, California
24 — Springfield, Virginia

KRLA ARCHIVES

PICTURES in the NEWS

NOEL HARRISON will be one of the stars of the brand new "Girl From U.N.C.L.E." series in the Fall, but he can't seem to get out of this refrigerator long enough to begin filming the show! C'mon Noel — you can do it. Now get out of that ice box!

AFTER SEVERAL MONTHS of rumor that they would go to England on tour, it looks as though Sonny and Cher will finally make it around the end of this month. They have finally completed work on their first film — "Good Times" — and Cher has plans for some recording sessions while she is in London. Wonder if the little fellow in the picture with Sonny and Cher will be touring with them. Or perhaps he is part of the background singers for their next disc!

OTIS REDDING is another American artist who has been anxiously awated by music fans in Great Britain, and the tour for which they had all been waiting is finally going to take place. Otis will tour England and Europe throughout the month of October.

GUESS WE'RE NOT the only ones who've been bugged by the air lines strike lately. Most recent victim is Dusty Springfield who has had to tentatively cancel her scheduled American visit for the month of September.

KRLA ARCHIVES

TEEN PANEL

Teen Immorality

BEAT Art: Henri Munsford

The BEAT's Teen Panel series has become one of the most widely discussed features in this or any publication for teenagers. We hoped to bring you something unique, and it's nice to know we've succeeded.

Teen panels are hardly anything new, and ours is different from the rest only because of the way the discussions are held. Because outside pressures prevent many people from making their personal views public, our Teen Panels meet in complete privacy on a "pen name" basis. Only five participants and one tape recorder are present.

This method has made it possible for our panelists to speak frankly. And, because their comments appear intact (only conversation that doesn't apply to the subject at hand is omitted), it is finally possible for someone to publish an **honest** *look at the teenagers of today.*

If you'd like to join in a future discussion, send your name, address, age and phone number on a postcard to BEAT Panel, 6290 Sunset, Hollywood, California, 90028. If you're selected as a panelist, we'll notify you by telephone and will not discuss the nature of the call with anyone but you personally.

* * *

The subject of this issue's discussion was suggested by "Caren," a 17-year-old reader of The BEAT. Her letter also included a request that she be allowed to participate on the panel if her topic was chosen.

We took her up on both offers.

She begins the discussion by telling the other panelists about the contents of her letter. Also participating are "Benje" – 16, "Don" – 17, "Susan" – 19 and "Jay" – 18.

Caren—"I told *The BEAT* that I'm tired of reading about 'teenage immorality.' Adult publications are full of articles on this subject, but the information they print isn't factual. It isn't even information—just a lot of speculation. It's either some writer's own opinion of something he knows nothing about, or the result of going around to a few clubs and talking to a few hippies and using them as a criterion to judge the rest of us. There are twenty million teenagers in this country alone. Adults are being led to think we're all alike, and all 'immoral.' No one is equipped to categorize this many people, especially where something as personal as sex is concerned. I thought that if five teenagers got together and expressed their own beliefs, people might realize how unrealistic the mass speculations really are."

Susan—"I don't believe such articles are trying to say we're all alike. What they're trying to point out is that this generation, *whatever* its members may feel as individuals, is not living up to the established moral code."

Jay—"Isn't that just as much of a generalization? There's no such thing as *a* moral code. Each church has its own code, each city and state and country has laws that affect personal behavior."

Susan—"Well, every major philosophy in this country has one vital point in common. They all agree that sex outside of marriage is immoral. That's the 'code' today's kids aren't living up to."

Caren—"I don't think you're any more qualified to speak for 'today's kids' than anyone else. This conversation is not going to go anywhere at all if we don't start being specific. We could sit here and argue for ten years and never arrive at an answer. I think it would be of a lot more value if each of us told what our own personal standards are."

Susan—"Fine. Then here's *my* viewpoint. I personally don't believe in sex before marriage. I don't feel this way because of religious reasons. I feel this way because I've seen people ruin their lives trying to make their own rules. The moral code we just discussed happens to coincide with my opinions, so I have no trouble following it. And I want to keep following it. I think sex is important, but I also think it's sacred. Too sacred to make a big game of."

Jay—"I think sex is too *uncomplicated* to make a big game of, but it's the biggest game in the history of mankind. Sex is nothing but an instinctive drive. Society made it complex and warped by trying to suppress it, and accept it for what it was. Instead they set up rules that everyone couldn't possibly live by. People are too different. Sex was too powerful a drive to be suppressed, so people found other ways to let off steam. Did you ever stop to think that, centuries ago, someone drew the first dirty picture? Today, what may have started as a scrawl on a cave wall is a multi-*billion* dollar industry. Sex is the big hype, the big deal. Books, magazines, movies pull at you from one side. Social and religious pressures pull at you from the other. No wonder so many people have sex hang-ups. It's all so out of proportion, and so stupid. This is the standard that's been passed down from generation to generation. I don't buy it. I think for myself. And *what* I think is my own business."

Caren—"I agree with Susan that sex is important, but I don't think it's sacred. Society has tried to make it sacred in order to control it, and this was probably a necessary move at the time. In those days, people weren't very civilized—not that we are now—and the majority of them probably weren't capable of controlling themselves. The human race has grown up since then—not enough, but enough to be able to make personal choices on their own. I've made my choice, and I choose to think that sex is a combination of something very natural and something very special. I don't believe in being promiscuous. Being the sort of person I am, I'd be unhappy if my life were a constant parade of sex experiences. But there are people who do live this way and it doesn't bother them a bit. They're not my problem. *I'm* my problem, and I don't do anything that *makes* me a problem to myself. I don't believe in adultery, either. And I don't think there'd be so much of it if people were more careful when they choose a marriage partner. I'd never marry someone unless I was absolutely certain we were compatible in every respect. In my opinion, sex is not the ultimate goal in a relationship. It's just a part of it, but it's an important part."

Then What?

Susan—There's only one way to find out whether two people are 'compatible in every respect,' and what happens if you discover that you aren't? Do you just go on to the next guy and start over? I don't mean *you*—I mean is this what you think a person should do if that happens?"

Caren—"Don't make it sound like a parade. You don't meet that many special people in your life. People who are special in every respect, I mean. I'm seventeen, and I've only met one so far, and it turned out that we weren't compatible in *any* way. But it was good experience for both of us. We both learned a lot about what we do and don't want from another person. I don't consider this a mistake, because it wasn't one. Someday I'll fall in love with someone else. It's that simple."

Susan—"What if the someone you fall in love with *does* consider it a mistake, and won't marry you because of it?"

Caren—"I rather doubt that I'll ever fall in love with a narrow person. I have enough trouble just tolerating them."

Susan—"I don't want to sound like I'm getting after you, so don't get mad. But I'm really interested in your outlook. What's your opinion of the girls who get into trouble because they don't wait for marriage? Do you think this kind of thing is all right?"

Caren—"I think these girls are stupid, and it's hardly *all right* to bring an unwanted human being into the world. Each person has a responsibility to himself. You don't have to take that kind of chance. I've never reached a point in my life where I stopped caring I can't answer for people who have. People have brains. It's up to each person to use them."

Benje—"I haven't thought much about sex. Well, I've *thought* about it a *lot*. I mean I haven't made up a list of things I do and don't believe in. But I read a wild bit the other day that really has me wondering. It was written by a doctor in New York who thinks he has it all figured out why the human race is such a mess. He thinks there are wars and crime, especially sex crimes, and so much unhappiness because the human sexual growth has been stunted. He said we're all twisted up and confused because we're not allowed to follow our natural urges. I guess it's a proven fact that your sex life affects your mental health. I know I've heard that said all my life. Anyway, this doctor sure thinks so, and he thinks people should start having a sex life whenever they start being interested in sex. I mean, he feels the world would be a healthier, happier place if such a thing was possible. But even he couldn't think of a way that it could be possible, because it goes against everything most people believe in. It's a wild idea, though. He could be right. It makes you think. There's something wrong with the way things are—if there weren't, people *could* live up to the rules with no problems, and there wouldn't be any market for that 'industry' Jay mentioned. Sex never has been confined to marriage, and it never will be. Not for everyone. I guess you just have to get to know yourself and do what's best for you."

Jay—"If all people could accept the fact that the rules can't apply to everyone, everyone can't apply to the rules, we'd stop kidding ourselves and getting all bent out of shape. Things would probably be chaotic if the rules suddenly didn't exist, because people who haven't bothered to think for themselves would have to start, and it takes awhile to learn how. But it would sure decrease the emphasis on sex. You'd think the people who try to mark it down would realize that they're only making it twice as irresistable. People seem to get bigger kicks when they're doing *anything* someone has told them not to."

Don't Mix

Benje—"That's true in one way, but again, not for everyone. I never even thought of this before, but one of the reasons the human race hasn't been able to confine sex to marriage could be because sex and marriage don't always mix. No, that's not what I mean. I mean it must be rough to suddenly develop a natural outlook toward sex just because you get married, when you've spent the first twenty-or-so years of your life being told it wasn't the thing to do. Parents are the cause of this a *lot* of times. My little sister is a perfect example. She's twelve, and when some smart mouth kid filled her in on the facts of life, my mother about had a stroke. She started crying and carrying on, and it scared my sister half out of her gourd. I suppose she'll get over it, but some people don't. I know a guy who's perfectly normal, a real groovy person, but he's scared you-know-whatless of fire because his house burned down when he was seven or eight. So many things can leave scars on you—inside scars. People are so weird."

Don—"I commend your mother for letting your sister know, right from the beginning, that sex is nothing to take lightly. Your sister will grow up a decent girl, and that's more than I can say for most girls today. I'd never marry a girl who wasn't decent. It's understandable that guys don't wait until they're married. But girls have *got* to wait if they want a good man to marry them. What guy would want second-hand merchandise? Why do you think brides wear white veils? To signify chastity. That's the whole concept of marriage."

Caren—"*What's* the whole concept of marriage?"

Don—"I just said it. Chastity."

Caren—"That's odd. I have been under the impression that the whole concept of marriage was comprised of many things like love and sharing and people belonging to each other, and having children."

Don—"Sure, that's all part of it, but marriage is built on a foundation of chastity."

Caren—"Chastity on the part of the bride."

Don—"Right."

Caren—"How about the groom?"

Susan—"I thought you were the one who said we'd never get anywhere arguing."

Caren—"I was. So I'll shut up in a second. Well? Can you answer my question?"

Don—"Yes. A good girl has enough purity for both of them, and this makes a man change and settle down to that one person."

Caren—"Oh. Well, think *this* over. The theory that premarital sex is okay for boys and not for girls has created nothing but chaos. It's the reason prostitution exists. It's the reason why girls who've 'made a mistake' fall apart from guilt and humiliation, and often end up making the same mistake every night of the week. Considering what your precious double-standard has done to the lives of innocent people, I don't think I have to tell you what you can do with it. That's all I'm going to say except this. Our conversation has proved exactly what I knew it would. We don't agree. We aren't alike. We all have individual viewpoints, and each of us lives up to what he believes in. Not one of us said 'I do so-and-so because I'm supposed to.' We're doing what we *want* to. And we aren't doing anything that generations before us didn't do. The only difference is, *we aren't afraid to admit it.*"

Susan—"I have a suggestion. Why don't we ask *The BEAT* if we can get together again and discuss that double-standard idea you brought up. The five of us have quite a mixture of viewpoints, and I'm sure we could exchange some pretty noisy opinions on the subject."

Caren—"Not to mention blows."

KRLA ARCHIVES

Rivers: The Fine Art Of Disappearing On A Chair

By Louise Criscione

I've come to the conclusion that Johnny Rivers divides his life between Whiskeys, cutting "live" albums and serving in the Army Reserves. Which isn't an awfully bad way to spend your life, I suppose, since he always sells-out his Whiskey dates; his albums continually do well. And he doesn't have any choice about the Army bit.

Johnny's funny, though; you never know quite what to expect from him. On stage, he's always rather formally attired. He seems to switch from his white to black tux but other than the color change there's never any marked difference in his stage clothes.

Two Rivers

But the Johnny Rivers on stage in the immaculate white tux and the Johnny Rivers off stage are two different people. I've never seen him in a fur coat ala' Sonny Bono but I did see him one night in an all white outfit which resembled those worn by judo experts—except it didn't have a belt.

The place was packed. The tiny tables were crammed with people, drinks and full chairs. So Johnny stood at the bar. No one bothered him. No napkins were thrust forward with the plea to "please sign it for me." The regular patrons of the club are used to seeing performers wander in and out. It happens every night and now they don't even look twice when someone like Brian Jones or Papa John or Mike Love strides in. But this is summer—our tourist season.

The night Johnny showed up several tables of tourists had managed to twist their way through the long hair, the short skirts and the hip-huggers. In their furs and heels and Madison Avenue suits they stood out like a crewcut Mick Jagger. Perhaps that's why they were so busy noting the long-haired group on stage or the funny way we "natives" looked that they failed to observe Johnny stationed rather obscurely in the corner. Or maybe they saw him but were afraid to ask for his autograph. They were conspicuous enough as it was.

Whatever the reason, Johnny spent an evening in relative calm. Actually, he's not very hard to miss. He sort of rivals Ringo in the height department but Ringo's hair outweighs Johnny's. It would be a big mistake to underestimate Johnny just because he doesn't stand a mighty six feet. What he lacks in inches he more than makes up for in talent, determination and a certain amount of temper.

There's a standing joke around the Hollywood area. Johnny always uses a stool when he performs and just as he goes to sit down on it someone is always heard to say: "Johnny's doing his disappearing act again!" Everyone then enjoys a good laugh and I suspect that inwardly Johnny laughs too.

Hidden

It *is* true that if you're unfortunate enough to be sitting in front of the dance floor, the minute Johnny sits down he disappears behind the wiggling heads of the dancers. But his voice is always there. And you can't miss that. He's clever in his choice of material. He continually sings songs which are recognizable to the audience, songs which they can sing along with.

If you've seen Johnny "live" and heard his Whiskey A'Go Go albums, you know there's no faking. Those voices you hear in the background are really there. They haven't been manufactured in a recording studio. They follow Johnny everywhere he goes. His performances are always sort of a Sing Along With Johnny and in today's wild, weird, improvised scene it's a nice change.

Johnny's determined. About a lot of things. But he seems to be especially concerned in giving an audience it's money's worth. That's why one night he walked off a stage because the sound system was way off and the audience couldn't hear him unless they were sitting on top of the speakers.

So, Johnny just left. As simple as that. Without even a word to the audience, he pulled his guitar plug out of the amp and walked off stage. After words with the club's owner and after the sound system had been repaired he came back. He'd missed an entire set because of the mike difficulty—something which he obviously thought was cheating his audience because he incorporated two sets into one extra long one.

Two Hours

And only when the perspiration was making a million tiny rivers down his face and when the heat of the lights became unbearable did he reluctantly pack up his guitar and leave. He'd been on stage for almost two hours straight. A long time in anybody's book.

The audience was his. They didn't want him to leave. But then, they hardly ever let Johnny leave the stage without thunderous claps of protest and throaty shouts of "More, more."

Yes, the way Johnny Rivers divides his life isn't bad at all. Fact is, it's quite good. Not to mention highly successful. And in the entertainment business, what else is there?

...JOHNNY DOIN' HIS DISAPPEARIN'

..."WHAT'S THAT YOU SAY?"

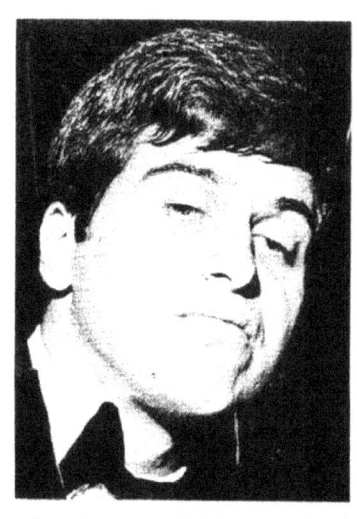

KRLA ARCHIVES

...THE KINKS (left to right) are Ray Davies, Dave Davies, Mick Avory and Pete Quaife.

Kinks: Modern Rebels

If you're a Kink, and you took a notion to go lazin' on a "Sunny Afternoon," you probably would. If you're a Kink, and you wanted to do almost anything... then you probably would.

But there are only four Kinks, and not many people—if any—can match their nonchalance and ignore the what-you're-supposed-to-do-and-say world around them.

Honest

The Kinks are 20th Century Rebels; they don't mince words and they don't bend their personalities for the sake of an image. If they don't like the shirt you're wearing they'll say something like, "We bloody well don't like that rotten shirt you've got on."

They aren't really rude—just frightfully honest. And while honesty today is sometimes considered a vice rather than a virtue, the Kinks' brash, straightforward personalities remain intact.

The Kinks are most outspoken concerning their own music. They speak with indifference about the fads and streaking changes in pop music, and sing only what pleases themselves.

"Changes in pop don't bother us, why should they?" asked Dave Davies. "We can dictate what we want to do. We don't have to go by the public fads anymore."

And in saying this, Dave pretty well summed up the Kinks' newest record, "Sunny Afternoon," which was number one in England and received a near status in the United States.

The record, biggest in a long line of hits for the Kinks, is one of the most original to be released by any group in a while. The song—like the group that sings it—has a kind of easy, free flowing pace to it, and shuns the commercial aspects of most songs released today.

They live from day to day, and haven't the faintest notion—nor do they seem to care about—what they'll be doing in several years.

"We don't care about five years from now," Dave said indifferently. "We'll probably be blown up. We've done everything we wanted to do, so it won't matter when we get blown up. We are a hit. What more is there?"

Not Much

Not too much really. Except, maybe, for another million dollars from record sales and public appearances. But on this subject, the Kinks seem even less concerned.

All four of the Kinks—Dave, Pete, Mick and Ray—live well but quite simply. They are no more extravagant with money than they are with flowery phrases of false compliments.

Their music, even more so than the money and fame, is the Kinks' chief motivation as pop singers.

"Playing and singing my own music is very important to me," said Ray Davies. "I think if I thought I could not improve musically, I would give it all up and become a tramp. The idea of tramping around the country with a healthy bank balance in time of difficulty appeals to me anyway."

For Pete Quaife, money looms as one of his major problems. Not the lack of it—but too much of it!

"I didn't have a bank account until a few months ago," confessed Pete. "I used to go through the week quite happily on one pound, but when you start earning hundreds a week, it seems to vanish into thin air."

It is said of many groups that they don't really change after they make it big. But most do change. The Kinks have not. They neither put on a cloak of humility nor do they reek with conceit. They leave tomorrow's worries for tomorrow and think only of the present.

And at the present, the Kinks need worry about very little.

The Beatles Own Gold 'Revolver'

The Beatles have done it again — earned a Gold Record for their "Revolver" album on the day of its release! This marks the tenth consecutive Beatle LP to receive a Gold Record on the day of release.

The "Revolver" album cover was designed by Klaus Voorman and does not have any meat or decapitated dolls anywhere in sight. Instead, it contains a montage of Beatle caricatures and pictures, both full-length and head shots. Hidden in one corner of the cover is a picture of Voorman. The album cover has been described by a student of art as the newest development in the arts — "Beatles Art" to be exact.

"Revolver" includes 11 Beatle-penned tunes, including the group's current single, "Yellow Submarine" b/w "Eleanor Rigby." The single is also expected to sell the necessary million dollars worth of copies to insure yet another Gold Record for the Beatles, who have made a habit out of collecting Goldies.

The songs, composers and soloists on "Revolver" are "Taxman," written and sung by George Harrison; "Eleanor Rigby," written by John and Paul and sung by Paul; "Love You To," written and sung by George Harrison; "Here, There and Everywhere," written by John and Paul and sung by Paul; "Yellow Submarine," written by John and Paul and sung by Ringo Starr; "She Said She Said," written by John and Paul and sung by John Lennon; "Good Day Sunshine," written by John and Paul and sung by Paul; "For No One," written by John and Paul and sung by Paul; "I Want To Tell You," written and sung by George; "Got To Get You Into My Life," written by John and Paul and sung by Paul; "Tomorrow Never Knows," written by John and Paul and sung by John.

Up Beat
By Eden

Starting off a brand new week with a brand new name, but don't worry 'cause we'll still be having a lot of heated "DISCussions" about the latest releases.

What do you think about the new Beatles' disc, "Yellow Submarine?" That's even better than "Rainy Day Woman," and it seems absolutely destined to become the instantaneous national anthem of every college and kindergarten classroom from Coast to Coast! It's a fun record though, and Ringo's voice never sounded more... Ringo!

My favorite so far, though, is still "Eleanor Rigby." Probably one of the greats ever from the talented quartet.

* * *

My personal pick hit for this week has to be the new single from The Association. Quickly on the heels of their first hit disc—"Along Comes Mary"—the boys are following up their chart success with the beautiful ballad, "Cherish."

This was written by the members of the group and it is undoubtedly one of the prettiest tunes around—lyrically and melodically. It should duplicate their latest success and head for the Top Ten immediately.

* * *

Everyone in the music industry these days seems to be talking about the new group, The Buffalo Springfield. Their first disc is "And Clancy Can't Even Sing." It's sort of slow, a little reminiscent of the Beau Brummels, and it could be this month's chart sleeper. Keep an ear glued to it.

* * *

"Black Is Black" by Los Bravos is really a good record, but I keep getting the feeling it could have been much better. One of the best features of the disc is the original and almost gospel-like harmony used at the end of each verse. It sounds like a good-sized hit for the first outing of this new group.

* * *

The Dave Clark Five have really surprised a lot of people with their latest — "Satisfied With You." It's amazingly good, and it might be another large hit for the quintet.

* * *

More surprises in store for Neil Diamond fans with his new 45er — "Cherry, Cherry." It's a hard-rocking, up-tempo tune which is far removed from his first hit, "Solitary Man."

This, too, is destined for chart-topping.

Bomb Title of the Week Award has to go to Lloyd Price's new disc, "The Man Who Took The Valise Off The Floor of Grand Central Station at Noon." I mean, what can you say after that!!

* * *

Tony Hatch has written and produced a number of hit singles for Petula Clark in the last couple of years, and now he has contributed his talents to the success of Peter and Gordon by penning their newest 45er—"To Show I Love You."

Unlike their last couple of records, there is nothing weird or unusual about this disc — it's just a very simple, pretty, easygoing love song.

* * *

The Turtles decided that "Outside Chance" wasn't going to be a hit after all, so they simply flipped the disc over and found themselves a new "A" side with "We'll Meet Again." This is another good-time song and might push the disc to the top yet.

* * *

I'm getting a good deal of mail in answer to my question about your favorite groups and artists, and you might be interested to know that the surfing craze is still very much alive. Several letters have come in praising the Beach Boys, the Sunrays, and Jan and Dean as well as anything else vaguely associated with the surfing craze.

Be sure and drop me a line to let me know who you're listening to.

* * *

Brian Wilson told me some weeks ago that "God Only Knows" — a beautiful cut off of their latest LP, "Pet Sounds," would be the new single. However, it seems that another cut off the same album — "Wouldn't It Be Nice" — is going out as the A-side.

That's okay, because both tunes are great. Who knows — might even be a double-sided Hit from the California smash-makers.

* * *

In order to be "in" this week, you have to be (1) female, and (2) record your rendition of "Alfie." Must be more recordings of this new tune than anything else right now.

Latest versions to be released include cuts by Cher — who will warble the tune beneath the opening credits in the movie — Joannie Sommers, and Cilla Black — who currently has the only hit version of the disc, riding high on British charts.

KRLA ARCHIVES

Open Letter To Mick Jagger

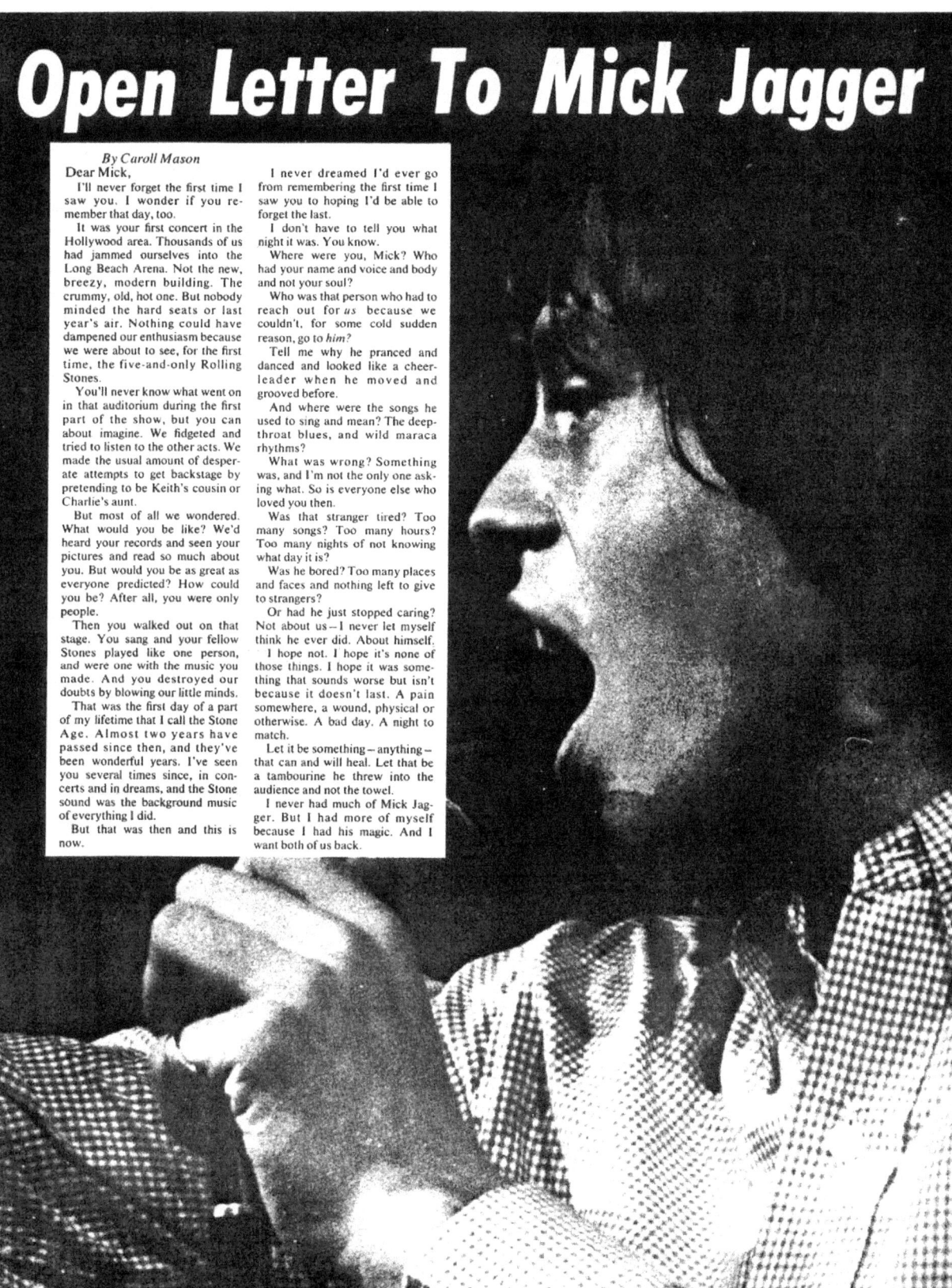

By Caroll Mason

Dear Mick,

I'll never forget the first time I saw you. I wonder if you remember that day, too.

It was your first concert in the Hollywood area. Thousands of us had jammed ourselves into the Long Beach Arena. Not the new, breezy, modern building. The crummy, old, hot one. But nobody minded the hard seats or last year's air. Nothing could have dampened our enthusiasm because we were about to see, for the first time, the five-and-only Rolling Stones.

You'll never know what went on in that auditorium during the first part of the show, but you can about imagine. We fidgeted and tried to listen to the other acts. We made the usual amount of desperate attempts to get backstage by pretending to be Keith's cousin or Charlie's aunt.

But most of all we wondered. What would you be like? We'd heard your records and seen your pictures and read so much about you. But would you be as great as everyone predicted? How could you be? After all, you were only people.

Then you walked out on that stage. You sang and your fellow Stones played like one person, and were one with the music you made. And you destroyed our doubts by blowing our little minds.

That was the first day of a part of my lifetime that I call the Stone Age. Almost two years have passed since then, and they've been wonderful years. I've seen you several times since, in concerts and in dreams, and the Stone sound was the background music of everything I did.

But that was then and this is now.

I never dreamed I'd ever go from remembering the first time I saw you to hoping I'd be able to forget the last.

I don't have to tell you what night it was. You know.

Where were you, Mick? Who had your name and voice and body and not your soul?

Who was that person who had to reach out for *us* because we couldn't, for some cold sudden reason, go to *him*?

Tell me why he pranced and danced and looked like a cheerleader when he moved and grooved before.

And where were the songs he used to sing and mean? The deep-throat blues, and wild maraca rhythms?

What was wrong? Something was, and I'm not the only one asking what. So is everyone else who loved you then.

Was that stranger tired? Too many songs? Too many hours? Too many nights of not knowing what day it is?

Was he bored? Too many places and faces and nothing left to give to strangers?

Or had he just stopped caring? Not about us — I never let myself think he ever did. About himself.

I hope not. I hope it's none of those things. I hope it was something that sounds worse but isn't because it doesn't last. A pain somewhere, a wound, physical or otherwise. A bad day. A night to match.

Let it be something — anything — that can and will heal. Let that be a tambourine he threw into the audience and not the towel.

I never had much of Mick Jagger. But I had more of myself because I had his magic. And I want both of us back.

KRLA ARCHIVES

Top 40 Requests

THIS WEEK	TITLE	ARTIST
1	YELLOW SUBMARINE	Beatles
2	ELENORE RIGBY	Beatles
3	FORTUNE TELLER	Rolling Stones
4	SUNSHINE SUPERMAN	Donovan
5	SUNNY	Bobby Hebb
6	UNDER MY THUMB	Rolling Stones
7	GOT TO GET YOU INTO MY LIFE	Beatles
8	THEY'RE COMING TO TAKE ME AWAY	Napolean XIV
9	SWEET PEA	Tommy Roe
10	CHERISH	Association
11	RED RUBBER BALL	Cyrkle
12	LITTLE RED RIDING HOOD	Sam the Sham & The Pharoahs
13	SUMMER IN THE CITY	Lovin' Spoonful
14	GOOD DAY SUNSHINE	Beatles
15	SUNNY AFTERNOON	Kinks
16	DIRTY WATER	Standells
17	SOMETIMES GOOD GUYS DON'T WEAR WHITE	Standells
18	HUNGRY	Paul Revere and the Raiders
19	THIS DOOR SWINGS BOTH WAYS	Herman's Hermits
20	JUST LIKE A WOMAN	Bob Dylan
21	SEVEN AND SEVEN IS	Love
22	OVER, UNDER, SIDEWAYS, DOWN	Yardbirds
23	SOMEWHERE MY LOVE	Ray Conniff
24	HANKY PANKY	Tommy James and the Shondells
25	THE WORK SONG	Herb Alpert and the Tijuana Brass
26	GUANTANAMERA	Sandpipers
27	STRANGERS IN THE NIGHT	Frank Sinatra
28	I SAW HER AGAIN	Mamas and Papas
29	WILD THING	Troggs
30	PAPER BACK WRITER/RAIN	Beatles
31	YOU CAN'T HURRY LOVE	Supremes
32	TURN DOWN DAY	Cyrkle
33	MOTHER'S LITTLE HELPER/LADY JANE	Rolling Stones
34	SATISFIED WITH YOU	Dave Clark 5
35	SUMMERTIME	Billy Stewart
36	DANGLING CONVERSATION/THE BRIGHT GREEN PLEASURE MACHINE	Simon and Garfunkle
37	DISTANT SHORES	Chad and Jeremy
38	LAND OF 1000 DANCES	Wilson Pickett
39	I COULDN'T LIVE WITHOUT YOUR LOVE	Petula Clark
40	BLOWING IN THE WIND	Stevie Wonder

LIMITED SUMMER BONUS FOR BEAT READERS —

$200 in Values — **Only $2 in Price!**

GO-GUIDE COUPON BOOK

More than 100 coupons for Free Admissions, Discounts up to 50% or 2 for 1 offerings. Activities and Products listed below, plus many others.

Movies	Revell
Clubs	Statewide Theatres
Dancing	So. Cal. Bowl. Assn
Sports	Troubador
Food	Ash Grove
Clothing	Orange Julius
Records	Hullabaloo
Jewelry	Gazzari's
Cosmetics	P.O.P.
Shows	Pasadena Civic
Fairs	Sports Show
Horseback Riding	L. A. Blades
Bowling	Ice House
Folk Music	World On Wheels
Plays	Independ. Theatres
Slot Car Racing	Vivian Woodward
Billiards	Fashion Tops
Skating	Mademoiselle

Dial F-U-N-T-E-E-N For More Information

ORDER NOW WHILE THEY LAST!

FUNTEEN GO-GUIDE
c/o KRLA BEAT
6290 Sunset, Suite 504
Hollywood, Calif. 90028

Please send me _____ copies of the 1966 FUNTEEN GO-GUIDE (Valid thru Dec. 31, 1966) at the special summer rate of only $2.00 each. I enclose $_____

NAME:
ADDRESS:
CITY: STATE: ZIP:

FUNTEEN BONUS COUPON OFFERINGS

All the Bonus Coupons printed in the back section of the Go-Guide are listed below:

NOW AVAILABLE TO MEMBERS ONLY:

A Supplement containing 30 additional coupons. Send 25c (for handling) plus a stamped, self-addressed envelope to

SUPPLEMENT
P.O. Box 1235, Beverly Hills, Calif.

Coupon	Merchant	Offering
"A"	International Import-Export Trade and Travel Fair, Long Beach Sports Arena	2 for 1 admission Nov. 8th – 13th
"B"	Discoteen — 5136 N. Citrus, Covina	2 for 1, $1 off with membership card
"C"	San Fernando Valley Teen Center, 17400 Victory Blvd.	2 for 1 admission
"D"	Drum City — Guitar Town, 15255 Sherman Way, Van Nuys; 5811 Jumilla, Woodland Hills; 6226 Santa Monica Blvd., L. A.	2 free "Crazy Fill" book covers for just dropping in. $5 gift certificate with $15 one-time or accumulated purchase.
"E"	Hobby-Land Hobby Shop, 1826 S. Robertson Blvd., L. A.	Free Gift plus 20% discount on all purchases, with card
"F"	Orange Julius, 8787 Santa Monica Blvd., W. Hollywood	Free Orange Julius with any purchase.
"G"	Gazzari's — 319 N. La Cienega	2 for 1 admission to Teen Night every Sunday (7 p.m. - 12 midnight)
"H"	Hullabaloo, 6230 Sunset Blvd., Hollywood	2 for 1 admission
"I"	Santa Monica Civic, Santa Monica	2 for 1 admission August 5 for MacGillivray's surfing film, "The Performers."
"J"	Michael's Jewelers, 7530 Woodman, Van Nuys	Free Beatle jewelry piece
"K"	Kookie Kapers — 7860 Santa Monica Blvd., L.A.	$5 certificate after $15 purchase
"L"	Dundee Donuts, Town & Country, 6332 W. 3rd., L.A.	Free donut for dropping in and free donuts with purchase
"M"	Northridge Valley Skateland, 18140 Parthenia, Northridge	2 for 1 admission, with or without skates
"N"	Ezra's Oasis — 316 N. La Cienega	"Most anything on the menu" at 2 for 1
"O"	Orange Julius, 6081 W. Pico, L.A.	2 Orange Juliuses for price of 1
"P"	Pasadena Civic Auditorium, 300 Green St., Pasadena	Free admission for member and 1 guest to dance any Saturday (8:30-11:30 p.m.) Dresses for girls, dress shirts, tie and slacks for boys. Same offer good at De Wald's Ballroom, 831 W. Las Tunas Dr., San Gabriel
"Q"	Orange Julius — 1715 Pico Blvd., Santa Monica	Free Orange Julius with any purchase
"R"	Valley Ice Skating Center, 18361 Ventura Blvd., Tarzana	2 for price of 1
"S"	Shirt Shack — 1908 Lincoln, Santa Monica	$5 gift certificate with $15 one-time or accumulated purchase. Member's friends may purchase on his accumulation.
"T"	Ice House — 24 N. Mentor, Pasadena	2 for 1 admission
"U"	Ice House — 234 S. Brand, Glendale	2 for 1 admission

Membership Card Admission: Cafe Danssa, 11533 Pico Blvd., West L.A. Sundays only — 2 for 1 admission.
Membership Card Admission: World On Wheels Show, Rose Bowl, Sunday, August 7. 8 a.m. til 5 p.m.
Membership Card Admission: Swinging Young Adults Club of Los Angeles. Dancing every Sunday, 2-10 p.m. Only 75c for members with card. Old Dixie Ballroom, 4269 S. Western.

SPECIAL ANNOUNCEMENT! All of the Statewide Theatre coupons in your Go-Gide are now good at any Statewide Theatre listed in the Guide. Coupons are interchangeable.

KRLA ARCHIVES

Win A Life Size Yellow Submarine

With the Beatles top new record, "Yellow Submarine" gurgling its way to the top of the charts, KRLA *BEAT* makes possible for its readers the ultimate in one-upsmanship. Be the first kid on your block to actually own a life-size "honest to goodness really works" yellow submarine six feet long, four feet wide, weighing 108 pounds.

This two-man sub is pedal operated and can navigate under water at three to four knots. (You never know when the Los Angeles riverbed will flood again and if there's a tie-up on the freeway, this sub will be the envy of your neighbors).

Because Paramount's great new mid-Atlantic action thriller "Assault on a Queen" is all about how some crazy mixed up kids (Frank Sinatra, Virna Lisi, Tony Franciosa and Richard Conte) float a German sub off the bottom of the ocean and hi-jack the Queen Mary, we thought we'd make a contribution to ending juvenile delinquency in their name—and the Beatles, of course. One thing is sure—a yellow submarine will really keep the kids off the streets.

See the contest blank on this page for details or listen to KRLA for contest details. Contest closes August 31, 1966.

YELLOW SUBMARINE YEAH, YEAH, YEAH!

KRLA BEAT
1401 S. Oak Knoll
Pasadena, Calif.

I agree with Frank Sinatra and Virni Lisi that every home should have a yellow submarine. If I win KRLA's groovy yellow submarine, I promise to give it tender, loving care and to scrape the barnacles off its sensitive little hull regularly.

NAME:_____

ADDRESS:_____

CITY:_____ ZIP:_____

TELEPHONE:_____

I estimate that there will be _____ underwater types who enter KRLA's yellow submarine contest.

(Winner will be selected on the basis of most accurate estimate of total number of contest entries. Contest closes **Aug. 31, 1966**. In case of tie, drawing will be held among those tied. Five runner-ups will receive pairs of passes to see Paramount's mid-ocean thriller, "Assault On A Queen" starring Frank Sinatra and Virni Lisi.)

KRLA'S Official Statement On The Beatle Controversy

If you remember your history, a group of British subjects came to America to avoid public censure of their religious beliefs. After many hardships, they won this religious freedom. Americans still enjoy this freedom. Therefore, we here at KRLA do not believe it is our right to question the religious beliefs of the Beatles or of any other talent. We are only interested in the quality of the entertainment they provide. We will continue to play Beatle recordings.

Drum City - Guitar Town
15255 Sherman Way, Van Nuys
5611 Jumilla, Woodland Hills
6226 Santa Monica Blvd. L.A.

2 free "Crazy Fill" book covers. $5 gift certificate with $15 one-time or accumulated purchase. Member's friends may purchase on his accumulation.
USE YOUR FUNTEEN BONUS COUPON "D"

Stan Freberg Joins KRLA

Freberg, Ltd., Stan Freberg's iconoclastic advertising organization, has been hired by radio station KRLA.

Although several stations have attempted to negotiate for his services, this represents the first time that Freberg has agreed to serve as a consultant to an individual radio station.

KRLA's acceptance as one of the nation's top rock stations makes an ideal target for Freberg's barbed satire. This, apparently, does not worry the station.

KRLA Station Manager, John Barrett, said, "Our approach has always been tongue-in-cheek. We recognize that the audience is listening for one thing...fun!" "Freberg," Barrett said, "has been given Carte Blanche to make these on-air-campaigns more fun."

Stan Freberg's company has produced successful advertising campaigns for such diverse clients as General Motors, Salada Tea, Orange Julius, Chun King Chow Mein, Mars Candy, Prince Macaroni and the United Presbyterian Church.

Asked where KRLA would fit in, Mr. Freberg answered, "Somewhere between Orange Julius and the United Presbyterian Church."

Danny Dassa Cafe Danssa
11533 W. Pico, L.A.   GR. 5-9940
International Folk Cafe
FUN CLUB MEMBERS — Two for price of one Sunday nite only — Just show Funteen card!

FINAL WEEK
GLENN YARBROUGH
ALSO
The Comedy of Jack Colvin and Yvonne Wilder
AT DOUG WESTON'S
Troubadour

RESERVATIONS
CR 6-6168
9083 SANTA MONICA BLVD.
L.A. NEAR DOHENY

SUPER DUPER MARVY FAB
KRLA BEAT SUMMER SPECIAL
$1.50 for the rest of the year!!
(new subscribers only)
$3.00 a year
SAVE 60%
on the bigger, better BEAT
Just clip and mail...

KRLA BEAT
Save 60%—Subscribe!

Mail to:
Beat Publications
6290 Sunset Blvd.
Hollywood 90028

Name_____
Address_____
City_____ State_____ Zip_____
☐ I want BEAT for the rest of the year at $1.50.
☐ I want BEAT for a year at $3.00.
☐ I want to extend my subscription for 1 year at $3.00.
I enclose ☐ cash ☐ check ☐ money order.

THEY STICK UP THE QUEEN MARY IN MID-ATLANTIC!

Six far-out fortune hunters re-float a sunken World War II sub and head for the heist of all time!

PARAMOUNT PICTURES in association with SEVEN ARTS and SINATRA ENTERPRISES presents

FRANK SINATRA **VIRNA LISI**
ASSAULT ON A QUEEN

CO-STARRING
RICHARD CONTE · ERROL JOHN · ALF KJELLIN and TONY FRANCIOSA AS "ROSSITER"

Screenplay by ROD SERLING · From the novel by JACK FINNEY · Produced by WILLIAM GOETZ
Directed by JACK DONOHUE · Music—DUKE ELLINGTON · TECHNICOLOR® PANAVISION®

OPENS AT THEATRES AND DRIVE-INS ALL OVER TOWN WED. AUG. 24TH.

KRLA ARCHIVES

BEAT SHOWCASE
(spotlighting new talent on the pop scene)

...SIR WALTER RALEIGH

Sir Walter Raleigh (really Dewey Martin) hails from Seattle, Wash., and until now has only appeared in that area. Before he began singing, he was a drummer for several stars, among them Roy Orbison. Sir Walter has recently released "I Don't Want To Cry."

...THE COOKIE FAIRIES

Take two teenage girls and mix well. Enter the Cookie Fairies. Take a box of cookies, leave it on the doorstep of their favorite drummer, who happens to be a Byrd, and he will say it is a present from his "friendly local cookie fairies." Hence the name. Carol Millsip and Candie Callaway, grads of Santa Barbara High, may have the spark to ignite their success — Gene Clark is writing their material.

...THINGS TO COME

This Chicago-based group has kids coming from miles around to see them. Admittedly influenced by the Byrds and Yardbirds, they say their originality far surpasses influence by others. Group features George Heatherton, bass; Ken Ashley, lead singer; Keith St. Michaels, rhythm; Cliff Harrison, drums.

...SOMETHING WILD

Something Wild is currently working central California with a comical and wild R & B show. Their style has been described as "rockin' blues," since a little bit of everything is thrown into their act. Most of their material is original, written by members Kal, Bill and Bill. Left to right in the above picture, Bill H. Payne, piano-organ; Bill "Pretty Boy" Evans, lead guitar; Red Libben, drums; Kal X. Blue, lead vocalist; Joe Geppi, bass.

...GRAINS OF SAND

A devoted fan club which even sports a sister club in England keep the Grains of Sand in good spirits — even when drummer Willie shaved off his beard and no one recognized him. Actually, the Grains of Sand are new for the second time around, having decided to hit the pop scene with a new image — mainly shorter hair and suits. The group has been making television and club appearances, and will release their second single in the near future. The first was "That's When Happiness Began" c/w "She Needs Me."

KRLA ARCHIVES

IN SEARCH OF FOLK
Legend Of Odetta

By Shannon Leigh

ODETTA — to those who know her, the name means *excellence*. It calls to mind the perfection, and class, and talent which is an integral part of this woman who has become a legend in her own lifetime.

Odetta is the artistic, *interpretive* artist who educates her audience — and cares *how* she educates them — as she entertains them. She was born in Birmingham, Alabama but moved North to Los Angeles at the age of six. Her background, then, was not the traditional "aesthetic sweat of the cottonfields-back-home," but she has achieved a crescendo of communication in the field of blues-oriented folk songs, nonetheless.

Glee Club

While still in junior high school, Odetta joined the school glee club as a coloratura soprano, then continued her singing when she entered high school. Here, she was coached by a voice teacher who was convinced that Odetta should be a contralto, as she was destined to become the next Marian Anderson. However, Odetta was not entirely reconciled to the idea of becoming the *next anyone*, and continued to develop her own unique vocal stylings.

After graduating from high school, Odetta worked during the days as a housekeeper, in order to finance her musical studies of art, songs and the classics in the evenings. It was during this period that Odetta accidentally fell into the world of folk music.

Appearing in her first professional performance — the West Coast production of "Finian's Rainbow" — she found herself traveling away from her home for the first time.

"I felt so melancholy that when I met a couple of Bay Area folk singers, I was probably a lot more receptive to their songs than I might otherwise have been. I remember that they sang the song, "I'm My Mother's Child," for instance, and it moved me deeply."

So deeply moved was she that Odetta began to explore this new musical idiom which she had discovered and in doing so, discovered a whole new freedom of creativity and expression with which she could work.

Her first public performance as a folk singer also came about in an accidental way, as she was unexpectedly introduced by a touring folk singer as she sat in the audience of the "Hungry i" in San Francisco. The introduction was so lavish, that Odetta was literally propelled — unexpectedly — into the spotlight, where she sang one song . . . and was immediately hired by the club's management.

The offer, however, eventually had to be withdrawn after the featured singer in the show began raising violent objections to the prospect of such formidable competition.

For the next year or so, Odetta performed in various coffee houses and night clubs on both the East and West Coasts, establishing a fine reputation for herself among audiences across the country, as well as among fellow artists, including Harry Belafonte and Pete Seeger.

Murderess

In California again, Odetta made her debut film performance in "Cinerama Holiday," then later appeared in the role of a murderess in her second film, "Sanctuary."

Odetta has now built up a following of ecstatic fans around the world, and her popularity is very graphically illustrated by the applause which greets her immediately as she enters the room — long before she ever approaches the stage.

Her fans have accorded her the status of a legend already, and the legend of Odetta is one of a highly talented, creative, proud, and sensitive artist. It is a legend which must continue indefinitely, for as long as the rich voice of Odetta continues to fill the ears of eager listeners around the world.

Dylan: Is He Weird?

By Eden

Millions upon millions of words have been written about this man, and usually — they are words of great eloquence, sentences highly stylized in their phrasing, paragraphs which run off to the weird. But it has come to be an accepted fact that when you read something which has been written *about* Bob Dylan, it must, of necessity, be *as* weird as the man himself.

Question Number One — is Dylan *really* so very weird? Or is it really just the people who are writing about this twenty-four year old enigma from Hibbing, Minnesota?

Over and over again in the infrequent interviews which Dylan grants to various publications, he has insistently demanded that he is *not* the genius he is said to be; that his songs were never meant to be great.

Dylan recently completed a very unusual world-wide concert tour which succeeded in creating more confusion and mixed reactions to the young American singer-poet-composer than anything else.

In his concert in Albert Hall in London, Dylan met once again with the problem of a booing, dissatisfied audience — an occurrence to which he is not entirely unaccustomed. He has heard the echoes of distaste before — in the Newport Folk Festival, for example — and he was readily able to cope with the situation, making quick use of his inimitable dry wit.

However, he made a speech to the audience which seemed only to further alienate it. He informed them after only the first two or three numbers that he would never again perform in Great Britain.

BOB DYLAN: Is he really the weird, genius-spokesman for pop music?

Then, he continued his tirade by attacking some of the British musical trade papers which had recently attacked him. Having had his fill of revenge, he then went on to explain to the people, "What you're hearing is just songs. You're not hearing anything else but words and sounds." Once again he denied the great value, or "genius" of his songs. Then he concluded, "I'm sick of people asking: 'What does it mean?' It means *nothing!*"

Despite this emphatic outburst, people will continue to search for a deeper meaning in Dylan. There have been accusations hurled at him of late insinuating that his recent writing is composed of nothing but "drug songs."

But Dylan has repeatedly denied this charge, saying that he never has written, nor will he ever write, a "drug song." Yet, music critics have pinned the responsibility for the initiation of the current "psychedelic" trend in pop music squarely on Dylan's shoulders.

It is a nearly impossible task to reach an accurate definition of *any* human being. Speaking in terms of Bob Dylan — it is *entirely* inconceivable. But some conclusions, at least, can be reached about this fascinating young man.

Whether or not you label it "genius," Bob Dylan is obviously a talented and creative poet and composer. He has been compared to Dylan Thomas in his use of startling chains of imagery; but Bob denies any relation — in name, or otherwise — to the great British poet. His work is only his own.

Dylan is definitely responsible for the current trend of better, more intelligent lyrics in popular music — and for that, if for nothing else, we are all in his debt.

He has wrought important changes in the moods and styles of contemporary music, and at least *begun* many of the trends which have taken shape in this field in the last year and a half.

His records are never musical masterpieces of sound — Dylan doesn't have a classically good voice. But they are always well-arranged, well-planned, and always interesting. They are also frequently hits.

Weird? Who is to say that Dylan is weird and we are not?

On what basis do we classify Dylan as "weird?" We must first know what "weird" is, and since "weird" to each individual is usually only that which he *isn't* — we are all probably a little bit weird to the next guy.

At any rate, Dylan tells us that he isn't weird — so, maybe he really *isn't*! For right now, what he is is an entertainer of great magnitude; an innovator, a creator of new styles of writing and recording who has achieved a very widespread influence in the field of popular music. And, most important of all — he is a human being.

Beyond that, we can only say that he is . . . Bob Dylan.

KRLA ARCHIVES

Wilson Picket Taught How's & Why's of R&R

"The Land of 1,000 Dances" and "The Midnight Hour." "If You Need Me" and "I Found A Love." Put them all together and what do you have?

A young singer who never even knew the meaning of rock 'n' roll, until he was out of his teens. You have Wilson Pickett—a musical midas who has mastered rock 'n' roll, rhythm and blues, spiritual singing and songwriting . . . all within a period of a few years.

If he wanted to, Wilson Pickett could probably master classical music. He has a flair for taking a song and giving it a twist of the unusual. And after four consecutive top sellers no one will argue with his method.

Wilson is as dedicated to rock 'n' roll and R&B today as he was dedicated to the spiritual singing he did most of his life.

Even with his belated start into his current type of singing, Wilson rose to one of the top men in the field. But not without a small amount of tutoring.

Wilson was "discovered" by a Detroit-based group called the Falcons. The group immediately recognized his raw talent and soul—derived from years of dedicated gospel singing—and set about to teach their diamond in the rough the fundamentals of rock 'n' roll.

Wilson's exciting, gospel type singing provides the basis for his current success in his relatively new field. When he sings a rock 'n' roll song he feels it, just as he felt the gospel songs he once sang.

Wilson, who now records for the Atlantic label, is as widely known for his songwriting as he is for his singing. And that's saying a lot.

Right away Wilson wrote two of his more memorable compositions, "I Found A Love," and "If You Need Me," which has become a rock standard and has been recorded by such outstanding artists as Solomon Burke, The Rolling Stones, Tom Jones and Bill Doggett.

. . . WILSON PICKET—lessons in R & R

Outsider Denies Filth In Music

"Music doesn't have anything to do with morals, especially rock music," said Tom King, leader of the Outsiders, in answer to *Time's* allegations that today's popular music is obscene and smutty.

The article in the national magazine has caused about as much controversy as Elvis' wiggling hips did in 1956, with teens rushing to defend their music and parents demanding to know why rock groups and artists are "polluting" their children's minds.

King, the author of "Time Won't Let Me," denies that today's singers and songwriters are contaminating the American youth. "There is no 'pollution' and, in fact, current rock 'n' roll songs are no dirtier than the imaginations of the people who are condemning them."

"Because you hear a song that says 'Let's Go Get Stoned,' doesn't mean you're going to do it. If you want to get stoned, you're going to do it no matter what the song says."

Adults came directly into Tom's line of fire as he brought up an interesting point. "Personally, I don't dig all the adult uproar. Did you ever think about all the adults that sit around countless hours watching murders, robberies and shootings on TV? They buy all their kids guns and introduce them to violence through television.

Is jealousy the real reason behind adults' condemnation of rock music? "I think they're envious of the younger generation," said Tom frankly. "The kids of today have their own music and that music not only helps them express their feelings but also to enjoy themselves."

As for the claim that rock is only the teens' way of escaping, Tom says: "Maybe it is, but don't adults try to escape, too. Trouble is they can't fully escape. They're bogged down with dreary jobs and bills, so the most they can do is go out and get stoned at the bowling alley or local bar. The next day they've got to come back to that dreariness.

"What really bugs me about all these hassles between adults and kids is that in every one of them we're always looked upon as the villains, the generation that is going to the dogs. I have news for you. I don't know if we're going to the dogs or not—but we sure are to Vietnam.

"Maybe next time it would be better for adults to remedy the world situation instead of just picking on a few songs."

Mama's & Papa's Wax Unique LP

Exclusively to *The BEAT* from Lou Adler, executive producer for Dunhill Records, this week comes news of the brand new album about to be released by the Mama's and Papa's.

The album will be the second to be released by the popular foursome, and will be entitled "Crash-on Screamon Singon All Fall Down."

Although the final decision had not been made as we went to press, tentative plans for the album called for a total of 14 tracks—something which is almost never done.

Some of the selections included in the new LP will be "The Dancing Bear," sung by Denny; "That Kind Of Girl," "Once Was A Time," which will be sung acapella by the entire group without *any* orchestration to accompany them; and "I Can't Wait."

Cass and John will sing a duet on one cut of the LP, while Cass will be soloing on two others. John has written a total of ten new songs for the album, one of which will be a surprise number. The only thing we can tell you about this track now is that it will be only one minute in length—but you will be surprised and pleased by what you will hear in those 60 seconds.

It is only just now that the world of pop has sufficiently recovered from the first onslaught by The Mama's and Papa's to be able to "believe their eyes and ears." But this exciting new release from the talented quartet should send us all reeling right back into *tubs of disbelief*. Another sensational album from the Mama's and the Papa's.

Jesus—'OK, But . . .'

(Continued from Page 1)

can swim and get a bite to eat."

Immediately after the statements by McCartney and Harrison, the Beatle management attempted to silence the outspoken singers. A London spokesman said the Beatles would refrain from comment to "avoid further confusion and misinterpretation."

The statement by Lennon has been construed into countless meanings and explanations by everybody from American Nazi party leaders to clergymen.

Statement True?

Could there, in actuality, be truth in Lennon's allegations? A Madison, Wis., minister thinks there is.

"There is much validity in what Lennon said," commented The Rev. Richard Pritchard of the Westminster Presbyterian Church. "To many people today, the golf course is also more popular than Jesus Christ."

The "Beatle Boycott" was begun in Birmingham, Ala., by two disc jockeys who took issue with Lennon's remarks in the Datebook Magazine article.

The disc jockeys asked listeners to send in their Beatle records, pictures, souvenirs and mop-top wigs for a huge "Beatle Bonfire." The burning was scheduled for Aug. 19—the night the Beatles were slated to appear in Memphis, Tennessee.

Even the Ku Klux Klan is jumping on the Beatle "Ban Wagon."

"In Tupelo, Miss., Dale Walton, Imperial Wizard of the Knights of the Green Forest, Inc., urged teenagers to "Cut their locks off" and send them to a "Beatle Burning" by the Ku Klux Klan on Aug. 15.

Similar bonfires have occurred across the nation, and the West Coast is no exception.

In Los Angeles, an angry mother and a number of teenagers lit the Beatle torch by publicly destroying Beatles' albums and records. A bonfire protesting Lennon's statements also burned in San Francisco.

But while the radio boycott of the Beatles was spreading—especially in the Midwest and the South—Station WSAC at Fort Knox, Kentucky, in the heart of the Bible Belt, started playing Beatle records for the first time.

"Perhaps the Beatles could be more popular than Jesus," a WSAC editorial said. "Perhaps that is what is wrong with society. And if they are, dear friend, you made them so. Not Jesus, not John Lennon and not the Beatles."

A few miles away, in Louisville, Station WAKY sided with the growing anti-Beatle forces. It provided ten seconds of silent prayer for it's listeners every hour, explaining that it replaced a Beatles' record.

Beatle Laws

But in Pennsylvania, an even sterner anti-Beatle movement is afoot.

State Senator Robert Fleming says he intends to file a resolution calling on talent agents in the state to refuse to book the British singing group and to cancel engagements already made.

Fleming said his resolution will also ask radio and television stations to stop playing Beatles' records and ask juke box operators to remove them from their machines.

As expected, the most heated resentment toward the Beatles occurred in the South and Midwest. And while there were a few isolated "Beatle Burnings" on the West Coast, California teens, for the most part, still supported the Beatles and resented banning of their records.

In sampling a cross section of West Coast youth, *The BEAT* found that 93 per cent of those questioned favored the continued airing of Beatles' records by radio stations.

Guilty Feelings

Several teens commented that Lennon's critics might "just have guilty feelings because maybe they don't go to church."

Others argued that the intellectual Beatle is perfectly within his rights—as granted in the American constitution—and besides, "What he said is very true."

There is, however, a moderate-sized group of California youth who took offense at Lennon's remarks. And they are just as staunch in their beliefs—if not more so—than the larger percentage of teens defending the Britons.

One youth in his late teens thought Lennon "should be punished for what he said." Another teenager, citing the Beatles' "Yesterday and Today" album as an example, said, "John Lennon has become too much of an authority on religion and not enough of one on music."

Many of the complaints against Lennon's comments were religious in nature. "Then let them die for us," quipped one youth.

Second Incident

Lennon's statement set off the second international controversy involving the Beatles in less than a month. The group was recently shoved, kicked and cursed at the Manila International Airport after the singers failed to keep a luncheon date with the Philippine's first lady.

But even that incident didn't have the effect of the statements made by Lennon.

It's beginning to look as though it's in vogue to be in questionable opinion. The Beatles—once again—are the pacesetters.

KRLA ARCHIVES

'We Don't Think Kids Are Following Us For Our Hair'

The last year and a half in the world of popular music has seen an amazing surge of popularity in the area of rhythm and blues. Although this kind of music is actually the base for all of our contemporary music — rock 'n' roll and otherwise — it has never been so widely accepted and popularized in the pop area as it is now. Spearheading this movement are the "soul" artists; performers who sing songs of great feeling and motion. Usually they are rhythm and blues oriented, and frequently the performers are Negro — hence, the so-called "Negro Sound."

Two young men who have helped to translate the traditional R&B into more modern pop terminology are the Righteous Brothers, who have long been identified as the most outstanding examples of "blue-eyed soul."

First Hit

The first hit record for the Righteous Brothers was a hard-rocker entitled "Little Latin Lupe Lu." It had a certain bluesy, "soul-sound" feel to it, and it was quickly followed with a succession of similar, and equally successful hit singles.

Then suddenly, the Righteous Brothers found themselves occupying the chart tops once again, but this time with a much different sort of sound. The tune was "Lovin' Feeling," which has since become a pop standard, and it opened up a whole new area of R&B music. It was a soulful sound which was entirely acceptable in the pop vein, and it established a standard which was rapidly copied by a number of artists, both pop and R&B.

We asked Bobby Hatfield how he felt about the new dominance of R&B in the pop field, and he explained: "Rhythm and blues isn't *dominating* — but it's certainly taking over! It's a *gas*, 'cause that's always been our bag."

Soul Is . . .

We went on to discuss soul music, and Bobby explained that he really couldn't find an accurate definition for the term — if, indeed, there *is* one.

He likened the idea of "soul music" to the concept of love, explaining that both were undefinable, but that both contain an element of great emotional feeling.

Bill Medley — or, "Willy," as Bobby calls him — agreed saying that "soul music is an emotional thing that you have to really feel."

Both boys have a quick smile and a great sense of humor, so when we questioned them about their "new hair-cuts" which have received so much publicity, Bobby just laughed and explained:

"When we got our hair cut, it's not supposed to be a whole new completely different bag! We just got our hair cut! We don't think that many kids are following us for our *hair!!!*

"You don't sell any records with your *hair* — it's what you sing in songs. We don't try to create any "new images" — if we get our hair cut, that's just where it *is!!*"

A Lot Of TV!

Looking to the future a little, we asked Bobby and Billy what plans they might have for television and for the movies in the coming weeks, and both immediately laughed and agreed:

"We both plan on watching a lot of television, and we'll probably go see quite a few more shows!" Forget about getting any straight answers from these two, right?

But Bobby came though and more seriously explained to *The BEAT*: "Actually, when we get back from our September tour, we're hoping to do a movie or a television special."

Both Bobby and Billy admit to being very interested in entering the field of motion pictures, and Bobby explained that a number of scripts have already been submitted to them for their approval, but they haven't completed reading any of them as yet.

New LP

The boys have their own recording company now — "Righteous Productions" — and they have just completed producing one of their first artists. Both Bobby and Billy have continued their song writing, and several of their tunes are included on their latest LP, "Go Ahead and Cry."

In addition to their albums, they have also done a good bit of writing for artists, but as Bobby explained: "We don't write for any *specific* artists, but as we write there may be many artists whom we feel could do a good job on different tunes."

Some of you may have heard three or four different single releases from the Brothers Righteous in the last two months, and we asked the boys the reason for this.

Bobby explained that it was because they are still connected, in one way or another, with several different recording companies. Technically, they are on Verve (M.G.M.) Records now, and their latest single on that label is "Go Ahead and Cry."

This is the record with the magnificent — and very *unusual* — choral introduction which everyone has been talking about.

New Direction?

Both Bobby and Bill quickly put down the idea that this represents a new direction in their music, and Bill explained that it was used because the introduction called for it and they were unable to sound like an entire chorus all by themselves.

In the meantime, the Righteous Brothers continue to create their own great and distinctive brand of R&R — "soul music" — and about the only thing which can be said for this blue-eyed soulful duo is, "that's *Righteous*, Brother..."

WAY BACK WHEN — The Brothers first made fashion news by introducing their collarless suits, just after dropping their "stingy brim" hats.

OTHER CHANGES include a trip to the barber. But, Bobby says, "You don't sell any records with your hair — it's what you sing in songs."

NICE SUIT YA GOT THERE — Even Bill notices the change in tailors they've gone through. Now it's only the very sharpest suits with the jazziest lapels and black bow ties for the popular Righteous Brothers.

KRLA ARCHIVES

For Girls only
by shirley poston

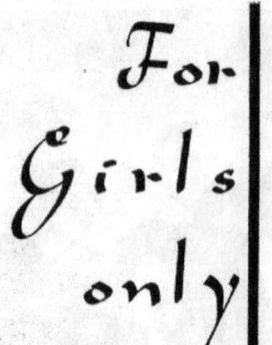

Start flinging things under the spare bed—I may be moving in soon. I've just finished giving my folks final proof that they're coming to take me away (bong, bong).

Moments ago, I had my hot hands on a letter filled with poems I wanted to print in this... this... words fail me. Anyhorse (hah?), I naturally misplaced it and had to search the entire house.

After loping through the living room for the twentieth time, my proud parents (oh, *definitely*) asked me what I was looking for (besides trouble).

When I told them I was trying to track down a letter, they asked if there was anything unusual about said letter. You know, a birthmark or something that might distinguish it from the other million envelopes that are flapping about the old homestead.

"No," I answered cleverly. "Wait a minute," I added. "It does have peanut butter all over the back of it, but that's not so unusual."

Well, that did it. Fortunately, I found the thingy in time and was able to race back to my (ex) room before they were able to haul the nets out of the closet.

If I thought it would do any good, I'd go back in there and try to explain that the *words* "peanut butter" were *written* all over the back of the envelope. And that this isn't unusual because the girl who wrote it *always* writes those words on the back of her letters. And maybe I'll try it just as soon as I finish re-inforcing the locks on my bedroom door.

Speaking of George, I mean envelopes, I can't announce the winners until next week. I'm having problems (I'll say) choosing the "top ten" because they're all so groovy.

Now, back to the peanut butter. Here are three of the poems I mentioned, which were penned by someone who would probably have a relapse (not to mention my 'ead) if I printed her name. (Coward!)

While others tone themselves
Down a little for fame,
He's just himself.
May no man be his master;
For he is his own, and mine,
And probably yours.
Maybe you've heard of him...
His name is bob dylan.

* * *

The carmel silver sweetness
Smoothy, large
Candy irridescence
Of kindness and sweet words
Coming from the lips...
Of a man they call Jagger.

* * *

Youth
Twenty years full
Young face
Curly hair
But his eyes tell of
Age and laughter
Through the reflection
Of sunlight and rainfall
And time...
Donovan is Truth.

Aren't those just great? They sure make *my* "poetry" sound like something that was scraped out from under a wharf. One of these years I'm going to make a book of all the poems that have been sent to me by both of my many readers. Please send more contributions! No, no, I won't use your names. (Re-cowards!)

And yes, yes, I am still going to send out those poems I promised, along with a detailed explanation of why it's taken so long, so prepare yourselves.

I hope I didn't tell you about this before, but my friends (which is not a typographical error) and I have made up a new drive-'em-off-their-twig-thingy. When someone you don't particularly dig asks you to do something, make up something really ridiculous that you have to do instead.

Abismal??

Like, if some abismal (abysmal?) (forget it) creep asks you out, tell him you have to stay home and give your kangaroo a bath, or iron your brother's pinafore, etc. The best one so far... sorry... so *far*. was an excuse offered by someone who shall remain nameless (if I want to remain alive.)

She was out on a date with a true twimp, and after dropping a series of hints (as in brick) that she wanted to get rid of him, she finally said she had to go home and *knit a movie*. Don't think *that* didn't do the trick!

Another goodie (as in dirty-rotten-trick), which really makes people wonder is to wait until there's a lull in a vastly boring conversation and say: "Come and get me, George. I can't stand another minute without you." Substitute the name of your own fave, of course.

That works best when you're having lunch with some of your mother's friends. Providing, of course, that you can run faster than your mother.

Crikeys! I don't know how long I've been forgetting to tell you this, but about a month ago, a boy called *The BEAT* office and asked for me. I wasn't there (make that *all* there), so he left a message.

In clipped British tones, he informed them that he was George Harrison and that he would like to know why I never write anything about him.

Honest! This really happened! Of course, I'm sure it wasn't the real George. (*Sure* I'm sure.) But I've stayed awake every night since, making up big whoppers about what would have happened if it *had* been him.

A lot of you have asked if I'm throwing any more snits this year so I can meet George again. Well, don't think it hasn't occured to me (hourly), but I've thought better of it. I'd be embarrassed to death after some of the stuff I've written about him. Besides, I might get carried away and take a large bite of him. As you (have the misfortune to) know, I'm not quite as sane and sensible as I was last year. (QUITE?) (QUITE!) (Doesn't it just carve you up when he sings "carve your number on my wall and maybe you will get a call from me?"—GASP!) (His wall isn't the only place I'd like to carve my number.)

Down, girl.

Hurling Tantrums

Besides, I'm too busy hurling tantrums so that one of you can meet your mind-blower. However, when I go to England this winter (dream on, dolt), I do plan to discuss a few things with George at great length. Ahem.

Here's one for everyone who thinks *they* have problems. I got a letter from a girl whose parents decided to move to another state the day after she got her Beatle concert tickets in the mail. They'll be leaving two days before the concert, which could explain a loud roar you may have been hearing of late. Godfrey, wouldn't that be *awful?*

And here's one I can't quite figure out. A sort-of-pen-pal of mine asked me the weirdest question in one of her letters. (Slight interruption: Sorry I haven't sent your pix back—I will instantaneously.)

She said—and I quote—"why do you smoke?"

Since the subject has never come up, in our letters or this (alledged) column, I'm beginning to wonder if the question wasn't a slip of the lip-er-pen.

Considering the way I write, she probably meant to ask *what*. Ta-ra (as in ra-boom-di-ay.)

Mrs. Miller Is Now Chairman

Mrs. Elva Miller, the music business' newest phenomena (?), has been doing so well for herself lately that she has now formed her own production company, Vibrato Productions.

Mrs. Miller, who has been making a small mint on her albums (people claim they don't know if they're buying the albums for jokes or for real) will act as chairman of the board.

Old Chinese Proverb?

The Leaves, playing San Francisco's Dragon A Go Go, found a modern-day proverb written inside the Chinese-owned club.

"All roads lead to the Dragon A Go Go. Blessed are those who come in; this is the land of sunshine and whisky," the inscription read.

But it was written in Hebrew!

THE WILD AFFAIR... On tour in jungles of Viet Nam.

The Wild Affair Touring Viet Nam

The Wild Affair is in Viet Nam on a goodwill tour, and those sounds you hear floating across the tropical rain forests may not be coming from sniper gun fire—but from the strings of amplified guitars.

Clad in uncustomary combat boots, loose fitting green fatigues and straw hats, the group is touring around the fringes of areas ripped by bloody fighting. Their demanding 17-day tour calls for two performances a day at air bases and field hospitals.

Surprised

The Wild Affair—one of the first American pop groups to visit the strife-torn country on a Government sponsored tour—were as surprised as they were happy when they first learned their visit had cleared the proper channels.

"It all happened so fast that we couldn't believe we were really going," said Denny Martin, newest member of the trio. "We talked to the GAC agency one day and the next day they called and told us we were going to Viet Nam. It was like a dream."

If it was like a dream the Wild Affair had a sharp awakening when they were greeted by nine different innoculation needles as they prepared for the disease infested jungles of Viet Nam.

Bad Reflection

But the yellow fever, cholera and other shots were only a part of the whirlwind procedures the boys undertook. They were confronted with stacks of regulations and briefings and as a parting comment by Air Force brass they were cautioned, "Don't do anything that would have a bad reflection on the United States."

In fact, the boys were kept so busy going through tour regulations they were left little time to consider the visit itself. A few days before they departed they were asked if they didn't think the trip would be a bit on the dangerous side.

A startled Rod Birmingham stared quizzically at his fellow troubadors and finally answered, "You know... we hadn't really thought about that, but I suppose it will be."

"Run And Hide"

"Well at any rate," laughed Chuck Morgan," we will be totally prepared to run and hide."

Aside from an occasional joke, the trio is taking the tour very seriously. The trip was their own idea, as "the least we can do."

Although the boys are all exempt from the draft, they are still concerned about the war in Viet Nam and especially about those who are fighting it. "I think tours of this sort help morale quite a bit," said Denny. "I know if I were over there fighting, seeing American entertainment would make me feel better."

Curious

Another reason they wanted to visit the trouble spot was to satisfy their own curiousity. "I think the reason there is so much criticism in the United States is because people don't know what is really going on over there," said Rod.

"While we're over there," he continued, "we are going to try to get an inside view of the war. We are going to talk to as many people as we can."

Diary

Denny, the historian of the group, is keeping a diary and taking pictures while in Viet Nam. The group's experiences and observations while in Southeast Asia will be printed in an up-coming issue of *The BEAT*.

KRLA ARCHIVES

Yardbirds From All Positions

By Louise Criscione

It really doesn't matter how you look at the Yardbirds. If you view them from overhead, the five shiny heads of freshly shampooed hair are the most obvious. The long, thin strands of blond which belong to Keith Relf catch the eye first. For many reasons. Light always attracts and Keith's hair is the lightest. But more than that, he is out of line. The one in the middle – the one nearest the audience. The lead singer. So, how could you miss noticing Keith first?

Jim McCarty you see next. He shares his brown hair color with Jeff Beck and Jimmy Page but you notice Jim because the off-white of his severely beaten drum skins glare up at you and his twirling drum sticks, perpetually in motion, make imaginary trails through the thick air.

A Rebel

Jeff Beck is an everpresent force. His rather unruly hair goes its own way despite all of Jeff's efforts to keep it in place. It's independent and listens to no one. It matches Jeff perfectly for he is the same kind of independent. A rebel, maybe. But a rebel with a musical cause. And that makes him okay.

Jimmy Page is the newest Yardbird and that's probably what makes his dark head stand out. Curiousity you could call it. You peer down on his unfamiliar brown hair and wonder. Will he fit in? Will he be accepted by Yardbird fans? Will he last? He tosses his head in sort of open defiance and you decide that in the Yardbird line-up he is very much at home.

Chris Dreja's fair hair compliments Keith's stark whiteness and the others' deep darkness. He stands the far opposite of Jeff and his light hair is cropped close for a Yardbird. It behaves and so does Chris. Perhaps it's afraid to move out of place but now it seems to have lost that initial shyness just as Chris has overcome his urge to remain in the background.

Five Faces

If you look at the Yardbirds from underneath, their faces stand out immediately. All completely different and yet all possessing the concentrated look of professional musicians. Keith's thin and fragile face is often hidden from his audience. He's not a movie star. He doesn't consider his face important. It's his voice and his soul which deliver. So, as he stands in the middle of the stage with the microphone and harmonica hiding his face, his soul and his deep-gutted feeling for the blues make everything else appear inconsequential and worth nothing.

Jeff's face stands naked before his audience. Every motion is shown there. Every chord brings a different expression to his face and every expression is unique. Ninety-nine percent of the time Jeff is not even aware that he has an audience. The only thing he feels is the electronic sound fighting its way out of his battered guitar.

Jim's face is one of constant change. Most of the time it is absorbed in his beat, the basis of the group he sits behind. But every so often it occurs to him that thousands of up-turned faces are noting his every move and then he breaks into an easy grin as he realizes the enjoyment the Yardbirds are giving to their audience in return for the claps of co-operation their audience is giving back to them.

The Boyish One

Chris' boyish face is nearly always shining and happy because Chris is nearly always aware of his audience. He smiles more frequently than the rest and throughout the night will occasionally pick an individual face to give his smile to. The only times he pushes the audience into the background of his mind is when he glances over to the rest of the group to make certain that everything is okay or when he steps back to adjust his amplifier. Then his face, too, becomes one of concentrated thought on the "sound" which belongs exclusively to the Yardbirds.

Jimmy is a musician in every sense of the word. Before joining the Yardbirds, Jimmy was a session musician with the reputation of being one of the best (if not *the* best) session men in England. His uppermost thoughts are of complete harmony between all the instruments on stage. This musical professionalism shows plainly through on his face and you can see right away that he's more than a performer – he's a performing musician.

If you look at the Yardbirds sideways, about the only things which stand out definitely are the shiny guitars and the glistening drums. Perhaps you'll notice a pair of flying maraccas or a bongo resting securely between Keith's knees. From the side, individuals are merely tall shadows – only the instruments are visibly there.

To really appreciate the music of the Yardbirds, you'd have to pull the curtain down to hide Keith, Jim, Chris, Jeff and Jimmy. That way you won't be distracted and you can fully *listen* to what they make their instruments say. Otherwise, your eyes tend to wander to Keith's flushed face, to Jim's quick smiles, to Jeff's flying fingers, to Chris' moving feet, to Jimmy's thumping bass. You see and you feel but you don't honestly listen.

So, watch the Yardbirds from "Over, Under, Sideways, Down." But while you're looking and feeling don't forget to close your eyes and really listen. Because, you see, that's what the Yardbirds are all about. And if you fail to listen, you've missed their whole point.

KRLA ARCHIVES

The Adventures Of Robin Boyd

©1965 By Shirley Poston

George, John, Paul and Ringo (A.I.G.A.A.R.) (As In Genies And Angel, Respectively) piled into the waiting Rolls Royce and Robin (A.F.F.) (As In Furious) flounced in after them.

"Horseradish," she moaned as the five of them sped down the driveway of the Bono residence.

George poked her, cracking a smile. "Gerroff it," he larfed. "It's not all *that* bad."

Robin snorted. "Then why can't you clean up your *own* bloomin' tea pot?" she snapped.

George glared. "I *told* you why! We don't have time. The four of us are on a special assignment, and I can't be askin' three visitors to stay in that *mess*."

John leaned over to say something about the tea pot not having been cleaned since they were in town *last* summer, but Robin scarcely heard him because her ears were standing straight up.

Assignment?

"Special assignment?" she echoed. (Should Robin ever find herself unemployed in later life, she can always get work as a parrot.)

George re-poked, cracking a rib this time. "Never you mind."

Robin's ears flattened. Oh well, she'd find a way to extract the information from George. However, she would have to find a phone booth first.

Peering in all four directions, Robin failed to discover one of the same, but she did succeed in discovering that she was once again up to her eyebrows in hot water. (Rather appropos for someone who's about to go into the tea-pot-cleaning business, don't you think?) (No, of course you don't, or you'd be reading something sensible.)

"HELP!!!" she blithered. "Not to be confused with the one I've seen 4,367½ times!" she added.

Whattt??

"WHATTT??" jumped George, John, Paul and Ringo. "Now," they added.

"*That!*" Robin cried, pointing to the car careening just behind them.

"And *that* and *that!*" she re-cried, pointing to the two cars careening on either side of them. "Not to mention *that!*" she finished, pointing to the car careening *toward* them!

George tried to leap to his feet and fell into the front seat instead. "*Hit the brakes, John!*" he bellowed.

John reached down and belted the pedal with a right cross. The Rolls ground to a halt.

"*Do* something!" Robin roared as sixty-eight sturdy Beatlemaniacs flang themselves out of their automobiles and pounced, "They think you're *them!*"

However, her suggestion fell on deaf ears (and very nearly hurt itself.) Hands were tangled in George's georgeous (ahem) dark hair. Several girls had a firm grip on John's sidies. Pauley, who had been dragged half way out of the car, was undergoing a series of toof-chipping smooches. And Ringo was almost hidden in a cloud of feathers. And what's *more*, all four of them were grinning.

Robin gasped. Those utter wretches! They were loving every minute of this! And they didn't have sense enough to know that if this touching scene continued for *another* of those moments, they might not live to talk (as in brag) about it.

Removing a stray foot from her mouth and chomping an unidentified fore-arm, Robin took a deep breath. Then, spitting out the flying wig she'd inhaled, she screeched the only thingy that came to mind. Which was "UP, UP AND *AWAY!*"

Robin, you see, read far too many comic books when she was a child (a week ago Thursday.) While other kidlets her age were wasting their time on fingerpainting projects, Robin was painting the town with the Masked Mover (her fave) and other caped swingers.

Rose Rolls

She had always figured that her early education would come in handy one of these days, and she was right. The very instant she uttered the aforementioned screech, the Rolls Royce rose into the air and hovered at an altitude of approximately six thousand feet.

"Gawd," she breathed proudly. "Help you," she added, turning to (not to mention on) her four smirking companions.

"What is the *matter* with you twits?" she raged. "Are you trying to get us all *deaded*?"

The foursome exchanged snickers. "It's good practice," John explained. "And, as I always say, practice makes perfect."

"You should *know*," Robin snarled. Then her ears did that thingy again (that's a standing joke.) "Practice for *what*?"

Socket Out

When no one bothered to give her the courtesy of a reply (George did yank her arm clean out of the socket, but that's another story), Robin curled her lip (using the rollers she always kept handy) and looked over the side of the car to make sure the aforementioned Beatlemaniacs were gone.

They were gone all right. Out of their gourds and into the nearest hospital.

Back To Earth

So, the coast being clear, she calmly ordered the Rolls to return to earth.

The next thing she knew, the car had disappeared and the four of them were standing in a strange (is not the *word*) place.

Robin's spine squeaked, as it always did when she got that I-Know-I've-Never-Been-Here-Before-But-I-Know-I've-Been-Here-Before-HUH? feeling.

She looked around fearfully. Suddenly the place fell into place (repetition re-rules.) Of course! This was an old set from "Help" (*to* be confused with the one she'd seen 4,367½ times.) It was the famous Beatle "apartment," to be exact. Or, to be even more specific, the *remains* of the famous Beatle "apartment," after nuclear warfare had been waged therein.

In other words (at this point, even Sanskit would be less confusing), the scene was not one but *several* mells of a hess.

I Did That

Robin's mouth dropped open. "How did we get *here*? Did *I* do it?"

George gave her a confused look (which she promptly returned because she already had one, thank you) (you're welcome, you're welcome.)

"You know," she explained. "Like I made the Rolls rise."

George re-looked confused. "I didn't know you could bake, too!"

"The Rolls *Royce*, you nerd," Robin frowned, wondering what he meant by that *too* stuff.

"My magnificent magic powers managed that mighty clever move!" George, John, Paul and Ringo mocked modestly. (Best not read that sentence aloud unless there's someone around to help untie your tongue.)

Robin's ego deflated suddenly, causing her to take a most unpleasant spin about the ex-room and land in a large pile of empty corn-flake cartons.

"Go wave a wand!" she thundered. "Over your am-day tea pot, for instance!"

Not Allowed

George pinched her angrily (which made it even madder.) "*Robin Irene Boyd*," he hissed. "We aren't *allowed* to use our powers for such thingys. And I think it's the *least* you can do after all the trouble we've re-gotten you out of!"

(Have you noticed how George is starting to talk like the aforementioned Robin Irene Boyd?) (So has George, and the situation is causing a lot of trundle-tossing.) (It is also keeping him awake nights.)

"You're Right"

Robin sat down wearily on a mountain of orange popsickle sticks. "I suppose you're right," she agreed grudgingly. "Besides, it couldn't be all *that* much work to clean up a mere *tea pot*."

Then she stood up briskly. "Well, when are we going to get out of this disaster area and proceed to our destination?"

"Hah?" they chorused.

Robin heaved a heavy sigh and prepared to translate. "Would you be so kind as to tell me when we will arrive at said pot?"

"Of *course*," soothed George, John, Paul and Ringo. "Would you believe about five minutes ago?" they added.

(To Be Continued Next Week)

Vinton Cover Girl Search

A unique major promotion campaign is being set in motion by Epic Records for the entire catalog of Bobby Vinton's albums. One part of the massive campaign is a contest running from August 15 through October 5.

The Grand-Prize winner, in addition to being featured on the cover of Vinton's next album, will fly to New York via TWA for an all-expense-paid weekend for two. Highlighting the weekend will be a dinner date with Bobby at the world famous Copacabana and a complete wardrobe of Irvington Place fashions.

The second prize winner will receive a $2,000 scholarship to the school of her choice; the Third, fourth and fifth prize winners will each receive a handsome Columbia 360 stereo system and the next 15 winners will receive Masterwork AM/FM shortwave portable transistor radios. The 500 remaining finalists will be awarded a copy of the Bobby Vinton Cover Girl album upon its release.

Entry blanks for the contest will be available free of charge from local Epic Record dealers throughout the United States.

In an unprecedented move, Epic is releasing two new Vinton albums to spearhead the all-out campaign. The albums, released simultaneously, are "More of Bobby's Greatest Hits" and "Bobby Vinton Live At the Copa."

Wayne Newton Sets Records

Wayne Newton tied an attendance record and set a record for most standing ovations during his three-week gig at the Fairmont Hotel's Venetian Room in San Francisco.

Two shows a night, every night were sold out during Newton's string of appearances. The supper club, which seats 420, has a $4.00 cover charge on weekends and $3.50 charge on week nights.

Newton also drew a standing ovation each night—the first time in the history of the club this has happened.

KRLA ARCHIVES

From The 'Perfect Society' Emerge The Temptations

By Eden

The Temptations are another of the fine Motown groups... but they are *not* just another group! Five talented and witty individuals involved in the creation of good music – whether it is rhythm and blues, pop, or country and western – and the communication of good will, would probably be a more accurate description of this successful quintet.

Individually, the Temptations sign in as Melvin Franklin – the 23 year old singer with a voice located 20,000 Leagues Beneath the Sea; David Ruffin, Otis Williams, Eddie Kendricks, and Paul Williams.

Between the five of them they play such instruments as the piano, drums, tuba and bass, and hope soon to incorporate these instruments into their act.

Humor, Class

There is something about the Motown artists, something distinctive which they all share, which can only be identified as "class."

And the Temptations have an abundance of this, as well as a fine group sense of humor. An interview with all five Temptations will always be interesting, informative, and somewhat unusual – but it will also be slightly *hysterical*, among other things, and spiced with a very gentle humor which the boys enjoy poking at themselves and anyone else around.

We began discussing the current trends of rhythm and blues in contemporary music, and Mel led off the conversation by booming: "Rhythm and blues, and how it's affecting the pop market: It's taking it over by storm, isn't it? It's *wonderful!*" After this proclamation, we proceeded to David, who explained: "I think *all* the music is coming, basically, toward rhythm and blues now."

Otis agreed with David, summing up: "To make a long story short – I think rhythm and blues is here to stay." Paul thought about all of this for a moment, then added his own contribution to the discussion.

"Rhythm and blues, as far as *pop* is concerned, stems mainly from *Motown*, the effect it has on it. When you say 'soul music,' I think it's just a blend with the rhythm and blues thing, which gives it the *feeling* and which can either send it pop or keep it rhythm and blues."

Paul had mentioned the Motown influence on pop and rhythm and blues, and this led us to a discussion of the much spoken of "Motown Sound." Once again we turned to Mel, who explained: "In my opinion, the Motown Sound is what I would call *perfection*, and we achieve it by striving *toward* perfection.

"I mean to say that we, the people at Motown, do our very best in our endeavors." This last statement, once pronounced, called forth an immediate reaction from the other four Temptations, who promptly jumped to their feet, hands on their hearts, facing Detroit.

The patriotic proceedings of the hour now dispensed with, we found ourselves discussing other sounds, including that particular sound with which the Temptations are identified.

Otis attempted to describe their sound for us: "I don't mean to sound vain or conceited, but I think it is good; it knocks me out. And a lot of people know our sound when they hear it due to that churchy sound."

Variety

One aspect of their music of which the Temptations can be justifiably proud is the variety and freshness which they maintain. They are always examining their music, and searching for ways in which to improve upon it, and this experimentation is one of their best features.

Mel explained this a little further as he told us of some of their current experimenting: "It's good in this business to be able to show versatility – this is one of the Temptations' traits, I'd like to believe – and we're planning, some time in the future, to interject the instruments that we play into our act, and be musicians as well as singers."

Other things up-coming for the group? "In the immediate future, we'll have the pleasure of having our own show – a complete band and everything. We're going to do some of the bigger TV spots – including two Dean Martin shows this Fall, and we're hoping to do the 'Hollywood Palace,' and the 'Ed Sullivan Show' and all of the rest." There are also tentative plans and very high hopes that the boys will be able to follow one of their sister groups in the Motown family – the Supremes – into the Copa, in New York, within the next two years.

All of the Temptations have a tremendous amount of respect for Smokey Robinson, who has been a friend-mentor-co-worker to all of them, and has coached them since they first began at Motown.

Smokey

David recalled the interest which Smokey took in the group, rehearsing, then later working with them on their album, "The Temptations Sing Smokey." There was a sincere feeling of gratitude in his voice as he spoke of his talented friend, then – bringing out the familiar sense of humor he shares with the other four – he asked: "Let's give Smokey a hand," and once again the five Temptations rose to their feet in applause.

In the Fall, the Temptations will be making their second trip to Europe along with their appearances in clubs and on TV in this country. They are also looking forward to getting into acting, if possible, and further into writing and producing at Motown.

Before we concluded our interview, Mel decided to give one more speech on the family at Motown, and in his deepest voice he boomed:

"It's a love, that has all the aspects of a perfect business machine, with that same warmth that you get at home with your sisters and brothers. It's something that's not really tangible; you *can't* really put down the Motown feeling in words. It's something that you'd really have to come there and witness. And everybody is really *sincerely* sincere about how they feel about each other. It's what I call a Perfect Society."

TWO FIFTHS of the Temptations, Paul, center, and Mel, work with the mike of Eden's tape recorder during her interview with them.

LATER ALL FIVE pour their smooth tones into the mikes of a sound system. The cowboy hats are part of their "Wagon Wheels" routine.

Shadows Of Knight Shun Beatle Sound

The Shadows of Knight say they don't want to sound like the Beatles.

You haven't just seen a misprint, or a slap against the Beatles or a quote from a group trying to get in solid with an 80-year-old audience.

It's just that the Shadows of Knight are looking for their own sound; they feel that most groups today copy the Beatles – with, of course, a few sartorial exaggerations – yet none can recapture the original excitement.

But if anybody can, the Shadows stand a good chance of creating a unique sound of their own.

The Beatle sound, in itself, is a masterpiece of musical innovation. It would take pure musical genius to parallel it. And this is where the musical knowledge and ingenuity of the Shadows of Knight comes in.

As a group the Shadows are five musically sophisticated young men who not only know music, but write it and speak with great intelligence.

The boys know not only about their own particular type of music, but of all types including classical and far-out jazz.

The music of the Shadows doesn't have its origin in Liverpool – but in the suburbs of Chicago.

The members of the group all hail from the Windy City, and it was there that the Shadows got their first big break. They didn't have to wait long for it, either.

The Shadows all hail from Chicago's Northwest suburbs. In a quiet, reserved little night spot called the Cellar the group made its start.

That is, everything was calm and quiet before the Shadows took over. By the end of the summer of 1965 the section of town was a happening place, and the sidewalks in front of the Cellar were crowded with Shadow fans.

After more than a year of playing teen clubs, dances and hops, the group got its first big break. An executive from a record company saw the Shadows perform and asked them if they wanted to make a record.

You guessed it...they consented. So their first hit, "Gloria," was born and released on the Dunwich label. It took Chicago – and the rest of the country – by storm. Local radio stations got more calls asking for that record than any other record in Chicago history.

The group followed with "Oh Yeah" and there was no question that they were going places.

The reason for the Shadows' instant success, undoubtedly, is their originality. The music of the Shadows of Knight – like the individual members – is anything but stereotyped.

Jim Sohn, lead singer, is the extrovert of the group, and answers to the title "the little hairy wild man." Warren is the group's perfectionist and handles the electronic equipment for the group.

Jerry is what is termed a "neatnik," and never appears without a coat and tie. His hair, always perfectly combed, sharply contrasts that of Joe, who is called the "sheep dog." Tom is extremely quiet and is the ladies man of the group.

Musically, the Shadows of Knight are just as individualistic. They would have to be to not want to sound like the Beatles.

...THE SHADOWS OF KNIGHT

KRLA ARCHIVES

...TERRY SLATER (LEFT) AND THE EVERLYS

Terry Slater Remembers 'The Good Days' of R&R

By Mike Tuck

The thin-faced Englishman across the table sat up straight in his chair and except for a few hundred years and a touch of mod clothing bore a strange resemblance to a British sentry perched in a crows nest atop a pirate ship.

If I were a child of literature I would not rest easy until I decided which character from "Horatio Hornblower" he most nearly resembled. When his salty smile revealed a gleaming row of uneven teeth I was positive he was the prankish boatswain.

But his slightly grizzled face, his long thin nose and a pair of stern peepers made him look more like prime captain material. His shaggy hair was blown back from a leathery face that was molded in a perenial squint as if to avoid the glaring sun that reflected from brimey water.

His expression revealed all the relief and fatigue of a lean pirate captain who had just brought his frigate and his men safely away from a battering storm and a long chase by the Spanish Armada.

But back to reality. Back to Terry Slater. My imaginative bubble dolefully burst as the would-be pirate quietly assured me the only ship he ever set foot on was an ocean liner from Liverpool to New York.

And, he said, the closest he had ever come to a battle was when some entranced teenagers trampled him in an attempt to reach his traveling mates, the Everly Brothers.

Terry Slater, the jolly bass guitarist for the Everlys, has an accent that drips with colloquialisms from the foggy isle.

As his initial windblown appearance had indicated he is what a literature professor would classify as a romantic, and he talks with wistful relish of bygone days when he and his group were knocking about Hamburg.

"Ah . . . them were the good days," he in his typical British grammar. "Them were the days before the Beatles and the Rolling Stones got their big starts, and they all played Hamburg. It was kinda the center of rock 'n roll and even though it wasn't a polished profession like it is today, it was still more exciting.

"Nobody had any money in their pockets back then but that's part of what made it so much fun. The living was hard and rough. All we lived on was cokes and hamburgers, but nobody seemed to care."

Terry Slater could still pass for one of the original colorful characters off a page from that era of rock 'n' roll history. He is with a world-renowned group now and he eats regular and money is the least of his worries. But you couldn't tell it by just talking to him.

He insists he is quite happy now, however, even though he at times is confronted with thousands of screaming people in plush auditoriums and has to make courtesy visits to such distasteful places as castles and foreign embassys.

The main reason for his happiness, he points out, is his close friendship and admiration for Phil and Don Everly.

"I've been good friends with Phil and Don for a long time — since about 1963 when they'd come to England and my group would back them up," he remembers.

"If it weren't for the Everlys," he allowed, "I wouldn't be here today. They're the ones that made it all right with the Government so I could come over here."

But Terry hasn't seen as much of the United States as he has seen of the rest of the world since he permanently joined the Everlys a year ago. They immediately went on a world-wide tour and are about to go on another.

And almost everywhere he's gone, the reaction has been the same. Crowds and screaming.

"Ya' know it's strange," he mused, "but the Everlys draw more crowds and better reactions in other countires than they do in the United States.

"In a gig in Canada, they were mobbed by not only teenagers but by grown men and women... One 45-year-old woman even fainted."

At this point, Terry noted a paradox between American audiences and American artists. "I prefer American artists," he said, "over English artists, because they seem to try harder. They are more anxious to please their audiences.

"Yet, the American audiences seem to appreciate it less. In England, if an artist had a hit ten years ago the audience will remember him and appreciate him."

He reflected for a moment upon what he had just said and again his lean face brightened. And I at last decided he more resembled the prankish boatswain.

Mel Carter's After Facets And Phases

By Carol Deck

Mel Carter's goal is *just* to "reach the ultimate in show business in every facet and phase of it" and to "be a name that everyone throughout this country and all the rest of the countries will be aware of."

That's a mightly large goal for anyone but this young Cincinnati singer's got a good start with a string of hits that includes "When A Boy Falls In Love," "Richest Man Alive," "Hold Me, Thrill Me, Kiss Me," "My Heart Sings," "Love Is All We Need," and his latest, "You, You, You."

Mel fell by The BEAT offices the other day and offered a few words on a few things dear to him—like his music.

He records mostly old standards, written 15 or 20 years ago. He doesn't feel there is much difference in the content of songs written then and now, but that the difference lies in how the songs are presented.

"Older songs say exactly what's happening today, but more elegantly."

People Listen

He does feel, however, that people are listening to lyrics more these days.

"Because of people like Dylan, Barry McGuire and Dean Martin, who are selling lyrics, teens listen to lyrics more than the beat now."

Mel, who was the late Sam Cooke's protege, has been very busy lately. Between taping television shows and taking dramatic lessons, he's just finished cutting an album that he calls "more of an album album."

The cuts on it are all from the "easy listening" charts and Mel says, "we didn't go in to do it commercially." He seems quite proud of this album, like maybe this is the *real* Mel Carter.

More Mels

And speaking of Mel Carters, he says he's finally accepted the fact that he can't separate Mel Carter the singer from Mel Carter in private life.

"You can't do it, at least not the way I wanted to do it. It takes more than 24 hours a day just to do and be what I want to do."

Somewhere in his busy schedule he's found time to take up the guitar too, but says he won't incorporate it into his act. "It's for something to do in my spare time."

The one thing he doesn't seem to find time for anymore is clothes designing. He used to design much of his own outfits, but no more. "My designs weren't keeping up with my image," he says. He kind of left himself behind in that field, so now he's gone on to other things.

Mel Carter wants to be a complete entertainer in every meaning of the word. The BEAT feels he's got the talent and the personality, and he's not rushing blindly into things—he's planning every step of the way.

So watch for him. He'll be up there with the Frank Sinatras and the Sammy Davis' someday.

...MEL CARTER

Pop Scene Quiz Answers

THE FIRST NAME GAME: 1—John (Beach Boys), 2—Cindy (Trini Lopez), 3—Caroline (Brian Wilson), 4—Michael (Dionne Warwick), 5—Johnny (Elvis Presley). MEMORY MAKERS: 1—"I'm Into Something Good," 2—"Do You Believe In Magic," 3—"Downtown," 4—"Jenny Take A Ride," 5—"This Diamond Ring," 6—"Like A Rolling Stone," 7—"Make It Easy On Yourself," 8—"She's Not There," 9—"Hold On To What You've Got," 10—"Heartbreak Hotel." MERRY OLD ENGLAND: 1—The Mindbenders, 2—North End Music Stores, 3—Noel is Rex's son, 4—The Beatles, 5—Bob Dylan, 6—Keith Relf, 7—German, 8—"Alfy," 9—The Animals, 10—Men's Wear. SPELL BOUND: 1—Tanega, 2—Temptations, 3—Pharoahs, 4—Knight, 5—Dionne, 6—Redding, 7—Garfunkel, 8—Lesley, 9—Pickett, 10—Johnny. BRAIN TEASER 1—Play and film "West Side Story" (Len Barry), 2—Movie "Flight of the Phoenix" (Brass Ring), 3—TV show filmed in Britain titled "Secret Agent" (Johnny Rivers or the Ventures), 4—Alkaseltzer TV commercial (T-Bones), 5—Old British music hall favorite (Herman's Hermits). SECOND TIME AROUND: 1—c, 2—e, 3—d, 4—a, 5—b. BEHIND THE SCENES: 1—d, 2—e, 3—a, 4—b, 5—d. FLIP SIDES: 1—j, 2—f, 3—d, 4—a, 5—i, 6—h, 7—e, 8—b, 9—c, 10—g. BEATLEMANIA: 1—Walter Shenson. 2—Buddy Holly. 3—Mary. 4—Malcolm Evans. 5—Paul is his middle name, first is James. 6—Cynthia accompanied the group to America in Feb. 1964. 7—"A Talent For Loving." 8—"Please Please Me." 9—Jimmy Nicholls. 10—"If I Needed Someone." 11—The Silkie. 12—Bernard Webb. 13—"That's My Life." 14—Chicago. 15—Pete Best. TRUE OR FALSE: 1—False (he's recording an album of Lennon poems). 2—true, for reasons of health. 3—false. 4—false (it's just the other way around). 5—false (it's Quintette). 6—true. 7—true. 8—true. 9—false (he's a staff sergeant which is three grades below first). 10—false (it's Denny not Danny). 11—false (they've received ten). 12—true. 13—false (6). 14—true. 15—false (John Sebastian). 16—false. 17—true. 18—false (among other things, he produced it). 19—true. 20—true. 21—false (Eric Burdon). 22—false (another DC5 flick begins soon). 23—true. 24—true (but it was corrected before too many copies went out—they had 15 letters in the presidents' names instead of 13). 25—false (poem was titled "This Bird Has Flown"). SCORING: If you have less than ten wrong answers, consider yourself a real expert. If you scored eighty right answers or over, you still know what's happening. 60 and up, you need to brush up on your pop knowledge, and we can't think of a better way to do it than to keep reading The BEAT.

Epstein Has New Partner

Brian Epstein and Nathan M. Weiss, old friends from business associations have opened their own management firm, Nemperor Artists Ltd., in New York.

Weiss, who manages the Cyrkle, had been in close contact with Epstein for some time.

KRLA ARCHIVES

...A SCIENCE FICTION PEEK INSIDE THE HUMAN BRAIN

...THE ONE-INCH MODEL OF A SUBMARINE WHICH ESCAPED THE BIRD

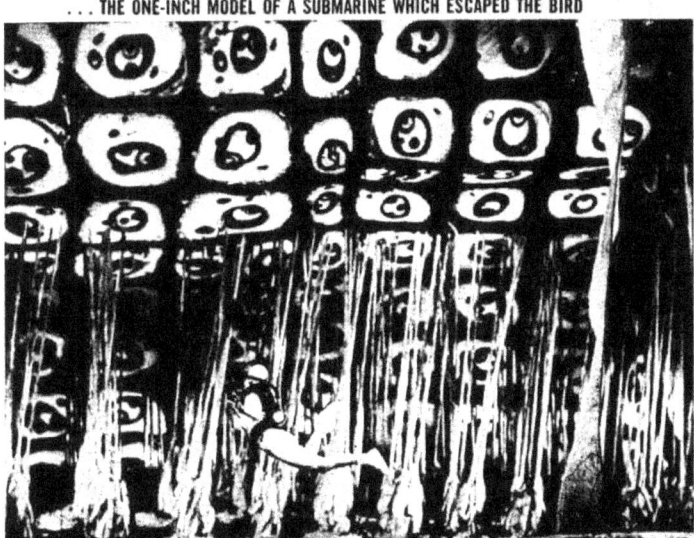

...THE SIX MILLION DOLLAR BRAIN

The BEAT Goes To The Movies

'FANTASTIC VOYAGE'

By Jim Hamblin
(The BEAT Movie Editor)

Briefly the story revolves around saving a scientist who came over "from the other side," to divulge all his knowledge of how to prolong the time in which matter can be reduced in size to microscopic dimensions. In an attempt on his life, he suffers brain damage, and the only way to save him is miniaturize a special submarine and put a crew inside his head to work on the problem.

The studio shot the story without any special effects, just actors, more than a year ago. Then they tried to see if they could successfully re-produce the inside of a blood vessel, and blood itself, and all the other things an atom-sized crew might see.

The result is a startling new concept in film-making. The special effects, upon which the film is completely dependent, are flawless. Special new techniques were designed to carry off the spectacular trip, and the company (20th Century-Fox) dropped a bundle doing it. But any studio that would spend so much money on Cleopatra certainly would not mind $6,600,000 on a picture almost certain to win Academy Awards for its technical excellence.

There are some funny stories connected with making the film, according to Saul David, the producer. Part of the filming required a tiny 1-1/4 inch model of the submarine. It was carefully handcrafted and painted meticulously, then casually set down on a studio workshop windowsill to dry. And a blue-jay swooped down, picked it up, and flew away with it! Several days were lost while craftsmen built another one.

The sets used for the lungs, the heart, the inner ear, and arteries, are painstakingly realistic, and about 5 million times bigger than the real thing. Experts from the UCLA Medical Center supervised construction.

Excellent cast includes Stephen Boyd, that lovely child Raquel Welch, as well as Arthur Kennedy, Arthur O'Connell, and Edmund O'Brien.

It is hard to call this simply a *science fiction* film. Who among us can say that tomorrow it may not all be a chilling and exciting reality?

* * *

AROUND AND WORTH SEEING:

ASSAULT ON A QUEEN: Sinatra is an unwilling partner in a daring plot to knock over the Queen Mary luxury liner. In last scene he hands survivors in raft a paddle, and notes well, "South America is thataway!" One of his best adventure flicks. (Paramount)

ALFIE: A sordid, very adult, not very cute movie about a confused but maybe happy man. Not for the young in years or the squeamish. Very much like a filmed version of the Keinholz art exhibit that upset Warren Dorn this year. Like us, you may never make up your mind about whether you like it. It is at the very least an interesting and often funny story. Best performance is by Paul McCartney's steady, Jane Asher. (Paramount)

BATTLE OF THE BULGE: A sweeping semi-type documentary of Hitler's last gasp. And with the possible exception of *Paths Of Glory*, the best war movie yet made. Stars Fonda, Dana Andrews, Robert Ryan, and 400 big mean tanks. (Warner Brothers)

WALK DON'T RUN: The smoothest of the old smoothies, Cary Grant, is still carrying bottles of milk around in his pajamas after all these years! Excellent comedy. (Columbia)

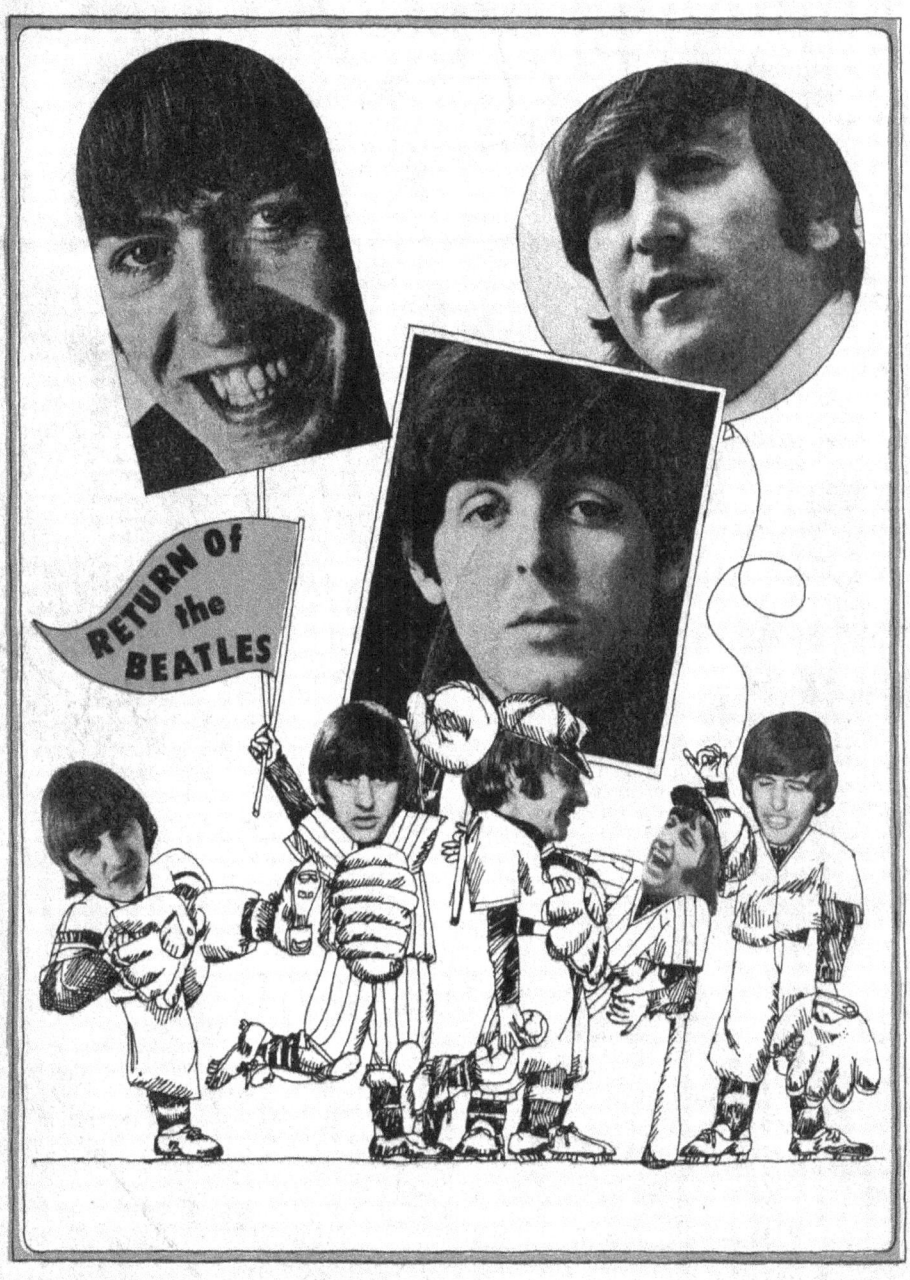

KRLA BEAT

Volume 2, Number 23 — September 10, 1966

Beatle Box Score: 14 Hits, One Error

Lennon: 'Sorry About the Mess'

With religious groups still condemning them and teens greeting them with mixed reactions, the Beatles are concluding their U.S. tour amidst apologies and attempted clarifications of John Lennon's statement on the condition of Christianity.

Lennon continually apologized for the furor caused by his statement that "the Beatles are more popular than Jesus," but insisted that he did not mean for his comment to be anti-Christian.

The intellectual Beatle said he merely was attempting to show that Christianity was on the decline—not that the Beatles were above Christ.

Losing Contact

"I do believe that Christianity is shrinking, that people are losing contact with it," he said at a recent press conference.

"However, I didn't mean it the way it sounded," he added. "I was using the Beatles as an example because that's what I'm most familiar with. I could have just as easily used cars or television."

Lennon said he was as surprised as he was worried when the statement had allegedly been taken out of context and printed in an American magazine.

"When I first heard of the uproar that the statement had created I didn't want to come to America at all," he said. "Then we decided we had better come and try to straighten the trouble out.

"I'm sorry about the mess it made."

Lennon said when he made the statement he never considered the way it might be misconstrued.

When asked if he was a Christian, Lennon replied that although he was brought up as one, he wasn't a practicing Christian. "But I don't have any un-Christian thoughts," he quickly added.

True Test

Meanwhile, teens across the nation continued to be violently divided on the Beatles' status in the world of rock.

The Beatles' tour however, rolled along without major incident. It was met by the customary hoardes of screaming teens who continued to proclaim the Britons as their idols.

And this, it is said, is the only true test of their popularity. So once again, the Beatles may be the first family of rock.

Home After Stormy Tour

England's all-star infield is back home after its blustery U.S. road trip—but not without the 14 consecutive victories skeptics said would be impossible.

After drawing the greatest mass reaction ever given a pop group, the Beatles capped their third tour of America in "the only state we really looked forward to," and the results must have been gratifying all the way around.

The Beatles frenzied near capacity crowds in Dodger Stadium and Candlestick Park — ending what some say will be their last U.S. visit — and it looked like a scene from the past.

For about an hour on their final stops they were the Beatles of old . . . laughing, singing, barely audible through the screams of those

(Turn to Page 21)

'We Love You— John AND God'

It was a moment many had predicted would never come. Swirling, reaching, screaming . . . the crowd was a contradiction — and a happy one.

It was the last hour in the United States for the Beatles. Flashbulbs popped. Beatlemaniacs — an uncountable number of them — craned, stretched and stood on their tip toes to get a glimpse of the foursome as it tunneled through the mass.

Placards, bobbing and twisting, protruded above the raucous gathering. One read, "We love you — John AND God."

The Beatles, surrounded by a reinforced brigade of uniformed policemen, were at last out of the terminal and heading slowly towards their private plane.

They were laughing, waving . . . occasionally reaching past their police escort to touch one of their admirers.

"It's them," shouted a 16-year-old girl in near hysteria. "We love you! We love you!" moaned a girl wedged next to her.

Finally they were climbing into their plane. They looked back momentarily, and were gone.

Inside the BEAT

- Those Soulful Beatles 2-3
- Letters to the Editor 4
- On the Beat 5
- Readers Write More 6
- News in Pictures 7
- "Sunny" Bobby 8
- The Songwriter's Songwriters 9
- A Big Bird & A Beatle 10
- Sir Douglas and His Quints 11
- For Girls Only 16
- Tough Young Rascals 17
- Pyschedelic Music 22-23
- And more, more, more, more, more

The BEAT is published bi-weekly by BEAT Publications, Inc., editorial and advertising offices at 6290 Sunset Blvd., Suite 504, Hollywood, California 90028. U.S. bureaus in Hollywood, San Francisco, New York, Chicago and Nashville; overseas correspondents in London, Liverpool and Manchester, England. Sale price, 15 cents. Subscription price, U.S. and possessions, $5 per year; Canada and foreign rates, $9 per year. Second class postage prepaid at Los Angeles, California.

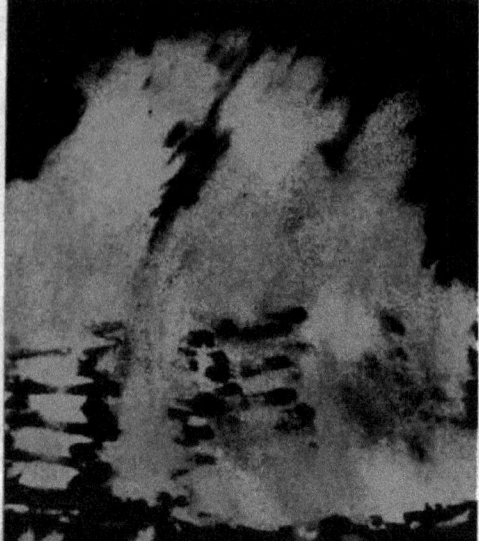

BURNING EMBERS . . . of resentment towards the Beatles still blaze in some regions of the country. Latest "flare up" was this massive bonfire in Longview, Texas. More than 7,500 righteous residents were on hand to toss Beatles records, wigs and other souvenirs into the blaze. In general, however, anti-Beatle sentiment was on a marked decrease, and the group departed "the land of the free" amidst the customary cheering, screaming and fainting.

Time Heals Wounds; Stations Lift Ban

Time heals many wounds.

And while the John Lennon controversy may never be completely forgotten, it has at least been softened by recent clarifications and explanations.

So now the Beatles are steadily regaining their stronghold.

Their records are again being played on major Hot 100 format stations around the country and their latest single, "Yellow Submarine" b/w "Eleanor Rigby," is rapidly climbing the charts.

Most of the stations playing Beatles records say public demand forced the action. Most radio station personnel said taking Beatles records off the air would greatly hurt their station's ratings.

One station in the midwest announced it was banning Beatle records — obviously thinking public opinion warranted it — and the ensuing results were nearly disastrous.

The next day, the station was presented with a petition containing 9,500 names. The petition was a threat to ban, not the Beatles, but the station.

JOHN . . . Singing, Not Talking.

The station quickly recognized its position, backed down . . . and "Yellow Submarine" was an hourly occurence.

BEATLES . . . Last hours in U.S.

KRLA ARCHIVES

Letters TO THE EDITOR

Lennon Vs. Christianity

(Ed. NOTE: The BEAT has received hundreds of letters, both pro and con, concerning John Lennon's remarks about Christianity. Unfortunately, we do not have nearly enough space to print all of the letters but we would like to thank each of you for writing. Perhaps, if in the future you concentrate on writing shorter letters, we will be able to print many more each week. Thanks again.)

Shut Mouths

Dear *BEAT*:
When a group of singers become stars, I feel that they take on the responsibility of when to make a statement of opinion and when to keep their mouths shut! This responsibility seems to have been overlooked in the last four or five months by our beloved (?) Beatles.

What has happened? When they were new to the world of fame they seemed to know their place and stayed in it. When a reporter asked a question on politics or religion they retorted with a cute quip and that was that. Now, it seems they have to give a five minute oration of what *they* think is wrong with the world.

I have been an avid Beatle fan ever since their first tour to America but I believe that these last few months have been the "straw that broke the camel's back."

I think it's about time somebody had a heart to heart talk to them to let them know that everyone does not enjoy hearing four young "men" say things that if given time to cool off or just think over would realize never should have been said.

I realize this will probably never be published but I just had to speak my mind as I know many people have my same opinion.

Sue Abbot

Dear *BEAT*:
I have read in our local paper that John has said that the Beatles are more popular than Christ. My mother thinks what he's saying is that most people aren't very religious these days—not saying it should go.

I don't think it's fair to condemn a whole group's future just because of what one member said. I thought that the Beatles, Rolling Stones, etc., were known and respected because they had no false fronts and spoke their minds often. The people who are burning their Beatle things will be sorry someday. In the years to come, the Beatles will always be known and respected for their musical and acting talent.

Also, why must people be continually trying to find fault with the Beatles. Can't they praise the group once in a while? They should think of the countless things the Beatles have done to help make the world happy.

They should be thankful there are four charming, talented guys like the Beatles together in a group.

Pattie Lockwood

Dear *BEAT*:
I hope you will print the following as an "open letter" to John Lennon. I will attempt to express my feelings for the banned album cover and John's attack on Christianity.

John, I have always respected you for the things you have accomplished and your fabulous career, even before George was my favorite.

When your album came out, I was shocked at the cover. I read in *The BEAT* how your fans made excuses for it. You have said: "The fans we have now were the real ones we had at the beginning." You implied that if they are true fans they will stick with you through thick and thin.

But your attack on Christianity was where I got off, buddy. Mr. Lennon, I am ashamed to say that I once liked you. I'm sorry the thought ever entered my head. If you think you're so great, that your fans will always love you, you have another think coming. You, sir, are no better than anyone else. From what source did you get the idea that you were more popular than Jesus?

If my guess is right, you got it out of your warped mind. If you think rock 'n' roll will outlive Christianity, you're nuts.

I can't wait to hear your poor fans' excuses for why you said this. They'll probably say it was for "shock value." You wasted what's left of your brain thinking that one up, if you did it for shock value—you got enough of that with the gory cover.

John, the sad thing about this Christianity bit is that you're not only going to lose your popularity but you're going to lose Paul's, Ringo's and George's. But don't worry too much. You've still got your wife.

Marilyn Iturri

Hurt By John

Dear *BEAT*:
You may not print this in your newspaper because it probably isn't that important to you—but it is to us.

We all read *The BEAT*. Also, we all liked the Beatles before all of this happened to them.

All of us have our own opinions about religion, as we know everyone does. But what John Lennon said about them being bigger than Jesus really hurt us.

How can anyone say that he or anyone is bigger than Jesus? Even if he doesn't mean it, he shouldn't have said it because it left a lot of people mad at them and very hurt because of them.

Diane DeCicco
Joe DeCicco
Florence DeCicco
Elizabeth Hunt
Donna Oldham
Becky Oldham

Is Religious

Dear *BEAT*:
I am tired of people taking potshots at the Beatles. There was nothing wrong with the album cover—we see the same thing in *Mad Magazine*.

As to the Manila situation, a couple of wisecracks never hurt anyone. Now to John's recent statement about Christianity.

What the papers printed was taken out of context. John *is* religious and was discussing religion privately.

Remember, *anyone* has the right to voice his opinion about anything. I'm still with the Beatles and so are my friends. Any station that bans Beatle records is wrong and is only hurting themselves.

Larry Schweikart
Harry McCoy
David Ruffin

Dear *BEAT*:
I'm writing about the controversy surrounding John. First, I'd like to express my opinion. Personally, I think John is right, although he could have put it in a less sarcastic way.

The Beatles, among other things such as golf, the beach, the show, etc., are more popular than the church. But it's a shame. And I think John was just stating a fact.

And, besides, if you were a *real* Beatle fan (such as I am), you wouldn't care about their religious beliefs.

Now, just take account of yourself for a minute. How many times a year do you go to church? Every week? Great, I can't think of anything better. But for those of you who go maybe five times a year—listen. How many hours have you spent listening, reading and watching the Beatles? Quite a few, I bet.

Now, truly, how many hours have you thought about church? I'll bet not half as much. Aren't you ashamed? I am. Not because I love the Beatles but because I don't spend the time I should on my religion.

So, you so-called true Beatle fans, stop complaining. John's like that and isn't that the reason we luv 'em?

Jeanne

Dear *BEAT*:
I think this whole Beatles vs. Christianity controversy has really been blown-up out of proportion. I believe it when John says that he meant that with the world situations as it is, the Beatles do seem to have a more loyal following.

The people who really are angry with John and denounce him firmly in this country are really like hypocrites. They make a big incident of what John said but when it comes to the pressing issues of such things as the rising number of divorces and how God, in whose name this country was founded, seems to be eliminated from everything in the United States, these "Christian" Beatle critics say nothing.

They are emphasizing the wrong issues. This may be because of their inability to cope with anything important or their refusal to face the truth and admit that something may be lacking in their own society. So, they must capitalize on someone else's good name because he is famous and loved by so many.

These people, so fast to ban and criticize, had better take a good look around in their own backyard before peering across the pond to criticize another's lawn.

JoAnn

Dear *BEAT*:
This is my first letter to your wonderful newspaper. And all I want to say is that "the Beatles STINK!"

After Mr. Lennon said they were more popular than God. Now, I seem to get the message Mr. Barry tried to get across to some of us, but we chopped the poor guy down.

What are the Beatles trying to pull? I don't think Mr. Lennon takes his religion very seriously. And I'm not just writing this letter because I go to church every Sunday but because I respect both the church and rock 'n' roll.

So, if Mr. Lennon thinks I'm going to bow down to him just for a couple of "Yeah, yeah" songs he can go to the London Bridge and jump off.

And I'm getting tired of reading all these letters you get everytime the Beatles get criticized for the things they do.

Their cry-baby fans start backing them up by saying that they are only human, that people don't want to accept them for what they are. Well, I've accepted them up to the ultimate.

So, I'm getting all my Beatle albums and pictures together and am going to have a bonfire of my own.

Ex-Beatles Fan

Want Out

Dear *BEAT*:
I just had to write this letter after reading the article in the newspaper about the Beatles. It stated that the Beatles said: "We are now more popular than Jesus."

It is quite evident that the Beatles are trying to kill themselves. First, it was their records that weren't up to usual, then that charming record cover, and now this statement about being more popular than Jesus. They're millionaires, they have all they want. They want OUT!

Plenty of kids will probably get mad about this letter saying that only people who aren't "true" Beatle fans will think this way. They'll probably make-up some excuse for the Beatles' behavior.

Well, all I can say to them is "forget it, kiddos," because the Beatles don't want you. They've got what they want and now they want out. Good-bye, Beatles.

Naomi Hardin

Dear *BEAT*:
So, John Lennon thinks he is more popular than Jesus now, does he? If he wants to be crucified I know quite a few people who would do it gladly.

You stated that the Beatles were entitled religious freedom. I agree with this but on the other hand, I think John Lennon had no right to criticize it the way he did. If he doesn't believe in Jesus, okay. He just doesn't have to show everyone that he thinks he's greater.

I have always liked the Beatles as pop artists and I shall always think this but I will never again respect John Lennon as I have in the past.

I feel no one has the right to think less of a person for what he believes in but he doesn't have the right to cut down a great, great number of people just to get his message across.

Brenda McNally

KRLA ARCHIVES

Whatever Happened To The

Beatlemania — a word which was non-existent until February of 1964. Now, it describes a very real emotional reaction to four talented entertainers.

Rubber Soul — until last year, a still-unconceived album title, which was destined to become a standard phrase used to describe a creation of exceptional excellence in the field of music.

Revolver — a brand new Beatle album, too-infrequently referred to as a second "Rubber Soul," and definitely a musical creation of exceptional excellence.

Beatlemania is no longer the wild, uncontrolled, hysterial phenomenon it was in the early days of 1964. It has simmered down a little now as its greatest exponents — the Beatlemaniacs — have grown up a little.

There is less screaming now and more appreciation; much more observation and attention is in evidence at current Beatle concerts.

But even that is somewhat sad. It is almost as though the enthusiasm — the uncontrolled exuberance — which became associated with Beatlemania from the beginning has died.

Enthusiasm

True, it isn't really the enthusiasm which has died — only the hysteria. And yet, it is the enthusiasm, the interest, the attention — which seems to be suffering from anemia. Beatlemaniacs have become somewhat jaded — just a little bit blasé' — and now at times they take the Beatles more or less for granted.

This summer has seen the birth of a great new album from the Fabulous Foursome, an album which involved weeks and weeks of long rehearsal, extensive arrangement, and hours and hours of recording. It is an album of which the Beatles should be justifiably proud, and yet it is receiving only a fraction of the attention and respect due.

In recent months, a number of albums released by other artists and groups have been labeled a "Rubber Soul in its field," indicating some form of high achievement.

But, there have been relatively few cries of a "second Rubber Soul" where the "Revolver" album is concerned — and these are the boys who *started it all!*

Oddly enough, several of the numbers included in the LP are already well on their way toward becoming contemporary standards, but the whole process is occuring with an amazing absence of fanfare and discussion.

Taxman

One of the best and most commercial George Harrison compositions for some time is the first cut on the album, "Taxman." It is also one of the best, most concise satirical comments on the British society and current tax situation (not to mention our own!) to come along from *anyone* for some time.

"Eleanor Rigby" must be destined to become a contemporary classic. Certainly the haunting melody is one of the most beautiful to be found in our current pop music, and the words — the universal description of the countless thousands of "lonely people" who are to be found everywhere — is both accurate and unforgettable. And need we mention the beautiful string arrangement — or is that something to be found in *every* run-of-the-mill pop release?

George has created a new extension of the music form which he introduced in "Rubber Soul" with his sitar arrangement for "Norwegian Wood," extending the Indian influence to his own composition — "Love You To." Well done and musically valid. Also musically unrecognized.

Love Song

"Here, There and Everywhere" is probably the most beautiful — or one of the most beautiful — love songs to be written and recorded in many, many years. It is also one of the least-mentioned, least-played cuts on the album. Fantastic new vocal arrangement from Paul here.

"Yellow Submarine" — the satirical "children's song" that *isn't;* "She Said She Said" — the up-tempo, semi-electronic lament; and "I Want To Tell You," the third Harrison composition on the LP, unusual, newly-melodic, and interesting — all of these receiving very little comment.

Of course, there have been a large number of attempts made at analyzing "Yellow Submarine," but as they are all highly hysterical and wholly inaccurate — they don't really count!

And then of course there is "For No One" — still another contender for the Contemporary Classic Hall of Fame. A fantastically beautiful

KRLA ARCHIVES

Beatle Soul?

BEAT Art: Carolyn La Vesque

and haunting love song, musically sighed as only Paul can.

Finally, "Tomorrow Never Knows" — a weird and polished electronic creation from John Lennon. Also, an unintended prophesy; tomorrow really doesn't ever know—if you don't believe that, just take a look at today.

The Beatles are returning for their third major American tour, but they won't be playing to stadiums sold out well in advance. Is their popularity really dying? Hardly. Fans are simply not interested in the mere "freak value" of the Beatles any more. They are no longer purchasing tickets priced high above their pocketbooks simply so they can catch a glimpse of the Beatles.

For Real

We've all seen them now. We know what they look like, we know they're for real. But this time around—we'd kind of like to hear what they have to say . . . and sing . . . and play.

And that's a pretty big order in a stadium which holds 50 or 60 thousand people. It's great if you want to watch nine faceless, nameless ball-players with only numbers for identification on their backs running about a field for a couple of hours. But, if you would be interested in seeing and *hearing* the performance of four of the most talented and most interesting performers in pop music today . . . it's pretty discouraging.

So, many promoters are somewhat discouraged, because they aren't selling tickets as they thought they would. This may slightly injure the Beatles' image — but it isn't through any direct fault of their own.

Political

Of course, there seem to be a large number of American individuals who are more interested in the Beatles' political views than the music which they are creating, and perhaps this is part of the reason why we are simply hearing about the "souls" of the Beatles rather than their "Rubber Soul."

It is always sad to see the diminishing of healthy, sincere enthusiasm, but it must be. If it were to continue, it would become only a monotone of emotion and be rendered eventually meaningless.

Impact

Perhaps there won't be quite as much screaming at Beatle concerts this year, and perhaps everyone isn't aware of the musical impact and importance of "Revolver"— but it is certain that "Revolver" has fired a shot which will be heard around the globe wherever people really care about the music they are listening to.

And the Beatles won't be soon forgotten either—at least not as long as there are Bibles resting beside the seats in air liners.

. . . THE MANY FACES OF MR. LENNON

. . . RINGO CAPTURED IN A PENSIVE MOOD

. . . PAUL—THAT'S ALL

. . . THE SMILE THAT FOLLOWS

KRLA ARCHIVES

On the BEAT
By Louise Criscione

The Beatles are here and they've succeeded in once again taking the spotlight from everyone and everything else. Despite fears of antagonistic crowds and security leaks, the four Beatles have spent a rather peaceful and harmless three weeks Stateside.

They arrived in Los Angeles two days earlier than originally expected when they touched down on the 24th for a press conference at Capitol Records — the scene of last year's Beatle press conference.

Last Tour?

Other than the religiouze issue (which has already been overplayed to the point of boredom) the only other serious problem facing Beatle fans is "will this be the last Beatle U.S. tour?" With those close to the scene predicting that it will indeed be the last major U.S. tour for John, Paul, George and Ringo.

However, the Beatles remain charmingly unpredictable so I wouldn't worry too much if I were you. If the Beatles want to make another Stateside tour next year, they will. And if they want this to be their last, you can bet your "Revolver" it *will* be their last. Anyway, enjoy them while they're here and fret about next year later.

Shoppers at the posh DeVos on the Sunset Strip were pleasantly surprised last week when they wandered in only to find all of the Mama's and Papa's as well as Mick Jagger and his girlfriend, Chrissie Shrimpton, spending wads on DeVos clothes.

Our *BEAT* photographer was on hand and next issue we'll have loads of proof on the entertainers shopping spree.

...PAUL McCARTNEY

Hangin' Around

Following the highly successful Stone tour, the boys hung around Hollywood for awhile. Bill Wyman sent for his wife, Diane, and son, Stephen and, of course, Mick sent for Chrissie.

Apparently, Charlie and Brian had enough sun to last them for awhile because they headed back to England while Keith reportedly flew off to New York to complete his vacation.

The Hollies are going to be movie stars. At least, they're going to give it a try. It's to be a Hollywood campus film with Alan Clarke and Graham Nash being eyed for large roles with the other Hollies appearing in the movies in lesser parts.

Negotiations have not been finalized yet and meanwhile the group is preparing to launch their next big American tour on September 12 and are being considered to head a giant college tour in November.

Wonder what the story behind Scott Walker's apparent suicide attempt is. The Walker Brothers' road manager, Bobby Hamilton, found Scott unconscious in his gas-filled London flat. He was rushed to the hospital and released the following day. But . . .

No More Ha Ha

Jerry Samuels, or Napolein XIV if you prefer, has admitted that after his follow-up album Napoleon will be officially dead. Says the recording engineer: "I will make records as a vocalist." But Napoleon and taking people away ha! ha! is not "out" and will never happen again. Thank God!

This doesn't exactly concern the pop world but I have to tell you about it anyway. You know, Richard Pryor, the young Negro comedian who is making quite a name for himself by appearing on the "Ed Sullivan" and "Merv Griffin" shows? Well, he has a twin — who *isn't* related?

It's true. There's a young actor hanging around Hollywood, Maurice Warfield, who looks exactly like Pryor. Anyway, he's been making the round and getting his name in all of the papers. People have been introducing him at clubs and inviting him to parties thinking he is Pryor.

But the cat was let out of the bag yesterday when Richard Pryor himself called us from Vegas to inform us of the joke. Only thing worrying Richard: "He does my routines as well as I do!" It could only happen in show business, right?

Herb Alpert's TJ Brass Smashing Office Records

Herb Alpert & his Tijuana Brass are setting a torrid pace on record sales with five of their albums on the LP charts, but it's their barnstorming road success that is drawing the most attention.

The musicians just completed an 11-day tour with all dates sold out in advance and grossing more than $500,000.

Beginning in Allentown, Pa., the popular group took in $160,000 for six shows and then journeyed into the Yale Bowl in New Haven, Conn., where they pulled in another $66,900.

Their next stop was at the Forest Hills Stadium in New York, where an additional $72,000 changed hands.

The group then headed for the Warm Memorial Auditorium in Syracuse, where the purse was $30,000. The following day, in a Kleinhans Theatre appearance in Buffalo, the group grossed $16,300.

Next, it was across the border into the O'Keefe Center in Toronto where a three-day stand grossed $46,999. The tour wound up at the Carter Barron Theatre in Washington, D.C., where the final $110,000 was taken.

The Move To Visit Vietnam

How's this for a switch in the strangely interwoven world of rock and roll and politics? While many entertainers are doing their very best to avoid Uncle Sam's eye, a British rock group, The Move, are negotiating with the American Government to *go* to Vietnam!

It's true. The Move would like very much to be the first English group, or entertainer, to travel to Vietnam to perform for our troops stationed there.

Johnny Rivers, Bobby Rydell, The Wild Affair and several other young entertainers have already made the trip to Vietnam but thus far no British pop artist has volunteered to go.

HERBIE ALPERT presents Tommy Boyce with his first A&M Record, "Sunday, The Day Before Monday." Boyce writes for the Monkees.

SAM THE SHAM IN FILM DEBUT

Sam the Sham is going to be an actor!

Sam has had the acting bug for quite a while now but the right script just failed to materialize for the bearded leader of the Pharoahs. Sam and his Pharoahs did make their motion picture debut a year ago in MGM's "When The Boys Meet The Girls."

However, it was a musical role which required no real acting ability. Sam would love to act in a western film but will have to be content in making his acting debut in "The Fastest Guitar Alive," which will also star pop singer Roy Orbison.

Filming begins on "The Fastest Guitar Alive" on September 8 and Orbison has already completed writing 10 songs which he will sing in the movie.

Sam Katzman will produce the film and was also the producer of "When The Boys Meet The Girls."

Things are on the up-swing for

Sam in the record department too, with his "Lil' Red Riding Hood" capturing the top spot on the nation's charts. It's been a long time since "Wooly Bully" but apparently Sam has found his way back and now hopes to fight his way to the top of the movie business as well.

And he most likely will. You know — you can't keep a good Texan down!

Yardbirds Lose Guitars And Amps—Vox To Rescue

A singing group without its musical instruments may as well forget about trying to stage a performance, and that's almost what happened to the Yardbirds recently when their equipment failed to reach its destination.

The Yardbirds, while on their 40-city U.S. tour, found themselves in Spirit Lake with neither amplifiers nor guitars. Their Vox equipment had been held up somewhere along the shipping route due to the air strike.

There was, however, a solution. T. Warren Hampton of the Vox promo department in Los Angeles arranged to have more equipment flown in from Chicago by private aircraft.

And as if this weren't enough, the Vox company assumed all expenses of the special air delivery.

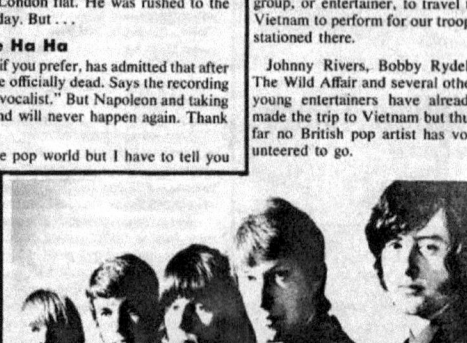

...YARDBIRDS POSE with their new member, Jimmy Page (extreme left).

KRLA ARCHIVES

Letters To The Editor
(Continued from Page 4)

Can't Compare

Dear *BEAT*:
Now that I've heard the entire story, I'd like to express my opinion. It seems that John was discussing religion and he observed that followers of Christianity are decreasing. That now, in this mixed up world, people actually worship other human beings. He observed that because of this they probably had more followers than Christ and that it was ridiculous.

Well, I agree. I'm not saying it's wrong to love the Beatles — I do, very much. But it *is* wrong to put them above Christ. But really, it's something that can't be compared.

Pam Kelsey

Beatles Sick Of Fame?

Dear *BEAT*:
For the past three or four issues, I have been calmly reading and tolerating people's opinions of the Beatles. Now, I would like to give mine.

To make a long story short, it's about time these so-called Beatle "fans" stopped thinking of themselves and started thinking about the four boys they keep trying to tell me they love so much. The Beatles are four wonderful human beings who have had their taste of fame and glory and are quite sick of it.

Their "fans" have treated them as if they were four dolls who must bow to every girl's command. Now, I ask you, is that right? Their "fans" have no right to command them like slaves.

But, I must say, their fans — their true fans — have been wonderful. They know the Beatles and they love them. What I'm truly sick of are these adults who sit in their ancient caves and just wait for the poor Beatles to do one little thing wrong so they can ban them, insult them, and would you believe it? Even beat them up!

I think these poor adults are too chicken to admit they're growing old and that they just don't fit in this generation. They keep telling us to stop trying to grow up so fast. If you adults want us to keep out of YOUR generation, how about keeping out of OURS!

One last thing. The Beatles are very wonderful people. Why? Because they don't lie to their public. They don't put on an act in front of us, just so we'll like them. Not very many people in show business have enough courage to be themselves in front of their public. The Beatle fans, their true fans, love them for what they are — *not* for what some penny-pinching magazine (*BEAT* not included) or adult tries to tell us.

We know what the Beatles are, and we love them. You can't change that, so stop trying!

Dale Hoover

Ridiculous Controversy

Dear *BEAT*:
I would like to thank you very much for printing so many wonderful articles about the Beatles, and I hope you will continue to do so as long as they are still the Beatles.

The Beatles have certainly changed a lot through these last two and one-half years. They have been wonderful changes. But now many of these fans have turned against the singers they once would maybe have even given up their lives for. Why?

Because controversies got started. The incident in Manila. Their appearance on Ed Sullivan. Their false accusations of no longer caring. And many, many more.

But the latest controversy about John's statement of over six months ago, which has lost them more fans than ever, was the most misinterpreted. People didn't (or didn't want to) take time to hear the true story and why he said it.

It is ridiculous the way these people are acting. John has his right to voice his beliefs and I think those anti-Beatle organizations should listen to him, maybe they'll learn something.

These people who turned against them were never true fans, because if they were they would accept them for their goods and also their faults.

These people don't even deserve the Beatles if they begged them back. Now there is more of the Beatles for us fans who still appreciate them.

I plan on staying a Beatle fan until they are gone and I hope that remaining Beatle fans feel the same way.

Pat Bartley

Big Mouth

Dear *BEAT*:
Those dearly beloved Beatles have really done it now! First came their distasteful LP and now John's big mouth. He, of all people, had the nerve to say: "We're more popular than Jesus now."

Don't get me wrong. Sure, I went out and bought all their albums, not to mention spending a fortune on magazines and books with information on the foursome.

But now you can count me out! I'll just sit and watch their disc zoom to the top and I'll pass up the newest magazines.

I'll also watch them go down the drain. Yes, all you Beatle fans, just wait. You'll be in for a Big Surprise!

E.B.F. (Ex-Beatle fan.)

Yellow Thingy

Dear *BEAT*:
I subscribe to *The BEAT* and love it the best of all the mags and newspapers in the world. I have but one small complaint. On the front of each *BEAT* there is a little yellow-fiendish-thingy that has my name and address on it, well . . . It just ruins those luscious, gorgeous pictures! Couldn't you put them somewhere else? At the top? On the bottom? In the corner? On the back? But not on the picture, please! I've tried to scrape it off but failed by making a hole in the page when I did so. All I can say is please. Think about it!

Unsigned

We have thought about it. But unfortunately we discovered that postal laws require the address stamp to be placed on the front of all publications going through the mail.
Editor

Mann Gentlemanly?

Dear *BEAT*:
Hooray for Gene Pitney and Gary Lewis! Boo for Len Barry and Barry Sadler . . . Boo for people who do the same song over and over (Len Barry, Four Tops, Nancy Sinatra Jr., etc.). Hooray for new gear style LP covers (Dylan and Beatles). Boo for the new, dreary Beatle cover — ungear . . . Hooray for *The BEAT* recognizing Gene Pitney's greatness! Boo for Jackie McGinty for bringing national fields into R&R . . . Hooray for "Double Shot (Of My Baby' Love)", "Gloria," "Satisfaction" and all realistic songs.

Hooray for Manfred Mann and all their songs! Why are only some versions of "If You Gotta Go, Go Now" banned? The Liverpool 5's version was played in Florida. Why was "With God On Our Side" banned? I don't know what a flamingo is, except a colorful tropical bird . . . As for "If You Gotta Go, Go Now," I admire it. It is a "gentlemanly," civilized song. I only wish most guys made a similar speech to girls, instead of being so aggressive!

Dorothy Boswell

MOM DEFENDS JOHN

Dear *BEAT*:
I hope I'm not too late to get my two cents worth into *The BEAT* concerning the current controversy raging over the heads of the Beatles. I'm not a teenager, but rather a mother of five, two of them teenagers already. I was never particularly interested in their choice of music, but after taking them to see the first Beatle movie I was completely captivated by everything about them. Their freshness, their talent, their obvious enjoyment of life and each other, all of it.

If there is anything worse than a teenage Beatlemaniac, it is an old one! We saw the movie many times so as not to miss one gesture or off-camera nonsense that had been overlooked before.

Our home was rocking with every album released and we couldn't get enough news about them.

People have tried to explain and reason out Beatlemania; there's no explaining it really. It is rather like a sickness but one you don't wish to recover from. Unlike popularity fads which come and go, they only served to carve their way deeper into our hearts as their fantastic, fabulous careers progressed. They didn't *force* their way in, we couldn't get enough.

It's been said that many idols have feet of clay and it is always a disheartening let-down when fans are forced to realize this and accept it.

But anyone who has ever professed to be a Beatle fan should hang his head in shame and disgrace if he is turning on them now. *However*, people are and what*ever* they do *they* are not to blame. The wild, screaming, insane fans, causing riots and near riots are behaving like people have never behaved before in the history of show business.

They are the ones to carry this blame. While they were loved like gods by millions, John, Paul, George and Ringo are people. They had human feelings and emotions like all of us. No amount of money in the entire world could ever compensate for the lives they have been forced to lead, and by whom?

Those adoring "fans" who ruined it all for them whenever they dared to venture out. It's been said before but what can money do, if you can't go out and see the cities and sights of a never before seen country?

Oh! We were unthinkably rude and indescribably thoughtless when they came to America. True, it came about as result of our "love" for them, but how I wish we had another chance to welcome them again and stand back and feast our eyes but keep our mouths shut.

They would still be the same Beatles they were in the beginning. And really, what has happened? An album cover? Rude remarks? And a religious issue.

I would challenge anyone to live through what they have and not turn surly and say much more than they ever have. We excuse all kinds of things in our artistic people, and if ever there were four geniuses it is the Beatles, maybe Paul and John a little more so because of the writing and composing.

They have *never* hurt anyone, they wouldn't want to. But they *have* had to endure more criticism and bad publicity and if one slip was made off that pedestal — POW!

I wish it was possible to get a letter to them. I'd like them to know how this fan, for one, really feels. I think they do care.

Some of the letters in this week's *BEAT* expressed some good thoughts, the phony fans have now been heard from, and I am glad to be able to count myself among the true ones.

So, true, they haven't stopped to remember what the Beatles have given us. Wonderful moments for over two years, in movies and in music. Has there ever been a thrill to equal what every heart experienced when we heard: "And now, here they are — the Beatles!" Not in my memory, there hasn't.

What have we given them? Money? Ha!

In conclusion, I wish to express the hope that this current trend of putting them down at the slightest provocation will die out. *Let up on them.* And maybe we can yet salvage those four unbelievable guys who got all this started.

Heartsick with worry they won't forgive us for what has been done to them.

JBL
SOUND IS WHERE IT'S HAPPENING!

Trini Lopez, Chet Atkins, Johnny Rivers, The Beach Boys, The Rolling Stones make it with JBL sound.

JBL is the sound of the scene at the top!

Fender, Jordan, Ampeg, Gretsch, Standel, Guild, Gibson, C. F. Martin, Sunn amplifier systems groove with JBL loudspeakers.

High notes that won't quit, thundering bass at peak volume from JBL F-Series loudspeakers. Write us for free information about use and installation.

▼

James B. Lansing Sound, Inc.
3249 Casitas Avenue
Los Angeles, California 90039

KRLA ARCHIVES

PICTURES in the NEWS

ROLLING STONES are not to be out-done in controversy, and have inadvertently begun to stir some up on their native shores of England. Manager Andrew Loog Oldham initiated court action against one of the largest pirate stations there, Radio Caroline. In retaliation, Caroline has placed a ban on **all** Stone records on all of their programming. They have also banned all Immediate Records and "Anyone associated with Andrew Oldham," which might involve the Beach Boys' material which is published by Oldham's company in Britain.

JOHN LENNON made headlines around the world with his widely misinterpreted statements concerning Christianity. Despite the controversy raging around him, however, John is going ahead with plans to appear in his first film effort without the other three Beatles, and will play the part of a soldier in "How I Won The War," scheduled to begin filming in Germany immediately after the Beatles' tour of America.

MICHELLE IS BACK! Of course, there are those who didn't even know she was gone in the first place!! It seems that Mama Michelle took a temporary leave of absence from the group, and in her place, Mama Jill made a very pretty stand-in. But, Michelle has returned to the group now and once again the Mama's and Papa's line up as John, Cass, Denny and Michelle — and that's quite a line-up for any group!

Roy Orbison To Movies

ROY ORBISON, one of the highest ranking record sellers of all time, is now going into the movies. Orbison, whose latest single, "It's Too Soon To Know," is climbing the charts, has set the final schedule of operations for the filming of his first motion picture, "The Fastest Guitar Alive." Orbison recently completed 10 songs which he will sing in the upcoming picture. Filming starts on September 8.

GARY LEWIS smilingly receives congratulations from Mama and Papa Lewis backstage in Kansas City, Mo., where he recently broke attendance records in that city as he made his legitimate stage debut in "Bye, Bye Birdie." Gary won raves for his portrayal of famous Birdie.

KRLA ARCHIVES

Bobby Hebb: 'The Beatles Are An Oak Tree-Mighty'

By Carol Deck

"It takes all kinds of trees to make a forest. And like the Beatles are an oak tree—tall and mighty. And maybe the Cyrkle are a palm tree. And the Ronnetts are a peach tree—very pretty. And maybe I'm a cherry tree."

That's the way Bobby Hebb explains his feeling about appearing on the Beatle tour.

"What's more important is the show, not the act," says Bobby when reminded that although it's somewhat of an honor to be asked to join the tour, it rarely does an artist much good because Beatle fans come to see Beatles and don't really pay much attention to whoever else is on the bill.

And, going back to his tree theory he says, "If people didn't like cherries, they wouldn't put them in cocktails."

Anyone appearing on the Beatle tour is bound to be asked repeatedly about the Beatles and John Lennon's recent comments on religion and Bobby Hebb takes these questions all in stride.

First Reaction

When first asked about Lennon's comment Bobby replied, "I don't discuss religion and politics at all. I have no comment."

But if pressed a little he will reveal his true feelings.

"All the fellows are men—their parents no longer speak for them and one doesn't speak for the group. The big question is 'was he kidding?' He could have been kidding."

First Cast

Then paraphrasing the Bible, Bobby concludes, "let the person who's never joked about religion be the first to cast a stone."

Bobby's an interesting man who's been in the music business for many years and has just gotten his first major hit with "Sunny," which he wrote and which has already become practically a standard.

His story, like most every R&B singer's, is one of starting at the very bottom, staying there for a long time, a couple of breaks, the first big success and the search for a follow-up.

Asked why he started singing in the first place, he'll pause a minute and say "It's the only job I could get right then. I had to satisfy those people in order to satisfy myself."

Important Pause

That pause before speaking is characteristic of Bobby. He always stops and thinks before saying anything and will quite often say, "That's important—give me a minute to think about it."

Then he'll sit back, chewing lightly on his fingernails, and compose his thoughts. Then out will come a complete thought and his true feelings on the matter—like his theory of the trees and the Beatle tour.

Trying to put into words his feelings about appearing with the Beatles' he gets a little stumped, but he thinks he's finally found a way of expressing it.

Flowing

"I guess I'll have to write an instrumental to express how I feel, 'cause the words just aren't there. Maybe later the words will flow."

Bobby's come a long way from watching his parents, both of whom are blind, sing and rehearse, and there's one very important part of his life that he hasn't forgotten.

He still spends two days a week working with mentally retarded children in New York whenever he's there. He doesn't talk about it a lot and forgot to mention it at all when his official biography was made up.

But there's pride in his eyes when he does talk about those kids. And on his right hand is a ring given to him by them before he left on this tour. It was their way of saying 'we know you'll be back.'

And he will.

...BOBBY HEBB—"Maybe I'm A Cherry Tree".

...CHRIS MONTEZ REMEMBERS the Beatles way back when.

Last Beatle Tour Believes Montez

By Rochelle Reed

Chris Montez dropped by the office this week to say 'hello' and fill us in on where he's been keeping himself lately.

As it turned out, the reason we haven't seen Chris recently is because he's been busy rehearsing a group to back him on a coming nationwide tour, plus recording and writing.

Chris is an extremely talented writer, and to prove it he composed "Cinco de Mayo" for the Tijuana Brass, which they recorded on their "Going Places" album. Herb Alpert returned the musical favor by arranging Chris' million seller, "Call Me."

We talked Chris into reminiscing about his 1963 tour of England with the Beatles. Would you believe Chris received billing OVER the Beatles, who hadn't yet played for the Queen, much less Ed Sullivan?

"We were always messing around and joking," Chris says about their stint together. "The Beatles were always in good humor."

"We talked mostly about the different members of the tour and the money we were getting for our appearances. The Beatles were always discussing how to spend it!"

One of the ways both Chris and the Beatles found of getting rid of their money was to spend it on clothes. In fact, Chris owns three pairs of boots handmade by Ringo's own bootmaker, but "I don't wear them anymore—they're almost out of style," he laments.

But how did Chris get the boots? Again, it was on the tour.

"Ringo, Paul and I were sitting around talking about boots, which had just begun to come into fashion. Ringo asked, 'How do you like mine?'

"They were really groovy. 'Where did you get them?' I asked. Ringo told me the name of the man who made them and the address of his shop. So I went there and had some made.

"They were only about ten dollars a pair—and for suedes! I bought blue, green and red ones. I really liked them."

Chris and the Beatles have remained good friends and whenever their paths cross, Chris visits them. The last time was when they were in Los Angeles for a concert and he went to the Bel Air home where they stayed. Chris will visit the Beatles again this year, if he is in town.

Though Chris readily admits he has no proof, or words from the Beatle's mouth, so to speak, he thinks the Beatles have done their last American concert.

"They're probably getting awfully tired," he says. "A tour isn't of *that* much importance anymore. They're well-established and probably want to go into different things."

Long hair, Chris says, is no doubt going the same way as the Beatles next tour—out. "I think everything will go back to normal in entertainment. Long hair is getting old."

Personally, Chris doesn't feel he has been hurt by performing without curly locks falling around his shoulders. "My audience is usually half teens and half adults," he says.

That couldn't be better for Chris. Someday, you see, he wants to be a dramatic actor and appeal to a much wider audience indeed. But until a movie studio calls him, he's content to sing "Call Me."

KRLA ARCHIVES

Holland & Dozier: Motown's Money

By Carol Deck

The Supremes strolled into the crowded club where the Temptations were playing and instantly everyone in the room knew they were there.

As attention went back and forth between the exciting group on stage and the lovely girls in the audience no on paid much notice to two young men sitting just a few tables from the Supremes.

And those who did, did so with amusement at the reaction of the crowd to the presence of the Supremes and the almost total ignorment of two of the three men who've been such a major part of the success of the Supremes, America's top female group.

A couple of days later, lounging around their hotel suite, Brian Holland and Lamont Dozier of the Holland-Dozier-Holland writing and producing team that has created many of Motown's biggest hits laughed easily about the lack of attention they usually get.

"We never care for fame and fortune, we take more pride in our work," said Brian.

They may not have much fame outside of people in the business but fortune is something else.

25 Million

They have been responsible for around 25 million sellers and probably many more that sold nearly a million.

The Holland-Dozier-Holland team came about several years ago after Brian and Lamont had both tried singing.

Lamont, born and raised in Detroit, used to sing with another record company. He continued singing after joining Motown but "that didn't work out too well," he says. "So I decided to hang my singing up for a while."

Brian joined Motown with the help of his brother Eddie — the other Holland in the team — who'd known Barry Gordy Jr., head of Motown, "when Berry was just managing artists."

Brian too was singing at first and worked a little for Jobete, Motown's publishing company, putting material to music.

Then Barry suggested that Brian and Lamont get together and try writing.

"But we were doing so much and it was hard writing lyrics too," said Lamont, so Brian's brother Eddie joined the team as the lyric writer.

Eddie, too, was a singer and had had a hit — "Jamie."

A short time later Lamont and Brian got together at a piano and wrote their first song, "Forever," and formed the producing team of Holland and Dozier.

Long String

Since then they've had a string of some of the biggest all time hits ever including "Where'd Our Love Go," "Come and Get These Memories," "I Can't Help Myself," and "Stop In the Name of Love."

They've written over 100 songs together and don't seem to miss singing at all. "What I'm doing now is much more of a challenge," says Brian.

Their latest smash is the Supreme's "You Can't Hurry Love," which they admit they knew at the time they cut it was a hit.

"We knew it would be big," notes Brian, "but we didn't know how big."

...DOZIER AND HOLLAND — 25 million sellers for Motown.

But Motown doesn't stand still and now Holland-Dozier-Holland are off in a new direction — movies. The move into movie production means a need for movie scores and a whole new field for this top writing-producing team.

The three of them are generally acknowledged as one of, if not *the*, top writing and producing teams in America, but they feel they haven't yet made it.

They feel Smokey Robinson of the Miracles is one of the top writers in the world, and their own goal is "to be the top."

If they keep up like they've been going where else is there for them but the top?

Up BEAT *By Eden*

One of the largest promotion campaigns for a pop group to be conducted since the coming of the Beatles is the one currently underway for The Monkees.

This brand new quartet will be the stars of a brand new TV series this Fall by the same name, and the first record to be released by the group — "Last Train To Clarksville" — sounds like a good vehicle to carry them to a successful destination on the charts.

Up-tempo, with a little bit of a Beatle sound to it, and very rocking — this is their first disc, and if the TV show proves half as popular, we have four new pop stars on our hands.

* * *

Troggs' latest — "With A Girl Like You" — may allow this new British group to join the ever-growing ranks of their musical countrymen who have established a trend of one-hit wonders on our charts in the last two years.

The disc is sort of ordinary pop stuff, and doesn't look like a hit followup to "Wild Thing" for the group.

* * *

Question of the week: Why isn't "Turn-Down Day" by the Cyrkle a very large hit already? Good, good record.

* * *

For all those currently hung-up in an attempt to discover "hidden meanings" and wonderful fairy tale material in the latest Beatle single — "Yellow Submarine" — here's a Number One clue for you: throw it into the same bag you've been keeping the Stones' "Mother's Little Helper" in lately, toss them around and see what you come up with then.

Comparison Number Two: "Taxman" ala Mr. G. Harrison, and "Sunny Afternoon" by the Kinks. Much duplication of subject matter going on, no?

* * *

Due to the pop success of Wilson Pickett's R&B version of "Land Of A Thousand Dances," Cannibal and the Headhunters (Whaawuzzatt?) have re-released their disking of the tune. Doesn't look like a hit on the second time around the groove though.

* * *

Marvin Gaye is doing it again with a new smash, "Little Darling." A very good record which should have both pop and R&B charts under control.

* * *

The Manfred Mann group has been one of the top British groups for some time, but just recently they lost their lead singer — Paul Jones — who decided to go into solo work.

The first release since Paul's departure is a cover of Dylan's latest, "Just Like A Woman." Lead vocal features the newest addition to the group, Michael D'Abo.

WALKER BROTHER SUICIDE ATTEMPT?

LONDON — Scott Walker, 21 year old member of the Walker Brothers trio, was found unconscious last week in his gas-filled London flat by the group's road manager, Bobby Hamilton.

According to Hamilton, Scott had visited manager, Maurice King, and then had returned home for "a few drinks" and to work on his song-writing. However, when Hamilton dropped by Scott's flat the door was locked and Hamilton, along with a porter, knocked down the front door.

Scott was unconscious when Hamilton entered and an ambulance was immediately summoned to take Scott to St. Mary's Hospital in Paddington.

He was given emergency treatment and discharged from the hospital the next day. And up to our press deadline no one connected with the Walker Brothers was talking.

The Walker Brothers are supposedly Britain's most popular American import. Gary, John and Scott have enjoyed tremendous success in England and have acquired the dubious distinction of having the wildest and most enthusiastic fans in all of Britain.

Their personal appearances are always sold-out and nearly everyone of them ends with fans rushing the stage and more times than not dragging along at least one Walker Brother with them. All members of the group have been injured by their "fans" and had lately taken to being under police escort from the minute they enter a city until they officially leave that city's limits.

Stateside, the American-born Walkers have tasted record success with "Make It Easy On Yourself," "My Ship Is Comin' In" and "The Sun Ain't Gonna Shine Anymore." However, they have failed to do any personal appearances here and at one time were reported to have expressed a desire never to return to the U.S.

Allegedly, the Walkers were also quoted as saying they were going to apply for British citizenship and give up their American citizenship. However, John Walker informed *The BEAT* that none of the Brothers were *about* to give up their U.S. citizenship although all of them *are* quite content living in England.

KRLA ARCHIVES

Sonny & Cher Finished; Off For European Visit

By Carol Deck

Sonny and Cher are gone.

The popular folk-rock duo have finally, after months of planning, left on their tour of England and Europe.

Following a farewell party thrown in their honor at a swank Hollywood hotel, the two, along with Harvey Kresky, one of their managers; Cher's sister and their arranger-conductor Harold Battiste, left for a four week tour of Europe.

The tour will hit England, France, Germany, Holland, Belgium, Sweden and Italy and will involve mostly television and what Kreskey refers to as "visiting."

They have only two live performances scheduled, both benefits for their favorite charity, the Braille Institute.

The shows take place Aug. 26 in the Astoria Theater in London and Sept. 12 in the Olympia in Paris.

The purpose of the trip is to visit areas where their greatest European fan mail comes from and to promote their movie, "Good Times."

Back in Sept.

They will return to Southern California Sept. 16 and will continue promoting the movie here.

The movie, which has been in the works for a full year, is scheduled for release before the end of the year.

Filming was completed a short while ago but Sonny didn't finish the musical score until less than week before leaving on this tour.

Rumors have been spreading that Sonny and Cher may have to move from their hill top Encino home in the San Fernando Valley due to annoying fans, and Kreskey has finally said that, although they do not want to move, "we're looking for a house."

The Bonos are a friendly couple and have been known to invite fans in and even feed them, but there is a limit to anyone's patience.

After having people knocking on the door at 4 and 5 a.m., trying to steal things and even siphoning gas out of their cars, Sonny and Cher have just about given up finding privacy there, particularly after a national magazine printed the address.

So after returning from this tour, and while in the midst of promotions for the movie, the couple may have to go through the rigors of moving again, thanks to the overanxious and unthoughtful fans.

MAMA CASS — A large bird who met a Beatle.

BEAT Photo: Chuck Boyd

...CHER — Forced to move.

BEAT Photo: Chuck Boyd

Cass Meets John

By Jamie McCluskey III

The Meeting of the Century has finally taken place. Yes, the Large Bird from America has finally made contact with the Chief Beatle of Blightyland — and the results are pretty wild!

Cass explains: "When I got over to England, I went through a lot of changes. First I thought — 'If I didn't meet him... it would be okay, you know, like — maybe it wasn't meant to be!' If he didn't make any opportunity to try and get to meet me, that maybe the time just wasn't right!

"I was over there for about three days before I met him. The first day we went to a club and Ringo was there. I mean, it was *really Ringo* sitting right there! I didn't know how to get over that! — so, I didn't speak to him, naturally! Later on, 'Monday, Monday' came on and he stood up and applauded John (Phillips). That was the first night.

"The second night we went to a discotheque called 'Dolly's,' and George Harrison was there, *and* Ringo. He came over and talked to me, and welcomed us to England and said that they hoped that they would get a chance to get together with us.

"Then, the third day, I went over to Mick's house — we were living right upstairs from Mick — and I just *casually* said, 'Oh! — is John Lennon around?' and he fell on the floor laughing! He said, 'Everybody's heard about it, that you want to meet John Lennon, and *he* knows — he's well aware of the fact! And everybody wants to be there 'cause they think it's going to be the meeting of the century!'

So, that night I had a date with Graham Nash of the Hollies, and we went to Dolly's. When I got home, I was very tired because of the whole thing about being in England excited me so much that I hadn't really slept since I'd been there, so I went to sleep.

"I hadn't been asleep for a half an hour and all of a sudden my door bursts open and Denny and John come running in. Denny started bouncing on my bed, and yelling, 'Cass — *get up, get up.* John and Paul are downstairs!!

"I went downstairs, and Paul was playing the piano and John got up and came over and said a few words, and I said a few words — we were sort of being sarcastic — and then we just sort of looked at each other and realized that we didn't want to be sarcastic that way, so we sat down and talked for a few hours."

And so the Meeting of the Century took place. Surprisingly enough Cass managed to hang onto her cool throughout the entire evening — in fact, she even played *Mama Cass* for the Beatle Boys, and entertained them just as though she were in her own home back in the States.

"They said they were hungry, and I had been shopping that day and I'd bought all sorts of typical English foods, like Cornish Pasties and things like that. I offered them some fresh fruit, but they said they weren't interested in that. And then I said, 'Well, how about some Cornish Pasties?' and they said, 'Cornish Pasties!!' — they couldn't believe it, 'cause that's like their favorite thing! They're like biscuits with meat in them.

"So, I went upstairs and fixed a big pot of tea and we had Cornish Pasties and little chicken sandwiches and things that I made, and they were very impressed!! Then we went up to the third floor, to John's (Phillips) suite and played our new record for them which they liked very much."

...SONNY — Completed score.

BEAT Photo: Robert Custer

DYLAN FAKE?

Amid heated charges of breach of contract and rumors of a "cop out," Bob Dylan has remained as elusive on the circumstances of his recent motorcycle accident as he is in his poetry.

The Wizard of Words was allegedly involved in a motorcycle accident severe enough to keep him from a scheduled appearance the following week.

Dylan's opponents say the "accident" was actually planned. They say he designed it specifically as a "cop out" to a scheduled performance which he did not wish to keep.

Columbia Records emphatically denied the charges. A spokesman told *The BEAT* that Dylan had definitely been injured and would be confined to bed for at least two months.

However, even Columbia spokesmen admitted that no official statement had come from either Dylan or his manager, Al Grossman. Both have remained unavailable for comment.

KRLA ARCHIVES

Sir Douglas: 'Adults Resent Groups'

Some English performers, it seems, have done nothing recently but knock America: the people, their attitudes, their way of life.

Many of us have been upset by the Britisher's comments, but the theme of the counter attack has not been a sparkling, positive defense of American practices, but rather, a lame retaliation... "Why do you come here? Just for the money?"

At last, The BEAT has found an American pop star willing to do more than accuse his English contemporaries of being mercenary.

By Doug Sahm

In an exclusive BEAT interview, Doug Sahm, leader of the hit-making Sir Douglas Quintet ("She's About A Mover" and "Rain, Rain, Rain") commented, "It's not the kids who treat pop performers badly.

"Young people are great everywhere—they like you no matter what you look like. They dig the music, whether it comes from Mick Jagger or James Brown or Fred Grind. If it's good, they dig it.

Adults Uptight

"It's the adults who get uptight. They can't accept that their children are not going to be exactly like them. They're fighting the way kids dress and act—and they're fighting it hard. But youth will win. Today's youth—or their children.

"Many of the criticisms from English groups are true. Hotels do discriminate against long-haired performers. Not just British artists, but Americans too.

"I can't begin to tell you how many places have turned us away because of our appearance.

"And I'm ashamed to say the situation is particularly bad in Texas—our home state!

"Adults are just not hip to new styles. In many places, we can't even walk down the streets without being stopped by a policeman. Any group will tell you this. Would you believe I went to my bank in San Antonio where I was born, to cash a check and the teller was convinced that I was trying to hold him up! How could I have money and wear clothes like that? he was asking.

"In fact, we refuse to play in the South any more—the ridicule and out-right violence is too much. It's a shame that in this country, of all countries, you can't wear your hair the way you want without suffering mental and physical abuse. And we do wash.

"Finally it got so bad that I cut my hair and had the rest of the group trim theirs too. It's still 'too' long by Texan standards, but it's shorter than I like."

Fun Hair

Doug referred to recent remarks about hair by his friend Jim McGuinn, who said: "Our (The Byrds) long hair is more fun than anything. We just like to look like this. We enjoy it because it represents to us sort of an artistic rebellion in a renaissance. The artists of the 14th Century and so on had long hair and were great artists and greatly appreciated by the public. In fact, everyone in the world at one time wore long hair. It wasn't until recently that it was cut off for, I think, military reasons, but I'm not sure.

"Anyway, we wear long hair because we like it. We feel that it's arbitrary what you wear, like clothing styles are always changing and people are always wearing different kinds of pants—pants without cuffs or with cuffs, coats with belts, coats with pockets and coats without pockets, coats with one vent in the back and coats with two vents in the back. It really gets absurd after a while because everything seems so arbitrary."

According to Doug, the scene has already changed in England: "There the whole situation is completely different. We were there for four weeks and never once met any unpleasantness. Everyone was so warm and friendly, no matter what age they were. They loved us *because* we were foreigners, and different. In restaurants, everyone would stand around mildly and listen to our accents—they were fascinated simply because we were Americans, and we were never stared at or put down.

"Most of the adults in Britain have recognized the fact that their children are people in their own right, not just carbon copies of themselves. *And* they discipline their kids.

"In the U.S. parents are still trying to hold the kids back spiritually and emotionally while at the same time loading them with money and a car to win their co-operation. In places like Southern California, it's not working. The teenagers are breaking loose. And California, apart from the sheriff's war on the hippies, is better than the rest of the United States.

Resentment

"Generally, over here, adults still resent the groups, primarily because they helped start this revolution in clothing and attitude. Besides, they never like the kind of music their children do. So... they heap all their anger onto one object. They need just this one symbol to absorb all their vengeance—rock 'n' roll.

"They can't do anything to their children—they're too busy griping about how much easier the kids have it today.

"So they take it out on music groups: in hotels, restaurants, airports, any public place anywhere.

"Really, they're unbelievably stupid. They think it's all right for them to dress in a way *we* don't like — baggy Bermudas, white knees and long black socks; but we can't dress in a way *they* don't like. Doesn't sound much like freedom in the home of freedom. Does anyone ever read the Constitution these days? I mean *really* read it?

"Well, maybe we all should have more compassion for the adult world. They're in the middle of three tragic wars: with Viet Nam, with the Negroes, and with their own children.

"But I think they'd be a lot happier if they would relax and let people dance and laugh and groove, wear their hair long and their pants tight or bell-bottomed anyway.

"Then maybe adults could concentrate on some *real* problems."

...SIR DOUGLAS: "In many places we can't even walk down the streets."

'in' people are talking about...

Boarding the last train to Clarksville as soon as they find out where Clarksville is... What the Beatles had in mind when they penned "Yellow Submarine" and who talked John into apologizing... The conversation that dangles... Mama Michelle being back with Papa John and what it all means to Jill... "Guantanamera" being banned in Detroit because of its affiliation with Cuba... The joker going wild and giving Brian a hit he thought he'd never find... Who lifted the intro to "I Can't Help Myself" and changed the words and the title but left all else the same and got a hit... Motown thinking Jewish... Bobby Hebb flipping out over "Got To Get You Into My Life"... Felix's pants... Tommy Roe hiding down in the boondocks.

PEOPLE ARE TALKING ABOUT lonely Eleanor... What makes the Temptations think beauty is only skin deep... Whether mother's little helper will aid or hinder the fortune teller... Who the Happenings used to be... The one in a million... The day being turned down... God only knowing and the Beach Boys not telling... How fantastic Bobby is... The work song to the tune of the green stuff... The monk wanting to know who dun it... Smitty wearing the plaid... Sonny and Cher actually leaving while the rest of 'em are trying desperately to get in... The Mindbenders turning to ashes... Who Mrs. Applebee is... Banning Napolean and re-instating Louis... Having a lonelier summer than the Shades thought they would after being so happy.

PEOPLE ARE TALKING ABOUT the Outsiders being respectable... What's happened to Herman... The way Buddy can't see without his glasses... Marianne trying to comeback and wondering if she'll make it... Tommy saying what I am... Mick and Chrissie shopping at DeVos and cruising in a limousine while fans thought the guys had split town... Dubs of kazoos and what Dave thought of that idea... Lou getting sore because neither his picture nor his musicians' pictures were chosen... How sweet it is... Not casting the first stone unless... Getting seasick with the Yardbirds... J. and J. and Northern stock going down... Eric's burden.

PEOPLE ARE TALKING ABOUT sunny afternoons, promotion men and which group out of the thousands are really going to make it... Kim Fowley's "Trip" and how in the world they think it's ever going to get airplay in the States... The Spoonful in the Village... Gary's symphony... The audience farce at Forrest Hills and how fed up the people at NBC were with the M's and P's ...The Who thinkin' the kids are okay... How they laughed when people tried to sell them on the idea of a TV show centered around a rock group and how they're now crying buckets because the Monkees are gonna make millions... Ethnic psychedelic Afro-Cuban folk rock and Mexican chiquaqua dogs.

PEOPLE ARE TALKING ABOUT what's gotten into Suzy Creamcheese and the Mothers... How they never dreamed Circus Boy would turn into a Monkee... Boo Goo Loo Baby and T.J. and his P.S. 13 Blues Band and wondering if they're kidding, or serious, or downright out of their minds.

KRLA ARCHIVES

Top 40 Requests

#	Title	Artist
1	FORTUNE TELLER	The Rolling Stones
2	YELLOW SUBMARINE	The Beatles
3	CHERISH	The Association
4	ELEANOR RIGBY	The Beatles
5	GOT TO GET YOU INTO MY LIFE	The Beatles
6	HERE THERE & EVERYWHERE	The Beatles
7	SUNNY	Bobby Hebb
8	SOMETIMES GOOD GUYS DON'T WEAR WHITE	The Standells
9	SUNSHINE SUPERMAN	Donovan
10	THEY'RE COMING TO TAKE ME AWAY HA HA	Napolean XIV
11	SWEET PEA	Tommy Roe
12	RED RUBBER BALL	The Cyrkle
13	YOU CAN'T HURRY LOVE	The Supremes
14	LITTLE RED RIDING HOOD	Sam The Sham & The Pharaohs
15	JUST LIKE A WOMAN	Bob Dylan
16	BLACK IS BLACK	Los Bravos
17	SUNNY AFTERNOON	The Kinks
18	GOD ONLY KNOWS	Beach Boys
19	SEE YOU IN SEPTEMBER	The Happenings
20	SUMMERTIME	Billy Stewart
21	WIPE OUT	The Surfaries
22	SUMMER IN THE CITY	The Lovin' Spoonful
23	SEVEN & SEVEN IS	Love
24	SOMEWHERE MY LOVE	Ray Conniff
25	GUANTANAMERA	The Sandpipers
26	TURN DOWN DAY	Cyrkle
27	SATISFIED WITH YOU	The Dave Clark Five
28	OVER, UNDER, SIDEWAYS, DOWN	The Yardbirds
29	I COULDN'T LIVE WITHOUT YOUR LOVE	Petula Clark
30	THE WORK SONG	Herb Alpert
31	LAND OF 1,000 DANCES	Wilson Pickett
32	DANGLING CONVERSATION	Simon & Garfunkle
33	STRANGERS IN THE NIGHT	Frank Sinatra
34	MAKE ME BELONG TO YOU	Barbara Lewis
35	LADY JANE/MOTHERS LITTLE HELPER	The Rolling Stones
36	BLOWING IN THE WIND	Stevie Wonder
37	HANKY PANKY	Tommy James & The Shondells
38	I SAW HER AGAIN	The Mama's & The Papa's
39	GO AHEAD AND CRY	Righteous Bros.
40	PAPERBACK WRITER/RAIN	The Beatles

ATTENTION!!!

High Schools, Colleges, Universities and Clubs:

CASEY KASEM MAY BE ABLE TO SERVE YOU!

Let Casey HELP You Put On A Show Or Dance

For information

Contact Casey at: HO 2-7253

LIMITED SUMMER BONUS FOR BEAT READERS —

$200 in Values *Only* **$2 in Price!**

GO-GUIDE COUPON BOOK

More than 100 coupons for Free Admissions, Discounts up to 50% or 2 for 1 offerings. Activities and Products listed below, plus many others.

Movies	Revell
Clubs	Statewide Theatres
Dancing	So. Cal. Bowl. Assn
Sports	Troubador
Food	Ash Grove
Clothing	Orange Julius
Records	Hullabaloo
Jewelry	Gazzari's
Cosmetics	P.O.P.
Shows	Pasadena Civic
Fairs	Sports Show
Horseback Riding	L. A. Blades
Bowling	Ice House
Folk Music	World On Wheels
Plays	Independ. Theatres
Slot Car Racing	Vivian Woodward
Billiards	Fashion Tops
Skating	Mademoiselle

Dial F-U-N-T-E-E-N For More Information

ORDER NOW WHILE THEY LAST!

FUNTEEN GO-GUIDE
c/o KRLA BEAT
6290 Sunset, Suite 504
Hollywood, Calif. 90028

Please send me _____ copies of the 1966 FUNTEEN GO-GUIDE (Valid thru Dec. 31, 1966) at the special summer rate of only $2.00 each. I enclose $_____

NAME:
ADDRESS:
CITY: STATE: ZIP:

FUNTEEN BONUS COUPON OFFERINGS

All the Bonus Coupons printed in the back section of the Go-Guide are listed below:

NOW AVAILABLE TO MEMBERS ONLY:

A Supplement containing 30 additional coupons. Send 25¢ (for handling) plus a stamped, self-addressed envelope to

SUPPLEMENT
P.O. Box 1235, Beverly Hills, Calif.

Coupon	Merchant	Offering
"A"	International Import-Export Trade and Travel Fair — Long Beach Sports Arena	2 for 1 admission Nov. 8th - 13th
"B"	Discotren — 5136 N. Citrus, Covina	2 for 1; $1 off with membership card
"C"	San Fernando Valley Teen Center 17400 Victory Blvd.	2 for 1 admission
"D"	Drum City — Guitar Town, 15255 Sherman Way, Van Nuys; 5611 Jumilla, Woodland Hills; 6226 Santa Monica Blvd., L. A.	2 free "Crazy Fill" book covers for just dropping in. $5 gift certificate with $15 one-time or accumulated purchase.
"E"	Hobby-Land Hobby Shop 1828 S. Robertson Blvd., L. A.	Free Gift plus 20% discount on all purchases, with card
"F"	Orange Julius, 8787 Santa Monica Blvd., W. Hollywood	Free Orange Julius with any purchase.
"G"	Gazzari's — 319 N. La Cienega	2 for 1 admission to Teen Night every Sunday (7 p.m. - 12 midnight)
"H"	Hullabaloo, 6230 Sunset Blvd., Hollywood	2 for 1 admission
		2 for 1 admission August 5 for MacGillivray's surfing film, "The Performers."
"J"	Michael's Jewelers, 7510 Woodman, Van Nuys	Free Beatle jewelry piece
"K"	Kookie Kapers — 7060 Santa Monica Blvd., L.A.	$5 certificate after $35 purchase
"L"	Dunkee Donuts, Town & Country, 6332 W. 3rd., L.A.	Free donut for dropping in and free donuts with any purchase
"M"	Northridge Valley Skateland 18140 Parthenia, Northridge	2 for 1 admission, with or without skates
"N"	Ezra's Oasis — 316 N. La Cienega	"Most anything on the menu" at 2 for 1
"O"	Orange Julius, 6001 W. Pico, L.A.	2 Orange Juliuses for price of 1
"P"	Pasadena Civic Auditorium 300 Green St., Pasadena	Free admission for member and 1 guest to dance any Saturday (8:30-11:30 p.m.) Dresses for girls, dress shirts, tie and slacks for boys. Same offer good at De Wald's Ballroom, 831 W. Las Tunas Dr., San Gabriel
"Q"	Orange Julius — 1715 Pico Blvd., Santa Monica	Free Orange Julius with any purchase
"R"	Valley Ice Skating Center 18361 Ventura Blvd., Tarzana	2 for price of 1
"S"	Shirt Stack — 1900J Lincoln, Santa Monica	$5 gift certificate with $15 one-time or accumulated purchase. Member's friends may purchase on his accumulation.
"T"	Ice House — 24 N. Mentor, Pasadena	2 for 1 admission
"U"	Ice House — 234 S. Brand, Glendale	2 for 1 admission

Membership Card Admission: Cafe Danssa, 11533 Pico Blvd., West L.A. Sundays only — 2 for 1 admission.

FUNTEEN OFFER: Free Orange Julius with purchase anytime. Just show Funteen card.

Membership Card Admission: Swinging Young Adults Club of Los Angeles. Dancing every Sunday, 2-10 p.m. Only 75¢ for members with card. Guys and Dolls A Go Go, 3617 Crenshaw Blvd., LA

SPECIAL ANNOUNCEMENT! All of the Statewide Theatre coupons in your Go-Guide are now good at any Statewide Theatre listed in the Guide. Coupons are interchangeable.

KRLA ARCHIVES

Inside KRLA
By Eden

Get ready, world, it's coming. Yes, your friendly neighborhood Norsemen at Valhalla are ever at the ready to serve you, and shortly you will be able to obtain your very own credit card for Valhalla Thor Thunderbolt Gas. Stay tuned to KRLA for details.

And speaking of the "men who wear the horns," one of them came prancing into our offices the other day for a little chat, and we thought we'd share it with all of you.

Our Viking representative is very typical of the friendly, smiling Norsemen who are waiting to service you and your car when you drive into Valhalla. His name is Svenson Shmorgasburger, he towers six feet, eleven inches above sea level, and boasts a blazing red beard and mustache surrounding his friendly Norse smile.

I asked Sven (his Norse-nickname) what he considered to be his most important function as one of the friendly, prancing Norsemen at Valhalla. He thought about that, for about half an hour, and then explained that he felt a great obligation to the customers of Valhalla, a deep responsibility for their well-being.

He went on, at length, to explain that when a car drives into the Valhalla Pump City station, he literally *rushes* out to greet the new customer. Removes him (or her) from his (or her) car and, true to his neighborly Norseman image, greets him (or her) with a huge bear hug—a symbol of Viking warmth and camaraderie.

You know, it gives me a warm feeling inside just to know that somewhere in the world—and fortunately, it's *here*—there are people like the friendly Vikings at Valhalla.

Oh yes, Sven also emphatically denied the continuing rumors being circulated by our competitors that the friendly Vikings at Valhalla have been attempting to sabotage their stations. Some people simply can't keep a tight rein on their jealousies!

Sven did assume responsibility for the large bronze spear found penetrating that large orange ball in the middle of Sunset Boulevard, and he admitted that he did *borrow* a few of the smaller orange globes to adorn his Viking horns—however, he made it quite clear that both acts were simply in keeping with the friendly Viking fellowship which is always to be found at Valhalla.

Johnny Hayes took a moment to chat with us the other eve, and informed *The BEAT* that he too was anxiously awaiting the first printing of Valhalla credit cards, already having become a loyal patron himself.

Johnny is very excited right now about his vacation coming up this Fall, 'cause he'll be traveling back to his home—Macon, Georgia—to visit his folks. And from what he tells me, Macon is nothing but fabulous at that time of the year. Autumn leaves and the whole scene, so immediately demanded a written promise that he would at least bring some *leaves* back to me! Ah for the life of a DJ!!!

DUE TO PUBLIC DEMAND, along with a little begging from The BEAT staff, The Association have pulled "Cherish," written by Terry Kirkman of the group, off their first album, "And Then Along Comes The Association," and have another hit on their hands. The guys will appear September 7 and 8 at The Carousel Theater in West Covina.

Funteen Moves Ahead to 1967

Funteen, Southern California's greatest fun and activity club, will be moving into 1967 with even more and better activities for the sophisticated young adults of today.

There will be no expiration date for the fabulous discounts offered in the Go-Guide Coupon Book to all members of Funteen, and membership will extend from the date applications are received by Funteen.

Funteen has also announced that a student advisory council will be organized to assist in the coming membership drive plans, all programs and activities and making Funteen into a better organization for all young adults through the age of 20.

Officers will be elected, committees appointed and co-ordinators chosen to represent each of the junior and senior high schools in the area.

Applications to serve on the council may be obtained by anyone between the ages of 13 and 20 by writing to P.O. Box 1235, Beverly Hills, California.

STUART WHITMAN / JANET LEIGH — This is Mrs. Rojack. Be glad you're not Mr. Rojack. *An American Dream* ...or is it a nightmare? Co-starring BARRY SULLIVAN · LLOYD NOLAN and ELEANOR PARKER · TECHNICOLOR · FROM WARNER BROS. NOW PLAYING! WARNER HOLLYWOOD THEATRE

Say you saw it in The BEAT

Danny Dassa Cafe Danssa — 11533 W. Pico, L.A. — International Folk Cafe

SUPER DUPER MARVY FAB KRLA BEAT SUMMER SPECIAL

$1.50 for the rest of the year!!
(new subscribers only)

$3.00 a year

SAVE 60% on the bigger, better BEAT
Just clip and mail...

KRLA BEAT
Save 60%—Subscribe!

Mail to:
Beat Publications
6290 Sunset Blvd.
Hollywood 90028

Name _____
Address _____
City _____ State _____ Zip _____

☐ I want BEAT for the rest of the year at $1.50.
☐ I want BEAT for a year at $3.00.
☐ I want to extend my subscription for 1 year at $3.00.
☐ I enclose ☐ cash ☐ check ☐ money order.

HERE IT COMES!! The International Teen World Festival
WHEN?? During Christmas Vacation
Contestants wanted for Miss Teen World!!! Dial "F-U-N-T-E-E-N" (386-8336) for details.
Attention All Fun Club members: 1 free admission with 1 paid (2 for 1) with AA coupon.

KRLA ARCHIVES

BEAT SHOWCASE
(spotlighting new talent on the pop scene)

JULIE DRISCOLL . . . an English lass, carries carrots in her handbag, wouldn't know what to do with Dior, gets attached to hotel rooms, paints surrealistic and sings. Her record: "I Didn't Want To Have To Do It" c/w "Don't Do It No More."

THE MAGICIANS . . . Columbia rock artists who sing and play so well that they get their sound across without having to rely on their amplifiers to make people listen. They've proved it in discotheques like the New York Phone Booth and Boston Unicorn. The group consists of lead guitar player Jake (Al Jacobs, really), drummer Alan Lee Gordon, lead vocalist Gary Bonner and bass guitarits John Towley. Their latest release is "I'd Like To Know."

THE PILGRIMS . . . take their name from the original pilgrims who landed at Plymouth Rock and founded for themselves freedom of self-expression. And history again repeats itself with the landing of the new Pilgrims on the pop music scene — a rock group who have found their own freedom of self-expression in music by composing all their own numbers. Left to right, top to bottom, the Pilgrims are Gary Giles, lead singer and percussionist; Tom Pergola, lead guitarist; Eddie Kobylarz, organist and Bob Severino, drummer.

KIM FOWLEY . . . honest. You aren't seeing things — it really is the inimitable Mr. Fowley himself. The "unofficial mayor of Sunset Strip" is in England, singing, writing, and causing a few comments about his style of dress . . . especially his Batman tee-shirts and Hawaiian print shoes. Kim recently wrote two songs for Manfred Mann.

KRLA ARCHIVES

For Girls only
by shirley poston

It's so weird how thing(ies) work out for the best.

Along about the time George got married (blither), a couple of you sent me a poem called "When England Went To War." I wanted to print it in my (poor excuse for a) column, but I thought it was a little too gory.

So, a few months later, I decided to make a rash promise. So, I did. I asked everyone who wanted a copy of the poem (plus a copy of John's "Toy Boy") to send me a SAE.

Ever since thin (hah?) . . . ever since then, I've been lurking around looking for a stray mimeograph machine and have been getting nowhere fast.

Without Them

After staying awake nights, wracked with guilt, I suddenly realized that it was probably *supposed* to happen this way. That I couldn't find a mimeo because I was supposed to print the poem in my column, no matter how gory it might be (the column, that is.) This way, a lot more people would get to read it, and maybe it would help a few of them realize what it would be like to be without the Beatles.

Don't panic or anything. I'm still going to send out "Toy Boy" just as soon as I can, but I think I'd better print the other poem this instant. And here goes . . .

WHEN ENGLAND WENT TO WAR
(Author Unknown)

*Life was hard, but wonderful too,
for the fabulous Liverpool four.
But all this was to change, you see,
when England went to war.*

*The Beatles were the first ones to enlist, and pay their country's debts.
Guitars were changed for rifles and guns for bayonets.*

•

*Fans held their breath, but cheered them on, and promised they'd never forget.
While long brown hair was pushed out of sight beneath a heavy army helmet.
When they were gone away to fight, in the hearts of fans there were fears.
And millions went to sleep at night with their cheeks still wet with tears.*

*John lay on his bunk one evening, softly singing a song.
George was writing a letter home "Dear Mom . . . nothing will go wrong . . ."
Ringo sat there deep in thought, homesick already and sad.
And Paul, dear Paul, feeling strangely afraid, wished to see his Dad.*

•

*But there was little time for such talk, as the British defended their home.
And soldiers died like fleas in mud, hard and all alone.
John was sent ahead to scout the enemy that night . . .
The others went too – for John to go alone just wouldn't be right.*

•

*They crawled so slowly in the dirt, but never to come back.
An enemy plane had spotted them, and everything went black.
Hours later, Ringo came to and put his hand to his bleeding head.
Remembering his mates, he turned to them, but John and George were dead.*

•

*Silhouetted against the sky, he saw a cross, but that wasn't all.
Looking up at it, Ringo also saw what was left of Paul.
Another plane passed over, but Ringo didn't run.
Three were gone and Ringo knew that now his time had come.*

•

*A shot was heard and the pain was felt as a bullet struck his side.
And there beneath the cross of honor, Richard Starkey died.
Time has passed, and years gone by, the shore still meets the waves.
And, in some far foreign land, lie four deserted graves.*

•

*But still there's one who cannot forget, though the years pass slowly on.
For back home, by an open window, Cynthia waits for John.*

I've sat here almost an hour since I typed that last line. I want to say something, and I just can't find the right words. But, I'll try. A lot of people might think that poem is soft, or maudlin or morbid. I don't think it's any of those things. Six months ago, "When England Went To War" made me cry. Now it terrifies me.

At War

Why? Because it was written way back before even Ringo and Mo, and everything in it is starting to come true. The Beatles *are* at war, over something for which a cross is symbolic, and I'm so afraid that if we don't help them, they're going to die in a worse kind of mud than the poem describes . . . the kind that people are *slinging* at them.

I don't know how we can help them, except to start loving them twice as hard and twice as loud. Maybe that will make the banners and burners realize that *nothing* can take away what the Beatles have given us, or make us give them up.

I suppose I'd better make it clear that I'm not saying we should all agree with John's viewpoints. If I don't, someone will probably start a movement to burn all the past chapters of Robin Boyd.

I'm just saying what difference does it make whether we agree *or* disagree? I don't agree with a lot of people about a lot of things, and in this particular case, John is one of those people. But hardly any two people *do* agree on something this personal. And wouldn't this world be a *marvelous* place if we started going around hating everyone who wasn't just like us.

The Beatles have proved to the world that they are talented musicians and honest human beings. I don't care if they think the moon is made out of green *cheese*, because that has nothing to do with their contributions as entertainers and individuals.

Shook Up

I'd better stop this raving, because that's all I'm doing. Sorry about that, but I'm so shook up I can't even think. In closing, I just want to add that I hope there's someone else in this world who isn't dragging their Beatle records off to the nearest bonfire just because of a misquoted, misinterpreted, garbled, out-of-context statement that is being exploited and blown way out of proportion by magazines that want only to make money, and people who can't get their name in the paper any other way.

He said it and I don't agree with what he said and I love him and three other people I could mention (and have been known to every five or six million.) And, at the moment, that love is about the only thing in this world that seems to make an ounce of sense.

Me included.

Lively Set For Vegas

The Lively Set, regulars on NBC-TV's Kraft Summer Music Hall, have been set for four weeks at the Casbar Theatre of the Sahara Hotel in Las Vegas beginning October 25.

They've also been signed for an additional month at the Casbar beginning December 25. However, the group's first single is not due to be released until late August, which means that the Lively Set is doing exceptionally well for a group without a record in the charts.

Williams C&W Head

HOLLYWOOD — The Academy of Country & Western music has elected Tex Williams as its first President and Eddie Dean as Vice-President.

The Southern California organization was formed last year and in February, 1966 it held its First Annual C&W Awards Show before a sell-out crowd and a $12,000 gross.

Williams stated that plans are currently being finalized for the Second Annual Awards Show (early 1967) which will be nationally televised.

The Rascals:

. . . FELIX CAVALIERE — Experience in himself.

By Lisa Stewart

From their conception in the mind of Felix Cavaliere, organist extraordinaire, to their birth at The Barge in Southampton, to their christening at the top discotheques in New York City, The Rascals have become a turning point in modern music.

In an age where the "English sound" was heading record sales and popularity charts everywhere, four guys with definite ideas in music and a goal to shoot for, have shown American teenagers and the entire music industry that the real sound is still in the United States where it first began.

Self-Contained

The group itself is a completely self-contained unit. They all write, sing, play, produce and are excellent businessmen. Much of their business accumen has come from watching and listening to their manager, entrepreneur Sid Bernstein. His excellent handling of the group has had a definite bearing in putting them where they are today.

Unlike many top groups, whose sound is due mainly to expert engineers and echo chambers, they have a sound which comes across as well, if not better, on stage as it does on recordings. What emerges from their instruments are the Rascals themselves. Every note they play or sing comes from inside. The music is filled with their drive, ambition, joys, sorrows, memories of the past and hopes of things to come in the future.

Their music and personalities are interchangeable – both frighteningly real and intricately woven together. Individually, though you seldom find them that way, the guys are complete opposites but this factor is a help, rather than a deterrent.

The Rascals are a visually fascinating group and one of the reasons for this is the dancing and on-stage antics of vocalist and number one tambourine man, Edward Franklin Joseph Brigati, Jr., more commonly referred to as Eddie. Eddie is as at home in jeans and a sweatshirt on a motorcycle or shooting the breeze with the guys he grew-up with, as he is holding his own conversationally etc., with the top echelon of show business. His is a frenetic and exuberant personality, which makes his presence known and himself remembered wherever he goes.

He can be charming and gentlemanly or he can be a rough, knockdown, "just one of the guys" kid. He changes as the occasion demands. But either way he is very real and never a phony. He has a quick and volitile temper but he is even quicker to forgive and forget and never lets down a friend who is depending on him. Some part of him is always in motion, whether it be feet, hands, mind or mouth. When the latter is in action, it can sing anything from a fast up-beat rocker, to a slow mournful and beautiful ballad. It is this unusual vocal versatility which more than makes up for the absence of a fourth instrument in the band.

When Eddie walks into a room there is an air of "what is he going to do next," because no one ever knows. You cannot anticipate him, for he doesn't even know. He may sit quietly, speaking now and then or he may completely dominate the conversation. He has a poise and assurance beyond his twenty years, which commands and receives the respect and attention of those around him. He may speak in the Jersey slang of his boyhood or he may suddenly quote Shakespeare with the perfect diction of an English actor. You never know.

On Top

In fact, where Eddie Brigati is concerned there is only one thing you can be absolutely sure of and that is . . . whether or not The Rascals are on top in ten or fifteen years, he will be.

Next on the list is Felix Cavaliere, singer, composer and organist. Fe, as he is known to his friends (the amount of which are virtually uncountable), is simply the perfect example of the Golden Rule. He is one of those rare people who always finds time to be nice to everyone – whether they be old friends or complete strangers. It is not unusual to hear a casual acquaintance describe him as a close friend because that is the impression he gives. It is not an act or an acquired mannerism but a gift.

New York Tough Guys Or . . . ?

An accomplished musician, he entered college to become a doctor but left when he found he could cure illness and give life to people another way—through his music and he does just that. There are few organists who can copy his intense and unique style of playing. When Fe performs he is lost in a world composed entirely of sounds. In those moments, nothing else exists.

Just watching him is an experience in itself. Musically, he is somewhat of a genius, understanding everything from classical to hot jazz and marveling in the beauty of it all.

Sounds fascinate him, be it cars, trains, birds or the spoken word and his ability to translate all of these into music makes him one of the top composers, in his field, today. Unlike the majority of long-haired R&B musicians, Fe can converse intelligently on any subject you care to bring up.

World Outside

In his spare time (of which there is not too much these days), he is a voracious reader, for he realizes that there *is* a world outside of music and one he must be prepared for. Prophetically speaking, there is a book called "Who's Who in Music," and if in a few years you care to look under the letter "C", you will find a listing for "Cavaliere, Felix (1942 – ?): Composer, singer, musician, producer, author, etc., etc., etc.

The only non-singing member of the group is drummer Dino Danelli and there are multitudes of people who will swear that he is the greatest drummer in the United States. If you have ever seen or listened to him, you will know why.

His sticks fly so fast you can hardly see them, much less follow them. They whirl around in his hands like batons, are thrown in the air, caught, and he never, never misses a beat. His movements have a strange mechanical quality, hard to describe but smooth as silk. He has a certain dignity about him when he performs. His amazing timing seems instinctive and a combination of this plus a superb sense of showmanship, make his intricate movements appear simple and uncomplicated.

Known to most as "the quiet Rascal," what he doesn't say with words, he says with his drums. He is one of the few drummers who can make that usually loud and un-melodic instrument, fascinatingly beautiful.

When Dino speaks he does so quietly and what he says is almost always about music and well worth listening to.

His other love is art and it is another field in which he excells. He spends much time studying art and gathering ideas and inspiration from both the old masters and the new modern artists. If he had not chosen music as his major profession, his paintings would probably be hanging in galleries all over the world. Sometime in the future you still may find them there.

As it is, he doesn't have as much time to spend painting as he would like to, for despite the national acclaim he has received musically, he is still not satisfied and practices constantly. This is a quality that will always keep him one jump ahead of everyone else.

Girls like his dark good looks and those highly arched eyebrows that give him a perpetually surprised look. They can always be found clustering around him, staring with looks of rapture and adoration.

Dino may not say much but he knows a lot.

For instance, exactly what he wants, where he's going and what he'll do when he gets there. And will he get there? Well, no one can foresee the future but considering the fact that he is just twenty-one and thought of by his rivals to be the best in the business, I would say that his chances are only slightly more than a definite, positive and emphatic YES.

Dylanesque

Last in the line-up but usually first on line is Gene Cornish. A voice that at times has a Dylanesque quality, a wildly off-beat sense of humor, a get-up-and-go attitude, an air of mystery and a guitar that literally soars, sings, cries and laughs are the component parts of Gene.

The air of mystery comes from the fact that he likes to keep his private life strictly private. Because he is famous and most of his movements are constantly in the public eye, the few hours he can keep to himself are precious to him. They are to be spent with those closest to him, who know Gene the person, not the Rascal.

Outwardly, he is somewhat of a comedian who is always there with the quick ad-lib, the funny line. But inside the smile there is a very serious side and an intelligent mind that is always filled with ideas on improvement both musically and promotionally.

It has been a long, hard and often hungry struggle for him to get where he is and he intends to move only one way—up. He is always aware of the new groups, the new sounds and the new gimmicks. He has a certain sense of the future and knows what will be considered "in" and "now" before it ever happens. Because of this, he is right there when it does.

Musically, Gene is one of the finest guitarists around. His music has a depth and sensitivity that reaches even the most callous of listeners. His musical ad-libs are always a topic of discussion among those who know sound.

Non-Italian

He can play anything from soft classical to the jazz and flamenco beat to the twangy melodies of the Southern banjo. It is always a constant source of amazement to me that he can play as he does and still manage to dance around the stage, at the same time. Being the only member of the group who is not Italian, he takes a lot of kidding from the other guys but they know, as does everyone who knows music and knows Gene, that he will be around and on top for a long, long time.

Now you know the Rascals, both individually and as a group and this is only the beginning. There is a secret to success and The Rascals have discovered it and we, the listening public, should be very glad that we have discovered them.

. . . **THE YOUNG RASCALS** (l. to r. Gene, Eddie, Dino and Felix) have discovered the secret.

. . . **DEVILISH GRIN** from Gene and concentration from Dino.

. . . **RASCALS HAM IT UP** with Buddy Hackett.

KRLA ARCHIVES

Woe Is Me!... The Major Is Stalked By Many Troubles

By Mike Tuck

Trouble just stalks some people. For Major Lance, it's like a black raincloud overhead that follows him everywhere he goes. He stands in an unceasing shower of bad luck, outrageous and pathetically comical situations.

Major Lance could be charged with breaking and entering for going to church. He's the kind of guy who could be convicted of assault and battery for shaking hands with somone.

But he's learned to live with it, and—as much as can be expected—to avoid some of it.

For one thing, he stays away from Mississippi.

"Our band was driving through there one time when this state patrolman stopped us," he remembered painfully. "He asks us where we're going and who we are."

A Real Band?

"We tell him we're a band and we're going to Jackson for a show. He says, 'You're a band? Let me hear you strum out a little tune.'

"We had to set up every piece of equipment right there on that highway and play him a song," the Major lamented.

The real trouble, however, didn't come until the scheduled show in Jackson. After a backwoods emcee had made a futile attempt at humor by introducing Major as Sargeant Bilko, fireworks began to explode.

"I finish my act and start to walk off stage when these two policemen grab me," he said. "I don't know what's going on and then this woman that looks like she's been hit with a truck comes running up and points her finger at me.

"She's yelling 'That's him, that's him.' I had never even seen that woman before. And anyway, she was so ugly I wouldn't even look at her in a storm," he concluded.

After two days behind bars, Major was finally cleared of the charges, but he vowed never to return to Mississippi.

Major took a huge gulp of coffee—we couldn't help but think it was to sooth his nerves—and continued recapping on his chain of misfortunes as BEAT reporters looked at each other in disbelief. His hard luck episodes go on and on and on.

Major Lance is a tightly wound individual with a sinewey, 155 pound frame. His face is one of drastic change: in a split second it transforms from a worried sulk to a beaming glow of content and self-approval.

Ironically, some of his broadest smiles come when he is explaining his woes. He mentioned the fact that he was once a professional fighter and right away we knew something bad—really bad—had to have happened to him.

A few years ago Major was a high ranking lightweight, having won 43 of 46 professional fights with the last 19 victories coming by knockouts. Then his raincloud of troubles burst.

He was suspended from boxing for life.

"Ya know, I got to thinking I was pretty good before that last fight. In fact, I was downright cocky," he admitted. "I just knew I couldn't be beat... why, I didn't even train for that last fight.

"We had a party planned for after the fight and I had two girlfriends sitting in ringside seats. I was up in the ring before the fight, prancing around, and every once in a while I would glance down and wink at those girls."

Wham

Then the fight started.

"He came out and I danced around him a little, just kind of playing with him. Then WHAM... he knocked me down. I got up, and he did it again," winced the Major.

"My eye was all swollen and I could barely see," he continued. "I was getting mad. He wasn't supposed to hit me like that. About that time I look down at ringside and those two girls are laughing.

"I got so mad I tried to take my gloves off. I couldn't get them off so I threw that guy up against the ropes and bit him. I was so mad I would have probably shot him if I'd had a gun."

Needless to say, the referee called the fight, and Major Lance was immediately notified it was his last professional fight. But the real blow came when Major returned from the dressing room after the fight.

His party had been cancelled and both girls had already left the arena—with the other fighter.

That's the type of thing that happens to Major Lance. If he could sing 24 hours a day he would probably be all right, because if there's one thing Major Lance is not it's an unlucky singer.

And besides, he adds, "singing keeps you out of trouble."

Top Major

The author of "The Monkey" and several other smashes is still one of the top people in the business, and his career is studded with instances of brilliance and gratification for Major.

Yet, he got into a singing profession by accident. He and another fellow were singing as amateurs and appeared on a Christmas program on a Chicago TV station. Several companies were half way interested in him after that, but he went to Wonderful Records to talk contract with an executive there.

"I could tell he wasn't really interested because he tried to put me off and told me to try over at Okey Records," he said. "He told me Okey was just hungry for young talent.

"So I went over there and they signed me. Right after that I had a big hit with 'The Monkey.' Now every time I see that fella from Wonderful I laugh at him."

We had dwelt with Major's troubles for so long it was time for him to leave. He gulped down the final bit of his coffee and politely excused himself.

Someone at the table he just left told him to "stay out of trouble" as he was walking away. Major Lance stopped slowly and glanced back, a pained expression covering his face.

... MAJOR LANCE

Teens Speak

In this issue, the members of The BEAT's Teen Panel discuss the problems of the American Negro. Rather than ask the panel to stick to one area of this many-faceted subject, we suggested that they exchange personal views and let the conversation evolve naturally.

Participating are Mike — 18, Linda — 16, Kris — 17, and Barry — 19.

Linda volunteered to begin the discussion.

* * *

Linda—"After I've said one sentence, you'll know why I wanted to start things off. I don't want anyone to hear my accent and immediately assume I'm against Negroes, because that isn't the way I feel."

Mike—"What part of the South are you from?"

Linda—"I'd rather not say. If it weren't for the privacy of no one knowing who we are, I couldn't be a member of this panel. I can't say where I'm from or my folks might pick up a copy of The BEAT and put two and two together. This way I can say what I feel without having to go through hell at home."

Kris—"Are your folks racially prejudiced?"

Ku Klux Klan

Linda—"Very. Not to the Ku Klux Klan extent or anything like that. But if they thought I'd even consider dating a Negro boy, I think they'd lock me in a closet for the next ten years."

Kris—"Are you saying that you would consider such a thing?"

Linda—"Not exactly. I'm still thinking about a lot of things, and I haven't really decided about this one in particular. But I am sick and ashamed about the way my part of the country—my *former* part, I should say—has acted toward Negroes. I'm embarrassed to be from the South, and I wish I didn't feel that way."

Barry—"I've never had the chance to talk about racial equality with anyone from your area. Would you say that the majority of whites in the South are prejudiced toward Negroes?"

Linda—"Yes they are, but not the way it's been made to sound. The majority of Southerners, and I *lived* there, don't run around burning crosses or murdering Civil Rights workers. They don't even *dislike* Negroes. They like them fine, just as long as colored people stay in their place and don't try to change things."

Barry—"How about young people? Do they feel the same way?"

How About... ?

Linda—"Not nearly so much. When the school I went to was de-segregated, hardly any of the kids protested. Most everyone was pretty cool about the whole thing. But some parents and other adults really got ridiculous. They stood out in front of the school and yelled at the Negro kids. It was awful. The whole school was ashamed of them. Maybe it helped though. A lot of the students didn't really believe in integration, but this stupidity probably made some of them realize that it was for the best. When good, responsible people stick up for a cause, it makes the cause seem worthwhile, but when a bunch of nuts turn out to support something, it makes you wonder about the thing they're fighting for or against. I know I started to wonder about the whole world in general when I heard those people screaming dirty words at kids."

Barry—"Did your parents make any attempt to protest the de-segregation of your school?"

Linda—"They went to a few meetings, not the Klan type of course, but when they saw that the meetings weren't going to do any good, they tried to make the best of things too. But they're still prejudiced. Because of the way they were brought up, I suppose. It's hard to change something that's existed since you were born. That's why it's taking the Negro so long to become equal, especially in the South where we have so many 'classes' of people, with them on the bottom of the totem pole."

Mike—"I think it's also because the Negroes—their leaders, anyway—are going about the cause all wrong. All the riots are just making the situation worse."

Linda—"I agree with that in a way. Well, I agree with the last part, period. But *nothing* seems to be doing much good. Compare the Negroes in the South with the same race in other parts of the country. Where I come from, Negroes wouldn't dare riot. They take a big chance just by participating in a non-violent march. But they're not really making much more progress than the rioters in the rest of the country. I don't mean that rioting is okay. It isn't. I just mean that whatever the *right* way is, I don't think anyone has found it."

More Harm

Barry—"I don't think Negroes *have* leaders. All they have are self-appointed Gods who usually do more harm than good. That's why riots happen. If Negroes want to revolt against society, and it's about time they did because no one is going to do it for them, someone needs to be in charge. This way, it's an Army without a general, and that ends up with a series of local battles instead of a full-scale war against the situation."

Kris—"That may be for the best, too. If the wrong person were 'in charge,' we might end up with a *real* war. That wouldn't solve anything. I'm all for the cause of equality myself, and for anything that's at least a step in the right direction. Even the rioting has had some good effects. It's at least made people in this country aware of what exists. I didn't know Negro ghettos existed until all the fighting started. I knew they lived in certain areas, but I didn't know how things *were* in those areas until the Watts trouble."

Mike—"That may be true, but it also made the rest of the world aware of the same elements. There are two major powers in the world today—Democracy and Commu-

KRLA ARCHIVES

Out On Problems Of U.S. Negro

nism. I think it's a pretty risky time for America to be involved in internal hassles. We're as much as saying that Democracy doesn't work. This country is founded on the constitution and on the fact that everyone has the rights it contains. How can we expect other countries to respect us when we so obviously can't live up to that constitution? America is getting to be the most hated country in the world, and I'm beginning to understand why. I used to think it was because of our higher economic levels and better education and that. But we worked hard for those things, and if other countries would do the same, they'd have them too. I don't think this is why America is so unpopular. It's because we say one thing and do another. We've been so busy working for material things, we've never taken time out to make our principles work. Each side is at fault. The people who allow or cause such situations to exist, and the people who try to fight the problem with molotov cocktails instead of common sense. If we keep this up, the Communists are going to take over the world without firing a shot. The problem is, how do you stop one thing and start another. I mean, how can you change millions of people?"

"You Can't"

Barry—"You can't. Each person has to do his own changing. That's why even a full-scale war wouldn't do the trick. Individuals have to revolt as individuals. White people who want to end prejudice have to eliminate it from their own personal worlds. Negroes who want a better life have to make one for themselves. Not as a race, as individuals. If enough whites and enough Negroes do this, prejudice will disappear in time. Not entirely, but it will become an isolated thing you can pack up and move away from."

Linda—"Yes, but that will take a long time. Too long. It's just natural to want the change now. There's one thing that may hurry up the process though. No, I'm positive it will. Every time I get really disillusioned about society, I remember that there are so many millions of young people in this country, and that so many of them are refusing to go along with the way things are. If the kids in the South are a hundred times more willing to accept the Negro as an equal than their elders are, this means—I hope—that kids elsewhere in the country are even more willing. I keep hearing that every generation in history has wanted to change life as they know it, but this generation seems to be dead-set on doing it instead of just talking about it and then forgetting the whole thing in later life. I'm not going to let that happen to me. I'm never going to be like my parents, in this particular respect, or the people who are so much more narrow than my own family. I have my own feelings about many things, and I'm trying my best to work out my thoughts on other subjects. If my folks had done this when they were teenagers—I mean actually stayed awake nights trying to arrive at beliefs and opinions instead of just accepting what they were told to believe—they wouldn't be the way they are. Well, maybe they did try to think for themselves, but I don't think it worked. I'm sure it didn't when they can honestly say they feel that Negroes—speaking of the race in general—don't have an equal capacity for intelligence. I'm only sixteen and I know better than that. It isn't just my opinion that some people are brighter than others and that race has absolutely nothing to do with it. It's a proven fact. And it's easy for me to accept it as a fact because my surroundings didn't succeed in conditioning me to think otherwise. My parents will never change their minds about Negroes. It's too late. But I learned the truth early enough so that it didn't conflict with things I'd believed all my life. I know other kids feel this way, too. I can understand adults not being able to change—I don't approve of this, but I can see how it can happen—but I can't understand them being down on teenagers for thinking for themselves. This generation is going in a better, more honest, more humanitarian direction, even if we do have long hair and kooky clothes. I'm sorry to rattle on so. I feel so strangely about this."

Kris—"Going back to something you said earlier, I've also wondered if I would date a Negro boy. Me being all rah-rah for the cause, I mean. I don't know whether I would either. If it were just me involved, I definitely would. If I met someone I wanted to go out with, that is. I wouldn't date a Negro just because he was one, just to prove that I'm not prejudiced. But I'm not the only one involved. My folks aren't really prejudiced, but they would die if I did anything 'scandulous.' They both have Negro friends where they work, close friends. But they're still against inter-marriage, and I know they'd think interracial dating was the first step toward that. I can see what Linda meant about teenagers helping the change to progress faster. In twenty years, I may have a daughter of my own. Considering the way I feel about this subject, she won't have to take my prejudices into consideration when she's choosing the people she wants to date. She'll be all on her own. It'll get easier with every generation. The way I feel now, I won't be upset if my daughter decides to date a Negro. By then, it won't be of personal harm to her because it won't have the social repercussions it does today. I'll only be concerned with the kind of boys she goes out with, not their color."

Hypocritical

Mike—"Don't you feel you're being a little hypocritical by not living up to your own rules now?"

Kris—"Not really. Barry was so right when he said that a person who believes in this cause has to keep prejudice from existing in his own private world. I can do a better job of that by setting a good example for my parents, and others in my own circle who may lean towards prejudice, than I would be  able to do by shocking them. Each person's world is different. I know mine pretty well. My folks are being helped by my feelings. It's making them see the narrowness of some of their own. I'd only hurt them, and hurt what I've accomplished so far, if I got involved in something I know they couldn't accept."

"Watch Her"

Linda—"That makes a lot of sense. I've thought about all this so much, and at times I get too furious to think straight. My folks are nothing compared to our relatives who still live down South. I've never come right out and admitted all of my feelings, but they know I don't agree with theirs. They just don't know to what extent. But I have this one aunt who is a real . . . well, it starts with B. When we moved to California, she said—not to my face, to one of my cousins who told me about it later—and I quote 'watch her—she'll come back married to the biggest, blackest nigger she can find.' I never told anyone about this before. It's almost as awful to repeat as it was for her to say. But, when I really get ticked off, I'd like to do just that, just to show her and everyone. I won't do it, of course. But just from listening to Kris, I see there are things I can do, and I intend to do them."

Barry—"If everyone who feels that way, right now, would start doing something about the situation, individually, the change wouldn't take very long at all. I'm willing to give something of myself to help, and you're willing to give something of yourself, and all we have to do is give it. Individual concern is of no help if you don't apply it."

Mike—"Well, I just hope we all hurry. I sound like I'm trying to press a panic button, but the whole world is watching while all this crap is going on in America. If it's up to the young people to solve the problem, we'd better get moving. It's insane the way things are now. They can't stay this way. If I thought they would always stay this way, I don't believe I'd go on living in this country, and I don't think this feeling is confined to just young people. All my life, I've heard about my dad's war record. He won a lot of medals, and has always been a real flag-waver. When I started to panic about being drafted, he really got shook. Finally, I just sat down and told him how I felt. It's different from the way it was when he joined the Army. He had something to fight against, and so do I. But he had something he believed in, to fight for. I don't have that. I hate to say this, but it's even worse to feel it. Things were probably even worse in America then—meaning the racial situation, but people weren't aware of it. I am aware of it, and I value my life too much to be willing to give it for something I don't believe in. I'm not being anti-American. I'm anti-hypocrisy. If there was an actual shooting war to decide whether this country would start practicing what it preaches, I'd enlist tomorrow! There aren't many things worth dying for, but to me, that's one of them. But I'll be damned if I'll willingly sacrifice myself to protect principles that seem to exist only on paper. If I have to go to war, and I will go if I'm called, I'm going to be fighting for the people I care about. Not to protect some slob of a cop in Mississippi so he can go on cracking the skulls of Negroes who want to vote. My God, how sick can you get? When I told all this to my dad, he couldn't say anything. There wasn't anything to say because I was making sense."

(Editor's Note: At this point in the conversation, the panelists went on to discuss their opinions about the draft, the war in Viet Nam, and other related subjects. A lack of space prevents us from printing the second half of their discussion now, but it will be continued in the next issue, so stay tuned.)

KRLA ARCHIVES

Mistaking The Four Monkees

By Louise Criscione

Just picture one very pretty princess who is about to become queen and one very jealous uncle who is determined to do her in before she reaches her eighteenth birthday. Then add four long-haired, unknown pop musicians who live together in a small but "tastefully" decorated apartment. The plot? Save the queen. The show? The Monkees. Result? A cross between Batman and Help.

In other words, a huge smash television show which no one (at least, not very many people) thought would come off. *The BEAT* ventured down to Screen Gems the other day to see this thing called The Monkees and our immediate reaction was – the show is out of sight! A complete about-face for us.

Doubtful

Approximately six months ago a gentleman appeared in the office to inform us of the show. We looked at him like he was absolutely out of his mind! A television show centered around a pop group sounded to us very much like another in a long line of hackneyed and thread-bare attempts at capturing the teen market on the screen.

Then a month or so ago teaser ads began appearing all over the country. "The Monkees is coming." "Everybody is going ape for the Monkees." "Monkee business is big business." All of which meant that somebody somewhere was prepared to spend a small fortune on four guys who had never worked together before.

Along about this time the Monkees traveled to the Stone camping grounds – the RCA studios in Hollywood – to record a single. They practically drove engineer, Dave Hassinger, (also from the Stone camp) out of his mind. They'd never recorded together before. In fact, except for Davy Jones it appeared that *none* of them had ever even cut a record! But no one was too sure about that fact so we'll just let it ride.

Anyway, when we learned that they were virtually amateurs at the art of recording we figured the record would come out sounding something like an infant group attempting to play a 12-string when they hadn't yet mastered a six-string!

Fooled Again

But we were fooled again when "Last Train To Clarksville" and "Take A Giant Step" were released. A two-sided smash and no one had even seen the television show yet!

We humbly bowed to the fact that the Monkees, despite their lack of experience as a group, had managed somehow to turn out a smash record. However, we were *not* prepared for total surrender. There was still the trite television show.

We *thought*. However, we were forced into a total surrender when we sat down in projection room 15 to view the latest attempt at teen humor. As the theme song poured out of the speakers and the four Monkees appeared on the screen in living, breathing color we admitted that there was a slim chance we had been wrong.

A half an hour later, we *knew* we had made a mistake! We know now that within a month after the show airs on NBC the Monkees will be the most talked-about "unknowns" in the country.

Probably the most familiar face among the Monkees belongs to David Jones, now known as Davy Jones but still the same English-born talent who appeared on Broadway in both "Oliver" and "Pickwick."

Most Popular

Davy tried the pop business several months ago, making the break from Broadway to Hollywood without much of a hit record but with mountains of determination. The rather short Davy will no doubt be the most popular Monkee. Because of his accent, his shiny hair, his blue eyes. Who knows?

Take a good look at Micky Dolenz and you know you've seen him before. He looks so familiar that you're bound to blow your mind trying to figure out *where* you've seen him before. Probably the next day it will hit you. He was once the blond-haired young boy who played Corky on the "Circus Boy" television series.

Micky's light blond hair has now changed to brown and he's grown quite a few inches since his "Circus Boy" days but the grin's still the same – and that's what gives him away.

Peter Tork and Michael Nesmith sort of share the honor of being totally unknown except to Greenwich Village and California folk addicts.

Ex-Folk

Peter is listed as "an ex-folk singer from the Village" and those familiar with ex-folk singers from the Village will probably recognize Peter but to the millions across the nation who will watch the Monkees, Peter will be a brand new face. Which isn't too awfully bad when you stop to consider that Peter doesn't have to face being type-cast *before* he's type-cast as one of the Monkees!

Mike "Wool Hat" Nesmith has the distinction of being known as someone who used to "live at the Troubador" – a local L.A. folk club. Meaning other than the California folks no one has ever heard of "Wool Hat." But after one look at the lank, typically Southern Mike you'll never forget him. At least, you won't *easily* forget him!

Fact is, you won't forget any of the Monkees. They're big business, you know. Also talented and fresh. *The BEAT* throws up the white flag. We surrender. We're crazy about the Monkees already!

...DAVY JONES – Most popular Monkee?

...THE MONKEES (l. to r.) Davy Jones, Micky Dolenz, Peter Tork and Mike Nesmith.

'PRIVILEGE' TAKING ADVANTAGE OF JOHN?

A movie being filmed in Birmingham, England, is taking advantage of the furor stirred by John Lennon's recent remarks on Christianity.

"Privilege," a biting satire condemning conformity, centers around a plot about a young singer pushed into heading an international Christian crusade.

Although the movie has no direct affiliation with the Beatles, it is particularly timely after the massive demonstrations against the Beatles because of Lennon's religious comments.

In the film, a full-scale evangelical rally staged by the Birmingham football grounds is climaxed by the teen crusade leader singing "Return to Christ" to thousands of local extras bearing "We want God" banners.

The Birmingham rally is described by directors of the film as the "largest mass demonstration of conformity since the Nuremberg rally staged by Adolf Hitler."

Besides satirizing religious fanaticism, the film is a free-swinging attack upon British television and press managers who turn singers into pop idols.

The film marks the debut for model Jean Shrimpton and former Manfred Mann group vocalist Paul Jones. Jones plays the part of the teen idol whose affections are directed towards Miss Shrimpton.

"Privilege" has been in the works since last February. Color filming is being done entirely on location and the film is scheduled to be completed late next month in London for a February release.

KRLA ARCHIVES

The Robbs Vs. The President

At first, I thought my eyes were deceiving me. It had to be a case of quadruple exposure or at least a severe attack of astigmitism.

But it wasn't that simple. The four identical looking gentlemen who just filed through the door were neither visual mirages nor imagination figments.

I had come to the interview prepared for the Robbs—three brothers and a cousin whom I suspected would be at least a slight similarity in appearance.

Instead, I was greeted by four young singers who looked more alike than some of Batman's impersonators. Right away they played their latest recording and their similarities were compounded.

On record, the Robbs give the impression of a single voice played simultaneously on four separate tracts. They easily have the most natural harmony of any group going.

The Robbs are a family of singers. They sing, they insist, "for the fun of it," and because they like each other's company. But somehow the old adage of "birds of the feather..." seems to fit their close knit group.

The Robbs' carefree attitude and tight personality interweaving probably accounts for the success of their last two records and their huge fan following on the "Where The Action Is" TV show.

It also accounts for their perserverence of singing even after a pathetically comical debut.

The Robbs' first public appearance came—you guessed it—in a Miami parade as the group played and sang on the back of a huge flat bed truck.

"We were riding along just fine," recalled Joe Robb, "when the driver of the truck 'accidentally' pulled the lever that causes the bed to empty its load.

"All of our equipment and all of us spilled down to the ground. We even had a piano that fell down on our drummer. By the way, he's not with the group anymore."

The Robbs' sense of humor is something else. And if I hadn't been forewarned that this calamity actually occured, it would have seemed natural to lump it with some of their other spoofings.

But this wasn't their only early misfortune. It was just a fitting beginning.

On our next appearance," continued Craig, "we were commissioned to play in front of a jewelry store. The chamber of commerce had hired us.

"But the guy in the jewelry store came running out and said we were hurting business. He gave us ten dollar each just to leave."

"Yeah," added Bruce, "we thought about coming back the next day and holding out for twenty."

But there is a serious side to the Robbs. This is most evident when they talk about their own music—even though it isn't what you would call serious music.

Dee Robb is the composer for the group, and when the conversation shifts to the group's songs, the speaker.

The Robbs' first record, "Race With The Wind," was labeled by many as a contemporary song, but Dee doesn't go along with that analysis entirely.

"When I write a song I do so because I'm in a particular mood," explained Dee. "They're usually happy or sad or express some other feeling. I don't try to get any great message across."

Dee's evaluation led to an extremely timely question. Just what is the role of today's pop singer?... just what should be the boundries of his dictates over the opinions and attitudes of the younger generation?

"I don't think singers have the right to assume the position of authorities on any subject except music," Dee said bluntly. "They should stick strictly to music and not try to be political or religious advisors.

"After all, President Johnson doesn't play the guitar."

Teens, Dee said, are easily influenced by their idols, and even songs that really have little philosophical intent are construed to have all sorts of meanings.

"What really bothers me is when I hear someone ask, 'Is this the way it really is... is this all that life means?'" said Dee. "A song is like a painting — it is an individual thing — and should mean different things to different people."

When the Robbs sing a song it means something to themselves—even though it isn't particularly aimed at driving a message across to the listener.

"We sing because it is fun to us," said Craig. "We just give 100 percent towards having fun."

And judging from the private life the Robbs lead, it is only natural that they should have fun singing.

...THE ROBBS

...BUFFALO SPRINGFIELD (l. to r.) Steve Stills, Richie Furay, Bruce Palmer, Dewey Martin and Neil Young

Buffalo Herding Clancy

By Louise Criscione

Nowadays Clancy can't even sing but the Buffalo Springfield have made it. And that's rather amazing in itself. Not because "Clancy" isn't a great record — it is. But because the Buffalo are even the Buffalo. And if you think that's mindblowing, you haven't heard *anything* yet.

The way the Buffalo came up with their name is even more unbelievable than the group. The story goes something like this — I think! They decided to form a group in the spring of '66. But they were too poor to afford rehearsal space, so they practiced at the edge of the road. And while they were practicing one day, a steamroller rolled past. The signs on the side of the roller eventually ended up on the walls of a Hollywood home. The signs read (just guess what?) "Buffalo Springfield." And that's how the Buffalo Springfield became the Buffalo Springfield.

Mind Blower

If you believe that story, your mind is already blown so you might as well continue on to the individual Buffalo because you're a lost cause anyway.

So, here goes. Steve Stills is the leader of the Buffalo Springfield — at least, *he* thinks he is. Steve's deep and throaty voice shares the vocal honors along with Neil and Richie.

Born in Dallas, Texas, Steve admits to a "gypsy childhood" which carried him through one southern city after another and even down into Central America. However, Steve calls New Orleans home. "Because, at least, I can remember the names of some of the streets there."

What musical star of magnetic proportions inspired Steve to enter the music business? Would you believe a respiratory infection? "I used to get up in the morning," declares Steve, "and yell very loud, once, sort of to clear everything up. Someone suggested I add pitch and tone..."

Thereupon, pitch, tone and the University of Florida were added to Steve's reperatory. However, Steve discovered that he preferred music to Political Science. So, the University was chucked and New York was "in."

You can't say that New York was a wasted experience for Steve. True, he didn't make it too awfully huge in the big city but he did meet Richie when they both played with the Au Go Go Singers. And then while he was on tour in Canada he met the leader of Neil Young and the Squires, who just happened to be one Neil Young, who latter became a Buffalo. But that's two years ahead of ourselves. And the story is confusing enough in chronoligical order!

Neil Young is the vocalist and lead guitarist for the Buffalo. His voice if funky but honest — and they say honesty is above all else. Neil says he's a "lover by nature." Also sensitive, poetic and extremely non-violent because "I used to get beat up a lot where I was a kid."

Mynah Birds

There he cut a record with The Mynah Birds but the lead singer got drafted, so Neil promptly bought a hearse in which he packed his guitars and a bass guitarist name Bruce and headed for California.

Beatles...
(Cont. from Page 1)

who proclaimed them their undying idols.

For about an hour there had never been a Manila... or a withdrawn album cover... or a seemingly insignificant quote lifted from context and blown out of proportion.

Critics had eagerly anticipated the Beatles' tour as ample proof that the Britons had fallen from the kingship of rockdom. If they have, then their U.S. tour — and especially their California performances — certainly didn't prove it.

Sandy Koufax and Juan Marcial seldom lure more customers to the erstwhile baseball parks. With tickets selling for $3.50 to $6, the Beatles played before huge crowds.

But it was the crowds' reactions — not their size — that was most convincing. There was no predicted air of uncertainty... no cautious skepticism.

It was just plain Beatlemania in one of its finest hours.

Being extremely popular in Westerville, Richie decided to tackle New York.

New York was not ready to be tackled, at least, not by one Richie Furay. He did meet a "gruff-voiced, smiling kid named Steve Stills" in New York and later joined the famous Au Go Go Singers and even managed to take a trip with the Singers to Texas — where they broke up.

It was back to New York for Richie and six months of dieting the hard way and working in Connecticut's factories. The sixth month ended, Richie received an urgent phone call from Steve. So, he immediately flew to California where he discovered the amount of success acquired by Steve on the West Coast — none. His decision to stay and be a Buffalo was probably the cause of many sleepness nights for Richie. Until "Clancy" came along, that is.

Dewey Martin is now the Buffalo drummer. Before that he was a baseball player, worked with the Grand Old Opry, Roy Orbison and Carl "Blue Suede Shoes" Perkins. He made the trip to L.A. with Faron Young, dug the climate so much that he came back in '64 with his fortune in his pocket — $30.

Needless to say, Dewey couldn't live on the climate alone and the $30 went so fast that he traveled up to Seattle and had a hit single with Sir Walter Raleigh and the Coupons.

That down the drain, Dewey returned to Southern California and worked with the MFQ and the Dillards before making it as a Buffalo Springfield.

Bruce Palmer insists upon being the group mystery man. However, he definitely stands out in a crowd since he is always seen wearing Indian clothes and beaded mocassins. He plays his bass guitar with his back to the audience and professes to be extremely camera-shy. Some say Bruce is from Liverpool, Canada and is 19 and 3/3 years old. Bruce himself doesn't say.

Dickie Davis is the non-playing member of the Buffalo. He escaped from the Eastern pre-school

(Turn to Page 23)

KRLA ARCHIVES

Psychedelic Music – Is

'Yes!' Says Group With Psych Sound

By Rochelle Reed

"People are ready for it now!" Paris Sheppard says. What is it that Paris feels people are ready for? A new music, a sound that may be the next musical innovation – psychedelic music.

Paris and Tony Scott, leaders of Fire and Ice, Ltd., are two of the forerunners of this new movement, or what could be a new movement. As of now, their music is still underground, played and understood by only a few. Old greats like the Beatles are experimenting with the psychedelic sound, while new groups are basing their entire repertoires on it.

Fire and Ice, Ltd. (the Ltd. was added when they heard of another group with the name Fire and Ice) have achieved the almost unheard of – being signed to Capitol without a reputation of merit or even a stable group. As this goes to press, it's anyone's guess as to exactly who are members of Fire and Ice, Ltd.

Back Up Group

This all came about when Capitol cut it's controversial documentary "LSD." Fire and Ice, Ltd. were the back up musicians on the album, for which they earned scale wages.

But one night a very high Capitol official heard the group as they tripped out (and this is meant as a mind trip induced by contemplation rather than one induced by the use of various drugs). The executive, his wife and some friends stayed at the studio almost all night, listening and dancing to the psychedelic spontaneous music of Fire and Ice, Ltd. In the end, the executive said, "Sign them!"

"They all agreed they went on a trip," Paris says of the evening. "At times they completely stood still, as if the music got them high." Which is precisely what it did, according to Tony and Paris. That's the entire idea of their music. "Lyrics float on top and weave in and out – words are an embellishment," Tony explains. "When we cut our album (The Happening), almost everything was improvised."

Paris feels this psychedelic state of music is a "twentieth centry attitude. It's happening all over – we're merely the first to get it together."

Born at 0

Paris Sheppard, flutist and vocalist, was "born at the age of zero," he explains brilliantly. After that Oscar winning performance, Paris began dancing as a child in shows, dressed in a white tuxedo and carrying a cane. In high school, Paris received the National Scholastic Press Association's scholarship award and had two of his paintings selected to tour the U.S., finally coming to rest in the Carnegie Museum in Philadelphia. A former art director at Kaiser Aluminum in Chicago, Paris also taught academic and professional courses in fine arts at the Ray-Vogue School in Chicago.

But a freer life called to Paris and he moved to San Francisco, where he became one of the voices of the beat generation. The blonde, blue-eyed painter-dancer-singer became a poet and was well-known for his spontaneous recitations in Bay Are coffeehouses. He found it easier to improvise than to prepare his material in advance – a quality that influences his music today.

Paris now sings, dances and plays a variety of instruments ranging from the reed flute to earth horn. And in his spare time, he designs men's sportswear.

Writes Naturally

Tony Scott is an English-born 29-year-old who has been in show business most of his life. An accomplished organist and pianist ("I prefer neither the organ nor the piano. They are both separate instruments, completely different. I prefer to write naturally and build electronically"), Tony moved to the U.S. when he was fourteen. But since then, he has lived in Italy, France and Africa.

When Tony was a child prodigy, he played classical music, but then switched to jazz. He is also involved in motion pictures and television as an actor and director – appearing on stage in both London and Hollywood.

Timothy Woods is the group's lead guitarist, and here because he was "tired of hearing the same thing over and over." Timothy hails from San Francisco, where he was playing with a band until Tony and Paris persuaded him to join Fire and Ice, Ltd.

Writes For Four

The group's drummer, Roy Durkee, trained to be a recording engineer, but then began writing material for the Four Freshmen. Roy plays guitar, drums, piano and trumpet.

But the most visually outstanding member of the group hasn't yet been mentioned. Barbara Jackson, Fire and Ice, Ltd.'s African drummer and tambourine player, choses to wear men's clothing and sports a shaved head.

From here on, it's anyone's guess as to who is in Fire and Ice. The prerequisites are that a member's mind is in tune with his leaders. And he must be genuinely interested in playing and having fun. Then he must be willing to be a member of the avant garde for what just might be the next sweeping change to hit the musical world, and the advent of an entirely new type of music.

THE NEXT BEATLES? – Paris Sheppard (left) and Tony Scott (right) stand over what may or may not be the Fire and Ice, Ltd. Barbara Jackson, sporting her bald head, kneels next to Tony.

PSYCHE-WHO?

Tune In, Turn On – Key To Real Understanding

"Psyche-WHO?" said one Sunset Strip teenager I captured in my relentless search for what might be called "what-in-the-heck-is-psychedelic-music?"

Other teens, or course, were more explicit, even mastering the pronounciation, but "psyche-who" seemed a good place to start.

First, psychedelic is pronounced psy-che-del-ic, and meaning-wise, boils down to mind-manifesting. Therefore, psychedelic music is mind-manifesting music. Simple, wasn't it?

But there is more. Mind-manifesting, although a nice sounding tongue-twister, doesn't say a whole lot. What it really means is that psychedelic music is free-form and spontaneous. Jazz is that way too. But psychedelic music breaks through the established structures of rock, jazz, folk and blues, incorporating them musically into one sound.

At first, psychedelic music is very difficult to listen to. It takes concentration and more concentration, so that you, the listener, can tell where a musician has been and where he is going. Maybe. A listener must put everything out of his mind and pay rapt attention, until the music seems to be an integral part of YOU, instead of someone else. A listener has to *tune in* and really communicate with psychedelic music.

A musician, playing psychedelic music, has to be *tuned in* with the rest of his band, following their every musical move, and in turn being followed. Finally, the right mood has been created and the musician's performance becomes effortless, for the instrument seems to almost play itself.

The direction music takes when played psychedelically depends on the backgrounds of the people performing. It will touch on many forms – jazz, rock, folk and often, if members of a group have a background in it, classical music has a way of weaving through the main sound pattern.

Lyrics in psychedelic music become like the frosting on a cake. The cake (music) is there and very good, but with frosting (lyrics) it becomes much better.

Lyrics, however, seldom tell a story in psychedelic music. Instead, they may be reactions to the music ("oh yeah, oh yeah") or just sounds, rather than words.

Most often, psychedelic music revolves around some title like "Under the Sea" and then proceeds to musically imitate the feeling that just such a trip would create.

And when the music has stopped and you feel like a human Ouija board, you can truthfully say you have been on a drugless, musical "trip." — R. Reed

KRLA ARCHIVES

It Next?

BRIAN...

GALE...

DENNY...

Q: DO YOU THINK PSYCHEDELIC MUSIC WILL BE THE NEXT BIG INFLUENCE ON POP MUSIC?

OH! WHAT THEY SAID...

Psychedelic music suffers from the label "psychedelic," which is often used to connote the use of drugs. Many entertainers, therefore, shy away from the use of "psychedelic" to describe their music. However, others feel that "psychedelic," with all it's connotations and misinterpretations, is still the best wrap-up term for the free, expanding type of sound.

Here's what they told *The BEAT:*

Frank Zappa, a Mother of Invention — "I don't play psychedelic music. It's for dopers. I don't want to be labeled that way.  **FRANK ZAPPA** We call our music the "new free music." ... Yes, I really do think this will be the next big influence on the pop scene ... music is now freed from the past."

Vocalist **Gale Garnett** — "I dig the concept but resent people who think they invented it. First, they must catch up with people like the Beatles ... No one bag will be dead right – some people think Pat Boone is their bag. But yes, psychedelic music is influencing the scene today."

Beach Boy **Brian Wilson** — (who resented summing up psychedelic in a few words) — "Psychedelic music will cover the face of the world and color the whole  **BRIAN WILSON** popular music scene. Anybody happening is psychedelic." Brian, by the way, has an apparent love for words. He coined "psychedelicate" during our conversation because it sounded great.

Papa Denny — "There is no such thing as psychedelic music. Have you heard any?"

Kenny Forssi, of Love — "No, psychedelic music is just like the sitar and Ravi Sankar. That influence played out before it gained any real impetus. Psychedelic music is accepted by only a few – it might take over but I don't think so."

Vocalist **Joey Paige** — "I like the idea and new concept of music. But I don't think teens know what it's all about. Frankly, I'm very concerned be-  **JOEY PAIGE** cause most musicians seem to use LSD. I personally don't need to take a trip. I'm happy with the world."

Terry Melcher, producer — "Psychedelic drugs are having an effect on music, but as for psychedelic music ...?"

John Beck, a Leave — "Psychedelic music has always been around. That's what music is all about. Psychedelic is just like saying music music — expanding on music. It's all very nebulus."  **JOHN BECK**

Herb Cohen is a producer who agrees with John Beck and feels the term "psychedelic" is totally useless because there is no such thing, or "only if you have no mind. There's nothing mind-bending or earth-shattering about it. No psyche is attached to it. I'm not putting it down, but most (current music labeled as psychedelic) gives the impression of a pseudo-narcotic state."

AND THE BEAT?

Carol Deck — "It's not exactly the sort of thing you can whistle in the shower. I think it's dull but it's where all music is going. But I don't like it – yet." Photographer Chuck Boyd  **CAROL** — "I think it's where all music is going, mainly because some of the big groups I've talked to think so. But some of it I just don't dig at all, although I do like some of the Beatles and Byrds music of that type."

Mike Tuck — "No, I don't think it will get too big. I think it's just a fad – another sound that's going around. People like to associate themselves with it because it's weird. But it's just another sound."  **MIKE**

Rochelle Reed — "Pscyhe-WHO?"

The Airplane Takes Off

By Carol Deck

In this business you meet so many new groups that they all tend to fade into one long line of starving but hopeful musicians and singers.

But every now and then, one comes along that has a little something special and you think to yourself, "Maybe this one will make it."

And you, as a reporter, try to do a little something for them, but you know they have to do most of it themselves, so you sit back and wait, doing what little you can.

And sometimes, very rarely, but sometimes, one of these groups does make it – they put out a successful record, play a number of big dates and people begin to talk about them and you no longer feel that you're the only person in his right mind who's ever even heard of them.

You remember the first time you heard of a group called the Jefferson Airplane. You thought the're coming up with weirder names every day, and the weirdest of all seem to be coming out of San Francisco, where this group's from.

You recall they were kind of far out – they're six quick witted people who talked circles around you and who wouldn't give you a straight answer to any question. But they were friendly and it was all in good fun, and you actually enjoyed the interview.

You went back and wrote a very complimentary article introducing the Jefferson Airplane to your readers, some of whom may have known more about the group then you did.

Then you began to hear things about them – mostly from the San Francisco area. And gradually you came to realize that they were pretty big around their home town.

They got a successful record out, played some impressive dates and a reporter for the San Francisco Chronicle started a one man campaign to make them the country's biggest group.

But still they were only happening around the Bay Area, even though they did get some national publicity through one short quote in Time magazine, but you found out later they weren't too happy about that.

Then you get a call saying they're recording again and wouldn't you like to come down and renew old acquaintances.

You troop down again, wondering if they've changed.

They have changed – in many ways – but all for the better. They were kind of far out before and you were afraid with a little success behind them, they'd really be weird now, but you discover that success has given them a little self confidence and they're now just being themselves and not putting anyone on anymore. They actually seem to be a little more down to earth.

There are other changes too. They have a new drummer – Spencer Dryden, who's from Los Angeles and who seems to fit in right with the others. They seem rather proud of the fact that they got him.

And you'd forgotten what a fantastic bass guitarist Jack is, so Marty reminds you by spending half the time raving about Jack and how the Byrds and Paul Butterfield were interested in him but he was a member of the Airplane and no one else could have him.

SPRINGFIELD WIN CLANCY

(Continued from Page 21)

world and came to California where he did lighting and stage managing at the Troubadour and was the road manager for the Back Porch Majority, Roger Miller and Barry McGuire.

He made Steve's acquaintance when Steve moved next door and ruined Dickie's eardrums with the aid of a powerful amp. When the Buffalo formed, Dickie was sort of adopted. He couldn't hear anything else anyway.

After two months at Hollywood's Whiskey, Brian Greene and Charlie Stone outbid 26 other record companies and ended up with the Buffalo. Says Steve: "I wanted Greene and Stone. I had seen these two way-out record producers riding around in their long limousine, one of them skinny and quiet, the other one with a beard and a carload of enthusiasm. They were just right for us."

And says Brian: "It was a natural for us. I haven't heard a group with so much talent since the Beatles."

So ends the saga of the Buffalo Springfield. And, actually, Clancy *can* sing.

LENNY'S BOOT PARLOR
1448 GOWER STREET
HOLLYWOOD, CALIFORNIA
90028

Guys & Gals!
Send For It!
Get It!
LENNY'S FREE CATALOG
with the latest in clothes and boots IS READY. Just your name and address on a 4c post card and it's yours.

KRLA ARCHIVES

Calendar of Happenings
WHISKY A GO GO
8901 SUNSET STRIP • 652-4202

• **SEPT. 1 – SEPT. 11**

BYRDS, BYRDS, BYRDS...

BYRDS, BYRDS...

NOW!

• **SEPT. 14 – SEPT. 24**

The CHAMBERS BROTHERS
THE HARD TIMES

COMING!

• **OCT. 5 – OCT. 15**

The Beau Brummels

COMING!

FOOD & FUN TILL 2 A.M. — AGE 18 & OVER WITH I.D.

KRLA ARCHIVES

America's Largest Teen NEWSpaper — 25¢

KRLA Edition BEAT

SEPTEMBER 24, 1966

Mick And Chrissie

A Mama and Papa

See Pages 15, 16 and 17

KRLA BEAT

Volume 2, Number 24   September 24, 1966

Walker 'Incident' Really 'Accident?'

Scott Walker is out of the hospital after the near fatal incident in his gas filled London flat, but the sullen American transport continues to remain mum on the circumstances that put him there.

Walker, who was found unconscious and required emergency treatment in a London hospital, wouldn't comment on speculations of suicide, but said the incident was caused by "a lot of pressures and a personal problem."

He also would not reveal what "the personal problem" was. But, Brian Sommerville, Walker's publicist, told reporters the incident was "obviously brought about by a fit of extreme depression aggravated by the effects of some tablets and drink he had taken."

The Walker Brothers' co-manager, Barry Clayman, tried to soften Sommerville's version. He said the whole thing was "an accident—entirely due to some pills he took and then an alcoholic drink."

The "accident" however, required Walker to have his stomach pumped—a rather uncommon procedure for someone who has simply inhaled too many gas fumes.

Since Walker's release from the hospital he has remained in unexpected high spirits—but a thread of tension is still evident in his speech.

"I think it woke a lot of people up, including myself," he told reporters gathered outside his home. "I'm still under a lot of tension, but I'm feeling a bit of relief."

Walker's hectic schedule, it is believed, had taken a heavy toll on him.

"I've learned to get over a lot of things, and I try not to let them get on top of me," he said. "I've been seeing the right doctor, and getting tranquilizers."

Since the incident, however, Walker said many of his worries are being obliterated. "The other guys are trying to help me. John is very helpful—especially on stage, doing things I worry about, like showing the band what to do.

"That's all being taken off my back."

Since his release from the hospital, Walker said he has been gratified by the letters and response from his fans.

"After the incident the fans were really great," he said. They sent loads of letters and gifts and flowers. I had a few letters from nuts saying 'how dare you,' but most of them were marvelous and sympathetic.

"I have a lot more respect for my fans than I did before. Some letters said: 'We love the Walker Brothers, but if there is that much pressure you should give it up.'

"But pressure wasn't the only reason. Nobody has the right reasons and I'm not telling anyone the right reasons."

JOHN LENNON, BACK HOME, TALKING AGAIN . . . "I hope to get to see more of America because it's the kind of place that might blow up some day, by itself, or with the help of some other country."

'American Scene Poor' — 'Benders

The Mindbenders have never been noted for their love of America. While they were here, the threesome commented in a BEAT interview that the only thing they liked about the U.S. was "the weather and the money."

But for once, the Mindbenders might be excused for their attitude about their former colonies. Once they returned home, they commented, "considering it was the home of pop music, the scene in America is pretty poor." But the Mindbenders last 22,000 mile tour was no ride to dreamland.

Air Strike

First, they were stranded by the air strike, which left them in Los Angeles when they were supposed to be in Portland, and San Francisco when they were supposed to be in Texas.

Then, they could only obtain a visa that would allow them to do concerts in states where each individual promoter applied for a separate permit. This meant they couldn't even stop to look at a radio station.

To top the whole thing off, the equipment they had to use "you wouldn't believe," said bass player Bob Lang. "Next time we go, we're going to take our own stuff, for a start. The drum kits were ropey as well," added Ric Rothwell.

"Some of our promoters were quite frightening," continued Eric Stewart, he intellectual-type of the group, and added that "the whole set-up wasn't as good as most visiting artists would envisage."

When we arrived at gigs, we'd ask them where the dressing rooms were. The usual reply was 'What dressing rooms?'"

"I don't think many of the promoters over there have realized that if they get a chance, the girls would maul us to bits. Some bloke met us at the ticket office and then walked us through the ballroom. We got about halfway before the bedlam started!" Eric continued.

Another concert, Ric said, was almost worse. "We got to one hall and went in by the side entrance. Just as we were looking for the dressing rooms, the supporting group suddenly stopped, turned round and said, 'And now from England, the fantastic Mindbenders!' The promoter gave us a shove and said 'You're on.' I was still carrying my sticks and clothes bag when I went on stage."

U. S. Huge

The vastness of America continued to fascinate the boys. Ric found this applied most to music. "Even if you've managed to get a number one record, it doesn't mean that they've heard of you all over the States. There are lots of specific areas where different kinds of music are popular."

And added Bob Lang, "on America, there is still a big parent thing. The kids aren't independent until they're over 21. Well, some are, but on the whole it's 21—whereas in England, the majority gain independence at sixteen and seventeen."

Eric Retains 'Animals'

Eric Burdon has been threatening to find himself another group for months now; one which would be, in fact, a back-up group for Burdon. Apparently, the "old" Animals were reluctant to stand in Eric's shadows and, thus, the amicable agreement whereby the group disband with Eric keeping the rights to the name "Animals" was reached.

Group Change

Following the completion of the Animals' Stateside tour, the group will return to England where the official personnel changes will be made.

Although Eric retains rights to the Animals name, he will lengthen it somewhat to include his own Therefore, the group will now be known as Eric Burdon and the Animals.

Immediately following the group changes, Eric and whoever will then make up the Animals will head for the recording studios as well as mking extensive television and radio promotion visits throughout England.

American fans are to get their first glimpse of the "new" Animals in late October when Eric and his crew return to the United States for a large college tour.

Those in the music business are a little surprised to find the Animals coming back to the U.S. on the heels of their last Stateside tour. Although the tour was highly successful, Eric was not at all happy with his American stay. He described American fans as "much wilder, less considerate, less hip and much louder" than their counterparts in England.

Threatened

Of course, it's no wonder Eric found the U.S. a little unbearable. Among other things, the Animals witnessed a Ku Klux Klan meeting, were threatened with race riots, had ice thrown at them, equipment sabotaged and were treated with a bomb threat.

Under these circumstances, one can easily see why Eric was quite fed-up with America and could hardly wait to return to England. However, he is, apparently, not so ed-up that he won't return in October!

BURDON — alone in spotlight.

Herman Beats Lennon In Solo Acting Role

While the Beatles were busy apologizing in America, Herman was quietly jumping ahead of John Lennon's gun by turning in a solo acting stint in London before the chief Beatle ever made it to Germany for "How I Won The War."

Admittedly, Herman's move was not nearly as dramatic as John's decision because while John is making a feature movie Herman's acting ability was put to the test in a television play.

But Herman will, perhaps, be seen by more people than John, as his play, "The Canterville Ghost," will be aired across the nation on November 2 on ABC-TV.

Herman secured a major acting role in the play which was filmed in London and also stars Michael Redgrave. However, the plot as well as Herman's role in the play are being kept a deep, dark secret in the hopes the curious will tune into the show on November 2.

Herman along with the Hermits are scheduled to begin filming their next MGM movie, "Mrs. Brown You've Got A Lovely Daughter," at the end of this year or early in '67.

While Herman's other film ventures have taken place in the United States, "Mrs. Brown" is now set for shooting at the Boreham Wood Studios in England.

Their next feature movie, to be made later in '67, will be a remake of the old Marx Brothers film, "A Day At The Races." However, it has yet to be decided if the actual shooting for this one will take place in Hollywood or England.

Inside the BEAT

Letters to the Editor	2
Monkees In Trouble	3
'In' People Are Talking About	4
Entire Beatle Coverage	6-9
Sonny & Cher Meet Press	11
Mick's Chrissie	15
Mama's and Papa's	16-17
Supreme's Special	21

The BEAT is published bi-weekly by BEAT Publications, Inc.; editorial and advertising offices at 6290 Sunset Blvd., Suite 504, Hollywood, California 90028. U.S. bureaus in Hollywood, San Francisco, New York, Chicago and Nashville; overseas correspondents in London, Liverpool and Manchester, England. Sale price 15 cents. Subscription price: U.S. and possessions, $5 per year. Canada and foreign rates, $9 per year. Second class postage prepaid at Los Angeles, California.

Letters TO THE EDITOR

Americans Sensitive?

Dear BEAT:
Well, it all happened a long time ago, when everyone started to complain about how the Beatles looked on the Ed Sullivan Show.

They complained about Paul's lip, about his appearance, about the sun glasses, about every little thing. Why was that? I just can't understand.

Another thing was John Lennon's comment on how they're much more popular than Jesus. Why would people stoop to such low things as to ban Beatle records? Why can't you Americans be like us English and take it as meant? John even apologized. Why? Because you Americans take everything the Beatles do the wrong way! You should know John by now but maybe John should learn more about *you* and why you're so sensitive about everything.

Yes, I said sensitive. Like about the banned Beatle cover on "Yesterday... And Today." I saw it and I think you're a bunch of... well, I'm just too polite to say it!

You Americans say you're hurt. Well, you only think of yourselves. If you had been real Beatle fans you wouldn't have (1) complained about how the Beatles looked on TV because maybe you look terrible once in awhile too; (2) thrown out your Beatle records because of John Lennon's remark about Jesus; or (3) said the Beatles hurt you. Did they hurt you by being different and not having to put out the same old cover with the same old stuff? Well, are you really hurt? Or is it that your foolish pride was hurt. Because why don't you take one big giant look and see who was hurt.

No, my friend, it wasn't you who was hurt—it was the Beatles, or have you forgotten them already? Have you forgotten that they have feelings too and while you're at it, look at yourself in the mirror after that. What do you see?

You hurt the Beatles because you didn't have faith in them and you wanted them to be perfect, to be God in other words, to perform miracles. Well, they are only human—but not like you 'cause they didn't try to hurt. They just wanted to be different, they wanted to prove to you that they were, and will always be, human. Now you don't care anymore and you're going to walk out on them because of it.

You shouldn't be hurt by them because they weren't trying to hurt; by John Lennon's remark, by the album cover, or by their performance on Ed Sullivan. You, instead, should be proud to be Beatle fans! You should be proud to have people who are still the same and haven't changed as idols.

No, they haven't changed—*you* must have! If you could hurt over such things that don't mean anything. And when you start changing, I'll be an American again.

Shelly Levy

Try To Find Yours

Dear BEAT:
I wonder how many of the people who have been condemning John Lennon for his remark about the Beatles being more popular than Jesus have actually taken the trouble to read the entire interview from which the remark is taken. The article in *Datebook* does not present the comment in the manner in which it is taken when read in context.

John appears, from the article, to be an extremely brilliant, somewhat frustrated and confused and a very lost individual. The world expects its Beatles to be perfect. They're not. John could not have known the consequences of his remark; he has always been honest about his agnosticism to his fans before and there is no reason why he should deceive us about his religious beliefs now.

Lennon is as entitled to his own opinions as everyone else is. Especially if the opinion is a mere expression of fact. How many people do you know who are truly religious and place religion above all else? Very, very few.

John's statement was not made out of conceit, rather a statement made as a result of the shock that Beatles or surfing or whatever could be allowed to separate the individuals from their God.

Sit up and take note of Lennon's statement before condemning him. No matter what your religion—Christian, Jewish, or even the dubious religion of those who do not know—the presence of a Supreme Being is the most important single factor of your existence. Try to find your God before you go out and buy your next Beatle record.

And act according to your beliefs; if you claim to be a Christian and condemn John, me or anyone else for their beliefs, you are a hypocrite. Christianity supposedly teaches love and brotherhood.

Jean Thielmann

Pious

Dear BEAT:
Isn't it time that the people of this country stop being so pious and phony? Regardless of whether one agrees or disagrees with John—one must respect him for his honesty. Regardless of whether he is right or wrong, he is not a phoney who would only say what he thinks all of his fans would like to hear.

For my own part, I find a lot of truth and humor in his statement. He prefaced his remark with two very important clauses: "It's a shame but..." and "It's ridiculous but..." and I am in full accord.

A nation that will plunk down $4.95 to buy a Beatle record quicker than it will plunk the same $4.95 into a collection plate at church does have its values mixed up and shouldn't take such great exception when the truth is pointed out to it. The fault is our own, not John Lennon's. His only crime is honesty.

Scott C. McDonald

Blasphemy?

Dear BEAT:
We want to tell everyone who is supporting the Ban The Beatles Records Campaign, that they are all being very narrow-minded. They should have the insight to look into the true meaning of a statement and then judge.

Hasn't anyone ever heard of free speech? To generally quote a Beatle, which seems to be the thing to do, "If Christianity's as good as they say it is, it should stand up to a bit of discussion."

Whether these people know it or not, they are frustrating to see them act this way. Sure, everyone is entitled to their own opinion, but carrying it to the point of trying to get a national ban of their records, and having bon fires from accumulated pixs, is carrying it a bit (to say the least) too far.

John Lennon is noted for his quotes and everyone has laughed them off before. But now he says something about Jesus and Christianity and everyone is jumping down his back crying "blasphemy."

Thank you for letting us say what we wanted to.

Georgia Reuss and Chris Salcido

Is Respect Important?

Dear BEAT:
I shall never in my ugly life turn on John for any reason. If he thinks different thoughts than I do, I'm not going to be offended. I can't say now if I respect him for his opinions, I honestly can't come along with a sure answer to that question now. I don't know if I respect him at all. I like him terribly, maybe even love him if it's possible, but I can't say I ever felt the feeling of respect for him.

The dictionary says to respect someone is to hold them in esteem or to appraise them for something they did. I never felt that way about John. He made it to the top from the bottom, he's made some awfully snobbish people cringe. He's been a trend setter—even if he doesn't admit it. For none of these things did I appraise him or hold him in esteem.

Respect puzzles me. Is it that important? I think so. In today's society if you don't have respect for yourself, respect from others and respect for others, you aren't such a good person it seems. Just liking someone isn't enough today.

I don't know, it bothers me. A lot of kids are mad at John for what he said. I am not. He's entitled to his own opinions. So is everyone else. I'm not going to get shook because someone I admire thinks differently than I do. I scoff at the kids that are going to burn their Beatle stuff.

I think it's just that John hit a nerve that has always been out in the open, yet everyone else was afraid to go near it.

John touched the nerve that no one dared to touch and now he's paying the consequences. I think it's unfair that he has to pay. Those people aren't mad because he lied about their point of view or because he insulted them. They, in my opinion, are mad and angry because the truth hurts. How many kids can quote volumes on the Beatles, and then again, ask anyone to name the disciples or 5 Bible stories and see if they can. That is what John was getting at.

He's been on a religious kick lately, reading a lot about it and forming opinions along the way. He realized that the people of today are letting their religion die and made the mistake of mentioning it.

Now I've decided. Now I respect John for saying what needed to be said. Maybe Christianity is a little more on it's feet now than it was before. I respect him for risking his future, and his name, to wake people up into the realization of what's going on.

I'm sorry that he, and the Beatles, have to reap all the ill feeling from his statement. I feel guilty because I know that what he said applies to me as well as all those others who are ranting about it and getting themselves into a tiff. But I'm glad it was said. I'm going to try harder now and get myself back on the right track.

Now, I not only like, admire and enjoy John Lennon. I respect him for saying something to help the entire world. The Beatles have done plenty but never before has anything they've done applied to so many and been of such help to so many.

Thank you, John Lennon. Someone ought to say it and I'd like to be the one to do so. I don't rate the honor but it does have to be said.

Julie Cook

A Great Bum

Dear BEAT:
We wish you would print this so people will know how two Beatle fans feel about John Lennon's statements.

The adults are the ones who are making a big deal about it. The adults think that even if the Beatles would say that they don't believe in God all their U.S. fans would follow suit.

Some disc jockeys in the U.S. have banned Beatle records. We don't think that is right. Because no matter what the Beatles say, they will always be talented. If they really are talented, nothing can stop them from being great and from people wanting to hear them.

John is outspoken and lives in part of the free world which includes freedom of speech. John was born with a terrific personality, the other Beatles might have been in a group but we doubt that they would have been such a great success without John.

John, no matter what he chose for an occupation, would have succeeded. If he would have chosen politics he could have been England's Prime Minister, a famous lion tamer, milkman, and maybe even a great bum. But he would have been a great "somebody." If the Beatles read this in *The BEAT*, we would like to say that we are not the only ones who feel this way. Beatles, we are behind you all the way!

Margie and Del Marin

Fakes Gone

Dear BEAT:
It's a good thing that Beatle John Lennon said what he didn't mean, for the Beatles will find that their fake fans have left them. They'll also discover that more people will accept them for their talents and not as a fad.

More people will stop screaming and more people will start listening and applauding. The Beatles are now "in." I have more faith in humanity than to believe people would throw a great deal of talent out the window because of a misinterpretation of words. The Beatles are a fad to some but to many they bring the pleasure of music. At last the Beatle fans can be counted.

Robert C. Schwent

Turtles Hungry

Dear BEAT:
In your August 27 issue you said that the Turtles were refused anything except water and menus at the L.A. International Airport coffee shop.

Well, it made me just plain sick. Some people must really think they are something special to let people go hungry just because they don't like the way they wear their hair or the way they look. Well, these people are snobs.

I think the Turtles are great. They can come to my house anytime for dinner.

Sandy

KRLA ARCHIVES

The Monkees In $6 Million Suit

The Monkees had their share of trouble before they ever even hit the television screen. A temporary injunction asking for $6,850,000 and a delay in the debut of "The Monkees" was sought by two plaintiffs who charge Screen Gems with lifting the idea for the new series from them.

The plaintiffs, David Gordon (director of public relations for United Artists TV) and David Yarnell (in charge of programming and production for RKO General) claim they approached, presented and worked with Screen Gems during the past five months on a series which was allegedly very similar in nature to "The Monkees."

According to Gordon and Yarnell, the idea they presented to Screen Gems was to be named "Liverpool, U.S.A." and was to be centered around a rock 'n' roll quartet, composed of English and American members. The show was to have combined elements of comedy and contemporary music.

Gordon and Yarnell charge that in November Screen Gems informed them that the corporation was not interested in "Liverpool, U.S.A.;" however, it is the contention of Gordon and Yarnell that "The Monkees" takes its concepts and storylines from "Liverpool, U.S.A." without permission.

Court action was filed in the New York State Supreme Court and names 14 defendants in the suit, including Screen Gems, RCA Victor, Burt Schneider and Bob Rafelson (producers of "The Monkees") and co-sponsors of the show, Yardley and Kellogg.

Red Baldwin, publicist for Screen Gems, told The BEAT that despite court action "We're ("The Monkees") going straight ahead."

As you undoubtedly know, "The Monkees" concerns the antics of a rock group composed of four members — three of which are American and one of which, Davy Jones, is English.

Screen Gems continues to pour money and time into promoting the color series and recently held a gigantic block party at the studio to introduce the press to The Monkees. During the outdoor festivities, continuous showings of two pilot films were being held in the projection rooms.

..."THE MONKEES" (l. to r.) Mike, Mickey, Davy and Peter face a six million dollar law suit in New York.

Simon, Garfunkle Back In England

Simon and Garfunkle have returned to England, the sight of a very successful tour for them early this year.

The duo will spend four days there and will tape two BBC-TV specials for transmission later.

Two personal appearances have been planned for them but hopes for a concert tour look dim.

"The Dangling Conversation" has just been released there.

Len To England

Len Barry's going to England. Following the recent controversary over Barry not wanting to appear with long-haired groups, he is returning to Britain this month for radio and television appearances to promote his latest single, "I Struck It Rich."

The record is set for release the day he arrives in England.

$1 Million's Worth Of Chug-a-Lugging

Roger Miller's first album, "Chug-a-lug, Dang Me," has finally chugged up to the million dollar mark in sales.

His two previous albums, "The Return of Roger Miller" and "The Golden Hits of Roger Miller" have already been certified as Gold Records and now the first one has caught up with the second two.

Miller has also been signed to his own television show which will air on NBC September 12.

Beatles In Air Fright

The Beatles are very nervous about flying, The BEAT has learned from several sources who spent a great deal of time with the foursome during their U.S. tour.

Their fright stems from the fact that the plane in which they toured America last year crashed and burned only four months after the group had used it.

This year, the plane in which the Beatle tour was flying threw sparks over Seattle.

The drummer for the Remains, who has a phobia about flying anyway, became nearly hysterical and had to leave the plane. Two members of the Ronettes decided to leave also.

The Beatles remained aboard, however, and continued their flight, but were reported "a little jumpy."

Hard Times Join 'Action'

The Hard Times have been added to the list of regulars on Dick Clark's "Where The Action Is."

Other regulars include Steve Alaimo, Tina Mason, Keith Allison, The Action Kids, Paul Revere and the Raiders and the Robbs.

The Robbs were the last group added to the roster of the daily nationwide pop show.

Gene Pitney Headed Home

Gene Pitney is in England on his way home to America from Italy.

But his visit in England will be brief and only for social purposes — he will not do any radio or television shows.

He will then return to America for a short while then go back to England for 10 days in October to promote his next single, "Cold Light of Day."

Georgie Fame To Vacation In U.S.

Georgie Fame will vacation in America the latter part of this month.

He will be in the country for a week and his only scheduled appointments are calls on radio and television stations in New York and Los Angeles.

Fame has just completed an extensive tour of England and a short trip to Zurich for a Swiss television appearance.

Herbie Buys CBS Studios

Herb Alpert's Tijuana Brass is moving into a new home — a million dollar Hollywood recording studio that was built by Charlie Chaplin more than fifty years ago and has since become a landmark.

Alpert and Jerry Moss, owners of A&M Records and Tijuana Brass Enterprises, announced the purchase of the CBS-La Brea studios from the Columbia Broadcasting System for a sum in excess of $1,000,000.

The studio, which has housed numerous famous tenants through the years, will provide needed space for the rapidly growing A&M organization which, within the past 18 months, has become one of the largest indpendent recording companies in the world.

Besides Charlie Chaplin's companies, the property has been occupied by Red Skelton's Van Bernard Productions.

After it's purchase by CBS, it's chief usage was as the production facility for Paisano Productions' television series, "The Perry Mason Show."

The studio is well equipped to handle Alpert's enterprises. It contains three sound stages, two office buildings, four other buildings for multiple usage, carpentry, electrical and special effects shops, scene docks and a fully equipped power plant.

Moss said that construction of a complete and comprehensive recording studio and a fully equip-

P. & G. Coming

Peter and Gordon are coming back to America on October 1.

Following a four-day tour of Ireland and a string of radio and television dates they'll fly here for a three-week tour.

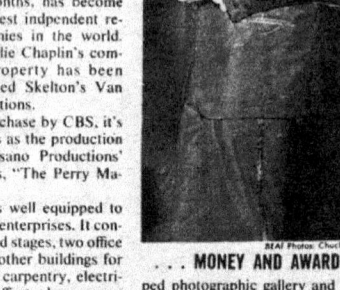

... MONEY AND AWARDS

ped photographic gallery and studio will begin shortly.

All existing facilities will be utilized for the Alpert and Moss companies' varied operations. Moss said that all A&M records and Tijuana Brass personnel would be moved into the facility by Nov. 1 of this year.

Well-known TV producer searching for new groups and songwriters. Contact Mr. Desmond (213) 463-6209

KRLA ARCHIVES

Letters To The Editor
(Continued from Page 2)

For Rascals How About Us?

Dear *BEAT*:

Could you print a fact sheet on the Young Rascals, or give me information as to where I could obtain one?

So far as I know, *The BEAT* is *the* publication that recognizes the Rascals for the four talented, groovy guys they are. But those recognitions have been few and far between, so . . . how about something new and groovy? More pictures of them, anything!! Please!!!!

A Rascal Fan

Dear Rascal Fan:

For a fact sheet how about looking through the back issues of *BEAT*, such as the Feb. 12, May 21 or Sept. 10 *BEAT*s.

The BEAT

Impartial?

Dear *BEAT*:

I am under the impression that a newspaper is supposed to maintain an impartial view of things, which isn't evident in *The BEAT*. I think that you are printing too much of a private opinion concerning the Beatles. I don't think that you should show so much of an opinion in your articles, which run about 2 to 1 – Beatles to Stones.

Recently, *The BEAT* has been building up the Beatles to a peak they can't possibly attain. Their talent has been fading away but The BEAT continues to give the opinion that they are as great as they were last year. *The BEAT* would probably be a much better paper if so much of a private viewpoint could be omitted.

Debby Nelson

P.S. I don't really expect you to print this because I probably have the wrong viewpoint to suit you.

John 8:4

Dear *BEAT*:

I don't think it was a coincidence that John 8:4 appeared after your headline in the August 27 issue of *BEAT*. As you know, John 8 is the chapter in the Bible in which Jesus rebukes the self-righteous accusers of another. He says that whoever is without sin may cast the first stone. When Jesus looks up the accusers are gone. How about it, Tommy Charles and Dough Layton, are you faultless enough to cast stones? Or are you just witch-hunting (with a five month old quote) for your own publicity?

Anne Kohler

P.S. If they were well enough informed to start such a movement, why didn't they know about this quote months ago? I did and I'm just a casual radio listener. I know you won't print this because it would make trouble for Charles and Layton, but after all, haven't they made enough trouble for John?

THANKS

Dear *BEAT*:

Thank you so much for your great coverage of the Beatles' stay in America. Please keep it up (especially the excerpts from their press conferences.) We luv ya for it.

April Orcutt

ANY BEATLE FRUITS?

Dear *BEAT*:

John Lennon, a member of the mop-haired foursome, better known as the Beatles, got the gang in dutch when he expressed his views relating to the popularity of Jesus Christ and Christianity versus the Beatles.

It's too bad his views were exercised in the public print, that his outlook has become cognizant to all. On the other hand, the cat is let out of the bag and the populace does know the true attitude of this self-esteemed group who would elevate themselves to such a lofty position.

Their agent, Brian Epstein, had the unfavorable duty to word wash up the mess and to condition the minds of the public that what John said was twisted, "displayed out of context." Naturally, a public disdain of John's statements could hit hard, where it hurts, in the pocketbook.

The mop-haired clique is really out of hand when such statements would nip and tear at the very foundations of a Christian civilization; one that has given so many benefits to society, despite those who have degenerated, misused it.

Has the Beatle group produced any good fruits that made for a better generation of young people? If the answer is in the positive, what are they? To me, their apparent pseudo-intellect is just as empty as their neurotic, sensual form of bedlam they label "music."

May their popularity go down – where it belongs.

G. B. Moultrhop

Stone Remark

Dear *BEAT*:

A chance remark by John Lennon – taken wholly out of context and thus given an entirely different meaning – has mushroomed into a terrible thing.

Being a fairly good Christian (and a Beatle fan), I too was quite shocked when I first heard about it. But now that I know what John really meant by what he said, I can't understand all the hullabaloo. Why doesn't all the fuss and ban the Beatles' records die now that John's true meaning is known?

One more point: If this remark – in or out of context – had been made by anyone else, even a Stone, nothing would've come of it. But let a Beatle say it and all heck breaks loose! It makes me angry; why can't we leave those poor guys alone? I guess it really must be open season on the Beatles.

Sylvia DuFresne

Disappointed By Raiders

Dear *BEAT*:

I would like to address this letter to Paul Revere and his Raiders. I didn't know where to send it, so I'm hoping you'll print it.

Dear Raiders:

Let me explain who I am. I'm one of those girls who you refused to give your autograph to. If that doesn't refresh your memory, it happened when you were at POP with the program "Where The Action Is." I'm not the only one who is disappointed with the Raiders. Out of all those teens in the group I came with '(a bus full) not one will say the Raiders were friendly.

You see, this was my first autograph hunt. To my knowledge, I was not being rude in my approach to get a Raider to sign his name. If I was, please accept my apologies. I hope you'll be polite enough to give me a reason for your behavior toward autograph hunters. I'm sure *The BEAT* will be happy to print your reply. Thank you.

Margie

'in' people are talking about...

The Hell's Angels helping the Beatles and wondering if top groups should hire the Angels to assist them in security . . . The Monkees' party and why they've let their hair grow so long . . . Why Sonny & Cher's fan mail has dropped considerably in the fan magazines' mailrooms . . . What made Carl Wilson decide to admit that he's married to Billy Hinche's (of Dino, Desi & Billy) 16 year old sister, Annie . . . Why Mick was chosen to play Ernie and wondering if the rockers will win and be left alive . . . Why Drake will not be re-joining the Raiders . . . Why we should all hurrah Hazel.

PEOPLE ARE TALKING ABOUT whether or not Spain will be the next "in" country and if Los Bravos is the start of something big . . . The real story behind the Richard Pryor-Maurice Warfield deal and who is doing all the phoning . . . Joan being aced out by Cass . . . Whether or not Bob Dylan really had his head shaved when he was in the hospital . . . How the Sandpipers are going to sing "Guantanamera" on stage when they are minus the girl who sang at their recording session . . . What Epstein would do if someone spelled Cyrkle, circle . . . How many different ways you can spell Eleanor . . . How cherished the Association are going to be in court.

PEOPLE ARE TALKING ABOUT the group which is a little too obvious in its imitation of the Yardbirds . . . Who got inside to do that Strip story for a national magazine . . . Why John went back to England and re-opened his mouth to the press . . . The changes that hurt in the Turtles . . . Why certain British groups continue to knock the U.S. while pocketing American money . . . Whether or not Jimmy Smith is really the Hoochie Coochie Man and if he isn't how come he's saying he is . . . The Chip who travels a lot . . . Where Renee will walk . . . What the 4 Seasons have under their skin . . . Billy Joe Royal's campfire girls . . . What does become of the broken hearted.

PEOPLE ARE TALKING ABOUT the headline in a national trade magazine which read: "Beatlemania Turns To "Beatle-waneia'," and quoted figures from their recent tour to justify the headline . . . The Jan & Dean discs which continue to flood the market . . . The new image Jackie . . . Johnny Rivers joining Herbie in the Spanish language . . . See See Rider and how many people are going to ride on it before it's never heard from again . . . How much advantage some publicists will take and how long groups are going to put up with it . . . How funny it is that most magazines are just now printing that Jill has joined the Mama's & Papa's when, in fact, she's just left the group . . . How ironic it is that Diana sings "Money" . . . The return of McGuire.

PEOPLE ARE TALKING ABOUT N.D. and how he is a tightrope walker but is afraid to fly . . . The sitar that soothes . . . Leslie wanting to be treated like a lady . . . If Bobby were a carpenter he wouldn't have nearly as much money . . . The German reporter who actually had the nerve to ask Ringo if it would damage his face if Zak threw some spaghetti in it . . . Who is really singing under the name "Grassroots" . . . Cannibal and the Headhunters re-releasing "Land Of A 1,000 Dances" and wondering how many more are going to come our way . . . How closely one of the "old" Animals resembles Brian Jones.

KRLA ARCHIVES

On the BEAT
By Louise Criscione

The Beatles have gone and the John Lennon controversy should really be over by now. But, of course, it's not. John has apologized repeatedly for "opening my mouth" and chooses to blame only himself "for not thinking what people a million miles away were going to say about it."

John went on to add that he was once an atheist but is now "more of a Christian than I ever was." John is not, and has never been, sorry that he said what he did. He is only sorry that it was so misinterpreted by Statesiders. He was apparently terribly upset over the furore his quote caused and, in fact, admitted that five years ago he would have simply chucked it all and refused to tour again.

Created Hate

But now, today, he couldn't do that because "I couldn't go away knowing that I'd created another little piece of hate in the world." So, he came and explained and apologized and let's hope that ends it.

John has already begun filming "How I Won The War" in which he plays a soldier in a platoon of eight men. There is talk that Richard Lester, director of the film, will ask John to trim his Beatle tresses a little more for the comedy; however, John has already submitted to the scissors and is unlikely to part with any more of his hair. The movie is being filmed in color and is scheduled for a May release by United Artists.

...JOHN LENNON

An ex-Yardbird and an ex-Animal are going to join forces in a new group which has not yet been named. Paul Samwell Smith, the alleged brains behind the Yardbirds, left the group on the grounds that he wanted to concentrate on writing and producing. However, he is now joining the group which will also include ex-Animal, Hilton Valintine. Their records will be independently produced by the group and their first single is due out in October. Oughta be wild – electronic soul, maybe?

A Knicker Mess

The Young Rascals are in the midst of a "knicker" controversy. Seems that the group started out with their knickers, used a knicker shot on the cover of their LP, and then decided to drop them. Fans on the East Coast are a little bit up-in-arms over the missing knickers while those on the West Coast are used to anything and, therefore, are not fazed by Eddie on stage in a combination of gold, turquoise, blue, black and red!

One New York City fan moaned, following a Rascal performance in Central Park, that "they don't look so happy without their knickers." What????? Anyway, it remains to be seen if the Rascals will go back to the knickers or stay in their sort of "come as you are" outfits. I, for one, vote that they get a hit record first and then worry about their clothes.

A hot rumor is flying that Jeff Beck, Yardbird guitarist extraordinaire, is soon to get his walking papers from the group. For one thing, his health is not too fantastic and his tonsils continue to flare up, causing the cancellation of the Yardbirds' San Diego appearance.

Based On Fact

The rumors of Jeff's departure have been making the rounds for several months now, partially based on fact and partially on fiction. However, this current crop is, unfortunately, based heavily on fact – though, groups as well as individuals are known to change their minds.

Wayne Fontana, formerly of "Game Of Love," and lately of only bombs, was married two weeks ago in England to 17 year-old Suzanne Davies who is from Wayne's hometown, Manchester. Ironically enough, Wayne has just finished waxing a song entitled, "Please Stop The Wedding." But no one paid any attention to his plea.

...ERIC BURDON

Apparently, Eric Burdon didn't dig this last Animal tour of the U.S. Says it was like a prison. Of course, they toured the South and ran into race riots, bomb threats and the Ku Klux Klan. Can't for the life of me imagine why Eric would want to go back to England, can you?

Donovan Is Coming Despite Loss Of His Permanent Visa

Donovan, whose "Sunshine Superman" has topped the American charts, is set for a Stateside visit during the latter part of September.

It's to be a rather short tour as the British folk singer will make only six personal appearances.

For a while it was feared that the tour would not materialize at all as Donovan had his permanent entry visa revoked because of a court case he's involved in here.

"But the American Embassy has stated that he can be granted a temporary visa for each visit," his manager Ashley Kozah said.

While in the U.S., Donovan will perform one concert each in Chicago, San Francisco and New York and three in Los Angeles.

Besides the concerts, he will undertake limited television promotion in conjunction with his latest album which is to be released shortly before his tour.

Stateside fans are anxiously awaiting their opportunity to see Donovan's new album which is to be released shortly before his tour.

Stateside fans are anxiously awaiting their opportunity to see Donovan's new "image" which was launched with "Sunshine Superman" and features Donovan in suits and ties rather than the more informal attire he has been noted for.

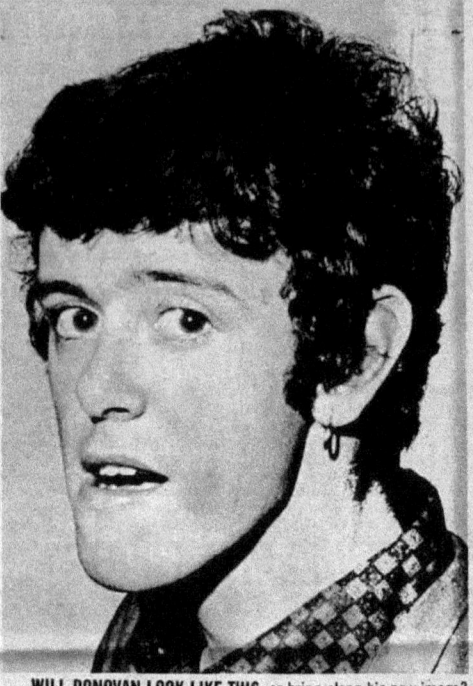
...WILL DONOVAN LOOK LIKE THIS, or bring along his new image?

Label Dispute Halts Trogg's American Visit

The Trogg's tour of America set for this month is off because of disputes over what label they are on in this country.

Both their first single and their first album have been released on two different labels in the U.S. and it appears that until someone finds out what label they are on they won't be coming over.

Instead they are going on a tour of Scotland.

There is hope they will make it here by the end of the year and their New York agent is negotiating for an appearance on "Ed Sullivan" for them.

Monkees Finish First P.A. Tour

The Monkees have just finished their first public appearance tour and are now back at work on their television show.

The group, created for the TV show "The Monkees," made their first public appearances together in Chicago, Boston and New York, then returned to the West Coast.

A heavy shooting schedule for the show will curtail most performances by the group for a while.

Their first record, "Last Train to Clarksville," has been released and appears to be on its way up.

Visas Are Denied Them; 'Dream' Halted In U.S.

After a three month visit in America, Them have left the country and returned to Ireland to get re-organized.

The group had some problems with the immigration authorities trying to get in the country, but with the help of BEAT readers and several lawyers they did enter America late last May.

Since then they have made numerous personal appearances, mostly in California, although they never did receive clearance to appear on television or do any recording.

While they were here their lawyers, both in America and England, successfully got them out of contracts with their old manager, producer and recording label, but could not get an extension of their visas which ran out August 31.

The lawyers also stopped the release of a record titled "Gloria's Dream" under the name Them. The record, actually recorded by several people that were in the group for a short time quite a while ago and sounds like "Gloria" revisited, is being released here under the name The Belfast Gypsies.

Just before Them left, Parrot Records released a single by them, "I Can Only Give You Everything" and "Don't Start Crying Now" – which was cut some years ago.

The guys knew nothing about the release of the record and didn't really think it was the strongest of their material, but didn't complain.

There have been some changes in the group since it first formed and it now consists of Van Morrison, Alan Henderson (the only two members left of the original group), Ray Elliott, Jim Armstrong and David Harvey.

Alan says he doesn't expect anyone to leave the present group but there are slight chances that additions may be made as part of their re-organization.

Before leaving they told The BEAT that they wished to express thanks to everyone who had helped them get into and stay in the country and to say how much they enjoyed it here.

They also expressed sincere regret at leaving California, which had become like another home to them, but they promised they'd go home, get organized, produce some more hits like their first ones – "Gloria," "Here Comes the Night," "Mystic Eyes" and "Baby Please Don't Go" – and be back soon, probably the first of next year.

KRLA ARCHIVES

Barrow Dispels Beatle Rumors

As Seen By A Beat Reporter After A Long Luvley Chat With Tony Barrow

On August 12, 1966, four Beatles arrived in these United States.

It was their fourth visit, but it felt more like their first. They hadn't known what to expect then, and they didn't know now.

The apprehension they felt was understandable. They had heard about the storm of controversy which had broken in our country, but they couldn't appraise the situation until they could see it for themselves.

So, they came and they saw.

At high noon on August 30, they boarded a plane at Los Angeles International Airport and went home smiling. For, once again, they had conquered.

Conquered really isn't the right term, though. This word is synonomous with winning, and it wasn't a question of that. It was more one of finding out how much they'd lost of what they'd already won years ago.

The reply came on fourteen different stages in fourteen different cities. From those platforms, the Beatles saw the same sea of faces and heard the same roar of welcome, and they knew they had lost absolutely nothing.

That answered their big question. Two days after the foursome had flown back to London, Tony Barrow, the Beatles' Senior Press Officer and *The BEAT's* London Correspondent, did his best to answer mine.

Tony had remained in Hollywood to attend to some of the countless post-tour details, among them this interview. When I met him that evening, at the comfortably-quiet restaurant in his hotel, I suppose he figured I was going to ask the question he has surely heard a thousand times these past few weeks, and he was right.

Coming Back?

After the usual pleasantries, my first words were: "Are they coming back next year?"

He didn't say yes, but he didn't say no (which was fortunate because I was prepared to plunge my pencil into my heart if he had.) What he did say was this: "Nothing is ever set twelve months in advance, but I see no reason why they won't be back."

He went on to say that two offers have already been made to book the Beatles in 1967 (one from Shea Stadium, the other from somewhere he didn't mention), but that there were no commitments as yet.

I then told him about the rumors which had prompted my question. I'd heard the Beatles were tired of touring, tired of performing, and anxious to devote their time to recording and making movies.

"Everyone is tired at the end of a tour," he said. "There's no fun in being jostled about and packing up every hour and riding around in florist's delivery trucks. But afterwards you look back and think of all the thousands of people who got to see you and it seems different then."

(A slight interruption – The Beatles solved a part of the packing-up problem by bringing along just two sets of on-stage costumes. In some cities they wore the forest green outfits we saw in Los Angeles and San Francisco; in others they wore gray-and-pink-striped suits. But they brought along fourteen different sets of matched shirts, and I imagine they had great fun hauling those around, not to mention the clothes they brought to wear off-stage.

Beatle Movie

The Beatles *do* plan to devote a lot of time to movies and recording. John's film began shooting the Saturday after he returned home, and the next Beatle movie ought to get underway just after the first of the year.

Tony had this to say record-wise: "Recording is a basic, long-term thing with the Beatles, and also the most rewarding and creative. I don't know that the writing of songs takes them longer than it used to, but they're progressing lyrically, they're more profound; they've passed through the I-love-you-and-you-love-me-stage. They do spend far more time working out how to present a song. They've passed through the three-guitars and-a-drum stage, too."

The following is a "transcript" of the remainder of our question and answer session. Hopefully, I have Tony's answers word for word. If not, I offer him my humblest apologies in advance. I also promise to learn how to read my own writing one of these days.

Q: At the Hollywood press conference, Paul said that the 'sound effects' in "Tomorrow Never Knows" were created by a series of tape loops. Would you explain what these are?"

A: "Tape loops are short pieces of recording tape joined back to back. For this particular record, they used tapes they'd been recording at home on their own equipment. Paul is the most prolific at this sort of thing.

Q: Why did the Beatles decide to appear at stadiums instead of places like the Hollywood Bowl?

A: Los Angeles is a good example of why. You either repeat the Bowl and disappoint the people who can't get in, or you look for somewhere larger. The Beatles played to more people at one performance in Dodger Stadium than they did with two shows last year at the Bowl.

Bomb Concerts

Q: I understand there weren't many complete sell-outs. Did they have any concerts they considered to be bombs?

A: "No – empty seats are nothing to go by. It's all in the way it's reported. You might see a headline that says *10,000 empty seats at Beatle concert*, but read on and you'll find there were 40,000 seats that weren't empty. Tickets weren't even printed for some seats, you know. The stages had to be put somewhere and it wouldn't have been fair to sell tickets in seating areas behind the stage. But, this kind of reporting isn't necessarily an attempt to knock the Beatles. It's just a turnabout so they'll have something new to say. How many ways can you say *Beatles a smash success?*

Q: Was this year's tour as financially successful as 1965's?

A: "It grossed more, and umpteen thousands more saw the Beatles."

Q: I read somewhere that only 12,000 attended the Candlestick Park concert in San Francisco. Could this be true?

A: "It must have been a misprint. I don't have the exact attendance figures, but I'd say there were at *least* twice as many."

Editors Note: Tony's guess was close. There were, in fact, over 25,000 at Candlestick Park.

Fire On Plane

Q: Was there a fire on the plane during the tour?

A: "Not *on* the plane, but as we were about to take off from Seattle, one of the engines backfired and flames did shoot out – we were in a DC6, I believe, and were used to electraplanes where this never happens."

A: Did the incident cause any commotion?

Q: "Two people did get off the plane to find other transportation. One of the Ronettes and the Re-

... TONY BARROW — Beatle press agent and columnist for **The BEAT.**

mains' drummer."

Q: Speaking of Seattle, what was *that* all about?

A: "We still don't know, and it hardly seems worth further investigation. Four or five days prior to our arrival there, a newsman telephoned me from Seattle – I don't know whether he was from a radio or TV station or from a newspaper, but he was in the news media – and quoted portions of the Paul-Jane rumor to me. Not the whole story, but the basic thing. I said it was absolutely not true. The story broke *after* an official denial had been made.

Q: Is it true that the bridal suite was reserved and a wedding cake actually ordered?

A: "Yes, the arrangements were made by a mysterious Mr. Bartholomew."

Q: Did a lot of people believe the rumor?

Where's Paul?

A: We left Seattle right after the concert, but even then everyone wasn't convinced. A local disc jockey who came back on the plane with us got on board, looked around and said 'Well, there you are . . . ' When asked what he meant, he said *'Where's Paul?'* At this point, Paul emerged from the john.

Q: This incident is mild compared to what happened at the outset of the tour. Do you think the uproar over John's comments ruined the tour for the Beatles?

A: "No. Once John was able to be here and explain himself, the majority of sane, sober people of average intelligence realized that John had made the kind of remark we might all make. That the church itself might make and then say let's *do* something about this. It wasn't an insult, it was a statement. According to an A.P. reporter, even the Vatican has taken it in the way it was intended."

Q: Were there any signs of anti-Beatle reactions across the country?

A: "Not in any way. Five 'klansmen' did show up in their gear in Washington D.C., but they went home in about fifteen minutes – it was dinnertime. They didn't seem to be anti-Beatle. I didn't hear this myself, but I understand second-hand that what they were shouting was 'Don't go in there, there are niggers.'"

Q: Good God – I mean, back to the subject of rumors for a moment. What was all this about the Beatles perhaps not leaving until September 9?

A: "I have no idea how this rumor started or why that particular date. Just yesterday, a reporter refused to believe they had left at all. He challenged me with 'Well, how come *you're* still here?' I asked 'How come *you* are?' 'I live here,' he said. And I said 'For the next couple of days, so do I – do you mind?'"

Brian Overdue

Q: Something else I've been curious about. The papers made it sound like Brian Epstein rushed to America solely for the purpose of defending John. Isn't it true that Brian was due to arrive in this country, for other reasons, the week previous to that – before the uproar had even started?

A: "Brian was due in New York the week before, but had to cancel his plans because of illness."

Q: Then he didn't come to

(Turn to Page 23)

Japanese Editor Tired Of Beatles

One of the members of the press who followed the Beatles on their American tour was Rumiko Hoshika, editor in chief of the Japanese monthly, "Music Life."

Rumiko, who stood quietly next to the bandstand during the Los Angeles concert, said her whole tour was "wonderful" but added that she, for one, was almost "tired of talking to the Beatles."

Sound impossible? Not really, since Rumiko has followed the foursome both here and in London. "It's so noisy and crowded everywhere," said Rumiko, laughing to show she really enjoyed the whole ordeal.

But even with every imaginable pass in her possession, it took Tony Barrow, the Beatles senior press officer, to get Rumiko's photographers on the field on Dodger Stadium. The stadium guards had the photographers detained in the dugout until just a few minutes before the Beatles rushed on stage.

Earlier in the tour, Rumiko asked George Harrison to write a note to her readers. George, as a joke, addressed the note to readers of "Music Laugh," rather than "Music Life." Rumiko, who confessed she has "big troubles" with English, didn't say whether she noticed it or not.

Are the Beatles still as popular in Japan as they were before the ill-fated Manila appearance. "Oh yes!" said editor in chief Rumiko.

KRLA ARCHIVES

Beatles Having A Love Affair

"... we pinch just as much as the rest of 'em." —Paul

"... we really don't need them anyway." —George

"... how do you know their legs are ugly?" —Ringo

"... she's great. I'm going to see her tonight." —John

BEAT Photo: Howard L. Bingham

By Louise Criscione

I rather think the Beatles are currently enjoying a two-sided love affair with California. Even when the "Jesus-Lennon" controversy was enjoying its peak and the Beatles were re-considering touring the U.S., George hastened to add that they were still looking forward to their California stop-off.

It's difficult to know why, exactly. It could be the weather—but I doubt it. After all, they could just as easily spend their free days in Miami. Yet, they continue to schedule their time off in California. I tend to think its' the relaxed atmosphere. And the "in" people who populate California. The Mama's and Papa's, Joan Baez, David Crosby. Find the Beatles and you find them.

Cancelled

When the Beatles finally did land in the U.S. this time and John had officially apologized for his "more popular than Jesus" comment, most of the press conferences originally scheduled were cancelled. And it's no small wonder.

They say, what price glory? And indeed the top price paid by the Beatles is having to deal with the press. There is the trade press, which technically is not too bad since they supposedly know what's going on. However, there is, unfortunately, the rest of the press. And "ignorant" is hardly the word.

They know there are four Beatles, they know they came from Liverpool and they know they are named John, Paul, George and Ringo. But more often than not, they still can't seem to fit the name with the face. Therefore, Paul becomes John, John becomes George and George becomes Paul. Only Ringo remains Ringo.

Still Kicks

I imagine the Beatles still get something of a kick out of being addressed as someone else. It's the trite questioning which must really irritate them.

Take for instance the press conference held at Capitol Records in Hollywood. You can bet the brilliance of the whole ordeal did not escape the Beatles.

Of course, the first question asked concerned the "comment controversy" and it was quite obvious to everyone that John was sick and tired of explaining. He gave a sigh, made a face and said simply: "I've explained it 800 times and I think it should be clear."

That, naturally, was not enough to suit the reporter. "Well, you made an apology before," persisted the reporter, "can't you say it again?" "No," replied John, "I can't because I can't remember what I said. Look, I could have used television or anything else. I used the Beatles because that's what I know the best."

I got the distinct impression that the reporter was still not satisfied but was forced to surrender only because the microphone had left his hand.

A Solo John

What made John decide to make "How I Won The War" minus the other Beatles? A relieved sort of smile spread across John's face—something which said "don't tell me someone is going to ask a *new* question; something which doesn't concern my quote, our money, or if this is to be the last tour."

"Well, you see, this man simply asked me if I'd like to make this movie," answered John, "and I said 'yes.' That's how it happened." And with both hands up, he added: "Really!" And the plot? "I don't know much about it. It's about the last World War," continued John. Would the other Beatles venture off into solo movies? "I've no idea. It just sort of came to me that quick," he finished up.

One reporter, who said he was hoping to stir up another controversy, asked the Beatles if they thought perhaps American girls didn't wear mini skirts because their legs were ugly. Ringo shot him down simply and expertly with: "If they don't wear mini skirts, how do you know their legs are ugly?"

How, indeed? Controversy down the drain, the frustrated reporter took to his seat. Actually, the only half-way controversial question was: "It was reported in the July 3 edition of the New York Times that one of you, it didn't say which one, told Maureen Cleave that 'show business is nothing but an extension of the Jewish religion.' Would you like to comment on that?"

Eyes pivoted on the platform holding the Beatles and rather reluctantly John admitted: "I said that one as well. No comment."

"I'm Sorry"

Again the pressure was focused on John, as he was asked if he was really sorry he had made that "Jesus" comment. Definitely tired now, John said: "I am, yes. Even though I didn't mean it that way, I'm sorry I ever opened my mouth."

Another reporter shot up and demanded to know how much money the Beatles make and if they're having trouble with American taxes. "We don't know about that," stated Paul. "We don't do the money side of it. We pay tax and things," he continued, "but we don't know how much. We'd be nervous wrecks by now if we did."

No doubt, the Beatles have learned their lesson. Say just one negative word and it explodes in your face all over the world. So, George found out when he made his famous "We're going to rest up before going to America to get beaten up again" remark.

Certainly he was asked about it at every ingle Beatle press conference and this one didn't want to be an exception. "I said that when we arrived back from Manila. We really weren't beaten up. We really just got shoved around a bit. Jouseled."

Don't Need Them

Is it a more enthusiastic fan or actually hostile individuals who attempt to mob them? "I think it's definitely enthusiastic fans," continued George. "The fan thing—I think they proved it themselves. We found out that the ones who can't make up their minds we really don't need anyway."

A truly profound and certainly devastatingly interesting question was next asked Ringo. "Do you carry around pictures of your son?" "No," shot back Ringo, "I don't carry around photographs of anyone."

A reporter did succeed in putting sort of a dubious feather in his cap when he managed to rather irritate the usually calm Paul by asking him to explain the Beatles' image as it stands today in the wake of the current crop of controversies. "I don't know," snapped McCartney, "our image is what we

(Turn to Page 23)

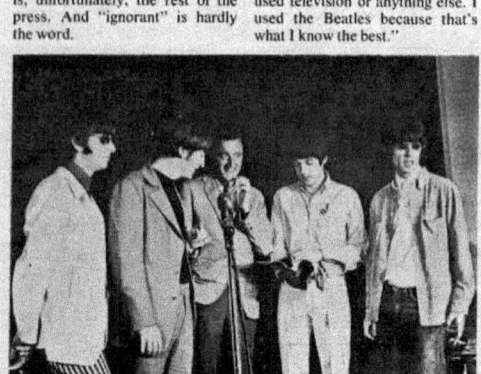

ROBERT VAUGHN whispers a few of his spy secrets to the Beatles.

YOLANDA HERNANDEZ, Stephanie Pinter, Debbie Pinter giving the Beatles initialed steak branding irons.

KRLA ARCHIVES

Baez And A Byrd

By Rochelle Reed

"This just stuns me!" said awed Byrd David Crosby, a Beatle mate. He was standing on the field of Dodger Stadium, gazing up at the stands and shaking his head in disbelief. The Los Angeles ballpark was jampacked that night, and from where David and I stood, it looked like the sky was raining people.

I couldn't have agreed with David more. I was stunned by the Beatles and the audience and by actually standing on the field right next to the bandstand. Guards, posted at every door, stairway, elevator and hall, had challenged anyone who attempted to get access to the dugouts, dressing rooms or field. Clever fans were using every excuse imaginable to get to the Beatles, but not one succeeded.

Bobby Helped

I almost hadn't made it. Once I'd gotten past the entire contingent of security officials upstairs, I was stopped at the dressing room door by another guard who must have ascertained that I looked too excited to be a member of the press. But about that time Bobby Hebb appeared, having heard of my plight, and convinced the guard that though I was a fan, I was also a reporter. And I was IN!

Bobby, "Sunny" as always, led me into the men's dressing room, stopping at the door to make sure everyone was clothed. It wasn't the Beatles' dressing room (they had their own) but the one for the rest of the acts.

I met the Cyrkle, who were sprawled on the floor playing silent songs with drumsticks or their hands. They were a very quiet group, not talking to each other a great deal. Tom, however, kept making comments about a woman being in the mens' dressing room. While he was pulling his suit out of a large case, he kept yelling "EEEEKKKK!!"

Bobby said the Remains were in the dugout, just about to go on, and that Howard and Chuck, BEAT photographers were there too. He pointed the way and then said he'd lead me instead.

"It's just great, the tour and everything," Bobby said, "and I go on pretty soon." He was excited but if he was nervous, he didn't show it.

I reached the dugout just in time to see the Remains run on stage and launch into their first number. Meanwhile, the road manager for the Ronettes said the girls were in their dressing room and why didn't I go back and say "hi."

I ventured back through the underground tunnel to the dressing room where the Ronettes, the only female act in the show were getting ready for their performance.

Or should I say, trying to. Estelle was sitting on a chair, combing her long black hair. "I went swimming today and my hair is a problem. That's one bad thing about swimming – your hair," she went on. Then, "Who are you?"

I identified myself and she continued chatting about the tour – "It's just been fabulous – and the weather and the Beatles' house.

"It's a beautiful mansion – we had dinner there last night with the rest of the acts," she said. Another Ronette lay on the couch alseep with cotton pads covering her sunburned eyelids. I lowered my voice but Estelle continued at full volume as she combed her long hair.

Promises

With promises of a full length interview later, I headed back to the dugout, where I sat down to watch the show while waiting for an escort across the field and up to the bandstand.

Bobby went onstage, his blue silk outfit almost glowing in the semi-darkness. A BEAT photographer and I were ushered across the field and into the second dugout, where we were greeted by Tony Barrow, the Beatles' senior press officer and BEAT columnist.

"The Beatles are in their dressing room," he said, gesturing behind him, but added that no one and that meant NO ONE could get to them. Meanwhile I glanced around to see who else was waiting there to see the British stars. I had ridden down to the field level in an elevator with character actor Don Knotts, and there in the dugout, pacing back and forth, was Batman Adam West, without his Batcape and clad in a grey suit with a yellow shirt.

2 Inches Tall

Then I walked out onto the field. From the bandstand, the stadium looked immense and I felt all of two inches tall. It was a fantastic sight and I rather wanted to stop and just stare with my mouth hanging open in awe.

During the time that I had been in both dugouts, I noticed a very slender girl with an olive complexion and barely shoulder length hair. Her short hair threw me off, however, and I kept saying to myself, "It just couldn't be."

But it was. Now that I was standing on the field, the slender girl in the houndstooth pants-suit walked up and said, "Hi!" How are you? Isn't this just great?"

"Oh yes," I answered, thinking to myself, "my gosh! it is!" About that time, someone said, "You know Joan Baez, don't you?"

I almost couldn't believe it. "You cut your hair!" I exclaimed, "I didn't recognize you." She nodded and with a wide sweep of her arm said, "Just look!"

By this time the Ronettes were on stage, looking very delicate in shiny gold dresses. We all knew it was time for the Beatles.

BEAT photographers were

KRLA ARCHIVES

Watch The Beatles

stationed strategically—one at the entrance from the dressing room and the other at the stairs to the stage. Luckily, the Beatles were acquainted with our photographers and always greeted them with smiles, waves and friendly comments.

George ran out first, then stopped. He continued on in a slow walk, carrying his guitar in front of him like a Bible. George and Joan Baez are good friends, and George sought out Joan as he walked and waved and smiled, and since I was standing with her, he waved my way too. Then came John, Paul and Ringo. They waved to everyone—the stands and the dugouts and the press people near the stage, even those of us without cameras.

The Beatles stopped to say a few words to the man who was to drive them out of the stadium and then ran on stage. They were dressed in tailored green suits and slim trousers. They wore black boots with their famous Cuban heels, except George, who wore brown suede boots without heels. Their shirts, which apparently looked blue polka-dotted from the stands, were actually cream colored and covered with large blue daisies with green leaves and stems.

'It's Great'

The roar of the crowd was deafening but I heard every word of every Beatle song. I was surprised to look around and see members of the press, who weren't madly shooting pictures, bouncing up and down with every beat. Joan Baez was dancing and kept saying "It's just great, just great!"

The Beatles waved while they played and John stamped his foot for a *BEAT* photographer, while Ringo smiled broadly for another.

Throughout the show, the Beatles traded comments with the people standing around the stage. Stars, press, anyone who could get a pass, crowded at the foot of the stage to watch the Beatles, who seemed to be standing on a pedestal rather than a bandstand.

Suddenly our single-minded devotion was shattered when fans at the far end of the stadium broke through police lines and attempted to rush across the field to the stage. The Beatles, who had just finished a song, stopped and stood very still. A chill went through the people standing around the stage. The Beatles hesitated a moment more, letting the screams sink in. John nodded, Paul shrugged his shoulders and they launched into "Baby's In Black." George, playing all the time, kept asking Joan Baez, "What's happening?"

A Useless Try

It was useless to try and explain. Besides, when the Beatles began playing, it calmed the nerves of almost everyone, most of whom weren't used to the idea that the Beatles could actually be in danger.

Thoughts began to turn to how the Beatles would get out of the ballpark. The press had learned that inside the tent labeled "dressing room" were actually two automobiles in which the Beatles would make their getaway. Everyone was anxious to see just precisely how this would work out.

Soon the Beatles launched into their last song. Paul looked down to where I was standing, yelled "Whooppee!!," rolled his eyes and continued belting out "Long Tall Sally." John stamped his foot and George waved. Ringo just beamed from ear to ear.

No sooner had they hit their last note then they bowed low and ran for it. Under the edge of the canvas, I could see Beatle boots and George's brown shoes. Then they disappeared and a gold Lincoln Continental, followed by a grey Ford filled with officials, roared out of the tent and towards the far gate. John and Ringo triumphantly waved white towels out of the back windows.

But just after they've gone through the blue gate at the far end of the field, the Beatles' car was engulfed by fans. I had wandered over there expecting to see the cars driving down the hill. Instead, I saw fans streaming down over a second wire fence and swarming onto the Continental. All I could see were the tail lights.

The police began pulling over-excited girls from the car while a second set of officers closed the outside wire gates. This left the car between the two sets of gates. The car began to back up and I stood there almost frozen as a few girls, who seemed to have lost all reason completely, kept throwing themselves against the car.

The Beatles were frightened for those few moments. As the car backed up to where I was standing, I could see that John was biting his cuff while Ringo, who had moments before been waving his white towel, had a corner of it in his mouth and was biting down hard.

John's Side

I was standing on John's side of the car, less than two feet from him. Apparently recognizing that I was press he waved in recognition and then widened his eyes and motioned as if to ask, "Is everything all right?"

I waved a victory sign to him and the rest of the Beatles saw and smiled. The car peeled back through the fence, made a half turn and sped back to the dugout, where the Beatles ran to their dressing room.

They left not long afterwards in an armored truck after an attempted getaway in an ambulance failed.

They spent the night in their Hollywood hillside home and flew to San Francisco the next day. The day after, they left the U.S. for England, where John Lennon will make a movie and the other Beatles will relax.

The remainder of us will be busy speculating as to whether or not they'll be back next year.

BEAT Photos: Howard L. Bingham

The Adventures of Robin Boyd

©1966 By Shirley Poston

It was a pleasantly uneventful day in the Boyd household.

Ringo Boyd (of 12-year-old sturdy frame and fame) was in her room banging contentedly away at her set of drooms. (Actually, it was a collection of empty oatmeal cartons, but why blow the poor kid's cool?)

The Boyd dog lay nearby. Although Ringo had thoughtfully stuffed it's ears with several vile-tasting carmels she'd bitten into while consuming a(nother) box of bon bons, the dog moaned plaintively after each "number."

Mrs. Boyd was in the kitchen preparing a nutritious luncheon of poached eggs and spinach (which she would pretend to eat and grab a cheeseburger later on her way to the market.)

Hole For Lunch

Mr. Boyd had ventured home for the weekend (he travels a lot, and considering that this was the *first* pleasantly uneventful day in the *history* of the Boyd household, he wouldn't have it any other way.) He was out in the back yard digging a hole under the rose bushes. (He would later bury his portion of the aforementioned nutritious luncheon in same and grab a cheeseburger.)

This then was the Boyd family, minus one. And all of them were curiously undisturbed by what was *causing* this to be a pleasantly uneventful day. Namely, the mysterious absence of the fourth member of the family (fifth, if you count the dog) (and considering the size of those teeth, it would be advisable.) Re-namely, Robin Irene Boyd.

Thanks to a temporary magic spell which had been cast over (as in net) the lot of them by four of Robin's friends (as in fiends), the family was blissfully unaware of her disappearance, not to mention her predicament.

Robin's Nest

And it was just as well.

It would be impossible to tell just *what* they might say if they knew that at this very moment, their one and only (thank Gawd) R.I.B. was *trapped* in the *tea pot* on the living room mantel. At any rate, it would surely be impossible to *print*.

Meaning, of course, that she was squalling at the top of her lungs.

"*Ratzafratz!*" she shrieked, poking savagely at the ceiling with the remains of a pole lamp. But she got nowhere at supersonic speeds (also faster than usual.)

When she'd first discovered that her three genies and one angel (George, John, Pauley and Ringo, respectively) (the utter twits) had trapped her in their am-day tea pot so they could go off on a special assignment concerning the *real* Beatles (pounce), she had flown into a rage.

Lid Flipper

Then she had come to her senses (a long trip, I tell you), and realized there was a way out of this dilemma. So what if the inside of the aforementioned A-D.T.P. *was* an exact replica of the Beatle domicile in "Help." It was still a tea pot, which meant it had a *lid!* And if Robin Irene Boyd wasn't the champion lid-flipper of all time, who *was?* (You might well arsk.)

She had since made every possible attempt to dislodge said lid, and had succeeded only in flipping her own. And, after her having flang every liftable *(hah?)* object in the room at the ceiling, the place was right back to what it had been before she'd been kind (not to mention stupid) enough to clean it up.

All was now lost. The pole lamp had been her last resort. It hadn't worked as a pogo stick (which particularly galled her because she was positive George would make her replace the spring she'd extracted from the couch), and it wasn't going to work as a battering ram either.

It was, however, very effective for bashing oneself over the bean, so she did this several times before stumbling into the kitchen to blither over a cuppa.

Snarling viciously, Robin shook and rattled pots and pans and rolled hysterically on the floor while she was waiting for the water to boil.

"*Boy, are they gonna get it,*" she vowed in gangster-type tones, plotting a series of horrifying deaths for her (un)faithful companions (especially George, who had *had* it) (this is news?).

Finally she got up and hurled a handful of something she hoped was tea into a nearby pot. Under any other circumstances, the tea-pot-within-a-tea-pot bit would have at least caused her mouth to curl at the corners. But not today. Today, her mouth wouldn't curl at the corners if she put it up on *rollers!*

Slamming a cup on the table, Robin tilted the pot and poured a stream of tea from the spout. Then she slammed the pot on the table. Then she slammed her *head* on the table!

Of course! Those utter wretches had probably *glued* the lid on so she wouldn't be able to escape. *However*, details did not number among the thingys George had a passion for (cough), and the chances were excellent that the *spout* had escaped his (alleged) mind!

It was then that Robin knew what she must do.

Drawing herself up to her full height (an awe-inspiring five-foot-two), she bellowed "*Liverpool.*"

At the very mention of the magic word, she immediately turned into a *real* robin and began winging wildly about. (About what?) (Get serious, kiddo.)

Nowhere Spout

She searched every inch of the abode, only to find that all was *still* lost. The spout was nowhere about.

At last she perched disgustedly atop a dart board (which featured a well-worn photo of two deejays from Alabama.)

Then it happened. When she tried to re-wing wildly, she couldn't budge an inch!

"Oh," she quipped cleverly, seeing what the trouble was. Her tail feathers were caught in a small hole in the wall just behind the dart board.

Removing her tailfeathers (from the small hole in the wall just behind the dart board, that is) (may repetition remain the fungus amongus 4-ever), she flapped furiously away for another spout hunt.

Suddenly, she fluttered to the floor. *A small hole in the wall just behind the dart board???* How dumb could she *be?* (Stick around and you may have the misfortune to find out.)

"*That was the spout, you lout!*" she shouted poetically. Then she went into action.

First she screeched "Ketchup," turned back into her sixteen-year-old self, and snatched the dart board off the wall. Then she re-"Liverpool"-ed and squeezed through the small hole.

That is to say, she sure as heck *tried.* But, after an exhausting experience of grunting, cramming, and cursing her worthless self for all the double orders of chips she'd been gobbling recently, she had to admit the truth. She was bigger about than the spout.

Greasy Robin

However, being the sort of person who does not give up easily, Robin refused to give up easily. Instead she careened to Ringo's automat, pecked the door open and wallowed in a peanut butter sandwich.

When she was thoroughly greased (not to mention nauseating), she tried the spout route again. And this time she made it up the olde tube (which was a nice change because she was used to going down it.)

She did have one moment of sheer panic just as she was about to emerge. *What if someone was in the living room?* She'd *never* be able to explain *this* one.

She thought of saying a quick prayer, but decided against it. Somehow it just didn't seem proper to address Higher Beings when one was covered with peanut butter in the spout of a tea pot.

Oh, well, she'd just have to chance it.

Hoping for the best, she gave a final squirm and plopped onto the mantel. Then she gave a sigh of relief. The living room was empty. (All except for the furniture, but that rather goes without saying, doesn't it?) (Not around *here*, baby.)

Happy that the Someone up there who had scarcely even been *tolerating* her of late was starting to like her again, Robin darted through an open window and took to the sky like a bat out of the opposite direction.

For a change, Robin knew exactly where she was going. She remembered, to the letter, what had been etched upon the glowing piece of parchment she'd found in John's bookcase.

She only hoped that she would make it to the chosen city in time, which was doubtful because the coating of peanut butter was cutting her speed down to a mere 4,500 miles per hour. Which was also just as well, because she was still trying to forget a most unpleasant incident when she had been picked up (I'll say) by an officer of the dread bird patrol (a blue jay with a silver helmet and a tendency to leer) for exceeding the 5,000 m.p.h. limit.

Special Assignment

Streaking toward her destination, Robin began to wonder what on earth she was going to do when she got there. The special assignment was a plan whereby her Beatle look-alikes would double for the far fabber foursome, thereby allowing the latter to get away in one (make that four) (yeah, yeh, yeah) piece. And where she fit into the action was an A-D good question.

But she was certain of one thing. She was going to have *nothing* to do with those imposters. After what those miserable clods had done to her, she was going to concentrate her efforts on the *realies!*

When Robin finally arrived on the scene, the concert was over. She could tell from the scramble below, as fans raced hysterically toward the backstage area.

From her vantage point, she also had a birds-eye view (clever, no?) (no) of what was happening on the other side of the fence.

And, as she saw four Beatles running towards a long black limousine parked at backstage left, she grinned fiendishly and prepared to *follow that car!*

Suddenly, she stopped so short, she almost lost her balance and landed in the esophogas (I flunked speling) of an open-mouthed Beatlemaniac far below. On account of because she also saw four *more* Beatles running toward a long black limousine parked at backstage *right!*

And, without her Byrd glasses (which had been smashed to smithereens the time she was locked in the glove compartment of Cher's speeding auto), she couldn't tell which was which. Not to mention which end was up.

(To Be Continued Next Issue)

NEW!! HAIR CONTROL FOR MEN WITH MOIST SPRAY ACTION

Shape Up
FOR HAIR CONTROL ALL DAY

Special BEAT OFFER
REG. $1.50
WITH COUPON
MAIL $1.00

includes tax and postage

Shape Up
The BEAT
6290 Sunset, No. 504
Los Angeles, Calif. 90028
Send ____ SHAPE UP
Enclosed is $____
Name____
Adress____
City____ State____ Zip____

KRLA ARCHIVES

...YES, THAT IS SONNY & CHER flanking Atlantic Records vice president, Nesuhi Ertegun, on the set of their "Good Times" which is now rescheduled for release in November.

Sonny: 'I Did What I Wanted To Do'

They stand close together beneath the glowing stage lights, each of them clasping a microphone tightly in one hand; both of them dressed very much alike; both of them watching the huge gathering of fans before them from beneath their long, shiny hair. And then, they sing: "I got *you*, babe!"

Sonny and Cher are the first to admit it, and their fans will all offer enthusiastic support: they really *do* have one another. The most famous married couple in all of popdom, there are those who might say that Sonny and Cher really have it *all*.

Have It All

The money, the fame, the bright lights, the fans, the glamour which follows closely behind success. Indeed, perhaps they *do* have it *all*—but if they do, then they are certainly sharing a vast majority of it with the people all around them.

They share the warmth and love and consideration which they have for one another with their many fans. Although it has at times caused them great inconvenience, Sonny and Cher have frequently flung wide-open the doors to their hilltop home, welcoming their curious, visiting fans inside.

More than once Sonny has cooked up one of his famous Italian feasts for a large number of "unexpected guests" who stopped by the Bono residence.

After an appearance in concert, or in a night club, both Sonny and Cher have always taken the time to try and speak with as many of their fans as possible, to sign the autographs which are requested, to pose patiently for the cameras which surround them from all sides.

Just recently Sonny and Cher put on a huge benefit concert at the Hollywood Bowl and succeeded in raising thousands of dollars for the American Braille Institute, one of their favorite charities.

On August 21, Sonny and Cher boarded a plane and began a month-long tour of Europe—a tour which should prove to be one of the most unusual ever.

People To People

The tour, which encompasses more than 20 personal appearances, and includes concerts, television appearances, radio shows, and people-to-people and press conferences, will be made in its entirety on a no-fee basis.

The itinerary lists nine cities in seven different countries, including England, France, Germany, Sweden, and Italy, and at no time will there be an artist charge incurred.

The main reason for the tour is to enable Sonny and Cher to meet their many European fans in person, and to keep their promise of eventually coming to these countries in person which they made in their first trip to England last year.

The couple will also promote their first motion picture, "Good Times," as well as the brand new album about to be released by Cher which will include a very secret single recording.

Charity Concerts

Once again, Sonny and Cher will be sharing with their friends, giving of their own time and efforts. And one of the most important appearances of their tour will be a gigantic charity concert given at the Astoria Theatre, Finsbury Park, in London.

They will give two complete performances in the same evening, and all proceeds of the huge concert will be given to the Braille Institute and to underprivileged children in that country.

They will duplicate this even with a similar concert to be given in the Olympia Theatre in Paris, also for the benefit of the French Braille Institute and underprivileged French children.

At a huge press conference held in one of the most elegant hotels in Hollywood just two days before they began their tour, Sonny and Cher greeted over one hundred members of the press, including a large representation of the foreign press, in an attempt to answer personally as many of their questions as possible.

Unfortunately, too many of the "senior citizens" of the press community could not respect the couple's choice in apparel, or appreciate their perogative to *make* that choice, and were much more concerned with pointing accusing fingers at the two, and making pathetic and unkind "jokes" about them.

Throughout the entire conference, Sonny and Cher remained polite, smiling, and cooperative, and attempted to answer *all* of questions, no matter how ridiculous they were.

Questioned at length about their "crazy clothing," one gentleman continually attacked Sonny with questions about the sort of clothes which the couple might wear to a "black tie affair."

Sonny simply smiled understandingly and explained, "We have *dress* 'crazy outfits' too!"

Later, in regard to the forthcoming movie, Sonny explained to the large gathering: "I'm very proud of the picture. I did what I wanted to do—I wanted to give a picture to the kids that didn't insult their intelligence; something that was *equal* to their intelligence."

Always Change

Again they were questioned about their unique style of dress, and asked if they would ever change? And again Sonny rose *above* the question with his honest, intelligent answer: "You always change as a person. As you do anything in life, your thoughts, and opinions are going to change with you."

And finally, they were asked if they would "condescend" to stop and see Princess Meg in London (the question was asked chidingly in reference to their unpleasant experiences after giving a Command Performance for the Royal Couple in Hollywood several months ago), and Sonny simply smiled and replied: "That's up to *her*—if she'd like to see us, we'll stop by and see her!!"

Yes, Sonny and Cher are quite willing to share themselves with *everyone*—even people who don't have a decent pair of bell-bottoms to their name!!!

KRLA ARCHIVES

Top 40 Requests

1. HERE, THERE AND EVERYWHERE ... The Beatles
2. FORTUNE TELLER ... Rolling Stones
3. GOT TO GET YOU INTO MY LIFE ... The Beatles
4. ELEANOR RIGBY ... The Beatles
5. CHERISH ... The Association
6. YELLOW SUBMARINE ... The Beatles
7. FOR NO ONE ... The Beatles
8. PSYCHOTIC REACTION ... The Count Five
9. GOD ONLY KNOWS ... Beach Boys
10. GOOD DAY SUNSHINE ... The Beatles
11. RED RUBBER BALL ... The Cyrkle
12. YOU CAN'T HURRY LOVE ... The Supremes
13. LAST TRAIN TO CLARKSVILLE ... The Monkees
14. SUNNY ... Bobby Hebb
15. SOMETIMES GOOD GUYS DON'T WEAR WHITE ... The Standells
16. SUNSHINE SUPERMAN ... Donovan
17. JUST LIKE A WOMAN ... Bob Dylan
18. BLACK IS BLACK ... Los Bravos
19. THE JOKER WENT WILD ... Brian Hyland
20. I'VE GOT YOU UNDER MY SKIN ... The 4 Seasons
21. SUMMERTIME ... Billy Stewart
22. SEE YOU IN SEPTEMBER ... The Happenings
23. SUNNY AFTERNOON ... The Kinks
24. SUMMER IN THE CITY ... Lovin' Spoonful
25. SOMEWHERE MY LOVE ... Ray Conniff
26. GUANTANAMERA ... The Sandpipers
27. MAKE ME BELONG TO YOU ... Barbara Lewis
28. LAND OF 1,000 DANCES ... Wilson Pickett
29. BEAUTY IS ONLY SKIN DEEP ... The Temptations
30. LIL' RED RIDING HOOD ... Sam The Sham
31. WHAT BECOMES OF THE BROKEN HEARTED ... Jimmy Ruffin
32. SEVEN AND SEVEN IS ... Love
33. I COULDN'T LIVE WITHOUT YOUR LOVE ... Petula Clark
34. HOW SWEET IT IS ... Jr. Walker
35. DANGLING CONVERSATION ... Simon & Garfunkel
36. GO AHEAD AND CRY ... The Righteous Bros.
37. TURN DOWN DAY ... The Cyrkle
38. BLOWIN' IN THE WIND ... Stevie Wonder
39. WORKIN' IN A COAL MINE ... Lee Dorsey
40. WIPE OUT ... Surfaris

Hair Cut For John

Alas, John Lennon's locks must go. Part of them, at least.

Lennon, preparing for the first solo film role for any of the Beatles, will have to undergo a hair trimming before appearing in "How I Won The War."

The hair cut, however, isn't expected to be a severe one.

"We have to do something about John's hair before every film," explained Dick Lester, who worked on both Beatle films and who will direct this one.

"But it will only be a trim."

John will play the part of Private Gripweed, a soldier in an imaginary British regiment during the second world war.

The movie, taken from the novel of the same name by Patrick Ryan, is expected to be premiered next summer.

"We may ask John and Paul to help with the sound track music later," said Lester. "But that depends on how the film shooting turns out."

Join the Dave Hull International Fan Club

Send $1.00 for one year to:
DAVE HULL FAN CLUB
634 sefton, monterey park, calif.
Monthly Bulletins, Photos, The Works!

ATTENTION!!!

High Schools, Colleges, Universities and Clubs:

CASEY KASEM MAY BE ABLE TO SERVE YOU!

Let Casey HELP You Put On A Show Or Dance

Contact Casey at:
HO 2-7253

Inside KRLA
By Eden

Okay—so you're hip to the fact that there just ain't *no way* we're gonna talk about anything but *Beatles* this column, right? Well, after all—what did you expect after the fantastic concert which the Beatles and KRLA presented at "Beatle Stadium" August 28 last?

All of the DJ's joined the thousands and thousands of Beatlemaniacs in KRLA-land who were able to attend the concert in agreeing that the Fabulous Foursome put on one of the best performances ever!

Lots of excitement in the last couple of weeks with Beatles in town, and the happiness and confusion at KRLA didn't die even when the Phenomenal Four left our town. 'Cause as they winged their way homeward, the Mama's and Papa's landed just long enough to answer our Request Lines and to give out some of their fantastic new LP's.

Remember, *your* votes on the Request Lines were responsible for the choice of the new single, and if you haven't heard the album in its entirely yet—run out and get several copies. It's really a groove!

Next day, Leslie Gore stopped in and shortly afterwards Gary Lewis and Company invaded our Happy Haunting Grounds.

Oh well—keep your requests coming in!

Danny Dassa
Cafe Danssa
11533 W. Pico, L.A. GR 8-9960
International Folk Cafe
FUN CLUB MEMBERS — Two for price of one Sunday nite only — Just show Funtee Card!!

COMPUTER DATING FOR HIGH SCHOOLS!

Computer dating, which up to now has been available only to college students, is here now for you, the high school student. MATCH DATE has designed its questionnaire to reflect the needs and desires of young adults between the ages of 14-18.

Matching people by computers has been very successful in colleges around the country; but now, MATCH DATE gives you, the high school student, the chance to go where the action is and join the excitement and adventure of computer dating.

MATCH DATE gives you the chance not only to list your interests and attitudes, but also to describe your ideal date. This mutual selection between you and your date makes for more fun-filled action. Meeting new people and making new friends also adds to the fun and adventure. Remember, if you tell your friends about MATCH DATE, and they join the fun, then the larger population gives you a better probability of finding your IDEAL MATCH DATE.

All you do is just fill out the questionnaire and mail it along with $3.00 to MATCH DATE, P.O. Box 69965, Los Angeles 90069. Our computer will then MATCH you with the FIVE or more members of the opposite sex with whom you are the most compatible. You will then receive their names, addresses, and telephone numbers, just as they will receive yours. Then, YOU ACT...

For your free questionnaire, fill out this form, or print the information on a piece of paper and mail it to: MATCH DATE, P.O. Box 69965, Los Angeles 90069. Questionnaires are also available by calling HO 9-5115.

Name _____ Age _____
Address _____ School _____
City _____ Phone _____
Mail to: MATCH DATE
P.O. Box 69965
Los Angeles 90069

KRLA BEAT SPECIAL
(NEW SUBSCRIBERS ONLY)

$3.00 a year

SAVE 60%
on the bigger, better BEAT

Just clip and mail...

KRLA BEAT
Save 60%—Subscribe!

Mail to:
Beat Publications
6290 Sunset Blvd.
Hollywood 90028

Name _____
Address _____
City _____ State _____ Zip _____

I want ☐ BEAT for a year at $3.00.
I enclose ☐ cash ☐ check ☐ money order.

KRLA ARCHIVES

KRLA AND BOB EUBANKS WISH TO THANK YOU ALL FOR MAKING THIS CONCERT THE MOST SUCCESSFUL IN THREE YEARS TONIGHT'S ATTENDANCE EXCEEDS LAST YEAR'S TOTAL BY MORE THAN 5000

KRLA'S BOB EUBANKS and Tony Barrow, Beatles' senior press officer, confer on the field of Dodger Stadium during the Beatles' performance.

FOUR WOODEN LETTERS, each over six feet tall, spell out KRLA on the front of the "Beatle Stadium" stage.

THE KRLA DISC JOCKEYS pose in front of the tent that held the get-a-way cars. l-r, Charlie O'Donnell, Dick Moreland, Casey Kasem, Bob Eubanks (promoter of the show), Dick Biondi and Dave Hull with his horn.

PAUL McCARTNEY, in the midst of one of their numbers, stands in front of marquee which spells out "KRLA Proudly Present The Beatles."

JERRY PAM, publicist, pauses for one quick quiet moment while the Beatles were on stage.

TIM MORGAN
at the **ICE HOUSE** Glendale
234 SO. BRAND
Reservations 245-5043
Thru Sept. 25 with
JEAN DURAND & LENIN CASTRO

NOW!

HIGH CAMP FROM LONDON!
PSYCHO-SIN-COPATIONS
OF
IAN WHITCOMB
AND HIS RAGTIME-ROCK BAND

"HE'LL TURN YOU ON AND MAKE YOU NERVOUS"

AT DOUG WESTON'S
Troubadour
9083 SANTA MONICA BLVD.
L.A. NEAR DOHENY
RESERVATIONS CR 6-6168

A-1

The 'ACTION MAN' Slacks

You'll find the swingin' A-1 styles at sharp men's stores that carry the latest!

PEGGERS® RACERS® TAPERS® CUSTOMS®
A-1 Kotzin Co., 1300 Santee St., Los Angeles, Calif. 90015

HERE IT COMES!! The International Teen World Festival
WHEN?? During Christmas Vacation
Contestants wanted for Miss Teen World!! Dial "F-U-N-T-E-E-N" (386-8336) for details.
Attention All Fun Club members: 1 free admission with 1 paid (2 for 1) with AA coupon.

KRLA ARCHIVES

PICTURES in the NEWS

JEFF BECK poses with girlfriend, Mary Hughes, under the skies of Catalina Island. Sources close to the Yardbirds are afraid that Jeff will soon be forced to leave the group due to ill health as well as a certain amount of undependability. However, the Yardbirds themselves are not talking and neither is Jeff — he's too busy squiring Mary around town.

BEACH BOYS enjoy that pause that refreshes before taking off for a rather short tour of England. It will be their first British tour and the Beach Boys will hit Finsbury Park Astoria, Totting Granada, Leicester de Montfort, Leeds Odeon, Manchester Odeon, Cardiff Capitol and Birmingham Theatre. Other European stop-offs for the Beach Boys will be in France, Germany, Austria, Denmark, Sweden and Holland.

MANFRED MANN as they stand today with (top) Tom McGuinness, (center) Klaus Voorman, Michael d'Abo, Mike Hugg and (bottom) Manfred Mann. Michael is replacing the Manfred's former lead singer, Paul Jones, and Klaus left the trio of Paddy, Klaus and Gibson to join the Manfred. He's also the one responsible for the cover of the Beatles' "Revolver" album. Latest disc is Dylan penned, "Just Like A Woman."

FOUR SEASONS (l. to r.) Frankie Valli, Tommy deVito, Bob Gaudio and Joe Lang smile as they hear the good news. Their "The 4 Seasons' Gold Vault of Hits" has been certified for a Gold Record, signifying sales of one million dollars for the LP. This makes the second 4 Seasons' Goldie for album sales; their first being for their "Rag Doll" album. On the singles scene, the Seasons' unique version of the Cole Porter oldie, "I've Got You Under My Skin," is smashing up the nation's charts — but then the 4 Seasons seldom miss!

KRLA ARCHIVES

...MICK JAGGER AND HIS STEADY GIRLFRIEND, Chrissie Shrimpton, point happily at the camera which caught them shopping at Hollywood's Devos.

Mick's Chrissie On Her Own

By Kimmi Kobashigawa

She is very tall—five feet, eight inches—very pretty, just 21 years old, the younger sister of Britain's top fashion model, and the girl friend of the lead singer of one of Britain's top pop groups. Her name is Chrissie Shrimpton.

Just recently, Chrissie flew into Los Angeles from London to join Mick as he and the Stones completed their latest American tour, and began an extensive series of recording sessions for the soundtrack of their upcoming motion picture.

On one of their leisure days, Mick and Chrissie decided to stroll into one of Hollywood's most "in" clothes spots for guys, and went on a shopping spree at DeVoss. Also in the hip haberdasherie that day were the Mama's and Papa's, and The BEAT's own trusty photographer who brought these fab pix back for you.

Chrissie Shrimpton is one of the most envied young girls in all the pop world—and yet, there was a long period of time when she might have traded her "position" with just about anyone. It isn't easy to have to live in the shadows of two very famous people, especially when they are the two people who mean the most to you.

But Chrissie seems finally to have adjusted to her "vicarious fame," and is now quite well-known as a personality in her own right. Of her former years of "overshadowing," Chrissie now says: "It doesn't mean much to me any more—about Mick and Jean. Being Mick Jagger's girlfriend and top model Jean Shrimpton's sister was awful for ages. I felt like a sort of non-person, with no personality of my own. Sometimes I wondered if I existed!"

But Chrissie has done a lot of growing up in the last couple of years, and she now admits that, "I no longer like or dislike being referred to as Mick's girl or Jean's sister. Now I take it as fact. It's true, after all."

Although she was acting as secretary to Stone's manager, Andrew Oldham, Chrissie now divides her time between some infrequent modeling sessions (unlike her sister, Chrissie doesn't really enjoy modeling, and explains that "I haven't much patience for photographs."), writing gossip columns for a number of teen magazines around the world, beginning a career in acting, and—of course—dating Mick.

While she was visiting Mick in Hollywood, Chrissie made quite a number of new friends in the American pop colony and it is possible that she might return for another visit, perhaps the next time that Mick is in town. And it seems quite certain that when she does, her friends will call her "Chrissie"—instead of "Mick's girl—you know, Jean's younger sister."

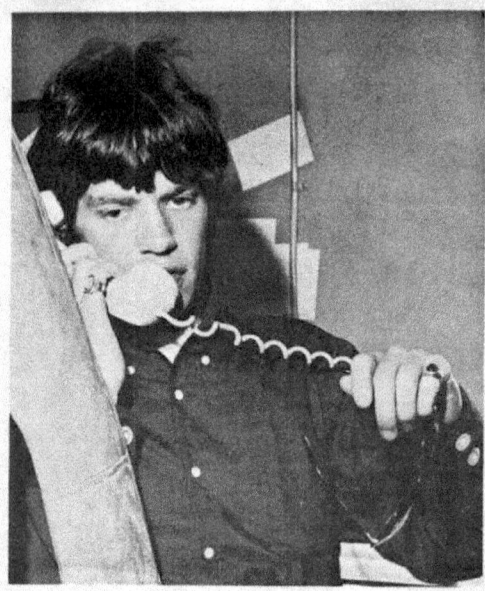

...WHO IS MICK TALKING TO so intently on the phone?

WOULD YOU BELIEVE it's Chrissie?

KRLA ARCHIVES

There Are Four of Them

John is a tall, thin, gaunt person who takes everything very seriously. He has played and sung his way around Greenwich Village and other areas with and without the other Mama's and Papa's. He has an unusually creative mind which is evident in the songs he has written.

Cass loves antiques, talks freely about art and Bob Dylan and has travelled the country in satirical revues. She occasionally wears gold-rimmed glasses and like the other Mama's and Papa's, lives for today. She is large and lovely, beneficial and broad-minded. What else... who knows?

Denny is a handsome young Canadian who is a nonconformist. He was originally clean-shaven but wore black leather. Now he wears expensive sports clothes — and a beard. Talking in terms of pin-ups and potential Lennons, Denny could play the role.

Michelle is certainly a mysterious but lovely Mama. She is a blonde vision-with-a-voice who doesn't say very much but just looks at you in a waif-like manner. She was once a model and in her own way still is.

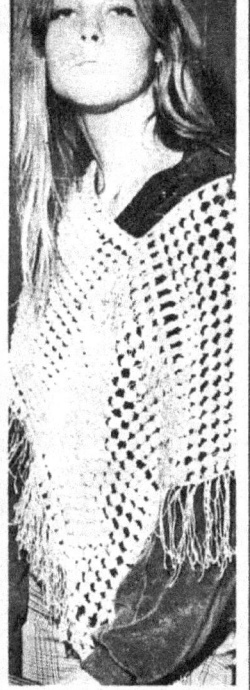

KRLA ARCHIVES

the MAMAS and PAPAS

BEAT Photos: Chuck Boyd

By Jamie McCluskey III

Okay, gang—can ya picture *this*?! The scene is the NBC television studios where the Rodgers and Hart television special is being filmed (the show will be aired next March.) We are seated in a huge dressing room downstairs which belongs to Dennis Dougherty, of the Mama's and Papa's.

Scattered recklessly all around the long make-up table is the largest selection of food you have ever seen. Super double-deck hamburgers, complete chicken dinners, steak sandwiches, several bags of French fries, about a dozen cokes and several cups of coffee, some potato chips, a few empty candy wrappers, and a large, gooey chocolate cream pie. And that's just the *table!!*

Scattered all around the room are the four Mama's and Papa's, several beards (of various colors, lengths, and styles!), a few Papa John hats—both on and *off* of various heads!—and a large selection of guitars and other instruments which are strewn all over the floor.

Okay, you've got the picture now, right? Right! Now we're going to do an interview, right? *Wrong!* Nobody, but nobody interviews a Mama or a Papa. At best—if you're *lucky*—they interview *you!!!*

Being basically foolish, we are going to *attempt* the first interview with Papa Denny, the handsome, irresistible, irrepressible, *unbelievably insane*, thoroughly irrational, and highly talented member of the group. At this point, the other human inhabitants of the room disappear, leaving us alone in the confusion.

Ready? Okay, we'll turn on the tape recorder and fire a few questions at Papa Denny. First we'll ask about the time and place of Denny's birth. Forget it! Cass immediately sticks her head in the doorway with the sage advice: "Don't tell her! It'll be all over the papers!"

"I was born in the year 1940, in a small city called Halifax—in the Province of Nova Scotia—in the Dominion of Canada—which is *North*—of this fair country of yours—which I have grown to love and know so well—in the few years that I have been here!"

He paused briefly, considered his words, and exclaimed: "I'm not in Canada now—I'm in California. I'm going to go to the *States* soon!!"

Okay—next question. What sort of education did you have, Denny? "Well, I didn't finish High School—but I started school!" Mmmhmmm! Well, aside from your obvious talents with the guitar, do you play any other instruments? "I played trombone for four years in a police boys' club band." Oh? Did you ever *study* music?

"Yes, for four years in a police boys' club band one time when I played trombone for four years!" Oh!!

Denny then proceeded to grab the microphone and loudly explain into it: "That's me licking chicken off of my fingers." At which point Michelle stuck her head in the door to ask if everything was okay.

"That was just me screaming for help," I loudly explained *off* of the microphone. "Oh," she nodded, as though it happened all the time, and vanished. "Oh!" I moaned in sheer disbelief!

Momentarily, three other M's and P's trooped back into the food-ridden room, threw themselves over, around, on top of, and beneath the existing furniture, and began to harmonize an East Indian melody, sounding very much like a three-part, human-style Sitar.

For the next fifteen minutes, the Fanatic Foursome proceeded to put one another on utilizing their own distinctive brand of humor which can be described in only one of two ways: Just "Mama's and Papa's" or absolute *insanity!!*

A shriek outside the dressing room alerted us that the now-frantic stage manager (who also couldn't quite "believe his eyes and ears!") wanted the four onstage for a taping. And as quickly as they had come—they were gone . . . I *think!*

However, their voices live on in a brand new album entitled "Mama's and Papa's." It's great—but then, so are they . . . "if you can *believe* your eyes and ears!!!! (If not—they're *still* pretty great!)

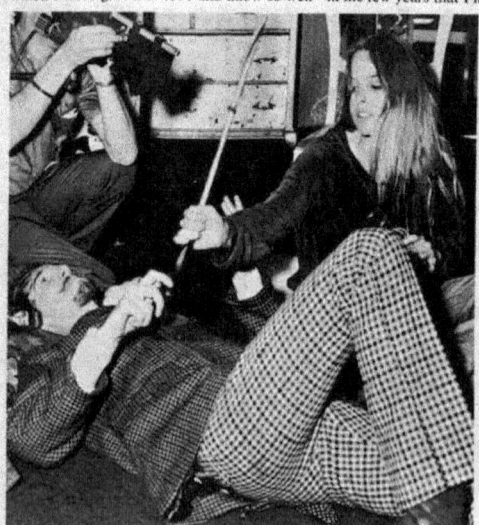

KRLA ARCHIVES

For Girls only
by shirley poston

I thought I'd do something different in this column. (Like speak English, for instance.)

I thought it would be too utterly neat for words to write "For Gawd's Sake" - urp - "For Girls Only" at a real live *Beatle concert*!

You know, while sitting in the grandstand, waiting for the marvelous, stupendous thingy to begin. So, in addition to the usual goodies I drag to Beatle concerts (binoculars, telescopes, tape records, eight boxes of Kleenex and three bottles of tranquilizers), I packed along a notebook and clutched an assortment of pencils in my trembling paw.

Well, I am in that aforementioned grandstand at his very moment, and I can see right now that my idea just isn't going to work. Because, so far, I've done everything in the world but *sit*. And I've discovered that it's very difficult to write while leaping several feet into the air every few seconds.

Too Early

I know it's too early for THEM (make that HIM) (make that GEORGE) (love to) (sorry about that, folks) . . . where was I? Oh yes, I know it's too early for them to arrive, but that doesn't stop me from losing consciousness every time someone so much as *coughs* anywhere in the stadium.

I guess that seeing someone you dig (a kind and gentle way of putting it, don't you think?) is the most exciting thingy in the entire world, but, in a way, it's even more exciting *before* you see them.

You know what I mean. That one feeling of being tied up in millions of knots and not being able to breathe properly and all that.

That's the way I feel right now, which may be the reason why all this gibberish doesn't make a whit of sense. (Make that one of the many reasons.)

Two Of Many

Although, I must say I came well prepared, thanks to two of both of my many readers. A few weeks ago, this groovy-looking package arrived at *The BEAT* office, addressed to yours truly.

Thinking perhaps it was George (GASP . . . he is somewhere breathing at this very moment and will soon be HERE breathing) (RE-gasp) (I can't stand it, I can't stand it) (down, girl and/or Shirl), in *rippp*).

You'll never guess what it was! Which is too bad because someone just screamed over by the dug-out and I can't remember a thing!

Oh yes, it was a "Star Kit." In it were six goodies that Mary Lou Robbins and Mary Erwin felt would come in handy, and were they correct!

First there was a GORGEOUS (ahem) (I can't stand it, I tell you) (he's coming *here*) (re-down) picture of George, with a note that read: "For your courage, confidence and cool." (None of which I have at the moment.) (Would you believe *ever*?)

Ban Spray

Second was a can of Ban spray deodorant, with another note that said: "*Shirley Poston Asks A Question:* If I use new Ban spray, will George Harrison make me his bride? *Answer:* No, but if you don't, your father might give you away anyroad." (When I showed it to him, he muttered something I didn't quite catch, but it sounded a lot like "an excellent suggestion.")

Then there was a tiny address book "for George's address and phone number so you can always get in touch with him." (I fear this is not the time to be thinking about the word *touch*.) (I'm just touched enough to make a mad dash for the stage if I don't keep myself firmly under control.) (Which would certainly be a first.)

Next came a really enormous pencil "for dear George to sign his valuable 'George Harrison' with." (Yes, yes, yes, and I get to say where.)

Prezzies?

The fifth and sixth prezzies were my special favorites. One was a bottle of smelling salts (which I have with me tonight) (you had better believe it), and the other was a pillow with a note that said: "This is for you to land on next time you shake hands with George (Pant) Harrison (Amen.) Try not to miss . . . we know you always fall hard for him and we can't afford another earthquake."

SPEAKING OF EARTHQUAKES, oh Gawd, Gawd, Gawd. They've just flashed on a sign! The Beatles are HERE! I can't write any more (I ever *could*?) I can't even think! He's in his dressing room, *dressing*! Oh, stomp, stomp, stomp, and forget it. I'll have to continue this after I get home tonight. Providing, of course, that I *live*.

Until then . . .

It is now just after midnight, and it's all over. I'm still not home, but a whole blithering gang of us have house to talk about the concert (not to mention gnash our teeth.)

I've just read over what I scribbled at the concert, and it sounds like it was written by a maniac. (*Welllllll?*) And here I'd really wanted to *say* something. You know, capture the magic of the moment on paper and all thot rot. And all I did was *rave*. (They don't call me the *Tower of Babble* for nothing.)

Well, if you think the first part of this mess is nothing but a lot of hysteria, wait until you read the *rest!* For, you see, I am no longer hysterical. I am now PANIC-STRICKEN.

I saw him, out there in that adorable green suit. And besides getting all the expected feelings, I suddenly came down with the weirdest sensation. I think a lot of you will understand exactly what I mean.

All of a sudden I just couldn't stand the distance another *second*. Him being so far away from me, I mean.

Olde Throat

I can see what makes people risk their lives and endanger their favorites just to get close for a minute. It shouldn't happen, but I can see why it does. Something just takes ahold of you right by the olde throat.

Well, I managed to keep from throwing myself at his feet, but I am not making any promises about what may happen during the next couple of days.

I cannot STAND for George (Moan) Harrison to be in this country without my at least talking to him or *something*. I don't know what I'm going to do, but I'm not going to just *sit* here. I just *can't*!

Don't worry, I won't do anything drastic.

I may be the retarded type, but underneath it all, I am extraordinarily sneaky.

Hmmmm. Come to think of it, the latter is even *worse* than the former. But, like I always say, no one is perfect.

Stay tuned for the further adventures of Shirley and George (stoke), and look out, G.P.H., because *here I come!*

Music—Not Name—4 Seasons' Secret

The Four Seasons are what their name implies—perennial. For a decade they have not only defied fad, but have also ignored the traditional crash to earth pop groups experience after a couple of hits.

The music of the Four Seasons has a sort of timeless interchangeability to it. "Sherry," for instance, would probably be as well received today as it was six years ago.

And "I've Got You Under My Skin," their latest release, would likely have enjoyed the same success in the early 1960's.

To understand the formula of the Four Seasons' unyielding success, you have to understand them as musicians. Dick Clark offers this explanation for their staying power with a variety of audiences:

"They're not a teenage group fresh up from the ranks. They have a good solid, well rehearsed act and sound which will be able to take them through night clubs and concert dates in both the teen and adult field."

Another secret of the Seasons is that they're not satisfied to be just a name—continuing to sell records on the basis of what they have done in the past.

So, to make sure this wasn't the case, early this year they released a single under the pseudonym "The Wonder Who."

The group already occupied the number one spot on the charts with "Let's Hang On," but "Don't Think Twice," released under the pseudonym, came very close to replacing it.

Another factor in the success of the group is their high degree of professionality.

Bob Gaudio, who has written the majority of the Season's material, says the group's schedule only allows them to record every three months.

This is particularly true because the Seasons, hearty perfectionists, spend a lot of time working on new material. "We never cut a song without a full scale conference first," said Bob.

There has been only one major change in the Seasons during their 11 year history as a group. And that came when 25-year-old Joe Long replaced retiring Nick Massi with the quartet.

Otherwise, the Seasons' lineup has remained the same with Tommy de Vito, Bob Gaudio, and Frankie Valli—the high pitched "sound" of the group that gives it a unique quality.

The group has been so close knit it came as a big surprise to most people last year when Frankie recorded without the other three Seasons.

Rumors immediately began to circulate that the group was about to split, but Frankie was the first to deny this speculation.

"You see," Frankie explained, "the Four Seasons are a corporation . . . a corporate body. We split everything into equal shares. So I make a hit single and it makes a lot of loot and . . . well, we all share in it.

"I figure that anything that can help the Seasons is just fine and dandy with me."

And with this kind of attitude, it's not hard to understand why they've weathered 11 years together. They will probably last 11 more.

GOING OVER AN ARRANGEMENT together during the latest 4 Seasons' recording session are (l. to r.) Joe Long, Frankie Valli, Bob Gaudio, producer Bob Crewe, conductor Arnie Schroeck and Tommy de Vito. The result? "I've Got You Under My Skin," naturally!!

KRLA ARCHIVES

BEAT SHOWCASE
(spotlighting new talent on the pop scene)

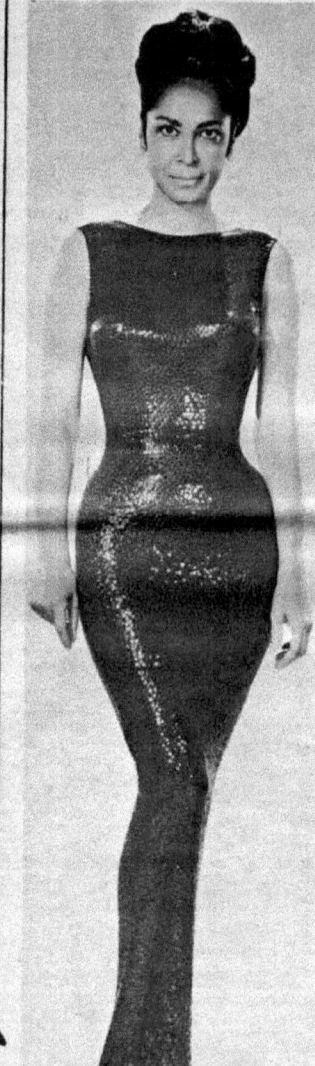

...a true beauty.
MARIA COLE
A year and a half after her husband's death, Maria Cole is once again launching the singing career she left behind 18 years ago to marry King Nat. Now, she says, it's a matter of "personal fulfillment." Her first album contains a large collection of ballads, which will surely renew the career of the former Duke Ellington songstress, and lend Maria a "great sense of accomplishment."

(l. to r.) Paul, Jorgen and Torben...handsome Danishmen.

THE LOLLIPOPS
Two brothers (Jorgen and Torben) and an uncle (Paul) might well be the next big sensation to hit the U.S. It stands to reason, since the handsome Danish boys have already swept the Scandanavian countries -- Sweden, Denmark, Finland and Norway. So many Americans have heard the group abroad that soon their records will be released Stateside. Though young in years (Paul, 18; Torben, 16; Jorgen, 15), the group are accomplished songwriters and speak, write and sing in English much of the time. If the boys are as charming as their picture, they'll be a hit indeed!

...first group signed to the newly formed Round Records.

CAPES OF GOOD HOPE
On the strength of their first single, "Shades" b/w "Lady Margaret," which is receiving enthusiastic reception, the Chicago-based Capes of Good Hope have high hopes of becoming one of the nation's hottest recording groups. From left they are: Mike Horn, Dick Toops, Yogi Landem (guess why!), Mike Jacobsen and Joel Cory.

KRLA ARCHIVES

Beatle Tour—'Like Playing In A Closet'

By Rochelle Reed

"Playing the Beatle tour was like performing in a closet with the lights off," confessed Briggs, one of the Remains who wandered up to *The BEAT* office the day after their last performance.

"It was a matter of an instrument being on or off," chimed in their road manager, "with no room for subtleties. Either the crowds could hear or they couldn't."

Apparently U.S. crowds could hear the group, because The Remains admitted reaction "was better than we'd thought it would be."

The BEAT was surprised to see The Remains at all, considering that they had just concluded 24 performances that at best could be described as "hectic."

Actually, we didn't see *all* The Remains. Briggs, Barry and Vern showed up, but N.D., their drummer, was somewhere between Hollywood and San Francisco.

"He didn't make it back," said Barry. "He got on the plane in San Francisco and then got off and said he just couldn't do it."

Flying Phobia

N.D. has a phobia about flying and left the plane once before when the craft threw sparks over Seattle. But N.D. used to be an acrobat and walk tightropes 300 feet off the ground. "Oh well," said Briggs, "that's N.D."

The three Remains, although tired, were almost radiating with new ideas for their act. "It's like closing a chapter in our careers," Barry said. "We're thinking about different directions we can take musically," Vern added. "Maybe we won't even play for awhile, just for a kick," chimed in Briggs, "we need time to think the whole thing out."

Vern admitted that the tour has made the group "hungrier for fame" than ever before. "It opened our eyes where they had been closed before," added Barry, and Briggs continued. "We learned that what's honest, both musically and personally, is best."

How did the Remains get on the tour in the first place? "A few people up there like us a lot," according to Briggs.

The Remains, who are noted for the true hard rock that they play, opened all the Beatle shows and then backed up Bobby Hebb and the Ronettes.

Never Back

"Backing was something we told ourselves we'd never do," Barry said, and said they almost refused the tour before deciding maybe the excitement and fame was worth it all.

"But we only had an hour and a half to practice with the other groups before we had to back them in our first show," Barry said, so they decided to not even try to simulate the backup sound that Bobby and the Ronettes use on their records.

Rather than sound like a poor imitation, Briggs explained, "we played our way and Bobby and the Ronettes liked it. At San Francisco, it turned into a way-out jazz session in the middle of 'Sunny.'"

The largest welcome for the tour, the group decided after much debate, was in Chicago, whereas Detroit holds the distinction of having the most junk thrown onstage. Memphis was infamous, the group said, because someone threw a cherry bomb at the platform.

But The Remains came through without any major hang ups and are now eagerly looking to the future and the "embelishments" they will make on their sound.

The group has a new album coming out, which they consider the best of what they used to do. It's called "Don't Look Back" after their hit single.

"Major diversity" is planned for their sound. Once known only as a hard rock blues band, they will now go softer and do the songs that they've always wanted to include in their repertoire.

"Right now our audience is growing up," says Briggs, "and

THE REMAINS — N.D., Vern, Briggs and Barry.

also calming down. They will appreciate talent even more than before."

So The Remains plan a search into who they really are, musically and personally. They credit the Beatles with giving them "a better insight in our search."

"They were everything I'd hoped they'd be," Barry said. "It's nice to know that the people who seem to be right think the way you do and like the things you like."

Barry became good friends with George Harrison, and the two spent many hours listening to sitar music that George brought over on tape. In Los Angeles, the two slipped out one night and visited many of the pop groups who call L.A. their home.

"It was great, really finding where these people are at," Barry said.

Though New England, mainly Boston, is home for the Remains, they hope to become more popular in other parts of the country. Until now, they have concentrated on college tours and large clubs in the East.

Barry Tashian, lead guitar player, has often been called "the white James Brown." William Brigg, or just Briggs as he is known, is a tall, sandy blond organist with the group. A talkative, bright-eyed musician, he would like to live in Balboa for awhile "without any shoes and not play at all, just for kicks."

"Crazy Things"

Vern Miller, the smallest of the Remains, was once a classical musician and plays just about everything, including guitar. He would like to branch out into electronic music. N.D. Smart II is the drummer for the group and as yet unmet by the *BEAT* staff. "He used to want to jump off bridges in Boston," the group explains, "and he does crazy, incredible things."

Anyway, N.D. is the most recent member of the group and used to play for Paul of Peter, Paul and Mary when he recorded alone.

The Remains now stand where many groups would like to—they have received the widest exposure any group could possibly hope for and "learned a lot." Though they are "hungrier for fame," they are also humbled a little. They are eager to attack their music and remake it to fit what they have become. Then, with minor embellishments and major diversity, they will put it to work.

AFTER THEIR ACT, The Remains backed Bobby Hebb and the Ronettes.

BEAT Photos: Howard L. Bingham

KRLA ARCHIVES

Taping A Television Special

The *BEAT* recently watched the filming of a Rogers and Hart Television Special scheduled for airing next March and featuring the Mama's and Papa's, Supremes, Petula Clark and Bobby Darin.

In sharp contrast to the casual funkiness of the Mama's and Papa's was the sleek elegance of the Supremes, who changed outfits and wigs between practically every number, and the always sharp looking Petula.

Since the show won't be aired until next year, the participants chosen were those who, in the estimation of the producers, would definitely still be stars at that time and The *BEAT* agrees—these are four of the top acts in the business and we see no downfall ahead for any of them.

THE TWO SOLO ARTISTS on the show, Bobby Darin and Petula Clark, get together on a large box to sing a duet of Rogers and Hart songs.

THE SUPREMES, attired in full length, sequined, multi-colored gowns are the stand-outs in the finale. The three beautiful Motown artists appear on the show in several different outfits — all absolutely gorgeous.

BOBBY DARIN JOINS THE SUPREMES in just one of the show's many great numbers. The entire program is a triubte to Rogers and Hart, who have composed and arranged so many of the great American standards.

OUR PET PETULA wows the audience on one of her solo numbers. Be sure to catch the show on NBC-TV shown sometime early next Spring.

KRLA ARCHIVES

Jerry Naylor's Learned A New Recipe For Success

Recipe of the week: take a large portion of a big beat sound, blend in a healthy amount of jazz and blues, flavor with a sprinkling of western sound... and serve.

The final product of this somewhat offbeat concoction will be one Jerry Naylor – and one of the most unique and original sounds be dished out by the record industry in some time.

Handsome, soft-spoken Jerry Naylor, currently hitting the charts hard with his "Almost Persuaded," had been doing standard, time-worn arrangements of rock 'n' roll for some time before he came up with his new twist.

The Hard Way

"Last year I recorded a couple of unsuccessful records with the standard rock sound," said Jerry. "I found, the hard way, that no identity was shown in these records and no one knew if I could sing or not.

"I still sounded like a 'group' on these records. I want identity and the only way to get that is to sing like Jerry Naylor." And for Jerry Naylor, identity does not consist of the current Liverpool sound.

But don't fool yourself by thinking that just because Jerry Naylor's songs have a slight western orientation he is out of the groove or in a different field than pop.

"Many people are recording country and western material today and doing it very successfully," he said. "Gene Pitney, Johnny Tillotson, Dean Martin, Al Martino, Vic Dana and Bobby Vinton are a few of them.

"And even the Beatles last year had a big hit with Buck Owens' 'Act Naturally.' So did Ray Charles when he did two other of Buck's compositions, 'Crying Time' and 'Together Again.'"

Jerry's contributions to the music world haven't gone unnoticed – or unappreciated. Since last January he has been touring throughout the United States, and his audience response and reviews have been what he calls "enthusiastically encouraging."

After a particulary commanding performance in San Francisco recently, several columnists even went so far as to compare him to Roger Miller, Bobby Darin, Jimmy Dean and Wayne Newton.

Actually, Jerry Naylor is a little bit of all of these entertainers. His act is surprisingly polished and he has a profound effect on live audiences.

Jerry's tour with Jimmy Dean last year can partially account for his tremendous on-stage show. The tour covered ten cities from New Mexico to Iowa – with the climax coming when the two taped a television spectacular before 7,000 people.

Chart Fight

Jerry's version of "Almost Persuaded" is catching on all across the nation — but not without a struggle. David Houston also has a version of the same song out and both artists are battling for pop markets throughout the country.

Even if Jerry's version of the song doesn't make it he still need not worry. The flip side of the record contains his own composition, "I'll Get My Lie The Way I Want To," which is picked to become a hit by many of the nation's top trade magazines and radio stations.

...JERRY NAYLOR

Up Beat By Eden

It's been a long, long time for the young man who started out singing a song called "Splish, Splash," – but Bobby Darin has come up with another giant-sized hit.

His latest release is a tune entitled "If I Were A Carpenter." The words are really great – simply stated and to the point – and the haunting meoldy ties it up to present a musical package which is hard to forget. Hope that pop people will remember to make this one a big hit.

* * *

Herb Alpert and the TJ Whatevers have returned to pay their monthly greetings to the top of the charts with their latest, "Flamingo." It really is a good disc, and just different enough to be another hit for the group.

* * *

"Only When You're Lonely" is the latest single by the Grass Roots. If you like this one – and many people do already – you may also have cast a positive vote for their previous hit,"Where Were You When I Needed You."

That's not at all unusual, considering that both records are very good – this last one being the better of the two musically. But what is unusual is the story behind these two bits o' wax, and it will probably surprise a lot of people.

Keep your ear on this one for the Top Ten – keep your eyes on the label, which lists the writers as Sloan-Barri, and the producers as Sloan-Barri – and tune into this column next issue around for a little surprise about the singers.

* * *

Mr. Frank Sinatra, in spite of his recent marriage, hasn't forgotten his duties as "Chairman of the Board," and has returned with a follow-up smash to his "Strangers in the Night," entitled "Summer Wind."

This one's a beauty, but unlike the first disc – it will probably be much larger on the "good music" stations.

* * *

Top teen fave-rave of the week – Len Barry – has returned to the pop race with "I Struck It Rich." Hmmmm – wonder if he means with the 35-and-above-crowd? Certainly couldn't be any of us scruffy "long-hair" types!

* * *

Two pretty new ballads have arrived this week from two consistent chart-toppers in Britain. One is by a talented young American who has been a huge star in Britain for several years while we have failed to fully recognize his talents on this side of the foam.

Gene Pitney's newest self-penned release is "Cold Light of Day." Listen for it. British subjects, Gerry and the Pacemakers, are back in the American chart-race in an attempt to dispel their one-hit wonder image, and they have a strong vehicle with their newest, "Girl on a Swing."

* * *

Do you remember the M.F.Q.? If so, you might remember a talented young man by the name of Chip Taylor (sometimes known as Chip Douglas), now a member of the Gene Clark Group – the leader of which used to be a member of the Byrds.

At any rate, Chip has written a great new song called "I Can Make It With You," which has been recorded by a girl named Jackie De Shannon who used to have a lot of hits, and was never in any group.

Unfortunately, Jackie's last two or three discs haven't been up to her usual high performance, and her rendition of this song isn't the best. The track is just a little bit obscure, and the sentiment seems almost affected. The record might get into the Top 20, but it will take a while.

* * *

New ones in the 45 RPM race this week include "What A Party," by Tom Jones; "I Really Don't Want to Know" by Ronnie Dove; "San Francisco Woman," by Bob Lind; and – believe it or not! – "Tarzan's Dance," by the Marketts.

Brand new record on the move this week is the latest by Tommy Roe – "Hooray for Hazel." Wild idea for an unusual lyric, and it even has a good beat! Hitsville for this one.

KRLA ARCHIVES

Beatles' Love Affair

(Continued from Page 7)

read in the papers. You people make up our image. We know what our *real* image is and it's nothing like our 'image'."

Back to John again and "did you meet Cass of the Mama's and Papa's?" "Yes," replied John with that fantastically teasing grin of his, "and she's great. I'm going to see her tonight."

Along about this time, a female reporter stood up and asked John if it was true he was going to make a movie without the other Beatles. And it was then that my opinion of John flew up a neat one hundred notches. Because rather than inform her that question had already been asked and answered a mere five minutes ago, he simply said, "yes."

Security?

Positively one of the more brilliant questions was concerning whether or not the Beatles really needed the tight security which seems to follow them everywhere. "What do you think?" thundered John. Silence soared all around the room until the man admitted he didn't think the Beatles could make it without security. Nodding, John answered: "We *wouldn't* make it. We couldn't make it."

"Sometimes we could," argued Paul. "But today we couldn't have made it," he continued in reference to the fans who stood outside Capitol and rushed the armored truck when it came into view.

Someone else wanted to know if the Beatles would draw an equal share of John's salary for "How I Won The War." "No," replied John, "we only share when we use the name 'Beatles.' If the name 'Beatles' is on a record then we all share but they don't make anything on my books."

Finally, the inevitable question of whether the Beatles would be back next year was asked. It's asked every year, and every year the Beatles give approximately the same answer. This time John did the honors: "We have no idea. We'll probably be back."

Then, of course, someone insisted on asking Paul the same question they've been asking ever since Walter Winchell made the premature announcement that Paul and Jane Asher were in fact married.

And, so once again, Paul answered: "I'll probably get married but I've no plans now."

Shot Down

During the rest of the press conference, the Beatles informed the world that the final script for their third movie had not yet been finished but when it is, and if they still like it, they will begin filming in January, that Lennon-McCart-

ney write most of their songs and that "it's an amicable arrangement" and finally Paul shot down a reporter for saying that other artists have stolen Beatle material.

"They don't *steal* them," stated Paul. "No, I know they don't," replied the reporter. "But you just said they did," answered Paul, "and, besides, we pinch just as much as the rest of 'em."

Another question of magnitude — who are John's favorite groups? "There are so many," said the Chief, "The Mama's & Papa's, the Spoonful, the Byrds, the Beach Boys."

Following the official press conference, the Beatles were presented with their 20th Gold Record by Capitol Records President, Alan Livingston, for their "Revolver" album.

Mr. Livingston made the announcement and then the huge curtains behind the Beatles parted, revealing a gigantic blow-up of the "Revolver" cover and four shining Gold Records.

The Beatles were notably as surprised as the rest of us when the records were presented and it was made known that with this 20th Gold Record they had received more Goldies than any other artist in the history of the recording industry.

Ringo aptly summed up the group's feelings by saying: "It's such a lovely surprise."

Three lucky girls who head up the Dallas Beatles' Fan Club were next on the agenda. They presented the four Beatles with initialed steak branding irons. About meeting the Beatles, Yolanda, Stephanie and Debbie chorused that "it was fantastic!" The Beatles themselves seemed to think it was rather fantastic too, as they busily set about branding each other with the steak irons!

On a whole, the Beatle press conference '66 style was very similar to the '64 and '65 editions. Probably a drag in the extreme for John, Paul, George and Ringo as the majority of reporters continue to ask the same monotonous questions as regularly as they collect their pay checks each week.

Humor — Tolerance

For their part, the Beatles handled the press as they would a small child — with humor, tolerance and an occasional straight answer where it was deserved.

And now they're back in England. Their third Stateside tour a success. Despite the bannings and burnings, they scored again. It *is* true that the wild, hysterical, follow-the-crowd Beatlemania which was born in '64 and ripe in '65 is a little tarnished in '66. There were fewer sell-outs but as George put it "we don't really need them anyway."

However, even with the not-so true fans gone the Beatles are still very much in the driver's seat, still the owners of the Pop Throne. Still the heads of their special world.

Will they be back again? Despite all the trade talk that they will not, I think we'll see them next year. Not in a major tour but rather in a few key cities. It's only a hunch, naturally, as no one knows what next year will bring. But I expect it to bring the Beatles back to California. After all, they wouldn't want to kill a love affair, would they?

...THE ALAN PRICE SET (l. to r.) Roy, Steve, John, Boots, Clive and Alan Price (center) have finally come up with a long awaited hit single here in America with their fantastic "I Put A Spell on You." Be sure to see the next issue of BEAT for an in-depth interview with the group written exclusively for The BEAT.

Tony Barrow Kills The Beatle Rumors

(Continued from Page 6)

America for the reason stated in the papers, which I thought made the situation sound even more serious.

A: "He was concerned, of course, and did want to see what was going on, but you can look at his time of arrival one of two ways — five days late or three days early."

Q: One last subject. Was there a press conference in every city?

A: "The Beatles saw the press in each of the fourteen cities they visited. In some cities, we were able to hold full-scale press conferences. In others, we were able to see only area newsmen due to time or space problems, etc."

Q: How did the press conferences go this year, and which did you consider the best of the lot?

New York Best

A: "Some were better than others — New York was the best. But an interesting thing happened around the country. Many newspapers used to just assign *a* reporter, but this year they sent along people with a more mature outlook. A number of drama and music critics attended. They seem to be accepting the Beatles on a more mature level. The Beatles themselves are far more mature. In experience, age, and intellectually as well."

Q: Weren't there two press conferences in New York?

A: "One was the regular confer-

ence, and the other was a junior press conference. It was held at the Beatles' request — they wanted to hear the fans' questions for a change — and they thoroughly enjoyed it. The 'reporters' were picked at random from the New York chapter of the official Beatles' fan club and listeners of WMCA."

Q: Did they scream during the press conference?

A: "They were a bit rowdy at first, but they settled down and it was a good conference. The idea worked, and it will definitely be repeated."

Q: Do you think it bothers the Beatles when they're asked at a press conference, what their music is trying to say? Creative people are often very sensitive about having their work questioned, even if they don't show it.

A: "The Beatles accept questions as they come. At a standard press conference, you get the standard range of writers. There are people like ourselves, who know all about pop music because it's our business. There are others who know very little about it, but are still some of the best journalists in the country. The Beatles take this into consideration, and don't let it bother them."

Plane To Catch

At this point, I noticed that Tony was looking rather nervously at his watch. He was leaving for London that same evening, and had a plane to catch, and when he

Cyrkle In Million $ Law Suit

A one million dollar lawsuit has been filed against the Cyrkle and managers Brian Epstein and Nathan Weiss.

Jerry Ross, whose Sheryl Records, Inc., formerly had the group under contract, is the plaintiff. He claims he still has the legal recording rights on the Cyrkle.

The group had recorded under the name "Rondells" for Sheryl and their records had previously been released on ABC.

The group's contract with Sheryl was dated Nov. 7, 1964, with renewal rights through 1969. The terms of the contract called for the group to record for Sheryl exclusively.

Ross claimed the group's contract had been renewed for at least one more year though November, 1966.

Weiss and Epstein became interested in the group early this year and signed as its managers. Epstein insisted the group's name be changed, and by courteousy of John Lennon, Cyrkle was decided upon.

Since that time the group has had two hit records, "Red Rubber Ball" and "Turn Down Day."

---

saw what time it was, he had to say goodbye.

I stayed at the table for awhile after he'd gone, hoping that my final words to him would turn out to be the truest ever spoken.

They were, of course, "see you next August."

KRLA ARCHIVES

KRLA ARCHIVES

America's Largest Teen NEWSpaper 25¢

KRLA Edition BEAT
OCTOBER 8, 1966

Monkees Taking Over

By Force Of 30,000,000
SEE PAGE 1

KRLA BEAT

Volume 2, Number 25 — October 8, 1966

Backers Found For Stones

The Rolling Stones have found a partner.

Decca Records, Ltd. has signed agreements to enter into a joint venture with the Stones to finance their forthcoming movie, "Only Lovers Left Alive." Financing the movie will cost an estimated $2,800,000.

Sir Edward Lewis, chairman of the British record company, negotiated with Allen Klein of the Stone management for the joint venture.

The Stones, who will receive more than $1,000,000 in their film debut, will begin shooting late this month.

Klein and Andrew Loog Oldham, Rolling Stones' manager, will produce the film for release by MGM.

The screenplay, patterned after the book by the same name, concerns the Mod generation taking over England.

The novel's plot remains the same in the screenplay, but alterations had to be made with several of the book's characters.

Monkees To Be TV's Beatles?

Will the Monkees be to television what the Beatles are to the recording industry — the biggest thing to hit the screen since commercials? Screen Gems thinks so and accordingly has signed Davy Jones, Mike Nesmith, Mickey Dolenz and Peter Tork (collectively known as the Monkees) to an exclusive seven year contract.

Says Steve Blaunder of Screen Gems: "We plan to give them the same publicity treatment as the Beatles in every respect. With 30,000,000 people watching them regularly Monday night they should be bigger than the Beatles."

Movies

The studio also announced that under the terms of the contract, they will produce one or more feature films starring the Monkees. The group's first film is scheduled for shooting during the summer of '67 when the television show takes it's "vacation" from filming. Other movies will be made depending on the success of the series.

However, that success seems assured. Screen Gems has spent a small fortune on the Monkees and, from all indications, it is paying off with big dividends.

Following the show's debut on NBC, The BEAT questioned roughly a hundred young people who had seen the show. The overwhelming majority of the teens were enthusiastically in favor of the Monkees, both as actors and as singers.

At random, then, here are some of the comments we received. "They're really groovy, I especially love Davy Jones. He's so darling."

"I thought the show was great. It's kinda like 'A Hard Day's Night' but it's even better 'cause it's in color and we can see it every week."

"I liked it but it was a little corny in parts. The guys are groovy, though, and I hope they have one of those interviews at the end of the show every week. That was the best part — except for the commercials. They were funny, too."

Fresh Idea!

"I dug it because it's a fresh, new idea for a television series. I think it's good for at least two years, maybe even longer. Of course, next year we'll probably have a show like that on every single station but like the Beatles, the Monkees will always be the most popular because they were first."

"I luv 'em. Mickey and Mike are so funny and Davy's so cute and Peter's just so... Anyway, even my parents liked the show and *(Turn to Page 5)*

THE MONKEES (l. to r.) Mike, Mickey, Davy and Peter have been signed to an exclusive seven year contract by Screen Gems with movies also in the offing. Their first feature film is scheduled for the summer of '67.

Herb Praised In U.S. Senate

Herbie Alpert and his Tijuana Brass received their biggest boost yet when Senator Thomas Kuchel praised the group on the floor of the U.S. Senate.

In part, Senator Kuchel said: "This team has contributed immeasurably to international understanding and promoted cordial relations with peoples around the globe.

"In a day when discordant sounds and irregular beats seemingly have a provacative attraction for unknown numbers, it is rewarding that a Southern California musical organization specializes in what may be called joyous music, affecting melody with humor and vigor and affection for life."

The Senator went on to say: "The effectiveness of their communication in what long has been recognized as a universal language was manifested a year ago when citizens of Mexico presented Mr. Alpert and his associates with a Good Neighbor Award. The citation saluted their influence in 'fostering better understanding and friendship' between our two adjoining Republics."

SENATOR AND MRS. KUCHEL greet Mr. and Mrs. Herbie Alpert outside the Senate chamber in Washington D.C. following Senator Kuchel's praise of Herb Alpert and the T.J. Brass on the floor of the Senate.

Inside the BEAT

Letters To The Editor	2
Neil Diamond In Competition	3
"In" People Are Talking	4
Sonny and Cher Meet Pope	5
Pics In The News	7
Wild Affair In Viet Nam	8
"Gassy" Brian Hyland	9
Cherishing The Association	10-11
Biggest Cat — James Brown	14

The BEAT is published bi-weekly by BEAT Publications, Inc., editorial and advertising offices at 6290 Sunset Blvd., Suite 504, Hollywood, California, 90028. U.S. bureaus in Hollywood, San Francisco, New York, Chicago and Nashville, overseas correspondents in London, Liverpool and Manchester, England. Sale price, 15 cents. Subscription price: U.S. and possessions, $5 per year; Canada and foreign rates, $9 per year. Second class postage prepaid at Los Angeles, California.

PETE TO LEAVE KINKS: REPLACED BY HAYDOCK

The BEAT has discovered that Pete Quaife, bass guitarist for the Kinks, may leave the group and join the BEA's advertisement department as a designer.

Quaife was injured in an auto accident over three months ago and has been unable to play since. There are strong indications, but no definite word, that his departure from the Kinks is because of his injuries.

Quaife is vacationing in Copenhagen and refused to comment on the alleged break with the group.

It seems unlikely that he would willingly give up singing for a career in commercial art. He once worked as a trainee on a men's magazine but says of the experience, "I was very much the flunky. I made lakes of coffee and did very little else. Finally, I left out of sheer boredom."

Amidst heavy speculation that Eric Haydock will soon be joining the Kinks, both Eric and the Kinks have denied interest in the merge.

A representative for both the Hollies and the Kinks, however, denied the rumors. "There's not a chance of it," said publicist Allan McDougal.

Eric recently left the Hollies when his former mates charged he took too much time off and missed too many engagements. He countered that the only time he took off was when his wife was having a baby.

He is still looking for a group — but says he will probably form a new group rather than join an established one.

"I'm looking for musicians at the moment," he said, "and I hope to have a group formed as soon as possible."

KRLA ARCHIVES

Letters TO THE EDITOR

Open Stone Letter

Dear Bill, Brian, Charlie, Keith and Mick:

When I heard "Play With Fire" or whatever it was that was pretty crummy but was your first hit anyway, you didn't appeal to me. And lately, when I still didn't quite open both ears and the strains of "Satisfaction" filled the radio waves, people would point at me, whisper that I didn't like the song and cry: "Look at that stupid girl!"

So, seeing that I was missing something, being the only one who wasn't under Mick's thumb, I came alive, joined the Pepsi generation, pulled the cotton out of my ears and let "Aftermath" blow every tissue of my mind.

A lot of people don't like your appearance — well, if they don't like it, they can look the other way.

"The Spider And The Fly" is the best you've ever done. I listen to it eating, drinking, sleeping, walking and doing odds and ends of other things. I tell everyone to keep fidelity in their heads (my cat calmly told me the other day to keep fidelity in *my* own head and leave his alone.)

If your movie ever gets to my town, I'll be sure to add my dollar seventy-five to the till. Only I hope it has a moral I can fathom. "A Hard Day's Night" was too deep for my younger generation brain.

I have one question, only one question, that I'd like to ask you if I ever saw you: Do you bite people? You must, 'cause we're all infected with it. Or maybe it's not an illness. Maybe it's just the feeling you get when you're under Mick's thumb.
Lyn

THANKS

Dear Shirley Poston:

Thank you for printing "When England Went To War." I, too, cried because of the bad and empty feeling that was a realization of how it would feel without my (our) Beatles. It was a stark, beautifully sad realization.

And I never would have gotten this so abruptly, so really, had I not read this poem — had you decided not to print it. I now have an idea of how life would be without the Beatles — the boys we sometimes take for granted ... Misery.
Terry Jacobsen

Witty 'In'

Dear BEAT:

I am also a fan of "In" People. And as every sidewalk wit I have a few additions to suggest.

Why the Pancake Man stepped on a girl ... Who really sent Dave those postcards and how John-John let it slip ... Why Eden went for that walk ... Jeremy's fantastic tab and who is signing his name there ... What fell besides sugar.

I hope you will use my contributions because the "In" people are really talking about them.
Jeni

SIX-PAGE PEACH

Dear BEAT:

Please enroll me as a faithful subscriber for one year trial (option on lifetime addiction.) Tucked away in this picturesque hole (Waterbury, Connecticut) I've little opportunity to contact the pop world which I find so fascinating. So, I enjoy The BEAT a great deal. Don't always agree with you but I like you.

Congratulations on your expansion — hope everything works out to your fondest expectations. As a feature, may I venture to suggest that you do a SIX-page highly-illustrated coverage of the epic of Jim McCarty's fake peach (which you so nastily gave us tempting references to in the most frustrating column in the rag, P.A.T.A.)? The question mark is due to the undeniable, lamentable fact that the previous meandering began as a question!!

I like also Shirley Poston and Louise Criscione (any friend of Keith Relf's is a friend of mine. And, she's got Jim's peach, hasn't she?)

Why don't you do articles on Michael Caine, mainly Tom Courtenay, Terence Stamp, actor-types who really *can* act!

Also a feature on an English Rep. company would be new, scoop-like, never-before and all those Cousin Brucie thingies (as in *Yech!*)

Since I work (?) as editor of my (highly-conservative, Catholic girls' school, literary-quality-before-readability) school rag, the fact that you manage to come out bi-monthly mystifies me.

We're trying for sweeping (as in soggy straw) changes, though.

Oh — Dick Lester is directing and Michael Crawford is starring in J.W. Lennon, MBE's new flic. In all decency, you should have mentioned that!

Please do a large, lots-of-pix interview with the Yardbirds. Only, please, more quotes, fewer author's opinions. (No, that shouldn't be author, but I like that word today.)

Good luck, don't take any wooden bananas, start mailing soon. Say hi to Jeff Beck, keep the flag waving, bury Barry Sadler, Lennon is right, and remember the pot of mystic, near-sighted purple geraniums.
Renee Beaulieu

'In' People Notes

Dear BEAT:

Some notes for your "In" column: How come some people who have grown needle-blase now get their kicks from slanting the news; all those righteous 11 year olds who would jump off bridges if they read what Dr. Shcoenfield had to say about it; the brilliance of "Revolver" from cover in; what 9,000 means; what 45,000 doesn't; how America was done proud because more people turned out to be anti-bigot than pro-Christian; why The BEAT mentioned Longview but didn't mention the reaffirmation in Memphis; why it's nice to be atheistic, obscene, and suggestive because that means you're number one; how if John wrote a song that started "the sky is blue," all the hippies would say "that's not what he really means"; why my 43 year old mother is knitting lip covers for Mick's Mobile Mouth, but wants to wait until Next Time so she can get them personally autographed; how we will all stop listening to the Robbs because they don't have any right and how it was all vindicated and forgiven when The BEAT included that "gasp" photo on the right side.
Anon (isn't everybody?)

BEAT Photo: Chuck Boyd

Work Of Art

Dear BEAT:

I'd like to thank Shirley Poston for her wonderful column in the September 10th issue of The BEAT. I think the poem "When England Went To War" is a work of art. It made me cry and it really scares me.

I've always stood by the Beatles. I love 'em. Now, I love 'em even more. Please thank Miss Poston for me. She's great!
Linda J.

P.S. I love Jesus too!

SIR DOUGLAS

Dear BEAT:

Your interview with Sir Douglas was really great — but also long overdue because the Sir Douglas Quintet is one of the best bands in the country and I haven't seen many articles on them lately.

Please write more about them soon and how about some information on the individual members of the group?
Wendy Norris

Orient BEAT

Dear BEAT:

I am enclosing a copy of part of a letter written to me by my pen pal in Japan. I have sent her three or four copies of The BEAT. You should be proud of yourselves.

Congratulations.
Kathy Kelso

"Thank you very much for the copies of The BEAT you sent me. Even though we do not hear your radio station here, I enjoyed their newspaper very much.

"All the children in my area took turns reading them, even though most of us cannot read English. I read to most of them. I wish we could hear your radio station here."
Satako

Dear Kathy:

Thanks for your letter and also for spreading The BEAT to Japan. Our thanks also for the good words from Satako — if we could only print The BEAT in Japanese we'd be in business!
The BEAT

Terry Knight

Dear BEAT:

I think I am fairly aware of the groups and the records that are popular out there in California because I have a lot of friends there to write to and also because I subscribe to The BEAT.

Your BEAT is the greatest except for one minor thing — you seem to be oblivious to one of the best-looking, most talented singing groups to come out in a very, very long time. (As a matter of fact, ever since the YOU-KNOW-WHO started in Liverpool.) Their two records have made it big all through the East, and I'm sure the same thing would happen in California if some radio station played them!

The name of the group is Terry Knight and the Pack and they're all from Detroit, Michigan. Terry Knight, the lead singer and composer of most of their material, is a fabulous looking, 22 year old former disc jockey. He used to work for *the* radio station in Detroit, CKLW. He left to live with the Rolling Stones for awhile, where he developed his singing style (looks a lot like Jagger's — not many people can pull that off successfully, but he can.)

Now they've been on a tour and are coming out with a third record which will undoubtedly be a smash. Just like the other two. The first was a song the Yardbirds also recorded on their last album, "Better Man Than I." It has a number one sound. So, does their second one, which is currently in the top 10. Terry wrote it and it's called "A Change On The Way." It's fabulous.

Please don't ignore all this — they're an outstandingly great group and deserve recognition from all over. Give it a try — someday you may be known as the paper who discovered Terry Knight and the Pack!
Ellen Bernstein

Dear Ellen:

Consider Terry Knight and the Pack formally introduced to BEAT readers! Thanks for the info and who knows — maybe someday *you'll* be known as the girl who discovered Terry Knight and the Pack!
The BEAT

Teeny-Bopper

Dear BEAT:

I have just about had it up to my John Lennon cap with these ungrateful rock 'n' roll singers! I am a teenie-bopper and proud of it! What's wrong with buying every Beatle and Gary Lewis album? I luv them. I went to the Beatle concert and screamed the whole time they were on stage. And I waited 5-1/2 hours at the airport the day they arrived. I buy every magazine with stories and pix of my fave foursome.

I don't smoke pot. I hear it rots your teeth or something. So, think twice, you guys, before you cut down teens. Because if it weren't for us, you wouldn't have any jobs!
Susan Creamcheese

KRLA ARCHIVES

On the BEAT
By Louise Criscione

Had a nice chat with the Monkees the other day and managed to come up with a real scoop for you Monkee fans, especially you Mickey Dolenz fans. "I'm gonna buy a helicopter! They're groovy, they're so out of sight!" exclaimed Mickey. "They fly right over the roofs and you can stick out your foot and hit people in the head!" And where is Mickey going to keep this helicopter of his? "On the roof." Naturally.

All kidding aside, though, the Monkees are really a great bunch of funny guys. They're one of the dying few who still get a kick out of signing autographs and talking to fans, etc. A groovy change from a lot of the swell-headed, in love with themselves groups which are making the scene today.

Two A Week

The ones who really amaze me, however, are Tommy Boyce and Bobby Hart. They write the material for the Monkees and are supposed to come up with two new songs for each segment! Which is a heck of a lot of writing, you must admit. And besides all the writing for the Monkees, Tommy records as a solo artist for A&M Records and Bobby has his own group. Gluttons for punishment? Maybe, but just think of all the money they must be making!

Brian Jones was supposed to have broken his hand so badly that he would be out of action for the next two months. It must have really put Andy Oldham uptight because the Stones were due on "Ed Sullivan" as well as starting a British tour and, of course, their movie, "Only Lovers Left Alive" is coming up in October.

... MICKEY DOLENZ

However, relief arrived when Brian was able to fly into New York for their "Sullivan" stint wearing only an elastic bandage and a Carnaby Street suit. Concerning the Stones on "Sullivan" the question of the week is: "How come Mick's barber forgot the back?"

The Association have definitely changed their stage act for the better. They've chucked most of those long comic routines they used to do. A wise move because the routines, while funny the first time you see them, get to be a real drag after you've seen the show several times.

Beautifully Round

Russ admitted to being a little uncertain about playing the Carousel Theatre because it was the first time the Association had played on a round stage. And that would scare anybody! But they came off beautifully and what with six group members, no matter where you were seated you could see *some* of their faces.

"Cherish" should be number one in the nation by the time you read this. Which only figures since I predicted it would never be a big hit! Only proving the point that fortune telling should be left to the Stones' fortune teller.

Poor Scott Walker. First the unfortunate "incident" in his London flat and now he took a tumble down the stairs of his new flat and was knocked unconscious! Some days it pays *not* to get up.

The funniest line of the year came from Sam The Sham. Said the bearded giant: "Mary Poppins is a junkie. I don't care what you say—nobody can fly *that* high with only an umbrella!"

For those of us who declared that Gary Lewis would be a one hit wonder—take note. Gary is celebrating his second year with Liberty Records. During the two years, Gary has chalked up two number one records, "This Diamond Ring" and "Everybody Loves A Clown" and has managed to sell five million dollars worth of singles. Like I said before—predictions to the fortune teller.

... GARY LEWIS

QUICK ONES: The Beatles have been awarded their 21st Gold Reocrd. "Yellow Submarine" b/w "Eleanor Rigby" has sold the necessary million. So, what's new?... Speaking of the Beatles, their tour partners, the Ronettes, are supposedly vacationing with the Beatles in Saint-Tropez ... Elvis and the Colonel anonymously donated $3,000 to the Playhouse Telethon.

Competition For Diamond

NEW YORK — Neil Diamond of "Solitary Man" fame has been signed by Associated Booking Corporation, winner of the heated competition surrounding Diamond.

The agency competition for Neil had been building up since his smash "Solitary Man" and came to such a head when "Cherry, Cherry" was released that Diamond found it necessary to "duck out of sight for a week" while his attorneys went through the negotiation hassle.

Associated has high hopes for Neil. Says Sol Saffian, who will handle Diamond at Associated: "We expect Neil Diamond to become an artist of major importance. He has proven himself as a song writer and recording artist of consistant quality but even more exciting is the fact that as a performer in a business of look-alike—soundalike acts he comes across as an individual, one who is able to develop a very personal rapport with his audience. We are very pleased to have this fresh new talent with us."

Although Neil has played with roughly 40 groups, he says he really got started about two years ago. "Before it was just to make a buck. I used to write poems and things and then I started putting them to music and I liked what I was able to do. I wrote for other people — Sonny & Cher, Bobby Vinton, Andy Williams, The Vogues, The Bachelors — but I really wanted to do it myself."

He did it himself with "Solitary Man", though ironically enough Neil didn't even want to record the self-penned song. "I wrote it just for myself," said Neil. "It was a personal thing to me and I didn't want to record it. After about three months of arguing I decided to do it."

Herb Alpert For Europe

Following the completion of their highly successful American tour, which grossed over $662,000 in only eight dates, Herb Alpert and his Tijuana Brass are set to embark on their first major European tour.

The tour opens in Paris at the Olympic Theatre with a simultaneous live television and radio broadcast which will be followed by another French network television show. Other tour stops will be for an Armed Forces concert in Munich, a television special in Brussels and a concert in Albert Hall, London.

The tour is slated to end with a bang when Herbie and his boys visit Monaco as the special guests of Prince Rainier and Princess Grace.

Stateside, the TJB's latest single "Flamingo," has already begun it's flight up the nation's charts and promises to be yet another in the long line of Alpert hits. In fact, the biggest feat in the American album market is in trying to knock one of Herbie's many albums out of the number one spot on the charts!

... NEIL DIAMOND — Object of agency competition.

BARRY SADLER STARTS A COLLEGE FOUNDATION

S/Sgt. Barry Sadler, who received national recognition for his "Ballad of The Green Berets," inaugurated the Barry Sadler Foundation in Washington, D.C.

At a luncheon of the Past Department Commanders Club of the American Legion Sadler donated a personal check for $20,000 The Honorable James V. Day, Chairman of the Federal Maritime Commission, accepted the check as seed money for the fund he will head. The purpose of the Barry Sadler Foundation is to provide full college scholarships for the children of servicemen of any branch of the military who are killed or wounded in the line of duty.

Having now gone public, the foundation plans to present four or five scholarships via national television in time for the Spring 1967 terms. Additonal full scholarships will be awarded every term.

Barry Sadler established the foundation because of the depth of his conviction that American servicemen are doing a necessary and noble job and that a college education should be available to everyone qualified.

When his physical ability to earn was impaired by a wound received in action in Vietnam, Sadler, who did not go to college, was faced with the very real and pressing problem of providing for his wife and young son. Through the phenomenal success of his "Green Berets," this problem was solved. Now, Sadler is a nationally known entertainer and although he can command large sums for his personal appearances, he still spends much of his time performing gratis for the army.

Various fund-raising committees have been established to explore ways to increase and perpetuate the fund. Donations from the public are now being accepted at the Barry Sadler Foundation, 200 West 57th Street, New York, New York, 10019.

During the same inauguration luncheon, Day presented Sadler with the club's First Annual "Our Favorite Soldier Award." The award, however, was not the first to come Sadler's way. He also holds an Armed Forces Expeditionary Medal, an Armed Forces Good Conduct Medal, a United States Air Force Meritorious Service Medal and is also the owner of the famed "Purple Heart."

KRLA ARCHIVES

Letters To The Editor
(Continued from Page 2)

Gene Clark

Dear *BEAT*:

Since you're always first with the latest, like the article on Gene Clark and his group, I thought I should write to you to find out what's happening both with the Byrds and Gene Clark.

I just read that there is no Gene Clark Group anymore.

Could you set all us Byrd lovers straight and tell us how they are getting along?

Unsigned

For the time being, at least, Gene is back with the Byrds. It happened at the Whiskey during the Byrds' engagement. David had a sore throat and Gene merely rejoined the group for the remainder of their Whiskey stand.

The BEAT

Big Hand

Dear *BEAT*:

I would like to devote this letter to everyone on the staff of *The BEAT*. Just imagine, you must receive hundreds of letters about the Beatles!

John this . . . George that . . . (And so on . . .) And I bet you read every one of them.

I really pity every one of you, even the mailman! You all deserve a *Great Big Hand!*

Marsha Hardin

Where's Jeff?

Dear *BEAT*:

I am a Yardbird fan and as one who follows them as much as I can I would like to ask this. Where is Jeff Beck? He has not played with the Yardbirds on this whole tour but I see him on the Strip with Mary Hughes. Is he no longer in the group and is the rumor true that he is married?

Barbara Sims

Jeff has been touring with the Yardbirds; however, due to his tonsils, Jeff has missed some dates. At the moment, he is still with the group but sources close to the Yardbirds predict that he will soon leave the group.

Jeff is in the process of obtaining a divorce.

The BEAT

AN APOLOGY TO BEATLES

Dear *BEAT*:

I'm going to make this short because you asked for shorter letters. But I hope I get my point across.

I wrote an open letter to John Lennon and called him a bunch of names for attacking Christianity. At the time, I had no idea that his statement was taken out of context. It wasn't five minutes after I read his statements that I began to write that "open letter."

Well, I jumped to the conclusion that that was what he said completely. I did not know that he said much more than that and the unfavorable things were all that hit the papers.

I still feel that Christianity isn't on the way out, even though it isn't as popular as it used to be. In my opinion, John should've kept his mouth shut. But maybe I should practice what I preach.

Maybe John and I are a matched pair. We both have sharp tongues and both regret what we said.

My apologies are extended now to anyone who is connected with the Beatles in any way and especially to John Lennon. I hope *The BEAT* will print this so that everyone will know how I feel about my letter that was put into print.

Marilyn Iturri

CHANGED ATTITUDES

Dear *BEAT*:

I have just read the letters to the editor. I want to say something about them now.

I am a Beatle fan. I have stuck with them through thick and thin. People have criticized me for liking the Beatles but that didn't matter. I love Paul more than any of the other Beatles. As a result whenever I see a picture of Paul and Jane Asher together I get a sick-weak feeling inside. I live everyday for Paul and I thought he did the same for his fans.

When the Beatles first came out, they were full of life. Everything they did seemed to be done out of their hearts. Now they do whatever has to be done because they have to do it. They also seem bored.

John and George are my major complaints. John uses his fans to push his ideas on. Such as the album cover, his books, his thoughts on a subject he knows little about, Christianity. What's more, he thinks he can convince his fans — no matter what. He doesn't seem to understand that whatever he says influences us. And whenever he shoots off his big mouth, we are bound to hear. When we don't agree he gets turbulent, and tries to use his so-called wit to ease his way out of the trouble he is in.

George could never be as bad, but he has changed. Ever since he has married, he has an "I don't care" attitude. He doesn't seem to care that he broke thousands of hearts and caused many tears. And when he smiles, he doesn't try to show you he still cares. It seemed at one time when he did smile, nothing could go wrong. But that has changed.

Paul and Ringo have changed too, but not so much. The Beatles with the worse attitudes are John and George. I agree with one letter, John must be mentally ill (if not all the time, once in a while.)

When the Beatles perform, they have no feeling for what they are doing. It seems they can't reach people like they used to.

I love Beatle music, but when I play "Paperback Writer" and compare it to "I Should Have Known Better," I begin to wonder.

I have written many letters but I have hope that the Beatles will see this one. Maybe they will, maybe they won't. But if they do, I'd like to say something. I still love you, even through all this. But please be as you were before — the Beatles who cared.

And always remember — Paul, I love you, no matter what. I may never meet you but I'll always know you. Fans like me care. Maybe some poeple will think that stupid and moronic, but I don't care, for they don't try to understand.

So, help me and people like me. Reach out and let us know you are there. I'd give my life to see you and the other Beatles as you were once. Please, help us.

R.D.

'in' people are talking about...

How nice it would be if a few of the other Beach Boys would follow Carl's lead and admit they're married . . . Jelly Belly and the instructions on the back of the jacket . . . Hurrying Love surfacing before the Submarine . . . The Hollies riding the bus stops instead of the bus . . . Tokens of Happenings . . . The 4 Tops reaching out and grabbing another one . . . How glad the Critters are to be so dicingly sad . . . Herbie's flamingo flying farther and higher than Manfred's bird . . . The throw-away train trip which became a hit record and how sweet it all is to Bobby and Tommy . . . Whether or not it is Sonny and Cher walking away from Renee and if it isn't why the cool people are sayin' it is . . . How Jackie couldn't make it but the Pozo-Seco's can . . . Where Johnny ever got the idea he lives on the poor side of town when all his neighbors are convinced they live in the diamond and ruby part of the city and deciding that maybe Johnny's trying to outsmart the tax collector.

PEOPLE ARE TALKING ABOUT repenting but deciding that if Russ hasn't why should they . . . What you get when you knock on wood . . . How we now possess Richard and the Young Lions, Teddy and the Panadas and the Abbey Tavern Singers and wondering how long we're going to have to wait until the Self-Adhesive Correction Tapes come along . . . Them outsmarting the Gypies . . . What gives between the short, dark-haired writer and the long, blonde-haired singer . . . How funny Keith's hair looks, sort of like a roller fell out during the night . . . The wind that blew the mind excursion . . . David Blue being the next Dylan, only with capitals . . . What's up with Jeff and how come he got so sore about the squiring bit but not about leaving . . . John's new hairdo and how long it's going to last . . . Frankie teaching the other Pharaohs to dance.

PEOPLE ARE TALKING ABOUT whether or not Pete is really serious about leaving the Kinks and how this would mark the first departure from the group and what they wouldn't give for a sunny afternoon . . . How long it's going to take before the fans discover that some of their faves are really phony, swell-headed types . . . How sad Mick looked after his Aston-Martin hurt itself in an accident . . . Going right over to the left banke . . . Who has been fiddling around . . . Counting to five before getting some psychotic reaction . . . The book called "The Penguin John Lennon" . . . Why Keith is trying to make it without a last name . . . How far up the Rascals are gonna come . . . How fast Tommy's hair grew back . . . The Spoonful and the tiger lily . . . Groovy Mickey, tired Davy, sensitive Peter and funny Mike and what's next, luv? . . . Who they're trying to fool with the Grass Roots and what they're going to do when people start demanding pictures.

PEOPLE ARE TALKING ABOUT the big Mama in her bikini in Palm Springs . . . Barry shaving and finding a face under all that beard . . . What the carpenter's union thinks of Bobby 'cause the hippies think it's a new psychedelic experience . . . The ease in reaching Herman because no one knew he was in town . . . How really great Sam is, despite the itchy beard . . . How groovy it would be if Frankie Valli, Lou Christie and Joey Paige formed a group . . .

How Lloyds of London will insure anything . . . The bank that opened the door to his heart and got a hit record out of the deal . . . What's going to happen when, and if, the Walkers come home . . . The real, yellow submarine parked in front of Capitol Records and how dirty it was that it didn't get a ticket because it wasn't licensed but was parked in a no parking zone anyway.

What Herman's role in "The Canterville Ghost" meant to the Hermits?

If the rumor that the group is going to break up is true or really just a rumor?

What Herman was doing in L.A.?

How Brian broke his hand? Whether he broke his hand or his fingers?

How he managed to play on Sullivan, or if he was really playing at all.

What his hand does to the Stones' tour, and who would they get to replace him if they had to?

KRLA ARCHIVES

Walker Brothers Coming Stateside?

The Walker Brothers, long self-exiled in Britain, may have to return to the States when their work permits expire March 31, 1967.

If an application for renewal is refused, as it was for P.J. Proby, the Walker Brothers might return to the U.S. for six months before applying for another English permit.

This might more than slightly upset the guys, who have enjoyed Beatle-size success in England but failed to stir more than a few hit records in America.

The group's manager, Maurice King, believes their work permits will be renewed, however. "I don't think there'll be any problems at all," he said.

"It's not definite yet that their work permit will expire," he added. "There's no hard and fast rule. The authorities were harder in the case of P.J. Proby, but I think they look on the Walker Brothers in a different light."

Some papers have reported that the Walker Brothers will tour the States anyway since their records are beginning to sell more than they used to here. But the group would have a difficult time imitating the success they have enjoyed in England, where their blonde, blue-eyed, typically American good looks have made them the heart-throb of many a British girl.

Meanwhile, they have just released a new single, "Another Tear Falls," written by Burt Bacharach-Hal David, and backed with "The Saddest Night In The World."

Proby Has New Single

P.J. Proby has another record ready for release, but somehow that isn't his primary concern at the moment.

His dog is.

Robert Marcucci, Proby's manager, said the singer is worried about the disappearance of his pet canine.

Lost Dog

"He left his St. Bernard dog in Buckingham with a friend in England before he left, and now it's been lost," he said.

Proby, meanwhile, has been a busy man. He just finished recording his single, which will be released shortly.

The title of his new single will be either "You Make Me Feel Like Someone" or "I Could Make It Alone," by Jerry Goffin and Carole King.

Not All

But recording isn't all Proby has been doing.

"We are also working on a motion picture and we are trying to get Proby to play an Errol Flynn role because he's got swashbuckling looks about him," said Marcucci. "We're negotiating now with Warner Brothers."

...PROBY LOSES DOG
BEAT Photo: Chuck Boyd

...SONNY GRINS AND CHER WAVES to the thousands of fans gathered at the Paris airport to greet them.

Sonny & Cher To Meet The Pope

Sonny and Cher have been awarded an audience with the Pope. The famous American duo were naturally thrilled at the prospect of meeting Pope Paul VI and their only worry at the moment is where to find a suitable dress for Cher. Protocal demands that when a woman meets the Pope she should appear before him in a long-sleeved, high-collared dress, preferably black. And on her head she should wear a veil.

Dress For Cher

Cher is noted for *never* wearing dresses, but for this special occasion Cher admitted that she was shopping for a dress and would appear before the Pope wearing the standard requirements.

Meanwhile Sonny and Cher's promotional tour of Europe is doing so well that the pair are expanding their stay to include stop-offs in Oslo, Helsinki, Bremen, Frankfurt and Antwerp.

While in London, Sonny and Cher chalked up a notable success when they headed a benefit show for the British Braille Institute drawing $40,000 for the English charity.

Their good will tour is costing the duo a pretty penny, not counting the cost of a 10-carat diamond which Sonny purchased for his wife in Amsterdam. However, it seems to be well worthwhile.

Sonny and his Cher were forced to slip into Hamburg 24 hours ahead of their original schedule when local police made a frantic plea to the couple to arrive early because they would not be able to handle the crowds of teenagers expected to storm the airport for the couple's arrival.

Paris was another huge success for Sonny and Cher. Thousands of cheering fans were on hand to greet the two when they touched down at the Paris airport and additional police had to be rushed in to assure Sonny and Cher safety from their over-eager following.

Safe in Paris, Tele-Hachette filmed a half hour special for French television, "The Musical World Of Sonny & Cher."

Another huge benefit performance by the duo took place at the Olympia Theatre in Paris. The proceeds of the sell-out show went to the French Braille Institute and was such a success that Sonny and Cher received a request for a return booking. They've been tentatively scheduled to return for a one-week stand at the famed Olympia next March with the proceeds of that one benefiting Sonny and Cher!

Armenian Songs

Discussions are now being held in order to decide if Sonny and Cher should record some upbeat Armenian folk songs on their next joint album. Cher is partly of Armenian descent.

On the Stateside record scene, Cher has just released her latest solo album, titled "Cher." "Little Man," Sonny and Cher's latest single, is doing very well and promises to be yet another smash for the couple.

The Monkees On Top?

(Continued from Page 1)
they promised not to laugh at me when I sit in front of the television and drool at them!"

"They're great. I dig the show. That's all."

"I wish it was on for an hour. It seems like it just comes on and then it's over. I also wish I had a color television."

And so the comments went—on and on and on. No one could think of anything particularly bad to say about the show, other than the fact that the plot was not all it could be. However, it was felt that the excellent camera work and the show's funny bits more than made up for the lack of script.

Therefore, the Monkees, according to your opinion, are "in" solidly as far as their television show is concerned and, from all reports, they're not bombing out as recording artists either. "Last Train To Clarksville" is making it's way up the charts all over the country and their first album, "The Monkees," is giving record stores a gigantic headache—you seem to be buying it faster than they can stock it!

KRLA ARCHIVES

Go Ahead . . .

Take Five!!
Products Of
LIBERTY RECORDS

KRLA ARCHIVES

PICTURES in the NEWS

DUSTY SPRINGFIELD, England's most popular female export, just put another feather in her pretty cap by being voted Top Girl Singer of the World by the international readership of "Melody Maker," one of Britain's pop trade papers. Runners-up in the category were Cilla Black, Petula Clark, Brenda Lee and Cher, respectively. Our congrats to Dusty.

HERMAN poses with his pretty co-star in "The Canterville Ghost," Tippy Walker. Herman and Tippy play the young romantic couple in the up-dated, musical version of the classic Oscar Wilde story which has been adapted by Burt Shevelove with music and lyrics by Pulitzer Prize winners, Sheldon Harnick and Jerome Bock. In the ABC "Stage '67" show, Herman portrays a modern young mod, the Duke of Chesire, and Miss Walker is the very conservative daughter of the American Ambassador to the Court of St. James. Tippy was previously seen in "The World Of Henry Orient."

GUESS WHO THESE TWO ARE! Would you believe that about 20 some years ago this is how the two Smothers Brothers looked? They are somewhat of a phenomen in the entertainment field because they manage to appeal to both the teen and adult audiences with their hilarious stage routines. They've begun something which could possibly set a brand new trend. Namely, teen press conferences throughout the United States where teen reporters from high school and college papers get a chance to fire their questions at Tom and Dick.

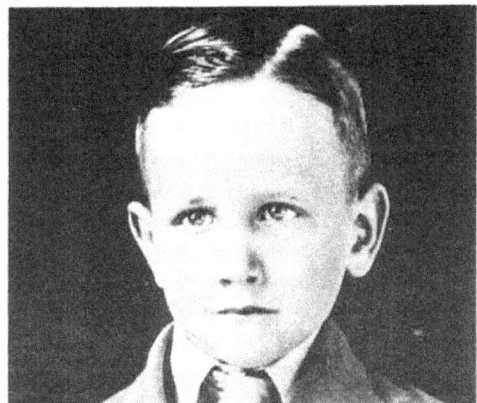

ROGER MILLER posed for this picture when he was an old man of four in Erick, Oklahoma. Of course, the downhome Mr. Miller never dreamed that it would one day be dug up and printed in **The BEAT**. Miller, whose current single is "My Uncle Used To Love Me But She Died," was one of the chosen few to debut this season with his own television program, "The Roger Miller Show."

KRLA ARCHIVES

A Wild Affair In Viet Nam

ONLY WAY TO TRAVEL... Denny Martin in the streets of DaNang.

Up BEAT
By Eden

Top of the list this week are Paul Revere and his Raiders with their brand new smash-hit, "The Great Plane Strike." It's a very different sound for the Raiders — something which you haven't heard from them before — and it's really great.

* * *

Still can't get over Bobby Darin's latest, "If I Were A Carpenter." Everyone else seems to be flipping out over this hauntingly beautiful tune, too, 'cause it's heading for the very top. Great lyric.

* * *

Awfully nice to see Joey Paige finally climbing the charts with his latest, "Merry-Go-Round". This is one of Joey's most commercial records, and it looks like he has a national hit on his hands this spin around.

* * *

Dionne Warwick has recorded Dusty Springfield's hit, "Don't Know Just What To Do With Myself," and you've gotta say that the girl's got *soul*! The arrangement is very much like her other Bachrach-David hits, and the results are beautiful. Should head for the Top Ten at least.

* * *

Seems as though Mr. Dick Clark has a knack for picking winners. He chose the Raiders for stardom and he was more than right. His latest group-pick has been the Robbs, who have become regulars on "Action," and their first record — "Next Time You See Me" — shows every indication of making them regulars on chart-tops everywhere. The request reaction to this new disc has been tremendous and it will probably be a big hit.

* * *

"Mr. Spaceman" is the new entry by the Byrds, but it sounds very much like one of their older hits, "Mr. Tambourine Man." Unlike the first record, however, this one probably won't make it. Too bad, 'cause the Byrds have really fallen out of their original groove in their last few records. The distinctive harmonies and unusual folk-rock instrumentations which made them popular seem to have all but vanished.

By Mike Tuck

Denny Martin held a primitive, menacing looking weapon in his hands and began explaining its lethal purposes in strife-torn Vietnamese jungles.

The weapon resembled a crude crossbow. A coarse, thick string hung loosely across its hand fashioned bow. Attached firmly to the stock was ammunition — three deadly arrows hewn from bamboo stalks.

The object looked like something a sadistic Neanderthal child would construct. It's sole purpose was to kill — not animals, but men.

"This belonged to a warrior in the Mountainyard tribe," said the Wild Affair's bass guitarist. "They poison the tips on these and the poison alone will kill within a matter of minutes.

"The Mountainyards are fighting the war in Viet Nam ... just like a lot of groups you don't hear about. Only the Mountainyards are on our side — fighting the Viet Cong."

Denny somehow looked out of his element as he grasped the crude weapon. Denny's customary role is cradling a guitar, not an object of such awful intent.

Goodwill Tour

But Denny and his group had just returned from a goodwill tour of U.S. military bases in Viet Nam, and he gained a lot of insight into the bloody war during his two week visit.

"I didn't really know what to think before we went over there," he said. "But now I feel very strongly about what the United States is doing.

"It's nothing anybody really wants to do — but everybody I talked to there thought it was something we *have* to do. A lot of guys said 'sure, I'd like to be home, but I know I'm needed over here.'"

Denny reached beneath his chair and retrieved a curious looking satchel. Vaulted inside were the momentos from his visit: a couple of citations, three letters from service men; a half-finished diary and some army decals.

He produced, after empting the bag's entire contents, a leather-encased certificate from the U.S. government and signed by Gen. Westmoreland.

In part, the certificate read: "For outstanding contribution to morale and welfare of the U.S. Armed Forces by touring the command, entertaining personnel of all branches of military service."

For the Wild Affair, the tour of Viet Nam was no lark. In their visits to army field hospitals they were confronted with soldiers — many of them still fuzzy cheeked — unconscious and dying.

Unlike many wars, bullets and explosions are only half the danger in Viet Nam. Savage tropical diseases also account for many casualties.

All three members of the Wild Affair — Denny, Rod Birmingham and Chuck Morgan — suffered mild cases of a common tropical disease.

But they still managed to appear at all 25 scheduled performances.

Although the group generally lived in comfortable style, traveling conditions were not always so fortunate.

Air travel is the only travel in Viet Nam. So when the group moved between air bases they had to take whatever was available ... cargo planes, flying boxcars, helicopters, single engined craft.

Inside, they were often wedged between cargo or seated on upturned Coke cases.

Denny said the group was kept under tight security during the tour, but he managed to break away occasionally and talk to the troops.

In general, Denny said, American soldiers in Viet Nam felt like this on the following subjects:

On U.S. chances of winning — "They think we *can* win and we *will* win. They feel like they're accomplishing something and it's only a matter of time. Right now it's just a war of patience."

On Barry Sadler — "I talked to one Green Baret who said his songs are good because they call attention to the Green Barets. But he said he neither liked the songs personally nor did he like Sadler."

A Big Joke

On U.S. dissent — "It doesn't bother them. Mostly, it's kind of a big joke to them."

On special entertainment shows — "The guys were really great. I think they appreciate — and need — this type of thing more than anything. They practically wouldn't let you off the stage."

"They like to laugh and they're always kidding around. We'd be in the middle of a performance and somebody would yell, 'hey, when are you guys gonna be over here?'

"We would usually tell them 'in about two months.'"

Generally, Denny said the tour was serious in nature. "But we had to keep laughing and telling jokes because that's what the guys wanted to see."

Would Denny be willing to go to Viet Nam strictly on a military basis? "Yes, I would," he said "just as soon as they call me."

His first trip to Viet Nam, he said, was "probably the most rewarding experience of my life.

"And if we're not drafted by next year, our group is going to try to go back for another tour."

JBL
SOUND IS WHERE IT'S HAPPENING!

Trini Lopez, Chet Atkins, Johnny Rivers, The Beach Boys, The Rolling Stones make it with JBL sound.

JBL is the sound of the scene at the top!

Fender, Jordan, Ampeg, Gretsch, Standel, Guild, Gibson, C. F. Martin, Sunn amplifier systems groove with JBL loudspeakers.

High notes that won't quit, thundering bass at peak volume from JBL F-Series loudspeakers. Write us for free information about use and installation.

James B. Lansing Sound, Inc.
3249 Casitas Avenue
Los Angeles, California 90039

"OUTSTANDING CONTRIBUTION"... Chuck, Rod and Denny receive citations for their Viet Nam tour.

KRLA ARCHIVES

'Gassy' Go Around With Brian Hyland

By Louise Criscione

"It's a gas!"

The speaker? Brian Hyland. The question? How does it feel? And life in 1966 feels good to Brian now. It did in 1960 too when he awoke the nation, actually the world, with his novel "Itsey Bitsy Teeny Weeny Yellow Polka Dot Bikini." The worldwide smash chalked up an impressive sales figure of over two million for the young Mr. Hyland.

But besides the money and the quick fame it didn't prove a thing. For a novelty record never proves talent, it merely proves good timing. It was Brian's next three hits which told the music world that here was another young, talented singer hoping to make it big. Not just for today. But for years.

World Tours

And, so Brian was big from 1960 to 1963. "Let Me Belong To You," "Ginny Come Lately," and "Sealed With A Kiss," soared up the nation's charts and with them came tours of England, Puerto Rico, South America, Japan and, of course, the United States.

Brian grew with the tours. In a lot of ways, but especially in the knowledge of human beings. Be they white, black, yellow or purple — people are people and you just can't get around it. "Kids are the same all over, they all like the beat," Brian learned. "One thing that's different," he said, "is the size of the audiences you run into abroad.

"I once did a show at a stadium in Buenos Aires, Argentina, during carnival time, and there were about 70,000 people there," Brian recalled. "Neil Sedaka and I were the headliners, together with local acts and there were people in the stadium that were so far away that they watched the entire show on closed circuit television."

Then Nothing

Caught up in the whirl of flash bulbs, screams, "can I have your autograph," reporters and television directors, the years between 1960 and 1963 flew past Brian so fast that he didn't know what had happened when 1964 arrived and with it no hit record materialized.

Surprise, horror, relief . . . who knows what Brian felt. But it is certain that he had quite a bit of time to think as '64 and '65 sped by and there was still no smash for Brian. But then in 1966 "The Joker Went Wild" and Brian once again found himself firmly entrenched in the merry go round they fondly call "show business."

With Brian, the person, nothing much has changed. He still looks basically the same, with sometimes long, sometimes short hair. "I had it long for awhile," Brian says. "Right now, it's short again but I like to keep changing. I figure it's good to keep changing in everything, you know?"

And going along with that theory, Brian has forsaken the lone star role and captured himself a back-up group, appropriately named, the Jokers. Brian still calls himself "a loner" but can't quite hide all the excitement in his voice when he talks about the Jokers.

The group members are all from Atlanta, Georgia and include a lead guitarist, a bass guitarist, an organist and a drummer. "I'll probably play a little guitar along with the group," Brian adds with an attractive grin.

And then, perhaps feeling that you'll get the impression he's not a loner after all, Brian says: "You know, show business is a 24 hour a day proposition and you get very little time to yourself. There's just not too much time to break away, so I like to whenever I can."

Writing Mood

Brian has learned the hard lesson that a performer who wishes to stay around after his hit record is dead cannot afford to limit himself to only one aspect of the business. Accordingly, Brian has branched out into the songwriting department. So far, he's penned approximately 25 songs. "I get in writing moods," he explained. "I'll maybe turn out five or six songs in about a week or ten days and then no more until I hit such a mood again."

Brian's a natural for the writing scene, primarily because of his keen desire to communicate with his audience. "I like to be able to communicate with my audience, no matter where I am performing," he says and goes on to admit that he once took foreign language lessons just so he could record his songs in German.

Firmly entrenched in the pop bag, Brian's interests really run to country and western music. "It's the words of country music I really dig," he says. "They're usually so real, you know, like life — they are realistic."

Film Interest

And then, of course, there are movies. "I also have an interest in films," Brian reveals. "I wouldn't mind an acting bit. I'd even like to get involved in films on the production end too." He's had plenty of opportunity to do those cameo song stints in movies but has turned them all down, preferring to wait for a good part in a good film.

But you can tell that Brian's first love is music when he admits that: "I guess what I'd most like to do is tour both here in the States and abroad with the group."

Although Brian's hair length goes up and down, depending on his mood, he hasn't yet gone the Carnaby Street route. "I like to wear just what I've always worn. You know, I really prefer wearing levis, knit shirts and loafers — and no socks, of course!"

Unfortunately, on stage the no socks bit won't go so Brian has neatly taken care of that problem by simply wearing boots, which he says "look really great with a suit."

Actually, it probably wouldn't matter much what Brian wore on stage because he has the art of audience communication down to a fine art. And "it's a gas," you know?

BRIAN HYLAND — Up and down but basically the same.

BRIAN POSES as the original Thinker!

Monkees Finish In 'Clarksville'

Would you believe it? RCA is spending money on someone other than Elvis Presley! The recepients of the latest bit of RCA promotion were the Monkees. The label, distributors of the Monkees' Colgems material, took the group on a ten day promotional tour which wound itself up in Del Mar, California where the city's name was officially changed to Clarksville for the day.

During the whirlwind tour, the four Monkees visited Chicago, Boston and New York. "We got mobbed in New York," Mickey Dolenz told The BEAT but when pressed for details admitted, "Well, we weren't exactly *mobbed*. But the girls tried to get us and we had to have guards and the whole bit. It was really groovy!"

Obviously excited about the group's newly-found popularity, Mickey continued: "We really don't know where it's at yet. I mean, like we just got back from the tour and then we got up this morning, flew down to San Diego, took a helicopter to Del Mar and now we're on a train to L.A.!"

The Monkees' tour was more to meet the press than anyone else, revealed Peter Tork. "Mostly we just talked to reporters. In one city we did about twenty minutes on stage but in each city we had special showings of one of the series' segments," said Peter.

Concerning the tour, about the only thing Davy Jones had to say was: "I'm tired." And it's no wonder! Besides the tour, the four Monkees have been keeping themselves busy filming their NBC television series and recording the new songs (skillfully penned for them by Tommy Boyce and Bobby Hart) which are included in each segment of "The Monkees."

Their first album, also titled "The Monkees," has just been released and neither Mickey, Davy, Mike nor Peter could seem to get over how fast the radio stations across the country were jumping on it. "You know, this morning," started Mickey but was forced to stop for a photographer. Photos taken, he tried it again: "Picture this. It's six in the morning, right? I'm in bed and the alarm goes off and the radio comes on and they're playing "The Monkees Theme." I think, 'what? I'm dreaming again!' But they're really playing it!"

Meanwhile, their debut single, "Last Train To Clarksville," is steadily climbing up the nation's charts and that, too, came as something of a surprise to the group. In fact, they couldn't decide whether to call it the "Last Train To Clarksville," or the "Last Train To Home, Girl."

"It's good we decided on Clarksville," laughs Peter. "Can't you just see the major saying: 'I now proclaim this the city of Home Girl?'"

Not quite — but we can see the Monkees taking over the world!

KRLA ARCHIVES

oh! but to cherish the ASSOCIATION

By Eden

Into the life of every reporter, some nuts must fall—and some *did* fall into mine. They call themselves The Association, and they definitely *are* associated in an underground conspiracy to overthrow, undermine, and completely drive insane *all* members of the press. And it's a pleasure!

Many, many months ago, these six, handsome, talented *nuts* fell into the lives of The BEAT staff—and we still haven't recovered! We *adopted* them—mainly 'cause they were basically *itinerant* at the time!—fed them, encouraged them, attended all of their performances, and continually told them that they would be stars, and someday their record would be Number One in Cashbox and Billboard.

They would always smile, and thank us, then proceed to camp out in our offices—which made it exceedingly difficult to put out a paper!

Then, one bright day, "Along Came Mary"—which immediately sent the boys on their way up the nation's charts with their first successful record. After that, they ate only *eight* meals a day in our offices instead of their usual ten.

Also, they slept under our work table only four days a week instead of nine. So we were able to put out the paper almost regularly once again.

This week, "Cherish" has jumped to the Number One spot on the national charts in Cashbox and Billboard. This week we are getting the paper out on time; there are no longer any sleeping bodies under our work table or slumped over our typewriters, and our supply of food lasts for an amazingly long period of time.

This week has also been pretty dull, 'cause The Association wasn't around. *But*—in an attempt to brighten things up just a little, they invited this reporter down to visit them at their rehearsals, and I am proud to report to you that they are just as nuts as ever. Success definitely *hasn't* changed them!!!

The Association is a group of musicians—*real* musicians, who give a great deal of thought to the music which they create, and are one of the few groups who can honestly make claims to true originality in their material.

Gary Alexander—the shortest member of the group, who divides

KRLA ARCHIVES

...THE ASSOCIATION (l. to r.) Gary, Russ, Jim, Brian, Ted and Terry have the number one record in the country with their "Cherish."

his time between the study of Eastern religions and looking like Dr. Zorba, explains their artistry this way:

"The whole thing has gotten into a new direction in song-writing. We come up with ideas in our songs that *I've* never heard before! They're totally original, and the ideas and concepts are based on our *lives* — the things we do every day, the things we see, and the people we know.

"There are musical moves in some of our songs that you just don't hear in pop music — at *all!*"

Jim Yester interrupted "Alex" here to add to the explanation further: "You have two different facets here — the kind of music you play onstage, and the kind of music you play when you're just playing for music's sake. And the two are getting closer together. After all, music is one of the only pure art forms if not *the* only one."

Renaissance

Just recently, Brian Wilson mentioned to *The BEAT* that he felt that a "Renaissance" was coming to pop music, and The Association agrees with this idea. However, Russ explained that "Pop music is in a *constant* state of Renaissance! Pop music is a reflection of everything that's happening." Gary agreed, saying "Pop music is the purest reflection of everything that's going on, and you can say *anything* in music."

And what *is* pop music? Well, Terry defines it as "Pop music is the reflection of the *Specific Now!*" And Jim scholarly informs us that "it comes from the old Latin Vox Populus — Voice of the People — let the people dig it!" Finally, Brian "Brank" Cole sums it up: "Pop music is popular because people dig it — if people dig it, then whatever they're buying at the time is indicative of the trend that it's going to. And, if you want to try to figure out what's going to happen in six months, it will take you *six months* to figure it out —

and by then it will have *happened!*"

Throughout the entire afternoon, any discussion we had was generously loaded with wisecracks in the background from any member of the group who wasn't answering a question. There were "Associates" sprawled across the seats (we were in a small theatre), Associates in the corner drinking cream soda pop, Associates all speaking simultaneously, faster than the speed of sound!

Jokers

I asked them to describe their sense of humor; do they play practical jokes on one another? Alex laughed and exclaimed: "We don't play *practical* jokes on each other ... we play *im*practical jokes on each other!! For instance — Russ will sneak up behind one of us and blast us in the back of the head with a water balloon!"

Brank, known as Brian to you, chimed in to relate the "classic" impractical joke to us: "Russell, at a party once, took a guy who had passed out from an over-indulgence in alcohol — put him in the bathtub, after removing some of his superflous outer clothing, bought *50* cans of Crisco — warmed them up so they wouldn't hurt him — and let him *sit* in the Crisco! When he woke up the next morning he was *encased* in Crisco in the bathtub! What a terrible thing to wake up to in the morning!!!!"

Blue-eyed drummer, Ted Bluchel popped in at this point to irreleventy explain: "I think that another direction in which all the popular groups will eventually head for is developing some kind of an entertainment style, besides just their music. We use almost a type of *theater* — we like to take them someplace besides just the musical world. We try to be as entertaining as we can be. We like to take them from laughing, to crying, to being angry, to being glad. Our act is an 'emotional trip through Association-land!'"

...BUT ALAS AND ALAC, they can't get Ted out of the phone booth and Brian can't even seem to bum a dime off his cohorts! Just goes to show what success will do!

KRLA ARCHIVES

Top 40 Requests

#	Title	Artist
1	NEXT TIME YOU SEE ME	The Robbs
2	FORTUNE TELLER	Rolling Stones
3	PSYCHOTIC REACTION	Count Five
4	WALK AWAY RENEE	The Left Banke
5	BUS STOP	The Hollies
6	TALK, TALK	Music Machine
7	CHERISH	The Association
8	GOD ONLY KNOWS	The Beach Boys
9	ELEANOR RIGBY	The Beatles
10	GOOD DAY SUNSHINE	The Beatles
11	LITTLE MAN	Sonny & Cher
12	MR. DIEINGLY SAD	The Critters
13	YELLOW SUBMARINE	The Beatles
14	HERE THERE & EVERYWHERE	The Beatles
15	IF I WERE A CARPENTER	Bobby Darin
16	YOU CAN'T HURRY LOVE	The Supremes
17	GOT TO GET YOU INTO MY LIFE	The Beatles
18	LAST TRAIN TO CLARKSVILLE	The Monkees
19	YOU ARE SHE	Chad & Jeremy
20	HAVE YOU SEEN YOUR MOTHER IN THE SHADOWS	Rolling Stones
21	BLACK IS BLACK	Los Bravos
22	WHAT BECOMES OF THE BROKENHEARTED	Jimmy Ruffin
23	SEE YOU IN SEPTEMBER	The Happenings
24	BEAUTY IS ONLY SKIN DEEP	The Temptations
25	THE JOKER WENT WILD	Brian Hyland
26	SUNSHINE SUPERMAN	Donovan
27	SUNNY	Bobby Hebb
28	WORKING IN THE COAL MINE	Lee Dorsey
29	FUNCTION AT THE JUNCTION	Shorty Long
30	SUNNY AFTERNOON	The Kinks
31	SOMETIMES GOOD GUYS DON'T WEAR WHITE	The Standells
32	REACH OUT	Four Tops
33	SUMMERTIME	Billy Stewart
34	HOW SWEET IT IS	Jr. Walker
35	JUST LIKE A WOMAN	Bob Dylan
36	LAND OF 1,000 DANCES	Wilson Pickett
37	WIPE OUT	The Surfaris
38	OPEN THE DOOR TO YOUR HEART	Darrell Banks
39	TURN DOWN DAY	The Cyrkle
40	THERE WILL NEVER BE ANOTHER YOU	Chris Montez

Inside KRLA
By Eden

ELLA FITZGERALD AND DUKE ELLINGTON recently wowed audiences at the popular Greek Theater following their return from an extensive European tour.

By Eden

Guests galore at the station in the last couple weeks, including such great guest phone operators as Bobby Hebb, the Cyrkle, the Robbs, Lesley Gore, Sam the Sham and the Pharoahs, Joey Paige, the Count Five and the Mamas and Papas. It's been pretty busy — and so have the request phones.

And speaking of requests, we've been receiving quite a few. For example, one loyal KRLA listener who is the head of a Northwestern Railroad Company has requested 3,000 gallons of Valhalla diesel fuel to fill his diesels with.

Talented composer-singer, Rod McKuen, has put in his request as well. He would like a credit card because he has become a regular user of Valhalla petroleum products. He says that he serves it to his guests mixed with tomato juice. He calls it a "Bloody Ethyl."

The brand new basketball season, featuring the lovable losers of KRLA-Land — the KRLApes — will get under way sometime in late September. For full information please contact Bill Slater.

Have you heard that Bob Eubank's brand new TV show — the Newlywed Game — has become the Number One-rated daytime game show ever on the ABC network? Leave it to our KRLAngels to get in there and win!

Pat Moore is really building up a huge audience during his Midnight-to-six "Graveyard" shift, but I recently overheard him complaining to Bill Slater that in all the time he has been on the air — Jamie McCluskey III hasn't proposed to him even *once!* Poor fella!!!

I received a request from a Newport KRLA listener to please tell Johnny Hayes that she turns her radio on every night just so she can hear his "groovy voice and fall in love with him all over again." Another request which came in from Pacoima Requested the Hullabalooer to play a duet with Herbie Alpert, *live* on the air — and *in tune!* And a young lady in Paramount wrote in a requesting about two inches of Mark Linday's Pony Tail. (I'm afraid I can't help you too much there, Andrea!)

BACK TO SCHOOL BEAT SPECIAL

$3.00 a year

Just clip and mail...

KRLA BEAT
Save 60% — Subscribe!

Mail to:
KRLA Beat #504
6290 Sunset Blvd.
Hollywood, Calif. 90028

Name _____
Address _____
City _____ State _____ Zip _____

☐ I want BEAT for a year at $3.00.
I enclose ☐ cash ☐ check ☐ money order.

Calendar of Happenings
Sept. 27 - Oct. 2

THE MOTHERS OF INVENTION...
with THE FACTORY
(You have to see to believe)

Oct. 5 - Oct. 15

THE Beau Brummels + THE DAILY FLASH

AGE 18 & OVER WITH I.D. WELCOME
FOOD & FUN TILL 2 A.M.

KRLA ARCHIVES

Ian Whitcomb—Doing What He Likes Best

By Carol Deck

Ian Whitcomb is well known for his high piched falsetto hits, "You Turn Me On" and "This Sporting Life," but those who came to see him at the Troubadour recently, saw a whole new side of Ian.

At the Troubadour he was given free rein to try something new and he grabbed the opportunity to do what he's always wanted to do— show off his rag time stuff.

Many people have wondered why Ian studied history in college and even went on to get his degree while his career was soaring. Why history, they asked.

But when they heard Ian give a brief history of each rag time song he sang, when it was written and what was going on in the world at that time, it became obvious.

The first part of his act was his usual rock act backed by Somebody's Chyldren. Although the crowded stage didn't give him as much room to move about as he could have used he still gave an exciting performance.

But then the group left, Ian took off his coat, sat down at a rented 1927 piano and you could feel his excitement at finally getting to do what he likes most.

In fact, opening night he got going on song after cute little rag time song and the first set ran over an hour long.

He bounced around on the piano, his mind working faster than his fingers on the keyboard remembering more and more songs that he hadn't performed in so long and he looked like he was about to burst because he couldn't do all of the hundreds that he knows.

One of the standouts of the show was a ditty called "I'm Shy

... IAN WHITCOMB

Mary Ellen, I'm Shy."

It was an entertaining bill that you don't get many places. There's just not a lot of good authentic rag time music around, but if Ian has anything to say about it, 1966 will be the year ragtime returns.

And he's starting it all with his latest album of strictly rag time songs and a new single, "Poor Little Bird."

THE STAFF AT KRLA have really gotten attached to the Mini-Surfer Capitol Records is giving away for the Beach Boys' birthday and will miss it when it's awarded to the winner. Giving it one last look over are, from left, Dave Hull, Dick Biondi, Johnny Hayes, Pat Moore, Charlie O'Donnell and Herb Whittaker from Capitol. Watch for lucky contest winners to be announced in a future issue of **The BEAT**.

KRLA Winners! Yellow Submarine

BARBARA METZLER of Gardena, California, was one of the 8,327 people who entered KRLA's Yellow Submarine Contest. But Barbara was different than the 8,326 other entrants—she won! Here is Barbara's version of the proper care and treatment of a real, live, floatable Yellow Submarine:

"I will float my Yellow Submarine into the nearest Val-Halla Petroleum Station and fill up Sebastian (my Sub's name). After Sebastian has been properly thunderbolted and I have had my fill of mead, I will put on my propeller hat and black cape. Then I will zip up and down the Hollywood Hills. And who knows? Maybe a spark of lightening will hit Sebastian and I'll have the first flyling Yellow Submarine. Also, may I request a pair of Val-Halla horns to put on Sebastian? Then I can buck traffic on Land, Sea and In the Air!"

Five runners-up receive pairs of passes to see Paramount's mid-ocean thriller, "Assault On A Queen," starring Frank Sinatra and Virni Lisi:

Donna Lewis, Alhambra
Weldon K. Booth, El Monte
Janie Borth, Saticoy
Paulette Mangano, Huntington Beach
Ken Peterson, Garden Grove

Saturday Afternoon Matinee
Oct. 1 - 1 Day Only
2 Shows, 1 p.m. and 3 p.m.

THE NEW GENERATION

Another Capitol Records' Great In Their Only L.A. Appearance. Call for reservations and prices.

Have You Discovered THE KNACK?
See It!
Experience It!

A New Show-Rock Thrill
A Capitol Records' Pick
For Stardom
Your Discovery

The Ice House Has
THE KNACK!
Oct. 4th to 9th

at the ICE HOUSE Glendale
234 So. Brand
Reservations — 245-5043

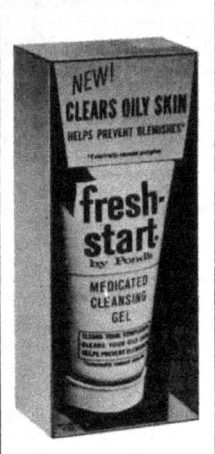

TEENAGERS WELCOME

COMING SOON
THE RAY BRYANT TRIO

NOW APPEARING THE FABULOUS
••• HUGH MASEKELA & QUARTET •••
CLUB TROPICANA
247 E. MANCHESTER, L.A. FOR RESERVATIONS CALL 758-7615

KRLA ARCHIVES

James Brown Says 'I'm A Dynamo!'

Mr. Soul Speaks Out On Himself His Music, His Points of View...

"...I'M NOT AS FAST as I want to be!"

"...WHEN I VISIT an all-girl school, they call me Mr. Brown."

By Rochelle Reed

"I've always been a little dynamo," James Brown said, nodding his head to punctuate the sentence. "I've always been outstanding at everything I've done. I've always made myself number one, two or three."

"Of course," he continued, "once in high school it amounted to breaking my leg—that's when I was playing football."

James hasn't found it necessary to break a leg to become number one in the rhythm and blues field. He's the undaunted King, so far and above his competition that they simply follow his footsteps and marvel.

You Tell 'Em

His shows are two hour periods of frenzied mass communication. The audience, which may have been sedate when they took their seats, turns into a singing, swaying, clapping mob, tracking Brown's each move with "You tell 'em, James Baby" and "Sock it to 'em, J.B."

This idol of thousands was once a school janitor. Now he owns a Lear jet, nearly one thousand suits and pairs of shoes, maintains several fantastic homes across the country, and could, right at this minute, write a check for $50,000 without blinking at the amount.

"I'm 75% business and 25% talent," he says, "and I'd tell a new singer just this — Be a businessman."

Now the man who never vacations except in a recording studio has a new bag: though he dropped out of school at 16, he's urging everyone to stay in, and not stop at high school, either.

"I was a drop-out at 16, but I was forced to," he says. "I had to work—it was different in my time. But now the only way to get a decent job is to finish high school, and even that's not enough today.

"School is your only weapon! If you don't finish, you might as well be dead."

Brown feels so strongly about education that he entitled his newest single, "Don't Drop Out." It's not a hype for any official body but Brown's true feelings on the subject. "It's not just a record," he explains, "it brainwashes kids to a good thing. But it will sell ten million copies because it's a good record and it has a new beat."

He's receiving a citation from the U.S. Vice President and from several Washington Youth Organizations. He's also starting a scholarship fund through the National Radio Announcers Association. But even before this, Brown has helped students.

"There was a girl who was the president of my fan club for several years and she was always loyal. When she finally graduated from high school, she didn't have anywhere to go. She was living with her aunt. So I got her into the best business school in New York City and got a paper signed so that they won't let her come home for a year, until she finishes. The kids who can should go away from home to go to school and get away from their so-called friends. Then you get a real education.

"I don't have an enemy, legitimately," Brown says, "because if they didn't like me, they wouldn't be jealous.

"You know," James continued, "A man's a man and a woman's a woman. But it's the man or woman that makes himself.

"When I was a kid, my father only made seven dollars a week. Can you imagine only seven dollars? Now I give him more than that. I take care of him and pay his bills. You know, he stopped school in the second grade. He can't write his name in a straight line. I begged him and begged him to go back to school."

"Poverty," says James, is what gives him his seemingly inexhaustible energy. That and "undying determination."

"I was always a good dancer, the best in my crowd. Even when I was little, the other kids would pay me a dime to dance for them. Near Augusta, there was a big army training center and the soldiers would get me up on a little stand when I was 10 years old and I'd sing and dance for them. And they'd throw pennies, nickels, dimes — sometimes even quarters —at me."

James used his extra money to help pay the rent for his family.

Now the fabulously wealthy Brown rates his best audiences as those in Los Angeles, New York, Atlanta, Chicago, Washington, New Orleans and Philadelphia. "And I can't complain about the other parts of the country. You know, I draw more people than any other artist!"

If Brown doesn't fill a concert occasionally, "I don't feel angry," he says. "I just feel maybe they had to do something more important. Maybe they had to go to school."

More Important

Few people miss Brown's performances, where he is backed by a 20 piece orchestra and ten other people in supporting acts. He is a firm employer and tolerates no tardiness or mistakes. If a member of his band misses a travel connection, he pays to get himself there. And then he gets a fine on top of it. If a performer makes a mistake, he is fined. Brown demands, and gets, perfection.

"When you pay money to see a show, you have the right to be entertained!" he announces. Brown himself performs—nonstop—for forty-five minutes. He never stops singing or dancing, even to introduce a song or say 'thank you.'

Brown and his band work so closely that he decides what number to do and the band follows in a split second. "We don't have to rehearse, we freshen up! We know what we want to do, we just get the feel of it."

Brown has a concept of immediacy that he defines as "Now!"

His fetish about speed causes him to say "Some people say I'm fast when I dance. I'm not as fast as I want to be."

"I'm looking for something else that nobody does. Mozart, Bach, Beethoven, Strauss, those cats all did it. I'm looking for it too."

And he'll keep looking for it. Brown might be in serious danger of running himself into the ground. His days and hours are periods of whirling motion, when he accomplishes the work of three men.

"I don't vacation," he says, "I don't want to get out of shape."

Could Brown leave his career long enough to get married? "I don't want to talk about that," he says.

All Of Brown

Brown will do lots of television specials in the next few months. Movies? "I don't think so. I never want to let people get all of James Brown. I always want to keep a little leverage—to hold something back. Like, when some kid jumps onstage, I stand back and let him dance."

Brown received a mixed reception when he toured Europe not long ago. Some people said they felt that the man they had idolized so long wasn't half as big as his image. But this isn't the way Brown says it was.

"They accepted me in Europe," he explains, "but it was pretty rough for a couple of days until I did the show 'Top of the Pops' and they gave me the whole show.

"Foreign countries want me back real bad now, but I'm having trouble finding the time to go. But let me say this: no place can compare to here! We don't know how much we've got. People who think they don't like it here should go outside the country and just look around. They won't believe how good we've got it.

"This is my home! I don't want to leave," he says.

What does Brown do with his wealth? "Well, I have my jet, and I have some income property. I feel I owe it to the people who believe in me not to throw my money around or spend it foolishly. How could they respect me as an entertainer if they knew that I threw away all my money foolishly?

"I don't have any problems with taxes, either," he says. "The kids respect me that way. When I visit an all-girl school, they all call me Mr. Brown. Then I say, 'No, you can call me James,' but they still call me Mr. Brown. Respect is more important to me than almost anything else."

How would James describe himself?

"I'm an intelligent human being. If I was a football player, I'd live the life of an athlete. If I was an executive, I'd live the life of an executive. I'm an entertainer, so I live the life of an entertainer. But I'd be a gentleman in athletics or business or what-have-you."

"I've been a pacesetter for the last five years, and I'll stay that way!"

KRLA ARCHIVES

Chad & Jeremy's
Newest Hit Album
Distant Shores
including **"You Are She"**
on
COLUMBIA RECORDS
at your
favorite Record Store

KRLA ARCHIVES

BEAT SHOWCASE
(spotlighting new talent on the pop scene)

The Unidentified Flying Objects have been described to *BEAT* by many people as the "only girl group who will really make it big." And they may. The girls hail from the East Coast but now live in Hollywood. Their sound is new and original, a folk rock blues mixture they describe as "lyrical rock," based on Lisa Kindred's strong voice. Left to right: Lisa Kindred, Helena Tribuno and Ann Sternberg. Sitting is drummer Laurie Stanton.

Five guys who call the West Coast their home form the Yellow Payges, a group that appears steadily in Southland clubs and shows. The Yellow Payges have conquered nervousness except before doing new songs and plan to capture the record world with their yet-to-be released single. Their leader, Danny Hortter, and several members of the group originally were the Driftones until adding drummer Danny Gorman, an unapproachable percussionist.

The Sparrow are a Canadian group who played New York's Arthur and remained perched at various discotheques around the U.S. Their first single, "Tomorrow's Ship" c/w "Isn't It Strange" is made stranger with unusual sounds they've created using their regular instruments. The group's consuming interest is sound: electronic, amplified, then soft and weird. From left, The Sparrow are Dennis Edmonton, Jerry Edmonton, John Kay and Goldy McJohn, with Nick St. Nicholas in the center.

Dave Heenan wandered into the *BEAT* offices one day to announce that he has arrived on the West Coast and tell us about himself. He went to school with the Animals, was a neighbor of the Beatles and formed a group in New York called the Mersey Lads, until all the other lads married. An R & B singer, he is looking for a group.

KRLA ARCHIVES

TEEN PANEL

War: Anti-American Or Anti-Hypocrisy

This is the second half of a teen panel discussion which began in the September 10 issue of The BEAT. The first half concerned the problems of the U.S. Negro. Midway in the discussion another topic came up. One of the panelists (Mike, age 18) conveyed his feelings on the subject of the draft, and the conversation then took a turn in that direction.

This portion of the discussion begins with a condensation of Mike's statement. Also participating are Linda—16, Kris—17, and Barry—19.

Mike—"The whole world is watching while this crap is going on in America (meaning the racial situation.) If I thought things would always stay this way, I don't believe I'd go on living in this country. My dad has a great war record and he got shook when I started to panic about being drafted. Finally, I told him how I feel. As a soldier, he had something to fight against, and so would I, but he had something to believe in and fight *for*. I don't have that. I'm not being anti-American, just anti-hypocrisy. It would be worth dying if it would help America practice what it preaches, but I won't willingly sacrifice myself to protect principles that seem to exist only on paper. If I'm drafted, I'll fight for the people I care about, not to protect some slob of a cop in Mississippi so he can go on cracking the skulls of Negroes who want to vote. When I told my dad this, he couldn't say anything, because I was making sense."

"I Get Sick"

Linda—"I wish you hadn't said that. I really wish you hadn't even brought it up. I get sick thinking about the Negro situation, but I get even sicker thinking about what you just said. I don't think I can even discuss war. Not intelligently. It makes me too ill."

Barry—"I wish *you* hadn't said *that*. You were able to discuss the racial situation objectively, and you're the first Southerner I've ever heard do that. Not that others don't; I just haven't heard them. So why can't you discuss this? Just because it makes you sick to think about it? That's a big part of what's wrong with the world. Half of the people are either too dumb or too chicken to talk about real problems, and the other half is too disgusted to bother. Things are in a mess and it's every person's responsibility to try and find a way to help. You *have* to think about it."

Linda—"Okay, so I think about it and talk about it. What good does that do? It doesn't change anything. You yourself said that individual concern is of no help if you don't apply it, and how can one person possibly change the world?"

Kris—"I could name you a few hundred people who have sure helped change it."

Barry—"And a few million more who don't have names because they helped on an individual level. The world *is* people, and if enough

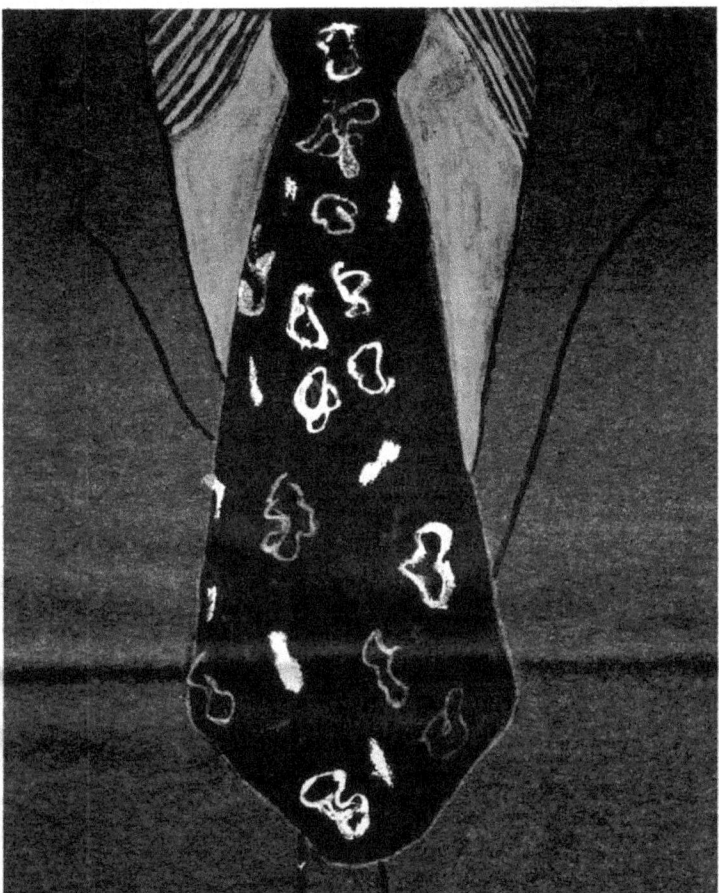

BEAT Art: Henri Munsford

people change, so will the world."

Linda—"I can't argue with that, but . . . I know what I'm thinking, but I can't get it out . . . what I mean is, there are different kinds of 'changes.' Some are a matter of choice, up to the individual. Like the racial problem. That can be solved by changing minds, or hearts, or attitudes. But if you're completely against war, you can't apply your theory."

Who Says?

Barry—"Who says you can't?"

Linda—"You can't apply it where it'll do any good. Not unless you're in a position to decide whether we will or won't go to war. There are less than a hundred people in the entire world who make these final decisions. What do they care what I think, or what anyone thinks? No matter how you feel, all you can do is what you're told. If there is a war, I mean. No one is going to come around and ask me or anyone else if it's all right to have a war."

Kris—"I understand what you're saying, but I think it's another subject entirely. From the one Mike brought up, that is. You're talking about war in general. He wasn't. He was speaking as an American who may have to fight to preserve our freedoms, and from what he said, I assume he doesn't feel this country is worth the trouble."

Mike—"I didn't say that. Anyway, I didn't mean it that way. America is the best country in the world in so many ways, but some of the people in it are making it the worst in other ways. I said I'd fight if I'm called, but I can't do it on a God-Bless-America flag-waving basis. It would be more God-*Help*-America. Everyone in my country doesn't have the freedoms I may have to die to 'preserve.' I'm not saying our principles aren't worth protecting and saving, but we're not living up to them as a nation. I don't feel guilty because I mind the thought of dying for words instead of actions."

Hypocritical

Kris—"I think you misunderstood me. I wasn't challenging you, or saying that the way you feel is wrong. This country is very hypocritical in many ways, and some of the people in it don't deserve to live here. Some of them don't deserve to live, period. But I don't think your feelings are anything new. When it comes right down to it, out on a battlefield, the majority of soldiers aren't giving their lives for *principles*. They're fighting to stay alive, and fighting so people they love can stay alive."

Linda—"If you get killed, you're just as dead no matter who or what you're fighting for. The who isn't the important thing. It's the *why* . . . why this kind of barbaric thing has to happen in a society that's smart enough to know better. It takes thousands of people to fight a war and only a few to prevent it. They make the rules and we play their games for them. War isn't an individual thing; it's mass murder."

Pacifists

Kris—"War is *becoming* a more individual matter. Maybe not the actual fighting, but in other respects. There's a lot of controversy over Viet Nam, for instance. There hasn't been a great deal of social protest in time of war before this. Now, people who don't feel we should be in Viet Nam are speaking up."

Mike—"Sure, but they're looked down on and called draft-card burners."

Kris—"Not all of them. Some very responsible people have spo-

ken out against American intervention. People in high places."

Linda—"And how about that big article in some magazine or other? The one about the way college students are shook up over being drafted right in the middle of their educations, or right after they've finished school and are starting a career. You should have seen some of the letters people wrote in after this was printed!. They were really down on anyone who wasn't all gung-ho over being in the service. Especially the veterans who wrote in. It was frightening. They had such a "we fought for you now it's your turn" attitude, just as though they accepted war as an inevitability. Something every generation has to face instead of something we should try to avoid. I can't understand that kind of attitude. Surely a person who has been in a war would want peace more than anyone else."

Mike—"It's doing a lot of good, isn't it? Especially for the guys who are over there dying. And how about the three servicemen who were just court-martialed and sentenced to five years at hard labor because their consciences wouldn't allow them to fight in Viet Nam?"

Social Protest

Barry—"Are you sure you've *tried* to understand? Try looking at this through the eyes of someone who's been through bloody hell and seen his friends getting their heads shot off. It's just human nature for them to think that pacifists and guys who admit they don't want to be drafted are a bunch of soft_____. They're not looking at the situation objectively, so they aren't seeing the reasons why the younger generation feels the way it does. There are a lot of those reasons—Mike's is a good one—just not wanting to fight for something you can't believe in, or just being sickened by the folly of war and not wanting any part of it. The best reason of all is having prepared yourself for something better, where you could really contribute something as a human being, and then being asked to give up what you're working for and join a fight you didn't start and can't finish. But they don't see it this way. They take the situation personally, and by doing that, they lose their perspective and can't see the situation from all sides."

Linda—"Maybe that does explain a part of the way some people feel about the non-gung-ho's, but what about their preoccupation with war? They make it sound like you're crazy if you *don't* want to get involved."

Barry—"The last war was theirs; this one is ours, and the two situations are entirely different. When they were called to the service, an act of aggression had been committed against the United States. There were no two ways about it. The protest couldn't be social because it had to be physical. The war now is more of a political gambit, and there's room for pro and con opinions. I should say, there's *cause*. Just cause. They're remem-

(Turn to Page 21)

KRLA ARCHIVES

...JIMMY RUFFIN

No 'Brother' Image For Jimmy Ruffin

Establishing yourself as an individual in the wake of an older brother's success isn't as easy as it sounds. For Jimmy Ruffin, breaking the "David's brother" label has been an uphill fight.

But Jimmy is steadily gaining recognition as an individual.

As a member of the famed Temptations, David has received most of the attention. He still does, although "What Becomes Of The Brokenhearted" is putting Jimmy in a spotlight all his own.

Gospel

No matter how much Jimmy strives for his own individuality, however, the two brothers have a lot of similarities.

Both spent their early years in the tradition of moving gospel singing. As a result, both brothers today possess the same feeling and ability for soul singing.

Both Jimmy and David have joined the fine Motown stable of performers—the company that has produced such groups as the Supremes and the Four Tops.

And finally, both have a record high on the music charts. "What Becomes of the Brokenhearted" is only a couple of notches behind the Temptations' "Beauty's Only Skin Deep" which is already in the top ten.

"What Becomes of the Brokenhearted" is Jimmy's third record. The first two bombed—but neither seemed to reflect Jimmy's real potential as does his latest release. The arrangement simply demonstrates Jimmy's versatility. Basically, Jimmy is a "soul" singer—and soul singers don't usually attempt easy flowing, "pretty" songs.

Jimmy's voice has the range for versatility. It can capture gusty, soulful moods and still do a smooth, sedate number like "What Becomes of the Brokenhearted."

Jimmy's talents as a soul singer can be traced to his childhood. Soul music has its origin in the church gospel singing of the deep south—and Jimmy had plenty of contact with this.

Jimmy's childhood was fixed about the traditions of Wednesday Night prayer meetings and Sunday Morning sermons. The church choir was as much a part of his early life as rock 'n' roll and radio are today.

Singing has become such a major part of his life that it is practically the sole topic of his thoughts and conversation. His goal, he says earnestly, is "to become the best entertainer I possibly can."

He is fast becoming a top entertainer.

His voice is slightly remindful of the ones of some of the all-time greats like Jimmy Rushing and Roy Brown.

Although his style is derived from the blues and the music of the church, there is a modern flavor to his songs.

Soul Label

His first job as a singer came in 1962, when he appeared at the Ebony Club in Muskegon, Michigan. At the close of his engagement he auditioned for Motown, was accepted and signed to the Soul label.

The idea of failure seems to have escaped his mind completely, and he says he has no plans should he not make it in show business.

He doesn't need to worry. Not only has he made it, but he has made it as an individual.

'Ooww' Sam's Chasing

By Rochelle Reed

"OOOOWWWW..." I heard as I knocked on the door, then "C'mon in!"

I considered fleeing down the hall and hiding in the linen closet, but instead I ventured into the lair of Sam the Sham, who has been scaring his recording, "Lil' Red Riding Hood" to the top of the charts.

Sam really didn't look like a big bad wolf at all. Actually, he looked more like a great, big, wiry part-Mexican lepricon. With an elaborately trimmed beard. And an earring in one ear.

Texas Mod

Well, Sam once wore a turban and a robe but "we used to get tripped up in them." So now he's clothed himself and the Pharoahs in something that closely approximates "Texas-Mod" and concentrated on doing a real stage act, instead of "just plunk! here's my record."

Sam's journeyed through almost every city in the U.S. with his act and left a number of Pharoahs behind. He's finally settled down with five young men he discovered in New York, gave onstage Texas accents, more Texas-Mod clothes and plenty of musical freedom. "I'm really proud of my Pharoahs," Sam says, and in turn, the Pharoahs do Sam proud.

Sam's onstage act, which used to involve simply standing and singing, has matured into a well-timed, ad-libbed show demonstrating the Pharoahs' talents as well as Sam's own.

But it was Sam's lack of talent at the organ that gave him the name Sam the Sham.

"I'm not an organist," he confesses, "I never could play very well. Other musicians in town, when they'd finished their shows, used to say 'Let's go down and watch the Sham instead of Sam."

And voila! Sam the Sham was born. But the Pharoahs? "It was the only name not taken by another group," he explained.

Sam's honesty about his organ playing has led him to add a few new members to his group. Plus the four musicians who travel with him now, he's adding a "real" organist, a baritone sax, a trumpet, and three girl singers, as yet unnamed. Sam was considering the Shamettes, (I shook my head a lot) but said maybe he'd think about it some more.

Sam plans to put even more life into his act. "Everyone's got to dance," he says emphatically, "if they can't, they'll have to learn."

It might be difficult to suddenly become as limber and twinkletoed as Sam and his Pharoahs. They manage to bend and jerk in directions most people just can't bend and jerk—and they play at the same time. "The girls will also dance and do routines," Sam added. (This we've got to see!)

Sam and the Pharoahs are masters of timing, something Sam says you learn "only from experience."

"We could provoke mass mania," he confides, "we could work people into a frenzie. But why? It's the small kids that get hurt."

"We got pulled off the stage in Baltimore, though," he adds, "and in New Orleans we did a show with the Byrds and Mitch Ryder. We weren't even top billing but the kids stormed the stage during our act.

"I didn't know what was happening," he went on. "It was dark and I sort of heard this rustling. Tony (bass guitarist) put his hand up to shade his eyes and look into the audience. All of a sudden I saw him jump up and give sort of a kick. I yelled 'Great Googagooba' (or something sounding like it) and ran. It's every man for himself when that happens!"

In Movie

Sam has just completed a short part in "Fastest Guitar Alive," a movie starring Roy Orbison as a singer-spy with a guitar that conveniently turns into a rifle with the push of a button.

"It was really a gas! I didn't want to sing, I wanted to act. I'm a guard on a train carrying a shipment of gold to the Mint. It takes place around the time of the Civil War."

And the beard and the hair and the earring? "They left me just like

...SAM TAKEN' IT EASY IN THE HAYSTACK.

KRLA ARCHIVES

Riding Hood By The Hair On His Chin!

I am. After all, I might have been a singer before I was an expressman.

Sam's acting, he says, is more real than put-on in one explosion scene. "They told us the explosion would go off on the count of four, and it went off on two. I really hit the ground and scrambled!"

Sam's nearly a natural for acting. "I like to play cowboys and Indians because I've played them before." He would be perfect if cast as Pancho Villa, and "I'd like to play it," he says.

Pass Word

About this time, Sam's manager rapped on the door, yelled "OOOOWWWW!!" ran in and pulled the whiskers on Sam's chin, singing "Not by the hair of my chinny chin chin."

Then he scrounged around and found a portable record player, slapped on a record and said, "You've got to hear this!"

It turned out to be a record named "By the Hair On My Chinny Chin Chin" which had just been released that day. Little Red Riding Hood, running from the wolf again, stops into the house of the three little pigs.

The disc is backed with an even funnier song—"I'm Out With The In Crowd"—something Sam says happens to him quite often.

"When I fly and ask at the desk if there are many empty seats, they always say 'oh yes' but as soon as I walk onto the plane, the 'occupied' signs start to pop into the seats. I have to stop and look at myself to see if I have leprosy or anything."

Laughing, joking Sam has a side to this personality that doesn't show onstage but pervades his offstage life: he's really a nice guy, the type you might want to take home to Mother. He's earnest, sincere, hard-working and sensitive.

Eligible Sam

Mother might also like the fact that 25-year-old Sam is one of rock 'n' roll's most eligible bachelors—wealthy and resembling Ricardo Montalban under all the hair.

If Sam had nine lives to live, "I'd give one to a really good friend," he says. If Sam had unlimited money he would buy a diamond ("I mean a *really* big one") and cut it up for all his friends.

His musicians must be "gentlemen first, then artists." Though Sam spent many months starving, he doesn't talk about it. "I don't sit around and complain about every little scratch. That's over."

... SAM CATCHES LITTLE RED RIDING HOOD BEHIND A TREE.

... CAN YOU SEE SAM AS PONCHO VILLA? HE CAN!

Sam was born on a Sunday and given the Spanish name for that day—Domingo. His last name is Samudio, which gave him the nickname Sam. He is Latin in his ideas of what constitutes men and women. For example, he feels that with man's intelligence, he should be able to out-wrestle a bear without having to hide behind a gun. "Now that," he says, "would really be something to talk about!"

Sam once said his ambition was to sing opera. Is it still?

Opera Star

"Oh yes," he says, and then explains that he thinks an ambition must be something that is really difficult for a person and thus it would be a true accomplishment. Singing opera, for Sam would be "about the hardest thing I could imagine."

But does that mean he wants hallowed halls to echo with strains of "Woolly Bully?" Not on your life. "I can still sing an aria," he says.

Sam doesn't pinch from other artists. "I may see what I don't want to do," he explains, but he seldom imitates others. That's because Sam specializes in never following what's "in" but doing "What's Out With The Out Crowd."

Opposite

"When I see music go really hard, I run over to the other side of the scene and do something soft." And vice versa. Sam, in the guise of Big Bad Wolf, wasn't really running after Little Red Riding Hood so much as running away from the sound that was flooding the airways at the time he cut the disc.

Did Sam have an alternate plan in mind in case he just didn't make it as a singer. "You bet," he says, practical as ever. "I was going to go to the Arkansas-Memphis Bridge—and jump!"

KRLA ARCHIVES

For Girls only

by shirley poston

I am about to swear an oath.

Oh, relax. It's not the kind you're thinking. What I mean is, I'm about to make you a solemn promise.

For the past few weeks, I have done nothing in this column (hah!) but gibber about one subject. Namely, the Beatles.

My gibbering is hardly anything new, if you have the misfortune to be one of both of my regular readers, but ordinarily, I at least have the good grace to gibber about *several* subjects.

Sooo...

Sooooo, this is the last week I am going to devote this entire space to Beatle blithering. If you'll bear with me just one more column (*double* hah!), we'll then get back to codes and envelope contests and other *fascinating* goodies (like orange popsickles and feet.)

I wouldn't Beatle-Blither this time, only you have just got to hear about the Shirley Poston (as in Smooth Move) of all time.

The last time you heard from me was just after the Beatle concert. I had just come down with a severe case of the panic-stricks (parddon?) and had decided that George *Pant* Harrison was not going to get out of town alive... I mean was not going to get out of town without my at least *talking* to him or something.

I imagine you're all just *dying* (as in yawn) to hear what I did about all this, which is just too bad because I'm going to tell you anycow (?).

First of all, picture the following scene...

Pacing

It is early on a Monday morn. A girl is pacing up and down in her room. There isn't much room to pace, but she has cleared three by three (three feet long and three inches wide) a path admist the rubble (envelopes, unanswered letters, records, Beatles' books, orange popsickle sticks, etc.) and is pacing all the same.

She looks as though she has not slept. This is because she has not slept. She has not slept because George Harrison is over on Curson Terrace and she *isn't*. And she is busy figuring out a way to get there (as in *or else*.)

Up to this point, she has had a number of ideas. Sampling Of Number Of Ideas: (1) Rent a kangaroo and hop over the security guards (2) Fell a tree and bash the door open. (3) Steal a tank and attack.

Somehow, these and other ideas didn't seem too rational, but this did not bother the aforementioned girl. She is used to this sort of thing(y).

Now, do you have the scene clearly in mind? That, then, is how my smoothest of all possible moves was born.

The idea came to me about 11 a.m. (by that time, I had reached the weeping-wailing-and-gnashing of-teeth state.)

It simply would not do for me to go lunging up to the Beatles' abode. (In other words, I couldn't think of a way to pull *that* plan off.) But was there anything wrong with my giving George a call?

Yes. I didn't have the telephone number.

That's where the pacing stopped and the racing began. First I made a list of everyone who would have those priceless digits in their hot hands. Then I checked the list to see which of the everyone's I knew the best.

Naturally, I didn't know *any* of them. However, I at least had a *speaking acquaintance* with one of the fortunate few, and knowing that she would probably never speak to me again after *this* day was over, I ran to the phone.

Shirley Who?

When I got through to the aforementioned, I trembled the following request:

"Hi... um... this is Shirley... er... could I take you to lunch?"

"Yes," she replied. "Shirley who?" she added.

"Poston," I quaked. "I write for *The BEAT*," I added.

"Oh," she said with hardly a trace of eagerness, as though she were wondering why I had chosen this particular time to become so friendly (and Lord knows she might well) (as in arsk.)

Anytoad (??), we arranged to meet later, and you are never going to *believe* what I did for the next two hours. I sat down and *wrote a speech*! I hate to admit that, but if you think *that's* ridiculous, stick around.

About one o'clock, armed with my memorized plea for George's (stomp) number, I staggered onward.

Wrong First

Everything went wrong right from the first. Instead of giving me a steely-eyed glare, she was extremely nice and that really threw me. In fact, when I sat down, she sort of gave me this *pat* (as in nicedoggie) and said: "What can I do for you, Shirley?"

"NOTHING!" I shrieked hysterically. "I mean, I just thought it would be nice for us to have lunch."

"Then why don't we? she said gently, so we did.

That is to say, *she* did. What *I* did was sort of mangle this poor hamburger while trying my best to keep from falling off my chair and writhing on the rug.

Finally, I knew the time had come, and taking one of Robin Irene Boyd's famous deep breaths, I prepared to launch into my speech. But before I got a word out, she gave me this weird look.

"Shirley," she said, and with good reason as this, oddly enough, is my name. "Have you been up to see George yet?"

"GEORGE?" I shrieked hysterically. "I mean, no, I *couldn't* do *that*."

She gave me another look. "Why not?" she arsked. "After all, you write about him constantly."

Putrid Purple

I blushed a deep and putrid purple. "Yeah, but some of the stuff I've *said* about him... oh, *you know*."

However, not one to let opportunity knock its fist to a pulp, I realized the time had re-come for my siege of begging, so I took another R.I.B. and began.

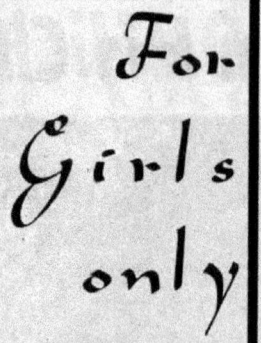

"Shirley," she interrupted. "I think you should at least *call* him. Here's the number," she added, handing me a bit of paper.

Well, if you don't think *that* one didn't about land me under the table, you've gotta be kidding. I hope you know what I mean. It was marvelous getting the number, but it was such a shock to my already-shattered nerves, I about had a *stroke*.

Godfrey, she even told me *when* to call him! That night about 1:30, when he'd just be getting back from the San Francisco concert, or the next morning before 11, because they'd be leaving for the airport just after that.

What To Say

But there was one thing she couldn't tell me, and that was *what to say* when I called him, and aye, that was the rub.

The rest of that day was a long series of additional strokes, and I alternated between writing another speech and leaping around the house like a spastic gazelle.

I didn't tell anyone about any of this, except my very best friend (who also may never speak to me again because she dropped the whole telephone on her foot, when I told her the news, and, to hear *her* tell it, is going to have to have it amputated) (her foot, not the phone.)

There's no possible way to describe what a MESS I was. Let it suffice to say that by midnight I'd completed my "George speech" and was sitting on my bed, hugging the telephone and twitching.

Now, are you READY for this? The next thing I knew, the telephone was ringing. After shooting seventeen feet into the air, I answered it. It was my best friend.

"Did you call him?" she moaned groggily.

"Not yet," I moaned groggily. "What time is it?"

"Five a.m." she replied.

"Oh my Gawd, Gawd, Gawd," I replied.

I know this is getting horribly long, but it's not over yet. The next thing I did (after throwing one of my most spectacular snits to date) was start writing another speech. (The one I'd prepared was a night speech, and wouldn't do at all for the crack of dawn—as in ten a.m.)

Ravings

Now, here is exactly what happened that next morning. By nine, I had my ravings memorized (which I would, of course, relate to George in well-modulated and seductive whispers) (oh, *sure* I would) (as in screech.)

At nine-thirty, I left for the office. (I *had* to be there for some reason or another that morning, on this day of *all* days yet.)

I had decided to let George sleep (nice of me, don't you think?) until a quarter after ten. At which time I crept nervous-wreckedly (oh comma brother) into an unoccupied office and clutched the telephone.

Then I opened my purse to take out my wallet, where I'd hidden the number from prying eyes (had my brother gotten his gloms on it, he'd have been selling it on street corners) (the number, the number.)

Then I opened my mouth and BELLOWED! My wallet wasn't in my purse! It *was*, I suddenly remembered, in my *bed*!

Down Five

Do I have to tell you that I fell down five flights of stairs, and drove like a raving maniac in the direction of the Poston Plantation (as in hovel)? Do I have to tell you that when I *got* there, it was *after* eleven, and that I literally pounced on that telephone?

I don't think I have to tell you these things. Nor do I think I have to tell you what happened then. But I will.

I dialed the number (fainting after each digit.) It rang. Someone answered.

"This is Shirley Poston," I croaked. "May I speak to George for five seconds?"

Gone!

The someone chortled. "You could have if you'd called five seconds sooner. He's a little too busy now."

"What's he doing?" I gargled.

"At the moment, he's leaping into a limousine," the someone replied.

"THEY'RE LEAVING?" I choked.

"They're *gone*," he answered.

Do I need to tell you that the remainder of my marbles are same? I hope not, because I can't *bear* to even discuss this another *second*.

I *am* now about to swear another oath.

And *this* time, it *is* the kind you're thinking!

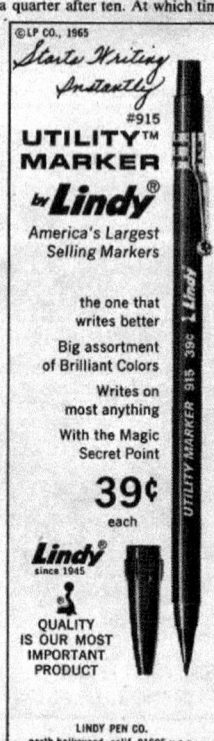

KRLA ARCHIVES

The Left Banke Need Clavinet

These days, the Left Banke are half way there.

They still haven't found the clavinet they've been combing the country for, but they have found another object of a search. They have a hit record.

You've heard their new record by now ("Walk Away, Renee") but it's quite possible you have never seen a clavinet. Or even heard of one.

A Clavinet

A clavinet, you see, is a sort of 18th century keyboard instrument that produces a sound similar to that of today's electric harpsichord.

Coming up with weird, antique instruments is the biggest kick among today's musicians. The Stones and the Beatles have incorporated such oddities as the sitar and the kazoo into their works.

But it took the Left Banke to come up with the Clavinet.

The unusual and unpredictable are trademarks with the Banke.

A prophecy that has almost become a bi-law in the recording profession says that when a group first breaks into the business they do so with a big, hard rock sound. You just don't start with a pretty melody.

But the Left Banke did.

"Walk Away, Renee" contains a smooth, softened blend of harmony you usually see attempted only by an established group. Within days after its release, the record was one of the most sought after in record shops.

The Left Banke are a weird array of individuals – a quintet with such varied interests you wonder if maybe the term "group" is a glittering generalization in their case.

Digs Poe

Take Tom Finn, for instance, who digs Edgar Allan Poe stories and once wanted to be a railroad engineer.

Or Steve Martin, who went to school in Spain and once had visions of becoming an actor. Or Jeff Winfield – the lead guitarist whose ambition is "to become an eccentric old man."

An amiable young man named Mike Brown is the leader of the group. He comes from a musical family, and his first love is writing music.

Mike's musical prowess is vast; he is proficient on the clavichord, organ, harpsichord and piano.

But music is only half the appeal of the Left Banke. Trying to guess what they'll do from one moment to the next is the other half.

...THE LEFT BANKE (l. to r.) Steve Martin, Mike Brown, George Cameron, Jeff Winfield (seated) & Tom Finn

Don't speculate on the type of clothing the group will be wearing the next time you see them. It's useless.

Their dress varies with the whim of the moment and one time you might see them in floppy bell-bottoms. The next time, they might be wearing tightly tapered pants with boots.

The Left Banke has one more basic prerequisite for success: 20-year-old George Cameron is from London.

And that, coupled with their musical skills and brash personal appeal, is all the Left Banke needs.

Pop Artist To Run For Cal. Governor

What with movie stars turning Senator and running for Governor, why shouldn't a pop artist get into the act too? According to Starbuck, there is absolutely no reason why the pop world should be left out of the Government bag and, accordingly, Starbuck is running for Governor!

Does he think he's a strong candidate? "I'm a strong candidate! Do you want to arm wrestle?" asked Starbuck. Well, was Mr. Starbuck ever in the service? "No," replied Starbuck, "you see I had a heart murmur. It said, 'don't go, don't go'."

Starbuck and his Rainmakers have a record out called "I Who Have Nothing" but says Starbuck: "You probably haven't heard it because they forgot to put the hole in the middle!"

Gazing into Starbuck's eyes, we decided that he didn't appear old enough to run for Governor of our fair State and dutifully said so. "Yes, that's true," answered a shattered Starbuck, "But, you see, I have a phony I.D."

We figured that would probably work, so we continued. Every candidate promises to do something if they're elected, that is, every candidate *except* our pop ambassador. "I promise," said Starbuck, "nothing!"

Well, does Mr. Starbuck consider himself a liberal or a conservative? "I'm sort of a conservative-liberal," he replied. But never fear, his campaign manager, Mr. Yellow Teeth, clarified the whole situation. "He's conservative with his money and liberal with everyone elses."

Wonderful, and what is Mr. Starbuck in favor of? "Personally, I'm in favor of free speech and free lunches."

While it's true that not every candidate is endorsed by a party, most of them are and we wondered who was backing Starbuck, the Democrats or the Republicans? "Shucks," moaned Starbuck, "I ain't been invited to either one."

The burning issue of the day seems to be our involvement in Viet Nam. Surely, Mr. Starbuck has an opinion on that subject. "We should declare war on North Viet Nam. We could pave the whole country and put parking stripes on it and still be home by Christmas."

What about unemployment? "The United States is the first country to have thought up the idea of making unemployment financially attractive," declared Mr. Starbuck.

The tax situation is one which has always been close to everyone's heart and even closer to their pocketbooks. Does Starbuck think taxes are too high? "Income taxes are fair," stated the candidate. "Rich or poor, you have an equal chance at poverty."

Carefully keeping in mind all of Starbucks' opinions and proposals, do you think he stands a chance of beating Brown or Reagan?

Should We Fight?

(Continued from Page 17)

bering war as a necessity, a 'fighting back' proposition."

Mike – "Isn't it possible that the difference lies in the people involved, and not in the wars at all? So much has happened in the past twenty years. It's hard for this generation to accept war because we're conditioned to a space-type age where there are so many more important things to do. I don't know how I'd have felt about the war in the 1940's, but this is the 1960's and war seems so simpleminded when we're about to send men to the *moon*. It's *ridiculous* really, when you think about it."

Communications

Barry – "There are a lot of differences. Another one is that the world is so much smaller now, because of advances in communications. When the Japanese attacked Pearl Harbor, I'll bet quite a few people said 'Pearl *who?*' Everything was so far away and so unreal. Today everyone knows what's going on everywhere – if they *want* to know. Everything is *not* very far away and it's very *real*. A person tends to think more about something if it's happening in a place they're aware of."

Fair?

Linda – "Can you honestly say you think it's fair to condemn anyone who wants something better and has worked to get it?"

Barry – "Why would you ask me a question like that?"

Linda – "Because you sound like you're sticking up for the people who do this."

Barry – "I'm not sticking up for anyone. I'm just trying to explain their side of it."

Linda – "They aren't trying to see it from our side. Why should we try to see it from theirs? No – don't even answer me. That was a stupid thing to say. I know it's hard for people to change. I said that myself earlier. The only way to get away from being narrow is to look at all sides. And we've got to do that – it's our only hope."

Folly Of War

Kris – "I wasn't going to say this, but I might as well *thoroughly* depress everyone. I was just thinking about a couple of remarks that have been made. About the folly of war and how ridiculous it really is. Did you ever stop to think that a lot of other things are just as ridiculous? Like racial prejudice, and basing your life on material things and money, and looking down on people who don't conform to your standards. The whole thing is really *absurd!* I just don't get it. Humans are capable of so much more than that; they've proved it in other ways. It's almost like the whole race has a part missing or something, and just can't function on all cylinders and make living really *work*."

Sermon Ends

Barry – "Well! Congratulations! You're about fifty years early, you've reached the point most people reach at about seventy when they're looking back on it all and wondering why in the hell they wasted so much of their time. You should be glad to feel that way. Realizing that hardly anything makes much sense is the first step to developing something that does. That concludes my sermon for the evening. We will now turn to hymn number twelve."

KRLA ARCHIVES

The Adventures of Robin Boyd

©1965 By Shirley Poston

After the final frantic fan had made a final frantic attempt to hurl herself into the limousine, the four figures in back relaxed against the leather seats.

For several moments, there was only silence. Then John broke it. (Fortunately, he had a sling with him). (Not to mention a shot). (As in sling-shot, as in sling-shot).

"I'd say something," he said, "but you'd all start thinking I'm daft."

George and Paul gave him looks. (They needn't have bothered—he already has plenty). (I'll say).

"That's no way to feel," Ringo soothed.

"Me Fingers"

"I know," said John. "I generally use me fingers." And, with this, he lapsed into another deep silence.

After awhile, George turned to Paul. "Would *you* start thinking he was daft if he said it?"

Paul shrugged. "Not at all. I started thinking he was daft years ago." Then he turned to John. "Go ahead and say it," he said gently.

John writhed uncomfortably. "You're certain it won't make any difference in our relationship?"

Paul, George and Ringo shook their heads solemnly.

John re-wrothe. "Here it is then... I smell peanut butter."

The other three exchanged expressionless glances.

"You could do a lot worse," Paul said at long last.

Peanut Butter

"You're getting it all wrong," John scowled. "I mean I smell peanut butter at this very moment."

"Oh," they replied in unison. Then the four of them re-relaxed against the leather in calm silence.

Calm, however, is not the *word* for the small bundle of feathers which was lurking beneath the driver's seat.

"*Am-day that George*," Robin thought furiously. If it hadn't been for him, she wouldn't have had to wallow in a peanut butter sandwich in the first place in order to squeeze through the spout of the tea pot in the second place, and she wouldn't be hiding under the seat smelling like something one fed to an elephant in the third place and John wouldn't have gotten an unnerving whiff of her in the fourth place, or something like that.

And that was only *part* of her problem.

Eenie, Meenie

When she'd arrived on the scene where the "special assignment" was to take place and seen four Beatles driving off to the left and four more Beatles driving off to the right, she'd suddenly realized that she had no mortal idea which was which.

So, after working the situation out mathematically (as in eenie, meenie, miney, etc.), she'd taken her chances and careened through an open vent in one of the limousines.

In all the flap of a post-concert Beatle getaway, she hadn't even been noticed, and she was now cowering under the aforementioned seat, trying to figure out whether she had hitched a ride with the real Beatles, or those wretched imposters (George, John and Paul of Genie fame, not mention Ringo the Angel).

And she was getting nowhere fast, because there was only one way to find out. Which was to eavesdrop in hopes that one of them would say something revealing (not to mention sensible).

Suddenly, Robin's ears stood at attention. They were talking again, and she quicked stopped all her internal blithering and listened.

John?

"John?"

"What is it you want, Ringo?"

Ringo gave an embarrassed cough. "I smell peanut butter too, by George!"

George looked to his left and then to his right. "It must be by someone else," he decided. Then they *re-re*-lapsed into silence.

"*Ratzafratz*," moaned Robin, muffling her beak in the carpet of the auto floor. Was this going to go on all night? What if she *was* in the company of the aforementioned wretches? If so, that meant the real Beatles were speeding off in another direction and she'd *never* be able to find them.

Suddenly, she spat out a large piece of lint and grinned feindishly. There *was* another way she could tell them apart. Maybe George The Harrison and George The Genie *did* look exactly alike, but surely there were any number of things they didn't *do* exactly alike!

In fact, there was *one* thing she was absolutely *certain* that no one in the *world* did quite like George Genie. And it was then that Robin knew what she must do.

Half-Wit

First she made every possible effort to gather her wits about her (as usual, she only found half of them). If her plan was to have any hope of working, she'd have to get it over and done with in a matter of seconds before they realized what was happening.

When she felt a little less rattled, she crept out from under the seat and peered up at the four figures in the darkened car.

Then, faster than a speeding bullet, she said "Liverpool," turned into her sixteen-year-old self, threw her arms around George's neck, kissed him so hard his teeth rattled, said "ketchup," turned back into a *real* robin and dashed back under the driver's seat. (Whew).

For a moment, all was silent again. Then George spoke up. "I have a question."

Ringo, Paul and John gave him their undivided attention, and he continued. "I would like to know if a bird just materialized out of nowhere, kissed me and then disappeared?"

Ringo, Paul and John shrugged. "So would we."

After another long and thoughtful spell of quiet, Paul peered closely at George. "I don't smell peanut butter *by* George," he announced. "I smell it *on* George."

Paul's Sleeve

George looked down at his splotched suit and wordlessly scrubbed at a few of the larger spots with Paul's sleeve.

Paul continued to peer. "You have some on your mouth, too," he offered helpfully.

George licked his lips. "I do, don't I."

Paul settled back, and then Ringo peered closely at George. "Do you have any more questions you'd like to ask us?"

George thought for a moment. "Not really... well, there is one more if it's not too much trouble... do any of you happen to have a bit of jelly along?"

"Would you like plum or raspberry?" John inquired.

"Peach, if you don't mind."

"I do mind," John replied, and a restful silence re-re-re-re-fell over the foursome.

Beneath Seat

Restful silence, however, is not the *word*(s) for what (not to mention who) was transpiring beneath the front seat.

Robin lay sprawled in an unladylike manner (make that an unlady*bird*like manner, panting hysterically.

The person she had attacked... er... no, come to think of it, attacked *is* the word for it, had not been *her* George. (But, should he ever decide he'd *like* to be, she would be more than happy to arrange it). That meant it was *them, them, THEM!* The *realies!* Robin Irene Boyd was in the same car with the real Be-*attles!* (Re-GASP!).

But why were they being so calm about what had just happened? And why had she done such a moronic thing anyway? And what was she going to do next?

But she never had to answer these questions. Because the next thing she knew, there was a terrible crash and everything went black.

(To Be Continued Next Issue)

Second Gold One For Dave Clark

...DAVE CLARK

The Dave Clark Five have been awarded their second Gold Record for their million-selling album, "The Dave Clark Five's Greatest Hits." Their first Gold Record was for the group's debut LP, "Glad All Over."

The DC5 recently completed their fifth highly successful cross-country tour and are currently riding in the top half of the nation's record charts with their latest single, "Satisfied With You."

Dave and the boys are scheduled to return Stateside in early October for yet another appearance on "The Ed Sullivan Show." The group has appeared on the show so many times that in the industry they have picked up the nickname, "Ed's house group."

On the album scene, the DC5's "Satisfied With You" LP has just been released but its sales pattern already indicates that it will be another major top-selling item in the country and possibly the object of the group's third Gold Record.

NEW!! HAIR CONTROL FOR MEN WITH MOIST SPRAY ACTION

Shape Up WITH MOIST SPRAY ACTION FOR HAIR CONTROL ALL DAY!

Now a moist grooming aid especially developed for a man's hair. SHAPE UP combines "Sure Control" with a naturalness and convenience never before available in a man's grooming aid. SHAPE UP is a new protein base formula... contains no lacquers, or shellac and is completely water soluable.

For neat, groomed, healthy looking hair use this Special Offer!
Reg. $1.50
With Coupon Only **$1.00**
Incl. tax & postage

Shape Up
The BEAT
6290 Sunset, No. 504
Los Angeles, Calif. 90028

Please send me _____ cans Shape Up at $1.00 each. I enclose $_____ in cash, check or money order.

Name _____
Adress _____
City _____ State _____ Zip _____

KRLA ARCHIVES

'Spell' Cast By Ex-Animal

By Carol Gold

The slim, blond young man at the organ throws his head back, tossing his flopping hair out of his tightly closed eyes. His face reflects the emotion of the music as he cries, "I put a *spell* on you!"

The young man is Alan Price and put a spell on you he does. With his band, the Alan Price Set, he is the leading figure in the "little big band" movement in Britain.

It's hard to believe when you watch and listen to this vibrant, hypnotic performer leading his swinging band of fine musicians that just 18 months ago, he turned his back on the pop world and in exhaustion left one of the world's top groups, the Animals.

Alan Price was the Animals' founder, backbone and soul. It was his arrangement and fantastic organ-playing, that, together with Eric Burdon's vocal made "House of the Rising Sun" the pop classic it is. But there are always problems in belonging to a group, especially in a big-name group. For Alan, the problem was flying. He is terrified of it—terrified to the point of physical illness. The Animals have always been the most widely-traveled group on the scene and this meant Alan had to fly. Tension grew and finally Alan went under.

In A Daze

The morning the Animals were due to take off on a 22-day tour, Alan called on their manager and said he couldn't face the trip. When he left, he was in a daze and doesn't remember anything that happened until he found himself on a train to Newcastle, his home. He was through with the Animals.

In fact, Alan felt he was through with music. "I said I was through and I meant it. For two or three months I thought of giving up music entirely. The disadvantages seemed to outweigh the advantages. But then I found the only way to sort myself out was to go back to it—music is what appeals most to me."

"Moral support was a necessity. You have to get self-confidence from somewhere and I didn't have any. I got it by talking to people like Zoot Money and Chris Farlowe." (They're leaders of groups in the same blues-jazz field as Alan.)

And slowly the Alan Price Set came to be. First to join was John Walters, an old friend of Alan's from Newcastle and a member of the jazz-blues-pop clique that spawned the Animals. John plays trumpet and is a jazz musician at heart. He was teaching school in Newcastle because, until the Price Set came along, trumpets were out on the pop scene. As far as he's concerned, playing with Alan is "as close to jazz as you can come."

Left Fame

Then came Boots Slade, who plays bass and can usually be found standing in the deepest shadows onstage, playing with a contented smile on his face. He left Georgie Fame to play with Alan.

And Clive Burrows, who plays baritone sax and is the Set's arranger. Clive is tiny and looks impish. When you get to know him, you find he *is* impish. Clive, who left Zoot Money's Big Roll Band to play with Alan is considered one of the top baritone players on the scene.

And Roy Mills, also tiny, almost hidden behind his drum kit. Roy does a drum solo that never fails to knock out the audience—he puts so much into it that by the end he's drenched with sweat and looks on the verge of collapse.

And the baby of the group, Steve Gregory, who plays tenor sax and just turned 21, to the accompaniment of much teasing from Alan and the Set.

What about their leader, the master pop organist, Alan Price? Alan is intense, energetic, moody, dedicated and possessed of a mischievous and wonderful sense of humor that delights in a send-up or a good laugh at himself. "Hi Lili," the Set's current British hit, is Alan's sense of tongue-in-cheek at work. He's one of the best-liked people in the music world, affectionately nicknamed Pricey by friends and fans.

"Thanks"

His music is his life—he can often be found sitting and playing around London just for the love of it.

Pricey isn't one to sit tight on a good thing, either. He's constantly trying to expand musically. Currently, he's hunting for a couple of girl singers to back the Set. He has visions of a true road show, complete with dancers. "I want the chicks to rave it up on stage with the band. The lads are too busy playing to do much leaping about," he says earnestly.

"All I ever wanted to do was play," he's told me.

It looks as though he'll be doing that for a long time to come—and more. He's been offered several movie contracts, not the least of which is from Warner Bros., who want to star him in a remake of "Rebel Without A Cause." I've never done any acting, but I'd like to. It's all part of the ego thing. But they'll have some trouble with my Geordie accent," he grinned, speaking at his usual top speed.

... The slim, blond, young man at the organ throws his head back, tossing his flopping hair out of his tightly-closed blue eyes, as his body sways with the rhythm and his fingers fly over the keyboard. He's the first person ever to leave a top group and make it on his own. His name is Alan Price.

... THE ALAN PRICE SET (l. to r.) Roy, Steve, John, Boots, Clive and Alan Price (center).

Angel Looks Like Elvis

... JIMMY ANGEL

You may not have noticed yet, but there's a minor revolution going on in rock 'n' roll—and more and more singers are joining its ranks.

It's not exactly a revolution, really. In essence, it is returning to the sounds and styles of the era of Elvis Presley — the era that launched rock 'n' roll as a legitimate, major form of music.

The latest singer to revert to this early style is Jimmy Angel, a handsome young Kansas product who has found a new home in sunny California.

Jimmy Angel even looks like Elvis. He sounds even more like Gene Pitney and says he likes them both.

"Everywhere I've gone the response to this type of music has been tremendous," said Jimmy. "So many of the top entertainers—Johnny Rivers among others—are doing it that it's just about becoming the thing to do."

Jimmy described his music as simply being "big beat" music. "We use a lot of bass and a lot of drums," he said.

Jimmy Angel is a good singer. He is on his way up but whether or not he sets on top in this unpredictable business is still anyone's guess.

But he believes in himself and when talking to him you get the idea that maybe his stern determination could be the deciding factor. He works hard at singing; for him it is more than just a nine to five job.

He once waited three days to audition for a prominent night club owner. On the fourth, the owner coldly told Jimmy he was too busy to hear him audition.

"I told him I wasn't going to leave until he heard me," Jimmy rememberd. "Finally, he said I could sing one number and that was it.

"After I finished that number he asked me to do another. I did, and after that he signed me for an engagement."

Jimmy has had some outstanding engagements in California—Los Angeles' Red Velvet, among others—but his show business interests aren't restricted to night club appearances only.

He has his eye on movies—and several producers have their eye on him.

"I've been talking to some people in Hollywood for about a month," he said. "Eventually, this is the field I want to end up in."

Indeed, he has all the physical necessities to become an actor. His rugged, sullen appearance and smooth, mellow voice would make him a natural for the screen.

Jimmy is currently working on new material for a record to be released soon. It will be his second record effort.

KRLA ARCHIVES

KRLA ARCHIVES

America's Largest Teen NEWSpaper 25¢

KRLA Edition BEAT
OCTOBER 22, 1966

BEAT Photo: Howard L. Bingham

GEORGE HARRISON, SITAR IN INDIA
SEE PAGE 1

ELVIS PRESLEY SHOWS HIMSELF
SEE PAGE 3

HERMAN HURT
SEE PAGE 1

KRLA BEAT

Volume 2, Number 25   October 22, 1966

Ike & Tina Smash Hit With Stones

Although it has been a full year since the Rolling Stones last toured their native country and they were, to say the least, a little uncertain of the reception they would receive this time around, they're a smash on their current English tour which kicked off at Alpert Hall in London.

Said Mick Jagger following their debut performance in London: "It's good to be touring again. I'm very surprised at the fans—I thought they'd be older but they all seem as young as ever. I never expected this sort of reception this time. It's a knockout."

Surprising

But what was even more surprising was the rousing acceptance by the British teens of the Stones' tour partners, the Ike and Tina Turner Revue. As you undoubtedly know, the Revue features 19 members and utilizes the best and wildest in American rhythm 'n blues.

England has long been noted for its love of American blues and yet when James Brown graced their shores several months ago, he was given an ice-cold reception and was the object of some heated contorversy as the English got their first glimpse of the great American entertainer.

Therefore, Ike Turner admitted to being just a bit worried about his first visit to England, especially since the Revue was slated for the Stones' tour.

"We were very nervous at first," said Ike, "but things seem to be working out all right and by the time we've done a few more dates we'll really start to swing." But his wife, Tina, stated that she was not at all worried about appearing in England as "it's just another job."

Outspoken Tina also had quite a few words to say about Phil Spector (whose record label they record for) and the current American record scene.

"The trouble is in the States now they play a disc because of the money that's been handed out. It doesn't matter anymore what the record sounds like. It hurt Phil's ego when 'River Deep, Mountain High' didn't go.

"He has quite a few difficulties in the States nowadays," continued Tina. "People think he's a nut and that he's strange. They don't understand him and, therefore, they think twice about promoting his records."

Spector Trouble

Tina admitted that she and Ike are having some troubles with Spector "because when we were supposed to be doing our follow-up he disappeared. I heard he was making films in Mexico or something."

Meanwhile, the Stones' tour rolls on with Ike and Tina getting loads of praise from everyone who sees the show. Said one British paper about Ike and Tina: "This must be one of the most exciting acts ever to come to Britain from America. They deserve to come back here and tour as star attractions."

Harrison Visits India

Beatle George Harrison and his wife Patti are currently in India, where George is learning to play the sitar.

George and Patti are reportedly registered at a Bombay hotel under the names of "Mr. and Mrs. Sam Wells."

George has not announced when they expect to return to Britain, but has indicated that it may be some time before the two go back. He holds "open" air tickets from Bombay to the U.K.

George's well-known interest in the Indian instrument caused a flood of sitar music in rock and roll, both in Beatle material and numbers by other groups.

John Lennon, on location for the shooting of "How I Won The War," will not return to London until the filming is completed in early November.

The whereabouts of Ringo Starr and Paul McCartney are assumed to be in London. Ringo said earlier that he wanted to spend more time with his wife Maureen and son, Zak.

...LEARNING SITAR IN INDIA

The Turtles Minus One

Following the current fad of musical chairs being played by a great majority of today's pop groups, the Turtles have changed members—again.

Latest to leave the Turtles is Chuck Portz, their bass player and one of the original group members. Chuck has decided to go back to school and leave the music business for the time being, anyway.

He was replaced by Chip Taylor, who was formerly in the now defunct MFQ and the equally defunct Gene Clark Group. Chip made his first appearance as a Turtle at the group's one-night appearance at the Carousel Theatre in Southern California.

Before losing Chuck, the Turtles had also lost their former drummer, Don, on the theory that Don wished to spend more time with his wife. Replacing Don was Johnny Barbata.

Dylan At Festival

Bob Dylan is going to make a personal appearance when he and Joan Baez headline the third annual Festival of the Roses in New York.

Dylan has been "in hiding" since he was injured in a motorcycle accident almost two months ago. Apparently, even his record company didn't know where the popular Dylan was keeping himself.

Naturally, since no one knows Dylan's whereabouts, speculation has been running rampant that Dylan was more seriously injured than initially suspected, that perhaps he would never make a personal appearance again and that the singer-composer's manage of curly, unruly hair had had to be shaved because of head injuries.

Dylan himself refused to reveal anything concerning the accident and as time went by, the rumors and speculations seemed to become more and more of a reality.

However, it has now been announced that Bob will indeed make at least one more personal appearance at the Festival of Roses. It's highly significant that Bob will star with Joan Baez as the two (who once were very, very close friends) have since had a parting of the ways with Miss Baez occasionally taking potshots at Dylan via the news media. No one ever thought that the two would ever agree to appear together on the same stage but time apparently does heal all wounds and so Dylan and Baez will once more divide the spotlight between them.

The foreign list of entertainers also appearing on the Festival includes Sandie Shaw, the British born miss who has had several big hits here in America.

Quaife's No Longer Kink

As predicted in the last issue of The BEAT, Pete Quaife has officially left the Kinks. Eric Haydock, ex-member of the Hollies, was rumored to be taking Pete's place with the Kinks but has apparently decided against the move and will concentrate on developing a group of his own.

Quaife was injured over three months ago in an auto accident and has never been well enough to re-join the Kinks. According to the Kinks' co-manager, Robert Wace: "It could be at least six months before he was well enough to rejoin the group and he has decided instead to make his career in other fields."

Speaking for the rest of the Kinks, Wace revealed that he felt Quaife may have made the wrong decision but added that "it was his decision."

John Dalton has been playing with the Kinks as Pete's replacement and will be staying with the group as a permanent member.

In the midst of the controversy surrounding Pete's split with the Kinks, they were scheduled to tour Iceland but cancelled out without any sort of explanation.

Herman Hurts Fingers In NY

Herman (Peter Noone) recently crushed three fingers on his right hand in an elevator door at a New York hotel. A minor operation was necessary, and was performed by a New York doctor.

Herman had just completed a three-week visit to America and was set to leave for England when the accident occurred on a Monday.

Herman's crushed fingers will not interfere with his scheduled appearances however—namely those set for Britain.

While in the States, Herman and the Hermits filmed an appearance on the Ed Sullivan Show. For the performance, his hair was trimmed fairly short on the back and sides.

On October 7, Herman and his group flew to Iceland, where they gave two shows at Reykjavik.

...HERMAN TANGLES WITH ELEVATOR

Inside the BEAT

Letters To The Editor............................2
On The Beat.......................................3
People Are Talking About.......................4
Count Five vs. Yardbirds........................5
Supremes Storm Japan..........................6
Pics In The News..................................7
Herman To Act?................................8-9
Beatles '66...11
Stone Talk...14
Zany Monkees....................................15
Beach Boys Married.............................17
Funny Men..19
Beat Showcase...................................21
For Girls Only.....................................22
BEAT Goes To The Movies...................23

The BEAT is published bi-weekly by BEAT Publications, Inc., editorial and advertising offices at 6290 Sunset Blvd., Suite 504, Hollywood, California 90028. U.S. bureaus in Hollywood, San Francisco, New York, Chicago and Nashville; overseas correspondents in London, Liverpool and Manchester, England. Sale price, 15 cents. Subscription price, U.S. and possessions, $5 per year; Canada and foreign rates, $9 per year. Second class postage prepaid at Los Angeles, California.

KRLA ARCHIVES

Letters TO THE EDITOR

SIR DOUGLAS POOR REP.

Dear *BEAT*:
I just read the article "Adults Resent Groups" by Doug Sahm in the September 10th issue and although I partially agree with the title statement, I think that the Sir Douglas Quintet is a very poor representative to be presenting the argument.

I'm eighteen years old, plan to be a singer and I thoroughly dig today's music – so don't think I'm prejudiced. However, last July I went to a concert which featured the Beach Boys, the Sir Douglas Quintet and the Association. Since I know the Association quite well, I went back stage before and after the show to see them.

The Beach Boys, of course, were not there until just before they went on but the members of the Sir Douglas Quintet were wandering around for quite a while. Well, I'll tell you, I had a hard time keeping a straight face. I wouldn't go so far as to say they looked obnoxious – but almost. And it wasn't that they had long hair or dressed "differently" but it was more the atmosphere around them.

They probably were physically clean but they just didn't give the impression of being clean. Or maybe it was the expressions on their faces or the way they slouched around not being at all friendly to anyone. But they didn't seem at all wholesome or like people that you would like to have stay in your hotel or eat in your restaurant if you owned one.

When the Quintet came on stage to perform, I actually felt sorry for them. They were the first on the program and the audience reaction to them the minute they walked on was sad. The girls laughed and the boys whistled and made rude remarks.

The point is, the image they're showing everyone – the too-long hair, the mismatched, rather silly clothing and the generally unhealthy aura – doesn't do what they'd like it to do. Instead of seeming like groovy, with-it guys, the look like a bunch of under-fed, homeless misfits. It's too bad because their sound is rather groovy – but after the first look, nobody cares.

One thing that was not brought out in the article is that not all long-haired singing groups are treated the way Sir Douglas describes. A perfect example of this took place at this same concert. In an almost complete contrast to the Sir Douglas Quintet, the Association, who followed them in the show, was like a breath of fresh air to the audience and to everyone connected with the show. They seemed to exude enthusiasm and the joy of life rather than boredom and depression. The contrast was unbelievable!

I don't think it's the long hair or the music they play or the age group they are associated with that turns adults against rock groups. If this were true, then groups like the Raiders, the Association, the Beatles and the Monkees wouldn't be as accepted by adults as they are. Rather, it's the attitude and general outlook that performers and non-performers have that alienates or attracts people.

Debbie Davis

English Retaliate

Dear *BEAT*:
Having just received the July 6th issue of *The BEAT* from an American pen pal, I was very shocked at the letter from Jackie McGinty describing the English as "two-faced" and insinuating their big-headedness. I missed the article by Jackie Genovese and I dread to think of the awful impression that these two people must have given to American teenagers about us.

Surely, intelligent readers must realize that there are good and bad in every nation, yes, including America. Jackie McGinty hadn't even lived in England and yet he or she assumed that they were an authority on English people. What a cheek! I am a 17 year old English girl and I *am* an authority on my fellow countrymen.

Many, many teenagers over here do not entirely concentrate on "liking what is good for the English, no matter who suffers" as J. McGinty suggests.

England is quoted as being "a nation of animal lovers" and we do not have a hundredth of the racial discrimination of the U.S. We are not angels by any means, but I don't think you've got any over there either.

I wish London had never been called "the swingingest city on earth" because it has caused nothing but jealousy and hard feeling. And, McGinty, do not judge others by your own standards and take a look around you before condemning a country that you obviously know nothing about.

Patsy Turner

P.S. Please print this as it is very important. Could you please find time to write back to me saying if you have printed it and what replies you received from other readers. I would be very grateful. I like your paper very much. Bye.

Well, what about it readers? Have anything to say to Patsy?
The Editor

MONKEES

Dear *BEAT*:
I'm just writing to thank you so much for putting the Monkees on the cover of *BEAT*. I think they're four of the grooviest guys around and I know that before long they'll be the biggest things on television.

I was privileged to meet them and I want to tell everyone how nice they are. They gladly take the time to talk to their fans and sign autographs. They seem to genuinely appreciate their fans – something that a lot of groups don't do.

I'd like to ask you one favor. I think Mike Nesmith is so funny and I'd give anything to see a picture of him alone. Could you please print one? I really would appreciate it.

Their album, "The Monkees," is out of sight – especially the hilarious "Gonna Buy Me A Dog." I don't care what anyone says – the Monkees are for me!

Lisa Graham

... NESMITH ALONE

Herman Is Happening

Dear *BEAT*:
In regards to the comment in the "In People Are Talking About" of September 10th of "What's happened to Herman?"

Nothing's happened to Herman – Herman's happening!!!

Susan Mills
Marsha Jump

SPECIAL FROM VIETNAM

Dear *BEAT*:
Once again I find myself without words to express myself. I guess the best way is to say thank you all very much for the *BEAT's*. This also goes for the rest of the guys in my PLT. We are out on a mission at this time and we were given mail and in it I received the papers which really gave us something to read for the first time in 40 days.

Instead of reading about people killing and us killing we were able to read about the stars and get the top songs. When I come back to the States, I would like to come visit your office and thank you myself for all you have done.

So, once again thank you from our hearts. Also, before I close this we all would like to say this – that the song "Green Berets" is a true song and not a song just to make money. It is all true because each one of us know it and in our books he is number one. So, anyone who calls his records trash, they just don't understand.

Thank you all so very much and if I make it out of here alive you have one member who will buy this paper for life. God bless you all.

SP4 George P. Feehon

Thanks for your great letter, George. We're glad that you and your friends dug The BEAT so much and, so, are sending you a free subscription. Good luck to all of you and we're looking forward to meeting you when you come home.
The Editor

Stone Woman

Dear *BEAT*:
I just saw a picture of the Rolling Stones which made me absolutely sick. All of the Stones were dressed up as woman in the picture. They look dumb enough as it is without going out of their way like this!

Don't get me wrong – I dig the Stones' music but why they have to stoop to something as low as dressing like woman is beyond me. Don't they think their music is good enough to sell without all these phony publicity deals?

Personally, I go for entertainers who make it without relying on fads or gimmicks. They're the ones who stay around after the fads have died. Don't these groups like the Daily Flash and all the rest of them who insist on growing shoulder-length hair realize that when hair is out they'll be out too?

On the other hand, groups like the Association and the Monkees will be around for a long, long time simply because they don't go overboard trying to be right "in" with everybody else.

Well, thanks for letting me have my say. I suppose you'll receive hundreds of letters protesting what I said but I don't care, I just had to say it anyway.

Eddie Clark

Australian Pen Friend

Dear *BEAT*:
Just recently we had a request from a young girl to have her name mentioned in *The BEAT* as wanting a penfriend and Tony McArthur from 4BC radio in Brisbane, Australia told me to drop you a line about it.

The girl is 16 years old and likes mod clothes, the Rolling Stones and all the latest dances and would like a girl penfriend of about the same age. Her name and address is: Judy Mooney, 266 Hamilton Road, Chermside, Brisbane, Queensland, Australia.

I hope this won't be an inconvenience to you.

Pam Stanley

Association Deserve It

Dear *BEAT*:
I don't want to waste any time so I'll get right to the point. Ninety per cent of what you print is old hat. You need something fresh. Why don't you set aside a place in your ever continuously growing *BEAT* for a column or two about "good" groups. Starting off, continuing and finishing up with the Association. I say no less than an entire page should be devoted to the top group in California. And no group deserves more of a write-up and a seven page layout than the Association.

Speaking from experience, they are the nicest, grooviest, talentedest, illustriously magnificent group of guys you could ever run across!

I do hope you will take my advice of an urgent cry from an urgent fan. Don't be un-Associated!

An Associated slugger

We took your advice and gave the nicest, grooviest, talentedest (?), illustriously magnificent group of guys we know, The Association, two full pages in the last BEAT. By the way, Gary Alexander read your letter and proclaimed that you're someone who "knows where it's at!"
The Editor

Monkee Talk

Dear *BEAT*:
Please have more articles on the fab Monkees. I think they're the best thing since Coke was invented. All the kids at my school dig them and watch their show every week. The next day all I hear is "Monkee talk."

I especially luv Davy Jones – he's really too much! So, please, please, print more pictures and articles about them. By the way, the picture of them on the cover of the last *BEAT* was great – it's hanging up in my bedroom.

Becky Chavez

Take a look at page 15 for more of those Monkee pics.
The Editor

KRLA ARCHIVES

On the BEAT
By Louise Criscione

Could it be that Cher is changing her bell-bottomed, flowing long-hair style for a more sophisticated image? It would seem that she is. She is now pulling her hair back from her face and is currently in New York shooting a full fashion layout for *Vogue!* And, if that is not enough, Cher purchased a $1500 Dior dress when she was in Europe. What next? Sonny in a suit?

Gassy Tom Jones may be a movie star yet. That is, if either 20th Century Fox or Columbia have their way about it. They've both made nice-sized film offers to Pussycat Tom. Fact is, Columbia has asked the award-winning playwright, Alun Owen (who wrote the script for "A Hard Day's Night") to write a script for Tom.

Not to be left behind, 20th is also planning a movie deal for Tom but refused to reveal any of the details.

Quick Tour

Meanwhile, Tom is preparing to make a quick tour of six countries in November. He'll visit Spain, Italy and South America (for appearances in Argentina, Uruguay and Brazil) before flying to the United States for television appearances.

The Rolling Stones are recording "live" again. The opening show on their current British tour was taped, as well as two others and will provide material for the Stones' next American album. Brian Jones is playing on the tour, despite injury to his hand but is performing "with some difficulty," according to a spokesman for the Stones.

...TOM JONES
BEAT Photo: Chuck Boyd

Change For Monkees

The Monkees' release of their much-in-demand album track, "I Wanna Be Free," as a single has been stopped. Suppose it was because fans are buying the album for the track, so why release it as a single? Besides, the song has already been covered by four different artists. The new Monkee single will, instead, be their theme song, "The Monkees."

Hilton Valentine wasted no time in recording a single following the Animals' split. It's his own composition, "My Friend," and was issued in America on the MGM label but has not yet been released in England.

Speaking of the Animals, Eric Burdon will have to hurry up on the decision of who he wants in his back-up group as he leaves on a British tour in a couple of weeks. Meanwhile, he's vacationing in Spain.

Found out who Question Mark and the Mysterian are. They come out of Detroit by way of Acapulco and are Bobby Balderamma, lead guitarist; Frank Rodriguez, organist; Eddie Serrato, drummer; and Frank Lugo, bass guitarist. And Question Mark? Well, he has chosen to remain anonymous and refuses to reveal his name, always wears sunglasses and is very much a loner although he is the acknowledged leader of the group.

Tops On Tops

It looks very much as if the swinging Four Tops will be tops in the nation with their fantastic "Reach Out I'll Be There." The Tops remain something of a rebellious group in the Motown stable as they appear on television in sports clothes while all other Motown artists wear suits, usually with diamond-studded cufflinks, etc.

...BILL COSBY

Bill Cosby, popular star of the "I Spy" television show and maker of piles of money (he's rated the number two entertainer in the booking annuals) is not above doing a bit of charity work. And, accordingly, Mr. Cosby has been named the Honorary Chairman for Watts Towers Community Art Center $250,000 Drive.

Congratulations are in order for Donovan. His "Sunshine Superman" has sold the necessary million and is now certified for a Gold Record. It marks the first time Donovan has won a coveted Goldie for a single, though his current American album, also dubbed "Sunshine Superman," is well on its way to a Gold Record.

Elvis At World's Fair?

If early reports hold true, Elvis Presley is slated to star in a ten-day pop music show which will be one of the many featured events at the 1967 World's Fair in Montreal, Canada.

Presley has made no official statement, confirming or denying the reports, but if such arrangements have been made, this marks another milestone in the career of Elvis The Ex-Pelvis.

Last In '58

El's last round of personal appearances occurred just before his induction into the Army in early 1958. His last concert in California was held in January of that same year, at the Pan Pacific Auditorium in Los Angeles.

At the close of his tour of duty, a more mature and less mobile version of the old Elvis staged a triumphant return to the famous-for-being fickle world of "showbiz." In his case, the old "out of sight, out of mind" adage couldn't have been less correct.

He bounced directly back to the top, and judging from the way he's remained there ever since, the "what goes up must come down" theory doesn't apply either.

The only un-smooth move Elvis seems to have made, in the eyes of many of his fans, was his decision to confine his talents to the boundaries of the recording studio and motion picture sound stage.

Benefits Only

Since his discharge from the service, Presley's only personal appearances have been at a non-publicized benefit which is held annually in his hometown of Memphis, Tenn. But even his no-tour, no-TV policy has failed to disband or diminish his loyal following.

His fans, however, haven't stopped hoping to see more of him, nor have they stopped asking. During the past year, a flurry of petitions have been circulated by avid Presley-ites, in hopes of convincing him that he sould be seen as well as heard.

Should the rumors of his World's Fair stint turn out to be fact, this will almost have to be the beginning of a brand new bag for the King.

If he doesn't make additional appearances out of choice, once his long-standing P.A. barrier has been broken, he may have to do so out of necessity.

Presley fans have waited nearly nine years for just such a miracle, and they well might stop asking for more and start demanding.

Playboys Play Manila, Orient

Gary Lewis and the Playboys will venture away from U.S. shores for the first time when they appear at the Loyola Palace in Manila at the end of this month.

On Oct. 26, Lewis and his Playboys will journey to Hong Kong for a number of shows at U.S. military installation bases.

In December, Gary Lewis, minus his Playboys, will find himself again at a military base, but this time without a musical purpose. He will serve two years in the Army.

...COMING OUT OF HIDING?

'POP' ARTISTS BREAK INTO THE JAZZ POLL

The multi-talents of today's young stars are slowly but surely bringing about integration in another area where it's long overdue.

Since the birth of rock and roll a decade ago, music has been segregated into two categories—"adult" and "teen."

But, since the *growth* of rock and roll, which was a long time stunted by songs that were an inane combination of up-beat and talking-down, this part of the music field no longer fits the categorization.

Today's artists are far too versatile not to have universal appeal. Even the tag no longer fits, and the term "rock and roll" is rapidly being replaced by the broader and far more apt title of "pop music."

The integration process is being evidenced in many ways. Among them is the cropping-up of so many "pop" names on this year's Playboy Magazine Jazz Poll voting ballot.

Conducted annually for the past eleven years, this concensus is probably the largest reader-participation music poll for adults in the world.

However, the age level of the voters didn't keep the Beatles, the Righteous Brothers, the Byrds and the Supremes from being nominated among the contenders for the top *Vocal Group* throne.

The *Male Vocalist* category looked like Olde Home Week for all-time greats who have always been popular with every age group, such as Tony Bennett, Frank Sinatra, Harry Belafonte and Dean Martin. But interspersed (in alphabetical order, which is how the nominees appeared in all categories) were such names as Bob Dylan, Ray Charles, Elvis Presley, Bobby Darin, Pat Boone, Roger Miller, Otis Redding, Brook Benton, Fats Domino and others who have been particularly successful with the younger half of the record-buying public.

The *Female Vocalist* nominations were largely composed of permanent members of the popularity club. Judy Garland, Lena Horne, Mahalia Jackson and Peggy Lee, for instance. But the list also included Petula Clark, Marianne Faithfull, Joan Baez, Ketty Lester and Dionne Warwick.

It will be interesting to see whether any of our "pop people" turn up as winners in a poll where the great majority of voters are adults. But, since the nominations were made by a board of jazz critics and editors, reps from the major recording companies and the winners of last year's poll (Louis Armstrong, Dave Brubeck, Barbra Streisand and Ella Fitzgerald, just to mention a few), it's rather interesting that they were nominated in the first place.

KRLA ARCHIVES

Letters To The Editor
(Continued from Page 2)

NICE CHANGE

Dear *BEAT*:
I hope this letter is a nice change from the many letters you must get on the many controversies in our mixed-up world. All I want to say is a word of congratulations to the writers and recording artists who are putting out such songs as "God Only Knows," "Mr. Dieingly Sad," "Cherish" and "Groovy Kind Of Love."

These are ballads with a beat and I love 'em. They'll never find a bit of filth in them. It's a nice and different change in today's pop music. These songs are what "happiness is" and make me happy every time I hear them. Although I like variety, I hope many more like those I mentioned are made. Only a crackpot could find them obscene.

Two and a half minutes of happiness

The No Talents

Dear *BEAT*:
I am writing to inform you of my opinions of certain no-talent groups. Such groups as the Knickerbockers, Swingin' Medallions and many other groups, local or otherwise, have no talent and should be put away. There are many groups that deserve the publicity you give the lousy guys. I'd hate to see the scene ruined by a bunch of mediocre performers. The public can demand and get good talent by boycotting those groups that offend our good taste.

I'd also like to give my opinion on the remarks some singers are making. I'm inclined to agree with them. How would you like a country if all you saw of it was hotel rooms and hot concert halls? The people they're meeting are probably sickening anyway. That's what we'd all want – to meet a bunch of phonies and giggling girls. I sure wouldn't.

Danny Shannon

Dare Ya To Print It

Dear *BEAT*:
I dare you to print this letter. I have read your *BEAT* many times and the only letters I have read are those that praise your paper, not once have you ever printed one that dared put it down.

First off, let me say that your paper isn't all bad. You have a few good articles in it from time to time but they are always on long-haired, no-talent groups such as the Robbs, while you almost ignore groups that are clean-cut and have talent, such as the Association. Not long ago you printed a full page article on the Robbs while in the same issue you had just a picture of the Association and I think printing *that* almost killed you.

The Association is one of the few groups who were able to make it without long hair and weird clothes. So, come on *BEAT*, print articles on talented groups for a change – like the Association.

Peggy Langlands

We're sorry you feel that way, Peggy. The Association is one of our favorite groups and, in fact, we were writing about them before they even had a record out! You must realize that while the Association have many fans, so do the "no talent" groups as you call them and we must try to include them all.

The Editor

Explanation For Raiders

Dear *BEAT*:
I would like to answer the letter that was written by Margie, the one who was "disappointed" by the Raiders.

Margie, you must understand that the Raiders are human beings and they at times become short-tempered just like any other person. I know that it must have hurt you very much because of their refusal but at least you have met them – something I have never done.

Maybe the Raiders were behind in their filming and didn't have time to sign autographs. Maybe before you saw them they had run into some other autograph hunters who were rude.

From reading your letter it seemed to me that you were more concerned with getting their autograph to show everyone than you were in just meeting them. Could this be true?

If you should meet them again, please keep in mind that they are on a time schedule with places to go and things to do. Please don't be too unjust to them; as I said before, they are human and everyone knows that humans are not perfect.

Debbie

INDIGNANT

Dear *BEAT*:
Since I've been in the States (about 2 months) I find that most kids are very indignant if they find out that you like another group and not *their* faves. In England, we don't choose friends for the groups they like but rather for the person themselves.

We also show respect for other people's opinions. I've been a Rolling Stones' fan since 1963 when they were just starting to get popular around the London area. I don't plan to change just to be friends with some people and I also advise everyone else not to change just to suit people or conform and be a carbon-copy of everyone else. Think!

Diane Bonner

Sonny & Cher

Dear *BEAT*:
This letter is in reference to the article, "Sonny & Cher Finished; Off For European Visit," which appeared in the September 10th edition of *The BEAT*.

It said that Sonny and Cher would probably have to move because of the "over-anxious and unthoughtful fans" who have been rude and unappreciative to them.

I don't know how anyone could steal things from their home and be so careless, especially after what Sonny and Cher have done for all of us. All of these so-called "fans" can't really love Sonny and Cher if they want to hurt them and destroy their property.

Sonny and Cher have never tried to hide from any of their fans, even their house isn't hidden like a lot of stars' homes are. They've never been anything but nice to all of their fans, at any time, no matter how busy they are.

So, please, if you want to go on being able to visit them like real Sonny and Cher fans, stop being so rude to them and stop taking advantage, as Sonny and Cher have been so nice. Don't make them have to move again and leave their beautiful new dream home, it's everything they've dreamed of, worked so hard for and so well deserve.

I hope it's not too late to stop them from moving.

A Real Sonny & Cher fan

'in' people are talking about...

The picture of the Rolling Stones dressed as 1940 American mothers and wondering whose "brain" thought that one up and if the Stones foresaw what remarks their acquaintances would make when they viewed it... Brian's tendons instead of bones... How well the Association went over at USC but how it's highly unlikely the university will ever be able to book another high class act due to inter-university squabbles... The chain letter which features Dick Clark, Dean Torrance and a bunch of other pop business people and wondering what the gimmick is and who started it... The latest in Elvis' rumors and deciding that someone, somewhere is spending his (or her) entire life making up rumors.

PEOPLE ARE TALKING ABOUT how long George Harrison is going to remain in India and wondering if he isn't by chance overdoing this Indian kick of his a bit and hoping he never gets hung-up on a musical instrument played in the Philippines... How the Cyrkle can be a circle when they have four members and are, therefore, a square... The Righteous two recording the "White Cliffs Of Dover" and wondering how long we'll have to wait for "Danny Boy" to make the charts. ... Whether or not the drummer for the Daily Flash is going to grow his hair down to his ankles or stop it at the knees... What a gigantic giggle the Beach Boys' marriage admits are because it was no secret in the first place although the B.B. tried their hardest to keep it that way.

PEOPLE ARE TALKING ABOUT how the Hollies were swimming up at the Big Mama's house... What Helen Noga means to Ted or if Russ was merely kidding his associate... Why Pete quit after all this time ... Why rumor has it that Los Bravos is really English when it's quite obvious to everyone that they're Italian... The on-again, off-again thing with Jeff Beck and the Yardbirds now being on again and wishing he'd make up his mind once and for all... Who? and the Mysterians really are and why they only believe in crying 96 instead of 100 tears... Eric possibly riding an old horse all the way to the top of the mountain... The 4 Tops reaching out like that and bagging a winner... How much Lee sounds like two other top groups... Keith rivaling Dylan in the hair department.

PEOPLE ARE TALKING ABOUT Tim Morgan forsaking his folk for rock and deciding he'd be a definite help... How we were responsible for introducing the Hollies to the Mama's and Papa's and wondering if we should call it a brain storm or a mistake... Whether or not the Left Banke have ever gone in the water and why they were *soooo* early... Watching Shane and congratulating themselves on cowboys going long-hair and how sweet it is to have won... Whatever happened to the Troggs and deciding their "Wild Thing" got the best of them ... How cool Tommy James is... How even orchestras are getting themselves amplified.

PEOPLE ARE TALKING ABOUT why Davy wants to be free when so many girls would luv to tie him up, including Heather ... How well Bobby Darin is doing as a carpenter and deciding it's probably not a half-bad profession after all... What's just like a woman... What the Mothers invented... All the attention being paid to the Strip and wondering when the world is going to discover North Beach... How Peter thinks you don't have to nudge a person just to get your point across and what a pleasant change it is... How ultra-groovy Sandy Koufax is and how many females have switched to baseball just so they can stare at him through a pair of binoculars... Whether or not it's good to be somebody's puppet. ... How it feels to have someone under your skin and wondering why the Seasons didn't sound so well on Sullivan... Why Lou thinks it's such a Hurtin' Thing and deciding that with his voice he can think anything he wants to.

KRLA ARCHIVES

UpBEAT
By Eden

Just cannot stop raving about the new Beach Boys' record, "Good Vibrations." Heard a special sneak-preview of the disc when the Beach Boys' leader-genius-producer, Brian Wilson, played the dub to me over the phone, and I just *could not believe it!*

This record has been months in the production and creation stages, and it is more than a brilliant follow-up to "God Only Knows" — which, by the way, has been described by many "insiders" in the disc-biz as a *perfect* record. Listen for "Vibrations" on your radio, 'cause it's about to be a gigantic smash hit.

* * *

Records like "Sunny," by Bobby Hebb, are part of the reason for which R&B has become more and more acceptable in the field of pop music. Now that Bobby has enjoyed his first nationwide hit, he seems determined to continue the winning streak with his latest release, "Satisfied Mind."

The song has been kicking around for some time now, but Bobby's shiny new rendition of it is one of the best ever. Easy-going, smooth-moving and catchy — all in all, a winner for sure.

* * *

Stones have another hit rolling for them... "Have You Seen Your Mother, Baby, Standing In The Shadow?" Hard-driving, fast-moving, and typically Stones.

Nothing exceptionally unique about this disc except the ads which the Stones have placed in the trades. Have *you* seen the *Stones, Baby, Laughing* in the Background???

* * *

Have you heard "The Great Airline Strike," the new smash by Paul Revere and the Raiders? Listen closely to the lyrics, they're very funny. You might also lay an ear lobe on the beginning of the record when the two jets come in for a landing.

If you listen closely enough, you'll notice that the bass guitar — which begins immediately after the planes (real World War II jets) — starts out on the same "note" which the planes land on. Credit here going out to the Raiders' talented producer, Terry Melcher.

* * *

Mitch Ryder and the Detroit Wheels released a beautiful soul-type of disc, called "Takin' All I Can Get." Unfortunately, it bombed — too much real R&B for the pop-oriented ears of America.

So they have gone back to their original hard-rock format and released a new disc entitled "Devil With A Blue Dress On & Good Golly Miss Molly." If you still have any breath left after you've said the title, this one could be a Top 20 item for the boys.

Count Five — Yardbird Copy?

It was a unanimous choice. When asked who they admired most in the music field, all five of the Count V listed the Yardbirds. And if you've heard the Count V's first record, "Psychotic Reaction," their preference for the English group probably needs no explanation.

Yardbird fans have noticed striking similarities between "Psychotic Reaction" and the Yardbirds' version of "I'm A Man."

'Bird Common

Certainly, there can be no denial the two songs have much in common. This stems from the Count V's longtime admiration of the Yardbirds. But the Count V has been experimenting for about two years now, and several of their innovations are evident in their new chart topper.

All five of the musicians are still in school. Sean Byrne and Ron Chaney attend San Jose City College; Kenn Ellner attends Los Altos Foothill College; and Craig Atkinson goes to San Jose State College.

"Mouse" Michalski is a senior at San Jose Pioneer High School.

Sean, who composes many of the group's songs, is now a "naturalized" American citizen, having come from Dublin, Ireland two years ago.

Overnight

The group has really undergone an overnight success. They have only been signed with a record company since August — and their hit with Double-Shot Records came about only after a Los Angeles disc jockey tipped the company off about the young group. "Psychotic Reaction," which instantly jumped to within the top ten best-sellers in the nation, has triggered an album by the same name.

Their music, like their attire, is wild and unattached. You might say it causes a "Psychotic Reaction."

...COUNTING TO A HAUNTED FIVE

RUDE IN AMERICA?

The Mindbenders returned to their native British shores after a successful American tour at the end of this summer. But even the success they enjoyed while in our country didn't improve their negative impressions of America.

After returning to England, they told the press there that, "American kids depend so much on their parents. British kids are far more independent. Here, teenagers have a mind and a life of their own, but American parents all want to appear hippy and with-it."

The Mindbenders were very well-received on this successful trip, however they still met with a few unpleasant people over here. One of the things the boys took objection to was the intolerance of some of the older Americans they encountered.

Ric Rothwell explained: "We found so many rude people over there. In the middle of the street people would shout at us to get our hair cut.

"But you should have seen the type of people who did the shouting! Great fat men who looked ridiculous in their Bermuda shorts and middle-aged women who were walking about in the middle of the afternoon with their hair in rollers."

The group has been asked to return to America this Fall for another tour, due to the success of their summer appearances here. But the Mindbenders have declined the offer thus far saying that they would prefer to work in their own country for awhile.

Until Jan. 1, 1967, you can have BEAT for

$1.00

Just clip and mail...

THE BEAT

Mail to:
The BEAT #504
6290 Sunset Blvd.
Hollywood, Calif. 90028

Name _____
Address _____
City _____ State _____ Zip _____

☐ I want BEAT for the rest of the year — only $1.
I enclose ☐ cash ☐ check ☐ money order.

...LOU RAWLS (HURTIN')

Lou's Single Hottest Yet

"Love Is A Hurtin' Thing," the new release by Lou Rawls, just can't go wrong.

Even if it bombs on the pop market — which seems unlikely at the moment — the record is still being aired on both R&B and "good music" stations, and can count on heavy sales in these areas.

It is the first release in many months to be played on the three type radio stations.

Already, it is the hottest selling record Rawls has produced since he began his Capitol recording career five years ago. Released only a month ago, the single has topped the 400,000 mark.

The demand for Rawls' latest album "Soulin'," which contains the single, has been equally impressive. The album sold 80,000 copies in the first nine days, and after two-and-a-half weeks it passed the 150,000 mark.

In their current pace, both the album and the single are destined easily to become million sellers.

KRLA ARCHIVES

U.S. Electronic Music 'In'?

By Anna Maria Alonzo

Electronic music—the sound of the times, the sound of 1966, the new sound which has created more controversy than almost any other form of "pop" music since the advent of the Beatles.

The first electronic "notes" to hit American ears were played by a British group called the Yardbirds. After their first two discs hit the chart-tops in a very normal fashion, the talented group suddenly changed course and created a new kind of pop music under the brilliant guidance of their exceptional lead guitarist, Jeff Beck.

"I'm A Man" was released and became an instantaneous smash. It was a good, strong, hard-driving beat record with all the usual ingredients of a pop hit. But along with the conventional hard-rock, the Yardbirds included a long electronic sort of "ad-lib" part in the end of the record—and a new trend was born.

The Who

Shortly afterward, Americans heard further electronic sounds emanating from other British groups, tops among them being The Who.

Back across the Surf on our own shores, home-grown groups like the Byrds were soaring high in pop charts with their own translation of the new electronic music, and they began releasing unusual records such as "Eight Miles High," and "5D."

Finally, the trend-setters themselves picked up the idea and modified it in their own inimitable style and we found the Beatles going electronic on us in their brand new "Revolver" album.

Although this unusual form of music has been called "new," it has actually been around for a lot longer than most pop-people might suspect.

Several years ago, the Beatles' talented producer, George Martin, released what was to be one of the first experimental electronic records to be cut in Great Britain. It was composed almost entirely of special electronic effects, collected from tapes used on one of the BBC radio programs in that country, and included almost no live musicians whatsoever. It was released under the name "Ray Cathode"—the word 'cathode' means 'negative pole'—and is still played occasionally today.

...LOVIN' SPOONFUL AMERICAN USERS OF ELECTRONIC MUSIC.

A short time after the release of George's "synthetic" record, RCA studios, in this country, released an entire LP of "songs" completely composed of various recorded frequencies. Every song on the album was of this "synthenature, and one cut in particular featured a "voice" composed of nothing but mechanical sounds.

It was strange and disembodied, but it even managed to "fake" an accent as it 'sang,' "Daisy, Daisy."

From these early, unusual beginnings, electronic music has undergone quite a bit of development, until now many "electronic" songs sound more like *music* than mere mechanical noise.

New techniques being employed by a vast number of groups now include the use of electronic feedback, tapes played in reverse, the sound of whirring machinery, whistles, bits of tape which have undergone some "surgery" in the editing room, and even drinking glasses tuned to a certain key!

Spoonful's City

In this country, the Lovin' Spoonful included the sounds of traffic in their recent hit, "Summer In The City." The newest smash released by Paul Revere and the Raiders begins with the sound of two jets coming in for a landing; the bass guitar which begins immediately afterward starts off on the same "note" as the one which the planes "landed" on!

The Beatles' "Revolver" included some electronic experimentation, notably illustrated by the "Tomorrow Never Knows" track. Originally, the sounds which are heard on the finished product were recorded by the Beatles themselves at various times on their own home equipment.

Later, they brought in "loops" of the sounds which they had recorded and wanted to use, which were then threaded onto one tape so that any one sound or any combination of sounds could be used during the actual recording.

Many, many people have asked how the shouting effects on "Yellow Submarine" were achieved, and the answer is simple. John Lennon plugged a hand mike through his guitar amplifier and called through it. These sounds were then recorded in the usual fashion.

In the future, to be sure, pop fans can look forward to a good deal more of the "new" electronic sounds. Experimentation—whether with voices, instruments, or machinery—is the keyword to success in the fast-paced world of pop music.

SUPREMES IN JAPAN

The Supremes have just touched down on American soil after a smash tour of Japan. When the three popular Supremes arrived in Japan they were greeted by waving members of the Supreme Fan Club of Japan.

Three smiling young Japanese men then presented Diana, Mary and Florence with large bouquets of flowers. Their reception at the airport was only an indication of things to come as the girls later learned when they traveled throughout Japan being greeted by enthusiastic throngs of fans wherever they went.

Highlight of the tour occurred at the Yokosuka Theater where the Supremes performed in two shows. The shows were sponsored by the Special Services with tickets selling at 75 and 50 cents. An unusually low price for concerts here in America but a rather large price to be paid in the Far East. However, both shows were complete sell-outs.

Following their Japanese tour, the Supremes flew to Las Vegas where they're appearing at the Flamingo Hotel. It's significant that the Supremes, commonly referred to as a "pop group," have made such headway in the music business that they are in demand in such "adult" spots as the Copabana in New York, the Fairmont in San Francisco and the top hotels in Las Vegas. Whenever a music poll of any nature is taken, the names of the Supremes are sure to find their way into the various categories.

Berlin Troops See TJ Brass

Herb Alpert and The Tijuana Brass presented an unusual tripartite concert for American, British and French occupation forces in West Berlin last week.

Three thousand troops from the U.S.A., England and France, plus high ranking West Berlin officials attended the show, which was held at the Berlin American Military Community in the Berlin Brigade Sports Center.

The West Berlin concert was under the sponsorship of the United States Commander in Berlin, Major General John F. Franklin, Jr., and the senior United States Army Commander in Berlin, Brigadier General James L. Baldwin.

Immediately following the group's return from Europe, they will head out on their first American college tour. It will kick off on November 14 at the Veteran's Auditorium in Des Moines, Iowa for Drake and Iowa State University students. November 15 will find the TJB at the Civic Auditorium in Omaha, Neb. for a concert for Omaha and Creighton University students.

The rest of the tour dates are Nov. 16, Pershing Memorial Auditorium, Lincoln, Neb. for University of Nebraska students; Field House, Wichita, Kansas for the University of Wichita students; Nov. 18, Gallagher Field House, Stillwater, Oklahoma for the Oklahoma State University student body; Nov. 19, Field House, Champaign, Ill. for the Illini. The tour will wind up at the Municipal Auditorium, Kansas City, Mo. for students of the University of Missouri and Metropolitan Junior College.

Herb's immense fan following continues to grow so much so that he is considered to be the top booking attraction in the United States, beating out all competition in all fields. The entertainer following on Herbie's tail is none other than the funny man and favorite spy of all-time, Mr. Bill Cosby. These two acts can be booked anywhere at anytime and be assured of a sell-out audience.

FARLOWE BY JAGGER

Another of the British imports is making it big in America, and this time it's a young man named Chris Farlowe. Already one of the most popular single performers in Britain, Chris is about to do it all over again on this side of the Big Pond.

His latest release, a cover version of the Stones' "Out Of Time," is rising rapidly on pop charts all over America, having already hit in Britain.

The disc was produced by Mick Jagger in London, and word comes to us this week that Mick will be teaming with Keith Richard to write the follow-up tune for Chris. Then he will go ahead and produce the disc as well.

America might well be in for another British pop star, but we might also find ourselves with a brand new producer.

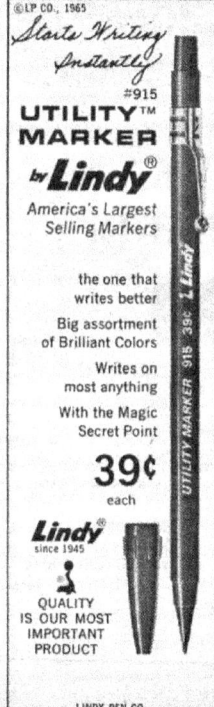

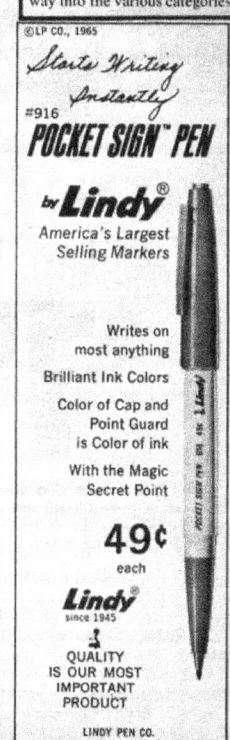

KRLA ARCHIVES

PICTURES in the NEWS

MARRIED MEMBERS OF THE DC5 decided to let their fans see pictures of their families. Here Lenny poses with his 22-year-old wife, Jill, and their year-old son, Grant. Quite a family picture, isn't it?

THE OTHER MARRIED DC5 MAN, Rick Huxley, gets into the act by posing with his 24-year-old wife, Eileen, their two sons, Mark David, age 4, and Darryl Richard, age 3. The dog is part of the family too.

ERIC BURDON returned to England and as predicted in **The BEAT**, the Animals have officially split up. Barry Jenkins will stay with Eric but Hilton Valentine is going solo, Chas Chandler is going to concentrate on agency work and Dave Rowberry is turning arranger. Eric admits that the break-up "is a gamble. But one I have to take if I'm going to progress at all."

Stones In Shadows

NO, YOU'RE NOT SEEING THINGS— Those are the Rolling Stones pictured on the right! The photo was taken early one morning in New York City with the Stones dressed as 1940 American mothers. It's a tie-in with the latest Stone single, "Have You Seen Your Mother, Baby, Standing In The Shadows."

Mick Jagger believes the picture will cause "scenes" in the U.S. but "actually there's nothing to upset people in the picture or the record. I don't think anybody will really complain. It's just a song and we just got dressed up as 1940 women."

Although begun in England, "Have You Seen Your Mother, Baby, Standing In The Shadows" was finished up in America as the English trumpet players "were a bit short of wind," according to Keith Richard.

The Stones have just embarked on a gigantic tour of Britain, following which they will begin shooting their first feature film, "Only Lovers Left Alive." Decca Records is set to finance the movie venture for over two million dollars, which should keep the Stones from begging on corners to gain the necessary coin for their first attempt at acting!

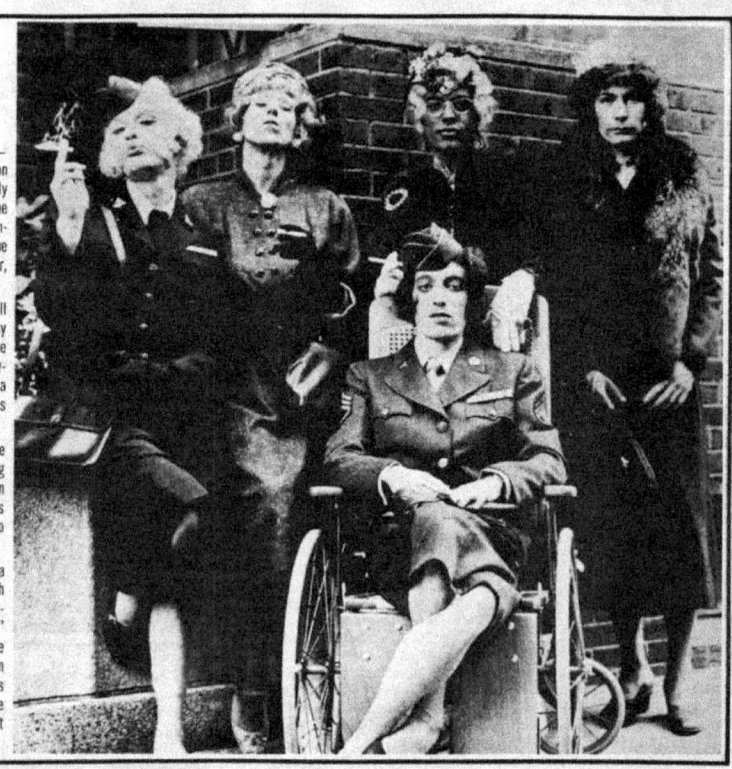

KRLA ARCHIVES

...JIM'S MISSING from picture but Jeff's been missing shows. Why?

Open Letter To Five Yardbirds

Once Upon there was this bird, a girl type one, really. Down deep she was a normal everyday kid. Except, she had fallen victim to a dread disease, known as "Yardbird" to laymen. Yardbird is a thing that starts in your ears, vibrates down to scruffy feet, and up, to resound somewhere in the general vicinity of the heart and comes out the soul.

Well, this bird waited a lifetime to see the disease, and one day the lifetime ended. Out of an allowance stepped one seventh row seat to one of the gassiest things of all time, a Yardbird show. Pow, Bang, Shezam and other cliques.

When this thing called Yardbird started to play, our little bird blew her little mind. Still, something wasn't groovy enough. The guy called Chris with the big smile was there, and so was a blond named Keith, and one groovy looking Jimmy, plus one very hard working drummer whose name was Jim.

But wait, that only adds up to four, unless I missed fourth grade. Ah, yes, a bloke name of Jeff Beck is in the hospital. "Poor kid," the people would say. "Good thing it wasn't Keith or the group would fall apart!" Listen closer, people. Are you sure that it was just another guitarist in the hospital? Is the fantastic group really together?

"No," says our little bird sadly, with tears in her eyes. And her soul, where the music should be, is empty, vacant. Why, says she, why go on without the most fantastic guitarist in the world? Why, Y-birds?

Everyone there were do-or-die fans anyway and they wouldn't have minded if you had set the concert date back a week, or even a month. Sure, some of the not-so-loyal might have grumbled, but that's all. Anything is better than having a piece of yourself missing — just gone.

Jimmy or Chris just couldn't replace that one spot, not that they didn't try, they did. The Yardbirds had done the impossible, they had turned noise into an object that lived. But now, just noise and soul.

Going out a person was heard to say, "The Yardbirds are dead, long live the Stones!" The Bird retorted, only this time not so loud.

But why should I care? Maybe because I am "that bird."

Best left - Unsigned

Herman To Fool Them

By Louise Criscione

Funny how someone comes along, walks into a scene he didn't make. Has a hit and hears that he'll never last 'cause he has no real talent, is too young, too naive.

He considers the possibility that they're right but in the end decides that today is groovy. His philosophy is simple – live today for today and worry about tomorrow some other day. But then tomorrow comes and it's as groovy as today, so after awhile he forgets all about what they said and concentrates on being himself and having a ball.

Basically

Such a someone is Pete Noone. Now known as Herman, leader of the Hermits, maker of hit records, drawer of huge crowds, object of a million young dreams. But basically still Pete Noone.

The boy they sort of snickered at and sort of dug. They made jokes because he was young and had hair covering his ears and was another in a long line of English imports. But at the same time, they sort of liked the kid who made all the funny faces. Because he appeared rather harmless, probably washed his hair, took a bath every now and again, and if shaved a little closer would look like any other young boy.

So, while not giving him long on top (if, indeed, he ever reached top), they didn't protest too loudly when their daughters bought his records, sighed at the television when he smiled and, in general, decided that he was the one they'd been waiting a good fifteen years for.

And so Herman walked into something good. But, of course, all the hot-shot, know-it-alls said it couldn't last. It wasn't Herman's scene. It belonged to older groups. It was owned by the Beatles and overseen by the Stones. On the surface it had no place for Herman.

But perhaps it was all for the best that Herman was born too late. While the Beatles and Stones were out of the age-reach of younger teens, Herman fit right in. He was one of the young, one of happening people who still enjoyed life with the number one in front of it.

Walks Alone

As the months sped by it became public knowledge that Paul had his Jane, Mick his Chrissie and Ringo, Charlie and Bill their wives. But Herman remained alone. Always in the States and for awhile in England.

But in Britain things are different. English fans accept girlfriends

...HERMAN IS ALWAYS SURROUNDED BY GIRLS! This pretty miss is his sister Suzanne. Herman also has a younger sister, Louise, and an older married sister, Diane, and his mom is expecting another baby.

KRLA ARCHIVES

And Leave Wax For An Acting Career

as inevitable. They don't even get *too* upset by marriages. Herman never made it as big in England as he did in America. Because he sang Cockney but was born in Manchester which is something like being born in the heart of New York City and then attempting to pass yourself off as a Texan. It won't go. People find out and they consider you something of a fraud but they admire your cheek and, therefore, will not condemn you entirely.

And so it was for Herman in England. His fellow Britains didn't particuarly dig him. But for the span of a hit record or two they dug a young singer named Twinkle. Who knows what was behind it but suddenly Herman and Twinkle were making the scene together.

Today Counts

Sources close to Herman say it was nothing but a publicity stunt, an easy way to obtain the much-needed British press. For both Twinkle and Herman.

Supposedly, Herman gifted Twinkle with an identification bracelet and she, in turn, gave Herman a matching I.D. bracelet. Said Twinkle in a British interview: "Herman and I don't think much of the future. We feel, now, that to love is in itself enough. Today does count after all and today with Herman is better than yesterday without him."

For his part, Herman remained surprisingly mum. Whether his management discovered that news of the "romance" was spreading to America and that U.S. fans didn't think much of the idea, or whether the romance (if it was a romance) cooled naturally, only Herman and Twinkle know. But whatever the reason for, or behind, the "affair" – it died. And was buried. Period.

But in it's place "Mrs. Brown's Daughter" was born and then a guy named "Henry VIII" and then a movie called "When The Boys Meet The Girls." And finally a huge contract with MGM and the promise of more movies, more money, more fame, more of everything.

Brain

For all his funny remarks and his attempt to project the "little boy" image, Herman has a quick-moving brain behind his conservative long hair. He spends most of his time in America. If you happen to catch him in a frank mood he'll tell you why. "In England to earn 300 pounds a night you have to travel miles around. But in America I have earned 8,000 pounds in one night. So why not go to America for a few weeks?

"In England, we're just a group, so why shouldn't we go to America where we are an *English* group?" Honestly, then, Herman spends his time in America for two reasons – more money and more fame. Disgusting, you say? Well, the truth often is and the truth of the matter is that money and fame are the two reasons why all performers are in the business. Whether they admit it or not. So, why not be honest about it?

... **DESPITE RUMORS OF A SPLIT,** the Hermits are still intact. (l. to r.) Karl Green, Herman, Lek Leckenby, Keith Hopwood and Barry Whitwam.

I get the definite impression, though, that Herman would much rather earn his money and fame as an actor. After all, that's where he started. And, in actual fact, that's what he is. Watch him closely and you can see the actor in him come out all over the stage. The faces he makes, his ad-lib remarks. He's stage left, follow the little red light, listen to the director, memorize your lines kid, and someday you'll be a star.

Unfortunately, Peter can't act in his movies. He's Herman, the head of the Hermits. He's a pop singer and in his movies he is not allowed to move out of that bag. But he's going to break the bag. Just watch and see.

In fact, he's already made a galgant attempt at it in the form of "The Canterville Ghost," which will be seen this season on "ABC-TV Stage '67." True, it's a musical but Herman appears minus the Hermits. And that's a stop toward longevity anyway you look at it.

The people who said Herman would never make it have been proven wrong. But, life being life, Herman's Hermits will one day fade away. And being smart, Herman knows it. He can't stand on a stage when he's pushing 30 and declare his undying love to Mrs. Brown's teenage daughter. People would say he was nothing but a lecherous old man.

On The Move

So, he has to move, progress. And since he's a natural born actor, it is only wise to move in the direction of the camera. And being wise, Herman is moving. It may take him years but someday he'll stand all alone. Only he won't be Herman anymore – he'll be a young man by the name of Peter Blair Denis Bernard Noone. It won't all fit up there on the marquee, so people will shorten it to Peter Noone.

And again he'll walk into a scene he didn't make but rather inherited. And people who go to movies but don't listen to records will say that he doesn't have any real talent, is too young, too naive. They'll say he'll never last. And maybe he won't. But whether he makes it or not, life today will always be groovy for Peter Noone. He's that kind of person. And tomorrow? It'll come – someday.

... **HERMAN DRESSED IN A TUX** and smiling happily with Lesley Gore.

KRLA ARCHIVES

High On A Hilltop
With The Hollies

By Carol Deck

High on a hilltop with the Hollies—what a way to spend an afternoon!

It all starts when you get a phone call.

"Hi, we're back in town. Why don't you come up. We're at Cass' place."

So you make the winding drive up to the A frame house belonging to Cass of the Mama's and Papa's, remembering all the way the last time you saw the Hollies.

They came up to the office one day and managed to throw the entire staff into such a state of confusion that we're still referring to it as the day Hurricane Hollies hit, but it was all in good fun and everyone had fun.

Cass isn't home when you arrive and Graham Nash greets you at the door. Inside the spacious modern house and scattered about the pool and patio are the rest of the group.

Graham introduces you to the newest Hollie, Bernie Calvert, who replaced bass player Eric Haydock.

There's something familiar about Bernie and you know immediately how well he fits in with the group, but he says it's actually "pretty nerve racking" joining an established group.

"It's a very responsible job. There's a lot to learn in a short time."

A Mountain Mover

Then Tony, who was on the phone when you arrived, strolls over, plops himself on a chair in front of you and starts to say something. But he's interrupted by the loud noise of construction work going on on top of the next hill over.

"The mountain was in my way," he shouts with a wave of the arm, "so I'm having it removed."

Actually they are building a golf course on it. If Cass takes up golf she won't have far to go.

Tony asks if you've heard the Everly Brothers album that contains several numbers written by the Hollies and then goes on to tell you how it all happened.

"We were doing the London Paladium and the Everlys were in a hotel next door. They called and said they were recording and were short of material. So Graham and I went around with a couple of guitars."

Then Allan pops over and wants to talk about *their* latest album instead. "It's an amalgamation of numbers we did three years ago. We're not very pleased with it actually," he says and the rest all add their agreement.

But their next album is something else. They've finished recording but it doesn't have a name yet and the cover picture is to be taken this afternoon, in fact the photographer is expected momentarily. They seem genuinely proud of this album.

Just then Cass arrives, yells something about keeping the door shut and goes off to the bedroom to rest.

Bobby's sitting on the couch examining the latest addition to his hat collection that now numbers over 50. This one's a black felt one he bought in Greenwich Village.

One Day

The guys were all in New York the night before and got one day off so they decided to fly out to the West Coast to visit friends.

Tony says these little one day vacations happen often "but we're usually too lazy to take advantage of them."

It's astoundingly hot up on top of that hill and Bernie brings you a coke as Graham strides over and asks if you don't want to ask him something too. He feels left out.

So you ask, "how long have you been growing the beard?"

"Oh, about two inches," he notes.

The beard wasn't there last time you saw Graham and now he looks more like a painter than a talented singer and composer.

"I don't know exactly why I started growing it," he says. "I started it while I was in Portugal on a holiday. I like it, it's growing on me."

All of the Hollies have nothing but praise for their hostess and her coharts, the Mama's and Papa's, and their new album.

General concensus among them is that "Dancing Bear" and "My Heart Stood Still" are the best things on the album.

The only criticism heard anywhere about the album is that some people are saying it's overproduced. "Rubbish," says Graham, "You can never overproduce.

"I put the Mama's and Papa's on the same level as the Beatles," he adds. "I'm not sure they are as big, but they're better."

Farewell

Then the photographer arrives and the guys have to change clothes for the picture session so you bid farewell and they promise to let you know whenever they're in town.

As you get up to leave you look around trying to freeze the Hollies in your mind.

Graham's on the phone (somebody's been on it constantly all afternoon), Allan is lying stretched out on the cool tile floor with his head on a large red pillow, Bobby's sitting on the couch drinking a coke, his mind obviously miles away, Bernie is outside sitting by the pool reading a book he borrowed from Cass and Tony is sprawled in the middle of a large white net hammock that stretches across the middle of the room.

Graham hangs up the phone and sits down on the opposite end of the hammock from Tony with a guitar in his hands. He starts picking out an idea he just had for a song and Tony adds his ideas.

Although you've seen the Hollies on stage, backstage, in your office and at recording sessions, you think maybe this is the way you'll always remember them.

TONY HICKS — Playing it casual, moving mountains.

GRAHAM NASH — Started growing in Portugal.

ALLAN CLARKE — Not pleased with the new album.

BOBBY ELLIOT — Still collecting hats.

THE HOLLIES at a party given for them at the Living Room in New York. From left, Bernie, Bobby, DJ Gary Stevens, Allan, Tony, Graham.

KRLA ARCHIVES

BEAT Photos: Howard L. Bingham

The Beatles—'66 Style

By Eden

Beatles . . . 1966. Another year, another summer, another American tour. Fifteen cities more are stricken with Beatlemania, and thousands have a relapse.

Beatles . . . 1966. Again the screaming headlines, glaring out into the streets from printed newspapers. Again the spoilers who must try to drag the Beatles down into their own mud-gutter level, and the jealous who seek to destroy all that which they can't own.

Beatles . . . 1966. Still hundreds of thousands are loyal to the Four. Still screaming mobs of happy teens, and quieter mobs of enthusiastic "adults."

Beatles . . . 1966. Four young men returning to our shores to revisit the lands they conquered, the hearts they won, three years ago. But they are four changed young men—four *mature* young men, who have assumed the heavy mantle of fame, and now have learned to wear it well . . . and learned to wear it with *class!*

JOHN . . .

Older now, even more mature.

A young man who *knows* where he's been, is *well-aware* of "where he's at," and is in *complete* control of where he's going. He's wearing a new hair-cut this year; he's had his famous golden-brown Beatle locks trimmed and they are a little shorter now than last time we saw him—very much reminiscent of the first time we were introduced.

He seems quite content now, very much at ease. His handsome face is in repose as he calmly answers questions cast at him, and he seems far more lucid, much more communicative than he has been for a while.

There are no signs of strain or over-tiredness; he seems to be at peace with himself for the first time in a year or so.

PAUL . . .

He, too, has been the object of some "growing pains" since we saw him last, and the results are pure success! The famous "cherubic look" of his is not so much in evidence this year, his face has become more manly, and he's not as likely to be mistaken for the mischievious little boy he has been reputed to be.

His words are still inimitably "Beatle," yet his answers are tinged with a little more sophisticated sarcasm this year. And still he remains the essence of courtesy when approached politely with a logical, intelligent question. He will trade his own sincerity of word and action for equal amounts of sincerity on the part of others. That's fair enough.

GEORGE . . .

More confident of his own abilities, more certain of just what those abilities are, now. He, too, looks much better this summer than we have ever seen him before. His hair has also been trimmed, and is kept quite neatly combed—not straggling about his face and neck as it was during our last meeting.

He seems somehow to have matured beyond his 22 years in the 12 months since we have seen him—and he wears his new maturity well.

Remarks around us filter back to our own quite sensitive ears, and we overhear less-interested people saying: 'I didn't know he was so intelligent!' Yes—he is. *We* knew it all along, but it's nice to see him using it so much more to his own advantage now.

RINGO . . .

The "little man from Dingle." The lovable little Beatle who seems to forever remain the same. He's a timeless personality in his own right, a very unique, one-of-a-kind sort of human being.

There has been little change in his large, sad blue eyes—save perhaps the blue-tinted spectacles with which he occasionally covers them now.

His reddish-brown hair still shines and falls softly about his famous face, and more than ever now he looks so like a cuddly little puppy dog, or a little boy who has lost his way home from school.

But this year, it is quite evident that Ringo is no longer lost—from anything. He seems to have found his niche in the life he calls his own — and, happily — he seems quite contented with his lot.

CONFERENCE . . .

Once again a tiny room is filled to brimming with the curious, the prying, the adoring, the cynics; the lightbulbs flashing, blinding, everywhere; the tape recorders whirring, recording every Beatle-sound; the TV cameras filming smiles, and gestures of the Four in front; the fans who only watch in awe.

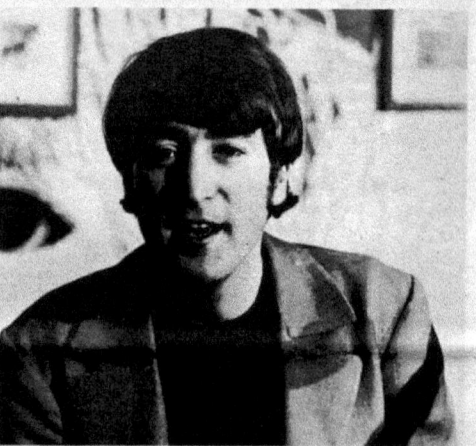

It's a hot room, a room too-full of people. Crowded over with reporters, pens-in-hand, a question at them ready. A room which somehow seems to be a vault to shelter us from the screaming reality of true Beatlemania just outside the guarded door. A room which temporarily will hold the non-reality of the curious who have come to see the freaks perform—and a room which eventually will see the curious become the caged and watched.

Four Beatles are within these walls—four Beatles who have grown immensely—both personally and professionally—in the last three years.

Four Beatles who have changed—for the better—confronted now by the pushing mass of humanity which hasn't changed enough.

CONCERT . . .

Relief! The things that they have been saying for months are absolutely *untrue!* The Beatles have in *no way* lost their golden, Midas touch. They are still the most phenomenal, exciting act on earth.

They have so much of what must be described as "class"—from their brand new outfits – hued a cross between *Lincoln* and "*Robin Hood*" green! — to the little bits of humor they share onstage.

There has been no let-up in the intensity of excitement—only an increase in the appreciation of their talents. The screams and applause are just as loud and long now—but they're mostly found at the end of songs, in appreciative *response* to the Beatles.

BEATLES . . . 1966. Still the most exciting, exceptional and influential foursome in the world of music. Still the largest, inexplicable phenomena of our times. Still the center of Happiness Production which they continually distribute 'round the world.

BEATLES . . . 1966 — Still John, Paul, George and Ringo!

BEATLES . . . 1966. Still the most exciting, exceptional and influential foursome in the world of music. Still the largest, inexplicable phenomena of our times. Still the center of Happiness Production which they continually distribute 'round the world.

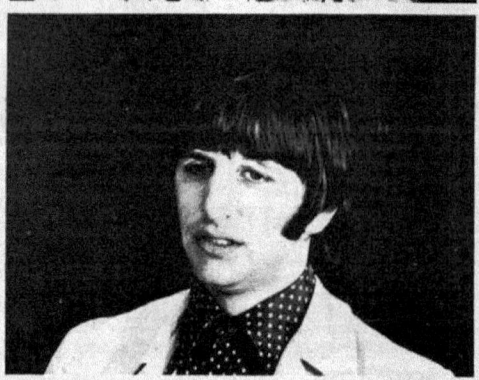

KRLA ARCHIVES

Top 40 Requests

1. NINETY SIX TEARS .... ? And The Mysterians
2. I WANT TO BE FREE .... The Monkees
3. DANDY .... Hermans' Hermits
4. WALK AWAY RENEE .... The Left Banke
5. CHERISH .... The Association
6. HAVE YOU SEEN YOUR MOTHER STANDING IN THE SHADOWS .... Rolling Stones
7. PSYCHOTIC REACTION .... Count Five
8. NEXT TIME YOU SEE ME .... The Robbs
9. CHERRY, CHERRY .... Neil Diamond
10. I'M YOUR PUPPET .... James and Bobby Purify
11. FORTUNE TELLER .... Rolling Stones
12. TALK, TALK .... Music Machine
13. REACH OUT .... The 4 Tops
14. THE GREAT AIRLINE STRIKE .... Paul Revere & The Raiders
15. THE LAST TRAIN TO CLARKSVILLE .... The Monkees
16. BUS STOP .... The Hollies
17. OUT OF TIME .... Chris Farlowe
18. GOD ONLY KNOWS .... The Beachboys
19. IF I WERE A CARPENTER .... Bobby Darin
20. YOU CAN'T HURRY LOVE .... The Supremes
21. YELLOW SUBMARINE/ELEANOR RIGBY .... The Beatles
22. WHAT BECOMES OF THE BROKEN HEARTED .... Jimmy Ruffin
23. BLACK IS BLACK .... Los Bravos
24. SEE SEE RIDER .... Eric Burdon
25. SEE YOU IN SEPTEMBER .... The Happenings
26. I GOT YOU UNDER MY SKIN .... The 4 Seasons
27. WORKING IN THE COAL MINE .... Lee Dorsey
28. POOR SIDE OF TOWN .... Johnny Rivers
29. THE JOKER WENT WILD .... Brian Hyland
30. OPEN THE DOOR TO YOUR HEART .... Darrell Banks
31. MR. DIEINGLY SAD .... The Critters
32. FLAMINGO .... Herb Alpert
33. TURN DOWN DAY .... The Cyrkle
34. BEAUTY IS ONLY SKIN DEEP .... The Temptations
35. LITTLE MAN .... Sonny & Cher
36. ALL I SEE IS YOU .... Dusty Springfield
37. SUNNY .... Bobby Hebb
38. THERE WILL NEVER BE ANOTHER YOU .... Chris Montez
39. SUNSHINE SUPERMAN .... Donovan
40. JUST LIKE A WOMAN .... Bob Dylan

Inside KRLA
By Eden

Leave it to KRLA to come up with the greatest contests ever, right? Right!! And they've really gone and out-done themselves this time, too.

Not only do we have the fantastic football game contest, in which you can win up to $10,000 dollars running, but now there is a brand new contest which offers you the *car of your choice.*

The new contest began Saturday, October 1, and will continue through the end of the month. And easier than this they don't come—or go! All you have to do is get yourself together, move on out of your habitation, and lay an eyeball or two on every single new '67 car.

That's right—look at *all* the models of *all* cars and then decide which one you want. When you've made your choice, record it for the ages on a 4c post card, along with your name and address, and dispatch it post haste to "'67 KRLA," right here in Sunny Pasadena, Calif.

Then if you are the lucky winner-type in this great contest, you will find the car of your choice, *whatever it is*—from a Rambler to a Cadillac—delivered to your very own front door.

Would you believe driven onto your *driveway?*

Dropping by KRLA to say hello lately have been Len Berry, the Robbs—great new group from "Action," and the Turtles—who have one of the most-requested new tunes on the KRLA Request List with their new smash, "Can I Get To Know You Better?"

By the way, have you listened to the new Pat Moore show yet? He's really a great addition to the midnight hours, so if you're one of those all-night freaks, forget about the candle-burning jazz and listen in on the Moore show instead. It gives you *Moore* of what you stayed *awake for!!!*

NOW!

THE LEGENDARY
MUDDY WATERS
AND HIS ORIGINAL CHICAGO BLUES BAND

AND INTRODUCING...

ELEKTRA RECORDING ARTIST
TIM BUCKLEY

AT DOUG WESTON'S
Troubadour
9083 SANTA MONICA BLVD.
L.A. NEAR DOHENY
RESERVATIONS CR 6-6168

Win $10,000 In KRLA'S Sweepstakes

You can win $10,000 every week in the KRLA $10,000 Football Sweepstake!

To win all you have to do is correctly guess the exact scores of the five games designated by the station. The games will be a combination of high school games, college and professional games.

The designated games will be announced each Monday, and repeated Tuesday and Wednesday on KRLA.

You can enter as often as you wish but entries must be on post card only.

Entries must be postmarked by midnight Wednesday and received at KRLA by noon Friday.

$10,000 will be offered each week throughout the football season and all you have to do to win it is guess the five scores exactly.

Stay tuned to KRLA for the designated games and you may win yourself a fortune.

Christmas Cheer Starts HERE

KRLA BEAT Gift Subscription — $3 a year
Each Additional Gift Subscription — only $1 a year

(We send you BEAT gift cards to mail to your friends—First issue will be sent in time for Christmas)

My name is _____
Address _____
City _____ State _____ Zip _____

☐ Send BEAT for Xmas (names listed below)
☐ I also want a BEAT subscription.
Total enclosed $ _____ for _____ subscriptions.
I enclose ☐ cash ☐ check ☐ money order.

Mail to:
KRLA BEAT #504
6290 Sunset Blvd.
Hollywood, Calif. 90028

Name _____
Address _____
City _____ State _____ Zip _____

Mail to:
KRLA BEAT #504
6290 Sunset Blvd.
Hollywood, Calif. 90028

Name _____
Address _____
City _____ State _____ Zip _____

Mail to:
KRLA BEAT #504
6290 Sunset Blvd.
Hollywood, Calif. 90028

Name _____
Address _____
City _____ State _____ Zip _____

Mail to:
KRLA BEAT #504
6290 Sunset Blvd.
Hollywood, Calif. 90028

Name _____
Address _____
City _____ State _____ Zip _____

KRLA ARCHIVES

Robbs Visit KRLA

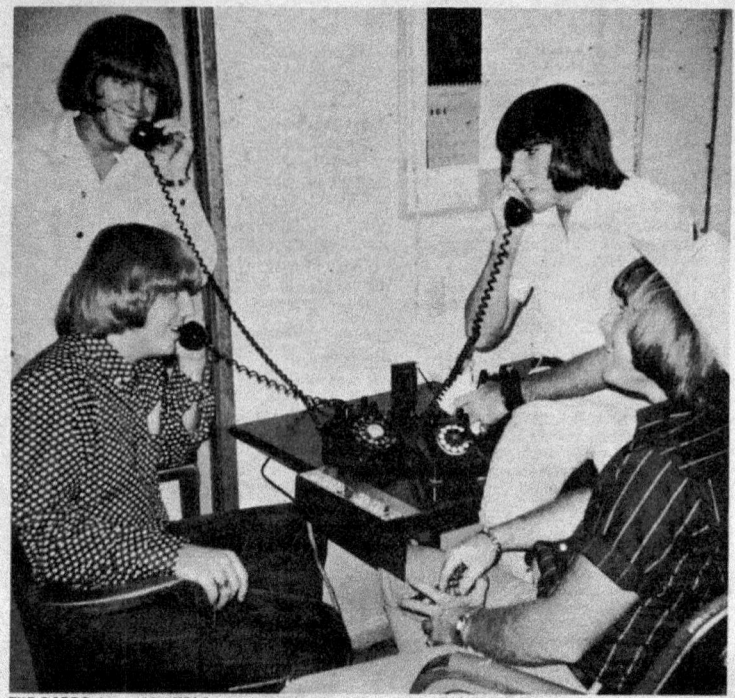

THE ROBBS dropped by KRLA to answer phones and would you believe the most requested song of the hour was their new one, "Next Time You See Me?" That's Joey Robb standing and Craig, Bruce and Dee, (l. - r.)

JOEY AND BRUCE sign autographs for a group of over a hundred fans who turned out to meet the guys when they arrived at KRLA's studios.

UNCLE DM, Dick Moreland, dropped into the phone answering room while the boys were there and he and Craig Robb layed an ear on, would you believe The Monkees' first album? How about the Robbs new single? How about the Robbs' first album, which isn't even finished yet?

Say you read it in The BEAT

THE DEEP SIX introducing their new Liberty album, "The Deep Six," at the Ice House in Glendale, Oct. 11-16.

the ICE HOUSE Glendale
234 SO. BRAND
Reservations 245-5043

WARREN BEATTY
SUSANNAH YORK

From London to the Riviera, a hair-raising tale of gallant love and truly desperate adventure!

KALEIDOSCOPE

the switched-on thriller!!!

A GERSHWIN-KASTNER PRODUCTION
CLIVE REVILL · ERIC PORTER
Written by ROBERT & JANE HOWARD CARRINGTON · Produced by ELLIOTT KASTNER · Directed by JACK SMIGHT
TECHNICOLOR® FROM WARNER BROS.

NOW PLAYING!
CALL THEATRE FOR SHOW TIMES
EXCLUSIVE ENGAGEMENT
WARNER HOLLYWOOD THEATRE
6433 HOLLYWOOD BLVD. at WILCOX · HO 6-5211

THE SONS OF ADAM
LAST APPEARANCE IN L.A. BEFORE TOUR

BIDO LITO'S
OPEN 10 P.M. NIGHTLY EXCEPT SUNDAY
HO 5-5235

18 & OVER

1608 COSMO ST. (NEAR SELMA) IN HOLLYWOOD

COVER CHARGE

THE NEW CLUB TROPICANA
247 E. MANCHESTER, L.A.

For Reservations — 758-7615
TEENAGERS WELCOME

NOW APPEARING
THE GENIUS OF
CHET BAKER
- also -
THE INCOMPARABLE
RAY BRYANT TRIO

KRLA ARCHIVES

MICK JAGGER
'That's Tough, Mom'

By Rochelle Reed

Keith Richard and Mick Jagger relaxed in the London hotel suite which their manager Andrew Loog Oldham was using as a temporary office and tossed off a few comments about the Stone scene as they see it.

First on their list was the well-publicized picture of the guys, taken on a New York street in early morning, with them posing in their version of wartime U.S. mothers.

A Giggle

"The photograph was just a laugh," Keith confessed, "there's no deeper interpretation to be placed on it than that. A photographer in New York took the picture as a giggle. We intend to bring it out in the U.S. as a cover for the single and on the flipside a photo of all of us dressed normally."

Sure enough, the pop picture does adorn the single jacket of "Have You Seen Your Mother, Baby, Standing In The Shadows?"

"We adopted the names of 'Molly' (Richards) and 'Sarah' (Jagger) for fun. I think Bill must get the 'king of queens' award for his portrayal of the bird in the bathchair (wheelchair to us) in the uniform. I mean just look at her. I mean, that's the one who pressed the button, isn't it?"

What Keith didn't tell us was the rest of the girlish names adopted as a gag by the five. Others are Flossie Jones, Penelope Wyman, and Millicent Watts!

The Stones have received a great deal of adverse comment about the shot from American mothers, but the guys don't seem overly perturbed. In fact, Mick and Keith showed a "that's tough" attitude about the whole thing.

But the Stones wanted to talk about music, not themselves, so they launched into a discussion of "Have You Seen Your Mother, Baby, Standing In The Shadows?"

"We tried trombones, saxes, nearly all permutations of brass before arriving at the trumpets," Keith explained when talking about the instruments backing their recording. "Everything but the trumpets dragged. If you have a question about the lyric," he added, "you must ask Mick — that's his department."

Mick, now pinpointed as the definite lyric writer on Stone records, looked up and nodded. "I get the ideas for the words by sitting down and following a train of thought — one thing just leads to another. This is simply about a boy and his bird. Some songs I write are just for a laugh. Others are extensions of ideas. This is a mixture of both.

"You must listen to it (Have You Seen Your Mother?) and place your own interpretation on the lyric. There is no attempt to present a controversial 'Mother' theme. 'Mother' is a word that is cropping up in a lot of numbers," he continued.

Then the two began to roll off remarks about their many best-selling discs, and how they do it all the time.

"We don't ask ourselves what is most commercial," Keith explained, "We simply say 'We like this best.' What we have liked over the past few years has proved to be what the young people like, so this is how to choose a single. This is probably the way that Mozart wrote. He wrote for himself. So do we. And it is a happy coincidence that what we like should also be what our public likes."

And what would happen if the guys liked something that no one else liked, say for instance, "Have You Seen Your Mother, Baby, Standing In The Shadow?"

"I'm not going to burst into tears if this doesn't go to number one," Mick said, "at least it is the best we could do and I am satisfied that we have given our best."

Then the two Stones broke their ban on themselves and hung out a few sentences on Brian Jones and his injured hand.

Insured Hands

"Brian was telling me that shortly before he broke the tendons in his hand someone had asked him if he had insured his hands," Keith said. "And just after that he broke his hand while climbing. Strange, isn't it?"

"He could play slowly with the hand while we were doing the Ed Sullivan Show," Keith continued. "I think he'll manage the tour all right."

Speaking of their tour, Mick decided to comment about the Walker-Troggs tour which was going on the road the same time as the Stones' show.

"I hope they have full houses," he said, "I hope we have full houses. I hope everyone has full houses," he finished generously.

But Keith was off on his own chain of thought.

"The Troggs are interesting," he said thoughtfully. "They are developing simplicity. We are trying to progress, but in a different direction — forward!"

Naughty Molly Richard!

Four Tops On The Four Tops

By Carol Deck

When four handsome young men from Detroit put out a record that immediately grabs everyone's attention, people soon want to know everything there is to know about those four guys.

Well, the Four Tops released "Reach Out I'll Be There," which is following "Ain't Too Proud to Beg" and "You Can't Hurry Love," other current Motown smashes up the charts, with the usual mighty Motown speed.

And people have been asking "What are the Tops really like?"

The BEAT went straight to the people who know the Tops better than anyone else in the world and asked that very question — we went to the Tops themselves.

That is, we went to three fourths of the Four Tops. At the time we talked with the three exciting young performers, their lead singer Levi Stubbs Jr. was in bed quite ill.

The other three — Renaldo Benson, Lawrence Payton and Abdul Fakir — however, were in great spirits as they sat sprawled about Motown's West Coast office intermittently answering phone calls from Detroit.

People often comment on the Tops names, particularly Abdul Fakir. Asked where his name came from, Abdul quips, "I got it from my father," but then seriously says, "it's East Indian."

If their real names confuse you, try keeping up with their nick names. Abdul is called Duke by the rest of the group and Renaldo is Obie.

The three came bursting into the office apologizing profusely for missing the interview which had been set up the day before. Motown acts rarely miss any appointment and these three knew that.

So we asked, "what are the Tops really like?" And they told us.

Lawrence describes Renaldo: "He's a great guy with a fantastic sense of humor. He smiles a lot, particularly when he speaks. On stage he's our little sunsport, besides that he's a nut."

Renaldo then offers his explanation for everything — "I had a very good education in starvation."

Renaldo describes Abdul: "He's cool, smart, understanding, patient very warm. Duke's very musical and creative. He's just a great guy."

Abdul on Lawrence: "He's cool, easy going. He doesn't bother no one and no one bothers him. Musically, I'd say he's a genius. He's behind all the Tops' success. He's a really swinging cat."

Renaldo backs up Abdul's praises of Lawrence: "He's a very warm person. Musically I think he's a genius too. He's also a great sports lover — any sport at all. And he's very dedicated, musically and otherwise.

Levi wasn't there, but he needed no defense. The other three had nothing but praise for their stricken leader.

"He's got one of the great voices of today," said Abdul. "He's a real lover of his fans and would do anything to make and keep his fans happy. Like right now, he should be in the hospital but he hasn't missed a show."

"He's a killer," added Lawrence, "one of the best singers I know. He's very sincere and goes out of his way to talk to his fans.

"Like the last time we played Philly. There were some wounded men brought out of a hospital to see our show and Levi braved 100,000 people to go back and to meet and talk to those guys. We all did but it was Levi's idea."

...THE FOUR TOPS REACHING OUT FOR NUMBER ONE?

KRLA ARCHIVES

If You Were A Monkee...

...YOU'D WRESTLE WITH HORSES,

...AUDITION TALENTED (?) NEWCOMERS,

...SING TO EMPTY COUCHES

...AND INSURE GOOD RELATIONS WITH THE SERVICE.

KRLA ARCHIVES

The Adventures of Robin Boyd

©1965 By Shirley Poston

After about half an hour of trying not to get any on her, Robin stopped watching the corny thriller she and George were looking at on the telly.

Leaning her head against her genie's arm, she closed her eyes.

"My, you have a strong shoulder," she sighed. "But scent isn't everything," she added waspishly when George shot her a *shurrup* look.

Re-leaning, Robin re-closed her eyes. So much had happened lately, this was really the first time she'd had a chance to think about it all, and she let her mind wander (she usually keeps it on a leash) back to that awful moment...

There she was, covered with peanut butter and cowering under the front seat of the Beatles' limousine. (If you're a new Robin Boyd reader, luck is with you, because why-and-what she was doing there is far too long a story to retell.) Suddenly, there was a terrible crash and everything went black.

Purple Rage

The next thing she knew, she was back to her sixteen-year-old self, back in the tea pot, and being backed up against a wall by a purple (with rage, that is) genie.

"Robin Irene Boyd!" he hisped furiously, shaking her until her *eyelids* rattled. "How *could* you?"

Robin jerked away from him. "I'm tick and sired — huh? — I mean *sick* and *tired* of missing all the *good* parts!" she screeched.

Then she gasped. "That crash! Was it an accident? Were the Beatles hurt?"

George re-shook her violently (which was already shaking enough, thank you) (here we go again). "There wasn't any crash!" he bellowed. "That was me lowering the boom on a moronic nit before she caused any *more* harm!"

Robin gulped. "I did get carried away, didn't I. Do they remember any of what I did?"

"No!" he re-bellowed, "but *I* do."

Robin tried to put her arms around him. "George, dear," she soothed. "I only kissed the *real* George to find out if he was him or you."

George grabbed her angrily (which is sooo cute when it's mad) by the hand and started walking her across the room. "I don't care *who* you kiss," he lied noisily. "I care that you don't pay one amday bit of attention to anything I tell you, and this time you aren't going to get away with it!"

"*George*," Robin said fearfully, trying to get out of his clutches. "Where are you taking me and what are you going to do?"

"I'm taking you *here*," he snapped, dragging her to a chair. "And I'm going to do *this!*" At which time he sat down, hauled her over his knee and whacked her backside until *his* eyelids rattled.

The minute he stopped the aforementioned whacking, Robin stopped screeching, jumped up, and kicked him right square in the left shin. Then she flang herself into a corner and blithered hysterically.

She kept it up, taking an occasional sidelong glance to see if he was weakening, until he weakened (repetition still reigns) and came over to her.

"Twit!" he said, looking down at her, but he said it rather fondly.

"Get away from me, you . . . you wife-beater," she sniffed. (This, of course was not the case (as in *yet*), but *girlfriend*-beater just didn't have the right amount of wallop to it.) (No pun intended.) (Or is it no pun accomplished?)

George stood his ground. "That's the way we do things in Liverpool," he said firmly. "Ask for it and you'll get it!" But, when she began to re-blither, he scowled and reached for her.

A Kiss

"Gerrup and give us a kiss," he ordered brusquely.

"I'd sooner kiss an unwashed Bulgarian," she snarled through a tangle of red hair.

However, since George rarely pays one am-day bit of attention to anything *she* tells *him* either, he yanked her to her feet and kissed her so warmly (not to mention well), she just couldn't resist returning the favor.

Of course, that was hardly the end of the incident. When the two of them finally stopped playing the olde All-Is-Forgiven scene (about a week later) (merely a joke, merely a joke), George made her re-clean up the tea pot, which she had re-destroyed in her attempts to escape by flipping the lid.

By the time she was finished (I'll say), John and Paul (as in Genie) and Ringo (as in Angel) appeared on the scene and Robin dutifully scurried off to the kitchen to make everyone a cuppa.

But she had a bit of trouble enjoying her portion of the potion. Seeing as how sitting down was not exactly *easy* after what she'd been through (as in smarts is not the *word*), she wrootched about uncomfortably and finally decided to drink her cuppa standing up.

"What's the difficulty?" John asked at last. "Got ants in yer... got stickers in yer knickers? he rephrased when George gave him a kick. (Which he later returned because he already had several.)

Larfing?

In spite of herself, Robin started to laugh, and she was still larfing a week later. Not that John's remark was all *that* foony. It was just that, during those next few days, she had more foon than she'd ever dreamed possible.

It wasn't *all* fun, of course. There were some very trying hours when George and company were off on more of their "special assignments." Trying not only because she missed her feindish foursome, but also because she was missing all the good parts again.

But, she managed to resist the temptation to join them by remembering two thingies.

One was the long talk she'd had with George, where he told her that the results would be *disastrous* for *all* of them if anything went wrong again. Especially if anyone (including the *real* Beatles) discovered that another foursome was doubling for them during particularly hysterical getaways, to throw off at least a part of the pursuing crowds. It had all been planned by George's Superior so that no one would see both sets of Beatles at the same time, and if there were any slip-ups, they would soon see the light(ning bolts, that is.)

And, when this failed to help her resist the irresistable urge to re-get involved, she was able to keep her beak in her own business by remembering that she had a most colorful set of bruises at the opposite end.

Still, she didn't mind being left out all that much because when the foursome was in town, they really made up for lost time.

Like the day at Disneyland, for instance. Having heard about the no-long-hairs-allowed ruling, the four of them mumbled a few magic words and showed up with shaved heads! And, as if that wasn't *enough*, they insisted on leaping out of their seats and flying over the "city" during the Peter Pan ride.

The biggest ball of all was the night the Beatles appeared at Dodger Stadium at Los Angeles. George had grudgingly but thoughtfully talked the other three into mumbling a few more magic words, and before Robin (who was sitting in the grandstand) (*sitting* is not the word either) knew what was happening, she disappeared into thin air and found herself standing right by the stage with her equally invisible companions. Just a few feet from the Beatles!

In fact, it was such a ball watching the concert from such close range, she nagged them into doing it all over again in San Francisco!

Robin very nearly died when the real Beatles left California for London. She hadn't been able to flap up to their abode even *one time!* Feeling that this would in no way conflict with any "special assignments," she did make a couple of olde college (Liverpool Art, to be exact) tries. But she found that one had very little success in such ventures when a jealous genie was keeping a rather firm hand on one. Particularly when that hand was directly on one's very *throat*.

She re-died when her own John, Paul and Ringo had to get back to their regular masters (or, as George puts it — at the top of his lungs, generally — *clients*.)

Just before they left, she hugged the dear Pauley so hard, she nearly collapsed one of his lungs. Then she brushed Ringo's wings for him, administering extra-loving care to the one she had mangled by slamming it in a car door. (Another long story you may have been fortunate enough to have missed.)

Unable to find a way to elude George long enough to give John a proper (as in im) goo-byee smooch (John has been known to admit it), she had to settle for a bit of kissie-cheek.

But, as the three of them disappeared, Robin smiled sneakily through her tears, almost positive that John had pinched her on the way out.

Hardly Dull

Even after their departure, things were hardly dull. There were new clothes to buy for school (and snits to throw for the money to buy them with), and there were friends to see who'd been gone for the summer (not to mention for years.) And, of course, there was her georgeous (ahem) George, who was so impressed by the way she was staying out of trouble, he even allowed her to visit his tea pot now and then (and when and if she'd finished her homework.)

In fact, that is where the two of them were at that very moment. And Robin's reverie ended as the aforementioned movie ended in a blaze of glory (not to mention baloney.)

George nudged her. "Are you sleeping?"

Robin shook her head, which, for a change, didn't rattle. "No — just thinking." She paused for a moment, then she looked deeply into his georgeous (re-ahem) dark eyes.

"George... so many incredible things have happened since I met you. I'll bet incredible-er things won't happen if I live to be two hundred, right?"

"More incredible," George corrected.

"Okay, okay, but will they or won't they?"

George chortled and gave her a pat, but he said nothing. Not because he didn't know the answer. Because he didn't want *her* to know it yet. For the first time in months, Robin was acting like a rational (well, *almost*), sensible (well, *sortof*) human (?) being.

And she would know soon enough that his unspoken reply was: "Baby, you haven't seen *any-thing* yet!"

NEW!! HAIR CONTROL FOR MEN WITH MOIST SPRAY ACTION

Shape Up

WITH MOIST SPRAY ACTION
FOR HAIR CONTROL ALL DAY!

Now a moist grooming aid especially developed for a man's hair. SHAPE UP combines "Sure Control" with a naturalness and convenience never before available in a man's grooming aid. SHAPE UP is a new protein base formula... contains no lacquers, or shellac and is completely water soluable.

For neat, groomed, healthy looking hair use this Special Offer!

Reg. $1.50
With Coupon Only **$1.00**
Incl. tax & postage

Shape Up
The BEAT
6290 Sunset, No. 504
Los Angeles, Calif. 90028

Please send me _____ cans Shape Up at $1.00 each. I enclose $_____ in cash, check or money order.

Name_____
Adress_____
City_____ State_____ Zip_____

KRLA ARCHIVES

like the Beat said...
the Beach Boys have wives

The BEAT has been saying it for months and the Beach Boys have been denying it for months but when too many people found out about it, they were forced to admit it. The Beach Boys are married. All except for Bruce Johnson, that is. The newest Beach Boy is still a bachelor but Brian, Dennis, Carl, Mike and Al are very much married.

Why the Beach Boys have denied their marital status as long as they have is anybody's guess. Several months ago, the then-married Brian Wilson stated: "Marriage has no bearing on a girl fan's adoration for an artist anymore. Two of our guys, Mike Love and Al Jardine, are already married." But what Brian forgot to mention—so was he!

...AL AND LINDA JARDINE

...CARL AND ANNIE WILSON

...MIKE AND SUZANNE LOVE

...DENNIS AND CAROL WILSON

...BRUCE JOHNSTON AND HIS MOTHER

KRLA ARCHIVES

Stevie Wonder Advances; No Longer Ray's 'Protege'

By Mike Tuck

Stevie Wonder, who plays five different instruments and dances as energetically and rhythmically as he sings, is probably a little more real than most people realize.

Stevie has been blind since birth, but I suspect only about one-third of those who enjoy his music know it. And it really doesn't seem to matter, because as a performer — as a person — his life is built around normalcy if not excellence.

Literally, Stevie's life is two-sided. The easy, jovial side is the most prominent, although in isolated moments he delves into deep, serious subjects.

Little?

However, he avoids seriousness if possible. I asked him about the "Little" tag he had for many years and a fellow in the corner picked it up and began to needle him about it.

"Now, just a minute," Stevie spun to the direction of Shelly Berger, head of Motown's West Coast office. "This 'Little' stuff has got to stop.

"I've been six feet tall for two years."

"That's okay," kidded a secretary, "I'm still going to get a belt after you. You're not that big yet."

"All right," the seated figure gave in, "I'm still 'Little' Stevie."

Onstage, Stevie injects an element of comedy into his act. "Now get yourself together," has become his wailing credo — one that has penetrated the language of the "hippy" set.

He sometimes even turns straight questions into jibes. "I play a lot of instruments," he answered my question. "Let's see, I play harmonica, piano, drums, bongos, radio and television.

"I like radio best."

His gift for mimicry is remarkable. He suddenly sat up in his chair and launched into an imitation. "This is ridiculous, this is ridiculous," he said in an excited, mocking fashion.

"Berry Gordy," chorused the contingency around him.

But in one aspect, Stevie is almost shy. This is his serious side — when he bashfully talks about subjects beyond his 16 years but still within his grasp.

He insists he leads a normal life. And although he is seldom around them, one of the things that concerns him most is the problems of his contemporaries in his own age group.

"I think the biggest problem facing young people today," he said, "is their fear that there won't be a tomorrow. I think the threat of war has done this to them.

"They think, 'well, if I won't be here tomorrow I might as well go out and do anything I want to today.' Then they go out and do all these crazy things.

"This is why I don't think you can compare this generation with the one of yesterday."

The only remedy to this, he thinks, is to offer teens more constructive things to do.

"I think teen clubs are a good idea," he said. "But they should be decent and have a wholesome atmosphere. And the people running them should treat the kids with respect if they expect respect in return."

Stevie's life, he tells you, has been a full one. "You know, I've been a lot of places and done a lot of things," he says in his stage act.

Offstage, he elaborates. "I really feel fortunate. I get to do a lot of things other people don't have a chance to do . . . and I enjoy doing them.

"No, I don't feel deprived at all." Singly dedicated, music has become the guideline in his life. He took up the harmonica and piano at four, and since has become entwined in the field where the only pre-requisites are rhythm and sense of hearing.

"Let me tell you about a dream I had when I was seven. It's kind of silly, I guess," he blushed.

"But I dreamed about this disc jockey in Detroit and he kept saying 'Little Stevie,' 'Little Stevie.'"

Stevie made his professional debut four years ago. At the time, he was being billed as a 12-year-old protege of Ray Charles. His admiration for the man known as "the Genius" was more than just a public relations handout.

Stevie even released an album entitled "A Tribute To Uncle Ray," in which he did his own version of several Ray Charles' songs. Since then, his esteem for Charles hasn't slackened, but he now disagrees with the "protege" image.

Admire Charlie

"I simply admire Mr. Charles," he said. "I probably always will; he's a great man. But I don't try to pattern myself after him. I have my own style."

His present style has undergone an almost unnoticed four-year evolution. His specialty — although he insists "I like absolutely all kinds of music" — is pulsating "soul" singing.

It is still his most popular with audiences. But he now attempts more sedate arrangements like "The Shadow Of Your Smile," which he does with remarkable polish.

Even in his own composing, which has produced several hits for other singers, he is prone to ballads. "That's all I've ever tried," he said.

...TANDYN ALMER — STRIP SONG

EDITOR'S NOTE:
The lights, the action, the hippies, the singers, the life on the Sunset Strip has been written up all over the world. Just recently, a national magazine devoted several pages in an attempt to describe what goes on in, around and by the Strip. But a young, successful (he penned the Association's "Along Comes Mary") songwriter by the name of Tandyn Almer has done the best job, in the fewest words. The following is Tandyn's birdseye view of what gives on the famous Sunset Strip.

Sunset Strip Soliloquy

Words and Music by Tandyn Almer

They're calling out the sheriff to bring his guns and tanks
   The neighborhood kids are up to their old pranks
And someone spiked the sugar bowls again down at Ben Franks
   And this time no one's around to doubt them
The Playboy Club is wretching 'cause someone gave them a tip:
   A bomb is going to explode next door inside The Trip
But the bomb turns out to be another Freudian slip
   By the folks who thought it'd be better off without them

False eyelashed and bell-bottomed as their flowing tresses stream
   The tennie-bopping groupie hang-out, freak-out chickies scream
For the sight of their shining hero which they hold in high esteem
   And would give their precious magic god's-eye-tooth for
The moon hangs low and heavy on the sidewalk super-scene
   It's been around the world a lot, but never has it seen
Such a generation lost in what remains to be unseen
   By the prying eyes of those who came much before

As far as the eye can wander, the tin river overflows
   With out-of-town and out-to-lunch hoodlums who make crude jokes
At the brite-attired patterns in the fadist colony droves
   Who parade and preen about in their proud contrivings
The line outside the Whisky is some eighty paces long
   Supposedly they've come to dig the singer and his song
But they hope to exit hay-loft bound with a friend to take along
   To help them forget their treadmill nine-to-fivings
And it's carnival nite most anytime in Hollywood's hippy-drome
   At six a.m. the party-crashers decide to make it home
All except for the obsessed irony of the poet and his poem
   Who hitch-hikes down the dead end street of strivings

USED BY PERMISSION COPYRIGHT 1966 DAVON MUSIC CORP.

...STEVIE WONDER meets Dodgers Maury Wills and Sandy Koufax at the airport.

KRLA ARCHIVES

Funny Men Coming Into The Teen Age

By Eden

"Everybody loves a clown"—another age-old adage from *The BEAT'S* trusty age-old Adage File. Old—but *true*; people *do* like a good guffaw now and then, and nowadays—teens seem to be laughing it up all over the place.

And what are they laughing about? And who are they laughing at? Well, while their parents are amusing themselves by laughing at the teens, the "youthful generation" is more appropriately amusing itself by laughing at some professional—and *non*-professional—funnymen.

Right at the top of the Teen Laugh List is a talented young comedian who has become widely acclaimed as a dramatic actor during this last TV season. Although Bill Cosby gained his show biz start in coffee houses, young-folk-type gatherings, and local TV shows—he has now gone on to a nationwide dramatic series. Even so, the bits of humor which he has initiated and made known to the public through the show has rapidly spread and become almost a household commodity.

His expressions—such as the "wonderfulness" thing, and various other unique speech humorisms he has started—have now become almost colloquialisms, and are used by people of all ages across the country.

In his night club and variety-TV show-guest spot-routines which are to be seen from time to time, Bill still enjoys looking back at his own childhood and teen age and poking gentle — but *hysterical* — fun at them. One reviewer who attended a Cosby concert recently remarked afterward that if Bill didn't already hold a degree in child psychology, he should. And that perhaps a few gentlemen who *did* hold such degrees could take a lesson from him!

Bill's Friend

A very funny man, Bill has already begun to be widely imitated, and one of the first comedians to strongly remind people of him was one of Bill's young friends, Richard Pryor.

Richard first came to the nation's attention when he received a break on the Merv Griffin show. Many people chuckled hysterically over their bedroom slippers while watching him on the late-night TV'er, then quickly picked up pen-and-whatever the next day to fire off a letter to Merv explaining how much Richard reminded them of Bill Cosby.

After a few more appearances on the show, people began to recognize Richard for his own individual talents, and his own unique brand of humor, and his fan club developed rapidly.

He is now one of the most popular comics in the country, and is rushing between TV guest appearances, to night club dates, to concerts, and then off to the movies, where he is about to appear in his first motion picture. Although he looks no older than 12, Richard is already well into his 20's and is also a married man.

Don Adams became a popular funnyman via the TV circuits when his series, "Get Smart" hit the air waves. For awhile there, it seemed as though the entire populace of these United States had completely lost their vocabulary, save for the immortal words, "Would you believe . . ." and "Sorry about that, Chief!" Marvelous how that was all you heard 24 hours a day from the mouths of babes, teens and adults! Even now, people still find themselves a little incredulous, frequently remarking: "Would you believe?!—whether they do or *not*!!

Wacky Phyllis

Another funny favorite of young people is wacky Phyllis Diller. Originally assaulting the public with her zany humor as a guest on shows such as the all-night Steve Allen laughathon, Phyllis quickly graduated to guest appearances on such *pop* shows as the Ed Sullivan show. Shortly thereafter, Phyllis became the leading lady of her very own detergent commercials and continued cackling it up through the suds.

Although Phyllis is the mother of five children and didn't "hit the big time" until she was already into her forties, she is now one of the most popular comediennes in America, with her own brand new TV series this Fall, and a couple of motion pictures to her credit. She also boasts the only laugh in the world that even Don Adams *wouldn't believe!*

Beach Party pictures have been the biggest rival to the consistently popular Elvis Presley pix in the last few years, and the funnyman in charge of the humor department in the surf-'n'-sand has been the King of Insult himself, Don Rickles. Although Don was previously confined to adult "lounges" in Las Vegas and other similar audiences, he has—through the miracle of wide-screen "surfavision"—become the popular, though *balding*, laugh-idol of millions of under-the-age-of-25'ers.

The Batman Bit

Apart from these individual laugh-makers, shows have also become very popular with teens, and probably the most successful to date has been the phenomenal "Batman" show. This one show has completely revamped the structure of humor in America, and "Bat Humor" has become not only "the thing"—but, the *only* thing.

The cartoon-characters-brought-to-life have become national heroes—the indefatigable twosome . . . the Dynamic Duo . . . ever at the ready to defend the innocent! But, holy laugh makers, Bat Man —you're going to have some mighty colorful competition this season with the Green Hornet riding around behind you!

Raiding Bats

In preparation for this new opposition, Bat Man has gone *pop*, and this season you will find people like Paul Revere and the Raiders appearing on the show. (Not singing—but *campaigning!*)

Other groups cashing in on the country's funny bone will be four young lads who call themselves The Monkees, and whose brand new TV show includes the use of what might be called "understated," or very "obvious" humor. This, too, might set a trend.

Even "Where The Action Is" will be employing some very funny visual laugh-thingies. All in all, it should be a laugh-filled, riotous season on the nation's TV sets. In fact, it might appear as though the funnymen are taking over!!

. . . **BILL COSBY** is one comedian who successfully turned actor.

. . . **BATMAN AND ROBIN** started the high-camp fad.

. . . **RICHARD PRYOR**

KRLA ARCHIVES

Computer dating, which up to now has been available only to college students, is here now for you, the **high school** student. MATCH DATE has designed its questionnaire to reflect the needs and desires of young adults between the ages of 14-18.

Matching people by computers has been very successful in colleges around the country; but now, MATCH DATE gives you, the high school student, the chance to go where the action is and join the excitement and adventure of computer dating.

MATCH DATE gives you the chance not only to list your interests and attitudes, but also to describe your ideal date. This mutual selection between you and your date makes for more fun-filled action. Meeting new people and making **new friends** also adds to the fun and adventure. Remember, if you tell your friends about MATCH DATE, and they join the fun, then the larger population gives you a better probability of finding your **IDEAL MATCH DATE**.

All you do is just fill out the questionnaire and mail it along with $3.00 to MATCH DATE, P.O. Box 69965, Los Angeles 90069. Our computer will then MATCH you with the FIVE or more members of the opposite sex with whom you are the most compatible. You will then receive their names, addresses, and telephone numbers, just as they will receive yours. Then, YOU ACT...

PRINT NAME: _____ AGE: _____

ADDRESS: _____ CITY: _____

PHONE: _____ AREA CODE: _____ SCHOOL: _____

SECTION 1: BACKGROUND

There are 24 questions to Section 1. Questions 1-13 ask you to describe certain characteristics of you and your MATCH DATE. Answer questions 1-13 in the blanks to the right of the questions. Questions 14-24 are to be answered TWICE. In the first blank, answer each question as it describes you. In the second blank, answer each question so that it describes your MATCH DATE to the computer. If your MATCH DATE'S characteristic is unimportant, enter the number zero (0) in the second blank. Make sure you fill in every blank with a number.

1. My sex is:
   1. Male
   2. Female

2. I am:
   1. Caucasian
   2. Negro
   3. Oriental
   4. Mexican
   5. Other

3. My date may be:
   1. Caucasian A. Yes B. No
   2. Negro A. Yes B. No
   3. Oriental A. Yes B. No
   4. Mexican A. Yes B. No
   5. Other A. Yes B. No

4. My religious background is:
   1. Protestant
   2. Catholic
   3. Jewish
   4. Other
   5. Unaffiliated

5. My date's religion may be:
   1. Protestant A. Yes B. No
   2. Catholic A. Yes B. No
   3. Jewish A. Yes B. No
   4. Doesn't matter A. Yes B. No

6. My age is closest to:
   1. 14
   2. 15
   3. 16
   4. 17
   5. 18

7. My date should be no younger than:

8. My date should be no older than:

9. My class is
   1. Freshman (9)
   2. Sophomore (10)
   3. Junior (11)
   4. Senior (12)
   5. Not in school

10. My school is
    1. Public
    2. Private
    3. Parochial
    4. Doesn't apply

11. My height is closest to:

12. The ideal height for my date is closest to:
    1. Under 5'
    2. 5'-5'2"
    3. 5'3"-5'5"
    4. 5'6-5'8"
    5. 5'9"-5'11"
    6. 6'-6'2"
    7. 6'3" or over

13. Physical attraction between my date and me is:
    1. Very important
    2. Moderately important
    3. Slightly important
    4. Unimportant

14. My hair is:
    1. Brown
    2. Blonde
    3. Black
    4. Red

15. My hair is:
    1. Long
    2. Average
    3. Short

16. My eyes are:
    1. Brown
    2. Blue
    3. Green
    4. Hazel
    5. Other

17. My build is:
    1. Light
    2. Medium
    3. Heavy

18. Social Club:
    1. Member
    2. Non-member

19. My family's income is:
    1. Under $5,000
    2. $5,000 - $7,499
    3. $7,500 - $9,999
    4. $10,000 - $14,999
    5. $15,000 - $20,000
    6. Over $20,000

20. Social Class:
    1. Upper
    2. Upper middle
    3. Middle
    4. Lower middle
    5. Lower

21. After high school, I plan to:
    1. Go to a junior college
    2. Go to a four year university
    3. Join the armed services
    4. Work full time
    5. Get married

22. My field of interest is:
    1. Humanities
    2. Natural Sciences
    3. Social Sciences

23. Which type of clothes do you generally wear:
    1. Mod
    2. Surf
    3. Ivy league
    4. Continental

24. My musical preference is:
    1. English sound
    2. Rock 'n Roll
    3. Folk-Rock
    4. Folk
    5. Jazz

SECTION 2: DATING THOUGHTS

In questions 25-33, answer the first blank so you describe your Dating Thoughts to the computer. Then answer the second blank so you describe your MATCH DATE'S answer to the computer. If your MATCH DATE'S answer is unimportant, enter the number zero (0) in the second blank.

25. I date:
    1. three times or more per week
    2. two times per week
    3. once per week
    4. once per two weeks
    5. once per month

26. I would prefer a first date at:
    1. a dance
    2. a movie
    3. a party
    4. a sporting event
    5. dinner

27. I prefer:
    1. single dating
    2. double dating

28. I usually am:
    1. going steady
    2. playing the field

29. I would kiss on the first date:
    1. certainly
    2. often
    3. rarely
    4. never
    5. depends on my date

30. Car:
    1. I have my own car
    2. I use the family's car
    3. I don't have the use of a car
    4. I don't drive

31. I like to dance:
    1. fast
    2. slow
    3. both
    4. neither

32. I drink:
    1. never
    2. occasionally
    3. frequently

33. I smoke:
    1. never
    2. infrequently
    3. moderately
    4. heavily

SECTION 3: DESCRIBING YOURSELF

In questions 32-42, describe yourself according to the characteristics on the left or right side on a one-to-five scale. Answer 1 if you are "definitely yes" the characteristic on the left. Answer 2 if you are "mostly yes" the characteristic on the left side. Answer 3 if you are undecided. Answer 4 if you are "mostly yes" the characteristic on the right. Answer 5 if you are "definitely yes" the characteristic on the right side.

34. Emotional / Not emotional
35. Talkative / Quiet
36. Athletic / Not athletic
37. Independent of family / Closely attached to family
38. Active in extracurricular activities / Not active
39. Politically concerned / Not politically concerned
40. Conformist / Non-conformist
41. Strong religious convictions / No strong religious convictions
42. School activities and organizations are: Important / Not important

SECTION 4: ATTITUDES

In questions 43-61, answer on a one-to-five scale. Place a "1" if your answer is "definitely yes". Place a "5" if your answer is "definitely no".

43. Is it difficult for you to limit the time and number of your telephone calls?
44. Do you study with the TV or the radio on?
45. Do you understand yourself better through dating members of the opposite sex?
46. Does your social life interfere with your classroom activities?
47. Do you believe in a God who answers prayer?
48. Are you independent of your family in spending money?
49. Should sex education be taught in public high schools?
50. Is your mind open about your personal faults?
51. Do you understand why your parents act as they do?
52. Are you willing to accept the consequences of a decision, right or wrong, that only affects yourself?
53. Do you feel that everyone has the right to protest against a law he disapproves of?
54. Do you believe cheating in school is for your benefit?
55. Is honesty always the best policy?
56. Do your actions reflect your feelings?
57. Can you control your actions?
58. Do the advantages of going steady outweigh the disadvantages?
59. Boys: Are you aggressive?
60. Girls: Do you consider yourself prudish?
61. Do you watch TV often?

SECTION 5: GENERAL INFORMATION

Answer questions 62-64 in the blank space provided. In question number 65, circle any of the numbers from 1-30 that describe your Special Interests or Hobbies. In question number 66, if you wish to reduce the probability of finding your MATCH DATE to a certain area, CIRCLE any of the numbers 1-20 where you would NOT accept a date from.

62. I attend church or synagogue:
    1. never
    2. once or twice a year
    3. less than once a month
    4. once or twice a month
    5. once a week or more

63. Grade Average:
    1. A— or above
    2. B
    3. B— or C+
    4. C
    5. C— or below

64. I study:
    1. more than average student
    2. the average amount
    3. less than average student

65. Special Interests or Hobbies:
    1. Water sports
    2. Tennis
    3. Bowling
    4. Golf
    5. Snow skiing
    6. Ice skating
    7. Gymnastics
    8. Boating
    9. Bicycling
    10. Horseback riding
    11. Fishing
    12. Hunting
    13. Automobiles
    14. Singing
    15. Acting
    16. Photography
    17. Movies
    18. Television
    19. Cooking
    20. Reading
    21. Playing cards
    22. Travel
    23. Writing
    24. Painting
    25. Literature
    26. Languages
    27. Politics
    28. Law
    29. Medicine
    30. Current Events

66. Which of the following areas would you NOT accept a date from:
    1. East San Fernando Valley
    2. West San Fernando Valley
    3. Chatsworth-1000 Oaks
    4. Sylmar-San Fernando
    5. Beverly Hills
    6. Hollywood
    7. East Los Angeles
    8. Pasadena-San Marino
    9. Santa Barbara
    10. Ventura-Oxnard
    11. Malibu-Santa Monica
    12. South Bay Cities
    13. Huntington Beach-Balboa-Laguna
    14. Oceanside-La Jolla-San Diego
    15. Alhambra-San Gabriel
    16. Covina-Pomona
    17. Santa Ana-Anaheim
    18. San Bernardino
    19. Big Bear-Arrowhead
    20. Lancaster-Palmdale
    21. San Francisco
    22. Oakland-Alameda
    23. Berkeley
    24. Richmond
    25. San Jose-Santa Clara
    26. Menlo Park-Palo Alto-Mt. View
    27. Castro Valley-Hollywood
    28. Daly City-San Bruno
    29. Stockton
    30.

Copyright 1966 by MATCH DATE

To receive your names by Nov. 15, you must return your questionnaire to Match Date by Nov. 1.
MAIL TO:
MATCH DATE
P.O. Box 69965
Los Angeles 90069

Name _____ Age _____
Address _____ School _____
City _____ Phone _____

KRLA ARCHIVES

BEAT SHOWCASE
(spotlighting new talent on the pop scene)

...LEE MALLORY
Berkeley-bred Lee Mallory is a 21-year-old currently leaping up record charts with his unique rendition of "That's The Way It's Going To Be." Lee's recording sounds a great deal like the six man Association, for whom he played guitar on their first album, but it's just Lee. Besides singing, Lee enjoys astrology and wears astrological keys, which he says, "Open anything that requires a key to open it now that I'm open."

...TIM BUCKLEY
A young man who looks like Dylan or Donovan but sounds more like McCormack or Mathis has just walked onto the folk-rock scene with his own album, appropriately titled "Tim Buckley." His single, "Wings," came off the press only two weeks ago. Currently, the 19-year-old singer is appearing at Los Angeles' Troubadour, having completed a stand in New York's Night Owl.

...THE KNACK
People have been telling *BEAT* that The Knack are going to be a habit, and indeed, they may be. The group is composed of two 17-year-olds, leader Mike Chain and bass Larry Gould, plus two 18-year-olds, lead guitar Dink Kaplan and drummer Pug Baker. They are dynamic, funny and refreshing, according to Capitol Records — they signed them!

KRLA ARCHIVES

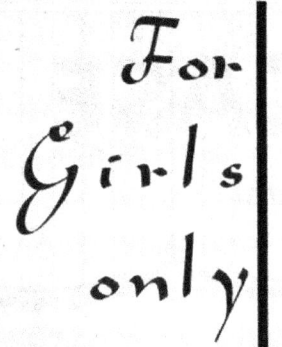

For Girls only

by shirley poston

I'm about to break another of my rash promises, and rave about one subject again. But, at least the subject I'm going to gabble about (Beatles, what else?) can be applied to other stars.

Remember when I said I'd tell you about our Beatle Birthday thingy before another B.B. rolled around? Naturally, I've waited until the last minute, but for those of you who have been crazy (and still are if you're reading this mess) enough to ask (for it), here is how my fiends (ahem) and I celebrate those special daze—sorry, days.

Lennon Day

If you hurry fast, maybe you can still try our scheme (not to mention the patience of the remainder of the world) on Lennon Day (be still, my beating heart). If not, save the whole idiotic plan—whoops—brilliant idea for another victim - er - star.

I've already told you about the first part, but bear with me as I try to repeat it, in English, if possible.

We start celebrating the night before by baking a rather strange birthday cake. That is, each person involved in the celebration bakes a one layer cake at home and brings same to the "party" the next day. Maybe that doesn't *sound* so strange, but it sure *looks* that way on account of before we don't decide beforehand what shape the cake will be, so we end up with an assortment of round, square, oblong, and triangular (triangular?) (oh, well) layers.

BeatlePageant

If the birthday occurs on a day when we don't have to get up at the crack of dawn, we gather at the stroke of midnight and usher in the holiday with our "Beatle Pageant."

If it isn't possible for us to get together then, we have the pageant just as soon as we *can* get together on the day of days. (Needless to say, the whole brilliant idea (as in idiotic scheme) works better if you can spend a whole day working at it, but all the activity can be crammed into one evening if necessary.)

I've tried to think of a way I can print the pageant, but it's just too long and too utterly ridiculous. (It just wouldn't do for the men in white, who are *already* on my trail, to hear *this* one.) (Nor would it be advisable to reveal said information to the postmaster.)

Anyrut, we have a separate pageant for each Beatle, which lasts about half an hour (the pageant, not the Beatle.) We have them all written down, and what we did when we were making them up was drink — I mean, pretend that we were angels who were deciding what the about-to-be-born Beatle was going to look like.

You know, selecting hair color and eyes and arms and legs (gasp) and all that.

Following the pageant we frost the cake. Then, after recovering from the hysterical fit we always have when we see how utterly insane it looks (not to mention the tantrums we have to throw to keep horrified parents from hurling us out of the kitchen) (not to mention the nearest window) . . . now I've lost my train of thought (actually, I *missed* it, years ago.)

Anygravel (*hah?*), we then affix the proper amount of candles and have our Official-Cake-Cutting Ceremony. At which time (to loud musical accompaniment) we cut the cake (using the term loosely) into exactly as many pieces as the Beatle in question is years old on that particular birthday.

Each piece must have its own candle, and if you don't think it's totally impossible to slice a tottering mass of cake, you're absolutely *right!* But it's close *enough* to impossible to have us rolling all over the linoleum, up to our ears in crumbs!

Parade Time

Still, we somehow manage (with the help of a lot of scotch tape) and then the fun really begins because it's "Parade Time."

After wrapping each piece of cake in neat (har) little bundles, we grab our "Happy Birthday Dear _____" (would you believe *George?*) (I would, if he told me the green was made out of moon cheese) (no, that's not it) (oh, well, maybe I'll think of it later) . . . anyway, we grab ths posters we made when we started all this nonsense almost three years ago (we have a different set of placards for each Beatle) (different is not the *word*) and rush into the street.

The object of all this is to find people who have the same first name as the Birthday Beatle, so we can give them a piece of cake!

Is Your Name

As you may have guessed, this isn't exactly easy, and often involves walking up to total strangers and saying "Is your name _____?" (Would you *re-believe* George?) (I would if he told me cheese is made out of green moon!) (No . . . that *still* isn't right.)

To even further complicate things, we have a rule that we MUST find a person for *each* piece of cake before the Beatle's birthday is over, and you can about imagine how hysterical the scene becomes if we still have fifteen pieces of cake along about 11:45 p.m.

Come to think of it, the scene is pretty hysterical from start to finish! Because of the signs and all, most people kind of get the idea and go along with the gag, but there are always a few who race wildly off into the sunset.

(One time a policeman stopped us and asked what we were doing. But, since it was Ringo's birthday we were celebrating, and the officer's name just happened to be Richard, things turned out fine.) (With the possible exception of his stomach. When we gave him his cake, that just turned, *period*.)

Sometime during the abovementioned hysteria, we pause to sing "Happy Birthday." We never plan in advance when we're going to do it. We just seem to know when the time is right. Like when we're standing on the busiest street corner in town and everyone is *already* pointing.

Finale

I remember that when I halfway told you all this before, I just couldn't figure out what part of the action was my special fave. Well, I've decided. The finale is definitely the part I dig (as in my own grave) most.

Unfortunately, this doesn't apply unless your birthday type person isn't from England, but you can always write your own words to the song we sing.

When we were looking for just the right finishing touch to our celebration, I just happened to remember a song from the days when I used to take piano lessons (at gunpoint, believe me.)

Ultra-Close

It's called (if this isn't the actual title, it's ultra-close) "He Is An Englishman." I don't know how to describe it except to say it is the *neatest*, funniest song in the world when it's being sung by people who couldn't warble their way out of a wet paper baggie!

If you've never heard of it, about the only way you can get a copy is to go to a music store and request same. Which is rather a panic in itself.

I know *I'll* never forget when I walked into a sheet music department and calmly asked the clerk: "Do you have the words and music of 'H.M.S. Pinafore' in stock? It's by Gilbert and Sullivan," I added nonchalantly.

He gave me an astonished look, and unable to bypass the opportunity, I drew myself up haughtily and said: "Just because I'm a teenager doesn't mean I'm an uncultured barbarian, sir."

He was so amazed, I bought the whole score when he finally found it. I'd intended to just copy off the song I wanted, but I just couldn't resist making him gape some more. (I, however, *did* resist telling him that he looked like he could use a few swigs of Beethoven's Fifth, and have never forgiven myself for passing up the chance.)

Beethoven's Fifth

You'll have to hear the song to imagine how positively moronic we sound as we sing same all the way home, but that's what we do, and if we live through it, we consider that particular birthday well celebrated and start praying for the next b-day to hurry!

Well, now that I've proved that I'm even nuttier than you thought I was, and encouraged you to put a little (more) insanity into your lives, I'd better excuse myself and start stirring up batter for John's cake. Not to mention trouble.

Whoops—nearly forgot. Three things I must tell you immediately (soon, too.)

1. Remember when I told you (in code) what was going to happen while the Beatles were in California? Well, it *did* happen! But do you think I got to *see* it happen? #*®÷✓!!! I realize you can't win 'em all, but at this point, I'll settle for winning *one!*

2. Speaking of winning, due to circumstances beyond my control (which I'll be more than happy to discuss sometime when you have a week), my snit-flinging failed to work in the Meet-Your-Fave-Contest, where the Beatles were concerned, that is. But there's still a chance it could happen, so tell you what I'm gonna do. I'm saving all the Meet-Your-Fave letters that applied to the Beatles for later, and will pick a winner from the letters of those who wanted to meet a star who isn't on the other side of the world. Then, when-and-if my alternate Beatle plan comes off, there'll be another winner. Soooo, everyone who wrote in should relax (as in nins and peedles) because there's still hope!

3. I carefully picked the winners of all my other outstanding (as in bettern *never* than *this* late) contests and put them in a safe place. They will be printed here just as soon as I find that safe place, which, incidentally, I never intend to leave.

Considering the contents of this column, I would like to close with a comment made by one of both of my many readers, which sort of sums up everything . . .

"Oh, the joy of being warped together!"

Stones' U.S. LP's Draw 20 'Golds'

The Rolling Stones are making a regular thing of having million-selling albums in the United States.

The Stones were recently awarded twenty gold discs, four each, which they earned for their last four U.S. albums. At the same time, they recorded their second "live" performance—this one intended for an album. Their first resulted in an EP.

The presentation and recording came during the Stones' concert at London's Royal Albert Hall. Engineers taped the entire act before a sell-out crowd of 5,000.

The Stones' first "live" recording came in March of last year when their performances in Greenford, Liverpool and Manchester were taped. Their EP was entitled "Got Life If You Want It."

The Stones' "live" album is expected to be issued only in America.

After the performance, Mick, Keith, Brian, Bill and Charlie hosted a party attended by more than a dozen prominent show business personalities.

The post concert party was filmed and presented later on a British TV show.

Wipe Out Woebegone Hair

Get with Shontex Dandrid Shampoo

Big FREE SAMPLE DEAL... NOW!

Like the price is right! Send for a freebee of the one shampoo guaranteed to give the go-go to woebegone hair, or your money back. Makes flaked-up limp, lifeless hair wake up, shape up! Or else. Mail coupon. Get free sample, plus certificate worth 50¢ off on purchase of Dandrid Shampoo at any store. This deal gets better and better! Do it!

Mail to: Shontex Dandrid Shampoo Deal
922 N. Vine St., Hollywood 90038

Send me my free sample of Dandrid Shampoo and my 50¢-off certificate for when I go to buy some at the store. I enclose 10¢ to cover cost of packaging and mailing, which is only fair for such a good deal.

Name: _____

Address: _____

City: _____ State _____ Zip _____

KRLA ARCHIVES

THE BEAT'S MOVIE REVIEW

"Not With My Wife, You Don't!"

By Jim Hamblin

Warner Brothers has come up with one of the funniest films yet to be made. Saul Bass, the man who creates the grooviest titles in the biz, has injected into this zany adventure many weird effects, all of which come off great. Beginning with an animated green-eyed monster right on through an hilarious spoof on fuzzy-looking Italian love scene movies, the picture starts great and never lets up.

As a matter of fact, if you go out for popcorn you may miss 5 or 6 good laughs. Better stock up before you go in. The story is about two jet fliers who are great buddies in Korea (with excellent combat footage, by the way) but are arch rivals at indoor sports. The Center of their continuing battle is Virna Lisi, the import whose third movie now puts her in the top money bracket.

Scott once again proves himself the most versatile and accomplished actor on the screen. HE'S GREAT!

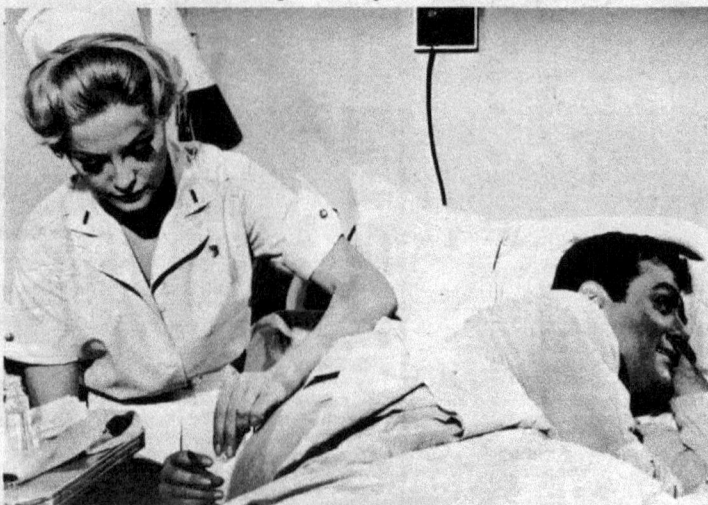

Says Scott, "If it weren't for the music, we'd all be arrested!"

GEORGE C. SCOTT

VIRNI LISI

TONY CURTIS

"THIS PROPERTY IS CONDEMNED"

This is easily the best yet of the Tennessee Williams stories made into films. Oddly, it is from what was originally a one-act play. Good color, good acting, well edited and a forceful story done in the usual sweaty South with the usual hatreds and beatings.

The star is obviously Natalie Wood. And no one can deny she works the hardest of any actress, on all her films.

In order to be authentic, the studio had to dig up some green Lucky Strike wartime cigarette packs, now the "newest" variety! Produced by Paramount Pictures.

"AN AMERICAN DREAM"

This picture is getting rather bad critical comment from most places. Perhaps because Eleanor Parker (the countess in Sound Of Music) does such a dramatic and forceful cameo performance that the rest of the picture would *have* to be a let-down.

Stuart Whitman does kinda shuffle through this one, mostly wrinkling his nose when a problem comes along.

But Janet Leigh also comes along, and she's pretty. The story, by author Norman Mailer, is a bit weird, and has an illogical conclusion. Basically we think it is a mediocre story done very well.

If you were to believe that police actually behave the way they do in this film, we need more Supreme Court decisions against them!

Recommended for all Les Crane fans.

KRLA ARCHIVES

America's Largest Teen NEWSpaper

25¢

KRLA Edition BEAT

NOVEMBER 5, 1966

THE ASSOCIATION PLAY THE COURT GAME

SEE PAGE 1

KRLA ARCHIVES

KRLA BEAT

Volume 2, Number 27 — November 5, 1966

KINKS BANNED IN SCANDINAVIA

If you have made plans for seeing the Kinks in concert this year, forget them. The group has already cancelled a handful of engagements and has no plans for accepting bookings for the remainder of the year.

Greatly concerned over problems in their schedule and their new recordings, Ray Davies of the Kinks flew to America last week for a conference with the group's U.S. business manager, Allen Klein.

But even the U.S. conference meant more cancellations. Davis' departure meant the group would have to nix their scheduled six-day tour of Austria and Switzerland.

The Kinks' haphazard appearance practices led the Musicians Union in Scandinavia to ban them here. Co-manager Robert Wace linked the ban to postponement of earlier engagements.

"This is obviously a reaction to the Kinks' cancellation engagements in Copenhagen last week," he said, "but there were no contracts for them to do these."

Association Sued By Former Publicist

DENY CONTRACT BINDING

A former publicist for the Association has filed suit against the group, charging fraud and breach of contract and asking for $100,000 in punitive damages.

Stan Zipperman, who left the group several months ago, filed the suit in Los Angeles Superior Court. The lengthy complaint, alleges, among other things, the following:

• Zipperman's contract for public relations and publicity services for the Association was improperly terminated.

• The Association induced Zipperman to execute the contract through fraud.

• It is well known in the industry that Zipperman was substantially responsible for the success of the Association.

Abundant Proof

Zipperman claims to have an abundance of proof to substantiate his allegations. In a prepared statement, he said the following:

"I am determined to take the case to court where all the true facts will come to light. To date, I have over one-hundred witnesses of top reputation in the industry who have volunteered to testify on my behalf."

Lee Colton, attorney for the Association, denied the contract was binding. He said there was no time limit specified on the contract, and the group had every legal right to terminate it when they felt Zipperman wasn't doing the job properly.

Colton said it was obvious the group wasn't simply trying to cut costs by firing their publicist, because an even more expensive publicist was hired after Zipperman's dismissal.

Talent Only

"Besides, it is talent that makes or breaks a group," Colton said in regard to Zipperman's claims for the success of the Association. "Lawyers, managers or publicists aren't as important to the success of the group as is talent."

Meanwhile, the Association and their new manager, Pat Collechio, are under fire from another direction.

Dean Fredericks, the group's original manager, has filed a Los Angeles Superior Court suit charging the Association with breach of contract. Fredericks, who claims he had the group tied to a seven-year contract, alleges the boys severed the pact six years early.

...THE ASSOCIATION ARE SAYING IT ISN'T SO.

Beach Boys Tops In English Polls

If English popularity pollsters have anything to do with it, the number one group in the world is right here in the United States.

An unexpected victory for America's Beach Boys came after English voters chose the Californians ahead of their own Beatles and Kinks.

World's Top

But while the British publication conducting the poll allowed its country doesn't at present possess the world's top group, it predicted the Beatles are well on their way to recapturing the position.

Still, vote tabulations indicated the Beatles have a good way to go before replacing the Beach Boys.

Behind the Beach Boys, Beatles and Kinks, the voters chose the following: the Small Faces, the Walker Brothers, Cilla Black, Dave Dee, Dozy, Beaky, Mick and Tich, the Spencer Davis Group and the Troggs.

The poll, however, may not be as accurate as it appears. The Rolling Stones were listed only as the number 12 most popular group in their native land.

The poll proved two things: groups are still the most dominant force in pop music and the Beatles are still holding their own.

The poll, taken weekly and tabulated on a basis of 30 points awarded the No. one position, 29 points for the No. 2, and so on, down to one point for No. 30, rated the Beatles No. 24 at the end of June.

'Revolver'

The publication said the impact of the Beatles No. 1 hit, Revolver, was the dominant factor boosting the group's popularity.

In a rating taking in the United States, meanwhile, the Beatles have a massive lead over the Rolling Stones are third, followed by the Mama's and Papa's and Simon and Garfunkel.

Monkee Lets Secret Slip

That harmonic accompaniment behind the Monkees on their TV show and deluge of records is coming from a source other than Mickey Dolenz, Davy Jones, Mike Nesmith and Peter Tork.

One of the Monkees admitted the well-kept secret last week in an interview with New York Times reporter Judy Stone. He said, however, the group does its own singing.

An unnamed Monkee is quoted as saying, "Studio musicians were used for the recordings, although all the boys do play guitars and Micky is learning to play drums."

The BEAT has learned three of the Monkees' back-up musicians are members of the New Order, a Warner Bros.' instrumental group. They are guitarist Jerry McGee, bassist Larry Taylor and drummer Bill Lewis.

BEATLES' SOLO CAREERS DETRACTING FROM GROUP?

With the Beatles all going separate, solo ways these days, Brian Epstein has announced the group may not release a customary disc during the Christmas season.

If they do not, it will be the first time since 1962 the Beatles haven't had a record at the top of the charts.

Epstein also announced Paul McCartney will soon be going the solo route. "It is not an acting role," the Beatles manager clued, "and an announcement can be expected soon."

The Beatles are also not expected to make a group appearance in England for the remainder of the year. Their last appearance there was in May.

Their failure to release a Christmas Season disc is the first major intimation that the boys' solo careers are detracting from their effectiveness as a group.

"We would naturally like to have another Beatles single before the end of the year," said an EMI spokesman, "but they have nothing in the can, so it is entirely dependent on whether they record again in time."

The Beatles are, however, expected to enter the recording studios in November to record songs and incidental music for their next film. The film is tentatively scheduled to begin production in January.

Inside the BEAT

Letters To The Editor 2
On The Beat 3
'In' People 4
Yardbirds Return 5
Highlights of Sonny & Cher's Tour 6
Association Speak 8
The Big Mama 9
Beach Boys Recording Session 10
Neil Diamond's Search 11
Lou Rawl's Black Pepper 15
Raiders On 'Screaming Kids' 17
Supremes In Vegas 19

Letters TO THE EDITOR

THANKS FOR TEEN PANEL

Dear BEAT:
Thank you! Thank you so much for putting in print what I've tried to put into words for so long. Your "Teen Panel" column is one of the best articles in the whole BEAT. Especially the September 10 and October 8 issues. You dared to print what you knew would be read by thousands of people, what some people don't have the courage and/or intelligence to even think about.

Maybe what we teens should do is open The BEAT to this page of your newspaper and "accidently" leave it where our parents could read it. Maybe then they'd be willing to talk to us and find out how some of us really feel. I hope so.

There's such a lack of communication between adults and kids that it's getting hard to live with each other!

I believe what Kris said was true: "About the folly of war and how ridiculous it really is. Did you ever stop to think that a lot of other things are just as ridiculous? Like racial prejudice and basing your life on material things and money and looking down on people who don't conform to your standards. The whole thing is really absurd!"

Thanks for an intelligent and really outa-sight newspaper!
Jana Covington

Where Is Bill Cosby?

...BILL COSBY 'SPYING' IN SPAIN

Dear BEAT:
I sure hope you can help me. I think Bill Cosby is so groovy. He is the one who really makes "I Spy" and is one of the few sincerely and honestly funny men in show business.

I'd like to write to Mr. Cosby and tell him how great I think he is but I don't know where to write to him. Can you tell me? I know that you are not allowed to give out his home address but I'd appreciate any address you'd be able to give me.

Also, you haven't had an interview with him in quite sometime. What's the matter? Please, talk to him again and print a huge article with lots of pictures.

Thank you very much for your time and trouble.
Judy Hamilton

You may write to Bill Cosby at 846 Cahuenga, Hollywood, California. Bill is currently in Spain for six weeks filming "I Spy" but as soon as he gets back we're going to interview him again. Okay?
The Editor

GREAT FAN

Dear BEAT:
My name is Liz Hamilton and I am a very great fan of the Monkees. I am very interested in starting a fan club and I would appreciate any information you could give me on how to go about starting a club. I watch their show every Monday night and I would not miss it for anything in the world.

If you don't know how I can start a fan club for the Monkees, I would appreciate any information you could give me on how to join a fan club that is already started.

Thank you for your time and trouble. I appreciate the time you have taken out to read this letter.
Liz Hamilton

For information on how to start a fan club for the Monkees, write to them at 1334 No. Beachwood Drive, Hollywood, Calif., 90028.
The Editor

CROWNED A BEATLE FAN

Dear BEAT:
I am a Beatle fan who would like to make a comment on a letter I just finished reading from R.D. about changing Beatle attitudes.

For one thing, I couldn't agree with her more. I have felt this way for months. When they came to San Francisco, gave a 33 minute concert and left, I was never so mad in my life. We get a chance to see them once a year and not even a dozen people got to talk to them. And the Beatles can do something about it if they wanted to. A few words to Tony Barrow would do the trick.

If anyone says I'm not a true Beatle fan I will truly and personally crown them. I have been one since February of 1964. Those were the good old days. When we knew they were the warmest guys we'd ever known. But they no longer seem that way any more. In fact, they don't even seem real to me. They seem to have thrown themselves into their private lives and come out only for records and a few personal appearances.

If the thought of fame never crossed their heads, if they didn't want to be bothered with fans and the likes, they should have quit after their first million.
Jill Anne Powell

Is Carl?

Dear BEAT:
I couldn't help but notice while I was reading "What 'In' People Are Talking About" the article that said Carl Wilson admitted he was married to Annie Hinche. Is it true that he is married to her? Why didn't we hear anything about the wedding? Or is it just a rumor?

Yes, it is true that Carl Wilson is married to Annie Hinche. The whole thing was supposed to be a secret but when too many people discovered that with the exception of Bruce Johnson all of the Beach Boys are married, they decided to admit it.
The Editor

MEET THE DYNAMICS

Dear BEAT:
Your fabulous newspaper always likes to hear about new talent so I would like to introduce you to six charming men, collectively known as Troy Marrs and the Dynamics.

First, there is Troy Marrs, lead singer. He loves guitars, girls and food in that order. His favorite pastime is playing practical jokes on people he doesn't know.

Eddie Horwitz, twenty year old piano and saxophone player, is a happy-go-lucky guy whose favorite hobby is calling up and requesting records on the radio.

Jim Keen is nineteen and plays the drums and, believe me, he lets you know about it! Sometimes you fear the worst for his poor drums.

Lead guitar player is David Smith and he concentrates wholeheartedly on perfecting his style. (Whatever it may be!)

Charlie Richmond plays bass guitar and seems to be quiet and shy on stage but off stage he does impersonations of everyone from Charlie Chaplin to Kirk Douglas.

Ken Kirksey is rather hard to describe because he is always hiding behind a huge pair of sunglasses!

Their first record, "Rhythm Message," was a big hit all over Southern Texas (by the way they are all from Houston) and they have a very bright outlook on the future. Maybe with the help of The BEAT it will be even brighter.

Thank you for listening.
Jo Anne Miller

MORE ON THE ASSOCIATION

Dear BEAT:
First, I want to thank you for the fabulous article on the Association in the October 8th issue of The BEAT. This group is one of the most talented groups ever to come along and I want to read more articles on them.

Success has ruined (or should I say "changed") some groups but the Association are still as nice as ever. I have talked to them before and after success and I can say it's a pleasure to know that they haven't changed.

Thanks again for the article. I hope to read more about them (the Association) in the future and please have pictures on them, too.
Name withheld by request

INFO ON THE PACK

Dear BEAT:
I was very happy to see the letter by Ellen Bernstein in your October 8 issue about Terry Knight. Though her state address was not listed, I guess she is from the Detroit area. Unfortunately, Terry is not very well known in my area, Louisiana, but I would like to add some to what Ellen wrote.

Terry had several records out before the two she mentioned and he has a new one out now, "I Who Have Nothing," and one of his own compositions, "Numbers." The label is Lucky Eleven, which is distributed by Cameo-Parkway Records.

I've met Terry once and this summer in Detroit I met some people who are friends of his as well as the presidents of his fan club, so I'm able to keep up with his activities. The members of his group, the Pack, are Curt Johnson, Donny Brewer, Herm Jackson and Bob Caldwell, all from Michigan except Bob, who is from Mississippi and Herm, from Kentucky. Terry is the oldest at 23 and Curt the youngest at 17.

Terry and the Pack have appeared in concert with the Dave Clark Five, the Strangeloves, the Beau Brummels, the Miracles, Marvin Gaye, Mitch Ryder, the McCoys and the Yardbirds.

They have an album coming out shortly which will include the Stones' "Lady Jane."

Terry produces his own records and is also independently producing a new group on the Cameo label, the Hard Times, from Atlanta, Ga. Terry and the Pack appeared on "Action" on September 23 and there should be several more appearances in the future.

Their fan club address is National Terry Knight and the Pack Fan Club, P.O. Box 4802, Detroit, Michigan, 48219. Anyone who writes should be sure to enclose a S.A.S.E. to insure a speedy reply. They are a terrific group and it's long past time for people everywhere to know they're around.
Jeri Holloway

KRLA ARCHIVES

On the BEAT
By Louise Criscione

Noel Harrison, popular television spy, is going back to where he came from—records. Don't get yourself all knotted up about it. Noel will, of course, continue to be the guy in "The Girl From UNCLE" but during the show's next breather Noel will record an album of original and previously unrecorded songs by Bob Lind. No doubt, uppermost in Noel's decision to record Lind material is his signing with Greene and Stone, who by coincidence we're sure (?) also manage Bob Lind.

Anyway, Noel is naturally elated with the solid success of "The Girl From UNCLE" and notes with genuine pleasure the fact that people no longer refer to him as "Rex Harrison's son." 'Course, his famous father hasn't hindered Noel's career but it's been a burr under Noel's skin ever since he started singing.

Supreme To Marry?
The Rumor of the Week has to be the one which is currently making the rounds concerning Supreme lead singer, Diana Ross, and her Motown boss, Berry Gordy. The rumor-mongers declare that Diana will soon wed Berry and leave the Supremes. Naturally, Motown is denying the whole thing but those close to the Motown stable admit that Diana and Berry are indeed going together.

However, the Supremes are Motown's top-selling act and it seems highly unlikely that Berry, the king of Motown, will pull Diana out of the hottest female group in the world. But then, love has been known to do strange things. Still, don't hold your breath until Diana becomes Mrs. Berry Gordy.

...NOEL HARRISON.

Surprise For Stones
The surprise of the month goes to the Rolling Stones. But it's a dubious honor and the Stones are not too terribly happy to accept it. Nonetheless, their latest single effort, "Have You Seen Your Mother, Baby, Standing In The Shadow?" has failed to make it to the number one spot in England. So what, you say? Well, it marks the first time since December, 1964 that a Rolling Stones' single has failed to become number one on the British charts.

As befits the Stones, they are not taking the insult lying down. Says Stones manager, Andrew Oldham: "We're offering no excuses. They are not necessary. In other charts the disc is climbing not falling. We make a point of never disputing the findings of any chart but from this distance, I must admit I like the look of the others better."

Before taking off for his British tour, Bobby Hebb was involved in a near-miss accident in a Boeing 707 jet in Bermuda. The popular American entertainer was returning from his stint at the Forty Thieves Club in Bermuda when the jet he was riding in blew a tire as the plane was taking off. The pilot brought the jet back down at the end of the runway and it was only after some terrifying moments that he was able to bring the plane under control. Thirty-five of the plane's passengers were injured but there were no fatalities and Bobby was, luckily, not among the thirty-five.

Trogg Trouble
Had to laugh at the Troggs' problems with "I Can't Control Myself" even though it's not actually that hilarious—especially to them. As you know, the disc is on the brink of total censorship in Australia and has been the object of heated controversy all over England. Allegedly, the lyrics are entirely too suggestive for air play but the Troggs claim the whole thing has been vastly misunderstood.

"It was done more as a tongue-in-cheek number," declared Troggs' guitarist, Chris Britton. However, their attempt at humor went soaring over everyone's head and all the Troggs got out of it was a lot of publicity. Which isn't bad, you know? Publicity helps to sell records and even if "I Can't Control Myself" is banned all over the world, there is still the black market where you can buy just about anything if you have the necessary money.

...CHRIS BRITTON.

Paul To Score Movie —Without John?

BEAT has learned that Paul McCartney may write the musical score for "Wedlocked Or All In Good Time," a film starring Hayley Mills. He will not work with John Lennon on the project.

If Paul actually does do the music for the picture, and indications are the he has already consented to the task, it will be the first time Paul has composed officially without the help of John.

It is also rumored that George Martin, Beatles A&R man, will help produce the soundtrack recording.

Paul's Mum
Paul is mum about the solo undertaking, as are other officials connected with the project.

Tony Barrow, Beatles Senior Press Officer, said: "No announcement is being made for some time."

Boulting Brother, the film company making "Wedlocked," stated: "It is premature to say anything." This probably means Paul has verbally agreed to do the musical score, but has not yet signed the papers.

Both Paul and John are under contract to their music company, and Dick James, Beatle publisher, said: "Any music writeen by either Paul or John must be published by Northern Songs."

The movie, "Wedlocked Or All In Good Time," is based on the play, "All In Good Time," written by Bill Naughton, author of "Alfie." Paul is believed to have seen the play when it was staged in the West End section of London.

Hayley's First
The picture will be a first for Hayley Mills, as well as for Paul McCartney. Hayley will play a married woman for the first time in her screen career.

In the film, she and her screen husband, Hywell Bennett, are forced to spend their honeymoon with her parents after an unscrupulous travel agent absconds with their money. The color picture has already been shot at the Shepperton Studios, with a few scenes filmed on location in northern England. It is set to premiere early next year.

USA Xmas For Herman

Herman's Hermits are coming back to the U.S. in time for Christmas!

The group will arrive in New York on December 21 and perform ten one-nighters across the country. The specific cities in which they will perform have not been announced yet.

The group is negotiating for an appearance on the Perry Como television special, to be filmed January 10. If this is arranged, their U.S. stay will be extended.

The Hermits are currently climbing up the English pop charts with their new single, "No Milk Today." The group released the disc in place of "Dandy," which was not issued there.

...WHILE JOHN'S AWAY, Paul will probably score a film.

'NOT RESPECTABLE NOW' SAY STONES

A different type of person is predominating the pop scene today, according to Keith Richard and Brian Jones, the Stones' most outspoken members.

"A new generation came to see us on tour with Ike and Tina Turner. Youngsters who had never seen us before, from the age of about 12, were turning up at the concerts. It was like it was three years ago when the excitement was all new."

So spoke Brian on the conclusion of the almost sell-out Stone tour, which also featured the Yardbirds and the Turner Revue.

"The tour has been an enormous success because its brought the young people back again," added Keith. "In the 'All Over Now' era, we were getting adults filling up half the theatre and it was getting all draggy and quiet.

"We were in danger of becoming respectable! But now the new wave has arrived, rushing the stage just like old times!"

"Young people are measuring opinion with new yardsticks and it must mean greater individual freedom of expression," he continued.

"Pop music will have its part to play in all this. When certain American folk artists with important messages to tell are no longer suppressed maybe we will arrive nearer the truth.

"The lyrics of 'Satisfaction' were subjected to a form of critical censorship in America. This must go. Lennon's recent piece of free speech was the subject of the same bigoted thinking. But the new generation will do away with all this – I hope," Keith concluded.

Keith and Brian also revealed that the girls acting in their movie, "Only Lovers Left Alive," will be unknowns, so that fans will be able to identify with the girls in the movie.

There will also be changes in the important motorcycle scenes of the film.

"The difficulty with motor-bikes in Britain is that the rockers have given them an evil image," Keith explained. "They've made them like factory hooters–you could say that the rockers have killed the motor-bike for Britain."

So instead, the Stones plan to substitute convertible sports cars for the motorcycles, or motor-bikes as they say in Britain.

KRLA ARCHIVES

Letters To The Editor
(Continued from Page 2)

BEAT Really Worth It!

Dear BEAT:
First, I've got to congratulate you on being the only teen newspaper or magazine worth subscribing to.
Now, I've got some questions and I sure hope you can answer them: 1) What address are letters to The BEAT staff supposed to be sent to? 2) Does Davy Jones of the Monkees know how to play the guitar? Did Davy attend an Army-Navy Academy at any time during 1966?
Thank you very much for your time and I hope you can answer my questions since answers would help very much in unraveling a mystery-thingy I've run into that would take too much room in your wonderful newspaper to explain.

Carol

First off, thanks for your congratulatory note. As for your questions—you may write to The BEAT at either 6290 Sunset Blvd., Hollywood, 28, California 90028 or #1 Nob Hill Circle, San Francisco, California. 2) Yes. 3) No.

The Editor

Wow! Stones

Dear BEAT:
I read Lyn's letter in the October 8th issue of The BEAT. I didn't agree with her all of the way.
All the Rolling Stones' songs have been great hits! This is the reason that when the Stones roll by they gather lots of fans for keeps.
I must agree that the "Aftermath" is a genuine treasure. Especially "Goin' Home" and "Under My Thumb." I'm sure with the rest of the Rolling Stones' fans that the "Aftermath" will be the greatest album of the year!
I had the pleasure of seeing the Stones perform this summer in Bakersfield, California, and believe me, the Stones give you your money's worth. Keep up the great work, Mick, Keith, Brian, Bill and Charlie.

Gloria Lopez

Where Do They Cut?

Dear BEAT:
Can you please tell me the name and address of the company the Beatles record under in England. I would appreciate any information you can give me.
Thank you.

Diane Giannini

The Beatles record for EMI in England. The address is 20 Manchester Square, London, England.

The Editor

MORE ELVIS

Dear BEAT:
Your newspaper is great but how's about more pictures, stories and etc. on our man Elvis— and I do mean Elvis Presley.
Thanks—I'll be looking for him in your next issues.

Anna Marie

BEAT Neglects Beatles, Stones?

Dear BEAT:
The BEAT is a really groovy magazine (newspaper) for the price and all the stuff it has in it. But please explain one thing to me. How come "brand" new groups like the Monkees, Association, etc., etc. get so much space in your paper? And the Beatles who used to really turn out some good music get more attention than ever.
Now, for instance, take the Stones—they have the best onstage act I've ever seen in my life. I don't think that any other group can create such wild audience reaction as the Stones can.
Not to mention their seven albums, which all rock-out. I don't think you do them justice at all in your magazine. So, please print more on them. They deserve it.

Noble Richardson

Cute Angel

Dear BEAT:
My girlfriend showed me your paper and I saw that article about Jimmy Angel. Tell us more, more, more. And if he sounds as good as Elvis!!!
When can we get his record? And where? I can't wait! Does he have a fan club? We think he's cuter than Elvis or Ricky Nelson.

Robin Dore
Marge Clark

Jimmy will have a record out in the very near future and in the meantime you can write to his fan club at 426 North Haviland, Whittier, California.

The Editor

Dreams Are A Gas

Dear BEAT:
I would like to say a few words to a certain R.D., who was the scribe of the letter "Changed Attitudes" in the October 8 BEAT.
R.D., you're a fool. You can't say John doesn't know anything about Christianity, when he is, and has, read quite extensively on the subject.
Your whole letter is a jumbled lot of contradictions. How? I mean really, how can you say you love a group no matter what and then turn around and call one of its members mentally ill?
So George wed—more power to him. I hope he is very happy and has all the kids he wants. So, he broke hearts and caused tears. The tears shed were a lot in joy and for some as a subconscious joy. Those shed out of anger or disappointment are those that belong to the chicks living in a dream.
Dreams are a gas but there is a limit. WOW! What did you expect him to do, tell Pattie to cool it because there are a million and one fans' hearts broken and tears shed? He loves her and, man, you just have to face this.
The Beatles will never be as they were at first. It's a mental as well as physical impossibility. Just like you can't be the same now as when you were five.
No, John's words don't influence me and I am a Beatlemaniac, nor do they influence my friends who also dig the Beatles. We have minds of our own and anything John or anyone else for that matter says is carefully judged and then decided upon. He doesn't use his fans to "push" over his ideas. If he wanted to do that he wouldn't have apologized for the Jesus bit.
The Beatles have said some pretty mean things about the U.S. but then the U.S. has been quite narrow-minded about some issues involving the Beatles and I needn't mention them.
R.D., you're living in another world and I pity you. You will never see the Beatles "as they were once" and they won't help. I hope for your sake this gets printed, and for others like R.D. For you've got to come to realization and now is as good a time as any.

Georgia Reuss

Hollies On Clark Tour

The Hollies have announced tentative plans to join Dick Clark's touring package of musicians in the United States this fall. The tour begins Nov. 11 and lasts 16 days.

The group, currently in the U.S. on a tour of their own, has raided U.S. charts with their hit, "Bus Stop," which was within this countries top five best-sellers.

The Hollies' present tour was threatened before the group ever left London. Issue of work permits came only hours before the group departed for the U.S.

It now appears plans for the Hollies' first Hollywood film have been nullified. "It looks as though this door is now closed," said a Hollies' agent.

'in' people are talking about...

"Dandy" being too dandified for the English ... Whether or not, now that they have a hit, the Music Machine will be able to afford two gloves apiece, and why their organist insists on being different ... Just exactly what song Gale Garnett unearthed and found to be as psychedelic as they come ... Dylan, and if a certain New York source was correct when he said the folk idol has half his head shaved, considering he won't make any personal appearances until next March ... The Turtles including BEAT as a permanent part of their act.
PEOPLE ARE TALKING ABOUT "Good Vibrations" giving just that to non-BB fans and knowing that Brian finally found a way to use the organ he got for Christmas ... What really inspired the Left Bank to write "Walk Away Renee" or were they joking with a BEAT reporter ... Diana Ross weighing 150 pounds like she told a Las Vegas audience ... What the Count V think of Gale ... The Daily Flash saying BEAT hates long hair, when among four staffers we measured over 79 inches worth.
PEOPLE ARE TALKING ABOUT the expression on Walt Disney's face when he sees Hayley playing a married woman. And he wouldn't even let her have but one on-screen kiss! ... Purple People Eaters and Little Blue Men and wishing they could hear them on the airways just once more, not to mention welcoming a visit from the friendly Witch Doctor ... What the Mothers of Invention were really saying on the LP and how to fix a phonograph so as to hear ... Mick Jagger and the wild sound he has on "Out Of Our Heads" at 45.
PEOPLE ARE TALKING ABOUT Henry Mancini writing a letter to an English magazine, which features rock and roll no less ... Lee Mallory being a nice guy with a friendly "hello" for all ... Olink buttons and the Associate who wears them ... Is it true Terry changed airplane seats when a woman wrinkled her nose at the button he was wearing? ... Whether eating too much pineapple turns hair green, or was the Honolulu rock group at the Whiskey putting everyone on.
PEOPLE ARE TALKING ABOUT the Everpresent Fullness wearing shoes and whether or not that makes them soleful ... Lou Rawls and black pepper, wondering which goes better with dinner. What would happen if Sandy K. cut a record — might be one way to make a hit ... Mamas and Papas back to England, figuring the English might just want to adopt Michelle ... Bye Bye Birdie bidding a final, corny goodbye to the pop scene after it's TV run ... The former USC football hero and student body president playing one of the Swine on the Monkees. BEAT being required reading at the largest California university and wondering what that will do to our subscriptions.
PEOPLE ARE TALKING ABOUT Barry at the Whisky and Barry cutting a record and wondering about Barry in general ... Sunset Strip suffering from over-exposure publicity-wise, and if it will become like the Village ... Mod being out, according to big department stores who have Carnaby Street clothing sections and believing they were just a little put-on all the way around ... Midwest surfers, hippies and mods, and whether they exist in Ruthven, Iowa ... Why Tommy Roe's friends call him Zip Zap ... Letting BEAT know what kind of walk Eden took.
PEOPLE ARE TALKING ABOUT the Purify Brothers being cousins and not brothers ... Pet trying to figure out who she is. Have You Seen Your Airplane, Mother, Standing In The Sky?, which is what you might come out with if you listen to the beginnings of both disks ... Pandora's Golden Heebee Jeebees, by none other than the Association, probably recorded live at Safeway, like we suggested.

Manfreds In Royal Show

The Manfred Mann will have the most elite audience of their careers in a concert at the Monte Carlo Opera House that will be attended by Prince Rainier and Princess Grace.

The show, which is part of the British Week festivities in the Principality, will take place Dec. 10. Julie Felix will be the only other artist in the program.

KRLA ARCHIVES

Yardbirds Coming Stateside Once More

The Yardbirds, who have been plagued with more than their fair share of problems, are returning to the U.S. to play independent dates as well as joining Dick Clark's Caravan Of Stars.

The announcement of the Yardbirds' return came as quite a shock because their last American tour was not exactly a resounding success due primarily to Jeff Beck's tonsil problem which resulted in the cancellation of several Yardbird dates.

Minus Jeff

And for the most part the dates which the Yardbirds did play were without Jeff. Jimmy Page and Chris Dreja did an admirable job of taking over for Jeff but fans who saw the Yardbird performances were visibly disppointed when the curtain parted and Jeff Beck failed to appear.

However, the Yardbirds are giving it one more try. This time with Jeff in tow. Their independent dates include Worcester, Massachusetts; San Francisco, California; Lima, Ohio; and Westport, Connecticut.

The majority of their U.S. stay will be as headliners on the Caravan of Stars. The Clark tour will take the Yardbirds to Amarillo, Texas; Harlingen, Texas; Corpus Christi, Texas; Beaumont, Texas; Alexandria, Louisiana; Magnolia, Arkansas; Decatur, Alabama; Little Rock, Arkansas; Kansas City, Kansas; Bartlesville, Oklahoma; Tulsa, Oklahoma; Chanute, Kansas; Davenport, Iowa; Terre Haute, Indiana; St. Louis, Missouri; Indianapolis, Indiana; Akron, Ohio; Athens, Ohio; Baltimore, Maryland; Prestonburgh, Kentucky; Bowling Green, Kentucky; Cookville, Tennessee; Martin, Tennessee; Detroit, Michigan; Richmond, Indiana; Pittsburgh, Pennsylvania; Beckley, West Virginia; Charleston, West Virginia; Winston Salem, North Carolina; Washington, D.C.; and Huntington, West Virginia.

It's notable that the Yardbirds will *not* appear in Southern California in either a Caravan show or an independent date. However, it is not difficult to ascertain why the Yardbirds will not perform in Los Angeles or San Diego.

First off, Dick Clark refuses to pull his Caravan into Los Angeles because when he has done so in the past the attendance has been low. It's a worn-out town, used to demanding and receiving the top names in the entertainment business. Anything less than the cream of the crop will not draw anywhere near capacity crowds.

The last time Clark put the Caravan into Southern California it was at Melodyland in Anaheim. The show, while entertaining and fast-paced, did not sell-out and probably was chalked up as a loser in Dick's book of winners.

Therefore, it is highly unlikely that the Caravan will again appear anywhere around Los Angeles.

Bomb

The Yardbirds took an independent date to play the Santa Monica Civic during their last visit to L.A. But they probably will not do it again. The concert did not sell-out and the Yardbirds themselves failed to put on the kind of show which their fans are accustomed to seeing from them.

The Yardbirds were set to play a gig in San Diego during August but due to Jeff's tonsils the show was cancelled. It was something the Yardbirds had no control over, perhaps, but still it left a bad taste in the mouth of those who had purchased tickets to the show.

... BRENDA LEE LOOKS AT DAVID MCCALLUM while David looks into space and two Yardbirds, Jim and Jeff, look at each other. The group is awaiting their cue to go before the television cameras on the National Arthritis Foundation telecast. The Yardbirds are due to soon return to the U.S. for a giant tour.

McCoys Named Teen Ambassadors By The Heart Association

NEW YORK: The McCoys, official Teen-Age Ambassadors of the American Heart Association, this week offered their fans an educational pamphlet put out by the American Heart Association. The pamphlet is a cigarette quiz aimed at teenagers.

The pamphlet, which asks "What's Your IQ On Smoking?" answers 12 questions which teens should ask themselves when they consider whether or not to start smoking.

The McCoys are the first contemporary pop group ever to be officially named Heart Ambassadors by the American Heart Association and have already given out 2,000 copies of the pamphlet which has been so well received that an additional 3,000 copies are now being printed up for distribution through radio and television stations as well as for continued use by the McCoy's fan clubs and before and after the group's personal appearances.

By now everyone is aware of the Medical Association's announcement that smoking can be linked to lung cancer. However, not many are aware that the death rate from heart attacks is definitely higher among cigarette smokers than among non-smokers.

The pamphlet in addition to asking 12 questions also answers them and in this way the Heart Association hopes to acquaint teens with the dangers of smoking. The pamphlet does not condemn smoking—it is aimed only at presenting the facts and causing teens to carefully think it over before they decide to smoke.

Some of the subjects discussed in the pamphlet are whether cigarettes hurt teens, whether filters make cigarettes safe, the risk involved in smoking if you do not inhale, the problem of gaining weight when smoking is stopped and the report to the Surgeon General of the United States Public Health Service on "Smoking and Health."

Ike & Tina Revue Extended 10 Days

Ike and Tina Turner, longtime favorites in England, were so successful on their first British tour that it was extended ten days.

The duo and their revue performed mostly one-nighters throughout the island, and appeared with the Troggs on Ready-Steady-Go, England's smash Friday night TV rock show.

During their stay, the husband-wife team released two singles for the English market. The first, "Goodbye, So Long," was released in the States a long time ago. The second, "A Love Like Yours," was withdrawn from the English release schedule, but then reinstated and finally issued.

Also issued was an album, "River Deep, Mountain High," which will not be released in the States.

Ike and Tina, plus the Ikettes and the rest of the 19-member revue, performed with the Stones and Yardbirds during their stay. Ike and Tina are married and have four sons.

... IKE   ... TINA

KRLA ARCHIVES

Highlights Of Sonny & Cher's Tour

Motion picture and recording stars Sonny & Cher returned to Los Angeles this week from a 30-day precedent-setting whirlwind trip to 12 cities and 9 countries in Europe highlighted by an audience with Pope Paul VI and three sold-out charity concerts in London and Paris for the benefit of the Variety Club Children's Fund and Braille Institute for the blind.

The popular couple uniquely eschewed all commercial engagements on their tour and instead financed the entire trip themselves and donated over $40,000 to the underprivileged and blind children in England and France, with funds raised through the charity concerts.

265 Million

Sonny & Cher greeted their European fans in person, via radio and press interviews, and an estimated 265 million persons viewed the colorful pair on top European television shows. They introduced Cher's new album for Imperial Records which includes the title tune from the soundtrack of the motion picture "Alfie." They also introduced their new hit single, "Little Man," which immediately jumped on to the "Top Ten" chart in England, and they talked about their forthcoming motion picture debut in Steve Broidy's production of "Good Times," which will premiere in Europe late this year.

Their first stop on the month-long trek was London where the popular singers were hosted to a round of press conferences and parties attended by no less than Frank Sinatra, Mia Farrow and Academy Award-winner Lee Marvin. The London highlight was their two complete concert performances given the same evening, at the Astoria Theater, Finsbury Park, for the benefit of the Variety Club's Children's Fund.

Sonny & Cher continued on from London to Amsterdam, Hamburg, Hanover, Bremen, Stockholm, Helsinki, Oslo, Copenhagen, Paris, Milan and Rome. In Paris, the two artists did a similar sold-out charity concert at the Olympia Music Hall for the Braille Institute for blind children.

Personal Highlight

The personal highlight for Sonny & Cher was their visit in a general audience with Pope Paul VI at Castel Gondolfo, the Pope's summer villa about 30 kilometers outside of Rome. In keeping with the tradition of their audience, Sonny wore a black six button suit, with a white shirt and tie, and Cher wore a black Chanel dress with a wide "middie" collar, white patterned stockings and her hair tied back with a large black bow. Cher also wore the traditional black lace mantilla on her head during the solemn visit with the pontiff. The audience took place at 9:30 a.m. and was the first time any American rock & roll artists had ever been in an audience with the Pope.

Cher's Vogue

Sonny & Cher left Los Angeles for Europe with some 32 pieces of luggage and trunks and their excess baggage charge came to over $5,000 during the entire tour. The stars returned to New York from Rome where they made a 4-day stop-over in order to have world-famous photographer Richard Avedon shoot a 2-day session of top fashion photographs of Cher for an upcoming issue of Vogue Magazine.

Sonny & Cher's tour set off an enormous barrage of press throughout Europe and gained fans for the stars numbered in the millions.

...SONNY & CHER ARRIVE STATESIDE WITH CHER SPORTING A NEW HAIRDO.

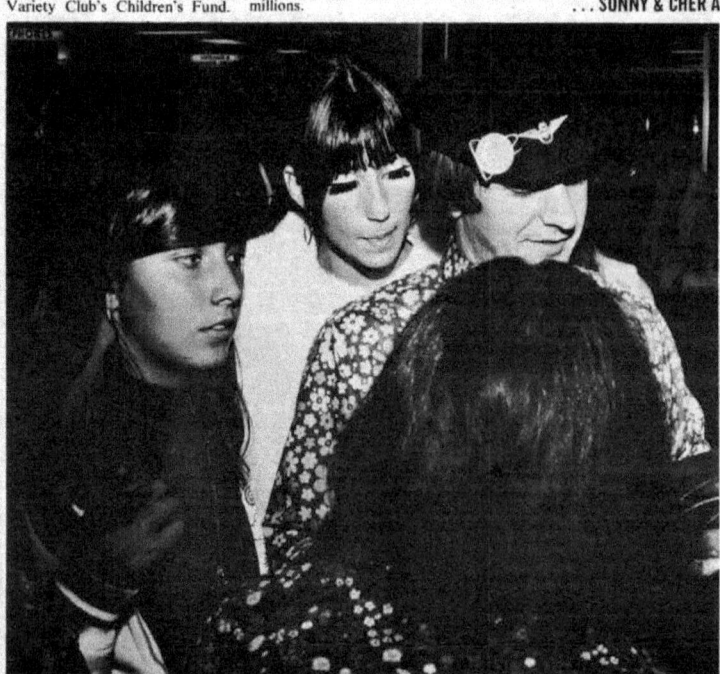

...MINGLING WITH THEIR FANS, SONNY & CHER SIGN AUTOGRAPHS AT KENNEDY INTERNATIONAL.

THE TROGGS HONORED BY AUSTRALIAN BAN?

It wasn't bad enough that the Troggs were faced with legal hang-ups over whether their material belongs to the Fontana or Atco-Atlantic labels here in the United States. Now their latest record is threatened with a total ban in Australia!

The ban in Australia is against Reg Presley's lyrics in "I Can't Control Myself." If the Australian Commercial Broadcasting Federation approves a decision to ban the Troggs' record, it will mark the first time a pop record has been banned by the Government in Australia.

The ban will mean not only that "I Can't Control Myself" will be forced off *all* radio and television stations in Australia but also that the disc may not be sold in record stores.

Speaking for the Troggs, Reg Presley said: "Naturally, we are disappointed but there is no point in getting angry about it." The record has also been met with sharp disapproval in England.

The Troggs may take some comfort from the fact that their fellow Britons, Dave Dee, Dozy, Beaky, Mick and Tich, are encountering their share of record problems in America.

The group with the totally unpronouncible name released a record Stateside titled "Bend It." However, the disc was banned by quite a few radio stations in the U.S. due to "suggestive lyrics."

Rather than take a chance of total censorship, Dave Dee, Dozy, Beaky, Mick and Tich have re-recorded "Bend It" with an entirely new set of lyrics for release in the U.S.

Tapes to be used of the group singing the controversial "Bend It" on American television shows had to be re-done in order to synchronize the new lyrics with the Troggs' actions on the tapes.

The whole mess only goes to show that the recording business is anything but peaceful—especially with many radio stations pulling out their "banning" sticks.

KRLA ARCHIVES

PICTURES in the NEWS

IT'S HARD TO BELIEVE BUT big bands are going rock 'n' roll! At least, one of them is. The world's first amplified orchestra debuted at the famous Royal Tahitian club last week. Here Bill Page, of Lawrence Welk fame, adjusts the amplifiers before the show. Says Mr. Page: "Amplification reduces the size of sound and at the same time each instrument has greater clarity and control." Sponsored by Jordon Amplifiers, it features amplified trumpet, trombone, tenor sax, baritone sax, soprano sax, clarinet, flute, electric piano and the drums.

THE RIGHTEOUS BROTHERS, Bobby and Bill, have long been one of the most popular duos in the recording business. Starting out in the teen market, it didn't take them long to graduate to the top clubs in the nation. But now they're going one step further and will make a movie for MGM! It's a one picture deal but if it goes over well there's a very good chance that the popular "Brothers" will make even more.

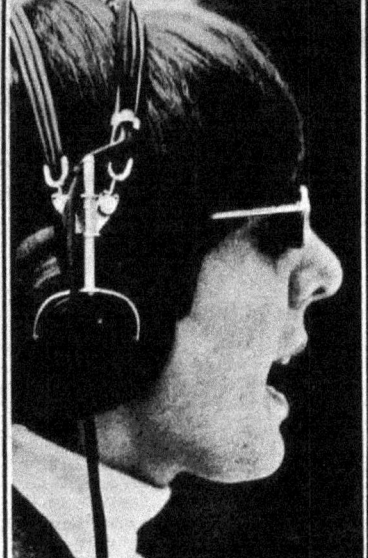

THE MONKEES ARE DEFINITELY GOING the movie route this summer, says Jackie Cooper, Screen Gems executive. The film will be made by Columbia but none of the details are yet available, though it is almost certain to follow in the footsteps of their popular television series format. A December 3 date has been set for the Monkees to appear in Oahu, Hawaii. On the record scene, the Monkees' "Last Train To Clarksville" is well into the nation's top ten singles and their album, "The Monkees," is making rapid progress in its bid to reach the top.

EVER WONDER WHAT SINGERS DO AFTER A SHOW? Well, wonder no more—they attend parties! And here's proof. Joey Paige, Eddie Brigati (of the Young Rascals) and Lou Christie take time out of the party happenings to grin into the camera for us. Lou is currently keeping himself busy running around the country doing personal appearances, Joey's been spending his time in the Marine Reseves and Eddie and his fellow Rascals are kept busy performing gigs on the East Coast.

KRLA ARCHIVES

Associates At It Again: Interviewing Themselves

By Jamie McCluskey III

As you may recall, some months ago this reporter ran into a short spell of extreme and uninterrupted *laziness* — which resulted in my "fudging of assigned duties" and allowing the members of the Association to simply interview *themselves!*

It all worked out very well actually — even The Boss was pretty cool about it, and I only had to wash *14* of the *21* windows in our 5th floor suite . . . from the *outside* — but there *was* one rather unfortunate consequence.

Associate Terry Kirkman somehow lost out on the whole deal. *I* still maintain that it was *his* fault entirely, 'cause he disappeared at just the moment when he was supposed to be quietly sitting in a corner conducting an in-depth interview with none other than *himself!*

Howsomever

Howsomever . . . in a concerted attempt to smooth over Terry's still ruffled feathers, I have finally given in and asked him to go ahead and interview himself. *But*, being basically sneaky — when his back was turned (to the corner where he was quietly conducting an in-depth interview with himself), I quietly asked each of his fellow Associates to make *marginal comments* on his interview!

So, following you will find Terry's interview, and sneaking along right behind that will be some of the carefully chosen critical remarks of his closest friends and *Associates*.

AUTOBIOGRAPHICAL NOTES — BY TERRY KIRKMAN:

Screaming yaggy voo I crossed the many borders between Kansas and California arriving here at 2 (years not o'clock).

Wallowing

Wallowing in the effort to escape my mid-western influences I finally splashed, wearing golashes, into the epitome of plasticity, Hollywood, at age 22 and was soon engulfed in the Association syndrome. I like the Association a lot, the Association likes a lot, and fortunately, a lot like the Association. We like *The BEAT* too. See, we're liberal. Are you?

"Are You"

Isaac Cohen, N.Y.C. cab driver influenced me greatly, with great relief, with his awareness of people and his general philosophy — After driving his cab for 34 years he still loves people particularly the young — Isaac Cohen believes in the young — all is not lost. Are you?

All in all no one could ask for more stimulating company than "the Pig," "the Brank," "the freak," "the Green Kid," or "the Birdman." We have nothing in common other than our desire to be honest with people and entertain — Amen!

Associates

GARY ALEXANDER:
I think we should all do a *latihan*.

TED BLUECHEL Jr.:
I only want mustard, onions, and relish on it!

JIM YESTER:
Yea, verility! As ye reap so shall ye rap! In the words of the immortal zilch, Gaye Ho!

JAMIE McCLUSKEY III:
EEEEEEEEEEEEE!!!!!!!!!!!

...TERRY KIRKMAN

...RUSS GIGUERE   ...TED BLUECHEL

...GARY ALEXANDER

...JIM YESTER

...BRIAN COLE

...KNICKERBOCKERS (L. to R.) Jimmy, Beau, Johnny, Buddy.

Knickerbockers Doing The Mod

By Mike Tuck

This article could be entitled "How To Win Teens and Influence People," or, "It's A Mod, Mod, Mod World."

The last exponents of gold-plated cuff links have turned their heads. Two-button suits are minus their last four defenders in the pop music world. Hair stylists have lost their final stronghold.

The Knickerbockers have changed scenery; they are now full-fledged modsters.

"It's been so long since I've seen a barber," Jimmy Walker was saying, "I've forgotten what one looks like." His hidden ears bore him out.

Mod Attire

The Knickerbockers' coat and tie days have ended. Mod attire — everything from flashy turtle-neck shirts to bell bottom trousers — have replaced their traditional continental suits and ties.

They're beginning to look like a pop group.

They had always performed and sounded like a top pop group, but their "clean cut" image had taken its toll.

"On our first tour," Buddy Randell recalled, "we seemed to go over real well with the audience but after the show, kids would approach us and ask, 'gee, why don't you guys have long hair?'"

"But on our last tour — to the South — people really seemed to dig the way we looked."

At what point would their hair become too long? "Our hair was always too long," Beau Charles answered. "As far as some people are concerned, anytime you don't have a crew cut your hair is 'too long.'"

The Knickerbockers' switch to London apparel has been more of a grasp for freedom than anything.

"We feel more comfortable in the clothes we wear now," said John Charles. "We're not as stiff and it's a lot easier to rock out."

The Knickerbockers have never had any noticeable trouble "rocking out." Their stage acts have always been periods of frenzied showmanship — the four participants in their own little groove yet still harmonizing.

"We were never really a quiet group. But because we looked conservative," Jimmy explained, "people naturally assumed our personalities were the same way."

With their new image, the Knickerbockers are not only aiming at the teen audience, but at adult night club assemblages as well. But if they have a preference between the two, they aren't giving it.

They are basically a teen group, but their harmony and musical skills have made them an attraction before older audiences.

"You can actually get away with more garbage with adults," said Beau. "Adults in clubs are different . . . they're wilder. They haven't cultivated a real taste for rock music so they dig anything with a good beat."

"A lot of times after a performance in a night club some guy will come up and say 'Ya know, I don't normally like rock 'n roll, but you guys are really good,'" said Buddy.

Bridging Gap

Successfully bridging the gap between the two audiences has led to part of the Knickerbockers' musical success.

Yet their music has never lost its sharp teen edge. Their first release, "Lies," sold more than 500,000 copies and has since become a standard with most rock groups.

They now have a new record on the charts, "Love Is A Bird," which amazingly was within the top 100 best-sellers only a week after its release.

Their style is all their own. On stage, however, they do realistic imitations of everybody from the Righteous Brothers to the Supremes.

KRLA ARCHIVES

THE BIG MAMA speakin' her mind!

By Barri

CASS ELLIOT: the *Big Mama*, the talented young lady who has stolen away the hearts and *ears* of thousands, the red-hot, rip-roarin', rock 'n rollin' Mama who belts the beat songs out like nobody's business.

In the last few months, Cass has gone from blissful anonymity to blossoming animosity, all by way of several hit records sung in harmony with one more Mama, two Papas, too.

Almost over-night, Cass has been confronted by a *new* kind of friend – the kind that comes *en masse*, in quantities of thousands bearing loyal fanship, and Cass has had to find a new understanding for this kind of friendship phenomena.

"I've met a couple of people who have said, 'I wish you'd meet my daughter – she'd really love to meet you!' or, 'I'd really like to meet you myself, and it's such a great thing for me.'

Dig 'Em

"I think – knowing how *I* felt about John Lennon – it enables me to *really* say, 'hello' to those kids, and not just stand there and be *fawned* over. I don't know whether years and years of tremendous fame will change my mind about that, but if somebody really digs you that much – boy, you *have* to dig them. If they really want to meet you that much, then you really want to meet them too. It sounds corny, but it's really true!"

Quite a flower, in the musical world now, Cassandra began blooming back in Baltimore, Maryland, September 19, 1943. As a child, she moved around a great deal with her family, and attended a number of different junior and high schools.

Her early musical training wasn't exactly extensive – "I studied piano from the time I was six – until I was *seven*," and today she denies any ability to read music, only picking out an occasional melody on the piano or the guitar.

Late Interest

With the normal childhood exception of wanting to be a "movie star," Cass recalls no burning aspirations which guided her formative years, explaining that she didn't really develop an active interest in show business until she was about 17-years-old.

In the meantime, she travled with her family, spent two months in a Washington university, and studied French for a year in night school. It was between her junior and senior year in high school, during the summer while she was studying French, that she had her first whiff of "grease paint."

"My best girlfriend was in a summer stock company and she didn't have a car and I did. So, after I finished at night school, I would drive out and pick her up.

"I started hanging out there on week-ends, and I met a guy there who was one of the juvenile leads and we started dating. When the season was supposed to close, they had done so well they decided to extend the season for another four weeks by doing one more play, and they needed sombody to play it – so I did it. It was a small part – I only had about four speaking lines!"

It was after her graduation from high school that Cass first thought seriously about becoming an actress, but that was a very short-lived dream.

"I stopped acting when my father died. I'd been in New York, and I was struggling, and my father died. He was ill so I had to come home. Things hadn't been going too well for me in New York anyway, I hadn't really *found my place*, so to speak, and I stayed home for a few months.

"Then I went on the road with the 'Music Man' in the Second National Company, and while I was on the road I met a very wise old lady who was in the show, who told me that I couldn't get very far without a college education, so I decided that I would go to college.

"I came back and went to the American University and I met a guy there named Tim who said, 'why don't you sing folk music, *or get out of town!*' So, I got out of town – went to Chicago – and sang folk music!"

From folk music, Cass sang her way out of and into a great many towns, and eventually into a group called the "Mama's and Papa's" and a spot called "Number One."

The M's and P's have established a certain trend in harmony in today's pop music, and already their unique vocal stylings are being widely copied.

Cass looks around her at the other things going on in pop, and comments on what might be coming next. "I don't know – but whatever it is, it's going to be musical. I don't think there's much room now for more gimmicks. I think people are more interested in what's going on.

"Our major concern has always been the music, and of course, the harmonies that we use in everything, the counterpoint, and things like that. So, I don't think that our views on harmony are going to change much. I mean, they might get a little more radical, a little more far out, as the music gets more far out – as it sometimes does – but I don't think we're going to pay any more attention to it than we do now, because we pay *so much* attention to it *now!*"

Farther Out

The music of the Mama's and Papa's probably *will* get a little farther out, a little farther *out* of the "norm" of pop music, and a good deal farther *into* the unusual and exceptional of *great* music. It will probably do this under the guidance of the sometimes-bearded, always be-capped, frequently oblivious, generally brilliant producer-mentor of the group, Lou Adler, in cooperation with the brilliant songwriting talents of John, and the exceptional vocal abilities of all four.

BEAT Photo: Chuck Boyd

KRLA ARCHIVES

...BEACH BOYS—All six of them showed up for this picture. Or were they corralled by Kimmi Kobashigawa and auctioned off as interviewers?

Beach Boys: *Instant Insanity*

By Kimmi Kobashigawa

It was a night like many other nights (where have we heard *that* before?!), except for the fact that I was attending a Beach Boys recording session on this particular evening.

I was going to also do what is commonly referred to in "cool" circles as an *interview* . . . but if anything, the BBV ended up interviewing *me!* Not to mention themselves, just about everything else in sight!

We got off to a really marvelous start when I asked bearded, furcapped Mike Love to describe the group's humor for us.

Good Humor

"I would like to talk to you about the group's humor," proclaimed Michael proudly, to which Bruce Johnston immediately added: "It's *good* humor . . . would you like a drumstick?!"

Michael groaned and continued: "That's a *splendid* example of the group's humor—it's inane, laugh-a-minute jocularity, carries us from the sands of Malibu, lolling on the beach by bikini-clad dolls, all the way to the mountains' heights where we filmed our classic tape to go along with one of our other million-selling hits . . . 'Mickey's Monkey!"

Bruce was lolling hysterically in the corner while Carl was reclined on the couch observing the whole scene.

Water Fights

I asked whether or not the boys played practical jokes on one another while on tour. In a bass voice extracted from somewhere deep within his cocoa-colored ski sweater, Mike informed me: "No—we just have water fights! Sometimes the water fights get a little rough!

"Sometimes we use toilet water, if we feel *nasty*—and if we feel *devilish*, a little *ice* water, or sometimes *scalding hot* water—if it's cold weather. There's art to water fights these days!"

Then Chief Beach Boy, Brian Wilson, clad in his fashionable blue-and-green competition-stripe *whatever*, appeared from behind a machine, wearing a pair of someone else's sunglasses, which prompted Mike to ask him for an interview.

Full Consent

Brian graciously consented and ace reporter Mike Love conducted the following in-depth interview:

"Have there been any changes in your music since 'Luau,' Brian?" "No," replied Brian, at length. Undaunted, Mike forged ahead. "There have been a lot of inquiries from the State Department, wondering if we'd do a tour on behalf of the 50th State, Hawaii, becoming involved in the States.

"You know, not *every* foreign nation actually knows that Hawaii is a *State* of the United States, and not just a domain or a territory, or a holding of the United States. So they were wondering if we'd do a tour of the Soviet satellites."

Way Too Big

"I'm *way* too big to even *consider* that," Brian explained. Mike decided to follow that line of thought for a moment, and promptly tripped over the very next question! "Do you believe that the Beach Boys are too big, or yourself are too great, for involvement in national and international affairs?"

Brian gave this a degree of thought, and replied, "It's going to be a while before we find out where we're at ourselves." "Oh" exclaimed Mike, in surprise and great interest. "Well," he continued brightly, "is that popular among the singing groups of the day—finding out just *where they're at?*"

Brian replied: "Exactly!" Like a good reporter, Mike attempted to pin Brian down to a more specific answer. "Could you elaborate just a *little bit* and tell me exactly what is the connotation of the obvious parenthetical, 'where it's at?'"

Speaking more directly, Brian explained: "First of all, it's a shame that you had to ask that question!" His feathers slightly ruffled, Mike asked, "Oh! Am I to understand that you're being *derogatory?*"

"No," replied Brian sincerely. "It's just a shame." "Do you think it's slightly demeaning (whatever *that* is!) of me to ask the question, or do you think that I am—as you would say—quote, 'straight'?"

Mike was interrupted here by a loud blast of music, being played back on a tape the boys had just completed recording, which immediately caused Brian to throw a violent explosion of temper around him, and he severely chastized the engineer for having interfered with our interview! "You've just ruined it! You've ruined our tape!" he cried, pointing at our trusty *BEAT* tape recorder.

Tape Session

This caused Mike to suddenly turn a serious face to our microphone in order to inform us: "For those of you who don't know— these frantic interruptions are because we are right in the middle of a real-live Beach Boy tape-cutting session . . . which is quite different from a vocal session!"

BEAT Reporter-for-an-hour, Mike Love, queried: "Brian, I understand you used to be a dance instructor at Mae Murray's. Is that right?"

Brian replied that he used to tap dance . . . on his toes! but had to give it up. Mike sympathized with him, explaining for our benefit: "Yes, Brian broke his toes. You should *see* his toes!—they look like a Black Belt Karate expert, they're so all-broken up from dancing on them!"

In a fit of passion, Brian grabbed the microphone away from Mike and conducted a little interview of his own. Turning to Al (who had somehow managed to hide out quietly in the corner beneath a chair all this time), he said, "Al—tell me a little bit about your shoes." "They're great!" Al offered. "They've got 'sole'!" Bruce added. "Awwwwwwwwwww!!" groaned the remainder of the Beach Boys in unison.

Finding the whole thing a bit difficult to believe, I grabbed my tape recorder and headed for the nearest looking-glass back to sanity . . . *I think!*

BRIAN WILSON was reported to have uttered a loud "Mooo" after this photo session. Due, of course, to his genuine cowhide vest!!

NEW!! HAIR CONTROL FOR MEN WITH MOIST SPRAY ACTION

Shape Up

WITH MOIST SPRAY ACTION FOR HAIR CONTROL ALL DAY!

Now a moist grooming aid especially developed for a man's hair. SHAPE UP combines "Sure Control" with a naturalness and convenience never before available in a man's grooming aid. SHAPE UP is a new protein base formula . . . contains no lacquers, or shellac and is completely water soluable.

For neat, groomed, healthy looking hair use this Special Offer!
Reg. $1.50
With Coupon Only **$1.00**
Incl. tax & postage

Shape Up
The BEAT
6290 Sunset, No. 504
Los Angeles, Calif. 90028

Please send me _____ cans Shape Up at $1.00 each. I enclose $ _____ in cash, check or money order.

Name _____
Adress _____
City _____ State _____ Zip _____

KRLA ARCHIVES

Neil Diamond's Searching For Tone

By Louise Criscione

Those who start young are more apt to make it since they've more time to profit from their errors. Such a person is Neil Diamond. Apparently placing great faith in the "early start" theory, Neil began writing songs while he was still in high school in Brooklyn. "I got a job for $50 a week writing songs for other people," reveals the darkly handsome Neil.

"I used to go to my office with school books under my arm. All I thought about was songwriting, even when I was in school. I used to sit in class and write down songs while my teachers thought I was taking notes. You know what happened? I passed all my courses but one. I flunked music!"

Three Weeks

Actually, Neil's musical ability began to take shape long before he ever reached high school. He started to play the guitar when he was 12 years old. And as early as that, the young Mr. Diamond began to project his independence. "I took lessons for about three weeks and then quit," he says. "They wanted to teach me notes. I wanted to learn to play from the heart and this they could never teach me."

However, by the time he had matured to the age of 14 he had given concrete thought to the value of music lessons and so started studying piano. "I took lessons for a month, much longer than the guitar. I gave up the lessons when I felt I had achieved the virtuosity necessary for my future career. And then I took up the comb and wax paper," laughs Neil.

Searching

They say everyone has his own special quirk, and independent though Neil may be, he admits to having his too. Accordingly, Neil changes pianos more often than most people change cars. "I'm searching for a tone and I haven't found it yet. I buy old upright pianos. I never spend more than $50 for them. Sometimes I just pay to have them moved. They really have the best tone. I've bought as many as 15 in one year. I'm supporting a moving company in New York. They're constantly moving them in and out because I only keep one piano at a time," assures Neil as you mention that his home must be getting a bit crowded what with 15 pianos residing there.

Hang-Up

Neil used to have the same hang-up with guitars until he found the one he uses now. "I saw this big, ugly, black guitar sitting in the window of a pawn shop on the Bowery in New York," says Neil. "It looked so sad there, something like a puppy dog. I didn't have enough money to buy it so I traded in two of my old guitars. I've never been sorry. This is my guitar. It has the sweetest tone you ever heard, just like it was made for me."

With the guitar business amply taken care of, Neil is now pawing his way through warehouses and other such interesting places in a desperate search for just the right piano. To accompany his guitar, no doubt. And he has specific piano rules all laid out. "It must be old. It must be an upright and it can't cost more than $50 to move. I once played an $8,000 concert grand," admitted Neil. "But the piano and I were terrible together. When I play, I play hard. How can you smash up an $8,000 piano?"

A gigantic myth has been perpetuated in the music business. It says that a composer can only write when he is duly inspired. Which is all fine until you take Neil into consideration. He wrote his "Solitary Man" and his equally successful "Cherry, Cherry," not to mention all the hits he has penned for such people as Bobby Vinton, Andy Williams, Jay and the Americans and Ronnie Dove. And there exists no such thing as "inspiration" as far as Neil is concerned.

Not Inspired

"I'm not inspired to write," Neil flatly states. "I write to express an emotion. I was feeling very lonely when I wrote 'Solitary Man.' It was an outgrowth of my despair." Neil goes on to say that he penned the song just for himself and fought against it being recorded. In fact, it took three months of arguing before Neil consented to record "Solitary Man" and even after it was cut he didn't want it released.

You know, of course, that in the end Bang Records won the fight and "Solitary Man" was released. Perhaps in the back (maybe even in the front) of Neil's mind he hoped that the record would never make it, that he'd never be forced to stand before an audience and sing something so personal to a sea of impersonal faces. But he lost. The record became a huge nationwide smash and as he sang it over and over it didn't hurt nearly as much as Neil had feared it would.

Lost It

"It's lost that personal feeling," Neil revealed following the news that "Solitary Man" was indeed a smash. "If you sing an emotional thing enough times it doesn't really mean the same thing anymore. It's a song I love and a song I love to sing but it doesn't stick me everytime I sing it. I'm very happy that they did put it out."

The story was completely reversed when Neil penned "Cherry, Cherry." "When I wrote 'Cherry, Cherry'," Neil says, "I was very happy and wanted the whole world to know." And within weeks of the record's release, practically the whole world *did* know. At least, the world which is addicted to pop music knew.

With the release of Neil's two hits, he found fan clubs sprouting up all across the nation. Letters poured in from every imaginable part of the country begging for pictures and news of this guy who claimed to be a solitary man. Naturally, Neil was elated with the homage being paid to him but at the same time he regarded this whole fan club thing with a somewhat wary eye.

He admitted to himself that he wanted fan clubs but not the run-of-the-mill kind which most artists possess. "I don't just want fans asking for autographed pictures, or news bits about me. I would like my fan clubs to meet with me after my performances. I like them to be there to share with me the elation I feel after a good show. Sometimes it gets lonely after the audience leaves," Neil says.

Lonely

It's hard to imagine someone as good looking and personable as Neil being lonely. But as the realization hits that Neil is, after all, as human as the next person, it's easy to see how Neil can be lonely even when surrounded by crowds.

He attempts, either consciously or unconsciously, to project the image of a serious and rather pensive individual. But the image loses all of its visual impact when Neil begins to talk. He's clever, funny, a tease, able to laugh at himself. His biggest fault, he frankly admits, is his ability to get lost in any city in the world.

Uniquely Neil

But uniquely Diamond, he recognizes his fault and has, through the years, rather learned to enjoy it. "I always get lost in every city. So, if I know I have to be somewhere and it's going to take a half an hour to get there I leave an hour and a half early! That way I know I'm gonna get lost but I enjoy it and see the sights!"

He still has the same ambition he's had since he started. Strangely enough, his big dream is not to have a number one in the nation,

...NEIL POSING IN HIS IMAGE

to earn a Gold Record or to sell-out the Copacabana. It's more difficult than any of those things. Neil wants to go to Russia!

Moscow Show

"What I'd really like to do," explains Neil with obvious enthusiasm, "is a rock 'n' roll show in Moscow because they're so restricted there that I have a feeling they'd really go out of their heads. It's that type of thing for me. It's sort of like when you let a guy out of prison and he sees the sun again.

"Of course, they wouldn't understand a word," says Neil philosophically, "but I'm really going to do that. I'm going to talk to some people and see if they'll let me go. They probably won't but I'm going to ask anyway."

I figure he'll actually make it to Russia someday. With his determination, are you kidding? He could probably make it to the moon before anyone else if he put his mind to it!

KRLA ARCHIVES

WHISKY A GO GO
8901 SUNSET STRIP • 652-4202

OCT. 19-30
Preview sound of their next album

age 18 & up welcome—food & fun till 2am

Cash, Car Given Away By KRLA

With the football campaign in mid-season and the new car season just beginning, KRLA is in the midst of a massive give-away program that involves literally thousands of dollars.

By entering one of KRLA's top contests listeners stand a good chance of winning either $10,000 cash or their favorite 1967 automobile.

The rules for KRLA's football contest are simple: jot down your guess of five weekly football games and send in your forecast to the station.

The contest spotlights five different games from the high school, college and professional ranks each week. The selected games, as well as guesses from KRLA sports director Danny Baxter, are broadcast over the station weekly.

"Each week we receive about 1,000 entries," a spokesman for KRLA said. "So far, we have had a lot of near misses but no one has guessed all five correctly."

Or, if Detroit's 1967 offerings are to your liking, write the name of your favorite automobile on a postcard and send it to the station. KRLA will have a mammoth drawing to determine the winner, who will be presented with his choice of automobiles.

The new car contest has stirred greater response than perhaps any other contest in KRLA history. So far, station officials say Mustang has been the prevalent choice among the thousands of entrees received.

But the choice has, to say the least, been varied. "We even had one request for a 1967 Excellcior" said a station representative.

WHISKY A GO GO
8901 SUNSET STRIP • 652-4202

OCT. 30—SUN. 4 P.M.
There will be

for ALL ages
SPECIAL MATINEE

age 18 & up welcome—food & fun till 2am

A NEW QUARTET? Well, not exactly. They're all accomplished entertainers by themselves but they're appearing together now at The Ice House in Glendale, 234 S. Brand, for a return engagement of the first folk-pop revue on the West Coast. They are, from left, Tim Morgan, Jean Durand, Lenin Castro, guitarist extraordinaire, and Spence, bass player. Whatever you do — make it to the Ice House to see them.

ATTENTION!!!

High Schools, Colleges, Universities and Clubs:

CASEY KASEM MAY BE ABLE TO SERVE YOU!

Let Casey HELP You Put On A Show Or Dance

For information
Contact Casey at:
HO 2-7253

WARREN BEATTY
SUSANNAH YORK

From London to the Riviera, a hair-raising tale of gallant love and truly desperate adventure!

KALEIDOSCOPE

the switched-on thriller !!!

A GERSHWIN-KASTNER PRODUCTION
CLIVE REVILL · ERIC PORTER
Written by ROBERT & JANE-HOWARD CARRINGTON · Produced by ELLIOTT KASTNER · Directed by JACK SMIGHT
TECHNICOLOR® FROM WARNER BROS.

SOON! AT A THEATER OR DRIVE-IN NEAR YOU

THE NEW CLUB TROPICANA
247 E. MANCHESTER, L.A.

For Reservations — 758-7615
TEENAGERS WELCOME

NOW APPEARING
THE GENIUS OF
CHET BAKER
- also -
THE INCOMPARABLE
RAY BRYANT TRIO

KRLA ARCHIVES

Top 40 Requests

1. GOOD VIBRATIONS .... Beach Boys
2. 96 TEARS .... ? and the Mysterians
3. I WANNA BE FREE .... Monkees
4. WALK AWAY RENEE .... Left Banke
5. CHERISH .... Association
6. DANDY .... Herman's Hermits
7. PSYCHOTIC REACTION .... Count Five
8. HOORAY FOR HAZEL .... Tommy Roe
9. RAIN ON THE ROOF .... Lovin' Spoonful
10. LAST TRAIN TO CLARKSVILLE .... Monkees
11. TALK TALK .... Music Machine
12. YOU ARE SHE .... Chad and Jeremy
13. WHY PICK ON ME .... Standells
14. NEXT TIME I SEE YOU .... Robbs
15. WINCHESTER CATHEDRAL .... New Vaudville Band
16. HAVE YOU SEEN YOUR MOTHER, BABY, STANDING
    IN THE SHADOW? .... Rolling Stones
17. STOP STOP STOP .... Hollies
18. I'M YOUR PUPPET .... James and Bobby Purify
19. SEE SEE RIDER .... Eric Burdon and the Animals
20. CAN I GET TO KNOW YOU BETTER .... Turtles
21. POOR SIDE OF TOWN .... Johnny Rivers
22. IF I WERE A CARPENTER .... Bobby Darin
23. CHERRY, CHERRY .... Neil Diamond
24. THE GREAT AIRPLANE STRIKE .... Paul Revere and the Raiders
25. REACH OUT, I'LL BE THERE .... Four Tops
26. BUS STOP .... Hollies
27. OUT OF TIME .... Chris Farlow
28. I JUST DON'T KNOW WHAT TO DO .... Dionne Warwick
29. WORKING IN A COAL MINE .... Lee Dorsey
30. MR. SPACEMAN .... Byrds
31. YOU CAN'T HURRY LOVE .... Supremes
32. SEE YOU IN SEPTEMBER .... Happenings
33. YELLOW SUBMARINE b/w ELEANOR RIGBY .... Beatles
34. LITTLE MAN .... Sonny and Cher
35. PAINT ME A PICTURE .... Gary Lewis and the Playboys
36. WHO AM I .... Petula Clark
37. ALL I SEE IS YOU .... Dusty Springfield
38. LOOK THROUGH MY WINDOW .... Mama's and Papa's
39. WHAT BECOMES OF THE BROKENHEARTED? .... Jimmy Ruffin
40. LOVE COME WHAT MAY .... Randy Fuller

A Beatle Fan Remembers That Day

THE WAY I SEE IT
By Laurie Sercombe

Beatle Days have a habit of falling on Sunday. I think that if I had to choose only one title for that day for the calendar and toss the others into oblivion, I would choose Beatle Day.

Beatle Day began with tradition this year when I awoke on August 28 to the sound of a 200-voice choir singing "The Lord Is Our Rock" on KRLA.

You see, Beatle Day for me starts at about 3:00 in the afternoon, when I don my new face, new dress, and new personality, and become a beauty of much cool.

Being so beautiful and all, I thought it seemed that the only vehicle worthy of my splendor would be a silver Jaguar or perhaps a voluptuous black limousine that would deliver me to the entrance of the stadium while guards held the door for me, and eager children in poor boys and bell-bottoms cried, "Look, look, it's Jane Asher!"

However, being slightly less than my dream, I boarded a bus at 6:00 with numerous commoners and was forced to remain incognito.

In spite of my worldly detachment, even I felt a lovely pang when Dodger Stadium came into sight. My eyes were blazed with excitement under their iridescent lashes and sultry green shadowing, even if it was beginning to run down my chin.

I stalked carefully from the humiliation of mass transport and into the realm of the Beatle Stadium.

I walked on to my seat. Looking out to the field, I broke into laughter at the sight of the large green tent with its blocked label, "DRESSING ROOM."

It reminded me of the part of "Help!" where the word "tiger" was used to aid all dolts in the identification of the animal on the screen. I glanced around expecting to see a sign reading "A stage" or "The grass," or even "A disc jockey."

At 8:00 the concert began. Well, actually it was 8:03, but considering the comparative advantages of KRLA, I am willing to overlook the fact. The Remains began the show. They were loud, that much I can say.

Bobby Hebb made a grand start by tripping on the steps as he climbed to the stage for his act. It wasn't quite as sensational as last year when one of the Headhunters' zippers was down, but it added that little something.

The Cyrkle and then the three Ronettes performed. Several times the already shaky attention of the audience was diverted by such events as the rumor that Jeremy Clyde was lurking somewhere close by.

Finally came the moment when Dave Hull was introduced. After honking his infamous horn into the microphone, he dramatically announced his pleasure in introducing for the third year the man who had made the show possible.

So everyone lined up onstage and tried with some class to do it right. But no one was watching them. All eyes were on the dugout. Simultaneously the Beatles appeared from nothing, and the disc jockeys disappeared into it.

They were great. My binoculars made them large enough to see Paul's tongue moving during the "la la la"s of "Nowhere Man." Oh bliss. Just to assure myself of the reality of the occasion, I aimed my binos at the side of the stage and located Byrd Dave Crosby and wondered if Shirley Poston was out there anywhere.

When George's amplifier needed assistance, everyone nearly went crazy with glee. I guess things like that make the Beatles seem more human. I thought how sad it was that one of them could not fall off the stage or get electrocuted by a microphone or something to *really* add a human touch.

Rats, it was over so quickly. They were gone as quickly as they'd come, waving their towels as they hopped from their golden carriages. There I stood, sweaty, wrinkled, with braces on my teeth, my super-cool fading rapidly. And happy, too.

WHISKY A GO GO
8901 SUNSET STRIP • 652-4202
OCT. 19th–30th
There will be more
LOVE
at the Whisky—
than ever before
age 18 & up welcome–food & fun till 2am

WHISKY A GO GO
8901 SUNSET STRIP • 652-4202
OCT. 19-30
have you been looking for
LOVE
They're here with the
Sons of Adam
age 18 & up welcome–food & fun till 2am

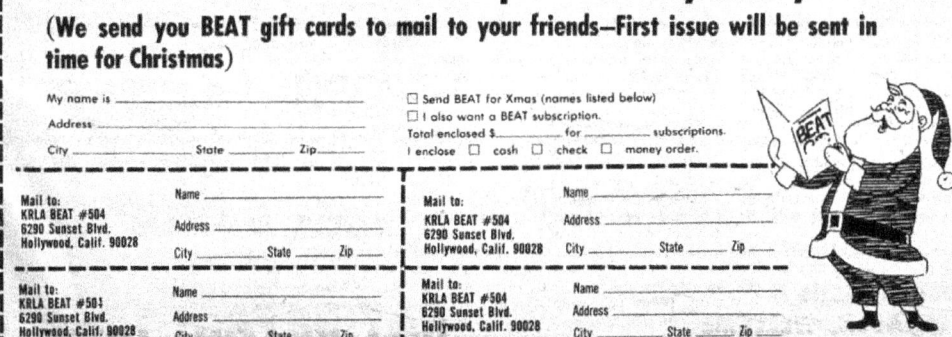

Christmas Cheer Starts HERE

KRLA BEAT Gift Subscription — $3 a year
Each Additional Gift Subscription — only $1 a year

(We send you BEAT gift cards to mail to your friends—First issue will be sent in time for Christmas)

My name is _____
Address _____
City _____ State _____ Zip _____

☐ Send BEAT for Xmas (names listed below)
☐ I also want a BEAT subscription.
Total enclosed $ _____ for _____ subscriptions.
I enclose ☐ cash ☐ check ☐ money order.

Mail to:
KRLA BEAT #504
6290 Sunset Blvd.
Hollywood, Calif. 90028

Name _____
Address _____
City _____ State _____ Zip _____

Mail to:
KRLA BEAT #504
6290 Sunset Blvd.
Hollywood, Calif. 90028

Name _____
Address _____
City _____ State _____ Zip _____

Mail to:
KRLA BEAT #504
6290 Sunset Blvd.
Hollywood, Calif. 90028

Name _____
Address _____
City _____ State _____ Zip _____

Mail to:
KRLA BEAT #504
6290 Sunset Blvd.
Hollywood, Calif. 90028

Name _____
Address _____
City _____ State _____ Zip _____

KRLA ARCHIVES

TEEN PANEL

Teens Making Own Rules?

Several issues ago, during one of the BEAT's panel discussions, one panelist set out to prove a theory.

It was her contention that teenagers are becoming more and more inclined to mae their own decisions where morality is concerned. She felt that whether a teenager followed the existing set of rules, or made up his own, he did so because he chose to, ad not because he felt he had to.

It was also her contention that no two people completely agree on the subject of sex, and that teenagers, who have been tagged an "immoral mass" by some, are nothing of the kind. She felt it was impossible for anyone to categorize that many people, particularly about something so personal, and something where each person differs.

To prove her theory, she suggested and then led a discussion in which four other teens participated and by the close of the conversation, her point had been made.

Disagreed

None of the five agreed; all had different opinions about sex. Some followed the code to the letter. Others had set up their own codes. But all five agreed on one thing—they were following the rules they lived by out of choice, and not out of fear or social pressures.

When this discussion was printed in The BEAT, it caused quite a stir. Her point had been proved, but on a small scale, and five teenagers can't be used as a yardstick to measure the other twenty million.

Many readers (adult and teen alike) have expressed an interest in hearing from other teenagers on this same subject, and the majority were particularly interested in how many teens are making their own rules.

Rather than sponsor another discussion and once again only have the viewpoints of a few participants, we had one of our reporters rove a bit and ask this question: "Do you live by your own standards, or do you follow the established moral code?"

Here are some of the answers we received...

'So Do Adults'

Ric – 17: "I live by a Standard Oil Station. Will that help?"

Virginia – 16: "Yes, I live by my own. So do adults, they just won't admit it."

Lynn – 18: "A lot of the standards I live by are part of the established moral code, but some of them are my own. It has to be that way. Certain things in life are up to you, and no one is qualified to make those decisions except yourself."

Joyce – 18: "I had to make my own set of values. I was brought up in a very strict church that was even against dancing and movies. They were so busy telling each other how to live, they forgot that a church is a place to worship. I finally told my folks I was going to leave home if I couldn't live my own life. We had terrible fights for awhile, but they finally agreed that I was being a hypocrite by pretending to believe in our church's rules when I really didn't. It was an awful period–I had to reconstruct my whole way of living, and I'd never been trained to think for myself. The church I go to now is more concerned with God than it is with gossiping. That's helped me a lot and I think my values are good ones."

Golden Rule

Kerry – 16: "This whole civilization is all stuffed up with a lot of meaningless do's and don'ts. The *Golden Rule* is about the only one that makes any sense. It can be applied to every person and every situation. I try to live by it and I'm a better person than I was when I was trying to follow everyone's rules."

Bob – 17: "If you're talking about sex, I think that's up to the person. I think it's criminal that it isn't up to the person. I'm going to law school after college and I've already started my thesis–it's on the Sex Statutes of the state of California. I can't believe those laws can exist in a contemporary society. You can't read them without wanting to throw up. No one has a right to dictate this part of a person's life.

"I'm not personally offended by moral codes–that's just people saying what you *shouldn't* do. But the laws that tell you what you *can* and *can't* do, in an area of human behavior is none of the government's business or anyone elses'–that's really gross. If you try to follow all the rules and find you aren't able to, which most people aren't, you can ruin your life with guilt, and you can also go to jail and have that record for the rest of your life.

I believe in making up your own mind and doing what's best for you. What really bugs me is that my opinion is *illegal* because of the 'bluelaws.' No wonder the world is in such a mess."

'Known Since 11'

Suzi – 16: "Actually, I haven't had much reason to concern myself with what I think you mean. I've known about sex since I was eleven, but I've never had to make a decision about it. I've never been that involved with anyone. When I do have to decide, I suppose I'll base part of my decision on what I've been taught and the rest on how I feel. Isn't that what everyone does really?

"People might think they do or don't do things because of rules and codes, but when you get right down to it, what you do or don't want to do as an individual is a big factor when you're making any kind of decision."

Anita – 17: "I try to live by the 'established moral code' and so far I've succeeded. But some of the peple who also follow it make me sick. So many use the 'code' for their own personal gains. You know, they make a big deal out of how pure and decent they are, just so people will look up to them and say 'wow, what a great person!'

"Politicians who use a moral issue to get attention make me

BEAT Art: Henri Munsford

even sicker. Sometimes you can just *tell* they're faking about what they're making a big stink about. I'ts just a way of getting votes and getting the public on their side, and it usually works. People don't want to put down someone who's on the 'good and clean side' because that puts you on the opposite side and no one wants to be considered dirty.

"The 'code' is okay, but people who misuse it ruin everything it stands for. They're a lot worse than the people who break the rules."

Personal Standards

Dennis – 14: "A teenager almost has to live by his own personal standards. Maybe we haven't been around long or been around that much, but you don't have to be old or experienced to see that the established *impersonal* standards aren't working."

Rodger – 19: "I don't think anyone lives by his *very own* personal code, unless he's a hermit. You live by the standards of whatever group you're a part of. You don't choose a group of friends just because you have similar interests. You make the choice because you also have similar attitudes. People you spend a lot of time with (out of choice) have an effect on your opinions because you exchange ideas. This exchange creates opinions and standards and opinions are the same thing.

"I also think you're 'standards' change a number of times during a lifetime because of having to adjust to new situations and surroundings and meeting new groups of people. You don't just go off in a corner and decide exactly how you're going to live and then go out and do it.

"And there is no *one* established moral code. There are thousands of them. The final decision of what to live by is up to the person, but a lot of other people and ideas contribute to that decision.

"Standards are a product of yourself and your environment. The only way a man can be an 'island unto himself' is to suffer amnesia so that the past influences would br wiped out of his mind and then go *live* on that island by himself."

Gil – 15: "Huh?"

Darlene – 16: "That 'code' was established by people who knew what was best, and by God's laws. How can anyone live with himself if he doesn't try to live up to it? Right is right and wrong is wrong. There aren't any two ways about it, so why try to kid yourself? Kids wouldn't be in so much trouble if they'd stop trying to change everything and learn to accept life as it is."

Claudia – 19: "I have my own standards. I have to. The established code brands my older brother as a sick person. I don't think I have to go into detail; let's just say he's 'diffeent.' Our family almost fell apart when we found this out, but when he told us he'd felt this way all his life, we realized we were being stupid. He's always been a kind, wonderful, responsible person and he still is. I can't go along with rules that say he's some kind of criminal or something. All this really changed my thinking. It changed my parents' too. All of us saw how narrow and how wrong some of society's thinking is."

Tom – 16: "I don't live by a set of standards, theirs or mine. I don't break the laws, but other than that I just do what I feel like. It's crazy to make up a list of rules and decide how you're going to handle certain situations before they even occur. You never know what you'll do until the time comes."

'I Should Start'

Randy – 15: "I try to do what I think is right. If that's living by my own standards, then I guess I do. I don't always agree with what other people think is right. I can't really answer this question. I haven't thought about it enough. Maybe I should start though."

Gordon – 19: "Why even talk about this? You keep hearing about the big 'moral revolution' that's going on among teenagers, but where is it? I don't see it happening. I just see life happening like it always has. The only difference is that it's more open. Why even talk about it? It's no big problem, like a lot of others are. We should be talking about them."

Janice – 17: "I certainly don't live by my own standards. I do what I'm supposed to, and when I'm in doubt about anything, I let my conscience guide me. Conscience goes hand in hand with the established moral code. They're both the same things and both against the same things. Even if you say you think it's okay to do something you really know you shouldn't, you feel guilty after you've done it. This should be proof enough that the existing rules are the right ones to follow."

KRLA ARCHIVES

LOU RAWLS
'Greatest Thing Since Black Pepper'

By Louise Criscione

They call it Blues but really it's a large spoonful of mother earth. All heaped up and occasionally spilling over. When it spills over it's out of sight because that's when you feel it. That's when you're alive. And if you can't feel it, you might as well just fold yourself right up. You're dead. It's kind of like dancing and not feeling the beat. Sort of bobbing up and down, hands and legs flying. But going nowhere because you're flying alone.

For decades now a certain segment of the American population has been alive with the blues. But only a small minority could feel it. The rest of us were dead. Then a wild thing happened. Another nation stole this thing called blues from us—only we were dead and didn't know it. They packaged it neatly in cellophane and long hair and sent it back across the ocean. And we dug it. Made them stars, gave them money, spent hours grooving to a sound which had been ours since long before we were born.

Wrong Ones

Slowly, almost like a turtle racing a horse, the realization hit that we were crediting the wrong people for the music that had now been changed to rhythm 'n' blues. Practically total integration took place and the pop charts and R&B charts, which had once been as different as Van Cliburn and Elvis Presley, became almost one.

As groups such as the Rolling Stones began talking about their early influences, the American teens became familiar with names which they had never heard before. American names. Muddy Waters, Howlin' Wolf, Rufus Thomas. But they were old and it was almost too late to give them the recognition they had deserved for so long. So, the search was on to find a new name, a younger man. But a man who had graduated from the old school of blues. One who would let his spoonful spill out so we could feel it too.

Enter Lou

That man was Lou Rawls. A product of Chicago, a guy who knew what it was like to play obscure clubs making little money and even less impact. For six years Lou beat the one-nighter, club to club route. And then in 1966 it all paid off. His timing was perfect. His phenomenally best-selling album, "Lou Rawls 'Live'," hit the market at the precise moment the American people were searching for that new someone.

Lou accomplished what was impossible. As a spokesman for Capitol Records commented: "He's successfully bridged the gap between rock 'n' roll and rhythm 'n' blues." The album zoomed to the top of the charts and the U.S. herald another "overnight" star. Lou probably laughed at the "overnight" tag. But not too loudly. As he remembered those six years of overnights which had finally brought him into national prominance and won for him the name "greatest soul singer ever."

Asked what teen music fans think of him—a 30-yer-old Negro blues singer—Lou grinned: "Man, they think I'm the greatest thing since Black Pepper!"

Becoming serious, Lou continued: "The acceptance by the kids has been great. Since that ' Live ' album hit, the concert halls have been filled with just as many kids as adults."

... LOU RAWLS AND HIS LOVELY WIFE, Lana, enjoy a night on the town.

And sure enough, Lou has just completed his second sell-out at the prestige-packed Carnegie Hall. Gazing into the Carnegie audience, one could easily spot a mingling of young, appreciative faces. Faces which grinned wider, hands which applauded longer and louder than their elder counterparts. Lou Rawls is "in." His latest single, "Love Is A Hurtin' Thing," is bounding up the charts with the momentum of a tumbling snowball. But why?

"I think," answered Lou, "it's because much of today's rock music was derived from the blues. Acts like the Beatles and Rolling Stones are singing the blues and they've shown that the kids not only can dance to it but they dig the sounds as well—and it sells.

"Five years ago, I was singing the same stuff at Pandora's on the Sunset Strip in Hollywood. The kids were digging it then and packing the place. But, it took groups like the Stones and Beatles to really put it across. They've paved the way for blues; made people aware that the blues songs make for good listening and dancing. They swing just as well as anything else."

Set Up

In addition to his smooth (but not *too* smooth) voice, his grasp of the blues and his obvious talent, Lou has furthered the cause of the monologue. "Monologues," says Lou, "are something I've been doing for years. They're all spontaneous and I always used them as an intro to the song. They're a perfect way to set it up. I never really thought people would dig them as much as they did. But I sure am happy about it."

It's fitting, then, that Lou uses a monologue on his newest album, "Soulin'," to introduce "It Was A Very Good Year." Because the year of 1966 *was* as Lou puts it, "a very, very good year."

And it was a very good year for Lou thanks to, among other things, America's teens. Lou believes that today's youth has picked up on his songs much quicker than the kids of ten years ago would have. "Kids today are quicker and smarter. They swing and have a ball just like the rest of us did, but today they're more aggressive. They know the only way they can survive is to be smart—and get off that corner and learn something."

Lou, who spent much of his Chicago childhood standing on the street corners, is doing his part to keep today's young generation off of those same corners. Accordingly, he's been working with such programs as "Teen Post" and "Operation Cool-Head." For almost every sell-out concert he's had, Lou has also staged a free one for teens.

Cooling Off

In Cincinnati, during the heat of the summer, more than 3,000 teens turned out to hear Lou sing. Centennial High School in Los Angeles was another "sell-out" for Lou as were about a half-dozen other schools in and around the country.

He's also doing his share to keep the drop-outs from chucking in their books by speaking in favor of education. But speaking in his own cool way. "When I was a kid," recalls Lou, "you'd hang around the corner and maybe make it. Survive with your 'mother' wit. Not today. Today you've gotta get it out of the books or else you're going to wake up one day and wonder, 'Where did it all go?'"

And Lou's goal? "I'm trying to reach everyone, young and old alike." But perhaps he had better find another goal. Lou Rawls has *already* reached everyone. And it feels great.

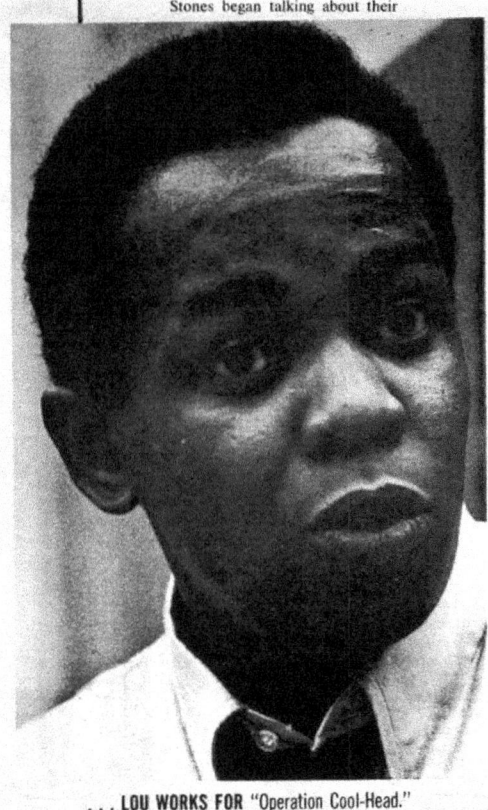

... LOU WORKS FOR "Operation Cool-Head."

KRLA ARCHIVES

DISCUSSION
By Eden

1966 will undoubtedly be recorded as "The Year of the Motown Sound" in pop history, as one after another of the Motown groups takes up residence in the Number One spot on the charts.

The Four Tops followed the Supremes' most recent smash into the Top Spot with "Reach Out, I'll Be There," and now the Supremes are planning an immediate return to their familiar old stamping grounds with their gigantic new smash, "I Keep Hangin' On."

Fortunately, the people at Motown finally seem to be getting out of the bag they fell into for the last year and a half, and have stopped trying to duplicate each hit on its follow-up record.

This new disc by the hitmaking trio reminds many of a message in *Morse code*, due to the unusual arrangement of the guitars. Probably the only message intended is simply "*Hitsville!!!*"

★ ★ ★ ★ ★

Speaking of hits, the Raiders seem to be trying to pull a Beatle thingie on us. Right in the middle of a rapid climb to the top with their latest winner – "The Great Airplane Strike of '66" – the five talented nuts are releasing still *another* chart-topper.

Title: "Good Thing," verdict: unbelievable! Or in the immortal syllables of Phil "Fang" Volk – *Outasite*!! Featured on the new platter are the winning elements of a good, strong beat; groovey harmonies; and some kinda soulful singer from one Mr. Mark Lindsay. All in all . . . "a very good, good, good, good thing!!!!"

★ ★ ★ ★ ★

One of the best "follow-up" records of this year has got to be "Secret Love," by Billy Stewart. For once, a singer has managed to maintain the "gimmick" which helped to make his initial disc successful, without producing just another sound-alike.

Great moving record which will probably have very similar paths to the tops of both the pop and R&B charts.

★ ★ ★ ★ ★

For those of you who have asked, the brand new "Action" theme song was recorded by Keith Allison, and it's being released as a single this week.

★ ★ ★ ★ ★

The Hollies' newie is "Stop Stop Stop." It has a lot of interesting production and unusual arrangement techniques going for it, but it doesn't seem to be headed in the same general direction as "Bus Stop."

This new disc lacks the instantaneous commercial appeal of the last record, and can be a little monotonous to listen to repeatedly.

★ ★ ★ ★ ★

"Why Pick On Me" by the Standells in brand new and probably not one of the best records around. Really sounds like a giant gimmick, but it may make it into the Top 20 as a dance item.

★ ★ ★ ★ ★

"I'm Ready For Love" is the very unusual new release from talented Motown artists, Martha and the Vandellas. Everyone keeps saying it sounds more like a Supremes-sort of record, but it really is Martha and Company.

Some Things are Nice to Have Around...

things you feel "at home" with

...the Utility™ ball pen

A good, practical pen for students. Fashionable, too.
There are twelve brilliant colors.
The color of the pen is the color of the ink.

Lots of students buy two or three at a time. Maybe because it's only 39¢
Maybe because it writes nice.
Or maybe they just like to have two or three or twelve around.

Lindy®

 manufactured by LINDY PEN CO., no. hollywood, calif. 91605, u.s.a.

KRLA ARCHIVES

Raider View: 'Lots Of Screaming Kids'

By Eden

Now, you'll have to admit that one thing is certainly true: Paul Revere and his zany Raiders are very definitely *"Where The Action Is!"* And, five more *active* guys you'll never find! As a matter of fact—that's just the problem: they're so active, it's almost *impossible* to find them all together and all in one place all at one time.

However, your faithful *BEAT* reporter loyally relinquished her *one-day-a-year-off* recently in order to travel to the ABC studios in Hollywood, which had been selected as that day's location for "Action."

And, lo and behold... —right inside the very self-same studios where "Shindig" once made its home was the entire cast and crew of "Action"—including *all five* of the Raiders.

Slapstick

We found Mark eating lunch in the commissary, and over a dish of cottage cheese we discussed the Raiders' famous humor. Mark explained that, "There's a lot of subtle humor that everybody misses, but we have a lot of slapstick comedy that *everybody* catches, I'm sure."

At one time famous for their practical joking, Mark explains that there is seldom enough time now to carry on this great "tradition." "I used to like to play practical jokes, but it seems that I haven't had too much time to be funny lately! I've been too busy being... busy!"

So many articles have been written lately pointing gloomy fingers at pop music and predicting its rapid demise. Is there really a lull in pop music? "No! It's stronger than ever! It's getting bigger and better than ever, and now popular music is *saying something* rather than just being a—to use the phrase of a friend—a 'heart beat that you can follow rhythmically with your body.' It all tells a story now; there's a 'heart beat,' but there's also a story behind it, or *with* it."

We are all familiar with happiness and hysteria associated with the concerts and appearances made by the Raiders, the pandemonium which accompanies their frequent tours around the country, the excitement which they generate wherever they go. But, I asked Mark what it might be like looking from the inside *out* on a Raider tour. What does *he* actually see.

"Lots of screaming kids!" he laughed through a mouthful of red jello. "No, but once in a while you see individuals in the crowd that you'd *really* like to go to talk to because they really look like they'd like to talk to *you*, or they've got something to say to you; or, maybe they look troubled and I'd like to straighten them out.

"There's a whole world out there; I see everything from poverty to pompous snobbery—and everything in between. I see a lot of things that I saw when I was growing up, and because I grew up in not a rich family at all—we were kind of poor—I can appreciate the poor side of it, and know what these kids are going through, and exactly what they feel like. But, I'm glad that I didn't have all the things that I wanted as a kid, because I sure appreciate more things now."

Changes

Its been a long road, and a lot of changes have come about in these last few years. The Raiders are now one of the top groups in the country, but basically—they have remained the same people they were when they began. Thinking about it for a while, Mark explained carefully: "Happiness is the satisfaction of knowing that you've done something for someone, or given someone something— whether it was a smile, or a thought, or a song, or a hug or a kiss, or a love, or *anything*.

"Sadness is the realization you've hurt someone, or a bad performance, or just *loneliness*, sometimes."

We left the commissary then and ran back to the studio where the "Action" shooting had resumed. Before the Raiders went on to film another number, we caught Harpo practicing guitar in a dressing room and stopped to chat for a few minutes.

Although he is the newest member of the group, Harpo has been singing for several years, and he looks back about three years to the different dances and clubs he used to play. "I don't miss it enough to leave the Raiders," he assures us, but still there are some things he misses. Mostly, the closer audience contact.

"Contact—eye contact with the people, and also being able to talk with them. But it's still fun!"

Harpo was also in one of his rare philosophical moods, and he considered for a moment the question which we had put to Mark earlier.

Then, slowly he explained: "Happiness, to me, is like, *life* and *people*. But sadness and happiness are very close, and to *really* have happiness you have to go through some sadness. And, there's sadness all around us."

Another subject to which "Harp" gave some serious thought was that of the responsibilities and obligations of a performer to his public. He explained: "I think he should be *true* to the people. If you're appealing to teen-agers, then I think that you shouldn't be a hypocrite—and that involves your press, and what you say. The people who bug me are the ones who play for teen-agers and then put them down.

"But, in our group, I don't think it is. I think our group is nicer, and much more open to people than any other group I've seen."

A little while later in the studio barber shop (Honest! Uncle Paul was actually having *his* hair cut!), Paul had a few thoughts of his own about the obligations between the performer and his audience. "I think that usually the public asks *too much*, because they don't have any idea how much pressure people have, or how busy people are.

Real Tyrant

"When people start making it, there's a thousand people pulling at them from every direction to do a million things. You usually smile and laugh and go along with it for about a month or two, and then lack of sleep, and lack of food, and lack of privacy, and a lack of people being understanding can turn you into a real tyrant.

"But, eventually, I think you get calloused-over and you start not letting all these things bother you and then you come back to your old, normal self.

People in the spotlight definitely do have a responsibility, and Paul agreed that they have a certain position in the social structure. "You're a standard-setter. I think you shouldn't promote anything or give the idea that you endorse anything unless you really give it some heavy thought, and make sure that it's really the right thing to do. Because, a lot of times, people do things they shouldn't do, and they won't stop and correct themselves, and they don't realize that other people are going to follow them.

"You have big responsibilities. You just don't stand around on public streets swearing or drinking whiskey and throwing bottles through windows because other kids are going to say, 'Well, man, if he does it and he's my idol, then that must be the answer.' You've got to be sure that you don't do anything that might be harmful to other people's personality, or hurt other people's feelings, or hard knocks against society.

"I think people can dress any way they want to, *but*—there's also a place and a time. If Mark tried to wear one of his famous stop-sign outfits to a wedding reception—especially if it was *my own*— I'd throw him out! You know, you've still got to conform to a *certain degree*.

"But, you should give it a little thought. Before you walk down the streets with nothing but your socks on, you should actually think, 'Now, what is the object in this? Is it really going to be accepted, is it really worth it just because I feel like doing this? Should I do whatever I feel like doing?"

Pretty strong words from a man who used to be one of the wildest kids in all of Idaho! But, Uncle Paul has done a lot of calming down and growing up and now he watches over his four Raiders—who *still* have a tendency to get a bit wild at times!

It was a long day, and an exciting one; the Raiders all have a lot more to say, but we'll have to save that for another time.

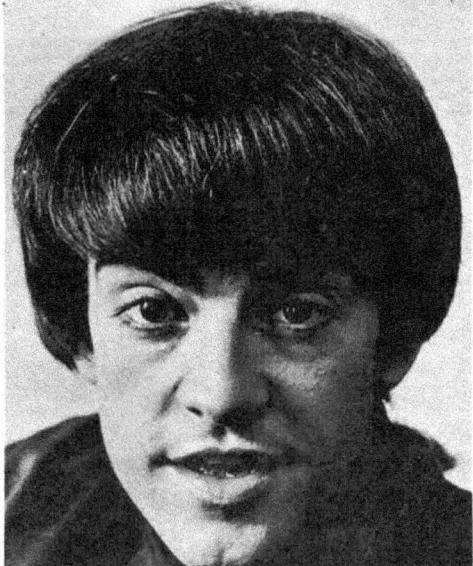

...MARK: "SUBTLE HUMOR EVERYBODY MISSES."

...HARPO: "EYE CONTACT WITH PEOPLE."

...PAUL: "YOU HAVE BIG RESPONSIBILITIES."

KRLA ARCHIVES

 # For Girls Only

By Shirley Poston

Let's hear it for Frances Phillips!

Who is Frances Phillips? She's one of the grooviest girls in this entire world, that's who (or is it whom?)

The other night, while I was lying awake feeling guilt-stricken because I *still* hadn't sent out those promised copies of John's "Toy Boy," I thought I'd read some more of the mail I'd picked up that day.

Would you believe that I found a great big package from the above-mentioned F.P., containing a whole big bunch of copies of the

After I'd finished blithering with joy, I read the letter she'd enclosed, and will quote from the part which explains this unexpected but wildly appreciated windfall.

"When I read your column in the September 10 BEAT, I felt like giving you some sort of standing ovation. You're so right about loving the Beatles and I agree with everything you said 100%. I was so pleased, in fact, I talked my father into letting me use the Xerox machine in his office to run off these for you. If I'm too late in getting them to you and you've already found a duplication machine, you can always use them to wallpaper your room."

I'm going to try not to get out the violins again, but I must say that was a wonderful thingy for her to do. And, since I hadn't found a spare mimeographer, and my room is already papered with pix of Gasp . . . I mean George (as in Gasp) (*that* kind of repetition will *always* rule), I raced for the pile of stabbed, un-dressed envelopes and sent "Toy Boy" on it's merrie way.

Frances also made me an associate member of the club she'd started to honor all Beatle compositions. It's called *Bernard Webb Fans Inc., Ltd.,* (which, as you know, is the name Paul used to write "Woman") and I think it's a really neat idea. I've written to Frances and asked if she'd like for me to print her address in my post —whoops—column in case a few (million) of youse would like to join too!

Speaking of the September 10 BEAT (thought I was gonna say George, diddinyah?) (so did I), I want to thank everyone who wrote me about the poem "When England Went To War." I really had a snit after I turned that column in. I was so worried that people might think it was stupid.

But, once again, it seems as though we think pretty much alike, and I didn't get one poison pen letter. A lot of you said the poem really made you think—not just about the Beatles—about a lot of things. It did me too.

Now that all the banning and burning ap-cray ('scuse, please) is over, I have to tell you about something that happened during the big controversy. It wasn't particularly amusing at the time (to me, anyway) because the person who made the comment had totally misunderstood John. Now that I know for sure that none of the abovementioned A.C. has made the slightest dent in the Beatles' popularity (if anything, I think they're more loved now), the bit is rather funny.

What happened was, a friend of mine heard an adult say: "I'll believe the Beatles are more popular than Jesus when I stub my toe and say 'Oh, *John Lennon!*'"

Before I get off the Beatle subject (as in don't hold your breath unless you happen to dig purple) I just have to read you a part of another letter. This one is from a girl who had just seen her first Beatle concert.

"I cried on the way home, but they were tears of love and contentment. I had a feeling of being complete. It was like God had finally finished me by joining my body and soul."

I don't think I've ever heard that magic feeling put into better words.

And now, a word about chain letters.

I just love such thingys, but I don't get to the office every day (Keeper won't let me out that often, you know.) So when someone sends me a chain letter, I end up breaking the chain because of the time limit involved.

Since I already have a guilt-complex over the rash promises I still haven't completely lived up to (*soon*, I tell you), pullease don't send chains. Unless they're the kind used to tie up people who are disorderly, disorganized, butter-fingered and an absolute slob about losing things in spite of the fact that I mean well (which I'm not very.)

Oh, back to the T.B. subject for a moment. I got a letter from someone who said she had *five hundred* copies of the poem, and has been ordered to get rid of them or else. Course, the someone signed her letter *Cynthia L. Lennon*, but surely you don't expect someone who signs their letters *Shirley Harrison* to find *that* one *bit* odd!

Anylover'slane (cough), if anyone else would like a copy of this poem, send a stabbed-undressed to Toy Boy—John Lennon, 680 S. Peckham Drive, Whittier, California, 90601.

Thanks, Cyn! You're a doll. (Your "Husband" is a little bit of all right, too, kiddo.)

Speaking to George—I mean speaking *of* letters, there's a BEAT reader in New Orleans who digs

(Turn to Page 19)

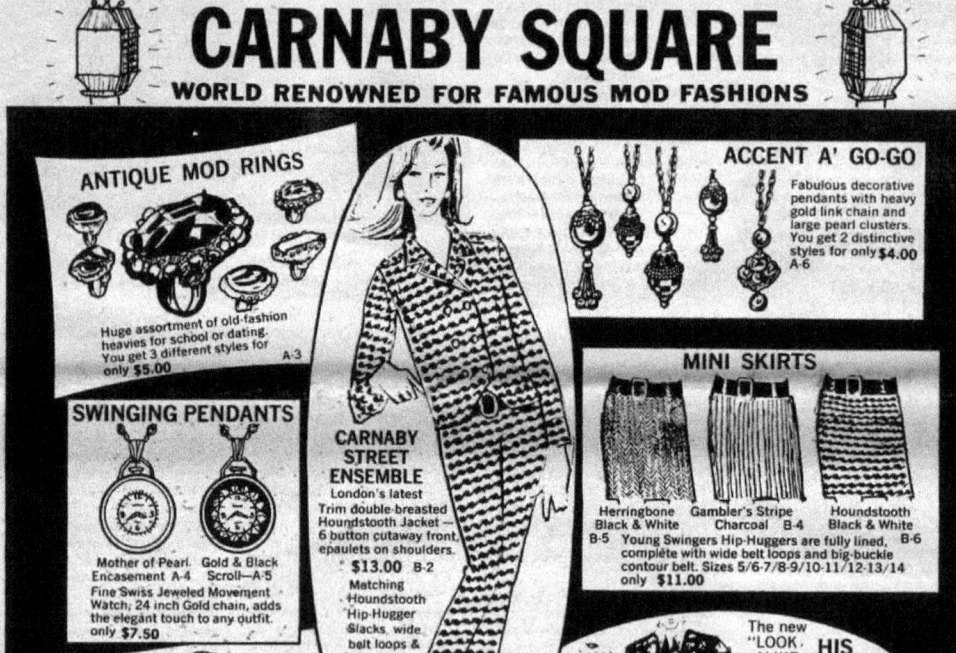

KRLA ARCHIVES

Supremes In Las Vegas

...DIANA

BEAT Photos: Howard L. Bingham

By Karen Price

People. All kinds of people from all walks of life. All with one thing in common—a desire to spend money in an effort to make more, maybe.

The place — The Flamingo in Las Vegas—crowded as usual.

Over there by the far table, a rather short but handsome young man dressed in blue with a blue golf hat on his head is gambling in the thousands of dollars.

But he can afford it. He's the head of one of the top Negro organizations in the nation.

Good Luck

Beside him are two attractive young girls—his good luck pieces. One is dressed in beige capris with a casual orange velour blouse. The other's in a loose fitting yellow shift.

A large crowd gathers around to watch. Why?

Because there's big money being played here and because the man in blue and his two good luck charms aren't just any Las Vegas customers.

The two girls are dressed pretty casual now but in just a few short hours they will emerge in high fashion wigs and classy full length gowns.

They'll be joined by another very beautiful young girl, a rather thin girl.

The three will walk onto the stage at the Flamingo and live up to their reputation as the world's number one female vocal act.

The girl in the beige and orange is Mary Wilson and Florence Ballard is in the yellow. The man in blue is their boss, Berry Gordy Jr., head of Motown Records, who incidentally won quite a lot this time at the tables.

Capacity Crowd

A short time later, after the capacity crowd has feasted on excellent steak dinners, Diana Ross joins Mary and Florence and The Supremes are appearing in Las Vegas, showplace of the world!

For this show they're wearing floor-length white satin sheaths with over-blouses of an interesting negligee type material—the color of polished steel, sort of blue-black.

They open with a quick and lively "Put On A Happy Face" and follow that with many of their biggest hits, "Baby Love," "Stop In The Name of Love," "You Can't Hurry Love" and many standards that most so-called pop groups wouldn't even attempt.

They do themselves proud on "With A Song In My Heart," "More," "Wonderful, Wonderful," an amusing version of "Queen Of The House!" and a medley of Sam Cooke numbers.

Diana practically brings the house down with "Somewhere" from "West Side Story." Throughout the entire performance she proves that there's nothing she can't sing—blues, comedy, pop and even torch songs.

There's a magic about these three that's unmatched anywhere.

Mary, the sexy one, is the kind of girl a guy would want to wine and dine in the best of style. She bounces vivaciously about the stage—a happy medium between Florence's quietness and Diana's exuberance.

Florence, the quiet one, is the kind of girl a guy takes home. She can stand perfectly still on stage and completely destroy every male in the first four rows with just her eyes—and she does.

Skinny One

And Diana, who calls herself the skinny one, is the kind of girl a guy just naturally wants to spend money on, in the best places in town. She's quite a showcase item with an extra helping of personality plus.

And the guy in blue who's always nearby, smiling like a proud papa, knows that he made no mistakes in signing these three Motown artists. They've made him a millionaire.

The Supremes in Las Vegas—a long way from their humble start in Detroit—nothing but successful, the greatest. What more can be said?

...MARY

...FLORENCE

For Girls Only . . .

(Continued From Page 18)

Californians and would luv to hear from some of the same, especially surfers. Her name is Connie Kumiski, and you can write her at 923 Opelousas Ave., New Orleans, Louisiana.

I don't seem to be able to get off the topic of letters. Have just thought of another goodie. It seems that one of both of my many readers had her name listed in the English (cheers) magazine "Rave," and she got three hundred replies!

If you don't already have a pen pale . . . urp . . . pal in God's Country, maybe you could talk her into giving you one of hers. If you wanna, write her in care of me and I'll send her the letters, or postcards or whatever. Put the initials K.P. on the front of the envelope so I'll know to forward them on.

As long as I'm still on the letter bit, I may as well mention this now. So many of you have commented that you think Robin Boyd should be made into a book, and I did make one feeble attempt to talk (as in stammersville) to a publisher, but do you have any *idea* how utterly impossible it is to discuss Robin with a *rational adult*?

He was very interested until he read a few chapters. Then, with a dazed and glazed look, he murmured: "I don't understand a *word* of it."

I already have quite a few letters from fellow R.I.B.-nuts, but maybe if I had more, I could get my point (and you know where *that's* located) across.

Hate to keep sending you off to the postoffice, but any comments about Robin would be appreciated. Then, next time I go somewhere to blush and quake a lot, I'll take the letters with me and maybe they'll help convince the Sane Set that *we* understand *every* word of it (a slight exaggeration) (*slight?*) (even *I* don't understand every word of it, and I *write* it) (using the term loosely), and she might end up in book form yetto!

Oh, a fabmary (*hah?*) thingy is happening. Someone is re-writing Robin from the beginning, only doing it from George's point of view. I've already received quite a few chapters (it's titled "The Adventures of George The Genie") and will try to get them all together and maybe print same someday soon!

Arp. I'm totally out of room, not to mention my mind. Goodbye forever (as in *promises, promises*.)

KRLA ARCHIVES

The Adventures of Robin Boyd

©1965 By Shirley Poston

Robin Boyd stomped gracefully through the front door and flang herself and her books onto the couch.

"Hullo," she said tiredly, addressing her mother and Ringo (of sturdy 12-year-old Boyd and bod fame) who were seated stiffly in arm chairs.

"And who are you? . . . I mean how are you?" she added, addressing the man who was pacing dolefully about the living room.

The man gave her a hurt look (which she returned because she already . . . oh, *you* know.) "I'm your father," he replied. "And I'm just fine."

"Just *fine*," her mother repeated sarcastically.

"Just *dandy-poo*," Ringo agreed, spearing her father with a Ludwig droomstick.

"Cut that *out*, Ringo," he snapped, moving out of his younger daughter's reach. "Don't we have enough problems already?"

Sit Down, Dear

Robin's ears flapped. "Problems?" she echoed.

Her father turned to her. "You'd better sit down, dear."

Robin, who was *lying* down at the time, shrugged and sat *up*, hoping that would do. "Yesss?" she hisped.

"Something has happened at work, dear," he said gently. "I've been transferred to another job and . . ."

"We're *moving*!" Ringo interrupted in a wail.

"Shurrup — I mean shut *up*, Ringo!" he ordered, returning his attention to his older daughter, who had just turned grotty-green.

"I've been made manager of a plant the company is building in . . . in another part of the country," he continued.

"In *South Dakota*," her mother snorted.

"*Pitchfork*, South Dakota," Ringo sobbed.

"Oh, come now. We won't be living in *Pitchfork*," her father soothed as Robin turned yick-yellow. "We'll be living in *East* Pitchfork."

Resisting the urge to snatch out a long strand of her red hair and hang herself from a rafter, Robin ground a pound of teeth. "When are we leaving?" she asked stonily.

"In two *weeks*," her mother and Ringo wept in unison.

"Oh_____!" Robin muttered, certain that her family wouldn't be familiar with this bit of Scouse she'd borrowed from George.

The family came to attention. "What does *that* mean?" they chorused.

Robin snarled, and without even thinking, she said "it means _____!"

Blammed Again

After her mother got through blamming her over the head with Ringo's droomstick, Robin decided to have a long rational talk (as in beg, rave, plead, and, if necessary, *bleed*) with her father.

So she did just that, and not being the sort to give up easily, she continued tantrumizing for five hours. But, 'twas all in vain (and it didn't do her any good, either.)

Finally she gave up, sogged off to her room, slammed the door and sat grimly on the edge of her bed until the rest of the family had retired (with full pensions, natch.)

When all was quiet, she sneaked (as in clomp) back into the darkened living room and tripped over to the tea pot.

Plant-Plant

Suddenly, she came to a shuddering halt. The few times she'd visited George's domicile, he'd just snapped his finger or some such and there they were inside the T.P. (not to be confused with teepee) (to, however, be confused with *whoopee*.) But she had no mortal (she preferred genies) idea how to get into the fiendish thingy on her own, with the possible exception of re-wallowing in a peanut butter sandwich and cramming herself back up the spout, but let's not start *that* again.

So, praying that no one would come into the room and see her rapping politely on the lid of a tea pot, she began rapping politely on the lid of a tea pot.

The next thing she knew, she was inside same and George was stubmling out of bed, clad in Ringo's blue pajamas. (George was wearing the pajamas, not the bed.) (Which rather goes without saying as George would look somewhat silly wearing a bed.)

"Oh, *George*," she cried, hurling herself at him. "My dad's making us leave California and move away and my life is ending I tell you!"

George patted her kindly (which promptly bit him.) "What are you gabbling about?" he asked sleepily.

"I *won't* live in *South Dakota* is what I'm gabbling about," Robin gabbled (not to mention garbled.)

George rubbed his yes. "South Da-whatta?"

Dakota!!

"*Dakota!*" screeched Robin. "It's a state (ho) that's ten million miles away from here (not to mention there and everywhere) (sorry, Pauley), and I won't, won't, *won't* go even if my dad's company *did* give him a plant!"

"All this fuss over a *plant?*" George asked incredulously, eyeing the potted (I'll say) palm in the corner.

"Not *that* kind," Robin bellered. "A *plant*-plant, as in building. Where they whatever those things are that they do!"

George scratched his head. "Just what *does* your father do?" he asked. (*Besides have the good sense to travel most of the time so he won't have to be around you Boyd-brains, that is,* he added mentally.)

Robin made an impatient (not to mention illegal) gesture. "How should I know? He works with dynamo's or dynamics or dinosaurs or something, but what difference does *that* make? Don't you even care that I'll go completely bonkers in South Dawhatta — I mean kota?"

Putting his arms around her, George rested his chin comfortably on the top of her head (just to the left of the point.) "It's not all that bad," he patted. "You'll still have me and your magic powers and . . . and . . ."

A Transfer?

Suddenly he pulled away from her. "Oh my *Gawd*," he moaned, but before she could ask what he was moaning *about* he said a strange word that sounded something like "grisp" and the two of them disappeared.

When they reappeared, they were standing in the middle of a deserted desert (you may have noticed what is continuing to rule.)

"*George!*" Robin said angrily, stamping her foot and sinking up to her hip-huggers in sand. "What's the *matter* with you? What are we doing *here?*"

George re-moaned. "I've got some bad news. I can't go to South Da-what's-its-face with you."

"*Whatttt?*" roared Robin.

"Let me *finish!*" George commanded. "I can't until I get a transfer."

"A *transfer?*" Robin re-roared. "How long will *that* take?"

"I don't know. Awhile, probably. There's this thingy about licenses or something — you have to get one from each state before you can be a resident genie, and they're not too keen on our kind in South Da-whosis."

Robin started to run around in hysterical circles, but George gave her a yank. (not to be confused with the one in the R.A.F.) (This one was in the A.R.M.) "I'm *still* not finished. *Your* powers won't work there either, not until I can get your permit changed."

At first, Robin just stood there like a stone, then she threw herself, not to mention the snit of the century.

It is not necessary to include all the gory details of those next few trying moments. Let it suffice to say that she lept wildly from dune to dune, bashed her head against rocks, kicked several cactii in the shins and shrieked a selection of sentiments that made George's Scouse sound like something straight out of the King Cousin's Songbook.

When she was finally too exhausted to continue, she dragged herself back to where George was waiting (im)patiently.

"Are you quite through?" he arsked.

"I'll say," she groaned as she sat down beside him and started to pick prickles out of her ex-feet (which now resembled a pair of totally teed-off porcupines.) "I can see why you brought me here. If I'd done that little number in the tea pot, I'd have had us splattered all over the living room."

George larfed half-heartedly. "Oh, dropinze dead," she snapped, giving *him* a look. But when he glowered and re-yanked, she remembered that a certain area of her anatomy was *still* black and blue from her most recent encounter with George's Liverpudlian temper., and she changed her tune in one large hurry.

"I only meant it's not foony, luv," she simpered, batting her lashes prettily. (Not as prettily as she thought, though, as one of them had fallen off during her war dance, but no one is perfect.)

Then she stopped talking for a moment and stared at him. They'd been apart before, but it was different this time (worse) because things were different now (better) (you better believe it.)

And wouldn't you just know that he would pick the most horrible night in her life to look so am-day georgeous (ahem) she couldn't *believe* it?

Not the sort to go wandering around the desert in his pajamas (make that Ringo's pajamas) (make that *anybody's* pajamas), George had solved that problem with another "grisp"-type word. He was now wearing slim faded levis and his long dark hair was brushing against the collar of a black turtle-neck shirt.

Willywackers

Feeling like throttling him for sitting there in the moonlight, giving her willywackers on the wezand when her very life was ending, Robin burst into tears.

"Oh, *George*," she blithered. "What am I going to do *without* you?"

George grinned that one grin and took her by the shoulders. "Just don't let me catch you doing *this* without me."

"*George Irene Boyd!*" Robin gasped shortly thereafter (would you believe six days?) (merely an attempt at humor, mom), which set them both to chortling. (And may do the same for you if the words "telephone booth" ring a bell.) (Sorry about that.)

But a few moments later, when Robin found herself at home in her trundle, she began to re-blither.

After she finally did get to sleep, she had a dream that she was never to forget as long as she lived. She dreamed that when the Boyds arrived in Pitchfork, they found the town consisted of one lonely Shell gas station. Which would have been bad enough, but to make things worse, when they drove up, someone was standing in front of the S.

(*To Be Continued Next Issue*)

BEAT BARGAIN!
(limited special offer)

$1.00

Just clip and mail . . .

THE BEAT

Mail to:
The BEAT #504
6290 Sunset Blvd.
Hollywood, Calif. 90028

Name_____
Address_____
City_____ State_____ Zip____

I want ☐ BEAT for the rest of the year — only $1.
I enclose ☐ cash ☐ check ☐ money order.

KRLA ARCHIVES

BEAT SHOWCASE
(spotlighting new talent on the pop scene)

THE W. C. FIELDS MEMORIAL ELECTRIC STRING BAND (and Marching Society for the Preservation of Long-haired Singers in the State of . . . oh well). Anyway, George Bee, who is really George Caldwell (second from the left) and a former member of The Bees, has announced to **The BEAT** staff that the W. C. F. M. E. S. Band, etc., has just cut a record, "Hippy Elevator Operator" b/w "Don't Lose The Girl."

THE CHYMES are three sisters (Candy, 14; Irise, 16; Stephanie, 17) from the San Fernando Valley who rated these words from lead Turtle Howard Kaylan: "The Chymes are three adorable girls and are a pleasure to work with. I feel very strongly that these girls have the talent and personality to really make a big impression on the music business today." Howard has written and produced a record for the group, "Quite A Reputation."

THE VAGRANTS wandered onto **The BEAT** Showcase pages from three thousand miles away, namely New York City where they are one of the highest paid, most popular groups in the area. The Vagrants (l to r, Jerry, Peter, Larry, Roger and Leslie) are composed of a variety of characters: Jerry Storch, the organist, was New York State Junior Bowling Champion; drummer Roger Mansour spent ten years in Haiti and five in France; Peter Sabatino, vocalist, met Jerry and Roger when all three were under fire in their high school principal's office for having long hair; guitarist Leslie West and bassist Larry West are brothers. The group is busy snowing New York and with the release of their next record, just may shine in California too.

KRLA ARCHIVES

Gale Makes 'New Adventures'

By Rochelle Reed

"I've got a warning for all *BEAT* readers!" announced Gale Garnett, who ventured up to the *BEAT* office to give us an insider's scoop on the pop scene here and abroad.

"Beware of the Kikieseisea Islands in Fiji. A Fijean sand fly there nests in the ends of hair. They're harmless but to get rid of them you have to burn off the ends of your hair.

"I fell asleep the last time I was in Fiji and woke up with sand flies nested in my hair. I had to have two inches burned off, and that ruined my hair so much I had to have two more inches cut off."

We tried to skip the obvious and not ask why, of all places, Gale had been in the Kikieseisea Islands of Fiji, because we knew she would have a good reason for being in the Kikieseisei Islands. And she did.

"I collect primitive art, you see," she threw in to soothe our itching curiousity.

Gale, who shelters a voice that is deep, rich and throaty, always puts her lung power to good use in an interview. She talks to you, which is especially surprising in the pop business where one of the games people play most often is titled, "Put On."

"I'm full of praise for my new arranger and new sound," Gale said when we had finished discussing sand flies. "It's a cross between a mind trip and religious music . . . a combination of organs and fuzz tone fender. It's guaranteed mind-expansion to an old lady, and at the same time, you can understand the words."

For instance?

"There's one song called 'I Make Him Fly.' This girl meets a guy and her parents put him down. But the girl says 'I make him fly,' and no one has ever said this to the guy before. Through him, you see, she can orbit."

"My arranger, Dick Rosmini — that R-o-s-m-i-n-i — is a gas!" Gale repeated for the one hundredth time, "I rank him next to Burt Bacharach.

"I was so tired of singing songs in concert and not being able to record them like I wanted. But I think we're gonna swing."

When Gale isn't swinging musically, as on her latest album, "New Adventures," she's swinging around the world. And the Kikieseisei Islands were just one stop.

"The big thing in England is floral shirts and matching ties, big ones. Everyone's in plastic — navy blue is very big."

Is it true that English teens are supposedly "more creative" than American teens, as they often proclaim?

"No," she said, "I don't think any 'group' is more creative than any other 'group.' They have creative individuals, but as a 'group' they aren't more creative."

Gale herself is quite creative, in her writing and singing, as well as her personal life. She left home when she was 14 and lived in Greenwich Village. But she doesn't think this should cause a wide-spread movement of teens to move away from Mom and Dad when they reach high school.

"First, you've got to be able to support yourself and not depend on your family for anything. I didn't take a nickel when I moved out. So many kids think it's an injustice when their parents say they aren't going to give them a dime when they leave.

"And when they leave, the only thing they should be bugged about is if they do something someone objects to — which applies to people of any age."

and furthermore . . .

Gale always has interesting comments. Here are a few . . .

Beatles — "I love the entire 'Revolver' album."

Rolling Stones — "I like 'Have You Seen Your Mother, Baby, Standing In The Shadows?' but I'm still decoding it."

Sonny and Cher — "I've never dug Sonny and Cher but their new record is a total gas. For one, Sonny's shut up and given Cher the complete lead."

Monkees — "I like 'The Last Train to Clarksville.' Peter is an old friend. He liked 'Sing In The Sunshine.' He lived in Greenwich Village then."

Tom Jones — "I did a concert with him in Paris at the Locomotive. Then I acted as girl guide for Tom and his band around Paris because none of them spoke any French."

Bobby Darin — "'If I Were A Carpenter' is the grooviest of 1966. I tend to like ballads more than anything else, but that song is really great."

Count V — "'Psychotic Reaction' is the cheapest trick I've heard. It's a sin. It's got the lyrics of a real mind trip, but it's no trip. It's just a cheap trick, a cheap idea. I don't like to have anyone tricked."

Herman — "'Dandy' is a fine, cute record."

Petula Clark — "I saw her opening at the Savoy in Paris. She's one of the few people in the pop scene that can perform live."

Bob Dylan — "'Just Like A Woman' I love. I don't like 'Born A Woman,' it's a whiney song."

Donovan — "'Sunshine Superman' won't get any award. The song meant nothing but I found it hard to get into."

James Brown and Ray Charles — "I love James Brown. No, I like James Brown very much but I love Ray Charles. Everyone has to take a chair behind him. Ray is where it's at."

Mary Quant — "She's got some very beautiful designs. I bought some that could only be described as 'sexy pioneer dresses.'"

GALE CAPTIONED THIS ONE: "Finding a friend in a Left Banke antique shop. I named her "Barbra Christian" because she looks like Streisand with a nose job!"

Lady Godiva Rides Again

By Mike Tuck

Gordon was sprawled across a lawn chair by the swimming pool when we finally located him. When awakened, he squinted into the sun, glanced around and slowly, very slowly made his way to a sitting position.

"We were originally in the U.S. on a tour," said Peter, "but about halfway through it we ran into some difficulties so we just decided to come out here and relax. We've always liked California, anyway."

The sun finally peeked through the Los Angeles smog and Peter and Gordon sought refuge under a nearby lawn umbrella. Sheltered, they both talked a little more freely.

Shocking Hair

Peter, who has a shock of red hair that can be dazzling on a bright day, is intelligent and, compared to his traveling mate, a little on the reserved side. Gordon is plainly an extrovert, and it's no trick to detect in him an element of spite — even when he's still half asleep.

"We were once having some trouble with our hotel manager," Gordon studied a cup of black coffee and said. "He got pretty nasty so at the end of our show that night we invited all the kids to come over to our room for a party."

"About 8,000 showed up. We stood on our balcony and threw autographed pictures to them while the manager went crazy."

The duo seems to get along together uncommonly well. They have been together since both were in school and would sneak out of the dormitories at night to play engagements at a small club.

"We were making $2 a night in those days," said Peter. "It was really hard because we would work long hours. Consequently, our grades began to drop."

Gordon & Peter

"But," Gordon raised his hand in triumph, "at least we were known as Gordon and Peter then."

Their career at the small club ended abruptly when Gordon was unable to appear one night and the club management discovered the two boys were still in school.

"Gordon was scaling the fence when he stuck a spike through his foot," Peter said. "His shoes filled with blood and he left great amazing footprints. He had to stay in bed for awhile after that."

"Just look at this," Gordon said, turning a size 12 foot upside-down. "I still have a hole in my foot."

When both boys were out of school and Gordon's foot had mended, the pair got their first break. They signed with a small-time agent, who "once knew a TV producer or something," and were immediately booked to a respectable club. Their salaries climbed to a totaled $150 weekly.

"Then one day a guy in a shiny suit spotted us. After our show he called us over and said 'I'm a recording manager for EMI.'

"We said, 'yes, we know,' and he asked us if we had ever made a record. Of course, we hadn't, and he asked us if we wanted to. Of course, we did.

"When we went to the studio," Peter said, "I guess we impressed them because we didn't take a lot of amps and equipment. All we took was a couple of old guitars.

"They liked the dubs we cut, too."

"Funny thing about that, though," Gordon picked up. "We recorded the exact same songs we did a couple of years earlier when we auditioned for EMI.

"Only they turned us down after the first audition."

The pair is extremely well-versed. Their schooling and public exposure has embedded in them a knowledge of a wide variety of subjects, and among them there is only one the pair is the least bit hesitant about discussing.

And that is the subject of Jane Asher, Peter's sister-actress who makes as many headlines by dating Paul McCartney as she does with her film roles.

"We do a lot of Lennon-McCartney songs," Peter said. "The only thing we resent is when people act like we would never have made it had it not been for my sister and Paul McCartney."

Peter and Gordon's first record, "World Without Love," was written by the Beatle composers. The disc sold nearly one-and-a-half million copies in England and the United States.

On the pop front, the duo now has a new single on the charts. "Lady Godiva" jumped to number 70 after only a week of sales. It appears to have great potential.

After two years as a top singing attraction Peter and Gordon haven't overlooked the possiblity that some unexpected day their popularity could dwindle.

"I wouldn't rule out the chance of going back to school," said Peter. "Or I might even go back into acting. I did this since I was about five, you know.

"But both of us like music very much and it's doubtful if we will ever leave it entirely."

...PETER

...GORDON

KRLA ARCHIVES

The BEAT Goes To The Movies

KALEIDOSCOPE

...SUSANNAH YORK EYES WARREN BEATTY

...WARREN BEATTY EYES SUSANNAH YORK

When Barney Lincoln (Warren Beatty), a good-looking, well-tailored and wealthy young American meets fetching dress designer Angel McGinnis (Susannah York) in London, "Kaleidoscope" might seem to be over before it begins. But a whirlwind plot snags debonaire Barney and "Mod" boutique owner Angel just in time for an exciting feature.

Barney Lincoln, you see, has something on his mind besides Angel— namely an ingenious plot for winning at chemin de fer in Monte Carlo. The plot isn't an altogether legal one either, since it consists of marking the plates which are used to print the famous Kaleidoscope playing cards used in all European gambling casinos.

But in Monte Carlo, Barney finds that his scheme has a flaw, namely Angel who happens to be there watching him rake in the money. Under an extenuating set of circumstances, Barney winds up involved in a Scotland Yard plan to undermine a large narcotics smuggling ring.

Highlight of the fast-moving movie is the up-to-date wardrobe worn by Susannah York, designed for her by the popular Carnaby Street team of Marion Foale and Sally Tuffin.

Warner Brothers premiered "Kaleidoscope" at the Warner Theater in Leicester Square, London, kicked off by an unbelievable round of parties, and promotions. Most interesting was a "Most Switched On Gear" contest, where one of the winners wore an entire suit made of fur. A mini-skirt meter stood nearby, admitting no one unless the hemline was four inches above the knee!

...AND THE EYES HAVE IT IN WARNER BROTHERS' "KALEIDOSCOPE"

...SWITCHED-ON CONTESTANTS

...SUSANNAH TRIES OUT IN PANTS-SUIT

...A CAMEL-WOOL SUIT

...AND A SATIN EVENING GOWN

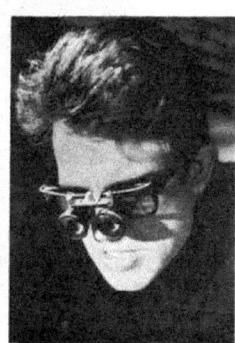

...BUT BEATTY DIGS HER IN ANYTHING.

www.ingramcontent.com/pod-product-compliance
Lightning Source LLC
Chambersburg PA
CBHW081125170426
43197CB00017B/2754